SECOND EDITION

Psychology
From Science to Practice

Robert A. Baron

Rensselaer Polytechnic Institute

Michael J. Kalsher

Rensselaer Polytechnic Institute

with

Rebecca A. Henry

Rensselaer Polytechnic Institute

Boston • New York • San Francisco
Mexico City • Montreal • Toronto • London • Madrid • Munich • Paris
Hong Kong • Singapore • Tokyo • Cape Town • Sydney

Senior Acquisitions Editor: *Stephen Frail*
Series Editorial Assistant: *Allison Rowland*
Marketing Manager: *Pamela Laskey*
Senior Production Editor: *Elizabeth Gale Napolitano*
Editorial Production Service: *Tonnya Norwood, NK Graphics*
Composition Buyer: *Linda Cox*
Manufacturing Buyer: *Joanne Sweeney*
Electronic Composition: *NK Graphics*
Interior Design: *Roy Neuhaus*
Photo Researcher: *Annie Pickert*
Cover Administrator: *Linda Knowles*
Cover Designer: *Roy Neuhaus*

For related titles and support materials, visit our online catalog at www.ablongman.com.

Between the time website information is gathered and then published, it is not unusual for some sites to have closed. Also, the transcription of URLs can result in typographical errors. The publisher would appreciate notification where these errors occur so that they may be corrected in subsequent editions.

Library of Congress Cataloging-in-Publication Data
Baron, Robert A.
    Psychology: from science to practice/Robert A. Baron, Michael J. Kalsher.—2nd ed.
        p. cm.
    Includes bibliographical references and indexes.
    ISBN 0-205-51618-1
    1. Psychology—Textbooks.   I. Kalsher, Michael J.   II. Title.

BF121.B325 2007
150—dc22   2006051524

Printed in the United States of America

10   9   8   7   6   5   4   3   2   Q-WC-V   11   10

Credits appear on page 644, which constitutes an extension of the copyright page.

To my granddaughter Samantha, whose sweet disposition and warm smiles truly brighten my world, and to the memory of my father, Bernard.

"One generation passeth away, and another generation cometh: but the earth abideth for ever...:

    (Old Testament, Ecclesiastes, 1:4,5)

R. A. B.

To the Montana crew that helps keep me grounded—Mom, Dad, John & Char, Patty & Paul—this book's for you! And a special thanks to PPK for reminding me of what friendship is all about.

M. J. K.

To Robert, whose love and support sustains me.

R. A. H.

Brief Contents

Contents

ONE

Psychology: What It Is . . . and What It Offers 2

TWO

Biological Bases of Behavior 38

THREE

Sensation and Perception: Making Contact with the World Around Us   72

FOUR

States of Consciousness   120

FIVE

*Learning: How
We're Changed by
Experience*   **158**

SIX

Memory and Cognition: Remembering, Thinking, Deciding, Creating 198

SEVEN

Human Development 244

EIGHT

Motivation and Emotion 296

NINE

Personality and Intelligence: Understanding Individual Differences 336

Contents

TWELVE

Psychological Treatments: Reducing the Pain and Distress of Mental Disorders   468

THIRTEEN

Social Thought and Social Behavior   502

FOURTEEN

Industrial/Organizational Psychology: Understanding Human Behavior at Work **540**

Preface

SEVENTY-FIVE YEARS OF TEACHING PSYCHOLOGY . . . AND THE LESSONS OUR STUDENTS HAVE TAUGHT *US* ABOUT DOING IT WELL

Seventy-five years: that's how long we (collectively) have been teaching psychology. And roughly 50,000—that's the number of students we have had in our own classes. We have certainly learned much from these experiences, which have involved teaching a very wide range of courses to many different kinds of students in highly varied settings. Among the most important lessons we have learned, though, are these:

1. **Most students find psychology fascinating,** *but* **. . . it is all too easy for an instructor (or a textbook) to dissipate these positive reactions through "information overload"—by presenting too much detail about too many topics.**

   When "information overload" occurs, students frequently wonder "Why am I being asked to read this stuff? What possible use is it to me?" or "Which of these things is *really* important?" And then, all too often, they conclude "This is more than I really want to know!" The result? Their enthusiasm for psychology wanes. (This is especially true for non-psychology majors or students who are returning to school from the workplace or military service.)

2. **A highly effective way to avoid such "information overload" is to present psychology in a truly** *balanced* **way—one that takes careful account of its scientific nature** *and* **its usefulness for solving practical problems.**

   In other words, by striking a good balance between the scientific and applied sides of psychology, the potential dangers of "information overload" can be reduced, students' initial enthusiasm can be maintained, and the transformational power of learning psychology realized.

3. **One of the most important things students gain from their first exposure to psychology is skill in** *thinking critically*—**about themselves, others, and the world around them. This is a crucial "take-away" from introductory psychology, and one that students can use for the remainder of their lives, regardless what career path they take.**

   While critical thinking can be taught in many different contexts, we believe that introductory psychology offers an especially useful one for transmitting this important skill to students. Why? Because nearly everyone has informal ideas about key aspects of human behavior. Yet, in most cases, they have not subjected these ideas to careful (critical) evaluation. Modern psychology, in contrast, applies the principles of critical thinking to all ideas or findings concerning human behavior, and so provides outstanding examples of critical thinking in action.

   These are some of the key lessons we've learned from our seventy-five years of teaching psychology. Now, we'll explain how we've tried to reflect them fully in this book.

HOW HAVE WE BUILT THESE LESSONS INTO THIS BOOK?

To build these lessons—which we view as *very* important ones—into this book, we have adopted three major goals. As explained below, these goals have shaped the nature and content of this book in many ways, and we have tried to follow them carefully from the very start.

GOAL 1: ATTAIN A GOOD BALANCE BETWEEN THE SCIENTIFIC AND PRACTICAL SIDES OF PSYCHOLOGY

We take the title of this book *seriously*; in fact, the title truly reflects our belief that a good balance between science and practice is essential to accurately communicating the nature of modern psychology to students. Reflecting this view, we have sought to explain the scientific foundations of psychology clearly and fully, while at the same time helping students understand *why* and *how* the knowledge psychology provides is so *useful*. To do this, we make sure that every chapter and every discussion explains not just the scientific side of psychology, but also how the information obtained in systematic research can be put to practical use—by society and by students themselves in their own lives and careers. This balance is especially important since, for many students, *this will be the only psychology text they ever read*. To achieve good balance between the scientific and practical sides of psychology, have taken the following steps:

- **Included Special Sections within Each Chapter Entitled** *Psychology Lends a Hand* **and** *Psychology Goes to Work.* These special sections are designed help students understand how they can actually use the findings and principles of psychology in their own lives and careers. **Psychology Lends a Hand** sections focus on ways in which students can use psychology to gain increased self-insight, to get along better with others, and to handle a wide range of life situations more effectively—everything from resisting sales pressure to being a better spouse or parent.

PSYCHOLOGY LENDS A HAND

Exceeding the Limits of Our Attention: Why Do Cell Phones Interfere with Driving?

The use of cellular phones in this country, and throughout the world, has skyrocketed. In 1990, approximately 4.3 million people in the United States used cell phones. By the end of 2005, that figure had ballooned to more than 200 million (Cellular Telecommunications & Internet Association, 2005). So what's the problem? A lot of people use their cell phone while driving—nearly 85 percent in one survey (Goodman et al., 1999). Unfortunately, talking on a cell phone while driving makes a motorist four times as likely to get into a serious crash (Insurance Institute for Highway Safety, 2005). Because of the danger they pose, several states and individual cities prohibit the use of hand-held cell phones while driving.

Redelmeier and Tibshirani (1997) reviewed the cell-phone records of nearly seven hundred people involved in motor-vehicle accidents and found that a significant portion of them (24 percent) had been talking on their cell phones just before the accident. One interpretation of this finding is that the use of cell phones distracts people, similar to the effects you might expect from doing other activities while driving, such as putting on make-up, eating or drinking, or listening to music. However, research has shown that the use of wireless devices causes far more accidents and near-accidents than other attention-grabbing distractions (National Highway Traffic Safety Administration, 2005).

Research suggests that the particular type of attention demanded by active listening or conversing is what makes it so dangerous (Spence & Read, 2003). In one recent study, Strayer and

colleagues (2005) asked some participants to perform a simulated driving task and others to perform the driving task while either talking on a cell phone or listening to the radio. To separate the effects of attention from manual manipulation of the phone itself, half the participants used a hand-held cell phone, while the other half used a hand-free phone. As shown in Figure 3.21, driving performance was worse among participants who talked on the cell phone compared to those who listened to the radio while driving. But contrary to what many people believe, the use of a hands-free cell phone did not lessen the negative effects compared to the use of a hand-held cell phone.

One interpretation of these findings is that people who use cell phones while driving notice traffic signals and other aspects of the driving environment, but fail to respond to them because of the competing demands of their phone conversation. As we'll see in Chapter 6, one possibility is that they are experiencing information overload—a bigger inflow of information than their cognitive systems can handle. However, another possibility is that the use of cell phones causes people to pay less attention to objects they encounter while driving. To test this possibility, Strayer and colleagues placed participants in a driving simulator and asked them to "drive" along routes that resembled city driving while using a hand-held or hands-free cell phone. In addition to measures of performance, their memory of objects (e.g., billboards) along the simulated driving route was also assessed. Participants who talked on a cell phone were less able to recognize these objects than

---

Here are a few examples of *Psychology Lends a Hand* sections:

Hypnosis: Effective Against Pain?

How to Give Feedback to Coworkers

Too Much Freud for Our Own Good?

How to Tell When Another Person is Lying

Becoming a More Transformational Leader

What Are the Risks of Long-term Cell Phone Use: Can You Hear Me Now?

Becoming a Very Happy Person

Laughter—the Best Medicine?

Psychology Goes to Work sections illustrate how students can use psychology to have a better and more successful career.

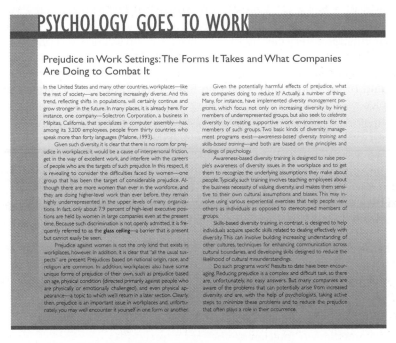

PSYCHOLOGY GOES TO WORK

Prejudice in Work Settings: The Forms It Takes and What Companies Are Doing to Combat It

In the United States and many other countries, workplaces—like the rest of society—are becoming increasingly diverse. And this trend, reflecting shifts in populations, will certainly continue and grow stronger in the future. In many places, it is already here. For instance, one company—Solectron Corporation, a business in Milpitas, California, that specializes in computer assembly—has, among its 3,200 employees, people from thirty countries who speak more than forty languages (Malone, 1993).

Given such diversity, it is clear that there is no room for prejudice in workplaces; it would be a cause of interpersonal friction, get in the way of excellent work, and interfere with the careers of people who are the targets of such prejudice. In this respect, it is revealing to consider the difficulties faced by women—one group that has been the target of considerable prejudice. Although there are more women than ever in the workforce, and they are doing higher-level work than ever before, they remain highly underrepresented in the upper levels of many organizations. In fact, only about 7.9 percent of high-level executive positions are held by women in large companies even at the present time. Because such discrimination is not openly admitted, it is frequently referred to as the **glass ceiling**—a barrier that is present but cannot easily be seen.

Prejudice against women is not the only kind that exists in workplaces, however. In addition, it is clear that "all the usual suspects" are present: Prejudices based on national origin, race, and religion are common. In addition, workplaces also have some unique forms of prejudice of their own, such as prejudice based on age, physical condition (directed primarily against people who are physically or emotionally challenged), and even physical appearance—a topic to which we'll return in a later section. Clearly, then, prejudice is an important issue in workplaces and, unfortunately, you may well encounter it yourself in one form or another.

Given the potentially harmful effects of prejudice, what are companies doing to reduce it? Actually, a number of things. Many, for instance, have implemented diversity management programs, which focus not only on increasing diversity by hiring members of underrepresented groups, but also seek to celebrate diversity by creating supportive work environments for the members of such groups. Two basic kinds of diversity management programs exist—*awareness-based diversity training* and *skills-based training*—and both are based on the principles and findings of psychology.

Awareness-based diversity training is designed to raise people's awareness of diversity issues in the workplace and to get them to recognize the underlying assumptions they make about people. Typically, such training involves teaching employees about the business necessity of valuing diversity, and makes them sensitive to their own cultural assumptions and biases. This may involve using various experiential exercises that help people view others as individuals as opposed to stereotyped members of groups.

Skills-based diversity training, in contrast, is designed to help individuals acquire specific skills related to dealing effectively with diversity. This can involve building increasing understanding of other cultures, techniques for enhancing communication across cultural boundaries, and developing skills designed to reduce the likelihood of cultural misunderstandings.

Do such programs work? Results to date have been encouraging. Reducing prejudice is a complex and difficult task, so there are, unfortunately, no easy answers. But many companies are aware of the problems that can potentially arise from increased diversity, and are, with the help of psychologists, taking active steps to minimize these problems and to reduce the prejudice that often plays a role in their occurrence.

Here are a few examples of *Psychology Goes to Work* sections:

The Harmful Effects of Noise At Work and At Play

Taking, Not Faking, Employment Tests

Abusive Supervisors and How to Deal With Them

Prejudice in Work Settings: The Forms It Takes and What Companies are Doing to Combat It

Using Behavioral Modeling and Mental Rehearsal to Teach Computer Skills

Job Stress: What Can You Do to Control It?

Drug Testing at Work: What Are Your Rights?

Using Memory Principles to Boost the Accuracy, Fairness, and Favorableness of Your Own Performance Appraisals

Choosing a Career: Some Steps That Can Help

Employee Assistance Programs: A Helping Hand From Your Employer

- **Illustrated the Scientific Foundations and Nature of Psychology by Presenting Cutting-Edge Research.** Since we also believe fervently that the scientific foundations of psychology are one of the things that make it uniquely valuable, we have sought to illustrate them clearly. To do so, we present, in every chapter, the most current findings available—*including many findings published in 2005 and 2006.* Calling readers' attention to this cutting-edge research serves to highlight psychology's scientific side. Moreover, throughout the book, we emphasize the following point: *it is psychology's scientific nature that makes it so uniquely valuable and useful.* A partial listing of the many topics added to this new edition is presented in the next section; here, we'll merely emphasize, again, that presenting *both* the scientific and practical sides of psychology has been a major theme throughout the book.

GOAL 2: BREADTH WITHOUT OVERLOAD

One thing we have definitely tried to do is present an exceptionally broad picture of modern psychology—to illustrate the tremendous range of truly fascinating topics and ideas it investigates. At the same time, however, we've made intense efforts to avoid overwhelming readers—most of whom are *not* psychology majors—with too much detail. To combine these goals, we have taken the following concrete steps:

- **Inclusion of a Separate Chapter on Industrial/Organizational Psychology.** Industrial/Organizational Psychology is an important field of psychology and one that illustrates very clearly the balance between science and practice we have sought. Often, though, it is not included in texts like this one. We have included a separate and informative chapter on I/O Psychology. This chapter, which comes at the end of the book, also serves an integrative function, demonstrating how principles presented in earlier chapters (learning, motivation, personality, persuasion) apply to the study of work behavior.
- **The Addition of Dozens of New Topics.** As noted above, we have included literally dozens of new topics and lines of research—ones that truly represent the "cutting edge" of our field. Together, these clearly illustrate its scientific nature and the major progress produced by this approach. Here is a partial listing of the topics and lines of research we have added to this new edition to emphasize the continued progress of scientific psychology:

New research findings on the nature of intuition.

New evidence concerning the functions of dreams.

The relationship between Circadian rhythms and both explicit and implicit memory.

The role of forgetting in interference between newly formed memories and existing ones.

The construction of memories (e.g., false memories, memories based on rumors).

Brain mechanisms in autobiographical memory.

Satisficing and maximizing as decision-making strategies.

New findings concerning the limits of human cognition

Research on gender bias in employee performance appraisal.

How to enhance interpersonal skills through training.

The role of cognitive processes in pain perception.

New research on self-esteem, including gender and ethnic differences, and the role of self-esteem in important life outcomes.

New research on the biological bases of personality, including new findings on neural centers involved in personality and the role of genetics.

New research on environmental effects on IQ, including compelling evidence debunking the "Mozart Effect."

New research on the role of stereotype threat in intelligence testing.

The role of neurotransmitters in disorders such as Alzheimer's disease and Parkinson's disease.

The role of the cerebellum in cognitive processes.

The use of brain-imaging techniques to identify emotion-location correspondence in the brain.

New research concerning the factors that contribute to happiness.

The psychological impact of large-scale disasters.

The effects of social support on the immune system.

New findings concerning the long-term health affects of using cellular phones.

The role of siblings in child development.

The role of mental activity in cognitive declines with aging.

Boomerang children and how they affect their parents.

The role of mirror neurons in autism.

The role of a perceptual tendency to focus on small details in obsessive-compulsive disorders.

The use of virtual environments in therapy.

The role of expressed emotion in relapse from recovery from mental disorders.

The role of missed opportunities in counterfactual thinking.

Similarity between pets and their owners.

Enhancing cooperation in teams.

Creating a satisfying work environment.

The benefits of fluency in more than one language.

The role of cognitive processes in pain perception.

Why using a cell phone while driving is more dangerous than other activities and why the use of hands-free phones may be no safer than hand-held models.

How conditioned taste aversion is being used to treat alcohol dependency.

New information showing how observational learning may help stroke victims regain lost motor function.

New findings concerning the social, economic, and cognitive factors that affect obesity.

New research suggesting that women can detect paternal qualities in men from facial cues.

The role of physical attractiveness in decisions concerning safe sex.

Findings concerning the healthful benefits of laughter.

The beneficial effects of lifestyle changes (e.g., healthy diet, relaxation techniques, working out) on brain function and enhancement of verbal skills.

The impact of primary prevention techniques on teen smoking.

- **Cross-Referencing among Chapters.** Another technique we use to achieve breadth without overload involves careful *cross-referencing* among chapters. By pointing out links between various topics and findings, we help students see psychology not as a set of independent lines of research or subfields, but as what it really is: a unified, integrated field in which new findings in one area often enrich progress in other areas or lines of research. Such cross-referencing occurs in every chapter and simply calls students' attention to links between information being presented currently, and related discussions in other sections of the text.
- **Recognizing the Needs of Non-Traditional Students: Other Steps to Avoid Information Overload.** To avoid the danger of too much detail, we asked ourselves the following question as we wrote every chapter and every major section of the text: "How much detail is needed to give students the "big picture"—to assure that they grasp the main ideas?" Then, once that point was reached, we stopped, rather than continue and run the risk of leaving students with the conclusion that they are learning more about a given topic than they really care to know! We fully realize that many readers of this book will *not* be psychology majors, and that many will be students outside the traditional mold. They will be working, have families, and perhaps have served in the military. We have kept this thought clearly in mind, and that, we believe, has helped us to avoid "information overload"—presenting more detail than necessary to assure that readers understand the main points.

Here's one example of how we followed this strategy: At many points in the text, we describe *specific research studies*. In doing so, we are careful to provide enough detail so that students can tell what was done, why the research was conducted, and what the major findings indicate. We do *not*, however, describe every aspect of the study and every possible issue relating to it. The result, we believe, is that students gain important insights into the nature of psychological research and its implications, without being swamped with too much detail—detail that is not really essential to their understanding of psychology.

GOAL 3: PROVIDE STUDENTS WITH LOTS OF EXPOSURE TO, AND PRACTICE IN, CRITICAL THINKING

As we noted earlier, we believe that skill in critical thinking is one of the most important things students gain from their first course in psychology. To make sure that critical thinking is an important theme of this text, we have taken several steps:

- **Every Major Section Ends with "Key Questions."** These provide a review of the major points covered and also serve as a starting point for critical thinking.

- **End-of-Chapter Exercises.** Each chapter ends with two different kinds of exercises designed to give students practice in critical thinking—primarily, with respect to psychology, but in a general sense, too. These exercises are titled *"Psychology: Understanding Its Findings,"* and *"Making Psychology Part of Your Life."* Together, they help to emphasize efforts to provide students with experience in thinking critically that are built into every chapter. These exercises can be used either as homework or as in-class exercises, and several can be assigned to groups to work on or discuss them together.

PSYCHOLOGY: UNDERSTANDING ITS FINDINGS

How Feelings Affect Our Judgment: A Personal Demonstration

Just how strong are the effects of our feelings (affective states) on our judgments? Very! Try this simple exercise to see for yourself.

1. Look through your photos and choose several that show people some of your friends have never met. Try to choose ones who are average-looking in appearance.
2. Now ask several of your friends to rate the attractiveness of the people shown in the photos on a scale ranging from 1 to 5 (1 = very unattractive; 2 = unattractive; 3 = average; 4 = attractive; 5 = very attractive).
3. Before you ask them to do the ratings, you have a task: Rate your friends' current moods: 1 = very negative; 2 = negative; 3 = neutral; 4 = good; 5 = very good.

4. After you have had several friends evaluate the photos, compare your ratings of their moods with the ratings they provided.

There is a very good chance you will find that the better your friends' moods, the higher they rated the people in the photos. Why? Because their moods biased their judgment—tilted them in the same direction as their current mood. This is a powerful demonstration of just how strong—and subtle—such effects can be. If you ask your friends, they will probably deny that their current moods had any bearing on their ratings!

MAKING PSYCHOLOGY PART OF YOUR LIFE

Practice in Forgiveness

Do you want to be happy? Then one skill you should practice is forgiveness—letting go of your anger and desire for revenge toward others who have harmed you in some way. Forgiving them is not only good for them, but also good for you! Start your practice with this exercise:

1. Remember some incident in your life when another person hurt you badly.
2. Now, rate how angry you felt toward this person at the time, and how much you wanted revenge against him. (Use a 5-point scale: 1 = not angry at all; 2 = a little angry; 3 = neutral; 4 = angry; 5 = very angry. Use the same numbers for rating your desire for revenge.)
3. Next, try to feel empathy for this person. Try to experience what he did when he harmed you—his feelings and emotions at the time.

terpret the cause of his behavior in a kind manner. Truly, we don't always know why other people do what they do, so perhaps you jumped to the wrong conclusion; perhaps this person didn't mean to harm you, or didn't realize how much he was harming you. Keep trying to come up with kind interpretations of his behavior until you find one that fits.
5. Finally, consider how often you thought about this past harm—ruminated about it. Did this make you happy or unhappy? In all likelihood, ruminating about this incident made you unhappy. So now, think of ways you can stop thinking about it—distract yourself, think about happier experiences, and so on.

To the extent you can make these steps work, you are on the way to developing your ability to forgive others, and that is an important step on the road to personal happiness.

Psychology: Understanding Its Findings exercises focus on giving students practice in thinking about and understanding the major ideas and concepts contained in the chapter they have just read. For example:

Can Hypnosis Solve Personal Problems?

Putting Fragrance to Work

How Feelings Affect Our Judgment: A Personal Demonstration

Making Psychology Part of Your life exercises, in contrast, show students how they can apply these ideas and concepts to their own lives. Here are the titles of a few of these exercises:

Avoiding Sunk Costs

Seeking Help at Work: Employee Assistance Programs

How You Can Get Other People to Like You

Do You Like Teamwork? Good Employees Come in All Forms

Interpreting the Results of Surveys: "To Believe or Not to Believe," That is the Question

On Becoming a Better Student: Using Study Habits

Managing Stress: Some Useful Tactics

Additional Steps Designed to Make This Book Easier to Read— and More Useful—To a Broad Range of Students

In addition to the features noted above—ones closely linked to our major goals— we have also taken a number of other steps designed to make the book useful— and, we hope—fun to read! These steps include the following:

■ An In-Text Study Guide.

To help students master the materials included in the text, we have also added an *in-text study guide*—a study guide that is built right into the book. This will save students the expense of buying a separate study guide, and will give them a very convenient way to improve their studying, and their understanding of psychology.

■ Inclusion of Many Pedagogical Aids.

Each chapter starts with an outline and is followed by an introduction that is as interesting and attention-grabbing as we could make it.

Some of these introductions focus on events and experiences in our own lives, while others use different approaches. All are designed to accomplish two goals: (1) seize students' attention, and (2) provide them with a brief overview of what follows—what topics and issues will be covered in the chapter.

In addition, all key terms are printed in **boldface type,** and are defined in the text and in marginal entries, as well as in a list of **Key Terms** *in the Glossary* at the end the book. Each major section is followed by **Key Questions,** which ask students to think about the major points just presented. Answers to these are provided at the end of each chapter in a **Summary and Review of Key Questions** section.

KEY TERMS

Agreeableness, p. 351
Anal stage, p. 343
Anxiety, p. 345
Archetypes, p. 345
Basic anxiety, p. 345
Behavioral activation system (BAS), p. 359
Behavioral inhibition system (BIS), p. 359
Collective unconscious, p. 345
Conscientiousness, p. 352
Content validity, p. 366
Criterion-related validity, p. 366
Cultural bias, p. 373
Ego, p. 342
Emotional intelligence, p. 373
Emotional stability, p. 352
Externals, p. 354
Extraversion, p. 351

Genital stage, p. 343
Heritability, p. 370
Humanistic theories, p. 345
Id, p. 342
Individual differences perspective, p. 338
Intelligence, p. 361
Internals, p. 354
Introverts, p. 345
IQ, p. 364
Latency stage, p. 343
Libido, p. 342
NEO personality inventory, p. 356
Neo-Freudians, p. 345
Neural plasticity, p. 368
Observational learning, p. 354
Oedipus complex, p. 343
Openness to experience, p. 352
Oral stage, p. 343

Pleasure principle, p. 342
Practical intelligence, p. 362
Psychoanalysis, p. 341
Psychosexual stages of development, p. 342
Reality principle, p. 342
Reliability, p. 365
Rorschach test, p. 357
Self-actualization, p. 349
Self-concept, p. 348
Self-efficacy, p. 354
Self-esteem, p. 350
Self-reinforcement, p. 354
Self-system, p. 353
Social cognitive theory, p. 353
Split-half reliability, p. 366
Stanford–Binet test, p. 363
Superego, p. 342
Test–retest reliability, p. 366

SUMMARY AND REVIEW OF KEY QUESTIONS

Personality: The Essence of What Makes Us Unique

• **What is personality?**
Personality consists of the unique and stable patterns of behavior, thoughts, and emotions shown by individuals.

• **How stable is it over time?**
Research findings indicate that personality is quite stable over time, although some people show more stability than others.

• **What is the interactionist perspective currently adopted by most psychologists?**
The interactionist perspective supports the view that our behavior in any given situation is a joint function of our personality and various aspects of the situation.

The Psychoanalytic Approach: Messages from the Unconscious

• **According to Freud, what are the three levels of consciousness?**
These levels are conscious, preconscious, and unconscious

gling to control the sexual and aggressive impulses of the id.

• **According to Rogers, why do many individuals fail to become fully functioning persons?**
Rogers believed that many individuals fail to become fully functioning people because distorted self-concepts interfere with personal growth.

• **In Maslow's theory, what is self-actualization?**
Self-actualization is a stage in which an individual has reached his or her maximum potential, and has become the best human being she or he can be.

• **What is self-esteem and how does it vary over time and across groups?**
Self-esteem is a person's overall feeling of worth. In general, self-esteem decreases during the teenage years and increases during adulthood, with males having higher levels than females on average. Self-esteem also varies by ethnic group, both within and outside the United States.

Another important feature is that all graphs and charts have been specially created for this book. Thus, they are all easy for students to read and understand; and all have *special labels* that call attention to the major points being illustrated. Overall then, we feel that our book will be very convenient for students to use and will, in this regard, be unusually "user-friendly."

■ Coverage of Diversity Issues is Integrated Into the Text—Not Merely Added On.

We feel that diversity and a multi-cultural perspective are key features of psychology at the present time. We fully reflect this fact by introducing diversity into the text at many points where it is relevant, and where interesting, new findings are available for discussion. As a result, diversity issues are *fully integrated* into the text, reflecting their importance in modern psychology. Here are some examples:

Diversity as a central theme in modern psychology (Chapter 1)
Gender differences in hearing loss with age (Chapter 3)
Cultural differences in pain perception (Chapter 3)

The role of automatic processing in racial prejudice (Chapter 4)

The influence of culture on decision making (Chapter 6)

Own-race bias in memory for faces (Chapter 6)

"Youth bulges" and their effects (Chapter 7)

Cultural differences in moral development (Chapter 7)

Differences in brain functioning between gays and heterosexuals (Chapter 8)

Cultural differences in life satisfaction (Chapter 8)

Ethnic and gender differences in self-esteem (Chapter 9)

The role of the "Big Five" dimensions of personality across many cultures (Chapter 9)

Gender differences in health beliefs (Chapter 10)

Gender differences in appreciation of humor (Chapter 10)

Cultural differences in suicide rates (Chapter 11)

Gender differences in the incidence and symptoms of depression (Chapter 11)

Multicultural approaches to therapy (Chapter 12)

Ethnic differences in reactions to drugs (Chapter 12)

Is dissonance universal across cultures? (Chapter 13)

The role of physical appearance in stereotypes (Chapter 13)

The role of diversity in team composition (Chapter 14)

A FULL RANGE OF ANCILLARY MATERIALS

We firmly believe that no text is complete—or useful!—without a full range of excellent ancillary materials. Thus, this text is accompanied by a complete teaching and learning package. The key parts are described below:

Instructor's Supplements

■ Instructor's Classroom Kit and CD-ROM, Volumes I and II

Our unparalleled classroom kit includes every instructional aid an introductory psychology professor needs to excel in the classroom. We have made our resources even easier to use by placing all of our print supplements in two convenient volumes. Each volume contains the Instructor's Manual, Test Bank, and slides from the PowerPoint Presentation, organized by chapter so that all resources are in one place. Electronic versions of the Instructor's Manual, Test Bank, PowerPoint presentation, and images from the text, all searchable by key terms, are made easily accessible to instructors on the accompanying Classroom Kit CD-ROM. In addition, the Classroom Kit includes a preface, a sample syllabus, and a table of contents for Allyn & Bacon's Introductory Psychology Transparency package, Digital Media Archive, and *Insights Into Psychology* video collection.

The Classroom Kit Includes:

■ Instructor's Manual

A wonderful tool for classroom preparation and management. Each chapter of the Instructor's Manual includes a Chapter-At-A-Glance Grid, with chapter topics linked to a variety of instruction ideas and other available supplements; learning objectives covering major concepts within the chapter; a detailed chapter overview; an annotated lecture outline organized by chapter headings and containing key terms, up to 20 lecture examples, 10 in-depth teaching demonstrations referencing top journals, critical thinking questions, and diversity topics; 10 Test Your Knowledge questions and a list of suggestions for student journal projects; a comprehensive list of Psychology and popular video and media; an up-to-date list of web links; and an appendix with over 150 pages of student handouts.

■ Test Bank

Featuring more than 150 questions per chapter, the Test Bank has been thoroughly revised and updated with challenging questions that target key concepts. Each chapter includes over 100 multiple choice, 20 true/false, 10 short answer, and 4 essay questions, each with an answer justification, page reference, a difficulty rating, and skill designation. The Test Bank is also available in TestGen 5.5 computerized version, for use in personalizing tests.

■ Powerpoint Presentation

An exciting interactive tool for use in the classroom. This dynamic, multimedia resource pairs key points covered in the chapters with images from the textbook to encourage effective lectures and classroom discussions.

■ MyPsychLab for Introductory Psychology

This interactive and instructive multimedia resource can be used to supplement a traditional lecture course or to administer a course entirely online. MyPsychLab is an all-inclusive tool: a text-specific e-book plus multimedia tutorials, audio, video, simulations, animations, and controlled assessments to completely engage students and reinforce learning. Fully customizable and easy to use, MyPsychLab for Introductory Psychology meets the individual teaching and learning needs of every instructor and every student. Visit the site at **www.mypsychlab.com.** Sample syllabi for integrating MyPsychLab into your course and ready-made homework sets for MyPsychLab are available for download at www.ablongman.com/catalog.

■ Insights Into Psychology Video or DVD, Vols. I–IV

These video programs include two or three short clips per topic, covering such topics as animal research, parapsychology, health and stress, Alzheimer's disease, bilingual education, genetics and IQ, and much more. A Video Guide containing critical thinking questions accompanies each video. Also available on DVD.

■ The Blockbuster Approach: A Guide to Teaching Introductory Psychology with Video

The Blockbuster Approach is a unique print resource for instructors who enjoy enhancing their classroom presentations with film. With heavy coverage of general, abnormal, social, and developmental psychology, this guide suggests a wide range of films to use in class, and provides questions for reflection and other pedagogical tools to make the use of film more effective in the classroom.

■ Interactive Lecture Questions for Clickers for Introductory Psychology

These lecture questions will jumpstart exciting classroom discussions.

■ Allyn & Bacon Digital Media Archive for Psychology, 5.0

This comprehensive source includes still images, audio clips, web links, animation and video clips. Highlights include classic Psychology experimental footage from Stanley Milgrim's Invitation to Social Psychology, biology animations, and more–with coverage of such topics as eating disorders, aggression, therapy, intelligence, and sensation and perception.

■ **Allyn & Bacon Introduction to Psychology Transparency Package**

The Transparency Kit includes approximately 230 full-color acetates to enhance classroom lecture and discussion – including images from all of Allyn & Bacon's Introduction to Psychology texts.

■ **Course Management**

Use these preloaded, customizable, content and assessment items to teach your online courses. Available in CourseCompass, Blackboard, and WebCT formats, the proprietary .zip file includes questions found in the Electronic Testbank.

Student Supplements

■ **MyPsychLab, Student Version, for Introductory Psychology**

This interactive and instructive multimedia resource is an all-inclusive tool, a text-specific e-book plus multimedia tutorials, audio, video, simulations, animations, and controlled assessments to reinforce learning. Easy to use, MyPsychLab for Introductory Psychology meets the individual learning needs of every student. Visit the site at www.mypsychlab.com.

■ **Study Card for Introductory Psychology**

Colorful, affordable, and packed with useful information, Allyn & Bacon/Longman's Study Cards make studying easier, more efficient, and more enjoyable. Course information is distilled down to the basics, helping students quickly master the fundamentals, review a subject for understanding, or prepare for an exam.

■ **Research Navigator Guide: Psychology, with access to Research Navigator™**

Allyn & Bacon's new Research Navigator™ is the easiest way for students to start a research assignment or research paper. Complete with extensive help on the research process and three exclusive databases of credible and reliable source material including EBSCO's ContentSelect Academic Journal Database, New York Times Search by Subject Archive, and "Best of the Web" Link Library, Research Navigator™ helps students quickly and efficiently make the most of their research time. The booklet contains a practical and to-the-point discussion of search engines; detailed information on evaluating online sources and citation guidelines for web resources; web links for Psychology; and a complete guide to Research Navigator.

■ **Companion Website for Introductory Psychology**

http://www.abintropsychology.com
This open access website Flash Card glossary terms, topically-organized online practice tests, and links to psychology-related resources on the Web.

Concluding Comments—And a Request for Help

Helen Keller (1903), who was both blind and deaf but who overcame these huge obstacles to lead a rich, full life, once remarked: *"Knowledge is happiness, because to have knowledge—broad, deep knowledge—is to know true ends from false, and lofty things from low."* We share her view and believe that knowledge is in fact one of life's great treasures. With that thought in mind, we have tried to write this book in a way that would provide a broad and useful introduction to the knowledge of modern psychology—its methods, tools, findings, and basic principles—but to do so in a style that would definitely *not* lose the "forest for the trees" by overwhelming students with excess detail. Have we succeeded? Only *you*, the students and colleagues who read this text can decide. With that thought in mind, we respectfully invite your comments and input. Please tell us what you like, and don't like, what should be added, and what should be reduced. We will listen *very* carefully to your suggestions and use them to move toward another of our key goals: making this book better and better in each new edition. Thanks in advance for your help!

Michael J. Kalsher
kalshm@rpi.edu

Robert A. Baron
baronr@rpi.edu

Rebecca A. Henry
henryr@rpi.edu

Acknowledgments

SOME WARM "THANK YOU'S!"

Writing is truly a solitary activity each of us must perform alone. But turning a manuscript into an actual book—that's something else entirely! It requires the talents and assistance of many people. We realize that fully, and want to take this opportunity to thank the many outstanding people who have helped us make *this* book a reality.

First, our sincere thanks to our editor, Stephen Frail. His commitment and enthusiasm were clearly key ingredients in bringing this book to fruition, and we look forward to working with him—and benefiting from his skills and talent—for many years to come.

Second, we want to thank Pam Laskey for her efforts on behalf of the previous edition and this new one, too. She has worked hard to get the text to colleagues who might find it suitable for their courses, and we appreciate her efforts in this and many other ways more than we can say.

Third, our sincere appreciation to Wendy Gordon, Director of Marketing at Allyn & Bacon. We were truly happy to learn that she had returned to the Allyn & Bacon fold, and are certain that her presence and her skill will contribute greatly to the success of this book in the months and years ahead.

Fourth, we want to extend out appreciation to the colleagues who read and commented on the manuscript for the second edition. We found their comments to be extremely helpful, and want to thank them for taking the time from their busy lives and schedules to share their expertise with us:

Robin Campbell, Brevard Community College

Nancy-Lee Devane, Community College of Rhode Island

Debra Parish, Tomball College

Nina Beaman, Bryant and Stratton College

Don Crews, Southwest Georgia Technical College

Myra Harville, Holmes Community College

Peggy Norwood, Red Rocks Community College

Christian Fossa-Anderson, DeVry University, South Florida

Larry Eisenburg, DeVry University, Long Island

James Rodgers, Hawkeye Community College

Wayne Shebilske, Wright State University

Deborah Evans, Ivy Tech Community College

Stuart J. McKelvie, Bishop's University

Wendy Domjan, University of Texas at Austin

Hugh Riley, Baylor University

Teraesa Vinson, Bronx Community College

Angelina MacKewn, University of Tennessee at Martin

June Breninger, Cascade College

Jay Brown, Southwest Missouri State University

We would also like to acknowledge our colleagues who reviewed manuscript for the first edition of this text:

Melinda Blackman, California State University, Fullerton

Lorry Cology, Owens Community College

Christian Fossa-Andersen, DeVry University, Southern Florida Campus

Debra Hollister, Valencia Community College

Jan Pascal, DeVry University, Kansas City

Carolyn Paul, DeVry University, Pomona

Paula Popovich, Ohio University

Lindsay Reid, DeVry University, Crystal City

Susan Siaw, California State Polytechnic University, Pomona

Joshua S. Spitalnick, University of Georgia

Keith Syrja, Owens Community College

Sheree Watson, University of Southern Mississippi

Adelia Williams, DeVry University, Arlington, Virginia

Michael Zickar, Bowling Green State University

Fifth, our personal thinks to Liz Napolitano, our Production Supervisor at Allyn & Bacon. Her experienced hand on the rudder was truly essential for keeping the book on schedule and assuring that the entire production process went smoothly and efficiently. We truly do appreciate her help—and patience!—in this complex task.

Sixth, our thanks to other talented people who contributed to various aspects of the production process: to Annie Pickert for photo research, and to Roy Neuhaus for the interior and cover design work.

To all of these truly exceptional people, and to many others, too, we extend our warmest personal thanks.

About The Authors

Robert A. Baron (Ph.D., Iowa, 1968) is the Dean R. Wellington Professor of Management and Professor of Psychology at Rensselaer Polytechnic Institute. He has held faculty appointments at Purdue University, University of Minnesota, University of Texas, University of South Carolina, University of Washington, Princeton University, and Oxford University (Visiting Fellow, 1982). He served as a Program Director at the National Science Foundation (1979–1981), and was appointed as a Visiting Senior Research Fellow by the French Ministry of Research (2001–2002) at the Universite des Sciences Sociales, Toulouse. He has been a Department Chair (1987–1993) and Interim Dean (2001–2002). Baron is a Fellow of both the American Psychological Association and a Charter Fellow of the Association for Psychological Science (APS).

Prof. Baron has published more than one hundred articles and forty chapters in edited volumes. He is the author or co-author of more than forty books including *Social Psychology* (11th ed.), *Behavior in Organizations* (9th ed.), and *Entrepreneurship: A Process Perspective* (2nd ed.). Prof. Baron holds three U.S. patents and was founder, President, and CEO of Innovative Environmental Products, Inc. (1993–2000). His current research focuses primarily on the social and cognitive factors that play a role in entrepreneurs' success. He is a long-time runner, and his hobbies include fine wood-working, music and cooking.

Michael J. Kalsher is Associate Professor of Psychology and Cognitive Science at Rensselaer Polytechnic Institute. Kalsher served as Chair of the Department of Cognitive Science at Rensselaer from 1997 through 2002. He received his Ph.D. in 1988 from Virginia Tech. Professor Kalsher is a member of both the American Psychological Society and American Psychological Association. He is also a member of the Human Factors and Ergonomics Society for which he currently serves as Chair of the Arnold M. Small Safety Lecture series.

Professor Kalsher has published more than fifty articles in professional journals, a number of chapters in edited books, and he has given more than one-hundred presentations at professional meetings.

Kalsher's company (Kalsher and Associates, L.L.C.) specializes in applying the principles of psychology to enhance human performance and workplace safety, including providing litigation support (e.g., as an expert witness) in product liability cases. Professor Kalsher's current research interests focus mainly on human factors issues, including development and evaluation of warnings and instructions, allocation of blame for consumer product injuries, and the use of emerging technologies to enhance communications in noisy environments (e.g., tanks, helicopters). Kalsher is a long-time runner and his hobbies include making fine wines.

Rebecca A. Henry is currently Visiting Associate Professor at Rensselaer Polytechnic Institute. She received her Ph.D. in 1989 from the University of Illinois and was on the faculty in the Department of Psychological Sciences at Purdue University for 14 years. She has published articles in several journals, including *Psychological Bulletin, Journal of Applied Psychology,* and *Organizational Behavior and Human Decision Processes (OBHDP)*. Professor Henry supervised over a dozen doctoral and master's students and served as the Director of Undergraduate Studies in the Department of Psychological Sciences at Purdue. While at Purdue she taught several undergraduate and graduate level courses and was honored as the Department's undergraduate teaching award nominee several times.

Professor Henry's research has spanned several topic areas in Industrial/Organizational Psychology, including group decision making, organizational citizenship, and ability testing. She currently serves on the editorial boards of *Psychology and Marketing* and *OBHDP*. Her hobbies include music and baking.

Psychology

ONE

Psychology: What It Is . . . and What It Offers

*I*t never fails. We are at a party talking to someone we've just met or on an airplane chatting with another passenger and they ask: "What do you do for a living?" When we tell them that we are psychologists, they usually react in one of three ways. Some people—we think of them as supporters—express great interest in psychology. Then, typically, they ask us questions about some aspect of human behavior—anything from "road rage" and why it occurs, to hypnotism (Is it real? Does it work?) or memory (Why do they forget other's names immediately after being introduced to them?). A second group of people, whom we describe as volunteer patients, react quite differently. They view meeting us as an opportunity for getting good (and free!) advice on personal problems. They quickly describe something that has been bothering them (or someone they know very well), and ask for our advice. We describe the third group as skeptics, and such persons let us know right away that, in their opinion, psychology is just "common sense" and is not something they take seriously. A few of these skeptics grudgingly admit that psychology might contain a grain of truth but, in their minds, it is not really useful; rather, it is just so much fluff that smart people, like themselves(!), tend to ignore.

What do these experiences tell us? Primarily, two things. First, since the first two groups (supporters and volunteer patients) are by far the majority, it is clear that most people are deeply interested in psychology and do believe that it can be helpful to them But the existence of the third group—the skeptics—reminds us that not everyone shares these views. On the contrary, some people have serious reservations about the value, scientific nature, and usefulness of psychology; they really don't believe it can tell them anything they don't already know.

In a sense, we have written this book for all three groups. For those in the first two groups, who already believe that psychology is interesting and valuable, it will offer a vast array of intriguing and potentially useful information about human behavior. For the skeptics, it will provide a solid basis for changing their minds. After reading this book, we predict that they will come to see psychology as much more interesting, valuable, and useful than they did before.

But this book is actually designed to do more than this. It also seeks to provide you with a *new perspective* on human behavior—your own and that of other people. Psychology, we strongly believe, offers far more than a collection of interesting facts; it also provides a new way of thinking about your own feelings, thoughts, and actions, and those of other persons. So after reading this book, we predict that you will never think about yourself, other people, and your relations with them in quite the same way as before. Further, we also predict that this new perspective will enrich your life in many ways.

At this point, we'd much prefer to turn immediately to the findings of our field, which—believe us!—are truly fascinating. Before doing that, though, it is important to complete several preliminary steps. Why? Because this will provide you with a framework for interpreting information presented later in the book, and one basic finding of psychology itself is this: new information that is *organized* is generally easier to understand, retain, and use than information that is *not* organized. To take account of this important fact, this first chapter will provide a framework for organizing the new information about psychology you'll encounter in later chapters. Specifically, we'll focus on three basic tasks.

First, we'll define psychology, say a few words about its origins, and describe some of the major issues with which it grapples (e.g., How much do we change over the course of our lives? To what extent is our behavior the result of our experiences in life, and to what extent does it reflect our genetic inheritance?). Second, we'll describe several major themes relating to human behavior that psychologists often consider in their efforts to understand specific topics—for instance, the question "To what extent is our behavior formed by our experience, and to what extent is it influenced by our genetic inheritance?" Third, we'll comment on the scientific nature of psychology, describing the *scientific method*, how psychologists use it, and how you, too, can put it to good use through *critical thinking*—a kind of thinking that will help you to evaluate many kinds of information more accurately and effectively. Fourth, we'll describe basic *research methods* used by psychologists in their efforts to increase our knowledge of human behavior. Since the vast majority of the information and findings reported in this book were acquired through the use of these methods, it is important for you to understand them.

After presenting all this basic background information, we'll consider another important issue: Why should *you* study psychology? In other words, what can you hope to gain from this experience? In our view, quite a lot. We believe—passionately!—that psychology is tremendously useful, and that this book's title is really accurate: knowing about psychology will truly be very helpful to you in your life and in your career. Finally, we'll conclude with an overview of the special features of this book—features designed to make it easier to read and use. Now, without further delay, let's turn to the questions of what modern psychology is, and how it got started.

FIGURE 1.1
Psychology: The Science of Behavior and Cognitive Processes
Modern psychology is concerned with all aspects of human behavior and human cognition—everything we do, feel, think, or experience.

THE FIELD OF PSYCHOLOGY: WHAT IT IS AND HOW IT STARTED

Suppose that you stopped fifty people on the street and asked them to define the field of psychology. What would they say? Probably many different things: "The field that studies the unconscious," "A branch of medicine that analyzes people," or even "Hypnotism, ESP, and stuff like that." If you posed this question to fifty psychologists, however, you'd obtain much greater agreement: almost all would note that **psychology** is best defined as *the science of behavior and cognitive processes*. Both parts of this definition are important. The first part suggests that psychologists view their field as basically *scientific* in nature. The second part, in contrast, calls attention to the fact that psychologists also view their field as being very broad in scope. Indeed, they perceive it as being concerned with virtually everything we do, feel, think, or experience (see Figure 1.1).

By the term *behavior,* in other words, they mean any observable action or reaction by a living organism—everything from overt actions (anything we say or do) through subtle changes in the electrical activity occurring deep inside our brains. If it can be observed and measured, then it fits within the boundaries of psychology. Similarly, by *cognitive processes*, psychologists mean every aspect of our mental life—our thoughts, memories, dreams, fantasies, reasoning, and so on—all aspects of the human *mind*.

Psychology was not always defined in this broad and inclusive way. During its formative years, major battles were fought among early psychologists who disagreed about many issues. One particularly divisive question was, "What should be the focus of the new field of psychology?" One group of early psychologists, known as **structuralists,** argued that psychology should focus on the human mind—its contents and structure. They suggested using the method of *introspection*, in which individuals reported on their own mental processes, as an excellent way to proceed.

In contrast, another group—and one that proved very important in shaping the nature of modern psychology—was known as the **behaviorists.** The most famous proponent of this view was John B. Watson, who took the extreme position that if something can't be observed directly (e.g., an idea, a mental image), it can't be in-

Psychology:
The science of behavior and cognitive processes.

Structuralism:
An early view of psychology suggesting that the field should focus on identifying the basic structures of the human mind.

Behaviorism:
The view that only observable, overt activities that can be measured scientifically should be studied by psychology.

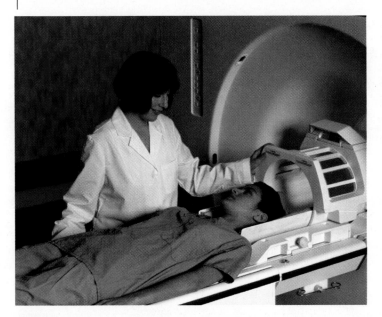
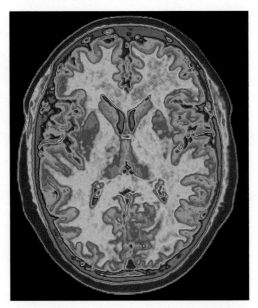

FIGURE 1.2
Observing Cognitive Processes: Technology Can Help
Even today, it is not possible to observe many aspects of cognition (e.g., ideas, memory) directly in the same way that we can observe overt actions. However, modern technology such as that shown here has recently provided amazing tools for observing the effects of mental events and processes in our brains.

cluded as part of psychology. As you can guess from our definition, this view, too, was gradually replaced by a much broader perspective that included many hidden events or processes (e.g., all our cognitive processes) within the range of modern psychology. While these processes or events can't be seen in the same way as overt actions (e.g., in the way you can see me typing these words), they are certainly important and can be measured—although, perhaps, in less direct ways. For instance, we can't, as yet, directly observe the events that occur when new information is entered into your memory. But we can certainly observe the effects of this process later, for instance, when you recall this information correctly (or incorrectly). As we'll see in Chapters 2 and 4 (and other chapters, too), modern technology is now providing the tools for observing the occurrence of mental processes within our brains (see Todd, Fougnie, & Martois, 2005; Figure 1.2). So clearly, psychology must include all aspects of cognition as well as overt behavior. This view is now accepted by virtually all psychologists.

The Origins of Modern Psychology: Multiple Strands Come Together

Have you ever seen the television program *Connections*? In it, the brilliant historian James Burke explains how seemingly unrelated and unconnected events and ideas can combine to produce major advances in technology—and in human welfare. For instance, he notes that the telephone did not suddenly emerge as an independent idea. On the contrary, its inventor, Alexander Graham Bell, simply combined unrelated technical advances in several fields (e.g., the production and measurement of sound; the nature and use of electricity) to develop the idea of the telephone—and the telephone itself.

In other words, new ideas often emerge out of existing ones that, when combined, produce something that really *is* new and different. This same process applies to the emergence of modern psychology. The idea of a scientific field that would study human behavior developed, logically, out of advances in several other fields that paved the way for its occurrence. One basis for the idea of a science of human behavior came from *philosophy* (more specifically, from the *philosophy of science*), which suggested that the methods of science can be applied to virtually anything in the natural world—including the task of understanding human behavior. Another important foundation was provided by the fields of biology and physiology, whose findings shed important new light on the nature and function of the nervous system, on how our senses operate, and on the relationship between physical stimuli (light, noise, heat) and how we sense them. Early psychologists used these advances as a basis for their own research on how we perceive the world around us—for instance, how physical energies from light or movement of molecules in the air are translated into our subjective experiences of color and sound. As we'll see in Chapter 3, these early psychologists found that physical energies of light or sound do *not* translate directly into our subjective experiences. For instance, a sound that is twice as loud, physically, as another one might not be perceived as twice as loud. So even at this very basic level, it soon became clear that the scientific study of human behavior would be filled with many intriguing surprises!

Additional foundation stones of modern psychology, especially in recent decades, involved advances in engineering and computer science. These fields provided psychologists with new tools to present stimuli to research participants in a very precise manner, and to measure the speed with which they responded to these stimuli. This, in turn, provided key techniques for investigating memory, thinking, and many other forms of mental activity that, as we noted above, can't be observed directly without such equipment. So in essence, modern psychology emerged gradually as a growing number of persons recognized that a scientific field that focuses on human behavior and human thought was not only possible—it was readily within their reach (see Figure 1.3).

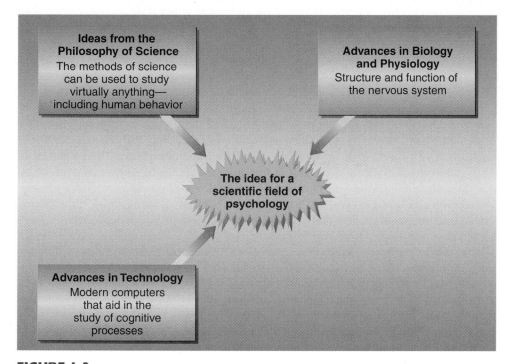

FIGURE 1.3
Modern Psychology: Some of Its Many Roots
Modern psychology derives from many different sources; some of them (but by no means all of them) are shown here.

PSYCHOLOGY: GRAND ISSUES, KEY PERSPECTIVES

More than ten years ago, one of us (Robert Baron) went to the thirtieth reunion of his high school class. He hadn't been to any previous reunions, so he knew he was in for an interesting time. Would he be able to recognize his former classmates? Would they be able to recognize him? The results were mixed. Everyone had changed physically, of course, but amazingly, Baron could still recognize many people. And even those who had changed so much that he couldn't recognize their faces still showed many of the traits he remembered from thirty years earlier. This experience calls attention to one of what might be termed psychology's "grand issues"—large-scale questions or themes that crosscut the field. This question has to do with *stability versus change*: to what extent do we remain stable over time, and to what extent do we change? We'll meet this issue again and again in this book as we address changes over time in cognitive abilities, physical functioning, personality, and other aspects of behavior.

A second, and closely related, theme centers around the following question: to what extent are various aspects of our behavior shaped by inherited tendencies and to what extent are they learned? This is usually known as the *nature-nurture* question, and we'll meet it repeatedly in future chapters. Does aggression stem primarily from innate tendencies or is it the result of experiences that "trigger" it in a given situation? Do we find certain persons attractive because we have built-in tendencies to find certain characteristics (e.g., smooth, clear skin) attractive, or because we learn, through experience, what our own culture sees as beautiful? As you'll soon see, the answer to such questions is *not* one suggesting that either experience or heredity dominates; rather, many aspects of behavior seem to represent the result of complex interactions between these factors. In any case, the nature or nurture question has recently come to the fore in psychology because of the development of a new field that focuses on the potential role of *evolution* in human behavior—evolutionary psychology. This field is so intriguing, and has stirred so much interest among psychologists, that we'll discuss it in more detail in a later section of this chapter.

Now for the third major theme. Answer quickly: Have you felt, in class, that if you thought about the professor, she or he would call on you to answer a question? Most people have, and as a result, try to think of other things when the teacher or professor is going around the room asking students to respond. But now ask yourself this: Do you *really* believe that "thinking can make it so"? Probably not. You know, rationally, that what you think about does not directly influence the external world. Yet you might still try to direct your thoughts away from the professor in such classroom situations. This, and many other examples from everyday life, suggest that we are definitely *not* completely rational. We know very well what is logical or reasonable in a given situation, but act otherwise. That's a third major theme you'll find throughout this book: *rationality versus irrationality*. Need more examples? Consider these: Have you ever underestimated the amount of time it would take you to complete a task? Have you ever let your liking for someone influence your judgments of his or her performance? If so, then you already have direct experience with the less than completely rational side of human nature. Psychologists are fascinated by these and other illustrations that show we are not always perfectly logical, because they often offer insights into how the mind works. We'll return to this theme as we examine such issues as decision making, eyewitness testimony, and how we form first impressions of other persons.

Keep an eye peeled for these three grand issues—they are central questions that have captured the attention of psychologists for decades and that have played an important role in shaping the questions asked by psychologists in their research.

Key Perspectives in Psychology: The Many Facets of Behavior

Cross-cutting the "grand issues" or themes described above are more specific perspectives concerning the nature of behavior and the factors that affect it. These perspectives refer to the specific ways in which psychologists attempt to understand complex aspects of behavior. To illustrate their basic nature, we'll use the following example. Imagine this scene: A young woman, wearing a beautiful silk costume embroidered with threads of gold, walks into the middle of a large arena, watched by a huge crowd. Suddenly, a large bull enters. The woman waves a red cape at the bull, and it charges directly at her. She steps gracefully out of the way at the last minute, and the crowd cheers with enthusiasm. Again and again the woman waves the cape and the bull charges. After many narrow but stylish escapes from then bull's horns, she kills the animal with one skilled and merciful stroke of a sword. The crowd goes wild with admiration (see Figure 1.4).

FIGURE 1.4
Contrasting Perspectives of Modern Psychology
Psychologists observing this scene could adopt any of several different perspectives in their efforts to understand it—behavioral, cognitive, biological, evolutionary, psychodynamic, and cultural. Each perspective would add to our understanding of these events.

How would a psychologist interpret this intriguing situation? The answer is, from many different perspectives—perspectives that cut across the three "grand issues" noted above (change versus stability, nature versus nurture, rationality versus irrationality). One, known as the *behavioral* perspective, would emphasize the overt actions occurring—the bullfighter's skilled performance, the bull's charges, the crowd's reactions. Another, the *cognitive* perspective, would focus on cognitive factors in this situation, such as the bullfighter's thoughts as the scene unfolds. What is going through her mind? What strategies does she plan? What does she think about killing the bull?

A third perspective would emphasize the *biological* factors that play a role in this situation. What are the emotions of the bullfighter as she faces the charging bull? What are the emotions of the crowd? What systems in her brain allow her to time her escapes so carefully that often she is literally inches from death? Closely related to this approach would be the *evolutionary* perspective, which would focus on such questions as whether the bull's tendency to charge moving, red objects is part of its inherited behavioral tendencies, and if so, what functions do this tendency serve. In other words, what evolutionary benefit does the bull gain from having these tendencies? The evolutionary perspective might ask whether choosing such a dangerous occupation reflects inherited tendencies for the bullfighter as well—perhaps a genetically determined desire for high levels of excitement, or a genetically determined desire for status, which gives high-status persons a wider choice among possible mates.

In contrast, a *developmental* perspective would focus on changes in behavior and cognitive processes that occur over the lifespan. Bullfighters, as you can probably guess, tend to be quite young: reflexes are fastest during youth, and the willingness to engage in high-risk, dangerous activities seems to be one that is stronger during the early part of life than during later phases. Will she continue her profession as she grows older? And do her plans concerning her career and future life play a role in her current performance (e.g., perhaps, if she is planning on marriage or children, she become more cautious). These are the kind of questions a developmental perspective would raise.

Yet another point of view that could be adopted by a psychologist observing this incident would focus on factors relating to hidden forces within the bullfighter's personality. This *psychodynamic* approach might focus on what aspects of the bullfighter's personality, and what motives—conscious or unconscious—played a role in her choice of this unusual and dangerous occupation.

Finally, a psychologist observing this situation could seek to understand it in terms of social or cultural factors. What is it about the young woman's culture that

TABLE 1.1	Major Perspectives in Modern Psychology
As shown here, psychology studies behavior from many different perspectives.	
Perspective	**Description**
Behavioral	Focuses on overt behavior
Cognitive	Focuses on cognitive processes such as memory, thought, reasoning
Biological	Focuses on the biological processes that underlie behavior
Evolutionary	Focuses on the possible role of evolved psychological mechanisms (inherited tendencies shaped by evolution) in human behavior
Developmental	Focuses on changes in behavior and cognitive processes over the life span
Psychodynamic	Focuses on the role of hidden, often unconscious processes (e.g., unconscious motives)
Cultural/Multicultural/Social	Focuses on the role of social and cultural factors and especially on differences between cultural, ethnic, gender, sexual preference, and racial groups

makes bullfighting so popular—and turns successful bullfighters into heroes? And why is it that in some countries the bull is killed at the end of the fight, while in others it is spared and returned to pasture? Interest in the effects of cultural and ethnic factors has recently become a major theme of modern psychology; in fact, this growing *multicultural perspective* is so important that we will consider it in detail in a later section (see Vazquez et al., 2006). For now, the main point to remember is this: Human behavior is extraordinarily complex and is influenced by many different factors. Thus, any aspect of behavior can be examined from many different perspectives. All these add to our understanding of behavior, so all will be represented throughout this book. (Table 1.1 summarizes these contrasting points of view or approaches.)

PSYCHOLOGY IN THE TWENTY-FIRST CENTURY: EXPANDING HORIZONS

Psychology is a tremendously diverse field. As shown in Table 1.2, psychologists specialize in many different aspects of behavior. As a result, there is always a lot going on and the field develops and changes in many ways at once. Among recent trends, however, three seem so important that they are worthy of special note. One is psychology's growing attention to the possible role of *evolution* in human behavior. The second is what we describe as the increasing "exportation" of psychology—a growing trend for other fields to use the principles and findings of psychology to help solve a wide range of practical problems. The third is psychol-

TABLE 1.2	Major Subfields of Psychology	

Psychologists specialize in studying many different aspects of behavior. The approximate percentage of all psychologists in each specialty is shown in this table; other subfields not listed separately make up the missing few percent.

Subfield	Description	Percentage
Clinical psychology	Studies diagnosis, causes, and treatment of mental disorders	43
Counseling psychology	Assists individuals in dealing with many personal problems that do not involve psychological disorders	10
Developmental psychology	Studies how people change physically, cognitively, and socially over the entire life span	5
Educational psychology	Studies all aspects of the educational process	6
Experimental psychology	Studies all basic psychological processes, including perception, learning, and motivation	14*
Cognitive psychology	Investigates all aspects of cognition—memory, thinking, reasoning, language, decision making, and so on	(Included under experimental)
Industrial/ organizational psychology	Studies all aspects of behavior in work settings	4
Psychobiology and evolutionary psychology	Investigates biological bases of behavior and the role of evolution in human behavior	1
Social psychology	Studies all aspects of social behavior and social thought—how we think about and interact with others	6

*Figure includes cognitive psychology.

ogy's increased attention to cultural and ethnic *diversity*, and adoption of a truly *multicultural perspective*.

Evolutionary Psychology: A New Perspective on "Human Nature"

Is there such a thing as "human nature"—a set of qualities or behaviors that define us as a unique species? Until about ten years ago, most psychologists would have expressed skepticism on this point. While they would certainly have agreed that our biological nature is, in part, inherited, many would have pointed to learning and the effects of experience rather than genes or evolution as the main sources of our behavior. In recent years, however, the pendulum of scientific opinion has swung in the opposite direction, and today most psychologists believe that genetic factors do play some role in many aspects of our behavior—everything from mate selection and mating strategies (e.g., why males express greater jealousy than females over sexual infidelity by their partners) through creativity and our desires for status and prestige (see Pinker, 1997).

One major reason for this shift in opinion is the development and rapid growth of the new field of **evolutionary psychology** (Buss, 1999, 2005). This new branch of psychology suggests that our species, like all others, has been subject to the process of biological evolution throughout its history, and that as a result of this process, we now possess a large number of *evolved psychological mechanisms* that help (or once helped) us to deal with important problems relating to survival. The theory of evolution, in its modern form, is quite complex, but basically it suggests that the members of any given species (including our own) show variation along many different dimension, and many of these variations can be passed on from one generation to the next. Over time, variations that help organisms survive and become parents of the next generation tend to become more common. This kind of change in the characteristics of a species over time is the concrete outcome of evolution.

Evolutionary psychology suggests that humans, like all other species on the planet, have always faced basic problems relating to survival: obtaining food, finding shelter, avoiding predators and other dangers, and combating disease. Over time, natural selection assured that variations that helped our ancestors to survive and to reproduce became increasingly common. Together, these inherited tendencies constitute our human nature, and often play an important role in shaping our behavior. Does this mean that our behavior is genetically determined and cannot be changed? Absolutely not! Rather, it suggests that as humans, we come equipped with a set of mechanisms that interact with the environment; it is this interaction that determines whether, to what extent, and in what form they are actually expressed (see Nelson & Demas, 2004). For instance, one evolved mechanism we possess is the ability to form calluses (hard patches of skin) on our hands and feet. Do we develop them? Only if we handle hard objects or walk on hard surfaces. If we spend our days turning the pages of books or walking on soft carpets, calluses never appear. Similarly, evolved psychological mechanisms provide only the *potential* for certain behaviors of tendencies to occur; whether they do or do not depends on external factors or experience. As for our ability to change, consider this: once we know that walking on hard surfaces will lead to the development of calluses on our feet, we can take steps to prevent them—for instance, wearing shoes with soft rubber soles or avoiding hard surfaces. So yes, evolutionary psychology suggests that our behavior is influenced by inherited mechanisms or tendencies, but *no*, it does *not* imply that it is determined solely by these mechanisms—far from it!

One more point that is sometimes misunderstood. The existence of evolved psychological mechanisms does *not* in any way imply that that our genes "force" us to act in certain ways, that we can't resist or change these impulses, or that our sole motivation in life is to reproduce. Rather, evolutionary psychology merely suggests that as humans, we come equipped with many mechanisms designed to help us survive in a complex and challenging world. These mechanisms are real, but they interact with the external environment and our experience, and leave tremendous room for individuality and change. Please note that evolutionary psychology is only one of many different perspectives in psychology, and we in no way wish to endorse it or emphasize it here. We describe it in some detail mainly because it has received a great deal of recent attention. (We'll consider the evolutionary approach again in Chapter 2, as part of our discussion of the biological bases of behavior.)

Evolutionary psychology: A new branch of psychology suggesting that because of evolution, humans possess a number of *evolved psychological mechanisms* that help (or once helped) us to deal with important problems relating to survival.

The Exportation of Psychology: From Science to Practice

Most people realize that several branches of psychology are *applied*—not only do they seek to acquire basic knowledge about human behavior, but they also attempt to put it to practical use. For instance, *clinical psychologists* help individuals deal with emotional and psychological problems, whereas *industrial/ organizational psychologists* focus on solving many practical problems relating to work (e.g., increasing motivation, evaluating employees' performance fairly and accurately). So, right from its beginnings, psychology has had a practical as well as scientific side. In recent years, however, application of psychology's knowledge about human behavior has expanded far beyond psychology itself. Many fields have found answers to some of their most important questions in the findings and principles of psychology and have begun to draw upon this knowledge to an increasing degree. In other words, as psychology has matured and become an ever-richer source of knowledge about human behavior, persons in other fields have recognized this fact and put it to good use. Please don't misunderstand: We are not referring here to people who are *not* trained psychologists but who try to use psychology anyway—for example, to design psychological tests, conduct therapy, or advise businesses about how to handle their employees. Rather, we are referring to much more legitimate uses of psychological knowledge, often with the help and guidance of trained psychologists who serve as "exporters" of the findings of their field. To mention just a couple of examples, in recent years, psychologists have helped anesthesiologists—doctors who specialize in putting patients to sleep safely before operations—to design equipment that greatly reduces the chance that patients will receive too much anesthetic and so be greatly harmed. Similarly, a growing number of psychologists have been working with colleagues in the field of business to help understand *entrepreneurship*—for instance, why some people but not others choose to become entrepreneurs, why some people but not others recognize opportunities for new products or services. With respect to this second question, recent findings indicate that part of the answer may involve *pattern recognition*—recognition of complex patterns of seemingly unrelated stimuli or events (Baron, 2006). Successful entrepreneurs are better at doing this than other people, and this helps them spot opportunities for new products or services. Pattern recognition is a basic kind of perception, and we'll discuss it again in Chapter 3. Since entrepreneurs create jobs and wealth not just for themselves for many other persons, too, obtaining answers to these questions is very important and can mean a better life for millions of people (see Figure 1.5, page 14).

This is just one example of what we mean by the "exportation" of psychology: many others exist, too, and we will highlight them throughout the text. The main point is simply this: in the twenty-first century, recognition of the practical as well as scientific value of psychology has increased greatly, with beneficial effects that few people would have predicted just two or three decades ago.

Growing Recognition of Diversity and Commitment to a Multicultural Perspective

There is no doubt that the United States and many other countries are undergoing a major social and cultural transformation. Recent censuses indicate that in the United States, the proportion of people who are of European descent continues to drop, while that of other groups continues to rise. At present, about 65 percent of the population identifies itself as being of European heritage (what was formerly called "white"), while fully 35 percent identifies itself as belonging to some other group (12 percent African American, 4.5 percent American Indian, 14 percent Hispanic, 4.5 percent Asian/Pacific Islander, and 7 percent some other group). This represents a tremendous change from the 1960s, when approximately 90 percent of the population was of European descent. Indeed, in several states (e.g.,

FIGURE 1.5
Studying the Psychology of Entrepreneurs: An Example of the "Exportation" of Psychology
Recently, a growing number of psychologists have turned the principles and findings of their field to the task of studying entrepreneurs. This research may yield important social benefits because entrepreneurs do not only create wealth for themselves: they also create good jobs for thousands of people.

California, New Mexico, Texas, Arizona), persons of European heritage are no longer a majority. In response to these tremendous shifts, psychologists have increasingly recognized the importance of taking cultural factors and differences into careful account in everything they do—teaching, research, counseling, and therapy.

Taking careful account of this fact, the American Psychological Association and Association for Psychological Science both have policies and guidelines designed to help psychologists to take account of diversity in all their professional activities. What does this mean? In essence, that psychologists should be aware of and sensitive to the fact that individuals' cultural, ethnic, and racial heritage often play key roles in their self-identity, and that this, in turn, can exert important effects on their behavior. This is in sharp contrast to the point of view that prevailed in the past, which suggested that cultural, ethnic, and gender differences are relatively unimportant. In contrast to that earlier and now discredited perspective, psychologists currently believe that such differences are *very* important, and must be taken carefully into account in our efforts to understand human behavior. As a result, psychology now adopts a **multicultural perspective**—one that carefully and clearly recognizes the potential importance of gender, age, ethnicity, sexual orientation, disability, socioeconomic status, religious orientation, and many other social and cultural dimensions.

This perspective has lead to major changes in the way psychologists teach, interact with clients, and conduct research (see Figure 1.6). For example, recent studies conducted by psychologists have focused on ethnic and cultural differences in everything from the use of numbers (Dingfelder, 2005) through cultural differences in binge drinking (Luczak, 2001), and ethnic differences in optimism and pessimism (Chang & Asakawa, 2003). In short, modern psychology has increasingly adopted a truly multicultural perspective, and this theme—and themes related to it—will be reflected throughout this book.

In addition, special efforts have been begun to increase the proportion of minority students in graduate programs in psychology, and so to increase diversity among psychologists. While some progress has been made (see Figure 1.7), much more change is necessary to assure that psychology not only studies diversity, but that it also reflects it in the backgrounds of psychologists!

Multicultural perspective:
A perspective that clearly recognizes the potential importance of gender, age, ethnicity, sexual orientation, disability, socioeconomic status, religious orientation, and many other social and cultural dimensions.

FIGURE 1.6
A Multicultural Perspective: A Guiding Theme of Modern Psychology
The United States and many other countries have become much more ethnically and culturally diverse in recent decades. As a result, psychologists build awareness of such diversity into everything they do—teaching, research, counseling, and therapy.

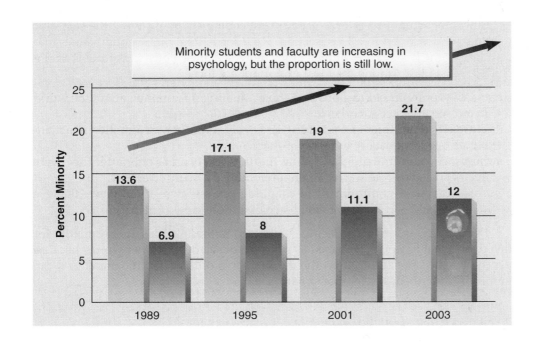

FIGURE 1.7
Diversity in Psychology Itself
The proportion of graduate students and faculty in psychology who come from minority groups is increasing, but there is still a long way to go. *Source:* Based on data in Maton et al., 2006.

KEY QUESTIONS

- What is the definition of psychology as it exists today?
- What ideas in philosophy and several branches of science (biology, physiology, computer science, physics) have contributed to the form and scope of modern psychology?
- What are the three "grand issues" about behavior addressed by psychology?
- What are the major perspectives adopted by psychologists and how do they differ?
- What is evolutionary psychology, and how does it contribute to our understanding of human behavior?
- What do the authors mean when they speak of "the exportation" of psychology?
- What is the multicultural perspective, and what role does it play in the activities of modern psychologists?

PSYCHOLOGY AND THE SCIENTIFIC METHOD

Remember the group of people we described earlier in this chapter as "skeptics"—people who believe that psychology is nothing more than "common sense"? Here's where we respond in detail to their doubts. In essence, our answer is simple: psychology is far more than common sense because the knowledge it provides rests firmly on the *scientific method*. Let's take a closer look at this method to see why it makes the knowledge gathered by psychologists much more valid and useful than is common sense.

The Scientific Method: Its Basic Nature

To many people, the term *science* conjures up images of people in white coats working around complex equipment in impressive laboratories. On the basis of such images, they then conclude that the word *science* applies only to fields such as chemistry, physics, and biology. Actually, this term simply refers to a special approach for acquiring knowledge—an approach involving the use of several key values or standards. Viewed in this light, the phrase *scientific method* means using these methods and adopting these values in efforts to study virtually *any* topic, including human behavior and human cognition. It is adoption of the scientific method that makes psychology a science—and that makes the information it acquires so valuable.

Since the actual procedures used by psychologists in applying the scientific method are described in a later section, we'll focus here on essential values and standards—the basic "rules of the game" by which all scientists, psychologists included, must play. Among the most important are these:

Accuracy: A commitment to gathering and evaluating information about the world in as careful, precise, and error-free a manner as possible.

Objectivity: A commitment to obtaining and evaluating such information in a manner as free from bias as humanly possible.

Skepticism: A commitment to accepting findings as accurate only after they have been verified over and over again, preferably by many scientists.

Open-mindedness: A commitment to changing one's views—even views that are strongly held—in the face of evidence that these views are inaccurate.

Psychology, as a field, is deeply committed to these values. It is primarily for this reason that it can be described as a branch of science. In other words, because psychology accepts and follows the requirements of the scientific method, it can indeed be described as scientific in nature.

Advantages of the Scientific Method: Why Common Sense Often Leads Us Astray

Earlier, we noted that knowledge gathered by means of the scientific method is superior, in several ways, to conclusions based upon common sense. Here, we'll explain why this is so. Two factors are most important in this respect. First, knowledge about behavior based on common sense is often inconsistent and contradictory. Consider the following statement: "Absence makes the heart grow fonder." Do you agree? Is it true that when people are separated they miss each other and so experience even stronger feelings of attraction? Perhaps, but what about *this* statement: "Out of sight, out of mind." It suggests exactly the opposite. Or how about this pair of statements: "Birds of a feather flock together" (people who are similar like each other) and "Opposites attract." We could continue, but by now you probably see the point: common sense is often an unreliable guide to human behavior.

This is not the only reason why we must be wary of common sense, however; another relates to the fact that, unlike Mr. Spock of *Star Trek* fame, we are *not* perfect information-processing machines. On the contrary, echoing the "rationality versus irrationality" theme mentioned earlier, our thinking is subject to many forms of error that can lead us badly astray. While these errors often save us mental effort and are generally helpful to us, they suggest the need for caution in relying on intuition or common sense when trying to understand human behavior. What are these errors like? We'll examine them in detail in later chapters, but let's take a brief look at some of the most important ones here.

■ **The confirmation bias: The tendency to verify our own views.**

If you are like most people, you prefer to have your views confirmed rather than refuted. Consider what this means when we attempt to use informal observation as a source of knowledge about human behavior. Since we prefer to have our views confirmed, we tend to notice and remember mainly information that lends support to these views—information that confirms what we already believe. This tendency, known as the **confirmation bias**, is very strong (see Johnson & Eagly, 1989), and when it operates, it places us in a kind of closed system where only evidence that confirms our existing beliefs is noticed, remembered, or accepted. Clearly, this is one tendency that can lead to error in our efforts to understand others and ourselves.

■ **The availability heuristic: Emphasizing what comes to mind first or more readily.**

Quick: are there more words in English that start with the letter *k* (e.g., king) or more words in which *k* is the third letter (e.g., awkward)? If you answered, "More words that begin with *k*," you are like most people. Actually, though, this answer is wrong—more words have the letter *k* in the third position. What's responsible for this type of error? A mental shortcut known as the **availability heuristic.** This shortcut, which is designed to save us mental effort, suggests that the easier it is to bring something to mind, or the more information we can think of about it, the greater its impact on subsequent decisions or judgments. In general, this tendency makes sense—when we can bring information about something to mind easily, it often *is* important. But the availability heuristic can also lead us into error. Why? Because sometimes what we can bring to mind most readily isn't especially important; it's just highly memorable because it is dramatic or unusual (see Rothman & Hardin, 1997). For instance, because airplane crashes are more dramatic and easier to remember than automobile accidents, many people believe that the chances of being killed in a plane are higher than those of being killed while in a car—a conclusion that is totally false. Judgments based on common sense or intuition are often strongly influenced by the availability heuristic, and they are often untrustworthy for this reason.

Confirmation bias:
The tendency to notice and remember primarily information that lends support to our views.

Availability heuristic:
A mental shortcut suggesting that the easier it is to bring something to mind, the more frequent or important it is.

"Stanley, we need to talk, so please don't interrupt."

FIGURE 1.8
Sunk Costs: Getting Trapped in Bad Decisions
Often, once we have made a decision, we have a strong tendency to stick with it, even if it is producing negative outcomes. This is known as *sunk costs* (or *escalation of commitment*) and may be one reason why many persons stick with decisions that are very bad ones, even in the face of mounting evidence that the decisions are poor. For instance, why do the two people shown here remain in this relationship, even though it does not seem to be working very well? Perhaps because of sunk costs.
Source: © The New Yorker Collection 2001 Robert Weber from cartoonbank.com. All Rights Reserved.

■ **Getting trapped in bad decisions: The dangers of "sunk costs."**

When one of us (Robert Baron) was a young associate professor, he owned a car that almost drove him to distraction. It was a powder-blue Toyota, and although Toyotas are famous for being reliable, this one was nothing but trouble. First it was engine problems; then the brakes; next the clutch. Finally, to add insult to injury, it began to rust—to the point where the doors had more metal patch than metal in them! When the problems first started, it made sense to repair them. After a while, though, it became clear that this car was a true lemon. The rational thing to do was simple: get rid of it. But Baron didn't do that; instead, he continued to pour more and more money into the car. Why? Partly because of a cognitive "trap" known as *sunk costs*. This refers to the fact that once we make a decision, we find it very hard to reverse it, even if it becomes increasingly clear that it was a bad one. The same mental trap occurs when people buy a stock and then fail to sell it as it continues to go down in value, or when they stay in bad relationships that are harmful to their mental health (see Figure 1.8). Why do we get trapped in this way? Partly because it is so hard to admit we made a mistake, and partly because we hope to make up for our past losses (the stock *will* go up; the car *will* become more reliable; the relationships will get better). The result? We throw good money, effort, or love after bad, right to the bitter end. Rational? Hardly!

We could continue because there are many other aspects of our thinking that can lead us astray. The main point, though, is clear: Because our thinking is subject to such potential sources of bias, we can't rely on informal observation or common sense as a basis for drawing valid conclusions about human behavior. We are on much firmer ground if we employ the scientific method, which is specifically designed to reduce such potential sources of error. By adopting the scientific method, therefore, psychologists vastly increase the probability that their efforts to attain valid information about human behavior will succeed. It is this commitment to the scientific method, more than anything else, that sets psychology apart from other efforts to understand human behavior, and makes its findings so valuable from the perspective of enhancing human welfare.

KEY QUESTIONS

- Why can psychology be viewed as a branch of science?
- What values are central to the scientific method?
- Why is common sense such an uncertain guide to human behavior?
- What are confirmation bias, availability heuristic, and sunk costs, and what role do they play in our efforts to understand human behavior?

The Scientific Method in Everyday Life: The Benefits of Critical Thinking

During an interview (June 9, 2005), Tom Cruise the movie actor was asked to comment on the fact that some people refer to psychiatry (note: *not* psychology) as a

"Nazi science." Here's what he said: *"Well, look at the history. Jung was an editor for the Nazi papers during World War II. Look at the experimentation the Nazis did with electric shock and drugging. Look at the drug methadone. That was originally called Adolophine. It was named after Adolf Hitler."*

What do you think of his reasoning? Does it make sense? Are you persuaded by his "arguments"? Even if you are a Tom Cruise fan, we doubt that you are persuaded, and for good reason. If you think carefully about his comments, you will readily see that they are largely based on opinion and rest on assumptions that are uncertain at best—and probably downright questionable. Did Carl Jung (a famous psychiatrist) really edit Nazi newspapers? And even if he did, does this constitute proof—as Cruise seems to imply—that Jung actually had something to do with the evil experiments the Nazis performed with electric shock and worse? And what about the drug methadone, which is used to treat alcoholism? Do you accept the view that it was originally named after Hitler?

If you see problems with these statements and are reluctant to accept them as a basis for drawing your own conclusions about psychiatry, methadone, or anything else, you are showing the kind of caution, skepticism, and concern with objectivity and evidence that are the basis for the scientific method—and for a kind of thinking known as **critical thinking**. Many definitions of critical thinking exist, but we feel the following one is very useful: *"Critical thinking is the use of those cognitive skills or strategies that increase the probability of a desirable outcome. It is used to described thinking that is purposeful, reasoned, and goal-directed—the kind of thinking involved in solving problems, formulating inferences . . . and making decisions when the thinker is using skills that are thoughtful and effective for the particular context . . ."* (Halpern, 2003).

In other words, critical thinking examines all claims and assumptions, carefully evaluates existing evidence, and cautiously assesses all conclusions. To the extent we use it, we become aware of the assumptions underlying information and arguments presented to us, judge the credibility of the source of these arguments, recognize efforts at persuasion when they occur, and carefully examine the validity of all conclusions. This may sound a little abstract, so here is what critical thinking involves in actual practice—a set of guidelines anyone can follow to think critically:

1. *Never jump to conclusions; gather as much information as you can before making up your mind about any issue.*
2. *Keep an open mind; don't let your existing views blind you to new information or conclusions.*
3. *Always ask "How?" as in "How was the evidence obtained?"*
4. *Be skeptical; always wonder about* why *someone is making an argument, offering a conclusion, or trying to persuade you.*
5. *Never be stampeded into accepting some view because others accept it.*
6. *Be aware that your own emotions can strongly influence your thinking, and try to hold such effects to a minimum.*

We, like many other psychologists, believe that critical thinking is very important, and want to encourage you to develop the habit of using it whenever and wherever you can. To help in this respect, we present specific critical thinking questions throughout the book, and special critical thinking exercises at the end of each chapter. Please give these materials careful attention, because although they involve some effort, it is effort very well spent, and you will soon be able to see the change in your own thinking in many contexts. Skill in critical thinking is one of the "extras" we had in mind when we claimed that you would learn much more from this book than a mere collection of interesting facts. In addition, you will sharpen your critical thinking skills, and be able to think more carefully, cautiously, and systematically about all aspects of human behavior—your own and that of others. That will be one of the key benefits you'll take away with you from your first encounter with psychology.

Critical thinking:
Thinking that is purposeful, reasoned, and goal-directed—the kind of thinking involved in solving problems, formulating inferences when the thinker is using skills that are thoughtful and effective for the particular context.

KEY QUESTIONS

- What is critical thinking?
- What role does it play in psychology?
- How can you use it in everyday life?

RESEARCH METHODS IN PSYCHOLOGY: HOW PSYCHOLOGISTS ANSWER QUESTIONS ABOUT BEHAVIOR

Now that we've explained what modern psychology is and have described the scientific method and its relation to critical thinking, it's time to turn to another key issue: How do psychologists actually perform the task of adding to our knowledge about human behavior? You'll soon see how, through the use of three basic procedures: *observation*, *correlation*, and *experimentation*.

Observation: Describing the World around Us

One basic technique for studying behavior, or any other aspects of the world around us, involves carefully observing it as it occurs. Such observation is not the kind of informal activity that we practice from childhood on. Rather, in science, it is **systematic observation** accompanied by *careful, accurate measurement*. One way in which psychologists use systematic observation is in *case studies*—an approach in which one or perhaps a few persons are studied carefully, often over long periods of time. Several famous psychologists have used this method. For instance, Sigmund Freud, one of the most famous psychologists of all time (although he was trained as a medical doctor), used a small number of cases as the basis for his famous theories of personality and mental illness. (We'll discuss these in Chapter 12.)

Is the **case method** really useful? In the hands of talented researchers, it does seem potentially useful. Moreover, when the behavior involved is unusual, the case method can sometimes be quite revealing, as we'll see in our discussion of mental disorders in Chapter 11. However, this method suffers from several important drawbacks. First, since all humans are unique, it is difficult to draw conclusions that can be generalized to all other people. Second, because researchers using the case method often have repeated contact with the people they study, there is the real risk that they will become emotionally involved with these people and so lose their scientific objectivity, at least to a degree. Because of such drawbacks, the case method is not widely used by psychologists today, although it *is* widely used in several fields such as management, which studies individual companies instead of individual people.

Systematic observation is also sometimes used in another, and very different way: to study behavior in the locations where it normally occurs. This approach is known as **naturalistic observation,** and it has been used to study a very wide range of behaviors by observing them in the locations and settings where they normally occur. For instance, this method has been used to study how and when people touch each other in public places. This was done by observing how people touch one another in airports, shopping malls, at sports events, and on the beach. Results, although far from conclusive (observational studies are not designed to reach that goal), offered important insights into such questions as who touches whom, how, and when (e.g., Argyle, 1988). In other research, naturalistic observation has been used to observe how alcohol changes the behavior of people in bars; does it make them more aggressive? More sensitive to real or imaginary "slights" from others? More receptive to romantic advances? To find out, psychologists (e.g., Murdoch & Pihl, 1988) have observed the number of drinks people consume and their reactions to others—for instance, do they get into arguments or fights

Systematic observation: A basic method of science in which the natural world, or various events or processes in it, are observed and measured in a very careful manner.

Case method: A method of research in which detailed information about individuals is used to develop general principles about behavior.

Naturalistic observation: A research method in which behavior is studied in the settings where it usually occurs.

FIGURE 1.9
The Survey Method in Action
The survey method can be used to measure people's views on almost any topic—from politics to the use of cell phones.

with them? As you can see, naturalistic observation can indeed provide important insights into behavior as it naturally occurs, in a wide range of settings. But do remember that it is useful mainly for formulating new ideas about some form of behavior—not for testing these ideas in a conclusive scientific way.

A third form of systematic observation—and one that is used much more frequently by modern psychologists—is the **survey method.** Instead of focusing in detail on a small number of people, researchers using this method obtain a very limited sample of behavior from large numbers of individuals, usually through their responses to questionnaires (surveys). Surveys are used for many purposes—to measure attitudes toward specific issues, voting preferences, and consumer reactions to new products, to mention just a few. Surveys can also be repeated over long periods of time to track changes in public opinion or other aspects of behavior. For instance, surveys of *job satisfaction*—individuals; attitudes toward their jobs—have continued for more than forty years. Similarly, changing patterns of sexual behavior have been tracked by the Kinsey Institute since the 1940s.

The survey method offers several advantages. Information can be gathered quickly and efficiently from many thousands of people. Further, since surveys can be constructed quickly, public opinion on new issues can be obtained almost as soon as the issues arise. For instance, suppose you wanted to find out how people feel about the use of cell phones in such public places as restaurants and theaters. Information on this topic could be gathered quickly—and accurately—by means of the survey method (see Figure 1.9). To be useful as a research tool, however, surveys must meet certain requirements. First, if the goal is to predict some event (for example, the outcome of an election), great care must be devoted to the issue of **sampling**—how the people who will participate in the survey are selected. Unless these people are representative of the larger population about which predictions will be made, serious errors can result.

Another issue deserving careful attention is the way in which the surveys are worded. Even changing a single word in a question can sometimes shift the meaning, and strongly influence the results. For example, recently, the governor of the state where we live reduced the number of state employees in the capital by 450. How did people react to these reductions? In one poll they were asked to indicate how they felt about the governor's "slashing" of the workforce, while in another they were asked to indicate how they felt about the governor's "pruning" of the

Survey method:
A research method in which large numbers of people answer questions about aspects of their views or their behavior.

Sampling:
With respect to the survey method, refers to the methods used to select persons who respond to the survey.

workforce. You can guess the results: the poll that used the word "slashing" indicated that the public was strongly against this action, while the one that used the word "pruning" produced the opposite result.

In sum, the survey method can be a useful approach for studying some aspects of human behavior, but the results obtained are accurate only to the extent that issues relating to sampling and wording are carefully addressed.

Correlation: The Search for Relationships

At various times, you have probably noticed that some events appear to be related to each other: as one changes, the other appears to change, too. For instance, you have probably observed that as people grow older, they often seem to gain weight; that when interest rates drop, the stock market rises; and that the older people are, the more conservative they tend to be in their political views. When such relationships between events exist, they are said to be *correlated* with each other (or that a *correlation* between them exists). This means that as one changes, the other tends to change, too. Psychologists and other scientists refer to aspects of the natural world that can take different values as *variables*, so from now on, that's the term we'll use.

From the point of view of science, the existence of a correlation between two variables can be very useful, because when a correlation exists, it is possible to predict one variable from information about one or more other variables. The ability to make such *predictions* is one important goal of science, and psychologists often attempt to make predictions about human behavior. To the extent predictions can be made accurately, important benefits follow. For instance, consider how useful it would be if we could predict from current information such future outcomes as a person's success in school or in various occupations, effectiveness as a parent, length of life, or likelihood of developing a serious mental disorder. For example, psychologists have often been asked by corporations to help predict which employees will make first-rate executives (Stambor, 2006). By drawing on information about several variables—the way in which they make decisions, their ability to set and reach goals, their "political savvy"—these psychologists are able to make accurate predictions. Since choosing the wrong person for a top-level job can be costly, this use of correlation has important practical value.

The occurrence of correlations between variables allows us to make such predictions. In fact, the stronger such correlations are, the more accurate the predictions that can be made. These facts constitute the basis for an important method of research—the **correlational method**. In this approach, psychologists or other scientists attempt to determine whether, and to what extent, variables are related to each other. This involves making careful observations of each variable and then performing statistical analyses to determine whether and to what extent the variables are correlated—to what extent changes in one are related to changes in the other. Correlations range from −1.00 to +1.00, and the more they depart from zero, the stronger the correlation. For example, a correlation of −.63 is stronger than one of +.31. Positive correlations indicate that as one variable increases the other increases, too. For instance, the greater the number of hours students study for their psychology tests, the higher their grades tend to be. Negative correlations indicate that as one variable increase, the other decreases. For example, the less satisfied people are with their jobs, the more likely they are to search for another one and to leave. As job satisfaction decreases, in other words, quitting increases. Now, let's examine a concrete example of how psychologists actually use the correlational method.

■ The correlational method of research: an example.

Suppose that a psychologist wants to study the following, intriguing question: What happens when individuals attempt to conceal their true feelings—their real emotions? That most of us do this often is apparent; for various reasons, we want to keep our feelings to ourselves and not let others know them. For instance, in

Correlational method of research:
A method in which researchers attempt to determine whether, and to what extent, different variables are related to each other.

stressful situations, most people want to appear "cool and calm." In situations in which a good friend asks us for our reaction to something they have just purchased, we may pretend to like it even if we don't, just to spare their feelings. That people can do a good job of concealing their true feelings is also clear; in fact, some individuals are so good at hiding their feelings that they make this the basis of their careers. Expert salespersons, for instance, are highly accomplished in hiding their own feelings while they pay careful attention to the feelings of customers.

But what are the effects of concealing one's feelings from others? The benefits of doing this successfully are obvious, but are there costs, too? Suppose that the psychologist doing this research predicts that when individuals hide or suppress their emotions, this consumes some of their "cognitive resources," thus leaving less for other tasks. Since our cognitive resources are limited (i.e., we can pay careful attention to only one task at a time), an interesting prediction follows: the more people suppress their emotions (conceal them from others) the worse they will do on other tasks. For instance, they will remember less of what other people say, and may also be less successful in "connecting" with them—in forming relationships with them. After all, they are too busy hiding their own feelings to pay careful attention to the people they meet or what these people say. To test this prediction (or **hypothesis**, which is an untested or unverified prediction), the psychologist asks individuals to indicate how often they hide their own emotions from others (three or more times a day; once a day; once a week; once a month), and also asks them how often they have problems remembering things other people have told them (every day; once a week; once a month, etc.). If a correlation occurs between these two variables, this would provide evidence for the psychologist's hypothesis: the more individuals suppress their emotions or feelings, the worse their memory for information presented to them by other people. (In this case, the correlation would be *negative*—as one variable increases, the other decreases.)

So far, so good. But watch out, for we are approaching a real danger zone—one in which many people seem to forget about the principles of critical thinking we described earlier. On the basis of the finding that as the amount of emotional suppression increases memory declines, many people would jump to the following conclusion: Suppressing one's emotions or feelings *causes* reductions in memory. This seems to make sense, but in fact, such conclusions would *not* be justified, because correlational research does not, by itself, provide strong or direct evidence about cause-and-effect relationships. Indeed, this is one of the major drawbacks of such research. In this case, we have found that as emotional suppression increases, memory declines, *but we do not know whether this effect stems from engaging in emotional suppression or from other factors.*

For instance, it is quite possible that the more people engage in emotional suppression, the more anxious or nervous they are. It could be these factors, not emotional suppression, that interfere with memory. In other words, memory suffers not because of the act of suppressing one's emotions, but because of other factors that are related to emotional suppression but that are not identical with it. Here's another example—one you may well have observed for yourself. Suppose it is found that the less hair men have on their head, the higher their income. (These two variables are correlated.) Does this mean that hair loss causes high incomes? Perhaps. But it is much more likely that both hair loss and income are related to a third factor—*age*. The older men are, the less hair they tend to have, but the higher their incomes because they have been working longer (see Figure 1.10, page 24). Because correlational research cannot resolve the issue of cause-and-effect, it is useful, but not as revealing as we might wish. For this reason, psychologists often use another research method, to which we'll now turn.

Hypothesis:
A testable prediction derived from a theory.

FIGURE 1.10
Correlation and Causation: Why They Are *Not* the Same
The less hair men have on their heads, the higher their income tends to be. Does this mean that hair loss causes men to earn more money? Hardly! It is much more likely that both hair loss and income are related to a third factor that underlies both: *age*.

KEY QUESTIONS

- What is naturalistic observation?
- What is the correlational method of research and how do psychologists use it?
- Why are even strong correlations between variables *not* evidence that changes in one cause changes in the other?

The Experimental Method: Knowledge through Systematic Intervention

The method we just mentioned—the one preferred by most psychologists—is known as **experimentation** or the **experimental method**, and it involves a strategy centering around intervention—making changes in the natural world to see what effects, if any, these changes produce. Specifically, the scientist systematically changes one variable, and the effects of these changes on one or more other variables are carefully measured. If changes in one variable produce changes in one or more other variables (and if additional conditions that we'll consider below are also met), it is then possible to conclude with reasonable certainty that there is indeed a causal relationship between these variables—that changes in one variable do indeed *cause* changes in the other. Because the experimental method is so valuable in answering this kind of question, it is frequently the method of choice in psychology, just as it is in many other fields. But bear in mind that there is no single "best" method of research; rather, psychologists choose the method that is most appropriate for studying a given topic and one that is consistent with practical and ethical constraints we'll soon consider.

■ **Experimentation: Its basic nature.**

In its most basic form, the experimental method in psychology involves two key steps: (1) the presence or strength of some variable believed to affect behavior is systematically altered, and (2) the effects of such alterations (if any) are carefully measured. The logic behind these steps is this: If the variable that is systematically changed actually influences some aspect of behavior, then individuals exposed to different levels or amounts of it should differ in their behavior. For instance, expo-

Experimentation
(the experimental method of research):
A method in which researchers systematically alter one or more variables to determine whether such changes influence some aspect of behavior.

sure to a low amount of the variable should result in one level of behavior, while exposure to a higher amount should result in a different level, and so on.

The factor systematically varied by the researcher is termed the **independent variable**, while the aspect of behavior is termed the **dependent variable**. In a simple experiment, then, different groups of participants are exposed to contrasting levels of the independent variable (such as low, moderate, high). The researcher then carefully measures their behavior to determine whether it does differ depending on the level of the independent variable to which research participants are exposed.

To illustrate the basic nature of experimentation, let's return to the possible effects of emotional suppression on memory discussed earlier. One way in which a psychologist could study this topic through the experimental method is as follows. First, the psychologist would have volunteers come to his laboratory and once there, would have them interact in pairs, making sure that the members of each pair do not already know each other. Some participants in the study would be asked to suppress their own emotions during this meeting, that is, they would be told to try to conceal their feelings from their partner during this meeting. Others would not be told to do this. Videotapes of the participants would be made to see whether they actually followed these instructions. (If they do, then persons told to suppress their emotions should show few if any changes in their facial expressions).

During the meetings between the two strangers, each would be given a script instructing them to present certain kinds of information to their partner (e.g., where they grew up, their current job or college major, the number of brothers and sisters they have, etc.). Then later, after the meeting is over, both groups of participants—those told to suppress their emotions and those not told to do this— would be tested for their memory of this information. If the people asked to suppress their emotions actually remember *less*, this would be evidence for the hypothesis that emotional suppression does interfere with memory. In this case, since emotional suppression was a variable in the study (some people were told to engage in it while others were not) the findings would also point to the conclusion that emotional suppression does indeed interfere with memory—in other words, when we suppress our own feelings so that others can't see them, this may cause reductions in our memory for what they say or do. This conclusion would only be tentative, though, unless two other conditions we will now describe were also met.

■ Experimentation: Two requirements for its success.

First, in order to provide to provide clear information on cause-and-effect relationships, an experiment must include **random assignment of participants to conditions**. This means that all participants in an experiment must have an equal chance of being exposed to each level of the independent variable. (In this case, they must have an equal chance of being told to suppress their own emotions or not being told to do this.) The reason for this rule is simple: If participants are *not* randomly assigned to each condition, it may later be impossible to tell whether differences in their behavior stem from differences they brought with them to the study, from the effects of the independent variable, or both.

Imagine that in the study on emotion suppression just described, all the people asked to suppress their emotions have just come from a long physical education class and are totally worn out. The people not told to suppress emotions, in contrast, came from regular classes that did not involve any physical exercise. Now, assume that those told to suppress their emotions show reduced memory. Is this because they suppressed their emotions, or simply because they are very tired? We can't tell. If, in contrast, these two groups of participants had been randomly assigned to each condition, a difference between the conditions *would* be revealing: it would suggest that suppressing one's emotions does interfere with memory.

The second condition essential for successful experimentation is this: To as great a degree as possible, all factors *other* than the independent variable that might also affect participants' behavior must be held constant. To see why this is so, consider what would happen in the study on memory suppression if those told to

Independent variable:
The variable that is systematically changed in an experiment.

Dependent variable:
The variable that is measured in an experiment.

Random assignment of participants to experimental conditions:
Assuring that all research participants have an equal chance of being exposed to each level of the independent variable (that is, of being assigned to each experimental condition).

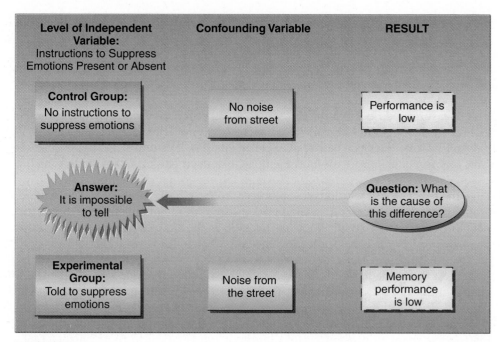

FIGURE 1.11
Confounding of Variables: A Fatal Flaw in Experimentation
In the experiment illustrated here, instruction to suppress one's emotions (the independent variable) is confounded with another variable—*noise from the street.* As a result of this confounding, it is impossible to tell whether any differences between the behavior of participants in these two conditions (control, experimental) stem from the independent variable, the confounding variable, or both.

Confounded (confounding):
Occurs when factors other than the independent variable in an experiment are permitted to vary across experimental conditions. When confounding occurs, it is impossible to determine whether changes in a dependent variable stem from the effects of the independent variable or from other, confounding variables.

suppress their feelings work in a room where there is loud construction noise from outside. Those not told to suppress their emotions, in contrast, work in a quiet room. Again, suppose the results indicate that those persons told to suppress their emotions later show poorer memory. Why? Again, we can't tell because the independent variable (instructions to suppress emotions) is **confounded** with another variable: the presence of noise from the street. So to the extent variables other than the independent variable are permitted to change in an experiment, the value of the study may be greatly reduced or even totally eliminated (see Figure 1.11).

When these two conditions are met, however, experimentation is highly effective and is, in fact, the crown jewel among psychology's research methods. Why, then, isn't it the only method used by psychologists? One reason is that the other methods do indeed offer several important advantages (e.g., the vast amount of information that can be collected quickly through the survey method; the high generalizability provided by **naturalistic observation**). Another is that, in many cases, practical and ethical constraints prevent some psychologists from using experimentation. For instance, suppose that 5 percent of all people asked to suppress their emotions are found to suffer harmful effects as a result of following these instructions—for instance, long-lasting reductions in memory. Could the psychologist conduct the experiment described above? No, because it would be on *very* shaky ethical grounds; there would be a risk of doing real harm to some participants. Admittedly, this is a far-fetched case, and it is very unlikely that anyone participating in this study would actually suffer any harmful outcomes. But the point is still clear: although experimentation is a powerful tool, it cannot be used to investigate all questions about behavior. In particular, it can't be used when exposing participants to systematic variations on one or more variables might put their health or welfare at risk. See Table 1.3 for an overview of the advantages and disadvantages of all the research methods described in this section.

TABLE 1.3   Various Research Methods: Advantages and Disadvantages

As shown here, psychologists use several different research methods. Each offers a mixture of advantages and disadvantages.

Method	Description	Advantages	Disadvantages
Systematic observation	Systematic study of behavior in natural settings	Behavior is observed in the settings where it normally occurs	Cannot be used to establish cause-and-effect relationships; often costly and difficult to perform
Case method	Detailed study of a small number of persons	Detailed information is gathered; individuals can be studied for long periods of time	Generalizability of results is uncertain; objectivity of researcher may be compromised
Surveys	Large numbers of persons are asked questions about their attitudes or views	Large amount of information can be acquired quickly; accurate predictions of large-scale trends can sometimes be made	Generalizability may be questionable unless persons surveyed are a representative sample of a larger population
Correlational research	Researchers measure two or more variables to determine if they are related in any way	Large amount of information can be gathered quickly; can be used in field as well as laboratory settings	Difficult to establish cause-and-effect relationships
Experimentation	The presence or strength of one or more variables is varied	Cause-and-effect relationships can be established; precise control can be exerted over other, potentially confounding variables	Results can be subject to several sources of bias (e.g., experimenter effects); generalizability can be doubtful if behavior is observed under highly artificial conditions

KEY POINTS

- What is the basic nature of experimentation?
- Why is random assignment of participants to conditions required in experiments?
- What is confounding of variables in an experiment?

PSYCHOLOGY: WHAT'S IN IT FOR YOU?

Why are you taking this course? When we ask our own students this question, they give us many different answers, including some that are quite routine: "It's required," or "I thought it might be interesting." But others provide answers indicating that they expect quite a lot from their first exposure to psychology. Some talk about gaining *self-insight*: "I want to understand myself better, and I think psychology can help." Others add that this enhanced insight, in turn, will make them happier, better-adjusted persons. Another group of students mentions what we term *enhanced life skills*—an improved ability to get along with other people (family, friends, romantic partners) and to deal with a wide range of everyday life situations (everything from raising children to resisting sales pressure). And a third group talks about their *careers*: they believe that psychology can help them to attain success (see Figure 1.12, page 28).

Are these reasonable goals? Will your first course in psychology, and this book, help you to gain self-insight and acquire useful life and career-related skills? We believe—fervently!—that it will. Psychology, in an important sense, has a dual

FIGURE 1.12
Enhanced Life and Career Skills: A Potential Benefit of Exposure to Psychology
Will learning about psychology equip you with skills that can contribute to your personal happiness and to success in your career? We believe the answer is: "Yes!"

nature: it is scientific in nature, and obtains its knowledge and findings through the scientific method. At the same time, though, it is strongly oriented toward application. As a result, it offers knowledge, principles, and information you can put to practical use in your own life *once you know and understand them*. And that is a major theme of this text; we want to help you (1) to understand the key findings and principles of modern psychology, so we will work hard to present these in as accurate, understandable, and up-to-date a manner as we can; and (2) to help you *apply* this knowledge to your own life—to acquire enhanced self-insight and specific, beneficial life and career skills.

In every chapter and every discussion, therefore, we will first summarize the key findings and principles obtained through systematic research and then explain what these findings mean to you and how, potentially, you can use them. Most texts do this to some extent, but we plan to carry such efforts further by emphasizing the fact that *every* branch of psychology and virtually every line of research can contribute to the quality and richness of your life. Here are a few examples of what we mean— ways in which psychology can help answer practical questions relating to your own life.

Perception (Chapter 3): How can you protect your own hearing from damage in today's noisy world?

Consciousness (Chapter 4): Why do we sleep? And how can you help yourself to get the best night's sleep possible?

Learning (Chapter 5): How can you enhance your self-control (e.g., your ability to hold your temper in check)?

Memory and Cognition: (Chapter 6): How can we improve our memories? Do some approaches to solving problems work better than others?

Human Development (Chapter 7): What steps can you take to make sure that you age gracefully—slowly, and without major declines in the quality of your life?

Motivation and Emotion (Chapter 8): How can you avoid the "obesity epidemic" and control your own weight? How you can use self-set goals to enhance your motivation—and performance?

Personality (Chapter 9): How can you tell whether you are suited for the job or career you want?

Social Psychology (Chapter 13): What are the best means for persuading others or exerting influence on them? How can you tell whether you are really in love?

Industrial/Organizational Psychology (Chapter 14): If you have to give another person negative feedback on their work, what is the best way to do it? What makes leaders effective?

In short, after reading this text, we hope that you will have not only have a broad acquaintance with the major findings and principles of psychology— you will also have begun the task of using this knowledge in your own life. In this sense, we agree strongly with the poet Kahlil Gibran (1960) who wrote: "A little knowledge that acts is worth infinitely more than much knowledge that is idle."

KEY POINTS

- What three things can you gain from psychology?
- Can you gain these from only some branches of psychology or from all of them?

USING THIS BOOK: AN OVERVIEW
OF ITS SPECIAL FEATURES

Although it is many years since we were students, we all remember the following fact very well: not all textbooks are equally useful or equally easy to read. For this reason, we have taken many steps to make this book one of the good ones—a book you will find convenient and easy to use, and one that is, we hope, interesting to read. Here is an overview of the steps we have taken to reach this goal.

Each chapter beings with an **outline** and ends with a **summary.** Within the text itself, key terms are printed in **dark type like this** and are defined. These terms are also defined in a running marginal glossary, and in a glossary at the end of the book. In addition, throughout each chapter, we call your attention to important points in special **Key Questions** sections. If you can answer these questions, that's a good sign that you understand the central points in each section. (They are answered for you at the end of the chapter.) As you'll soon notice, all figures are clear and simple, and most contain special labels and notes designed to help you understand them.

Two special sections focus on our key theme of helping you to understand the key findings of psychology *and* to use them in your own life. These sections are headed **Psychology Lends a Hand** and **Psychology Goes to Work,** and both occur at the end of major sections of the text. The first type (see page 30 for an example) focuses on explaining how you can use the findings of psychology to deal with a wide range of important life situations (e.g., using basic principles of learning to train your pet; how to tell when another person is lying or being truthful). The second type (Psychology Goes to Work) focuses on applying the findings of psychology to work settings, and your career (e.g., dealing with abusive bosses; coping with the problems of dual careers). Together, these sections will get you started on the road toward that new perspective we mentioned at the start of this chapter—the perspective of modern psychology.

Each chapter is followed by several kinds of exercises, all designed to give you practice not just in understanding psychology, but in actually *using* it, too. **Psychology: Understanding Its Findings** exercises focus on helping you to understand the major points covered in the chapter. **Making Psychology Part of Your Life** exercises, in contrast, are designed to help you apply this information to your life and your career.

We hope that together these features will help to make reading this book a stimulating and enjoyable experience. In any case, we are definitely confident about one thing: in the pages that follow, you will discover something we first learned several decades ago: Psychology is indeed fascinating, enjoyable, and . . . useful!

PSYCHOLOGY LENDS A HAND

How to Study Psychology—or Any Other Subject—Effectively

Among the topics that psychologists know most about are learning, memory, and motivation. (We'll examine these in Chapters 5, 6, and 8.) Fortunately, all these topics are directly relevant to one activity you must perform as a student: studying. You must be motivated to study, must learn new materials, and must remember them accurately after they have been mastered. Knowledge gained by psychologists can be very useful to you in accomplishing these tasks. Drawing on what psychology knows, here are some useful tips to help you get the most out of the time you spend studying.

- *Begin with an overview.* Research on memory indicates that it is easier to retain information if it can be placed within a cognitive framework. So when you begin to study, try to see "the big picture." Examine the outline at the start of each chapter and thumb through the pages once or twice. That way, you'll know what to expect and will form an initial framework for organizing the information that follows.
- *Eliminate (or at least minimize) distractions.* In order to enter information into your memory accurately, you must devote careful attention to it. This means that you should reduce all distractions; try to study in a quiet place, turn off the television or radio, put those magazines out of sight, and unhook your phone. The result? You will learn more in less time. *Don't do all your studying at once.* All-nighters are very inefficient. Research findings indicate that it is easier to learn and remember new information when learning is spaced out over time rather than when it is crammed into a single long session. So try to spread your study sessions out; in the final analysis, this will give you a much greater return for your effort (see Figure 1.13).
- *Set specific, challenging, but attainable goals.* One of the key findings of industrial/organizational psychology is that setting certain kinds of goals can increase both motivation and performance on many different tasks. This principle can be of great help to you in studying, and it's relatively easy to apply. First, set a concrete goal for each session—for example, "I'll read twenty pages and review my class notes." Merely telling yourself "I'll work until I'm tired" is less effective because it fails to give you something concrete to shoot for. Second, try to set challenging goals, but ones you can attain. Challenging goals will encourage you to "stretch"—to do a little bit more. But impossible ones are simply discouraging. Because you are the world's greatest expert on your limits and your work habits, you are the best judge of what would be a challenging but attainable goal for *you*. Set such goals when you begin, and the results may surprise you.
- *Reward yourself for progress.* As you'll see in Chapter 5, people often perform various activities to attain external re-

FIGURE 1.13
All-Nighters: Not the Best Strategy for Studying
Psychological research indicates that we learn more efficiently—and remember more of what we learn—when we spread our work sessions out over time. For this reason, as well as several others, all-nighters are the not the best or most efficient way to study.

wards, ones delivered to them by others. But in many cases, we can provide our own rewards. We can pat ourselves on the back for reaching goals we've set or for other accomplishments, and this "pat on the back" can take many different forms: eating a favorite dessert, watching a favorite TV program, visiting friends. Again, you are the world's greatest expert on what you enjoy, so you can readily choose rewards that are appropriate. Whatever you choose, though, be sure to reward yourself for reaching your goals.

- *Engage in active, not passive studying.* As you probably know, it is possible to sit in front of a book or a set of notes for hours without accomplishing much—except daydreaming! To learn new information and retain it, you must do mental work—that's an inescapable fact of life. You must think about the material you are reading, ask yourself questions about it, relate this new information to things you already know, and so on. The **Key Questions** sections in each chapter are designed to help you do this, but in the final analysis, it's up to you. To the extent you really try to answer them, and engage in other forms of active learning, you will absorb more information, more efficiently.

We know: following these guidelines sounds like a lot of . . . work! But once you master them, the whole process will get easier. You will learn and remember more, get better grades, improve the value of your own education—and do it more efficiently than ever before. So in this case, a little extra effort is well justified.

SUMMARY AND REVIEW OF KEY QUESTIONS

The Field of Psychology: What It Is and How It Started

- **What is the definition of psychology as it exists today?**
  Psychology is the science of behavior and cognitive processes.

- **What ideas in philosophy and several branches of science (biology, physiology, computer science, physics) have contributed to the form and scope of modern psychology?**
  Philosophy supplied the idea that virtually any aspect of the natural world can be studied by the methods of science. Biology and physiology provided new insights into the function of the nervous system and brain. Computer science provided means to study cognitive processes, and physics offered equipment to scan the human brain as it performs many complex functions.

Psychology: Ground Issues, Key Perspectives

- **What are the three "grand issues" about behavior addressed by psychology?**
  The three issues are stability versus change, nature versus nurture, and rationality versus irrationality.

- **What are the major perspectives adopted by psychologists and how do they differ?**
  Major perspectives in psychology include the behavioral, cognitive, biological, psychodynamic, social, and evolutionary approaches. These perspectives focus on different aspects of behavior, but are complementary rather than competing in nature.

Psychology in the Twenty-First Century: Expanding Horizons

- **What is evolutionary psychology, and how does it contribute to our understanding of human behavior?**
  This is a new branch of psychology that suggests that humans have been subject to the process of biological evolution and as a result, possess many *evolved psychological mechanisms* that influence our behavior.

- **What do the authors mean when they speak of "the exportation" of psychology?**
  They are referring to a growing tendency for other fields to use the findings and principles of psychology to solve a wide range of practical problems.

- **What is the multicultural perspective, and what role does it play in the activities of modern psychologists?**
  This refers to increased sensitivity to and recognition of the importance of cultural, ethnic, racial, and other differences. Psychologists now include this perspective in all their activities—teaching, research, and counseling or therapy.

Psychology and the Scientific Method

- **Why can psychology be viewed as a branch of science?**
  Psychology can be viewed as a branch of science because psychologists adopt the scientific methods in their efforts to study human behavior.

- **What values are central to the scientific method?**
  Values central to the scientific method include accuracy, objectivity, skepticism, and open-mindedness.

- **Why is common sense such an uncertain guide to human behavior?**
  Common sense often suggests inconsistent and contradictory conclusions about behavior, and is influenced by several important forms of bias.

- **What are confirmation bias, availability heuristic, and sunk costs, and what role do they play in our efforts to understand human behavior?**
  These are cognitive errors we make in thinking about the world around us. They often lead us to false conclusions about human behavior.

- **What is critical thinking?**
  Such thinking closely examines all claims and assumptions, carefully evaluates existing evidence, and cautiously assesses all conclusions.

- **What role does it play in psychology?**
  Critical thinking is a basic aspect of the scientific method and is an integral part of efforts by psychologists to understand behavior.

- **How can you use it in everyday life?**
  You can use it to assess claims about human behavior made in newspaper and magazine articles, on television shows, and in many other contexts.

Research Methods in Psychology: How Psychologists Answer Questions about Behavior

- **What is naturalistic observation?**
  This involves carefully observing behavior in the settings where it normally occurs.

- **What is the correlational method of research and how do psychologists use it?**
  This is a basic method of research in which two or more variables are carefully observed to see if changes in one are related to changes in the other. Psychologists use it to make predictions about one variable from observations of another variable.

- **Why are even strong correlations between variables *not* evidence that changes in one causes changes in the other?**
  Even strong correlations don't necessarily indicate causality because changes in both variables may stem from the influence of some other variable.

- **What is the basic nature of experimentation?**
  In experimentation, researchers produce systematic changes in one variable (the independent variable) to observe whether these changes affect another variable (the dependent variable).

- **Why is random assignment of participants to conditions required in experiments?**
  Because if participants are *not* randomly assigned to each condition, it may later be impossible to tell whether differences in their behavior stem from differences they brought with them to the study, from the impact of the independent variable, or both.

- **What is confounding of variables in an experiment?**
  Confounding occurs when or more variables other than the independent variable are permitted to vary during an experiment.

Psychology: What's in It for You?

- **What three things can you gain from psychology?**
  You can acquire enhanced self-insight, and skills useful in many life situations and in your career.

- **Can you gain these from only some branches of psychology or from all of them?**
  All branches of psychology offer knowledge that is useful.

KEY TERMS

PSYCHOLOGY: UNDERSTANDING ITS FINDINGS

Designing an Experiment

Earlier in this chapter we noted that experimentation is the research method preferred by psychologists—when it can be used. As a result, much of the information presented in this book is based on this method. Try the following exercise to gain some first-hand experience with the joys—and challenges!—of designing an experiment. Here's the hypothesis: **One effective way to get people to say "yes" to a request is to flatter them first, then make the request.**

Now, design an experiment to test this hypothesis. To do this, follow these steps:

Define the independent and dependent variables and indicate how you will measure them.

Decide how you will change the independent variable systematically to determine whether it produces effects on the dependent variable.

Describe the various conditions of your study (e.g., no flattery, a small amount of flattery, a lot of flattery).

Who will be the participants? Why will they participate? How long will the study take?

What would it mean if results offered support for your hypothesis? Could the information be put to practical use?

MAKING PSYCHOLOGY PART OF YOUR LIFE

Interpreting the Results of Surveys: "To Believe or Not to Believe," That Is the Question

Surveys are reported very frequently in newspapers, the evening news, and magazines. Should you accept their results as accurate? This is a complex question, but one you should consider carefully in the light of information presented in this chapter. Here's an example of what we mean:

Suppose that one day you came across an article in a newspaper describing the results of recent survey. The survey indicated that among married or cohabiting couples, the more often the man in the couple said "Yes, dear" to the woman (i.e., agreed with her or gave the woman her way), the happier the couple was. How would you go about interpreting these results—deciding whether to believe them? In other words, now that you know something about the "basics" of psychological research, what questions would you ask yourself about these results? (Hint: One might be "Who were the participants?" Another might be "Are they a representative sample of all couples?")

Make a list of the questions you would ask and then try to decide which are crucial to your accepting the results of the study as valid. This is precisely the kind of procedure you should use *whenever* you learn about the findings of a survey. Merely accepting them as accurate because they appear in a newspaper or magazine can be misleading—and dangerous. As we noted in this chapter, results can be viewed as being accurate and informative only to the extent surveys meet specific requirements.

If you are using MyPsychLab, you have access to an electronic version of this textbook, along with dozens of valuable resources per chapter—including video and audio clips, simulations and activities, self-assessments, practice tests, and other study materials. Here is a sampling of the resources available for this chapter.

EXPLORE

Psychologists at Work
Correlations Do Not Show Causation

WATCH

The Beginnings of Psychology
The Complexity of Humans

SIMULATE

Distinguishing Independent and Dependent Variables

If you did not receive an access code to MyPsych Lab with this text and wish to purchase access online, please visit www.MyPsychLab.com.

STUDY GUIDE

CHAPTER REVIEW

The Field of Psychology: What It Is and How It Started

1. Most people believe in the usefulness of modern day psychology. (True-False)
2. The text authors assert that the best definition of psychology is
   a. the scientific study of living organisms.
   b. the rational analysis of unconscious mental functions.
   c. the science of behavior and mental processes.
   d. that branch if medicine that analyzes people.
3. The most famous advocate of the behaviorist viewpoint was
   a. John B. Watson
   b. Charles Darwin
   c. John Baron
   d. Sigmund Freud
4. The _____ point of view used _____ to study the human mind.
   a. physiological; the method of introspection
   b. evolutionary; measures of reaction time
   c. structural; the method of introspection
   d. behavioral; interviews
5. Which of the following pairs of terms DO NOT belong together?
   a. structuralist psychology; method of introspection
   b. behavior; any observable action in a living organism
   c. cognitive processes; all aspects of the human mind
   d. scientific psychology; ESP
6. Which of the following is considered to be an important foundation for modern psychology?
   a. Ideas from the philosophy of science.
   b. Advanced ideas and techniques from computer science and engineering.
   c. Studies from biology on the workings of the nervous system.
   d. All of the above are correct.

Psychology: Grand Issues, Key Perspectives

7. Prof. Baron's experiences at his 30th high school reunion illustrate the theme of
   a. nature versus nurture
   b. stability versus change
   c. conscious versus unconscious function
   d. rationality versus irrationality
8. The theme of _____ is a key issue in the study of aggression.
   a. nature versus nurture
   b. stability versus change
   c. conscious versus unconscious function
   d. rationality versus irrationality
9. A person who dreams about falling from a building is doomed to experience their dream. (True-False)
10. Which of the following is an example of the rationality versus irrationality theme?
    a. Considering the intelligence level of a person at age ten versus age seventy.
    b. Determining the degree to which genes control our selection of a mate.
    c. A woman who rejects an attractive male because his great-grandfather served time in prison.
    d. An employee who consistently underestimates how much time it will take to complete a project.
11. The _____ perspective would strongly consider the personality and hidden motives of a person in explaining their behavior.
    a. psychodynamic   c. cognitive
    b. multicultural   d. evolutionary
12. The behavioral of a person can be explained from many different perspectives (True-False).
13. Match up the appropriate perspective with the key question addressed by that psychological perspective.
    _____. This approach looks to the role of social factors in explaining behavior.
    _____. This approach considers personality factors in explaining human behavior.
    _____. This approach considers the extent to which inherited tendencies may determine behavior.
    _____. Changes in thought over the lifespan are the focus of this approach.
    _____. The focus of this approach is on the behaviors that occur in a specific situation.
    _____. The focus of this approach is on the thoughts of a person in a specific situation.
    _____. This approach considers brain function as mediating behavior.
    a. cognitive   e. developmental
    b. multicultural   f. psychodynamic
    c. biological   g. evolutionary
    d. behavioral

Psychology in the 21st Century: Expanding Horizons

14. Evolutionary psychology argues that human behavior is unchangeable because it is determined by our biological heritage. (True-False).
15. Which of the following is consistent with the evolutionary perspective?
    a. Our thought processes are fixed and unchangeable.
    b. Our genetic heritage can play a key role in mate selection, but not higher processes such as creativity.
    c. Psychological mechanisms are subject to evolutionary pressure.
    d. Humans are only motivated by their evolved psychological mechanisms.
16. Which pair of terms DO NOT belong together?
    a. evolutionary psychology; psychological mechanisms
    b. applied psychology; evolved psychological mechanisms
    c. applied psychology; strategies to help people deal with emotional crises
    d. industrial/organizational psychology; applied psychology

17. Which of the following is an example of "exportation of psychology"?
    a. An engineering team uses research from cognitive psychology to design a new flight control panel for an aircraft cockpit.
    b. A disaster relief organization uses research from clinical psychology to help survivors of a hurricane avoid stress disorders.
    c. An unscrupulous student photocopies a psychology introductory text and sells these pages to other students.
    d. A and B are correct.
18. Over the last 40 years, the proportion of the population comprised of people of European descent has continued to rise.   (True-False)
19. Which of the following factors would be considered by a psychologist adopting a multicultural perspective?
    a. Religious orientation.
    b. Sexual orientation.
    c. Gender.
    d. All of the above are correct.

Psychology and the Scientific Method

20. Match up each term with the appropriate definition of the term.
    _____. An approach to acquiring knowledge.
    _____. The view that a research finding is accepted only after it has been established repeatedly by different scientists.
    _____. The idea that a scientist can change his/her views in response to new evidence.
    _____. The view that information is to be gathered using care, precision, and effort to avoid error.
    _____. The notion that scientists avoid bias when evaluating research information.
    a. Accuracy
    b. Objectivity
    c. Skepticism
    d. Open-Mindedness
    e. Science
21. Psychologists are wary of knowledge derived from "common sense" because
    a. it is difficult to export such knowledge for public use.
    b. this source can be unreliable.
    c. this source of knowledge is reliable but sometimes not useful.
    d. such knowledge is difficult to evaluate.
22. The tendency of a person to notice information that is consistent with their own view of an issue is know as the
    a. cognitive dissonance bias.
    b. availability heuristic.
    c. critical thinking trap.
    d. confirmation bias.
23. Match up the appropriate mental processing error with its correct definition.
    _____. The failure of people to reverse a bad decision even after substantial negative feedback.
    _____. The tendency of a person to make a judgment based on information that is easily recalled.

_____. Our tendency to notice and remember information that is consistent with our own view.
    a. Availability heuristic
    b. Cognitive dissonance.
    c. The "sunk costs" cognitive error.
    d. Confirmation bias.
24. Which of the following DO NOT belong together?
    a. scientific method;   objective observations
    b. critical thinking;   cognitive bias
    c. Tom Cruise;   questionable views on psychiatry
    d. critical thinking;   considering the credibility of a source of information
25. Critical thinking refers to the use of a set of skills that can be used to evaluate existing evidence for a claim and to cautiously assess all conclusions.   (True-False)
26. Which of the following situations would be an example of critical thinking?
    a. A scientist whose children suffer from a life-threatening disease pushes hard to have a new vaccine approved for use in humans, even though the vaccine has not been thoroughly tested.
    b. A juror in a court case listens to the evidence while under the influence of alcohol.
    c. A psychologist creates a new theory of emotion regulation based on their own life experiences.
    d. A juror in a court case notes that the prosecution introduced conflicting evidence against the defendant and refuses to vote guilty, thus holding out against pressure from the other 11 jurors.

Research Methods in Psychology: How Psychologists Answer Questions about Behavior

27. The form of observation that involves the careful monitoring of a single person over a period of time is known as a(n)
    a. developmental design.
    b. case study.
    c. correlational study.
    d. survey procedure.
28. The process of systematic observation involves
    a. brief measures of behavior.
    b. sampling behaviors on a random basis.
    c. careful, accurate measurement.
    d. the use of computers to model human mental function.
29. Match up the appropriate research method with the best example of that method (continues on page 36.)
    _____. A psychologist administers a drug to one group of subjects and a placebo pill to another group and then assesses their driving skill.
    _____. A clerk at the local district attorney's office notes that a number of recent homicides involves the use of alcohol and draws the conclusion that alcohol causes homicide.
    _____. A corporate sales agent makes calls to wealthy clients asking about their views on future investing trends, specifically those involving the product sold by her company.

_____. A developmental psychologist charts the changes in cognitive ability shown by her two children from ages 1–14. These form the basis for her new theory on adult cognitive function.
   a. Survey method.
   b. Correlational study.
   c. Case study.
   d. Experimental method.
   e. Developmental design.

30. A correlation coefficient of _____ would represent the strongest relationship of one variable to another variable.
   a. −0.25
   b. 0.00
   c. +0.79
   d. +0.75

31. Because psychologists have advanced training in statistics, they are able to use correlational data to draw causal inferences such as "Variable A is caused by Variable B". (True-False)

32. The independent variable of an experiment is
   a. also known as a "correlated variable."
   b. systematically varied by the experimenter.
   c. measured by the experimenter.
   d. is assumed to be under the control of the dependent variable.

33. Which of the following conditions will invalidate the results of an experiment?
   a. Randomly assigning subjects to either the control or experimental condition.
   b. Setting up a hypothesis to be tested by the experiment.
   c. Deciding on how best to measure the experiment outcomes.
   d. Setting the values of the independent variable, but allowing other experimental conditions to be uncontrolled.

34. A serious problem with using the case method is that the researcher will bond with their subjects of study and lose their impartiality. (True-False).

Psychology: What's in It for You?

35. The authors expect that students will gain _____ from reading the textbook.
   a. self-insight
   b. expertise at treating the issues of family members
   c. some knowledge and a few like-skills
   d. All of the above are correct.

IDENTIFICATIONS

1. Identify the term that belongs with each of the concepts below (place the letter for the appropriate term below in front of each concept).

Identification   Concept:
_____ 1. The view that asks as to the extent to which our behaviors are shaped by environmental factors as opposed to inherited tendencies.
_____ 2. Only those things that can be directly observed are worthy of study in psychology.
_____ 3. The source of knowledge that is the basis for statements such as "birds of a feather flock together" as opposed to "opposites attract".

_____ 4. The cognitive error made by Prof. Baron over a decade to rescue his car.
_____ 5. Science of behavior and cognitive processes.
_____ 6. A view that emphasizes the overt actions of people in a situation.
_____ 7. An early view in psychology which sought to identify the basic structures of the mind.
_____ 8. The historian who argues that advances in technology can occur from the combination of what appear to be unrelated and unconnected events.
_____ 9. The variable that is assumed to controlled by a causal factor in an experiment (and is measured by the experimenter).
_____ 10. This doctor formulated a theory of personality based on his experiences with cases in his medical practice.

Identification:
a. Behavioral perspective
b. Dependent variable
c. John Watson
d. Sigmund Freud
e. Sunk costs
f. Availability heuristic
g. Nature versus nurture
h. Common sense
i. Psychology
j. Structuralism
k. James Burke
l. behaviorism
m. Independent variable

FILL IN THE BLANK

1. Structural psychologists used _____ to probe the contents of the mind.
2. The three grand themes used by the authors in this textbook include _____, _____, and _____.
3. Three recent trends noted in psychological research include _____, _____, and _____.
4. Evolutionary psychology proposes that modern-day humans retain _____.
5. The perceptual ability of a person to recognize complex patterns of what appears to be unrelated information is known as _____.
6. _____ refers to a special approach for the acquisition of knowledge.
7. The notion that scientists avoid bias when evaluating research information is known as _____.
8. The _____ refers to the human tendency to notice and to remember information that supports our personal views.
9. The notion of _____ refers to a cognitive trap in which people find it hard to reverse a mental decision, even as evidence mounts that the decision was an error.
10. The types of cognitive skills that are important for the scientific method form are known as _____.
11. The three basic procedures used by psychologists to gain knowledge about human behavior are _____, _____, and _____.
12. The _____ method studies a few persons in great detail, perhaps over many years.

13. One advantage of the correlational method is its ability to generate _____ about future human behavior.
14. A major disadvantage of the correlational method is its inability to specify a _____ relationship between two variables.
15. The _____ variable is measured by the experimenter whereas the _____ variable is systematically varied.
16. The key issues required in order for an experiment to show a cause-and-effect relationship are _____ and _____.

COMPREHENSIVE PRACTICE TEST

1. The majority of persons in the US have a deep distrust and skepticism about psychology. (True-False).
2. Research on genetic predispositions for homosexuality can be viewed as an instance of the theme of
   a. inherited psychological mechanisms.
   b. stability versus change.
   c. rationality versus irrationality.
   d. nature versus nurture.
3. Which of the following statements are consistent with the evolutionary perspective?
   a. Genetic factors play a major role in human behavior.
   b. Human behavior is minimally influenced by our genetic heritage.
   c. Humans have inherited behavioral tendencies that in the past helped their ancestors to survive and to reproduce.
   d. Evolved psychological mechanisms can dominate our behavior.
4. The multicultural perspective would pay special attention to factors in a person such as
   a. Age.
   b. Gender.
   c. Ethnicity.
   d. All of the above are correct.
5. The core value issue in science of _____ refers to the view that information is to be gathered using care, precision, and effort to avoid error.
   a. accuracy
   b. objectivity
   c. skepticism
   d. open-mindedness
6. Which of the following represents a guideline for critical thinking?
   a. Do not let your emotions cloud your judgment.
   b. Be skeptical.
   c. Never jump to a conclusion.
   d. All of the above are correct.
7. A researcher who used the case method to develop a theory of personality was:
   a. John B. Watson
   b. James Burke
   c. Charles Darwin
   d. Sigmund Freud

8. Which of the following is an advantage of the survey method?
   a. Surveys require little attention to wording and thus can be quickly prepared and administered.
   b. A survey will generate correlations which in turn can be used to establish causality.
   c. Information can be gathered quickly by a survey from thousands of people.
   d. Surveys are a type of experimental method.
9. Correlational research can allow us to use outcomes of one variable based on its relationship with another variable to make predictions. (True-False)
10. There is a negative correlation between the age of a man and the remaining hair on his head (True-False).
11. The _____ can be used by a scientist to establish a cause-and-effect relationship between two variables.
    a. case method
    b. survey method
    c. experimental method
    d. correlational method
12. The dependent variable of an experiment is
    a. also known as a "correlated variable."
    b. systematically varied by the experimenter.
    c. measured by the experimenter.
    d. is assumed to be a confounding factor..
13. The requirement that each subject in an experiment has the same likelihood of being in the control or the experimental group is accomplished by
    a. random assignment of subjects to conditions.
    b. matching the subjects on some third variable.
    c. letting the subjects know what condition they are in prior to the experiment.
    d. placing those subjects that show up first in one group while the late-comers go into the other group.
14. _____ refers to the difficulty wherein a causal conclusion cannot be drawn about the independent variable because some other variable has changed during the experiment.
    a. Confabulation
    b. Observational bias
    c. Confounding
    d. Confirmation bias
15. Whether or not subjects have been randomly assigned to control and experimental conditions is less important than is controlling for confounding variables. (True-False).

CRITICAL THINKING

1. Explain what is meant by the multicultural approach to psychology and how this approach has implications for psychological research, applied clinical psychology, and the teaching of psychology.
2. Describe the key steps of an experiment. Include in your answer a definition of the dependent and independent variables as well as an explanation of the importance of random assignment of subjects to experimental conditions.

TWO

Biological Bases of Behavior

Although originally from the western United States, I (Michael Kalsher) have lived most of my adult life in upstate New York. Since my parents and siblings and their families remain out West, I try to visit them often, especially since my parents are now well into their eighties. This situation has provided an interesting opportunity to observe the effects of aging, particularly in my dad. Because my visits are relatively infrequent, these changes are more apparent to me than they are to my siblings, who see my parents often. Physically, my dad is in good health. He still drives, has a healthy appetite, reads a lot, and walks several miles each day with my mom. Unfortunately, he has not been so fortunate when it comes to declines in his cognitive abilities. Most of the changes have been predictable. For example, he has difficulty hearing, his short-term memory is not what it once was, and he functions best when he sticks to a regular daily routine. In other ways, however, the changes have been less predictable. For example, when I call them, my mother alerts me as to how "with it" he is before I speak with him on the phone. Some days we visit about a wide range of topics, from what's happening with our favorite sports teams to what's going on with the stock market. On other occasions, however, he becomes confused easily, and our conversation is restricted to relatively simple topics, such as the weather and what he plans to do that day. What is especially interesting to me is that the cognitive declines have not been linear or fixed in nature; instead, my dad tends to have both good days and bad days, and it is difficult to predict when each will occur. In fact, some days I can tell that he isn't really sure who I am. This also proves true when I visit. Because I'm not a regular part of his predictable daily routine, he occasionally has to be reminded who I am, even when I'm physically present. During a recent trip out West, I took my dad's truck to the car wash, and while I was gone, he inquired as to who that "nice young man" was who took his truck!

The point of this story, of course, is to illustrate that the changes in my dad's cognitive functions stem from complex basic biological processes common to all people. In fact, almost all psychologists agree that everything we think, feel, or do has a basis in biological processes and events—primarily, in activities occurring in our brains and other portions of the nervous system (see Figure 2.1). Are you reading and understanding these words? If so, it is the result of activity in your brain. Do you feel sleepy? If so, it is the result of activity in your brain and other biological events. Can you remember what your psychology professor looks like? What it felt like to have your first kiss? The sound of your first-grade teacher's voice? Again, your ability to do so is the result of activity in several areas of your brain.

Given this basic fact, it seems only fitting to begin our study of psychology by considering the biological processes that underlie all aspects of our behavior. But please note: Our goal is not to make you an expert in these events. This is a course in psychology, not biology, and we promise not to forget it. But as you'll soon see, we really can't obtain full answers to many questions about behavior without attention to biological factors—especially activity in our brains.

This is not the only reason why psychologists are interested in the biological events and foundations of behavior, however. In addition, they realize that understanding these roots may often suggest effective treatments for behavioral problems. As we'll see in Chapter 11, much progress has been made in understanding the biological causes of mental disorders—depression, schizophrenia, and anxiety disorders, to name just a few. Such knowledge, in turn, has led to the development of effective drugs for treating these disorders (we examine these in detail in Chapter 12). Similarly, growing understanding of the biological mechanisms that

FIGURE 2.1
All Aspects of Behavior Have Biological Roots
In an ultimate sense, everything we do, feel, think, or experience is related to biological processes occurring in our bodies—and especially in our brains and nervous systems.

play a role in drug addiction is now pointing the way toward more effective treatment of this serious problem.

There's still one more reason for beginning our study with biology, and it has to do with scientific progress. Modern technology has provided impressive new tools for studying the living brain—for seeing where activity is centered as people solve problems, listen to music, reason, or memorize new information (see Mason & Just, 2004). These new tools, which are described in a later section, have done for psychologists what the microscope did for biology and medicine, and what the telescope did for astronomy: They have provided researchers with new ways of examining events and processes that were previously hidden from view. The result has been nothing short of a revolution in our understanding of how the brain works and the role it plays in the complex forms of behavior that make us human. So, get ready for some amazing surprises. We are truly on the verge of obtaining a much fuller understanding of the mysteries of the human mind than ever before.

To provide you with an overview of these exciting new discoveries, we'll first examine the structure and function of *neurons*, the building blocks of the nervous system. Next, we'll turn to the structure and function of the *nervous system*, devoting special attention to the brain, the marvelous organ that is ultimately responsible for consciousness—and for the fact that you are now reading and understanding these words. After this, we will move psychology to center stage by examining important links between the brain and behavior—what we currently know about the neural bases of speech and other *higher mental processes*—reasoning, problem solving, and so on. As we'll soon see, the modern tools we mentioned earlier have provided new insights into all these topics. Finally, we'll examine the role of *genetic factors* in human behavior, and the possible role of evolution in our behavior—a topic investigated by the field of *evolutionary psychology*. To start at the beginning, let's turn now to *neurons*—the building blocks of which, ultimately, our consciousness is composed.

NEURONS: BUILDING BLOCKS OF THE NERVOUS SYSTEM

You are driving down a winding country road when suddenly your friend, who is sitting next to you, shouts, "Watch out for the deer!" Immediately, you experience strong anxiety, step on the brake, and look around in every direction. The process seems automatic, but think about it a moment: How did information from your ears get "inside" and trigger your emotions and behavior? The answer involves the activity of *neurons*—cells within our bodies that are specialized for the tasks of receiving, moving, and processing information.

Neurons: Their Basic Structure

Neurons are tremendously varied in appearance, but most consist of three basic parts: (1) a *cell body*, (2) an *axon*, and (3) one or more *dendrites*. **Dendrites** carry information toward the cell body, whereas **axons** carry information away from it. Thus, in a sense, neurons are one-way channels of communication. Information usually moves from dendrites or the cell body toward the axon, and then outward along this structure. A simplified diagram of a neuron and its basic structure is shown, magnified, in Figure 2.2 on page 42. Scientists estimate that the human brain contains more than 100 billion neurons.

In many neurons, the axon is covered by a sheath of fatty material known as *myelin*. The myelin sheath (fatty wrapping) is interrupted by small gaps (places where it is absent). Both the sheath and the gaps in it play an important role in the neuron's ability to transmit information, a process we'll consider in detail shortly. Near its end, the axon divides into several small branches. These, in turn, end in

Neurons:
Cells specialized for communicating information; the basic building blocks of the nervous system.

Dendrite:
The part of the neuron that conducts action potentials toward the cell body.

Axon:
The part of the neuron that conducts action potentials away from the cell body.

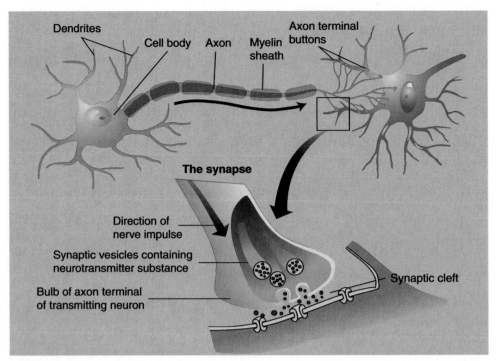

FIGURE 2.2
Neurons: Their Basic Structure
Neurons vary in form, but all possess the basic structures shown here: a cell body, an axon (with axon terminals), and one or more dendrites.

Axon terminals:
Structures at the end of axons that contain transmitter substances.

Synapse:
A region where the axon of one neuron closely approaches other neurons or the cell membrane of other types of cells, such as muscle cells.

Action potential:
A rapid shift in the electrical charge across the cell membrane of neurons. This disturbance along the membrane communicates information within neurons.

Synaptic vesicles:
Structures in the axon terminals that contain various neurotransmitters.

Neurotransmitters (transmitter substances):
Chemicals, released by neurons, that carry information across the synapse.

round structures known as **axon terminals** that closely approach but do not actually touch other cells (other neurons, muscle cells, or gland cells). The region at which the axon terminals of a neuron closely approach other cells is known as the **synapse.** The manner in which neurons communicate with other cells across this tiny space is described next.

Neurons: Their Basic Function

We just noted that neurons closely approach but do not actually touch other neurons. How, then, does one neuron communicate across this gap? Generally, like this: When a neuron responds to some stimulus either from inside or outside the nervous system, it generates a tiny electrical reaction known as the **action potential,** which then travels along the axon to the axon terminals. Within the axon terminals are many structures known as **synaptic vesicles.** Arrival of the action potential causes these vesicles to approach the cell membrane, where they empty their contents into the synapse (see Figure 2.3). The chemicals thus released—known as **neurotransmitters**—travel across the tiny synaptic gap until they reach specialized receptor sites in the membrane of the other cell.

These receptors are complex protein molecules into whose structure neurotransmitter substances fit like chemical keys into a lock. Specific neurotransmitters can deliver signals only at certain locations on cell membranes, thereby introducing precision into the nervous system's complex communication system. After binding to their receptors, neurotransmitters either produce their effects directly or function indirectly through the interaction of the neurotransmitter and its receptor with other substances.

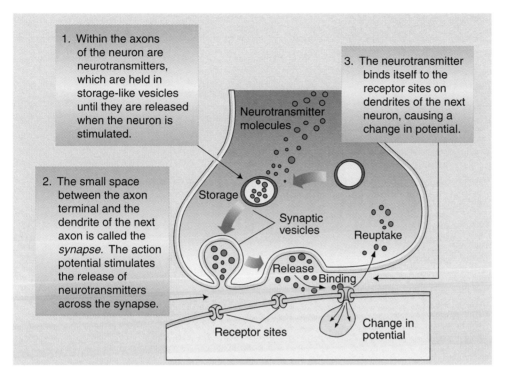

1. Within the axons of the neuron are neurotransmitters, which are held in storage-like vesicles until they are released when the neuron is stimulated.

3. The neurotransmitter binds itself to the receptor sites on dendrites of the next neuron, causing a change in potential.

2. The small space between the axon terminal and the dendrite of the next axon is called the *synapse*. The action potential stimulates the release of neurotransmitters across the synapse.

Neurotransmitter molecules

Storage

Synaptic vesicles

Reuptake

Release

Binding

Receptor sites

Change in potential

FIGURE 2.3
Synaptic Transmission
The axon terminals found on the ends of axons contain many *synaptic vesicles*. When an action potential reaches the axon terminal, these vesicles move toward the cell membrane. Once there, the vesicles fuse with the membrane and release their contents (*neurotransmitters*) into the synapse.

Neurotransmitters produce one of two effects. If their effects are *excitatory* in nature, they make it more likely for the neuron they contact to fire. If, instead, their effects are *inhibitory*, they make it less likely that the neuron will fire. What happens to neurotransmitters after they cross the synapse from one neuron to another? Either they are taken back for reuse in the axon terminals of the neuron that released them, a process known as *reuptake*, or they are broken down by various enzymes present at the synapse—in a sense, chemically deactivated.

It is important to note that our comments so far greatly simplify things by describing a situation in which one neuron contacts another across a single synapse. In fact, this is rarely, if ever, the case. Most neurons actually form synapses with many others—ten thousand or more in some cases! Thus, at any given moment, most neurons are receiving a complex pattern of excitatory and inhibitory influences from many neighbors. Whether a neuron conducts an action potential or not, then, depends on the total pattern of this input—for example, whether excitatory or inhibitory input predominates. Further, the effects of excitatory and inhibitory input can be cumulative over time, in part because such effects do not dissipate instantaneously. Thus, if a neuron that has recently been stimulated, but not sufficiently to produce an action potential, is stimulated again soon after, the two sources of excitation may combine so that an action potential is generated.

In one sense, then, neurons serve as tiny *decision-making* mechanisms, firing only when the pattern of information reaching them is just right. The fact that individual neurons affect and are, in turn, affected by many others strongly suggests that it is the total pattern or network of activity in the nervous system that is

TABLE 2.1   Neurotransmitters: An Overview

Neurons communicate with one another across the synapse through neurotransmitters. Several of these are listed and described here.

Neurotransmitter	Location	Effects
Acetylcholine	Found throughout the central nervous system, in the autonomic nervous system, and at all neuromuscular junctions.	Involved in muscle action, learning, and memory.
Norepinephrine	Found in neurons in the autonomic nervous system.	Primarily involved in control of alertness and wakefulness.
Dopamine	Produced by neurons located in a region of the brain called the substantia nigra.	Involved in movement, attention, and learning. Degeneration of dopamine-producing neurons has been linked to Parkinson's disease. Too much dopamine has been linked to schizophrenia.
Serotonin	Found in neurons in the brain and spinal cord.	Plays a role in the regulation of mood and in the control of eating, sleep, and arousal. Has also been implicated in the regulation of pain and in dreaming.
GABA (gamma-amino-butyric acid)	Found throughout the brain and spinal cord.	GABA is the major inhibitory neurotransmitter in the brain. Abnormal levels of GABA have been implicated in sleep and eating disorders.

crucial. As we will see in later discussions, it is this intricate web of neural excitation that generates the richness and complexity of our conscious experience.

Neurotransmitters: Chemical Keys to the Nervous System

The fact that transmitter substances produce either excitatory or inhibitory effects might seem to suggest that there are only two types. In fact, there are many different neurotransmitters, and many more chemical substances, that can mimic the effects of neurotransmitters—for instance, many drugs produce their effects in this way. Several known neurotransmitters and their functions are summarized in Table 2.1. Although the specific role of many transmitter substances is still being studied, we are now fairly certain about the functions of a few. Perhaps the one about which we know most is *acetylcholine*. It is the neurotransmitter at every junction between motor neurons (neurons concerned with muscular movements) and muscle cells. Anything that interferes with the action of acetylcholine can produce paralysis. South American hunters have long used this fact to their advantage by dipping their arrow tips in *curare*, a poisonous substance that occupies acetylcholine receptors. As a result, paralysis is produced, and the unlucky animal dies quickly through suffocation.

Some evidence suggests that neurological difficulties from conditions such as Alzheimer's disease and Parkinson's disease result from a degeneration of cells that produce acetylcholine. Examinations of the brains of persons who have died of Alzheimer's, for instance, show unusually low levels of this substance. Treatment of Alzheimer's disease and Parkinson's disease now includes drugs that increase the level of acetylcholine by decreasing levels of the enzyme that breaks it down. The results are improved memory, attention, and performance of daily activities (Atri et al., 2004).

■ **Drugs and neurotransmitters.**

Have you ever taken a painkiller? A drug to help you sleep? One to make you more alert? If so, you may have wondered how these drugs produce their effects. The answer is that, in many cases, they do so by altering the process of synaptic transmission. Drugs that change our feelings or behavior are similar enough in chemical structure to natural neurotransmitters to occupy the receptor sites normally occupied by the neurotransmitters themselves (see Kalivas & Samson, 1992). In this respect, drugs can produce two basic effects: They can mimic the effects of the neurotransmitter, in which case they are described as being **agonists,** or they can inhibit the effects normally produced by the neurotransmitter, in which case they are described as being **antagonists.** Many painkillers (analgesics) occupy receptor sites normally stimulated by endorphins; thus, they block pain and produce a temporary "high." Addicting drugs such as opium, heroin, and crack also occupy these sites and produce more intensely pleasurable sensations than endorphins. This seems to play a key role in their addicting properties.

KEY QUESTIONS

- What do neurons do and what are their basic parts?
- What are action potentials? How do neurons communicate with one another?
- What are the effects of neurotransmitters?
- How do drugs produce their effects? What are agonists? Antagonists?

THE NERVOUS SYSTEM: ITS BASIC STRUCTURE AND FUNCTIONS

If neurons are building blocks, then the **nervous system** is the structure they erect. The nervous system is actually a complex network of neurons that regulates our bodily functions and permits us to react to the external world in countless ways, so it deserves very careful attention. But remember: This is *not* a course in biology, so the main reason to focus on the nervous system is to understand its role in all aspects of our behavior.

The Nervous System: Its Major Divisions

Although the nervous system functions as an integrated whole, it is often viewed as having two major portions—the **central nervous system** and the **peripheral nervous system.** These and other divisions of the nervous system are presented in Figure 2.4 on page 46.

■ **The central nervous system.**

The central nervous system (CNS) consists of the brain and the spinal cord. Because we'll soon describe the structure of the brain in detail, we won't examine it here. The spinal cord runs through the middle of a column of hollow bones known as vertebrae. You can feel them by moving your hand up and down the middle of your back.

The spinal cord has two major functions. First, it carries sensory information from receptors throughout the body to the brain and conducts information from the brain to muscles and glands. Second, it plays a key role in various **reflexes.** These are seemingly automatic actions evoked rapidly by particular stimuli. Withdrawing your hand from a hot object or blinking your eyes in response to a rapidly approaching object are common examples of reflex actions. Spinal reflexes offer an obvious advantage: They permit us to react to potential dangers much

Agonist:
A chemical substance that facilitates the action of a neurotransmitter at a receptor site.

Antagonist:
A chemical substance that inhibits the impact of a neurotransmitter at a receptor site.

Nervous system:
The complex structure that regulates bodily processes and is responsible for all aspects of conscious experience.

Central nervous system:
The brain and the spinal cord.

Peripheral nervous system:
That portion of the nervous system that connects internal organs and glands, as well as voluntary and involuntary muscles, to the central nervous system.

Reflexes:
Seemingly automatic actions evoked rapidly by specific stimuli.

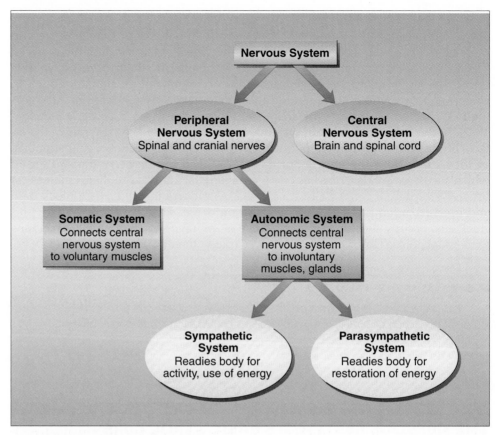

FIGURE 2.4
Major Divisions of the Nervous System
As shown here, the nervous system consists of several major parts.

more rapidly than we could if the information first had to travel all the way to the brain.

■ The peripheral nervous system.

The peripheral nervous system consists primarily of nerves, bundles of axons from many neurons that connect the central nervous system with sense organs and with muscles and glands throughout the body. Most of these nerves are attached to the spinal cord; these spinal nerves serve the body below the neck. Other nerves known as *cranial nerves* extend from the brain. They carry sensory information from receptors in the eyes and ears and other sense organs; they also carry information from the central nervous system to muscles in the head and neck.

As you can see in Figure 2.4, the peripheral nervous system has two subdivisions: the **somatic** and **autonomic nervous systems.** The somatic nervous system connects the central nervous system to voluntary muscles throughout the body. When you engage in almost any voluntary action, such as ordering a pizza or reading the rest of this chapter, portions of your somatic nervous system are involved. In contrast, the autonomic nervous system connects the central nervous system to internal organs and glands and to muscles over which we have little or no voluntary control—for instance, the muscles in our digestive system.

We can't stop dividing things here, because the autonomic nervous system, too, consists of two distinct parts. The first is known as the **sympathetic nervous system.** In general, this system prepares the body for using energy, as in vigorous physical actions. Thus, stimulation of this division increases heartbeat, raises

Somatic nervous system:
The portion of the nervous system that connects the brain and spinal cord to voluntary muscles.

Autonomic nervous system:
Part of the peripheral nervous system that connects internal organs, glands, and involuntary muscles to the central nervous system.

Sympathetic nervous system:
The portion of the autonomic nervous system that readies the body for expenditure of energy.

blood pressure, releases sugar into the blood for energy, and increases the flow of blood to muscles used in physical activities. The second portion of the autonomic system, known as the **parasympathetic nervous system,** operates in the opposite manner. It stimulates processes that conserve the body's energy. Activation of this system slows heartbeat, lowers blood pressure, and diverts blood away from skeletal muscles (e.g., muscles in the arms and legs) and to the digestive system. Figure 2.5 on page 48 summarizes many functions of the sympathetic and parasympathetic divisions of the autonomic nervous system.

Before concluding, we should emphasize that while the autonomic nervous system plays an important role in the regulation of bodily processes, it does so mainly by transmitting information to and from the central nervous system. Thus, it is the central nervous system that runs the show.

KEY QUESTIONS

- What structures compose the central nervous system? What is the function of the spinal cord?
- What two systems make up the peripheral nervous system?
- What are the roles of these two systems?
- What are the functions of the sympathetic and parasympathetic nervous systems?

The Endocrine System: Chemical Regulators of Bodily Processes

Although the nervous system is our primary system for moving and processing information—for responding to the world around us and to our own internal states—another exists as well. This is the **endocrine system,** which consists of a number of *glands* that release chemicals called **hormones** directly into the bloodstream. These hormones exert profound effects on a wide range of processes related to basic bodily functions. Of special interest to psychologists are *neurohormones*—hormones that interact with and affect the nervous system. Neurohormones, like neurotransmitters, influence neural activity. Because they are released into the circulatory system rather than into synapses, however, they exert their effects more slowly, at a greater distance, and often for longer periods of time than do neurotransmitters.

One major part of the endocrine system is the **pituitary gland.** It is sometimes described as the *master gland* of the body, for the hormones that it releases control and regulate the actions of other endocrine glands. This gland is also closely connected to important regions of the brain that play a role in emotion—areas we'll discuss in the next section. Another important part of the endocrine system is the *adrenal glands*, which sit on top of the kidneys. In response to messages from the autonomic nervous system, the adrenal glands release *epinephrine* and *norepinephrine* (also known as *adrenaline* and *noradrenaline*). These hormones help the body handle emergencies by increasing heart rate, blood pressure, and sugar in the blood.

KEY QUESTIONS

- What is the endocrine system?
- What are some of its major parts?

THE BRAIN: WHERE CONSCIOUSNESS DWELLS

Clearly, modern computers are impressive and are getting better. At present, though, none comes even close to matching the amazing abilities packed within the roughly three pounds of tissue that make up the human brain. Computers can

Parasympathetic nervous system:
A portion of the autonomic nervous system that readies the body for restoration of energy.

Endocrine system:
A system for communication within our bodies; it consists of several glands that secrete hormones directly into the bloodstream.

Hormones:
Substances secreted by endocrine glands that regulate a wide range of bodily processes.

Pituitary gland:
An endocrine gland that releases hormones to regulate other glands and several basic biological processes.

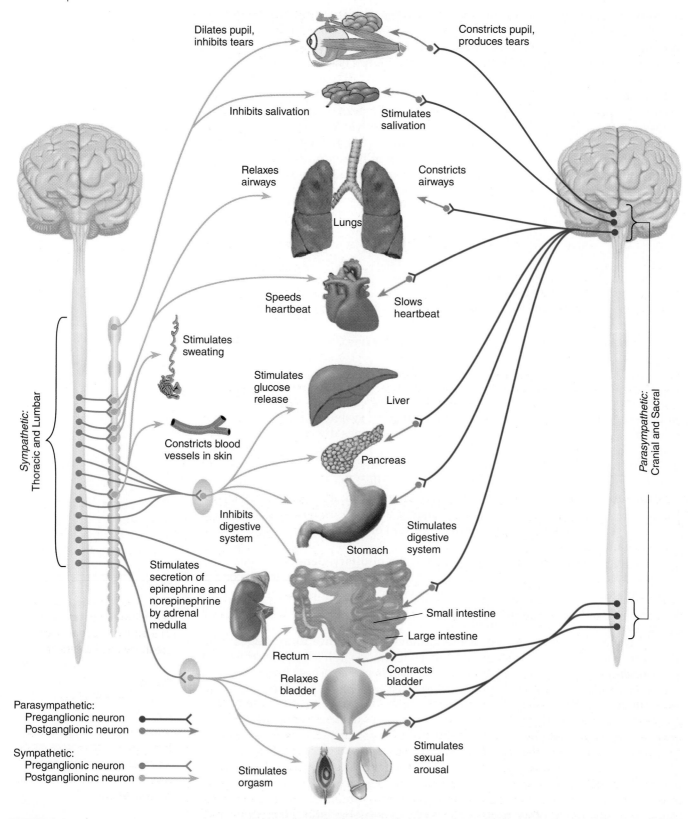

Dilates pupil, inhibits tears

Constricts pupil, produces tears

Inhibits salivation

Stimulates salivation

Relaxes airways

Constricts airways

Lungs

Speeds heartbeat

Slows heartbeat

Stimulates sweating

Stimulates glucose release

Liver

Constricts blood vessels in skin

Pancreas

Inhibits digestive system

Stomach

Stimulates digestive system

Stimulates secretion of epinephrine and norepinephrine by adrenal medulla

Small intestine

Large intestine

Rectum

Contracts bladder

Relaxes bladder

Sympathetic: Thoracic and Lumbar

Parasympathetic: Cranial and Sacral

Parasympathetic:
Preganglionic neuron
Postganglionic neuron

Sympathetic:
Preganglionic neuron
Postganglioninc neuron

Stimulates orgasm

Stimulates sexual arousal

FIGURE 2.5
The Autonomic Nervous System: An Overview
The autonomic nervous system consists of two major parts, the sympathetic and parasympathetic nervous systems. Some of the functions of each are shown here.

Source: Nell R. Carlson, *Foundations of Physiological Psychology,* 4/e © 1999. Published by Allyn and Bacon, Boston, MA. Copyright © 1999 by Pearson Education. Reprinted by permission of the publisher.

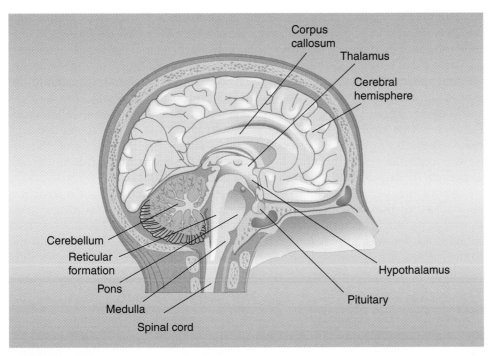

FIGURE 2.6
Basic Structure of the Human Brain
In this simplified drawing, the brain has been split down the middle, from the front of the head to the back, the way you would cut an apple in half through its core, to reveal its inner structure.

"crunch numbers" at amazing speeds, but they cannot do many things we take for granted: recognize thousands of different faces, speak one and perhaps several languages fluently, add just the right amount of salt or pepper to a dish we are cooking. Nor can they experience the emotions we label "love," "hate," and "sorrow." So clearly the human brain is truly a marvel.

Although the brain is complex, it can be divided into three major parts that are concerned with (1) basic bodily functions and survival; (2) motivation and emotion; and (3) our higher mental processes, including language, planning, problem solving, and reasoning.

The Brain Stem: Survival Basics

Let's begin with the basics: the structures in the brain that regulate the bodily processes we share with many other life forms on earth. These structures are located in the *brain stem*, the portion of the brain that begins just above the spinal cord and continues into the center of this complex organ (see Figure 2.6).

Two of these structures, the **medulla** and the **pons,** are located just above the point where the spinal cord enters the brain. Major sensory and motor nerves pass through these structures on their way to higher brain centers or down to effectors (muscles or glands) in other parts of the body. In addition, both the medulla and the pons contain a central core consisting of a dense network of interconnected neurons. This is the **reticular activating system,** and it has long been viewed as a part of the brain that plays a key role in sleep and arousal—a topic we'll discuss in greater detail in Chapter 4. The medulla contains several *nuclei*—collections of neuron cell bodies—that control vital functions such as breathing, heart rate, and blood pressure, as well as coughing and sneezing.

Medulla:
A structure in the brain concerned with the regulation of vital bodily functions, such as breathing and heartbeat.

Pons:
A portion of the brain through which sensory and motor information pass and that contains structures relating to sleep, arousal, and the regulation of muscle tone and cardiac reflexes.

Reticular activating system:
A structure within the brain concerned with sleep, arousal, and the regulation of muscle tone and cardiac reflexes.

Cerebellum:
A part of the brain concerned with the regulation of basic motor activities.

Midbrain:
A part of the brain containing primitive centers for vision and hearing. It also plays a role in the regulation of visual reflexes.

Hypothalamus:
A small structure deep within the brain that plays a key role in the regulation of the autonomic nervous system and of several forms of motivated behavior, such as eating and aggression.

Thalamus:
A structure deep within the brain that receives sensory input from other portions of the nervous system and then transmits this information to the cerebral hemispheres and other parts of the brain.

Limbic system:
Several structures deep within the brain that play a role in emotional reactions and behavior.

Hippocampus:
A structure of the limbic system that plays a role in the formation of certain types of memories.

Amygdala:
A limbic system structure involved in aspects of emotional control and formation of emotional memories.

Cerebral cortex:
The outer covering of the cerebral hemispheres.

Behind the medulla and pons is the **cerebellum** (refer again to Figure 2.6), which is primarily concerned with regulating motor activities, serving to orchestrate muscular activities so that they occur in a synchronized fashion. The cerebellum also plays a role in certain cognitive processes, including language, reading, internal speech, and speech perception (Ackermann et al., 2004). Damage to the cerebellum results in jerky, poorly coordinated muscle functioning. If such damage is severe, it may be impossible for a person to stand, let alone walk or run. Damage to this structure has also been shown to impede word recognition and reduce cognitive flexibility (Berger et al., 2005; Mathiak et al., 2002). Cerebellar abnormality in the cerebellum has been linked to dyslexia and attention-deficit/hyperactivity disorder (ADHD) (Fawcett & Nicolson, 2003).

Above the medulla and pons, near the end of the brain stem, is a structure known as the **midbrain.** It contains an extension of the reticular activating system as well as primitive centers concerned with vision and hearing. The midbrain also contains structures that play a role in the pain-relieving effects of opiates and the control of motor movements by sensory input.

The Hypothalamus, Thalamus, and Limbic System: Motivation and Emotion

Ancient philosophers identified the heart as the center of our emotions. While this poetic belief is still reflected on many valentine cards, modern science indicates that it is wrong. If there is indeed a center for our appetites, emotions, and motives, it actually lies deep within the brain in several interrelated structures, including the *hypothalamus, thalamus,* and *limbic system.*

Although the **hypothalamus** is less than one cubic centimeter in size, this tiny structure exerts profound effects on our behavior. First, it regulates the autonomic nervous system, thus influencing reactions ranging from sweating and salivating to the shedding of tears and changes in blood pressure. Second, it plays a key role in *homeostasis*—the maintenance of the body's internal environment at optimal levels. Third, the hypothalamus seems to play a role in the regulation of eating and drinking, signaling us when to begin eating or drinking and when to stop. We'll consider this role in detail in our discussion of motivation and emotion (Chapter 8). The hypothalamus also plays a role in other forms of motivated behavior, such as mating and aggression. It exerts this influence, at least in part, by regulating the release of hormones from one of the endocrine glands, the *pituitary gland*.

Above the hypothalamus, quite close to the center of the brain, is another important structure, the **thalamus.** This structure consists of two football-shaped parts, one on each side of the brain. This has sometimes been called the great relay station of the brain, and with good reason. The thalamus receives input from all our senses except olfaction (smell), performs some preliminary analyses, and then transmits the information to other parts of the brain.

Finally, we should consider a set of structures that together are known as the **limbic system.** The structures that make up the limbic system play an important role in emotion and in motivated behavior, such as feeding, fleeing from danger, fighting, and sex. The largest of these structures, the **hippocampus,** plays a key role in the formation of memories (see Eichenbaum & Bunsey, 1995; Marshuetz, 2005), a topic we'll consider in Chapter 6. The **amygdala,** also part of the limbic system, is involved in aspects of emotional control. Damage to this structure can produce striking differences in behavior; for example, a typically docile cat may become uncontrollably violent.

The Cerebral Cortex: The Core of Complex Thought

Now, at last, we come to the part of the brain that seems to be responsible for our ability to reason, plan, remember, and imagine—the **cerebral cortex.** This outer surface of the brain is only about one-eighth of an inch thick, but it contains bil-

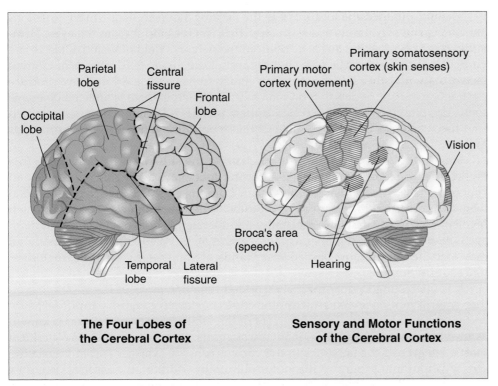

FIGURE 2.7
Major Regions of the Cerebral Cortex
The cerebral cortex is divided into four major lobes (*left drawing*). Specific areas in these lobes are
concerned with sensory and motor functions and with our higher mental processes (*right drawing*).

lions of neurons, each one connected to thousands of others. The cortex is divided
into two nearly symmetrical halves known as the *cerebral hemispheres*. Thus, many
of the structures described subsequently appear in both the left and right cerebral
hemispheres. As we'll soon see, however, this similarity in structure is not entirely
matched by similarity in function. The two hemispheres appear to be somewhat
specialized in the functions they perform.

In humans, the cerebral hemispheres are folded into many ridges and
grooves, which greatly increase their surface area. In other organisms, there are
fewer folds or no folds at all. The result is that the human cortex covers much
more area than does the cortex in other species. Each hemisphere is usually described, on the basis of the largest of these grooves or fissures, as being divided
into four regions or lobes: frontal, parietal, occipital, and temporal.

The **frontal lobe** occupies the area of the brain nearest the face and is bounded
by the deep *central fissure*. Lying along this fissure, just within the frontal lobe, is
the *motor cortex*, an area concerned with the control of body movements (see
Figure 2.7). Damage to this area does not produce total paralysis. Instead, it often
results in a loss of control over fine movements, especially of the fingers.

Across the central fissure from the frontal lobe is the **parietal lobe.** This area
contains the *somatosensory cortex*, to which information from the skin senses—
touch, temperature, pressure, and so on—is carried (see Figure 2.7). Damage to
this area produces a variety of effects, depending in part on whether injury occurs
to the left or right cerebral hemisphere. If damage involves the left hemisphere, individuals may lose the ability to read or write, or they may have difficulty knowing where parts of their own bodies are located. In contrast, if damage occurs in
the right hemisphere, individuals may seem unaware of the left side of their bodies. For example, a man may forget to shave the left side of his face.

Frontal lobe:
The portion of the cerebral
cortex that lies in front of the
central fissure.

Parietal lobe:
A portion of the cerebral cortex, lying behind the central
fissure, that plays a major role
in the skin senses: touch, temperature, and pressure.

The **occipital lobe** is located near the back of the head. Its primary functions are visual, and it contains a sensory area that receives input from the eyes. Damage to this area often produces a "hole" in the person's field of vision: Objects in a particular location can't be seen, but the rest of the visual field may remain unaffected. As with other brain structures, injury to the occipital lobe may produce contrasting effects, depending on which cerebral hemisphere is affected. Damage to the occipital lobe in the right hemisphere produces loss of vision in the left visual field, whereas damage to the occipital lobe in the left hemisphere produces loss of vision in the right visual field.

Finally, the **temporal lobe** is located along the side of each hemisphere (see Figure 2.7). The location makes sense, for this lobe plays a key role in hearing and contains a sensory area that receives input from the ears. Damage to the temporal lobe, too, can result in intriguing symptoms. When such injuries occur in the left hemisphere, people may lose the ability to understand spoken words. When damage is restricted to the right hemisphere, they may be able to recognize speech but may lose the ability to recognize other kinds of sound—for example, melodies, tones, or rhythms.

It is interesting to note that when added together, areas of the cortex that either control motor movements (motor cortex) or receive sensory input (sensory cortex) account for only 20 to 25 percent of the total area. The remainder is known as the *association cortex* and, as its name suggests, it is assumed to play a critical role in integrating the activities in the various sensory systems and in translating sensory input into programs for motor output. In addition, the association cortex seems to be involved in complex cognitive activities such as thinking, reasoning, remembering, language, recognizing faces, and a host of other functions. We'll return to several of these in the next major section.

KEY QUESTIONS

- What structures compose the brain stem? What are their functions?
- What are the functions of the hypothalamus and thalamus?
- What is the role of the cerebral cortex?

Two Minds in One Body? Our Divided Brain

The two hemispheres of the brain appear to be mirror images of each other. Yet, a large body of evidence suggests that, in fact, they are specialized to perform somewhat different functions, although they do not compete with each other as implied in the humorous example in Figure 2.8. In general terms, the left hemisphere is the *verbal* hemisphere—it is specialized for speech and other verbal tasks. In contrast, the right hemisphere specializes in the control of certain motor movements, in synthesis (putting isolated elements together), and in the comprehension and communication of *emotion*. Two kinds of evidence point to these conclusions: (1) studies of people whose cerebral hemispheres have been isolated from each other either through accident or (more typically) surgery performed for medical reasons, and (2) studies of the rest of us—people in whom the two cerebral hemispheres are connected in the normal way.

■ Research with split-brain persons.

Under normal conditions, the two hemispheres of the brain communicate with each other almost exclusively through the **corpus callosum,** a wide band of nerve fibers that passes between them (Cherbuin & Brinkman, 2006; Gazzaniga, 2000). Sometimes, though, it is necessary to cut this link for medical reasons—for example, to prevent the spread of epileptic seizures from one hemisphere to the other. Such operations largely eliminate communication between the two hemispheres, so they provide a unique opportunity to study the effects that result. Study of individuals who have undergone such operations provides intriguing evidence for

Occipital lobe:
A portion of the cerebral cortex involved in vision.

Temporal lobe:
The lobe of the cerebral cortex that is involved in hearing.

Corpus callosum:
A band of nerve fibers connecting the two hemispheres of the brain.

the view that the two hemispheres of the brain are indeed specialized to perform different tasks (Gazzaniga, 1984, 1985; Sperry, 1968). Following surgery, patients report viewing their disconnected hemispheres as having their own personality, each with its own distinct and often conflicting characteristics, such as likes, dislikes, opinions, aspirations, and morals (Zaidel, 1994; Iacoboni et al., 1996). They also describe frustration between their two hands, complaining for instance that the left hand is performing in a strange and unfamiliar way, even slapping the right hand. A right-handed person might be unable to put a name to an item held in the left (Bogen, 1993; Zaidel, 1994). While one hand is trying to put on clothes, the other might be busy trying to take them off!

Consider, for instance, the following demonstration. A man whose corpus callosum has been cut is seated before a screen and told to stare, with his eyes as motionless as possible, at a central point on the screen. Then the word *tenant* is flashed across the screen so that the letters *ten* appear to the left of the central point and the letters *ant* appear to the right. What does the man report seeing? Before you guess, consider the following fact: Because of the way our visual system is constructed, stimuli presented to the *left* visual field of each eye stimulate only the *right* hemisphere of the brain; items on the *right* side of the visual field of each eye stimulate only the *left* hemisphere.

"You'll have to forgive Sidney. The left and right hemispheres of his brain are currently engaged in a struggle for dominance..."

FIGURE 2.8
The Two Hemispheres of the Human Brain
The left and right hemispheres are specialized for different functions, and unlike the characters in this cartoon, the hemispheres do not compete with each other.
Source: From www.nearingzero.net. Reprinted by permission of Nick Kim, Cartoonist

Now, what do you think our split-brain person reports? If you said, "ant," you are correct. This would be expected, because only the left hemisphere, which controls speech, can answer verbally. However, when asked to *point* to the word he saw with his left hand (which is controlled by the right hemisphere), the man reacts differently: He points with his left hand to the word *ten* (part of the word *tenant*). So the right hemisphere has indeed seen and recognized this stimulus; it can't describe it in words, but it *can* point to it. While the left hemisphere is better at verbal tasks, the right hemisphere is superior in other respects—in copying drawings, recognizing faces, and expressing emotion.

■ **Research with persons whose hemispheres are connected.**

Additional evidence for specialization of function in the two hemispheres is provided by research on persons whose corpus callosum is intact—the great majority of us. For instance, consider the following kind of research, conducted with people who are about to undergo brain surgery. First, they are asked to describe traumatic emotional events (e.g., a near-fatal traffic accident). Not surprisingly, they do so in vivid terms. Then, as preparation for surgery, they receive a drug injected into an artery that leads to the right hemisphere; as a result, this hemisphere is anesthetized. When asked to describe the same events again, they do so in much less intense terms. This provides support for the view that the right hemisphere plays a key role in the experience and expression of emotions (see Ross, Homan, & Buck, 1994).

Research involving individuals who have sustained damage to the right hemisphere has yielded similar findings. Whereas most people are readily able to judge the emotional states of others from viewing their face and/or hearing the tone of their voice, individuals who sustain damage to the right hemisphere frequently cannot (see Figure 2.9, page 54). Their interpersonal skills and social behavior, such as responding appropriately to social cues, can also be adversely affected (Perry et al., 2001; Adolphs, 2002). The right hemisphere also appears to be home to our ability to process humor. People with damaged right hemispheres don't seem to "get" humorous stories, and not surprisingly, they fail to exhibit facial expressions consistent with amusement, such as smiling after hearing a funny joke

FIGURE 2.9
The Right Brain Hemisphere of The Brain and Humor
The right hemisphere appears to play a key role in our ability to process humor. People with damaged right hemispheres don't seem to "get" humorous stories and they fail to exhibit appropriate facial expressions, such as smiling after hearing a joke.

(Shammi & Stuss, 1999). People who experience this type of damage also have difficulty interpreting the relationship between a verbal comment and its context, such as sarcastic remarks, irony, satire, and metaphoric language (Coulson et al., 2005; Shamay-Tsoory et al., 2005).

Finally, evidence for this view is provided by studies using a technique known as *PET scans;* such scans reveal the levels of activity in different portions of the brain occurring as individuals perform various tasks—the more active the area, the more vivid the color. Research with this technique indicates that when individuals speak or work with numbers, activity in the left hemisphere increases. In contrast, when they work on perceptual tasks—for instance, tasks in which they compare various shapes—activity increases in the right hemisphere (see Springer & Deutsch, 1985). Interestingly, additional research suggests that while individuals are making up their minds about some issue, activity is higher in the left than in the right hemisphere (Sharp, Scott, & Wise, 2004). However, once logical thought is over and a decision has been made, heightened activity occurs in the right hemisphere, which seems to play a larger role in global, nonanalytic thought—for instance, overall reactions of the "I like it" or "I don't like it" type.

In sum, a large body of evidence suggests that, in a sense, we *do* seem to possess two minds in one brain: The two cerebral hemispheres are specialized for performing somewhat different tasks. Why does such specialization exist? From an evolutionary perspective, the answer might be, "Because it is beneficial and increases our chances of survival." For instance, because the right hemisphere specializes in responding to emotion-provoking events (e.g., dangers in the world around us), it can respond very quickly—more quickly than if the two hemispheres were identical in function.

Now that we've examined the structure of the brain and the functions of its major parts, we are just about ready to explore its complex role in many forms of behavior. Before discussing this topic, however, we'll pause to briefly examine the methods used by psychologists to study brain–behavior links.

How Psychologists Study the Nervous System and the Brain

While many procedures for studying the nervous system exist, most fit under three major categories: observing the effects of *damage* to various parts of the brain; *recording neural activity;* and techniques for studying the *intact, living brain.*

■ Observing the effects of damage.

The world, unfortunately, can be a dangerous place. Many people sustain damage to their brains in automobile or industrial accidents; many others develop illnesses that damage their brains directly, or that lead to medical procedures (e.g., surgery) that produce such effects. While these events are tragic for the persons who experience them, they provide psychologists with an invaluable research opportunity. By observing the symptoms or deficits shown by such people, it is sometimes possible to determine which portions of their brains are involved in various forms of behavior. For instance, consider a person who shows the following, baffling set of symptoms: If one object is held in front of her, she can name it. If two objects are held in front of her, however, she can name one of them but not the other. In addition, she can recognize that one wooden block is larger than the other, but when asked to pick one up, she fails to adjust the distance between her fingers and thumb according to the size of the object. What is responsible for these strange symptoms? By studying a number of persons who show them, psychologists have determined that they involve damage to an area of the brain on the border between the parietal and occipital lobes (see Broussaud et al., 1996; Goodale et al., 1994). In many instances, then, studying persons who have experienced damage to areas of their brains can provide valuable information.

Where people are concerned, psychologists must wait for naturally occurring damage or medical procedures to see what effects result from harm to the brain. With laboratory animals, in contrast, it is possible to produce such damage to study the effects that occur. Although this may sound cruel, it is, of course, done under highly humane conditions and produces no pain in the subjects (the brain has no pain receptors). Moreover, such research is performed only when the information to be acquired can contribute to human welfare (e.g., to develop new treatments that are best for reducing chronic pain).

■ Recording a neural activity.

A second way to study the brain concerns recording the electrical activity that occurs within it. This can involve recording the activity of individual neurons (with tiny *microelectrodes* implanted into the brain) or of brain regions (with larger *macroelectrodes*). In both cases, changes in patterns of activity that occur in response to specific stimuli, or during various activities, are recorded. Changes in response to specific stimuli or events are referred to as *event-related brain potentials*, or ERPs for short. The results can often help identify the specific functions of different regions of the brain. With humans, electrodes cannot generally be implanted in the brain, so recordings are made from the outside of the scalp (the *electroencephalogram*).

■ Images of the intact, functioning brain.

In recent years, advances in technology have provided an array of valuable new techniques to study the brain as it actually functions. Many of these exist, but here we'll briefly describe two of the most important. The first of these is **magnetic resonance imaging,** or **MRI.** This technique is based on the fact that hydrogen atoms, found in all living tissue, emit measurable waves of energy when exposed to a strong magnetic field. In MRI, these waves are used as a basis for constructing extremely clear images of the brain. A recent development is *functional MRI,* in which images can be scanned much more quickly than in the past.

A second important technique is **positron emission tomography,** or **PET.** As discussed in an earlier section, PET scans peer into the functioning brain by measuring blood flow in various neural areas, or by gauging the rate at which glucose, the brain's fuel, is metabolized. Individuals undergoing PET scans are injected with small amounts of harmless radioactive isotopes attached to either water or glucose molecules. Blood flow (containing the radioactive water molecules) is greatest in the most active areas of the brain. Similarly, glucose is absorbed by brain cells in proportion to their level of activity, with the most active cells taking in the greatest amount of glucose. As a result, PET scans allow scientists to map activity in various parts of a person's brain as she or he reads, listens to music, or engages in a mental activity such as solving math problems. For instance, look at the PET scans in Figure 2.10 on page 56. The top row shows brain activity while a person is in a relaxed state; the lower scans show the same person's brain while he is clenching and unclenching his fist. Scans can be made while people perform almost any activity imaginable, or can be made to compare people having various mental disorders with people who do not show such disorders. As you can guess, PET scans provide psychologists with an extremely valuable tool.

Now that we've described the basic methods used by psychologists to study the brain, let's see what recent research using such methods has revealed.

Magnetic resonance imaging (MRI):
A method to study the intact brain in which images are obtained by exposing the brain to a strong magnetic field.

Positron emission tomography (PET):
An imaging technique that detects the activity of the brain by measuring glucose use or blood flow.

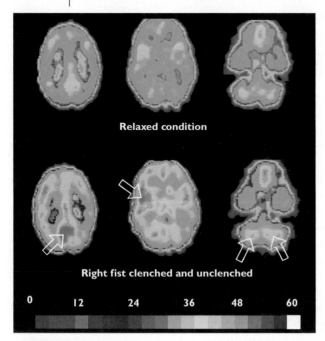

Relaxed condition

Right fist clenched and unclenched

0   12   24   36   48   60

FIGURE 2.10
PET Scans: An Example
PET scans reveal the amount of activity occurring in different parts of the brain as individuals perform various tasks. The scans in the top row were made while the individual was at rest. The ones in the bottom row were made as he clenched his right fist and then unclenched it. Clearly, this motor action was associated with increased activity in many parts of the brain. (The brighter the color, the more activity, as shown in the color chart below the photos.)
Source: Courtesy of Brookhaven National Laboratory.

These methods have definitely lived up to their promise, and have added tremendously to our knowledge of the intricate—and intimate—links between the brain and behavior.

KEY QUESTIONS

• Who are "split-brain" persons? What evidence do they provide for specialization of function in the two cerebral hemispheres?
• What evidence from persons with intact brains supports such specialization?
• What methods are used by psychologists to study the brain and its role in behavior?

THE BRAIN AND HUMAN BEHAVIOR: WHERE BIOLOGY AND CONSCIOUSNESS MEET

Armed with the new techniques and procedures described previously, psychologists and other scientists have begun to understand how the brain functions to produce human consciousness—our perceptions of the world around us, our thoughts, memories, and emotions. As you can probably guess, the findings of this research are complex, but they also tell a fascinating story.

How the Brain Functions: A Modern View

Do modern computers provide a good model of how the human brain works? As we'll see in Chapter 6, such a model has been useful in the study of memory, because our brains and computers do seem similar in certain respects. Both can receive information, enter it into storage (memory), and retrieve it at a later time. But computers and the human brain are different in at least one fundamental way. Computers are *serial* devices: They work on information one step at a time. In contrast, our brains appear to process information in a *parallel* fashion; this means that many *modules*—collections of interconnected neurons—process information in different ways simultaneously. These modules may be scattered at widely different locations in the brain. Moreover, each may work on a different aspect of a task. The more complex the task, the greater the number of modules that are called into operation. The result is that even very complex tasks can be handled very quickly, because different aspects of them are performed at the same time.

To discover how the brain handles its myriad information processing tasks so efficiently, scientists have used brain-imaging techniques, including *f* MRIs, to observe the activity in people's brains and determine how different regions interact as they perform simple tasks (Chialvo, 2004). To allow a more fine-grained view of how the interaction between different areas occurs, each brain image (in a continuous stream of images) is divided into a matrix of thousands of tiny three-dimensional cube-shaped areas termed *voxels*. The image intensity at each voxel usually indicates the amount of brain activity at that site. Results thus far seem to indicate that the brain is organized into networks in which most of the component areas have only a few connections; a few of the areas, however, have connections to many others (Eguiluz et al., 2005). These latter "superconnected" areas appear to act as hubs, much like the Internet or a gossipy friend, helping to get the information out quickly and widely. The result of this organization is, of course, increased speed and efficiency in carrying out cognitive tasks.

Plasticity of the Human Brain: How the Brain Is Shaped by Experience

Now that we've described how the brain functions, it's important to consider another basic fact about it: its *plasticity*. Psychologists use this term to refer to the fact that the brain can be altered by experience. So, for example, if you learn a new skill, such as how to play a musical instrument, changes occur in the structure of your brain—changes that can, potentially, be observed and measured. Similarly, our capacity to retain information in memory, too, is related to structural changes in the brain. Many factors, aside from experience, are capable of producing such changes, including various drugs, hormones, illness, and stress (Kolb, Gibb, & Robinson, 2003). What kinds of changes are produced by these and other aspects of our life experiences? Changes are made in the number of neurons in various parts of our brain, and in the length of dendrites and dendritic "spines," areas where neurons form synapses with many other neurons. For instance, when animals are placed in complex, stimulating environments, either as juveniles, in adulthood, or even in old age, they experience structural changes in their brains. The precise nature of these changes, though, may vary with their ages—thus illustrating how complex the interplay between our brains and the external world actually is (see Kolb, Gibb, & Gorny, 2003). For additional information concerning how such changes occur in the brains of people as well, please see the **Psychology Lends a Hand** section on page 58.

Plasticity of the brain also extends to what happens after injuries. If the areas damaged are not too extensive or crucial, functions that are lost can be recovered, as other neurons and other regions of the brain "take over" the tasks performed by the damaged areas. For instance, after suffering serious strokes that damage motor areas of their brains, many patients can no longer work. After undergoing months of physical therapy, however, they may regain this ability as other, nearby regions "learn" to perform the necessary functions.

The Brain and Human Speech

The brain's capacity to produce and understand speech is truly remarkable. Consider those individuals fluent in more one language. In recent studies, bilinguals performed memory tasks more efficiently than their monolingual counterparts (Bialystok et al., 2004). In 2003, the U.S. Census Bureau reported that nearly 18 percent of Americans spoke a language other than English in their homes (U.S. Census Bureau, 2003). With the rapid growth of the Hispanic population (an increase of 58 percent from 1990 to 2000), it's not surprising that Spanish seems to be the language most on the rise in the United States. English-speaking children are acquiring the ability to speak Spanish from the increased number of Hispanic and Latin American caregivers immigrating to the United States. A rise in the number of adoptions from Asian countries has created an increase in bilingualism in homes where parents desire to maintain a connection to a child's roots. Children of couples who speak different languages readily become bilingual when each parent speaks only his or her native tongue to the child. The good news for bilinguals is that the positive effects continue into old age, and seem to thwart some of the deterioration of cognitive processes that occurs with normal aging (Bialystock et al., 2004). In recent decades, psychologists and other scientists have gained a much clearer picture of the regions of our brains that play a key role in speech. We say "regions" because, in fact, several areas are important, and it is the integrated functioning of all of them that allows us to produce and understand speech.

PSYCHOLOGY LENDS A HAND

The Potential Role of Brain Plasticity in Cognitive Processes

As we've noted previously, an important characteristic of the brain is its plasticity; the fact that it can be changed through experience. Until recently, much of the evidence supporting this idea has been based on studies of animals. More recently, researchers have employed brain-imaging techniques to investigate plasticity in the brains of humans. In one recent study, Shaw and colleagues (2006) used magnetic resonance imaging (MRI) to scan the brains of several hundred children at several points while they were growing up, from the ages of about six to twenty. When the researchers divided the children into groups according to their intelligence, they noticed intriguing differences in the pattern of changes that occurred in the frontal cortex—the area of the brain involved in abstract reasoning, planning, and other complex thought processes. The smartest boys and girls started with relatively thin cortexes that grew thicker at a rapid pace, peaking at about age eleven (please refer to Figure 2.11). The cortex of these children subsequently thinned out quickly during early adolescence. In the children of average intelligence, cortical thickness peaked earlier, at about age eight, and then declined gradually. By age nineteen, the groups converged, with all the children having cortexes of roughly equal thickness.

The researchers propose that the distinctive growth pattern observed in the smartest children reflects extended development of neural circuits that underlie critical components of intelligence, such as reasoning, planning, and other aspects of analytical thinking. This would suggest that the brains of highly intelligent children are more plastic or have a greater capacity for memory compared to children of average intelligence.

It is also likely, however, that environmental factors may have contributed to differences in the children's brain development, as the researchers concede that many of the smartest kids were also from the wealthiest families. Thus, differences in nutrition, quality of education received, family size, and how the children spent their leisure time may have also played a role. Since people's intelligence is affected by the intelligence of those they associate with, other factors, such as the quality of conversation during family chats, may be important, too (Dickens & Flynn, 2001). In short, features present in the environments in which the smartest children were raised may have differentially stimulated the pattern of their brain development relative to the children of average intelligence who were raised in less advantaged circumstances.

So what can we take away from all this? Clearly, heredity plays an important role in determining intelligence and many other individual differences, and the markedly different patterns of cortical growth observed for children of superior and average intelligence seems to support this view. However, the results also indicate that providing children with an enriched rather than intellectually impoverished atmosphere can help them attain the highest reaches of their natural ability. Here are a few useful tips to help your children achieve their greatest intellectual potential:

- Monitor your child's diet. The benefits of good nutrition are varied and many.
- Choose intellectually stimulating topics of conversation for family time. Make your children think.
- Promote fascinating and thought-provoking reading material for leisure time.
- Solve a mystery or memorize a famous poem together.
- Make puzzles, brainteasers, and word games a part of free time. Strategy games such as chess get the gears turning.
- Don't give away the ending! Have a child provide an imaginative alternative ending to a short story.
- Pick out educational television programs to view together and discuss afterward.
- Schedule quality one-on-one time with a child to allow her to express her views, ask questions, and brainstorm.

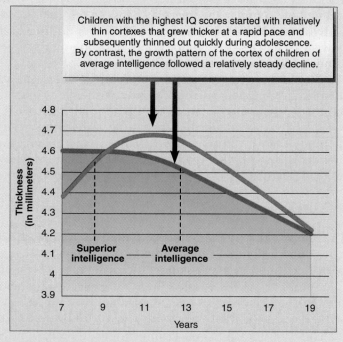

FIGURE 2.11

Brain Plasticity and Intelligence: Some Recent Findings
Different patterns of cortical growth were apparent between children of superior intelligence and children of average intelligence. Researchers propose that the distinctive growth pattern in the smartest children reflects extended development of neural circuits that underlie components of intelligence. However, environmental factors may also play an important role.
Source: Based on data from Shaw et al., 2006.

Let's start with speech production. Here, a region in the frontal lobe near the primary motor cortex, known as **Broca's area,** is crucial. Damage to this area disrupts the ability to speak, producing a condition known as *Broca's aphasia*. People with Broca's aphasia produce slow, laborious speech that does not follow normal rules of grammar. In addition, persons with Broca's aphasia can't seem to find the word they want, and even if they do, have difficulty pronouncing the word. What do all these symptoms mean? One interpretation is that this portion of the brain, and the regions immediately around it, contain memories of the sequences of muscular movements in the mouth and tongue that produce words. When it is damaged, therefore, the ability to produce coherent speech is impaired.

Broca's area has long been recognized as the center of language production, but other research points to the role of this region in functions other than speech and articulation, such as motor activation, motor imagery, and rhythmic perception (Embick & Poeppel, 2003). It also seems to play a part in understanding action, imitating motor activities, sequencing of events, and speech-related hand and facial gestures (Nishitani et al, 2005).

Although the primary therapy for those with Broca's aphasia has been speech and language rehabilitation, studies are under way with prospects of attaining a more successful recovery of language motor skills. The experiments involve surgically implanting a small electrode and administering electric current to the cortex in conjunction with the language rehabilitation. Because unimpaired parts of the cortex seem able to adjust for the missing motor functions, researchers are hopeful that the electrical stimulation during the language therapy will trigger new connections and help regain lost motor functions (U.S. National Institutes for Health, 2005).

The task of speech comprehension—understanding what others say—seems to be focused largely in another region of the brain located in the temporal lobe. Damage to this region—known as **Wernicke's area**—produces three major symptoms: inability to recognize spoken words (i.e., to tell one from another), inability to understand the meaning of these words, and inability to convert thoughts into words. Together, these symptoms are known as *Wernicke's aphasia*. Careful study of these symptoms has revealed that they stem from somewhat different kinds of damage to the brain. For instance, if Wernicke's area alone is damaged, pure word deafness occurs—individuals can't understand what is said to them and they can't repeat words they hear; that's the first major symptom listed above. They aren't deaf, however; they can recognize the emotion expressed by the tone of others' speech (e.g., that they are angry or sad), and can hear other sounds, such as doorbells or a dog barking. Further, they can understand what other people say by reading their lips. Other kinds of damage produce the other symptoms mentioned (e.g., inability to convert thoughts into words).

Putting these and related findings together, the following model of human speech has emerged. The meanings of words involve our memories for them—what they represent (objects, actions), and such memories are stored in sensory association areas outside Broca's and Wernicke's areas. *Comprehension* of speech involves a flow of information from Wernicke's area to the posterior language area and then to sensory association areas and back again. In contrast, speech *production* involves the flow of information from sensory association areas to the posterior language area and then to Broca's area. This is probably an oversimplification of a highly complex process, but it is consistent with current knowledge about the role of the brain in speech. Figure 2.12 on page 60 summarizes this model of human speech.

The Brain and Higher Mental Processes

Try this simple problem: Maria has longer hair than Takesha. Takesha has longer hair than Brianna. Does Maria have longer hair than Brianna? The answer is obvious, but how do you obtain it so effortlessly? The basic theme of this chapter

Broca's area:
A region in the prefrontal cortex that plays a role in the production of speech.

Wernicke's area:
An area in the temporal lobe that plays a role in the comprehension of speech.

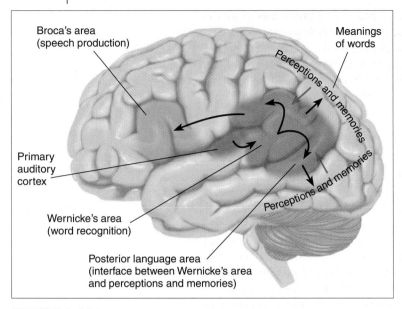

FIGURE 2.12
The Neural Basis of Human Speech: One Model
Existing research suggests that *comprehension* of speech involves the flow of information from Wernicke's area to the posterior language area and then to sensory association areas and back again. (The meanings of words may be stored in sensory association areas.) Speech *production* involves the flow of information from sensory association areas to the posterior language area and then to Broca's area. *Source:* Neil R. Carlson, *Foundations of Physiological Psychology*, 4/e © 1999. Published by Allyn and Bacon, Boston, MA. Copyright © 1999 by Pearson Education. Reprinted by permission of the publisher.

("Everything psychological is ultimately biological") suggests that reasoning, problem solving, planning, and all our *higher mental processes* must involve events occurring in our brains. But what parts of our brains? And what kind of events? These are among the questions investigated by psychologists in their efforts to understand the role of the brain in all aspects of human behavior (see Johnson et al., 2004; Robin & Holyoak, 1995). As an example of this research, let's consider findings concerning the neural foundations of one important kind of reasoning.

Relational reasoning, is illustrated by the hair-length example. In essence, reasoning depends on the ability to manipulate mental representations of relations between objects and events in our minds: You don't have to see Maria, Takesha, and Brianna to know that Maria's hair is longer—you can tell just from reasoning about them. But here's the crucial point: While you can tell that Maria's hair is longer than Takesha's directly from the sentence "Maria's hair is longer than Takesha's," there is no statement comparing Maria and Brianna, so here you must mentally integrate available information to attain the correct solution. This ability, many experts believe, may underlie several of our higher mental processes. For instance, consider planning. To formulate effective plans, we must be able to arrange many goals and subgoals according to their importance, and this, again, involves being able to mentally manipulate information so that we can see, for instance, that goal C is more important than goal D, which, in turn, is more important than goal F (see Delis et al., 1992).

Now for the key question: Does any part of the brain play a special role in such reasoning? A growing body of evidence suggests that the *prefrontal cortex*—part of the association areas of the brain—is a likely candidate (see Graham & Hodges, 1997; Waltz et al., 1999).

KEY QUESTIONS

- What is the modern view of how the brain functions?
- What is brain plasticity and why is it important?
- What evidence suggests that processing of visual information occurs in a parallel fashion?
- What is the modern view of speech production and speech comprehension?
- What portions of the brain are involved in relational reasoning?

HEREDITY AND BEHAVIOR: GENETICS AND EVOLUTIONARY PSYCHOLOGY

My son Ryan and I (Michael Kalsher) have always looked very much alike and many people point this out when they see us together (you can judge for yourself in the photo in Figure 2.13, page 62). The fact that we do often resemble people to whom we are closely related illustrates the powerful impact of **heredity**—biologically determined characteristics—on our physical appearance and traits. But what about be-

Heredity:
Biologically determined characteristics passed from parents to their offspring.

havior? Does heredity affect the ways in which we behave and think, too? A growing body of evidence suggests that it does, although the relationship between heredity and complex forms of behavior is very complex. Let's take a look, first, at the basic processes through which we inherit the predisposition or potential for a wide range of characteristics from our parents. After that, we'll consider some of the evidence for the impact of heredity on complex and important forms of behavior.

Genetics: Some Basic Principles

Every cell of your body contains a set of biological blueprints that enable it to perform its essential functions. This information is contained in **chromosomes,** structures found in the nuclei of all cells. Chromosomes are composed of a substance known as DNA, short for deoxyribonucleic acid. DNA, in turn, is made up of several simpler components arranged in the form of a double helix—something like the twisting water slides found by the sides of large swimming pools. Chromosomes contain thousands of **genes**—segments of DNA that serve as basic units of heredity. Our genes, working in complex combinations and together with forces in the environment, ultimately determine many aspects of our biological makeup.

Most cells in the human body contain forty-six chromosomes, existing in pairs. When such cells divide, the chromosome pairs split; then, after the cells have separated, each chromosome replicates itself so that the full number is restored. This kind of cell division is known as **mitosis.** In contrast, sperm and ova—the male and female sex cells, or gametes—contain only twenty-three chromosomes. Thus, when they join to form a fertilized ovum from which a new human being will develop, the full number (forty-six) is attained. For each of us, then, half of our genetic material comes from our mother and half from our father. In general, the members of each pair of chromosomes look very similar—with one exception. One chromosome pair is directly linked to biological sex: Females possess two chromosomes that are "full-size" and contain one thousand or more genes (X chromosomes). Males, in contrast, possess an X chromosome and a much shorter Y chromosome, which contains fewer than one hundred genes. Because there is only one Y chromosome, it cannot divide like other chromosomes during mitosis. Rather, it bends in half and reproduces in this manner (Wade, 2003).

These basic mechanisms explain why persons who are related resemble one another more than persons who are unrelated, and also why the closer the familial tie between individuals, the more similar they tend to be physically. The closer such links, the greater the proportion of chromosomes and genes family members share. And because genes determine many aspects of physical appearance, similarity increases with closeness of relationship. Thus, siblings (children of the same parents) tend to be more alike than cousins (the children of siblings). In the case of identical twins, or *monozygotic* twins, a single fertilized egg splits in two and forms two embryos; in contrast, nonidentical, or *fraternal*, twins grow from two eggs fertilized by two different sperm. Because identical twins share all their genes, they are usually remarkably similar in appearance. They are surprisingly similar in other respects as well, including—amazingly!—their religious beliefs, their television viewing preferences, and even how they express their grief (see Segal & Bouchard, 1993).

While genes may strongly affect our physical characteristics, their relationship to psychological characteristics and to behavior is often highly complex. Genes do not *control* behavior or other aspects of life directly. Rather, they exert their influence indirectly, through their impact on chemical reactions in the brain or other organs. Moreover, as we'll soon see, these reactions may be strongly influenced by environmental conditions. In short, our genes equip us with predispositions to develop or show certain patterns of behavior or traits, but the environments in which we live play a major role in determining whether, and to what extent, such tendencies become reality. To make matters even more complex, most human traits are determined by more than one gene. Hundreds of genes acting in concert with

Chromosomes:
Threadlike structures containing genetic material, found in nearly every cell of the body.

Genes:
Biological "blueprints" that shape development and all basic bodily processes.

Mitosis:
Cell division in which chromosome pairs split and then replicate themselves so that the full number is restored in each of the cells produced by division.

FIGURE 2.13
The Role of Heredity in Physical Appearance
Do this father (Michael Kalsher) and his son (Ryan) look alike? Many people frequently comment on the resemblance. Do you agree? If so, this is a clear illustration of the role of genetic factors in physical characteristics such as facial appearance.

environmental forces may be involved in shaping complex physical or cognitive abilities (Lerner, 1993; McClearn et al., 1991). So, while there is increasing evidence for the role of genetic factors in many aspects of human behavior, heredity is only part of the total story.

Disentangling Genetic and Environmental Effects: Research Strategies

If both heredity and environment influence human behavior, the next question is obvious: How do we separate these factors to determine the relative contribution of each to any particular aspect of behavior? This question relates, of course, to the *nature–nurture controversy* described in Chapter 1, and psychologists use a number of different methods to address it. Two of these, however, have proven to be most useful: *twin studies* and *adoption studies*.

Twin studies are helpful in disentangling the relative roles of genetic and environmental factors in a given form of behavior because identical twins share the same genes, while fraternal twins do not. Under normal conditions, however, both kinds of twins are raised in environments that, if not identical, are at least very similar. After all, pairs of twins are normally raised in the same homes, attend the same schools, and so on. Thus, if a given aspect of behavior is strongly influenced by genetic factors, we'd expect identical twins to resemble each other more closely in this respect than fraternal twins. If an aspect of behavior is *not* influenced by genetic factors, however, we would not anticipate such resemblances. As we'll see in Chapter 11, psychologists have used this approach to investigate the role of genetic factors in many forms of mental disorder and have found that, indeed, genetic factors *do* play a role in several of these (e.g., phobias, autistic disorders, depression, schizophrenia; see Merkelbach et al., 1996).

A major problem with such twin studies, however, is obvious: The environments in which they are raised are often *not* identical. This is especially true for fraternal twins who may differ in sex, and so are treated quite differently by parents and other persons. For this reason, twin studies, while revealing, cannot provide conclusive evidence on the relative role of genetic and environmental factors. Actually, *no* single type of study can provide such evidence, but a second research approach—*adoption studies*—does seem to come closer to this goal. Such research focuses on identical twins who are separated very soon after birth and are adopted into different homes. Because the twins have identical genes, differences between them with respect to various aspects of behavior can reasonably be attributed to environmental factors. We'll describe research using this approach at several points in this book, and as we'll see in those discussions, adoption studies involving identical twins provide compelling evidence for the role of genetic factors in many aspects of human behavior. Even when they are raised in sharply contrasting environments, identical twins show remarkable degrees of similarity in everything from various aspects of their personalities, to attitudes and values, hobbies, career choices, and even job satisfaction (see Figure 2.14; Lykken et al., 1992; Hershberger, Lichtenstein, & Knox, 1994).

One might think that because of their high degree of similarity, identical twins might also choose similar mates. However, existing evidence seems to cast doubt on this possibility. In a study testing opinions of a twin's choice of spouse, about two-thirds of male twins reported indifference to or actual dislike of their twin's spouse. When the spouses were questioned, only about one in ten said they could have fallen in love with their own spouse's identical twin and about one in three actively disliked the twin. It seems that other factors may exert more influence over a twin's mate selection than the many shared genetic predispositions (Lykken & Tellegen, 1993; Rushton & Bons, 2005).

Based on findings from twin studies and adoption studies, psychologists have been able to arrive at estimates of what is known as **heritability** for various traits. This term refers to the extent to which variations among individuals with respect to a given aspect of behavior or a given trait are due to genetic factors. So, if it is found that heritability for a given trait is 0.50, this suggests that 50 percent of the differences between individuals in this trait is due to genetic factors. For instance, suppose it was found that the heritability of intelligence is 0.50 (it actually is). This means that 50 percent of the variation in intelligence among individuals in the population for which heritability has been estimated is due to genetic factors. It does *not* mean that half of each person's intelligence is determined by genetic factors and half by environmental factors. So, heritability estimates should be treated with caution. Still, they do provide a rough index of the extent to which genetic factors influence any aspect of behavior, and so are of considerable interest.

FIGURE 2.14

Identical Twins: More Than Mere Look-Alikes

Growing evidence suggests that identical twins are highly similar with respect to many aspects of behavior—not just in the way they look. Moreover, this is so even if they are separated very early in life and raised in different environments. These findings suggest that genetic factors play a role in a much wider range of human behavior than was once believed.

We just mentioned that intelligence (at least the kind measured by IQ) has a heritability index of 0.50. This might lead you to conclude that scientists should be able to identify specific genes that contribute to a high IQ. Efforts to do this, though, have run into major obstacles. While it appears that some genes (probably many) are related to intelligence, each makes a very small contribution. Thus, it is primarily the complex interplay between these genes, and between genes and the environment, that determines intelligence. For instance, a very small difference in intelligence produced by genetic factors may be magnified, over time, by differences in experience, as we noted in the **Psychology Lends a Hand** feature earlier in this chapter. A child who starts out with slightly above-average intelligence may spend more time reading and thus may receive more praise from teachers than a child who starts out with average intelligence. These experiences may serve to magnify the first child's initially small advantage in intelligence. Similarly, children raised in environments that stimulate and challenge them intellectually may develop higher IQs as a result of these experiences (Begley, 2003). Smaller family size allows parents and other significant adults to enrich a child's learning. How children spend their leisure time may also sharpen their cognitive capacities (e.g., reading or playing complex games such as chess). Technological advances in the machinery and gadgets we regularly use, such as computers and digital devices, may also be boosting the demands on our thought-processing abilities (Dickens & Flynn, 2001).

So, clearly, single genes do not determine anything as complex as intelligence. Rather, such multifaceted traits are shaped by intricate interplay between genetic and environmental forces. (We'll describe these in detail in Chapter 6.)

Heritability:
The extent to which variations among individuals, with respect to a given aspect of behavior or a given trait, are due to genetic factors.

Evolutionary Psychology: Genes in Action

Do you recall our discussion of the new field of **evolutionary psychology** in Chapter 1? To refresh your memory: This field suggests that our species, like all others on the planet, has been subject to the process of biological evolution throughout its history. As a result, we now possess a large number of *evolved psychological mechanisms* that help (or once helped) us to deal with important problems relating to survival. These have evolved because organisms vary greatly in many different ways, and some of these variations can be passed from one generation to the next through genes. Because some of these variations give individuals

Evolutionary psychology:
A new field of psychology, suggesting that as a result of evolution, humans now possess a large number of evolved psychological mechanisms that help (or once helped) us deal with important problems relating to survival.

PSYCHOLOGY LENDS A HAND

Promoting Prosocial Behavior to Reduce Aggression

As we've noted repeatedly throughout this chapter, heredity and environment play important complementary roles in the development and expression of many forms of complex behavior. Research shows this is true for both *prosocial behavior*—our propensity to be concerned for the welfare of others—and aggression. Genetically determined factors, such as high testosterone levels in boys, can give rise to aggression, but parents' response to their child's aggressive behavior can have an impact on the expression of that tendency (Rushton, 2004). Children who exhibit genetically influenced antisocial behavior that is met by positive, warm, nurturing discipline tend to demonstrate more prosocial behavior and less aggressive behavior than those who are met with parental harshness and strict punishment. Indeed, hostile-reactive behavior on the part of a parent can actually *promote* antisocial behavior, even in a child who might not otherwise be prone to behave in that manner. And children who seem to be just plain "born difficult" can adversely affect the home environment by increasing negative emotions in parents who might naturally have pleasant temperaments.

During adolescence, when physiological changes are at their peak, it is especially important for parents to use reason to avoid power struggles and exert a positive sway toward constructive behavior. Children who are provided with structure, including a consistently applied set of rules for their behavior, are more likely to mirror their parents' principles and values and lean toward empathy, compassion, selflessness, and cooperation (Knafo & Plomin, 2006). Over the long run, evidence indicates that parents who are caring role models—that is, ones who display positive, affectionate, and empathic behavior toward their children—may promote increased levels of prosocial behavior even in children who possess a tendency to engage in antisocial behavior.

The main point of this discussion is simply this: Just because a tendency or behavior stems, in part, from genetic factors in no way means that it cannot be modified. Remember: The nervous system and brain show a high degree of plasticity. As a result, new experiences and information can modify the underlying structures that shape our behaviors. So, while biology is important, it is not destiny where humans are concerned. Change is always possible, and adaptability may, in fact, be the most useful evolved psychological mechanism we possess!

who possess them an advantage in terms of reproduction, natural selection ensures that, over time, these variations become more common in the species. But watch out: Just because a characteristic or behavioral tendency exists among members of a species (including our own) does *not* guarantee that it is useful (adaptive). On the contrary, it may simply exist because it is linked, genetically, to something else that *is* useful (de Waal, 2002). For instance, consider the structure of the human back: Because it is not well suited for our upright posture, many people suffer serious back problems (slipped disks, neck pain). Why, then, do we continue to have the back structure we do? Perhaps because the advantages conferred by an upright posture are so great that they outweigh these problems. This illustrates the fact that just because something exists in a species does *not* guarantee that it is useful or adaptive; it may, in fact, be the "by-product" of something else that *is* adaptive.

We examined some examples of evolutionary psychology in Chapter 1, so here we'll simply note that this perspective has been used to shed light on a wide range of behaviors, everything from *dominance motivation*—why people often desire to attain positions of high status in their societies (see Ellis, 1995)—through the tendency to help others—to show *prosocial behavior*, a tendency we explore in greater detail in the **Psychology Lends a Hand** feature above. In fact, recent studies suggest that even our preference for fair treatment may reflect a genetic component. Consider research by Brosnan and de Waal (2003), conducted with monkeys. Pairs of monkeys working in full view of each other were first rewarded with tokens that they could then trade for slices of cucumber. After the monkeys had learned to do this, conditions were changed so that one was rewarded with grapes while the other continued to receive cucumbers. Because monkeys strongly prefer grapes to cucumbers, the key question was this: Would the under-rewarded monkeys (the ones still receiving cucumber) object? In fact, they did; many refused to exchange their tokens for this inadequate reward, and some even threw the cucumber away after receiving it! One interpretation of these findings is that the desire for fairness is "built into" our primate nature (although, of course, other explanations exist, as well; for instance, perhaps the monkeys had already learned to value fairness through their past experience). We'll return to the role of perceived fairness in work settings in Chapter 14.

In sum, evolutionary psychology provides a unique and intriguing perspective on the question of *how* our genes can, over time, shape our behavior. Whether the explanations it provides will turn out to be valid, however, can be determined only by further, careful research. If a tendency to behave in some way is an evolved psychological mechanism, does this mean it cannot be changed? Absolutely not! For an example of how behaviors that may partly reflect genetic factors may be altered, please see the **Psychology Lends a Hand** section on the previous page.

KEY QUESTIONS

- How do psychologists seek to separate the role of genetic and environmental factors in many forms of behavior?
- What is heritability?
- Why is it true that the existence of a trait or behavior among members of a species does not guarantee that the trait or behavior is useful or adaptive?
- How can behaviors that stem, at least in part, from genetic factors be changed?

SUMMARY AND REVIEW OF KEY QUESTIONS

Neurons: Building Blocks of the Nervous System

- **What do neurons do and what are their basic parts?**
  Neurons are cells specialized for receiving, processing, and moving information. They are made up of a cell body, an axon, and one or more dendrites.

- **What are action potentials? How do neurons communicate with one another?**
  Action potentials are rapid changes in the electrical properties of the cell membranes of neurons. They constitute a mechanism by which information travels through the nervous system. Graded potentials occur in response to a physical stimulus or stimulation by another neuron; they weaken quickly and their strength is directly proportional to the intensity of the physical stimulus that produced them. Neurons communicate across tiny gaps (synapses) that separate them by means of neurotransmitters.

- **What are the effects of neurotransmitters?**
  Neurotransmitters produce one of two effects: Excitatory effects make it more likely that a cell will fire; inhibitory effects make it less likely that the cell will fire.

- **How do drugs produce their effects? What are agonists? Antagonists?**
  Many drugs produce their effects by influencing synaptic transmission. *Agonists* are drugs that mimic the impact of neurotransmitters at specific receptors; drugs that inhibit their impact are termed *antagonists*.

The Nervous System: Its Basic Structure and Functions

- **What structures compose the central nervous system? What is the function of the spinal cord?**
  The central nervous system includes the brain and the spinal cord. The spinal cord carries sensory information from receptors of the body to the brain and carries information from the brain to muscles and glands. It also plays an important role in reflexes.

- **What two systems make up the peripheral nervous system?**
  The peripheral nervous system consists of the somatic and autonomic nervous systems.

- **What are the roles of these two systems?**
  The somatic nervous system connects the brain and spinal cord to voluntary muscles throughout the body; the autonomic nervous system connects the central nervous system to internal organs and glands and to muscles over which we have little voluntary control.

- **What are the functions of the sympathetic and parasympathetic nervous systems?**
  The sympathetic nervous system prepares the body for using energy, whereas the parasympathetic nervous system activates processes that conserve the body's energy.

- **What is the endocrine system?**
  A communication system that operates by releasing hormones into the bloodstream.

- **What are some of its major parts?**
  The endocrine system includes the pituitary and adrenal glands, plus several others.

The Brain: Where Consciousness Dwells

- **What structures compose the brain stem? What are their functions?**
  The brain stem—including the medulla, pons, and cerebellum—is concerned primarily with the regulation of basic bodily functions. The cerebellum, however, may be involved in higher cognitive processes, such as learning.

- **What are the functions of the hypothalamus and thalamus?**
  The hypothalamus is a brain structure involved in the regulation of motivated behavior and emotion. The thalamus serves as a relay station, directing incoming messages to appropriate brain regions.

- **What is the role of the cerebral cortex?**
  The cerebral cortex is the hub for such higher mental processes as thinking, planning, reasoning, and memory.

- **Who are "split-brain" persons? What evidence do they provide for specialization of function in the two cerebral hemispheres?**
  These are people whose cerebral hemispheres have been isolated from each other through surgery. Evidence they provide suggests that the left hemisphere is specialized for verbal tasks while the right hemisphere is specialized for perceptual tasks and expression and recognition of emotions.

- **What evidence from persons with intact brains supports such specialization?**
  PET scans of people whose cerebral hemispheres have *not* been isolated reveal that when they speak or work with numbers, activity in the left hemisphere increases. When they work on perceptual tasks, activity increases in the right hemisphere.

- **What methods are used by psychologists to study the brain and its role in behavior?**
  These methods involve examining the effects of damage to various portions of the brain or nervous system, recording and stimulating neural activity, and obtaining images of the intact, living brain.

The Brain and Human Behavior: Where Biology and Consciousness Meet

- **What is the modern view of how the brain functions?**
  The brain processes information in parallel, in many modules.

- **What is brain plasticity and why is it important?**
  Plasticity refers to how the structure and functioning of the brain are influenced by experience. Plasticity is im-

portant because it is these changes that permit us to learn, remember information, and adapt to an ever-changing world in many different ways.

- **What evidence suggests that processing of visual information occurs in a parallel fashion?**
  Evidence indicates that visual information about object identification is processed separately from information about where an object is or how we can react to it.

- **What is the modern view of speech production and speech comprehension?**
  Speech *production* involves the flow of information from sensory association areas to the posterior language area and then to Broca's area. *Comprehension* of speech involves a flow of information from Wernicke's area to the posterior language area and then to sensory association areas and back again.

- **What portions of the brain are involved in relational reasoning?**
  Such reasoning seems to occur primarily in the prefontal cortex.

Heredity and Behavior: Genetics and Evolutionary Psychology

- **How do psychologists seek to separate the roles of genetic and environmental factors in many forms of behavior?**
  They do this primarily with twin studies and adoption studies.

- **What is heritability?**
  The extent to which variations among individuals with respect to a given aspect of behavior or a given trait are due to genetic factors.

- **Why is it true that the existence of a trait or behavior among members of a species does not guarantee that the trait or behavior is useful or adaptive?**
  Presence of a trait or behavior does not guarantee that it is useful or adaptive because the trait or behavior may simply be a "by-product" of something else that *is* useful.

KEY TERMS

Action potential, p. 42
Agonist, p. 45
Amygdala, p. 50
Antagonist, p. 45
Autonomic nervous system, p. 46
Axon, p. 41
Axon terminals, p. 42
Broca's area, p. 59
Central nervous system, p. 45
Cerebellum, p. 50
Cerebral cortex, p. 50
Chromosomes, p. 61
Corpus callosum, p. 52

Dendrite, p. 41
Endocrine system, p. 47
Evolutionary psychology, p. 63
Frontal lobe, p. 51
Genes, p. 61
Heredity, p. 60
Heritability, p. 63
Hippocampus, p. 50
Hormones, p. 47
Hypothalamus, p. 50
Limbic system, p. 50
Magnetic resonance imaging (MRI), p. 55

Medulla, p. 49
Midbrain, p. 50
Mitosis, p. 61
Nervous system, p. 45
Neurons, p. 41
Neurotransmitters (transmitter substances), p. 42
Occipital lobe, p. 52
Parasympathetic nervous system, p. 47
Parietal lobe, p. 51
Peripheral nervous system, p. 45
Pituitary gland, p. 47

PSYCHOLOGY: UNDERSTANDING ITS FINDINGS

Do People Inherit Their Personalities?

Have you ever heard someone say, "She's really outgoing, just like her father," or "He's very organized, just like his mother"? Statements like this suggest that genetic factors play a role in personality. Do you think this is true? Suppose you were interested in obtaining evidence on this intriguing issue. How would you go about it? In other words, what kind of research would you conduct to find out whether some aspects of personality can be inherited? Here are some steps to help you get started:

1. State the hypothesis you want to test.
2. Identify the aspects of personality you want to measure.
3. Formulate a list of environmental variables that might affect these aspects of personality.
4. Identify methods you could use to separate the effects of these factors from the effects of genetic factors.

MAKING PSYCHOLOGY PART OF YOUR LIFE

Observing Your Own Evolved Psychological Mechanisms

Evolved psychological mechanisms are inherited patterns of behavior or behavior tendencies that help the members of a given species to survive and reproduce. Many people find it difficult to accept that many aspects of their behavior—everything from their choice of a mate through their desire for status—may stem, at least in part, from genetic factors. How do you feel about this possibility? Before making up your mind, try the following exercise.

1. Think about two key areas of life: love (seeking romantic partners) and food (what you like to eat). For each, make a list of your preferences (i.e., what you are seeking in romantic partners; foods you like to eat).
2. Now for each item on your list, consider the following question: Could this preference stem from genetic factors? In other words, could having this preference be beneficial in terms of survival and reproduction?
3. Examine the pattern of your answers; do you find many aspects of your behavior and preferences that could, indeed, reflect evolved psychological mechanisms?

If you are using MyPsychLab, you have access to an electronic version of this textbook, along with dozens of valuable resources per chapter—including video and audio clips, simulations and activities, self-assessments, practice tests, and other study materials. Here is a sampling of the resources available for this chapter.

WATCH

Action Potential

Humor & Brains

Brain Building

Forebrain

EXPLORE

The Nerve Impulse and Afferent and Efferent Neurons

The Action Potential

The Autonomic Nervous System

The Endocrine System

SIMULATE

Split-Brain Experiments

If you did not receive an access code to MyPsych Lab with this text and wish to purchase access online, please visit www.MyPsychLab.com.

STUDY GUIDE

CHAPTER REVIEW

Neurons: Building Blocks of the Nervous System

1. Biological processes are involved in the capacity of humans to feel, think, and to move. (True-False)
2. The progress made by scientists in understanding the role of brain processes in behavior has led to
   a. development of new drugs for treating depression.
   b. new ways to examine the role of the brain in behavior.
   c. a better understanding of mental disorders.
   d. All of the above are correct.
3. Which of the following is NOT a component of most neurons?
   a. Glial branches
   b. Cell body.
   c. Dendritic branches
   d. Axonal branches
4. The key function of a neuron is to
   a. control the movements of our body.
   b. process information.
   c. receive sensory messages from the environment.
   d. All of the above are correct.
5. Identify the correct sequence of flow of information in a neuron.
   a. action potential (AP) in axon -> AP travels to axon terminals -> AP induces synaptic vesicles to spill transmitter molecules into the cleft -> transmitter activates next neuron
   b. AP induces synaptic vesicles to spill transmitter molecules into the cleft -> transmitter causes AP in dendrite
   c. transmitter activates next neuron -> AP travels along the dendritic branches -> synaptic vesicles in the soma then spill transmitter molecules into the space around the soma
   d. action potential (AP) in axon -> AP travels to dendritic terminals -> AP induces synaptic vesicles to spill transmitter molecules into the cleft -> transmitter activates next glial cell
6. Myelin is a(n) _____ found wrapped around the _____.
   a. type of connective tissue;   soma of the nerve cell
   b. fatty material;   axon
   c. muscle fiber;   dendritic branches
   d. membrane;   glial cells
7. The _____ is the small gap between an axon terminal and the membrane of the next neuron.
   a. vesicle
   b. synapse
   c. fissure
   d. neural breach
8. A neurotransmitter that has a(an) _____ action on the a neuron receptor makes it _____ likely that the neuron will undergo an action potential.
   a. inhibitory;   more
   b. excitatory;   less
   c. excitatory;   more
   d. None of the above are correct.

9. The end fate of a neurotransmitter molecule is
   a. to diffuse into the bloodstream.
   b. to be taken back into the axon terminal.
   c. to be degraded by enzymes in the synapse.
   d. B and C correct
10. Neurotransmitter A facilitates the rate at which humans consume alcohol in a social setting. You would expect that a drug that blocks the reuptake of Neurotransmitter A in brain tissue would cause people to drink less alcohol.   (True-False).
11. Indicate the correct match between a specific drug/neurotransmitter and the major action/function of that drug.
    _____. This compound can paralyze an animal.
    _____. This is the neurotransmitter at the junction of nerve cells onto muscle fibers.
    _____. This neurotransmitter acts to suppress neural activity in the brain.
    _____. Mood and eating are controlled by this neurotransmitter.
    _____. Low levels of this transmitter are noted in the brains of Alzheimer's disease persons.
    _____. Schizophrenia may result from excessive brain levels of this transmitter.
    _____. This transmitter in involved in maintaining alertness.
    _____. Parkinson's disease is caused by degeneration of neurons containing this transmitter.
    a. dopamine
    b. acetylcholine
    c. curare
    d. serotonin
    e. GABA
    f. norepinephrine
    g. glutamate
12. A drug that blocks the enzyme that normally breaks down acetylcholine would be expected to improve memory. (True-False)
13. A drug that binds to neural receptors but does not activate these receptors is a(n)
    a. agonist.
    b. sympathetic agent.
    c. antagonist.
    d. analgesic.

The Nervous System: Its Basic Structure and Function

14. The brain and spinal cord form the _____ nervous system.
    a. peripheral
    b. central
    c. somatic
    d. automatic
15. Spinal reflexes allow us to rapidly withdraw from painful situations. (True-False).
16. Which of the following do NOT belong together?

a. spinal cord;   reflex actions
b. central nervous system;   parasympathetic division
c. spinal cord;   vertebral column
d. central nervous system;   brain and spinal cord

17. The _____ nervous system allows the brain to control the body's muscles.
    a. somatic
    b. central
    c. peripheral
    d. spinal

18. We usually are unaware of and have little control over the actions of our somatic nervous system. (True-False)

19. Which of the following is true of the sympathetic nervous system (SNS)?
    a. The SNS is responsible for that drowsy feeling we get after eating a large meal.
    b. The SNS acts to conserve bodily energy.
    c. Activation of the SNS prepares the body for vigorous physical action.
    d. Drugs that activate the SNS are used to lower blood pressure.

20. Activation of the parasympathetic nervous system results in
    a. the expenditure of energy.
    b. increased flow of blood to the muscles.
    c. the inactivation of the process of digestion.
    d. the conservation of bodily energy.

21. _____ are released by _____ into the _____.
    a. Neurotransmitters;   neurons;   bloodstream
    b. Neurohormones;   glands;   synapse
    c. Hormones;   neurons;   synapse
    d. Hormones;   glands;   bloodstream

The Brain: Where Consciousness Dwells

22. Match up the brain structure with its appropriate function.
    _____. Prepares the body for a vigorous fight.
    _____. Damage to this structure would impair memory.
    _____. Death can occur after damage to this collection of nuclei.
    _____. This region modulates fighting, feeding, mating, and emotion.
    _____. Control of the muscles of the body.
    _____. All sensory systems (but smell) send inputs to this region.
    _____. This diffuse neural network plays an important role in sleep and arousal.
    _____. Damage to this region can greatly increase aggressive tendencies.
    a. Somatic nervous system
    b. Adrenal gland
    c. Reticular activating system
    d. Hippocampus
    e. Thalamus
    f. Sympathetic nervous system
    g. Medulla
    h. Amygdala
    i. Hypothalamus

23. The function of the cerebellum is to coordinate muscle actions. (True-False)

24. The capacity of the body to maintain its internal environment is known as
    a. physiological control.
    b. homeostasis.
    c. set-point theory.
    d. biomedical stasis.

25. The surface of human cortex
    a. is convoluted by grooves and bulges.
    b. is divided into two symmetrical halves.
    c. is convoluted with grooves and bulges.
    d. All of the above are correct.

26. The region of cortex that controls body movements is located within the _____ lobe
    a. occipital
    b. temporal
    c. frontal
    d. parietal

27. Damage to the _____ lobes of the brain would be expected to impair _____.
    a. frontal;   the sense of touch
    b. occipital;   vision
    c. parietal;   hearing
    d. temporal;   motor function

28. You might expect that a person who loses the ability to recognize musical rhythms after a head injury may have damage involving the
    a. right temporal lobe.
    b. left parietal lobe.
    c. right parietal lobe.
    d. left temporal lobe.

29. The right hemisphere specializes in the communication of emotion.   (True-False)

30. Anesthesia directed to the right hemisphere would
    a. reduce the emotional intensity of recalled traumatic memories.
    b. interfere with the use of the person's right hand.
    c. produce an inability to speak.
    d. reduce the emotional intensity of recalled traumatic memories.

31. PET studies indicate that speaking or working with numbers _____ the activity of the _____.
    a. increases;   left hemisphere
    b. decreases;   right hemisphere
    c. decreases;   left hemisphere
    d. increases;   right hemisphere

The Brain and Human Behavior: Where Biology and Consciousness Meet

32. Which of the following can alter the physical structure of the brain?
    a. A series of environmental experiences.
    b. Exposure to stress.
    c. Serious illness.
    d. All of the above are correct.

33. Broca's aphasia involves _____ after damage to the _____.
    a. poor speech comprehension;   parietal lobe
    b. slow speech production;   left frontal lobe
    c. poor word choice;   temporal lobe
    d. emotionless speech;   corpus callosum

34. Which of the following symptoms are representative of Wernicke's aphasia?
    a. Slow speech production and grammar difficulties.
    b. An inability to spell words.
    c. An inability to recognize a word or to understand word meaning.
    d. An inability to write words.

Heredity and Behavior: Genetics and Evolutionary Psychology

35. The basic units of heredity are the genes located on chromosomes.   (True-False).
36. Which of the following is true of the 23rd pair of chromosomes?
    a. Females have two Y chromosomes.
    b. Males have one X and one Y chromosome.
    c. Females have two X chromosomes.
    d. Females have one X and one Y chromosome.
37. Twin studies indicate that genetic factors play a role in
    a. phobias.
    b. depression.
    c. schizophrenia.
    d. All of the above are correct.

IDENTIFICATIONS
Identify a key function for each brain structure listed below
1. _____. Frontal lobes.
2. _____. Medulla.
3. _____. Cerebellum.
4. _____. Amygdala.
5. _____. Hypothalamus.
6. _____. Hippocampus.
7. _____. Pons
8. _____. Parietal lobes.
    a. This region receives information about the skin senses.
    b. This structure can control eating.
    c. Damage to a portion of this region can produce a loss of control of fine movements.
    d. A region that contains dense interconnected neurons; located just in front of the medulla.
    e. A portion of the brain stem that controls vital functions such as breathing.
    f. A structure involved in the regulation of emotion.
    g. This structure coordinates movements.
    h. A structure involved in memory.

FILL IN THE BLANK
1. _____ are the building blocks of the nervous system.
2. Information is carried from the neuron _____ toward the _____.
3. Packets of neurotransmitter molecules are stored within _____ at the axon terminals.
4. Drugs that increase brain levels of _____ improve memory.
5. The central nervous system consists of the _____ and the _____.
6. The _____ division of the autonomic nervous system functions to conserve energy.

7. Three key functions of the brain are _____, _____, and _____.
8. Damage to the cerebellum results in _____.
9. _____ refers to the capacity of the body to maintain the internal environment at an optimal level.
10. A major relay structure for sensory signals en route to the cortex is the _____.
11. Motor cortex is located within the _____ lobe.
12. The processing of sound is accomplished within the _____ lobe.
13. The _____ hemisphere plays a key role in the experience of emotion.
14. Recordings of the brain electrical activity from the scalp are made using an _____.
15. Unlike computers, the human brain processes information in a _____ fashion.
16. _____ area is the key region of brain for the production of speech.
17. _____ twins have the same complement of genes.
18. The extent to which variation of a trait in a group of person reflects genetic factors is termed _____.

COMPREHENSIVE PRACTICE TEST
1. The _____ is that portion of the neuron that receives electrical signals from the cell body.
2. The activity of an excitatory synapse onto a neuron can be cancelled out by an inhibitory synapse.   (True-False)
3. _____ neurons control the activities of our bodies.
4. Sensory neurons directly control muscle contraction. (True-False)
5. Which of the following is NOT a part of the central nervous system?
    a. Medulla
    b. Pons
    c. Cerebellum
    d. Autonomic nervous system
6. Synaptic vesicles contain neurotransmitter molecules. (True-False)
7. Activation of the sympathetic nervous system results in
    a. the expenditure of energy.
    b. increased flow of blood to the muscles.
    c. the inactivation of the process of digestion.
    d. All of the above are correct.
8. Which of the following pairs are synonymous?
    a. dopamine;   ephedrine
    b. adrenaline;   epinephrine
    c. epinephrine;   norepinephrine
    d. pituitary gland;   adrenal gland
9. Match up the correct brain structure with its function.
    _____ This region controls vital functions and lies just in front of the spinal cord.
    _____ This lobe contains the primary visual cortex.
    _____ Damage to this lobe can impair hearing.
    _____ Circuits in this lobe receive information from the skin senses.
    _____ This set of structures controls emotionality and motivation.
    _____ A portion of this lobe contains the primary motor cortex.

a. Limbic system.
b. Parietal lobe.
c. Occipital lobe.
d. Frontal lobe.
e. Temporal lobe.
f. Brain stem

10. PET scans of human brain activity take advantage of the fact that
    a. some humans have accidentally damaged their brains.
    b. hydrogen atoms emit energy when exposed to a strong magnetic field in a scanner.
    c. active brain tissue uses more glucose or has greater blood flow through the region.
    d. the brain emits small electric charges which can be measured from the scalp.

11. _____ are used to record the electrical activity of individual neurons.

12. The function of the corpus callosum is to _____.

13. Damage to the _____ impairs the ability to process humor.
    a. corpus callosum
    b. right hemisphere
    c. frontal lobes
    d. limbic system

14. The _____ is key for the _____ of speech.
    a. parietal lobe; comprehension
    b. occipital lobe; production
    c. temporal lobe; comprehension
    d. right hemisphere; production

15. The process by which bodily cells divide to form two new cells each with a full complement of chromosomes is known as
    a. mitosis.
    b. genetic fusion.
    c. replication.
    d. meiosis.

16. The heritability of intelligence is about
    a. 0.05.
    b. 0.25.
    c. 0.50.
    d. 0.95.

CRITICAL THINKING

1. Neurotransmitters are released by nerve cells into the synapse and can stimulate receptors on other neurons. Describe the processes by which the action of transmitter is terminated and explain how drugs might be used to alter these processes in order to correct imbalances of transmitters in the brain.

2. Explain how twin studies and adoption studies can be used to determine the relative heritability of a particular trait (say, manic-depression).

THREE

Sensation and Perception: Making Contact with the World around Us

*R*ecently, while attending a conference, I (Michael Kalsher) was pleasantly surprised to run into a colleague whom I hadn't seen in years. We were both on our way to sessions, but agreed to meet for "happy hour" later that day to catch up on our lives. As my friend and I were being led to our table, I noticed a pianist in the corner of the lounge playing light jazz. Although our conversation had soon relegated the music to the background, our attention was suddenly drawn back to the pianist when he hit a "sour" note while playing a song. On hearing the mistake, my friend looked in the direction of the offending note and casually muttered, "It should have been a B-flat," then returned to our conversation as if nothing had happened. Bewildered by her response, I interrupted to ask how she knew that. After all, although I could tell that the note was clearly "sour," I was skeptical that she could have so effortlessly diagnosed the problem that precisely. She explained that she has perfect pitch, *the capacity to identify any tone or to sing any specified note.* Seeing the skeptical look on my face, she said, "Here, I'll show you," at which point she dragged me by the arm over to the pianist. After explaining the situation to him, she turned her back to the pianist and asked him to play a note, which he did. Without seeing which note he played, she smiled coyly and announced, "That was an F-sharp." The pianist nodded, and then proceeded to play a wide range of individual notes for my friend to judge. Time after time she was correct. At this point, all I could do was shake my head and smile, impressed by my friend's special ability.

FIGURE 3.1
Experiencing the World Around Us: The Role of Sensory and Perceptual Processes

The ability to interact successfully with the world around us, such as making correct judgments about aspects of the physical environment around us, is the result of complex processes occurring within the nervous system. Performer Alicia Keys is known to have perfect pitch, the capacity to identify any tone or to sing any specified note.

Sensation:
Input about the physical world provided by our sensory receptors.

Perception:
The process through which we select, organize, and interpret input from our sensory receptors.

Sensory receptors:
Cells of the body specialized for the task of *transduction*— converting physical energy (light, sound) into neural impulses.

Why do we start with this example? Because we believe it helps to illustrate that the world around us is complicated, even for relatively simple events, such as the musical incident just described (see another example in Figure 3.1). Moreover, the processes that help us make sense of the sights, sounds, smells, tastes, and feelings that constantly bombard us are not as simple or direct as common sense might suggest. Careful psychological research conducted during the past one hundred years has shown that we do not understand the external world in a simple, automatic way. Rather, we actively construct our interpretation of sensory information through several complex processes.

To clarify how we make sense of the world around us, psychologists distinguish between two key concepts: *sensation* and *perception*. The study of **sensation** is concerned with the initial contact between organisms and their physical environment. It focuses on describing the relationship between various forms of sensory stimulation (including electromagnetic, sound waves, pressure) and how these inputs are registered by our sense organs (the eyes, ears, nose, tongue, and skin). In contrast, the study of **perception** is concerned with identifying the processes through which we interpret and organize this information to produce our conscious experience of objects and relationships among objects. It is important to remember that perception is not simply a passive process of decoding incoming sensory information. If this were the case, we would lose the richness of our everyday stream of conscious experiences.

The complementary processes of sensation and perception play a role in virtually every topic to be considered in later chapters. For these reasons, we will devote careful attention to them here. We'll begin by exploring in detail how the receptors for each sensory system transform raw physical energy into an electrochemical code. As we'll soon note, our sensory receptors are exquisitely designed to detect various aspects of the world around us. We'll also consider the possibility of subliminal perception—perception without any underlying sensation. Next, we'll turn our attention to the active process of perception. Here, the focus will be on how the brain integrates and interprets the constant flow of information it receives from our senses. We will conclude by examining evidence concerning the possibility of extrasensory perception or *psi*.

SENSATION: THE RAW MATERIALS OF UNDERSTANDING

The sight of a breathtaking sunset, the enticing aroma of a favorite dish, the smooth feel of a baby's skin, the rush you experience while thundering down a steep incline on a roller coaster: Exactly how are we able to experience these events? As you may recall from Chapter 2, all these sensory experiences are based on complex processes occurring within the nervous system. This highlights an intriguing paradox. Although we are continually bombarded by various forms of physical energy, including light, heat, sound, and smells, our brain cannot directly detect the presence of these forces. Instead, it can respond only to intricate patterns of action potentials conducted by *neurons,* special cells within our bodies that receive, move, and process sensory information. Thus, a critical question is how the many forms of physical energy impacting our sensory systems are converted into signals our nervous system can understand.

Highly specialized cells known as **sensory receptors,** located in our eyes, ears, nose, tongue, and elsewhere, are responsible for accomplishing this coding task. Thus, sights, sounds, and smells that we experience are actually the products of **transduction,** a process in which the physical properties of stimuli are converted into neural signals that are then transmitted to our brain via specialized sensory nerves. To illustrate how our nervous system makes sense out of the surging sea of physical energies in our environment, we'll focus on two critical concepts: *thresholds* and *sensory adaptation*.

Sensory Thresholds: How Much Stimulation Is Enough?

Our receptors are remarkably efficient, but they do not register all the information available in the environment at any given moment. We are able to smell and taste certain chemicals but not others; we hear sound waves only within a certain range of frequencies; and our ability to detect light energy is restricted to a relatively narrow band of wavelengths. The range of physical stimuli that we and other species can detect, however, is uniquely designed to maximize survival potential. Because human survival is tied to our unique capacity for spoken language, it is not surprising that our auditory system is best at detecting sound frequencies that closely match the frequencies of human speech (Goldstein, 2002).

For more than a century, psychologists have investigated the sensory capabilities of the various sense organs. An important goal of this area of research, termed **psychophysics,** has been to establish the relationship between physical properties of stimuli, such as brightness and loudness, and people's psychological experience of them. A casual observer might assume such a relationship to be a direct one. In other words, given a stimulus of sufficient intensity, we should always be able to detect its presence. This suggests that at levels above a certain intensity, a person would always report detecting the stimulus. In practice, this pattern of results almost never occurs. Why? One reason is that our sensitivity to stimuli changes from moment to moment. Bodily functions change constantly to maintain the body's internal environment at optimal levels, a state termed *homeostasis*. It is not surprising that because of these changes, the sensitivity of our sensory organs to external stimuli also varies. For this reason, psychologists have coined the term **absolute threshold** to describe our sensory threshold and define it as the smallest magnitude of a stimulus that can be reliably discriminated from no stimulus at all 50 percent of the time (Wolfe et al., 2006).

■ **Sensory thresholds: Some complications.**

Our discussions to this point seem to indicate that sensory thresholds are not really "fixed," but instead change in response to a number of factors, including fatigue, lapses in attention, and moment-to-moment fluctuations that occur within our nervous system. Additional research suggests that *motivational factors,* or the rewards and costs associated with detecting various stimuli, may also play an important role.

According to **signal detection theory,** complex decision mechanisms are involved whenever we try to determine if we have or have not detected a specific stimulus (Erev, 1998; Swets, 1992). An important point to remember is that stimuli (signals) are usually embedded in the context of other competing stimuli, or background "noise." Obviously, the challenge is to distinguish signal from noise. Two concepts—*sensitivity* and *bias*—help to explain how these signals are either detected or missed. *Sensitivity* refers to a person's ability to distinguish between a faint stimulus (the signal) and the background (the noise). *Bias* refers to a person's willingness to report noticing the stimulus—in other words, how strong the stimulus needs to be before the person says he or she detected it.

To illustrate the relationship between these two concepts, consider the following example. Imagine that you are a radiologist and while scanning a patient's X-ray you think you detect a faint spot on the film, but you're not quite sure (see

Transduction:
The translation of a physical energy into electrical signals by specialized receptor cells.

Psychophysics:
A set of procedures psychologists have developed to investigate the relationship between physical properties of stimuli and people's psychological experience of them.

Absolute threshold:
The smallest amount of a stimulus that we can detect 50 percent of the time.

Signal detection theory:
A theory suggesting that there are no absolute thresholds for sensations. Rather, detection of stimuli depends on their physical energy and on internal factors such as the relative costs and benefits associated with detecting their presence.

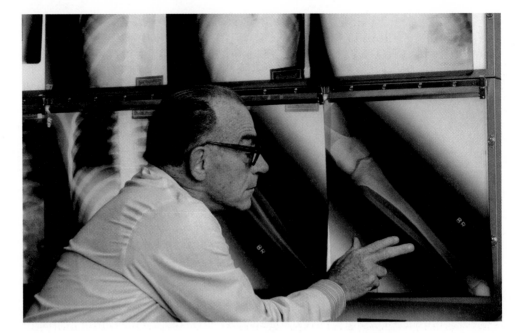

FIGURE 3.2
Signal Detection Theory: Separating Sensitivity from Motivational Factors
Signal detection theory seeks to explain why people detect signals in some situations but miss them in others. It does so by attempting to separate sensitivity from motivational factors.

Figure 3.2). What should you do? If you conclude that the spot is an abnormality, you must order more scans or tests—an expensive and time-consuming alternative. If further testing reveals an abnormality, such as cancer, you may have saved the patient's life. If no abnormality is detected, though, you'll be blamed for wasting resources and unnecessarily upsetting the patient. Alternatively, if you decide the spot is *not* an abnormality, then there's no reason to order more tests. If the patient remains healthy, then you've done the right thing. However, if the spot really is cancerous tissue, the results could be fatal. As you can see, deciding whether we have detected a given stimulus is not always easy and involves much more than a simple determination of the relationship between amount of physical energy present in a stimulus and the resulting psychological sensations. Your decision is also likely to be influenced by the rewards and costs associated with each choice alternative.

■ Difference thresholds: Are two stimuli the same or different?

A good cook tastes a dish, adds salt to it, then tastes it again to judge the change. This illustrates another basic question relating to our sensory capacities: How much change in a stimulus is required before a shift can be noticed? Psychologists refer to the amount of change in a stimulus required for a person to detect it as the **difference threshold.** Obviously, the smaller the change we can detect, the greater our sensitivity. In other words, the difference threshold is the amount of change in a physical stimulus necessary to produce a **just noticeable difference (jnd)** in sensation. As it turns out, our ability to detect differences in stimulus intensity depends on the magnitude of the initial stimulus; we easily detect even small changes in weak stimuli, but we require much larger changes before we notice differences in strong stimuli. For example, if you are listening to music at a low sound intensity, even small adjustments to the volume are noticeable. But if you crank up the volume, much larger changes are required before a difference is apparent. We are also more sensitive to changes in some types of stimuli than to changes in others. For example, we are able to notice very small shifts in temperature (less than one degree Fahrenheit) and in the pitch of sounds, but we are somewhat less sensitive to changes in loudness or in smells (Galanter, 1962).

It is important to note that the vocabulary that people use to describe stimulus

Difference threshold:
The amount by which two stimuli must differ in order to be just noticeably different.

Just noticeable difference (jnd):
The amount of change in a physical stimulus necessary for an individual to notice a difference in the intensity of a stimulus.

intensity and intensity differences appears to be influenced by the type of stimuli being judged (Bartoshuk, Fasat, & Snyder, 2005). For example, a woman giving birth is likely to describe the pain she is experiencing as "very strong," but she may also use the same terms to describe a particularly strong cup of coffee. The intensities of the two experiences are clearly different. Therefore, it is useful to think of sensory descriptors in terms of the position they might occupy on an imaginary elastic ruler; their relative positions on the ruler are fixed, but the ruler itself can be stretched or compressed to fit the domain of interest (Bartoshuk et al., 2002).

■ Stimuli below threshold: Can they have an effect?

The possibility of **subliminal perception** has been a source of controversy for many years. Subliminal perception occurs whenever stimuli presented below the threshold for awareness influence thoughts, feelings, or actions. Subliminal perception first captured the public's attention in the 1950s when a marketing executive announced he had embedded subliminal messages like "Eat popcorn" and "Drink Coke" into a then-popular movie. Supposedly, the embedded messages were flashed on the screen in front of movie audiences so briefly (a fraction of a second) that audience members were not aware of them (Brean, 1958). Although the executive later confessed to the hoax (no messages were actually presented), many people remained convinced that subliminal messages can be powerful sources of persuasion.

An important question raised by this, and other subsequent incidents, is whether we can sense or be affected by stimuli that remain outside our conscious awareness. We'll return to this question in Chapter 4, where we discuss intuition and related processes. The most direct answer to this question has come from studies that have used *visual priming*, in which participants are "primed" with brief exposures (often less than one-tenth of a second) to words or simple pictures. The duration of the exposure is long enough to be detected by the nervous system, but too brief for people to be consciously aware of a picture's or word's presence. Participants are usually unable to name the visual primes, but their reactions to stimuli presented subsequently (e.g., words or pictures) do seem to be affected.

Studies have shown that subliminally presented visual stimuli can have small but measurable effects on many aspects of our cognition and emotion, including our liking of ambiguous stimuli and words (see Greenwald, Draine, & Abrams, 1996; Murphy & Zajonc, 1993), our attraction to members of the opposite sex (Bargh et al., 1995), and even our attitudes toward people (Kawakami, Dovidio, & Dijksterhuis, 2003). Repeated exposure to the same subliminal stimuli tends to strengthen their effects, and the positive effect resulting from such exposure can become associated with other unrelated stimuli (Monahan, Murphy, & Zajonc, 2000).

But can subliminally presented visual stimuli exert measurable affects on behavior? Recent findings seems to suggest the answer is *yes*, but indirectly. To illustrate how this might happen, Winkielman and colleagues (2005) measured whether subliminal presentations of "happy," "neutral," and "angry" faces would affect behavior; in this case, how much beverage (lemon-lime drink) participants in the study poured and consumed. The researchers selected drinking because changes in basic affective and motivational processes induced through visual priming are most likely to influence very basic forms of behavior, such as eating and drinking. The results showed that subliminally presented smiles caused *thirsty* participants to pour and consume more of the beverage than either the neutral expressions and frowns (see Figure 3.3, page 78). No such differences were apparent among participants who were *not* thirsty. In other words, visual priming produced measurable changes in pouring and drinking only among participants who were already motivated to do so (the thirsty ones). As might be expected, the subliminal messages by themselves were insufficient to produce changes in behavior directly (Jostman et al., 2005).

Subliminal perception: The presumed influence on the behavior of a stimulus that is below the threshold for conscious experience.

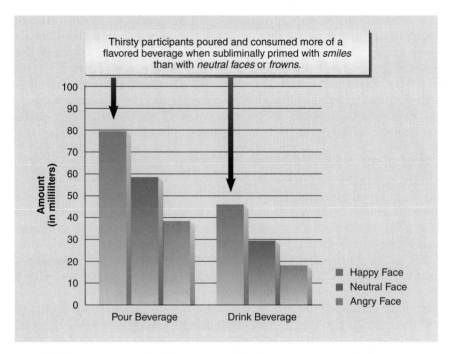

FIGURE 3.3
Subliminal Perception and Visual Priming
Although participants were unaware of seeing the visual primes they were exposed to (either happy, sad, or neutral faces), thirsty participants subliminally exposed to smiles poured and consumed more beverage than participants exposed to either neutral faces or frowns. Thus, despite their brief duration, these stimuli were registered at some level within the nervous system.
Source: Based on data from Winkielman, Berridge, & Wilbarger, 2005.

Some researchers speculate that subliminal perception may have evolved as a tool to help humans and other animals avoid predators. This intriguing idea is based on evidence showing that people are slightly better at detecting *negative* than positive stimuli when both are presented subliminally (Dijksterhuis & Aarts, 2003). Applied to prey animals, such as deer and rabbits, this makes sense, because being even a few milliseconds late in detecting a would-be predator could prove fatal, while being a little late in detecting possible food sources would not be so bad.

Taken together, these findings seem to confirm that the priming stimuli used in studies of subliminal perception—despite their brief duration—are registered at some level within the nervous system. However, several cautions are warranted. First, we should emphasize that speculation concerning the possible evolutionary role of subliminal perception is just that. Additional research is needed to confirm or refute this possibility. Second, the effects of visual priming are generally small, and most laboratory studies show that the effects of priming are short-lived. Finally—and perhaps most important—no evidence currently supports the possibility that subliminal messages are a powerful means of persuasion.

Unfortunately, these facts have not slowed the explosion of self-help materials that offer to help people lose weight, stop smoking, get smarter, or improve their sex lives. Manufacturers of such materials continue to insist that the effectiveness of these products is due to the presence of subliminal messages. Are these claims true? Systematic evidence seems to cast doubt on this possibility. Instead, any improvements people experience are more likely the result of other factors, such as motivation and expectations (Greenwald, 1991; Urban, 1992).

Sensory Adaptation: "It Feels Great Once You Get Used to It!"

I have vivid memories of summer camping trips I took as a young boy with my friends. On particularly hot afternoons we would cool off with a dip into an icy mountain lake or stream. Although the initial shock of the icy water was overpowering, it eventually felt refreshing. This experience illustrates the process of **sensory adaptation,** the fact that our sensitivity to an unchanging stimulus tends to decrease over time. When we first encounter a stimulus, such as the hot water evident in the steamy example depicted in Figure 3.4, our temperature receptors fire vigorously. Soon, however, they fire less vigorously, and through the process of sensory adaptation, the water then feels just right.

Sensory adaptation has some practical advantages. If it did not occur, we would constantly be distracted by the stream of sensations we experience each day. We would not adapt to our clothing rubbing our skin, to the

FIGURE 3.4
Sensory Adaptation
At first, the water feels . . . well, hot! But later, it feels soothing due to sensory adaptation.

feel of our tongue in our mouth, or to bodily processes such as eye blinks and swallowing. However, sensory adaptation is not always beneficial and can even be dangerous. After about a minute, for example, our sensitivity to most odors drops by nearly 70 percent. This drop in sensitivity is useful in everyday situations in which we encounter unpleasant but harmless odors, such as cooking odors or a roommate's smelly sneakers. Sensory adaptation can be maladaptive, however, by reducing our sensitivity to odors that signal danger, such as the smell of a gas leak in a home heated by natural gas or the smells that emanate from other harmful chemicals. In general, though, the process of sensory adaptation allows us to focus on important changes in the world around us, and that ability to focus on and respond to stimulus change is usually what is most important for survival.

Now that we've considered some basic aspects of sensation, let's examine in detail each of the major senses: vision, audition, touch, smell, taste, and the kinesthetic and vestibular senses.

KEY QUESTIONS

- What is the primary function of our sensory receptors?
- What does the term *absolute threshold* refer to?
- Why is signal detection theory important?
- What is a difference threshold?
- Can subliminal messages affect our behavior?
- What is the role of sensory adaptation in sensation?

VISION

Light, in the form of energy from the sun, is part of the fuel that drives the engine of life on earth. Thus, it is not surprising that we possess exquisitely adapted organs for detecting this stimulus: our eyes. Indeed, for most of us, sight is the most important way of gathering information about the world. Figure 3.5 on page 80 shows a simplified diagram of the human eye.

Sensory adaptation: Reduced sensitivity to unchanging stimuli over time.

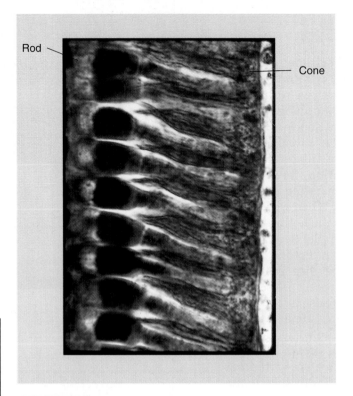

FIGURE 3.5
The Human Eye
Light filters through layers of retinal cells before striking receptors (rods and cones) located at the back of the eye and pointed away from the incoming light. The rods and cones stimulate bipolar cells, which in turn stimulate the ganglion cells. The axons of these cells form the fibers of the optic nerve.

Cornea:
The curved, transparent layer through which light rays enter the eye.

Pupil:
An opening in the eye, just behind the cornea, through which light rays enter our eye.

Iris:
The colored part of the eye that adjusts the amount of light that enters by constricting or dilating the pupil.

Lens:
A curved structure behind the pupil that bends light rays, focusing them on the retina.

Retina:
The surface at the back of the eye containing the rods and cones.

Cones:
Sensory receptors in the eye that play a crucial role in sensations of color.

Rods:
One of the two types of sensory receptors for vision found in the eye.

The Eye: Its Basic Structure

How is light energy converted into signals our brain can understand? The answer lies in the basic structure of the eye. It is in the eye that light energy is converted into a neural code understandable to our nervous system. Light rays first pass through a transparent protective structure called the **cornea** and then enter the eye through the **pupil,** a round opening whose size varies with lighting conditions: The less light present, the wider the pupil opening (see Figure 3.5). These adjustments are executed by the colored part of the eye, termed the **iris,** which is actually a circular muscle that contracts and expands to let in varying amounts of light. After entering through the pupil, light rays pass through the **lens,** a clear structure whose shape adjusts to permit us to focus on objects at varying distances. When we look at a distant object, the lens becomes thinner and flatter; when we look at a nearby object, the lens becomes thicker and rounder. As we age, the lens tends to lose its flexibility, causing older people to have trouble reading and seeing nearby objects. Light rays leaving the lens are projected onto the **retina** at the back of the eyeball. As illustrated in Figure 3.6, the lens bends light rays in such a way that the image projected onto the retina is actually upside down and reversed, but the brain reverses this image, letting us see objects and people correctly.

The retina is a postage-stamp-sized structure that contains two types of light-sensitive receptor cells: about 5 million **cones** and about 120 million **rods** (Gold-

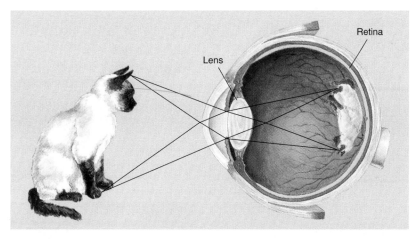

FIGURE 3.6
The Upside Down and Reversed Image Projected onto the Retina
The lens bends light rays entering the eye so that the image projected onto the retina is upside down and reversed: Light rays from the top of an object are projected onto receptors at the bottom of the retina, and light rays from the left side of an object are projected onto receptors on the right side of the retina. Our brain rearranges this information and enables us to see the object correctly.

stein, 2002). Cones, located primarily in the center of the retina in an area called the **fovea,** function best in bright light and play a key role both in color vision and in our ability to notice fine detail. In contrast, rods are found only outside the fovea and function best under lower levels of illumination, so rods help us to see in a darkened room or at night. At increasing distances from the fovea, the density of cones decreases and the density of rods increases. Once stimulated, the rods and cones transmit neural information to other neurons called *bipolar cells*. These cells, in turn, stimulate other neurons, called *ganglion cells*. Axons from the ganglion cells converge to form the **optic nerve** and carry visual information to the brain. Interestingly, no receptors are present where this nerve exits the eye, so there is a **blind spot** at this point in our visual field. We usually remain unaware of our blind spot because the brain automatically "fills in" the spot with an extrapolation of the surrounding image. Refer to Figure 3.7 to check out your own blind spot.

FIGURE 3.7
The Blind Spot
You can demonstrate the existence of your own blind spot. First, close your right eye and align the cross with your left eye. While looking at the cross with your left eye, move the book slowly toward you (or your eye toward the page). When your eye is six to twelve inches from the book, the circle should disappear. This is the point at which the image of the circle is falling on the blind spot.

Fovea:
The area in the center of the retina in which cones are highly concentrated.

Optic nerve:
A bundle of nerve fibers that exit the back of the eye and carry visual information to the brain.

Blind spot:
The point in the back of the retina through which the optic nerve exits the eye. This exit point contains no rods or cones, and is therefore insensitive to light.

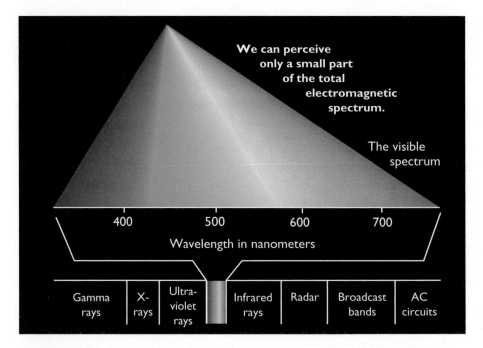

FIGURE 3.8
The Electromagnetic Spectrum
Visible light, the part of the electromagnetic spectrum we can detect, occupies only a narrow band in the entire spectrum.

Light: The Physical Stimulus for Vision

Let's consider some important facts about light, the physical stimulus for vision. First, the light that is visible to us is only a small portion of the electromagnetic spectrum. This spectrum ranges from radio waves at the slow- or long-wave end to cosmic rays at the fast- or short-wave end (see Figure 3.8).

Second, certain physical properties of light contribute to our psychological experiences of vision. **Wavelength,** the distance between successive peaks and valleys of light energy, determines what we experience as **hue** or color. As shown in Figure 3.8, as wavelength increases from about 400 to 700 nanometers (a nanometer is one-billionth of a meter), our sensations shift from violet through blue (shorter wavelengths), green, yellow, orange (medium wavelengths), and finally red (longer wavelengths). The intensity of light, the amount of energy it contains, is experienced as **brightness.** The extent to which light contains only one wavelength, rather than many, determines our experience of **saturation;** the fewer the number of wavelengths mixed together, the more saturated or "pure" a color appears. For example, the deep red of an apple is highly saturated, whereas the pale pink of an apple blossom is low in saturation.

Basic Functions of the Visual System: Acuity, Dark Adaptation, and Eye Movements

The human visual system is remarkably sensitive and can detect even tiny amounts of light. However, another important aspect of vision is **acuity,** the ability to resolve fine details, as on the familiar chart at an eye doctor's office. If you wear eyeglasses or contact lenses designed to improve your visual acuity, chances are that your visual deficit stems from a slight abnormality in the shape of your eye or the cornea (Wolfe et al., 2006). If your eyeball is too long or the cornea is too

Wavelength:
The peak-to-peak distance in a sound or light wave.

Hue:
The color that we experience due to the dominant wavelength of light energy.

Brightness:
The physical intensity of light.

Saturation:
The degree of concentration of the hue of light. We experience saturation as the purity of a light.

Acuity:
The visual ability to see fine details.

stiffly curved, you suffer from **nearsightedness,** in which you see near objects clearly, but distant objects appear blurry. This occurs because the image entering your eye is focused slightly in front of the retina rather than directly on it. Similarly, in **farsightedness,** your eyeball is too short, or the cornea too flat, and the lens focuses the image behind the retina. Fortunately, recent advances in laser surgery have made it possible to correct certain visual acuity problems by changing the shape of the cornea.

Another aspect of visual sensitivity is **dark adaptation,** the increase in sensitivity that occurs when we move from bright light to a dim environment, such as a darkened movie theater. Initially, we find it difficult to see. Why? When we're exposed to bright light, a pigment inside the retinal cells is bleached. When we move from bright light to dark, the cones and rods become temporarily nonfunctional until the pigment is regenerated. This occurs much more rapidly for cones than for rods, so in essence, dark adaptation is a two-step process. During the first few moments, the cones are more sensitive. Thus, we rely on them to see until the rods catch up and then surpass the cones in terms of light sensitivity. The cones reach their maximum sensitivity in about five to ten minutes. The rods overtake the cones in sensitivity in about seven to ten minutes, but take about thirty minutes to complete this process (Goldstein, 2002). When completely dark-adapted, the eye is about 100,000 times more sensitive than the light-adapted eye.

Eye movements also play a role in visual acuity. To appreciate the importance of the ability to move your eyes, just imagine how inefficient it would be to read a book or play your favorite sport if your eyes were stuck in one position. In order to change the direction of your gaze, you would have to move your entire head. Eye movements are of two basic types: *version movements,* in which the eyes move together in the same direction, and *vergence movements,* in which the lines of sight for the two eyes converge or diverge. As we'll discover later in this chapter, vergence movements are crucial to our ability to perceive distance and depth.

Color Vision

A world without color would be sadly limited, for color—vivid reds, glowing yellows, restful greens—is a crucial part of our visual experience. For many people, though, some degree of color deficiency is a fact of life. Nearly 8 percent of males and 0.5 percent of females are less sensitive than the rest of us either to red and green or to yellow and blue (Nathans, 1999). And a few individuals are totally color-blind, experiencing the world only in varying shades of white, black, and gray.

Today's Internet technology has created a new set of problems for people afflicted with a color deficiency because they are frequently unable to perceive much of the text or images presented on certain web sites (Arditi, 2005). This presents a real challenge to web page designers, who must construct sites with color schemes that are legible to people with a color deficiency. Arranging for a high degree of contrast between images and text and the background on which they are presented can help make the information more discernible to people with color deficiency (Wolfmaier, 1999). People with color vision deficiencies also face other more serious problems, such as discerning product use and warning information on hazardous products. The labeling on these products is frequently difficult to read, especially when there is low contrast between the safety-related information and the background on which it is printed, or when the colors used are not easily distinguishable from one another (see Figure 3.9, page 84).

Two leading theories have been proposed to explain our rich sense of color. The first, **trichromatic theory,** suggests that we have three different types of cones in our retina, each of which is maximally sensitive, though not exclusively so, to a particular range of light wavelength—a range roughly corresponding to blue (400–500 nanometers), green (475–600 nanometers), or red (490–650 nanometers).

Nearsightedness:
A condition in which the visual image entering our eye is focused slightly in front of our retina, rather than directly on it. Therefore, near objects can be seen clearly, while distant objects appear fuzzy or blurred.

Farsightedness:
A condition in which the visual image entering our eye is focused behind, rather than directly on, the retina. Therefore, close objects appear out of focus, while distant objects are in clear focus.

Dark adaptation:
The process through which our visual system increases its sensitivity to light under low levels of illumination.

Trichromatic theory:
A theory of color perception suggesting that we have three types of cones, each primarily receptive to different wavelengths of light.

FIGURE 3.9
Technology and Color Blindness

Today's Internet technology has created problems for people afflicted with a color deficiency because they frequently have difficulty perceiving much of the text or images on certain web sites. Similar problems are created by the labeling on certain dangerous products when the labels lack contrast or use colors that are not easily discernible to people afflicted with color deficiencies.

Negative afterimage:
A sensation of complementary color that occurs after staring at a stimulus of a given hue.

Opponent-process theory:
A theory that describes the processing of sensory information related to color at levels above the retina. The theory suggests that we possess six types of neurons, each of which is either stimulated or inhibited by red, green, blue, yellow, black, and white.

Careful study of the human retina suggests that we do possess three types of receptors although, as Figure 3.10 shows, there is a great deal of overlap in each receptor type's sensitivity range (DeValois & DeValois,1975; Rushton, 1975). According to trichromatic theory, the ability to perceive colors results from the joint action of the three receptor types. Thus, light of a particular wavelength produces differential stimulation of each receptor type, and it is the overall pattern of stimulation that produces our rich sense of color. This differential sensitivity may be due to genes that direct different cones to produce pigments sensitive to blue, green, or red (Mollon, 1993; Nathans et al., 1986).

Trichromatic theory, however, fails to account for certain aspects of color vision, such as the occurrence of **negative afterimages**—sensations of complementary colors that occur after staring at a stimulus of a given color. For example, after staring at a red object, if you shift your gaze to a neutral background, sensations of green may follow. Similarly, after staring at a yellow stimulus, sensations of blue may occur.

The **opponent-process theory** addresses these aspects more effectively by accounting for what happens after the cones in the retina transmit their information to other cells of the retina (e.g., the bipolar and ganglion cells) and to a structure in the thalamus termed the *lateral geniculate nucleus* (Goldstein, 2002). This theory suggests that we possess specialized cells in these structures that play a role in sensations of color (DeValois & DeValois, 1993). Two of these cells, for example, handle red and green; one is stimulated by red light and inhibited by green light, whereas the other is stimulated by green light and inhibited by red. This is where the phrase *opponent process* originates. Two additional types of cells handle yellow and blue; one is stimulated by yellow and inhibited by blue, while the other shows

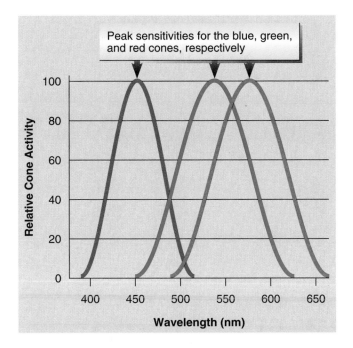

Peak sensitivities for the blue, green, and red cones, respectively

FIGURE 3.10

Three Types of Receptors Contribute to Our Perception of Color

Color vision appears to be mediated by three types of cones, each maximally sensitive, but not exclusively so, to wavelengths corresponding to blue, green, and red.

Source: "Retinal Mechanisms of Color Vision" by E. F. MacNichol, pp. 119, 133 from *Vision Research.* Copyright © 1964. Reprinted with permission from Elsevier.

the opposite pattern. The remaining two types handle black and white—again, in an opponent process manner. Opponent-process theory can help explain the occurrence of negative afterimages (Jameson & Hurvich, 1989). The idea is that when stimulation of one cell in an opponent pair is terminated, the other is automatically activated. Thus, if the original stimulus viewed was yellow, the afterimage seen would be blue (see Figure 3.11, page 86). Each opponent pair is stimulated in different patterns by the three types of cones. It is the overall pattern of such stimulation that yields our complex and eloquent sensation of color.

Although these theories competed for many years, we now know that both are necessary to explain our impressive ability to respond to color. Trichromatic theory explains how color-coding occurs in the cones of the retina, whereas opponent-process theory accounts for processing in higher-order nerve cells. We'll now turn to a discussion of how visual information is processed by the brain.

Vision and the Brain: Processing Visual Information

Our rich sense of vision does not result from the output of single neurons but instead from the overall pattern of our sensory receptors. In other words, there is more to vision than meets the eye. But how, then, do the simple action potentials of individual neurons contribute to our overall conscious experience? To help answer this question, let's consider how the brain "invents" our visual world.

Our understanding of the initial stages of this process was greatly advanced by the Nobel Prize–winning series of studies conducted by Hubel and Wiesel (1979). These researchers conducted studies on **feature detectors**—neurons at various levels in the visual cortex. Their work revealed the existence of three types of feature detectors. One group of neurons—known as **simple cells**—responds primarily to bars or lines presented in certain orientations (horizontal, vertical, etc.). A second group—**complex cells**—responds maximally to moving stimuli such as a vertical bar moving from left to right, or to a tilted bar moving from right to left. Finally, **hypercomplex cells** respond to even more complex features of the visual world, such as length, width and even aspects of shape, such as corners and angles. Since then, researchers have identified additional specialized neurons (Gross, 2005). Some respond to specific shapes, whereas others respond only to shapes

Feature detectors:
Neurons at various levels within the visual system that respond primarily to stimuli possessing certain features in the visual cortex.

Simple cells:
Cells within the visual system that respond to specific shapes presented in certain orientations (e.g., horizontal, vertical).

Complex cells:
Neurons in the visual cortex that respond to stimuli that move in a particular direction and that have a particular orientation.

Hypercomplex cells:
Neurons in the visual cortex that respond to complex aspects of visual stimuli, such as width, length, and shape.

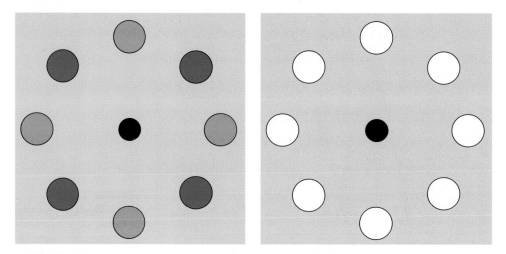

FIGURE 3.11
Negative Afterimages: Sensations of Complementary Colors
To understand what negative afterimages are, look at the left side of the figure and convince yourself that the outside circles are *not* colored. Now stare at the black dot on the left. After twenty seconds or so, shift your focus to the black spot on the right. What do you see? If you have normal color vision, the outside circles on the right should now appear to be colored. This is a negative afterimage.

combined with a color or a texture. For example, Tanaka and colleagues (1991; 1993) identified a type of cell that responds to a model of an apple, but stops responding if the apple's stem is removed.

Important clues about the specialized nature of visual processing in the brain have come from studying people with brain damage. Damage to the temporal lobe, for example, can cause a rare condition termed **prosopagnosia,** in which people lose the ability to recognize familiar people (even themselves!) by their faces, but still retain relatively normal vision in other respects. Studies using brain-imaging techniques have shown that pictures of faces activate neurons in a structure within the temporal lobe of the brain called the *fusiform face area* (FFA) (see Bentin et al., 2002; Kanwisher et al., 1997). Studies like this further highlight the specialized nature of the visual system.

Some evidence suggests the nervous system may have evolved such structures to enhance an animal's ability to survive. Neurons in the visual cortex of newborn monkeys, for example, signal information about the direction in which objects are moving and the distance between them—qualities key to a monkey's survival (Chino et al., 1997). This evidence suggests that such specialization may be "built in." However, other research seems to indicate that experience, or learning, is also important (Gross, 2005). Gauthier and colleagues (2000) have attempted to determine whether practice in recognizing nonface objects increases the activity of neurons in the FFA. The researchers first determined the level of activity in the FFA that occurred in response to faces and to computer-generated objects called *Greebles.* As predicted, neurons in the FFA initially responded strongly to the faces but weakly to the Greebles. Participants then received intensive training to help them become experts in recognizing each of the many different Greebles and their names. After the training, neurons in the FFA responded about as well to Greebles as to faces. Apparently, neurons in this area possess a plasticity that allows them to respond not just to faces, but also to other stimuli—ones that are seen often and are behaviorally important (see Kolb et al., 2003).

Taken together, these findings highlight the fact that "seeing" the world is a complex process—one that requires precise integration across many levels of our visual system. They also highlight the practical usefulness of such findings; for example, they help to explain why we are more apt to remember a person's face

Prosopagnosia:
A rare condition in which brain damage impairs a person's ability to recognize faces.

than his or her name. They also help to explain how people and other animals are able to "tune in" to relevant danger signals in their respective environments.

KEY QUESTIONS

- What are the basic structures of the eye and what is the physical stimulus for vision?
- What are the basic functions of the visual system?
- How do psychologists explain color perception?
- Why is visual perception a hierarchical process?
- What are the basic building blocks of visual perception?

HEARING

The melody of a baby's laughter, the roar of a jet plane, the rustling of leaves on a crisp autumn day—clearly, we live in a world full of sound. And, as with vision, human beings are well equipped to receive many sounds in their environment. A simplified diagram of the human ear is shown in Figure 3.12 on page 88; refer to it as you proceed through the discussion.

The Ear: Its Basic Structure

Try asking a friend, "When did you get your pinna pierced?" The response will probably be a blank stare. **Pinna** is the technical term for the visible part of our hearing organ, the *ear*. However, this is only a small part of the entire ear. Inside the ear is an intricate system of membranes, small bones, and receptor cells that transform sound waves into neural information for the brain. The *eardrum*, a thin piece of tissue just inside the ear, moves ever so slightly in response to sound waves striking it. When it moves, the eardrum causes three tiny bones within the *middle ear* to vibrate. The third of these bones is attached to a second membrane, the *oval window*, which covers a fluid-filled, spiral-shaped structure known as the **cochlea.** Vibration of the oval window causes the fluid in the cochlea to move. Finally, the movement of fluid bends tiny *hair cells*, the true sensory receptors of sound. The neural messages they create are then transmitted to the brain via the *auditory nerve*.

Sound: The Physical Stimulus for Hearing

In discussing light, we noted that relationships exist between certain of its physical properties, such as wavelength and intensity, and psychological aspects of vision, such as hue and brightness. Similar relationships exist for sound, at least with respect to two of its psychological qualities: *loudness* and *pitch*.

Sound waves consist of alternating compressions of the air, or, more precisely, of the molecules that compose air. The greater the *amplitude* (magnitude) of these waves, the greater their loudness to us (see Figure 3.13, page 89). The rate at which air is expanded and contracted constitutes the *frequency* of a sound wave, and the greater the frequency, the higher the **pitch.** Frequency is measured in terms of cycles per second, or hertz (Hz). Humans can generally hear sounds ranging from about 20 Hz to about 20,000 Hz, but are most sensitive to sounds between 2,000 and 4,000 Hz, the range of frequencies that is most important for understanding speech (Goldstein, 2002).

Older adults progressively lose sensitivity to sound, particularly for higher sound frequencies. This form of hearing loss, termed *presbycusis*, affects males more severely than females, and may be due, at least in part, to long-term exposure to workplace noise or other loud noises. Declines in hearing among the elderly also interact with declines in cognitive functioning, making it difficult for

Pinna:
The external portion of our ear.

Cochlea:
A portion of the inner ear containing the sensory receptors for sound.

Pitch:
The characteristic of a sound that is described as high or low. Pitch is mediated by the frequency of a sound.

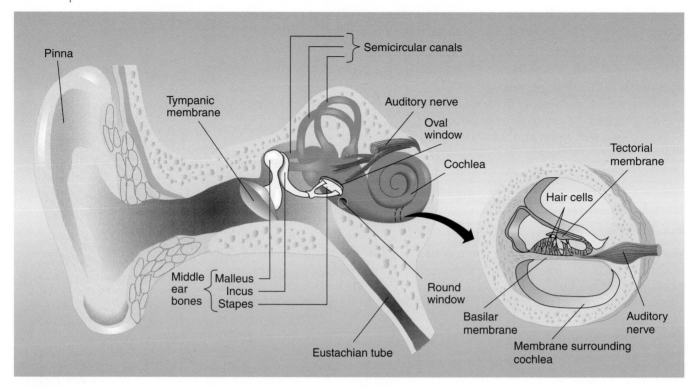

FIGURE 3.12
The Human Ear
A simplified diagram of the human ear. Sound waves (alternating compressions and expansions in the air) enter through the external auditory canal and produce slight movements in the eardrum. This produces movements in the fluid within the cochlea. As this fluid moves, tiny hair cells shift their position, thus generating the nerve impulses we perceive as sound.

older people to do tasks most of us take for granted, such as remembering new information and keeping pace with everyday rapid speech (Wingfield et al., 2005). To illustrate this, consider a recent study by McCoy and colleagues (2005). These researchers compared word-list recall in two groups: older adults who had *good* or *poor* hearing. All participants listened to lists of words being spoken. At random points, they were asked to recall the last *three* words they had heard. Both groups performed equally well in recalling the last word, but recall for the two words that preceded it was significantly poorer for the group with hearing loss, even though all the words were delivered at the same volume (see Figure 3.14, page 90). Why should this occur? The researchers reasoned that the extra effort the older adults with hearing loss had to expend to hear the words came at the expense of other cognitive resources needed to encode the words in memory (see Chapter 6 for additional information on memory).

A third psychological aspect of sound—its **timbre**—refers to a sound's quality. This quality depends on the mixture of frequencies and amplitudes that make up the sound (refer to Figure 3.13). In general, the timbre of a sound is related to its complexity—how many different frequencies it contains. However, other physical aspects of the sound source may be involved as well, so the relationship is not simple.

Pitch Perception

When we tune a guitar or sing in harmony with other people, we demonstrate our ability to detect differences in pitch. Most of us can easily tell when two sounds have the same pitch and when they are different. As noted previously, some lucky individuals have **perfect pitch,** the ability to name or produce a note of particular pitch in the absence of a reference note. The prevalence of perfect pitch is about 1

Timbre:
The quality of a sound resulting from the complexity of a sound wave that, for example, helps us distinguish between the sound of a trumpet and that of a saxophone.

Perfect pitch:
The ability to name or produce a note of particular pitch in the absence of a reference note.

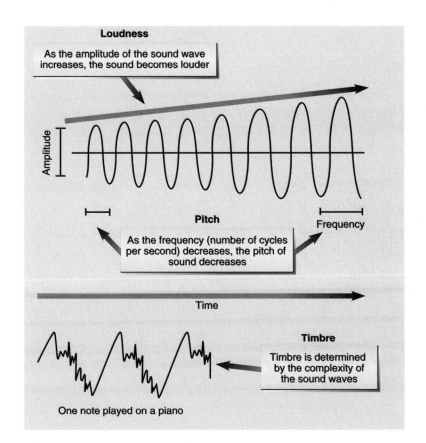

FIGURE 3.13
Physical Characteristics of Sound
Our perception of sound is determined by three characteristics. *Loudness* depends on the amplitude, or height, of the sound waves; as amplitude increases, the sound appears louder. *Pitch* is determined by the frequency of the sound waves—the number of sound waves that pass a given point per second. *Timbre* refers to the quality of the sound we perceive and is the characteristic that help us to distinguish the sound of a flute from the sound produced by other musical instruments.

in 10,000 among people in the United States, but is greater among skilled musicians than those without any musical training and among people in countries where tone languages are spoken (Deutsch, Henthorn, & Dolson, 2004). In a tone language, such as Mandarin Chinese, Somali, or Vietnamese, the same word takes on different meanings depending on the way it is spoken. So, for example, among Mandarin speakers, the same word—say, "ma"—can mean "mother," "hemp," "horse," or a reproach, depending on the particular pitch, or combination of pitches, used to pronounce it. Although perfect pitch appears to occur in families, suggesting a genetic component, cultural differences such as this seem to indicate that learning, or experience, also plays a role in the development of pitch perception.

Interestingly, scientists may have pinpointed the part of the brain responsible for perfect pitch by using brain-imaging techniques such as PET (see Chapter 2) to determine which parts of the brain are most active when people with perfect pitch perform a pitch-naming task. Studies using these techniques show that the most active area of the brains of skilled musicians performing the task is an area of the right frontal cortex called the planum temporale (Wilson & Reutens, 2002).

Sensory mechanisms that work at a more basic level are also involved in pitch perception, and we'll discuss these next. **Place theory** (also called the *traveling wave theory*) suggests that sounds of different frequencies cause different places along the *basilar membrane* (the floor of the cochlea) to vibrate. These vibrations, in turn, stimulate the hair cells—the sensory receptors for sound. Observations have shown that sound does produce pressure waves and that these waves peak, or produce maximal displacement, at various distances along the basilar membrane, depending on the frequency of the sound (Narayan et al., 1998; von Bekesy, 1960). High-frequency sounds cause maximum displacement at the narrow end of the basilar membrane near the oval window, whereas lower frequencies cause maximal displacement toward the wider, farther end of the basilar membrane. Unfortunately, place theory does not explain our ability to discriminate very low

Place theory:
A theory suggesting that sounds of different frequency stimulate different areas of the basilar membrane, the portion of the cochlea containing sensory receptors for sound.

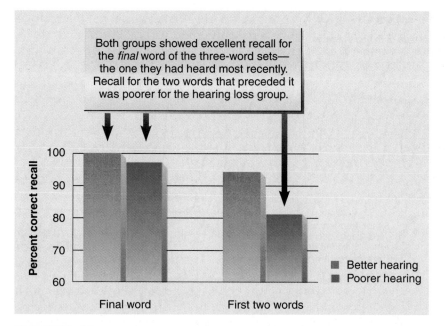

Both groups showed excellent recall for the *final* word of the three-word sets— the one they had heard most recently. Recall for the two words that preceded it was poorer for the hearing loss group.

FIGURE 3.14
How Hearing Loss Interacts with Other Cognitive Processes in the Elderly
Participants in both groups of elderly people showed excellent recall for the final word of three-word sets they listened to, but recall of the first two words was poorer for the hearing-loss group than for participants with better hearing. All the words were delivered at the same volume.
Source: Based on data from McCoy et al., 2005.

frequency sounds whose frequencies differ by as little as 1 or 2 Hz, because displacement on the basilar membrane is nearly identical for these sounds.

A second explanation, termed **frequency theory,** suggests that sounds of different pitch cause different rates of neural firing. Thus, high-pitched sounds produce high rates of activity in the auditory nerve, whereas low-pitched sounds produce lower rates. Frequency theory seems to be accurate up to sounds of about 1,000 Hz—the maximum rate of firing for individual neurons. Above that level, the theory must be modified to include the *volley principle*—the assumption that sound receptors for other neurons begin to fire in volleys. For example, a sound with a frequency of 5,000 Hz might generate a pattern of activity in which each of five groups of neurons fires 1,000 times in rapid succession—that is, in volleys.

Because our daily activities regularly expose us to sounds of many frequencies, both theories are needed to explain our ability to respond to this wide range of stimuli. Frequency theory explains how low-frequency sounds are registered, whereas place theory explains how high-frequency sounds are registered. In the middle ranges between 500 and 4,000 Hz, the range we use for most daily activities, both theories apply.

Sound Localization

You are walking down a busy street when suddenly a familiar voice calls your name. You instantly turn in the direction of this sound and spot one of your friends. How do you know where to turn? Research on **localization**—the ability of the auditory system to locate the source of a given sound—suggests that several factors play a role.

The first is that we have two ears, placed on opposite sides of our head. As a

Frequency theory:
A theory of pitch perception suggesting that sounds of different frequencies (heard as differences in pitch) induce different rates of neural activity in the hair cells of the inner ear.

Localization:
The ability of our auditory system to determine the direction of a sound source.

result, our head creates a *sound shadow*, a barrier that reduces the intensity of sound on the shadowed side. Thus, a sound behind us and to our left will be slightly louder in our left ear. The shadow effect is strongest for high-frequency sounds, which have difficulty bending around the head (Phillips & Brugge, 1985). The placement of our ears also produces a slight difference in the time it takes for a sound to reach each ear. Although this difference is truly minute—often less than one millisecond—it provides an important clue to sound localization.

What happens when sound comes from directly in front or directly in back of us? In this instance, we often have difficulty determining the location of the sound source, because the sound reaches our ears at the same time. Head movements can help resolve a problem like this. By turning your head, you create a slight difference in the time it takes for the sound to reach each of your ears—and now you can determine the location of the sound and take appropriate action (Moore, 1982).

In summary, our auditory system is ideally constructed to take full advantage of a variety of subtle cues. When you consider how rapidly we process and respond to such information, the whole system seems nothing short of marvelous in its efficiency. However, as with anything in life, too much of a good thing can often be harmful! This also holds true for sound. Currently, about 30 million Americans are affected by hearing loss, and 50 million have *tinnitus*, an early indicator of hearing loss (Dangerous Decibels, 2006). The use of modern conveniences such as stereo headsets, electric blow dryers, and leaf blowers are partly to blame. So, too, is living near or working in a noisy environment. For additional information on the harmful effects of sound in the workplace, refer to the **Psychology Goes to Work** section on page 92.

KEY QUESTIONS

- What is the physical stimulus for hearing?
- What is perfect pitch?
- How do psychologists explain pitch perception?
- How do we localize sound?

TOUCH AND OTHER SKIN SENSES

The skin is our largest sensory organ and produces the most varied experiences: everything from the pleasure of a soothing massage to the pain of an injury. Actually, there are several skin senses, including touch (or pressure), warmth, cold, and pain. Microscopic examination has revealed several different receptor types that differ in terms of the type of stimulation to which they respond best. Because each receptor is specialized to respond to different types of stimulation, stimulating the skin usually activates a number of receptor types, some more strongly than others, depending on the stimulus. Therefore, our overall perception of particular objects is determined by the total pattern of nerve impulses reaching the brain.

Have you ever wondered why certain areas of your body are more sensitive than others? As it turns out, the receptors in skin are not evenly distributed; the touch receptors in areas highly sensitive to touch, such as the face and fingertips, are much more densely packed than receptors in less sensitive areas, such as our legs. Additionally, areas of the skin with greater sensitivity also have greater representation in higher levels of the brain.

In most instances we discover the texture of an object through active exploration—using our finger tips or other sensitive areas of our body. Psychologists distinguish between *passive touch*, in which an object comes in contact with the skin, and *active touch*, in which we place our hand or other body part in contact with an object. We are considerably more accurate at identifying objects through active than through passive touch, in part because of feedback we receive from the movement of our fingers and hands when exploring an object (Wolfe et al., 2006). Let's now turn to a discussion of how the sense of touch helps us experience pain.

Pain: Its Nature and Control

Nociceptor:
A sensory receptor that responds to stimuli that are damaging.

Pain plays an important adaptive role; without it, we would be unaware that something is amiss with our body or that we have suffered some type of injury. Sources of pain, such as intense pressure, extreme temperature, or burning chemicals stimulate receptors called **nociceptors.**

Actually, two types of pain seem to exist. One can best be described as quick and sharp—the kind of pain we experience when we receive a cut. The other is

PSYCHOLOGY GOES TO WORK

The Harmful Effects of Noise: Turn Down the Sound at Work and at Play!

The National Institute of Occupational Safety and Health (NIOSH) estimates that more than 30 million U.S. workers are regularly exposed to hazardous noise. Not surprisingly, high levels of ambient noise are one of the most prevalent environmental stressors in the workplace. Here are some facts that can help you avoid hearing loss, both at work and at home.

How Much Noise Is Too Much?

Long-term exposure to even moderate noise levels—ones louder than 85 decibels (dB)—can produce stress-related disorders and permanent hearing loss. A *decibel* is a unit that measures the intensity of sound. A normal conversation is about 60 dB; noisy restaurants and office environments clock in at about 90 dB. However, one-time exposure to extremely loud noises, such as the sound of a gun firing at close range (165 dB), can produce permanent damage. The use of earplugs snugly fitted into the outer ear canal can reduce the level of noise by 15 to 30 dB. Compare this with the 7 dB reduction achieved by cramming cotton balls or tissue paper into the ear canal (American Academy of Otolaryngology, 2006).

Personal Sound Systems: The Facts

One of the biggest offenders when it comes to hearing loss is personal sound systems—especially those with headphones (see Figure 3.15). These devices produce sounds as loud as 105–120 dB if turned up to maximum levels. Older personal sound systems distorted the sound when played at maximum volume; however, today's technology has enabled the new digital players to produce high-quality sound from low volume to full blast. Now it's easy to listen to 100 decibels and be unaware of the dangerous level. How long can you safely listen to 115 decibels?

Experts say that this level is risky after only twenty-eight seconds! Unfortunately, many listen to their personal sound systems at high levels for hours on end—both at work and at play.

Steps to Protect Hearing While Listening to Personal Stereo Systems

Consider the following tips to reduce the chances of experiencing permanent hearing loss.

- Buy a personal stereo system with an *automatic volume limiter* that limits the output of the system to safe levels. Some manufacturers (e.g., Apple®) provide software updates at their web sites that allow customers to set their personal maximum volume limit, as well as the limit on their children's digital players.
- Don't turn it up when you are in a noisy setting to "block out" the noise. This will only add to the noise and increase the risks of hearing loss.
- Follow this simple rule of thumb: If you cannot hear other people talking when you are wearing headphones, or if other people have to shout to you to be heard at three feet away while the headphones are on, the sound could be damaging to your hearing.
- Don't discard the "earbud" headphones that come with most MP3 players. You can protect your hearing with their use, as they rest in the "bowl" of the ear. Unfortunately, optional accessories that tout their "great sound quality" go directly into the ear canal and can cause much more damage to hearing.
- Limit the amount of time you use the personal stereo system with headphones. Unlike the Walkman of the 1980s, which forced listeners to pause the music to turn over the cassette or

dull and throbbing—the pain we experience from a sore muscle or an injured back. The first type of pain seems to be transmitted through large myelinated sensory nerve fibers (Campbell & LaMotte, 1983). You may recall from Chapter 2 that impulses travel faster along myelinated fibers, and so it makes sense that sharp sensations of pain are carried via these fiber types. In contrast, dull pain is carried by smaller unmyelinated nerve fibers, which conduct neural impulses more slowly. Both fiber types synapse with neurons in the spinal cord that carry pain messages to the thalamus and other parts of the brain (Willis, 1985).

Gate-control theory:
A theory of pain suggesting that the spinal cord contains a mechanism that can block transmission of pain to the brain.

■ **Pain perception: The role of physiological mechanisms.**

The discovery of the two pain systems described above led to the formulation of an influential view of pain known as the **gate-control theory** (Melzack, 1965; 1988). Gate-control theory suggests that there are neural mechanisms in the spinal

---

psychology goes to work (continued)

change batteries, today's large-capacity MP3 players allow the user to listen to music for many hours with no break in the action.

- If you notice any ringing in your ears, or that speech sounds are muffled after wearing a personal stereo system, discontinue its use and have your hearing checked by a qualified audiologist.

Personal Stereo Systems: Blessing or Curse?

It is highly likely that the MP3 player is here to stay. But is there a place for it in the workplace? Many workers claim it boosts their productivity, motivates them to work faster, or lifts their spirits on a bad day. Yet not all management welcomes the portable music players with open arms, claiming that employees who use them are often rude, unprofessional, and distracted. If the volume level is high, it can distract and annoy coworkers as well. And what about safety? Workers with headphones might be unable to hear warning alarms, moving machinery, or strangers approaching them. The solution seems to be straightforward: If using your player at work has the potential to causes these, or similar problems, leave it at home.

Source of Sound	Sound Intensity (in decibels, or dB)
Rocket launch	180 dB
Gunshot	165 dB
Firecrackers or jet engine at takeoff	140 dB
Noisy squeak toys	135 dB
Ambulance siren	120 dB
Stadium football game	117 dB
Stereo headset (turned to high setting)	112 dB
Chain saw and some children's toys	110 dB
Noisy restaurant or office environment	90 dB
City traffic	85 dB
Ringing telephone	80 dB
Vacuum cleaner	75 dB
Normal conversation	60 dB
A whisper	30 dB

Long-term exposure to sound intensities at or above these levels can produce permanent hearing loss

FIGURE 3.15
Decibels in Everyday Life
Examples of sound intensities (in decibels) that are a part of modern daily life. It is important to note that long-term exposure to relatively moderate sound intensities (85 dB and above) can contribute to permanent hearing loss.

cord that sometimes close, thus preventing pain messages from reaching the brain. Apparently, pain messages carried by the large fibers cause this "gate" to close, while messages carried by the smaller fibers—the ones related to dull, throbbing pain—cannot. This may explain why sharp pain is relatively brief, whereas an ache persists. The gate-control theory also helps to explain why vigorously stimulating one area to reduce pain in another sometimes works. Presumably, countermeasures such as rubbing the skin near an injury, applying ice packs or hot water bottles, and even acupuncture stimulate activity in the large nerve fibers, closing the spinal "gate" and reducing sensations of pain. The gate neurons that block pain transmission can apparently also be activated by applying pressure, cold, or other noxious stimulation to sites distant from the pain source. For example, pain from electrically stimulating a tooth can be reduced by applying uncomfortable stimulation to the hand (Motohashi & Umino, 2001).

Gate-control theory has been revised to account for the importance of several brain mechanisms in the perception of pain (e.g., Fields & Basbaum, 1999; Weissberg, 1999). For example, our current emotional state may interact with the onset of a painful stimulus to alter the intensity of pain we experience. The brain, in other words, may affect pain perception by transmitting messages that either close the spinal "gate" or keep it open. The result: When we are anxious, pain is intensified, and when we are calm and relaxed, pain may be reduced.

■ Pain perception: The role of cognitive processes.

Research shows that pain may exert its unpleasant effects, in part, by interrupting ongoing thought and behavior and redirecting our attention to the pain (Eccleston & Crombez, 1999). The extent to which we experience pain results from a dynamic interplay between characteristics of the pain (e.g., its intensity, novelty, predictability) and the context in which we experience pain. Cognition, or thought, plays a critical mediator role, determining the extent to which we focus on pain relative to these factors and the degree of threat that they pose to us. This cognitive activity may help explain why procedures that *redirect* our attention are effective countermeasures for pain.

Hypnosis, for example, has been shown to be effective in reducing the effects of pain, apparently by activating a supervisory attention-control system in the brain that shifts the focus of our attention *away* from the pain (Crawford, Knebel, & Vendemia, 1998). (See Chapter 4 for additional information on hypnosis.) A more high-tech method of distraction—playing immersive virtual reality games—has been used successfully to help alleviate the pain experienced by young burn victims (Hoffman et al., 2000). To promote healing, burn wounds must be scrubbed regularly, which causes the patient significant pain, and medication cannot totally block it. However, burn victims who play an immersive virtual reality game during the painful procedure rate their pain significantly lower than when playing a less realistic 2-D video game (see Figure 3.16). Finally, researchers have discovered that coughing—definitely a no-frills method of distraction—can be an effective means of reducing the pain that accompanies an injection. By coughing at the time the needle pierces the skin, a patient may be distracted from the ache, but evidence also points to a quick rise in blood pressure when coughing, which apparently helps lessen the discomfort of the injection (Ahmed et al., 2004; Usichenko et al., 2004).

A group of therapies, collectively termed *cognitive-behavioral procedures* (see chapter 12), have also been shown to be effective in counteracting the effects of pain. These procedures are based on how our thoughts, feelings, and beliefs can dramatically influence our perceptions of pain (Stroud et al., 2000; Turk & Okifuji, 2002). To illustrate this, consider a study in which participants were led to believe they would be helping to test a new topical anesthetic for its pain-reducing effect (Montgomery & Kirsch, 1996). The fictitious pain reliever (placebo) was actually a harmless, but medicinal-smelling mixture dispensed from a bottle labeled "Trivar-

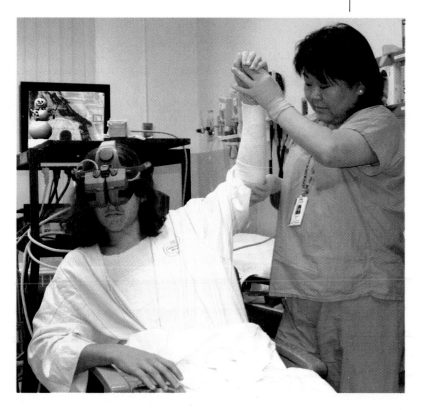

FIGURE 3.16
The Role of Cognitive Processes in Pain Perception
Cognition plays a critical role in determining the extent to which we focus on pain and helps explain why procedures that redirect our attention are effective countermeasures for pain. One high-tech method of distraction—playing immersive virtual reality games—has been used to help alleviate the excruciating pain experienced by young burn victims during the painful recovery process. (Left: Courtesy Hunter Hoffman; right: photo by Gretchen Carrougher. © Hunter Hoffman.)

icane: Approved for research purposes only." The researchers applied the mixture to either the left or right index finger of each participant. After waiting a brief period of time to allow the "medication" to take effect, the researchers delivered equal intensities of a painful stimulus (pressure) to both the left and right fingers. As predicted, the placebo was effective in reducing the participants' perceptions of pain; ratings of pain intensity and unpleasantness were significantly lower for "treated" fingers than for "untreated" fingers.

Taken together, these results illustrate the important role cognitive processes play in determining the extent to which we experience pain. They also form the basis for designing procedures to help people learn to tolerate pain. This is particularly important for people who are allergic to pain medications, or in instances of chronic pain, in which the long-term use of such substances could become addicting.

■ **Pain perception and culture.**

Although we commonly view pain as something automatic and universal, large cultural differences in the interpretation and expression of pain do exist. But what is the basis for these differences? At first glance, it is tempting to conclude that differences in pain threshold—physical differences—are the cause. However, no consistent evidence supports this view (Zatzick & Dimsdale, 1994). Instead, observed cultural differences in the capacity to withstand pain seem to be perceptual in nature and to reflect the effects of social learning (Morse & Morse, 1988; Sargent, 1984). To illustrate this point, consider a study by Clark and Clark (1980). These researchers gave electric shocks to a group of Western participants and a group from Nepal (a country in Southeast Asia, between India and China). Participants were asked to indicate the intensities at which they experienced faint and extreme pain, respectively. Both groups began to detect the shocks at about the same intensity, but the Nepalese participants required much higher intensities before they indicated they were experiencing either faint or extreme pain. Similar findings have been observed in many other studies and in different cultures. In sum, the evidence

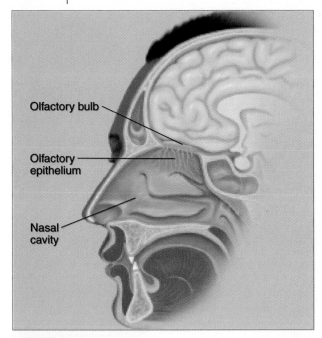

FIGURE 3.17
The Receptors for Smell
Receptors for our sense of smell are located in the olfactory epithelium, at the top of the nasal cavity. Molecules of odorous substances are dissolved in moisture present in the nasal passages. This brings them into contact with *receptor cells*, whose neural activity gives rise to sensations of smell.

suggests that pain may be universal—at least in some respects—and that differences in pain perception result from the powerful effects of social learning, not from physical differences among various groups of people.

KEY QUESTIONS

- What is the physical stimulus for touch?
- Where does the sensation of pain originate?
- What role do cognitive processes play in the perception of pain?
- What role does culture play in pain perception?

SMELL AND TASTE: THE CHEMICAL SENSES

Although smell and taste are separate senses, we'll consider them together for two reasons. First, both respond to substances in solution—that is substances that have been dissolved in a fluid or gas, usually water or air. That is why they are often referred to as the *chemical senses*. Second, in everyday life, smell and taste are interrelated.

Smell and Taste: How They Operate

The stimulus for sensation of smell consists of molecules of various substances (odorants) contained in the air. Such molecules enter the nasal passages, where they dissolve in moist nasal tissues. This brings them in contact with receptor cells contained in the *olfactory mucosa* (see Figure 3.17). Humans possess about 20 million of these receptors split between our right and left nostrils. A bloodhound, by contrast, possesses about 220 million. Indeed, dogs can sense odors at concentrations nearly 100 million times lower than humans can (Krestel et al., 1984; Willis et al., 2004). Nevertheless, our ability to detect smells is impressive. In a "scratch-and-sniff" survey, for example, six different odors were embedded separately onto panels about 1.75 by 1.25 inches in size. Less than one ounce of each odor was needed to place the smells onto 11 million copies of the survey (Gibbons, 1986; Gilbert & Wysocki, 1987). Yet, despite the tiny amounts deposited on each survey, people were easily able to detect the smells.

Interestingly, there are a small number of individuals (fewer than fifty) throughout the world termed "Noses" who possess an unusually well-developed sense of smell. As you might expect, their special talents are highly prized by manufacturers of various scented products, including perfume and wine. A Nose can apparently identify and classify hundreds of scents, as well as detect the percentage of ingredients blended. Prospective Noses begin their smell education by memorizing four hundred raw materials by smell. The palette of a Nose can eventually expand to as many as two thousand scents. Noses also claim they can "smell" a scent as soon as they hear its name.

Our olfactory senses are restricted, however, in terms of the *range* of stimuli to which they are sensitive. Just as the visual system can detect only a small portion of the total electromagnetic spectrum, the olfactory receptors can detect only certain substances termed *odorants*. Each molecule of an odorant has a particular size and weight; humans seem to be able to smell odorants with molecular weights ranging from fifteen to about three hundred (Carlson, 1998). This explains why we can smell alcohol, but not table sugar. The molecules that comprise alcohol fall within this range (46), whereas the ones that comprise table sugar do not (342).

Several theories have been proposed for how smell messages are interpreted by the brain. *Shape-pattern theory* suggests that odorant molecules and olfactory receptors have different shapes and that an odorant will be detected to the extent that the odorant's molecules fit into a particular receptor (Amoore, 1970; 1982). According to this view, substances differ in smell because they have different molecular shapes. An alternative to shape-pattern theory, termed *vibration theory*, proposes that because of atomic structure, every smell molecule has a specific vibrational frequency (Turin, 1996). According to this view, molecules that produce the same vibrational frequencies should have the same smell, whereas molecules with different vibrational frequencies should smell different.

Unfortunately, support for each of these theories has been mixed. Shape-pattern theory cannot explain why nearly identical molecules can have extremely different fragrances, whereas substances with very different chemical structures can produce very similar odors (Engen, 1982; Wright, 1982). Similarly, vibration theory cannot account for several puzzles of olfactory perception, such as why some individuals are unable to smell a particular substance but otherwise have normal smell perception, and why *stereoisomers*—molecules comprised of the same atoms, but arranged differently—smell completely different.

Recent evidence seems to indicate that the brain's ability to recognize odors may be based on the overall pattern of activity produced by the olfactory receptors (Zou & Buck, 2006). According to this view, different scents activate different arrays of olfactory receptors in regions in the *olfactory cortex*—the part of the brain that handles smell and recognizes specific odors. More research will be needed to determine precisely how the brain accomplishes this task.

We'll now turn to a discussion of the other chemical sense—*taste*. The sensory receptors for taste are located inside small bumps on the tongue known as *papillae*. Within each papilla is a cluster of *taste buds* (Figure 3.18, page 98). Each taste bud contains several receptor cells. Humans possess about ten thousand taste buds. In contrast, chickens have only twenty-four, while catfish would win any "taste-bud counting contest"—they possess more than 175,000, scattered over the surface of their body. In a sense, they can "taste" with their entire skin (Pfaffmann, 1978).

For decades, scientists have agreed that we have four basic food tastes: sweet, salty, sour, and bitter. Recent research, however, seems to indicate there could be several more. Scientists are currently investigating the possibility of a fifth candidate, *umami,* which is evoked by the amino acid glutamate, a substance found in meats, meat broths, and monosodium glutamate (MSG). Glutamate contributes significantly to the "savory" taste of many natural foods, including fish and cheese (Damak et al., 2003; Nelson et al., 2002). Emerging evidence also hints at the possibility of a sixth basic taste: *fattiness.* It was generally accepted at one time that the fat in food doesn't have any taste, but instead provides textural cues or is detected through the smell it imparts to foods. However, research now shows that when these factors are controlled, people and other animals can still detect fat. Studies of rats have shown that fats cause electrical changes in taste cells, evidence that there is a "fat" detection system at work. Preliminary research with humans has revealed similar findings (see Matte, 2001).

Interestingly, findings like these may help to explain why people do not seem to find fat-free food alternatives as satisfying as their full-fat counterparts. They also give rise to the following important question: Given the fact there are only a relatively small number of basic tastes, why do people generally believe they can distinguish many more flavors than the ones just described? The answer lies in the fact that we are aware not only of the taste of the food but also of its smell, its texture, its temperature, the pressure it exerts on our tongue and mouth, and many other sensations. When these factors are removed from the picture, only the basic tastes remain (see Figure 3.18, page 98).

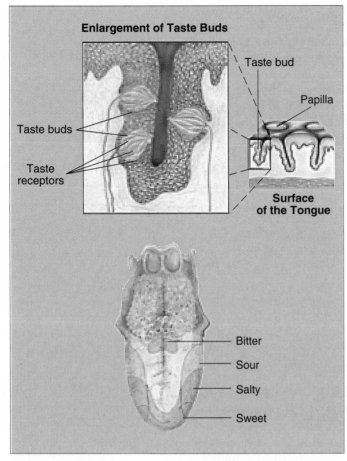

Enlargement of Taste Buds

Taste bud

Papilla

Taste buds

Taste receptors

Surface of the Tongue

Bitter

Sour

Salty

Sweet

FIGURE 3.18
Sensory Receptors for Taste
Taste buds are located inside small bumps on the surface of the tongue known as papillae. Within each taste bud are a number of individual receptor cells.

Smell and Taste: Some Interesting Findings

Perhaps because they are more difficult to study, smell and taste have received far less attention from researchers than vision and hearing. However, this does not imply that these senses are not important. Indeed, individuals who have lost their sense of smell (a state known as *anosmia*) often become deeply depressed; some even commit suicide (Douek, 1988).

Despite the relative lack of research effort, many interesting facts have been uncovered about smell and taste. For example, it appears that we are able to discriminate thousands of odors and training seems to enhance this ability further. Professional perfumers and wine tasters can distinguish as many as 100,000 odors (Dobb, 1989). It is important to note, however, that we rarely smell pure odorants in everyday life; most of the smells we encounter are mixtures of odorants that we perceive as unitary wholes. For example, there is no such thing as a "bacon" odorant. Instead, the smell we recognize at bacon is comprised of many different individual chemicals.

Although we are good at detecting whether an odor is present or if two odors are the same or different, we are not very good at applying a verbal label to odors (Engen, 1986). When asked to identify thirteen common fragrances (such as grape, smoke, mint, pine, and soap), individuals were successful only 32 percent of the time. Even when brand-name products or common odors are used, accuracy is still less than 50 percent. Some research suggests that we lack a well-developed representational system for describing olfactory experiences (Engen, 1987). In other words, we may recognize a smell without being able to name the odor in question—sometimes called the *tip-of-the-nose* phenomenon (Lawless & Engen, 1977; Richardson & Zucco, 1989).

Actually, although our ability to identify specific odors is limited, our memory of them is impressive (Schab, 1991). Once exposed to a specific odor, we can recognize it months or even years later (Engen & Ross, 1973; Rabin & Cain, 1984). This may be because our memory for odors is often coded as part of memories of more complex and emotional life events (Herz, 1997; Stevenson & Boakes, 2003).

Knowledge about the chemical senses—especially smell—can also have important practical implications. Commercial success has led to numerous claims regarding the potential benefits of fragrance. For example, practitioners of a field called *aromatherapy* claim that they can successfully treat a wide range of psychological problems and physical ailments by means of specific fragrances (Tisserand, 1977). Aromatherapists claim, for example, that fragrances such as lemon, peppermint, and basil lead to increased alertness and energy, whereas lavender and cedar promote relaxation and reduced tension after high-stress work periods (Iwahashi, 1992). Can fragrance influence human behavior in measurable ways? Research indicates the answer is "yes." But whether specific fragrances produce contrasting effects is still uncertain. Although some findings support this claim, others do not. A study by Diego and colleagues (1998) provides some supporting evidence. Participants in this study were exposed to either lavender, supposedly a "relaxing" odor, or rosemary, presumably an "alerting" odor. Results showed that participants exposed to the rosemary fragrance were indeed more alert following the exposure, as gauged by self-report measures and changes in their electroencephalograph (EEG) patterns. And although both fragrances led to *faster* performance on a math computation task, only participants exposed to the lavender fragrance showed improved *accuracy*.

Findings from other research, however, seriously question the claim that specific odors produce specific effects (see Baron, 1997; Baron & Bronfen, 1994; Baron & Thomley, 1994). Research conducted by Robert Baron and colleagues suggests that any fragrance people find pleasant enhances their mood slightly, and that these positive feelings then influence their cognition and behavior. The specific fragrance doesn't seem to matter, as long as it is one people find pleasant.

Nevertheless, even these more limited effects may have practical applications. For example, Baron and Kalsher (1996) showed that participants' performance on a simulated driving task was significantly enhanced by the presence of a pleasant ambient lemon fragrance, suggesting that the use of fragrance may be an inexpensive but effective tool for maintaining alertness in people engaged in potentially dangerous activities, such as driving. So no, pleasant fragrances don't seem to have the powerful and highly specific effects aromatherapists claim, but yes, they do seem to influence behavior in interesting and potentially important ways.

KEY QUESTIONS

- What is the physical stimulus for smell and where are the sensory receptors located?
- Where are the sensory receptors for taste located?
- What are the practical benefits of using pleasant ambient fragrances?

KINESTHESIS AND VESTIBULAR SENSE

One night while driving, you notice flashing lights on the roadside ahead. Because traffic has slowed to a crawl, you get a close look at the situation as you pass by. A state trooper is in the process of administering a sobriety test to the driver of the car he has pulled over. The driver's head is tilted back at an angle, and he is trying to touch his fingers to his nose but is having great difficulty doing so. This example illustrates the importance of our *kinesthetic* and our *vestibular senses*—two important but often ignored aspects of our sensory system.

Kinesthesia is the sense that gives us information about the location of our body parts with respect to one another and allows us to perform movements—from simple ones like touching our nose with our fingertips, to more complex movements required for gymnastics, dancing, or driving an automobile. Kinesthetic information comes from receptors in joints, ligaments, and muscle fibers (Matlin & Foley, 1997). We also receive important kinesthetic information from our other senses, especially vision and touch. To demonstrate how your kinesthetic sense system draws on other senses, try the following experiment: Close your eyes for a moment and hold your arms down at your sides. Now, without looking, touch your nose with each of your index fingers—one at a time. Can you do it? Most people can, but only after missing their nose a time or two. Now, try it again with your eyes open. Is it easier this way? In most instances it is because of the added information we receive from our visual sense.

Whereas kinesthesia keeps our brain informed about the location of our body parts with respect to one another, the **vestibular sense** gives us information about body position, movement, and acceleration—factors critical for maintaining our sense of balance (Schiffman, 1990).

The sensory organs for the vestibular sense are located in the inner ear (see Figure 3.19, page 100). Two fluid-filled *vestibular sacs* provide information about the body's position in relation to the earth by tracking changes in linear movement. When our body accelerates (or decelerates) along a straight line, as when we are in

Kinesthesia:
The sense that gives us information about the location of our body parts with respect to one another and allows us to perform movement.

Vestibular sense:
Our sense of balance.

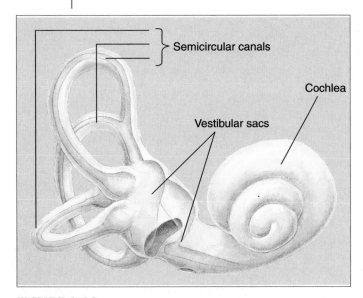

FIGURE 3.19
The Structures Underlying Our Sense of Balance
Shown here are the organs of the inner ear that comprise the vestibular sense. Structures in the two *vestibular sacs* provide information about the positions of the head and body with respect to gravity by tracking changes in linear movement, whereas those in the *semicircular canals* provide information about *rotational acceleration* around three principal axes.

a bus that is starting and stopping, or when we tilt our head or body to one side, hair cells bend in proportion to the rate of change in our motion. This differential bending of hair cells causes attached nerve fibers to discharge neural signals that are sent to the brain.

Three fluid-filled, *semicircular canals,* also in the inner ear, provide information about rotational acceleration of the head or body along the three principle axes. Whenever we turn or rotate our head, the fluid in these canals begins to move and causes a bending of hair cells. Because these structures are arranged at right angles to one another, bending is greatest in the semicircular canal corresponding to the axis along which the rotation occurs. Note that the vestibular system is designed to detect *changes* in motion rather than constant motion. For example, it helps us to detect the change in acceleration that accompanies take-off in an airplane but not the constant velocity that follows. We also receive vestibular information from our other senses, especially vision—a fact that can produce "queasy" consequences if the information from these senses are in conflict. For example, many people and their children become ill after participating in theme park rides that incorporate 3-D imagery and movement, such as the Spider Man, Jimmy Neutron, and Shrek attractions at Universal Studios in Orlando, Florida (see Figure 3.20).

KEY QUESTIONS

- What information does the kinesthetic sense provide to the brain?
- What information does the vestibular sense provide to the brain?

PERCEPTION: PUTTING IT ALL TOGETHER

Up to this point, we have focused on the sensory processes that convert raw physical stimulation into usable neural codes: vision, hearing, touch, taste, smell, and the kinesthetic and vestibular senses. You may now be wondering how this array of action potentials contributes to the richness of conscious experience. Stop for a moment and look around you. Do you see a meaningless swirl of colors, brightnesses, and shapes? Probably not. Now, turn on the radio and tune it to any station. Do you hear an incomprehensible babble of sounds? Certainly not—unless, of course, you've tuned to a foreign-language station. In both cases, you "see" and "hear" more than the raw sensations that stimulate the receptors in your eyes, ears, and other sense organs; you see recognizable objects and hear understandable words or music. In other words, transmission of sensory information from sensory receptors to the brain is only part of the picture. Equally important is the process of perception—the way in which we *select, organize,* and *interpret* sensory input to achieve a grasp of our surroundings. The remainder of this chapter concerns some basic principles that influence perception.

Perception: The Focus of Our Attention

Based on the preceding discussion, you may realize that your attention, or mental focus, captures only a small portion of the visual and auditory stimuli available at

FIGURE 3.20
Sensory Conflict and Nausea: A Case of Mismatched Sensory Information
Many people get more than they bargained for after participating in theme park rides that incorporate 3-D imagery and movement, especially when the information that is conveyed to different sensory modalities is in conflict—they get sick!

a given moment, while ignoring other aspects. But what about information from our other senses? By shifting the focus of our attention, we may suddenly notice smells, tastes, and tactile sensations that were outside our awareness only moments ago. For example, if you're absorbed in a good book or watching a suspenseful movie, you may be unaware of the sound of someone knocking at the door, at least temporarily.

One thing is certain—we cannot process all the available sensory information in our environment. Thus, we *selectively attend* to certain aspects of our environment while relegating others to the background (Johnston & Dark, 1986). **Selective attention** has obvious advantages, since it allows us to maximize information gained from the object of our focus while reducing sensory interference from other irrelevant sources. We are, however, faced with many everyday situations in which we must cope with multiple conflicting inputs. Think back to the last time you were at a crowded party with many conversations going on at once. Were you able to shut out all voices except for the person you were talking to? Probably not. Our attention often shifts to other aspects of our environment, such as a juicy bit of conversation or a mention of our own name (Moray, 1959). This is often referred to as the **cocktail party phenomenon,** and it illustrates one way in which we deal with the demands of divided attention.

Although we control the focus of our attention, at least to some extent, certain characteristics of stimuli can cause our attention to shift suddenly. Features such as contrast, novelty, stimulus intensity, color, motion, and sudden change tend to attract our attention (Donderi, 2006). Psychologists often refer to this phenomenon as *pop-out*. As you might expect, the ability to shift the focus of our attention to detect such changes plays a crucial survival role in aspects of our everyday life by alerting us to immediate natural dangers in our environment.

As we've seen throughout this section, attention plays an important role in our ability to safely navigate the world around us. However, many aspects of modern living have begun to test the limits of our attentional capabilities. Perhaps the most widespread of these is the use of cell phones while driving. For a discussion on the dangers of using these devices while driving, please see the **Psychology Lends a Hand** section on page 102.

Selective attention:
The process of focusing on a particular quality, object, or event for relatively detailed analysis.

Cocktail party phenomenon:
The effect of not being aware of other people's conversations until something of personal importance, such as hearing one's name, is mentioned and then suddenly hearing it.

P S Y C H O L O G Y   L E N D S   A   H A N D

Exceeding the Limits of Our Attention: Why Do Cell Phones Interfere with Driving?

The use of cellular phones in this country, and throughout the world, has skyrocketed. In 1990, approximately 4.3 million people in the United States used cell phones. By the end of 2005, that figure had ballooned to more than 200 million (Cellular Telecommunications & Internet Association, 2005). So what's the problem? A lot of people use their cell phone while driving—nearly 85 percent in one survey (Goodman et al., 1999). Unfortunately, talking on a cell phone while driving makes a motorist four times as likely to get into a serious crash (Insurance Institute for Highway Safety, 2005). Because of the danger they pose, several states and individual cities prohibit the use of hand-held cell phones while driving.

Redelmeier and Tibshirani (1997) reviewed the cell-phone records of nearly seven hundred people involved in motor-vehicle accidents and found that a significant portion of them (24 percent) had been talking on their cell phones just before the accident. One interpretation of this finding is that the use of cell phones distracts people, similar to the effects you might expect from doing other activities while driving, such as putting on make-up, eating or drinking, or listening to music. However, research has shown that the use of wireless devices causes far more accidents and near-accidents than other attention-grabbing distractions (National Highway Traffic Safety Administration, 2005).

Research suggests that the particular type of attention demanded by active listening or conversing is what makes it so dangerous (Spence & Read, 2003). In one recent study, Strayer and colleagues (2005) asked some participants to perform a simulated driving task and others to perform the driving task while either talking on a cell phone or listening to the radio. To separate the effects of attention from manual manipulation of the phone itself, half the participants used a hand-held cell phone, while the other half used a hand-free phone. As shown in Figure 3.21, driving performance was *worse* among participants who talked on the cell phone compared to those who listened to the radio while driving. But contrary to what many people believe, the use of a hands-free cell phone did not lessen the negative effects compared to the use of a hand-held cell phone.

One interpretation of these findings is that people who use cell phones while driving notice traffic signals and other aspects of the driving environment, but fail to respond to them because of the competing demands of their phone conversation. As we'll see in Chaper 6, one possibility is that they are experiencing information overload—a bigger inflow of information than their cognitive systems can handle. However, another possibility is that the use of cell phones causes people to pay less attention to objects they encounter while driving. To test this possibility, Strayer and colleagues placed participants in a driving simulator and asked them to "drive" along routes that resembled city driving while using a hand-held or hands-free cell phone. In addition to measures of performance, their memory of objects (e.g., billboards) along the simulated driving route was also assessed. Participants who talked on a cell phone were less able to recognize these objects than

Perception: Some Organizing Principles

Look at the illustration in Figure 3.22. Instead of random smatterings of black and white, you can probably discern a familiar figure in each. But how does our brain allow us to interpret this confusion as a dog and a horseback rider? The process by which we structure the input from our sensory receptors is called *perceptual organization*. Aspects of perceptual organization were first studied systematically in the early 1900s by **Gestalt psychologists**—German psychologists intrigued by certain innate tendencies of the human mind to impose order and structure on the physical world, and to perceive sensory patterns as well-organized wholes, rather than as separate isolated parts (*Gestalt* means "whole" in German). These scientists outlined several principles that influence the way we organize basic sensory input into whole patterns (gestalts). Some of these are described below.

■ Figure and ground: What stands out?

By looking carefully at Figure 3.23 on page 104, you can experience a principle of perceptual organization known as the **figure-ground relationship.** What this means, simply, is that we tend to divide the world around us into two parts: *figure*, which has a definite shape and a location in space, and *ground*, which has no shape,

Gestalt psychologists: German psychologists intrigued by our tendency to perceive sensory patterns as well-organized wholes, rather than as separate isolated parts.

Figure-ground relationship: Our tendency to divide the perceptual world into two distinct parts—discrete figures and the background against which they stand out.

participants who did not. Once again, the use of a hands-free cell phone did not improve performance relative to a hand-held phone. Interestingly, eye-tracking data revealed that both groups of drivers had exhibited similar patterns of scanning aspects of the simulated driving environment, including billboards. Thus, participants who were talking on a cell phone while driving looked at these objects, but really didn't "see" them. Merely listening to the radio did not exert the same negative effects. The fact that people often fail to notice objects appearing in front of their eyes when they are preoccupied with an attentionally demanding task has been termed **inattentional blindness** (Mack & Rock, 1998; Most et al., 2005). The bottom line is that when drivers become involved in a cell phone conversation, it makes them less able to process and react effectively to information in the driving environment.

To avoid the possibility of injuring yourself, or someone else, while driving, consider the following driving safety tips:

Don't use your cell phone while driving. Talking on a cell phone—even a hands-free one—while driving is dangerous, because of the type of attention it demands. If you must use your cell phone, pull off the road into a safe place before dialing *or* answering your cell phone.

Avoid other competing activities. Talking on a cell phone is not the only problem; eating, drinking, and applying make-up are also dangerous activities, because they divert attention away from driving.

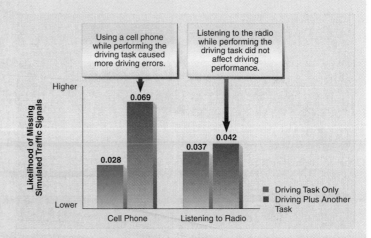

FIGURE 3.21

The Dangers of Talking on Cell Phones While Driving: Attention Appears to Be the Key

As shown here, performance on the simulated driving task was worse among participants who talked on the cell phone compared to those who listened to the radio while driving. The use of a hands-free cell phone did not alleviate the negative effects of talking on the cell phone while driving. *Source:* Based on data from Strayer et al., 2005.

Drive defensively. As the information in this section shows, a significant portion of people now use cell phones while driving—even in states where it is against the law. This could affect their driving, so plan ahead for the unexpected. Always be prepared to react to the other driver.

Inattentional blindness:
The inability to perceive features in a visual scene if they are not being attended to.

FIGURE 3.22

Perceptual Organization

Look carefully at each of these figures. What do you see? Our perceptual processes often allow us to perceive shapes and forms from incomplete and fragmented stimuli.

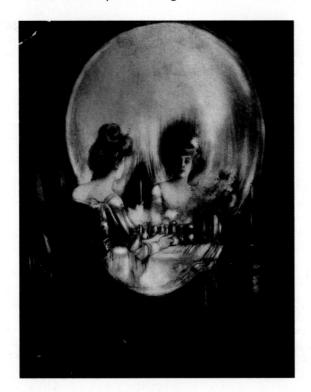

FIGURE 3.23
A Demonstration of Figure-Ground Relationship
Because this is an ambiguous figure, your perceptions may switch back and forth between these two possibilities.

seems to continue behind the figure, and has no definite location. The figure-ground relationship helps clarify the distinction between sensation and perception. While the pattern of sensory input generated in our receptors remains constant, our perceptions shift between the two figure-ground patterns in Figure 3.23; thus, we may see either a man's ear or a woman, but not both simultaneously. Note that the principles of perceptual organization apply to the other senses, too. For instance, consider how the figure-ground relationship applies to audition: During a complicated lecture, you become absorbed in whispered gossip between two students sitting next to you; the professor's voice becomes background noise. Suddenly you hear your name and realize the professor has asked you a question; her voice has now become the sole focus of your attention, while the conversation becomes background noise.

■ Grouping: Which stimuli go together?

The Gestaltists also called attention to a number of principles known as the **laws of grouping**—basic ways in which we group items together perceptually. Research suggests that these principles play a key role in visual perception; they help explain how small elements become perceptually grouped to form larger objects, and how a scene is segmented into relevant regions to help us recognize individual objects (Sekuler & Bennett, 2001). Several of these laws are illustrated in Figure 3.24. As you can see from this figure, they do offer a good description of our perceptual tendencies.

Still, some observers have questioned whether these principles are innate—as the Gestaltists contended—or the product of learning and experience. Proponents of this latter view have suggested these principles may apply only to people who have had experience with geometrical concepts. To illustrate this, let's consider a classic study by Luria (1976). Luria presented stimuli like those depicted in Figure 3.25 to several groups of participants that included uneducated people from remote villages and students in a teachers' school. Luria reasoned that if Gestalt principles were innate, then all participants—regardless of education

Laws of grouping:
Simple principles that describe how we tend to group discrete stimuli together in the perceptual world.

Laws of Similarity
Tendency to perceive similar items as a group

Laws of Proximity
Tendency to perceive items located together as a group

Laws of Common Region
Tendency to perceive objects as a group if they occupy the same place within a plane

Law of Good Continuation
Tendency to perceive stimuli as part of a continuous pattern

Law of Closure
Tendency to perceive objects as whole entities, despite the fact that some parts may be missing or obstructed from view

Laws of Simplicity
Tendency to perceive complex patterns in terms of simpler shapes

FIGURE 3.24
Laws of Perceptual Grouping
We seem to possess strong tendencies to group stimuli together in certain ways. Several of these *laws of grouping* are illustrated here.

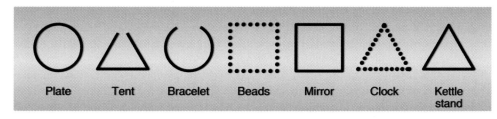

FIGURE 3.25
Gestalt Principles: Innate Principles or a Product of Learning?
People with formal education tend to refer to these shapes as circles, squares, triangles, and other geometric forms. In contrast, people from cultures without formal education perceive them in terms of their resemblance to familiar objects in their environment.
Source: Based on data from Luria, 1976.

level—should perceive the objects in similar ways. The results showed that the students tended to identify the shapes by category (e.g., circle, triangle, square), regardless of the "completeness" of the stimuli or the presence of other features (e.g., color)—a tendency that may have emerged from their experience with two-dimension drawings of three-dimensional objects. In contrast, the participants with no formal education tended to name the shapes according to familiar objects they resembled. Apparently in their eyes, a circle resembled a plate or the moon—not the abstract categories named by the students. This type of evidence indicates that the Gestalt principles may not be universal, but instead depend on the effects of learning and experience (see Matsumoto, 2000; Quinn et al., 2002). In any case, principles of perceptual organization are readily visible in the natural world and they are effective in helping us organize our perceptual world.

Constancies and Illusions: When Perception Succeeds—and Fails

Perception, we have seen, is more than the sum of all the sensory input supplied by our eyes, ears, and other receptors. It is the active selection, organization, and interpretation of such input. It yields final products that differ from raw, unprocessed sensations in important ways. Up to now, this discussion has focused on the benefits of this process. But perception, like any other powerful process, can be a double-edged sword. On the one hand, perception helps us adapt to a complex and ever-changing environment. On the other hand, perception sometimes leads us into error. To see how, let's consider *constancies* and *illusions*.

■ **Perceptual constancies: Stability in the face of change.**

Try this simple demonstration. Hold your right hand in front of you at arm's length. Next, move it toward and away from your face several times. Does it seem to change in size? Probably not. The purpose of this demonstration is to illustrate the principles of perceptual **constancies**—our tendency to perceive aspects of the world as unchanging despite changes in the sensory input we receive from them. The principle of **size constancy** relates to how the perceived size of an object remains the same when the distance is varied, even though the size of the image it casts on the retina changes greatly. Under normal circumstances, such constancy is impressive. Consider, for example, seeing a friend we are meeting for lunch walking toward us, though still several blocks away. Distant objects—including cars, trees, and people—cast tiny images on our retina. Yet, we perceive them as being of normal size. Two factors seem to account for this tendency: size-distance invariance and relative size.

The principle of *size-distance invariance* suggests that when estimating the size of an object, we take into account both the size of the image it casts on our retina and the apparent distance of the object. From these data we almost instantly calculate the object's size. Only when the cues that normally reveal an object's distance are missing do we run into difficulties in estimating the object's size (as we'll see in our discussion of illusions that follows). We also notice the **relative size** of an object compared to objects of known size. This mechanism is especially useful for estimating the size of unfamiliar things.

But size is not the only perceptual feature of the physical world that does not correspond directly with the information transmitted by our sensory receptors. The principle of **shape constancy** refers to how the perceived shape of an object does not alter as the image it casts on the retina changes. For example, we all know that coins are round, yet we rarely see them that way. Flip a coin into the air: Although you continue to perceive the coin as being round, the image that actually falls onto your retina constantly shifts from a circle to various forms of an ellipse.

The principle of **brightness constancy** refers to how we perceive objects as constant in brightness and color, even when viewed under different lighting conditions. Thus, we will perceive a sweater as dark green whether we see it indoors or

Constancies:
Our tendency to perceive physical objects as unchanging, despite shifts in the pattern of sensations these objects induce.

Size constancy:
The tendency to perceive a physical object as having a constant size, even when the image it casts on the retina changes.

Relative size:
A visual cue based on a comparison of an object of unknown size to one of known size.

Shape constancy:
The tendency to perceive a physical object as having a constant shape, even when the image it casts on the retina changes.

Brightness constancy:
The tendency to perceive objects as having a constant brightness when they are viewed under different conditions of illumination.

FIGURE 3.26
Illusions of Size
In the Ponzo illusion, the line in the distance appears larger, although both lines are actually the same size.

see it outdoors in bright sunlight. Brightness constancy apparently prevails because objects and their surroundings are usually lighted by the same illumination source, so changes in lighting conditions occur simultaneously for both the object and its immediate surroundings. As long as the changes in lighting remain constant for both object and surroundings, the neural message reaching the brain is unchanged. Brightness constancy breaks down, however, when changes in lighting are not equivalent for both the object and its surroundings (Sekuler & Blake, 1990).

Although most research on perceptual constancies has focused on size, shape, and brightness, constancy pervades nearly every area of perception, including our other senses. For example, imagine listening to background music while riding on an elevator. One of your favorite "oldies" begins, but recorded by a different group. You can't believe what they've done to "your song." Nonetheless, you are still able to recognize it, despite differences in its loudness, tone, and pitch.

Whatever their basis, perceptual constancies are highly useful. Without them, we would spend a great deal of time and effort reidentifying sensory information in our environments each time we experienced the information from a new perspective. Thus, the gap between our sensations and the perceptions provided by the constancies is clearly beneficial.

■ Illusions: When perception fails.

We've seen that perception organizes sensory information into a coherent picture of the world around us. Perception can also, however, provide false interpretations of sensory information. Such cases are known as **illusions,** a term used by psychologists to refer to incorrect perceptions. Actually, there are two types of illusions: those due to physical processes (e.g., mirages) and those due to cognitive processes. Our focus will be on the latter type of illusion.

Countless illusions related to cognitive processes exist, but most fall into two categories: illusions of *size* and illusions of *shape* or *area* (Coren et al., 1976). Figure 3.26 contain an example of size illusions and as you can see, the effects are powerful. But, why do illusions occur? Some evidence suggests that illusions

Illusions:
Instances in which perception yields false interpretations of physical reality.

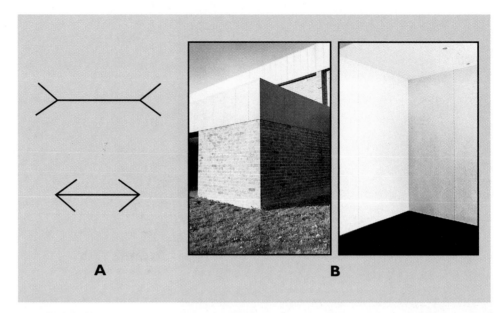

FIGURE 3.27
The Müller–Lyer Illusion
In the Müller–Lyer illusion, lines of equal length (A) appear unequal. The line with the wings pointing outward looks longer than the line with the wings pointing inward. Now carefully examine the vertical line in each of the photographs (B). Which line is longer? Most people perceive the vertical line in the photo on the right as longer, although careful measurement shows they are exactly the same length.

generally have multiple causes (Schiffman, 1990). One explanation is provided by the *theory of misapplied constancy.* It suggests that when looking at illusions, we interpret certain cues as suggesting that some parts are farther away than others. Our powerful tendency toward size constancy then comes into play, with the result that we perceptually distort the length of various lines (see Figure 3.26). Learning also plays an important role in illusions, as shown in the *Müller–Lyer illusion* in Figure 3.27. Past experience tells us that the corner shown in the figure on the right is usually farther away than the corner in the figure on the left. Therefore, although the size of the retinal image cast by the vertical lines in both figures is identical, we interpret the vertical line as longer in the figure on the right. Moreover, learning seems to affect the extent to which our perception is influenced by illusions: Many visual illusions decline in magnitude following extended exposure—although they do not disappear entirely (Greist-Bousquet, Watson, & Schiffman, 1990).

Another type of illusion is that of *shape* or *area.* A powerful example of this type of illusion is provided by the *Ames room,* originally created by ophthalmologist Adelbert Ames. Characteristics of the Ames room leads us to perceive people as being very different in size (see photo in Figure 3.28 on page 109). The reason for this misperception of size lies in the unusual shape of the room. When an observer looks into an Ames room, the room *appears* normal and rectangular, but its true shape is cleverly distorted (see diagram in Figure 3.28 on page 109). The floor, ceiling, some walls, and the far windows are actually trapezoidal surfaces. Although the floor appears level, it is actually at an incline (the far left corner is much lower than the near right corner). The two corners appear to be the same size and distance away, but the left corner is actually twice as far away from the observer as the right corner. What's happening in the Ames room? Because we think we are looking into a normal rectangular room, and because the two people appear to be at the same distance, we perceive the person on the left to be much smaller.

A

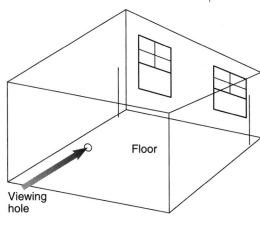

B

FIGURE 3.28
The Ames Room
(A) An observer looking into this Ames room might conclude that the person on the right is much taller than the person on the left, even though they are about the same height. (B) From an observer's perspective, the Ames room appears normal and rectagular. However, the trapezoidal shape of the windows, floor, and some walls and sloping ceiling and floors provide misleading cues. Because these cues lead observers to believe the two people are the same distance away, they perceive the person on the right to be much larger than the person on the left.

Like illusions of size or area, *shape illusions* can also exert powerful influences on our perception. Several well-known examples of these, including the *Poggendorf* and *Hering–Helmholtz* illusions, are presented in Figure 3.29 on page 110.

One final point: Illusions are not limited to visual processes. Indeed, there are numerous examples of illusions for our other sensory modalities, including touch and audition (Shepard, 1964). One well-known illusion that you can demonstrate for yourself is that of touch temperature. First, place one hand in a container of hot water and the other hand in cold water. Then, place *both* hands in a container of lukewarm water. Most people experience a dramatic difference in perceived temperature between the two hands; the hand initially placed in hot water feels the lukewarm water as cool, whereas the hand initially placed in cold water feels it as hot. How do we explain this illusion? When we touch an object, the temperature of the area of our skin in contact with it shifts toward that of the object's surface. So, when we perceive an object to be warm or cool, our experience stems partly from the temperature difference between the object and our skin, not solely from the actual temperature of the object.

K E Y   Q U E S T I O N S
- Why is selective attention important?
- What role do the Gestalt principles play in perceptual processes?
- What are perceptual constancies?
- What are illusions?

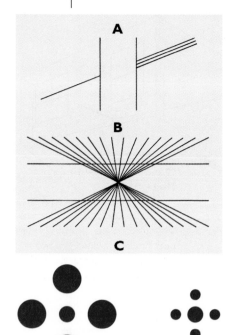

FIGURE 3.29
Illusions of Area or Shape
Illusions of shape or area, too, can be quite powerful. In drawing A, known as the Poggendorf illusion, which of the three lines on the right continues the line on the left? Check your answer with a ruler. In drawing B, known as the Hering–Helmholtz illusion, are the horizontal lines straight or bent in the middle? Again, check for yourself. Finally, in the third, are the sizes of the center circles the same or different? When you check, you'll see why sometimes you can't believe what you think you see!

Bottom-up approach:
Suggests that our ability to recognize specific patterns, such as letters of the alphabet or objects, is based on simpler capacities to recognize and correctly combine lower-level features of objects, such as lines, edges, corners, and angles.

Top-down approach:
Approach to pattern recognition that starts with the analysis of high-level information, such as our knowledge, expectancies, and the context in which a stimulus is seen.

Some Key Perceptual Processes: Pattern and Distance

Perception is a practical process since it provides organisms with information essential to survival in their normal habitat. The specific nature of this information varies greatly with different species. Nonetheless, it is probably safe to say that virtually all living creatures need information concerning (1) What's out there? and (2) How far away is it? Humans are no exception to this general rule, and we possess impressive perceptual skills in both areas.

■ Pattern recognition: What's out there?

The fact that you are able to read the words on this page depends on your ability to recognize small black marks as letters and collections of such marks as words. How do we accomplish this task? Research on this issue suggests the following two possibilities, termed the *bottom-up* and *top-down theories* of pattern recognition.

As their names imply, these adopt somewhat opposite perspectives on the basic question of how we recognize patterns of visual stimuli. The **bottom-up approach** to pattern recognition suggests that our ability to recognize specific patterns, such as letters of the alphabet or objects, is based on simpler capacities to recognize and correctly combine lower-level features of objects, such as lines, edges, corners, and angles. One theory, termed *recognition-by-components*, proposes that objects are represented in terms of a set of simple geometric components called *geons* (Biederman, 1987). According to this view, common objects are readily recognized given only two to three geons in the proper alignment. Another view, termed *feature integration theory*, proposes that object perception occurs according to a sequence of stages (see Triesman, 1998). A third, termed the *computational approach*, treats the visual system as if it were a computer that has been programmed to assemble basic features within the visual scene (Marr, 1982). Although each approach differs in many respects, they all converge on the idea that pattern recognition is constructed from simpler perceptual abilities through a discrete series of steps.

In contrast, the **top-down approach** emphasizes how our knowledge and expectancies play a critical role in shaping our perceptions. We often proceed in accordance with what our past experience tells us to expect, and therefore we don't always analyze every feature of most stimuli we encounter. Although top-down processing can be extremely efficient (think about the speed with which you can read this page), it can also lead us astray. Nearly everyone has had the experience of rushing over to another person who appears to be an old friend, only to realize he or she is actually a stranger. In such cases, our tendency to process information quickly from the top down can produce errors.

Which of these views is correct? Current evidence seems to indicate that perception often involves both bottom-up and top-down processing working together. To illustrate this point, consider the plight of pharmacists who must interpret the messy handwriting evident in many doctors' prescriptions. To decipher a prescription, a pharmacist might begin with bottom-up processing, which is based on an analysis of the lines and squiggles that comprise the writing. However, top-down processing also comes into play as he uses his knowledge of the names of drugs—and perhaps his experience with a particular doctor's writing—to solve the problem.

■ Distance perception: How far away is it?

Our impressive ability to judge depth and distance occurs because we make use of many different cues in forming such judgments. These cues can be divided into

FIGURE 3.30
Monocular Cues to Depth Perception
As illustrated, artists make effective use of a variety of monocular cues to convey a sense of depth in their paintings. In this scene, the two falling figures appear all too real!

two categories, *monocular* and *binocular,* depending on whether they can be seen with only one eye or require the use of both eyes (see Figure 3.30).

Monocular cues to depth or distance include the following:

1. *Size cues:* The larger the image of an object on the retina, the larger it is judged to be; in addition, if an object is larger than other objects, it is often perceived as closer.
2. *Linear perspective:* Parallel lines appear to converge in the distance; the greater this effect, the farther away an object appears to be.
3. *Texture gradient*: The texture of a surface appears smoother as distance increases.
4. *Atmospheric perspective:* The farther away objects are, the less distinctly they are seen—smog, dust, and haze get in the way.
5. *Overlap* (or interposition): If one object obscures another in the visual field, it is seen as being closer than the one it obscures.
6. *Height cues* (aerial perspective): Below the horizon, lower objects in our field of vision are perceived as closer; above the horizon, higher objects are seen as closer.
7. *Motion parallax:* When we travel in a vehicle, objects far away appear to move in the same direction as the observer, whereas close objects move in the opposite direction. Objects at different distances appear to move at different velocities.

We also rely heavily on **binocular cues**—depth information based on the coordinated efforts of both eyes. Binocular cues for depth perception stem from two primary sources:

1. *Convergence:* To see close objects, our eyes turn inward, toward each another; the greater this movement, the closer such objects appear to be.
2. *Retinal disparity* (binocular parallax): Our two eyes observe objects from slightly different positions in space; the difference between these two images is interpreted by our brain to provide another cue to depth.

The list of monocular and binocular cues is by no means exhaustive. By using the wealth of information provided by these and other cues (Schiffman, 1990), we can usually perceive depth and distance with great accuracy.

KEY QUESTIONS

- What are the bottom-up and top-down approaches to pattern recognition?
- How are we able to judge depth and distance?

Monocular cues:
Cues to depth or distance provided by one eye.

Binocular cues:
Cues to depth or distance resulting from having two eyes.

PSI: PERCEPTION WITHOUT SENSATION?

Have you ever wondered if we have a "sixth sense"? In other words, can we gain information about the external world without using our basic senses? Many people believe we can and accept the existence of **extrasensory perception (ESP)**—literally, perception without a basis in sensation. The first and most basic question we can ask about ESP is, "Does it really exist?" This question has been recast by Bem and Hornton (1994) in terms of a hypothetical process known as **psi.** These researchers define psi as unusual processes of information or energy transfer that are currently unexplained in terms of known physical or biological mechanisms.

Psi: What Is It?

Parapsychologists, those who study psi and other *paranormal events,* or events outside our normal experience or knowledge, suggest that several distinct forms of psi (or ESP) exist. One form of psi is *precognition,* the ability to foretell future events. Fortune-tellers and psychics often make their livings from the supposed ability to make such predictions. *Clairvoyance,* the ability to perceive objects or events that do not directly stimulate your sensory organs, is another form of psi. While playing cards, if you somehow "know" which one will be dealt next, you are experiencing clairvoyance. *Telepathy,* a skill used by mind readers, involves the direct transmission of thought from one person to the next. Another phenomenon often associated with psi is *psychokinesis,* the ability to affect the physical world purely through thought. People who bend spoons or move objects with their mind or perform feats of levitation (making objects rise into the air) claim to have powers of psychokinesis.

Psi: Does It Really Exist?

The idea of a mysterious sixth sense is intriguing, and many people are passionately convinced of its existence (Bowles & Hynds, 1978). But does it really exist? Most psychologists are skeptical about the existence of psi for several reasons. The first reason is the repeated failure to replicate instances of psi; that is, certain procedures yield evidence for psi at one time, but not at others. Indeed, one survey failed to uncover a single instance of paranormal phenomena that could be reliably produced after ruling out alternative explanations such as fraud, methodological flaws, and normal sensory functioning (Hoppe, 1988). Moreover, it appears that the more controlled studies of psi are, the less evidence for psi they have provided (Blackmore, 1986).

Second, present-day scientific understanding states that all aspects of our behavior must ultimately stem from biochemical events, yet it is not clear what physical mechanism could account for psi. In fact, the existence of such a mechanism would require restructuring our view of the physical world.

Third, much of the support for psi has been obtained by people already deeply convinced of its existence. As you might expect, scientists are not immune to being influenced in their observations by their own beliefs. Thus, while studies suggesting that psi exists may represent a small sample of all research conducted on this topic, perhaps only the few experiments yielding positive results find their way into print; perhaps the many "failures" are simply not reported.

In short, no reliable evidence supports the existence of psi or extrasensory perception. So the next time you read about or see people on television who claim they can read minds, tell the future, or bend objects with their minds—don't be fooled! Instead, think about other more tangible ways they might have accomplished these feats.

Extrasensory perception (ESP):
Perception without a basis in sensory input.

Psi:
Unusual processes of information or energy transfer that are currently unexplained in terms of known physical or biological mechanisms. Included under the heading of psi are such supposed abilities as telepathy (reading others' thoughts) and clairvoyance (perceiving objects that do not directly stimulate sensory organs).

Parapsychologists:
Individuals who study ESP and other paranormal events.

KEY QUESTIONS

• How do most psychologists view the possibility of extrasensory perception or psi?

SUMMARY AND REVIEW OF KEY QUESTIONS

Sensation: The Raw Materials of Understanding

- **What is the primary function of our sensory receptors?**
  Sensory receptors transduce raw physical energy into neural impulses, which are then interpreted by our central nervous system.

- **What does the term *absolute threshold* refer to?**
  The absolute threshold is the smallest magnitude of a stimulus that can be detected 50 percent of the time.

- **Why is signal detection theory important?**
  Signal detection theory helps to separate sensitivity from motivational factors.

- **What is a difference threshold?**
  Difference threshold refers to the amount of change in a stimulus required for a person to detect it.

- **Can subliminal messages affect our behavior?**
  Research using visual priming suggests that stimuli that stimulate the sensory receptors, but remain outside conscious awareness, produce measurable effects on cognition and behavior. However, research fails to support the use of subliminal messages as tools of persuasion.

- **What is the role of sensory adaptation in sensation?**
  Sensory adaptation serves a useful function by allowing us to focus on important changes in our environment.

Vision

- **What are the basic structures of the eye and what is the physical stimulus for vision?**
  Light rays first pass through the cornea and then enter the eye through the pupil. Adjustments to lighting conditions are executed by the iris. The lens is a clear structure whose shape adjusts to permit us to focus on objects at varying distances. Light rays leaving the lens are projected onto the retina at the back of the eyeball. The physical stimulus for vision is electromagnetic wavelengths that stimulate the rods and cones in the retina.

- **What are the basic functions of the visual system?**
  The basic functions of the visual system include acuity, dark adaptation, and eye movements. Acuity refers to the ability to see fine details. Dark adaptation refers to the increase in sensitivity that occurs when we move from bright light to a dim environment. Various types of eye movements are crucial to our ability to track moving objects and to perceive distance and depth.

- **How do psychologists explain color perception?**
  Our rich sense of color stems from mechanisms at several levels of our nervous system. Two leading theories that explain how we perceive color are trichromatic theory and opponent-process theory.

- **Why is visual perception a hierarchical process?**
  Visual perception is a hierarchical process because increasingly complex visual information is analyzed and compiled at successive stages, eventually yielding a coherent and flowing visual world.

- **What are the basic building blocks of visual perception?**
  The basic building blocks of visual perception begin with feature detectors—neurons in the visual cortex that respond when particular types of stimuli, with characteristic features, are detected.

Hearing

- **What is the physical stimulus for hearing?**
  The physical stimulus for hearing is sound waves that stimulate tiny hair cells in the cochlea.

- **What is perfect pitch?**
  The ability to name or produce a note of particular pitch in the absence of a reference note.

- **How do psychologists explain pitch perception?**
  Place theory and frequency theory help explain how we perceive pitch.

- **How do we localize sound?**
  The sound shadow created by our head causes sound to reach one ear slightly sooner than the other. This small time difference helps us to localize the source of sound.

Touch and Other Skin Senses

- **What is the physical stimulus for touch?**
  The physical stimulus for touch is a stretching of or pressure against receptors in the skin.

- **Where does the sensation of pain originate?**
  Sensations of pain originate in receptors called nociceptors.

- **What role do cognitive processes play in the perception of pain?**
  Our thoughts, feelings, and beliefs appear to play an important mediator role, determining the extent to which we focus on pain.

- **What role does culture play in pain perception?**
  Observed cultural differences in the capacity to withstand pain seem to be perceptual in nature and reflect the effects of social learning.

Smell and Taste: The Chemical Senses

- **What is the physical stimulus for smell and where are the sensory receptors located?**
  The physical stimuli for sensations of smell are molecules that stimulate receptors in the nose.

- **Where are the sensory receptors for taste located?**
  The sensory receptors for taste are located in papillae on the tongue.

- **What are the practical benefits of using pleasant ambient fragrances?**
  The use of pleasant fragrances can increase alertness among people engaged in potentially dangerous activities, such as driving.

Kinesthesia and Vestibular Sense

- **What information does our kinesthetic sense provide to the brain?**
  Kinesthesia informs the brain about the location of body parts with respect to one another.

- **What information does the vestibular sense provide to the brain?**
  The vestibular sense provides information about body position, movement, and acceleration.

Perception: Putting It All Together

- **Why is selective attention important?**
  Selective attention reduces the interference from irrelevant sensory sources.

- **What role do the Gestalt principles play in perceptual process?**
  The Gestalt principles of perceptual organization help us to structure the input from our sensory receptors.

- **What are perceptual constancies?**
  Perceptual constancies are principles describing our ability to perceive aspects of the world as unchanging, despite variations in the information reaching our sensory receptors, such as information about size, shape, or brightness.

- **What are illusions?**
  Illusion is a term used by psychologists to refer to errors in interpreting sensory information.

- **What are the bottom-up and top-down approaches to pattern recognition?**
  The bottom-up approach suggests that pattern recognition stems from our ability to recognize and combine basic visual features. In contrast, the top-down approach emphasizes the role that knowledge, expectations, and the context in which stimulation occurs play in shaping our perceptions.

- **How are we able to judge depth and distance?**
  Judgments of depth and distance result from both binocular and monocular cues.

PSI: Perception without Sensation?

- **How do most psychologists view the possibility of extrasensory perception or psi?**
  Most psychologists remain highly skeptical about its existence and await the results of further careful research.

KEY TERMS

Absolute threshold, p. 75
Acuity, p. 82
Binocular cues, p. 111
Blind spot, p. 81
Bottom-up approach, p. 110
Brightness, p. 82
Brightness constancy, p. 106
Cochlea, p. 87
Cocktail party phenomenon, p. 101
Complex cells, p. 85
Cones, p. 80
Constancies, p. 106
Cornea, p. 80
Dark adaptation, p. 83
Difference threshold, p. 76
Extrasensory perception (ESP) p. 112
Farsightedness, p. 83
Feature detectors, p. 85
Figure-ground relationship, p. 102
Fovea, p. 81
Frequency theory, p. 90
Gate-control theory, p. 93
Gestalt psychologists, p. 102

Hue, p. 82
Hypercomplex cells, p. 85
Illusions, p. 107
Inattentional blindness, p. 103
Iris, p. 80
Just noticeable difference (jnd), p. 76
Kinesthesia, p. 99
Laws of grouping, p. 104
Lens, p. 80
Localization, p. 90
Monocular cues, p. 111
Nearsightedness, p. 83
Negative afterimage, p. 84
Nociceptor, p. 92
Opponent-process theory, p. 84
Optic nerve, p. 81
Parapsychologists, p. 112
Perception, p. 74
Perfect pitch, p. 88
Pinna, p. 87
Pitch, p. 87
Place theory, p. 89
Prosopagnosia, p. 86

Psi, p. 112
Psychophysics, p. 75
Pupil, p. 80
Relative size, p. 106
Retina, p. 80
Rods, p. 80
Saturation, p. 82
Selective attention, p. 101
Sensation, p. 74
Sensory adaptation, p. 79
Sensory receptors, p. 74
Shape constancy, p. 106
Signal detection theory, p. 75
Simple cells, p. 85
Size constancy, p. 106
Subliminal perception, p. 77
Timbre, p. 88
Top-down approach, p. 110
Transduction, p. 75
Trichromatic theory, p. 83
Vestibular sense, p. 99
Wavelength, p. 82

PSYCHOLOGY: UNDERSTANDING ITS FINDINGS

Putting Fragrance to Work

Research by the authors (Baron and Kalsher) showed that a pleasant ambient fragrance (a lemon scent) exerted an alerting effect on participants performing a simulated driving task. Other research by Baron indicates that fragrance can improve our mood; the specific fragrance doesn't seem to matter as long as it is one that people find pleasant. Try the following exercise to put scent to work for you.

Most of us have at least one time during the day when we feel less alert. Kalsher's happens to occur at about 4 P.M.; yours may be different. To identify your alertness "peaks" and "valleys," use the scale below to record your level of alertness at several points during the day. You can also use it to rate your mood. Next, find a fragrance that you like and introduce it into your living space at a time when your alertness level is relatively low. Does the fragrance increase your alertness? Does it improve your mood? If so, by how much? Did your alertness or mood change more in response to a particular scent than to another? Keep a diary for a week or two to track the effects of one or more fragrances on your alertness. Your friends may want to try this, too.

Alertness:

Low						High
1	2	3	4	5	6	7

Mood:

Bad						Good
1	2	3	4	5	6	7

MAKING PSYCHOLOGY PART OF YOUR LIFE

Managing Your Pain: Some Useful Tips

As a long-time sports enthusiast, I (Michael Kalsher) am very familiar with the predictable muscular aches and pains that occasionally result from overdoing it. When I run too far or overdo it while weight lifting, I can usually count on muscle soreness—or worse—the following day. Although these and other types of minor injuries definitely have a physical component, the degree to which we experience pain can be influenced by many factors, including how we think about the pain. Although you should do everything to avoid getting injured (e.g., stretching before you run or work out), here are a few things that you can do to lessen the impact of the minor aches and pains that accompany exercise.

1. Use *counterirritants*. As we learned in this chapter, there are neural mechanisms in the spinal cord that sometimes close, thereby preventing pain messages from reaching the brain. Counterirritants can help close the gate and are particularly useful to relieve the sharp pain that occurs when we stub our toe or close a door on our finger. To use this technique, vigorously rub the surrounding area right after the injury occurs.

2. Use deep massage or apply ice packs or heat to help soothe the more generalized pain that results from sore, achy muscles should you overdo it during a run or workout.

3. Use *cognitive-behavioral techniques* to change the way you think about the pain
   - Dwelling on negative thoughts usually intensifies your perceptions of pain. Try replacing negative thoughts with positive ones.
   - Distraction is another effective technique. Try focusing your attention away from the pain, by getting involved with another activity that attracts your interest.
   - Induce an emotional state incompatible with pain—for example, laughter. Expose yourself as quickly as possible to something—or someone—you find humorous. If no one is around, think of something that makes you laugh.

4. **Caution!** Remember that pain serves a useful purpose that should definitely not be ignored. Indeed, use pain as a guide to hasten your recovery.

If you are using MyPsychLab, you have access to an electronic version of this textbook, along with dozens of valuable resources per chapter—including video and audio clips, simulations and activities, self-assessments, practice tests and other study materials. Here is a sampling of the resources available for this chapter.

EXPLORE

Five Well-Known Illusions

Frequency and Amplitude of Sound Waves

WATCH

Ear Ringing

Brain Pain

Sensory Receptors in the Skin Managing Pain

SIMULATE

Gestalt Laws of Perception

Experiencing the Stroop Effect

Methods of Constant Stimuli

If you did not receive an access code to MyPsych Lab with this text and wish to purchase access online, please visit www.MyPsychLab.com.

STUDY GUIDE

CHAPTER REVIEW

Sensation: The Raw Materials of Understanding

1. The key distinction between sensation and perception is that perception involves
   a. the detection of stimuli in the outside world.
   b. the interpretation of sensory input.
   c. a passive process.
   d. the study of how receptors transform sensory signals into action potentials.

2. _____ refers to the process by which _____ convert sensory stimuli into action potentials.
   a. Homeostasis;   neurons
   b. Perception;   cortical neurons
   c. Adaptation;   receptors
   d. Transduction;   sensory receptors

3. The auditory system of a human can best detect
   a. sound frequencies that are close to those of speech.
   b. small differences in the location of sound coming from the left or right of a person.
   c. sounds that are similar to those made by a gun as it is cocked for firing.
   d. sound frequencies above 20,000 hertz.

4. Another name for a sensory threshold is the
   a. relative threshold.
   b. subliminal threshold.
   c. absolute threshold.
   d. the homeostatic threshold.

5. The key goal of signal detection theory is to
   a. eliminate the noise in a sensory system.
   b. distinguish a sensory signal from the background noise.
   c. increase the bias of a sensory observer.
   d. decrease the sensitivity of a sensory observer.

6. Signal detection theory suggests that _____ and _____ interact to determine whether a person reports the detection of a stimulus or not.
   a. noise;   stimulus modality
   b. bias;   sensitivity
   c. sensation;   perception
   d. sensory modality;   stimulus thresholds

7. Bias refers to how willing a person is to report detecting a stimulus.   (True-False).

8. Which of the following stimuli would be expected to show the smallest just-noticeable difference?
   a. The pitch of a jet engine waiting at the terminal gate.
   b. The smell produced by an open sewer.
   c. The temperature of an object on your kitchen table.
   d. The loudness of a car stereo.

9. _____ refers to the capacity of the nervous system to perceive a stimulus presented at an intensity that is below threshold.
   a. Stimulus adaptation
   b. Subliminal perception
   c. Unconscious processing
   d. Supraliminal sensation

10. Studies using visual priming suggest that exposure to brief stimuli
    a. can change our attraction for members of the opposite sex.
    b. are likely to influence our purchasing of cars and deodorant.
    c. can alter our perception of ambiguous figures.
    d. is a quick way to boost concession sales at a movie theatre.

11. Subliminal messages do not have the power to directly control behavior.   (True-False)

12. Which of the following is true of sensory processing?
    a. Our ability to detect a stimulus remains constant over time.
    b. Humans are better able to detect positive subliminal stimuli than negative subliminal stimuli
    c. Perception is not subject to change from motivation or from bias.
    d. Exposure to a constant stimulus can lead to sensory adaptation.

Vision

13. The portion of the eye through which varying amounts of light can enter the eye is the
    a. pupil.
    b. retina.
    c. orbits.
    d. cornea.

14. The _____ focuses light onto the retina of the eye.
    a. pupil
    b. retina
    c. lens
    d. cornea

15. Match up the component of the eye with its appropriate definition.
    _____. This structure focuses light onto the retina.
    _____. These photoreceptors are sensitive to light, but not color.
    _____. This structure contains the photoreceptors and is located at the back of the eye.
    _____. A circular muscle of the eye that contracts to vary the amount of light entering the eye.
    _____. Light enters the eye through this aperture.
    _____. This portion of the retina contains color-sensitive photoreceptors.
    _____. The outer transparent layer that covers the eye.
    a. retina
    b. pupil
    c. iris
    d. lens
    e. cornea
    f. fovea
    g. cones
    h. rods

16. The blind spot of eye is
    a. that portion of the retina where there are no photoreceptors.
    b. produced when the pupil closes after intense light.
    c. that portion of the retina where there are no ganglion cells.
    d. a result of sensory adaptation.
17. Which of the following pairs of terms do NOT belong together?
    a. rods;   sensitive to low levels of light
    b. blind spot;   lack of photoreceptors
    c. rods;   most prevalent in the central retina
    d. cones;   provide excellent visual acuity
18. The wavelength of visible light is measured in
    a. nanometers.
    b. meters.
    c. decimeters.
    d. millimeters.
19. The attribute of _____ best corresponds to the intensity of a light.
    a. brightness
    b. color
    c. limen
    d. hue
20. A key advantage of opponent-process theory is the capacity to explain negative afterimages.   (True-False)
21. The studies of Hubel and Wiesel noted that neurons in the visual cortex function as
    a. face detectors.
    b. color detectors.
    c. feature detectors.
    d. modules that decode afterimages.
22. Prosopagnosia is
    a. a rare form of color blindness.
    b. the inability to recognize a familiar face.
    c. a memory disorder associated with aging.
    d. an inability to perceive depth cues.

Hearing

23. Sound waves are transduced within the _____ by movements that bend hair cells which trigger action potentials within the _____.
    a. cochlea;   auditory nerve
    b. pinna;   cochlea
    c. middle ear;   acoustic nerve
    d. oval window;   cochlea
24. The _____ is another name for the eardrum.
    a. tympanic membrane
    b. basilar membrane
    c. acoustic membrane
    d. oval membrane
25. The loudness of a sound is related to
    a. the amplitude of a sound wave.
    b. the purity of the sound wave.
    c. the frequency of vibration of a sound wave.
    d. which part of the basilar membrane is vibrated by the sound wave.

Touch and Other Skin Senses

26. Which of the following is true of the skin senses?
    a. Pain is considered to be a skin sense.
    b. Touch receptors are densely packed in the skin of the face and fingertips.
    c. Multiple receptors are found in the skin.
    d. All of the above are correct.
27. Pain is adaptive in the sense that it motivates us to avoid tissue damage.   (True-False)
28. "Dull" pain involves _____ whereas "sharp" pain involves
    a. pain from a cut to the skin;   pain from a sore muscle
    b. activation of small unmyelinated fibers;   activation of large myelinated fibers
    c. closing of the spinal gates;   opening of the spinal gates
    d. release of serotonin within the spinal cord;   a focus away from pain stimuli
29. Human capacity to tolerate pain is largely a reflection of physical differences among people rather than cognitive or cultural factors.   (True-False)

Smell and Taste: The Chemical Senses

30. A bloodhound can detect odors at lower concentrations than can a human because
    a. humans have more olfactory receptors than do bloodhounds.
    b. bloodhounds devote more of their cortex to the processing of odor information.
    c. bloodhounds have more olfactory receptors than do humans.
    d. bloodhounds are given greater training at odor detection.
31. The most recent explanation of odor recognition involves
    a. different odorants have shapes that match different receptors.
    b. different odor molecules that activate different patches of receptors along the olfactory mucosa.
    c. odor molecules that have a frequency of vibration that determines the smell generated by that molecule.
    d. the overall pattern of activation of olfactory receptors.
32. The "savory" quality associated with cheese and fish is related to activation of taste cells that code for
    a. the presence of glutamate in a foodstuff.
    b. fattiness.
    c. sugars and acids.
    d. bitterness.
33. After reading the section on aromatherapy, imagine that your new job is to make recommendations to the government on how to use aromatherapy for airport security screeners. You would most likely recommend that containers of _____ fragrance be placed at checkpoints so as to _____.
    a. lemon;   decrease alertness
    b. lavender;   increase accuracy and alertness
    c. rosemary;   decrease alertness
    d. peppermint;   increase EEG measures of arousal

Kinesthesis and Vestibular Sense

34. Our kinesthetic system senses the _____ based on inputs from _____ receptors. (*continues on page 118.*)
    a. spatial position of our body parts;   joints, muscle, and visual
    b. relative temperature of our body;   skin

c. position of the sun;   visual

d. relative contraction of our muscles;   ligament and muscle

Perception: Putting It All Together

35. Psychologists refer to the capacity of certain environmental features to attract our attention as the _____ phenomenon.
    a. tip-of-the-mind
    b. distraction
    c. pop-out.
    d. egocentric
36. The literal meaning of "gestalt" is whole.   (True-False)
37. A key clue used by humans in estimating the size of an unfamiliar object is
    a. our ability to see it as we walk toward the unfamiliar object.
    b. the size of the retinal cue provided by the unfamiliar object.
    c. the binocular disparity produced as we look at the object with our two eyes.
    d. a comparison of the size of that object with objects of known size.
38. Indicate which form of perceptual constancy is best illustrated by each situation.
    _____. Your new blue car remains the same color when viewed in your garage or at the beach.
    _____. A dime appears to be the same size when viewed on the ground as in your hand.
    _____. A door frame is rectangular when viewed from the side or from straight-on.
    a. Size constancy
    b. Shape constancy
    c. Texture constancy
    d. Figure-ground constancy
    e. Brightness constancy

Psi: Perception without Sensation

39. Which form of ESP involves the ability to view future events?
    a. Psychokinesis.
    b. Clairvoyance.
    c. Precognition.
    d. Telepathy.

IDENTIFICATIONS

Identify the term that belongs with each of the concepts below (place the letter for the appropriate term below in front of each concept).

Identification   Concept:
_____ 1. The smallest magnitude of a stimulus that can be reliably discriminated from no stimulus.
_____ 2. The process by which a sensory stimulus is converted into neural impulses.
_____ 3. The study of the relationship between the physical properties of stimuli and our psychological experience of those stimuli.
_____ 4. Light wavelength results in this psychological experience
_____ 5. A German word meaning "whole."

_____ 6. How willing a person is to report detecting a stimulus
_____ 7. A type of photoreceptor that is sensitive to color.
_____ 8. The capacity of the body to maintain its own internal environment.
_____ 9. The capacity of a person to perceive a stimulus presented at an intensity that is far below threshold.
_____ 10. The form of ESP that involves ability to move objects at will.
_____ 11. Cells in the visual cortex that respond best to bars of light at a particular orientation.

Identification:

    a. Psychokinesis.
    b. Absolute threshold.
    c. Gestalt.
    d. Difference threshold.
    e. Cone
    f. Psychophysics.
    g. Subliminal perception
    h. Bias
    i. Hue
    j. Homeostasis.
    k. Transduction
    l. Simple

FILL IN THE BLANK

1. The concept of _____ refers to the ability of a person to distinguish between a faint stimulus and the background noise.
2. The observation that our sensory receptors stop firing in response to a constant stimulus is known as
3. The _____ admits light into the eye.
4. The human eye is sensitive to light wavelengths between _____ and _____ nanometers.
5. _____ refers to the inability to recognize a familiar face.
6. The timbre of a sound refers to _____.
7. A person with musical ability would show high levels of activity within the _____ while performing a task involving identification of pitch.
8. _____ are sensitive to stimuli that damage the body.
9. Perhaps the simplest means of distraction to alleviate pain involves _____.
10. The substances that are detected by our olfactory receptors are termed _____.
11. The receptors for the vestibular sense are located within the _____.
12. Perception involves our capacity to _____, _____, and _____ sensory input.
13. Research on figure-ground relationships was the focus of the _____.
14. The _____ approach to pattern perception argues that objects are represented by a set of simple geometric components.
15. Linear and aerial perspective are examples of _____ for depth perception.
16. You would expect that the forms of ESP known as _____ or _____ would be key talents for a poker player.

COMPREHENSIVE PRACTICE TEST

1. Perception is a passive process   (True-False)
2. The smallest magnitude of a stimulus that can be reliably discriminated from no stimulus is the
   a. liminal threshold.
   b. relative threshold.
   c. subliminal threshold.
   d. absolute threshold
3. Sensory adaptation involves _____ in firing rate of _____ in response to a constant stimulus.
   a. an increase;   cortical cells
   b. a reduction;   sensory receptors
   c. an increase;   sensory receptors
   d. a reduction;   cortical cells
4. The fovea contains of an equal mixture of cones and rods (True-False)
5. The amount of light entering the eye is regulated by the size of the
   a. lens.
   b. pupil.
   c. optic orbits.
   d. cornea.
6. Which of the following pairs of terms do NOT belong together?
   a. brightness;   light intensity
   b. hue;   light intensity
   c. lens;   focus of light onto retina
   d. receptor;   stimulus transduction
7. The trichromatic color theory has difficulty explaining why
   a. any color can be produced by the appropriate mixture of three colors.
   b. some persons are color blind.
   c. color is a useful aspect of human vision.
   d. staring at a red square and then looking at a white surface will give rise to the perception of a green square.
8. The perceived pitch of a sound stimulus is related to
   a. the amplitude of a sound wave.
   b. the purity of the sound wave.
   c. the frequency of vibration of a sound wave.
   d. which part of the basilar membrane is vibrated by the sound wave.
9. A sound frequency less than 1000 Hz is coded for within the cochlea by
   a. phase shifts of the basilar membrane.
   b. place coding along the basilar membrane
   c. "volleying" the firing rates of successive sets of auditory neurons
   d. frequency of firing of acoustic neurons.
10. Touch receptors are sparsely located in the skin of the face and fingertips. (True-False)
11. Pain intensity can be reduced by
    a. hypnosis.
    b. playing a virtual-reality game.

c. coughing during a pain stimulus.
d. All of the above are correct.
12. If one compared the processes involved in audition and in smell, the detection of the smell of bacon would most closely resemble the concept of
    a. volley theory.
    b. place coding.
    c. sound timbre.
    d. sound intensity.
13. The Poggendorf illusion is an example of a touch illusion involving competing temperature cues.   (True-False)
14. Match up the monocular depth cue with its best definition or example.
    _____. As you ride in a train and look out the window, objects in the far distance appear to move in the same direction as your train while objects just below the window move in the opposite direction.
    _____. An object that is judged to be larger than other objects is judged to be closer.
    _____. As you move your head closer to a gold ball its surface appears to be more and more pitted.
    _____. A railroad track that converges to a point in a scene will appear to be far away.
    _____. An object viewed above the horizon that is higher appears to be closer to you.
    _____. Objects that are interposed between another object and the viewer are seen as closer.
    _____. A car viewed through the smog-filled air of Los Angeles or Houston will appear to be farther away from the observer.
    a. Linear perspective.
    b. Atmospheric perspective.
    c. Overlap.
    d. Size cues.
    e. Motion parallax.
    f. Aerial perspective.
    g. Texture gradient.
15. _____involves the ability to move objects at will.
    a. Psychokinesis
    b. Clairvoyance
    c. Precognition
    d. Telepathy

CRITICAL THINKING

1. Describe three means by which humans are able to modify their experience of pain and explain the functional significance of these pain processes.
2. Summarize the common attributes of how different sensory systems process environmental signals into neural impulses.

FOUR

States of Consciousness

I (Robert Baron) have always been blessed with very good health, so the events that happened to me on the evening of September 13, 2004, seem—even now—like some kind of very bad dream. I was about to cook some food on our grill when, with no warning, my head seemed to literally explode. I am not prone to headaches, so the sudden pain took me totally by surprise. "Wow!" I said to my wife, Rebecca, "I feel as though my head is exploding . . ." And in fact, it was. That evening, I experienced a very serious ruptured brain aneurysm; a blood vessel inside my brain had become enlarged, and then suddenly burst. Blood is toxic to brain tissue, so although I didn't realize it, my life was in great danger. Fortunately for me, Rebecca phoned 911 and when the ambulance arrived, she insisted, against my protests, that I be taken to a nearby hospital. If she hadn't, and if the doctors there hadn't sent me for immediate surgery, I would not be writing these words. But I did survive, and even more amazing, came back to being very much the same person I was before this frightening experience. Looking back, though, I will never, ever forget what it was like to be in a tremendously altered state of consciousness for several weeks in which, to put it simply, I could not really think! The trauma to my brain both from the aneurysm and the three operations I underwent was truly major, and the result was that although I never lost the ability to speak, I knew—at some dim level— that I was living in a dense, gray fog. I could answer questions and hold a conversation, but what I said often made no sense. And when asked to solve simple puzzles, such as "connect the dots" or "move through a maze without crossing any lines," I failed miserably. Perhaps the worst part was that I knew, at some level, that something was terribly wrong and that I could no longer reason or think logically. So each night after my wife, brother, and friends left the hospital, I would lie awake trying to coax my brain into working in the ways that it did before. Despite my best efforts, though, nothing seemed to help and gradually I began to give up hope. But then, one night, something truly miraculous happened: I was trying to figure out how my wife and I could drive from the hospital to a restaurant we really liked. This sounds simple, but I had tried it before many times and never succeeded. That night, though, it was different: Somehow, I was able to "see" the route we could take in my mind's eye, and I knew that it would work, too! I was overjoyed, and as I fell asleep that night, exhausted by these efforts, I kept thinking to myself: "I'm coming back . . . I'll be me again . . ." And, I'm happy to say, I was right!

FIGURE 4.1
Changing States of Consciousness: A Part of Daily Life
During the course of each day, we experience several different states of consciousness.

States of consciousness:
Varying degrees of awareness of ourselves and the external world.

We truly hope that *you* never have an experience like this—it is simply too painful. But I did learn some very important lessons from it, and several of these have to do with the topic of this chapter—**states of consciousness**—varying levels of awareness of ourselves, our behavior, and the world around us (see Figure 4.1). As you already know from your own experience, we all undergo major shifts in consciousness every day—for instance, from being wide awake and mentally alert to being deep asleep, and from being acutely aware of actions we are performing (e.g., giving a speech in front of a group) to performing actions on "automatic," without any conscious attention to them (e.g., brushing our teeth). Because these shifts are so profound, psychologists have been studying them for several decades. To provide you with an overview of the knowledge they have gathered, we'll proceed as follows.

First, we'll examine *biological rhythms*—naturally occurring, cyclical changes in many basic bodily processes and mental states that occur over the course of a day or longer periods of time. While this topic is also related to personal health and could be discussed in Chapter 11, some of the changes produced by biological rhythms involve shifts in consciousness, so it makes sense to consider them here. Next, we'll consider some aspects of *waking consciousness*—changes in consciousness that occur while we are awake. In this context, we'll discuss the difference between *automatic* and *controlled processing*, and also the fascinating topic of intuition—what some psychologists have described as "offstage thought," cognitive events and processes that are real and definitely occur, but of which we are not fully aware (Myers, 2002). After examining these topics, we'll turn to what is, perhaps, the most profound shift in consciousness we experience on a daily basis: *sleep*. Here, we'll consider the nature of dreams and what functions, if any, they may serve. Then, we'll turn to the topic of *hypnosis*, what it is, the effects it produces, and its possible uses. We'll conclude by examining *consciousness-altering drugs* and how they produce their effects.

BIOLOGICAL RHYTHMS: TIDES OF LIFE—AND CONSCIOUS EXPERIENCE

Are you a morning person or an evening person? When do you feel most alert and energetic? Whatever your answer, it's clear that most of us experience regular shifts in these respects each day. Psychologists and other scientists refer to such changes as **biological rhythms**—regular fluctuations in our bodily processes and in consciousness over time. Many of these fluctuations occur during the course of a single day and are therefore known as **circadian rhythms** (from the Latin words for "around" and "day"). Others occupy shorter periods of time (e.g., many people become hungry every two or three hours). And still others occur over longer periods, such as the mating seasons shown by many animals—they mate only at certain times of the year—and the female menstrual cycle, which is roughly twenty-eight days. Since circadian rhythms have the most direct relationship to consciousness, however, we'll focus primarily on these.

Circadian Rhythms: Their Basic Nature

Most people are aware of fluctuations in their alertness, energy, and moods over the course of a day, and research findings indicate that such shifts are closely related to changes in underlying bodily processes (e.g., Moore-Ede, Sulzman, & Fuller, 1982). Daily cycles occur in the production of various hormones, core body temperature, blood pressure, and several other processes. For many people, these functions are highest in the late afternoon and evening and lowest in the early hours of the morning. However, large individual differences in this respect exist, so the pattern varies greatly for different people. In addition, circadian rhythms seem to shift with age; as people grow older, their peaks often tend to occur earlier in the day. Adolescents, however, appear to be the exception to this general pattern; their circadian rhythms shift toward later cycles. That's one reason why many junior high and high school students want to stay up late: They feel most activated and alert just when their parents or other adults are saying "Lights out." This suggests that middle schools, which start their days earlier than elementary schools, should actually do the opposite to give students a chance to get much needed sleep! (Greene, 2006).

As you might expect, these cyclic fluctuations in basic bodily functions—and

Biological rhythms:
Cyclic changes in bodily processes.

Circadian rhythms:
Cyclic changes in bodily processes occurring within a single day.

TABLE 4.1 Are You a Morning Person or a Night Person?

If you answer "day" to eight or more of these questions you are probably a morning person If you answer "night" to eight or more, you are probably a night person.

Answer each of the following items by circling either "day" or "night."

1.	I feel most alert during the	day	night
2.	I have most energy during the	day	night
3.	I prefer to take classes during the	day	night
4.	I prefer to study during the	day	night
5.	I get my best ideas during the	day	night
6.	When I graduate, I plan to find a job during the	day	night
7.	I am most productive during the	day	night
8.	I feel most intelligent during the	day	night
9.	I enjoy leisure-time activities most during the	day	night
10.	I prefer to work during the	day	night

Source: Based on items from Wallace, 1993.

Suprachiasmatic nucleus:
A portion of the hypothalamus that seems to play an important role in the regulation of circadian rhythms.

Morning people:
Individuals who experience peak levels of energy and physiological activation relatively early in the day.

Night people:
Individuals who experience peak levels of energy and physiological activation relatively late in the day.

our subjective feelings of alertness—are related to task performance. In general, people do their best work when body temperature and other internal processes are at or near their personal peaks. However, this link appears to be somewhat stronger for physical tasks than for mental ones—especially physical or cognitive tasks that require considerable effort (Daniel & Potasova, 1989).

If bodily processes, mental alertness, and performance on many tasks change regularly over the course of the day, it seems reasonable to suggest that we possess some internal biological mechanism for regulating such changes. In other words, we must possess one or more *biological clocks* that time various circadian rhythms. While there is not as yet total agreement on the number or nature of these internal clocks, existing evidence points to the conclusion that one structure—the **suprachiasmatic nucleus (SCN),** located in the hypothalamus—plays a key role in this respect (Lewy et al., 1992; Moore & Card, 1985).

Individual Differences in Circadian Rhythms: Are You a Morning Person or a Night Person?

Before reading further, please answer the questions in Table 4.1. How did you score? If you answered "day" to eight or more questions, the chances are good that you are a **morning person.** If you answered "night" to eight or more questions, you are probably a **night person.** Morning people feel most alert and active early in the day, while night people experience peaks in alertness and energy in the afternoon or evening. Such differences are more than purely subjective. Studies comparing morning and evening people indicate that the two groups differ in several important ways. Morning people have a higher overall level of adrenaline than night people; thus, they seem to operate at a higher overall level of activation (see Akerstedt & Froberg, 1976). Similarly, morning people experience peaks in body temperature earlier in the day than night people (Wallace, 1993).

That these differences in alertness and bodily states translate into important effects on behavior is indicated by research demonstrating that students who are morning people earn higher grades in early-morning classes, while those who are evening people receive higher grades in classes offered later in the day (e.g., Guthrie, Ash, & Bandapudi, 1995). So, if you are a morning person, try to take your classes at that time, but if you are an evening person, it's better to sign up for afternoon or evening classes. If you follow this strategy, the result may be higher grades.

Disturbances in Circadian Rhythms: Jet Lag and Graveyard- or Swing-Shift Work

Under normal conditions, the existence of circadian rhythms poses no special problems; we simply adjust our activities to these daily fluctuations in energy and alertness. For instance, to take account of my own "down" period around 2 P.M., I (Robert Baron) try to schedule less-demanding tasks for that time of day. There are two situations, however, in which external conditions cause our circadian rhythms to get badly out of phase with events in our lives: rapid travel across several time zones, and working the graveyard shift.

When we fly across several time zones, we may experience considerable difficulty in adjusting our internal clock to the new location—an effect known as *jet lag*. People suffering from jet lag feel tired, dull, and generally miserable. Research on circadian rhythms indicates that in general, it is easier to reset our biological clocks by delaying them than by advancing them. In other words, we experience less disruption when we fly to a time zone where it is *earlier* than the one in which we normally live, than when we fly to one where it is *later*. So, for instance, if you live on the East Coast of the United States and fly to California, where it is three hours earlier, you simply stay up a few extra hours, and then go to sleep. In contrast, if you live in California and fly to the East Coast, where it is three hours later, you may experience greater disruption and take longer to adjust your internal clock.

Why is this so? One explanation is suggested by how light acts as a *zeitgeber*, resetting our biological clock. If you travel from New York to, say, Paris, and start out in the evening (most flights depart at that time), you fly into darkness and then, just when you are really tired and about to fall asleep, dawn occurs, and the cabin is filled with brilliant sunlight (see Figure 4.2, page 126). Certain portions of your brain respond, and reset your biological clock to morning. But you haven't really had a night's sleep, and aren't really prepared for a new day. As a result, you feel awful and it may take you several days to get back to normal. If you fly west, however, you leave in daylight and arrive in daylight, and so don't experience the same unsettling effects. You "gain" several hours, and just stay up a little longer than usual—although after you fall asleep, you may wake up very early because your biological clock is indicating that it is much later in the day than it is in your new location.

A second cause of difficulties with respect to circadian rhythms occurs in *graveyard-shift work*, which requires individuals to work at times when they would normally be sleeping (for instance, 11 P.M. to 7 A.M.). This is an important issue, because about 20 percent of all employees in the United States and several other

FIGURE 4.2
Zeitgebers and Jet Lag: When Dawn Comes Too Early

Passengers flying across several time zones to the east (e.g., from New York to Paris or London) often start their journey in the evening. Just when their biological clocks are signaling "time to sleep," the plane flies into a new dawn. The bright light acts as a *zeitgeber*, resetting their biological clocks and contributing to their fatigue.

Seattle
6:00 A.M.

You fly to a later time zone: jet lag is **strong**

You fly to an earlier time zone: jet lag is **weak**

New York
9:00 A.M.

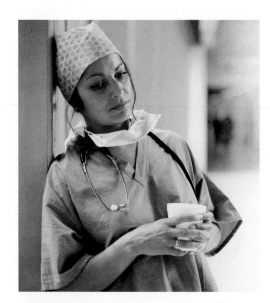

FIGURE 4.3
The Graveyard Shift: Often It Disturbs Biological Rhythms

Tens of millions of employees work at night all around the world. This often disturbs their biological rhythms and can contribute to both reduced performance and the occurrence of accidents.

countries work at night (usually from 11 P.M. until 7 A.M.; Fierman, 1995). To make matters worse, those who work the graveyard shift or the swing shift often face a schedule in which they work on one shift for a fairly short period (say, a week), get two days off, and then work on another shift. The results are, for many people, quite unsettling, and the reason is clear: Such individuals have to reset their biological clocks over and over again, and this process is draining, both physically and psychologically (see Czeisler, Moore-Ede, & Coleman, 1982). These effects, in turn, have been linked to poorer job performance, increased industrial and traffic accidents (see Figure 4.3), and adverse effects on health (Lidell, 1982; Meijmann, van der Meer, & van Dormolen, 1993). So clearly, when biological clocks meet work schedules, the results can be very serious.

Recent evidence suggests that some of the discomfort—and dangers—of graveyard- and swing-shift work can be reduced by resetting our biological clocks. One scientist (David Glass) has obtained promising results with *neuropeptides*, substances found naturally in our brains and other portions of the nervous system (see Chapter 2). However, this work is still in the experimental stage, so there is not yet a pill you can take to reset your biological clock in some specific way. Such pills may be coming, though, so stay tuned for further developments (Economic Times, 2006)! Until such medicine is available, how can you minimize the discomfort and other adverse effects of jet lag and shift work? For the advice offered by psychology, see the following **Psychology Lends a Hand** section.

KEY QUESTIONS

- What are biological rhythms? What are circadian rhythms?
- How do "morning" people and "night" or "evening" people differ?
- What steps can you take to counter the effects of jet lag and work on various shifts?

P S Y C H O L O G Y   L E N D S   A   H A N D

Coping with Jet Lag and the "Blahs" of Graveyard-Shift Work: Some Techniques That Can Help

The fatigue, reduced alertness, and inability to concentrate that often occur when our circadian rhythms are disrupted can have adverse effects on our health, cause accidents, and greatly reduced performance on many tasks. In short, they are *serious*. What can we do about these problems? While there are no simple, no-fail techniques, psychological research points to the following steps to avoid jet lag:

1. *Prepare for the trip:* Get as much sleep as possible during the days before a trip so that you don't start out fatigued.
2. *Drink plenty of water:* The air on jet planes is very dry, and this causes you to become dehydrated unless you drink more than normal. Being dehydrated, in turn, seems to magnify the discomfort produced by jet lag. So drink plenty of water.
3. *Try to sleep on the plane:* We know—this is easier to say than do. But if you can block out light and noise (e.g., by wearing a mask to cover your eyes and "noise-canceling" earphones) you stand a better chance of sleeping—and that will be a big help.
4. *Try to sleep when you arrive* (west-to-east travel), or *Stay up a little longer* (east-to-west travel): These actions will help you reset your biological clock, and that can be a "plus."
5. *Avoid alcohol and other drugs:* While a glass of wine or a tranquilizer may help you to feel relaxed, these drugs often interfere with normal circadian rhythms, and this can intensify the negative effects produced by jet lag. So if at all possible, don't give in to the temptation to try them. (Alcohol, by the way, causes even more dehydration, so this is another reason to avoid it.)

To reduce the effects of graveyard- or swing-shift work:

1. *Stay on one shift as long as possible:* While it may not be under your control, if your job permits, stay on a single shift. Changing to another one, especially after you have adjusted to the first, can magnify the problems.
2. *Try to stay on the same schedule even on the weekend:* Many people who work unusual hours (e.g., they start very early in the day, or work from midnight until morning) try to get back on a fully normal schedule during the weekend. The result? When Monday comes around, they are wiped out! So, avoid the temptation to sleep late on Saturday and Sunday; if you stay a little closer to your regular schedule during the weekend, you will find it much easier to return to it when the work week starts.
3. *Try exposure to very bright light* (if you have to work at night): Exposure to very bright light when you begin to feel sleepy can help reset your circadian rhythm so that it more closely matches the requirements of your job (see Hoput, Boulus, & Moore-Ede, 1996).

While none of these procedures will totally solve the problem of disrupted circadian rhythms, research conducted by psychologists suggests that they can help, so give them a try—they may well prove useful.

WAKING STATES OF CONSCIOUSNESS: FROM CONTROLLED PROCESSING TO . . . INTUITION

All professors have had the following experience: They stand in front of a class, lecturing (on a topic they think is very interesting), and all the students in the room follow them with their eyes; some even nod their heads in agreement. Then, the professor asks one particular student for her or his opinion. Sometimes, this person answers immediately and it is clear that the student *has*, in fact, been thinking about the professor's words. In other cases, though, the chosen student looks blank and it is clear that she or he has not heard (or at least, not *processed*) one word uttered by the professor, and has, instead, been thinking about other things. Yet, as a result of long practice, this person gave every outward sign of paying careful attention.

Experiences like this tell us that, throughout the day, we experience major shifts in consciousness. Sometimes we are paying close attention to whatever task we are performing, and at other times we—like the students in our classes—are operating on "automatic"—for instance, looking carefully at the professor and seeming to listen when our thoughts are far, far away. Psychologists have studied these shifts in our waking states of consciousness from several perspectives, and here we'll focus on two. One has to do with the extent to which we actually pay careful attention to whatever task we are currently performing or, instead, carry it out on what amounts to "automatic pilot." The other, and more recent line of research, has carefully examined the topic of *intuition*—cognitive activity that seems to occur outside the realm of conscious awareness, but still can have powerful effects on our thought and our behavior (Gladwell, 2005; Winerman, 2006). If you have ever used phrases such as "I don't know . . . I just had a good feeling about him . . . ," or "My gut-level reaction was really negative . . . ," you are already familiar with intuition and the many ways in which it can influence our lives. But get ready for some surprises: Psychologists have discovered many fascinating things about this topic. Now, however, we'll return to the two basic modes of thought we mentioned earlier.

Controlled and Automatic Processing: Two Basic Modes of Thought

Often, we perform two tasks at the same time—for example, brushing our teeth while our thoughts wander far and wide, or talking to another person as we drive a car. How can we do this? The answer is that there are two contrasting ways of controlling ongoing activities—different levels of attention to, or conscious control over, our own behavior (see Folk & Remington, 1996; Logan, 1985, 1988).

The first level uses very little of our *information-processing capacity*, and seems to occur in an automatic manner with very little conscious awareness on our part. For this reason, psychologists refer to it as **automatic processing.** It *does* seem to be automatic, and sometimes we can perform several activities of this type at once (see Shiffrin & Schneider, 1977; Shiffrin & Dumais, 1981). Every time you drive while listening to the radio, you demonstrate such automatic processing; both activities can occur simultaneously because both involve automatic processing (see Figure 4.4).

In contrast, **controlled processing** involves more effortful and conscious control of thought and behavior. While it is occurring, you direct careful attention to the task at hand and concentrate on it. Processing of this type consumes significant cognitive resources; as a result, only one task requiring controlled processing can usually be performed at a time.

Research on the nature of automatic and controlled processing suggests that these two states of consciousness differ in several respects. First, behaviors that have come under the control of automatic processing are performed more quickly and with less effort than behaviors that require controlled processing (Logan, 1988). In addition, acts that have come under automatic processing can be initiated without conscious intention; they are triggered in a seemingly automatic manner by specific stimuli or events (e.g., Norman & Sallice, 1985). In fact, it may be difficult to inhibit such actions once they are initiated. If you ever played "Simple Simon" as a child, you are well aware of this. After following many commands beginning "Simple Simon says do this . . . ," you probably also responded to the similar command, "Do this . . ." Why? Because your imitation of the leader's actions was under automatic control, and you obeyed even when you should have refrained from doing so.

Another example of this kind of automatic processing is provided by our ability to respond to others' facial expressions in an automatic manner—even if we can't recognize them overtly (Ohman, 2002). For instance, if individuals are exposed to faces showing angry, neutral, or happy expressions, and the exposure time is so brief that they cannot recognize these expressions (they can't report which ones they have seen), they still show reactions in their own facial muscles that mimic these expressions. For instance, when they see happy faces, electrical

Automatic processing: Processing of information without minimal conscious awareness.

Controlled processing: Processing of information involving relatively high levels of conscious awareness.

activity occurs in muscles that pull the corner of the mouth upward, as in smiles. And when they see angry faces, activity occurs in muscles that play a role in frowning (Dimberg, Thunberg, & Elmehed, 2000). Findings such as these indicate that important aspects of our behavior do reflect automatic processing.

Is either of these types of processing—controlled or automatic—superior? Not really. Automatic processing is rapid and efficient, but can be relatively inflexible—precisely because it is so automatic. Controlled processing is slower, but is more flexible and open to change. In sum, both play an important role in our efforts to deal with information from the external world. One final point: Automatic and controlled processing are not hard-and-fast categories, but rather ends of a continuous dimension. On any given task, individuals may operate in a relatively controlled or a relatively automatic manner. In general, we match the level of our processing to the demands of the situation and so are almost totally unaware of such shifts. In fact, it is often a shock to realize that our behavior is "on automatic" in a situation where we should be paying more careful attention to what is happening around us.

We should briefly mention that research suggests that automatic processing may play a role in racial and ethnic prejudice. Apparently, many people have negative stereotypes of various groups (ones based on race, ethnicity, sexual preference, religion, etc.), but are not aware of these views (see Kersting, 2006; Kawakami & Dovidio, 2001). Yet the stereotypes can be activated in an automatic manner by various events (e.g., some stimulus linked to members of that group—for instance, a symbol of their religion, or mention of a food associated with their culture). Once activated, these stereotypes can, although they are not conscious, result in subtle forms of bias against the groups in question (Towles-Schwen & Facio, 2001). In short, beliefs we don't recognize, which are triggered or primed automatically and of which we are not aware, can have important effects on our behavior.

FIGURE 4.4
Automatic Processing: Sometimes It Can Be Dangerous!
Actions with which we are very familiara can often be performed with very little overt attention to them—on "automatic pilot." Unfortunately, this fact often encourages us to take on more than we can actually handle. In other words, we perform so many different actions at once that we exceed our own attentional capacity. As shown in this photo, that can be downright dangerous.

Intuition: Thought Outside Consciousness Awareness

Imagine the following scene: In a restaurant, twenty small tables have been set up with two chairs facing each other (see Figure 4.5, page 130). At a signal, men and women sit down on opposite sides of the table and begin conversations. Three minutes later, a loud bell is sounded, and each man shifts to another table, where he begins talking to another woman. At the end of the evening, all involved turn in cards on which they indicate whether they want to see a certain person they have met again.

What we have just described is a popular trend known as speed dating. The advantages are obvious: Each participant can meet many new people in a single evening. But such procedures raise an intriguing question: Can we really make useful decisions about how much we might like others—or anything else!—in such a rapid manner, and on the basis of so little information? In other words, can we trust our **intuition,** which many psychologists now define as rapid thought that happens outside our consciousness awareness (see Myers, 2002). Overall, findings are mixed. Growing evidence suggests that under some conditions, we can trust such rapid, and largely nonconscious, judgments. For instance, in several studies, students have watched brief clips of graduate assistants lecturing to their

Intuition:
Refers to cognitive events and processes of which we are not fully aware and that we cannot readily describe in words.

FIGURE 4.5
Speed Dating: Intuition in Action?
In speed dating events, participants meet others for a few minutes. On the basis of these brief conversations, they decide whether they want to see each of the people they've met again. Can we really make accurate decisions in this rapid manner? Some research findings indicate that we can—although perhaps less accurately than we often believe.

classes and then rated the assistants on several dimensions (e.g., competence, confidence, etc.). The students doing the rating were *not* in classes taught by these assistants. Yet, their ratings were very similar to ratings given by the assistants' own classes at the end of the semester (e.g., Ambady, 1993; Winerman, 2006). This suggests that students can form accurate impressions of teachers' performance even on the basis of very scanty evidence. If that's true, then speed dating might really work, because the same basic process—forming an accurate impression of another person on the basis of a very brief exposure to him or her—is at work.

But although intuition can indeed be helpful in many contexts, it can also lead us seriously astray, especially when we trust such "gut level" feelings rather than logic. For instance, consider the following study (Epstein, 1994). Participants were given a choice: They could try to draw a red bean from a jar containing ten beans (nine white, one red), or a jar containing hundred beans (ninety-three white and seven red). Which would they prefer? Logic suggests that the odds of drawing a red bean are greater in the jar with ten beans (10 percent), but most people preferred to draw from the larger jar, with one hundred beans. Why? Because their intuition told them that since there were seven red beans in that jar, they had a better chance of drawing one. In cases like this, intuition and logic point in different directions—and often, we tend to follow intuition, since it is related to our feelings rather than to our reason. (Recall that earlier, we noted that this may also be one effect of engaging in automatic processing—and in a sense, intuition *is* automatic in nature—it is not under our conscious control.)

Even worse, thought processes of which we are unaware can often be a source of racial, ethnic, or religious bias, even when the people involved disapprove of such bias. (Recall that earlier, we noted that this may also be one effect of engaging in automatic processing—and, in a sense, intuition *is* automatic in nature: it is not under our conscious control.) A large body of research findings indicate that many people who are not aware of racial, gender, or ethnic bias—or strongly deny having any!—show signs of it in their actions, or at least in their thinking (see Bar-Haim et al., 2006). One method of studying such "intuitive" or nonconscious bias

FIGURE 4.6
Do We Really Possess a "Sixth Sense?" And Does it Involve our Intuition?
When shown the two photos here (one after the other) and asked to report when (1) they sensed a change and (2) when they actually noticed a change, many persons reported "sensing" changes (the disappearing sail) several seconds before they reported being able to describe these changes. This suggests that one aspect of intuition was at work.
Source: Photos courtesy Dr. Ronald Rensink.

involves the *implicit association test*. In this test, individuals are told to respond as quickly as possible to pairs of concepts such as "good" and "white" and "bad" and "black." Implicit bias—bias of which people are unaware—is shown by differences in the speed of their responses. For instance, if someone is biased toward blacks, they may respond more quickly when "black" is paired with "bad" than when it is paired with "good." This procedure has been used with literally thousands of people, and the results indicate that bias does indeed often lurk in thought processes that are not conscious. Thus, it's entirely possible for someone to say—honestly—"I'm not biased and have no prejudice," but to show traces of such reactions in the speed of their reactions.

But what about another aspect of intuition: Does it provide the proverbial "sixth sense" often mentioned in common sense? In other words, can we sometimes be aware of events or stimuli before we can put such awareness into words? Research by one psychologist—Ronald Rensink (2004)—suggests that this may be so. Rensink was studying what is known as *change blindness*—our inability to recognize even very large changes in a scene, and while doing so, he found that although many persons could not report seeing changes he made in scenes presented to them, they *could* report sensing that *something* was different (e.g., one scene showed a statue with a wall behind it, and the change involved removing the wall). Although participants couldn't accurately report *what* had changed, they did report having the sense that something was different in the scene. Specifically, when asked to push one key to indicate that they had noticed *some* kind of change, and to push another key when they noticed a change they could identify, many persons pushed the first key several seconds before they pushed the second one. This suggests that they noticed that something had changed before they could pinpoint this change or describe it accurately (see Figure 4.6).

These findings and many others indicate that, often, our thoughts, decisions,

FIGURE 4.7
Intuition? Perhaps!

What's going on here? Is Noreldo actually reading his cat's mind? Or is he merely responding to thought processes of which he is, perhaps, unaware—for instance, his dim perception that the cat's food dish is empty and that the cat is sitting next to the dish! You decide. But in this case, as in many others, we would lean toward an explanation in terms of intuition—thought processes occurring outside conscious experience.

Source: © The New Yorker Collection 1990 Gahan Wilson from cartoonbank.com. All rights reserved.

judgments, and overt behavior are influenced by *intuition*—by cognitive processes that exist, but which we cannot readily describe. (Another amusing example is provided by the cartoon in Figure 4.7.) Such processes can assist us in some contexts (e.g., when we need to make very rapid, accurate judgments), but can also lead us badly astray in many others, when our thinking and decisions should, in fact, be governed by logic and facts rather than our "gut-level" feelings. Whatever its effects, though, there is currently little doubt among psychologists that intuition exists and represents one important aspect of our states of consciousness.

One final point: It's important to distinguish between intuition and automatic processing. Actions performed automatically are ones that we *can* describe in words. As a result of long practice, such actions are now performed so effortlessly that we hardly realize we are doing them and don't think about them consciously. But we could still describe them in words if asked to do so. Intuition, in contrast, refers to cognitive processes and events that we cannot readily describe in words, and perhaps never could describe. This is a key distinction between automatic processing and intuition.

KEY QUESTIONS

- What is the difference between automatic processing and controlled processing?
- What is intuition?
- Does intuition provide the proverbial "sixth sense"?

SLEEP: THE PAUSE THAT REFRESHES?

"Oh sleep, it is a gentle thing, beloved from pole to pole . . ." (Samuel Taylor Coleridge, 1834)

Whether sleep is gentle or not, we certainly spend a lot of time in its embrace. In fact, if you think for a moment about the question, "What single activity occupies more of your time than any other?" the answer, for most people, is clear: **sleep,** which psychologists define as a process in which important physiological changes and slowing basic bodily functions are accompanied by major shifts in consciousness. How much do we sleep? Most people spend fully one-third of their entire lives asleep (Dement, 1975; Webb, 1975), so clearly sleep is a state of consciousness well worthy of careful study. But why do we sleep so much? What important functions does it serve? And what are dreams? These are key questions on which we'll focus. To get started, though, let's first consider the question of how psychologists study sleep.

The Basic Nature of Sleep

Everyone would agree that when we sleep, we are in a different state of consciousness than when we are awake. But what is sleep really like? To find out, psychologists carefully monitor changes in the electrical activity occurring in people's brains and muscles as they fall asleep. Recordings of electrical activity of the brain

Sleep:
A process in which important physiological changes (e.g., shifts in brain activity, slowing of basic bodily functions) are accompanied by major shifts in consciousness.

are known as the **electroencephalogram (EEG),** while those for muscles are known as **electromyogram (EMG).** Research using these methods indicates that as people fall asleep, they move through four distinct stages during which faster activity in the brain is gradually replaced by slower activity (**alpha waves** replace faster *beta waves*). Then, as we fall more deeply asleep, activity slows still further, and **delta activity** appears. This may represent a synchronization of neurons in the brain, so that an increasingly large number of neurons fire in unison (see Figure 4.8, page 134). Such sleep is known as slow-wave sleep.

About ninety minutes after we begin to fall asleep, something quite dramatic often happens: We enter a very different phase of sleep known as **REM (rapid eye movement)** sleep. During this phase, the electrical activity of the brain quickly comes to resemble that shown when people are awake. Slow delta waves disappear and fast, low-voltage activity returns. Sleepers' eyes begin to move about rapidly beneath their closed eyelids, and there is an almost total suppression of activity in body muscles (as measured by the EMG).

These shifts in brain activity and bodily processes are accompanied, in many cases, by one of the most dramatic aspects of sleep: *dreams.* Individuals awakened during REM sleep often report dreaming—although it is now recognized that we can dream during non-REM (NREM) sleep, too (McNamara, 2004). Periods of REM sleep continue to alternate with the other stages of sleep throughout the night. The duration is variable, but the REM periods tend to increase in length toward morning. Thus, while the first REM period may last only five to ten minutes, the final ones—from which many people awake—may last thirty minutes or more (Hartmann, 1973; Kelly, 1981).

In sum, the picture of sleep that has emerged from scientific research is of a gradual movement through deeper and deeper stages of sleep, punctuated, irregularly, by periods of REM sleep, during which we dream and show brain activity that is more like that when we are awake than when we are deeply asleep.

Why Do We Sleep? The Many Functions of Sleep

Almost by definition, any activity that fills almost one third of our lives must be important. As one well-known sleep researcher put it: "... Sleep is costly. When an animal sleeps it's not taking care of its young, it's not protecting itself, it's not eating, it's not procreating. If sleep doesn't serve an absolutely vital function, it is the biggest mistake evolution ever made" (Rechtschaffen, cited in Azar, 2006). But what, precisely, are the functions of sleep? Several possibilities exist, and together they suggest that sleep is indeed an important state of consciousness. Among the major theories proposed are these: sleep (1) helps babies learn about their own bodies and acquire control over movement of their limbs; (2) may help us to store new information and memories; (3) may provide our brains with time to replenish energy stores; and (4) may provide our brains with an opportunity recuperate from the stress and learning activities of the preceding day. Let's take a closer look at each of these possibilities.

■ **Sleep and mapping the body.**

Infants of many different species—including our own—spend a great deal of time asleep, and during this sleep, they tend to squirm around and show many twitches and sudden spasms. This suggests that one possible function of sleep is that it helps the nervous system get organized. Infants must learn to control their limbs and to control their reflexes—very rapid movements we discussed in Chapter 2. During the day, there is little opportunity for such learning to occur, because there is simply too much input from the outside world. During sleep, however, infants can use twitches and sudden movements as the basis for learning to control these movements—and their bodies—more effectively. In a sense, these activities, which occur mainly during

Electroencephalogram (EEG):
A record of electrical activity within the brain. EEGs play an important role in the scientific study of sleep.

Electromyogram (EMG):
A record of electrical activity in various muscles.

Alpha waves:
Rapid, low-amplitude brain waves that occur when individuals are awake but relaxed.

Delta activity:
High amplitude, slow brain waves (3.5 Hz or less) that occur during several stages of sleep, but especially during stage 4.

REM sleep:
A state of sleep in which brain activity resembling waking restfulness is accompanied by deep muscle relaxation and movements of the eyes. Most dreams occurring during periods of REM sleep.

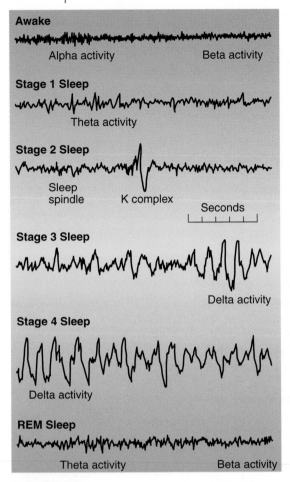

Awake

Alpha activity   Beta activity

Stage 1 Sleep

Theta activity

Stage 2 Sleep

Sleep
spindle   K complex   Seconds

Stage 3 Sleep

Delta activity

Stage 4 Sleep

Delta activity

REM Sleep

Theta activity   Beta activity

FIGURE 4.8
States of Sleep

As shown here, there are four distinct stages of sleep, each characterized by changes in the electrical activity of our brains. In addition, another stage of sleep—REM sleep—is markedly different, and during this stage activity in our brains closely resembles, in some respects, the activity that occurs when we are awake.

sleep, help infants to understand their own bodies and to map them more completely. Many research findings offer support for this view (see Blumberg & Lucas, 1994), so it seems to be at least one possible function of sleep.

■ **Sleep and the storage of new information and memories.**

The view that sleep permits us to consolidate memories is an old one in psychology; in recent years, however, growing evidence in support of this view has been obtained. For instance, consider a recent study by Stickgold (2005). He trained participants to tap out a number sequence on a keyboard by practicing this task. They gradually improved their performance, but soon reached a peak. Participants were then divided into two groups. One was sent home to sleep and then retested on the same task twelve hours later. The other group was simply retested with no sleep intervening. Results indicated that the people who slept improved by fully 20 percent on the key-tapping task, even though they had not practiced any more. The group that had not slept, however, showed no improvements. Other studies have found similar effects on other tasks, and seem to indicate that the more REM sleep people get, especially early in the night, the more they improve. Why do such effects occur? Apparently because sleep boosts brain cell plasticity—the ability of neurons in the brain to form new connections with other neurons (see Chapter 2). Whatever the mechanisms, sleep does seem to help boost the benefits of learning new things.

■ **Sleep as a source of replenishment and repair.**

Life, nearly everyone would agree, is filled with challenge. During each day, we must grapple with many problems and handle many sources of stress. These events take a toll on our brains, which are called on to work long and hard for many hours. Sleep, it is has been suggested, is nature's way to provide our brains with the rest needed to replenish depleted energy, and to provide an opportunity to make necessary repairs. This, too, is an old idea, but, once again, one supported by a growing amount of new evidence. With respect to repair, it is now clear that intense activity in our brains often produces *free radicals*—molecules that can damage cells within the body. To combat these free radicals, our bodies produce neutralizing enzymes, including one called *superoxide dismutase* (SOD). These enzymes destroy the damaging free radicals, and research findings indicate that they are depleted after sleep-deprivation (Siegal, 2002). Sleep restores the levels of SOD, and so helps the brain protect itself from damage.

Additional evidence indicates that energy stores, too, are replenished during sleep and that, moreover, sleep encourages the growth of new neurons (Winerman, 2006). Sleep deprivation, in contrast, reduces the number of new cells formed, and this can be harmful to the brain in several ways.

These are not the only possibilities concerning the potential functions of sleep. Another is that sleep removes organisms from "harm's way"—it keeps them safe during periods when they are not well equipped to protect themselves (e.g., during the night for people, during the day for bats or owls). Which of these proposed functions of sleep are most important? At the present time, we do not have enough evidence to reach a firm conclusion. And there may be no reason for choosing one possible role over another. As one noted sleep researcher (McGinty, 2000; cited in Winerman, 2006) put it, "Even something as simple as breathing has multiple functions; so it's quite likely that something as complex as sleep is in the same boat," a suggestion quite consistent with the fact that we spend so much of our lives in this altered state of consciousness!

KEY QUESTIONS

- How do psychologists study sleep?
- What are the major stages of sleep?
- What happens during REM sleep?
- What are the possible functions of sleep?

Effects of Sleep Deprivation

Another way to identify the functions of sleep is to see what happens when we are deprived of it. Everyone has had the experience of feeling completely miserable after a sleepless night, so it seems reasonable to focus on sleep deprivation as a possible source of information about the functions of sleep. So what *are* the effects of sleep deprivation? Among humans, even prolonged deprivation of sleep does not seem to produce large or clear-cut effects on behavior for many people. For example, in one famous demonstration, seventeen-year-old Randy Gardner stayed awake for 264 hours and 12 minutes—eleven entire days! His motivation for doing was simple: He wanted to earn a place in the *Guiness Book of Records,* and he did. Although Randy had some difficulty staying awake this long, he remained generally alert and active throughout the entire period. After completing his ordeal, he slept fourteen hours on the first day, ten hours on the second, and less than nine on the third. Interestingly, his sleep on these nights showed an elevated proportion of slow-wave (stage 3 and 4) sleep and REM sleep, but did not show a rise in early stages (1 and 2). So it was as if his brain focused on making up the deprivation in slow-wave and REM sleep, but could get along fine without compensating for the losses in stages 1 and 2. Randy suffered no lasting physical or psychological harm from his long sleepless period. But please don't consider trying to beat Randy's record: There are potential risks in long-term sleep deprivation, including an increased chance of serious accidents and harm to personal health.

That long-term deprivation of sleep can be harmful to human beings is suggested by several recent findings. First, growing evidence suggests that sleep deprivation is associated with physiological changes (e.g., lowered glucose tolerance, elevated activity in the sympathetic nervous system) that mark increased wear and tear on our bodies (see Spiegel, Leproult, & Van Cauter, 1999). These findings suggest that sleep does indeed serve a restorative function. Second, Cacioppo and colleagues (2002) have found that lonely people—individuals who have few if any friends and few social ties of any kind—show poorer quality sleep than people who are not lonely. While the total time of sleep for lonely people and those who are not lonely is about the same, lonely people show lower *sleep efficiency:* They are asleep a smaller percent of the time they are in bed, and spend more time awake after initial sleep onset (see Figure 4.9, page 136). These findings suggest the possibility that one reason lonely people show poorer health is that they experience poorer sleep.

Sleep Disorders: No Rest for Some of the Weary

Do you ever have trouble falling or staying asleep? If so, you are in good company: Almost 40 percent of adults report that they sometimes have these problems—known, together, as **insomnia** (Bixler et al., 1979). Further, such problems seem to increase with age and are somewhat more common among women than men. While many people report insomnia, it is not clear that the incidence of this problem is as high as these self-reports might suggest. When the sleep habits of people who claim to be suffering from insomnia are carefully studied, it turns out that many of them sleep as long as people who do not complain of insomnia (Empson, 1984). This does not mean that these people are "faking"; rather, it is possible that although they attain an amount of sleep that falls within normal limits (six and a half hours or more per night), this is not enough to meet their individual needs.

Insomnias:
Disorders involving the inability to fall asleep or maintain sleep once it is attained.

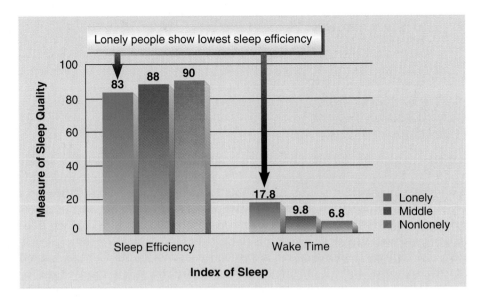

FIGURE 4.9
Loneliness and Sleep Quality
Lonely individuals show lower sleep quality than people who are not lonely. As a result, they may be sleep deprived. This, in turn, may contribute to their relatively poor health.
Source: Based on data from Cacioppo et al., 2002.

Narcolepsy:
A sleep disorder in which individuals are overcome by uncontrollable periods of sleep during waking hours.

Cataplexy:
A symptom of narcolepsy (a sleep disorder) in which individuals fall down suddenly.

Somnambulism:
A sleep disorder in which individuals actually get up and move about while still asleep.

Night terrors:
Extremely frightening dream-like experiences that occur during non-REM sleep.

Apnea:
A sleep disorder in which sleepers stop breathing several times each night, and thus wake up.

Further, the quality of their sleep may be disturbed in ways not yet measured in research. Still, such arguments aside, it does appear that many people who believe that their sleep is somewhat inadequate may actually be getting a normal amount. While insomnia is the most common sleep disorder, it is not the only one. Several other disorders, some related to REM sleep and some to slow-wave sleep, exist. Let's consider some in each category.

■ **Disorders associated with REM sleep.**

Perhaps the most dramatic disturbance of REM sleep is **narcolepsy,** a disorder in which sleep occurs at inappropriate—and often unexpected—times. Persons suffering from narcolepsy often have sleep attacks in which they experience an irresistible urge to sleep during waking activities. They sleep from two to five minutes, and then awake, refreshed. I once had a colleague who had sleep attacks in class. He would stop lecturing, put his head down on the desk, and—much to the amusement of his students who made many jokes about "putting himself under"—sleep.

Another symptom of narcolepsy is **cataplexy,** in which the individual falls down suddenly and without warning. Often, such people will remain fully conscious, but their muscles are paralyzed, as during REM sleep. And sometimes they experience vivid dreams while in this state: In other words, they are dreaming while awake!

■ **Disorders associated with slow-wave sleep.**

Perhaps the most dramatic disorder associated with slow-wave sleep is **somnambulism**—walking in one's sleep. This is less rare than you might guess; almost 25 percent of children experience at least one sleepwalking episode (see Figure 4.10; Empson, 1984). A second related disorder is **night terrors.** Here, individuals—especially children—awaken from deep sleep with signs of intense arousal and powerful feelings of fear. Yet they have no memory of any dream relating to these feelings. Night terrors seem to occur mainly during stage 4 sleep. In contrast, nightmares, which most of us have experienced at some time, occur during REM sleep and can often be vividly recalled. Both somnambulism and night terrors are linked to disturbances in the functioning of the autonomic system, which plays a key role in regulating brain activity during sleep.

Another disturbing type of sleep disorder is **apnea.** People suffering from sleep apnea actually stop breathing when they are asleep. This causes them to wake up, and since the process can be repeated hundreds of times each night, apnea can seriously affect the health of people suffering from it. Apnea is more common among chronic snorers than other people, by the way. The causes of sleep disorders are as varied as the complex neural and chemical systems that regulate sleep itself; thus, discussing them here would lead us into many complex topics well beyond the scope of this book. Suffice it so say that sleep disorders have their roots in the mechanisms and brain structures that regulate arousal, slow-wave sleep, and REM sleep. (See Chapter 2.)

Dreams: "Now Playing in Your Private, Inner Theater . . ."

What is the most dramatic aspect of sleep? For many people, the answer is obvious: **dreams**—jumbled, vivid, sometimes enticing, and sometimes disturbing images that fill our sleeping minds. What are these experiences? Why do they occur? Let's first consider some basic facts about dreams, and then turn to the answers to these questions provided by psychological research.

■ Dreams: Some basic facts.

Here are some the answers to intriguing questions about dreams provided by psychological research:

1. *Does everybody dream?* The answer seems to be "yes." While not all people remember dreaming, EEG recordings indicate that everyone experiences REM sleep.
2. *How long do dreams last?* Dreams run on "real time": The longer they seem to last, the longer they really are (Dement & Kleitman, 1957).
3. *Do dreams occur during all stages of sleep?* Most dreams seem to occur during REM sleep, but growing evidence indicates that dreams occur during NREM sleep too; as noted below, however, the content of dreams during these sleep stages may differ considerably.
4. *When people cannot remember their dreams, does this mean that they are purposely forgetting them, perhaps because they find the content disturbing?* Probably not. Research on why people can or cannot remember their dreams indicates that this is primarily a function of what they do when they wake up. If they lie quietly in bed, actively trying to remember the dream, they have a good chance of recalling it. If, instead, they jump out of bed and start the day's activities, the chances of remembering the dream are reduced. While we can't totally rule out the possibility that some people actively try to forget their dreams, there is little evidence for its occurrence.
5. *Do dreams foretell the future?* There is no scientific evidence for this belief.
6. *Do dreams express unconscious wishes*? Again, there is no convincing scientific evidence for this view.
7. *Do dreams serve any useful function?* This is still open to debate, but below, we'll describe some evidence suggesting that dreams may be more than just meaningless images speeding through our minds as we sleep—images caused by random activity in our nervous systems.

Now that we've considered some basic facts about dreams, let's turn to several views concerning their nature and function. Many different views concerning dreams have been offered and all may provide insights into understanding the nature of dreams.

■ Dreams: The psychodynamic view.

One view of dreams is that they are a mechanism for expressing unconscious wishes or impulses. Such beliefs can be traced largely to Freud, who popularized the view that dreams reveal the unconscious—thoughts, impulses, and wishes

FIGURE 4.10
Sleepwalking: One Disorder of Slow-Wave Sleep
About 25 percent of children show one or more episodes of *somnambulism*, walking in their sleep. I remember having such experiences myself as a child; I'd suddenly awaken to find that, without being aware of this fact, I had gotten out of bed and walked into another room. These episodes stopped by the time I was about ten years old.

Dreams:
Cognitive events, often vivid but disconnected, that occur during sleep. Most dreams take place during REM sleep.

that lie outside the realm of conscious experience. In dreams, Freud believed, we give expression to impulses and desires we find unacceptable during our waking hours. Freud based this view on careful analysis of his patients' dreams and reported that, often, he gained important insights into the causes of their problems from their dreams. These views are not supported by convincing scientific evidence, however. There is no clear or convincing scientific evidence that dreams offer a unique means for exploring the unconscious. So this view is not accepted by most psychologists.

■ Dreams: The physiological view.

If dreams aren't reflections of hidden wishes or impulses, what are they? Another answer is provided by what is sometimes known as the *physiological view* of dreams (Hobson, 1988). According to this perspective, dreams are simply our subjective experience of what is, in essence, random neural activity in the brain. Such activity occurs while we sleep simply because a minimal amount of stimulation is necessary for normal functioning of the brain and nervous system, and our dim awareness of this stimulation is the basis for dreams (Foulkes, 1985; Hobson, 1988).

A logical extension of this view suggests that the activity of which we try to make sense is not actually random; rather, it occurs primarily in the two systems of the brain that are most active when we are awake—the visual system and the motor system. As this view suggests, dreams are usually silent, but are filled with visual images. And although many contain images of movement, few people report experiencing smells, tactile (touch) sensations, or tastes in their dreams (Carlson, 1999).

■ Dreams: A cognitive view.

Another, and closely related, explanation of dreams suggests that they represent our cognitive systems' efforts to interpret activity in our brains while we are sleep. This perspective (Antbrobus, 1991) suggests that two facts about REM sleep are crucial to understanding the nature of dreams: (1) during REM sleep, areas of the brain in the cerebral cortex that play a role in waking perception, thought, and regulation of motor processes are highly active; (2) at the same time, there is massive inhibition of input from sensory systems and muscles (these are suppressed during REM sleep). As a result, the cortical structures or systems that normally regulate perception and thought have only their own activity as input, and this forms the basis for the imagery and ideas in dreams.

■ Dreams: Do they have any meaning?

Now, taking account of all these different views concerning the nature of dreams (especially the physiological and cognitive perspectives), we can pose the following question: do dreams have any meaning, or are they merely our brains' interpretation of random activity occurring while we sleep? This question is still open to debate, but two kinds of evidence indicate that dreams may have some real meaning. First, there is some evidence for real connections between dreams and important events in our lives. People attempting to make important changes in their own behavior—for example, to quit smoking or drinking—often report having **dreams of absent-minded transgression**—DAMIT for short (see Gill, 1985)—in which they suddenly notice that they have absentmindedly slipped back into the habit they wish to break—they are smoking or drinking without having planned to do so. This realization leads to feelings of panic or guilt in the dream. In many cases, the dreamers awake at that point feeling quite disturbed. Interestingly, having such dreams is positively related to success in breaking the habits in question (e.g., in giving up smoking; Hajek & Belcher, 1991). So this kind of dream, at least, does seem to be related to important events in our daily lives.

Second, recent findings (McNamara et al., 2005) suggest that the content of dreams occurring during REM and NREM sleep differ, and do so in ways reflecting the origins of these two kinds of sleep in different portions of the brain. During

Dreams of absent-minded transgression: Dreams in which people attempting to give up the use of tobacco, alcohol, or other drugs see themselves slipping into the use of these substances in an absentminded or careless manner.

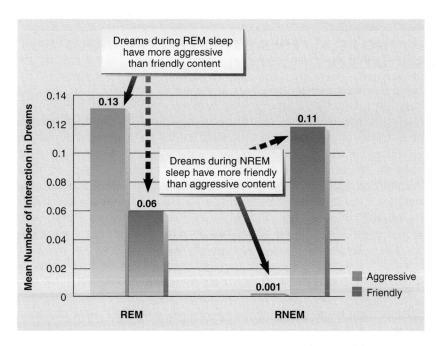

FIGURE 4.11
Dreams During REM and NREM Sleep: They Differ in Content
As shown here, dreams occurring during REM sleep contain more aggressive than friendly content. In contrast, dreams occurring during NREM sleep show the opposite pattern. These differences seem to reflect activation of different portions of the brain during these two kinds of sleep, and suggest that dreams may indeed have some meaning.
Source: Based on data from McNamara et al., 2005.

REM sleep, areas of the brain related to emotion (the hypothalamus, amygdala, and limbic systems) tend to be active, while during NREM sleep, other areas of the brain not so closely related to emotion (e.g., the forebrain and cortical sites) are active. This suggests that perhaps dreams during REM sleep would contain more emotion-related content—for instance, more themes relating to aggressive actions. In contrast, dreams occurring during NREM sleep would have more nonaggressive, friendly content. A study conducted by McNamara and colleagues (2005) confirms these predictions. These researchers arranged for volunteer subjects to be awakened during REM and NREM sleep and to describe any dreams they were having. The dreams were then analyzed for different kinds of content—the relative frequency of aggressive and nonaggressive actions, efforts to befriend another person, physical aggression, sexuality. As you can see from Figure 4.11, results indicated that as predicted, dreams occurring during REM sleep had much more aggressive than friendly content, while the opposite was true for dreams occurring during NREM sleep. That these differences exist, and mirror the portions of the brain active during each kind of sleep, suggests that dreams are not simply our brains' efforts to interpret basically random activity. Rather, they may actually be linked to important events and experiences in our lives. The precise nature of these connections remains unknown, but for now, it seems reasonable to suggest that dreams may indeed have meaning—we simply don't yet know how to interpret them!

KEY QUESTIONS

- What are the effects of sleep deprivation?
- What are important disorders of REM sleep? Of slow-wave sleep?
- How do the psychodynamic, physiological, and cognitive views of dreams differ?
- Do dreams have any meaning?

HYPNOSIS: ALTERED STATE OF CONSCIOUSNESS . . . OR SOCIAL ROLE PLAYING?

Have you ever seen a professional hypnotist at work? If so, you may have been very impressed by the strange effects this person seemed to produce. For instance, the hypnotist may have placed several seemingly normal women and men into a deep trance and then, while they were in this state, given them instructions about how they should behave when they woke up. And sure enough—they seemed to obey the hypnotist's instructions when this performer snapped his or her fingers and awakened the willing "victims." For instance, if told to bark like a dog each time the hypnotist uttered the words "Good boy," that's what they did. Or if told to imagine they were a juggler when the hypnotist snapped her fingers, they would begin juggling imaginary objects when the hypnotist gave this signal.

But is **hypnosis**—a special type of interaction between two people in which one (the hypnotist) induces changes in the behavior, feelings, or cognitions of the other (the subject) through suggestions—(Kihlstrom, 1985; Patterson & Jensen, 2003) actually real or not? Or is merely a clever hoax? Psychologists have studied this question from many angles, so let's see what their research indicates.

Hypnosis: How It's Done and Who Is Susceptible to It

Let's start with two basic question: How is hypnotism performed? Is everyone susceptible to it? With respect to the first, standard techniques for inducing hypnosis usually involve *suggestions* by the hypnotist that the person being hypnotized feels relaxed, is getting sleepy, and is unable to keep his or her eyes open. Speaking continuously in a calm voice, the hypnotist suggests to the subject that he is gradually sinking deeper and deeper into a relaxed state—not sleep, but a state in which the person will be highly susceptible to suggestions from the hypnotist, suggestions concerning the way he feels, his thoughts, and his behavior. Another technique involves having the subject concentrate on a small object, often one that sparkles and can be rotated by the hypnotist (Figure 4.12). The result of such procedures, it appears, is that some people (emphasize the word *some*) enter what appears to be an altered state of consciousness that is definitely not sleep— EEG recordings from hypnotized people resemble those of normal waking, not any of the sleep stages described earlier (Wallace & Fisher, 1987).

Now for the second question: Can everyone be hypnotized? The answer seems clear. Large individual differences in hypnotizability (or *hypnotic suggestibility*) exist. About 15 percent of adults are highly susceptible (as measured by their response to a graded series of suggestions by the hypnotist); 10 percent are highly resistant; the rest are somewhere in between. What makes people highly susceptible to hypnotic suggestions? Research findings suggest that four characteristics are important: *expectancy*—the extent to which individuals believe that they will respond to hypnotic suggestions; *attitudes* toward hypnosis—the more positive these are, the more they will respond to suggestions; *fantasy proneness*—highly hypnotizable individuals often have vivid fantasies; and *absorption*—the tendency to become deeply involved in sensory and imaginative experiences. The greater the extent to which individuals possess these characteristics, the greater their susceptibility to hypnosis.

Hypnosis: Contrasting Views about Its Nature

Now, let's turn to more complex questions: What is the basic nature of hypnosis? What kind of changes in consciousness, if any, does it produce, and how does it work? Careful research on hypnosis has led to the formulation of several contrasting views concerning this issue.

Hypnosis:
An interaction between two people in which one (the hypnotist) induces changes in the behavior, feelings, or cognitions of the other (the subject) through suggestions. Hypnosis involves expectations on the part of subjects and their attempts to conform to social roles (e.g., the role of the hypnotized person).

FIGURE 4.12
Hypnosis: How It Is Performed
Hypnotists sometimes ask the people they are hypnotizing to concentrate on a small object that hypnotists rotate or move in some other way.

■ The social-cognitive or role-playing view.

One of these approaches, the **social-cognitive** or **role-playing** view, suggests that, in fact, there is nothing strange or mysterious about hypnosis. On the contrary, the effects it produces stem, in large part, from a special type of relationship that is created between the hypnotist and the subject. According to this perspective, people undergoing hypnosis have seen many movies and read stories about hypnosis, have clear ideas about what it involves, and what, supposedly, will happen to them when hypnotized. These views lead them to play a special *social role*—that of *hypnotized subject*. This role implies that they will be "in the hypnotist's power," unable to resist this person's suggestions. When they are then exposed to hypnotic inductions from the hypnotist—instructions to behave in certain ways or to experience specific feelings—they tend to obey, since this is what the social role they are enacting indicates *should* happen. (e.g., Lynn, Rhue, & Weekes, 1990; Spanos, 1991).

It's important to note that this view does *not* suggest that persons undergoing hypnosis are consciously faking. On the contrary, they sincerely believe that they are experiencing an altered state of consciousness and that they have no choice but to act and feel as the hypnotist suggests (Kinnunen, Zamansky, & Block, 1994). But these behaviors and experiences are due mainly to their beliefs about hypnosis and the role of the hypnotic subject, rather than to the special skills of the hypnotist or their entry into an altered state of consciousness.

■ The neodissociation and dissociated control views.

Two additional views suggest that hypnosis does actually produce an altered state of consciousness. One of these, the **neodissociation theory**—contends that hypnosis induces a split or dissociation between two basic aspects of consciousness: an *executive or central control function*, through which we regulate our own behavior, and a *monitoring function*, through which we observe it. According to Hilgard (1986, 1993), the most influential supporter of this view, these two aspects of consciousness are normally linked. Hypnosis, however, breaks this bond and erects a cognitive barrier—referred to as *hypnotic amnesia*—that prevents some experiences during hypnosis from entering into normal consciousness. The result is that people who are hypnotized are, indeed, in a special altered state of consciousness in which one part of their mind accepts and responds to suggestions from the hypnotist, while the other part—which Hilgard terms "the hidden observer"—observes the procedures without participating in them. Because of this split in consciousness, these two cognitive mechanisms are no longer in direct contact with each other. So,

Social-cognitive or role-playing view:
A view suggesting that effects produced by hypnosis are the result of hypnotized people's expectations about and their social role as the "hypnotized subject."

Neodisassociation theory:
A theory suggesting that hypnotized individuals enter an altered state of consciousness in which consciousness is divided.

for example, if hypnotized people are told to put their arms into icy water but instructed by the hypnotist that they will experience no pain, they will obey and will indeed report no discomfort. However, if asked to describe their feelings in writing, they may indicate that they *did* experience feelings of intense cold (Hilgard, 1979). In other words, they have the experience of pain, but it is not available to their conscious thought as it would be normally, when they are not hypnotized.

More recently, Bowers and colleagues (e.g., Bowers, 1992; Woody & Bowers, 1994) have modified this view by proposing the **theory of dissociated control.** According to this theory, hypnotism does not necessarily involve a division of consciousness. Rather, it simply weakens control by the central function over other cognitive and behavioral subsystems. Thus, these subsystems can be invoked directly by the hypnotist's suggestions in an automatic manner that is *not* mediated by normal cognitive mechanisms.

Which of these views is more accurate—the social-cognitive view or the theories emphasizing dissociation? Existing evidence offers a mixed and complex picture (see Reed et al., 1996; Kirsch & Lynn, 1998; Noble & McConkey, 1995). Until recently, though, direct and convincing evidence for the view that hypnosis produces important changes in consciousness was lacking, and most evidence offered support for the social-cognitive view (Green & Lynn, 1995; Kirsch & Lynn, 1998). For instance, most of the unusual or bizarre effects observed under hypnosis can readily be explained in terms of hypnotized people's beliefs in the effects of hypnotism and their efforts—not necessarily conscious—to behave in accordance with these expectations. In addition—and this, perhaps, is the key argument—the effects of hypnotic suggestion can often be produced in the absence of hypnosis.

Here's what we mean: In a typical study on the effects of hypnosis, a hypnotic-induction ritual is first performed and then people are given various suggestions—they are told they will not be able to move certain muscles (they will experience paralysis), that they will not be able to remember certain kinds of information (they will experience amnesia), or they will perceive stimuli that aren't really there (hallucinations). If these effects are observed in their behavior, it is concluded that hypnosis has worked. In fact, though, the same kind of effects can often be produced *without the hypnotic ritual* (e.g., Braffman & Kirsch, 1999). In other words, "hypnotic effects" can occur even though no one has been hypnotized.

For instance, consider research conducted by Raz and his colleagues (e.g., Raz, Kirsch, Pollar, & Nitkin-Kaner, 2006). In these studies, individuals perform what is known as the *Stroop* task. This task involves reading the names of colors (e.g., red, blue) printed in various colors of ink. The color names and the actual colors of the ink can be *congruent* (the word "red" printed in red ink) or *incongruent* (the word "red" printed in blue or green.) Not surprisingly, when asked to name the colors they see, persons performing this task respond more slowly when the words and ink colors do not match (are incongruent) than when they match.

Here's how hypnotism enters the picture. In research using the Stroop task to study hypnosis, some individuals are hypnotized and told that what they will see will be meaningless symbols printed in various colors. Others are given the same information, but *without being hypnotized*. Then, both groups are tested in the Stroop task. Results indicate that the hypnotized participants told they will be seeing "meaningless symbols" respond more quickly than people not given this suggestion. In other words, the size of the Stroop effect—slower responding to incongruous pairs of words and colors—is reduced by the hypnotic suggestion. So far, these findings seem to offer support for the view that hypnosis does indeed produce important changes in consciousness. But—and this is the key point—*similar reductions in the Stroop effect also occur for subjects who are not hypnotized, but merely given the suggestion that they will see "meaningless symbols" printed in various colors.* In other words, hypnosis is not necessary to produce these effects; all that's needed is a clear suggestion to this effect (see Figure 4.13). As Raz (2006, page 27) puts it: "We now have evidence . . . that highly hypnotizable people do not need to be hypnotized in order to benefit from suggestion." In other words, the suggestion alone is enough.

Dissociated control, theory of:

A theory suggesting that hypnotism weakens control by the central function over other cognitive and behavioral subsystems, thus permitting these subsystems to be invoked directly by the hypnotist's suggestions.

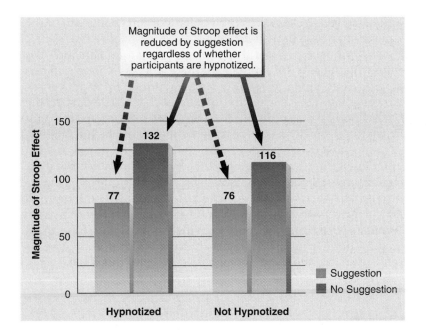

FIGURE 4.13
Hypnotism: Evidence for the Social-Cognitive View
Does hypnotism produce important changes in consciousness? While some evidence suggests that it does, other findings indicate that hypnosis itself is not crucial; the effects it produces are based largely on powerful *suggestions* by the hypnotist to the people being hypnotized, not on the induction of a "trance" or other special state of consciousness. For instance, as shown here, telling individuals that they will see meaningless symbols printed in various colors reduces the magnitude of the Stroop effect regardless of whether these persons are hypnotized or merely given this suggestion in a waking state.
Source: Based on data from Raz et al., 2006

But Yet . . . Evidence That Hypnotism Does Involve More Than Suggestion

So where does all this leave us? Does hypnotism actually produce altered states of consciousness? This remains a complex issue, but to be entirely fair, we should note that recent findings offer some evidence for the view that hypnotism is real and does produce altered states of consciousness. For instance, in the research on the Stroop effect described above, when people are hypnotized and told that they will see only "meaningless symbols," not only is the magnitude of the Stroop effect reduced; in addition, areas of the brain that are active when individuals try to deal with conflicting information are less active than if these people have not been hypnotized (Raz, 2005). So hypnotism seems to change brain activity relative to what it would be without a hypnotic induction.

In other studies (e.g., Oakley, 2004), hypnotized people who were told that they would feel heat-related pain in the absence of any hot object showed activity in areas of the brain (the thalamus, cingulate cortex) in which people who actually do touch a hot object show such activity. In other words, hypnotically induced pain produced the same pattern of brain activation as real pain!

Finally, consider one more intriguing study—research that used very different procedures from the ones we have been considering. In this research (Wheatley & Haidt, 2005), participants were hypnotized and told that they would feel a flash of disgust whenever they read an arbitrary word (e.g., often; take). Then, they read descriptions of stories in which characters engaged in moral transgressions (e.g., cousins who had sexual relations, a congressman who took bribes, a student who stole library books). Each story was written in two versions—one version contained the word that subjects had been told would cause them to feel a flash of disgust and one version did not. Participants then rated how morally wrong the behavior described in each story was. Results indicated that those who read the stories containing the word for which a hypnotic suggestion concerning disgust had been established rated the behavior of the characters in the stories as more wrong. Further, when offered free cookies at the end of the study, those who read these words took and ate a smaller number, thus suggesting that they were experiencing stronger feelings of disgust. In short, there were strong indications, once again, that hypnosis produced more than a mere willingness to accept the hypnotist's suggestions; in fact, it seemed to produce important changes in participants' moral judgments and even in their appetites.

In the face of such evidence, we feel that it is appropriate to conclude that hypnotism is definitely not fake. It can produce dramatic effects—changes in people's behavior or perceptions that are often quite astounding. So in this sense, hypnosis is real. However, hypnotic suggestibility may not be unique or special in any way. Rather, it is, perhaps, simply an enhancement of nonhypnotic suggestibility. In short, all hypnosis does is to provide a context in which tendencies to be suggestible are amplified (Kirsch & Braffman, 2001). So be on guard: A scientific approach to this intriguing topic suggests that hypnotism is not nearly as mysterious—or mystifying—as many people believe. On the contrary, it can be readily understood in the context of cognitive processes that have nothing to do with trances or magical powers possessed by hypnotists. (Does hypnosis have any beneficial uses? In other words, can it be more than just an intriguing form of entertainment? A growing number of psychologists believe that it does. Please see the **Psychology Lends a Hand** section below for a discussion of this issue.)

PSYCHOLOGY LENDS A HAND

Hypnosis: Effective against Pain?

While there is still considerable debate over the nature of hypnosis and how it operates, there is no doubt that it can produce amazing changes in the behavior, thinking, and perceptions of at least some people—especially, those who are highly susceptible to hypnosis. This raises an intriguing question: Can this potentially powerful tool be used to enhance human welfare? Local newspaper ads are often filled with promises of precisely such benefits—ads for "therapists" who claim that they can, by means of hypnosis, help smokers give up their harmful habit and assist overweight persons to shed excess pounds. Our advice about such claims is simple: Approach them with caution! Hypnotism is definitely *not* as effective for such purposes as the ads state, and in fact, can be downright dangerous.

There is another potential use of hypnosis, however, that has received much attention from psychologists, and for which there does seem to be some convincing evidence: When used appropriately, hypnosis can sometimes be an effective tool for reducing pain (see Patterson, 2004). As you might guess, though, it is better for combating some kinds of pain than others, and must be combined with other treatments to be effective.

Hypnosis has been used to treat two basic kinds of pain: *acute* pain and *chronic* pain. Acute pain is usually temporary, and is often the result of medical procedures. In contrast, chronic pain stems from many different causes and lasts for months or even years. A recent review of all available evidence suggests that hypnosis is generally more effective for treating acute pain (e.g., pain produced by care for burns, childbirth, bone marrow operations) than for treating chronic pain (e.g.,

headache pain; Patterson & Jensen, 2003). The reasons for this difference seem relatively clear.

When individuals experience acute pain, hypnosis can be used to give them suggestions of comfort, relaxation, and well-being—feelings that help to counter the pain they experience during dental care, surgery, cancer care, or childbirth. In contrast, when individuals experience chronic pain, they may also be experiencing feelings of depression and anxiety, plus a strong belief that the only cure for them is physical, and long-lasting causes of pain (e.g., atrophied muscles). Moreover, they may be rewarded by others for expressing their pain, by increased attention and sympathy. This means that hypnotic suggestions of comfort or relaxation are not sufficient to reduce chronic pain. For such pain, hypnosis must be combined with other treatments designed to counter depression, reduce anxiety, and change individuals' perceptions about the causes of their pain.

Pain itself is a complex reaction, so efforts to reduce it must take account of this basic fact. It seems reasonable to say, though, that evidence now exists that at least for some people and some kinds of pain, hypnosis *can* be effective. It is especially useful in treating acute pain brought on by specific events (e.g., medical procedures), but can also be helpful to treating chronic pain if it is combined with other approaches—drugs, therapy, counseling. By "demystifying" hypnosis, and determining when it can be helpful, psychologists have begun to turn this unusual and often dramatic means of changing our states of consciousness into a tool useful for alleviating human suffering. Stay tuned for more developments, because they are certain to come.

- What is hypnosis?
- How do the social-cognitive, neodissociation, and dissociative control views of hypnosis differ?
- What do most psychologists conclude with respect to the question of whether hypnosis is real?
- Can hypnosis be used to control pain? For what kinds of pain is it most useful?

CONSCIOUSNESS-ALTERING DRUGS: WHAT THEY ARE AND WHAT THEY DO

Have you ever taken aspirin for a headache? Do you drink coffee or soft drinks to "get a lift"? If so, you are in good company: Each day, hundreds of millions of people around the world use drugs to change the way they feel—to alter their moods or states of consciousness. Much of this use of consciousness-altering drugs is completely legal—soft drinks and coffee are freely available everywhere, and many other drugs are consumed under a doctor's supervision. Often, though, people use drugs that are illegal, or use legal ones to excess. The effects of doing so can be both dramatic and tragic, so in this final section, we'll consider several issues relating to the use of consciousness-altering drugs.

Consciousness-Altering Drugs: Some Basic Concepts

Let's begin with some basic issues. First, what are **drugs**? One widely accepted definition states that they are compounds that, because of their chemical structure, change the functioning of biological systems (Grilly, 1989; Levinthal, 1999). Consciousness-altering drugs, therefore, are drugs that produce changes in consciousness (Wallace & Fisher, 1987).

Unfortunately, when people consume consciousness-altering drugs on a regular basis, they often develop *dependence* on these drugs—they come to need the drugs and cannot function without them. Two types of dependence exist. One, **physiological dependence** occurs when the need for the drug is based on biological factors, such as changes in metabolism. This type of dependence is what is usually meant by the term drug addiction. However, people can also develop **psychological dependence,** in which they experience strong desires to continue using the drug even though, physiologically, their bodies do not need it. As we'll soon see, several psychological mechanisms probably contribute to such dependence.

Continued use of a drug over a prolonged period of time often also leads to drug **tolerance**—a physiological reaction in which the body requires larger and larger doses to experience the same effects. For example, I once had a friend who drank more than twenty cups of coffee each day. My friend didn't start out this way; rather, he gradually increased the amount of coffee he consumed until he reached this very high level (see Figure 4.14, page 146). In some cases, one drug increases tolerance for another; this is known as **cross-tolerance.**

Why do people use consciousness-altering drugs? For several different reasons. First, many consciousness-altering drugs have *rewarding properties*—taking them makes the users feel good or reduces negative feelings and sensations. Second, many people—especially teenagers—use consciousness-altering drugs because it is the "cool" thing to do. Their friends use these drugs, and they believe that if they do, too, this will enhance their social image. (see Sharp and Getz, 1996). Third, people sometimes use consciousness-altering drugs because doing so has become a form of automatic behavior (in the sense of automatic versus controlled processing). Using a specific drug may be an automatic response to internal cues such as feeling tired or depressed. Similarly, drug use may become an automatic reaction to external cues—for example, being in an environment in which they have enjoyed this drug in the past, such as a bar (Tiffany, 1990). In sum, the use of consciousness-altering drugs

Drugs: Compounds or substances that, because of their chemical structure, change the functioning of biological systems.

Physiological dependence: Strong urges to continue using a drug based on organic factors such as changes in metabolism.

Psychological dependence: Strong desires to continue using a drug even though it is not physiologically addicting.

Tolerance: Habituation to a drug so that larger and larger doses are required to produce effects of the same magnitude.

Cross-tolerance: Increased tolerance for one drug that develops as a result of taking another drug.

FIGURE 4.14
Drug Tolerance: All Too Easy to Acquire
People who drink one cup of coffee after another may ultimately find that they have developed a high degree of *tolerance* for caffeine, an active ingredient in coffee. If they can't have their normal quota, they may experience headaches and other negative symptoms.

Drug abuse:
Instances in which individuals take drugs purely to change their moods, and in which they experienced impaired behavior or social functioning as a result of doing so.

Depressants:
Drugs that reduce activity in the nervous system and therefore slow many bodily and cognitive processes. Depressants include alcohol and barbiturates.

stems from many factors—which is one reason why combating **drug abuse** is such a difficult task.

KEY QUESTIONS

• What are drugs? What is drug abuse?
• What are physiological and psychological dependence on drugs?
• Why do people use consciousness-altering drugs?

Consciousness-Altering Drugs: An Overview

While many different drugs affect consciousness, most seem to fit under one of four major headings: *depressants, stimulants, opiates,* or *psychedelics and hallucinogens.*

■ Depressants.

Drugs that reduce both behavioral output and activity in the central nervous system are called **depressants.** Perhaps the most important of these is alcohol, probably the most widely consumed drug in the world. Small doses seem, subjectively, to be stimulating—they induce feelings of excitement and activation. Larger doses, however, act as a depressant. They dull the senses so that feelings of pain, cold, and other forms of discomfort become less intense. Large doses of alcohol interfere with coordination and normal functioning of our senses, often with tragic results for motorists. Alcohol also lowers social inhibitions, so that after consuming large quantities of this drug, people become less restrained in their words and actions, and more likely to engage in dangerous forms of behavior, such as aggression (see Pihl, Lau, & Assad, 1997). In fact, recent findings indicate that exposure to advertisements for alcohol can produce such effects, even if the alcohol is not consumed! (This may occur because ads for alcohol trigger hostile thoughts and associations even in the absence of alcohol itself; Bartholow & Heinz, 2006.) Alcohol seems to produce its pleasurable effects by stimulating special receptors in the brain. Its depressant effects may stem from how it interferes with the capacity of neurons to conduct nerve impulses, perhaps by affecting the cell membrane directly.

Growing evidence suggests that alcohol abuse may have a strong genetic component. Two major patterns of alcohol abuse exist; one group of abusers drinks consistently at high levels (steady drinkers); people in this group usually have a history of antisocial acts—fighting, lying, and so on. In contrast, another group of abusers can resist drinking alcohol for long periods of time, but if they do, they cannot control themselves and go on true binges. The first of these patterns of alcohol abuse seems to be strongly influenced by heredity, while the second pattern of alcohol abuse—binge drinking—seems to be influenced by both heredity and environment. Binge drinking seems to be related to variations in the ALDH2 gene (aldehyde dehydrogenase). Not everyone has this gene, and people who do are less likely to engage in binge drinking than those who do not.

Interestingly, the frequency of binge drinking also varies across different ethnic groups. For instance, on one revealing study (Luczak et al., 2001), binge drinking rates in three groups of college students—Chinese, Korean, and those of European heritage—were compared. In addition, information was obtained on whether participants in the study possessed the ALDH2 gene. Results indicated that binge drinking was more common among Whites, less common among Koreans, and least common among Chinese students. In addition, for the Chinese and Korean students, possessing the ALDH2 gene was an added protective factor against binge drinking.

FIGURE 4.15
**Coca-Cola: Did It Ever
Contain Cocaine?**
Ads like this one suggest that
Coca-Cola can greatly enhance
energy and alertness, but despite
this claim, Coca-Cola never actually contained cocaine, a powerful
stimulant.

Barbiturates, which are contained in sleeping pills and relaxants, constitute a
second type of depressant. Initially, high doses of barbiturates can produce feelings of relaxation and euphoria—a kind of drunkenness without alcohol. They
often go on to produce confusion, slurred speech, memory lapses, and reduced
ability to concentrate. Wide swings of emotion, from euphoria to depression, are
also common. Extremely large doses can be fatal, because they result in paralysis
of the brain centers that regulate breathing.

Because some barbiturates induce sleep, people often try to use them to treat
sleep disorders, such as insomnia. However, these drugs do not seem to produce
normal sleep. They suppress REM sleep, and this sleep stage may rebound
sharply after individuals stop taking the drugs.

■ **Stimulants.**

Drugs that produce the opposite effects of depressants—feelings of energy and activation—are known as **stimulants.** Included in this category are **amphetamines**
and **cocaine.** Both of these stimulants inhibit the reuptake of the neurotransmitters
dopamine and norepinephrine. As a result, neurons that would otherwise stop
firing continue to respond. Such drugs raise blood pressure, heart rate, and respiration—signs of activation produced by the sympathetic nervous system. In addition, stimulants yield short periods (twenty to forty minutes) of pleasurable
sensations during which users feel extremely powerful and energetic. As the
drug wears off, however, users often experience an emotional "crash" involving
anxiety, depression, and fatigue.

Coca-Cola is one of the most popular soft drinks in the world, so you may find
the following question interesting: Was cocaine ever really present in Coca-Cola?
Despite advertising claims about Coke's energizing effects (see Figure 4.15), the answer is no (Levinthal, 1999). Since 1903, when "Coke" was first made, the Stepan
Company in New Jersey has had the task of removing cocaine from high-grade

Barbiturates:
Drugs that act as depressants,
reducing activity in the nervous system and behavior
output.

Stimulants:
Drugs that increase activity in
the nervous system (e.g., amphetamines, caffeine, nicotine).

Amphetamines:
Drugs that act as stimulants,
increasing feelings of energy
and activation.

Cocaine:
A powerful stimulant that produces pleasurable sensations
of increased energy and self-
confidence.

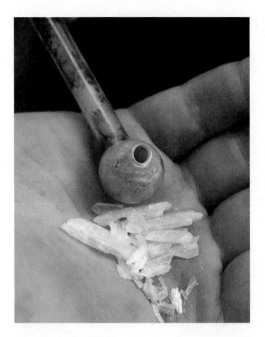

FIGURE 4.16
Crystal Meth: Another Dangerous "Street" Drug
The flow of dangerous new drugs to "the street" seems endless. One is known as *crystal meth*, and it seems to be even more dangerous than the drugs that preceded it.

coca leaves. The remainder, known as "decocanized flavor essence" was then sent to the Coca-Cola Company to flavor the world-famous drink. Many soft drinks do contain caffeine, however, often in doses as high as that found in coffee or tea. So you can get a lift from Coke or Pepsi, but not because they contain cocaine.

Cocaine is usually consumed by *snorting*, a process in which it is inhaled into each nostril. There it is absorbed through the lining of the nose directly into the bloodstream. Cocaine can also be swallowed, usually in liquid form, but this produces weaker effects. When cocaine is heated and treated chemically, a form known as **crack** is produced. This can be smoked, and when it is, the drug affects the brain almost instantly. This produces a high during which individuals experience powerful feelings of energy, confidence, and excitement. Repeated use of cocaine often produces strong psychological dependence on it: Users feel that they can't get along without it. And crack appears to have much stronger effects of this type. In order to obtain the drug, heavy users turn to prostitution, theft, and anything else they can think of that will provide enough money for the next dose.

Another dangerous stimulant on the streets is crystal meth (sometimes known as ice, krank, or tina). It is made from highly volatile, toxic substances that are combined to give what some experts describe as "a mix of laundry detergent and lighter fluid." Like other stimulants, crystal meth (which is snorted, injected, or smoked in a pipe; see Figure 4.16), results in strong feelings of excitement and well-being. Blood pressure rises, and the drug can sometimes produce hallucinations and strange, aggressive behavior. Perhaps the greatest risk, though, is the tendency for users to engage in dangerous sexual practices—ones that put them at risk for contracting several serious diseases (e.g., HIV). The drug is highly addictive; the relapse rate of 92 percent is higher than that for cocaine.

Other stimulants in common use include caffeine, found in coffee, tea, and many soft drinks, and *nicotine*, found in tobacco. Many experts view nicotine as highly addicting, and it is difficult to argue with this view when more than 50 percent of people who have been operated on for lung cancer continue to smoke after their surgery (Carlson, 1999).

■ Opiates.

Another group of drugs in widespread use are the **opiates.** These drugs include opium, morphine, heroin, and related synthetic drugs. Opium is derived from the opium poppy. (Do you remember the scene in *The Wizard of Oz* where Dorothy and the Cowardly Lion fall asleep in a field of beautiful poppies?) Morphine is pro-

Crack:
A derivative of cocaine that can be smoked. It acts as a powerful stimulant.

Opiates:
Drugs that induce a dreamy, relaxed state and, in some persons, intense feelings of pleasure. Opiates exert their effects by stimulating special receptor sites within the brain.

duced from opium, while heroin is derived from morphine. Opiates produce lethargy and a pronounced slowing of almost all bodily functions. These drugs also alter consciousness, producing a dreamlike state and, for some people, intensely pleasurable sensations. While opiates have legitimate uses—for instance in treating chronic, intense pain (e.g., in cancer patients)—they can pose serious risks. Heroin and other opiates are extremely addicting, and withdrawal from them often produces agony for their users. Growing evidence indicates that the brain produces substances (opioid peptides or endorphins) closely related to the opiates in chemical structure and also contains special receptors for them (Phillips & Fibiger, 1989). This suggests one possible explanation for the pain experienced by opiate users during withdrawal. Regular use of opiates soon overloads endorphin receptors within the brain. As a result, the brain ceases production of these substances. When the drugs are withdrawn, endorphin levels remain depressed. Thus, an important internal mechanism for regulating pain is disrupted (Reid, 1990). To make matters worse, tolerance for such opiates as heroin increases rapidly, so physiological addiction can occur very quickly. So to reiterate: Although opiates have legitimate medical uses, when used outside this context they can be highly dangerous.

■ Psychedelics and hallucinogens.

Perhaps the drugs with the most profound effects on consciousness are the **psychedelics,** drugs that alter sensory perception and so may be considered mind-expanding, and **hallucinogens,** drugs that generate sensory perceptions for which there are no external stimuli. The most widely used psychedelic drug is *marijuana.* Use of this drug dates back to ancient times; indeed, it is described in a Chinese guide to medicines from the year 2737 B.C.E. Marijuana was widely used in the United States and elsewhere for medical purposes as late as the 1920s. It could be found in almost any drugstore and purchased without a prescription. It was often prescribed by physicians for headaches, cramps, and even ulcers. Starting in the 1930s, however, the tide of public opinion shifted, and by 1937 marijuana was outlawed completely in the United States. When smoked or eaten—for example, in cookies—marijuana produces moderate physiological effects: increased heart rate (up to 160 beats per minute), changes in blood pressure (the direction seems to depend on whether the individual is sitting, standing, or lying down), and dilation of blood vessels in the eye, thus producing bloodshot eyes. Short-term psychological effects include heightened senses of sight and sound, and a rush of ideas, which leads some individuals to conclude that marijuana increases their creativity. Unfortunately, marijuana also interferes with the ability to carry out tasks involving attention and memory, and reduces ability to judge distances. This latter effect can lead to serious accidents when users of the drug drive a car or operate machinery. Other effects reported by some, but not all, users include reduced inhibitions, feelings of relaxation or drowsiness, and increased sexual pleasure. Most of these effects seem to vary strongly with expectations—what marijuana users believe will happen to them. In the United States, many people believe that marijuana will make them sexually aroused, and they report such effects. In India in contrast, marijuana is believed to be a sexual depressant, and this is what users report. So as we have noted throughout this text, cultural factors often exert powerful effects on behavior.

Because marijuana is still illegal in many nations, it is produced by unreliable sources who frequently blend it with other substances; the result is that users never know exactly what they are getting—and this can be dangerous. There is also some evidence suggesting long-term use of marijuana can impair the immune system, thus making people who use it over long periods of time more susceptible to various diseases.

More dramatic effects are produced by *hallucinogens*—drugs that produce vivid hallucinations and other perceptual shifts. Of these, the most famous drug is **LSD** (lysergic acid diethylamide), or acid. After taking LSD, many people report profound changes in perceptions of the external world. Objects and people seem

Psychedelics:
See *Hallucinogens.*

Hallucinogens:
Drugs that profoundly alter consciousness (e.g., marijuana, LSD).

LSD:
A powerful hallucinogen that produces profound shifts in perception; many of these are frightening in nature.

to change color and shape; walls may sway and move; and many sensations seem to be more intense then normal. There may also be a strange blending of sensory experiences so that colors produce feelings of warmth or cold, while music yields visual sensations. Such effects may sound exciting, but many others produced by LSD are quite negative. Objects, people, and even one's own body may seem distorted or threatening. Users may experience deep sorrow or develop intense fear of close friends and relatives. The effects of the drug are unpredictable, so users have no way of predicting how it will affect them.

Finally, we should mention *designer drugs*—drugs that are designed to resemble already existing illegal drugs. One of the most famous of these is *MDMA* or *ecstasy*. Users of MDMA report that it increases their awareness of their own emotions, changes in visual perception, and feelings of closeness to others (which is why it is sometimes called the "hug drug"). Prolonged use may lead to confusion, fatigue, nausea, and depression (Cloud, 2000). MDMA is often used in rave parties, and has been used by up to 40 percent of all teenagers.

■ **Drug use and abuse: A concluding comment.**

Efforts to reduce or eliminate the use of illegal consciousness-altering drugs have continued for many decades, and in general, results have been mixed. Drug use continues with three key results: (1) the drugs sold to millions of people cannot be checked by the government for purity; (2) the prices of such drugs are very high; and (3) the profits from their sale enriches organized crime. Does this mean we should adopt a new policy—one that, perhaps, makes some of these drugs legal (and therefore, places them under supervision of the government)? This is a complex question and we have no simple answers, but it is one with which many societies will have to grapple in the future because clearly, it will not simply go away. (Use of drugs in work settings raises additional, complex issues. For discussion of these, see the **Psychology Goes to Work** section below.)

PSYCHOLOGY GOES TO WORK

Drug Testing at Work—What Are Your Rights?

Several years ago, the driver of a New York City subway train feel asleep at the controls because he had consumed a large amount of alcohol. The result: Five passengers were killed and two hundred injured. Incidents like these suggest that the use of drugs at work can have devastating effects. Faced with these possibilities, many large companies have adopted *random drug testing*, in which a random sample of employees is tested each day to determine whether they are using illegal drugs. Court rulings on the legality of such testing vary from state to state in the United States, but in general, employers can adopt random testing if they have a legitimate reason for doing so (e.g., to protect the public or other employees). If you are selected for such testing, what should you do? You should probably agree unless you have a special reason for objecting—for instance, you are taking drugs, prescribed by your doctor, that may show up in the tests. The weight of law is generally on the employer's side, because of legislation

such as the Drug-Free Workplace Act, which requires employers to assure that their work environments are drug-free. But you should agree only if you know that the drug testing procedures are fair. This means: (1) every employee has an equal chance of being tested (e.g., names are selected randomly by a computer program); (2) tests are done by at least two different laboratories, as a check on accuracy; and (3) blood or urine samples are sealed and stored properly until collected for testing. If you have doubts on any of these points, *object strongly*. The law protects you from unfair or sloppy testing that may be done to obtain grounds for firing certain employees rather than to protect the health and safety of all employees. Your best protection? Don't even think about using drugs while at work, and avoid illegal drugs anywhere, at any time. The health and career you protect will be your own—not to mention the lives and well-being of others, too.

KEY QUESTIONS

- What are the effects of depressants?
- What are the effects of stimulants? Opiates? Psychedelics? Hallucinogens?

SUMMARY AND REVIEW OF KEY QUESTIONS

Biological Rhythms: Tides of Life— and Conscious Experience

- **What are biological rhythms? What are circadian rhythms?**
  Biological rhythms are regular fluctuations in our bodily processes. Circadian rhythms are biological rhythms that occur within a single day.

- **How do "morning" people and "night" or "evening" people differ?**
  Morning people feel most alert and energetic early in the day. Evening people feel most alert and energetic late in the day.

- **What effects do jet lag and work on various shifts have on circadian rhythms?**
  Both jet lag and some shift work produce disturbances in circadian rhythms.

Waking States of Consciousness: From Controlled Processing to . . . Intuition

- **What is the difference between automatic processing and controlled processing?**
  In automatic processing, we perform activities without directing conscious attention to them. In controlled processing, we direct conscious attention to various activities.

- **What is intuition?**
  Intuition is defined by psychologists as thought processes occurring outside conscious awareness.

- **Does intuition provide the proverbial "sixth sense"?**
  While some evidence indicates that we can "sense" changes in the external world before we can identify them, this is no way suggests that intuition offers another sense, distinct from our other senses.

Sleep: The Pause That Refreshes?

- **How do psychologists study sleep?**
  Sleep is often studied by examining changes in the EEG and EMG.

- **What happens during sleep?**
  During sleep, we pass through four major stages of sleep and a very different stage known as REM sleep.

- **What happens during REM sleep?**
  During REM sleep the EEG shows a pattern similar to that of waking, but the activity of body muscles is almost totally suppressed. Most dreams occur during REM sleep.

- **What are the functions of sleep?**
  Sleep appears at serve several major functions, including helping to map the body and regulate reflexes, enhance storage of new information and memories, and replenish and repair the brain and other portions of the nervous system.

- **What are important disorders of REM sleep? Slow-wave sleep?**
  Disorders of REM sleep include narcolepsy, cataplexy, and catatonia. Disorders of slow-wave sleep include insomnia, somnambulism, night terrors, and apnea.

- **How do the psychodynamic, physiological, and cognitive views explain dreams?**
  The psychodynamic view suggests that dreams reflect suppressed thoughts, wishes, and impulses. The physiological view suggests that dreams reflect the brain's interpretation of random neural activity that occurs while we sleep. The cognitive view holds that dreams result from how the many systems of the brain are active during sleep, while input from muscles and sensory systems is inhibited.

- **Do dreams have any meaning?**
  Growing evidence indicates that dreams are indeed related to important events in our lives, and that their content may reflect differences in the functioning of various portions of the brain.

Hypnosis: Altered State of Consciousness . . . Or Social Role Playing?

- **What is hypnosis?**
  Hypnosis involves a special type of interaction between two people in which one (the hypnotist) employs suggestions to induce changes in the behavior, feelings, or cognitions of the other (the subject).

- **How do the social-cognitive, neodissociation, and dissociative control views of hypnosis differ?**
  The social-cognitive view suggests that the effects of hypnosis stem from the hypnotized person's expectations and efforts to play the role of hypnotized subject. The neodissociation view suggests that the effects of hypnotism stem from a split in consciousness between the executive cognitive function and a monitoring function. Dissociative control theory suggests that hypnotism weakens control by the central function over other cognitive and behavioral subsystems.

- **What do most psychologists conclude with respect to the question of whether hypnosis is real?**
  On the basis of scientific evidence, most psychologists have concluded that the effects produced by hypnosis are real, but that they stem primarily from the ability possessed by some people to produce dramatic alterations in their own experience or behavior—nonhypnotic suggestibility—rather than from special properties of hypnosis itself.

- **Can hypnosis be used to control pain? For what kinds of pain is it most useful?**
  Growing evidence suggests that hypnosis can be used to reduce pain. It is more effective for acute than chronic pain, but can also help to reduce chronic pain when used along with other pain-reducing techniques (e.g., forms of therapy designed to reduce anxiety and depression).

Consciousness-Altering Drugs: What They Are and What They Do

- **What are drugs? What is drug abuse?**
  Drugs are substances that, because of their chemical structure, change the functioning of biological systems. Drug abuse involves instances in which people take drugs purely to change their moods, and in which drugs produce impaired behavior or social functioning.
- **What are physiological and psychological dependence on drugs?**
  Physiological dependence involves strong urges to continue using a drug based on organic factors, such as

changes in metabolism. Psychological dependence involves strong desires to continue using a drug even though it is not physiologically addicting.

- **Why do people use consciousness-altering drugs?**
  People use consciousness-altering drugs for several reasons: the drugs make them feel good or eliminate negative feelings; they experience social pressure to use the drugs; using them has become automatic behavior.
- **What are the effects of depressants?**
  Depressants (e.g., alcohol) reduce both behavioral output and neural activity.
- **What are the effects of stimulants? Opiates? Psychedelics? Hallucinogens?**
  Stimulants produce feelings of energy and activation. Opiates produce lethargy and pronounced slowing of many bodily functions, but also induce intense feelings of pleasure in some people. Psychedelics such as marijuana alter sensory perception, while hallucinogens such as LSD produce vivid hallucinations and other bizarre perceptual effects.

KEY TERMS

Alpha waves, p. 133
Amphetamines, p. 147
Apnea, p. 136
Automatic processing, p. 128
Barbiturates, p. 147
Biological rhythms, p. 123
Cataplexy, p. 136
Circadian rhythms, p. 123
Cocaine, p. 147
Controlled processing, p. 128
Crack, p. 148
Cross-tolerance, p. 145
Delta activity, p. 133
Depressants, p. 146
Dissociated control, theory of, p. 142

Dreams, p. 137
Dreams of absent-minded transgression, p. 138
Drug abuse, p. 146
Drugs, p. 145
Electroencephalogram (EEG), p. 133
Electromyogram (EMG), p. 133
Hallucinogens, p. 149
Hypnosis, p. 140
Insomnias, p. 135
Intuition, p. 129
LSD, p. 149
Morning people, p. 124
Narcolepsy, p. 136
Neodisassociation theory, p. 141

Night people, p. 124
Night terrors, p. 136
Opiates, p. 148
Physiological dependence, p. 145
Psychedelics, p. 149
Psychological dependence, p. 145
REM sleep, p. 133
Sleep, p. 132
Social-cognitive or role-playing view, p. 141
Somnambulism, p. 136
States of consciousness, p. 122
Stimulants, p. 147
Suprachiasmatic nucleus, p. 124
Tolerance, p. 145

PSYCHOLOGY: UNDERSTANDING ITS FINDINGS

Can Hypnosis Solve Personal Problems?

Have you ever seen an ad for a hypnotist who claims to be able to help people lose weight, stop smoking, or get over their shyness? We see them every so often in our local newspaper. What do you think? Taking account of the information in this chapter on hypnotism, do you think it can produce such beneficial changes? If so, why? If not, why?

Now, whatever your own opinion, try this question on several of your friends—especially ones who have *not* read this chapter. What do *they* think? We predict that they will have more faith in the effectiveness of hypnotism than you do. To make this study more useful, ask them to answer the following questions:

1. Do you think hypnotism is real—that once hypnotized, people will do whatever the hypnotist tells them to do?

Definitely No				Definitely Yes
1	2	3	4	5

2. Do you think that hypnotism can help people to lose weight?

Definitely No				Definitely Yes
1	2	3	4	5

3. Do you think hypnotism can help people to stop smoking?

Definitely No				Definitely Yes
1	2	3	4	5

4. Do you think hypnotism can help people get over being shy?

Definitely No				Definitely Yes
1	2	3	4	5

Add the responses of your friends to see how they feel, in general, about the usefulness of hypnotism.

MAKING PSYCHOLOGY PART OF YOUR LIFE

Do You Trust Your Own Intuition?

Recent research in psychology suggests that intuition has a basis in fact: It involves thought and knowledge that can strongly affect our behavior, but of which we are not fully aware. How much faith do you put in *your* intuition? To find out, answer the following questions by giving yourself a number from 1 (very low) to 7 (very high) for each. Insert your numbers in the spaces to the left of each item.

1. How good are you at forming first impressions of other persons? In other words, can you do this quickly and accurately?
2. Do you ever feel very lucky on particular days?
3. Do you ever "sense" a change in some situation before you actually notice it (i.e., can consciously report it)?
4. How often do you have strong "gut level" feelings about events, so that in a sense, you can "tell" how they will turn out?

5. Suppose you had to interview several people for a job. How successful would you be at this task?

Now, add your numbers and divide by five to find your "intuition score." If you scored 4.0 or higher, welcome to the club: You, like most of us, trust your own intuition. You believe that you do indeed "know" things you can't put into words and accept this knowledge as useful, even though you can't describe it. If you scored 2.0 or lower, in contrast, you have very little faith in your own intuition. There's no "good" or "bad" result on this informal test. Rather, all that matters is that you understand both the nature and limits of intuition and avoid accepting it as an infallible guide for your own behavior or decisions.

If you are using MyPsychLab, you have access to an electronic version of this textbook, along with dozens of valuable resources per chapter—including video and audio clips, simulations and activities, self-assessments, practice tests and other study materials. Here is a sampling of the resources available for this chapter.

EXPLORE

 Theories of Dreaming

WATCH

 Lucid Dreaming
Sleep Apnea
Hypnosis

If you did not receive an access code to MyPsychLab with this text and wish to purchase access online, please visit www.MyPsychLab.com.

STUDY GUIDE

CHAPTER REVIEW

Biological Rhythms: Tides of Life- and Conscious Experience

1. The neural event that caused the hospitalization of Professor Baron was
   a. the formation of a clot within his spinal cord.
   b. the occurrence of an epileptic stroke.
   c. a ruptured aneurysm within his brain.
   d. a severe migraine headache.
2. An example of "automatic" processing is driving our car while listening to the radio.   (True-False)
3. A(n) _____ rhythm fluctuates over a period of 24 hours.
   a. circadian
   b. seasonal
   c. ultraradian
   d. menstrual
4. Which of the following is true of circadian rhythms (CRs)?
   a. The period of a CR is about 28 hours.
   b. Human core body temperature shows a CR.
   c. Teenagers show a shift to a CR that peaks early in the day.
   d. Most people do their best work when their body temperature is at its lowest daily value.
5. The _____ of the hypothalamus is a key component of the neural systems that control our internal rhythms.
   a. ventromedial nucleus
   b. nucleus accumbens
   c. area postrema
   d. suprachiasmatic nucleus
6. College students would do well to ensure that their course schedules match the time of day at which they show peak levels of activation.   (True-False)
7. Circadian rhythms are less likely to be disrupted by "jet lag" when
   a. we fly towards the east.
   b. our travel takes us to the south.
   c. we travel in a westward direction.
   d. our travel takes us to the north.
8. Most people do their best work when their body temperature is at its lowest daily value.   (True-False)
9. Which of the following is NOT expected to help a person cope with jet-lag?
   a. Try to sleep on the plane.
   b. Drink plenty of alcohol while on the plane.
   c. Try to stay up longer after you arrive.
   d. Start the trip rested rather than tired.
10. A person who works the graveyard shift should attempt to go back to a normal schedule on the weekend. (True-False).

Waking States of Consciousness: From Controlled Processing to Intuition

11. _____ refers to cognitive processing that affects our behavior without reaching the level of consciousness.
    a. Preconscious processing
    b. Unconscious motivation
    c. Intuition
    d. Daydreaming
12. When we imitate the facial expressions of others, we are showing the power of
    a. automatic processing.
    b. social roles.
    c. controlled processing.
    d. preconscious processing.
13. An advantage of controlled processing relates to its
    a. speed.
    b. flexibility.
    c. ability to control social interactions.
    d. efficiency.
14. The cognitive process known as intuition can contribute to social problems such as
    a. religious bias.
    b. racial bias.
    c. ethnic bias
    d. All of the above are correct.
15. It is possible for a person to consciously despise racism while at the same time showing implicit racial bias. (True-False)
16. A key difference between intuition and automatic actions is that
    a. the cognitive processes of intuition are easily translated into words.
    b. we can use words to describe our actions.
    c. intuition precedes an automatic action.
    d. automatic actions precede intuition.

Sleep: The Pause that Refreshes?

17. Humans spend the greatest amount of their lives devoted to the behavior known as
    a. work.
    b. play.
    c. sleep.
    d. school.
18. The various stages of sleep are easily distinguished by
    a. whether we dream on color or in black and white.
    b. our patterns of respiration as we sleep.
    c. our thought patterns during the night.
    d. the electrical activity of our brain and muscles.
19. Which of the following is NOT a feature of REM sleep?
    a. Suppression of muscle activity.
    b. The presence of beta waves in the EEG record
    c. As the night goes on, we spend less time in REM sleep.
    d. Rapid eye movements
20. Humans first enter REM sleep and then transition to non-REM sleep.   (True-False)

21. A key function of REM sleep is to
    a. rest the body.
    b. reduce the number of new cells formed in the brain.
    c. promote learning.
    d. keep us away from night-time dangers.
22. REM sleep is often accompanied by dramatic movements of the arms and legs.   (True-False)
23. A key aspect of human narcolepsy relates to
    a. sleeping at inappropriate times.
    b. an inability to sleep at night.
    c. walking and talking while asleep.
    d. the occurrence of vivid nightmares.
24. The _____ view of dreams was proposed by _____.
    a. pharmacological;   Robert Hobson
    b. physiological;   Timothy Leary
    c. psychodynamic;   Sigmund Freud
    d. random noise;   Simon Fraser

Hypnosis: Altered State of Consciousness or Social Role Playing?

25. Hypnosis is defined as a form of
    a. brain dysfunction brought on by fever.
    b. social interaction in which one person induces changes in the behavior and thoughts of another.
    c. a game played at social functions.
    d. meditation associated with brain alpha wave activity.
26. Match up the characteristic that makes a person susceptible to hypnosis with its formal definition.
    _____. Having a vivid imagination facilitates undergoing hypnosis.
    _____. Having a positive attitude toward hypnosis makes it easier to enter a hypnotic trance.
    _____. The characteristic in which a person believes they will respond to hypnotic suggestions
    _____. The ability to be deeply involved in sensory experiences.
    a. Expectancy.
    b. Absorption.
    c. Fantasy proneness.
    d. Role-playing expertise
    e. Attitudes
27. The _____ view of hypnosis suggests that hypnosis reflects a weakening of cognitive and behavioral subsystems by the central function.
    a. social-playing
    b. dissociated control
    c. neodissociation
    d. cortical dysfunction
28. Hilgard argues that hypnosis is nothing but a form of social role-playing.   (True-False)
29. A key finding in support of the social-cognitive view of hypnosis is that
    a. hypnotized persons can be instructed to be unable to move their major muscles.
    b. giving hypnotic instructions to a non-hypnotized person has no effects.
    c. hypnotic effects involving paralysis and memory can be induced without inducing hypnosis.
    d. some people will experience amnesia for the time they were in a hypnotic trance.

30. Which of the following is NOT consistent with the social-cognitive view of hypnosis?
    a. Hypnotically induced pain activates the same brain regions as does real pain.
    b. Some people will experience amnesia for the time they were in a hypnotic trance.
    c. The effects of hypnosis are due to the power of suggestion.
    d. The effects of hypnotic suggestion can be induced without inducing hypnosis.
31. The text authors conclude that hypnosis is an elaboration of our tendencies for suggestibility.   (True-False)

Consciousness-Altering Drugs: What They are and What They Do

32. A consciousness-altering drug is one that
    a. has effects that do not involve the brain.
    b. changes the functioning of biological systems.
    c. cannot produce tolerance or dependence.
    d. produces a change in our capacity to think, feel, and move.
33. A person who has a(n) _____ for a drug will show _____.
    a. psychological dependence;   a need for the drug based on bodily reactions without the drug
    b. physiological dependence;   a need for the drug based on psychological factors
    c. pathophysiological drug habit;   an interest in the drug if it is available for the right price
    d. psychological dependence;   a wanting for the drug without a biological need for the drug
34. People abuse consciousness-altering drugs because such use
    a. activates the reward circuits of the brain.
    b. may be an automatic response to internal states such as stress.
    c. is deemed by their friends as "cool".
    d. All of the above are correct.
35. A(n) _____ drug suppresses activity in the central nervous system and reduces ongoing behavior.
    a. opiate
    b. depressant
    c. antidepressant
    d. antiopiate
36. A person whose genetic background includes the ALDH2 gene is more likely to engage in binge drinking that a person who does not have this gene.   (True-False)
37. Which of the following is NOT a feature associated with the misuse of a stimulant drug?
    a. Sedation and reduced behavioral output.
    b. A feeling of euphoria,
    c. An intense feeling of energy.
    d. Activation of the sympathetic nervous system.
38. A key reason as to which drugs such as cocaine or crystal meth are highly addictive is
    a. that eating these drugs results in rapid drug entry into brain.
    b. that smoking these drugs rapidly changes brain chemistry.

c. that such drugs induce physiological and psychological dependence.

d. A and C are correct.

39. The view that nicotine is addictive is supported by the observation that 50% of smokers who have had lung cancer surgery continue to smoke after the surgery. (True-False)

40. Which of the following is NOT an example of an opiate drug?
    a. Heroin.
    b. Morphine.
    c. Opium.
    d. Nicotine

41. A drug that alters sensory perception is considered to be a(n)
    a. stimulant.
    b. psychedelic.
    c. hallucinogen.
    d. psychotomimetic.

IDENTIFICATIONS

Identify the term that belongs with each of the concepts below (place the letter for the appropriate term below in front of each concept).

Identification   Concept:

_____ 1. A type of work schedule that can generate symptoms of jet-lag.

_____ 2. A stage of sleep that involves suppression of muscle activity

_____ 3. A highly addictive stimulant.

_____ 4. A social interaction in which one person induces changes in the behavior and thoughts of another.

_____ 5. A drug that alters appetite and sexual pleasure.

_____ 6. Driving our car while listening to the radio.

_____ 7. A form of sleep in which movement is possible.

_____ 8. This structure is a key component of the neural systems that control our internal rhythms.

_____ 9. A rhythm that fluctuates over a period of 24 hours.

Identification:
    a. Automatic processing
    b. Non-REM sleep
    c. Circadian
    d. Beta waves
    e. Hypnosis
    f. Suprachiasmatic nucleus
    g. Marijuana
    h. Shift work
    i. Crack cocaine
    j. REM sleep

FILL IN THE BLANK

1. _____ refers to our varying degrees of awareness of ourselves and the world around us.

2. The _____ is an instrument used to electrical potentials from muscles during sleep.

3. As the night goes on, the relative length of _____ increases in each successive sleep cycle.

4. A drug that induces arousal and may be addictive is a(n) _____.

5. A college student who has the ALDH2 gene is less likely to _____.

6. _____ is the most widely used psychedelic drug.

7. _____ is a sleep disorder in which sleep intrudes into the day hours

8. A non-drug treatment for pain involves the use of _____.

9. The ability to be deeply involved in sensory experiences is known as _____.

10. Mating capacity in certain mammals shows a _____ rhythm.

11. A(n) _____ drug suppresses activity in the central nervous system and reduces ongoing behavior.

12. A(n) _____ drug alters sensory perception.

13. Heroin is produced from _____.

14. _____ requires less effort than does controlled processing.

15. Depressants can be used in order to treat _____.

COMPREHENSIVE PRACTICE TEST

1. Circadian rhythms are most likely to be disrupted by "jet lag" when
    a. we fly towards the east.
    b. our travel takes us to the couth.
    c. we travel in a westward direction.
    d. our travel takes us to the north.

2. Which of the following is a key issue associated with graveyard or shift work in the United States?
    a. An intense feeling of being tired.
    b. Improved job performance for people whose schedules vary across the week.
    c. Reduced secretion of neuropeptides in the brain.
    d. Adverse health effects.

3. A key difference between automatic and controlled modes of processing is that
    a. controlled processing occurs without effort.
    b. automatic processing is a conscious form of thought.
    c. controlled processing is faster than is automatic processing.
    d. automatic processing requires less effort than does controlled processing.

4. Controlled processing occurs without effort. (True-False)

5. Which of the following does NOT belong together?
    a. REM sleep;   movements of the eyes
    b. non-REM sleep;   eye movements
    c. non-REM sleep;   moderate muscle tone
    d. awake state;   fast, low voltage EEG waves

6. Humans spend about a third of their life asleep. (True-False)

7. Prolonged sleep deprivation in humans results in
    a. psychosis that does not respond to drug treatment.
    b. physiological changes associated with physical wear and tear.
    c. illness and death.
    d. major perceptual distortions.

8. Which of the following is NOT true of dreams?
    a. Dreams do not foretell the future.
    b. Everyone dreams.

c. Dreams occur in real-time.

d. Most dreams occur during non-REM sleep.

9. Which of the following is true of hypnosis?

a. Almost 90% of the population can be placed into a hypnotic state.

b. Hypnosis is most easily induced in a person who is already relaxed by alcohol consumption.

c. The EEG recording of a hypnotized person resembles that of non-REM sleep.

d. People who have positive attitudes toward hypnosis are more susceptible to being hypnotized.

10. Match up the correct term with its definition.

_____. A stage of sleep featuring beta waves in the EEG but suppression of motor activity.

_____. A type of sleep in which a person fails to breathe while asleep.

_____. A sleep disorder in which sleep intrudes into the day hours.

_____. A form of brain activity characterized by slower waveforms.

_____. Fast waves that are low voltage.

_____. A measure of sleep problems related to the fraction of time in bed that a person is asleep.

a. Narcolepsy

b. Beta waves

c. Sleep efficiency

d. Alpha waves

e. Sleep apnea

f. REM sleep

11. Which of the following is a feature associated with use of a stimulant drug?

a. Activation of the sympathetic nervous system.

b. A feeling of euphoria,

c. An intense feeling of energy.

d. All of the above are correct.

12. A common problem associated with the use of depressants to induce sleep is

a. that these drugs rapidly move the sleeper into REM sleep for much of the night.

b. some people experience a paradoxical arousal reaction and are unable to sleep.

c. that these drugs suppress REM sleep which can sharply rebound when the person does not take the sleeping medication.

d. that low doses can depress breathing leading to death.

13. The withdrawal symptoms noted in heroin users is caused by

a. the fact that heroin use suppresses the secretion of brain endorphins so that during withdrawal brain endorphin levels are low.

b. the conversion of morphine into heroin in the brain.

c. the pain of being in county jail.

d. the fact that heroin use increases the secretion of brain endorphins so that during withdrawal brain endorphin levels are high.

14. Which of the following is an example of an effect of marijuana on human cognition?

a. Interference with memory.

b. Feelings of jitteriness and insomnia.

c. Reduced sexual pleasure.

d. Enhanced ability to judge distances while driving.

15. Alcohol would be classified as a _____ at low doses, but as a _____ at higher doses.

a. depressant;   depressant

b. psychedelic;   stimulant

c. stimulant;   depressant

d. stimulant;   psychedelic

CRITICAL THINKING

1. Describe three hypotheses as to the function(s) of sleep.

2. Discuss the physiological and psychological factors that predispose humans to use and abuse psychoactive drugs.

FIVE

Learning: How We're Changed by Experience

*T*he first and only time a friend of mine (Michael Kalsher) ate cream of potato soup was in the fourth grade. That was the day her babysitter served it up for lunch from the familiar red-and-white Campbell's™ soup can. There was just something about that concoction that my friend knew she didn't like from the very first bite. Because of the babysitter's "waste not, want not" mentality and her enforcement of the "no dessert until your bowl is empty" motto, my friend slurped up every last bit of the bowl's contents, but unfortunately for her, felt it come up in the back of her throat almost as quickly as it went down. Today, some forty years later, my friend remains unable to stomach the thought of cream of potato soup, and whenever a waitress announces that it's the soup of the day, or someone at the table actually orders it, she experiences an unpleasant feeling, sometimes accompanied by a bad taste in her mouth. She can't even be tempted by savory homemade potato soup, even when it contains some of her favorite foods such as mushrooms, clams, or sausage. Interestingly, though, she still enjoys eating potatoes, as long as they're mashed, baked, or fried.

Have you or someone you know had a similar experience, but perhaps with a different type of food or beverage? If so, you already know how powerful the effects of such experiences can be. In fact, in that one short lunch hour, my friend underwent a lifelong change in her eating habits as the result of a single negative learning experience.

As illustrated by this example, the learning process is important to all organisms, including people, because it helps us acquire important skills and adapt to changing conditions in the world around us. In this chapter, we'll examine several basic principles that help to explain how many forms of behavior are affected by experience. Psychologists refer to these effects on behavior as learning. Specifically, they define **learning** as any relatively permanent change in behavior, or behavior potential, produced by experience. Several aspects of this definition are noteworthy. First, the term *learning* does not apply to temporary changes in behavior such as those stemming from fatigue, drugs, or illness. Second, it does not refer to changes resulting from maturation—the fact that you change in many ways as you grow and develop. Third, learning can result from *vicarious* as well as from direct experiences; in other words, you can be affected by observing events and behavior in your environment as well as by participating in them (Bandura, 1986). It is important to note that the effects of learning are not always apparent, emphasizing the need to differentiate learning from performance. This highlights the importance of including changes in "behavior potential" in the definition of learning. Finally, the changes produced by learning are not always positive in nature. As you well know, people are as likely to acquire bad habits as good ones.

There can be no doubt that learning is a key process in human behavior. Indeed, it appears to play an important role in virtually every activity we perform. Although the effects of learning are diverse, many psychologists believe that learning itself occurs in a few basic forms: *classical conditioning, operant conditioning,* and *observational learning*. We'll begin with *classical conditioning,* a form of learning in which two stimulus events become associated in such a way that the occurrence of one event reliably predicts the occurrence of the other. Classical conditioning is the basis for many learned fears and also helps explain how we acquire aversions to certain foods or beverages as was evident in the "potato soup episode" described earlier. Next, we'll turn to *operant conditioning,* a form of learning in which organisms acquire associations between behaviors and the stimuli that precede (antecedents) or follow (consequences) them. Here, we'll see how basic operant principles have been instrumental in changing behavior in several important domains ranging from innovative instructional practices and traffic safety to pain control. Finally, we'll explore *observational learning,* a form of learning in which organisms learn by observing the behaviors—and the consequences of the behaviors—of others around them.

CLASSICAL CONDITIONING: LEARNING THAT SOME STIMULI SIGNAL OTHERS

Imagine the following situation. You're visiting friends. It's 7 A.M. and you are drifting somewhere between sleep and waking. In the next room you hear a soft click. Then, almost immediately, you are practically knocked out of bed by a loud noise. You are about to rush out of the room to find out what's happened, when you figure it out: Your friends have switched on the bathroom fan, and, being old, it is extremely noisy. You try to go back to sleep, but your heart is pounding so hard that you decide to get up. Because you are staying with your friends for two weeks, the same events are repeated each morning. Would there be any change in your behavior during this period? The chances are good there would be. Gradually, you might begin to respond not just to the sound of the fan, but to the soft click as well. The reason is simple: Because it is always followed by the noisy fan,

Learning:
Any relatively permanent change in behavior (or behavior potential) resulting from experience.

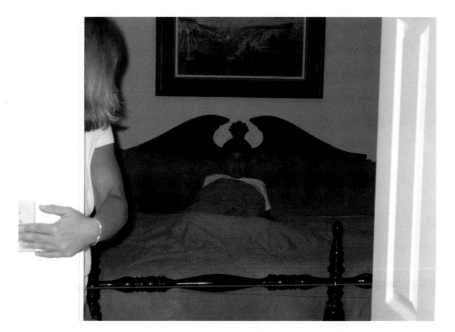

FIGURE 5.1
Classical Conditioning: A Simple Example
At first, the soft "click" of the switch that turns on a noisy bathroom fan would have little effect on your behavior. After the click (a conditioned stimulus, or CS) has been paired with a loud noise (an unconditioned stimulus, or UCS) on several occasions, you might begin to react to the click alone (conditioned response, or CR).

the click comes to serve as a signal for the onset of this loud, irritating sound. In other words, hearing the click, you expect the fan noise to follow, and you react accordingly—you are startled and you experience increased arousal (see Figure 5.1).

This simple incident provides an everyday example of **classical conditioning,** the first type of learning that we will consider. In classical conditioning, a physical event—termed a **stimulus**—that initially does not elicit a particular response gradually acquires the capacity to do so because of repeated pairing with a stimulus that *can* elicit the response. Learning of this type is quite common and seems to play a role in such varied reactions as strong fears, taste aversions, drug tolerance and withdrawal, and even racial or ethnic prejudice (Baron, Byrne, & Branscombe, 2005; Mineka & Zinbarg, 2006; Siegel, 2005). Classical conditioning became the subject of careful study in the early twentieth century, when Ivan Pavlov, a Nobel Prize–winning physiologist from Russia, identified it as an important behavioral process (Pavlov, 1928).

Pavlov's Early Work on Classical Conditioning

Pavlov did not actually set out to investigate classical conditioning. Rather, his research focused on the process of digestion in dogs. During his investigations he noticed a curious fact: The dogs in his studies often began to salivate when they saw or smelled food but *before* they actually tasted it. Some even salivated at the sight of the pan where their food was kept or at the sight or sound of the person who usually brought it. This suggested to Pavlov that these stimuli had somehow become signals for the food itself: The dogs had learned that when the signals were present, food would soon follow.

Pavlov quickly recognized the potential importance of this observation and shifted the focus of his research accordingly. The procedures that he now developed were relatively simple. On *conditioning trials,* a neutral stimulus that had previously been shown to have no effect on salivation—a bell, for example—was presented. This was immediately followed by a second stimulus known to produce a strong effect on salivation: dried meat powder placed directly into the dog's mouth. The meat powder was termed the **unconditioned stimulus (UCS),** because its ability to produce salivation was automatic and did not depend on the

Classical conditioning:
A basic form of learning in which one stimulus comes to serve as a signal for the occurrence of a second stimulus. During classical conditioning, organisms acquire information about the relations between various stimuli, not simple associations between them.

Stimulus:
A physical event capable of affecting behavior.

Unconditioned stimulus (UCS):
In classical conditioning, a stimulus that can evoke an unconditioned response the first time it is presented.

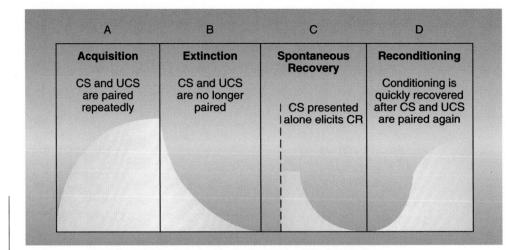

FIGURE 5.2
Acquisition and Extinction of a Conditioned Response
During *acquisition*, the strength of the conditioned response rises rapidly to a point and then levels off (*panel A*). The process of *extinction* begins once the conditioned stimulus is no longer paired with the unconditioned stimulus (*panel B*). As shown in panels C and D, extinction can be disrupted through the processes of *spontaneous recovery* and/or *reconditioning*. Finally, although not shown in the figure, if no subsequent conditioned stimulus–unconditioned stimulus pairings occur, the conditioned response will decrease once again.

Unconditioned response (UCR):
In classical conditioning, the response evoked by an unconditioned stimulus.

Conditioned stimulus (CS):
In classical conditioning, the stimulus that is repeatedly paired with an unconditioned stimulus.

Conditioned response (CR):
In classical conditioning, the response to the conditioned stimulus.

Acquisition:
The process by which a conditioned stimulus acquires the ability to elicit a conditioned response through repeated pairings of an unconditioned stimulus with a conditioned stimulus.

Delay conditioning:
A form of forward conditioning in which the onset of the unconditioned stimulus (UCS) begins while the conditioned stimulus (CS) is still present.

Trace conditioning:
A form of forward conditioning in which the onset of the conditioned stimulus (CS) precedes the onset of the unconditioned stimulus (UCS) and the presentation of the CS and UCS does not overlap.

dog's having learned the response. Similarly, the response of salivation to the meat powder was termed an **unconditioned response (UCR);** it, too, did not depend on previous learning. The bell was termed a **conditioned stimulus (CS),** because its ability to produce salivation depended on its being paired with the meat powder. Finally, salivation in response to the bell was termed a **conditioned response (CR).**

The basic question was whether the sound of the bell would gradually come to elicit salivation in the dogs because of its repeated pairing with the meat powder. In other words, would the bell elicit a CR when it was presented alone? The answer was clearly *yes*. After the bell had been paired repeatedly with the meat powder, the dogs salivated upon hearing it—even when the bell was not followed by the meat powder.

Classical Conditioning: Some Basic Principles

Let's turn now to the principles that govern the occurrence of classical conditioning.

■ Acquisition: The course of classical conditioning.

In most instances, classical conditioning is a gradual process in which a conditioned stimulus gradually acquires the capacity to elicit a CR as a result of repeated pairing with a UCS. This process—termed **acquisition**—proceeds quite rapidly at first, increasing as the number of pairings between CS and UCS increases (see Figure 5.2). However, there is a limit to this effect; after a number of pairings of CS and UCS, acquisition slows down and finally levels off.

Although psychologists initially believed that conditioning was determined primarily by the number of CS-UCS pairings, we now know that this process is affected by other factors. As shown in Figure 5.3, one such factor is *temporal arrangement* of the CS-UCS pairings. Temporal means time-related: the extent to which a CS precedes or follows the presentation of a UCS. The first two temporal arrangements shown, **delay conditioning** and **trace conditioning,** are examples of what is

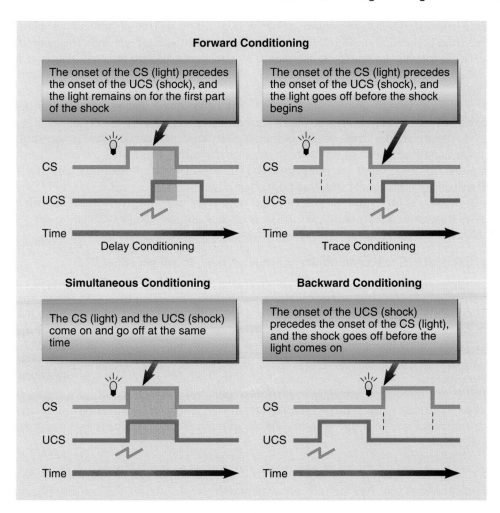

FIGURE 5.3
Temporal Arrangement of the CS and UCS Affects the Acquisition of a Conditioned Response
Four CS-UCS temporal arrangements commonly used in classical conditioning procedures are shown. *Temporal* refers to timing: the extent to which a conditioned stimulus precedes or follows the presentation of an unconditioned stimulus. *Delay conditioning* generally produces the most rapid rate of learning. *Simultaneous* and *backward conditioning* are usually the least effective procedures.

termed *forward conditioning*, because the presentation of the CS (light) always precedes the presentation of the UCS (shock). They differ, however, in that the CS and the UCS overlap to some degree in *delay* conditioning but not in *trace* conditioning. Two other temporal arrangements are **simultaneous conditioning,** in which the conditioned and unconditioned stimuli begin and end at the same time; and **backward conditioning,** in which the UCS precedes the CS.

Delay conditioning is generally the most effective method for establishing a CR, because in delay conditioning, the CS helps predict forthcoming presentations of the UCS (Lieberman, 1990). To illustrate this point, consider the following example: You are taking a shower when suddenly the water turns icy cold. Your response—a startle reaction to the cold water—is a UCR. Now imagine that just before the water turns cold, the plumbing makes a slight grinding sound. Because this sound occurs just before and overlaps with the onset of the icy water, delay conditioning can occur. If this situation is repeated several times, you may acquire a startle reaction to the slight grinding sound; it serves as a CS. In contrast, suppose you do not hear the sound until after the water turns cold, as in backward conditioning, or until the precise instant at which it turns cold, as in simultaneous conditioning. In these cases, you would probably not acquire a startle reaction to the grinding sound, because it provides no information useful in predicting the occurrence of the icy water.

Several additional factors also appear to affect conditioning. In general, conditioning is faster when the *intensity* of either the CS or UCS increases (Kamin, 1965). In other words, conditioning is more likely when conditioned stimuli stand out, relative to other background stimuli. Second, conditioning also depends on the

Simultaneous conditioning:
A form of conditioning in which the conditioned stimulus (CS) and the unconditioned stimulus (UCS) begin and end at the same time.

Backward conditioning:
A type of conditioning in which the presentation of the unconditioned stimulus (UCS) precedes the presentation of the conditioned stimulus (CS).

time interval between presentations of the two stimuli. Extremely short intervals—less than 0.2 second—rarely produce conditioning. In animal research, the optimal CS-UCS interval seems to be between 0.2 and 2 seconds; longer intervals make it difficult for animals to recognize the CS as a signal for some future event (Gordon, 1989). Finally, *familiarity* can greatly affect conditioning. In contrast to the laboratory, in which stimuli selected for study are often novel, many of the potential conditioning stimuli found in the environment are familiar to us. Thus, our day-to-day experiences often teach us that certain stimuli, such as the background noise usually present in an office setting or the odors ordinarily present in our homes, do not predict anything unusual (Lubow, 1998). Interestingly, psychologists' understanding of this last point has important practical implications. Research shows, for example, that children who have uneventful encounters with a dentist prior to a traumatic (painful) experience are less likely to develop dental anxiety than are children with fewer uneventful encounters (Kent, 1997).

■ **Extinction: Once conditioning is acquired, how do we get rid of it?**

Suppose you and your coworkers have been working night and day to prepare a proposal crucial to the survival of the marketing firm for which you work, and things are not going well. During the past week the president of the company has chewed you out at least a dozen times. Now, whenever you hear his approaching footsteps, your heart starts racing and your mouth gets dry, even though he has not yet reached your office. Fortunately, the company's directors are impressed by the proposal, and your boss is no longer angry when he enters your office. Will you continue to react strongly to his footsteps? Probably not. Gradually, his footsteps will cease to elicit the original CR from you. The eventual decline and disappearance of a CR in the absence of an *un*conditioned stimulus is known as **extinction.**

The course of extinction, however, is not always smooth (see Figure 5.2). Let's consider the behavior of one of Pavlov's dogs to see why this is true. After many presentations of a bell (CS) in the absence of meat powder (UCS), the dog no longer salivates in response to the bell. In other words, extinction has occurred. But if the CS (the bell) and the UCS (the meat powder) are again paired after the CR of salivation has been extinguished, salivation will return very quickly—a process termed **reconditioning.**

Or suppose that after extinction, the experiment is interrupted: Pavlov is caught up in another project that keeps him away from his laboratory and the dog for several weeks. Now will the sound of the bell, the CS, elicit salivation? The answer is yes, but the reaction will be in a weakened form. The reappearance of the reaction after a time interval is referred to as **spontaneous recovery.** If extinction is then allowed to continue—that is, if the sound of the bell is presented many times in the absence of meat powder—salivation to the sound of the bell will disappear relatively quickly compared to extinction of the initial CR.

■ **Generalization and discrimination: Responding to similarities and differences.**

Suppose that because of several painful experiences, a child has acquired a strong conditioned fear of hornets: Whenever she sees one or hears one buzzing, she shows strong emotional reactions and heads for the hills. Will she also experience similar reactions to other flying insects, such as flies? She almost certainly will, because of **stimulus generalization,** the tendency of stimuli similar to a CS to elicit similar CRs. The more closely new stimuli resemble the original CS—in this instance, hornets—the stronger the response will be. As you can readily see, stimulus generalization often serves a useful function. In this example, it may indeed save the girl from additional stings. The red lights that we encounter at certain intersections while driving also illustrate the important function served by stimulus generalization: Even though these signals often vary in brightness, shape, or location, we learn to stop in response to all of them, and it's a good thing we do.

Extinction:
The process through which a conditioned stimulus gradually loses the ability to evoke conditioned responses when it is no longer followed by the unconditioned stimulus.

Reconditioning:
The rapid recovery of a conditioned response (CR) to a CS-UCS pairing following extinction.

Spontaneous recovery:
Following extinction, reinstatement of conditioned stimulus–unconditioned stimulus pairings will produce a conditioned response.

Stimulus generalization:
The tendency of stimuli similar to a conditioned stimulus to evoke conditioned responses.

Although stimulus generalization can serve an important adaptive function, it is not always beneficial and in some cases can be dangerous. For example, because of many pleasant experiences with parents and other adult relatives, a young child may become trusting of all adults through stimulus generalization. Unfortunately, this process will not be beneficial if it extends to certain strangers. You can understand why stimulus generalization can be maladaptive—even deadly. Fortunately, most of us avoid such potential problems through **stimulus discrimination**—a process of learning to respond to certain stimuli but not to others. A few years ago a friend was severely bitten by a dog. Until that incident she had no fear of dogs. Because she was so frightened by the attack, I was concerned that the incident would generalize to other breeds of dogs—perhaps even to her own dog. Fortunately, because of stimulus discrimination, this didn't happen; she becomes fearful only when she encounters the breed of dog that bit her (see Figure 5.4).

KEY QUESTIONS

- What is learning?
- What is classical conditioning?
- Upon what factors does acquisition of a classically conditioned response depend?
- What is extinction?
- What is the difference between stimulus generalization and stimulus discrimination?

Classical Conditioning: The Neural Basis of Learning

Now that we've discussed the basic principles of classical conditioning, let's turn to another question that has puzzled scientists for many years: What is the neural basis of this and other kinds of learning? Psychologists have started to unravel this mystery, at least for some forms of learned behavior (Brembs, 2003; Daum & Schugens, 1996; Schoenbaum et al., 2003; Woodruff-Pak, 1999).

Research with animals, for example, has resulted in nearly complete identification of the neural circuitry that underlies eyeblink classical conditioning (Steinmetz, 1996; Thompson et al., 1997). To establish eyeblink classical conditioning, scientists repeatedly pair the presentation of a stimulus that does not ordinarily cause us to blink, say a tone or a light (a CS), with one that does, say a puff of air to the eye (a UCS). People and other animals quickly learn to blink in response to the light or tone (a CR). The site essential to the acquisition and performance of this type of CR is the cerebellum. When the cerebellum of animals is surgically destroyed, previously learned associations can be severely disrupted, and the ability to learn new associations eliminated altogether (Thompson & Krupa, 1994). Other brain structures known to be involved in eyeblink conditioning include the hippocampus, amygdala, and brain-stem areas that project to or receive information from the cerebellum (Rorick-Kehn & Steinmetz, 2005; Christian & Thompson, 2005).

Studies of humans who have sustained damage to the cerebellum or related structures reveal a similar pattern of results. These persons blink normally (UCR) in response to a puff of air to the eye (UCS), indicating that their motor functions and ability to respond to external stimulation remains intact. However, efforts to establish a CR to, say, a light or a tone are usually unsuccessful (Daum & Shugens, 1996; Topka et al., 1993).

Because the neural circuitry underlying eyeblink classical conditioning is so well known, behavioral researchers have begun to use this procedure to investigate a variety of basic processes in humans (see Ivkovich et al., 1999; Clark & Squire, 1999), including the biological correlates of certain mental disorders. For example, we know that the symptoms experienced by people with *obsessive–compulsive disorder* arise from learned associations that are maladaptive and particularly resistant to extinction. Obsessive–compulsive disorder is characterized by intrusive, unwanted, and uncontrollable thoughts, images, compulsions, or

FIGURE 5.4
The Adaptive Function of Stimulus Discrimination
People who have undergone traumatic experiences, such as being bitten by an unfamiliar dog, sometimes become fearful of *all* dogs because of *stimulus generalization*—the tendency of stimuli similar to a conditioned stimulus to elicit similar conditioned responses. Fortunately, many people are able to avoid such problems through *stimulus discrimination*—the process of learning to respond to certain stimuli (the breed of dog that bit the person), but not others.

Stimulus discrimination:
The process by which organisms learn to respond to certain stimuli but not to others.

urges that are often accompanied by repetitive behaviors or mental acts that the person feels driven to perform (see Chapter 11 for additional information). Interestingly, eyeblink classical conditioning appears to proceed much more quickly in individuals who exhibit these tendencies than in those who do not, suggesting that some people may be biologically predisposed to establish associations between feelings of fear and anxiety and otherwise neutral objects (Tracey et al., 1999). Clearly, these findings will play an important role in designing more effective treatments for obsessive–compulsive disorder or, conversely, in learning how to prevent the development of the maladaptive associations that characterize this disorder altogether.

More recent research with humans has identified the parts of the brain involved in the acquisition, storage, and expression of learned fears, which, in turn, may help psychologists develop more effective ways to treat them (see Cheng et al., 2003; LeDoux, 2000). Although scientists are just beginning to understand the complex relationship between brain functions and behavior in humans, it is clear that our knowledge of the neural basis of learning is expanding at a rapid pace, and that it has important practical applications—for instance, in developing better treatments for various forms of psychological disorders.

Classical Conditioning: Exceptions to the Rules

When psychologists began the systematic study of learning at the turn of the twentieth century, they saw their task as that of establishing general principles of learning— principles that applied equally well to all organisms and to all stimuli. Beginning in the 1960s, however, some puzzling findings seemed to indicate that not all organisms learn all responses or all associations between stimuli with equal ease.

The most dramatic evidence pointing to such conclusions was reported by Garcia and colleagues (Braverman & Bronstein, 1985; Garcia, Hankins, & Rusiniak, 1974). In perhaps the most famous of these studies, Garcia and Koelling (1966) allowed two groups of rats to sip saccharin-flavored water from a device that emitted a bright flashing light and a loud clicking noise (conditioned stimuli) whenever the rats licked the water. While both groups were drinking, one group of rats was exposed to X-rays that later made them sick (a UCS); the other group received painful shocks to their feet (also a UCS). Traditional principles of classical conditioning suggest that *both* groups of rats should have learned to avoid all three stimuli—the flavored water, the bright light, and the clicking noise. After all, for both groups, these stimuli were followed by a strong UCS (either X-rays or a painful shock). But this was not what Garcia and Koelling found. Rats exposed to the painful shock learned to avoid the light and noise but not the flavored water; rats that were made to feel ill learned to avoid the flavored water but not the light or noise (see Figure 5.5). In short, it seems that rats—and other organisms—are predisposed to associate nausea and dizziness with something they've consumed (the flavored water) and to associate pain with something they've seen or heard (the bright light and clicking noise). Similar findings from many different studies suggest that acquisition of a CR does *not* occur with equal ease for different stimuli.

Further research has also shown that in regard to conditioning, important differences exist among species. Because of these **biological constraints on learning,** types of conditioning readily accomplished by some species are only slowly acquired by others. And often, the types of conditioning most readily accomplished by one species are the very ones it needs to survive in its normal habitat (Shettleworth, 1993). For example, rats eat a varied diet and are most active at night. Thus, it is especially useful for them to be able to associate specific tastes with later illness, because in many cases they can't see the foods they eat. In contrast, birds depend heavily on vision for finding food. For a bird it is more useful to be able to form associations between visual cues and later illness (Wilcoxon, Dragoin, & Kral, 1971).

Biological constraints on learning:
Refers to how all forms of conditioning are not equally easy to establish with all organisms.

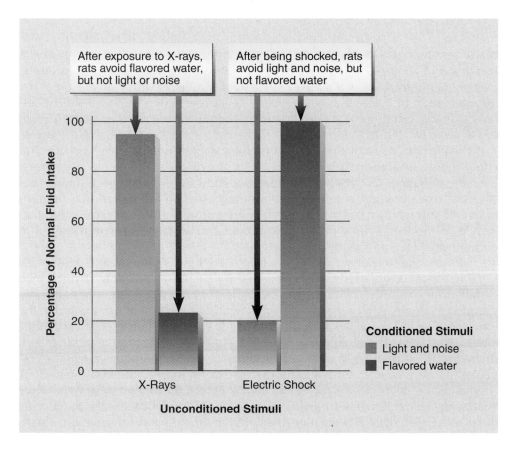

FIGURE 5.5
Biological Constraints and Characteristics of the CS and UCS Affect the Acquisition of a Conditioned Response
Rats quickly acquired an aversion to a flavored water when it was followed by X-rays that made them sick, but they did *not* readily acquire an aversion to the flavored water when it was followed by an electric shock. In contrast, rats learned to avoid a light-noise combination when it was paired with shock but *not* when it was followed by X-rays. These findings indicate that classical conditioning cannot be established with equal ease for all stimuli and for all organisms.
Source: Based on data from Garcia & Koelling, 1966.

Another intriguing outcome that emerged from Garcia and Koelling's study is also noteworthy: Although the rats who received the X-rays did not get sick immediately, they still acquired an aversion to the taste of the flavored water. This finding contradicted the widely held belief that classical conditioning can occur only if the UCS follows the CS within a very short interval. **Conditioned taste aversions** are important for survival because they inhibit the repeated ingestion of dangerous and toxic substances in animals' natural environments. The way in which these powerful associations are formed differs from most classical conditioning in several important respects. First, a conditioned taste aversion can usually be established with a single CS-UCS pairing, termed *one-trial learning*, in contrast to the many pairings involved in most Pavlovian conditioning. Second, conditioned taste aversions have been reported when the CS was presented hours before the occurrence of the UCS. In contrast, most instances of conditioning require a CS-UCS interval of not more than a few seconds. Finally, conditioned taste aversions are extremely resistant to extinction; in fact, they may last a lifetime, as illustrated by the potato soup example described at the beginning of this chapter. Fortunately, researchers have discovered ways to help people avoid developing conditioned taste aversions and we'll discuss these later in this chapter.

Conditioned taste aversion:
A type of conditioning in which the UCS (usually internal cues associated with nausea or vomiting) occurs several hours after the CS (often a novel food) leading to a strong CS-UCS association in a single trial.

KEY QUESTIONS
- Where in the brain does classical conditioning take place?
- Is classical conditioning equally easy to establish with all stimuli for all organisms?
- How do we acquire conditioned taste aversions?

Classical Conditioning: A Cognitive Perspective

Many psychologists believe that classical conditioning involves more than just formation of a simple association between stimuli. We now know, for example, that regular pairing of a CS with a UCS provides subjects with valuable *predictive* information; it indicates that whenever a CS is presented, a UCS will shortly follow. Thus, as conditioning proceeds, subjects acquire the *expectation* that a CS will be followed by a UCS.

The idea that cognitive processes involving expectation play a role in classical conditioning is supported by several types of evidence (Kirsch et al., in press; Rescorla & Wagner, 1972; Stewart-Williams & Podd, 2004). First, conditioning fails to occur when unconditioned and conditioned stimuli are paired in a random manner. With random pairings, subjects cannot acquire any firm expectation that a UCS will indeed follow presentation of a CS. Therefore, for conditioning to occur, the CS-UCS pairing must be consistent.

Second, the cognitive thesis is supported by a phenomenon known as *blocking*—the fact that conditioning to one stimulus may be prevented by previous conditioning to another stimulus. For example, suppose that a dog is initially conditioned to a tone. After repeated pairings with presentation of meat powder, the tone becomes a CS, capable of causing the dog to salivate. Then a second stimulus, a light, is added to the situation. It, too, occurs just before the presentation of food. If classical conditioning occurs in an automatic manner, simply as a result of repeated pairings of a CS with a UCS, then the light, too, should become a CS: It should elicit salivation when presented alone. In fact, this does not happen. Why? Again, an explanation in terms of expectancies is helpful. Because the meat powder is already predicted by the tone, the light provides no new information. Therefore, it is of little predictive value to the subjects and fails to become a CS.

The idea that cognitive processes play a role in classical conditioning is also supported by studies of mental imagery (Dadds et al., 1997). Research suggests that the cognitive processes underlying the generation, manipulation, and scanning of mental images closely mirror the processes involved in perceiving actual physical stimuli (Kosslyn, 1994). Studies using brain imaging techniques indicate that areas of the brain known to be involved in visual processing are also active during visual imagery tasks (Farah, 1988; Kosslyn & Thompson, 2003).

Mental images of physical stimuli also appear to elicit reactions that closely resemble the ones elicited by their physical counterparts (see Figure 5.6). For example, asking people to *imagine* drinking a sour solution causes them to salivate as if they were actually drinking it; in contrast, asking people to drink a glass of water does not (Barber, Chauncey, & Winer, 1964).

FIGURE 5.6
Cognitive Processes and Classical Conditioning
As illustrated by this example, mental images of certain stimuli can sometimes elicit reactions that closely resemble the ones elicited by their physical counterparts, evidence of the powerful role of cognitive processes in conditioning.

Classical Conditioning: Turning Principles into Action

Before concluding, we should call attention to how knowledge of the basic principles of classical conditioning has been put to many practical uses to help people. One of the earliest applications of classical conditioning was in the treatment of learned fears, or **phobias,** an issue we'll discuss in Chapter 12. These principles have also been applied to other important problems, and we'll consider these next.

■ Classical conditioning and drug overdose.

Knowledge of conditioning processes has helped to explain some instances of drug overdose. For example, it is well known that certain drugs become less effective over time. But why does this occur? One possibility is that when a person uses drugs in a particular context repeatedly, the stimuli in that environment become conditioned stimuli and so elicit a CR (Siegel, 2005; Siegel & Ramos, 2002). For certain addictive drugs, this CR can be just the opposite of the UCR. Such learned responses have been termed *conditional compensatory responses*, or CCRs.

This suggests that environmental cues associated with the environment in which drugs are consumed serve as conditioned stimuli and prepare drug users' bodies partially to counteract the effects of the drug. Drug users who have nearly died following drug use commonly report something unusual about the environment in which they took the drug (Siegel, 1984). Often these environmental differences are quite subtle, a fact that emphasizes the powerful effects produced by conditioning. These results have important implications for drug treatment, because the environments to which former drug users return often contain cues that may produce drug-related CRs, such as withdrawal symptoms and drug cravings (Ehrman et al., 1992). Researchers have compared relapse rates among treated drug users who have either returned to environments rich in drug-associated cues or relocated to an environment very different from that in which they used drugs. The relocated patients generally show far less relapse (Siegel & Ramos, 2002).

■ Classical conditioning and the immune system.

Research also indicates that it is possible to alter the immune system through classical conditioning (Ader et al., 1993; Husband et al., 1993). In one study, Alvarez-Borda and colleagues (1995) used classical conditioning to enhance specific immune functions in rats. On conditioning day, one group of rats was allowed to drink a distinctive beverage—saccharin-flavored water (the CS)—before receiving an injection of a substance (the UCS) known to raise the level of certain antibodies in their systems. A second group of rats received only water before receiving the same injection. As predicted, both groups showed an enhanced immune response (UCR) to the injection. Then, after the effects of the injection had faded (more than a month later), the researchers tested to see if conditioning had taken place. Half the rats that had been exposed to saccharin-flavored water during conditioning were again exposed to saccharin-flavored water, while the other half received only water. The group that had received only water during conditioning also received water during the test trial. The researchers' predictions were supported: Reexposure to the saccharin-flavored water (the CS) resulted in a significant elevation of antibodies in these rats, even though no further injections (the UCS) were given. In contrast, there was no enhanced immune response in the other groups; measurements indicated that antibody levels in these rats were not significantly different from levels assessed prior to conditioning.

Research suggests that conditioning can be also effective in enhancing aspects of the immune systems of humans (Miller & Cohen, 2001). Together, these results show that conditioning can exert powerful effects on the immune system—even in the absence of the original substance that produced it. As you may have guessed already, the implications of these results are enormous. Indeed, they offer

Phobia:
An irrational conditioned fear of some object or event.

tremendous hope to people whose health is compromised due to depressed immune systems—for example, persons who are HIV-positive or have AIDS.

■ **Classical conditioning and learned taste aversions.**

As we've noted previously, conditioned taste aversions are important for survival because they help animals to avoid repeated ingestion of dangerous and toxic substances in their natural environments. Research shows that food or beverage aversions are very common among humans, too, as was evident in the potato soup example at the beginning of this chapter.

Conditioned taste aversions create serious problems for some people. For example, radiation and chemotherapy used to treat cancer often cause nausea or vomiting as a side effect (Burish & Carey, 1986). Thus, cancer patients may acquire taste aversions to food ingested before therapy sessions. Research shows that even thinking about the sight or smell of these foods can produce anticipatory nausea and vomiting in some patients.

Fortunately, patients receiving chemotherapy can reduce the likelihood of developing a conditioned taste aversion. First, they should arrange their meal schedules to decrease the chances of establishing an association between ingestion of the food and illness; the interval between their meals and chemotherapy should be as long as possible. Second, patients should eat familiar food, avoiding new or unusual foods before therapy. Because familiar foods have already been associated with feeling good, it is less likely that cancer patients will acquire an aversion to them. Finally, because the strength of a CR is related to the intensity of the CS, patients should eat bland foods and avoid strongly flavored ones; foods with strong odors, such as chocolate and coffee, may frequently become the targets for aversions (Bernstein, 1999).

Interestingly, conditioned taste aversion has also been used to treat alcohol dependency. How? By pairing environmental stimuli associated with ingestion of a beverage containing alcohol with a substance that makes the people involved sick. Participants who agree to this type of therapy are given a solution to drink that makes them sick. Just before the nausea is expected to occur, they are then offered a drink of their preferred alcoholic beverage to smell, swirl around in their mouth, and spit out. The nauseous feelings they experience, which can last up to several hours, become associated with the sight, smell, and taste of the alcohol. This basic procedure is repeated across several days and participants are exposed to many different types of beer, wine, and distilled sprits to generalize the conditioned aversion to a range of alcoholic flavors. Subsequently, stimuli that once prompted a desire to consume alcohol now result in nausea. Indeed, the mere sight or smell of an alcoholic beverage can bring on a strong aversive reaction in people who undergo this treatment (Howard, 2001). It is important to note, however, that the procedures just described are not equally effective for all people exposed to it. A number of factors—including level of alcohol dependence and prior experience with nausea and vomiting after consuming alcohol—tend to reduce its effectiveness. As you can see, classical conditioning may be a very basic form of learning, but it is also powerful, frequent, and general, and as a result, often has strong effects on important aspects of our behavior.

KEY QUESTIONS

• How do modern views of classical conditioning differ from earlier perspectives?
• What is blocking?
• How can classical conditioning principles solve problems of everyday life?

FIGURE 5.7
Operant Conditioning: Learning Based on Consequences
Operant conditioning is a form of learning in which behavior is maintained, or changed, through consequences. The views politicians express are often shaped by the reactions of those who listen—or by the results of polls.

OPERANT CONDITIONING: LEARNING BASED ON CONSEQUENCES

When a local politician started his campaign for state office, his speeches contained many remarks about the need for higher spending. He would note, with considerable passion, that the state's schools were in serious trouble, its roads and bridges were falling apart, and that the salaries paid to its employees were below the national average. The crowds he addressed, however, weren't favorably impressed by these views. Whenever he mentioned raising taxes, many people would shake their heads, boo, or get up to leave. Now, several months later, his speeches have an entirely different flavor. He rarely, if ever, mentions the need for higher spending. Instead, he emphasizes efficiency—getting full value from every tax dollar spent. And when he makes such remarks, people smile, applaud, and cheer (see Figure 5.7).

What happened here? Why did this politician change the nature of his speeches? The answer should be obvious: As many politicians do, he changed his remarks in response to the consequences they produced. Statements that yielded hisses and boos from voters decreased in frequency, while those that yielded applause and cheers increased. In other words, he learned to perform behaviors that produced positive outcomes and to avoid behaviors that yielded negative ones. This process is known as *operant conditioning* and it is the second major form of learning we will consider.

The Nature of Operant Conditioning: Consequential Operations

In situations involving **operant conditioning,** the probability that a given response will occur changes depending on the consequences that follow it. Psychol-

Operant conditioning:
A process through which organisms learn to repeat behaviors that yield positive outcomes or that permit them to avoid or escape from negative outcomes.

ogists generally agree that these probabilities are determined through four basic procedures, two of which strengthen or increase the rate of behavior and two of which weaken or decrease the rate of behavior. Procedures that *strengthen* behavior are termed *reinforcement*, whereas those that *suppress* behavior are termed *punishment*.

■ Reinforcement.

There are actually two types of **reinforcement:** positive reinforcement and negative reinforcement. *Positive reinforcement* involves the impact of **positive reinforcers**—stimulus events or consequences that strengthen responses that precede them. In other words, if a consequence of some action increases the probability that the action will occur again in the future, that consequence is functioning as a positive reinforcer. Some positive reinforcers seem to exert these effects because they are related to basic biological needs. Such *primary reinforcers* include food when we are hungry, water when we are thirsty, and sexual pleasure. In contrast, other events acquire their capacity to act as positive reinforcers through association with primary reinforcers. Such *conditioned* reinforcers include money, status, grades, trophies, and praise from others.

Preferred activities can also be used to reinforce *less*-preferred activities, a principle referred to as the **Premack principle.** If you recall hearing "You must clean your room before you can watch TV" or "You must eat your vegetables before you get dessert" when you were growing up, then you're already familiar with this principle. As you can guess, the Premack principle is a powerful tool for changing behavior.

Please note that a stimulus event that functions as a positive reinforcer at one time or in one context may have a different effect at another time or in another place. For example, food may serve as a positive reinforcer when you are hungry, but not when you are ill or just after you finish a large meal. Also, at least where people are concerned, many individual differences exist. Clearly, a stimulus that functions as a positive reinforcer for one person may fail to operate in a similar manner for another person. We will return to this important point later on in this chapter.

Negative reinforcement involves the impact of **negative reinforcers**—stimuli that strengthen responses that permit an organism to avoid or escape from their presence. Thus, when we perform an action that allows us to *escape* from a negative reinforcer that is already present or to *avoid* the threatened application of one altogether, our tendency to perform this action in the future increases (see Figure 5.8). Some negative reinforcers, such as intense heat, extreme cold, or electric shock, exert their effects the first time they are encountered, whereas others acquire their impact through repeated association.

Many examples of negative reinforcement can be found in our everyday lives. To illustrate this, imagine the following scene. On a particularly cold and dark winter morning, you're sleeping soundly in a warm, comfortable bed. Suddenly, the alarm clock across the room begins to wail. Getting out of your cozy bed is the last thing you want to do, but you find the noise intolerable. What do you do? If you get up to turn off the alarm—or, on subsequent mornings, get up early to avoid hearing the sound of the alarm altogether—your behavior has been *negatively* reinforced. In other words, your tendency to perform actions that allow you to escape from or avoid the sound of the alarm clock has increased. Another everyday example of negative reinforcement occurs when parents give in to their children's tantrums—especially in public places, such as restaurants and shopping malls. Over time, the parent's tendency to give in may increase, because doing so stops the screaming. In short, the parent's behavior has been negatively reinforced.

To repeat, then, *both positive and negative reinforcement are procedures that strengthen or increase behavior.* Positive reinforcers are stimulus events that

---

Reinforcement:
A procedure by which the application or removal of a stimulus increases the strength of a specific behavior.

Positive reinforcers:
Stimuli that strengthen responses that precede them.

Premack principle:
The principle that a more preferred activity can be used to reinforce a less preferred activity.

Negative reinforcers:
Stimuli that strengthen responses that permit the organism to avoid or escape from their presence.

strengthen responses that precede them, whereas negative reinforcers are stimulus events that strengthen responses that lead to their termination or avoidance.

■ Punishment.

In contrast to reinforcement, **punishment** refers to procedures that weaken or decrease the rate of behavior. As with reinforcement, there are two types of punishment: positive punishment and negative punishment. In *positive punishment*, behaviors are followed by stimulus events termed *punishers*. In such instances, we learn not to perform these actions, because aversive consequences—punishers—will follow. And this highlights a point about which there is often much confusion. Contrary to what common sense seems to suggest, punishment is *not* the same as negative reinforcement. Here is an example to illustrate the difference. Imagine that you are driving home in a hurry, exceeding the speed limit. A sick sensation creeps into your stomach as you become aware of flashing lights and a siren. A state trooper has detected you speeding. Your eyes bug out when you see how much the ticket will cost you, and after paying that fine, you now obey the posted speed limit. This is an example of the impact of *punishment*—an unpleasant outcome follows your speeding, so the chances that you will speed in the future *decrease*. Now imagine that a year later you are again caught speeding. Apparently the punishment suppressed your speeding behavior only temporarily. Because you are a past offender, the judge handling your case gives you an interesting choice: either attend a month-long series of driver education classes or lose your driver's license. To avoid losing your license, you attend every class. This is an example of *negative reinforcement*: You attend the driver education classes to *avoid* an aversive event—the loss of your license.

In *negative punishment*, the rate of a behavior is weakened or decreased because it is linked to the loss of potential reinforcement (Catania, 1992; Millenson & Leslie, 1979). For example, parents frequently attempt to decrease the frequency of certain behaviors of their teenagers (e.g., hitting younger siblings or talking back to their parents) by temporarily denying them access to reinforcers, such as driving the family car on weekend dates. Negative punishment is also commonly referred to as "time-out," a procedure you may have experienced as a youngster growing up. Thus, both positive and negative punishment are procedures that weaken or decrease behavior. For more information on how parents can put the procedures described here to good use in helping their children develop into happy, healthy adults, please refer to the following **Psychology Lends a Hand** section on page 174.

Thanks to his new rotting carcass cologne, Bill never had problems finding a seat on the subway.

FIGURE 5.8

Negative Reinforcement: A Simple Example

Negative reinforcement involves the impact of negative reinforcers—stimuli that strengthen responses that permit an organism to avoid or escape from their presence. In this example, the other subway riders are moving away to *escape* the stench of Bill's new cologne. On future rides, they may *avoid* getting close to Bill altogether.

Source: Close to Home © 2006 John McPherson. Reprinted with permission of Universal Press Syndicate. All rights reserved.

KEY QUESTIONS

- What is operant conditioning?
- What are examples of primary reinforcers? Of conditioned reinforcers?
- Which operant techniques strengthen behavior? Weaken behavior?
- How do negative reinforcement and punishment differ?

Punishment:
A procedure by which the application or removal of a stimulus decreases the strength of a behavior.

PSYCHOLOGY LENDS A HAND

Spare the Rod, Spoil the Child? The Wisdom of Using Punishment with Children

One of the most controversial issues concerning the use of punishment centers on whether parents should use corporal punishment with their children; in other words, whether parents should spank them for their misbehavior. A large body of research spanning more than fifty years seems to cast doubt on both the appropriateness and effectiveness of corporal punishment as a disciplinary tool (Gershoff, 2002). Why? There are several reasons that we'll explore here.

Problems Associated with the Use of Punishment

Although corporal punishment can be effective at temporarily suppressing problem behaviors or getting children to comply with their parents' requests, there can also be significant negative side effects associated with its use.

One problem is that, over time, milder forms of punishment can escalate into physical abuse (see Wolfe, 1987; Zigler & Hall, 1989). Why does this happen? Earlier in this chapter we learned that when behavior is rewarded it tends to be repeated. If a parent punishes misbehavior with a spanking and the behavior stops, the parent's use of corporal punishment is negatively reinforced by the termination of the child's misbehavior; the child's cessation of the misbehavior is negatively reinforced by the termination of the parent's punishment. In such a scenario, we would predict that both parental punishment (perhaps at increasing levels of severity) and the child's compliance to it will continue.

A second problem is that some children might become angry after experiencing physical punishment, particularly if they believe they were punished unfairly or inappropriately (Izard, 1991). Children's anger at being spanked can erode bonds of trust and closeness and lead them to withdraw or avoid their parents. In some instances, they may even retaliate against the parents. Such acts of aggression may become particularly dangerous as children get older—and stronger.

A third potential problem with the use of physical punishment is that it models aggression. As we'll learn a bit later in this chapter, modeling and imitation are thought to be key learning mechanisms by which children become aggressive. Because children see aggression modeled, in the form of corporal punishment, and rewarded, in the form of their own compliance with it, they learn that aggression is an effective way to manipulate other people's behavior.

The Use of Punishment as a Disciplinary Tool

Psychologists and other professionals are still divided on the question of whether the potential benefits of using corporal punishment outweigh the risks. Those opposed to its use argue that corporal punishment is not only ineffective, but also harmful (see American Academy of Pediatrics, 1998; Straus, Sugarman, & Giles-Sims, 1997; Straus & Stewart, 1999).

Proponents of corporal punishment suggest that it can be used effectively in some circumstances—for example, if a child's behavior is aggressive or is a threat to his or her own or others' safety (see Baumrind, 1996; Larzelere, 1998). They defend their position by pointing to research documenting the conditions under which punishment is effective (see Domjan, 2000). To be effective, punishment must be immediate, consistent (applied after every offense), sufficiently intense (at least for the first offense), and delivered without warning.

Unfortunately, these conditions are usually difficult to meet. To illustrate this last point, consider a situation in which a child throws a tantrum in a shopping mall because his parents refuse to purchase a toy that he wants them to buy. Are they likely to follow each of the conditions outlined above? Probably not, in part because of the public attention they might draw from their actions. Parents may instead choose to give in to the child's tantrums by buying the toy, threatening him with a later punishment (e.g., "Just wait until we get home!"), or leaving the store altogether. Should they choose to punish the child on the spot, there is a chance they may be overly harsh, particularly if they are angry at the time.

Please note that these results do not mean that all children who experience corporal punishment turn out to be aggressive or suffer other lasting adverse effects. Research by Baumrind

Operant Conditioning: Some Basic Principles

In classical conditioning, organisms learn associations between stimuli: Certain stimulus events predict the occurrence of others that naturally trigger a specific response. In addition, the responses performed are generally *involuntary*. In other words, they are *elicited*—pulled out of the organism—by a specific UCS in an automatic manner; for example, salivation to the taste of food, blinking the eyes in response to a puff of air.

In operant conditioning, in contrast, organisms learn associations between particular *behaviors* and the consequences that follow them. Additionally, the responses involved in operant conditioning are more voluntary and are *emitted* by organisms in a given environment. To understand the nature of this form of conditioning, then, we

P S Y C H O L O G Y   L E N D S   A   H A N D

(1996) seems to indicate that the consequences of spanking vary, depending on the quality of the parent–child relationship. Children who have a warm relationship with their parents, have not experienced any violence in the home, and are spanked only as a last resort tend not to suffer any long-term consequences. Additional evidence indicates that although a large majority of Americans are spanked as children (Straus & Stewart, 1999), most people do not suffer any long-term effects from it.

What Can Parents Do to Address Problem Behaviors?

So, given the potential drawbacks of using punishment, what can parents do to get their children to behave appropriately? Fortunately, there are a number of effective alternatives to corporal punishment. One procedure that works particularly well with young children is time-out (from reinforcement). As the name implies, time-out means removing a child from toys or activities that she likes whenever she misbehaves. In practice, this typically means placing the child in a chair in a quiet corner for a few minutes (under supervision, of course!), then giving the child the opportunity to behave appropriately once time-out has ended. With older children, corrective action may take the form of removing privileges for a prescribed period of time, contingent on the cessation of the misbehavior or the performance of desired behavior (e.g., doing their homework).

You might have noticed that the procedures just described are examples of negative punishment (see the earlier section on punishment). Procedures involving positive reinforcement are also effective (see Figure 5.9). Please remember, however, that all people—including children—have different likes and dislikes, so it is important to select rewards that are appropriate and appealing. One technique for handling this issue with young children involves a system in which they earn tokens (secondary reinforcers) for instances of good behavior. Over time, they can accumulate and then trade these in for valued activities (e.g., miniature golf, going to the movies) or toys. Older children often receive a weekly al-

lowance, which, again, can be made contingent on meeting their responsibilities (e.g., completion of their homework and chores)—and, of course, good behavior. Regardless of age, children generally appreciate receiving genuine praise for their good deeds, so it is important that parents regularly acknowledge and encourage desirable behaviors. By consistently reinforcing appropriate behavior, so goes the argument, it is less likely that problem behaviors will occur.

FIGURE 5.9
Positive Approaches to Discipline
Psychologists have developed numerous approaches to parenting that focus on rewarding "good" behavior, including praise and the use of secondary reinforcers that children can exchange for valued activities and toys. The idea is that by consistently reinforcing appropriate behavior, problem behaviors are less likely to occur.

must address two basic questions: Why are certain behaviors emitted in the first place? Once they occur, what factors determine the frequency with which they are repeated?

■ **Shaping and chaining: Getting behaviors started and then putting them all together.**

Many of the behaviors that we perform each day require little conscious effort on our part. But what about new forms of behavior with which we are unfamiliar? How are these behaviors initially established? The answer involves a procedure known as shaping.

In essence, **shaping** is based on the principle that a little can eventually go a long way. Subjects receive a reward for each small step toward a final goal—the

Shaping:
A technique in which closer and closer approximations to desired behavior are required for the delivery of positive reinforcement.

FIGURE 5.10
A Demonstration of Shaping and Chaining
The dual processes of shaping and chaining help to explain the development of complex behavior. Please note, however, that *complex*, is a relative term—relative to the abilities and limitations of each organism.

target response—rather than only for the final response. At first, actions even remotely resembling the target behavior—termed *successive approximations*—are followed by a reward. Gradually, closer and closer approximations of the final target behavior are required before the reward is given. Shaping, then, helps organisms acquire, or construct, new and more complex forms of behavior from simpler behavior.

What about even more complex sequences of behavior, such as the routines performed by certain animals? (See Figure 5.10.) These behaviors can be cultivated by a procedure called **chaining,** in which trainers establish a sequence, or chain, of responses, the last of which leads to a reward. Trainers usually begin chaining by first shaping the final response. When this response is well established, the trainer shapes responses earlier in the chain, then reinforces them by giving the animal the opportunity to perform responses later in the chain, the last of which produces the reinforcer. Shaping and chaining obviously have important implications for human behavior. For example, when working with a beginning student, a skilled dance teacher or ski instructor may use shaping techniques to establish basic skills, such as performing a basic step or standing on the skis without falling down, by praising simple accomplishments. As training progresses, however, the student may receive praise only when he or she successfully completes an entire sequence or chain of actions, such as skiing down a small slope.

Shaping and chaining techniques can produce dramatic effects. In one study, researchers investigated whether shaping could help cocaine users kick their drug habit (Preston et al., 2001). For eight weeks, cocaine users in a methadone maintenance program were given the opportunity to earn vouchers that were exchangeable for goods and services that were consistent with a drug-free lifestyle (e.g., movie passes, exercise equipment). Half the participants (the abstinence group) were rewarded for cocaine-free urine samples only, whereas the other half (the shaping group) were rewarded for each urine specimen with a 25 percent or more decrease in cocaine metabolite during the first three weeks and then only for cocaine-free urine specimens during the last five weeks. The results showed that during the last five weeks, cocaine use was lower among participants in the shaping group, suggesting that shaping was useful in helping them to curb their drug use.

■ **The role of reward delay in impulsiveness and procrastination.**

Operant conditioning usually proceeds faster as the *magnitude* of the reward that follows each response increases. But the effectiveness of rewards can be dramatically affected by *reward delay*—the amount of time that elapses before the reward is delivered. In general, longer delays produce poorer levels of performance (Capaldi, 1978). Children, for example, will often choose smaller, immediate rewards over rewards of greater value that they must wait to receive, a tendency sometimes referred to as *impulsiveness* (Green, Fry, & Myerson, 1994; Logue, 1988). Adults frequently engage in impulsive behavior, too, even when the long-term consequences for their impulsiveness are deadly. Smokers and heavy drinkers, for instance, choose the immediate pleasures they derive from smoking or consuming alcoholic beverages over the potentially negative consequences they may suffer later on, such as cancer (Rachlin, 1995; Steele & Josephs, 1990).

The processes underlying impulsive behavior just discussed also seem to describe another type of behavior with which you may be familiar: *procrastination*— the tendency to put off until tomorrow what we should do today. The decision fac-

Chaining:
A procedure that establishes a sequence of responses that lead to a reward following the terminal or final response in the chain.

ing procrastinators is whether to perform a smaller, less effortful task now or a larger, more effortful task later. Although the most efficient decision in terms of time and effort is obvious—do the less effortful task now—research shows that people, and animals, often choose the more delayed alternative, even when it leads to more work (see Mazur, 1996).

Research seems to indicate that procrastination can even exert negative effects on our health, including higher levels of stress and illness. In one semester-long study of college students, researchers told students at the beginning of the term that they would be required to write a term paper and were given a completion deadline (Tice & Baumeister, 1997). Procrastinators were identified by their scores on standardized measures designed to assess this tendency. The researchers also obtained several measures of stress, health, and performance at several points during the semester. As expected, students who were late in handing in the required paper scored much higher on the procrastination scales than students who handed their papers in on time. Moreover, procrastinators did not benefit from the extra time available to them to absorb course-related information, as they received significantly lower grades on the paper and exams than nonprocrastinators.

The results also revealed intriguing differences between procrastinators and nonprocrastinators in terms of their reported levels of stress and illness. Procrastinators reported significantly fewer symptoms of illness at the beginning of the term than nonprocrastinators. However, this relationship was reversed at the end of the term, when procrastinators reported significantly more stress and symptoms of illness than nonprocrastinators. These results seem to suggest that procrastination can be explained, at least in part, by people's tendency to follow the path of least resistance. In other words, we tend to procrastinate because of the short-term benefits that it provides to us. Unfortunately, as this study illustrates, these benefits are later outweighed by the negative effects that procrastinating exerts on many aspects of our performance and health.

■ **Schedules of reinforcement: Different rules for delivery of payoffs.**

Through experience, you may already realize that, under natural conditions, reinforcement is often an uncertain event. Sometimes a given response yields a reward every time it occurs, but sometimes it does not. For example, smiling at someone you don't know may produce a return smile and additional positive outcomes. On other occasions it may be followed by a suspicious frown or other sign of rejection. Similarly, putting coins into a soda machine usually produces a soft drink. Sometimes, though, you lose the money.

In these cases, the occurrence or nonoccurrence of reinforcement seems to be random or unpredictable. In many other instances, though, it is governed by rules. For example, paychecks are given out on certain days of the month; free pizzas or car washes are provided to customers who have purchased a specific amount of products or services. Do such rules—known as **schedules of reinforcement**—affect behavior? Decades of research suggest that they do. Many different types of schedules of reinforcement exist (Ferster & Skinner, 1957; Honig & Staddon, 1977). We'll concentrate on several of the most important ones here.

The simplest is called the **continuous reinforcement schedule** (CRF), in which every occurrence of a particular behavior is reinforced. For example, if a rat receives a food pellet each time it presses a lever, or a small child receives twenty-five cents each time he ties his shoes correctly, both are on a continuous reinforcement schedule. As you might imagine, continuous reinforcement is useful for establishing or strengthening new behaviors.

Other types of schedules, however, termed *partial* or *intermittent reinforcement*, are often more powerful in maintaining behavior. In the first of these, known as a **fixed-interval schedule,** the occurrence of reinforcement depends on the passage of time; the first response made after a specific period has elapsed brings the reward. When placed on schedules of this type, people generally show a pattern in

Schedules of reinforcement:
Rules determining when and how reinforcements will be delivered.

Continuous reinforcement schedule:
A schedule of reinforcement in which every occurrence of a particular behavior is reinforced.

Fixed-interval schedule:
A schedule of reinforcement in which a specific interval of time must elapse before a response will yield reinforcement.

which they respond at low rates immediately after delivery of reinforcement, but then gradually respond more and more as the time when the next reward can be obtained approaches. A good example of behavior on a fixed-interval schedule is provided by students' studying habits. After a big exam, little if any studying takes place. As the time for the next test approaches, the rate of studying increases dramatically.

Reinforcement is also controlled mainly by the passage of time in a **variable-interval schedule.** Here, though, the period that must elapse before a response will again yield reinforcement varies around some average value. An example of behavior on a variable-interval schedule of reinforcement is provided by employees whose supervisor checks their work at irregular intervals. Because the employees never know when such checks will occur, they must perform in a consistent manner to obtain positive outcomes, such as praise, or to avoid negative ones, such as criticism. This is precisely what happens on variable-interval schedules: Humans and other animals respond at a steady rate without the kind of pauses observed on fixed-interval schedules. An important procedure that is arranged according to a variable-interval schedule is random drug testing of individuals in safety-sensitive jobs—people whose impaired performance could endanger the lives of others, such as airline pilots, air-traffic controllers, or operators at nuclear reactor sites. Because they cannot predict the day on which the next test will occur, these individuals may be more likely to refrain from using drugs that can either impair or unfairly enhance their work performance.

Reinforcement is determined in a very different manner on a **fixed-ratio schedule.** Here, reinforcement occurs only after a fixed number of responses. Individuals who are paid on a piecework basis, in which a fixed amount is paid for each item produced, are operating according to a fixed-ratio schedule. Generally, such schedules yield a high rate of response, though with a tendency toward a brief pause immediately after reinforcement. Salespeople who receive a commission for each sale, or those who collect beverage containers, office paper waste, and other recyclable materials for the money they bring, are behaving according to a fixed-ratio schedule.

Finally, on a **variable-ratio schedule,** reinforcement occurs after completion of a variable number of responses. Because organisms confronted with a variable-ratio schedule cannot predict how many responses are required before reinforcement will occur, they usually respond at high and steady rates. The effect of such schedules on human behavior is readily apparent in gambling casinos, where high rates of responding occur in front of slot machines and other games of chance.

Variable-ratio schedules also result in behaviors that are highly resistant to *extinction*—ones that persist even when reinforcement is no longer available. This phenomenon is known as the *partial reinforcement effect* and seems to occur for the following reason. Under a variable-ratio schedule, many responses are not followed by reinforcement. Many golfers are well acquainted with the partial reinforcement effect; for each great shot they hit, they hit many more poor ones, yet they continue to play the game. Suppose that a golfer fails to hit even one good shot over the course of an entire season—will she continue to play? The chances are good that she will. When reinforcement is infrequent and intermittent in its delivery, people or other organisms may continue to respond because it is difficult for them to recognize that reinforcement is no longer available (Mowrer & Jones, 1945).

As summarized in Figure 5.11 and evident throughout the preceding discussion, different schedules of reinforcement produce distinct patterns of responding. Each schedule helps describe how the delivery of consequences affects our behavior.

■ **Stimulus control of behavior: Signals about the usefulness (or uselessness) of responses.**

People and other organisms readily learn to pay attention to cues in the environment that reliably signal certain consequences for their actions. Children may learn, for example, that when their father whistles, it is an indication he is in a good

---

Variable-interval schedule:
A schedule of reinforcement in which a variable amount of time must elapse before a response will yield reinforcement.

Fixed-ratio schedule:
A schedule of reinforcement in which reinforcement occurs only after a fixed number of responses have been emitted.

Variable-ratio schedule:
A schedule of reinforcement in which reinforcement is delivered after a variable number of responses have been performed.

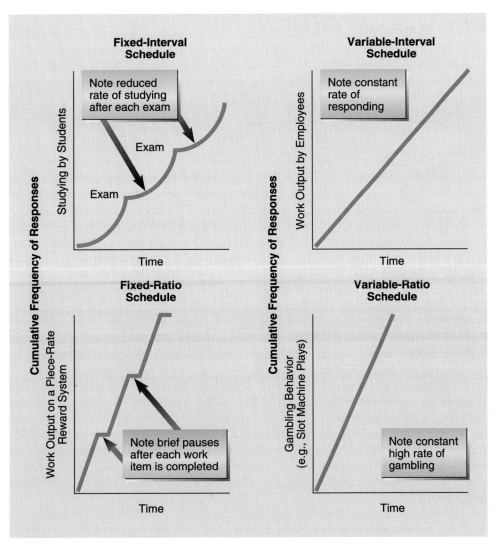

FIGURE 5.11

Schedules of Reinforcement: A Summary of their Effects

Rates of responding vary under different schedules of reinforcement. Note that the steeper the line in each diagram, the higher the rate at which responses are performed.

mood and therefore more likely to respond favorably to requests for money or permission to do something fun with their friends. Aspects of the father's mood, such as whistling or singing, are actually signals: He is likely to give in to requests when he is in a good mood (e.g., when he is whistling), but unlikely to do so when he is in a bad mood or not feeling well. Over time, they learn to make requests only in the presence of these signals—termed **discriminative stimuli.** In short, their behavior has come under **stimulus control** of the sound of his whistling (or related cues): They are obeying the signal as to whether they should ask for something they want now or wait until he is in a better mood (Skinner, 1938).

Stimulus control has important practical applications, too. For example, graphic discriminative stimuli, such as the ones depicted in Figure 5.12 on page 180, have been developed to prevent accidental poisonings and electrocution among small children who cannot yet read warning labels or understand the dangers of many household products. How do Mr. Yuk and Mr. Ouch stickers work? Initially parents place the stickers on all poisonous products and electrical outlets in their home and explain to their children that Mr. Yuk and Mr. Ouch mean "No, don't touch." Then, each time a child attempts to handle a product or get too near an electrical outlet containing the sticker, he or she receives a scolding. Soon these symbols come to signal unpleasant consequences, and children quickly learn to avoid objects labeled with these stickers. Clearly, stimulus control has important implications for solving a variety of problems in everyday life.

Discriminative stimulus:
Signals the availability of reinforcement if a specific response is made.

Stimulus control:
When a behavior occurs consistently in the presence of a discriminative stimulus.

FIGURE 5.12
Using Stimulus Control to Prevent Accidental Poisonings
Stimulus control can help solve important problems of everyday life—in this case, preventing accidental poisonings among very small children.
Source: Mr. Yuk is a registered trademark of Children's Hospital of Pittsburgh and is reprinted with permission.

Learned helplessness:
Feelings of helplessness that develop after exposure to situations in which no effort succeeds in affecting outcomes.

Hypohedonia:
A genetically inherited impairment in the ability to experience pleasure.

KEY QUESTIONS

• What are shaping and chaining?
• How does reward delay affect operant conditioning? What are the effects of procrastination?
• What are schedules of reinforcement?
• When is the use of continuous reinforcement desirable?
• What is a discriminative stimulus?

Operant Conditioning: A Cognitive Perspective

Do cognitive processes play a role in operant conditioning as they do in classical conditioning? This continues to be a point on which psychologists disagree. Operant psychologists have contended that there is no need to introduce cognition, or mental processes, into the picture: if we understand the nature of the reinforcers available in a situation and the schedules on which they are delivered, we can accurately predict behavior. But many other psychologists believe that no account of operant conditioning can be complete without attention to cognitive factors (see Colwill, 1993; Kirsch et al., in press). Several types of evidence support this conclusion.

■ **Learned helplessness: Throwing in the towel when nothing seems to work.**

Perhaps the most dramatic evidence is the existence of a phenomenon known as **learned helplessness:** the lasting effects produced by exposure to situations in which nothing an organism does works—no response yields reinforcement or provides escape from negative events. After such experiences, both people and animals seem literally to give up. And here is the unsettling part: If the situation changes so that some responses *will* work, they never discover this fact. Rather, they remain in a seemingly passive state and simply don't try (Seligman, 1975; Tennen & Eller, 1977). Although we still do not have a complete understanding of why learned helplessness occurs, it seems impossible to explain it entirely in terms of contingent relations between individual responses and the consequences they produce.

Research on learned helplessness seems to suggest that its onset stems partly from our perceptions of control; when we begin to believe that we have no control over our environment or our lives, we stop trying to improve our situations (Dweck & Licht, 1980). For example, many children growing up in urban slums perceive they have little control over their environment and even less hope of escaping it. As a result of learned helplessness, they may simply resign themselves to a lifetime of disenfranchisement, deprivation, and exclusion. Please note, however, that not all people respond in this way. Indeed, a large number of studies show that even people whose early lives were ravaged by traumatic experiences, such as the early death of a parent, divorce, war, or extreme poverty, often grow up optimistic and resilient (see Haggerty et al., 1994; Seabrook, 1995; Stewart et al., 1997). This suggests that other factors must also be involved.

Researchers speculate that genetic factors may also play a role in learned helplessness. One such factor is a genetically inherited impairment in the ability to experience pleasure termed **hypohedonia** (Meehl, 1975). This tendency may cause children who inherit it to interpret the feedback they receive for their actions quite differently from children who do not. Apparently, these individuals experience the rewarding consequences they receive from their actions as if they were on an extinction schedule. This peculiar tendency to misinterpret rewarding feedback may lead to perceptions of lack of control and helplessness (Hamburg, 1998). When normal children make mistakes while practicing a skill, such as playing soccer, it is typical for them to experience frustration, anger, and disappointment. However, when they eventually perform the skill correctly, it usually results in feelings of satisfaction and pride. Over time, the steady accumulation of positive experiences leads them to believe, for example, that they are good at soccer, that it is not as difficult as they initially thought, and that they will likely want to continue to play soccer. When children with inherited hypohedonia make the same mistakes, they are likely to experience similar negative feelings but to feel them more intensely. And unfortunately, when they eventually perform the skill successfully, they may not experience the same positive feelings enjoyed by their unaffected peers. They may instead experience a carryover of the frustration, anger, and disappointment elicited by previous mistakes. Over time, the steady accumulation of negative feelings may lead them to believe that they are not good at soccer, that soccer is hard, and that they will continue to perform poorly in the future. They may also generalize these expectations to other task domains, which in turn may increase the likelihood these children will eventually experience learned helplessness, particularly if they are faced with difficult circumstances later in life.

■ **Evidence that it's all relative: The contrast effect.**

Some evidence suggests that our behavior is influenced not only by the level of rewards we receive, but also by our evaluation of rewards relative to our experiences with previous rewards. Studies have shown that shifts in the amount of reward we receive can dramatically influence performance, a temporary behavior shift termed the *contrast effect* (see Crespi, 1942; Flaherty & Largen, 1975; Shanab & Spencer, 1978). When laboratory animals are shifted from a small reward to a larger reward, there is an increase in their performance to a level greater than that of subjects consistently receiving the larger reward. This increase is known as a *positive contrast effect*. Conversely, when subjects are shifted from a large reward to a smaller reward, their performance decreases to a level lower than that of subjects receiving only the smaller reward—a *negative contrast effect*. But positive and negative contrast effects are transient. Thus, the elevated or depressed performances slowly give way to performance levels similar to those of control animals that receive only one level of reward.

The existence of contrast effects indicates that level of reward alone cannot always explain our behavior, and that experience with a previous level of reward—and consequent expectancies—can dramatically affect our performance. Contrast effects also help explain certain instances of our everyday behavior. For example, following an unexpected raise in salary or a promotion, a person is initially elated, and his or her performance skyrockets—at least for a while. Then, after the novelty wears off, performance falls to levels equal to that of others already being rewarded at the same level.

■ **Tolman's cognitive map: A classic study in the history of psychology.**

Finally, evidence suggests that cognitive processes play an important role in learning among animals, as well. In a classic study by Tolman and Honzik (1930), rats were trained to run through a complicated maze. One group, the reward group, received a food reward in the goal box at the end of the maze on each of its daily trials. A second group, the no-reward group, never received a reward. The third group, the no-reward/reward group, did not receive a food reward until the eleventh day of training. As illustrated in Figure 5.13 on page 182, rats in the reward group showed a steady improvement in performance, decreasing the number of errors they made in reaching the goal box. Rats in the no-reward group showed only a slight improvement in performance. Rats in the no-reward/reward group showed performance similar to those in the no-reward group—for the first ten days. However, their performance improved dramatically immediately after the introduction of the food reward. In fact, their performance was as good as that of rats who had been rewarded for their performance all along.

How do we account for these results? An explanation based on reinforcement alone is not sufficient; the change in performance of the third group was too sudden. Obviously, the rats had learned something in the previous trials. Tolman and others point to these data, and to the results of other studies (e.g., Colwill &

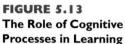

FIGURE 5.13
The Role of Cognitive Processes in Learning
Performance for rats in the no-reward/reward group improved dramatically immediately after the introduction of the food reward. Because the improvement was so dramatic, these data suggest that the animals "learned" something during previous trials—even though they received no reward for their efforts. Tolman used this as evidence for the importance of cognitive processes in learning, suggesting that the rats may have formed a "cognitive map."
Source: Based on data from Tolman & Honzik, 1930.

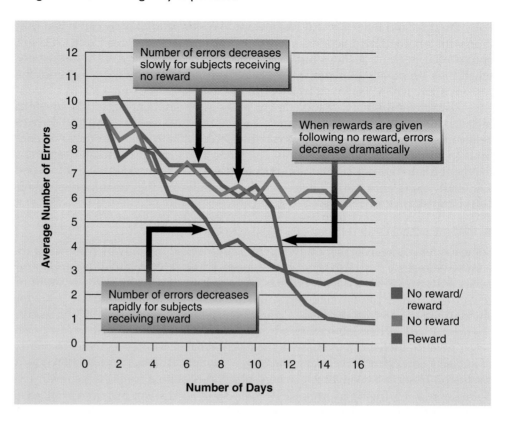

Rescorla, 1985, 1988), as evidence for the importance of cognitive processes in learning. In fact, Tolman theorized that the rats may have formed what he termed a *cognitive map*—a mental representation of the maze. Although the existence of such maps has not yet been clearly established, a growing body of evidence supports the view that animals do, in fact, form mental representations of their environment (Capaldi, Alpetekin, & Birmingham, 1997; Capaldi & Birmingham, 1998).

Applying Operant Conditioning: Solving Problems of Everyday Life

Because positive and negative reinforcement exert powerful effects on behavior, procedures based on operant conditioning have been applied in many practical settings—so many that it would be impossible to describe them all here. An overview of some of these uses will suffice, though.

First, principles of operant conditioning have been applied to the field of education. One of the most impressive operant-based teaching techniques involves the use of computers in the classroom—often termed *computer-assisted instruction,* or *CAI.* Research indicates that intelligent software can be programmed to successfully monitor, assess, diagnose, and remediate each student's performance on a variety of tasks (Salas & Cannon-Bowers, 2001). The success of CAI as a learning tool can be traced, at least in part, to how it provides students with immediate and consistent feedback regarding their performance. CAI and other emerging technologies, such as desktop video conferencing and Internet-based training, also offer the ability to reach anybody, anywhere, at nearly any time. The benefits of these new instructional approaches are becoming increasingly apparent (Rudestam, 2004). They allow groups of learners previously unable to obtain formal education, whether because of distance from the academic institutions or because of scheduling problems, to participate. Online classes minimize social stereotyping, or opinions formed of others on the basis of gender or ethnicity. Forums or discussion groups require students to post feedback and support for the contributions of others and allow for equal participation by all.

But does the use of technology in the classroom enhance its effectiveness beyond more traditional instructional practices? When the criterion is comprehension or achievement, various approaches to education, including those that incorporate the use of technologies, fare equally well (see Boling & Robinson, 1999; Andrews et al., 1999). However, if students' satisfaction with the learning experience is important, then the use of technology-enhanced instruction is usually preferred.

Operant conditioning principles have also played an important role in procedures developed to promote traffic safety. For example, research has consistently shown that newly licensed teen drivers are overrepresented in traffic crashes. In fact, the per-mile fatal crash rate among sixteen-year-old drivers is three times that of eighteen-year-olds and ten times that of adults (McKnight & Peck, 2002). How can learning principles help? Traffic safety experts have used learning principles to develop graduated driver licensing (or GDL) programs (Waller, 2002; Williams, 2002). In GDL programs, teen drivers are given provisional licenses that allow them to drive unsupervised, but subject to requirements that reduce their exposure to risky situations, such as late-night driving and transporting other teens. Advancement to full licensure is made contingent on compliance with the program's requirements and evidence of safe driving (e.g., no traffic violations and the consistent use of their safety belt while driving). Evaluation research has shown a reduction in teen crashes in states where GDL has been implemented (Shope & Molnar, 2002).

Peer pressure has been shown to be an effective tool in influencing driving habits as well. A campaign known as "Speak Out" was instituted in Norway to change adolescent drivers' safety-related attitudes and behavior, urging teenage passengers to confront their peers' unsafe driving habits. The campaign also aimed to dissuade passengers from riding with drivers who did not heed the advice. The result of this program, based on negative reinforcement, was a substantial decrease in traffic accident deaths of sixteen- to nineteen-year-olds, an estimated five per year in one county alone (Amundsen et al., 1999).

Researchers have also used operant conditioning principles to help reduce the occurrence of aggressive driving, sometimes termed "road rage." In one innovative study, Geller and Dula (2003) created a system designed to promote positive—rather than negative—communication between drivers. The goals of the system, termed the "Courteous Code," included reducing driver frustration and anger and increasing prosocial driving behaviors. To test their ideas, the researchers exposed drivers in one community to the "code" via a multimedia blitz comprised of billboards and roadside signs, flyers, newspaper advertisements, and radio announcements; a second community that did not receive the media blitz served as a control site. As illustrated in Figure 5.14 on page 184, drivers in the intervention group were instructed to use their vehicle's hazard lights or a specially designed device termed the "Polite Lite" to make requests, thank other drivers for courtesies they extended, or apologize for the infractions they committed while driving. Drivers in both groups were given the opportunity to win prizes for maintaining driving diaries in which they recorded instances of aggressive and courteous behavior, as well as the emotions they experienced while driving, such as anger toward another driver. Results showed that drivers trained to use the "code" reported significantly more instances of positive driving behavior, such as using their turn signals, and fewer instances of aggressive behaviors, such as refusing to allow other drivers into traffic or making negative remarks about other drivers compared to drivers in the control group. Drivers in the intervention group also scored lower on a measure of aggressive driving.

As a final example, operant conditioning combining behavioral and cognitive therapy has proven effective with individuals who suffer from chronic pain. Research begun in the 1960s led to the use of behavioral techniques for managing debilitating pain (Fordyce, 1973). Evidence from these studies indicates that the actions of sympathetic family members and medical personnel can actually reinforce negative pain behavior. Behavioral strategies such as ignoring the grumbling and complaints and praising the successes can help patients "unlearn" their pain and change their response to it (Patterson, 2005). Adjusting pain medicine so that

FIGURE 5.14
Operant Conditioning in Action: Reducing Aggressive Driving
Learning principles have been applied to develop programs that provide drivers with a positive means of communication—using one's hazard lights or a special device termed the "Polite Lite" to make requests, thank other drivers for polite behavior, or apologize for a driving infraction. Preliminary research indicates that drivers taught to use the "code" engaged in more prosocial driving behaviors and fewer negative behaviors than drivers in a control group.
Source: Geller and Dula (2003). Used with permission.

it is time-based rather than pain-based reduces the tendency to overmedicate and encourages alternative methods of pain relief. Because exercise can frequently diminish pain, a program of positive reinforcement for increased activity using rest periods as rewards is often instituted (Fordyce, 1973).

Cognitive approaches to change the way patients perceive their pain are used for those who view their pain as hopeless, as something over which they have no control. Development of coping skills and reinforcement of the positive belief that people can successfully manage their pain can help to redirect their attention from the pain, even though its intensity might not lessen (see Kalsher et al., 1986). Individuals can anticipate upcoming episodes of pain and divert their focus to a positive one (Cole, 1998). Although complete pain relief may not be always be possible, a patient's increased role in its control and the subsequent constructive enhancement of their self-worth can significantly decrease its damaging effects (Lebovits, 2002).

KEY QUESTIONS

• What evidence supports the involvement of cognitive factors in operant conditioning?
• Why is knowledge of operant conditioning important?

OBSERVATIONAL LEARNING: LEARNING FROM THE BEHAVIOR AND OUTCOMES OF OTHERS

A few years ago, I (Michael Kalsher) became interested in learning to make wine. Fortunately, there is a store near my home that sells equipment and ingredients for this purpose so I asked the owner for advice on how to get started. As he makes wine right at the store, he offered to let me watch him as he performed the various steps involved over the course of about a month. After observing him, I was able to successfully make my first batch of wine—a tasty mild white wine called pinot grigio (see Figure 5.15). You, too, have probably encountered numerous situations in which you have acquired new information, forms of behavior, or even abstract rules and concepts from watching the actions of other people and the consequences they experience. Such **observational learning** is a third major way we learn, and it is a common part of everyday life (Bandura, 1977, 1986). Indeed, a large body of evidence suggests it can play a role in nearly every aspect of behavior.

More formal evidence for the existence of observational learning has been provided by hundreds of studies, many of them performed with children. Perhaps the most famous of these studies are the well-known "Bobo doll" experiments

Observational learning:
The acquisition of new forms of behavior, information, or concepts through exposure to others and the consequences they experience.

FIGURE 5.15
Observational Learning: Acquiring New Skills by Watching the Behavior of Others
Observational learning is an important form of learning in which people acquire new information and skills by watching other people in action. Here, I (Mike Kalsher) am attempting to make wine by reading the instructions from a wine-making kit. Learning to perform tasks such as this can often be facilitated by watching a more experienced person perform the action first.

conducted by Bandura and colleagues (see Bandura, Ross, & Ross, 1963). In these studies one group of nursery-school children saw an adult engage in aggressive actions against a large inflated Bobo doll. The adult who was serving as a model knocked the doll down, sat on it, insulted it verbally, and repeatedly punched it in the nose. Another group of children was exposed to a model who behaved in a quiet, nonaggressive manner. Later, both groups of youngsters were placed in a room with several toys, including a Bobo doll. Careful observation of their behavior revealed that those who had seen the aggressive adult model often imitated this person's behavior: They, too, punched the toy, sat on it, and even uttered verbal comments similar to those of the model. In contrast, children in the control group rarely if ever demonstrated such actions. While you may not find these results surprising, they may be significant in relation to the enduring controversy over whether children acquire new ways of aggressing through exposure to violent television programs and movies. We'll return to this issue shortly. For the moment, let's consider the nature of observational learning itself.

Observational Learning: Some Basic Principles

Given that observational learning exists, what factors and conditions determine whether, and to what extent, we acquire behaviors, information, or concepts from others? The following four factors appear to be the most important (Bandura, 1986).

First, in order to learn through observation, you must direct your *attention* to appropriate *models*—that is, to other people performing an activity. And, as you might expect, you don't choose such models at random but focus most attention on people who are attractive to you; on people who possess signs of knowing what they're doing, such as status or success; and on people whose behavior seems relevant to your own needs and goals (Baron, 1970).

Second, you must be able to *remember* what the people have said or done. Only if you can retain some representation of their actions in memory can you perform similar actions at later times or acquire useful information from them.

Third, you need to be able to convert these memory representations into appropriate actions. This aspect of observational learning is termed *production*

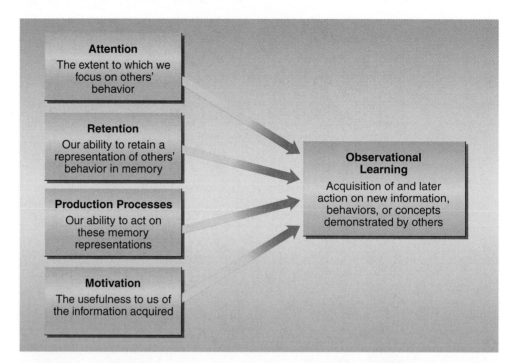

FIGURE 5.16
Key Factors in Observational Learning
Observational learning is affected by several factors or sub-processes. The most important of these are summarized here.

processes. Production processes depend on: your own physical abilities—if you can't perform the behavior in question, having a clear representation of it in memory is of little use; and your capacity to monitor your own performance and adjust it until it matches that of the model.

Finally, *motivation* plays a role. We often acquire information through observational learning but do not put it into immediate use in our own behavior. That is why we define learning as a relatively permanent change in behavior, or *behavior potential,* produced by experience. You may have no need for the information, as when you watch someone tie a bow tie but have no plans to wear one yourself. Or the observed behaviors may involve high risk of punishment or be repugnant to you personally, as when you observe an ingenious way of cheating during an exam but don't want to try it yourself. Only if the information or behaviors acquired are useful will observers put them to actual use. Figure 5.16 summarizes factors affecting observational learning.

As you can see, observational learning is a complex process—far more complex than mere imitation—and plays an important role in many aspects of behavior. This point is perhaps most forcefully illustrated by the controversy that has persisted in psychology, and in society as a whole, since the early 1960s: whether children, and perhaps even adults, are made more aggressive by long-term exposure to violence on television shows, in movies, or on the Internet.

Observational Learning and Aggression

After analyzing thousands of hours of programming on cable and broadcast television, the *National Television Violence Study* (1998) reported that approximately 60 percent of television programs contained some form of violence, with a typical one-hour episode containing a minimum of six violent events. Estimates indicate that the average American eighteen-year-old has seen approximately 200,000 acts of violence on TV alone (American Academy of Pediatrics, 2001)!

But does merely watching violence on television lead people to commit similar acts? A large body of research indicates that aggression may indeed be learned through observation (Baron & Richardson, 1994; Centerwall, 1989; Snyder, 1991; Wood, Wong, & Chachere, 1991). Apparently, when children and adults are ex-

FIGURE 5.17
Observational Learning and Aggression
Experts continue to worry that exposure to violence on television and in movies may encourage children to perform violent acts. Research on this topic suggests that the negative effects of exposure to violence may be most pronounced for individuals who are highly aggressive by nature.

posed to new ways of aggressing against others—techniques they have not previously seen—they may add these new behaviors to their repertoires (see Figure 5.17). Later, when angry, irritated, or frustrated, they may put such behaviors to actual use in assaults against others. Research also suggests that the negative effects of exposure to violence may be most pronounced for individuals who are highly aggressive by nature. Bushman (1995), for example, showed that participants who scored higher on a measure of aggressive tendencies were more likely to choose a violent film to watch, more likely to *feel* angry after watching it, and more likely to commit aggressive acts after viewing videotaped violence than were their less aggressive counterparts.

Of course, exposure to media violence, whether on the evening news or in movies or television programs, has other effects as well. It may convey the message that violence is an acceptable way to handle interpersonal difficulties, particularly if children identify with the violent characters; after all, if heroes and heroines can do it, why not viewers (Huesmann et al., 2003)? It may elicit additional aggressive ideas and thoughts, convincing viewers, for example, that violence is even more common than it actually is (Berkowitz, 1984). And it may also lessen emotional reactions to aggression and the harm it produces, so that such outcomes seem less upsetting or objectionable (Thomas, 1982).

More than 50 percent of the violent events depicted in programs studied included acts of aggression that would be debilitating or fatal had they occurred in real life. Combined with the fact that approximately 40 percent of violent incidents were presented along with humor, producing a connection between positive feelings and hurting others, this creates a very real potential for viewers to become desensitized toward violence or to trivialize it (NTVS, 1998).

It is especially alarming that data now point to a link between exposure to violent programming during childhood and an increase in antisocial behavior in young adults. A fifteen-year longitudinal study (Huesmann et al., 2003) has reported a positive relationship between the amount of violence viewed and adult aggression. The results show that males exposed to a large amount of television violence during childhood have a crime conviction rate three times higher than other men. Aggressive behavior becomes not only an acceptable, but also often an attractive way to deal with conflict and achieve goals in those who have been fed a steady diet of violent media.

Evidence indicates that television violence doesn't have to encourage aggressive behavior (NTVS, 1998). Displaying the negative consequences of violent behavior has been shown to be effective in influencing its occurrence. Unfortunately, results of the television violence study show that more than a third of the plots in violent programming show no punishment for the "bad guys," potentially increasing the risk of imitation by viewers.

As much as a 22 percent increase in adolescent aggressive behavior has been attributed to playing violent video games (Anderson, 2000). These games allow virtual participation in the violence, rewarding the player each time he responds aggressively, making it more likely for the player to learn violence through its imitation. Players not only are taught how to be aggressive, but studies also show that arousal is increased as well as feelings of anger or hostility (Anderson & Bushman, 2001). Because young children often cannot differentiate between fantasy and reality, this puts them at risk for embracing aggression as the norm.

Before we conclude this section on observational learning and aggression, let's touch on one more subject that may be particularly relevant: the effects of music with violent lyrics on behavior. Research experiments conducted with college students (Anderson et al., 2003) determined that violent songs produced feelings of hostility and an increase in aggressive thoughts in those students who favored rap and heavy metal music. Specifically, the heavy metal fans had more negative attitudes toward women. In addition, there appears to be a correlation between rap and heavy metal preference and lower academic achievement, antisocial behavior at school, illegal drug use, arrests, and sexual activity (Took & Weiss, 1994).

All the above factors become especially disturbing when you consider that the average American child between age two and eighteen spends more than six and a half hours *every day* using some type of media, ranging from watching television, videos, or films, to playing video games, surfing the Internet, or listening to music (American Academy of Pediatrics, 2001). No other activity besides sleep occupies as much of a child's day. An additional negative side effect of violent television and video games is an increase in nightmares. A recent study showed that 25 percent of the first-graders participating had a TV violence–related nightmare at least once a month, with 10 percent experiencing a nightmare weekly (Van den Bulck, 2004).

Observational Learning and Culture

As we've already noted, observational learning plays an important role in many aspects of behavior. Much of our understanding of the world around us—including our language and customs—comes to us by observing the behaviors of others around us. Psychologists using applied principles of observational learning are helping companies throughout the world prepare their employees for the business environment of the twenty-first century—an environment that requires a broad range of skills and the ability to interact effectively with people from other cultures (Adler & Bartholomew, 1992; Feldman & Tompson, 1993). Dramatic differences in language, customs, and lifestyle often lead to unintended misunderstandings among people from different cultural backgrounds. Behaviors that are acceptable in one country may be quite offensive to people from another country.

To soften the effects of culture shock, experts in the area of cross-cultural training have advocated an experiential approach based on behavioral modeling (Black & Mendenhall, 1990). Trainees watch films in which models exhibit the correct behaviors in a problem situation. Then they participate in a situation role play exercise to test their knowledge. Finally, they receive constructive feedback regarding their performance.

Some evidence suggests that this approach can be quite effective. In one study,

Harrison (1992) compared the effectiveness of several approaches to cross-cultural training: One group of participants received culture-relevant information only; another received behavioral modeling training only; a third received both components; and a fourth, the control group, received no training. The results showed that participants who received both forms of training—information and behavioral modeling—performed best on measures of culture-specific knowledge and on a behavioral measure.

These findings illustrate the important role that observational learning plays in alleviating the effects of culture shock. It initially enables us to perform behaviors appropriate to our own cultures, but later helps us to adapt to the demands of a rapidly changing world. For additional examples of how observational learning can be applied in the workplace, please refer to the following **Psychology Goes to Work** section.

PSYCHOLOGY GOES TO WORK

Using Behavioral Modeling and Mental Rehearsal to Teach Computer Skills

As we've noted throughout this section, observational learning is an important form of learning that enables people to acquire new information and behaviors by watching the actions of others. The value of observational learning as an important workplace training tool is becoming increasingly apparent. Training programs that incorporate behavior modeling have already been applied to enhance important work-related skills in a number of important domains, including supervisory, communications, sales, and customer service (see Wexley & Latham, 2002). Behavior modeling has been shown to be particularly beneficial in the development of interpersonal skills on the job. Recent workplace studies used videos depicting sample positive *and* negative scenarios, allowing trainees to see the unfavorable response presented side by side with the favorable in various work-related situations (Taylor et al., 2005). The evidence further pointed to the longer-lasting effects that behavior modeling has over information received verbally. And the effects improved even more when rewards were given whenever training was transferred to the work environment.

Given the rapid deployment of computer technologies in the workplace and elsewhere, training programs that incorporate behavioral modeling are currently being used to train employees to use computer software (Galvin, 2001). Emerging evidence suggests that the effectiveness of behavior modeling can be enhanced even further when trainees visualize how they will apply their new skills before actually instituting them, a process termed *symbolic mental rehearsal* (SMR). To illustrate this, let's consider the results of a study by Davis and Yi (2004). All participants in the study first watched video segments depicting a person performing specific tasks on a computer (manipulating a Microsoft Excel™ spreadsheet). For half the participants, the researchers paused the video at the end of each training segment and had them summarize the computer operations they had just seen by writing down key points of the demonstration. These participants were also asked to mentally rehearse the key learning points they had written. Then, all the participants completed a knowledge test and performed the computer tasks they had watched on the videotape. As shown in Figure 5.18, participants who

had written down key points of the demonstration and mentally rehearsed these steps outperformed their counterparts who had merely watched the video. These results illustrate the usefulness of observational learning as a training tool. However, they also highlight that mentally rehearsing modeled behavior can enhance a person's ability to perform the actions themselves.

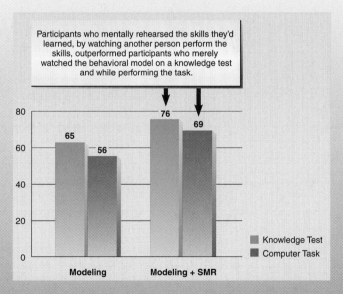

FIGURE 5.18

Enhancing the Effectiveness of Behavioral Modeling Through Mental Rehearsal

Participants who mentally rehearsed the computer skills they had seen modeled by another person outperformed participants who merely watched the skills being performed.

Source: Based on data from Davis & Yi, 2004.

Observational Learning: Some Practical Applications

As you can see from the previous discussions, the effects of observational learning on our behavior can indeed be powerful—and not always for the good. For example, observational learning may contribute to the development of unhealthy behaviors, including smoking, especially among adolescents (Hahn et al., 1990). Because acceptance by peers is so important to people in this age group, it is possible that observing peers who smoke contributes to their own decisions to start smoking (Hawkins, Catalano, & Miller, 1992). Some evidence seems to indicate that this is true (e.g., Aloise-Young, Graham, & Hansen, 1994).

Fortunately, another large body of evidence shows that peer influence can also be used to promote more productive behaviors. In one interesting study, Werts and colleagues (1996) examined whether children with mild retardation enrolled in a regular classroom could acquire skills by having their peers who didn't have disabilities model skills for them. The to-be-learned skills included spelling their name, using a calculator to perform simple arithmetic, and sharpening a pencil. The results revealed that the children with disabilities learned the skills in a relatively short period of time (less than a month). It is noteworthy that the time the peers spent modeling the behaviors averaged about five minutes per day, suggesting that observational learning can be an efficient tool in the learning process.

Observational learning may also offer new hope for stroke victims. Studies are under way (U.S. National Institutes of Health, 2005) that test a patient's ability to relearn impaired skills through repeated observations of motor tasks being performed by others. After viewing a particular motor function, say finger tapping, for several minutes on a video screen, individuals are asked to imitate the movement the moment the film is stopped. The researchers then use *f*MRI (refer to Chapter 2) to monitor brain activity related to motor learning in stroke patients and in healthy control subjects to see whether stroke patients process visual-motor information the same way people who have not suffered a stroke do. The researchers' hope is that observational learning will be sufficient to increase the level of activity in the premotor cortex area of the brain—the area of the brain that enables motor learning—and eventually help people regain motor skills lost as a result of a stroke.

To summarize, then, observational learning plays an important role in many aspects of behavior.

KEY QUESTIONS

- What is observational learning?
- What factors determine the extent to which we acquire new information through observational learning?
- In what forms of behavior does observational learning play a role?
- In what ways can observational learning be used to solve problems of everyday life?

SUMMARY AND REVIEW OF KEY QUESTIONS

Classical Conditioning: Learning That Some Stimuli Signal Others

- **What is learning?**
  Learning is any relatively permanent change in behavior (or behavior potential) produced by experience.

- **What is classical conditioning?**
  Classical conditioning is a form of learning in which neutral stimuli (stimuli initially unable to elicit a particular response) come to elicit that response through their association with stimuli that are naturally able to do so.

- **Upon what factors does acquisition of a classically conditioned response depend?**
  Acquisition depends on the temporal arrangement of the CS-UCS pairings, the intensity of the CS and UCS relative to other background stimuli, and the familiarity of potentially conditioned stimuli present.

- **What is extinction?**
  Extinction is the process through which a conditioned stimulus gradually ceases to elicit a conditioned response when it is no longer paired with an unconditioned stimu-

lus. However, this ability can be quickly regained through reconditioning.

- **What is the difference between stimulus generalization and stimulus discrimination?**
  Stimulus generalization allows us to apply our learning to other situations; stimulus discrimination allows us to differentiate among similar but different stimuli.

- **Where in the brain does classical conditioning take place?**
  Research shows that the cerebellum, a structure in the brain involved in balance and coordination, plays a key role in the formation of simple forms of classically conditioned responses. Other brain structures known to be involved include the hippocampus, amygdala, and brainstem areas that project to or receive information from these structures.

- **Is classical conditioning equally easy to establish with all stimuli for all organisms?**
  Because of biological constraints that exist among different species, types of conditioning readily accomplished by some species are acquired only slowly—or not acquired at all—by others.

- **How do we acquire conditioned taste aversions?**
  Conditioned taste aversions are usually established when a food or beverage (conditioned stimulus) is paired with a stimulus that naturally leads to feelings of illness (unconditioned stimulus). Conditioned taste aversions can be established after a single CS-UCS pairing.

- **How do modern views of classical conditioning differ from earlier perspectives?**
  Modern views of classical conditioning emphasize the important role of cognitive processes. Research shows that conditioning is a complex process in which organisms form mental representations of the relationships among a variety of factors.

- **What is blocking?**
  In blocking, conditioning to one stimulus is prevented by previous conditioning to another stimulus.

- **How can classical conditioning principles solve problems of everyday life?**
  Basic principles of classical conditioning have been used to solve a variety of everyday problems, including explaining instances of drug overdose, enhancing aspects of the immune system, reducing the likelihood that cancer patients will develop a conditioned taste aversion, and treating alcohol dependency by pairing environmental stimuli associated with ingestion of a beverage containing alcohol with a substance that makes them sick.

Operant Conditioning: Learning Based on Consequences

- **What is operant conditioning?**
  In operant conditioning, organisms learn the relationships between certain behaviors and the consequences they produce.

- **What are examples of primary reinforcers? Of conditioned reinforcers?**
  Primary reinforcers include food, water, and sexual pleasure; conditioned reinforcers include money, status, and praise.

- **Which operant techniques strengthen behavior? Weaken behavior?**
  Both positive and negative reinforcement strengthen or increase behavior. In contrast, positive and negative punishment are procedures that suppress or weaken behavior.

- **How do negative reinforcement and punishment differ?**
  Both negative reinforcement and punishment involve aversive events. They differ, however, in terms of their effects on behavior. Negative reinforcement is a procedure in which behaviors that allow an organism to escape from an aversive event, or to avoid it altogether, are *strengthened*. Punishment is a procedure in which an aversive event *weakens* the behavior it follows.

- **What are shaping and chaining?**
  Shaping is used to establish new responses by initially reinforcing behaviors that resemble the desired behavior, termed *successful approximations*. Chaining is a procedure used to establish a complex sequence or chain of behaviors.

- **How does reward delay affect operant conditioning? What are the effects of procrastination?**
  When asked to choose between a smaller-but-sooner and a larger-but-later reward, people often choose the former option, a tendency termed *impulsiveness*. People exhibit a similar tendency when faced with a choice between performing a smaller, less effortful task now and performing a larger, more effortful task later on: They *procrastinate*, choosing the more delayed alternative, even when it leads to more work, lower performance, and illness.

- **What are schedules of reinforcement?**
  Schedules of reinforcement are rules that determine the occasion on which a response will be reinforced. Schedules of reinforcement can be based on time or event, fixed or variable. Each schedule of reinforcement produces a characteristic pattern of responding.

- **When is the use of continuous reinforcement desirable?**
  A continuous reinforcement schedule is desirable for establishing new behaviors; partial or intermittent schedules of reinforcement are more powerful in maintaining behavior.

- **What is a discriminative stimulus?**
  Discriminative stimuli signal the availability of specific consequences if a certain response is made. When a behavior occurs consistently in the presence of a discriminative stimulus, it is said to be under stimulus control.

- **What evidence supports the involvement of cognitive factors in operant conditioning?**
  Studies of learned helplessness and the presence of a genetically inherited impairment in the ability to experience pleasure, contrast effects, and memory of reward events support the conclusion that cognitive factors play an important role in operant conditioning.

- **Why is knowledge of operant conditioning important?**
  Procedures based on operant conditioning principles can be applied to address many problems of everyday life—for example, in improving classroom instructional technology, in promoting traffic safety, and in helping people who suffer from chronic pain.

Observational Learning: Learning from the Behavior and Outcomes of Others

- **What is observational learning?**
  Observational learning is the acquisition of new information, concepts, or forms of behavior through exposure to others and the consequences they experience.

- **What factors determine the extent to which we acquire new information through observational learning?**
  For observational learning to be effective, we must pay attention to those modeling the behavior, remember the modeled speech or action, possess the ability to act on this memory, and have the motivation to do so.

- **In what forms of behavior does observational learning play a role?**
  Observational learning plays an important role in many types of behavior, including aggression.

- **In what ways can observational learning be used to solve problems of everyday life?**
  Observational learning can play an important role in work settings; for example, in training workers to interact more effectively with people from different cultural backgrounds. It can also play a role in helping people to acquire new information and behaviors such as computer skills. Finally, observational learning may offer new hope to stroke victims by helping them to relearn impaired skills through repeated observations of motor tasks being performed by others.

KEY TERMS

Acquisition, p. 162
Backward conditioning, p. 163
Biological constraints on learning, p. 166
Chaining, p. 176
Classical conditioning, p. 161
Conditioned response (CR), p. 162
Conditioned stimulus (CS), p. 162
Conditioned taste aversion, p. 167
Continuous reinforcement schedule, p. 177
Delay conditioning, p. 162
Discriminative stimulus, p. 179
Extinction, p. 164

Fixed-interval schedule, p. 177
Fixed-ratio schedule, p. 178
Hypohedonia, p. 180
Learned helplessness, p. 180
Learning, p. 160
Negative reinforcers, p. 172
Observational learning, p. 184
Operant conditioning, p. 171
Phobia, p. 169
Positive reinforcers, p. 172
Premack principle, p. 172
Punishment, p. 173
Reconditioning, p. 164
Reinforcement, p. 172

Schedules of reinforcement, p. 177
Shaping, p. 175
Simultaneous conditioning, p. 163
Spontaneous recovery, p. 164
Stimulus, p. 161
Stimulus control, p. 179
Stimulus discrimination, p. 165
Stimulus generalization, p. 164
Trace conditioning, p. 162
Unconditioned response (UCR), p. 162
Unconditioned stimulus (UCS), p. 161
Variable-interval schedule, p. 178
Variable-ratio schedule, p. 178

PSYCHOLOGY: UNDERSTANDING ITS FINDINGS

Using Learning Principles in Everyday Life

Throughout this chapter, we have discussed several basic principles of learning and shown their usefulness for solving a variety of important problems of everyday life. You may recall from our discussions that one of these procedures—punishment—while useful in certain specific situations, can often have a host of negative side effects. Do the following exercises to see how alternatives to punishment can be useful in your own life.

1. Think of situations in which you may have inadvertently used punishment (e.g., saying something negative to a friend to get them to stop an annoying behavior) or have been on the receiving end of someone else who has used this technique with you. Now, try to think of other proce-

dures we have discussed that might have been more effective alternatives. (Hint: You may want to consider procedures for rewarding behaviors that are incompatible with the undesirable behavior—a procedure that psychologists refer to as *differential reinforcement of other behavior,* or DRO.) Now, try these procedures the next time the occasion arises. Were they effective?

2. Are there certain goals that you would like to accomplish? For example, developing better study habits or learning to budget your money more effectively? Write each goal on a piece of paper and then think of how the learning principles we have discussed could be used to reach your goals. (Hint: Do you think the shaping, stimulus, control, and schedules of reinforcement might be useful concepts?) Be sure to track your progress!

MAKING PSYCHOLOGY PART OF YOUR LIFE

On Becoming a Better Student: Using Learning Principles to Improve Your Study Habits

Over the years, we've all noted that many students report that the job of "student" is a difficult one. Why? The reasons they offer are varied, but the most common answer seems to suggest that their difficulties stem, at least in part, from poor study habits. Many of the learning principles in this chapter can be useful in helping to enhance study skills—we've included a few of these here. Following these tips may lead to better academic performance and an enhanced learning experience.

1. **Shaping—one step at a time.** Your current study habits did not develop overnight. It is therefore reasonable to expect that developing new ones will also take time. Trying to do too much at first can punish your efforts and quickly lead to failure. To avoid this pitfall, start slowly. You may want to begin, for example, by establishing a fixed time each day for studying. Over time, you can slowly increase the amount of time you spend studying.

2. **Use contingent rewards to maintain your study behavior.** As the information in this chapter suggests, many forms of behavior (including studying) are governed by their consequences. But remember, where people are concerned, many individual differences exist. A stimulus that functions as a reinforcer for one person may fail to operate in a similar manner for another person, or at a different time. So, choose rewards that are meaningful to you and make access to these rewards contingent on successful completion of your study goals. It is also important to select rewards that are consistent with these goals (e.g., taking time out to exercise or seeing a movie with

friends), not ones that could serve to undermine your study efforts (e.g., consuming alcohol, staying out too late on a school night). Over time, you may find that the positive feedback you receive from your instructors may also help to maintain your motivation to study.

3. **Don't procrastinate.** As you probably know, many people follow the path of least resistance, and this holds true for studying. Doing a little bit of studying on a regular basis will more than offset the pain—and perhaps poor performance—that will come your way should you choose to put off studying or doing your homework until the last minute.

4. **Arrange your environment wisely.** Research on concurrent schedules of reinforcement and the matching law has helped to clarify why particular events are reinforcing at certain times and in certain contexts, but not others. Applied to studying, this suggests that sitting down to study on a particular night may not seem so bad if nothing else is going on. So, plan ahead and avoid scheduling your study sessions during periods that compete with other more desirable activities (e.g., a social event or favorite television program). Or better yet, make your participation in these activities contingent on completion of your homework or studying, a practical application of another principle we discussed earlier, the Premack principle.

5. **Ask for help.** Many students get into trouble because they don't ask their instructors for help. If you are having difficulty understanding an assignment or the material in a particular class, make an appointment with the course instructor and ask for help. You'll be surprised at how quickly doing so can get you back on track!

If you are using MyPsychLab, you have access to an electronic version of this textbook, along with dozens of valuable resources per chapter—including video and audio clips, simulations and activities, self-assessments, practice tests and other study materials. Here is a sampling of the resources available for this chapter.

EXPLORE

Three Stages of Classical Conditioning
The Shaping Process
Bandura's Study on Observational Learning

WATCH

B.F. Skinner Speaks
Bandura's Bobo Doll Experiment

SIMULATE

Forms of Learning
Classical Conditioning
Schedules of Reinforcement

If you did not receive an access code to MyPsychLab with this text and wish to purchase access online, please visit www.MyPsychLab.com.

STUDY GUIDE

CHAPTER REVIEW

Classical Conditioning: Learning That Some Stimuli Signal Others

1. Which of the following would NOT represent a change in behavior related to learning?
   a. An elderly man with Alzheimer's disease is unable to recall where he parked his car.
   b. Your ability to control your car is changed after consuming that fifth beer.
   c. The capacity of an infant to move changes from crawling to walking.
   d. All of the above are correct.
2. An aversion to food may be acquired through the process of
   a. operant conditioning.
   b. classical conditioning.
   c. behavioral potentiation.
   d. maturation.
3. _____ refers to a form of learning in which we monitor the behaviors of others.
   a. Social learning
   b. Observational learning
   c. Classical conditioning
   d. Operant conditioning
4. Which of the following scientists is known for their research on classical conditioning?
   a. Gregor Mendel.
   b. Eduardo Tolman.
   c. Ivan Pavlov.
   d. Charles Darwin.
5. In Pavlov's experiments on learning, the unconditioned stimulus was usually
   a. orange juice.
   b. a metal pan.
   c. a tone.
   d. meat powder.
6. Indicate the correct match between a classical conditioning term and its definition.
   _____. A temporal arrangement in classical conditioning in which the CS overlaps with the UCS.
   _____. The response of an organism to the conditioned stimulus.
   _____. A neutral stimulus that does not elicit a response prior to conditioning.
   _____. A temporal arrangement in classical conditioning in which there is a time gap between the CS and UCS.
   _____. A stimulus that does not require conditioning to induce a response.
   _____. A response elicited by a stimulus (does not require conditioning)
   _____. A temporal arrangement in classical conditioning in which the UCS comes on before the CS.
   a. conditioned stimulus
   b. unconditioned response

   c. delay conditioning
   d. unconditioned stimulus
   e. backward conditioning
   f. conditioned response
   g. trace conditioning
7. The form of classical conditioning in which the UCS appears before the CS is known as _____ conditioning.
   a. trace
   b. delay
   c. backward
   d. forward
8. Which of the following is a factor that speeds up the process of conditioning a CR?
   a. The temporal arrangement between the CS and UCS.
   b. The intensity of the CS or UCS.
   c. The delay between the CS and the UCS.
   d. All of the above are correct.
9. A(n) _____ stimulus is unlikely to support the formation of a CR.
   a. intense
   b. visual
   c. familiar
   d. auditory
10. Spontaneous recovery refers to the situation in which a CR is extinguished, the CS and UCS are again paired, and the CR rapidly returns.   (True-False)
11. The reappearance of an extinguished CR after some time interval is termed
   a. extinction.
   b. delayed acquisition.
   c. reverse acquisition.
   d. spontaneous recovery.
12. An antibody is formed within the body to attack a particular protein on the surface of a cell. If the antibody attaches itself to proteins that precisely match the original, it is said to have specificity. If the particular protein was a CS, we would say that the antibody was exhibiting stimulus
   a. habituation.
   b. discrimination.
   c. recovery.
   d. generalization.
13. The _____ must be intact in order to establish an eye blink CR to a puff of air in the eye.
   a. spinal cord
   b. cingulate gyrus
   c. cerebellum
   d. occipital cortex
14. The key event behind classical conditioning is that an organism develops an expectation that the UCS will follow the CS.   (True-False)
15. The possibility that a cancer patient undergoing chemotherapy will develop a CTA can be reduced by
   a. eating many frequent meals.
   b. eating novel flavors.
   c. consume strongly flavored foods.
   d. eat familiar but bland foods.

16. A novel application of classical conditioning would be to condition a flavor aversion in a(n) _____ between the taste of _____ with a drug that induces nausea.
    a. alcoholic;   alcohol
    b. anorexic;   candy bars
    c. heroin addict;   marijuana
    d. obsessive-compulsive;   bland foods

Operant Conditioning: Learning Based on Consequences

17. An operant response that leads to a favorable consequence
    a. is usually suppressed.
    b. will occur more frequently.
    c. weakens brain reward circuits.
    d. is classified as a punisher.
18. The concept of negative reinforcement is best illustrated when a(n)
    a. hungry rat presses a lever for a food pellet.
    b. addict injects heroin to get high.
    c. man ingests an aspirin to end a painful headache.
    d. child is sent to their room after throwing a tantrum at lunch.
19. Which of the following best illustrates the concept of punishment?
    a. A man ingests an aspirin to rid himself of a strong headache.
    b. A hungry rat obtains a food pellet after pressing a lever.
    c. A woman injects heroin into her veins to obtain a "rush."
    d. A curious child reaches to touch a red hot cooking pan.
20. Match up the operant conditioning term with its appropriate definition or example of the term.
    _____. A procedure that strengthens behavior.
    _____. A man with a painful headache takes a pain pill.
    _____. A stimulus that acts as a positive reinforcer and that is related to a biological need.
    _____. A teenager who fails to clean their room cannot use the family car for a date.
    _____. A situation in which a response that produces a favorable outcome is more likely to be repeated.
    _____. A procedure that suppresses behavior.
    _____. "You can watch television only after you eat your spinach!"
    a. Conditioned reinforcer
    b. Punishment
    c. Premack principle
    d. Reinforcement
    e. Negative reinforcement
    f. Negative punishment
    g. Primary reinforcer
    h. Positive reinforcement
21. An example of _____ is when a child is given a piece of candy whenever their behavior is close to that desired by their parent.
    a. conditioned punishment
    b. shaping
    c. classical conditioning
    d. modeling
22. Responses in operant conditioning are voluntarily made by the organism.   (True-False)
23. The effectiveness of a reward in operant conditioning is increased when
    a. there is a long delay between the response and the reward.
    b. the magnitude of the reward is decreased.
    c. the reward involves electric shock.
    d. the magnitude of the reward is increased.
24. A person who is high in the procrastination trait would be expected
    a. have better grades than nonprocrastinators.
    b. to be mellow at the end of a semester.
    c. to be sicker at the end of a semester than persons low in this trait.
    d. turn in work early to avoid deadline pressures.
25. In a continuous reinforcement schedule, a reward is given
    a. after every tenth response.
    b. after some time interval has elapsed.
    c. on average, after every third response.
    d. after every response.
26. A person who is paid for each widget they make in a factory is operating under a _____ schedule of reinforcement.
    a. fixed interval
    b. variable ratio
    c. fixed ratio
    d. variable interval
27. _____ refers to an inability to experience pleasure in daily living.
    a. Hyperhedonia
    b. Neuroleptemia
    c. Hypohedonia
    d. Hypodepression
28. A proven cognitive method by which to reduce your pain experience is to complain more about the pain.   (True-False)

Observational Learning: Learning From the Behavior and Outcomes of Others

29. A key aspect of observational learning is
    a. monitoring the behaviors of appropriate models.
    b. having the motivation to perform the behavior.
    c. being able to remember the actions/statements of other persons.
    d. All of the above are correct.
30. By the age of 18, it is likely that you will have observed some 200,000 acts of violence while viewing television. (True-False)

IDENTIFICATIONS
Identification   Concept:
_____ 1. A situation in which a response that leads to an aversive stimulus will be suppressed.
_____ 2. "You can   only play that video game after you study the chapter on learning."
_____ 3. A form of classical conditioning in which an organism learns to avoid a flavor previously paired with illness.

_____ 4. The most effective means to establish a CR.

_____ 5. His work on taste aversion reshaped the field of classical conditioning.

_____ 6. Eye blink conditioning cannot be done in the absence of this brain structure.

_____ 7. A scientist who studied classical conditioning in dogs.

_____ 8. A form of conditioning that has been used to promote immune function.

_____ 9. Smoking and gambling are examples of this type of behavior.

_____ 10. A relatively permanent change in behavior due to experience but not illness or fatigue.

Identification:
a. Premack principle.
b. Learning.
c. Negative reinforcement.
d. Conditioned taste aversion.
e. Amygdala.
f. Impulsive behaviors.
g. Ivan Pavlov.
h. Punishment.
i. Delay conditioning.
j. John Garcia.
k. Cerebellum.
l. Classical conditioning.

FILL IN THE BLANK

1. Learning can be viewed as occurring in the forms of _____, _____, and _____.

2. The temporal arrangement whereby the UCS occurs before the CS is termed _____.

3. A _____ involves a recurring, unwanted and uncontrollable thought.

4. A noteworthy aspect of a conditioned taste aversion is that this learning is resistant to _____.

5. An environmental cue associated with the use of an addictive drug can create a _____ that is opposite in form to that of the drug state.

6. _____ conditioning is the most effective method to establish a CR.

7. A(n) _____ signals the availability of a reinforcer for a particular response.

8. Smoking and drinking are considered to be examples of _____.

9. Behaviors that are reinforced by a _____ schedule of reinforcement are highly resistant to extinction

10. Gambling is an example of a behavior maintained by a(n) _____ schedule of reinforcement.

11. The reappearance of an extinguished CR after some time interval is termed _____.

12. _____ refers to a cognitive learning deficit in which a history of being unable to avoid/escape unpleasant circumstances leads a person to stop responding and to be passive.

13. _____ refers to the tendency to put off some behavior to a later date.

14. _____ conditioning refers to the situation in which the UCS appears before the CS.

15. A(n) _____ schedule of reinforcement that is useful for maintaining already established behaviors.

COMPREHENSIVE PRACTICE TEST

1. Psychologists define _____ as a long-lasting change in behavior induced by experience.
   a. education
   b. wisdom
   c. learning
   d. maturation

2. _____ refers to a form of learning in which we monitor the behaviors of others.
   a. Social learning
   b. Observational learning
   c. Classical conditioning
   d. Operant conditioning

3. The unconditioned response in Pavlov's experiments was usually
   a. salivation.
   b. running speed.
   c. consuming the meat powder.
   d. eye movements.

4. A bell was sounded by Pavlov and then two minutes later a plate of meat powder was presented to the dog. We would term this temporal arrangement as _____ conditioning.
   a. trace
   b. delay
   c. backward
   d. forward

5. Delay conditioning is the most effective method to establish a CR. (True-False)

6. The progressive decline of a CR in the absence of the UCS is termed
   a. extinction.
   b. fading.
   c. reverse acquisition.
   d. habituation.

7. A(n) _____ involves a repetitive thought whereas a(n) _____ refers to a repetitive behavior.
   a. delusion; obsession
   b. obsession; compulsion
   c. hallucination; delusion
   d. compulsion; delusion

8. A woman eats a novel ice cream before undergoing a session of chemotherapy in which she develops nausea. A few days later she passes up an opportunity to eat the same flavor of ice cream because the flavor makes her nauseous. Garcia would suggest that she has developed a(n)
   a. form of gastritis.
   b. homeostatic malaise.
   c. form of anorexia nervosa.
   d. conditioned taste aversion.

9. Conditioned aversions (CTA) are distinct from most forms of classical conditioning in that
   a. a CTA is extremely resistant to extinction.
   b. it usually requires many trials to establish a CTA.
   c. a CTA will not be formed if the interval between the taste and the illness is more than a few minutes.
   d. All of the above are correct.

10. A key function of operant conditioning is to allow us to
    a. adjust our behavior according to its consequences.
    b. allow us to learn new motor behaviors.

c. remember the events of our lives.

d. predict the occurrence of a future stimulus.

11. Which of the following DO NOT belong together?

   a. positive reinforcement;   a procedure that strengthens behavior

   b. primary reinforcers;   praise about a job well done

   c. conditioned reinforcers;   course grades

   d. negative reinforcement;   a procedure that suppresses behavior

12. Punishment is another term for negative reinforcement. (True-False)

13. Many companies try to ensure abstinence from drug taking by doing drug testing of employees using a _____ schedule.

   a. fixed interval

   b. variable ratio

   c. fixed ratio

   d. variable interval

14. Match up the schedule of reinforcement with its definition or example (a schedule may fit more than one answer).

   _____. In this schedule, the first response after some time interval has elapsed is reinforced.

   _____. Factory workers that are paid on a per piece basis are on this schedule.

   _____. In this schedule, every response is reinforced.

   _____. The pursuit of gambling at a slot machine is maintained by this schedule.

   _____. The likelihood of a politician meeting their campaign promises is governed by this schedule.

   _____. In this type of schedule, not every response is reinforced.

_____. An example of this schedule is a security guard that makes their rounds of a building on an irregular schedule.

   a. Fixed interval.

   b. Variable interval.

   c. Fixed ratio.

   d. Continuous reinforcement.

   e. Intermittent reinforcement.

   f. Variable ratio

15. The "Speak Out" program in Norway asks teenage passengers to confront unsafe driving habits in their peers. The program is based on the learning concept of

   a. computer-aided instruction.

   b. timeout.

   c. intermittent punishment.

   d. negative reinforcement.

16. A positive contrast effect occurs when a subject is shifted from a(n)_____ reward to a(n) _____ reward.

   a. smaller;   larger

   b. continuously available;   intermittent

   c. larger;   smaller

   d. immediate;   delayed

CRITICAL THINKING

1. Discuss two lines of research that support the cognitive interpretation of classical conditioning.

2. Discuss the implications of the work of John Garcia for the fields of classical conditioning and learning.

SIX

Memory and Cognition: Remembering, Thinking, Deciding, Creating

*E*ven today, several decades later, I (Robert Baron) can remember many of the teachers I had in high school. My memories for most of them are pleasant, but for one—my eleventh-grade trigonometry teacher— these thoughts still, so many years later, give me negative sensations in the pit of my stomach. As I recall, this teacher—Mr. Hoffman—was tough as nails. He would write on the board and then, with his back turned, call on members of the class to answer questions—hard ones. Even worse, he would choose specific students, order them to the front of the room, and then tell them to solve various problems, ones most of us found very difficult to handle. Perhaps the worst thing he did, though, was to walk up and down the rows whenever he gave us a test—which was often. He would stand next to individual students and stare down at the backs of their heads as they tried to work. The result was that most of us were terrified of Mr. Hoffman and his class, and dreaded the time of day when we had to see him. I vividly recall sitting in my seat as Mr. Hoffman patrolled the rows, and silently trying to think of other things. Why? Because I was convinced that if I thought about Mr. Hoffman, he would immediately choose me for painful grilling. And I also recall one day when, during an exam, he stood behind me. I had studied hard and I knew the material well, but with him standing next to me, staring down at my back, I panicked—and seemed to forget everything. I tried to stay calm, telling myself, "Hey . . . you know this stuff . . . don't give up." But it was no use; my memory seemed to go blank. Only when he finally moved away was I able to remember how to solve the problems on the test. It *was too late, though, and I can still picture the day he returned the test and my humiliation when he said: "Well, Mr. Baron . . . the worst yet! Try studying next time . . . !"*

As this incident from my own dim past reminds me, there are indeed many instances when our memory seems to let us down—when we forget information we *know* we should remember, but simply can't. And it also drives home another key point: In many cases, our thinking is far from totally rational! Would thoughts of Mr. Hoffman really cause him to call on me? Even as a sixteen-year-old, I knew that wasn't so, but that knowledge didn't stop me from trying!

In this chapter, we'll focus on key aspects of the cognitive (mental) side of life: memory, thinking, decision making, and creativity. As humans, we are truly blessed with remarkable systems for remembering, interpreting, and using information we acquire from the experience of living. But these systems, good as they are, are definitely *not* perfect—far from it. So in addition to describing the basic nature of memory and other key aspects of our cognitive systems, we'll also call attention to their limitations and drawbacks. (Please recall that we discussed *intuition*—cognitive events and processes of which we are not fully aware—in Chapter 4.)

Cognition, which psychologists use to refer to all of our higher mental processes, has been a key topic of interest in our field for decades. To provide you with a useful overview of the fascinating findings that research on this topic provides, we'll proceed as follows. We'll begin with **memory**—our system (or really systems) for retaining information. Here, we'll first consider the nature of human memory, examining each of its major components and how they operate. Then, we'll examine *forgetting*—how and why information is lost from memory, and the related topic of how information stored in memory is sometimes distorted or changed over time so that it becomes less accurate (see Wixtel, 2006). After that, we'll consider the role of memory in *everyday life*—for instance, memory for emotional events and experiences. Then, to conclude our discussion of memory, we'll briefly consider memory *impairments* and what these tell us about the biological basis of memory.

Following this discussion of memory, we'll turn to other key aspects of cognition—*thinking, decision making*, and *creativity*. Before examining these topics, though, we'll first describe some basic *limits* of cognition and why, together, these assure that we can't really be as rational or accurate as we would like (Morewedge, Gilbert, & Wilson, 2005).

Cognition:
The mental activities associated with thought, decision making, language, and other higher mental processes.

Memory:
Our cognitive system(s) for storing and retrieving information.

HUMAN MEMORY: HOW WE REMEMBER, WHY WE FORGET

Because we can't observe memory directly (even with modern brain scans), psychologists have found it useful to construct *models* of it—representations of how it functions and the systems it must include to produce the kind of effects that it does—for instance, long-term storage of vast amounts of information, and shorter-term storage of small amounts of information, such as a phone number you dial but then promptly forget (see Anderson, 1993; Baadley & Hitsch, 1994; Raajimakers & Shiffrin, 1981). Many different models have been proposed, but one that has proven to be very useful is known as the **information-**

processing approach (Atkinson & Shiffrin, 1968). We'll first briefly describe this model and then explain how, in the light of new evidence, it can be expanded.

Memory: An Information-Processing Model—and Beyond

The information-processing model of memory mentioned earlier starts with the suggestion that there are certain similarities between computer memory and human memory. For instance, both computer memory and human memory must perform three basic tasks: **encoding**—converting information into a form that can be entered into memory; **storage**—somehow retaining information over varying periods of time; and **retrieval**—locating and accessing specific information when it is needed at later times.

For computers, encoding involves complex programs that convert what you type on the computer keyboard into codes the program can process. For humans, encoding involves converting information supplied by our senses into neural information that can be processed in our brains. Storage presents a more complex picture. Computers generally contain two kinds of systems for storing information: *random-access memory*—what's open on your desktop at any given moment—and a hard drive, a larger and more permanent memory in which information is stored for longer periods of time. The information-processing model of memory suggests that, in contrast, human memory involves *three* distinct systems for storing information. One of these, known as **sensory memory**, provides temporary storage of information brought to us by our senses. If you've ever watched someone wave a flashlight in a dark room and perceived trails of light behind it, you are familiar with the operation of sensory memory. A second type of memory is known as *short-term memory* (or, more recently, *working memory*). Short-term memory holds relatively small amounts of information for brief periods of time, usually thirty seconds or less. This is the type of memory system you use when you look up a phone number and dial it. Our third memory system, *long-term memory*, allows us to retain vast amounts of information for very long periods of time. It is this type of memory system that permits you to remember events that happened a few hours ago, yesterday, last month—or many years in the past. And it is long-term memory that allows you to remember factual information such as the capital of your state, the name of the president, and the information in this book.

With respect to retrieval, both computers and human memory must be able to find information that has previously been stored. Computer memory requires that you precisely specify the location of information for it to be found. In contrast, you can often find information in your own memory even on the basis of partial information ("I know his name . . . it rhymes with "home" . . . Oh yeah, *Broam!*") Also, when information is lost from computer memory, it is often lost permanently, or at least becomes very difficult to restore. In contrast, information we cannot retrieve from our own memories is often still present, and sometimes pops into mind at a later time, when we are not actively trying to find it.

How does information move from one memory system to another? While there's not complete agreement about this important point, much evidence suggests that information in sensory memory enters short-term memory when it becomes the focus of our attention—when we notice it or concentrate on it. In contrast, information in short-term memory enters long-term storage through *elaborative rehearsal*—when we think about its meaning and relate it to other information already in long-term memory. Unless we engage in such cognitive effort, information in short-term memory quickly fades away and is lost. (See Figure 6.1, page 202 for a summary of the information-processing model.)

While this basic model of memory has proven very useful in efforts to understand how we store and later remember information, it definitely has important limitations. Computers deal with only one kind of information (electronic signals). In contrast, our brains (and our minds) deal with many—input from our senses,

Information-processing approach:
An approach to human memory that emphasizes the encoding, storage, and later retrieval of information.

Encoding:
The process through which information is converted into a form.

Storage:
The process through which information is retained in memory.

Retrieval:
The process through which information stored in memory is located.

Sensory Memory:
A memory system that retains representations of sensory input.

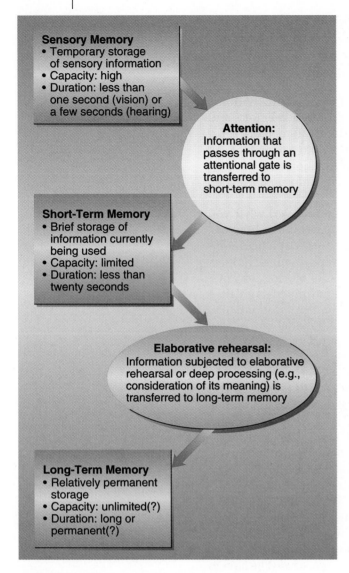

FIGURE 6.1

Human Memory: The Information-Processing View

One view of memory (the information-processing perspective) suggests that we possess three basic memory systems: sensory memory, short-term memory, and long-term memory. Each system must deal with the tasks of encoding information, storing it, and retrieving it when needed.

Source: Based on suggestions by Atkinson & Shiffrin, 1968.

emotion, language, and a system that seems to keep track of causal relations but doesn't always use language. Each of these kinds of information seems to be handled by a different system, which has its own functions, processes, structures, and forms of memory, and may well involve different areas of the brain (Rubin, 2005). So a truly modern model of memory suggests that it actually rests on the complex interplay among several basic systems and, as a result, cognition—the way in which our minds work—is more complex than what a computer or information-processing model suggests. Having said that, though, we should note, again, that the information-processing model has proven very useful and, for that reason, we'll use it as a guide in several sections of this chapter.

KEY QUESTIONS

- According to the information-processing model, what key tasks are performed by memory?
- What are sensory memory, short-term memory, and long-term memory?

Our Different Memory Systems

As you already know from your own experience, our memories hold many kinds of information. Some of it is factual and relates either to (1) *general information* you can remember—for instance, "The earth is round, like a basketball," and "George Washington was the first president of the United States"; or (2) events and experiences in your life that you can recall (e.g., "I remember my last trip to the dentist and how much it hurt!" "That was a great meal I had with my friend Juanita last week."). But your memory holds much more than factual information. Can you play a musical instrument? Ride a bicycle? If so, you realize that you also have another, distinctly different type of information stored in memory—information that allows you to perform such activities. And here's the interesting point: While you can verbally state that your friend is moving or that Hawaii is in the Pacific Ocean, you really can't describe the information that allows you to play the piano or guitar, to ride your bicycle without hands (don't do it!), or type without thinking of individual keys, as I'm doing right now (see Figure 6.2). And what about information in memory that tells you when to do something—for instance, take your medicine, leave for school or work, and so on? This is yet another kind of information stored in memory until it is needed. So memory actually holds several kinds of information. We'll now examine the memory systems that allow us to store these different kinds of information.

■ **Working memory: The workbench of consciousness.**

Have you ever had the following kind of experience? You obtain some useful piece of information—a telephone number, a computer password, a word in a foreign language—and can use it right after you see or hear it. But then, a few minutes later, it is totally gone and you can't remember it no matter how hard you try. What's going on here? What happened to that wonderful system we term "mem-

FIGURE 6.2
Memory for Different Kinds of Information
We store many kinds of information in memory—factual information about the world around us and information that permits us to perform many kinds of skilled actions. Although we can readily describe the first type of information, we usually find it difficult to put the second type into words.

ory"? The answer involves the operation of what psychologists first described as *short-term memory*, but now often describe by the phrase **working memory.** Working memory is a system for holding small amounts of information for short periods of time. In fact, it can hold only about seven separate items. The amount of information working memory stores can be greatly increased, though, by **chunking**—combining separate items in some way. For instance, consider the following list of letters: IBFIMBWBMATWIAC. After hearing or reading it once, how many could you remember? Probably no more than about seven (that's the general limit of short-term storage of independent bits of information). But imagine that, instead, the letters were presented as follows: FBI, IBM, BMW, TWA, CIA. Could you remember more now? In all likelihood you could, because now you could combine them into meaningful *chunks*—acronyms for famous organizations. Because of the process of chunking, short-term memory can hold larger amounts of information than the limit of seven to nine separate items would suggest.

■ Working memory: Short-term storage with a very important plus.

From what we've said so far, you might conclude that short-term memory is simply a system for storing small amounts of information for a very limited period of time. In fact, though, this aspect of our memory involves much more. Active processing of information occurs in it as well—processing that may well determine how well we can perform very complex tasks such as reading, playing a musical instrument, or reasoning (Engle et al., 1999). This is why psychologists now prefer the term *working memory* to describe this system; this phrase indicates that something *active* is happening, and in fact, it is. Not only does working memory store information, but it also involves other mechanisms. First, it may involve a mechanism of attention—one that permits us to determine *what* information is retained in short-term storage and what information is ignored or actively blocked from entry (Baddeley, 1992)

Second, recent findings (e.g., Ericsson, 2006) indicate that working memory may also include a mechanism that permits us to draw very efficiently on information stored in another memory system, **long-term memory**—our system for storing huge amounts of information for long periods of time. The more efficiently we can draw on such information, the better we can use it for whatever tasks we are currently performing—from taking a test to giving a speech. In fact, as individuals become experts in a given field (sports, medicine, science, whatever), they seem to acquire an enhanced form of working memory for that field—something some researchers describe as *long-term working memory*, because it involves very close ties to long-term memory (e.g., Ericsson & Kintsch, 1995). In short, working memory is much more than just a system for holding on to small amount

Working memory (previously known as *short-term memory*): A memory system in which information we are processing at the moment is held. Recent findings suggest that it involves more complex levels and forms of processing than was previously believed.

Chunking: Combining separate items in some way.

Long-term memory: A memory system for the retention of large amounts of information over long periods of time.

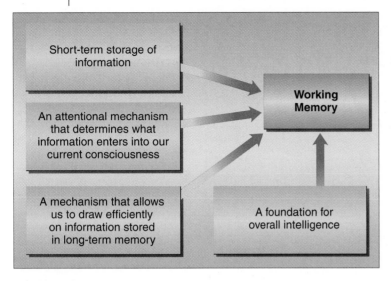

FIGURE 6.3
Working Memory: Its Basic Nature
Recent research indicates that *working memory* provides much more than a system for short-term storage of small amounts of information. It also includes a mechanism for determining what information becomes the focus of our attention and so enters into consciousness; may contribute to our ability to perform many complex cognitive tasks; and may form an important foundation for our overall intelligence.

of information temporarily. It also seems to play a key role in determining what information enters our consciousness, either from the external world or from our own memories.

Now, here's the truly interesting part: The more effectively an individual's working memory operates (and there are several good measures of such performance), the better the person tends to do on complex cognitive tasks such as following directions, understanding complex written passages, writing, reasoning, and even writing computer programs (Engle, 2001). In fact, findings indicate that working memory capacity (one measure of its performance) is closely related to overall intelligence—which, as we'll see in Chapter 9, provides one measure of the effectiveness of our cognitive systems. For instance, in one recent study (Friedman et al., 2006), participants performed a task that required them to update their working memories rapidly—to delete information they no longer needed and add information they did need. Their scores on this task were then related to measures of their intelligence. As expected, a strong positive correlation was found between performance on the updating task (which is an index of the operation of working memory) and overall intelligence. This suggests that working memory does indeed play a key role in many aspects of our cognition, and is much more than a temporary "holding area" for information (see Figure 6.3).

KEY QUESTIONS

- What is the difference between short-term memory and working memory?
- Why is working memory much more than a system for holding small amount of information for short periods of time?

Memory for Factual Information: Episodic and Semantic Memory

Now that we have examined the nature of working memory, we'll turn to several aspects of long-term memory—our memory system (or, really, systems) for retaining large amount of information for long periods of time. We'll begin with the systems that permit us to retain factual information. Such information consists of our general knowledge about the world, which is stored in **semantic memory,** and of events that happened to us personally, which is stored in **episodic memory.** Let's take a closer look at both kinds of memory.

■ Episodic memory: Some factors that affect it.

As a student, you have lots of first-hand experience with the functioning of episodic memory. Often, you must memorize definitions, terms, or formulas. Such information is stored in episodic memory because we know that we learned it at a specific time, in a specific place (e.g., a course in college). What can you do to improve such memory? Research on semantic memory suggests that many factors influence it, but among these, the most important are the *amount and spacing of practice.* The first finding seems fairly obvious; the more often we practice information, the more of it we can retain. However, the major gains occur at first, and

Semantic memory:
A memory system that stores general, abstract knowledge about the world—information we cannot remember acquiring at a specific time and place.

Episodic memory:
Memory for factual information that we acquired at a specific time.

FIGURE 6.4
Retrieval Cues: Usually—But Not Always—Helpful!
Retrieval cues, stimuli associated with information stored in memory, are often helpful in bringing such information to mind. They don't have to be this obvious to work!
Source: © King Features Syndicate.

then further improvements in memory slow down. For this reason, spacing (or distribution) of practice is important, too. Spreading out your efforts to memorize information over time is helpful. For instance, two sessions of thirty minutes are often better, in terms of retaining information, than one session of sixty minutes.

Another factor that has a powerful effect on retention is the kind of processing we perform. When we study a list of words, we can simply read them or, alternatively, we can think about them in various ways. As you probably know from your own studying, it is possible to read the same pages in a text over and over without remembering much of the information they contain. However, if you actively try to understand the material and think about it (e.g., its meaning, its relationship to other information), you stand a better chance of remembering it when the exam booklets are handed out.

Another, and very important, factor that influences episodic memory involves what are known as **retrieval cues**—stimuli that are associated with information stored in memory and so can help bring it to mind at times when it cannot be recalled spontaneously. Many studies suggest that such cues can often help us remember; indeed, the more retrieval cues we have, the better our ability to remember information entered into episodic memory (see Tulving & Watking, 1973)—and they don't have to be as obvious as the ones shown in Figure 6.4 to work! For instance, many studies demonstrate the existence of what is known as **context-dependent memory,** which refers to how material learned in one environment or context is easier to remember in a similar context or environment than it is in a very different one. For instance, believe it or not, deep-sea divers who memorize a list of words while fifteen feet below the surface remember these words better when tested in this same setting than when tested on the beach (Baddeley & Godden, 1975).

External cues relating to a given environment or location are not the only ones that can serve as aids to memory, however; a growing body of evidence indicates that our own internal states can sometimes play this role, too. The most general term for this kind of effect is **state-dependent retrieval,** which refers to how it is often easier to recall information stored in long-term memory when our internal state is similar to that which existed when the information was first entered into memory. For example, suppose that while studying for an exam, you drink lots of coffee. Thus, the effects of caffeine are present while you memorize the information in question. On the day of the test, should you also drink lots of coffee? The answer appears to be "yes," and not just for the boost in alertness this may provide. In addition, being in the same physical state may provide you with retrieval cues that may help enhance your performance (Eich, 1985). The basic principle that underlies all these effects is sometimes described as the **encoding specificity principle:** Retrieval of information is successful to the extent that the retrieval cues match the cues the learner used when acquiring the to-be-remembered information. The more these are similar, the more memory is facilitated.

Retrieval cues:
Stimuli associated with information stored in memory that can aid in its retrieval.

Context-dependent memory:
Refers to how information entered into memory in one context or setting is easier to recall in that context than it is in others.

State-dependent retrieval:
Occurs when aspects of our physical states serve as retrieval cues for information stored in long-term memory.

Encoding specificity principle:
Retrieval of information is successful to the extent that the retrieval cues match the cues the learner used during the study phase.

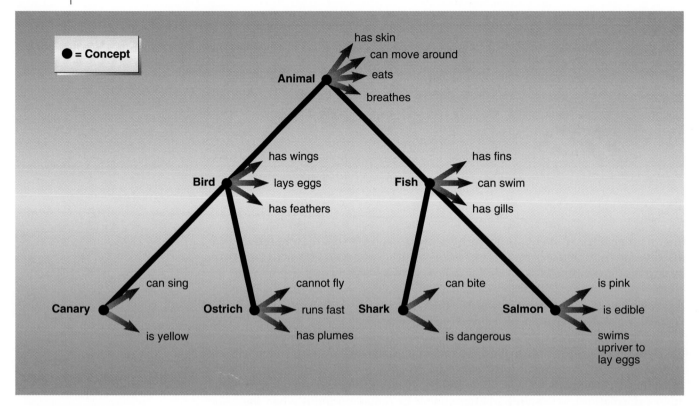

FIGURE 6.5
Semantic Networks
Semantic memory contains many concepts that seem to exist in networks reflecting the relationships among them. One such network is shown here.

■ **Semantic memory: How information is organized in memory.**

Now let's turn to semantic memory—memory for general information about the world. Since each of us already possesses a very large amount of information in semantic memory, psychologists have focused primarily on how such information is organized, rather than on how it is entered into memory in the first place. One important basis of such organization is in terms of **concepts**—mental categories for objects or events that are similar to one another in certain ways. For instance, the words *bicycle, airplane, automobile,* and *elevator* are included in the concept for *vehicles* or *means of transportation.* The words *shoes, shirts, jeans,* and *jackets* are included in the concept *clothing.*

Concepts in semantic memory seem to exist in networks reflecting the relationships between them—semantic networks. One such network is shown in Figure 6.5. As you can readily see, this shows a hierarchy of concepts: *Animals* includes both *birds* and *fish,* and *birds,* in turn, includes ostriches and canaries. Similarly, *fish* includes *sharks* and *salmon.* However, unless the person whose semantic memory is represented here is confused, it does *not* contain *porpoises,* because they are mammals, not fish.

KEY QUESTIONS

- What are episodic memory and semantic memory?
- What are retrieval cues and what role do they play in memory?
- What are concepts and what role do they play in semantic memory?

Memory for Skills: Procedural Memory

Concepts:
Mental categories for objects or events that are similar to one another in certain respects.

Can you ride a bicycle? Most people can. But now, can you state, in words, how you perform this activity? You would probably find that difficult. And the same principle applies to many other skills we have acquired—for instance, can champion golfer Tiger Woods explain how he hits a golf ball so far? Again, not very readily. Situations like this one indicate that often we have information in memory that we can't readily put into words. Our ability to store such information is known as **procedural memory,** or sometimes as *implicit memory* (both semantic and episodic memory, in contrast, as described as being aspects of *explicit memory*—we can intentionally recall such information and can readily put it into words). Both terms are informative: We often know how to perform some action but can't describe this knowledge to others, and what we can't put into words is, in one sense, implicit.

Evidence for the existence of procedural memory is provided by the way in which many skills are acquired. Initially, as we learn a skill, we think about what we are doing and can describe our actions and what we are learning verbally. As we master the skill, however, this declarative (explicit) knowledge is replaced by procedural knowledge, and we gradually become less and less able to describe precisely how we perform the actions in question (Anderson, 1993). Do you recall our discussion of intuition in Chapter 4? Clearly, knowledge stored in procedural memory is closely related to what many psychologists mean by this term—knowledge or cognitive processes that can't readily be expressed in words.

Interestingly, recent findings indicate that our ability to use information stored in implicit (procedural) memory may be related to our circadian rhythms—another topic we discussed in Chapter 4. While you might guess that we would be best at remembering and using such information when we are at our personal "peak" (e.g., early in the day for morning people, late in day for evening people), the opposite seems to be true: We are actually better at remembering and using such information when we are "off-peak." In contrast, we *are* better at remembering information in explicit (episodic or semantic) memory when we are at our circadian-rhythm peaks. These effects are shown clearly by the results of a study by May, Hasher, and Foong (2005). Participants in this research were tested for both kinds of memory at times when they were at their circadian-rhythm peaks and when they were not at these peaks. Results indicated that explicit memory was better at peak times during the circadian cycle, but implicit memory was better at "off-peak" times (see Figure 6.6, page 208). Why? Perhaps because we are more relaxed during "off-peak" hours and so more receptive to information that is "offline" and not explicit. Whatever the reason, these findings provide further, intriguing evidence for the existence, and importance, of information stored in procedural or implicit memory—information that we can't readily put into words, but that strongly affect our behavior.

What about memory itself—can it be viewed as a skill that can be improved? Absolutely; in fact, some techniques for improving memory are described in the **Psychology Goes to Work** section on page 216.

KEY QUESTIONS

- What is procedural memory?
- Is there a link between circadian rhythms and our ability to use explicit and implicit (procedural) memory?

Forgetting: Largely a Matter of Interference—but What *Kind* of Interference?

When are we most aware of memory? Typically, when it fails—when we are unable to remember information that we need at a particular moment. Often, it seems to let us down just when we need it most—for instance, during an exam, as described in the opening story to this chapter. Why does this occur? Why is information entered into long-term memory sometimes lost, at least in part, with the passage of time? Many explanations have been offered, so here we'll focus on the ones that seem most accurate.

Procedural memory
(implicit memory): A memory system that retains information we cannot readily express verbally—for example, information necessary to perform various skilled motor activities such as riding a bicycle.

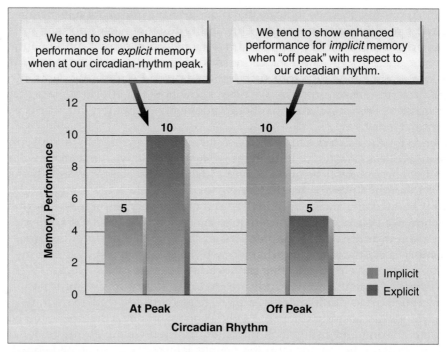

FIGURE 6.6
Procedural Memory: When Can We Use it Best?
As shown here, recent findings indicate that while we are best at remembering and using *explicit* memory (information in semantic or episodic memory) when we are at our circadian-rhythm peaks, the opposite may be true for *implicit* (procedural) memory: we are better at remembering and using such information when we are *not* at our circadian peaks.
Source: Based on data in May, Hasher, & Foong, 2005.

The earliest view of forgetting was that information entered into long-term memory faded or decayed with the passage of time. While this seems to fit with our subjective experience, many studies indicate that the amount of forgetting is *not* simply a function of how much time has passed; rather, what happens during that period of time is crucial (e.g., Jenkins & Dallenbach, 1924). For instance, in one unusual study, Minami and Dallenbach (1946) taught cockroaches to avoid a dark compartment by giving them an electric shock whenever they entered it. After the subjects had mastered this simple task, they were either restrained in a paper cone or permitted to wander around in a darkened cage at will. Results indicated that the insects permitted to move about showed more forgetting over a given period of time than those who were restrained. So, what the roaches did in between learning and testing for memory was more important than the mere passage of time. On the basis of such findings, psychologists rejected the notion that forgetting stems from passive decay of memories over time and turned, instead, to the view that forgetting primarily involves various forms of *interference*—some kind of competition between information in memory and new information (Wixtel, 2005). But what kind of interference, and how does such interference produce forgetting? Those are the issues we'll now examine.

■ Forgetting and interference.

One possibility is that forgetting stems mainly from *interference* between items of information stored in memory. Such interference can take two different forms. In **retroactive interference,** information currently being learned interferes with information already present in memory. If learning how to operate a new computer program causes you to forget how to operate one you learned previously, this would be an example of retroactive interference. In **proactive interference,** in contrast,

Retroactive interference:
Occurs when new information being entered into memory interferes with retention of information already present in memory.

Proactive interference:
Occurs when information previously entered into memory interferes with the learning or storage of current information.

previously learned information present in long-term memory interferes with information you are learning (and trying to remember) at present. Suppose you learned how to operate one DVD player; now you buy a new one, which requires different steps for recording a television program. If you now make mistakes by trying to operate it in the same way as you did your old DVD, this would constitute proactive interference (see Figure 6.7).

A large body of evidence offers support for the view that interference plays a key role in forgetting from long-term memory (see Tulving & Psotka, 1971). But precisely what kind of interference is crucial? Until recently, the dominant view involved what was known as *cue overload:* Interference occurs because several memories are linked to the same retrieval cue (Wixted, 2004). Thus, when we encounter that cue, several different memories can, potentially, be activated. The more similar these memories are to one another, the greater the interference and the more forgetting occurs. This is demonstrated in many laboratory studies in which the more similar are the words or nonsense syllables participants learn, the more interference occurs among them and the poorer is participants' later recall of these materials (Gruneberg, Morris, & Sykes, 1988).

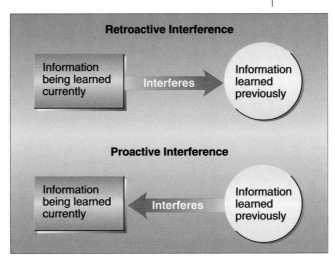

FIGURE 6.7
Retroactive and Proactive Interference
In *retroactive interference*, information currently being learned interferes with the retention of information acquired previously. In *proactive interference*, information learned previously interferes with the retention of new information currently being acquired and put into memory.

Recently, though, an alternative view has been proposed. This view suggests that interference does not really involve cue overload (which is primarily related to the process of retrieval), but rather, interference between *newly formed* memories and *previously formed* ones (interference involving *storage* of information in memory). In other words, this new approach is similar to the idea that memories must be consolidated in the brain in order to persist (an old idea in psychology), and suggests that the process of forming new memories may weaken or even eliminate previously formed memories if they have not had sufficient time to consolidate (see Wixtel, 2005). What evidence supports this view? Perhaps the most impressive is that after individuals take drugs that reduce the rate at which new memories are formed—for instance, alcohol, tranquilizers (e.g., Valium, Xanax)—their memory for information they learned just prior to taking the drugs is *enhanced*. In other words, the drugs, which prevent the formation of *new* memories (among other effects they produce), actually reduce forgetting.

Additional evidence for this view is provided by studies indicating that these drugs block certain kinds of activity in areas of the brain (e.g., the hippocampus) known to play a role in the formation of new memories. Again, to the extent such activity is reduced, new memories can't be formed—and forgetting is actually *reduced* (Wixtel, 2005). Overall then, interference does indeed seem to be a key factor in forgetting, but it may be interference between newly formed memories and existing ones that is crucial—not interference produced by similarity between materials being learned or between different memories linked to the same retrieval cue. To put it simply, we forget information we once knew because new information somehow removes or weakens it, especially if the new information arrives before the earlier information has had a chance to become firmly established or consolidated.

KEY QUESTIONS

- What is proactive interference? Retroactive interference? What role do they play in forgetting?
- According to recent findings, what kind of interference plays a crucial role in forgetting?

Memory Distortion and Construction: How Memories Are Sometimes Changed—or Created

What happens to information once it is stored in memory? Our discussion up to this point seems to suggest two possible outcomes: It is stored in a permanent, unchanging form, or it is forgotten. But this is not the entire story. A growing body of evidence suggests a third possibility: Information entered into memory is *altered* in various ways over time. Such changes take many different forms, but most fall under two major headings: memory *distortion*—alterations in information stored in memory (e.g., we tend to remember what we *want* to remember)—and memory *construction*—the addition of information that was not actually entered into memory (e.g., the construction of false memories; Toglia, Neuschatz, & Goodwin, 1999). While both changes are important, memory construction is so surprising and dramatic that we'll focus primarily on it here.

■ **Memory construction: Creating memories for events we never experienced.**

Memory construction involves the creation of memories for events we never experienced or actions we never performed. Unfortunately, it is far from rare. In fact, growing evidence indicates that many factors and situations lead us to create memories—to construct them in our minds even though they do *not* in any way reflect reality. Further, the findings of recent research suggest that such false memories can be triggered by several kinds of events or experiences (see Garry & Gerrie, 2005).

First, such false memories can be produced by *rumors*—public communications that have no factual basis (Rosnow, 2001). The power of this source to create false memories is illustrated dramatically by research carried out by Principe and her colleagues (Principe et al., 2006). These researchers arranged for preschool children to be exposed to a false rumor—a rumor suggesting that a rabbit had escaped from a magician and was loose in the school. (The children heard one adult tell this information to another adult.) Other children were not exposed to this rumor directly—they simply heard it from classmates. A third group actually saw a rabbit loose in the school, and a final (control) group was not exposed to the rumor—the students in this group were not classmates of the children who heard the rumor when it was originally spread. A week later, the children in all four groups were interviewed and asked whether they knew about the rabbit, and whether they themselves had seen it. As shown in Figure 6.8, results were dramatic. As expected, nearly all the children who saw the rabbit themselves knew about it and reported that it had escaped. In addition, though, many of the children who heard the rumor either from the adults or from their classmates not only knew about it, but *also reported having seen it themselves!* In other words, the rumor not only spread among the children—it also led many of them to believe that they had seen the rabbit, an event that, for most of them, never occurred. Clearly, this is dramatic evidence that false memories can often be generated by rumors—even ones that have no basis in reality.

But rumors are not the only source of false memories. In addition, they can be stimulated by photos (Garry & Gerrie, 2005) and by reports in the mass media. For instance, during and immediately after the Iraq war of 2003, the media often printed various claims (e.g., the presence of weapons of mass destruction in Iraq), and then retracted or denied these initial reports. Presumably, when people hear such retractions, they will delete the false information from their memories and no longer accept it as accurate. In fact, though, the results of research conducted by Lewandoswky and colleagues (Lewandowsky et al., 2005) indicates that once false information is received, it often serves as the basis for memories that are *not* eliminated when the information is withdrawn or denied. These researchers found that among Americans who largely supported the Iraq war (at least initially), statements that were later retracted were seen as true *even after they had been withdrawn or denied.* Among citizens of Germany and Australia—countries in which most people were *not* strongly in factor of the war—retracted statements were later recognized as being false. This suggests a key fact about memory: Often, we believe or remember what we *want* to believe or remember. As a result, Americans who wanted to justify the war continued to believe in "weapons of mass destruction" and atrocities by the Iraqi army, even after initial media reports of such items or events were withdrawn. Germans and Australians, in contrast, had weaker desires to justify the war, and so quickly rejected the retracted statements as false.

Perhaps the most disturbing instances of false memories, however, arise with respect to claims concerning *child sexual abuse*, in instances where individuals report memories of such treatment even though it never actually occurred (see Acocella, 1998). Unfortunately, a growing body of research evidence suggests that false memories of such abuse are both persistent and convincing—the people involved strongly believe that they are real (Brainerd & Reyna, 1998; Reyna & Titcomb, 1996). Accuracy for reporting such events is increased when they are especially traumatic for the victims—when, for instance, the victims describe these experiences as the most

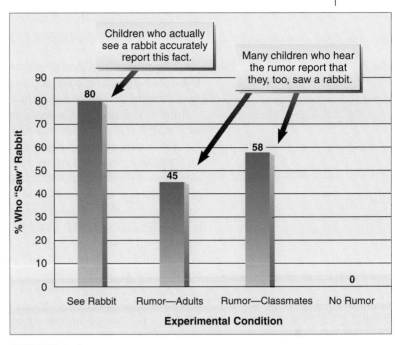

FIGURE 6.8
Rumors as a Source of False Memories
Many children who heard the rumor that a rabbit was loose in their school, but who had never seen the rabbit, came to believe that they *had* seen it—almost as many, in fact, as among those who really *did* see a rabbit in the school. In contrast, children not exposed to this rumor did not report false memories of having seen the rabbit. This is a dramatic illustration of the construction of false memories by rumors.
Source: Based on data from Principe et al., 2006.

traumatic ones of their entire life (Alexander et al., 2005); further, and contrary to popular belief, most people who actually experience such abuse do *not* attempt to repress it, or voluntarily forget it (McNally, Ristuccia, & Perlman, 2005). But the fact remains that in some cases, at least, individuals who report childhood sexual abuse never actually experienced it. Why, then, do they claim to "remember" such horrible experiences? For many different reasons. For instance, such "memories" are suggested to them by well-meaning therapists or by vivid reports of other case in the mass media (McNally, 2004). Whatever the reason, false memories of such events can certainly be damaging both to the people who are falsely accused of having engage in abusive actions and to the people who wrongly "remember" having experienced these events.

■ **Eyewitness testimony: Is it as accurate as we believe?**

Another very dramatic example of the power of false memories is provided by research on **eyewitness testimony**—evidence given by people who have witnessed a crime. Such testimony often plays an important role in many trials, and at first glance, this makes a great deal of sense. What better source of information about the events of a crime than the persons who actually saw them? After reading the previous discussions of distortion and construction in memory, however, you may already be wondering about an important question: Is such testimony accurate?

The answer provided by careful research is clear: Eyewitnesses to crimes are far from perfect. In fact, they often falsely identify innocent persons as criminals (Wells, 1993), make mistakes about important details concerning a crime (Loftus, 1991), and sometimes report "remembering" events they did not actually see (Haugaard et al., 1991). Why do such errors occur? Not, it appears, because the witnesses are purposely "faking" their testimony. On the contrary, most try to be

Eyewitness testimony:
Information provided by witnesses to crimes or accidents.

as accurate as possible. Rather, these errors occur because of several factors that produce distortions in memory: *suggestibility*—witnesses are sometimes influenced by *leading questions* and similar techniques used by attorneys or police officers; and errors with respect to *source monitoring*—eyewitnesses often attribute their memories to the wrong source. For instance, they identify a suspect in a line-up as the person who committed a crime because they remember having seen this individual before, and assume this was at the scene of the crime; in fact, his or her face may be familiar because they saw it in an album of "mug shots."

Revealing research on the role of false memories in eyewitness testimony has been conducted by Loftus and her colleagues, as well as by many other researchers. (e.g., Loftus, 1997, 2003). Initially, this research involved efforts to distort or change memories through the power of suggestion or leading questions—for instance, asking participants whether they had seen a "Stop" sign in a photo of an accident scene when in fact, only a "Yield" sign had been present. In response to such suggestions and leading questions, many individuals did in fact report false memories—memories for events that did not happen and that they did not in fact witness (Loftus, 1997).

More recently, such research has been extended and demonstrates that not only can memories be changed by suggestion and related processes—totally false memories can be created. In one especially dramatic demonstration of this fact, (Braun, Ellis, & Loftus, 2002), participants were asked to read a false ad for Disneyland that featured Bugs Bunny—who is *not* a Disney character and could probably never be present at Disneyland because because he belongs to a competing company. After reading the false ads (or control ads that did not mention Bugs Bunny), participants in the study were asked about their own childhood experiences at Disneyland. Fully 16 percent of those who had read the false Bugs Bunny ads stated that they had personally met Bugs at Disneyland—a totally impossible event! If they saw several fake ads, this percentage rose even higher. Clearly, findings such as these—which have been repeated in many different studies—indicate that people can indeed be led to believe that they had experiences they could not possibly have had. Further, false memories tend to be believed and accepted as accurate just as strongly as real ones (McNally et al., 2004). The implications of such false memories for the legal system are both obvious and unsettling for as Loftus (2004, page 147) has noted, they show, dramatically, that: ". . . humans are the authors or creators of their own memories, and can also be the authors of creators of someone else's memory." As a result, serious questions can be raised about the accuracy of eyewitnesses and the great emphasis placed on their reports by the legal system.

KEY QUESTIONS

- What is memory construction and how does it occur?
- What factors potentially reduce the accuracy of eyewitness testimony?

Memory in Everyday Life: Autobiographical Memory and Memory for Emotions

Much of the research described so far has involved the performance of relatively artificial tasks: memorizing nonsense syllables or lists of unrelated words. Sometimes, we perform tasks like these outside the laboratory; for instance, as a student, you sometimes memorize lists of terms or definitions. In general, though, we use memory for very different purposes in our daily lives. Let's see what psychologists have discovered about how memory functions in natural contexts.

■ Autobiographical memory: Remembering the events of our own lives.

How do we remember information about our own lives? Such **autobiographical memory** (which falls under the more general heading of *episodic memory*), has long

Autobiographical memory:
Memory for information about events in our own lives.

been of interest to psychologists (see Wagenaar, 1986). One question that has been addressed in this research is, "When do autobiographical memories begin?" In other words, when are our earliest memories about our lives or ourselves formed? This is a tricky question to answer because very young children lack the verbal skills required for storing memories in words. Thus, when later asked to remember such information, it is not available to them in verbal form. What is *your* earliest memory? For most people, such memories date from their third or fourth year of life although a few people report even earlier memories (Usher & Neisser, 1995). This fact raises an interesting question: Can we remember events from before this time—from the first two years of our lives, before we could even talk? And if we can't, why not? Why does such **infantile amnesia** (Howe & Courage, 1993) occur?

Actually, recent research findings indicate that infantile amnesia may not, in fact, exist. Growing evidence suggests that we *can* remember events from very early periods in our lives. However, as noted above, we didn't possess fully developed language skills at the time such memories were formed, so we can't report them in words (Bauer, 1996). The memories do exist, however: they just can't be readily put into words (e.g., Meyers et al., 1987).

Other factors, too, may contribute to our inability to report memories from the first two years of our lives. One possibility is that autobiographical memory is absent early in life because we do not possess a clear *self-concept* until sometime between our second and third birthdays (Howe & Courage, 1993). Without this concept, we lack the personal frame of reference necessary for autobiographical memory.

Whatever the precise mechanisms involved in our inability to verbally report memories from our early lives, it appears that we can store information from this period in memory. So by and large, the term *infantile amnesia* is misleading because in fact, certain types of memory are indeed present even in very early childhood. We simply can't describe them in words, as we can for memories stored later.

Here's another interesting finding concerning infantile amnesia: the results of several recent studies (e.g., Winerman, 2006) indicate that persons who are "mixed-handed" (who do things with both their right and left hands), may have better episodic memory for events early in life (events that happened to them personally) than persons who are strictly right-handed. The reason seems clear: semantic memories are encoded and retrieved from the left hemisphere of the brain. Episodic memories, such as memories for early childhood, are encoded in the left hemisphere but retrieved in the right hemisphere. Persons who are mixed-handed have better connections between the two hemispheres of the brain, so this gives them an advantage in recalling early episodic memories (Christman, 2004). One of us (Robert Baron) is mixed-handed: he writes with his left hand but does many other things right-handed. Perhaps this is one reason why he has such vivid memories of events that occurred to him in early childhood—more vivid than his brothers, who are not mixed-handed.

Other findings indicate that autobiographical memories are "special" in several other respects, though, is suggested by recent research employing neuro-imaging techniques (e.g., studies using MRI). This research indicates that when individuals recall autobiographical memories, certain areas of the brain are more active than they are when the same people try to recall semantic memories (general information about the external world; Rubin, 2005). For instance, in one intriguing study, students took pictures of locations around their college campus. Later, they viewed these pictures, and other students who had not taken them saw the same photos. As they looked at the photos, their brains were scanned by functional magnetic resonance imaging. Results indicated that the students' brains showed greater activity in several areas when they had taken the photos themselves than when they merely looked at photos taken by others. This provides very basic evidence for the view that autobiographic memories are indeed "special"—they are

Infantile amnesia:
Our supposed inability to remember experiences during the first two or three years of life.

processed differently by the brain than semantic memories that are not directly relevant to our lives and experiences.

■ Memory for our own emotions: Coping with the present by reconstructing the past.

Another question relating to memory in everyday life is this: how accurately can we remember emotions we had in the past? This is an important question, because often our emotions provide important guides for our behavior. For instance, if we meet someone and leave with the feeling that we don't like that person, we will probably avoid them in the future, even if we can't remember *why* we didn't like them. Similarly, to treat people suffering from psychological problems such as depression, therapists often need to know how strong these emotional reactions were in the past. So, how accurate *are* we in recalling our own emotions? In general, quite accurate: When individuals rate their emotions and later try to recall them, the two ratings generally agree (Levine & Safer, 2002). However, factors exist that can strongly distort the memories of our own emotions.

First, our current emotional state can produce such effects. For instance, when people who have lost a spouse are asked to rate the intensity of their grief in the past, their answers are more closely related to their current levels of grief than to the grief they reported years earlier—the time they are trying to remember (Safer, Bonano, & Field, 2001; Safer, Levine, & Drapalski, 2002). Second, we tend to cope with present problems by reconstructing the past—by changing our memories of our emotions. For instance, after going through a very painful experience, many people report that they have gained wisdom or insight. In fact, though, this change is often less than they imagine: To feel better about the event, they disparage their wisdom or insight *before* the event, remembering it as less than it really was (McFarland & Alvaro, 2000). Similarly, patients who have successfully completed therapy overestimate their pre-therapy distress, thus perceiving greater positive change than actually occurred (Safer & Keuler, 2002). The basic principle seems to be that we really do reconstruct the past—change our memories of our emotions—to maximize our current happiness or satisfaction. In such instance memory distortions can have beneficial effects, even if they rest on an illusory foundation (see Figure 6.9).

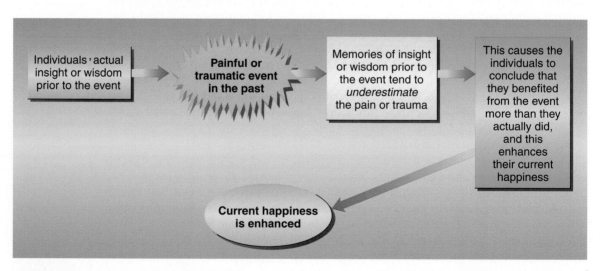

FIGURE 6.9
Adjusting Memories of our Past Emotions to Maximize Current Happiness
After experiencing painful or traumatic events, individuals often accentuate the benefits they have gained from these events by disparaging their knowledge or insight prior to the event. This allows them to conclude that they benefited from it even more than they actually did.

■ **The effects of mood on memory.**

Earlier, in our discussion of retrieval cues, we noted that our internal states can serve as a cue for information stored in memory: It is often easier to recall information stored in long-term memory when our internal state is similar to that which existed when the information was first entered into memory. The effects of mood on memory are closely related to such *state-dependent retrieval* because our moods can be another internal state that serves as a retrieval cue. How can mood influence memory? In two related but distinct ways. First, memory can be enhanced when our mood state during retrieval is similar to that when we first encoded some information; this is known as **mood-dependent memory.** For instance, if you entered some information into memory when in a good mood, you are more likely to remember this information when in a similar mood once again; your current mood serves as a kind of retrieval cue for the information stored in memory. Note that you will remember this information, whatever it is—positive, negative, or unrelated to mood. For instance, if you learned a list of definitions while in a good mood, you will remember them better when in a good mood again, although they have nothing to do with producing your mood.

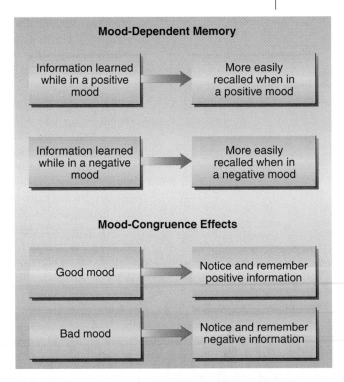

FIGURE 6.10
Effects of Mood on Memory
Memory is enhanced when our mood at the time of retrieval is the same as that at the time information was first entered into memory (i.e., encoded); this is *mood-dependent memory.* We also tend to notice and remember information consistent with our current mood; this is the *mood-congruence effect.*

Second, we are more likely to store or remember positive information when in a positive mood and negative information when in a negative mood—in other words, we notice or remember information that is consistent with our current moods (Blaney, 1986); this is known as **mood-congruence effects.** A simple way to think about the difference between mood-dependent memory and mood-congruence effects is this: In mood-dependent memory, mood serves as a retrieval cue, helping us to remember information we acquired when we were in that mood before—this information may be almost anything, such as the list of definitions we mentioned earlier. In mood-congruence effects, we tend to remember information consistent with our present mood—positive information when we feel happy, negative information when we feel sad (see Figure 6.10). For instance, suppose you are feeling very happy and then are asked how much you enjoyed a particular class you took last year. The chances are good that you will report more enjoyment than you would if you were in a bad mood when you were asked to rate this class.

One reason why mood-congruence effects are important is that they may be closely related to depression (see Chapter 11). Specifically, they help explain why people with depression have difficulty in remembering times when they felt better (Schachter & Kihlstrom, 1989). Their current negative mood leads them to remember unhappy past experiences, and this information causes them to feel more depressed. In other words, mood-congruence effects may push them into a vicious, closed circle in which negative feelings breed negative thoughts and memories, which result in even deeper depression. (The fact that memory is subject to forgetting and to many forms of construction and distortion suggests that the task of *performance appraisal* is a difficult one. What can *you* do to help assure that the performance appraisals you receive at work are fair and accurate? For some hints, see the **Psychology Goes to Work** section on page 216.)

■ **Diversity and memory: Own-race bias in remembering faces.**

One memory task we often face in everyday life is that of recognizing people we have met before. While faces are certainly distinctive, we meet so many people in

Mood-dependent memory:
Refers to the finding that what we remember while in a given mood may be determined, in part, by what we learned when previously in that same mood.

Mood-congruence effects:
Refers to the finding that we tend to notice or remember information congruent with our current mood.

so many different contexts that sometimes our memory plays tricks on us and we mistakenly believe we have met someone before, or, conversely, forget that we *have* met them. This is not at all surprising, but more disturbing is that we often find it easier to remember people belonging to our own racial or ethnic group than people belonging to other ones. Many studies confirm this fact; a review of dozens of separate studies involving more than five thousand participants suggests that people are indeed more successful in recognizing people they have met (or whose photos they have seen) who belong to their own race much better than people who belong to another race (Meissner & Brighman, 2001). Moreover, this seems to be true whether they have actually met these people or merely seen photos of them (Ludwig, 2001). Even more unsettling is that such effects are stronger for people who are high in racial prejudice than for people who are low in such prejudice (Brigham & Barkowitz, 1978; Meissner & Brighman, 2001).

Why do such effects occur? Perhaps because, at least until recently, many people had more frequent contact with members of their own race than with members of other races. Thus, they became more familiar with the physical traits of their own race, and so had better retrieval cues for recognizing individual faces. The role of experience in such cross-race recognition or memory is clearly illustrated

PSYCHOLOGY GOES TO WORK

Using Memory Principles to Boost the Fairness, Accuracy, and Favorableness of Your Performance Appraisals

In most organizations, employees receive *performance appraisals*—evaluations of their work—once or twice a year. These appraisals serve as the basis for setting raises and selecting people for promotion, and as a source of valuable feedback that can help employees improve. In other words, they are *important*. But think about how they are done: Once or twice a year, your boss must remember your performance over a period of several months. And then, she or he evaluates it on the basis of these memories. Given the many errors and distortions to which memory is subject, this can be a very tricky task! Are there steps you can take to help assure that what your boss remembers is really an accurate picture of your performance and contributions—and one that fully takes account of your important contributions? Here are some we think may be useful.

- **Ask your boss to keep a record of your most important contributions:** If your boss agrees, he or she will have a written record of what you contributed, and will not have to try to retrieve this information from memory. If your boss is too busy, offer to provide such a summary yourself.

- **Try to make sure that your boss is in a good mood when he or she prepares your appraisal.** Mood-congruence effects suggest that when people are in a good mood, they tend to remember positive information—and that's certainly what you want to happen!

- **Try to make sure that when you perform very well, your boss notices:** Only information that is noticed can be entered

into memory, so when you do something specially good, this is *not* the time to be modest! Call it to your boss's attention so that she or he can enter it into memory, and retrieve it when the time for appraisals comes around.

- **Be sure to start out strong on any new job:** First impressions count because once they are formed, they are entered into memory and tend to persist unless something important or dramatic happens to change them. So, if you start out well, your boss will form a favorable mental framework for you and your performance—and this will make it easier for her or him to remember your good contributions when doing your appraisal.

- **Try to provide your boss with clear retrieval cues for your own good performance:** You want to be sure that when the time comes, your boss will be able to remember examples of very good performance on your part. That means you should try to link these instances with cues that will remind your boss of your good work. For instance, you can notice something important that happened at a time when your boss commented on your good work—something that happened the same day or week. Reminding your boss of that event may help to remind her or him of your good work, too.

By following these steps, you can increase the chances that your boss will remember favorable information about you when preparing your evaluation—and that can be an important boost to your career.

by a study conducted by Bar-Haim and colleagues (2006). These researchers observed the amount of time three-month-old infants looked at color photographs of members of their own race or another race. Some of the infants lived in a very homogenous racial environment (Ethiopian infants living in Africa; Caucasian infants living in Israel), while others lived in an environment in which they had exposure to people of various races (Ethiopian infants living in Israel). Results indicated that the infants who lived in a homogeneous racial environment did spend more time looking at members of their own race than the other race (the Caucasian Israeli infants looked more at Caucasian faces, while the African Ethiopian infants looked more at African faces; see Figure 6.11). However, the infants who lived in a heterogeneous environment (African infants in Israel) did not show this effect. So even by three months of age, infants demonstrate a same-race preference reflecting the environment in which they are raised. Fortunately, the increasing diversity of the United States and many other countries may lead to a decrease in the magnitude of such effects; after all, as individuals have increasing exposure to and contact with people in many ethnic and racial groups, they may come to recognize them all with equal accuracy. And then the detestable phrase, "They all look alike to me . . . ," may finally be abolished.

KEY QUESTIONS

- What is autobiographical memory? When does it begin?
- Why do we sometimes distort memories of our own prior emotional states?
- What are mood-dependent memory and mood-congruence effects?
- What is own-race bias in memory for faces?

FIGURE 6.11
Own-Race Bias in Memory for Races: It Stems Primarily from Environmental Factors
Infants raised in a racially homogenous environment spent more time looking at photos of members of their own race than at another race. However, infants raised in a racially heterogeneous environment did not show this preference for photos of their own race. This suggests that the same-race bias stems primarily from infants' experience with members of various races.
Source: Y. Bar-Haim, T. Ziv, D. Lamy, and R. Hodes, 2006, "Nature and Nurture in Own-Race Face Processing," *Psychological Science*, 17(2), p. 159. Reprinted with permission from Blackwell Publishing.

Memory and the Brain: Evidence from Memory Impairments and Other Sources

Let's begin with a basic assumption: When information is entered into memory, *something* must happen in our brains. Given that memories can last for decades, it is only reasonable to suggest that this "something" involves relatively permanent changes. But where, precisely, do these occur? And what kind of alterations do they involve? Thanks to the development of tools and methods such as those described in Chapter 2, answers to these questions are beginning to emerge (see Paller, Kutas, & McIsaac, 1995). Let's see what research on these issues has revealed.

■ Amnesia and other memory disorders: Keys for unlocking brain-memory links.

One way to investigate the biological bases of memory is to study individuals who have experienced loss of memory—**amnesia**. Amnesia is far from rare, and can stem from accidents that damage the brain, from drug abuse, or from operations performed to treat medical disorders. Two major types exist. In **retrograde amnesia**, memory of events prior to the amnesia-inducing event is impaired. Thus, people suffering from such amnesia may be unable to remember events

Amnesia:
Loss of memory stemming from illness, accident, drug abuse, or medical operation.

Retrograde amnesia:
Loss of memory of events that occurred prior to an amnesia-inducing event.

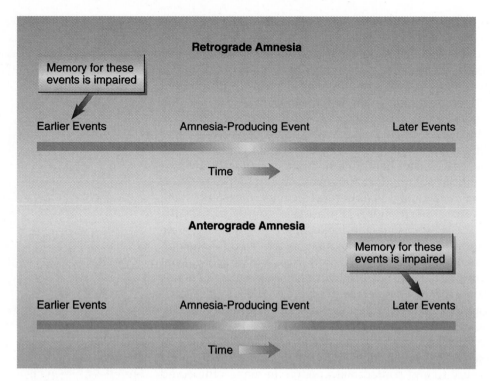

FIGURE 6.12
Two Kinds of Amnesia
In *retrograde amnesia*, memory of events prior to the amnesia-inducing event is impaired—people forget things that happened to them in the past. In *anterograde amnesia*, memory of events occurring after the amnesia-inducing event is impaired—people can't remember things that happen to them after the onset of their amnesia.

from specific periods in their lives. In **anterograde amnesia,** in contrast, individuals cannot remember events that occur *after* the amnesia-inducing event. For example, if they meet someone for the first time after the onset of amnesia, they cannot remember this person the next day, or, in some cases, a few minutes after being introduced (see Figure 6.12).

■ **S.P.: An example of the dissociation between working memory and long-term learning.**

One of the most important findings to emerge from studies of people with amnesia is this: They often retain factual information stored in memory, but can no longer enter new information into long-term storage. S.P., a patient described by the Swiss psychologist A. Schnider (Schnider, Regard, & Landis, 1994), provides a vivid example of such effects. S.P. was sixty-six years old when he suffered a major stroke. An MRI indicated that the stroke had affected S.P.'s medial temporal lobes, the left hippocampus, and many other adjoining areas. After the stroke, S.P. showed a pattern demonstrated by many other people with damage to the hippocampus: He seemed unable to enter information into long-term memory. If he left a room for a few moments, he could not find his way back to it. He could not remember physicians who examined him, or people he met for the first time. (He did, however, recognize his wife and children.) He could talk, read, and write, and repeat words on a list as they were read, but could not remember the words after the list was completed. In short, he showed profound anterograde amnesia. Inter-

Anterograde amnesia:
The inability to store in long-term memory information that occurs after an amnesia-inducing event.

estingly, he *could* enter new information into procedural memory: His performance on tasks such as drawing geometric figures without directly looking at them improved with practice, although he couldn't remember performing the task or explain how he got better at it. This case, and many others like it, point to the importance of the *hippocampus* in memory. Damage to this structure seems to interfere with the ability to transfer information from working memory to a more permanent kind of storage. However, since damage to this structure does *not* eliminate the ability to acquire procedural knowledge (i.e., new skills), it does not seem to be involved in this kind of memory.

■ **Amnesia as a result of Korsakoff's syndrome.**

Individuals who consume large amounts of alcohol for many years sometimes develop a serious illness known as **Korsakoff's syndrome.** The many symptoms of Korsakoff's syndrome include sensory and motor problems as well as heart, liver, and gastrointestinal disorders. In addition, it is often accompanied by both anterograde amnesia and severe retrograde amnesia—patients cannot remember events that took place many years before the onset of their illness. Careful medical examinations of such people's brains after their death indicate that they have experienced extensive damage to portions of the thalamus and hypothalamus. This suggests that these portions of the brain play a key role in long-term memory.

■ **The amnesia of Alzheimer's disease.**

One of the most tragic illnesses to strike humans in the closing decades of their life is **Alzheimer's disease.** This illness occurs among 5 percent of all people over age sixty-five, including famous people such as former President Reagan. It begins with mild problems, such as increased difficulty in remembering names, phone numbers, or appointments. Gradually, though, patients' conditions worsen until they become totally confused, are unable to perform even simple tasks like dressing or grooming themselves, and experience an almost total loss of memory. In the later stages, patients may fail to recognize their spouse or children. In short, people suffering from Alzheimer's disease suffer a wide range of memory impairments: Semantic memory, episodic memory, memory for skills, working memory, and autobiographical memory are all disturbed. As one memory expert puts it (Haberlandt, 1999): "Along with their memories, the patients lose their pasts and their souls."

Careful study of the brains of deceased Alzheimer's patients has revealed that in most cases they contain tiny bundles of *amyloid beta protein*, a substance not found in similar concentrations in normal brains. Growing evidence (Yankner et al., 1990) suggests that this substance causes damage to neurons that project from nuclei in the basal forebrain to the hippocampus and cerebral cortex (Coyle, 1987). These neurons transmit information primarily by means of the neurotransmitter *acetylcholine*, so it appears that this substance may play a key role in memory. Further evidence that acetylcholine-based systems are important is provided by the fact that the brains of Alzheimer's patients contain lower than normal amounts of acetylcholine. In addition, studies with animal subjects in which the acetylcholine-transmitting neurons are destroyed suggest that this does indeed produce major memory problems (Fibiger, Murray, & Phllips, 1983). However, very recent evidence suggests that other neurotransmitters are also involved, so the picture is more complex than was previously assumed.

■ **Memory and the brain: A modern view.**

So what can we conclude from this evidence? Several things. Memory functions do show some degree of localization within the brain. The hippocampus plays a key role in converting information from a temporary state to a more permanent one, and in spatial learning; however, it does not seem to play a role in procedural memory, because damage to the hippocampus leaves such memory largely intact.

Korsakoff's syndrome:
An illness caused by long-term abuse of alcohol that often involves profound retrograde amnesia.

Alzheimer's disease:
An illness primarily afflicting individuals over the age of sixty-five involving severe mental deterioration, including severe amnesia.

The frontal lobes play a role in working memory, executive functions in working memory, and in the encoding and retrieval of factual information from long-term memory. Damage to these areas disrupts these key functions, but may leave other aspects of memory intact.

Why does damage to various brain structures produce amnesia and other memory deficits? Several possibilities exist. One is that damage to these areas prevents consolidation of memories after they are formed (see Squire, 1995). Another is that when information is stored in memory, not only the information itself but its context, too—when and how it was acquired—is stored. Amnesia may result from an inability to enter this additional information into memory (Mayes, 1996).

What about memories themselves—where are they located and what, precisely, are they? Over the years, the pendulum of scientific opinion concerning this issue has swung back and forth between the view that memories are highly localized within the brain—they exist in specific places—to the view that they are represented by the pattern of neural activity in many different brain regions. At present, most experts on memory believe that both views are correct, at least to a degree. Some aspects of memory do appear to be represented in specific portions of the brain, and even, perhaps, in specific cells. For instance, cells have been identified in the cortex of monkeys that respond to faces of other monkeys and humans, but not other stimuli (Desimone & Ungerleider, 1989). So there do appear to be "local specialists" within the brain. At the same time, networks of brain regions seem to be involved in many memory functions. So in reply to the question, "Where are memories located?" the best available answer is—there is no single answer. Depending on the type of information or type of memory being considered, memories may be represented in individual neurons, the connections between them, complex networks of structures throughout the brain, or all the above. Given the complexity of the functions memory involves, this is not surprising; after all, no one ever said that the task of understanding anything as complicated and wonderful as human memory would be easy!

One final comment: Although we don't yet have clear or definite answers to basic questions about the links between the brain and memory, we are certainly making progress. New research tools such as techniques for scanning the intact, functioning brain (e.g., PET scans, *f*MRI) have armed psychologists and other scientists with important tools for unraveling the biological bases of memory. So stay tuned: Rapid progress is occurring now, and will certainly continue in the future. (How can you improve *your* memory? For some suggestions, see the following **Psychology Lends a Hand** section.

KEY QUESTIONS

- What are retrograde amnesia and anterograde amnesia?
- What role do the hippocampus and frontal lobes play in long-term memory?
- What are Korsakoff's syndrome and Alzheimer's disease? What do they tell us about the biological bases of memory?
- What does current research suggest about the location of the memory trace and its nature?

COGNITION: THINKING, DECIDING, AND CREATING

If memory provides the systems for storing information—for retaining it for future use—then *cognition* refers directly to such use. Psychologists use this term to refer to all our higher mental processes—thinking, reasoning, making decisions, solving problems, and showing creativity. We'll examine several of these aspects of cognition in this chapter; another key aspect of cognition—*language*—will be discussed in Chapter 7. Before turning to these intriguing topics, though, we'll briefly address another, and very basic issue—the limits of cognition—restrictions

PSYCHOLOGY LENDS A HAND

Improving Your Memory: Some Useful Steps

How good is your memory? Your answer probably is: "Not good enough!" At one time or another, most of us have wished that we could improve our ability to retain facts and information. Fortunately, with a little work, almost anyone can improve her or his memory. Here are some tips for reaching this goal:

1. **Really think about what you want to remember**: If you wish to enter information into long-term memory, it is important to think about it. Ask questions about it, consider its meaning, and examine its relationship to information you already know. In other words, engage in "deep processing." Doing so will help make the new information part of your existing knowledge frameworks—and increase your chances of remembering it at a later time.

2. **Pay careful attention to what you want to remember**: Unless you pay careful attention to information you want to remember, it stands little chance of really getting "in"—into long-term memory. So be sure to direct your full attention to information you want to remember. True—this involve a bit of hard work. But in the long run, it will save you time and effort.

3. **Minimize interference**: Interference is a major cause of forgetting, and in general, the more similar materials are, the more likely they are to produce interference. In practical terms, this means that you should arrange your studying so that you *don't* study similar subjects one right after the other. Instead, work on subjects that are unrelated; the result may be less interference between them—and, potentially, better grades.

4. **Engage in distributed learning/practice**: Don't try to cram all the information you want to memorize into long-term storage at once. Rather, if at all possible, space your studying over several sessions—preferably, several days. This is especially true if you want to retain the information for long periods of time rather than just until the next exam!

5. **Use visual imagery and other mnemonics**: You've probably heard the saying, "A picture is worth a thousand words." Where memory is concerned, this is sometimes true—it is often easier to remember information associated with vivid mental images (see Gehrig & Toglia, 1989). You can put this principle to use by adopting any one of several different *mnemonics*—tactics for improving memory. One of these, the *method of loci*, involves linking points you want to remember

with visual images, arranged in some familiar order. For instance, suppose you want to remember the points in a speech you will soon make. You can imagine walking through some familiar place, say your home. Then form a series of images in which each item you wish to remember is placed in a specific location. Perhaps the first point is, "The greenhouse effects are real." You might imagine a large, steamy greenhouse right outside your front door. The next point might be, "Cutting down the rain forest is increasing the greenhouse effect." For this one, you might imagine a large cut-down tree in your living room. You'd form other images, in a different location, for the other points you want to make. Then, by taking an imaginary walk through your house, you can "see" each of these images, and so remember the points in your speech.

6. **Give yourself extra retrieval cues**: Remember the concept of state-dependent retrieval? As we noted previously, you can use this principle to provide yourself with extra retrieval cues, and so help to enhance your memory. For instance, if you studied for a test while in one physical state, try to be in the same state when you take it—this may help. Similarly, use the principle of mood-dependent memory. If you learned some material while in a given mood and then want to remember it, try to put yourself in the same mood. This is not as hard as it sounds: You can often vary your mood by imagining happy or sad events. To the degree that your mood now matches your mood when you learned the information, your memory for it may be improved.

7. **Develop your own shorthand codes**: To learn the names of the planets in our solar system, many children use the *first-letter technique*, in which the first letter of each word in a phrase stands for an item to be remembered. So, the sentence "Mary's Violet Eyes Make John Stay Up Nights Pondering" (for Mercury, Venus, Earth, Mars, Jupiter, Saturn, Uranus, Neptune, and Pluto) is very helpful. This can be a very useful technique for remembering other lists of items, too, so use it whenever you can.

We could list additional techniques, but most would be related to the points already described. Whichever techniques you choose, you will learn that making them work does require effort. In memory training, as in any other kind of self-improvement, it appears, "No pain, no gain" holds true.

on their capacity to accomplish key tasks and their surprising susceptibility to a wide range of errors.

The Limits of Human Cognition: Why We Aren't—and Can't Be—as Rational as We'd Like

In a sense, human cognition is nothing short of a marvel: It has allowed us to travel in space, produce beautiful art, develop rich and varied cuisines, and conquer many deadly diseases. Clearly, our abilities to think, reason, use language,

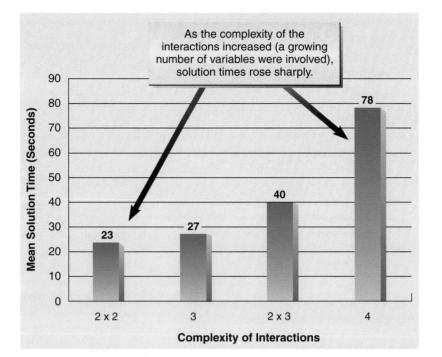

FIGURE 6.13

Testing the Limits of Human Cognition

Research findings indicate that there are clear limits to our ability to process information. We can handle up to three different variables at once, but beyond that, our ability to deal with new information is quickly exceeded.

Source: Based on data from Halford et al., 2005.

and solve problems are one of the greatest strengths of our species. Yet, wonderful as these skills are, they are far from perfect. All our cognitive processes have clear limits on what they can accomplish and are subject to many potential sources of error and bias. With respect to limits, it is now apparent that regardless of how intelligent and motivated we are, it is impossible—perhaps for biological reasons—for us to handle more than a certain amount of information at any one time. Evidence for this is provided by many different findings (see Hummel & Holyoak, 2003). Perhaps the most dramatic illustration of the limits of our cognitive systems, though, is provided by research indicating that although we can readily think about two different factors at the same time, three is "pushing the envelope," and four is just about—or even beyond—our limit.

Evidence pointing to such conclusions is provided by an ingenious study by Halford and colleagues (2005). These researchers asked participants in the experiment to think about a very familiar kind of item: cakes. Specifically, they were asked to examine graphs supposedly presenting information about how much other people liked various kinds of cakes. The information on the graphs represented two, three, or four different aspects of the cakes. For instance, the cakes were chocolate or carrot, either fresh baked or frozen, iced or plain, and low-fat or high-fat. The graphs showed complex interactions between these variables—suggesting, for instance, that people liked carrot cake better when it was fresh and iced than when it was fresh and not iced, but liked chocolate cake better when it was fresh and *not* iced, and so on. Participants then answered questions about these interactions.

The major results were clear: When faced with interactions between two variables, participants could interpret the graphs very well—they could handle this amount of information quickly and accurately. When the interactions involved three variables (e.g., kind of cake, iced, high- or low-fat), though, they began to make errors. And when the interactions involved four variables (kind of cake, iced or not, high- or low-fat, fresh or frozen), their performance dropped sharply (see Figure 6.13). In short, four variables was about at the limits of human information processing capacity—the limits of cognition. That's an important point to keep in mind in our increasingly complex and multifaceted world!

■ Potential errors and biases in cognition: Thinkers
   (deciders, problem-solvers)—beware!

Limits on our cognitive capacity are not the only problem we face, however. In addition, it is also clear that our cognitive processes are subject to powerful and pervasive sources of error. We described some of these in Chapter 1, where we called attention to the **confirmation bias**—our tendency to notice and remember mainly information that confirms our current beliefs, and *escalation of commitment*—the tendency to get trapped in bad decisions (sunk costs). These are only the tip of the iceberg, though, because many other potential sources of error exist, too.

One of the most powerful of these errors is the *optimistic bias*—the tendency to expect things to turn out well even when there is no rational basis for such expectations. Because of this bias, most people expect to experience greater happiness, greater success, and better health than other people; in other words, most of us expect that we will be better than average on many important dimensions. Further, we predict higher chances of success in most things we do than is rationally justified (e.g., Baron & Shane, 2007). While this strong tendency toward optimism may be good for our psychological health, it does not necessarily help us to make excellent decisions or to think clearly and rationally about important issues. One especially common form of the optimistic bias is known as the *planning fallacy*—the tendency to believe that we can accomplish more in a given period of time than we actually can. You have probably observed this tendency in your own thinking. Unless you are very unusual you probably underestimate how long it will take you to complete various tasks, and also overestimate the amount you can get done in a given period of time.

Another kind of error is known as the **hindsight bias,** which refers to our tendency to believe that whatever happens, we actually expected it all along and are not surprised—in other words, a tendency to believe that we know more than we really do (Hawkins & Hastie, 1990). Why does this occur? Perhaps because of our strong desire to put ourselves in a favorable light; one way to do that is to assume that we actually knew what was going to happen all along. Whatever the basis for this effect, it is quite strong and provides another illustration of how our cognitive processes are far from completely rational. We could go on to describe many other examples, but we'll save some of these for our later discussions of key aspects of cognition (e.g., decision making). The major point, though, should be clear: Our cognitive processes provide us with truly magnificent tools for making sense of the world around us, but they definitely *do* have their limits, and are subject to many different kinds of errors.

KEY POINTS

- Are there limits to human cognition? If so, what are they?
- What potential errors can affect the accuracy of our cognitive processes?

Thinking: The Foundation of Consciousness

What are you thinking about right now? Hopefully, the words on this page! But perhaps your thoughts have wandered and you are thinking about a vacation, tonight's dinner, a friend, or a new romantic interest. Whatever thoughts are in your mind right now, it is clear that consciousness presents a rapidly shifting pattern of diverse ideas, impressions, and feelings. Let's now take a closer look at these various components of thought.

Many early psychologists grappled with the following question: "What are the contents of the human mind?" While this turned out to be largely a scientific dead end, psychologists now generally agree that thought involves three basic components: *concepts*, other cognitive frameworks for understanding the external world, and *images*.

Confirmation bias:
The tendency to pay attention primarily to information that confirms existing views or beliefs.

Hindsight bias:
The tendency to assume that we would have been better at predicting actual events than is really true.

As we noted in our discussion of memory, *concepts* refer to mental categories for objects or events that are somehow similar to each other in certain respects. Consider, for instance, the words *bicycle, airplane, automobile,* and *elevator*; all included in the concept *vehicle.* Similarly, the words *shoes, shirts, jeans,* and *jackets* are all included in the concept *clothing.* As you can see, the objects within each of these concepts differ greatly, but are similar to one another in certain underlying respects (e.g., all vehicles are used to move people from one place to another). In a sense, then, concepts act as a kind of "filing system" in memory, and once established, can help us to store new information. Concepts generally take one of two major forms. **Logical concepts** are ones that can be clearly defined by a set of properties. For instance, all *vehicles* move people or objects from one place to another, and all have a way to start and stop. Something that does *not* move things or people around and is stationary itself would probably not fit under the concept "vehicle." Other concepts, however, are harder to define—they are "fuzzy" around the edges. For instance, are viruses living things? Many biologists would say that they are because they can reproduce. Others, however, might disagree, since they can be dried and stored in a bottle for long periods of time. These are known as **natural concepts.** Both logical and natural concepts play important roles in our thought, and we use both to organize vast amounts of information about the world.

Concepts are not the only "filing system" we have, however. In addition, we also construct other cognitive frameworks to help us deal with large amounts of information stored in memory, or entering our minds from the outside world. One of these is known as **prototypes,** and refers to mental representations of the most typical member of a concept. For instance, consider the prototype for *house,* one that most people have. This cognitive framework is broad enough so that everything from a grass hut to a huge mansion would fit within the prototype *house,* but shopping malls, skyscrapers, and sports arenas would not (see Figure 6.14). Why? Because they lack some of the key features included in the prototype for *house;* for instance, they are not generally a place where people live—sleep, cook, eat their food, and so on. Prototypes are an important framework we all use. In fact, in thinking about the world, we often compare new experiences with existing prototypes to determine whether they fit. In other words, prototypes, like concepts, help us to organize information and often play a key role in our thinking (e.g., Baron, 2006).

When you read the words "automobile," "rock star," or "ocean waves," do you form mental pictures of them in your mind? Probably you do, because **images**—mental "pictures" of the external world—are another important aspect of our thought. People report using images for understanding instructions they receive, for making predictions about future events, for understanding past events, and even for changing their own behavior (e.g., they imagine themselves losing weight or winning some prize; Taylor et al., 1998). So clearly images, too, are an important component of thought.

One final comment: In a sense, thinking forms the backdrop for all our cognitive processes. It continues all the time (at least, all the time we are awake), and is often the basis for our feelings and actions. So understanding some of its basic features is a very useful way to start our discussion of specific cognitive processes.

Logical concepts:
Concepts that can be clearly defined by a set of rules or properties.

Natural concepts:
Concepts that are not based on a precise set of attributes or properties, do not have clear-cut boundaries, and are often defined by prototypes.

Prototypes:
The best or clearest examples of various objects or stimuli in the physical world.

Images:
Mental "pictures" of the external world.

KEY POINTS

- What are concepts?
- What are images?

Decision Making: Choosing among Alternatives

Do you sometimes find the task of making decisions hard work? Most people do—and for good reason. Choosing between alternatives, which is the essence of

FIGURE 6.14
Prototypes: Frameworks for Thinking About the World
All the structures shown here could be described as "buildings," but only the ones on the top fit into the prototype for *house*—only they provide places where people live, sleep, cook their food, and so on. Prototypes and other cognitive frameworks for understanding the world are important aspects of our thought.

decision making, is often difficult. And recent research by Schwartz (2004a) suggests that having a large number of choices or options can be bewildering! Too many products to choose from, too many careers, too many lifestyles—choice, like almost anything else, can be overdone (see Figure 6.15, page 226). Regardless of our reactions to the options and choice in our lives, though, we must usually forge ahead and make decisions. How do we do this? What factors influence our choices? And how can be do a better job with respect to this important aspect of cognition? We'll now take a closer look at each of these issues.

■ Decision making: Some basic strategies. Are you a maximizer or a satisficer?

When you have to make an important decision, do you search carefully through all the possible alternatives looking for the one that is best—the perfect choice? Or do you, instead, search through the alternatives until you find one that is "good enough"—one that you find acceptable, even though you fully realize that it is not perfect? Research findings indicate that in making decisions, we tend to adopt one or the other of these two strategies. The first is known as **maximizing,** since it is focused on finding the very best alternative (people who prefer this strategy are known as *maximizers*). The second is known as **satisficing,** because it involves

Decision making:
The process of choosing among various courses of action or alternatives.

Maximizing:
A strategy for reaching decisions in which every possible alternative is considered to choose the one that is best.

Satisficing:
A strategy for making decisions in which the first acceptable alternative is chosen.

FIGURE 6.15
Making a Decision Is Hard Work—and Too Many Choices Can Make It Harder
Modern life offers many people (especially those living in high-developed countries) a huge number of choices. This means that the task of making decisions is even more complex and challenging than it was in the past.

searching not for something that is perfect or best, but for a choice that is merely acceptable (Schwartz, 2004b) (people who prefer this strategy are known as *satisficers*).

The really interesting thing about these two strategies is that they offer a very mixed pattern of costs and benefits. Maximizers engage in very careful and diligent comparison of all existing alternatives; this means that, all things being equal, they tend to make good decisions—better ones than satisficers. On the contrary, since maximizers are seeking perfection (or, at least, the very best possible choice), they tend to be dissatisfied with their decisions. Satisficers, in contrast, are generally pleased with their decisions since they have chosen alternatives that are, as far as they are concerned, "good enough."

Direct evidence for precisely these effects has been reported recently by Iyengar, Wells, and Schwartz (2006). These researchers asked graduating seniors at several colleges to complete a questionnaire that measured their tendency to be a maximizer or a satisficer. Then they asked them to report on how much effort they were putting into their job search. Several months later, they asked all study participants to indicate how satisfied they were with the jobs they had obtained. Results were directly consistent with predictions. Maximizers reported applying for more jobs and generally searching more diligently than satisficers. They also obtained higher starting salaries—$44,515—than satisficers—$38,085. But despite this fact, they also reported being less satisfied with the jobs they accepted than were satisficers.

So, as we noted earlier, both strategies—maximizing and satisficing—offer a mixed bag of advantages and disadvantages. Maximizers work harder at making decisions and, as a result, often experience higher outcomes. But they are also less satisfied with their own choices, and the outcomes they receive, than are satisficers. This suggests that perhaps the best overall strategy is to maximize when we are making very important decisions—ones that influence our lives—but to satisfice in most other cases. At the least, though, we should all be aware of these different approaches to decision making and consider them carefully when making our own choices.

■ Potential sources of error in decision making.

Earlier, we noted that making decisions is hard work. Because it is, we often use tactics designed to reduce our effort. These can certainly work, but as is true with most shortcuts, they also have a "downside"—increased likelihood of errors. One set of mental shortcuts we often use to reduce the effort involved in making decisions is known as **heuristics.** These are mental "rules of thumb" we apply to complex information to make decisions about it easier. We discussed one of these—the **availability heuristic**—in Chapter 1, where we noted that this heuristic involves the tendency to judge the importance or likelihood of events in terms of how readily examples of them can be brought to mind. In other words, the more easily we can think of something and the more information about it we can remember, the more important or frequent we tend to think it is. This can be true, but in many cases it is not. For instance, because reports of airplane crashes are covered in great detail in the news, most of us can bring vivid images of them to mind. This leads many people to conclude that the risks of dying in an airplane crash are greater than are the risks of dying in a traffic accident when, in fact, exactly the opposite is true.

Another heuristic we often use in making decisions is known as *representativeness*. It refers to our tendency to assume that the more something resembles objects belonging to some category or concept, the more likely it is to fit within that category or concept. For instance, suppose you have a next-door neighbor who has a great vocabulary, is constantly bringing large piles of books to her home, is shy, and dresses very conservatively. You don't know what she does for a living, but if asked to guess, you might say, "I think she's a librarian." Why? Because she seems similar to other people you've known in this occupation. You'd be much less likely to guess that she is a manager in a business, because she doesn't seem to fit your image of that group. In this case, you are using the **representativeness heuristic** to reach your decision, and you may be right. But you may also be wrong, and for a very important reason. Are there more business managers or librarians? There are probably fifty times as many managers as librarians. So in a sense, guessing she is a manager would be more likely to be correct, just because the number of people in that field is much higher. In other words, the representativeness heuristic ignores *base rates*—the relative frequency of various objects or events—and this can get us into trouble! The bottom line about heuristics, then, is this: They can often save us lots of effort in making decisions, but can lead to serious errors (Dhami, 2003). So use them with caution and always be aware of their impact.

■ Framing.

The way information is presented can influence decisions. Suppose you go to a grocery store and pick up a package of ground beef. It says "75% lean." That sounds pretty good, so you buy it. Next week, you shop at another store and when you pick up a package of ground beef, it says, "25% fat." Would you find that less appealing? Rationally, both labels provide the same information, but research on decision making suggests that many shoppers would react more favorably to the "75% lean"

Heuristics:
Mental rules of thumb that permit us to make decisions and judgments in a rapid and efficient manner.

Availability heuristic:
A cognitive rule of thumb in which the importance or probability of various events is judged on the basis of how readily they come to mind.

Representativeness heuristic:
A mental rule of thumb suggesting that the more closely an event or object resembles typical examples of some concept or category, the more likely it is to belong to that concept or category.

FIGURE 6.16
Framing: Its Role in Decision Making
The way information is framed can influence decisions. The package of meat on the top reveals fat content in a different way than the package of meat on the bottom. Yet, the fat content is just about the same in each. Which would you buy?

packages than to the "25% fat" packages (see Figure 6.16). Why? Because, as we've said before, our cognitive processes are *not* completely rational and, in many cases, the way information is presented to us—how it is **framed**—is important.

Here's an example of a slightly different kind of framing. Suppose the government is trying to encourage people to wear their seat belts. This could be done in two ways. The ads in magazines could emphasize the positive effects of wearing safety belts: "People who wear their safety belts are much more likely to survive accidents without serious injury than people who do not." Alternatively, the ads could emphasize the negative effects of *not* wearing safety belts: "People who don't wear their safety belts are much more likely to suffer serious harm in accidents than people who do wear their belts." Which approach would be more effective? Research findings indicate that such framing does matter: Messages that stress the negative effects of *not* taking some action tend to be more successful than ones that emphasize the potential benefits of taking those actions (e.g., Frisch, 1993).

Why do framing effects occur? Apparently because the way information is framed leads us to think about situations differently. In other words, thinking about the glass as "half full" is *not* the same as thinking about it as "half empty." And if we see situations as different, it is not surprising that we make different decisions. So, to repeat: Good as our cognitive systems are, they are *not* perfect and we are definitely *not* totally rational!

■ **Escalation of commitment: Getting trapped in bad decisions.**
Have you ever heard the phrase "Throwing good money after bad"? It refers to how, in many situations, people who have made a bad decision—one that is yielding negative outcomes—tend to stick to it even as the evidence for its failure mounts. They may even commit additional time, effort, and resources to a failing

Framing:
Presentation of information concerning potential outcomes in terms of gains or in terms of losses.

course of action in the hope of somehow turning it around. This tendency to become trapped in bad decisions is known as *sunk costs* or **escalation of commitment,** and is very common. It happens to investors who continue to hold stocks that fall sharply; to people in troubled relationships and who often remain in them when all their friends urge them to withdraw; and to people with old cars who continue to make one repair after another (see Staw, Barsade, & Koput, 1997). (We covered this briefly in Chapter 1, but it is so important that we think it is worth discussing briefly again.)

Why do such effects occur? Why do people tend to stick to decisions even if they are producing negative results? For several reasons. First, sticking with a decision is, initially, quite rational. Giving up too quickly can be a mistake, and if the decision was made carefully to start with, it makes sense to continue with it, at least for a while. As losses mount, though, other processes that are *not* so rational come into play. People are unwilling to admit that they made a mistake, because doing so will cause them to lose face and look foolish. Similarly, those who made the initial decision want to justify their actions, and the best way to do so is to continue on the present course and somehow make it turn out well.

Fortunately, there are ways to reduce escalation of commitment—for instance, by making it clear that people won't be blamed or made to feel foolish for backing away from a bad choice. We'll consider ways to reduce escalation of commitment, and other potential sources of error in decision making, in the **Psychology Lends a Hand** section on page 231.

■ Arousal and "auction fever."

Before concluding, we want to touch briefly on one more factor that plays an important role in decision making—emotional arousal. Perhaps the best way to illustrate the powerful impact of this factor is by looking at what happens in auctions. Have you ever taken part in an auction? If so, you know that some very unexpected things can occur. When bidders battle one another for an item up for sale, the excitement often rises, and the bidders may quickly run the price up to levels that no one expected, and that far exceed initial predictions (see Figure 6.17, page 230). Moreover, bidders caught up in the process may greatly surpass the limits they set for themselves when they started. Here's one example: A few year ago, the city of Chicago sponsored a public art auction of three hundred life-sized fiberglass cows. Bidding took place both on the Internet and live, and results were amazing: The cows sold for almost seven times the initial estimate (almost $3.5 million)!

What happens in auctions that often leads bidders to make what appear to be very poor decisions? Research by Ku, Malhotra, and Murnighan (2005) suggest that high levels of *arousal*—and especially competitive arousal—may be crucial. When arousal is high, people generally find it very difficult to think clearly and to consider all their options carefully. Rather, they respond quickly—and often this leads them to make very bad choices. For this reason, people taking part in an auction, especially an auction that involves direct competition among bidders, often get swept up in the process; they are aroused and want to win—and don't care how much it costs them to do so. So they experience what is sometimes known as *auction fever*, and bid repeatedly until they far exceed their own limits and the actual value of the items being sold. Evidence that this is actually what happens is provided by careful study of live and Internet auctions (Ku et al., 2005). In such auctions, it has been found, there is more overbidding when there are few, not many, bidders—because these bidders begin to compete with one another. Further, more overbidding occurs late during the auctions, when competition has become truly fierce, and more overbidding occurs in live auctions, where arousal is often increased by the crowd, than in Internet ones. Overall, then, it seems clear that high levels of arousal can often interfere with effective decision making. That's an important point to keep in mind when *you* are making decisions: Remaining calm, cool, and collected may help you to make the best choices.

Escalation of commitment:
The tendency to become increasingly committed to bad decisions even as losses associated with them increase.

FIGURE 6.17
Competitive Arousal: Why Auctions Often Run Wild
High levels of arousal often interfere with effective decision making. In auctions, competition among bidders may add to such arousal, thus producing situations in which the peopole involved make very bad decisions; for instance, they may bid much more than the items for sale are really worth.

■ **Cultural differences in decision making.**

Throughout this discussion, we've focused on decision making as a process and described several factors that can strongly affect it. Before concluding, we want to emphasize the fact that *cultural factors,* too, often play a key role in decisions. For instance, in cultures described as *individualistic,* such as the United States and many European countries, decisions are often made by individuals—*they* make the choices and choose how they'd like to proceed. In more *collectivistic cultures,* such as China, Japan, and many African nations, individually made decisions are rare. Instead, most decisions are made in groups and mainly by consensus (Adler, 1991).

In addition, cultural factors strongly influence the *speed* with which decisions are made. In the United States, people who are in charge are expected to make decisions quickly; in fact, being described as "decisive" means just that—being able to reach decisions *fast*. In other cultures, decisions are expected to take longer—and actually do. For instance, in Egypt, the more important the issue, the longer the decision is expected to take (Greenberg & Baron, 2007). Finally, cultures also decide who should made decisions. Overall, then, it's important to realize that decision making occurs against a backdrop of culture, and can't be viewed independently of such factors. (How can you improve your own decision making? See the following **Psychology Lends a Hand** section for some tips.)

P S Y C H O L O G Y   L E N D S   A   H A N D

Making Good Decisions: Avoiding Major Pitfalls

Making good decisions is, perhaps, one of the most important ingredients in having a happy life. Mistakes can be costly and get us off the track toward the success and happiness we all want. Fortunately, the findings of research on decision making can be a big help in this respect. No, these findings can't tell you what options to choose in every situation—life is too complicated for that to be true. But they *can* help you to avoid some of the major pitfalls—the factors that are most likely to lead you to decisions you may later regret. Here are some guidelines that we think you will find helpful. Following them may well help you to make the decision that are right for you and your personal goals.

1. **Be aware of mental shortcuts—they can prove costly!** As we noted earlier, it is all too easy to make decisions in terms of heuristics—rules of thumb that reduce the effort required to make decisions. Following these "rules," however, can sometimes get us into serious trouble. For instance, just because you can think of some information doesn't mean that it is necessarily important or reliable. In fact, there is evidence that we tend to remember mainly what is atypical or unusual—these things stand out in our memories (see Morewedge, Gilbert, & Wilsom, 2005). But the fact that they are atypical can be a problem because since they are, the availability heuristic operates and we assume that they are important and informative, when in fact they are not. The overall principle, then, is, "Don't let heuristics lead you to making decisions based on only a small amount of information—that can be very costly!"

2. **Watch out for framing effects!** Advertisers, politicians, and many other people who want to influence our decisions understand the power of framing very well: They often present information to us in a way that will lead us to make the choices they *want* us to make. For instance, they will emphasize the benefits or "pluses" of the products or programs while down-

playing the "negatives." For instance, many products say, in large words, on the label "Low Fat!" or "All Natural!" They don't proclaim "High Chemical Content" or "Lots of Filler." Be aware of framing because it is very common and can, if we ignore it, strongly affect our decisions.

3. **Beware of sunk costs:** It is all too easy to get trapped in our own bad decisions. Once we have invested time, effort, or emotion in something (an old car, a bad relationship), it is very difficult to admit that we made a mistake and back away from this decision. Instead, we often tend to continue investing *more* time, money, or love in what is essentially a losing proposition. Fortunately, there are ways to break this cycle. First, it's often useful to have someone who did *not* make the initial decision (a good friend, family member) tell you candidly whether he or she thinks you should continue with this decision or reverse it. He or she is not as invested in the initial decision as you, so he or she can be more accurate. Second, you should face the costs of continuing squarely and openly; ultimately, *you* will have to pay them, so confronting this fact may help you to realize that getting out is better than continuing. Finally, realizing that admitting an error is a *good* thing, not something that makes you look foolish, is very important. Once you recognize this fact, you may find it easier to stop "throwing good money/love/effort after bad."

4. **Try to make important decisions when you are calm:** High levels of arousal—or high levels of emotion—are definitely *not* helpful for making good decisions. In fact, strong arousal can get in the way and make it much harder to choose the right options. So, if at all possible, don't make important decisions on the spur of the moment or when you are feeling tense or excited. Usually, it is better to make such choices when you are calm and can think more clearly and systematically

KEY QUESTIONS

- What are maximizers and satisficers?
- What is framing?
- What is "auction fever"?
- Do cultural factors influence decision making?

Creativity: Generating the Extraordinary

Suppose you were asked to name people high in creativity: Who would be on your list? When faced with this question, many people come up with names such as Albert Einstein, Leonardo da Vinci, Thomas Edison, and Sigmund Freud. These famous persons worked in very different domains, so what do they have in common? Essentially, this: All created something almost everyone agreed was *new*—theories, ideas, inventions that did not exist before. Newness by itself, though, is not enough. Most researchers who study **creativity** define it as involving two key

Creativity:
The ability to produce work that is both novel (original, unexpected) and appropriate (it works—it is useful or meets task constraints).

aspects: The items or ideas produced are novel (original, unexpected) *and* appropriate or useful—they meet relevant constraints. In other words, they can actually *work* and do what they are designed to do.

In a sense, creativity is the crowning jewel of our cognitive processes. From it comes new knowledge, products, and other advances that can improve the quality of human life. But what are its origins? What are its foundations, and since it offers many benefits, how can we encourage it? The answers seem to involve basic aspect of cognition that, together, provide the foundations for creative thought and ideas.

■ **The building blocks of creativity: Concepts.**

As we noted earlier, the amount of information stored in long-term memory is vast, so to make it easier to retrieve and use this information, we organize it in various ways by creating internal frameworks to hold it. *Concepts,* one kind of mental framework that we described in detail earlier, are especially helpful in understanding creativity. In fact, concepts have both positive and negative implications for creativity.

On the plus side of the ledger, these internal cognitive structures enhance our ability to retrieve the vast amount of knowledge present in long-term memory, and this gives us better access to the raw materials from which new ideas can emerge. On the downside, however, the fact that knowledge is organized in memory in terms of concepts often constrains our thinking, assuring that it stays pretty much within what have sometimes been described as *mental ruts.* In other words, the internal structures we have created for ourselves are so strong that we find it very difficult to escape from, or think outside, them. Here's a striking example.

In the mid-1970s, engineers and scientists at Sony Corporation were charged with the task of developing music CDs. They made great progress but ultimately gave up for the following reason: The CDs they produced stored fully eighteen hours of music, and that was viewed as being too large to be marketable. Why did the CDs hold so much? *Because the engineers made them the same size and shape as existing LP records!* Although they were brilliant scientists and engineers, they simply could not escape from the mental ruts created by their past experience to realize that the new CDs could be *any size they wished!*

Here's yet another, and perhaps even more amazing, example of how cognitive organization can interfere with creativity. The Inca of South America had a very advanced civilization—one whose achievements astounded the Spaniards who first encountered them. But one invention they did not possess was wheeled vehicles; items to be transported were loaded on animals or dragged on poles—no carts or wagons existed. Yet—and here's the really surprising fact—Inca children played with models of wheeled carts. So the Inca had the *idea* of putting wheels on vehicles, but for some reason they viewed this design as suitable only for toys! This is a very dramatic illustration of the power of mental ruts to constrain human thought.

If the impact of mental ruts can be this strong, you may be wondering, how do people ever escape from them so that creativity can occur? The answer seems to involve how concepts can sometimes be *expanded,* thus paving the way for creativity. This can occur in several ways. First, concepts can be *combined,* with the result that something very new is generated. For instance, consider the concept of the "phone-camera." The concept of "phone" has been combined with the concept of "camera" to produce something that never existed before, but quickly gained tremendous popularity (see Figure 6.18).

Concepts can also be *expanded.* This is often what happens with new products—even ones that represent a major breakthrough. For instance, the first railroad cars looked very much like the horse-drawn carriages they replaced. The concept of "carriage" had been expanded to include a vehicle for moving people, but what resulted was very similar to the original concept in appearance, if not means of propulsion.

A third way in which concepts can be changed or expanded is through *analogy*. Analogies involve perceiving similarities between objects or events that are otherwise dissimilar. For instance, the inventor of *Velcro*, a product used just about every day, noticed how seeds clung to his clothing with minute hooks. He then reasoned, "Why not use the same basic process to make things stick together?"—and Velcro was born. When concepts are stretched through analogy, creativity is encouraged and important advances can result.

Basically, then, creativity seems to involve instances in which we escape from mental ruts by stretching the concepts we already possess, combining them in new ways, or applying them in new contexts. The result can be something that is both new and useful—and those are the basic qualities of true creativity.

FIGURE 6.18
Creativity: Its Cognitive Foundations
Creativity often seems to stem from the expansion or combination of concepts. The result of such expansions or combinations is something that is both new and useful—the key characteristics of creativity. The item shown here is based, in part, on the combination of existing concepts (e.g., "phone" and "camera").

■ Mental ruts, culture, and problem solving.

By the way, we should note that the tendency to organize information stored in memory in terms of concepts plays a key role in another important aspect of cognition, **problem solving**. In problem solving, we attempt to develop responses that permit us to reach desired goals. And, unfortunately, such efforts are often slowed or even blocked by what is known as **functional fixedness**—a powerful tendency to think of using objects only in the ways they have been used before. For instance, suppose you were given the following objects—a candle, a box of matches, and thumbtacks—and were then and told to somehow attach the candle to a wall so that it stands upright and burns normally, using only these objects. Because of functional fixedness, most people tend to think of such solutions as tacking the candle to the wall or attaching it with melted wax. They are used to using these objects in these ways, so they can't readily imagine other uses for them. A much better solution is to tack the box holding the matches to the wall, and then place the candle inside it.

Interestingly, if the match box is shown empty, it is much easier to solve this problem, because then it is seen not as a box for holding matches, but as a box useful for holding *anything*. As you might guess, the particular mental ruts we develop are often strongly influenced by our culture. This is clearly illustrated by a study conducted with an isolated group living in the Amazon region of Ecuador, people who have very little exposure to manufactured items and many aspects of modern technology (German & Barrett, 2005). The researchers who performed this study reasoned that because members of this group have little exposure to a wide range of products, they might be especially susceptible to functional fixedness. To test this hypothesis, they asked members of the group to solve two simple problems in which the items included were arranged either in ways that suggested their function or in ways that did not suggest their function (see Figure 6.19, page 234). For instance, one problem involved using six Styrofoam cubes, a battery, a pencil eraser, and a rubber band to build a tower tall enough to reach a very high spot. In the *function-demonstration condition*, the blocks were shown inside the box; in the *control condition*, they were shown on the ground outside the box. The correct solution involved using the box as a platform on which to build a tower with the other objects, but as predicted, participants in the study were much slower to hit on this solution when the box was shown as a container for the cubes (right-hand photo) than when it was not. These findings, and those of many other studies, indicate that our tendency to organize information and to think about the world in terms of specific concepts (e.g., a box as a *container* rather than a *platform*), can often interfere with our efforts to solve various problems.

Problem solving:
Efforts to develop or choose among various responses to attain desired goals.

Functional fixedness:
The tendency to think of using objects only as they have been used in the past.

FIGURE 6.19
Cultural Factors in Problem Solving: An Example Involving Functional Fixedness
When individuals perceive various objects as having a definite function, it is harder for them to imagine other uses for these objects. This is known as *functional fixedness* and can interfere with successful problem solving, where flexibility is a key ingredient. The tasks shown here were recently used with an isolated group living in the Amazon region of Ecuador. These people, who lived in an environment with few manufactured items and little or no technology, were especially subject to functional fixedness. When they were shown the objects being used in a particular way, they were very slow at identifying problem solutions that required them to use these objects in different ways.
Source: T. P. German and H. C. Barret, "Functional Fixedness in a Technologically Sparse Culture," *Psychological Science, 16*(1), p.1. Reprinted with permission from Blackwell Publishing.

■ Encouraging creativity: The confluence approach.

Now that we have considered the origins of creativity in basic aspects of cognition, we'll turn to another question: How can it be enhanced? Since creativity offers major benefits, this is truly an important question with practical implications. One framework that offers useful suggestions is the **confluence approach** (Sternberg, 2004; Sternberg & Lubart, 1995). This theory suggests that creativity emerges out of the confluence (i.e., convergence) of several basic resources:

- *Intellectual abilities*—the ability to see problems in new ways, the ability to recognize which ideas are worth pursuing coupled with persuasive skills—being able to convince others of the value of these new ideas (a combination of successful and social intelligence).
- *A broad and rich knowledge base*—a large store of relevant information in memory; without such knowledge, the cognitive foundations for creative thought are lacking.
- *An appropriate style of thinking*—a preference for thinking in novel ways, and an ability to "see the big picture"—to think globally as well as locally; in essence, a propensity for escaping from mental ruts.

Confluence approach:
An approach suggesting that for creativity to occur, multiple components must converge.

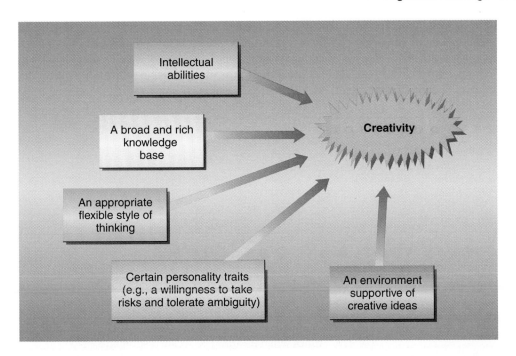

FIGURE 6.20
**Creativity: The Confluence
Approach**
The confluence approach suggests that creativity stems from
the convergence of several factors. The most important of these
include certain intellectual abilities, a broad and rich knowledge
base, an appropriate style of
thinking, certain personality attributes, and high intrinsic motivation.
Source: Based on suggestions by
Sternberg & Lubart, 1995.

- *Personality attributes*—such traits as a willingness to take risks and to tolerate ambiguity.
- *Intrinsic, task-focused motivation*—creative people usually love what they are doing and find intrinsic rewards in their work.
- *An environment that is supportive of creative ideas*—one that does not impose uniformity of thought and one that encourages change.

To the extent these factors are present, the theory suggests, creative thought can emerge (see Figure 6.20). A large body of evidence offers support for this view, so it appears to be quite useful, and it also suggests several techniques for enhancing your own creativity.

First, and most important, it is clear that new ideas do *not* emerge out of a vacuum. Rather, they derive from combining, stretching, or viewing existing information in a new way. This means that to be creative, it is essential to have lots of information at your disposal. There are many ways to gain a broad and rich knowledge base, but research findings indicate that among the most useful are having varied work experience (e.g., the more jobs people have held, the more likely they are to become self-employed); having lived in many different places; and having a broad social network—many friends and acquaintances who can share their knowledge with you. All these factors increase the amount of information individuals have at their disposal and make them more creative.

Second, as the confluence approach suggests, you should cultivate a style of thinking that helps you break out of mental ruts. This is more difficult than it sounds, because it is always easier to think in routine ways than to question our own beliefs. One way to do so is to make sure that the people with whom you spend time are *not* all very similar to you. To the extent they are, you will tend to agree with one another about most issues, and will *not* challenge one anothers' beliefs. If, instead, you count among your friends people from different backgrounds and occupations, and who have contrasting views on a wide range of issues, this can help you develop flexible, open modes of thoughts—and these, in turn, can enhance your creativity.

Third, you should try to work in environments that encourage rather than discourage creativity. In many work settings—and in many schools—creativity is discouraged. But in the very best companies and schools, it is encourage. The more time you can spend in such settings, the better from the point of view of enhancing your own creativity. In sum, there are a number of steps you can take to increase your own creativity. To the extent you make these part of your daily life, you will become more creative.

KEY QUESTIONS

- What is creativity?
- What role do concepts play in creativity?
- What other factors influence creativity?

SUMMARY AND REVIEW OF KEY QUESTIONS

Human Memory: How We Remember, Why We Forget

- **According to the information-processing model, what key tasks are performed by memory?**
  Encoding, which involves converting information into a form that can be entered into memory; storage, which involves retaining information over time; and retrieval, which involves locating information when it is needed.

- **What are sensory memory, short-term memory, and long-term memory?**
  Sensory memory holds fleeting representations of our sensory experiences. Short-term memory holds a limited amount of information for short periods of time. Long-term memory holds large amounts of information for long periods of time.

- **Our Differing Memory Systems**

- **What is the difference between short-term memory and working memory?**
  Short-term memory refers to our memory system for storing limited amount of information for relatively short periods of time. Working memory refers to short-term storage of information *plus* a mechanism to focus attention on and determine what information will be processed and what will be ignored or suppressed.

- **Why is working memory much more than a system for holding small amounts of information for short periods of time?**
  It is much more than a temporary storage system because working memory also determines what information enters into our consciousness, and also strongly influences our ability to perform many complex tasks.

- **Memory for Factual Information: Episodic and Semantic Memory**

- **What are episodic memory and semantic memory?**
  Episodic memory contains factual information individuals relate to their own lives and experiences. Semantic memory holds factual information of a more general nature.

- **What are retrieval cues and what role do they play in memory?**
  These are stimuli that are associated with information stored in memory and so can help bring it to mind at times when it cannot be recalled spontaneously.

- **What are concepts and what role do they play in semantic memory?**
  These are mental categories for objects or events that are similar to one another in certain ways. They seem to be arranged in hierarchical networks in semantic memory.

- **Memory for Skills: Procedural Memory**

- **What is procedural memory?**
  This is memory for information we cannot readily put into words, such as various skills.

- **Is there a link between circadian rhythms and our ability to use explicit and implicit (procedural) memory?**
  Recent findings indicate that we tend to show enhanced performance for *explicit* memory at peak times during our circadian rhythm, but peak performance for *implicit* memory at off-peak times.

- **Forgetting: Largely a Matter of Interference—but What *Kind* of Interference?**

- **What is proactive interference? Retroactive interference? What role do they play in forgetting?**
  Retroactive interference occurs when information being learned currently interferes with information already present in memory. Proactive interference occurs when information already present in memory interferes with the acquisition of new information.

- **According to recent findings, what kind of interference plays a crucial role in forgetting?**
  Recent findings indicate that interference between newly formed memories and existing ones that have not had a chance to fully consolidate may be crucial.

- **Memory Construction: How Memories Are Sometimes Changed—or Created**

- **What is memory construction and how does it occur?**
  Memory construction involves the creation of false memories—memories for events we never experienced. It is often produced by rumors and can also derive from reports in the mass media.

- **What factors potentially reduce the accuracy of eyewitness testimony?**
  The accuracy of eyewitness testimony is reduced by suggestibility, leading questions, and errors in source monitoring—attributing memories to the wrong source.
- **Memory in Everyday Life: Autobiographical Memory and Memory for Emotions**
- **What is autobiographical memory? When does it begin?**
  Autobiographical memory contains information about our own lives. It begins every early life, although most people can't describe memories from the first two years of life.
- **Why do we sometimes distort memories of our own prior emotional states?**
  We sometimes distort memories of our own prior emotional states to increase our present happiness by, for instance, perceiving that we benefited more than we really did from painful or traumatic events.
- **What are mood-dependent memory and mood-congruence effects?**
  When our mood during retrieval is similar during encoding, memory may be enhanced; this is mood-dependent memory. We tend to remember information consistent with our current mood; this is mood congruence.
- **What is own-race bias in memory for faces?**
  This refers to a tendency to recognize people belonging to our own racial or ethnic group more readily and accurately than people belonging to other racial or ethnic groups.

Memory and the Brain: Evidence from Memory Impairments and Other Sources

- **What are retrograde amnesia and anterograde amnesia?**
  Retrograde amnesia involves loss of memory of events prior to the amnesia-inducing event. Anterograde amnesia is loss of memory for events that occur after the amnesia-inducing event.
- **What roles do the hippocampus and frontal lobes play in long-term memory?**
  The hippocampus seems to play a crucial role in the consolidation of memory—the process of shifting new information from short-term to longer-term storage. The frontal lobes appear to play a key role in various aspects of semantic memory.
- **What are Korsakoff's syndrome and Alzheimer's disease? What do they tell us about the biological bases of memory?**
  Korsakoff's syndrome is produced by long-term alcoholism, and often involves severe forms of amnesia. It indicates that the hypothalamus and thalamus play important roles in memory. Alzheimer's disease produces increasingly severe deficits in memory. It calls attention to the role of the neurotransmitter acetylcholine in memory.
- **What does current research suggest about the location of the memory trace and its nature?**
  Current research suggests that the memory trace may involve individual neurons, connections between them, and complex networks of neurons and brain structures. It may involve changes in the structure and function of individual neurons, or complex networks of neurons.

Cognition: Thinking, Deciding, Creating

- **Are there limits to human cognition? If so, what are they?**
  There are definite limits to the amount of information we can process at any given time. It appears that we can process information about three different variables, but four or more variables exceed our limits.
- **What potential errors can affect the accuracy of our cognitive processes?**
  Many potential errors can affect our cognitive processes. These include the confirmation bias, the hindsight bias, and escalation of commitment, among others.
- **Thinking: The Foundation of Consciousness**
- **What are concepts?**
  Concepts are mental categories for objects or events that are similar to one another in some way.
- **What are images?**
  Images are mental pictures of the external world.
- **Decision Making: Choosing among Alternatives**
- **What are maximizers and satisficers?**
  Maximizers are individuals who attempt to identify the best alternative when making decisions. Satisficers, in contrast, seek to identify an alternative that is "good enough."
- **What is framing?**
  Framing refers to the way in which information is presented. This can strongly influence decision making.
- **What is "auction fever"?**
  This refers to the effects of high levels of arousal on decision making, especially in an auction setting. High levels of arousal often interfere with making effective decisions.
- **Do cultural factors influence decision making?**
  Absolutely. Cultural factors determine who makes decisions, whether decisions are made by individuals or groups, and the amount of time decision-makers have to make their choices.

Creativity: Generating the Extraordinary

- **What is creativity?**
  Creativity involves developing something *new* that is often *useful*.
- **What role do concepts play in creativity?**
  Concepts are, in a sense, the foundation of creativity. In fact, creativity often emerges out of the combination of expansion of existing concepts,
- **What other factors influence creativity?**
  Several other factors play a role in creativity, including living and working in an environment that supports creativity, having a broad and rich store of knowledge, and the possession of certain personality characteristics.

KEY TERMS

Alzheimer's disease, p. 219
Amnesia, p. 217
Anterograde amnesia, p. 218
Autobiographical memory, p. 212
Availability heuristic, p. 227
Chunking, p. 203
Cognition, p. 200
Concepts, p. 206
Confirmation bias, p. 223
Confluence approach, p. 234
Context-dependent memory, p. 205
Creativity, p. 231
Decision making, p. 225
Encoding, p. 201
Encoding specificity principle, p. 205
Episodic memory, p. 204
Escalation of commitment, p. 229

Eyewitness testimony, p. 211
Framing, p. 228
Functional fixedness, p. 233
Heuristics, p. 227
Hindsight bias, p. 223
Images, p. 224
Infantile amnesia, p. 213
Information-processing approach, p. 201
Korsakoff's syndrome, p. 219
Logical concepts, p. 224
Long-term memory, p. 203
Maximizing, p. 225
Memory, p. 200
Mood-congruence effects, p. 215
Mood-dependent memory, p. 215
Natural concepts, p. 224

Proactive interference, p. 208
Problem solving, p. 223
Procedural memory, p. 207
Prototypes, p. 224
Representativeness heuristic, p. 227
Retrieval, p. 201
Retrieval cues, p. 205
Retroactive interference, p. 208
Retrograde amnesia, p. 217
Satisficing, p. 225
Semantic memory, p. 204
Sensory memory, p. 201
State-dependent retrieval, p. 205
Storage, p. 201
Working memory, p. 203

PSYCHOLOGY: UNDERSTANDING ITS FINDINGS

Human Memory and Computer Memory: The Same or Different?

Each year, computers get faster and have larger memories. In fact, right now we can both place everything we have ever written—every book, every article, every lecture note—on a tiny faction of the hard drives in computers. So, computer memory is certainly impressive. But is it as good as human memory? To answer this question, it is important to understand differences as well as similarities between human and computer memory. We think that comparing these two systems for storing information will help you to more fully understand what psychologists have learned about the nature of memory. So please list (1) the ways in which human memory and computer memory are similar, and (2) the ways in

which they are different. After you complete these tasks, answer the following question: In what ways is human memory superior to computer memory, and vice versa?

_____

_____

_____

_____

_____

_____

_____

MAKING PSYCHOLOGY PART OF YOUR LIFE

Avoiding Sunk Costs

Getting trapped in bad decisions is one of the most damaging cognitive errors we can make, because it can lead us to invest our time, energy, emotion, and personal resources in courses of action that are doomed to fail. For this reason, it's important to recognize situations that pose the danger of getting us trapped in bad decisions. This exercise will help you do accomplish this goal.

First, think of a situation in your life that is producing disappointing outcomes—some situation in which no matter what you do, you can't seem to "win." This can be spending increasing amounts of money on an old car in which one thing after another needs repair, working in a job where your efforts are neither recognized nor appreciated, or continuing

to invest time and effort in a personal relationship (romantic, work) that is _not_ going well.

Now, write down three things:

1. The initial decision that first involved you in this situation (e.g., the decision to repair the car, or take the job).
2. What, at that time, you expected would result from this decision.
3. What, instead, you have actually experienced—and are still experiencing

Next, ask yourself these questions:

a. Did I make a mistake initially?
b. If I stay in this situation, will things improve—or are they likely to continue to produce negative outcomes?

c. What can I do to change the situation?

d. Should I admit that I made an error and get out?

If you follow these procedures carefully and are totally honest with yourself, you may be in a position to better decide whether you are the victim of "sunk costs." And if you are, we wish you the strength and resolve to escape as quickly and painlessly as possible.

If you are using MyPsychLab, you have access to an electronic version of this textbook, along with dozens of valuable resources per chapter—including video and audio clips, simulations and activities, self-assessments, practice tests and other study materials. Here is a sampling of the resources available for this chapter.

EXPLORE

Key Processes in Stages of Memory

Encoding, Storage, and Retrieval in Memory

How to Be a Critical Thinker

WATCH

What Happens with Alzheimers

Exercise Your Brain

Giftedness

SIMULATE

Serial Position Curve

The Mind's Organization of Conceptual Knowledge

How Good Is Your Memory for Stories?

If you did not receive an access code to MyPsychLab with this text and wish to purchase access online, please visit www.MyPsychLab.com.

STUDY GUIDE

CHAPTER REVIEW

Human Memory: How We Remember, Why We Forget

1. The memory task by which information is transformed into a storable form is termed
   a. retrieval.   c. encoding
   b. storage.   d. maturation.
2. Human memory in similar to the random access memory used in a computer.   (True-False).
3. The process of _____ is used to transfer information from short-term memory to long-term memory.
   a. attentional focus
   b. random access storage
   c. elaborative rehearsal
   d. encoding
4. Human working memory can retain about _____ separate items.
   a. 3   c. 10
   b. 7   d. 12
5. The process of chunking allows us to
   a. extend the duration of sensory memory.
   b. transfer information directly into long-term memory.
   c. expand the capacity of our short-term memory.
   d. extend the capacity of long-term memory.
6. The process of _____ determines what information is retained in short-term memory.
   a. attention
   b. random access storage
   c. elaborative rehearsal
   d. encoding
7. Match up the appropriate concept with the correct definition or best example of the concept.
   _____. Also known as short-term memory.
   _____. A process that retains information within short-term memory.
   _____. A neural representation of sensory input.
   _____. A process by which we think about new information and relate it to that of long-term memory.
   _____. A failure to recall previously learned information.
   _____. A strategy that increases the capacity of working memory.
   a. forgetting   d. sensory memory
   b. working memory   e. attention
   c. chunking   f. elaborative rehearsal
8. _____ memory relates to our knowledge of the world.
   a. Sensory   c. Episodic
   b. Nondeclarative   d. Semantic
9. Our knowledge of the world involves _____ memory, whereas _____ memory involves our personal experiences.
   a. episodic;   sensory
   b. semantic;   sensory
   c. semantic;   episodic
   d. episodic;   semantic

10. Which of the following is a key factor for improving the efficiency of episodic memory?
    a. Studying all of the material for an exam on the night before the exam.
    b. Reading the material while in a crowded coffee shop.
    c. Regularly reading and reviewing exam material at different times during the semester.
    d. Studying the material while under the influence of a drug reported to facilitate memory.
11. A student who studies for an exam while under the influence of methamphetamine would due well to
    a. reduce their dosage during the days before the exam.
    b. not take the drug prior to the exam.
    c. take the exam in an environment very different from the conditions under which they studied for the exam.
    d. remember to take the drug during the exam to ensure the presence of retrieval cues related to the drug.
12. Semantic memory involves our ability to recall general information about the world,   (True-False)
13. Semantic memory is organized into hierarchies of _____.
    a. impressions   c. views
    b. concepts   d. models
14. _____ memory is another name for procedural memory.
    a. Implicit   c. Sensorimotor
    b. Semantic   d. Explicit
15. Episodic memory and semantic memory are considered to involve implicit memory.   (True-False)
16. Which of the following is an example of implicit memory?
    a. Your memory of your first day in school.
    b. Your ability to recall your last birthday.
    c. Your ability to ride a bike.
    d. Your recall of the name of the capital of Wyoming.
17. Our ability to remember information from _____ memory is best when we are at the _____ of our circadian rhythm.
    a. semantic;   "off-peak"
    b. implicit;   "off-peak"
    c. explicit;   "off-peak"
    d. procedural;   "peak"
18. Which of the following is NOT true of memory?
    a. Humans can talk about their episodic and semantic memories.
    b. Riding a bike is an example of implicit memory.
    c. Forgetting increases as a function of time since we learned the information.
    d. Memory function can vary with our circadian rhythms.
19. _____ is said to occur when a new memory interferes with an old memory.
    a. Analytical dementia
    b. Korsakoff's syndrome
    c. Retroactive interference
    d. Proactive interference
20. Studies with drugs that slow down memory consolidation support the view that interference effects in memory operate at the level of memory consolidation. (True-False).

21. A person whose memory has been altered to reflect what they want to remember would be said to have undergone memory _____.
    a. distortion   c. construction
    b. consolidation   d. forgetting
22. Memory construction involves the addition of information so as to create a false memory.   (True-False)
23. A key source for the creation of a false memory is
    a. personal experience.
    b. distortions that reflect our personal motivations.
    c. the harmful effects of drugs such as alcohol.
    d. rumor.
24. An example of suggestibility as a problem in eyewitness testimony is
    a. when a person forgets the source of their memory.
    b. when an attorney asks a leading question of the witness.
    c. when a therapist suggests that an incident occurred for the witness during their childhood,
    d. All of the above are correct.
25. Match up the appropriate concept with the correct definition or best example of the concept.
    _____. An eyewitness error made when a person forgets where they saw a person or event.
    _____. The testimony of a person in court as to what they saw and heard during a crime.
    _____. A general issue in memory whereby false memories are created.
    _____. A personal characteristic of an eyewitness by which leading questions can create testimony errors.
    a. Memory construction.   c. Eyewitness testimony.
    b. Suggestibility.   d. Source monitoring.
26. _____ memory involves our memories of our personal lives.
    a. Autosensory   c. Homeostatic
    b. Autobiographical   d. Semantic
27. Infantile amnesia involves a(n)
    a. general inability of adults to remember any details from the first two to three years of life.
    b. inability of an infant to recall facial features.
    c. infant's ability to recall their last meal.
    d. a rare form of amnesia caused by a severe stroke involving the hippocampus.
28. A key explanation for infantile amnesia is that we lack fully developed language skills before age 4 and thus cannot report our early memories in words. (True-False)
29. Autobiographical memories are reported
    a. in 6 month old infants.
    b. to involve semantic rather than episodic memory systems.
    c. to activate brain areas different from those activated by semantic memories.
    d. A and B are correct.
30. James had separated from his fiancée just before final exams. While studying for the exams, he spent much time ruminating about how badly he was treated by the fiancée. What conditions would be optimal for James to do well on his final exams?
    a. James does not think about her during the exams.
    b. Just before the exams, James should look for someone else who makes him quite happy.

c. James should keep his old fiancée in mind during the exams.
d. James should study for the exams, consume alcohol to forget the fiancée, and then take the exams.
31. _____ refers to the fact that we are _____ to notice and remember information that is consistent with our current mood.
    a. Mood-dependent memory;   more likely
    b. Mood congruence;   more likely
    c. Mood-dependent memory;   less likely
    d. Mood congruence;   less likely
32. Which of the following is true of infantile amnesia?
    a. Infantile amnesia refers to the inability to recall information during the first four years of life.
    b. Left handed people are able to report events during the first month of life.
    c. Mixed handed people are better able to recall information from early in life.
    d. Right handed people are able to report events during the first month of life.
33. A positive aspect of increasing the racial diversity of the population we live in is that exposure to such diversity will
    a. eliminate bias, racism, and hatred for those of other races.
    b. increase our same-race facial recognition preference.
    c. reduce our same-race facial recognition preference.
    d. increase racial conflict.
34. Which of the following would be expected of Patient S.P.?
    a. He would be unable to remember the faces of his family.
    b. He can read but not write.
    c. He could learn new phone numbers but not new street addresses.
    d. He could learn a new procedural memory.
35. An important cause of the memory disorder known as _____ involves brain damage induced by _____.
    a. Alzheimer's disease;   adult alcoholism
    b. Parkinson's disease;   fetal alcohol exposure
    c. Korsakoff's syndrome;   adult alcoholism
    d. Pickwickian syndrome;   fetal alcohol exposure
36. Alzheimer's disease occurs in approximately _____ percent of the population over the age of 65.
    a. 75   c. 25
    b. 55   d. 5
37. Alzheimer's disease involves a loss of the transmitter _____ within the _____.
    a. acetylcholine;   basal forebrain
    b. dopamine;   amygdala
    c. dopamine;   basal forebrain
    d. acetylcholine;   amygdala

Cognition: Thinking, Deciding, and Creating

38. The term cognition refers to the capacity of humans to think, reason, solve problems, and create.   (True-False).
39. Humans are capable of simultaneously considering _____ mental variables without making errors.
    a. two   c. four or more
    b. three   d. five or more
40. The cognitive error known as _____ involves the tendency to overestimate what we can accomplish in a period of time.
    a. optimistic bias   c. planning fallacy
    b. hindsight bias   d. confirmation bias

41. An example of confirmation bias is
    a. a person who expects to have a good retirement but has not saved any money.
    b. a politically conservative person who only watches Fox News.
    c. the person who is habitually late turning in their work assignments.
    d. the person who voted for Candidate A, but then says "I knew it" when Candidate B wins the election.
42. Match up the appropriate concept with the correct definition or best example of the concept.
    _____. A person who is habitually late turning in their work assignments.
    _____. The tendency to assume that we are better at predicting the future than is really true.
    _____. A person who does not save for retirement but expects to have a good retirement.
    _____. Our tendency to be trapped in bad decisions.
    _____. A politically conservative person who only watches Fox News.
    a. Escalation of commitment.
    b. Confirmation bias.
    c. Optimistic bias.
    d. Hindsight bias.
    e. Planning fallacy.
43. A(n) _____ would be an example of a(n)
    a. prototype; natural concept
    b. image; fuzzy concept
    c. fuzzy concept; logical concept
    d. logical concept; prototype
44. A person who seeks the very best from all available alternatives
    a. is a satisficer.
    b. will always be happy with their choices.
    c. would be classified as a maximizer.
    d. is satisfied with "good enough".
45. A heuristic is a mental short-cut that allow us to make quick decisions.   (*True-False)
46. The major flaw for the representativeness heuristic is that
    a. it focuses on what is easy to remember or to notice.
    b. it fails to consider the relative frequencies of an event, object or person.
    c. it can lead to staying in a bad situation when it would be better to leave.
    d. All of the above are correct.
47. Competitive _____ can result in bad decisions as when a bidder pays too much for an object at an auction.
    a. framing   c. prototypes
    b. heuristics   d. arousal

IDENTIFICATIONS
Identify the term that belongs with each of the concepts below (place the letter for the appropriate term below in front of each concept).
Identification   Concept:
    _____ 1. A highly aroused person overbids for an item.
    _____ 2. The inability to enter new information into long-term memory.
    _____ 3. Damage to this region would impair the formation of new long-term memories.

    _____ 4. A person who chooses the best out of a large number of possible alternatives.
    _____ 5. A way of presenting information in terms of potential gains or losses.
    _____ 6. Creativity emerges from the combined action of several basic mental resources.
    _____ 7. Memory for the details of our personal life.
    _____ 8. Out tendency to be trapped in a mental rut when thinking about how to use an object.
    _____ 9. A mental short-cut used to make rapid decisions.
    _____ 10. The type of intelligence used to solve everyday problems.
    _____ 11. A person who does not save for retirement but expects to have a good life.
    _____ 12. A neurotransmitter molecule that is key to memory.
    _____ 13. A chronic capacity to overestimate how much time is needed to finish a task.
    _____ 14. The capacity to produce a novel and useful idea or invention.
    _____ 15. The best example of an object in the physical world.
Identification:
    a. Functional fixedness.
    b. Prototype.
    c. Framing.
    d. Creativity.
    e. Confluence approach to creativity.
    f. Acetylcholine.
    g. "Auction fever"
    h. Anterograde amnesia.
    i. Optimistic bias.
    j. Hippocampus.
    k. Heuristic.
    l. Planning fallacy.
    m. Maximizer.
    n. Practical intelligence.
    o. Autobiographical memory.

FILL IN THE BLANK
1. _____ refers to all of our higher mental processes.
2. The process of _____ is used to transfer information from short-term memory to long-term memory.
3. Our knowledge of the world involves _____ memory.
4. Episodic memory and semantic memory are considered to involve _____ memory.
5. _____ is said to occur when a new memory interferes with an old memory.
6. Large amounts of information are stored within _____.
7. A person who seeks the very best from all available alternatives would be classified as a(n) _____,
8. Your ability to swing a tennis racket would be an example of _____.
9. Drugs that block formation of new memories within the _____ may reduce forgetting.
10. False memories can be created by exposure to _____, _____, or _____.
11. _____ refers to our lack of memories for the time when we were three years old or younger.

12. _____ can be clearly defined by a set of properties.
13. The process of _____ allows us to increase the capacity of working memory.
14. A _____ is a mental short-cut that allow us to make quick decisions.
15. The _____ approach argues that many sources of information converge for creativity.
16. Autobiographical memory involves memory for details of _____.
17. In a test of eyewitness memory, 16% of those persons who read a false ad about Disneyland reported that they had personally met _____ when they visited Disneyland as a child.

COMPREHENSIVE PRACTICE TEST

1. An example of sensory memory is
   a. the perceived trails of light as a flashlight is waved in the dark.
   b. when information is encoded into a permanent version for storage.
   c. your capacity to remember a phone number.
   d. your ability to recall your first day in grade school.
2. Which of the following would reflect a problem involving short-term memory?
   a. A person perceives trails of light as a flashlight is waved in the dark.
   b. A woman looks up a phone number but cannot remember it by the time she opens her cell phone.
   c. A freshman cannot remember where he parked his car after a night of drinking.
   d. A ninety year old cannot recall their first day in grade school.
3. Which of the following DO NOT belong together?
   a. sensory memory;   30 second duration
   b. short-term memory;   working memory
   c. long-term memory;   large capacity
   d. short-term memory;   elaborative rehearsal
4. "Cramming," the night before an exam has been shown by science to be the most effective method to learn new information.   (True-False)
5. Which of the following terms belong together?
   a. semantic;   explicit
   b. implicit;   procedural
   c. episodic;   explicit
   d. All of the above are correct.
6. The process of chunking allows us to extend the duration of sensory memory.   (True-False)
7. State-dependent retrieval involves _____ recall of information when our _____ state during recall matches that present when we first learned the information.
   a. better;   internal
   b. better;   external
   c. poorer;   internal
   d. better;   external
8. Forgetting increases as a function of time since we learned the information.   (True-False)
9. You find that the information you learned last summer about calculus is interfering with your ability to learn the basic concepts of statistics. This is an example of

a. proactive interference.
b. Korsakoff's syndrome.
c. retroactive interference.
d. dementia.

10. The mood congruence effect may offer an explanation as to why _____ persons have difficulty in remembering times when they felt better.
    a. psychotic   c. obsessive
    b. depressed   d. traumatized
11. Which of the following is a factor that can create false memories?
    a. Media reports.
    b. Interactions with a mental health therapist.
    c. Rumors.
    d. All of the above are correct.
12. A person who has experienced traumatic childhood abuse usually does not attempt to forget these memories. (True-False)
13. A person suffering from anterograde amnesia
    a. would have major sensory deficits.
    b. would be unable to remember a telephone number for even 5 seconds.
    c. would be unable to recall childhood events.
    d. are unable to enter new information into long-term memory.
14. The capacity limit of human information processing is about seven variables.   (True-False)
15. _____ can be clearly defined by a set of properties.
    a. Natural concepts   c. Logical concepts
    b. A schema   d. An image
16. Match up the appropriate concept with the correct definition or best example of the concept.
    _____. You decide that a man wearing a black shirt with a white collar must be a hotel bellman (as opposed to a priest or clergy) because that is how a bellman was dressed when you took a trip to Chicago 15 years ago.
    _____. A way of presenting information in terms of potential gains or losses.
    _____. A person believes they are more likely to die in a plane crash than a car wreck.
    _____. Our tendency to be increasingly committed to a bad decision even as we lose more money.
    _____. The tendency to overpay when bidding for a highly desired item.
    _____. A person who settles for "good enough" from a list of alternatives.
    a. Satisficer.   d. Availability heuristic.
    b. Auction fever.   e. Framing.
    c. Sunk costs.   f. Representativeness heuristic.

CRITICAL THINKING

1. Discuss the three major systems that comprise human memory and suggest an explanation as to why there are differences among the temporal characteristics of these systems.
2. Describe three means by which we can overcome the limits placed on us by our "mental ruts".

SEVEN

Human Development

*M*y birth certificate indicates that I (Robert Baron) was born at 8 A.M. on a Monday, and my mother has often said to me: "That was really the right time for you to be born, because you have been a busy person all your life." In fact, she often describes how, as a child, I could keep myself occupied with various tasks (e.g., playing with toy cars, blocks) for hours on end. And even today, people who know me would probably say, "He's not really happy unless he's busy." When I go on vacation, I like to see new sights and visit new places—not merely rest. And I have always felt that it is important to be productive until the very end of one's career—so, there will be no "slipping gradually into retirement" for me! I like to be busy! These days, however, my mother also makes another and very different observation: "You are much calmer than you were in the past," she often remarks. "You never lose your temper and are much more easygoing . . ."

O K, we can almost hear you saying, "So this author has always liked action, and he's getting mellow with age. . . . So what?" Actually, quite a lot, because in a sense, these two patterns—stability and change—are the main themes of this chapter, which is focused on *human development*—how we change throughout life's journey, and also how, in some respects, we stay very much the same. We noted in Chapter 1 that these patterns, stability and change, are one of psychology's "grand themes," and that we would meet them over and over again. We'll do so here, and in Chapter 9 as well. To reflect both of these themes, this chapter will proceed as follows.

In the first portion we'll concentrate on changes during **childhood**—the years between birth and adolescence. Then, in later sections, we'll examine changes occurring during *adolescence* and *adulthood*. For each of these phases of life, we'll examine change (and stability) with respect to physical attributes, cognitive processes, and social behavior and relations—in other words, we'll focus on physical, *cognitive,* and *social* development. Given that these three aspects of our lives are intimately interconnected, the fact that we will sometimes discuss them separately reflects our desire to present these topics clearly, and definitely *not* that any clear or sharp boundaries exist among them.

PHYSICAL GROWTH AND DEVELOPMENT DURING CHILDHOOD

When does human life begin? In one sense, this is a philosophical or religious issue. From a purely biological point of view, though, your life as an individual began when one of the millions of sperm released by your father during sexual intercourse fertilized an *ovum* deep within your mother's body. As you probably recall from our discussion of genetics in Chapter 2, the ovum has twenty-three pairs of chromosomes, one member of each pair from our mother and one from our father. One of these pairs determines biological sex, with females possessing two X chromosomes (XX) and males possessing one X and one Y (XY).

The Prenatal Period

After fertilization, the ovum moves through the mother's reproductive tract until it reaches the womb or *uterus.* This takes several days, and during this time the ovum divides frequently. Ten to fourteen days after fertilization, it becomes implanted in the wall of the uterus, and from then on is known as the **embryo.** By the third week the embryo is about one-fifth of an inch (one-half centimeter) long, and the region of the head is clearly visible. By the end of the eighth week the embryo is about one inch long and a face as well as arms and legs are present. By this time, too, all major internal organs have begun to form and some, such as the sex glands, are already active. The nervous system develops rapidly, and simple reflexes appear during the eighth or ninth week.

During the next seven months the developing child—now called a **fetus**—shows an increasingly human form. The external genitals take shape, fingernails and toenails form, hair follicles appear, and eyelids that open and close emerge. By the end of the twelfth week the fetus is 3 inches (7.6 centimeters) long and weighs about three-fourths of an ounce (21 grams). By the twentieth week it is almost 10 inches (25 cm) long and weighs 8 or 9 ounces (227–255 g). The eyes are formed and are sensitive to light by about the twenty-fourth week.

During the last three months of pregnancy, the fetus gains about eight ounces each week. By the seventh and eight months, it appears to be virtually fully

Childhood:
The years between birth and adolescence.

Embryo:
The developing child during the first eight weeks of life.

Fetus:
The developing child during the last seven months of pregnancy.

formed. However, if born prematurely, it may experience difficulties in breathing. At birth, babies weigh more than 7 pounds (3.17 kilograms) and are about 20 inches (50.8 cm) long (see Figure 7.1). (These numbers have increased slightly in recent years.)

Prenatal Influences on Development

Under ideal conditions, development during the prenatal period occurs in an orderly fashion and the newborn child is well equipped at birth to survive outside its mother's body. Unfortunately, however, conditions are not always ideal. Many environmental factors can damage the fetus and interfere with normal patterns of growth. Such factors are known as **teratogens,** and their impact can be devastating (e.g., Bookstein et al., 1996).

FIGURE 7.1
The Newborn: Starting Life's Journey
Holding their newborn infant for the first time is one of the most profoundly moving experiences many parents ever have.

■ **Infectious agents.**

The blood supply of the fetus and that of its mother come into close proximity in the **placenta,** a structure within the uterus that protects and nourishes the growing child. As a result, disease-producing organisms present in the mother's blood can sometimes infect the fetus. Tragically, diseases that exert only relatively minor effects on the mother can be very serious for the fetus. For example, *rubella,* or German measles, can cause blindness, deafness, or heart disease in the fetus if the mother contracts this illness during the first four weeks of pregnancy. Other diseases that can be transmitted to the fetus include chicken pox, mumps, tuberculosis, syphilis, and herpes (Samson 1988).

Since the early 1980s, two other illnesses, genital herpes and AIDS (acquired immune deficiency syndrome) have been added to this list. Genital herpes is usually transmitted during birth, when the newborn comes into contact with lesions present in its mother's genitals. When newborns contract this disease, they may suffer many harmful effects, ranging from paralysis and brain damage, to deafness and blindness; the disease is fatal for many babies (Rosenblith, 1992). AIDS, in contrast, can be transmitted to the fetus prior to birth, as well as during the birth process. About 20 percent of women who carry the AIDS virus in their bodies transmit it to their infants (Mattheson et al., 1997). Tragically, few babies born with AIDS survive until their first birthday.

■ **Prescription and over-the counter drugs.**

The use of drugs by the mother can also exert important effects on the fetus. Excessive use of aspirin, a drug most people take without hesitation, can result in harm to the fetus's circulatory system (Kelsey, 1969). Caffeine, the stimulant found in coffee, tea, and many soft drinks, can slow fetal growth, contribute to premature birth (Jacobson et al., 1984), and produce increased irritability in newborns whose mothers have consumed it in large amounts (Schikedanz et al., 1998).

■ **Alcohol.**

In the past, it was widely believed that moderate consumption of alcohol by expectant mothers had no harmful effects on the fetus. Now, in contrast, it is widely recognized that virtually *any* alcohol consumption by expectant mothers can produce harmful effects. That's one reason why all bottles of wine, beer, and spirits sold in the United States have a warning sticker on them. For instance, existing data suggest that alcohol consumption by pregnant women can potentially produce

Teratogens:
Factors in the environment that can harm the developing fetus.

Placenta:
A structure that surrounds, protects, and nourishes the fetus.

retardation, learning disorders, and retarded growth among newborns (e.g., Streissguth et al., 1995; Williams et al., 1994).

If pregnant women consume large quantities of alcohol—and especially if they engage in binge drinking—their children may be born with a disorder known as **fetal alcohol syndrome** (FAS; Julien, 1992). This includes a smaller than normal head size, deformities of the face, irritability, hyperactivity, retarded motor and mental development, heart defects, limb and joint abnormalities, feeding problems, and short attention spans (e.g., Bookstein et al., 1996). These problems persist, and as children with FAS grow older, they have increasing difficulty interacting with others and may develop serious behavioral problems (e.g., Becker et al., 1994).

How much alcohol must a pregnant woman consume, and how often, before such effects are produced? This is a complex question, but since alcohol has no benefits for the fetus and since even small amounts may be harmful, the safest answer seems to be: none. In other words, pregnant women should abstain from drinking *any* alcohol whatsoever.

■ Smoking.

While the proportion of adults who smoke has decreased in the United States and several other nations, this figure is increasing in many parts of the world. Moreover, the proportion of *women* who smoke seems to be on the rise. From the point of view of fetal development this is unfortunate; smoking by pregnant women is related to many harmful effects for the fetus and newborn child. These include decreased birth weight and size and increased risk for miscarriage and stillbirth (Wen et al., 1990). Maternal smoking may also interfere with cognitive development in early childhood (Cunningham et al., 1994), perhaps in part because smoking raises the level of carbon monoxide in the mother's blood, and this harmful substance, rather than oxygen, is carried across the placenta to the fetus.

In sum, many factors can adversely affect development during the prenatal period, and prospective mothers should carefully consider the potential risks before engaging in actions that may put their unborn children at risk.

Physical Development during Our Early Years

Physical growth is rapid during infancy. Assuming good nutrition—something we'll discuss below—infants almost triple in weight (to about twenty pounds or nine kilograms) and increase in body length by about one-third (to twenty-eight or twenty-nine inches, seventy-one to seventy-four cm) during the first year alone.

■ Reflexes.

Newborns possess a number of simple **reflexes** at birth—inherited responses to stimulation in certain areas of the body. If these are present, the baby's nervous system is assumed to be intact and working normally; if they are not, this is often a sign that something is seriously wrong. One of these reflexes, the *Moro reflex*, is triggered by a loud sound or a sudden dropping back of the infant's head. It involves a series of actions in which the baby first throws out his or her arms, then fans his or her fingers, and lets out a cry before bringing the arms back over his or her chest. Another is the *palmar grasping reflex*, which is elicited by pressing or stroking the palms of the newborn's hands. The baby closes its hand and holds tightly. This reflex might well be useful in helping babies cling to their mothers as the mother moves about. These and other reflexes are summarized in Table 7.1.

■ Locomotor development.

As anyone who has observed newborns well knows, infants have limited ability to move around at birth. This situation changes quickly, and within a matter of a few months they become quite mobile. They can sit and crawl, and most begin to walk by the time they are fourteen or fifteen months old. Motor development pro-

Fetal alcohol syndrome:
A disorder found in newborns whose mothers have consumed large amounts of alcohol during pregnancy.

Reflexes:
Inherited responses to stimulation in certain areas of the body.

TABLE 7.1   Reflexes in the Newborn

Newborns show all the reflexes described here at birth or very shortly thereafter.

Reflex	Description
Blinking	Baby closes eyes in response to light
Rooting	When cheek is touched or stroked, baby turns toward touch; moves lips and tongue to suck
Sucking	When nipple of other object is placed in mouth, baby sucks
Tonic neck	When baby is placed on back with head turned to one side, baby stretches out arm and leg on side baby is facing
Moro	Baby throws out arms and fans fingers, extends neck, and cries in response to loud noise or sudden drop of head
Babinski	When baby's foot is stroked from heel to toe, toes fan out
Grasping	When palms of hand are stroked, baby closes fingers around the object in a strong grasp
Stepping	Baby makes stepping motions if held upright so one foot just touches a surface

ceeds from the head toward the limbs, so that at first infants can hold up their head, then their chest, then they can sit, and so on. Figure 7.2 on page 250 summarizes several milestones of motor development. It's important to note that the ages shown are merely *average* values, so departures from them are trivial unless they are very late.

■ Learning abilities of newborns.

Can newborns show the kinds of learning discussed in Chapter 5? Absolutely. Research findings indicate that they can be classically conditioned, but primarily with respect to stimuli that have survival value for babies. For example, infants only two hours old can learn to associate gentle stroking on the forehead with a sweet solution, and after these two stimuli have been paired repeatedly, they suck in response to stroking (the conditioned stimulus; Clarke-Stewart, Friedman, & Koch, 1985).

Newborns can also show operant (instrumental) conditioning. For example, they readily learn to suck faster to obtain exposure to certain stimuli—visual designs or music and human voices (Sansavini, Bertonicini, & Giovanelli, 1997). Similarly, findings indicate that unborn fetuses show an *increase* in heart rate in response to the sound of their mothers' voice, but a *reduction* in heart rate in response to the sound of a stranger's voice (Kisilevsky et el., 2003). In sum, the ability to show basic kinds of learning is clearly present even before birth.

■ The devastating—and persistent—effects of malnutrition.

It is estimated that throughout the world, hundreds of millions of children are malnourished—they are receiving a diet that is far below what they need for good growth and development. The immediate effects of malnutrition are obvious: Infants do not grow normally and show many other negative effects in their movements and health. Perhaps even more disturbing than these immediate effects, however, are what appear to be the long-term, persistent results of malnutrition. Recent findings (see Adelson, 2005) suggest that when infants receive an inadequate diet, not only their physical growth, but also their brains and their later learning abilities may be adversely affected.

Birth
Fetal posture

1 month
Lift head
(2 weeks to 2 months)

2 months
Lift chest
(1½–3 months)

3 months
Reach and miss
(2–4 months)

4 months
Sit with support

5 months
Sit on lap,
grasp object

6 months
Sit in high
chair, grasp dangling object

6 months
Sit alone
(5–6½ months)

8 months
Stand with help

8 months
Stand holding furniture
(5–9 months)

8 months
Pull to stand
(6–9 months)

10 months
Creep on hands
and knees

11 months
Climb stairs

11 months
Walk when led

11 months
Stand alone
(10–13 months)

12 months
Walk alone
(11–13½ months)

FIGURE 7.2
Milestones of Locomotor Development
As shown here, infants make rapid progress in their ability to move around. Please note that the ages shown are only *averages*. Most children will depart from them to some extent, and such variations are of little importance unless they are extreme.
Source: From J. A. Schickedanz, D. I. Schickedanz, P. D. Forsyth & G. A. Forsyth, *Understanding Children and Adolescents,* 3/E. Published by Allyn and Bacon, Boston, MA. Copyright © 1998 by Pearson Education. Reprinted by permission of the publisher.

Much of this research has been conducted with birds (see Pravosudov, Lavenex, & Omanska, 2006), and has involved feeding one group a restricted diet, only two-thirds of what the chicks would normally eat. Other birds are offered a full diet. After a month, both groups are given all they can eat, and the key question is: Will this early malnutrition produce lasting effects that don't vanish when malnutrition ends? The answer is *yes*. For instance, the chicks fed the restricted diet show reductions in the size of important areas of the brain (e.g., the hippocampus). In addition, when tested for their ability to find hidden food, the birds that had been malnourished early in life performed more poorly. In short, eating enough later in life didn't make up for early malnutrition. Of course, we don't know if the same effects occur for humans. If they do, however, then infant malnutrition is even more tragic and devastating than was previously believed.

KEY QUESTIONS

- What environmental factors (teratogens) can adversely affect the developing fetus?
- What are reflexes and which ones do infants possess at birth?
- What learning abilities are shown by newborns?

PERCEPTUAL DEVELOPMENT DURING CHILDHOOD

How do infants perceive the world around them? Do they recognize form, see color, and perceive depth in the same manner as adults? Infants can't talk, so it is necessary to answer such questions through indirect methods, such as observing changes in behaviors they *can* perform when exposed to various stimuli—for instance, differences in sucking responses, in heart rate, or in the amount of time they spend looking at various stimuli. Developmental psychologists reason that if infants show different reactions to different stimuli, then they can, indeed, distinguish between them, at some level. For example, it has been found that after infants have seen a visual stimulus several times, they spend less time looking at it when it is presented again than they do at a new stimulus they have never seen before. This provides a means to determine whether infants can detect a difference between two stimuli. If they can, then after seeing one repeatedly, infants should spend less time looking at it than at a new stimulus. If they cannot tell the two stimuli apart, then they should look at both equally.

Studies based on this reasoning have found that newborns can distinguish between different colors (Adams, 1987), odors (Balogh & Porter, 1986), tastes (Granchrow, Steiner, & Daher, 1983), and sounds (Morrongiello & Clifton, 1984). Moreover, infants as young as two or three days old have been found to show contrasting patterns of sucking to what seem to be quite subtle differences in the sounds of human speech. For instance, by the time they are only a few months old, they can tell the difference between their own name and other names—even ones that are quite similar (see Mandel, Jusczyk, & Pisoni, 1995). Perhaps most surprising of all, newborns can even keep track of time, showing increases in heart rate just before an event they are expecting to happen actually does happen (Colombo & Richman, 2002).

Infants also show impressive abilities with respect to recognizing *form* or *pattern*. Although they can't see very clearly at birth (their vision is about 20/400, which means that they can see clearly at twenty feet what an adult can see at four hundred feet), they show marked preferences for patterns and contrasts in visual stimuli. In now classic research on this topic, Fantz (1961) showed babies six months old a variety of visual patterns. By observing how long they looked at each, he determined that the babies had a clear preference for patterned as opposed to plain targets, and that they seemed to prefer the human face over all

FIGURE 7.3
The Visual Cliff: Apparatus for Testing Infant Depth Perception
Infants six or seven months old will not crawl out over the "deep" side of the visual cliff. This indicates that they can perceive depth. Even two-month-old infants show changes in heart rate when placed over the "deep" side, so perception of depth may be present even at this young age.

other stimuli tested. Later research indicated that recognition of faces may develop even earlier. By two months of age, infants prefer a face with features in normal locations over one with scrambled features (Maurer & Barrera, 1981). By six months, they can distinguish their mother's face and that of a stranger, and even distinguish one stranger's face from another (Lewkowicz, 1996).

The ability to perceive depth, too, seems to develop rapidly. Early studies on *depth perception* employed an apparatus known as the *visual cliff* (Gibson & Walk, 1960). The patterned floor drops away on the deep side of the cliff, but a transparent surface continues across this drop, so there is no drop in the surface—and no real danger (see Figure 7.3). Yet, human infants six or seven months old refuse to crawl across the deep side to reach their mothers, indicating that they perceive depth by this time. Does this ability appear prior to this age? Since younger infants can't crawl across the cliff even if they want to, this research method can't answer that question. But other research, using different methods, indicates that depth perception may first appear when infants are only two months old—infants of this age show a change in heart rate when presented with the visual cliff (see Campos et al., 1970; Yonas, Arterberry, & Granrud, 1987).

In sum, shortly after birth, infants have sophisticated abilities to interpret complex sensory input. How do they then integrate such information into cognitive frameworks for understanding the world? This is the question we will consider next, in our discussion of cognitive development.

KEY QUESTIONS

- What perceptual abilities are shown by infants?
- What evidence indicates that infants can keep track of time?

COGNITIVE DEVELOPMENT DURING CHILDHOOD: CHANGES IN OUR ABILITY TO UNDERSTAND THE WORLD AROUND US

Do children think, reason, and remember in the same manner as adults? Until well into the twentieth century, it was widely assumed that they do. However, this view was vigorously challenged by the Swiss psychologist Jean Piaget. On the basis of careful observations of his own and many other children, Piaget concluded that in several respects, children do *not* think or reason like adults: Their thought processes are not just different *quantitatively* (e.g., slower or less effective), they are different *qualitatively*—in their basic nature. Because Piaget's theory of

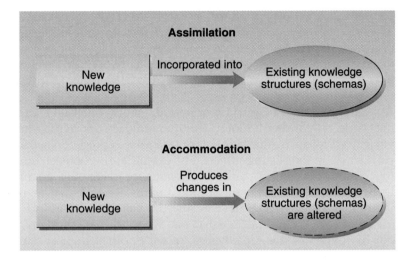

FIGURE 7.4
Assimilation and Accommodation
According to Piaget, children build increasing knowledge of the world through two processes: *assimilation*, in which new information is incorporated into existing schemas (cognitive frameworks), and *accommodation*, in which existing schemas are modified in response to new information and experiences.

cognitive development contains many valuable insights and has a major, lasting impact on the study of cognitive development, we'll consider it in detail here. As we'll soon see, though, several aspects of it have been strongly challenged by research findings.

Piaget's Theory: An Overview

One of the most central assumptions of Piaget's theory is the suggestion that children are active thinkers who are constantly trying to construct an accurate understanding of the world around them (see Siegler & Ellis, 1996). How do they go about building such knowledge? According to Piaget, through two basic processes. The first of these is **assimilation,** which involves the incorporation of new information or knowledge into existing knowledge structures known as **schemas.** As we noted in Chapter 6, we all create cognitive frameworks to hold and organize information, and schemas are one of these. The second process is known as **accommodation,** and involves modifications in existing knowledge structures (schemas) as a result of exposure to new information or experiences. Here's an example of how these processes operate.

A two-year-old child has seen many different kinds of cats and on the basis of such experience, has built up a schema for them: They are relatively small, four-legged animals, with tails and fur coats. Now she sees a squirrel for the first time and through *assimilation* includes it in this mental structure. As she encounters more and more squirrels, however, she begins to notice that they differ from cats in several respects: They move differently, climb trees, have much bushier tails, and so on. On the basis of this new experience, she gradually develops another schema, one for squirrels; this illustrates *accommodation*—changes in our existing knowledge structures resulting from exposure to new information (see Figure 7.4). Piaget believed that it is the tension between these two processes that encourages cognitive development. But don't lose sight of the key fact: According to Piaget, these changes occur because, in essence, children are constantly trying to make better and more accurate sense out of the complex world around them (Baillorgeon, 2002). Let's now take a closer look at several specific stages of cognitive development Piaget described.

■ **The sensorimotor stage: Figuring out ways to make things happen.**
Piaget suggested that the first stage of cognitive development lasts from birth until somewhere between eighteen and twenty-four months. During this period, termed the **sensorimotor stage,** infants gradually learn that there is a relationship

Cognitive development:
Changes in cognitive abilities and functioning.

Assimilation:
In Piaget's theory of cognitive development, incorporation of new information into existing mental frameworks (schemas).

Schemas:
Cognitive frameworks representing our knowledge about specific.

Accommodation:
In Piaget's theory of cognitive development, modifications in existing knowledge structures (schemas) as a result of exposure to new information or experiences.

Sensorimotor stage:
In Piaget's theory, the earliest stage of cognitive development.

between their actions and the external world. They discover that they can manipulate objects and produce effects. In short, they acquire a basic grasp of the concept of *cause and effect*. For example, they learn that if they make certain movements—for instance, shake their leg—specific effects follow (for instance, toys suspended over their crib also move), and they begin to "experiment" with various actions, to see what effects they will produce.

Throughout the sensorimotor period, Piaget contended, infants seem to know the world only through motor activities and sensory impressions. They have not yet learned to use mental symbols or images to represent objects or events. This results in some interesting effects. For example, if an object is hidden from view, four-month-olds will not attempt to search for it. For such infants, "out of sight" is truly "out of mind." By eight or nine months of age, however, they *will* search for the hidden objects. They have acquired a basic idea of **object permanence**—the idea that objects continue to exist even when they are hidden from view. (But see our discussion of this topic below; recent findings suggest that here, as in many other respects, Piaget greatly *underestimated* the abilities of infants, who often show signs of understanding a great deal about the physical world when they are only two or three months old [Baillorgeon, 2004].)

■ The preoperational stage: Growth of symbolic activity.

Sometime between the ages of eighteen and twenty-four months, Piaget suggested, toddlers acquire the ability to form mental images of objects and events. At the same time, language develops to the point at which they begin to think in terms of words. These developments mark the transition to Piaget's second stage—the **preoperational stage.** During this stage, which lasts until about age seven, children are capable of many actions they could not perform earlier. They begin to demonstrate **symbolic play,** in which they pretend that one object is another—for instance, that a pencil is a rocket, or a wooden block is a frog. But although they can use mental symbols in play and other contexts, their thinking remains somewhat immature in that it is still inflexible, illogical, fragmented, and tied to specific contexts. For instance, children of this age show what Piaget described as **egocentrism**—the inability to understand that others may perceive the world differently than they do (Piaget, 1975). For example, if two-year-olds are shown a card with a picture of a dog on one side and a cat on the other, and the card is placed between the child and the researcher, many do not seem to realize that they and the adult see different pictures. (In this case, too, Piaget seems to have underestimated the abilities of young children; more recent findings indicate that even very young children can appreciate the fact that others have different perspectives than they do [see Birch, 2005].)

Children in the preoperational stage also seem to lack understanding of relational terms such as *lighter, larger, softer*. Further, they lack *seriation*—the ability to arrange objects in order along some dimension. Finally, and most important, they lack what Piaget terms the principle of **conservation**—knowledge that certain physical attributes of an object remain unchanged even though the outward appearance of the object is altered. For example, imagine that a four-year-old is shown two identical lumps of clay. One lump is then flattened into a large pancake as the child watches. Asked whether the two lumps still contain the same amount of clay, the child may answer, "No." In other words, the term *pre*operational is really appropriate, because during this stage of cognitive development, infants can't perform many of the mental operations that they perform with relative ease during later stages.

■ The stage of concrete operations: The emergence of logical thought.

By the time they are six or seven (or perhaps even earlier, as we'll see below), most children can solve the simple problems described above. According to Piaget, their mastery of conservation marks the beginning of a third major stage, known as the stage of **concrete operations.**

Object permanence:
Understanding of the fact that objects continue to exist, even when they are hidden from view.

Preoperational stage:
In Piaget's theory, a stage of cognitive development during which children become capable of mental representations of the external world.

Symbolic play:
Play in which children pretend that one object is another object.

Egocentrism:
The inability of young children to distinguish their own.

Conservation:
Understanding of the fact that certain physical attributes of an object remain unchanged, even though its outward appearance changes.

Concrete operations:
A stage in Piaget's theory of cognitive development occurring roughly between the ages of seven and eleven. It is at this stage that children become aware of the permanence of objects.

TABLE 7.2 Major Stages in Piaget's Theory

According to Piaget, we move through the stages of cognitive development described here.

Stage	Age	Major Accomplishments
Sensorimotor	0–2 years	The child develops basic ideas of cause and effect and object permanence.
Preoperational	2–6 or 7 years	The child begins to represent the world symbolically.
Concrete operations	7–11 or 12 years	The child gains understanding of principles such as conservation; logical thought emerges.
Formal operations	12–adult	The adolescent becomes capable of several forms of logical thought.

During this stage, which lasts until about the age of eleven, many important skills emerge. Children gain understanding of relational terms and seriation. They come to understand *reversibility*—the fact that many physical changes can be undone by a reversal of the original action. Children who have reached the stage of concrete operations also begin to engage in what Piaget described as *logical thought*. If asked, "Why did you and your mother go to the store?" they reply, "Because my mother needed some milk." Younger children, in contrast, may reply "Because afterwards, she came home."

■ **The stage of formal operations: Dealing with abstractions as well as reality.**

At about the age of twelve, Piaget suggested, most children enter the final stage of cognitive development—the stage of **formal operations.** During this period, major features of adult thought make their appearance. While children in the earlier stage of concrete operations can think logically, they can do so only about concrete events and objects. In contrast, those who have reached the stage of formal operations can think abstractly; they can deal not only with the real or concrete but also with possibilities—relationships that do not exist, but can be imagined. During this final stage, children become capable of what Piaget termed **hypothetico-deductive reasoning.** This involves the ability to generate hypotheses and to think logically about symbols, ideas, and propositions (see Kuhn & Dean, 2005).

One final—but crucial—point: People who have reached the stage of formal operations are *capable* of engaging in advanced forms of thought, but there is no guarantee that they will actually do so. Such thinking requires lots of cognitive effort, so it is not surprising that adolescents, and adults, too, often slip back into less advanced modes of thought. Table 7.2 provides a summary of the major stages in Piaget's theory.

Piaget's Theory: A Modern Assessment

All theories in psychology are subject to careful scientific test, so what do research findings indicate about Piaget's theory? Essentially, that it is highly insightful in many respects, but should be revised to take account of new findings. The most important of these revisions concerns how Piaget greatly underestimated the cognitive abilities of infants and preschoolers. They are, in fact, capable of performing more tasks—and more complex ones—at younger ages than he suggested. To illustrate this point, we'll now take a closer look at one of the abilities that Piaget underestimated—*object permanence*. (We'll comment on another of Piaget's ideas—that young children don't realize that others may see the world differently than they do [egocentrism]—in a later discussion.)

Formal operations (stage of):
In Piaget's theory, the final stage of cognitive development.

Hypothetico-deductive reasoning:
A type of reasoning first shown by individuals during the stage of formal operations. It involves formulating a general theory and deducing specific hypotheses from it.

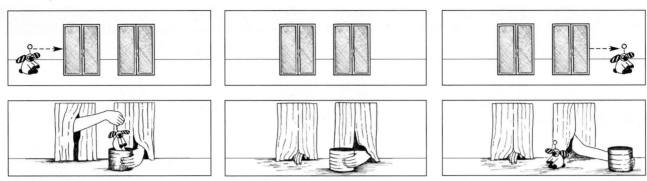

FIGURE 7.5
Infants' Understanding of the Physical World
Contrary to what Piaget proposed, even very young infants possess understanding of basic principles of the physical world. Evidence pointing to this conclusion is provided by studies in which young infants are shown both *expected* and *unexpected* events. For instance, in the top drawings, a toy disappears behind one screen and then later reappears from behind another one. Infants look longer at such unexpected events than at ones that are expected (e.g., the toy disappears behind one screen and then reappears from behind the same screen). This indicates that they do understand that physical objects continue to exist continuously—in other words, contrary to what Piaget proposed, they do have basic understanding of object permanence. (The second row illustrates another type of unexpected event known as *containment*.)
Source: Baillorgeon, 2004, p. 90.

■ **Infants' understanding of the physical world.**

As you may recall, Piaget concluded that infants younger than eight or nine months old did not realize that objects have an existence that continues even when they are removed from sight. However, recent findings indicate that even infants as young as two and a half months have some understanding of the fact that objects continue to exist even if they cannot see them (Baillorgeon, 2002; Lipton & Spelke, 2006). Evidence pointing to this conclusion—and to the more general conclusion that even young infants have a good grasp of basic principles relating to the physical world (e.g., *solidity*—two objects can't occupy the same space at the same time)—is provided by research using the *violation-of-expectation method*. In this technique, infants are shown an *expected* event, which is consistent with what they expect to happen, and an *unexpected* event—one that violates their expectations. If the infants look longer at the unexpected than the expected event, this indicates that they possess the expectation being investigated and could detect the violation of this expectation in the unexpected event.

Three basic events used in such research are *occlusion* events—one object is placed or moves behind a nearer object; *containment* events—an object is placed inside a container; and *covering events*—in which a rigid cover is lowered over an object (Baillorgeon & Wang, 2002). For instance, the top drawings in Figure 7.5 illustrate an occlusion event in which infants' expectations are violated. A toy is placed behind a screen and then, later, reappears from behind another screen. Infants look longer at this unexpected event than they do at an expected one—for instance, the toy is placed behind one screen and then reappears from behind the same screen. Here's another example: a toy is placed inside a container and then, when the container is moved, the toy is shown behind it. Again, infants look at this kind of unexpected event longer than at expected ones—for instance, the toy is placed in the container, the container is moved, and then the toy is taken out of the container (see Figure 7.5, second row).

Many studies using these methods indicate that even infants only two and a half months old have clear expectations about basic aspects of the physical world; for instance, they expect that objects will continue to exist even if they can't see them. They do get better in terms of understanding various aspects of the physical world as they grow older (Baillorgeon, 2004), but overall, it seems clear that Piaget greatly underestimated infants' basic grasp of the world around them (Markson & Spelke, 2006).

Even though some of Piaget's suggestions have been called into question by recent research, it is clear that his theory changed the way in which psychologists think about cognitive development in basic and important ways. And since theories are *made* to be revised and improved, this is simply an illustration of the scientific method at work!

KEY QUESTIONS

- What are the major stages in Piaget's theory, and what cognitive abilities do infants, children, and adolescents acquire as they move through these stages?
- In what respects does Piaget's theory appear to be in need of revision?

Beyond Piaget: Children's Theory of Mind and Research on the Information-Processing Perspective

While Piaget certainly added much to our understanding of children's thought, recent research has investigated topics that were not included in his work. One of these involves children's **theory of mind**—their growing understanding of their own mental states and those of others. A second is the application of an *information-processing* perspective to various aspects of cognitive development.

■ Children's theory of mind: Thinking about thinking.

As adults, we possess a sophisticated understanding of the process of thinking. We realize that our own thoughts may change over time and that we may have false beliefs or reach false conclusions. Similarly, we realize that other people may have goals or desires that differ from our own and that they may sometimes try to conceal these from us; further, we realize that given the same information, they may reason to conclusions different from our own. In other words, we understand quite a bit about how we and other people think. What about children? When—and how—do they acquire such understanding? This has been a major focus of recent research on cognitive development.

Let's begin with what might seem to be a fairly simple aspect of such thinking—children's ability to recognize that others can hold beliefs different from their own, and that these beliefs can be false. Do they understand this basic fact? Piaget thought that they did not, and termed this effect *egocentrism*. And to some extent, he was correct: Until children are about four years old (e.g., Naito et al., 1994), they often think that if they know something or see something, others must know it or see it, too. They don't realize that other people can have a different perspective.

Why does this tendency exist? In part, because young children—and even adults, too!—suffer from what is known as the **curse of knowledge**—an inability to separate our own knowledge from what we think others know. In other words, because we *know* something, we have difficulty realizing that others don't. Here's an example: Young children (four or younger) are told that one child places candy in a basket and then leaves. While she is away, another child moves the candy to a box. Children are then asked: Where does the first child look when she comes back and wants her candy? Prior to age four, most children suggest that she will look in the box—where the second child placed it. They don't seem to realize that *they* know this is the location of the candy, but the first child does not because she was out of the room when the candy was moved. After age four, they answer that the first child will look in the basket, where she placed it.

This inability to realize that others don't necessarily know what we know is very clear among young children, but recent findings indicate that it may exist among adults, too! In fact, it may be one reason for the *hindsight bias*—the tendency

Theory of mind:
Refers to children's growing understanding of their own mental states and those of others.

Curse of knowledge:
Refers to how we tend to be biased by our own knowledge when judging the perspective of people who know less about some topic than we do.

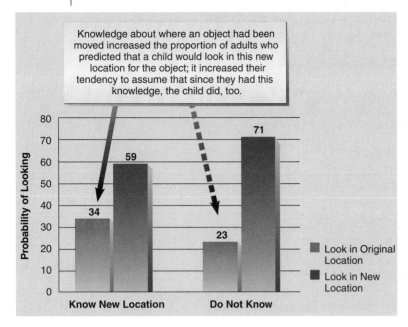

Knowledge about where an object had been moved increased the proportion of adults who predicted that a child would look in this new location for the object; it increased their tendency to assume that since they had this knowledge, the child did, too.

FIGURE 7.6

The Curse of Knowledge: It Occurs among Adults, Too

Children younger than age four often seem to assume that if they know something, others know it, too. For instance, if they see one child place candy in a basket and another child move it to a box, they will guess that the first child will look in the box when she returns and searches for her candy. While this tendency to show the *curse of knowledge* decreases with age, it is still present in adults. In the study illustrated here, adults estimated the probability that a child would look for an object (a violin) in a given location after placing it there. Half the adults were told *where* the object had been moved by a second child and half were simply told that it had been moved, but not where. Surprisingly, when they knew *where* the object had been moved, a higher proportion of adults guessed that the first child would look for the violin in the new location—even though she could not possibly know it had been moved there.

Source: Based on data from Birch & Bloom, 2005.

for current knowledge to influence our memories about what we knew or did in the past so that often, we assume that we knew more than we really did at the time (Birch, 2005). For instance, in one study (Birch & Bloom, 2004), adult participants were given the same problem used with children: one child hides candy, another moves it while the first is gone, and then participants in the research are asked, "Where will the first child look for the candy she previously hid?" Four containers instead of two were used and a violin, rather than candy, was the object that was hidden and then moved. Participants estimated the probability that the first child would look in each location (the original one, or the new one). To study the effects of knowing the outcome, half were told that the violin had been moved to a specific container while the others were simply told it had been moved but not told where. Results were very clear: a higher proportion of the adults in the study guessed that the first child would look for the violin in the place where the second child had moved it if they knew its new location. When they did not know where the second child had placed the violin, however, fewer guessed that the first child would look for it in this location (see Figure 7.6). In other words, the tendency to show this aspect of egocentrism (a lack of understanding of others' knowledge of perspective) seems to stem, at least in part, from the fact that even as adults, we can't totally discount the impact of our own knowledge on what we think others know.

■ An information-processing perspective—and increasing reliance on heuristics and other potential sources of error.

Another way in which recent research on cognitive development has moved beyond Piaget's theory involves application of an **information-processing perspective.** This perspective seeks insights into cognitive development in terms of children's growing abilities with respect to basic aspects of cognition such as attention, memory, and **metacognition** (thinking about thinking and being able to control and use one's own cognitive abilities strategically). For instance, as they grow older, children acquire better strategies for retaining information in working (short-term) memory. Five- and six-year-olds are much less likely than adults to use *rehearsal*—repeating information to themselves as they try to memorize it. By the time children are eight years old, however, they can do this much more effectively.

In a similar manner, children acquire increasingly effective strategies for focusing their attention, for using **scripts** and other mental frameworks (schemas; Fivush et al., 1992), and greater understanding of *metacognition*—for instance, how to regulate and control problem-solving processes and memory (Frederiksen, 1994). Research conducted from an information-processing perspective has helped link the process of cognitive development more closely to basic research on cognition, so it, too, is very useful.

Information-processing perspective (of cognitive development):

A perspective emphasizing the importance of information processing in cognitive development.

Metacognition:

Awareness and understanding of our own cognitive processes.

Scripts:

Mental representations of the sequence of events in a given situation.

- What is the "curse of knowledge" and what does it tell us about young children's cognitive abilities?
- To what does the term *children's theory of mind* refer?
- According to the information-processing perspective, what does cognitive development involve?
- What role do heuristics and other potential sources of error play in cognitive development?

Language: Learning to Communicate

No discussion of cognitive development would be complete without attention to **language**—the system we use to communicate information through the use of specific symbols (e.g., words, gestures) and rules for combining them. Because language is such a key aspect of human cognition—and human behavior—it has received a great deal of attention from psychologists. While we can't possibly cover more than a small part of our current knowledge of language here, we can at least provide a good general picture of how this crucial skill develops.

■ The development of language: Some basics.

Throughout the first weeks of life, infants have only one major means of verbal communication: crying. Within a few short years, however, children progress rapidly to speaking whole sentences and acquire a vocabulary of hundreds or even thousands of words. What mechanisms play a role in this remarkable process? And how, and at what ages, do children acquire various aspects of language skills?

■ Theories of language development: Some contrasting views.

One view, the social learning approach, proposes that speech is acquired through a combination of operant conditioning and imitation. Presumably, children are praised or otherwise rewarded by their parents for making sounds approximating those of their native language. Moreover, parents often model sounds, words, or sentences for them. Together, it is contended, these basic forms of learning contribute to the rapid acquisition of language.

A sharply different view, proposed by the noted linguist Noam Chomsky (1968), suggests that language acquisition is at least partly innate. Human beings, he contends, have a *language acquisition device*—a built-in neural system that provides them with an intuitive grasp of grammar—they can use it without understanding its formal rules. In other words, humans are prepared to acquire language and do so rapidly for this reason. Chomsky points out, for example, that children throughout the world go through similar stages in language development at about the same age and in a way that mirrors their motor development.

As you might expect, more recent theories of language development tend to emphasize the importance of both innate mechanisms and learning. The most recent of these, termed the *constrained statistical learning framework*, suggests that we acquire language through the use of statistical features of linguistic input that help us discover structure, including sound patterns, words, and grammar (Newport & Aslin, 2000; Saffran, 2003). According to this view, the similarities in language development patterns noted by Chomsky and others may not be the result of innate linguistic knowledge but, instead, a more generalized set of *learning mechanisms* inherent in humans, and perhaps other species (see Hauser, Newport, & Alin, 2001).

To illustrate how this might work, consider the difficulties faced by infants confronted with the complexities of language. One of the most significant challenges they face is learning *word segmentation*; in other words, learning where the boundaries are between words in fluent speech. Why is this a problem? In part,

Language:
The system we use to communicate information to others through the use of specific symbols (words, gestures), and the rules for combining them.

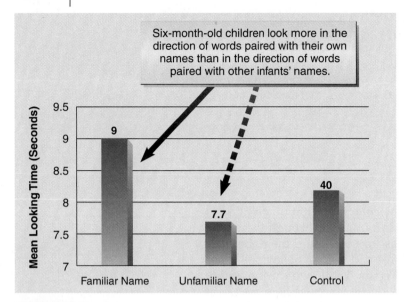

Six-month-old children look more in the direction of words paired with their own names than in the direction of words paired with other infants' names.

FIGURE 7.7

Word Segmentation: Using Familiar Words as Markers

How do children learn to segment speech—to divide one word from another? Research studies indicate that one way they accomplish this task is by using familiar words as *markers* that help them divide one word from another. As shown here, six-month-old infants learned to recognize unfamiliar words that had been paired with their own names; the names helped them recognize that these words were distinct parts of speech.

Source: Based on data from Bortfeld et al., 2005.

because experienced speakers do not consistently mark word boundaries with detectable pauses—they keep going! This is why it is often difficult to learn a foreign language: People speaking it seem to be talking very fast, and it is hard to tell where one word ends and another begins. How do children master this difficult task? One answer is they use familiar words to help them segment speech—to divide it into recognizable words or parts. This is illustrated clearly in research conducted by Bortfeld and colleagues (2005).

In this study, six-month-old infants heard an adult read sentences of two types: One type of sentence contained the infant's own name and an unfamiliar target word (e.g., for an infant named Maggie: *Maggie's bike had big black wheels; Maggie's cup was bright and shiny*). The other type of sentence contained another infant's name and the same unfamiliar word (e.g., *Hannah's bike; Hannah's cup*). Later, the infants were tested for recognition of the unfamiliar words paired with their own name or another infant's name by presenting these words and seeing how long they looked in the direction of the words. It was expected that they would look longer toward the sources of these words if they had been paired with their own names than with another infant's names. (Control words were not paired with either name.) As you can see from Figure 7.7, this is precisely what happened. These findings indicate that infants do indeed use familiar words—for instance, their own names—as a kind of "entering wedge" for segmenting speech, for telling where one words ends and another begins. That's a very basic aspect to learning a language, so understanding how it works is very helpful in terms of understanding language development generally.

■ **Basic components of language development.**

Another important aspect of language development involves the development of **phonological awareness**—sensitivity to the sound structure or oral (spoken) language. For instance, as children develop this ability, they can blend sounds together, separate words into their basic sounds, recombine the sounds of words, and judge whether two words have sounds in common. In short, phonological awareness relates to the ability to recognize, discriminate, and manipulate the sounds in one's language (Anthony & Francis, 2005). Current evidence indicates that such awareness develops in much the same manner across different languages, and involves intelligence, memory, and vocabulary, as well as experiences with oral and written language. In general, phonological awareness develops as follows.

At some point between three and six months, babies begin babbling. At first *babbling* contains a rich mixture of sounds, virtually every sound used in human speech. Indeed, research suggests that babies only a few months old can distinguish sounds from many different languages (Werker & Desjardins, 1995). This makes sense since humans are born with the capacity to learn any language. By nine or ten months, however, the range of babbling narrows and consists mainly of sounds used in the language of the child's native culture. From this point to the production of the first spoken word is a relatively short step, and most children accomplish it by their first birthday.

Phonological awareness: Sensitivity to the sound structure of oral (spoken) language.

Between the ages of one and two, children's vocabularies increase rapidly; for instance, by the time they are eighteen months old, many toddlers have a vocabulary of fifty words or more. Not surprisingly, these words include the names of familiar objects important in the children's own lives—foods (*juice, cookie*), animals (*cat, dog*), toys (*block, ball*), body parts (*ear, eye*), clothing (*sock, hat, shoe*), and people (*Momma, Dadda*).

There is considerable variability in the size of a child's vocabulary and the rate at which vocabulary increases. Not surprisingly, exposure to spoken words—reflected, for example, in the amount of time parents spend speaking to their child—is an important factor in vocabulary size and rate of growth (Huttenlocher et al., 1991).

■ **The role of gestures in language development.**

I (Robert Baron) had no pets when I was a child, but now—mainly because of my wife's preferences—I have ownership with her of a very pretty white cat named Gentil (which means "nice" or "kind" in French). Since I had never lived with a cat before, I had a lot to learn, but one thing I noticed at once was that Gentil could correctly understand my *gestures*. If I stood in a doorway and pointed inside, she would look inside and enter; if I brought out a treat, placed it on the floor and then pointed to it, she would look where I pointed—and find the treat very quickly. And when I taught her the go upstairs in response to the word "up," I moved my arms upward and pointed my body toward the stairs—and she caught on quickly. These informal experiences suggest that *gestures*—movements of various body parts to convey meaning—may indeed be an important aspect of communication, and such communication can be across different species (to my cat!) as well as within it. Clearly, we use gestures frequently in our daily lives, but—and this is the key question—do they play any role in language development? Research findings indicate that they do. In fact, gestures may, in an important way, pave the way for speech, preceding it and helping young children communicate with their caregivers even before they have a large vocabulary. That this is so is clearly indicated by research conducted by Iverson and Goldin-Meadow (2005).

These researchers observed young children in a study that continued from the time the children were ten months old until they were twenty-four months old. During each observation session, the children were at home with their primary caregiver (e.g., their mothers), and observations were made during a snack or at mealtime as they ate or played with toys. The children's use of three kinds of gestures were recorded. One kind is *deictic gestures*—gestures that indicate references in the immediate environment (e.g., holding up an object in front of an adult or pointing at it); *conventional gestures*—ones that have a culturally defined meaning, such as nodding the head to indicate "yes"; and *ritualized reaches*—in which children reach toward an object, often while opening and closing their palms. The children's use of words, too, was recorded, and the key question was this: would their use of gestures precede their use of various words, and perhaps the development of two-word sentences—an important step in language development? Results were clear: Gestures did precede the use of words and also preceded the transition to two-word sentences. In other words, children showed understanding of the meaning of many words in their gestures—for instance, by pointing to the correct item—before they could actually say the words or use them in sentences. This suggests that gesture may actually facilitate language development. How? Perhaps by signaling caregivers that children are ready for certain kinds of instruction, or by reducing demands on memory (pointing to an object may require less memory than producing the word for that object). Whatever the precise mechanisms, it is clear that gestures do play an important role in language development and this role may even continue into middle childhood (Singer & Goldin-Meadow, 2005).

■ Semantic development: The acquisition of meaning.

A child's vocabulary increases rapidly after age two, with many new words being learned each day. Thus, by the time children are six, most have a vocabulary of several thousand words. Children don't simply learn new words, however; they also learn new types of words—ones that allow them to communicate a much richer range of thoughts and ideas. Thus, they acquire understanding of negatives such as *no* and how to use these in sentences. Similarly, they acquire many adjectives and prepositions—words that allow them to be more specific in describing their own thoughts and the world around them. They start with simple adjectives such as *little*, *good*, and *bad*, but soon move on to ones with more specific meaning, such as *high*, *low*, *narrow*, and *wide*, and prepositions such as *in front of* and *behind*. Children also learn to use question words—words that allow them to ask for information from others in efficient and specific ways: *Why? When? Who? Where?* These are key words children acquire between the ages of two and three.

While children increase their vocabulary very rapidly, they often demonstrate several interesting forms of error. One such error involves *overextensions*—a tendency to extend the meaning of a word beyond its actual usage. For instance, eighteen-month-olds may use the word *raisin* to refer to all small objects—flies and pebbles as well as raisins themselves. Similarly, they may use *meow* as a shorthand word for all small furry animals—dogs as well as cats. They also show *underextensions*—limiting the meaning of a word more than is appropriate. For instance, they may think that the word *cat* refers to the family's pet cat and to no others.

KEY QUESTIONS

- What processes play a role in language acquisition?
- What is phonological awareness?
- What role do gestures play in learning acquisition?
- What advances do children make in understanding the meaning of words and language?

MORAL DEVELOPMENT: REASONING ABOUT "RIGHT" AND "WRONG"

Is it ever right to cheat on an exam? To mislead consumers through false advertising? To lie to other people? To claim exaggerated deductions on your income taxes? As adults we often ponder such *moral questions*—issues concerning what is right and what is wrong in a given context (see Figure 7.8). And as adults, we realize that such matters are often complex. Whether a given action is acceptable or unacceptable depends on many factors, including the specific circumstances involved, legal considerations, and our own personal code of ethics.

How do children deal with such issues? They, too, must make moral judgments. Is their reasoning about such matters similar to that of adults? This is the key question addressed in research on **moral development**—changes in the ability to reason about what is right and what is wrong in a given situation (see Carpendale & Krebs, 1995; Carlo et al., 1996). While many different views of moral development have been proposed, the most famous is a theory offered by Lawrence Kohlberg (1984).

Kohlberg's Stages of Moral Understanding

Building on earlier views proposed by Piaget (1932, 1965), Kohlberg studied boys and men and suggested that human beings move through three distinct levels of moral reasoning, each divided in two phases. To determine the stage of moral development people had reached, Kohlberg asked them to consider imaginary situ-

Moral development: Changes that occur with age in the capacity to reason about the rightness or wrongness of various actions.

FIGURE 7.8
Moral Judgment: Telling Right from Wrong
Throughout life, we must decide whether various actions are "right" or "wrong." What do you think of the actions of Dogbert in this cartoon? Very likely you would conclude that they are *wrong*. How does our ability to make such decisions change with age? This is the issue investigated in research on *moral development*.
Source: Dilbert: © Scott Adams/Dist. by United Feature Syndicate, Inc.

ations that raised moral dilemmas. Participants then indicated the course of action they would choose, and explained why. According to Kohlberg, it is the explanations, *not* the decisions themselves, that are crucial, for it is the reasoning displayed in these explanations that reveals individuals' stage of moral development. One such dilemma is as follows:

> A man's wife is ill with a special kind of cancer. There is a drug that may save her, but it is very expensive. The pharmacist who discovered this medicine will sell it for $2,000, but the man has only $1,000. He asks the pharmacist to let him pay part of the cost now and rest later, but the pharmacist refuses. Being desperate, the man steals the drug. Should he have done so? Why?

Let's consider the kind of reasoning that would reflect several of the major stages of moral reasoning described by Kohlberg. (An overview of all the stages he described is presented in Table 7.3 on page 264.)

■ **The preconventional level.**

At the first level of moral development, the **preconventional level,** children judge morality largely in terms of consequences: Actions that lead to rewards are perceived as good or acceptable; ones that lead to punishments are seen as bad or unacceptable. For example, a child at this stage might say: "The man should not steal the drug because if he does, he'll be punished."

■ **The conventional level.**

As children's cognitive abilities increase, Kohlberg suggests, they enter a second level of moral development, the **conventional level.** Now they are aware of some of the complexities of the social order and judge morality in terms of what supports the laws and rules of their society. Thus, a child at this stage might reason: "It's OK to steal the drug because no one will think you are bad if you do. If you don't, and let your wife die, you'll never be able to look anyone in the eye again."

■ **The postconventional level.**

Finally, in adolescence or early adulthood many, though by no means all, individuals enter a third level known as the **postconventional level** or principled level. At

Preconventional level (of morality):
According to Kohlberg, the earliest stage of moral development, one at which individuals judge morality in terms of the effects produced by various actions.

Conventional level (of morality):
According to Kohlberg, a stage of moral development during which individuals judge morality largely in terms of existing social norms or rules.

Postconventional level (of morality):
According to Kohlberg, the final stage of moral development, one at which individuals judge morality in terms of abstract principles.

TABLE 7.3 Kohlberg's Theory of Moral Development: An Overview

According to Kohlberg, we move through the stages of moral development (and reasoning) described here.

Level/Stage	Description
Preconventional Level	
Stage 1: Punishment-and-Obedience Orientation	Morality judged in terms of consequences
Stage 2: Naive Hedonistic Orientation	Morality judged in terms of what satisfies own needs or those of others
Conventional Level	
Stage 3: Good Boy–Good Girl Orientation	Morality judged in terms of adherence to social rules or norms with respect to personal acquaintances
Stage 4: Social Order–Maintaining Orientation	Morality judged in terms of social rules or laws applied universally, not just to acquaintances
Postconventional Level	
Stage 5: Legalistic Orientation	Morality judged in terms of human rights, which may transcend laws
Stage 6: Universal Ethical Principle Orientation	Morality judged in terms of self-chosen ethical principles

this stage, people judge morality in terms of abstract principles and values rather than in terms of existing laws or rules of society. People who attain this stage often believe that certain obligations and values transcend the laws of society. The rules they follow are abstract and ethical, not concrete like the Ten Commandments, and they are based on inner conscience rather than external sources of authority. For example, a person at this stage of moral development might argue for stealing the drug as follows: "If the man doesn't steal the drug, he is putting property above human life; this makes no sense. People could live together without private property, but a respect for human life is essential." In contrast, if they argue for not stealing the drug, they might reason: "If the man stole the drug he wouldn't be blamed by others, but he would probably blame himself, since he has violated his own standards of honesty, and hurt another person for his own gain."

Evidence Concerning Kohlberg's Theory

Do we really pass through the series of stages described by Kohlberg? Some findings are consistent with this view. Individuals do generally seem to progress through the stages of moral reasoning Kohlberg described, moving to increasingly sophisticated modes of thought (e.g., Walker, 1989). Other evidence, however, suggests that Kohlberg's theory, while providing important insights, requires major revisions in several respects.

■ **Consistency of moral judgments.**

Kohlberg's theory, like other **stage theories,** suggests that as people grow older, they move through a successive series of discrete stages. If that is true, then it would be predicted that individuals' moral reasoning across a wide range of moral dilemmas should be consistent—it should reflect the stage they have reached. Do people show such consistency? The answer appears to be "no." Research on this issue (see Ward & Krebs, 1996) indicates people do not show a high degree of consistency reflecting a specific stage of moral reasoning, as Kohlberg's theory predicts.

Stage theory:

Any theory proposing that all humans move through an orderly and predictable series of changes.

Second, we should note that Kohlberg's research focused entirely on males; he basically ignored females—a serious flaw soon noted by other researchers (e.g., Gilligan, 1982) who pointed out—strongly!—that in many cultures, women face quite different challenges and have very different life experiences than men.

■ **Cultural differences and moral development.**

A second problem with Kohlberg's theory is neither the stages Kohlberg described, nor steady progression through them, appear in all cultures. In cross-cultural studies carried out in many countries (Taiwan, Turkey, Mexico), it has sometimes been found that people from tribal or rural village backgrounds are less likely to reach stage 5 reasoning than people from more advantaged backgrounds (see Nisan & Kohlberg, 1982; Simpson, 1974). These findings suggest that Kohlberg's work may, to an extent, be "culture-bound": It is biased against people from ethnic groups and populations different from the ones he originally studied. Whether, and to what degree, this is true remains uncertain, but it *is* clear that cultural factors play an important role in shaping moral development, and should be taken fully into account in our efforts to understand this important topic.

KEY QUESTIONS

- What are the major stages of moral development described by Kohlberg's theory?
- Do cultural factors have any impact on moral development?

SOCIAL DEVELOPMENT DURING CHILDHOOD: FORMING RELATIONSHIPS WITH OTHERS

Cognitive development is a crucial aspect of human growth, but it does not occur in a social vacuum. As infants and children are acquiring the capacities to think and reason, they are also gaining the basic experiences, skills, and emotions that permit them to form close relationships and interact with others effectively in many settings. In this section, we will examine several aspects of such **social development.**

Temperament: Individual Differences in Emotional Style

Do you know anyone who is almost always energetic, cheerful, and upbeat? How about the other extreme—someone who is usually reserved, quiet, and gloomy. Psychologists refer to such stable individual differences in attention, arousal, mood, and reactivity to new situations as **temperament** (see Guerin & Gottfried, 1994; Plomin, 1993). Growing evidence suggests that these differences are present very early in life—perhaps at birth (e.g., Kagan & Snidman, 1991; Seifer et al., 1994). What are the key dimensions of temperament? Most experts agree that they involve *positive emotionality*—the extent to which infants show pleasure and are typically in a good, happy mood; *distress-anger*—the extent to which infants show distress and the emotion of anger; *fear*—the extent to which infants show fear in various situations; and *activity level*—their overall level of activity or energy.

Large individual differences occur in these dimensions, and these are sometimes easy to spot even during brief interactions with infants (see Figure 7.9, page 266). On the basis of such differences, some researchers (Thomas & Chess, 1989) have suggested that infants can be divided into three basic groups: *easy children* (about 40 percent)—infants who are generally cheerful, adapt easily to new experiences, and quickly establish routines for many activities of daily life; *difficult children* (about 10 percent)—infants who are irregular in daily routines, slow to accept new situations or experiences, and show negative reactions more than other

Social development:
Changes in social behavior and social relations occurring over the life span.

Temperament:
Stable individual differences in the quality or intensity of emotional reactions.

FIGURE 7.9
Individual Differences in Temperament Present Very Early in Life
Research findings indicate that individual differences in *temperament*—in arousal, mood, attention, and reactivity to new situations—are present early in life, perhaps even at birth. These differences tend to persist and can exert strong effects on later social development.

infants; and *slow-to-warm-up children* (15 percent)—infants who are relatively inactive and apathetic and show mild negative reactions when exposed to unexpected events or new situations. The remaining 35 percent of infants cannot be readily classified under one of these headings.

How stable are such differences in temperament? Research findings suggest that they are only moderately stable early in life—from birth until about twenty-four months. After that time, however, they appear to be highly stable (e.g., Lemery et al., 1999). Individual differences in temperament are at least partially genetic in origin (e.g., Lytton, 1990). Indeed, some findings indicate that genetic factors may account for 50 to 60 percent of the variations in temperament (Kagan, 1998). Different aspects of temperament may be influenced by genetic and environmental factors to varying degrees, however (see Magai & McFadden, 1995). Whatever the relative role of genetic and environmental factors in temperament, individual differences in such emotional style have important implications for social development. For example, a much higher proportion of difficult than of easy children experience behavioral problems later in life (Chess & Thomas, 1984).

Attachment: The Beginnings of Love

Do infants love their parents? They can't say so directly, but by the time they are six or seven months old, most appear to have a strong emotional bond with the people who care for them (Ainsworth, 1973; Lamb, 1977). This strong affectional tie between infants and their caregivers is known as **attachment** and is, in an important sense, the first form of love we experience toward others. What are the origins of this initial form of love? How can it be measured? These are among the questions developmental psychologists have sought to answer in their research on attachment.

■ **Patterns of attachment.**

That infants form strong attachments to the people who care for them is obvious. But attachment is not the same for all infants. In fact, several distinct patterns ap-

Attachment:
A strong affectional bond between infants and their caregivers.

pear to exist. Most infants show **secure attachment;** they feel safe around their caregiver (e.g., their mother), enjoy exploring new environments—often using their caregiver as a "safe home base"—and are sociable and playful. In contrast, other infants show **insecure/avoidant attachment.** They don't rely on their care-givers for security, and often avoid close contact with them. They explore new environments, but don't seem to view their caregiver as a source of safety and comfort. A third group of infants show a pattern known as **insecure/ambivalent attachment.** These infants often engage in continuous efforts to maintain contact with their caregiver, and often cling to them in new situations. They are inhibited and show many signs of fear.

How do these different patterns develop? Research findings suggest that they derive out of complex interactions between infants' temperament and the treat-ment they receive from caregivers. If a child has an easy temperament (is gener-ally cheerful and adaptable), and the caregiver provides sufficient attention, responsiveness, and approval, secure attachment is likely to develop. If, in con-trast, the child has a fearful, inhibited temperament and the caregiver offers little attention and approval, insecure/ambivalent attachment may develop. In short, attachment is reciprocal: It depends on both the child *and* the caregiver.

■ The long-term effects of attachment.

Do these different patterns of attachment have effects that persist beyond infancy? A growing body of evidence indicates that they do. During childhood, youngsters who are securely attached to their caregivers are more sociable, better at solving certain kinds of problems, more tolerant of frustration, and more flexible and per-sistent in many situations than children who are insecurely attached (Beksly & Cassidy, 1994; Pastor, 1981). Further, securely attached children seem to experi-ence fewer behavioral problems during later childhood (Fagot & Kavanaugh, 1990).

Perhaps even more surprising, some findings suggest that differences in at-tachment style as an infant may have strong effects on the kind of relationships in-dividuals form when they are adults (see Hazan & Shaver, 1990). People who showed insecure/avoidant attachment to their caregivers as infants have a diffi-cult time forming intimate bonds with romantic partners; they didn't trust their caregivers as infants, and they are reluctant to trust spouses or lovers when they are adults. Similarly, people who showed insecure/ambivalent attachment to their caregivers as infants seem to be ambivalent about romantic relationships, too: They want them, but they also fear them because they perceive their partner as distant and unloving. In contrast, people who were securely attached to their caregivers as infants seek closeness in their adult relationships, and are comfort-able with having to depend on their partners (Shaver & Hazan, 1994). In a sense, then, it seems that the pattern of our relationships with others is set—at least to a degree—by the nature of the very first relationship we form, attachment to our caregivers.

■ Culture and attachment.

While attachment of infants to their caregivers is universal, research findings indi-cate that culture may strongly affect the outcome of this process. For instance, Cole (1999) compared patterns of attachment in three countries—the United States, Germany, and Japan. Results indicated significant differences across the three cultures in terms of the proportions of children who were securely, avoidantly, and ambivalently attached to their caregivers. Secure attachment was higher in Japan and the United States than in Germany, while avoidance attach-ment was highest in Germany, and ambivalent attachment was higher in Japan. Contrasting child-rearing practices seem to account for these differences. German parents, more than American and Japanese parents, try to encourage indepen-dence rather than clinging dependence at an early age; this results in more

Secure attachment:
A pattern of attachment in which infants actively seek contact with their caregiver and take comfort from her presence when she returns.

Insecure/avoidant attachment:
A pattern of attachment in which children don't cry when their caregiver leaves in the *strange situation* test, and are slow to greet their caregiver when this person returns.

Insecure/ambivalent attachment:
A pattern of attachment in which children seek contact with the caregiver before sep-aration but then, after this person returns, first seek this person but then resist or re-ject his or her offers of com-fort.

FIGURE 7.10
Culture and Attachment
As shown here, patterns of attachment between infants and their caregivers differ across cultures. These differences appear to reflect contrasting patterns of child-rearing practices in the countries involved.
Source: Adapted from Cole, 1999.

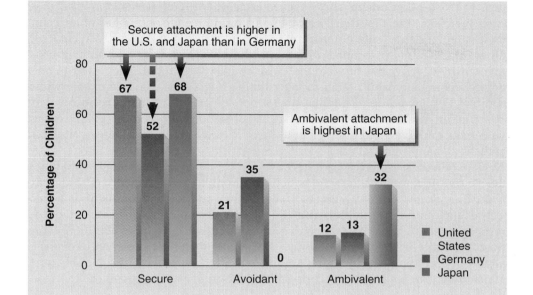

FIGURE 7.10
Culture and Attachment
As shown here, patterns of attachment between infants and their caregivers differ across cultures. These differences appear to reflect contrasting patterns of child-rearing practices in the countries involved.
Source: Adapted from Cole, 1999.

avoidant attachments. In contrast, in Japan, infants are rarely away from their parents; in both the United States and Germany, they are often placed in child-care facilities. As a result, anxious-ambivalent attachment is more common in Japan than in the other two cultures (see Figure 7.10). So, once again, we can see that cultural differences have important implications for basic aspects of human behavior—or, in this case—human development.

■ Contact comfort and attachment: The soft touch of love.

Before concluding, it's important to consider an additional factor that seems to play an important role in attachment. This is *close physical contact* between infants and their caregivers. Such contact—known as *contact comfort*—involves the hugging, cuddling, and caresses infants receive from their caregivers, and it seems to be an essential ingredient in attachment. The research that first established this fact is a "classic" in the history of psychology, and was conducted by Harry Harlow and colleagues (Harlow & Harlow, 1966).

In this research, baby monkeys were exposed to two artificial "mothers." One consisted of bare wire, while the other possessed a soft terrycloth cover. The wire mother, but not the soft one, provided milk. According to basic principles of conditioning, the monkeys should soon have developed a strong bond to the cold, wire mother, but in fact the opposite happened. The infants spent almost all their time clinging tightly to the soft cloth-covered mother and left her to visit the wire mother only when driven by pangs of hunger (see Figure 7.11).

On the basis of these and related findings, Harlow concluded that a monkey baby's attachment to its mother rests, at least in part, on her ability to satisfy its need for *contact comfort*—direct contact with soft objects. The satisfaction of other physical needs, such as that for food, is not enough.

Do such effects occur among human babies as well? Some studies seem to suggest that they may. For example, two- and three-year-old children placed in a strange room play for longer periods of time without becoming distressed when they have a security blanket present than when it is absent (Passman & Weisberg, 1975). In fact, they play almost as long as they do when their mother is in the room. These findings suggest that for blanket-attached children, the presence of this object provides the same kind of comfort and reassurance as that provided by their mothers. So, human infants, too, may have a need for contact comfort, and the gentle hugs, caresses, and cuddling they obtain from their mothers and other caregivers may play a role in the formation of attachment.

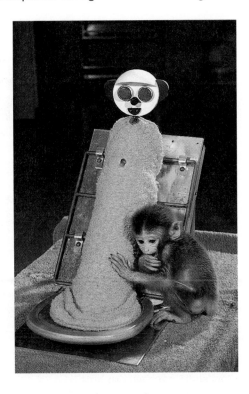

FIGURE 7.11
Harlow's Studies of Attachment
Although the wire "mothers" used in Harlow's research provided monkey babies with nourishment (note the bottle of milk) the babies preferred the soft, cloth-covered mothers that provided contact comfort but no nourishment.

Siblings and Friends: Key Factors in Social Development

Do you have brothers or sisters (siblings is the most general term)? If so, you will not be surprised to learn that they often play an important role in shaping social development. A large body of evidence indicates that older siblings often serve as teachers and guides, helping their younger brothers and sisters to acquire new skills and increased understanding of other people (e.g., Maynard, 2002). And having younger siblings—as I (Robert Baron) do—often teaches the older siblings about responsibility. When I was a child, I was often asked by my parents to "watch" my younger brothers—and I did. The result, I think, is that I learned a lot about being conscientious and accepting responsibility. Fortunately for me, my brothers tell me that I was a pretty good older sibling—and we still have very warm relations even today (see Figure 7.12, page 270).

Siblings also exert indirect effects on one another through their impact on their parents. It is often suggested that parents are "tougher" on their first children than on ones that arrive later in life. While this may or may not be true, there is considerable evidence that children influence their parents as well as vice versa. For instance, a highly successful first child may give parents so much pleasure that they become more secure, and that may make them better parents for later-born children (Brody, 2004). In contrast, when older siblings have posed serious problems for their parents, the parents may experience reductions in self-esteem, depression, or other difficulties that interfere with their effectiveness. So clearly, siblings influence one another indirectly, through their impact on parents, as well as directly.

Another important influence on children's social development is friends—other children of their own age with whom they play and interact. After they are about five years old, children in many countries start attending school. Their experiences in this setting play an important role in their social and emotional development, because schools are places in which children not only acquire information and cognitive skills; they also provide them with the opportunity to learn, and practice, many social skills. In school settings, children learn to share, to co-operate, to work together in groups to solve problems, and they acquire growing

FIGURE 7.12
Siblings: Often, They Play an Important Role in Social Development
Older siblings often serve as teachers or guides to their younger brothers and sisters. The older siblings, in turn, learn much about responsibility from their interactions with their younger siblings. This was certainly true for one of the authors, shown here with his two younger brothers.

Friendships:
Mutual dyad relationships between children involving strong affective ties.

Emotional development:
Changes in the experience or expression of emotions throughout the life span.

experience in forming and maintaining **friendships**—mutual dyadic relationships involving strong affective ties (Berndt, 2002).

Friendships play an important role in social development. Research findings indicate that high-quality friendships—ones marked by intimacy, loyalty, and mutual support—enhance children's social adjustment. Children who have more of these are liked by other children to a greater extent, are more sociable, and assume more leadership roles than those who have fewer friendships or ones lower in quality (Ladd et al., 1996), apparently because such friendships give children an opportunity to learn and practice skills needed for effective interpersonal relationship—social skills that are helpful not only during childhood, but also throughout life. Friendships also contribute to **emotional development,** giving children opportunities to experience intense emotional bonds with someone other than their caregivers, and to express these feelings in their behavior.

Another effect of friendship quality is that the higher such quality, the greater the influence friends have on one another. This is beneficial when friends show mostly positive characteristics or social behaviors, but can "backfire" and prove harmful when close friends show negative characteristics or engage in negative social behaviors. In other words, being close friends with someone who is shy or withdrawn can lead children to develop similar behaviors, and being close friends with someone who engages in delinquent behaviors can, perhaps, increase such tendencies (see Poulin, Dishion, & Haas, 1999). So, truly, friendship is a double-edged sword that can produce harmful as well as beneficial effects.

In sum, siblings' and children's experiences with friends in school and other settings play a key role in their development; indeed, since these experiences shape their later capacities to get along with others, to form friendships with them, and to love, it is clear that such social development shapes the course—and quality—of children's future lives. (While many problems threaten children's healthy development, one that has become increasingly harmful in recent years is *obesity*: More and more children around the world are seriously overweight. Can psychology help solve this problem? For information suggesting that it can, see the **Psychology Lends a Hand** section on page 272.)

KEY QUESTIONS

- What is temperament and what role does it play in later development?
- What is attachment?
- How does attachment influence later social development?
- What role do children's friendships play in their social and emotional develpment?

FROM GENDER IDENTITY TO SEX CATEGORY CONSTANCY: HOW CHILDREN COME TO UNDERSTAND THAT THEY ARE FEMALE OR MALE

When do children first recognize that they are a girl or a boy? And how do they come to understand what this aspect of their identify means? These are important aspects of development, so we'll focus on them here. Before beginning, though, it's important to clarify the meaning of two terms: **gender** and **biological sex.** Biological sex is straightforward: It refers to the whether an individual is, biologically speaking, a male or female (e.g., Does this person possess two X chromosomes or one X and one Y?). Gender, in contrast, refers to a given society's beliefs about the traits and behavior supposedly possessed by males and females. Thus, it includes what psychologists term **gender stereotypes**—beliefs about traits possessed by males and females and the differences between them (see Eagly & Wood, 1999; Unger & Crawford, 1993)—and **gender roles**—expectations concerning the roles males and females should fill and the ways in which they are supposed to behave (see Deaux, 1993). Such expectations come into play as soon as a nurse or physician announces, "It's a boy!" or "It's a girl!" And they continue to influence us, and our behavior, throughout life. For instance, parents often choose different colors for the clothing or rooms of female and male infants, and even play with them in different ways—rougher and more vigorous for males than for females (e.g., Martin & Ruble, in press). If you want to see this process in action, just visit a nearby Toys "R" Us or other large toy store. In the past, these stores made efforts to eliminate separate sections for girls and boys. But recently, they have shifted back to distinct departments for each gender (see Figure 7.14, page 273). Why? In part because boys and girls are starting to choose gender-related toys at an earlier and earlier age—perhaps because of their early experiences with peers in day care and preschools, and their early exposure to the media (Bannon, 2003). Whatever the reason, toys—like many other aspects of life—tend to drive home the point that one's gender is *important*.

Children's Growing Sophistication with Respect to Gender

The first step on the path toward sex-category constancy is children's recognition that they belong to one sex or the other—that they are a boy or a girl. Such **gender identity** occurs quite early in life; by the time they are two, many children have learned to label themselves appropriately and consistently. At this time, however, they are uncertain as to whether they will always be a boy or a girl. Such **gender stability** is usually in place by the time they are four.

It is not until they are about six or even seven, however, that children acquire **gender consistency**—the understanding that even if they adopted the clothing, hairstyles, and behaviors of the other sex they would still keep their current sexual

Gender:
A society's beliefs about the traits and behavior of males and females.

Biological sex:
Whether an individual is, biologically speaking, a male or a female.

Gender stereotypes:
Cultural beliefs about differences between women and men.

Gender roles:
Beliefs about how males and females are expected to behave in many situations.

Gender identity:
Children's understanding of the fact that they are male or female.

Gender stability:
Children's understanding that gender is stable over time.

Gender consistency:
Children's understanding that their gender would not change even if they adopted the behavior, dress, and hairstyles of the other gender.

PSYCHOLOGY LENDS A HAND

Helping Children Avoid the Dangers of Obesity

Believe it or not, 9 million children in the United States are overweight, and the problem is growing in many other countries too—including China and Japan, countries that, in the past, have never experienced this important threat to personal health. In fact, obesity has increased to virtually epidemic proportions in the United States, where a majority of all adults—and a growing number of children—are seriously overweight (see Figure 7.13). The link between childhood obesity and adult obesity seems clear: 50 percent of obese adults were obese as school-age children (Williams et al., 1992). So the problem seems to start early, and is then carried over to adulthood. Given that obese children are at risk for the same physical illnesses as adults, this is a serious issue. Can anything be done to solve this disturbing problem? Research by psychologists (see Chamberlin, 2006) suggests that several steps can be helpful:

- *Teaching parents to understand their children's nutritional needs.* Many parents overestimate the amount of food their children need. That's why they often urge a child to "take another bite" or "clean your plate if you want dessert." The result is that youngsters tend to overeat, and—perhaps more important—to ignore the internal cues that say "Enough!" A key task for parents who want to help their children to avoid being overweight, then, is to recognize just how much food children need and to resist the temptation to coax them into eating more.
- *Acquiring healthy eating habits.* One psychologist (Debra Haire-Joshu) has developed a program to help parents encourage healthy eating by their youngsters. She terms it the "High-5 Kids" approach. The goal is to encourage parents to eat five servings a day of the healthiest foods—fruits and vegetables.

This means making sure that such foods are present in the home and that the parents themselves demonstrate positive reactions to them. It's hard to get your child to eat carrots, for example, if you say "Ugh!" every time you see one! Healthy eating, it is generally agreed, is one the surest ways to avoid obesity, and training in this skill should begin early.

- *Contracting.* This involves procedures in which parents and children pay money into a program when it begins; they receive it back as they attend the sessions—and make progress in weight control.
- *Banning soda machines and fast food in schools.* Right now, many schools have soda machines in the halls or lunchroom, and sell fast-food snacks to students. A bill introduced in the U.S. Congress known as the Childhood Obesity Act is designed to remove these "temptations" from schools and to encourage physical activity among children by providing more parks, walking trails, and gyms. The bill is now being debated and if it is passed, may be a major help to parents who want to help their children eat a healthy diet.
- *Exercise.* This is the other side of the weight-loss equation, and many studies indicate that obese children exercise less than others. Teaching children new ways to burn calories (new games, new activities) can be a big plus in helping them shed extra pounds.

Through a combination of the steps outlined above, parents—and society in general—can help prevent children from becoming overweight. Since being obese carries important risks for personal health and psychological well-being, it may indeed be worthwhile to fight—and win—this battle against excess calories.

FIGURE 7.13
Childhood Obesity: A Growing Threat to the Health of Children
A growing number of children in many different countries are seriously overweight. Several techniques based on psychological research can help to combat this threat to children's health and well-being.

FIGURE 7.14
Gender Identity: A Key Aspect of Development
Increasingly, toy stores are establishing separate departments for boys and girls. Why? Spokespersons for the stores say it is in response to stronger preferences among both girls and boys for gender-related toys. Whatever the reasons, it is clear that children's gender identity is an important aspect of their social development.

identity. At this time they can answer correctly such as questions: "If Jack were gentle and cooked dinner, would Jack be a boy or a girl?"

Gender Development: Contrasting Explanations of How It Occurs

That children move toward full understanding of their own sexual identity as they grow older is clear. But how, precisely, do they acquire such knowledge? Several explanations have been offered. One of these—*social-learning theory*—emphasizes the role of learning—especially the impact of *modeling* and *operant conditioning* (see Chapter 5). According to this theory, children are rewarded (e.g., with verbal praise) for behaving in accordance with gender stereotypes and gender roles—the ways in which boys and girls are expected to behave. Further, because children have a tendency to imitate models they perceive as being similar to themselves, they tend to adopt the behaviors shown by their same-sex parents (see Bandura, 1986; Baron, 1970). As children become increasingly aware of their own behavior and these similarities, the idea that they belong to one gender or the other emerges with growing clarity. It is as if they reason: "I act like Daddy, so I'm a boy," or "I act like Mommy, so I'm a girl."

A second view of gender development—*cognitive development theory*—suggests that children's increasing understanding of gender is just one reflection of their steady cognitive growth. For instance, below the age of two, children lack a clear concept of self, so they can't identify themselves consistently as a boy or a girl. Once they acquire a concept of self, they can do this and begin to show gender constancy. Later, as they acquire increasing ability to classify objects as belonging to specific categories, they begin to form an idea of gender stability: They realize that they belong to one category and won't shift to the other. Gradually, then, children acquire the understanding that they belong to one sex or the other, and as a result of this understanding, strive to adopt behaviors they view as consistent with this identity. This is the opposite of what social-learning theory proposes; this theory suggests that first children imitate the behavior of same-sex models, and *then* they develop sexual identity. Cognitive development theory suggests that first they develop their gender identity and then they adopt behaviors consistent with this identity.

A third, and highly influential view, known as **gender schema theory,** has been proposed by Bem (1984, 1989). Bem noted that knowledge of one's sex or gender is far more important than knowledge that one has blue or brown eyes, or even that one belongs to a particular race or religious group. This reasoning led her to propose that children acquire *gender schemas*—cognitive frameworks reflecting experiences with their society's beliefs about the attributes of males and females, such as instructions from their parents, observations of how males and females typically behave, and so on. Gender schemas develop, in part, because adults call attention to gender even in situations where it is irrelevant—for instance, teachers say "Good morning, boys and girls!"

Once a gender schema forms, it influences children's processing of many kinds of social information (Martin & Little, 1990). For example, children with firmly established gender schemas tend to categorize the behavior of others as either masculine or feminine. Similarly, they may process and recall behaviors consistent with their own gender schema more easily than ones not consistent with it. In short, for children possessing such schemas, gender is a key concept or dimension, one they often use in attempts to make sense out of the social world, and one that becomes linked, in important ways, to their self-concept. This link between gender and one's self-concept is also emphasized in other, related views about gender identity (see Spence, 1993.)

While these three theories emphasize different aspects of gender development, all seem to provide important insights into this process. Thus, as is true of other aspects of development, several interrelated processes appear to influence children's progress toward full **sex-category constancy**—full understanding of their sexual identity.

KEY QUESTIONS

- What is gender constancy? Gender stability? Gender consistency?
- What is sex-category constancy?
- How do social learning theory, cognitive development theory, and gender schema theory explain gender development?

ADOLESCENCE: BETWEEN CHILD AND ADULT

When does childhood end and adulthood start? Since development is a continuous process, there is no simple answer to this question. Rather, every culture decides for itself just where the dividing line falls. Many cultures mark this passage with special ceremonies. In many countries, however, the transition from child to adult takes place more gradually during a period known as **adolescence**—the topic on which we'll focus next.

Physical Development during Adolescence

The beginning of adolescence is signaled by a sudden increase in the rate of physical growth. While this *growth spurt* occurs for both sexes, it starts earlier for girls (at about age ten or eleven) than for boys (about age twelve or thirteen). Prior to this spurt, boys and girls are similar in height; in its early phases, girls are often taller than boys; after it is over, males are several inches taller, on average, than females.

This growth spurt is just one aspect of **puberty,** the period of rapid change during which individuals of both genders reach sexual maturity (see Figure 7.15). During puberty, the *gonads,* or primary sex glands, produce increased levels of sex hormones, and the external sex organs assume their adult form. Girls begin to

---

Gender schema theory: A theory indicating that children develop a cognitive framework reflecting the beliefs of their society concerning the characteristics and roles of males and females. This *gender schema* then strongly affects the processing of new social information.

Sex category constancy: Complete understanding of one's sexual identity, centering around a biologically based categorical distinction between males and females.

Adolescence: A period beginning with the onset of puberty and ending when individuals assume adult roles and responsibilities.

Puberty: The period of rapid change during which individuals reach sexual maturity.

FIGURE 7.15
Adolescence: The Dawn of Sexual Maturity
During adolescence, members of both sexes move rapidly toward sexual maturity.

menstruate and boys start to produce sperm. In addition, both sexes undergo many other shifts relating to sexual maturity. Most girls begin to menstruate by the time they are thirteen, but for some this process does not start until considerably later, and for others it may begin as early as age seven or eight. Most boys begin to produce sperm by the time they are fourteen or fifteen, but again, for some the process may start either earlier or later.

Cognitive Development during Adolescence

Physical growth is obvious during adolescence, but another aspect of physical change is less obvious: During this period, the brain, too, continues to develop in important ways. First, it produces a large number of new neurons (gray matter; see Chapter 2) followed by a "pruning" of these cells so that only the most important remain, and then, myelination of neurons increases (white matter), providing better insulation of established neuronal connections. By late adolescence, then, teenagers have fewer, stronger, and more selective connections between their neurons than when they were children. These changes are reflected in shifts in adolescents' cognitive abilities. Contrary to what Piaget suggested, however, these changes are gradual rather than sudden, and do not involve primarily a shift to logical thought or **propositional thinking** ("If . . . then . . ."). Rather, they involve more subtle changes relating to enhanced *executive control*—they monitor and manage their own information processing (e.g., Kuhn & Franklin, 2006).

What cognitive changes, specifically, occur during adolescence? Several of great importance. First, processing speed continues to increase so that adolescents can accomplish many cognitive tasks more quickly than can children (Kuhn, 2006). Second, adolescents show improved ability to manage their own learning, to take steps necessary to enhance their understanding of complex information and events. Third, adolescents are better at decision making. In particular, they can override our "gut-level," intuitive (experiential) system for making decisions and use a systematic, analytic approach to a greater degree (Kuhn, 2006). Finally, adolescents are far superior to children in thinking about their own cognition—in directing it into questions and issues of greatest important to them, and keeping it

Propositional thinking:
Reasoning during the stage of formal operations, in which individuals can assess the validity of verbal assertions even when they refer to possibilities rather than actual events.

focused on these issues and topics. This does not imply, however, that adolescents—or even adults!—think primarily in logical or analytical ways. As we noted earlier, human cognition, even among adults, is far from perfect—and far from completely rational. It is subject to many potential errors (e.g., Diamond & Kirkham, 2005), and is often strongly influenced by intuition—information or knowledge we can't readily put into words (see Chapter 4). We've mentioned this fact before, but it is so important that we want to emphasize it again.

KEY QUESTIONS

- What physical changes occur during puberty?
- How does the brain develop during adolescence?
- What changes in cognitive abilities occur during adolescence?

Social and Emotional Development during Adolescence

It would be surprising if the major physical and cognitive changes occurring during adolescence were not accompanied by corresponding changes in social and emotional development. What are these changes like? Let's see what research has revealed.

■ Emotional changes: The ups and downs of everyday life.

It is widely believed that adolescents are wildly emotional—they experience huge swings in mood and turbulent outbursts of emotion. Are these views correct? To a degree, they are. In several studies on this issue, large numbers of teenagers wore beepers and were signaled at random times throughout an entire week. When signaled, they entered their thoughts and feelings in a diary. Results indicated that they did show more frequent and larger swings in mood than those shown by older people (see Csikszenthmihalyi & Larson, 1984). Moreover, these swings occurred very quickly, sometimes within only a few minutes. Older people also show shifts in mood, but these tend to be less frequent, slower, and smaller in magnitude.

Other widely accepted views about adolescent emotionality, however, do *not* appear to be correct. For instance, it is often assumed that adolescence is a period of great stress and unhappiness. In fact, most adolescents report feeling quite happy and self-confident, *not* unhappy or distressed (Diener & Diener, 1996). Moreover, and again contrary to common views, most teenagers report that they enjoy good relations with their parents. They agree with them on basic values, future plans, and many other matters (Bachman, 1987).

■ Social development: Friendships and the quest for identity.

While friendships are important during childhood, they often take on added significance during adolescence. Most adolescents are part of extensive **social networks,** consisting of many friends and acquaintances, and these people have profound effects on them, shaping their attitudes, values, and behavior. One motive for forming friendships during adolescence seems to be the developing *need to belong*—to feel that one is accepted and is part of a social group. This need strengthens during early adolescence and leads many preteens and teenagers to reject parental influence and to identify with their peers. Thus, they adopt the dress, phrases, and overall style of their chosen peer group, sometimes to the point where parents worry that they have surrendered their unique identity entirely. Within a few years, however, this tendency subsides and teenagers begin to conform less to their peers.

Friendships and social success also play an important role in another key aspect of social development during adolescence—the quest for a *personal identity*. This process is a key element in a famous theory of psychosocial development

Social network:
A group of people with whom one interacts regularly.

FIGURE 7.16
Youth Bulges and Revolution
Research findings indicate that the larger the proportion of children and teenagers in the population of a country and the less civic knowledge they have (i.e., the less their understanding of how their government operates), the greater the political instability in that country.

proposed by Erik Erikson (1950, 1987), a theory well deserving of a closer look. Before turning to that theory, though, we think it's important to mention one additional aspect of social development during adolescence (and early adulthood, too): the temptation, faced by many adolescents, to openly rebel!

■ **Youth bulges, knowledge, and . . . rebellion.**

Sometimes, teen "rebellion" goes far beyond arguments with parents or teachers; in fact, in various countries, and at different times, most active *rebels*—people who seek to overthrow, or at least radically change, the existing government—are young. Usually, they are in their teens or early twenties. Why? Is this period during life one when we are most susceptible to discontent, anger, and the desire for change? Perhaps. But recent research on this issue (see Hart et al., 2004) suggests that it may involve other factors, too. One of these is what is known as a *youth bulge*—a large proportion of children and teenagers in the population. Another is a low level of understanding of how the current government operates, and of the legal and civic rights of individuals. Together, these factors may create a volatile mix, in which young people, having little understanding of the political process, and seeing many others of their age around them, become especially susceptible to the lure of charismatic leaders. The result? They take to the streets and help make rebellion (see Figure 7.16).

Evidence for this reasoning is provided by the finding (Hart, Atkins, & Youniss, 2005) that the greater the proportion of the population in a country below the age of fifteen, the lower its political stability. And contrary to the view that rebels are often highly educated people who have fully developed political philosophies (Ginges, 2005), the proportion of youngsters enrolled in school is *not* related to political stability. In sum, it appears that a combination of social factors (lots of young people in a society) and cognitive factors (a lack of civic knowledge, tendencies to accept simple ideologies) may truly be a dangerous mix—and set the stage for a very dangerous kind of adolescent rebellion! Now, back to the theory we mentioned earlier—one proposed by Erikson.

■ **Erikson's eight stages of life.**

Erikson's theory deals with development across the entire life span, so we could have introduced it in our discussion of childhood. Since adolescence is in some ways a bridge between childhood and adulthood, though, it makes sense to examine the theory here.

Erikson's theory is, like Piaget's, a *stage theory*: It suggests that all human beings pass through specific stages or phases of development. In contrast to Piaget,

TABLE 7.4 Erikson's Eight Stages of Psychosocial Development

According to Erikson, we move through eight stages of psychosocial development during our lives. Each stage centers around a specific crisis or conflict between competing tendencies.

Crisis/Phase	Description
Trust versus mistrust	Infants learn either to trust the environment (if needs are met) or to mistrust it.
Autonomy versus shame and doubt	Toddlers acquire self-confidence if they learn to regulate their bodies and act independently. If they fail or are labeled as inadequate, they experience shame and doubt.
Initiative versus guilt	Preschoolers (aged 3–5) acquire new physical and mental skills but must also learn to control their impulses. Unless a good balance is struck, they become either unruly or too inhibited.
Industry versus inferiority	Children (aged 6–11) acquire many skills and competencies. If they take pride in these, they acquire high self-esteem. If they compare themselves unfavorably with others, they may develop low self-esteem.
Identity versus role confusion	Adolescents must integrate various roles into a consistent self-identity. If they fail to do so, they may experience confusion over who they are.
Intimacy versus isolation	Young adults must develop the ability to form deep, intimate relationships with others. If they do not, they may become socially or emotionally isolated.
Generativity versus self-absorption	Adults must take an active interest in helping and guiding younger persons. If they do not, they may become preoccupied with purely selfish needs.
Integrity versus despair	In the closing decades of life, individuals ask themselves whether their lives had any meaning. If they can answer yes, they attain a sense of integrity. If they answer no, they experience despair.

however, Erikson is concerned primarily with social rather than cognitive development. He believed that each stage of life is marked by a specific crisis or conflict between competing tendencies. Only if individuals negotiate each of these hurdles successfully can they continue to develop in a normal, healthy manner.

The stages in Erikson's theory are summarized in Table 7.4. The first four occur during childhood; one takes place during adolescence; and the final three occur during our adult years. The initial stage, which occurs during the first year of life, centers on the crisis of *trust versus mistrust*. Infants must trust others to satisfy their needs. If these are not met, they fail to develop trust in others and remain forever suspicious and wary.

The next crisis occurs during the second year of life and involves *autonomy versus shame and doubt*. During this time, toddlers are learning to regulate their own bodies and to act in independent ways. If they succeed in these tasks, they develop a sense of autonomy. But if they fail, or if they are labeled as inadequate by people who care for them, they may experience shame and doubt their abilities to interact effectively with the external world.

The third stage unfolds during the preschool years, between the ages of three and five. The crisis at this time involves what Erikson terms *initiative versus guilt*. During these years, children are acquiring many new physical and mental skills. Simultaneously, however, they must develop the capacity to control their impulses, some of which lead to unacceptable behavior. If they achieve a good balance between feelings of initiative and feelings of guilt, all is well. However, if initiative overwhelms guilt, children may become too unruly; if guilt overwhelms initiative, they may become too inhibited.

The fourth and final stage of childhood occurs during the early school years, when children are between six and eleven or twelve years of age. This stage involves the crisis of *industry versus inferiority*. During these years, children learn to make things, use tools, and acquire many of the skills necessary for adult life. Children who successfully acquire these skills form a sense of their own competence; those who do not may compare themselves unfavorably with others and suffer from low self-esteem.

Now we come to the crucial stage in Erikson's theory for this discussion of adolescence: the crisis of *identity versus role confusion*. At this time of life, teenagers ask themselves, "Who am I?" "What am I *really* like?" "What do I want to become?" In other words, they seek to establish a clear *self-identity*—an understanding of their own unique traits and what is really of central importance to them. These, of course, are questions individuals ask themselves at many points in life. According to Erikson, it is crucial that these questions be answered effectively. If they are not, individuals may drift, uncertain of where they want to go or the kind of person they wish to become. (We'll return to later stages in Erikson's theory in our discussion of adult development.)

KEY QUESTIONS
- Are widely accepted ideas about adolescent emotionality correct?
- According to Erikson, what is the most important crisis faced by adolescents?

DEVELOPMENT DURING OUR ADULT YEARS

If you live an average number of years, you will spend more than 70 percent of your life as an adult. Obviously, we continue to change and develop during this major portion of our lives. We'll now examine some of the most important of these changes. Before doing that, however, we'll return to the final three stages in Erikson's theory.

Erikson's Theory Revisited: The Crises of Adult Life

During adulthood, Erikson suggests, we pass through three major crises. The first of these involves the crisis of *intimacy versus isolation*. During late adolescence and early adulthood, individuals must develop the ability to form deep, intimate relationships with others. This does not mean simply sexual intimacy; rather, it involves the ability to form strong emotional attachments to others. In short, this first crisis of adult life centers around the capacity to *love*—to care deeply for others. People who fail to resolve it successfully will live in isolation, unable to form truly intimate relationships.

Erikson labeled the second crisis of adult life the crisis of *generativity versus self-absorption*. This refers to the need for individuals to overcome selfish, self-centered concerns and to take an active interest in helping and guiding the next generation. For parents, such activities are focused on their children. After the children are grown, however, the tendency toward generativity may involve serving as a **mentor** or guide for members of the younger generation, helping them in their careers and lives. People who do not become parents can express generativity by providing help and guidance to young people—students, younger coworkers, nieces and nephews, and others. Individuals who successfully resolve this crisis and turn away from total absorption with their own lives discover new meaning. People who do not resolve this crisis successfully become absorbed in their own lives and gradually cut themselves off from an important source of growth and satisfaction.

Mentor:
Older and more experienced individuals who help to guide young adults.

Erikson termed the final crisis of adult development *integrity versus despair*. As people reach the final decades of life, they look back and ask: "Did my life have any meaning?" "Did my being here really matter?" If they are able to answer "Yes," and to feel that they reached many of their goals, they attain a sense of *integrity*. If, instead, they find their lives to be lacking on such dimensions, they may experience intense feelings of *despair*. Successful resolution of this final crisis can have important effects on how individuals come to terms with their own mortality—the inevitable fact of death—and on their psychological and physical health during the final years of life.

In sum, according to Erikson and others who view adult development in terms of discrete phases or stages, development during our adult years follows an orderly plan, reflecting the fact that at different times in our lives, we all experience the same problems, events, challenges, or—as Erikson puts it—crises. The way in which we deal with each of these turning points then determines the course and nature of our lives from then on.

Physical Change during Our Adult Years

That we change physically during our adult years is obvious; if you ever look through family albums and see photos of your parents—or yourself!—at different ages, such change is clear. In addition to these shifts in appearance, however, many other physical changes occur during adulthood. Here is a brief overview.

■ Physical change during early adulthood.

Physical growth is usually complete by the time people leave their teens, but for some parts of the body, the process of aging actually begins long before this. For example, the lenses in our eyes begin to lose flexibility by the time we are only twelve or thirteen years old, and for some people, the tissues supporting their teeth begin to recede and weaken even before they have attained physical growth. So aging, like growth, is a continuous process that starts very early in life. In general, however, physical change is slow and very gradual during our early adult years.

■ Physical change during midlife.

By the time they are in their forties, however, most people are all too aware of the age-related changes occurring in their bodies. The amount of blood pumped by the heart decreases noticeably and the walls of the large arteries lose flexibility. As a result, less oxygen can be delivered to working muscles within a given period of time, and even people who exercise regularly become aware of some decline in this respect. They simply can't do quite as much as they once could. The performance of other major organ systems, too, declines, and an increasing number of people experience difficulties with digestion. Other changes are readily visible when middle-aged people look in the mirror: thinning and graying hair, bulges and wrinkles in place of the smooth skin of youth. Huge individual differences exist in the rate at which such changes occur, however. While some people in their forties and fifties closely match common stereotypes concerning middle age, others retain much of their youthful appearance and vigor.

Among the most dramatic changes occurring during middle adulthood is the **climacteric**—a period during which the functioning of the reproductive system, and various aspects of sexual activity, change greatly. While both sexes experience the climacteric, its effects are more obvious for females, most of whom experience **menopause**—cessation of the menstrual cycle—in their late forties or early fifties. During menopause the ovaries stop producing estrogens, and many changes in the reproductive system occur: thinning of the vaginal walls, reduced secretion of fluids that lubricate the vagina, and so on. Since females no longer release ova, pregnancy is no longer possible. In the past, menopause was considered to be a

Climacteric:
A period during which the functioning of the reproductive system and various aspects of sexual activity change greatly.

Menopause:
A cessation of the menstrual cycle.

stressful process for many women, but it is now recognized that for most, this process occurs with no significant difficulties.

Among men the climacteric involves reduced secretion of testosterone and reduced functioning of the *prostate gland*, which plays a role in semen formation. In many men, the prostate gland becomes enlarged, and this may interfere not only with sexual functioning, but with urination as well. Men often experience reduced sexual drive at this time of life, and although sperm production decreases, many can still father children.

■ Physical changes in later life.

Average age in many countries is currently rising at a steady pace, so clearly, it is important to have a clear picture of the physical changes that occur during our later decades of life. Research on this topic offers a mixed but somewhat encouraging picture. A very large proportion of Americans in their sixties and seventies report excellent or good health, and these are not simply overoptimistic self-reports. It appears that most people younger than age eighty *are* in reasonably good health and are not much more likely than middle-aged people to suffer from *chronic illnesses*—ones that are long-term, progressive, and incurable (U.S. Department of Health and Human Services, 1989). Further, even in their seventies and eighties, a large majority of people do not receive hospital care during any given year (Thomas, 1992). In short, the picture of older people that emerges, at least in developed countries like the United States, is quite encouraging.

One additional point should not be overlooked: While many physical changes do occur with increasing age, it is crucial to distinguish between those that are the result of **primary aging**—changes caused by the passage of time and, perhaps, genetic factors—and of **secondary aging**—changes due to disease, disuse, or abuse of our bodies. Let's briefly examine some of the physical changes that result from primary aging. They include declines in our sensory abilities (vision, hearing, smell, taste), and a general slowing in the speed of responding (Spirduso & Macrae, 1990). Recent findings indicate that hearing loss that occurs with increasing age may be especially damaging. Such loss results from several sources (e.g., loss of hair cells on the basilar membrane; Chapter 3), but whatever its source, it is particularly large for high-frequency sounds. Since these play a key role in understanding speech, this can be a serious problem (Tun, O'Kane, & Wingfield, 2002).

In addition to interfering with the capacity to understand others' words, the hearing loss that occurs with age may have other important effects. For instance, it may cause individuals to focus an increasing portion of their information processing capacity on identifying the words or sounds they hear. This, in turn, leaves less of these resources for other tasks. This is clearly illustrated in research by Wingfield, Tun, and McCoy (2005). These researchers asked people with and without significant hearing loss to listen to lists of fifteen words. The lists were stopped at random points, and participants were asked to recall just the last three words they had heard on the list. As shown in Figure 7.17 on page 282, both groups showed excellent recall for the last word in each three-word set. However, people with hearing loss showed much worse recall of the other two words. These findings suggest that the information-processing capacity used to recognize the final word reduced the ability of people with hearing loss to enter the earlier two words into memory. In other words, they were so busy trying to hear each word as it was presented that they had less capacity left for entering information into memory. Clearly, then, age-related declines in our sensory abilities have important and far-reaching implications.

KEY QUESTIONS

- How do stage theories and contextual theories account for adult development?
- What physical changes occur during early and middle adulthood?
- What physical changes occur in later life?

Primary aging:
Changes in our bodies caused by the passage of time and, perhaps, genetic factors.

Secondary aging:
Changes in our bodies due to disease, disuse, or abuse.

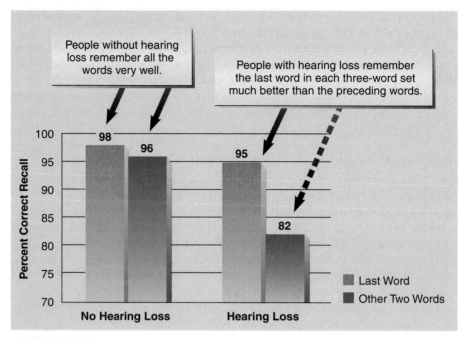

FIGURE 7.17
Hearing Loss: How It Can Impair Information-Processing Capacity
Participants in the study shown here either had significant hearing loss or did not. Both groups were exposed to lists of words, and then asked to recall the last three words they heard on these lists. Those without hearing loss remembered both the last word and the other two words in each three-word set very well. Those with hearing loss, in contrast, showed reduced memory for the first two words in each set. This suggests that the information-processing capacity they used to understand each word reduced the capacity they had for entering these words into memory.
Source: Based on data in Wingfield, Tun, & McCoy, 2005.

Cognitive Change during Adulthood

What about our cognitive abilities? Do these change as we grow older? Since our cognitive abilities rest, ultimately, on biological processes (see Chapters 2 and 6), it is reasonable to expect some declines with increasing age. As we grow older, however, we also gain in experience, practice with various tasks, and our overall knowledge. Can these changes compensate for inevitable biological decline? The issue of whether, and how, our cognitive functioning changes with age, therefore, is quite complex.

■ **Aging and memory.**

First, let's consider the impact of aging on memory. Research on working (short-term) memory indicates that older people are able to enter about as much information in this system as young people are (Poon & Fozard, 1980). However, some findings suggest that the ability to transfer information from working memory to long-term memory may decrease with age (Hunt, 1993). Turning to long-term memory, it appears that there may be some declines in episodic memory (memory for events relating to an individual's life and experience) with increasing age, while semantic memory (general knowledge) remains largely intact. Procedural memory—the information necessary to perform many skilled actions—seems to be the most stable of all.

Other evidence indicates that although older people enter as much information as younger ones into memory, they later make poorer use of this information, failing to retrieve details they actually did initially notice (Koutstaal, 2003). Overall, though, it appears that unless we experience serious illness (e.g., Alzheimer's disease), many of our cognitive abilities remain largely intact.

■ Aging and intelligence: Decline or stability?

In the past, it was widely believed that intelligence increases into early adulthood, remains stable through the thirties, but then begins to decline as early as the forties. This view was based largely on cross-sectional research that compared the performance of people of different ages on standard tests of intelligence. However, more recent research on aging and intelligence has often employed a *longitudinal* design, in which the same people are studied for many years. The results of studies using such procedures have yielded a more positive picture. Instead of declining sharply with age, many intellectual abilities seem to remain quite stable across the entire life span. In fact, they show relatively little change until people are well into their sixties, seventies, or beyond. Moreover, some abilities even seem to increase (see Schaie 1986, 1990, 1994). Only on tasks involving speed of reasoning are there consistent declines in performance. Since drops in performance may reflect decreased reaction time—which is known to decline with age (see Funkel et al., 1998; Shimamura et al., 1996)—there is little if any indication of a general decrease in intelligence with age.

■ Fitness: An effective means to prevent—or even reverse—cognitive decline.

Before concluding, we should call attention to one highly encouraging fact: Recent studies indicate that becoming physically fit can greatly improve cognitive functioning in older people. For instance, a review of many different studies (Colcombe & Kramer, 2003) on this topic indicates that a combination of aerobic and strength training can significantly boost scores on a wide range of cognitive tasks for people in their sixties and seventies. In fact, people who participated in programs designed to boost their physical fitness have been found to perform much better than those who did not, and this different was especially great for complex tasks (controlled and executive processes). These findings suggest that becoming physically fit is not only beneficial to our health—it can also help us to preserve our precious cognitive abilities (see Figure 7.18, page 284).

■ Mental exercise: Does it help, too?

If physical exercise can help prevent declines in our cognitive abilities, shouldn't mental exercise do the same—or even more? This is a very reasonable hypothesis and is widely accepted. Unfortunately, though, careful research designed to test this idea has yielded only weak support for it. Various kinds of cognitive training do produce short-term benefits—of that there is no doubt (see Kramer & Willis, 2002). However, none of these activities seem to produce long-term slowing in the decline in cognitive capacities with increasing age. Further, it appears that even people who engage in strenuous mental activity—for instance, expert chess masters—show declines in some aspects of cognitive capacity with growing age. Presumably, their vigorous mental exercise should prevent such declines if mental exercise is beneficial. Overall, then, existing evidence in support of the "use it or lose it" idea with respect to cognitive capacities is weak (Salthouse, 2006). Despite this fact, one expert on this topic suggests that people should still seek mental stimulation as they age. It might not slow any declines they experience, but as he puts it (Salthouse, 2006): "such activities are enjoyable . . . and engagement in cognitively demanding activities serves as an existence proof—if you can still do it, then you know that you have not yet lost it" (84–85). Where does all this leave us? With a fairly encouraging overall pattern. Yes, some cognitive processes do decrease with age—especially ones closely related to speed of responding. But others remain quite stable over many years, and others may actually increase as individuals gain in experience. Further, becoming physically fit can slow or even

FIGURE 7.18
Physical Fitness in Later Life: Many Benefits
Research findings indicate that people who remain physically fit as they grow
older not only live longer and experience better physical health: in addition, their
cognitive abilities, too, seem to benefit!

reverse any declines we do experience. Our overall conclusion: Aging is inevitable, but our minds can—and often do—remain active until the very end of life.

KEY QUESTIONS

- What changes in memory occur as we age?
- How does intelligence change over the life span?
- What are the effects of becoming physically fit on cognitive functioning?

Social and Emotional Development during Adulthood

Do we continue changing socially and emotionally during our adult years? Definitely! Here's an overview of some of the most important of these changes.

■ Adjusting to major life changes: Parenthood, careers, divorce, aging parents, and retirement.

When they are young, many people tend to believe that as they age, they will also grow much wiser: They will come to understand the profound mysteries of life better and better. In one sense, this is true: We *do* acquire many kinds of wisdom as we move through life's journey. But because we also experience profound changes, each period during our adult lives is filled with new events and challenges; as a result, we go on learning—and improvising!—throughout life. What are these changes? They are unique for every individual, but most of us experience changes such as these: the joys—and demands—of parenthood (Hock et al., 1995), many shifts in our careers as we move from one job and work setting to another (Levinson, 1986), the pain of divorce or marital separation, and the dilemma of caring for our parents as they age and become increasingly frail. And recently, a growing number of parents have had to deal with a new issue: **boomerang children**—children who are young adults but, because of economic factors (the high costs of housing in many areas) and the prolonged education required for many fields, come home to live with their parents. In many cases, this is a source of pleasure and joy to the parents; they enjoy having their children with them, even if they are grown. In other instances, through the desire of boomerang children to live their lives the way they wish, can come into conflict with the values and lifestyles of their parents—with negative effects for both sides (e.g., Furman, 2005; Gaston, 2006). The problem is a large one, by the way: more than eighteen million young adults live with their parents in the United States alone (Gaston, 2006).

Other challenges during our adult lives center around the *empty-nest* syndrome (Birchler, 1992), in which parents must learn to adjust to the absence of their grown children who are off starting families of their own, and, ultimately, their own retirement and aging. None of these challenges is easy, and the result is that development is truly a continuous process. (Many theories of adult development emphasize the importance of careers [see Levinson, 1986]. If careers are indeed an important factor in our lives, a crucial question arises: How should we choose them? For suggestions based on psychological research, see the **Psychology Goes to Work** section on page 287.)

KEY QUESTIONS

- What are some of the key challenges we face during our adult years?
- How should you choose your career?

DEATH AND BEREAVEMENT

Since ancient times, human beings have searched for the "Fountain of Youth"— some means of prolonging youth, and life, indefinitely. Sad to relate, such dreams have remained unfulfilled; life and health can be prolonged, but there is no way to live forever. In this section, we'll consider key questions relating to the close of life: (1) How do terminally ill people react to their own impending death? And (2) How can we cope with the death of persons we love?

Meeting Death: Facing the End with Dignity

What is death? The answer to this question is more complex than you might suspect. First, there are several kinds of death. Physiological death occurs when all physical processes that sustain life cease. Brain death is defined as a total absence of brain activity for at least ten minutes. Cerebral death means cessation of activity in the cerebral cortex. And social death refers to a process through which other people relinquish their relationships with the deceased (Thomas, 1992).

Second, there are complex ethical issues connected with death. Should individuals have the right to die when they choose? Should physicians be allowed to grant such requests? These are complex questions, only partly within the realm of science. We raise them here simply to remind you that death involves much more than a biological event.

But given that death is the inevitable end of life, how do persons confronted with their own impending death react? Perhaps the most famous study of this subject was conducted in the late 1960s by Elizabeth Kubler-Ross (1969). She studied terminally ill cancer patients and, on the basis of extensive interviews with them, concluded that they pass through five distinct stages.

Boomerang children: Young adults who live at home with their parents, often after first attempting to live alone.

The first is denial. In this phase, patients refuse to believe that the end is in sight. "No, it can't be true," they seem to say. This stage is soon replaced by a second—*anger*. "Why me?" dying persons ask. "It isn't fair." In the third stage, patients show what Kubler-Ross terms *bargaining*. They offer prayer, good behavior, or other changes in lifestyle in exchange for a postponement of death. Unfortunately, such efforts cannot alter medical realities, so when it becomes apparent that their best efforts to make a deal with death have failed, many dying persons enter a stage of *depression.*

That's not the end of the process, however. According to Kubler-Ross, many people ultimately move into a final stage she labels *acceptance*. At this stage, dying persons are no longer angry or depressed. Instead, they seem to accept their impending death with dignity, and concentrate on saying good-bye to important persons in their lives, and putting their affairs in good order.

Although these findings are comforting and appealing, they have not been confirmed by other researchers (e.g., Arnoff & Spilka 1985; Metzger, 1980). It is also important to note that Kubler-Ross worked with a special group of individuals: people who were middle-aged and had suddenly learned that their lives would be cut off prematurely by cancer. This raises important questions about whether her findings can be generalized to other persons—especially older individuals for whom death is a less unexpected event. In view of these points it seems best to view Kubler-Ross's conclusions with caution. They are intriguing, and hold out hope that many of us can meet death in a dignified manner. However, they cannot be viewed as scientifically valid unless they are confirmed by further research.

Bereavement: Coming to Terms with the Death of Loved Ones

Funerals, it is often said, are for the living. And in a key sense, this is true: when individuals die, they usually leave behind them several persons who loved them dearly and must now cope with their loss. Because bereavement is a very profound experience and one almost everyone has, it has been the subject of increasing attention from psychologists (Norris & Murrell, 1990). Their work suggests that bereavement is a process in which individuals move through a discrete series of stages. The first is *shock*—a feeling of numbness and unreality. This is followed by stages of *protest* and *yearning*, where they resent the loss of their loved one and fantasize about this person's return. These reactions are often followed by deep *despair*, which can last a year or more—a period when bereaved persons feel that life is not worth living. Finally, bereaved persons usually enter a state of *detachment and recovery*, in which they separate themselves psychologically from the loved person who has died (e.g., Hart et al., 1995), and go on with their lives. Even during this stage, however, painful bouts of grieving may recur on birthdays, anniversaries, and other occasions that remind the bereaved person of his or her loss.

Bereavement is especially strong in cases where death is sudden and unexpected. Such deaths are described as *high-grief* experiences. In contrast, when death is expected, grief may be less pronounced (*low-grief* deaths). One type of death seems to leave especially deep and long-lasting scars: the death of a child. Parents who go through this agonizing experience may never recover from it entirely; they continue to experience what is known as *shadow grief* for their entire lives (Knapp, 1987).

Fortunately, a large majority of grieving persons do ultimately recover from the pain of their loss and go on to resume their lives. But often, they can't do it without help from their friends and relatives so when someone you care about faces bereavement, do try to help. Here are some steps that may help reduce their pain:

PSYCHOLOGY GOES TO WORK

Choosing a Career: Some "Steps That Can Help"

Our careers—the sequence of work experiences we have over time—play a key role in our lives. Not only are they the source of the income that allows us to live in certain ways, but they are also a key part of our self-identity. Not convinced? Just ask several people you know who are working, "Who are you?" Many will reply in terms of their career or occupation (e.g., "I'm a police officer," "I'm a salesperson," "I'm a teacher."). So choosing an appropriate career—one in which you will be happy and fulfilled—is a very important task. How should you perform it? While we can't provide a complete answer here—only a highly trained counseling or occupational psychologist can do that—we can at least give you some pointers of what to do and what *not* to do.

- **First, recognize the careers have changed—radically!** In the past, people started their careers young, and generally stayed on the same "track" for many years. Now, the situation is entirely different. Lifetime employment with one company is a thing of the past. People move from one company or industry to another, and they often do many different jobs during their working lives (McClelland, 2001). So don't expect the kind of career your parents or grandparents had: In many cases, it doesn't exist!

- **Recognize that careers take many different forms.** Suppose your parents own a family business and you decide to work in it. In that case, your career might involve one job for years or decades—maybe for good! But careers come in many different forms these days. Another pattern might be to work in one field and move up, by steps, as you gain experience; this is known as a *linear* career. A third pattern is to move from one occupation to another, each requiring different skills. This is known as a *spiral career*, and an increasing number of people

have it. The key point? Keep your options open and recognize that your career can evolve in ways you did not at first expect.

- **Concentrate on learning new skills.** Perhaps the most important thing you can do in planning your career (e.g., in deciding whether to move from one job or field to another) is to ask yourself: What new skills will I learn? Will these increase my potential value in the job market? If the answers to these questions are "yes," this is probably a good move for you to make. If they are not, think again.

- **Try to obtain a close match between your personal characteristics and preferences and your career.** One big mistake many people make is that of "falling in love" with a particular field without considering whether they are really suited for it. Different jobs and occupations require different characteristics. For instance, to be a good salesperson, you must be outgoing and sociable; a very shy or inhibited person will probably not succeed in this role. Similarly, to be a good accountant, you must be neat and orderly, at least to a degree. So, consider your personal characteristics carefully and try to choose a job or career that is consistent with them. (We will describe one way of doing this in the Making Psychology Part of Your Life exercise at the end of this chapter.)

No, these steps won't guarantee that you will end up in a career that's perfect for you. But they will, at least, point you in the right direction, and get you thinking about the key issues. Good luck! And remember: Careers are *not* set in stone—on the contrary, since you will certainly change in the years ahead, so, too, may your career.

- Continue your contacts with the grieving person: Phone calls, social invitations, notes—signs that you are thinking of the grieving person—can make a real difference. They indicate to grieving persons that they are not alone.

- Sometimes, just be present: Often, it appears, the best thing you can do for a grieving person is *listen:* let them express their grief. Many grieving people often find expressing their feelings to someone who is sympathetic is a very big help.

- Don't tell them that things will get easier: While this is true, research findings indicate that many grieving persons react to such statements with resentment: they interpret them as a sign that you don't really understand because to them, it seems as though their loss is irreparable—one they can never get over (e.g., Rigdon, 1986).

Through these behaviors, you can help make the bereavement process a bit less unbearable for persons you care about. Of course, nothing you or anyone else does can ever take the place of the person who is gone. But as one Italian saying puts it, "Vita continua"—"Life goes on"—so helping people pick up the pieces and continue is one of the kindest things you can ever do.

KEY QUESTIONS

* According to Kubler-Ross, what stages do terminally ill persons pass through when confronting their own death?
* What are the major stages of bereavement?

SUMMARY AND REVIEW OF KEY QUESTIONS

Physical Growth and Development

* **What environmental factors (teratogens) can adversely affect the developing fetus?**
Infectious agents, drugs, alcohol, and smoking by prospective mothers are all among teratogens that can harm the development fetus.

* **What are reflexes and which ones do infants possess at birth?**
Reflexes are inherited responses to stimulation in certain areas of the body. Infants possess several reflexes, including the Moro reflex, the palmar grasping reflex, and the sucking reflex.

* **What learning abilities are shown by newborns?**
Newborns seem capable of basic forms of learning, including classical conditioning and operant conditioning.

Perceptual Development during Childhood

* **What perceptual abilities are shown by infants?**
Infants can distinguish among different colors, sounds, and tastes, and they prefer certain patterns, such as the human face.

* **What evidence indicates that infants can keep track of time?**
Infants show increased heart rate at the precise times when a stimulus previously presented at specific times would normally occur again.

Cognitive Development during Childhood: Changes in Our Ability to Understand the World around Us

* **What are the major stages in Piaget's theory, and what cognitive abilities do infants, children, and adolescents acquire as they move through these stages?**
During the sensorimotor stage, infants acquire basic understanding of the links between their own behavior and the effects it produces—cause and effect. During the preoperational stage, infants can form mental representations of the external world, but show egocentrism in their thinking. During the stage of concrete operations, children are capable of logical thought and show understanding of conversation. During the stage of

formal operations, children and adolescents can think logically.

* **In what respects does Piaget's theory appear to be in need of revision?**
Piaget's theory is inaccurate in that it seriously underestimates the cognitive abilities of young children.

* **What is the "curse of knowledge" and what does it tell us about young children's cognitive abilities?**
The *curse of knowledge* refers to how we tend to be biased by our own knowledge when judging the perspective of people who know less about some topic than we do.

* **To what does the term *children's theory of mind* refer?**
This refers to children's growing understanding of their own mental states and those of others.

* **According to the information-processing perspective, what does cognitive development involve?**
It involves children's growing abilities with respect to basic aspects of cognition (e.g., attention, memory, metacognition).

* **What role do heuristics and other potential sources of error play in cognitive development?**
As children's cognitive abilities increase, they also acquire heuristics and other cognitive biases.

* **What processes play a role in language acquisition?**
Several basic forms of learning (instrumental conditioning), innate language systems, and the statistical structure of a given language may all play a role in this process.

* **What is phonological awareness?**
This refers to the sound structure of an individual's language, and involves being able to recognize, discriminate, and manipulate the sounds in one's language.

* **What role do gestures play in learning acquisition?**
Gestures appear to precede children's use of specific words and also their shift to two-word sentences—a major milestone in language acquisition.

* **What advances do children make in understanding the meaning of words and language?**
Their vocabularies expand rapidly, and they gradually come to understand the use of adjectives, question words, and negatives (e.g., *no*).

Moral Development: Reasoning about "Right" and "Wrong"

- **What are the major stages of moral development in Kohlberg's theory?**
  At the first, or preconventional, level, morality is judged largely in terms of its consequences. At the conventional level, morality is judged in terms of laws and rules of society. At the third, or postconventional, level, morality is judged in terms of abstract principles and values.

- **Do cultural factors have any impact on moral development?**
  Cultural factors do appear to influence moral development. Depending on the society in which they live, individuals learn to make moral judgments on the basis of different criteria.

Social Development during Childhood: Forming Relationships with Others

- **What is temperament and what role does it play in later development?**
  Temperament refers to stable individual differences in the quality or intensity of emotional reactions. It plays a role in shyness and in the later occurrence of several kinds of behavioral problems, and may even influence the nature of adult romantic relationships.

- **What is attachment?**
  Attachment refers to infants' strong emotional bonds with their caregivers.

- **What role do children's friendships play in their social and emotional development?**
  Friendships help children to develop socially and emotionally, and often help them avoid loneliness.

From Gender Identity to Sex Category Constancy: How Children Come to Understand That They Are Female or Male

- **What is gender identity? Gender stability? Gender consistency?**
  Gender identity refers to children's ability to label their own sex and that of others accurately. Gender stability is children's understanding that sex identity is stable over time. Gender consistency is children's understanding that their sex identity won't change even if they adopt the clothing, hairstyles, and activities of the other sex.

- **How do social learning theory, cognitive development theory, and gender schema theory explain gender development?**
  Social learning theory emphasizes the role of operant conditions and modeling. Cognitive development theory emphasizes the role of children's growing cognitive abilities. Gender schema theory emphasizes the role of gender schemas.

Adolescence: Between Child and Adult

- **What physical changes occur during puberty?**
  Puberty, the most important feature of physical development during adolescence, is a period of rapid change and growth during which individuals attain sexual maturity.

- **How does the brain develop during adolescence?**
  During adolescence, the brain first produces a large number of new neurons and then "prunes" these to retain only the most useful ones. Myelination (insulation) of neuronal connections, too, increases.

- **What changes in cognitive abilities occur during adolescence?**
  During adolescence, processing speed increases, and adolescents become better able to manage their own cognitive processes and learning, to make decisions, and to think analytically.

- **Are widely accepted ideas about adolescent emotionality correct?**
  Adolescents do show larger swings in mood or emotion than adults, but contrary to popular views they are generally quite happy and get along well with their parents.

- **According to Erikson, what is the most important crisis faced by adolescents?**
  Erikson suggests that this is a crisis involving identity versus role confusion, which concerns establishment of a clear self-identity.

Development during Our Adult Years

- **What physical changes occur during early and middle adulthood?**
  Reduced physical functioning and decreased vigor plus changes in appearance appear during middle adulthood. In addition, both women and men experience changes in their reproductive systems during midlife.

- **What physical changes occur in later life?**
  Among the many physical changes occurring in later life are declines in sensory abilities and a slowing of reflexes.

- **What changes in memory occur as we age?**
  Working memory does not decline with age, but moving information from it to long-term storage may become somewhat slower. Recall of information from long-term memory does decline somewhat, but such effects are greater for meaningless information than meaningful information.

- **How does intelligence change over the life span?**
  There may be some declines in some aspects of intelligence with age, but these are smaller and more limited in scope than was once widely believed.

- **What are the effects of becoming physically fit on cognitive functioning?**
  Becoming fit has been found to enhance many forms of cognitive functioning, especially ones involving executive functions—planning and sequencing of mental procedures.

- **What are some of the key challenges we face during our adult years?**
  These include marriage, parenthood, career changes, divorce, the "empty-nest syndrome," caring for aging parents, and our own aging and retirement.

- **How should you choose your career?**
  While many factors should be considered, p
  most important is obtaining a good match
  personal characteristics and the career y

Death and Bereavement

- **According to Kubler-Ross, what stages do terminally ill persons pass through when confronting their own death?**
 Kubler-Ross reported five stages: denial, anger, bargaining, depression, and acceptance.

- **What are the major stages of bereavement?**
 These include shock, protest and yearning, disorganization and despair, and finally detachment and recovery.

KEY TERMS

PSYCHOLOGY: UNDERSTANDING ITS FINDINGS

While the view that young children are just "miniature adults" is no longer widely accepted, many parents act as though they believe it: They often try to "reason" with their children about why the children should (or should not!) engage in certain actions, and often try to explain highly abstract ideas or principles to them (e.g., fairness, justice, loy-alty). According to Piaget's theory of cognitive development and modern findings about children's cognitive abilities, why do these efforts often fail? At what age *can* children begin to reason like adults and understand abstract principles and ideas? And until they can, what techniques should parents use to influence their children's behavior?

YCHOLOGY PART OF YOUR LIFE

inding a Good Match for
istics

 on choosing a career indicates
d most successful—when the

careers they choose provide a close match to their personal characteristics and preferences. What are your characteristics and what careers would fit them best? These are complex questions that can't be answered fully in a brief exercise. But to get you started in the right direction, follow these steps:

perhaps the
between your
u select.

1. **Rate your own standing on the following clusters of traits** (use a 5-point scale, where 1 = very low; 2 = low; 3 = average; 4 = high; 5 = very high):
   a. Practical, stable
   b. Analytic, introverted, reserved, precise
   c. Creative, impulsive, emotional
   d. Sociable, outgoing, need affection
   e. Confident, energetic, assertive
   f. Dependable, disciplined, orderly

2. Now, to increase the accuracy of your assessments, have three friends who know you well rate you on the same dimensions.
3. Next, consider the pattern of your traits: On which are you highest? Next highest? Lowest?
4. A major theory of career choice—Holland's *theory of vocational choice* (Holland, Gottfredson, & Holland, 1990) suggests that people high on each of the clusters of traits above can be described by the terms shown in the table below, enjoy certain kinds of environments or activities, and would most prefer the jobs listed:

Cluster label	Preferred environments or activities	Preferred jobs
Realistic	Working with hands, machines, tools	Auto mechanic; mechanical engineer
Investigative	Discovering, collecting, analyzing, and problem solving	Systems analyst; dentist; scientist
Artistic	Creating new products or ideas	Novelist; advertising copy-writer
Social	Serving or helping others, working in teams	Social worker, counselor, nurse
Enterprising	Leading others, achieving goals	Manager, politician, stockbroker
Conventional	Performing systemic manipulation of data or information	Accountant, banker, actuary

The jobs shown are only examples. Can you think of others that would provide you with a good match to your personal traits?

If you are using MyPsychLab, you have access to an electronic version of this textbook, along with dozens of valuable resources per chapter—including video and audio clips, simulations and activities, self-assessments, practice tests and other study materials. Here is a sampling of the resources available for this chapter.

EXPLORE

The Embryonic Period

Cross-sectional and Longitudinal Research Designs

Piaget's Stages of Cognitive Development

Ages and Stages of Cognitive and Moral Development

SIMULATE

Kohlberg's Stages of Moral Reasoning

Adult Attachment

Identity Status

Baumrind's Parenting Styles

If you did not receive an access code to MyPsychLab with this text and wish to purchase access online, please visit www.MyPsychLab.com.

STUDY GUIDE

CHAPTER REVIEW

Physical Growth and Development during Childhood

1. Human life begins when a(n) _____ from a father fertilizes an _____ within the mother.
   a. X chromosome;   Y chromosome
   b. Y chromosome;   X chromosome
   c. sperm;   ovum
   d. ovum;   sperm
2. Uterus is another name for the mother's womb.   (True-False)
3. A fetus will show simple reflexes by the _____ week of life.
   a. third   c. ninth
   b. fifth   d. twelfth
4. Pregnant women are advised to abstain from heavy use of alcohol during the first trimester. (True-False)
5. The _____ reflex is triggered by a sudden drop of the infant's head and involves _____.
   a. Babinsky;   loud crying
   b. palmar grasping;   grasping of the mother's hair
   c. suckling;   movements of the mouth and tongue
   d. Moro;   the infant throwing out its hands and then crossing its arms across its chest.
6. A learning capacity evident in a newborn infant involves
   a. operant conditioning of salivary responses.
   b. classical conditioning of fear responses.
   c. operant conditioning of fetal heart rate in response to stroking of the forehead.
   d. classical conditioning involving survival stimuli.
7. A serious outcome of early malnutrition is
   a. a greater risk of developing obesity following the end of malnutrition.
   b. reduced volume of the hippocampus, regardless of subsequent nutrition.
   c. mental retardation and blindness.
   d. a greater risk of developing of dementia in later life.

Perceptual Development during Childhood

8. Newborns can distinguish between different
   a. colors.   c. sounds.
   b. tastes.   d. All of the above are correct.
9. The visual acuity of a newborn is
   a. 20/20   c. 20/100
   b. 10/50   d. 20/200
10. By the age of _____ months, an infant would be expected to _____.
    a. three;   have just developed taste perception
    b. nine;   distinguish between their own name and other names
    c. six;   be able to distinguish their mother's face from that of a stranger
    d. ten;   perceive depth
11. Indicate the approximate age (in months) at which an infant is capable of each perceptual function.
    _____. The capacity to keep track of time.
    _____. The ability to distinguish their mother's face from that of a stranger.
    _____. The capacity to distinguish between different colors.
    _____. The ability to perceive depth.
    _____. The ability to distinguish between their own name and other names.
    _____. The capacity to distinguish between different tastes.

Cognitive Development during Childhood: Changes in Our Ability to Understand the World around Us

12. Which of the following scientists developed a theory of cognitive development based on observations of his/her children?
    a. B.F. Skinner.   c. Jean Piaget.
    b. Noam Chomsky.   d. Robert Baron
13. Piaget argued that mental schemas change to new information during the process of _____.
    a. mental homeostasis   c. accommodation
    b. assimilation   d. schema expansion
14. Piaget argued that the conflict generated by assimilation and accommodation fuels cognitive development. (True-False)
15. Recent studies by Baillorgeon have confirmed Piaget's view that 3 month old infants do not have a concept of object permanence.   (True-False)
16. We would expect that the "curse of knowledge" would be most evident in
    a. bilingual children.
    b. a forty year old adult.
    c. children younger than four years of age.
    d. monolingual children.
17. The information processing perspective suggests that cognitive development involves changes in children's cognitive abilities including attention, memory use, and metacognition.   (True-False)
18. Noam Chomsky argued that language skills develop through _____ which he defines as _____.
    a. social learning;   the modeling of language by the parents.
    b. an innate mechanism;   a set of wired-in neurons
    c. classical and operant conditioning;   a general set of learning mechanisms
    d. a language acquisition device;   a neural system programmed to acquire language
19. The use of _____ by caregivers promotes language development in children.
    a. word repetition   c. physical gestures
    b. baby-talk   d. All of the above are correct.

Moral Development: Reasoning about "Right" and "Wrong"

20. Our changing capacity to reason about what is right and wrong in a given situation is known as
    a. creative justice.   c. ethicality.
    b. moral development.   d. norm adjustment.

21. A person who argues that moral decisions must be based on societal laws is at the _____ level of moral development.
    a. concrete
    b. preconventional
    c. social justice
    d. conventional
22. Cross-cultural studies have generally supported the existence of Kohlberg's stages of moral development. (True-False)
23. Match the Kohlberg level of moral development with the each description below.
    _____. "Killing another person is not good because life is sacred for all persons."
    _____. "I took the money to buy drugs to get high"
    _____. "Mexican citizens should be allowed to enter this country because having a job is a basic human right."
    _____. "Selling heroin to children was wrong because I got caught and now am in prison."
    a. Preconventional level
    b. Conventional level
    c. Postconventional level

Social Development during Childhood: Forming Relationships with Others

24. _____ involves a stable individual difference in arousal, mood, and reactivity in new situations.
    a. Emotional intelligence
    b. Emotivation
    c. Behavioral homeostasis
    d. Temperament
25. Your cousin has just had baby which you will meet in a few minutes. Based on reading the temperament section of this book, your best guess is that your cousin's new child will have a(n) _____ temperament.
    a. "difficult"
    b. "easy"
    c. inconsistent
    d. "slow-to-warm-up"
26. A person's temperament is highly stable after the second year of life. (True-False)
27. Cross-cultural studies suggest that _____ attachment is highest in _____.
    a. secure; Germany
    b. ambivalent; Japan
    c. secure; Sweden
    d. avoidance; Germany
28. Another name for the close physical interaction between infant and caregiver is _____.
    a. tactile synergism
    b. somatotemperament
    c. contact comfort
    d. physical homeostasis

From Gender Identity to Sex Category Constancy: How Children Come to Understand That the Are Female or Male

29. Whether a person has an XX or a XY chromosome pattern refers to
    a. gender.
    b. biological sex.
    c. gender roles.
    d. gender identity.
30. Which of the following do NOT belong together?
    a. gender stereotypes; expected differences in traits between males and females
    b. gender identity; XX or XY chromosomes
    c. gender roles; expected patterns of behavior for males versus females
    d. biological sex; XX or XY chromosomes
31. Cognitive development theory argues that children imitate their same-sex models and as a consequence develop their own gender identity. (True-False)
32. Match up the appropriate concept with the correct definition or best example of the concept.
    _____. The recognition by a child that they belong to one sex or the other.
    _____. Whether a person has an XX or XY chromosome pattern.
    _____. A set of expected patterns of behavior for males versus females
    _____. A set of expected differences in traits between males and females
    _____. A cognitive framework incorporating social beliefs about male and female attributes.
    a. Gender role.
    b. Social-learning theory
    c. Gender schema
    d. Biological sex.
    e. Gender identity.
    g. Gender stereotypes

Adolescence: Between Child and Adult

33. Which of the following is an example of a cognitive change noted during adolescence?
    a. Adolescents show faster processing speeds than do children.
    b. Adolescents are better able to manage their own learning than are children.
    c. Adolescents are better than children at decision making.
    d. All of the above are correct.
34. The participation of young people in open rebellion against the government is a function of
    a. There is a large proportion of adolescents in the population.
    b. Adolescents are less susceptible to discontent and anger.
    c. Adolescents have just completed classes in civics.
    d. Adolescents are susceptible to influence by charismatic government leaders.

Development during Our Adult Years

35. The focus of Erikson's theory is _____ development across the life span.
    a. maturational
    b. cognitive
    c. biological
    d. social
36. According to Erikson, an adolescent who asks questions such as _____ is undergoing the crisis of identity versus role confusion.
    a. "Who will feed me?"
    b. "Who am I?"
    c. "Is this all there is?"
    d. "I cannot be 70!"
37. An example of a secondary cause of aging would be
    a. the passage of time.
    b. adopting a healthy lifestyle.
    c. your genetic heritage.
    d. a bodily disease.
38. During the process of primary aging, changes in _____ result from _____.
    a. vision; improved diet and exercise
    b. hearing; having to concentrate to hear what others are saying

c. hearing;   loss of hair cells on the basilar membrane
d. taste;   loss of hair cells

39. A major change in cognitive function during aging includes
   a. improved reaction time.
   b. a slight impairment in information transfer from short-term to long-term memory.
   c. impaired short-term memory function.
   d. reduced intelligence.
40. There are approximately 18 million young adults who could be classified as "boomerang" children. (True-False)

Death and Bereavement

41. The refusal of a dying person to recognize their impending death is termed the
   a. bargaining stage.   c. denial stage.
   b. boomerang stage   d. anger stage.
42. Parents who lose a child are more likely to show "shadow grief" for their entire lives.   (True-False)

IDENTIFICATIONS

Identify the term that belongs with each of the concepts below (place the letter for the appropriate term below in front of each concept).

Identification   Concept:

_____ 1. A strong affectional bond between and child and caregiver.

_____ 2. The developing child during the last 7 months of pregnancy.

_____ 3. Shared social beliefs about how males and females should behave in most situations.

_____ 4. Environmental factors that can harm a developing fetus.

_____ 5. Whether a person has an XX or XY chromosome pattern.

_____ 6. Understanding that the physical properties of object do not change in spite of a change in appearance.

_____ 7. Bodily changes that occur as a function of time and of genetics.

_____ 8. A trait in which a person is unable to see the point of view of others.

_____ 9. The earliest stage of Piaget's theory of development.

_____ 10. The inability to separate what we known from what we believe others to know.

_____ 11. A ball hidden under blanket continues to exist.

_____ 12. A point in life at which a female ceases her menstrual cycle.

_____ 13. The refusal of a dying person to recognize their impending death.

_____ 14. A period of life in which sexual and reproductive function undergo great changes.

_____ 15. A 30 year old son who lives at home with his parents.

Identification:
   a. Climacteric.
   b. Conservation.
   c. Curse of knowledge.
   d. Menopause.
   e. Biological sex.
   f. Primary aging.
   g. Sensorimotor.
   h. Teratogen.
   i. Boomerang child.
   j. Gender roles.
   k. Object permanence.
   l. Attachment.
   m. Denial stage.
   n. Fetus.
   o. gocentrism.

FILL IN THE BLANK

1. The focus of developmental psychology is on _____, _____, and _____ development.
2. A fetal disorder involving retarded growth, brain damage; and facial malformations is known as _____.
3. A fertilized egg that has been implanted in the uterine wall is termed a(n) _____.
4. Depth perception in an infant that can crawl is best studied using a(n) _____.
5. The _____ reflex allows an infant to better hold onto its mother.
6. _____ refers to the cognitive process in which new experiences are fitted into an existing schema.
7. The increasing capacity of a child to understand their own mental states and those of others is _____.
8. Conservation, reversibility, and logical thought are key characteristics
9. _____ refers to understanding and strategically controlling one's own cognitive abilities.
10. The most common type of temperament is that of the _____ child.
11. The use of _____ by a child interacting with their caregiver may improve the child's language skills.
12. A moral judgment based on whether an actor is punished or rewarded is made at the _____ level.
13. A person reaches sexual maturity after _____.
14. _____ is noted in the offspring of mothers who consume much alcohol during pregnancy.
15. A person at the _____ level uses abstract principles to reach moral judgments.
16. _____ refers to our awareness and use of our own cognitive processes.
17. _____ reflects changes in our body due to disease, disuse, or abuse.

COMPREHENSIVE PRACTICE TEST

1. A(n) _____ is an environmental factor that can damage or impair normal growth and development of a fetus.
   a. teratogen   c. dermatogen
   b. endotoxin   d. ionophore
2. Which of the following DO NOT belong together?
   a. AIDS; teratogen
   b. rubella; fetus is infected during birth
   c. FAS; binge drinking of alcohol
   d. decreased birth weight; maternal smoking
3. Which of the following behaviors is elicited in a newborn showing the Babinski reflex?
   a. Their toes will fan out.
   b. The baby makes a stepping motion.

c. The fingers of the baby close around an object.

d. The infant moves it lips toward an object as if to suck.

4. Which of the following body structures would be expected to first undergo motor development?

   a. The infant's feet.

   b. The legs of the infant.

   c. The infant's head.

   d. The hands and toes of the infant.

5. Newborns can keep track of time   (True-False)

6. In the process of accommodation, a child

   a. modifies their existing knowledge structures to handle new information.

   b. ignores new information to preserve their old mental schemas.

   c. integrates new ideas into old schemas.

   d. a child's growth accelerates during the period prior to puberty.

7. Match up the appropriate concept with the correct definition or best example of the concept.

   _____. Understanding that the physical characteristics of an object remain the same as it outward appearances change.

   _____. The view that objects continue to exist when they cannot be seen.

   _____. The first stage of cognitive development in Piaget's theory.

   _____. That stage during which children can make mental representations of the external world.

   _____. A child's inability to take the perspective of others.

   _____. The highest level of thought in Piaget's system.

   _____. The process by which new information is integrated into a knowledge structure.

   _____. A set of knowledge structures are modified to incorporate new information.

   a. Operational thought.

   b. Sensorimotor stage.

   c. Assimilation.

   d. Object permanence.

   e. Preoperational thought.

   f. Accommodation.

   g. Egocentrism.

   h. Conservation.

8. Most eighteen month infants have a vocabulary of more than five hundred words.   (True-False)

9. The key aspect of preconventional moral judgment is whether

   a. the specific action in question leads to some sort of punishment or a reward.

   b. the action in question is one that helps others.

   c. the action is rejected by societal laws.

   d. a specific action is consistent with the person's ethical standards.

10. Which of the following DO NOT belong together?

   a. secure attachment;   a social and playful child

   b. insecure attachment;   child feels safe around the caregiver

   c. avoidant attachment;   child avoids close contact with the caregiver

   d. ambivalent attachment;   a child who is inhibited and shows signs of fear

11. Harlow found that isolated monkeys spent much of their time

   a. feeding from the cold wire-"mother".

   b. playing in their home cage.

   c. clinging to the wire-"mother".

   d. clinging to the terry-cloth covered "mother".

12. We would expect that a child will have achieved gender consistency

   a. before they understand gender roles.

   b. in adolescence.

   c. by the age of seven.

   d. by the age of two.

13. Which of the following is NOT an example of a physical change noted during midlife?

   a. The development of wrinkled skin.

   b. Reduced physical capacity for physical work.

   c. Improved digestion.

   d. Reduced function of the reproductive systems.

14. Which of the following is an example of a primary effect of aging?

   a. Muscle cramping due to lack of exercise.

   b. Cancer brought on by overeating.

   c. Reduced sexual function caused by alcoholism.

   d. reduced sensory function.

15. Retaining physical fitness is a key factor for improving cognitive function during aging.   (True-False)

16. Match up the appropriate concept with the correct definition or best example of the concept.

   _____. A form of bereavement caused by an unexpected death.

   _____. A process of healing shown by persons who have experienced the death of a loved one.

   _____. A stage proposed by Kubler-Ross in which people try to postpone death by offering good works.

   _____. A stage proposed by Kubler-Ross in which the person is resigned to their impending death.

   _____. A form of bereavement in which death was expected.

   a. A low-grief death.

   b. Bargaining.

   c. Anger.

   d. A high-grief death.

   e. Acceptance.

   f. Bereavement.

17. Which of the following is a factor that can produce a "boomerang child"?

   a. The high cost of housing.

   b. The desire of a parent to have their child back in the house.

   c. The prolonged nature of higher education.

   d. All of the above are correct.

CRITICAL THINKING

1. Explain the implications that temperament is stable after the age of two for our personal functioning as adults.

2. Describe the developmental changes that occur during midlife and how these changes can be modified in an aging person.

EIGHT

Motivation and Emotion

In 1991, I (Michael Kalsher) completed the Pittsburgh Marathon, the first of three marathons I ran during the first half of the 1990s. My initial motivation to start running was definitely not to run that far— 26.2 miles to be exact—but rather to find an activity that I could enjoy and would help me to lose the excess weight I had gained in graduate school. At first, I was content to jog two to three miles several times per week because it was sufficient to help me reach my goal of shedding weight and getting into shape. Then, a graduate student who had been observing my progress encouraged me to think about training for a marathon and handed me a book written for that purpose. Initially, such a feat seemed to be out of reach—until I started to execute the training program that was organized around one progressively longer, slow run each week. As the weekly long runs approached and then surpassed twenty miles, it became clear that the key to running a marathon was less about being athletic and more about developing and then sticking with an effective training regimen.

Although it's now been more than ten years since my last marathon, I'm currently in the process of training for another one. Why? Not because I need to lose weight, get fit, or prove that I can do it, but because of something I saw on TV! While channel surfing, I stumbled on to a documentary about a man and a woman, both in their seventies, who had trained for and completed an iron-man triathlon—a contest in which participants swim 2.4 miles, bike 112 miles, and then run a marathon. Although it took each of them about twenty hours to do so, both reached the finish line. Watching two people who are clearly much older than I am complete a race that is significantly more

arduous than merely running a marathon has motivated me to resume training
for another long-distance race, and perhaps one day, to train for and complete
a triathlon.

Why do we start with this personal anecdote? Because it helps illustrate the essential nature of the two major topics we'll consider in this chapter: *motivation* and *emotion*. Psychologists use the term *motivation* to refer to the internal processes that *activate, guide,* and *maintain* behavior (often, over long periods of time); the operation of such processes is certainly apparent in my interest in participating in long-distance runs. Why, after all, would I commit to the months of training needed to complete another 26.2-mile race when I have easily maintained my weight and stayed in shape during the past decade by running much shorter distances? And why would watching two elderly people complete a triathlon on TV exert such profound effects on my personal behavior? When it is difficult to explain someone's behavior in terms of the immediate situation or with respect to obvious rewards and punishments, psychologists often seek the explanation in terms of motivation—internal processes that *energize* behavior, *guide* it, and cause it to *persist* over time (see Figure 8.1). In the case of my motivation to participate in more long-distance races, these internal factors energize and guide my efforts to seek out and adhere to advice that will improve my training, and ultimately my running, and I suspect they will cause me to engage in such behavior for many years. What are these internal processes like? We'll soon examine them in detail, but should note here that they include *goals, intentions,* and *desires*—processes that certainly exist and often strongly affect behavior (see Figure 8.1) but are difficult to observe directly.

Emotion, in contrast, refers to complex reactions consisting of (1) physiological responses such as changes in blood pressure and heart rate; (2) the subjective feelings we describe as happiness, anger, sorrow, or disgust; and (3) expressive reactions that reflect these internal states, such as changes in facial expressions or posture. Such reactions are apparent in the pleasure I feel when I've met my goal of completing a long-distance run in a specific amount of time or in the strong disappointment I experience if I do not, and in the communication of these feelings in my facial expressions and words. Emotions play a crucial role in many aspects of behavior, including personal health (see Chapter 10) and psychological disorders (see Chapter 11). In addition, they exert strong effects on many aspects of cognition, affecting the way we process information and shaping our judgments and decisions in important ways (see Forgas, 1995, 1998; Zeelenberg et al., 2006).

In this chapter, we'll describe what psychologists have learned about both of these important topics. Starting with *motivation*, we'll consider contrasting theories about its basic nature. Why should you be interested in these theories? Because they provide important insights into understanding your own motivation and, perhaps, how to change it. Next, we'll examine two important forms of motivation: *hunger* and *sexual motivation*. In addition, we'll also consider a motive that, as far as we can tell, is unique to human beings: *achievement motivation*—the desire to excel. We'll also consider *intrinsic motivation*—motivation that does not stem from external rewards—and *forgiveness*—replacing desires for revenge with compassion and other positive reactions.

After that, we'll turn to the topic of *emotion*, beginning, again, with a brief overview of theories concerning its nature. Then we'll turn to the biological bases of emotion. Third, we'll consider the expression and communication of emotion—how emotional reactions are reflected in external behavior. We'll then shift focus

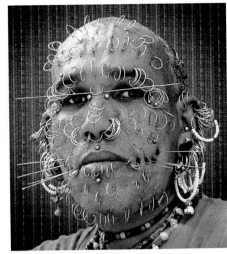

FIGURE 8.1
MOTIVATION: USEFUL IN ANSWERING THE QUESTION "WHY"?
We often wonder why other people behave as they do—especially in situations in which rewards for their actions are not readily apparent. The concept of motivation is often helpful in understanding such behavior. Can you guess why the people shown here are engaging in the activities they are performing? In other words, what are the motives behind their actions?

to *affect* (or affective states)—relatively mild subjective feelings and moods. Here, we'll consider the complex relationships between emotion and cognition—how feelings shape thoughts and thoughts shape feelings. Finally, we'll examine one important kind of affective state—personal happiness.

MOTIVATION: THE ACTIVATION AND PERSISTENCE OF BEHAVIOR

Consider the following events:

- A group of young women and men hurl themselves out of a plane. Then, as they fall toward earth, they join hands and form a circle. After that, they divide into pairs and swing round and round each other in a kind of dance. Only at the last minute do they open their parachutes and glide safely to the ground.

- Employees of a large company remain on strike for many weeks, even though the settlement, no matter how large, will not be enough to compensate them for the wages and benefits they have lost during the strike.
- An individual spends long hours working on complex word puzzles that require a great deal of concentration. He receives no rewards for solving these puzzles; in fact, he is often frustrated by being unable to solve them.

How can such actions be explained? On the face of it, they are puzzling. Why would people voluntarily jump out of planes and risk their lives playing games as they fall toward earth? Why would workers remain on strike, even though such actions offer no chance of real economic gains? Why would someone exert so much effort solving complex puzzles? One answer to such questions is this: These actions occur because the people involved are *motivated* to perform them. In other words, they are responding to their own **motivation**—internal processes that can't be directly observed in the situation but that serve to activate, guide, and maintain their actions. Whenever the causes of a specific form of behavior can't be readily observed in the immediate situation or in terms of obvious rewards or punishments, psychologists believe that it is useful to explain them in terms of motives. But what, precisely, are these motives? And how do they influence behavior? Let's see what psychologists have to say about these issues.

Theories of Motivation: Some Major Perspectives

Many theories of motivation have been proposed over the years—more theories, in fact, than we could possibly examine here. The views described here, however, are the ones that have received the most attention and may be most relevant to understanding—and changing—your own motivation.

■ Drive theory: Motivation and homeostasis.

What do being hungry, thirsty, too cold, and too hot have in common? One answer is that they are all unpleasant states that cause us to do something to reduce or eliminate them. This basic fact provides the basis for a major approach to motivation known as **drive theory.** According to drive theory, biological needs arising within our bodies create unpleasant states of arousal—the feelings we describe as hunger, thirst, fatigue, and so on. To eliminate such feelings and restore a balanced physiological state known as **homeostasis,** we engage in certain activities (Winn, 1995). Thus, according to drive theory, motivation is basically a process in which various biological needs push (drive) us to actions designed to satisfy these needs (see Figure 8.2). Behaviors that work—ones that help reduce the appropriate drive—are strengthened and tend to be repeated (see Chapter 5). Those that fail to produce effects are weakened and will not be repeated when the drive is present once again.

In its original form, drive theory focused primarily on biological needs and the drives they produce. Soon, though, psychologists extended this model to other forms of behavior not so clearly linked to basic needs, such as drives for stimulation, status, achievement, power, and forming stable social relationships (see Baumeister & Leary, 1995). For many people, these are important motives, and they engage in vigorous efforts to satisfy them. So although these drives may not be based on biological needs, they, too, can serve as powerful sources of motivation.

Drive theory persisted in psychology for several decades, but at present, most psychologists believe it suffers from several major drawbacks. Contrary to what drive theory suggests, humans often engage in actions that *increase* rather than reduce various drives. For example, people sometimes skip snacks when hungry to lose weight or to maximize their enjoyment of a special dinner. Similarly, many people watch or read erotic materials to increase their sexual excitement, even when they don't anticipate immediate sexual gratification. In view of such evi-

---

Motivation:
Internal processes that activate, guide, and maintain behavior over time.

Drive theory:
A theory of motivation suggesting that behavior is "pushed" from within by drives stemming from basic biological needs.

Homeostasis:
A state of physiological balance within the body.

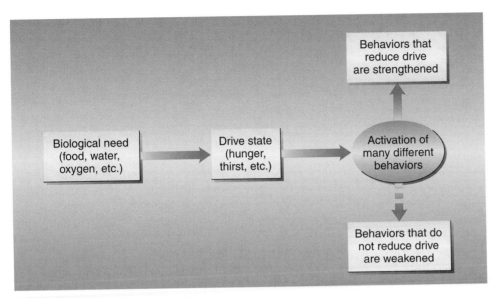

FIGURE 8.2
Drive Theory: An Overview
According to drive theory, biological needs lead to the arousal of drives, which activate efforts to reduce them. Behaviors that succeed in reducing drives are strengthened and are repeated when the drive is aroused again. Behaviors that fail to reduce the drive are weakened and are less likely to recur when the drive is aroused once again.

dence, most psychologists now believe that drive theory, by itself, does not provide a full explanation of human motivation.

■ Expectancy theory: A cognitive approach.

Why are you reading this book? Not, we'd guess, to reduce some biological need. Rather, you are probably reading it because doing so will help you to reach important goals: to gain useful and interesting knowledge, to earn a high grade on the next exam, to graduate from college. In short, your behavior is determined by your thoughts about future outcomes and how your current actions can help you get wherever it is that you want to go in life. This basic point forms the basis for another major theory of motivation, **expectancy theory.**

This theory suggests that motivation is not primarily a matter of being pushed from within by various urges or drives; rather, it is more a question of being *pulled* from without by expectations of attaining desired outcomes. Such outcomes, known as **incentives,** can be almost anything we have learned to value—money, status, and the approval of others, to name just a few. In other words, while drive theory focuses mainly on the factors that push or (drive) us toward certain actions, expectancy theory focuses more on the outcomes we wish to obtain. Why do people engage in complex, effortful, or even painful behaviors, such as working many hours on their jobs, studying long into the night, performing exercises that are, at least initially, painful? Expectancy theory answers: Because they believe that doing so will yield the outcomes they wish to attain, as illustrated in Figure 8.3 on page 302. Certainly, you can think of instances in which this principle applies to your own behavior. For instance, why do you—or people you know—study, work, or exercise hard? Not because these activities are intrinsically enjoyable. You perform them because you believe that doing so will produce the outcomes you want—better grades, success in your career (or at least a steady income!), and better health. So expectancy theory does seem to provide important insights into motivation: why we do what we do in many situations.

Expectancy theory has been applied to many aspects of human motivation, but perhaps it has found its most important applications as an explanation of *work*

Expectancy theory:
A theory of motivation suggesting that behavior is "pulled" by expectations of desirable outcomes.

Incentives:
Rewards individuals seek to attain.

FIGURE 8.3

The Role of Incentives in Motivating Behavior

According to expectancy theory, people perform certain behaviors because they believe doing so will yield outcomes they wish to attain. As illustrated by this example, the outcomes that people desire often vary considerably!

Source: CartoonStock.com. Reprinted with permission.

motivation—the tendency to expend energy and effort on one's job (Locke & Latham, 2002). We'll consider several aspects of work motivation (especially job satisfaction) in Chapter 14, but here, we simply want to note that research findings in the field of *industrial/organizational psychology* indicate that people will work hard at their jobs only when they believe that doing so will improve their performance (known as *expectancy* in the theory), that good performance will be recognized and rewarded (known as *instrumentality* in the theory), and that the rewards provided will be ones they want (known as *valence*).

■ **Goal-setting theory.**

Another theory of motivation that emphasizes the importance of cognitive factors rather than drives or arousal is known as **goal-setting theory,** and it can be illustrated by the following example. Suppose that you are studying for a big exam. Do you ever tell yourself, in advance, that you won't stop until you have read a certain number of pages, memorized some specific number of definitions, or solved a fixed number of problems? The chances are good that you do, because most people realize that they often accomplish more when they have a concrete goal than when they do not. This basic fact is central to *goal-setting theory* (see Locke & Latham, 2002), which suggests that motivation can be strongly influenced by goals.

Additional findings, however, indicate that goal setting works best under certain conditions. It is most effective in boosting performance when the goals set are highly *specific*—people know just what they are trying to accomplish; the goals are *challenging*—meeting them requires considerable effort; and the goals are perceived as *attainable*—people believe they can actually reach them. Setting goals also works best when people receive feedback on their progress toward meeting the goals and when they are truly and deeply committed to reaching them. This last point is quite important; if goals are set by someone else and the people who are expected to meet these goals aren't committed to doing so, then setting goals can be totally ineffective, and may even backfire and *reduce* motivation. Finally, contextual factors play an important role in the activation and management of goals (Bargh et al., 2001; Shah, 2005). In everyday life, we typically pursue goals in particular settings, with particular individuals, and while doing specific activities. This suggests that it is important to arrange contexts in which each of these components, collectively termed *attainment means*, contributes to goal achievement. According to Shah (2005), doing so facilitates goal-setting in several important

Goal-setting theory:

The view that motivation can be strongly influenced by goals.

PSYCHOLOGY LENDS A HAND

Managing Your Motivation

Motivation, almost everyone agrees, is a key ingredient in success. Highly motivated people can often outperform those who are more skilled, experienced, or talented because, to put it simply, they try harder! Can psychology help you to boost your own motivation at times when you'd like to do so? Absolutely. By applying the principles of several theories of motivation, you can increase your own ability to exert sustained effort toward attaining various goals or outcomes. Here, briefly, are some of the steps that can be very helpful in this regard:

1. **First, figure out what you want.** There's an old saying that suggests you really can't get anywhere unless you first know where you want to go. So the initial step should be figuring out what's really important to you. Success? Security? Love? Leisure time? Status? A useful exercise is to list the things you want most in life and then to rank them from most important down. Once you are clear about what you really want, move on to the next step.

2. **Next, identify specific actions that can help you to reach these goals.** Reaching important goals generally means performing various tasks better than we are performing them right now. And remember: Increased effort does not always produce better performance; sometimes, it's just "spinning our wheels." For this reason (suggested by expectancy theory), you should be careful to put your effort where it will pay off—where it will actually help you to do better. For instance, if you want better grades, simply spending more time studying will not necessarily work. Rather, you have to figure out better

ways to study—ones that will help you to understand the materials in your courses. Bottom line: Invest your effort where it is most likely to produce concrete results.

3. **Set concrete, challenging, but achievable goals for yourself.** Rome, it is often said, was not built in a day. Similarly, you can't expect to attain everything you want in life right away; real progress toward important goals takes time. And to get there, you should begin by setting goals that are challenging (they are a real stretch), that are specific (they indicate precisely what you want to achieve), and that will also allow you to measure your progress toward them. Say, for instance, that you want to get along with other people better than you do now. One goal might be to be less openly critical of them, because no one likes receiving harsh, negative feedback. Begin by observing how many times each day you say something critical to other people. Then, choose a concrete goal: For instance, you will reduce this by 25 percent over the next two weeks. Monitor your progress as you work toward reaching this goal. When you do attain it, give yourself a reward—and then set a higher goal for the next round. The main point is that because you are setting the goals, and can measure your progress toward them, using goal-setting can really be a helpful motivational tool.

Good luck! Psychologists believe people can change almost anything about themselves they wish—if they really want to change and are willing to exert the effort. So start today and you may be truly happy with the results!

---

ways. First, it helps to ensure that the resources needed to achieve our goals are available and sufficient. Second, it focuses our attention on particular goals to the exception of competing ones, a process psychologists have termed *goal shielding*. Finally, it enhances our commitment to pursuing and attaining the goal.

In summary, when all these conditions are met, setting goals is a highly effective way to increase motivation and performance (Kozlowski & Bell, 2006; Wright et al., 1994). For ideas on how you can use it in your own life, see the **Psychology Lends a Hand** feature above.

■ Maslow's needs hierarchy: Relations among motives.

Suppose that you were very hungry and very cold; could you study effectively under these conditions? Probably not. Your hunger and feelings of cold would probably prevent you from focusing on the task of learning new materials, even if the materials were quite interesting to you. Observations like this suggest that human motives may exist in a *hierarchy*, so that we must satisfy those that are more basic before moving on to ones that are less linked to biological needs. This point is central to a theory of motivation proposed by Maslow (1970). Maslow places *physiological needs*—such as those for food, water, oxygen, and sleep—at the base of the **hierarchy of needs.** One step above these are *safety needs*; needs for feeling safe and secure in one's life. Above the safety needs are *social needs*, including needs to have friends, to be loved and appreciated, and to belong (see Baumeister & Leary, 1995).

Hierarchy of needs:
In Maslow's theory of motivation, an arrangement of needs from the most basic to those at the highest levels.

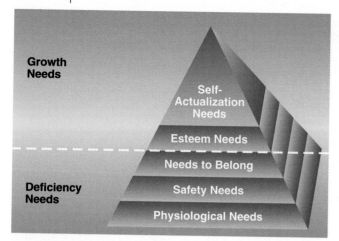

Growth Needs

Self-Actualization Needs

Esteem Needs

Needs to Belong

Deficiency Needs

Safety Needs

Physiological Needs

FIGURE 8.4

Maslow's Needs Hierarchy

According to Maslow (1970), needs exist in a hierarchy. Only when lower-order needs are satisfied can higher-order needs be activated, and serve as a source of motivation.

Maslow refers to physiological, safety, and social needs as *deficiency needs.* They are the basics and must be satisfied before higher levels of motivation, or *growth needs,* can emerge. Above the social needs in the hierarchy he proposes are *esteem needs,* the need to develop self-respect, to gain the approval of others, and to achieve success. Ambition and the need for achievement, to which we'll return later, are closely linked to esteem needs. Finally, at the top of the hierarchy are *self-actualization needs.* These involve the need for self-fulfillment—the desire to become all that one is capable of being (see Figure 8.4).

Maslow's theory is intuitively appealing, but research designed to test it has yielded mixed results. So overall, the idea that needs arise, and are satisfied, in a particular order has not been confirmed. For this reason, Maslow's theory should be viewed mainly as an interesting but unverified framework for understanding motivation. (See Table 8.1 for an overview of the theories of motivation discussed in this section.)

KEY QUESTIONS

- According to drive theory, what is the basis for various motives?
- According to expectancy theory, why do people engage in tasks requiring effort?
- Under what conditions will setting goals increase motivation and performance?
- What are the basic ideas behind Maslow's needs hierarchy theory?

Hunger: Regulating Our Caloric Intake

A Greek proverb states: "You cannot reason with a hungry belly; it has no ears." This statement suggests—eloquently!—that **hunger motivation,** the urge to obtain and consume food, is a powerful one, and if you have ever had the experience of going without food for even a single day, you know how strong feelings of hunger can be and what a powerful source of motivation they can provide. But where do such feelings come from? And how do we regulate the amount of food we consume so that for some people, body weight remains fairly stable over long periods of time, while for others, the "battle of the bulge" is quickly lost? Let's see what psychologists have discovered about these and related questions.

■ The regulation of eating: A complex process.

Consider the following fact: If you consume just twenty more calories than your body needs for fuel each day (less than the number in a single small carrot), you can expect to gain about two pounds per year—twenty pounds in a decade. How do people keep caloric input and output closely balanced and avoid such outcomes? One answer, of course, is that in many cases, they don't: People do gain weight despite their best efforts to avoid doing so. Indeed, we are living in the midst of what seems to be an epidemic of obesity. Since the early 1970s, the percentage of Americans twenty years and older who are either overweight or obese has risen from 17 percent to nearly 65 percent, and the number of obese people in the developed world has now matched the number of those suffering from hunger (National Center for Health Statistics, 2002). The practice of overeating seems to be starting at an early age. It's estimated that the average American child views about ten thousand TV ads annually, more than 90 percent of which promote fast food and sweets (Horgen et al., 2001). Experts estimate that 16 percent of children and adolescents ages six to nineteen years are overweight (National Center for

Hunger motivation:

The motivation to obtain and consume food.

TABLE 8.1 Theories of Motivation: An Overview

The theories summarized here are among the ones that have been most influential in psychology.

Theory of motivation	Key assumptions	Strengths/Weaknesses
Drive theory	Biological needs produce unpleasant states of arousal that people seek to reduce.	People sometimes try to *increase* their drives, not reduce them.
Arousal theory	Arousal (general level of activation) varies throughout the day and can motivate many forms of behavior; people seek optimal arousal, not low arousal.	Arousal is only one of many factors that influence motivated behavior.
Expectancy theory	Behavior is "pulled" by expectations of desired outcomes rather than "pushed" from within by biologically based drives.	Focus on cognitive processes in motivation is consistent with modern psychology; widely used to explain *work motivation*.
Goal-setting theory	Setting specific, challenging, but attainable goals can boost motivation and performance, especially when individuals are committed to reaching the goals and receive feedback on their progress.	Highly effective in increasing performance, but mechanisms that explain these effects are still somewhat uncertain.

Health Statistics, 2002). We'll return later in this chapter to several factors that may be contributing to these trends. Now, though, let's focus on the question of why, for some people, a balance is struck between needs and caloric intake so that weight remains relatively stable. What mechanisms contribute to this balance?

Part of the answer involves the *hypothalamus,* which plays a role both in eating and satiety (knowing when we've had enough). The regulation of eating involves much more than this, however. It seems to involve a complex system of regulatory mechanisms located not only in the hypothalamus, but in the liver and other organs of the body as well. These systems contain special *detectors,* cells that respond to variations in the concentration of several nutrients in the blood. One type of detector responds to the amount of *glucose,* or blood sugar. Other detectors respond to levels of *protein,* and especially to certain amino acids. This is why we feel full after eating a meal high in protein, such as a steak, even though the level of glucose in our blood remains relatively low. Finally, other detectors respond to *lipids,* or fats. Again, even if glucose levels are low, when the amount of lipids circulating in the blood is high, we do not feel hungry.

Complex as this may sound, it is still not the entire picture. In addition, eating and hunger are also strongly affected by the smell and taste of food and by feedback produced by chewing and swallowing. As we consume food, information from taste and smell receptors, and from muscles in our mouths and throats, provide feedback that helps us determine when we have eaten enough (Tataranni, P. A. et al., 1999).

The sight of food, too, is important. Foods that are attractive in appearance are hard to resist and may overwhelm the regulatory mechanisms just described, leading us to overeat (Rozin, 1996). Cognitive factors, too, play a role. Findings reported by Rozin and colleagues (1998) indicate that memories about when we last ate can influence whether we decide to eat and how much we consume at any given time, quite apart from what internal cues from our bodies may be telling us. In this research, researchers offered several meals in a row to two individuals who had suffered extensive bilateral damage to the hippocampus and amygdala—structures that play a role in memory. As a result of these injuries, these people could not remember recent events. Both individuals were offered a meal at lunch time. A few minutes after eating it, they were offered a second meal, and then, a

FIGURE 8.5
Many Factors Contribute to Our Eating Habits—And Ultimately to Weight Gain
Weight gain is determined by the interaction of many factors, including genetic predisposition, eating habits, environmental factors, socioeconomic factors, attentional processes, and our own bodies' reaction to weight gain. Several of these factors are illustrated by this scene of a family "pigging out" on high-calorie foods while living the life of "couch potatoes."

few minutes after eating that one, were offered yet a third meal. Results indicated that both people consumed the second meal, and that one of them ate part of the third meal as well. Yet, both rated their hunger as lower after consuming the first meal than before it. Why, then, did they eat again? Apparently because they could not remember that they had just eaten! Findings such as these underscore the main point we want to make: Many mechanisms operating together influence hunger motivation and eating.

■ Factors in weight gain: Why many people experience difficulty in the long-term regulation of body weight.

There can be little doubt that at the present time, "thin is in," at least in most Western cultures. As a result, consumers in many countries spend huge sums each year on books and other products related to weight loss. Despite these efforts, however, many people can't seem to prevent their weight from increasing. As a result, there is a widening gap between people's desired weight (most want to be slim) and their actual weight. What factors are responsible for this trend? Research findings point to several (refer to Figure 8.5).

First, part of the problem involves the effects of learning. Many people acquire eating habits that are very likely to produce excess pounds. They learn to prefer high-calorie meals that are rich in protein and fats—Big Macs, for instance. Further, they learn to associate the act of eating with many different contexts and situations. If you feel a strong urge to snack every time you sit down in front of the TV or a movie screen, you know what we mean. The desire to eat can be classically conditioned (see Chapter 5); cues associated with eating when we are hungry can acquire the capacity to prompt eating when we are not hungry.

Second, genetic factors interact with these changes in diet and can, for many people, intensify them. Genes can affect a person's appetite, satiety cues, rate of metabolism, and how the body stores fat. Consider the situation faced by our ancestors: Periods of plenty alternated with periods of famine. Under these conditions, people who were efficient at storing excess calories as fat during times of plenty gained an important advantage: They were more likely to survive during famines and to have children. As a result, all of us living today have some tendency to gain weight when we overeat—much to our dismay!

Third, environmental and cultural factors appear to play an important role. In recent years, the portion size of many foods has increased dramatically. When we were teenagers, a Coke or Pepsi was eight ounces; now, one-liter bottles (about thirty-two ounces!) are being offered as a single serving. Similarly, McDonald's hamburgers were originally small and thin and contained about two hundred calories; now, most people purchase double cheeseburgers or Big Macs containing four hundred or five hundred calories. Because people tend to eat their entire portion of food, no matter how big it is, this, too, may be a factor in the rising rate of obesity. The term "serving size" actually seems to differ culturally. Take, for example, a serving of yogurt. In the United States, a standard carton of yogurt contains eight ounces, whereas in France, just a little over half that amount constitutes one serving. New research by Geier and colleagues (2006) tested American's propensity to "super-size" by making differing sizes of snacks available (at no cost) to people in various public settings. For example, large Tootsie Rolls on one day, small ones on another day, or whole soft pretzels some of the time compared to pretzels cut in half at other times. Snackers consistently consumed significantly more when larger portions were available. Because people might limit themselves to one serving, so as not to be perceived as gluttonous, smaller servings could, of course, result in less eating, and potentially contribute to a decline in obesity.

Fourth, socioeconomic factors can affect obesity. A study of adolescents (Wardle et al., 2004) found that individuals from more affluent households held different attitudes toward weight than their less affluent counterparts and were more apt to have engaged in healthier approaches to weight control. The more affluent adolescents also had higher levels of dietary self-discipline. Similarly, what happens to your eating habits when you're in a group of people? Do you eat more or less? Research indicates that the behavior of a person's companions can cause him or her to make adjustments in food intake, so as not to be perceived in a negative light, such as lacking self-control (Herman et al., 2003). When groups of people eat together, such as at large family gatherings, there is usually much more available food and people typically eat over longer periods of time. In these situations, it's not surprising that many people tend to overeat.

Fifth, overeating can take place when we are trying to escape from a negative experience or personal failure or are engrossed in highly cognitive activities, such as reading, doing computer work, or engaging in stimulating conversation (Ward & Mann, 2000). Why? When our minds are actively engaged in another activity, we are less likely to pay attention to cues that usually guide how much we eat.

One final factor—and perhaps the most discouraging of all—involves the human body's reaction to weight gain. Common sense might suggest that when we gain weight, internal mechanisms that tend to return us to our initial, healthy weight might spring into action. In fact, the opposite seems to be true. Such mechanisms do exist, and they normally serve to regulate our weight within a specific range (our current *set point*). Unfortunately, growing evidence suggests that once we gain a significant amount of weight, our sensitivity to a chemical produced by our bodies that reduces appetite and speeds metabolism (*leptin*) actually *decreases*. The result: Once we start to gain weight, it becomes harder and harder to stop (Gladwell, 1998). The process *can* be halted if we lose weight and maintain the loss for several years, but this requires more willpower and discipline than many people seem to possess.

Taking all these factors together, it is not surprising that many people experience difficulties in regulating their weight over the long term. There are simply

FIGURE 8.6
Sexual Motivation: One of Our Most Powerful Motives
Judging from ads in magazines, on billboards—virtually everywhere!—sexual motivation is a very strong motive for human beings.

too many variables or conditions that, acting together, overwhelm the mechanisms that establish and maintain a balance between our internal needs and the food we consume.

KEY QUESTIONS

• What factors play a role in the regulation of eating?
• What factors override this system, so that many people fail to maintain a stable weight?

Sexual Motivation: The Most Intimate Motive

Suppose that voyagers from another planet arrived on earth and visited large cities in many different countries. What would they see? Among other things, large numbers of advertisements designed to attract attention through the use of sex-related images (see Figure 8.6). In fact, so common are such displays that the alien visitors might quickly conclude that humans are obsessed with sex. While advertisements may well exaggerate our interest in sex, it is clear that **sexual motivation**—our motivation to engage in sexual activity—is a powerful one. Let's see what psychologists have discovered about it.

■ **Hormones and sexual behavior.**

As we saw in Chapter 7, the onset of puberty involves rapid increases in the activity of the sex glands, or **gonads.** The hormones produced by these glands have many effects on the body, and for many species, they strongly affect sexual motivation. In fact, sex hormones exert what are usually termed *activation effects*—in their presence, sexual behavior occurs, and while in their absence, sexual behavior does not occur or takes place with a very low frequency. For example, in rats, the

Sexual motivation:
Motivation to engage in various forms of sexual relations.

Gonads:
The primary sex glands.

species for whom the link between sex hormones and sexual behavior has been most extensively studied, females show receptivity to males only at times during their menstrual cycle when concentrations of certain sex hormones are high. Once these levels drop—regardless of whether mating has resulted in fertilization—females are no longer receptive to males. Additional evidence for a link between sex hormones and mating is evidenced when, for many species, removal of the ovaries totally eliminates female sexual receptivity to males. Removal of the testes in males produces similar, though somewhat less clear-cut, results. In many species, then, hormones produced by the gonads play a key role in sexual motivation (Wallen, 2001).

Humans, and to some degree other primates, are an exception to this general pattern. Although findings indicate that many women report substantial changes in sexual desire over the course of their menstrual cycle, these changes do not occur at times when hormones, such as estrogen, are at peak levels (Zillmann, Schweitzer, & Mundorf, 1994). On the contrary, peaks of sexual desire or interest seem to occur when such hormones are at relatively low levels. Further, many women continue to engage in and enjoy sexual relations after *menopause*, when the hormonal output of their ovaries drops sharply. And, in men, there is little evidence of a clear link between blood levels of sex hormones such as *testosterone* and sexual responsiveness (Byrne, 1982).

These findings seem to suggest that sex hormones play little role in human sexual motivation. However, recent evidence indicates that, in fact, such hormones may exert subtle effects on our behavior. For instance, several studies indicate that women find masculine faces—and men who show good self-presentation skills (e.g., high levels of eye contact)—more appealing during ovulation (when women are most likely to become pregnant) than at other times (Gangstead et al., 2004; Penton-Woak & Perrett, 2000). Similarly, in another intriguing study, female participants were asked to decide whether faces shown on a computer screen were males or females. Results indicated that for male faces, women performed this task more quickly when they were at high risk for conception (when female sex hormones were high) than at other times in their menstrual cycles (when sex hormones were low). For female faces, no such differences emerged (Macrae et al., 2002).

Apparently women can also detect paternal qualities in men from facial cues. In one study, Roney and colleagues (2006) asked women to examine photos of men's faces and then rate them according to how masculine, attractive, and kind they appeared, plus whether they thought the men liked children. Then, the women rated the men's attractiveness as short-term romantic partners or as long-term partners for relationships, such as marriage. Each man had been tested for testosterone levels and for his interest in children. Results showed that the women were quite accurate at predicting both testosterone levels and interest in children by looking at the men's faces, and these factors played key roles in how attractive the women found the men. The men with higher testosterone levels were generally picked out of the group as more masculine than men with lower testosterone levels, which the women preferred for potential short-term relationships. Those men perceived as "liking kids" were rated higher by women for potential long-term partners, and interestingly, were the same men who had registered the greatest interest in children on a pre-photo-shoot survey.

Findings such as these suggest that sex hormones do play some role in human sexual behavior. In general, though, the link between these hormones and sexual motivation appears to be far less clear and less compelling for humans than is true for many other species. In sum, while sex hormones are not as clearly linked to sexual motivation in humans as in other species, there is some evidence that other substances produced by our bodies do play a role in such motivation, and even in romantic love. Thus, there does appear to be a biochemical side to love, but we are only just beginning to understand it.

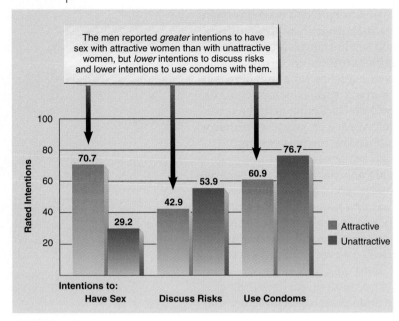

FIGURE 8.7
Physical Attractiveness and Safe Sex: A Deadly Combination?
Participants reported greater intentions to have sex with the attractive females, but lower intentions to take precautionary behaviors, despite the fact they rated the level of risk associated with having sex with attractive and unattractive women as being equal.
Source: Based on data from Kruse & Fromme, 2005.

■ Human sexual behavior: An evolutionary perspective.

A very different approach to understanding human sexual motivation, and especially to understanding potential differences between women and men in this respect, is provided by evolutionary psychology—the view that many aspects of our behavior reflect, at least in part, the effects of evolution. One question evolutionary psychology has addressed is: Do women and men differ in their sexual behavior or, more specifically, in what are known as *mating strategies*—the ways in which they choose sexual partners? In the past, it was widely assumed that they do. For instance, there was a general belief that men seek variety—they want to have as many different sexual partners as possible—while women are less interested in having many partners and instead prefer stable, long-term relationships. Although these views are almost certainly an exaggeration, research findings indicate that they may contain a grain of truth. For instance, when asked how long they would have to know someone before consenting to sexual relations with them, men name much shorter periods of time than do women (Buss & Schmitt, 1993). Similarly, men indeed report that they would like to have more sexual partners in the future than do women (Schmitt, 2003). Not surprisingly, physical attractiveness also influences both men's and women's decisions regarding choice of potential sexual partners (see Fletcher et al., 2004; Li & Kenrick, 2006). However, intriguing new findings seem to indicate this tendency may have a definite downside! In one recent study, Kruse and Fromme (2005) showed men photos of attractive and unattractive women and then had them evaluate the women in terms of desirability and the likelihood they would have sex with them. Additionally, the men were asked about the level of risk associated having sex with both the attractive and unattractive women and the likelihood they would take precautionary actions. As expected, the men found the attractive women more desirable and they reported greater intentions to have sex with them as compared to the unattractive women (see Figure 8.7). But surprisingly, the men reported they would be *less* likely to practice safer sex behaviors, such as discussing sexual history and using condoms, with the *attractive* women, despite the fact they viewed the risks associated with having sex with the attractive and unattractive women as being equal (Kruse & Fromme, 2005). One explanation for these findings stems from people's tendency to overgeneralize their perceptions of other people based on their physical appearance. Specifically, research indicates that people tend to assume that individuals who are physically attractive also possess more positive personal characteristics than do unattractive individuals (Eagly et al., 1991). Thus, the men may have been acting in accordance with the mistaken belief that what is beautiful is also good (see Dion, Berscheid, & Walster, 1972).

To summarize then, there seem to be some differences between males and females where short-term sexual strategies are concerned (Buss, 1999). But why is this the case? Many different possibilities exist, including the fact that cultural beliefs simply cause people to answer questions about their sexual preferences in accordance with such views. In other words, men report that they want many partners because this is consistent with the gender stereotype for men, and women report that they want fewer partners because this is consistent with the gender stereotype for women. Another possibility is suggested by evolutionary psychology.

The evolutionary view—which, we should add, is quite controversial—suggests that by having sex with many different women, men can father a large number of children, many more than if they had sex with only one woman. In contrast, no matter how many lovers a woman has, she can have only one child at a time. Moreover, the investment in having a child is much greater for women than it is for men: Women are the ones who are pregnant for nine months. Evolutionary psychology suggests that because of this, natural selection has tended to produce a stronger preference for sexual variety among males than among females. The reasoning behind this suggestion is as follows: Men who prefer many different mates produce more offspring than men with a weaker preference for sexual variety. As a result, a preference for variety has become widespread among males. In contrast, women who prefer sexual variety do not necessarily produce more children, so a preference for sexual variety is not as strongly favored by natural selection.

But there is a serious flaw in this reasoning that you may already have noticed: How could there have evolved a strong desire for sexual variety if no women ever showed an interest in such behavior? After all, having sex requires two partners, so some women, at least, must also have found variety enticing! How do evolutionary psychologists respond to this objection? By suggesting that by having multiple partners, women could gain valuable resources from them (e.g., food, gifts); alternatively, by having many lovers, a woman could perfect her love-making skills, and so perhaps replace her current mate with a more desirable one (Buss, 1999).

We should add that although the evolutionary perspective on human sexual behavior is intriguing, it is only one of many approaches and is quite controversial. So it is probably best to view it as interesting "food for thought" rather than as a firm basis for answering complex questions about our sexuality.

■ Sexual orientation.

While a large majority of human beings are exclusively **heterosexual** (they engage in sexual relations only with members of the opposite sex), some are **bisexual** (they seek partners from their own as well as the other sex), and still others are exclusively **homosexual** (they seek partners only from their own sex) (Laumann et al., 1994). What factors influence or determine **sexual orientation**? In other words, why are some people exclusively homosexual while most others are exclusively heterosexual? This is a complex question and one to which no one—psychologists included—can yet offer a complete answer. Initially, however, emphasis was on environmental factors. For example, psychodynamic theory suggested that homosexuality resulted from having an overprotective mother and a distant, ineffectual father. Other views emphasized factors ranging from being separated from members of the opposite sex during childhood (e.g., attending all-boy or all-girl schools) to sexual abuse by parents or other adults. Decades of research have failed to yield clear support for any of these suggestions (Breedlove, 1994). Indeed, large-scale studies of thousands of homosexuals have failed to find any consistent differences between them and heterosexuals in terms of early life experiences. There is some indication that extremely feminine behavior in young boys or extremely masculine behavior in young girls predicts later development of homosexuality (Bailey & Zucker, 1995), but aside from that, findings relating to the role of various environmental factors have been far from conclusive.

Evidence is growing, however, for the role of genetic and other biological factors in homosexuality. For example, Green (1987) followed forty-four extremely feminine boys for fifteen years—from early childhood until they were young adults. Fully three-fourths later became homosexual or bisexual. In contrast, only one boy from a group of typically masculine boys became homosexual. Moreover, efforts by parents

Heterosexual:
A sexual orientation in which individuals prefer sexual relations with members of the other sex.

Bisexual:
A sexual orientation in which individuals engage in sexual relations with members of both sexes.

Homosexual:
A sexual orientation in which individuals prefer sexual relations with members of their own sex.

Sexual orientation:
Individuals' preference for sexual relations with their own sex, the other sex, or both.

or professionals (psychologists, psychiatrists) to alter the behavior of the feminine boys made little or no difference. Such findings point to the possibility that some individuals have a biological predisposition toward homosexuality or bisexuality.

Other findings indicate that there may be subtle differences between the brains of heterosexual and homosexual individuals. For instance, the anterior commissure, a bundle of nerve fibers that allows communication between the two hemispheres of the brain, is larger in homosexual men than in heterosexual men or women (Allen & Gorski, 1992). Similarly, the hypothalamus is smaller in homosexual men than in heterosexual men (LeVay, 1991). Twin studies, too, point to the role of genetic and biological factors in homosexuality. If one identical twin is homosexual, there is a greater than fifty-fifty chance that the other twin, too, will be homosexual. Among fraternal twins, this figure drops to only 22 percent (Bailey & Pillard, 1991). Homosexual men also seem to differ in some cognitive abilities from heterosexual men, falling in between heterosexual men and heterosexual women in their performance on visual/spatial ability tests (Witelson, 1991). Finally, emerging evidence suggests that the prevalence of homosexuality differs substantially depending on how the term is defined (see Savin-Williams, 2006).

Taking all available evidence into account, it seems reasonable to conclude that sexual orientation is not simply a matter of preference or free will; rather, it may stem, at least in part, from biological and genetic factors that are not directly under individuals' control and that operate outside their conscious awareness. How these factors exert their influence in shaping sexual preference, however, remains to be determined.

KEY QUESTIONS

- What role do hormones play in human sexual motivation?
- How does evolutionary psychology explain differences in the mating strategies of women and men?
- What factors appear to play a role in determining sexual orientation?

Achievement Motivation: The Desire to Excel

Hunger and sex—these are motives we share with many other forms of life. Some motives, however, appear to be unique to our own species. In this section, we'll focus on one such motive—**achievement motivation** (often termed "need for achievement")—the desire to accomplish difficult tasks or to excel. That individuals differ greatly in the desire for achievement is obvious, but what are the effects of these differences? Let's see what psychologists have discovered about this issue. (Several methods for measuring such differences exist, but the details of them are not central to this discussion, so we won't describe them here.)

■ Effects of achievement motivation.

Everyone has known people they would describe as high or low in achievement motivation, and some of the differences between these people are far from surprising. For instance, as you might expect, persons high in achievement motivation tend to get higher grades in school, earn more rapid promotions, and attain greater success in running their own businesses than people low in such motivation (Andrews, 1967; Raynor, 1970). In fact, some evidence suggests that entrepreneurs—people who start their own businesses—are higher in achievement motivation than most other people, and are also higher in this respect than managers—people who prefer to work for large, existing companies (see Collins, Hanges, & Locke, 2004; Shane, 2003).

People high in achievement motivation differ from people low in this motive in other respects, too. First, people high in achievement motivation tend to prefer tasks that are moderately difficult and challenging. The reason they tend to avoid

Achievement motivation: The desire to accomplish difficult tasks and meet standards of excellence.

very easy tasks is obvious: Such tasks don't pose enough challenge for people high in achievement motivation. But why do they prefer tasks that are moderately challenging to ones that are extremely difficult? Because the chance of failing on extremely difficult tasks is too high, and such people want success above everything else (Lee, Sheldon, & Turban, 2003).

Another characteristic of people high in achievement motivation is that they have a stronger-than-average desire for feedback on their performance: They want to know how well they are doing so they can adjust their goals to make them challenging, but not impossible. Because of this desire for feedback, people high in achievement motivation tend to prefer jobs in which rewards are closely related to individual performance—merit-based pay systems. They generally don't like working in situations in which everyone receives the same across-the-board raise, regardless of their performance (see Turban & Keon, 1993).

Finally, as you might expect, people high in achievement motivation tend to excel in performance under conditions in which their achievement motive is activated (see McClelland, 1995). Situations in which they are challenged to do their best, in which they are confronted with difficult goals, or in which they compete against others are "grist for the mill" of high-achievement people, and they generally rise to the occasion in terms of excellent performance.

KEY QUESTIONS

- What is achievement motivation?
- What are the effects of achievement motivation on behavior?

Intrinsic Motivation: How, Sometimes, to Turn Play into Work

Individuals perform many activities simply because they find them enjoyable. Hobbies, gourmet dining, lovemaking—these are a few of the actions that fit within this category. Such activities may be described as stemming from **intrinsic motivation:** We perform them because of the pleasure they yield, not because they lead to external rewards. But what happens if people are given external rewards for performing these activities—if, for example, they are paid for sipping vintage wines or for pursuing their favorite hobby? Research findings suggest that they may then actually experience reductions in intrinsic motivation. In other words, they may become *less* motivated to engage in such activities. Why? Here is one explanation: When people consider their own behavior, they conclude that they chose to perform the activities in question partly to obtain the external reward provided, not only because they enjoyed these activities. To the extent they reach that conclusion, they may then view their own interest in these activities as lower than was previously the case. In short, when provided with an external reward for performing some activity they enjoy, they shift from viewing their own behavior as stemming from intrinsic motivation ("I do it because I enjoy it") to perceiving it as stemming from external rewards ("I do it partly because of the external rewards I receive"). (See Figure 8.8 on page 314 for a summary of these suggestions.)

Many studies support this reasoning. In such research, some participants were provided with extrinsic rewards for engaging in a task they initially enjoyed, while others were not. When later given an opportunity to perform the task, those who received the external rewards showed reduced motivation to do so (Deci, 1975; Lepper & Green, 1978). These results have important implications for anyone—parents, teachers, managers—seeking to motivate others by means of rewards. If the target people already enjoy various activities, then offering them rewards for performing these activities may lower their intrinsic motivation and so actually reduce rather than enhance their performance!

Fortunately, additional evidence suggests that this is not always the case, and that intrinsic and extrinsic motivation are not necessarily incompatible (Deci & Ryan, 1985; Rigby et al., 1992). If external rewards are viewed as signs of recognition

Intrinsic motivation:
Motivation to perform activities because they are rewarding in and of themselves.

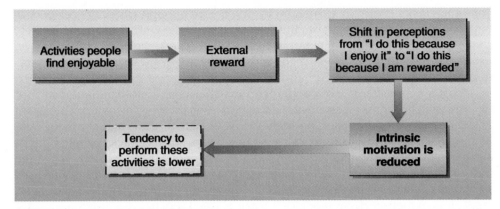

FIGURE 8.8
Intrinsic Motivation: How it Operates
When individuals receive external rewards for performing activities they enjoy, they may conclude that they perform them at least in part to gain the external rewards. As a result, their intrinsic motivation to perform these activities is reduced.

for competence rather than as bribes (Rosenfeld, Folger, & Adelman, 1980), and if the rewards provided are large and satisfying, intrinsic motivation may be enhanced rather than reduced (Lepper & Cordova, 1992; Ryan, 1982). But providing others with extrinsic rewards for performing activities they enjoy does run the risk of undermining their intrinsic motivation, so this is a fact that anyone wishing to motivate others should always keep in mind.

KEY QUESTIONS

- What is intrinsic motivation?
- Why is intrinsic motivation sometimes reduced when individuals receive external rewards for performing activities they enjoy?

Forgiveness: When Compassion Replaces the Desire for Revenge

Almost everyone has experienced intense desires for revenge: Another person harms us in some manner, and we conclude that retaliating against them would be appropriate. Seeking to "pay them back" seems only natural, and we often feel it may accomplish more than just make us feel better—it may produce positive outcomes as well. But, in fact, seeking revenge often has harmful effects for everyone concerned. The people who seek it may feel better temporarily, but their actions may start an upward spiral of retaliation, revenge, further retaliation, and so on, in which all parties are at growing risk. For these reasons, *forgiveness*—giving up the desire to punish those who have hurt us and seeking, instead, to act in kind, helpful ways toward them—may be highly beneficial. In fact, research on this topic suggests forgiveness often has more positive effects than seeking revenge (see McCullough et al., 2001). Recent research seems to indicate that a surprisingly high percentage of people are willing to forgive people who have wounded them—75 percent in one study (Wade et al., 2005).

Why are some people able to forgive more readily than others? In part because of their own traits. Research findings indicate that people who forgive differ from people who find it hard to forgive in several important ways. First, they are higher in *agreeableness* (a tendency to trust others and want to help them) and higher in *emotional stability* (low vulnerability to negative moods or emotions), two aspects of personality we'll examine in detail in Chapter 9 (Berry et al., 2001, 2005). Second, they tend to possess higher levels of self-esteem and greater self-confidence (Wade & Worthington, 2005). Finally, some research suggests that people who forgive are more spiritually or religiously inclined than people who are less likely to forgive (McCullough, 2001).

What do such people do to forgive their former enemies? They experience empathy toward them, sharing or at least understanding the feelings and emotions that caused the transgressors to harm them. In addition, they make generous attributions about the causes of their enemies' behavior, concluding that they had good reasons for acting as they did, even though this harmed them in some way. And they avoid ruminating about past transgressions; once these are over they put them out of their minds and concentrate on other things (McCullough, 2001). Success in granting forgiveness can be fostered by having people recall occasions when they were the offender; recalling the liberating feelings they experienced when someone else forgave them can increase the willingness to offer the same gift to another wrongdoer. It is important to note, however, that forgiveness and reconciliation do not always go hand in hand. Forgiveness can change the way a person views the offender and/or the offending behavior, but forgiveness may not result in restoration of a damaged relationship (Wade & Worthington, 2005).

How forgiveness is thought about and practiced varies according to one's culture (McCullough, Pargament & Thoresen, 2000). For example, in collectivist societies such as the People's Republic of China, willingness to forgive is influenced more by societal needs, such as a perceived need to preserve social harmony, and less by personality variables or religiosity as in Western cultures (Fu, Watkins, & Hui, 2004). Overall, most psychologists have concluded that forgiveness is indeed a better strategy for happiness than maintaining anger and strong desires for revenge. In sum, there seems to be a large grain of truth in the proverb stating, "To err is human, to forgive, divine."

KEY QUESTIONS

- Why are some people able to forgive more easily than others?
- How do they forgive people who have harmed them?

EMOTIONS: THEIR NATURE, EXPRESSION, AND IMPACT

Can you imagine life without emotions—without joy, anger, sorrow, or fear? Perhaps, but what would such an existence be like—a life without any feelings? Because emotions play such a critical role in enriching and informing our lives, few of us would choose such an existence.

But what, precisely, are emotions? The closer we look, the more complex these reactions seem to be. There is general agreement among scientists who study emotions, however, that they involve three major components: (1) physiological changes within our bodies—shifts in heart rate, blood pressure, and so on; (2) subjective cognitive states—the personal experiences we label as emotions; and (3) expressive behaviors—outward signs of these internal reactions (Tangney et al., 1996; Zajonc & McIntosh, 1992).

In this discussion, we'll first look at several contrasting theories of emotion. Then we'll consider the biological basis of emotions. Third, we'll examine how emotions are expressed. Next, we'll turn to **affect**, temporary and relatively mild shifts in current mood, examining the complex interplay between affect and cognition. We'll conclude with a brief look at what psychologists have discovered about personal happiness (*subjective well-being*).

The Nature of Emotions: Some Contrasting Views

Many different theories of emotions have been proposed, but among these, three have been most influential. These are named after the scientists who proposed them: the *Cannon–Bard, James–Lange,* and *Schachter–Singer* theories.

Affect:
Temporary and relatively mild shifts in current feelings and mood.

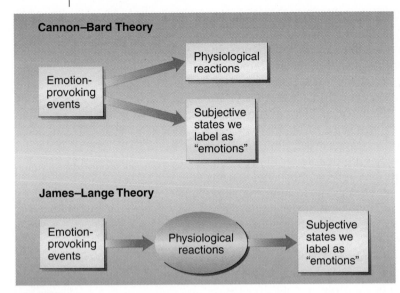

FIGURE 8.9
Two Major Theories of Emotion
According to the Cannon–Bard theory, emotion-provoking stimuli simultaneously evoke physiological reactions and the subjective states we label as emotions. According to the James–Lange theory, emotion-provoking events produce physiological reactions, and it is our awareness of these changes in bodily states that we label as emotions.

Cannon–Bard theory:
A theory of emotion suggesting that various emotion-provoking events simultaneously produce subjective reactions labeled as emotions and physiological arousal.

James–Lange theory:
A theory of emotion suggesting that emotion-provoking events produce various physiological reactions, and that recognition of these is responsible for subjective emotional experiences.

Facial feedback hypothesis:
A hypothesis indicating that facial expressions can produce changes in emotional states.

■ The Cannon–Bard and James–Lange theories: Which comes first—action or feeling?

Imagine that in one of your courses you are required to make a class presentation. As you walk to the front of the room, your pulse races, your mouth feels dry, and you can feel beads of perspiration on your forehead. In short, you are terrified. What is the basis for this feeling? Contrasting answers are offered by the Cannon–Bard and James–Lange theories of emotion.

Let's begin with the **Cannon–Bard theory,** because it is consistent with our own commonsense beliefs about emotions. This theory suggests that various emotion-provoking events induce *simultaneously* the subjective experiences we label as emotions and the physiological reactions that accompany them. In the situation just described, the sight of the audience and of your professor, pen poised to evaluate your performance, causes you to experience a racing heart, a dry mouth, and other signs of physiological arousal and, at the same time, to experience subjective feelings you label as fear. In other words, this situation stimulates various portions of your nervous system so that both arousal, mediated by your *autonomic nervous system* (discussed in Chapter 2), and subjective feelings, mediated by your cerebral cortex and other portions of the brain, are produced.

In contrast, the **James–Lange theory** offers a more surprising view of emotion. It suggests that subjective emotional experiences are actually the *result* of physiological changes within our bodies. In other words, you feel frightened when making your speech *because* you notice that your heart is racing, your mouth is dry, and so on. As James himself put it (1890, page 966), "We feel sorry because we cry, angry because we strike, and afraid because we tremble." (See Figure 8.9 for a comparison of these two theories.)

Which of these theories is more accurate? Until recently, most evidence seemed to favor the Cannon–Bard approach: Emotion-provoking events produce both physiological arousal and the subjective experiences we label as emotions. Now, however, the pendulum of scientific opinion has moved toward greater acceptance of the James–Lange approach—the view that we experience emotions because of our awareness of physiological reactions to various stimuli or situations. Several lines of evidence point to this conclusion. First, studies conducted with modern equipment indicate that different emotions are indeed associated with different patterns of physiological activity (Levenson, 1992). Not only do various emotions feel different, it appears they also result in somewhat different patterns of bodily changes, including contrasting patterns of brain and muscle activity (Ekman, Davidson, & Friesen, 1990; Izard, 1991).

Second, support for the James–Lange theory is also provided by research on the **facial feedback hypothesis** (Laird, 1984). This hypothesis suggests that changes in our facial expressions sometimes produce shifts in our emotional experiences rather than merely reflecting them. In addition, other research suggests that changing our bodily postures (see Flack, Laird, & Cavallaro, 1999) or even the tone of our voices (see Siegman & Boyle, 1993) may influence emotional experiences. In view of such findings, the facial feedback hypothesis has been renamed

TABLE 8.2 Theories of Emotion: An Overview

The theories summarized here are among the ones that have received the most attention from researchers.

Theory of Emotion	Basic Assumptions
Cannon–Bard theory	Emotion-provoking events induce, simultaneously, the subjective experiences we label as emotions and the physiological reactions that accompany them.
James–Lange theory	Subjective emotional experiences result from physiological changes within our bodies (e.g., we feel sorry because we cry, frightened because we run away from something, etc.).
Schachter–Singer (two-factor) theory	Emotion-provoking events produce increased arousal; in response to these feelings, we search the external environment to identify the causes behind them. The factors we identify then determine the label we place on our arousal and the emotion we experience.

the *peripheral feedback effect*, to suggest that emotions can be influenced by more than simply facial expressions. Although there are many complexities in examining this hypothesis, the results of several studies offer support for its accuracy (see Ekman, Davidson, & Friesen, 1990). These findings suggest that there may be a substantial grain of truth in the James–Lange theory (Zajonc, Murphy, & Inglehart, 1989). Though subjective emotional experiences *are* often produced by specific external stimuli, as the Cannon–Bard view suggests, emotional reactions also can be generated by changes in and awareness of our own bodily states, as the James–Lange theory contends (Ekman, 1992).

■ **Schachter and Singer's two-factor theory.**

Strong emotions are a common part of daily life, but how do we tell them apart? How do we know that we are angry rather than frightened, or sad rather than surprised? One potential answer is provided by a third theory of emotion. According to this view, known as the **Schachter–Singer theory,** or sometimes as the **two-factor theory,** emotion-provoking events produce increased arousal (Schachter & Singer, 1962). In response to these feelings, we then search the external environment to identify the causes behind them. The factors we then select play a key role in determining the label we place on our arousal, and so in determining the emotion we experience. If we feel aroused after a near-hit in traffic, we will probably label our emotion as "fear" or perhaps "anger." If, instead, we feel aroused in the presence of an attractive person, we may label our arousal as "attraction" or even "love." In short, we perceive ourselves to be experiencing the emotion that external cues tell us we *should* be feeling. This contrasts with the James–Lange theory, which suggests that we focus on internal, physiological cues to determine whether we are experiencing an emotion and what this emotion is. The Schachter–Singer theory is a two-factor view because it considers both arousal and the cognitive appraisal we perform in our efforts to identify the causes of such arousal.

Many studies provide support for the Schachter–Singer theory (Reisenzein, 1983; Sinclair et al., 1994), so it does seem to provide important insights into the process through which we label our own emotions. (See Table 8.2 for an overview of the theories discussed in this section.)

Schachter–Singer theory (two-factor theory):
A theory of emotion suggesting that our subjective emotional states are determined, at least in part, by the cognitive labels we attach to feelings of arousal.

Two-factor theory (of emotion)
See Schachter–Singer theory.

KEY QUESTIONS

• How do the Cannon–Bard and James–Lange theories differ?
• What is the Schachter–Singer theory of emotion?

The Biological Basis of Emotions

As we noted earlier, emotions are complex reactions involving not only the intense subjective feelings we label as "joy," "anger," "sorrow," "fear," and so on, but also outward expressions of emotions and the ability (or abilities) to understand emotional information (e.g., the ability to "read" the emotional reactions of others). Research on the biological and neural bases of emotions indicates that different portions of the brain may play a role in each of these components. Research concerning the neural basis of emotion is complex, so here we'll simply try to summarize a few of the key findings.

First, it appears that the right cerebral hemisphere plays an especially important role in emotional functions (see Coulson et al., 2005; Harrington, 1995). Individuals with damage to the right hemisphere have difficulty understanding the emotional tone of another person's voice or correctly describing emotional scenes (Heller, 1997; Heller, Nitschke, & Miller, 1998). Similarly, healthy people with no damage to their brains do better at identifying others' emotions when such information is presented to their right hemisphere rather than to their left hemisphere (it is exposed to one part or the other of the visual field; see Chapter 3) (see Ladavas, Umilta, & Ricci-Bitti, 1980). The right hemisphere also seems to be specialized for the expression of emotion; patients with damage to the right hemisphere are less successful at expressing emotions through the tone of their voice than are people without such damage (Borod, 1993).

In addition, there appear to be important differences between the left and right hemispheres of the brain with respect to two key aspects of emotion: *valence* (the extent to which an emotion is pleasant or unpleasant) and *arousal* (its intensity). Activation of the left hemisphere is associated with approach, response to reward, and positive affect (i.e., feelings), while activation of the right hemisphere is associated with avoidance, withdrawal from aversive stimuli, and negative affect (Root, Wong, & Kinsbourne, 2006). Further, anterior (frontal) regions of the hemispheres are associated primarily with the valence (pleasant–unpleasant) dimension, while posterior regions are associated primarily with arousal (intensity). These findings have important implications for understanding the neural basis of various psychological disorders. Consider, for instance, depression and anxiety—disorders we'll examine in detail in Chapter 11. Both involve negative feelings or emotions, but depression is usually associated with low arousal (depressed people lack energy), while anxiety is associated with high arousal (if you've ever experienced anxiety right before an exam, you know this very well!). This leads to interesting predictions: People suffering from depression should show reduced activity in the right posterior region, while people suffering from anxiety should show increased activity in that brain region (see Figure 8.10). These predictions have been confirmed in several studies (see Heller, Etienne, & Miller, 1995). Insight into the neural mechanisms that underlie such disorders can be an important first step toward developing effective treatments for them, so our growing knowledge of the neural bases of emotions has important practical as well as scientific implications.

Newer research using brain imaging techniques (refer to Chapter 2) to map the neural circuitry that underlies specific categories of emotion, however, has produced somewhat mixed results (Barrett, 2006). On the one hand, a large number of studies that have attempted to identify unique brain activation patterns for specific emotions, including fear, anger, sadness, disgust, and happiness, have been largely unsuccessful (see Murphy et al., 2003; Phan et al., 2002). Instead, the patterns of brain activation for different emotions appear to overlap. On the other hand, researchers have been more successful in identifying emotion-location correspondence in specific brain structures. In particular, the *amygdala* (see Chapter 2) has been found to become active when individuals are experiencing negative emotions, particularly fear (see Hamann et al., 2002; LaBar et al., 1998, 2003) and sadness. For example, Wang and colleagues (2005) used *f* MRI to measure brain ac-

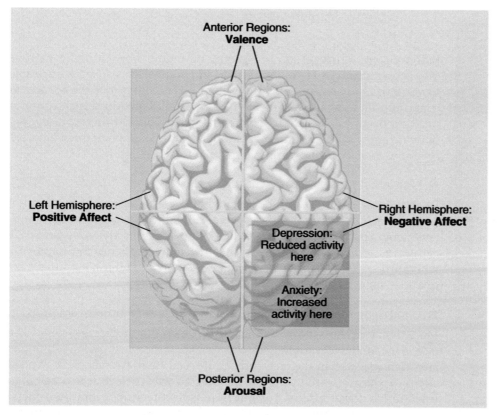

**Anterior Regions:
Valence**

**Left Hemisphere:
Positive Affect**

**Right Hemisphere:
Negative Affect**

**Depression:
Reduced activity
here**

**Anxiety:
Increased
activity here**

**Posterior Regions:
Arousal**

FIGURE 8.10

Role of the Cerebral Hemisphere in Emotion—and In Psychological Disorders
Growing evidence indicates that activation of the left cerebral hemisphere is associated with positive emotions, while activation of the right hemisphere is associated with negative emotions. Further, activation of anterior (frontal) portions of both hemispheres is associated with the valence (pleasantness—unpleasantness) of emotions, while activation of the posterior (rear) portions of the hemispheres is associated with arousal—the intensity of emotions. Together, these findings suggest that depressed people should show reduced activity in the right posterior regions, while anxious persons should show increased activity in these regions. These results have been confirmed in recent studies.

tivity in a group of participants as they were performing a computer task. Participants were instructed to press a computer key each time they saw a "target" stimulus (a circle), but not when they saw other *distractor* stimuli that included photos of people exhibiting either sad or emotionally neutral facial expressions. The results showed higher levels of activity in the amygdala and related structures in response to the sad photos than to either the neutral photos or to the circles. Please note, however, that other brain-imaging studies have reported that the left amygdala may also be activated by *positive* stimuli and the positive emotions they induce (see Hamann et al., 2002). In addition, it appears that the amygdala plays a role in memories for emotion-producing stimuli or experiences (Gallagher, 2000). So, it participates both in the occurrence of emotional arousal and in subsequent memory for the stimuli that elicited it. Stay tuned for further developments as psychologists continue to use modern techniques to improve our understanding of the neural circuitry that underlies emotion—it's sure to come!

KEY QUESTIONS

- What roles do the left and right cerebral hemispheres play in emotions?
- What is the role of the amygdala in emotions?

FIGURE 8.11
Nonverbal Cues: External Guides to Internal Reactions
People often reveal their emotions through nonverbal cues—facial expressions, body movements or postures, and other observable actions.

The External Expression of Emotion: Outward Signs of Inner Feelings

Emotions are a private affair. No one, no matter how intimate with us they are, can truly share our subjective inner experiences. Yet, we are able to recognize the presence of various emotions in others, and we are able to communicate our own feelings to them as well. How does such communication occur? A large part of the answer involves **nonverbal cues**—outward signs of others' internal emotional states shown in their facial expressions, body postures, and other behaviors (see Figure 8.11).

■ **Nonverbal cues: The basic channels.**

Several decades of research on nonverbal cues suggests that this kind of communication occurs through several different *channels* or paths simultaneously. The most revealing of these involve *facial expressions* and *body movements and posture*. (We'll also consider nonverbal cues in Chapter 13, where we examine its role in *social thought*—how we think about and try to understand other people.)

■ **Unmasking the face: Facial expressions as clues to others' emotions.**

More than two thousand years ago, the Roman orator Cicero stated, "The face is the image of the soul." By this he meant that feelings and emotions are often reflected in the face and can be read there from specific expressions. Modern research suggests that Cicero was correct: It is possible to learn much about others' current moods and feelings from their facial expressions. In fact, it appears that six different basic emotions are represented clearly, and from an early age, on the human face: anger, fear, sadness, disgust, happiness, and surprise (Ekman, 1992). In addition, some findings suggest that two other emotions—contempt (Rosenberg & Ekman, 1995) and pride (Tracy & Robins, 2004)—may also be quite basic. However, agreement on what specific facial expression represents these emotions is less consistent than that for the six emotions just mentioned.

For many years, it was widely assumed that basic facial expressions such as those for happiness, anger, or disgust are universal: They are recognized by people all over the world as indicating specific emotions (see Ekman & Friesen, 1975). Other research, however, has called this assumption into question (see Russell, 1994). The findings of several studies indicate that while facial expressions may indeed reveal much about others' emotions, such judgments are also affected by the context in which such expressions occur and various situational cues. For instance, if individuals are shown a photo of a face expressing what would normally be judged as fear, but are also read a story suggesting that this person is actually showing anger, many describe the face as showing *anger*—not fear (Carroll & Russell, 1996). Findings such as these suggest that facial expressions may not be as universal in terms of providing clear signals about underlying emotions as was previously assumed.

Newer research on this topic has asked a somewhat different question: Do facial expressions merely reflect the person's emotional feelings or are they an evolved mechanism designed to convey important information useful in predicting the displayer's future behavior? One cross-cultural study tested this idea by showing American, German, and Swiss participants photos of people's facial expressions intended to convey six basic emotions (anger, disgust, fear, happiness, sadness, and surprise) (Horstmann, 2003). The participants' task was to decide whether the facial expressions were signaling a person's emotional feelings or his or her behavioral intentions—what the person was going to do next. Results showed that for all the emotions except *anger*, participants consistently chose emotional feelings as the primary message signaled by the facial expressions. When

Nonverbal cues:
Outward signs of others' emotional states. Such cues involve facial expressions, eye contact, and body language.

shown the angry face, however, participants frequently stated that the person in the photo was about to engage in an aggressive act or they were conveying a warning, such as "back off" or "move away." These results seem to suggest that additional information, such as body movement or posture, may be necessary for observers to make accurate judgments about another person's intentions. We'll consider this possibility in the next section. Emotions communicated by the face are also affected by whether a person uses a direct or averted gaze. In general, joy, love, and anger are more often expressed with a direct gaze, whereas fear, sadness, and disgust are usually conveyed with an averted gaze (Adams & Kleck, 2005).

■ Gestures, posture, and movements.

Try this simple demonstration: First, remember some incident that made you angry—the angrier the better. Think about it for a minute. Now try to remember another incident—one that made you feel happy—the happier the better. Did you change your posture or move your hands, arms, or legs as your thoughts shifted from the first incident to the second? The chances are good that you did, for our current mood or emotion is often reflected in the posture, position, and movement of our bodies. Together, such nonverbal behaviors are sometimes termed **body language,** and they can provide several kinds of information about others' emotions.

First, frequent body movements, especially ones in which a particular part of the body does something to another part, such as touching, scratching, or rubbing, suggest emotional arousal. The greater the frequency of such behavior, the higher a person's level of arousal or nervousness seems to be (Harrigan et al., 1991). Larger patterns of movements involving the whole body can also be informative. Such phrases as "she adopted a threatening posture" and "he greeted her with open arms" suggest that different body postures can be suggestive of contrasting emotional reactions (Aronoff, Woike, & Hyman, 1992).

Recent research (Meeren et al., 2005) indicates that when body language is compatible with facial expression, recognition of those expressions is improved. But when the two are conflicting, an observer's attention will tend to shift toward the emotion they see conveyed by the body. Participants in the Meeren study were asked to direct their attention to facial expressions of computer-created images; in some of these, facial expressions matched body language, while in others they did not. They were then asked to name the emotion pictured. When the photos were mismatched, for example, a fearful face paired with an angry body, the study participants judged the emotions based on the *body language* portrayed, even though they were asked to focus on the face.

Finally, more specific information about others' feelings are often provided by **gestures**—body movements carrying specific meanings in a given culture. In the United States, for example, shrugging one's shoulders means "I don't know." Similarly, a thumb pointing upwards means "Good" or "OK." Gestures often only have meaning in a given culture, so it is wise to be careful about using them while traveling in cultures different from your own: You may offend the people around you without intending to do so! (We'll return to nonverbal cues in Chapter 13 in our discussion of social thought, because the information nonverbal cues provide is often very valuable in the context of our efforts to understand others.)

Body language:
Nonverbal cues involving body posture or movement of body parts.

Gestures:
Movements of various body parts that convey a specific meaning to others.

KEY QUESTIONS

- What emotions are shown by clear facial expressions? What do research findings indicate about the universality of such expressions?
- What information about others' emotions is conveyed by body language?

Emotion and Cognition: How Feelings Shape Thought and Thought Shapes Feelings

Earlier, we asked you to recall incidents that made you feel angry and happy. When you thought about these events, did your mood also change? The chances are good that it did. In many instances, our thoughts seem to exert strong effects on our emotions. This relationship works in the other direction as well. Being in a happy mood often causes us to think happy thoughts, while feeling sad tends to bring negative memories and images to mind. In short, there are important links between *emotion* and *cognition*—between the way we feel and the way we think. Let's take a brief look at some of the evidence for such links (see Forgas, 1995a; Forgas & Fiedler, 1996).

We should clarify one important point before proceeding: Throughout this discussion, we'll focus on *affect*—relatively mild feelings and moods—rather than on intense emotions. The boundary between affective reactions and emotions is somewhat fuzzy, but because most research has focused on the effects of relatively modest shifts in mood—the kind of changes we experience many times each day as a result of ordinary experiences—these will be the focus here.

■ How affect influences cognition.

The findings of many studies indicate that our current moods can strongly influence several aspects of cognition. We have already examined the influence of affect on memory in Chapter 6 (mood-dependent memory), so, here, we'll focus on other ways in which moods or feelings influence cognition. One such effect involves the impact of our current moods or *affective states*, as they are often termed, on our perception of ambiguous stimuli. In general, we perceive and evaluate these stimuli more favorably when we are in a good mood than when we are in a negative one (Isen & Baron, 1991; Isen, 1991). For example, when asked to interview applicants whose qualifications for a job are ambiguous—neither very strong nor very weak—research participants assign higher ratings to applicants when they (the interviewers) are in a positive mood than when they are in a negative mood (see Baron, 1987, 1993).

Another way in which affect influences cognition is through its impact on the style of information processing we adopt. A growing body of research findings indicates that a positive affect encourages us to adopt a flexible, fluid style of thinking, while a negative affect leads us to engage in more systematic and careful processing (see Stroessner & Mackie, 1992). Why? Perhaps because we interpret negative affect as a kind of danger signal, indicating that the current situation requires our full attention (see Edwards & Bryan, 1997).

Our current moods also influence another important aspect of cognition—creativity. The results of several studies suggest that being in a happy mood can increase creativity—perhaps because being in a happy mood activates a wider range of ideas or associations than being in a negative mood, and creativity consists, in part, of combining such associations into new patterns (see Lyubomirsky, King, & Diener, 2005).

Sometimes, we do not even have to experience affective states for them to influence our thinking. Research findings indicate that when making decisions, we often anticipate the emotions we might experience as a result of the outcomes the various choices will produce. We then tend to choose the decision that will maximize our future anticipated positive reactions (e.g., pleasure; Mellers, 2000). The results of many studies are consistent with this view, so it seems to provide an important insight into how our feelings—even anticipated ones—can shape our judgments and decisions (Mellers & McGraw, 2001).

Finally, we should mention research indicating that positive emotions or affective states can trigger upward spirals toward emotional well-being and happiness. Why? Because when individuals feel happy, they tend to adopt what is known as *broad-minded coping*—strategies for dealing with life's problems that are highly adaptive. Such strategies include trying to think of different ways to deal with the problem, taking a step back from the situation to be more objective, and so on. Some evidence (see Fredrickson & Joiner, 2002) indicates that when individuals feel happy, they tend to deal with their problems in these adaptive ways, and this, in turn, makes them happier. The result? An upward spiral toward increasing happiness and adjustment (see Figure 8.12). In other words, experiencing positive emotions and feelings is more than just a "temporary fix" for life's troubles: It may also help us to deal with them more effectively.

■ **How cognition influences affect.**

Most research on the relationship between affect and cognition has focused on how feelings influence thought. However, there is also compelling evidence for the reverse—the impact of cognition on affect. We have already mentioned one aspect of this relationship in our earlier discussion of the two-factor theory of emotion proposed by Schachter and Singer (1962). As you may recall, their theory suggests that often we don't know our own feelings or attitudes directly. Rather, because these internal reactions are often somewhat ambiguous, we look outward—at our own behavior or other aspects of the external world—for clues about our feeling's essential nature. In such cases, the feelings we experience are strongly determined by the interpretation or cognitive labels we select.

A second way in which cognition can affect emotions is through the activation of schemas containing a strong affective component. For example, if we label an individual as belonging to some group, the schema for this social category may suggest what traits he or she probably possesses. In addition, it may also tell us how we feel about such people. Thus, activation of a strong racial, ethnic, or religious schema or stereotype may exert powerful effects on our current feelings or moods.

Third, our thoughts can often influence our reactions to emotion-provoking events. In other words, we use cognitive mechanisms to regulate our emotions or affective states. In general, we use two different tactics: *reappraisal*—cognitive reevaluation of a potentially emotion-eliciting situation to regulate (e.g., decrease) its emotional impact; or *suppression*—a form of response modulation in which we actively inhibit ongoing, emotion-expressive behavior. In other words, reappraisal occurs early, before we are experiencing affect or emotion, while suppression occurs later. Both can be useful means for regulating our emotions or feelings, but because it occurs earlier, reappraisal may sometimes be more effective. Reappraisal decreases the experience of emotion, reduces behavioral expressions of emotion, and may also reduce physiological reactions to emotion-provoking events. In contrast, suppression occurs later, so it does not change the emotional experience and may actually increase physiological reactions (because of the effort being expended to suppress the emotion). But it will strongly suppress outward expressions of emotion. These predictions have been confirmed by several studies (see Gross, 2001).

In sum, as our everyday experience suggests, there are many links between affect and cognition. The way we feel—our current moods—influence the way we think, and our thoughts, in turn, often shape our moods and emotions.

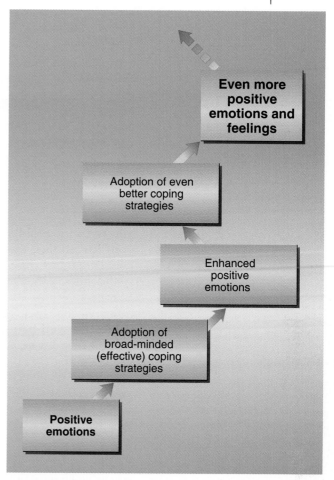

FIGURE 8.12

Positive Emotions: An Important Step on the Road to Happiness

Recent evidence suggests that when people experience positive emotions, they adopt more effective techniques for dealing with the problems they face. This, in turn, causes them to experience more positive feelings and emotions. The result? An upward spiral toward emotional well-being and personal happiness.

Source: Based on suggestions by Fredrickson & Joiner, 2002.

KEY QUESTIONS
- In what ways do our affective states influence cognition?
- In what ways does cognition influence our affective states?

SUBJECTIVE WELL-BEING: CAUSES AND EFFECTS OF PERSONAL HAPPINESS

Suppose you were asked the following questions: "How happy are you?" and "How satisfied are you with your life?" If you were then prompted to answer these questions using a scale that ranged from 1 (very unhappy; very unsatisfied) to 7 (very happy; very satisfied) how would you reply? If you're like most people, you would probably indicate that you are quite happy and quite satisfied with your life. In fact, the results of many studies, including large-scale surveys of people in many different parts of the world, indicate that about 80 percent of respondents say they are very happy and satisfied (Diener, Lucas, & Scollon, 2006; European Values Study Group and World Values Survey Association, 2005). In other words, they report relatively high levels of what psychologists term **subjective well-being**—individuals' global judgments of their own life satisfaction (Diener, Lucas, & Oishi, 2002). Moreover, this seems to be true across all age groups and gender, at all income levels above grinding poverty, among people considered relatively unattractive as well as people considered attractive (Diener, Wolsic, & Fujita, 1995), and in all racial and ethnic groups (see Myers & Diener, 1995). Given that most people report being happy, let's consider some of the factors that appear to contribute to happiness.

■ Factors that influence happiness.

As we've already noted, research indicates that, overall, most people report being relatively happy and satisfied with their lives. Why? We don't know for certain, but it appears that humans generally have a strong tendency to look on the bright side of things—to be optimistic and upbeat in a wide range of situations (see Diener & Suh, 1998). But does this mean that everyone is happy, no matter what their life circumstances? Not at all; a number of factors have been found to influence subjective well-being (Diener & Seligman, 2002). First, happy people report experiencing higher levels of positive emotion and lower levels of negative emotion than less happy people (Lyubomirsky, King, & Diener, 2005). According to psychologist Barbara Fredrickson, high levels of positive emotion lead people to think, feel, and act in ways that help to broaden and build their emotional, physical, and social resources (see Fredrickson, 2001; Fredrickson & Joiner, 2002). Second, good social relations with other people—close friends, family, romantic partners—appear to be necessary for being very happy. Finally, happy people tend to be more extroverted but lower in neuroticism (they exhibit greater emotional stability), and they exhibit fewer signs of mental disturbance (e.g., depression, family conflict, hypochondriasis—the tendency to imagine illnesses they don't have). In short, a combination of factors contributes to give people this priceless gift (see Figure 8.13).

Additional findings (Diener et al., 1999) suggest that personal happiness may be influenced by other factors, too. One of these involves having goals and the resources—personal, economic, and otherwise—necessary to reach them. Many studies indicate that people who have concrete goals, especially goals that they have a realistic chance of reaching, and who feel (realistically or otherwise) that they are making progress toward these, are happier than people lacking in such goals (Cantor & Sanderson, 1999).

External conditions over which individuals have varying degrees of influence also play a role in happiness. In general, married people tend to be happier than single people, although this varies with how a particular culture views marriage

Subjective well-being: Individuals' global judgments of their own life satisfaction.

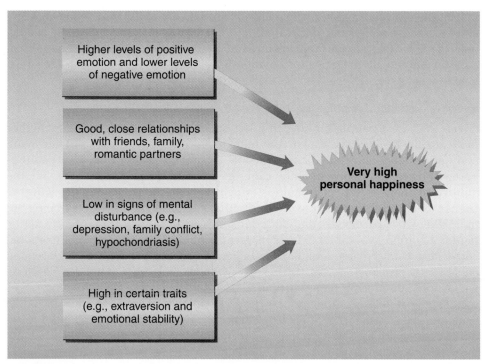

FIGURE 8.13
Very Happy People: How They Differ from Others
As shown here, many factors contribute to the happiness enjoyed by very happy people.
Source: Based on findings reported by Diener & Seligman, 2002, and Lyubomirsky, King, & Diener, 2005.

(Diener et al., 1998), and people who are satisfied with their jobs and careers tend to be happier than those who are not (see Weiss & Cropanzano, 1996). People with religious beliefs who attend church regularly report greater life satisfaction than self-described atheists (Ferriss, 2002). Not surprisingly, people who live in wealthy countries are generally happier than those in poor nations, although additional considerations, such as political stability and human rights, appear to moderate the relationship between wealth and happiness (Diener & Diener, 1995). For example, a cross-cultural study of life satisfaction determined that the African Maasai, a tribe of herdsmen with no electricity or running water, and northern Greenland's Inughuit people, who dwell in a somewhat brutal climate, rated their life satisfaction level at 5.8 (7.0 was the highest possible rating; Biswas-Diener et al., 2004). Interestingly, this is the same rating given by people on *Forbes* magazine's list of "richest Americans." In addition, although income has continued to rise in the United States over the past fifty years (the Gross Domestic Product [GDP] has tripled over that period), the incidence of depression here has increased tenfold, evidence that material wealth is only one of many determinants of well-being (Diener & Seligman, 2004; Easterbrook, 2003).

Surprisingly, though, other factors we might expect to be related to personal happiness do not seem to affect it. Very happy people do *not* differ from average or very unhappy people with respect to perceptions of how much money they have compared to others, their own physical attractiveness, their use of tobacco and alcohol, or the amount of time they spend sleeping or exercising. Finally, there appear to be no substantial differences in happiness between men and women, and personal happiness does not appear to decline with age (see Charles et al., 2001). Why do people remain happy as they get older? One possibility is that older people learn to structure their lives and pursue goals in ways that complement age-related declines in their physical and cognitive capabilities, which in turn tends to maintain high levels of subjective well-being. Other findings indicate that relative to younger people, older people attend to and remember emotionally *positive* information more than they do emotionally negative information (Carstensen & Mikels, 2005). Let's turn next to what psychologists have learned about the benefits of happiness.

■ Some benefits of happiness.

Given that most people report being happy, an important question is whether there are any benefits associated with high levels of happiness. A rapidly growing body of evidence shows that happy people tend to fare better than their counterparts who are less happy in many different ways, including their work life, the quality of their social relationships, and their health (Lyubomirsky, King, & Diener, 2005). With regard to work, individuals high in subjective well-being are more likely to experience better work outcomes, including increased productivity, higher quality of work, higher income, greater job satisfaction, and organizational citizenship, and they are less likely to engage in counterproductive work-related behaviors (Borman et al., 2001; Weiss et al., 1999; Wright & Cropanzano, 2000). As we've noted previously, happy people also tend to have more friends and stronger social support networks than do less happy people (see Lyubomirsky, Sheldon, & Schkade, 2005; Pinquart & Sorensen, 2000). And finally, happy people tend to report better health and fewer unpleasant physical symptoms and deal with illness more effectively when it does occur (Lyubomirsky, King, & Diener, 2005).

Additional health-related benefits associated with higher levels of well-being include increased resistance to cold and flu viruses (Cohen et al., 2003), better pain management (Keefe et al., 2001), a lower incidence of depression (Maruta et al., 2000), improved recovery from surgery (Kopp et al., 2003), and even longer life. With respect to this last point, Maruta and colleagues (2000) reported that people with an optimistic outlook on life tended to outlive their more pessimistic counterparts by an average of eight years. In short, the evidence is clear: Higher levels of happiness are associated with many beneficial outcomes.

■ Can we increase personal happiness?

Because of the many benefits associated with happiness, researchers have begun to investigate ways to increase it—but only recently. Why? Because previous research seemed to point to the conclusion that happiness—like many dispositional traits—is relatively fixed. Therefore, many psychologists adopted the view that people possess a happiness *set point* that remains relatively stable throughout life, and as a result, assumed it is relatively resistant to change. Studies consistently show, for example, that subjective well-being tends to be stable over time (Eid & Diener, 2004). Additional research involving twins provided evidence for the existence of a set point by showing that happiness is, at least in part, a genetically inherited characteristic; it showed that identical twins tend to be more similar in their levels of happiness than fraternal twins or other less closely related family members (Tellegen et al., 1988). A third source of evidence came from the idea that emotions, including happiness, are maintained within a genetically determined range through a process termed the *hedonic treadmill* (Brickman & Campbell, 1971, 1978). Support for this view comes from studies showing that after experiencing both good and bad emotionally significant events, such as winning a lottery or sustaining a permanent injury, people tend to return to a neutral emotional set point (see Fredrick & Loewenstein, 1999).

Although a large part of happiness is clearly genetically determined and fairly stable throughout life, emerging evidence has opened the door to new thinking about the nature of happiness and the potential for change. Research has revealed that happiness varies considerably across individuals (Diener & Lucas, 1999) and researchers have begun to pinpoint the conditions most likely to give rise to sustainable changes in happiness (Diener, Lucas, & Scollon, 2006). These, and related, findings have fueled efforts to develop interventions geared toward increasing aspects of happiness and well-being among people. A currently influential model proposed by psychologist Sonja Lyubomirsky summarizes the three primary types of factors that determine happiness: namely the *set point*, life circumstances , and intentional activity (Lyubomirsky, Sheldon, & Schkade, 2005). As shown in Figure 8.14, genetic factors appear to account for about 50 percent of happiness (Lykken & Tellegen, 1996; Tellegen et al., 1988) and external circumstances account for approximately 10 percent (Diener et al., 1999). This suggests that a significant amount of happiness—up to 40 percent—is determined through a person's thoughts and actions, and therefore subject to change. Interventions targeting intentional activity have been shown to produce relatively lasting effects on happiness. For example, careful research has confirmed that relatively simple behavioral interventions, such as asking participants to exercise regularly or to be kind to others, and

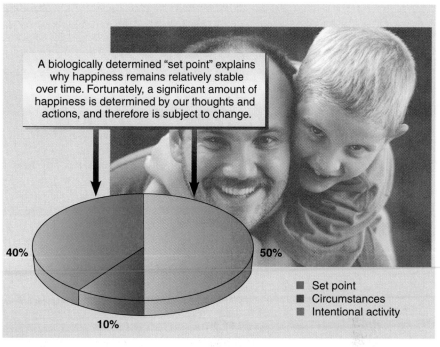

FIGURE 8.14
Factors that Contribute to Happiness and Their Proportion
A currently influential model showing the primary factors thought to determine happiness and the relative contribution of each factor.
Source: Based on findings reported by Lyubomirsky, Sheldon, & Schkader, 2005.

cognitive interventions, such as having people pause to count their blessings, can exert lasting effects on measures of happiness (Lyubomirsky, King, & Diener, 2005; Seligman et al., 2005). In sum, a growing body of evidence suggests we can increase our level of happiness through interventions that target *intentional activity*—a term used to describe things that people think and do in their daily lives. For additional suggestions for becoming a happier person, see the following **Psychology Lends a Hand** section.

KEY QUESTIONS

- Where do most people stand with respect to personal happiness?
- What are key differences between people who are very happy and people who are unhappy?

SUMMARY AND REVIEW OF KEY QUESTIONS

Motivation: The Activation and Persistence of Behavior

- **According to drive theory, what is the basis for various motives?**
  Drive theory suggests that motivation is a process in which various biological needs push (drive) us to actions designed to satisfy them.
- **According to expectancy theory, why do people engage in tasks requiring effort?**

Expectancy theory suggests that people exert effort on tasks because they believe doing so will yield results they want to attain.

- **Under what conditions will setting goals increase motivation and performance?**
  Setting goals will increase motivation and performance when the goals are specific and challenging, yet attainable, and when individuals are committed to them and receive feedback on their progress.

PSYCHOLOGY LENDS A HAND

Becoming a Very Happy Person

Almost everyone wants to be happy—of that there can be no doubt. And although different people define happiness in contrasting ways, most would agree that being happy involves such things as experiencing positive emotions much of the time; having good relations with friends, family, and romantic partners; having a successful, rewarding job or career; and having hobbies and interests that one can enjoy in leisure time. But describing these goals is a lot easier than reaching them. Are there steps you can take to increase the chances that you will get there—that you will be a very happy person?

Drawing on research on personal happiness and in the new field of positive psychology, we can offer the following suggestions:

- **Start the upward spiral going.** Experiencing positive emotions appears to be one way of "getting the ball rolling," so to speak. Positive emotions help one adopt effective ways of coping with life's unavoidable problems, and this, in turn, can generate even more positive emotions. So the hardest step, as in many tasks, may be the first: Once you begin experiencing positive feelings, it may quickly become easier to experience more of them.

- **Build close personal relationships.** Although no single factor can grant you personal happiness, it is clear that one of the most important ingredients in being happy is having good, mutually supportive relations with friends, family members, and romantic partners. Developing and maintaining good relationships requires a lot of hard work, but the rewards appear to make this effort well worthwhile. In fact, this may be the single most important thing you can do to increase your own happiness. So start thinking more about the people who are important to you and how you can make them happy. The result may be a major boost to your own life satisfaction.

- **Build personal skills that contribute to being happy.** Very happy people possess a number of personal characteristics that contribute to their happiness. If you already possess them, great; if not, you can work at building them. These characteristics include being friendly and outgoing (extroverted), agreeable (i.e., approaching others with the belief that you will like and trust them), and emotionally stable. So, figure out where you stand on these dimensions, and then begin working on them—preferably with the help of close friends.

- **Get into shape!** All of us (the authors) have followed a disciplined workout regimen for many years, and we continue to exercise regularly. Sure, this is good for our personal health, but even more important, every time we do it, it makes us feel good! It's not simply "runner's high"—you can get such effects even from relatively short workouts. The principle is simple: When your body is working well, it produces substances that tend to put you in a good mood. The result? A boost to your happiness. So by all means, get in shape: Your moods as well as your emotions are likely to improve.

- **Stop doing counterproductive things.** Because everyone wants to be happy, we all take many steps to enhance our positive emotions. Some of these—like the ones listed in this feature—are helpful. Others (e.g., abusing drugs, worrying about anything and everything, trying to be perfect, setting impossible goals for yourself, etc.) are not. They may work temporarily (see Chapter 10 for more discussion), but in the long run, they will not contribute to your personal happiness. So start now to eliminate them from your life.

Good luck! And may you soon become one of those fortunate, very happy people!

- **What are the basic ideas behind Maslow's need hierarchy theory?**
Maslow's theory suggests that needs exist in a hierarchy and that higher-level needs cannot be activated until lower-level ones are satisfied.

- **What factors play a role in the regulation of eating?**
Eating is regulated by complex biochemical systems within the body involving detector cells in the hypothalamus and elsewhere, and is also affected by the sight of food, feedback from chewing and swallowing, cognitive factors (e.g., memories about when we ate last), and cultural factors.

- **What factors override this system, so that many people fail to maintain a stable weight?**
Many factors tend to override this system, including the impact of learning, responses to food-related cues, genetic factors (a predisposition to gain weight), the growing size of food portions, and reduced sensitivity to leptin once we gain significant amounts of weight.

- **What role do hormones play in human sexual motivation?**
Recent findings indicate that sex hormones play some role in human sexual behavior, but this role is smaller and more subtle than is true for many other species.

- **How does evolutionary psychology explain differences in the mating strategies of women and men?**
Evolutionary psychology suggests that men can have more offspring by having many sexual partners and make little investment in each, while women cannot increase their offspring by having many sexual partners, and make a major investment in each child. As a result, men show a stronger preference for many different partners.

- **What factors appear to play a role in determining sexual orientation?**
The weight of available evidence suggests that genetic and biological factors play a key role in determining sexual orientation.

- **What is achievement motivation?**
Achievement motivation is the desire to meet standards of excellence or outperform others.

- **What are the effects of achievement motivation on behavior?**
Individuals high in achievement motivation tend to excel in school and in running their own businesses. They do especially well in situations that activate their high need for achievement.

- **What is intrinsic motivation?**
Motivation to perform some activity simply because it is enjoyable.

- **Why is intrinsic motivation sometimes reduced when individuals receive external rewards for performing activities they enjoy?**
When individuals receive rewards for performing activities they enjoy, they conclude that they perform these activities not solely because they like them, but also because of the external rewards they receive.

- **Why are some people able to forgive more easily than others?**
Because they possess certain traits that assist them in forgiving others (e.g., they are high in agreeableness and in emotional stability).

- **How do they forgive people who have harmed them?**
They forgive by experiencing empathy toward people who harmed them and by making generous attributions about the causes of their harmful actions.

Emotions: Their Nature, Expression, and Impact

- **How do the Cannon–Bard and James–Lange theories differ?**
The Cannon–Bard theory suggests that emotion-provoking stimuli simultaneously elicit physiological arousal and the subjective cognitive states we label as emotions. The James–Lange theory suggests that emotion-provoking stimuli induce physiological reactions and that these form the basis for the subjective cognitive states we label as emotions.

- **What is the Schachter–Singer theory of emotion?**
The Schachter–Singer theory suggests that when we are aroused by emotion-provoking stimuli, we search the external environment for the causes of our feelings of arousal. The causes we select then determine our emotions.

- **What roles do the left and right cerebral hemispheres play in emotions?**
Activation of the left hemisphere plays a role in positive emotions; activation of the right hemisphere plays a role in negative emotions. Anterior regions of the hemispheres are associated primarily with the valence (pleasantness or unpleasantness of emotions), while posterior regions are associated primarily with arousal (intensity).

- **What is the role of the amygdala in emotions?**
The amygdala seems to contain neural mechanisms specialized in interpreting emotional information relating to threat or danger, such as signs of fear or anger on the part of others.

- **What emotions are shown by clear facial expressions? What do research findings indicate about the universality of such expressions?**
Research findings indicate that clear facial expressions exist for anger, fear, sadness, disgust, happiness, and surprise. Recent findings indicate that such expressions, while informative, may not be as universal in meaning as was previously assumed.

- **What information about others' emotions is conveyed by body language?**
Body language provides information about others' overall level of arousal, about their reactions to us, and about specific reactions they may be having.

- **In what ways do our affective states influence cognition?**
Affective states can influence our perception of ambiguous stimuli, our memory, decisions, and judgments we make, the style of information processing we adopt, and our creativity.

- **In what ways does cognition influence our affective states?**
Cognition can influence the labels we place on emotional states and can activate schemas containing strong affective components. In addition, cognitive processes such as reappraisal and suppression allow us to regulate our emotional reactions.

Subjective Well-Being: Causes and Effects of Personal Happiness

- **Where do most people stand with respect to personal happiness?**
Most people are relatively high in personal happiness, perhaps because of a strong human tendency toward optimism.

- **What are key differences between people who are very happy and people who are unhappy?**
Very happy people have closer relationships with friends, family members, and romantic partners; are higher on several personal traits (e.g., extroversion, emotional stability); and are lower in signs of mental disturbance.

KEY TERMS

PSYCHOLOGY: UNDERSTANDING ITS FINDINGS

How Feelings Affect Our Judgment: A Personal Demonstration

Just how strong are the effects of our feelings (affective states) on our judgments? Very! Try this simple exercise to see for yourself.

1. Look through your photos and choose several that show people some of your friends have never met. Try to choose ones who are average-looking in appearance.
2. Now ask several of your friends to rate the attractiveness of the people shown in the photos on a scale ranging from 1 to 5 (1 = very unattractive; 2 = unattractive; 3 = average; 4 = attractive; 5 = very attractive).
3. Before you ask them to do the ratings, you have a task: Rate your friends' current moods: 1 = very negative; 2 = negative; 3 = neutral; 4 = good; 5 = very good.

4. After you have had several friends evaluate the photos, compare your ratings of their moods with the ratings they provided.

There is a very good chance you will find that the better your friends' moods, the higher they rated the people in the photos. Why? Because their moods biased their judgment—tilted them in the same direction as their current mood. This is a powerful demonstration of just how strong—and subtle—such effects can be. If you ask your friends, they will probably deny that their current moods had any bearing on their ratings!

MAKING PSYCHOLOGY PART OF YOUR LIFE

Practice in Forgiveness

Do you want to be happy? Then one skill you should practice is forgiveness—letting go of your anger and desire for revenge toward others who have harmed you in some way. Forgiving them is not only good for them, but also good for you! Start your practice with this exercise:

1. Remember some incident in your life when another person hurt you badly.
2. Now, rate how angry you felt toward this person at the time, and how much you wanted revenge against him. (Use a 5-point scale: 1 = not angry at all; 2 = a little angry; 3 = neutral; 4 = angry; 5 = very angry. Use the same numbers for rating your desire for revenge.)
3. Next, try to feel empathy for this person. Try to experience what he did when he harmed you—his feelings and emotions at the time.
4. After doing that for a while, try to understand why he did what he did to you. And here is the hard part: Try to in-

terpret the cause of his behavior in a kind manner. Truly, we don't always know why other people do what they do, so perhaps you jumped to the wrong conclusion; perhaps this person didn't mean to harm you, or didn't realize how much he was harming you. Keep trying to come up with kind interpretations of his behavior until you find one that fits.
5. Finally, consider how often you thought about this past harm—ruminated about it. Did this make you happy or unhappy? In all likelihood, ruminating about this incident made you unhappy. So now, think of ways you can stop thinking about it—distract yourself, think about happier experiences, and so on.

To the extent you can make these steps work, you are on the way to developing your ability to forgive others, and that is an important step on the road to personal happiness.

If you are using MyPsychLab, you have access to an electronic version of this textbook, along with dozens of valuable resources per chapter—including video and audio clips, simulations and activities, self-assessments, practice tests and other study materials. Here is a sampling of the resources available for this chapter.

EXPLORE

Expectancy Theories

Maslow's Hierarchy of Needs

Physiological, Evolutionary, and Cognitive Theories of Emotion

The Effects of the Hypothalamus on Eating Behavior

Evolutionary Drive, Arousal, Cognitive, and Humanistic Theories of Motivation

WATCH

Sex & Mating Behavior

The Challenger Disaster

Food and the Brain

SIMULATE

Recognizing Facial Expressions of Emotions

If you did not receive an access code to MyPsychLab with this text and wish to purchase access online, please visit www.MyPsychLab.com.

STUDY GUIDE

CHAPTER REVIEW

Motivation: The Activation and Persistence of Behavior

1. Motivation refers to processes that activate, guide, and maintain behavior.   (True-False)
2. _____ motivation does not involve external rewards.
   a. Incentive
   b. Hunger
   c. Sexual
   d. Achievement
3. The view that the body monitors and maintains internal states at relatively constant levels is known as
   a. homeostasis.
   b. incentive motivation.
   c. internal invariance.
   d. achievement motivation.
4. A key problem for drive theories of motivation is to explain why
   a. hungry rats will race down an alleyway for food.
   b. thirst is an unpleasant feeling.
   c. humans engage in behaviors that increase arousal.
   d. All of the above are correct.
5. The _____ approach to motivation argues that our behavior is pulled by _____.
   a. homeostatic;   incentives
   b. incentives;   biological needs
   c. drive;   cognitive attributions
   d. expectancy;   incentives
6. A drive is thought to "push" behavior, while an incentive is thought to "pull" behavior.   (True-False)
7. An example of an incentive is
   a. a cool drink for a thirsty person.
   b. the approval of other persons.
   c. an unconscious impulse to kill others.
   d. a type of arousal that feels uncomfortable.
8. Goal-setting is NOT effective in a situation where
   a. goals are highly specific.
   b. a person knows the exact nature of the goal.
   c. goals are attainable.
   d. a person does not view the goal as challenging.
9. Maslow argued that _____ needs include _____.
   a. homeostatic needs;   drives and incentives
   b. deficiency;   social, safety, and physiological needs
   c. social needs;   desire for self-respect and for success
   d. physiological;   the need to feel safe and warm
10. An example of a deficiency need would be
    a. the desire for the approval of others.
    b. the desire for food and water.
    c. a desire for success and achievement.
    d. the desire to "be all that one can be."
11. Researchers have verified that basic physiological and safety needs are met before satisfying esteem needs. (True-False).
12. As of the year 2002, about _____ of U.S. adults are classified as either overweight or obese.

a. 95%
b. 65%
c. 35%
d. 15%
13. The _____ is a key brain structure for the regulation of eating and of satiety.
   a. frontal cortex
   b. cerebellum
   c. corpus callosum
   d. hypothalamus
14. Research by Paul Rozin suggests that factors relating to _____ can lead to _____ food intake.
   a. hypothalamic;   decreased
   b. cognitive function;   decreased
   c. memory;   increased
   d. taste and smell;   altered
15. Which of the following is NOT a factor that contributes to the increasing body weight of Western cultures?
   a. impaired memory for what we ate in our last meal.
   b. An increase in portion sizes.
   c. A learned preference for high-calorie meals.
   d. A biological heritage that favors the tendency to store excess calories as fat.
16. Body weight is determined by biological factors but not socioeconomic factors.   (True-False).
17. Which of the following is an example of an environmental factor that tends to increase calorie consumption?
   a. Having been born to a wealthy family.
   b. Eating your meals at a restaurant that offers a free upgrade to a Super-Sized meal.
   c. Eating dinner at a "Smith" family reunion.
   d. All but A are correct.
18. The capacity of the body to inhibit eating (satiety) is _____ as we _____ body weight.
   a. increased;   gain
   b. decreased;   lose
   c. decreased;   gain
   d. increased;   lose
19. A key factor in the regulation of body weight is the chemical leptin which acts to inhibit appetite and speed up metabolism.   (True-False).
20. An example of an activational effect of a hormone would be
   a. male rats are sexually active after castration.
   b. administration of female hormones to a male rat induces female sexual behavior.
   c. the sexual behavior of a female rat is suppressed by ovarian hormones.
   d. female rats are sexually inactive after removal of the ovaries.
21. Adult women tested during the ovulatory phase of the menstrual cycle show
   a. increased interest in masculine faces.
   b. decreased sexual motivation.
   c. an inability to judge the sex of faces displayed on a computer screen.
   d. a preference for men who do not "like kids".

22. The perceptual capacity of a human female is altered across her menstrual cycle (True-False).

23. Mating strategies in human males include
    a. a preference for stable long-term relationships.
    b. few romantic liaisons.
    c. a preference for many future sexual partners.
    d. avoidance of attractive female partners.

24. Evolutionary psychology suggests that natural selection produces a mating strategy for _____ that involves _____.
    a. men; gaining valuable financial resources
    b. men; having many sexual partners
    c. women; expanding their options by having many partners
    d. women; low interest in sex and children

25. Current research indicates that a homosexual orientation
    a. is the result of parental experiences such as an overprotective mother.
    b. can be influenced by genetic and biological factors.
    c. can be changed by psychotherapy.
    d. results from childhood sexual abuse.

26. The best way for a parent to encourage a hobby in their child is to pay them for that activity. (True-False).

27. Which of the following is true of forgiveness?
    a. A person with low self-esteem would be expected to be very forgiving.
    b. People who are forgiving are less likely to be spiritual.
    c. Most people are unlikely to forgive a person who has harmed them.
    d. People who are forgiving are more likely to have an agreeable personality.

Emotions: Their Nature, Expression, and Impact

28. A(n) _____ is a psychological state that involves subjective feelings, a physiological response, and a behavioral response.
    a. mood
    b. emotion
    c. motive
    d. incentive

29. Which statement below is most consistent with the Cannon-Bard theory of emotion?
    a. An emotion-evoking event first induces physiologic reactions followed by subjective reactions.
    b. The brain interprets the pattern of physiologic reactions as an emotion.
    c. Subjective experiences and physiologic reactions occur at the same time to an emotion-evoking event.
    d. Facial expressions can induce changes in emotional experience.

30. A key difference between the Cannon-Bard and the James-Lange theories of emotion is that
    a. the Cannon-Bard view suggests that awareness of peripheral physiologic signals can influence our emotions.
    b. the James-Lange view suggests that an emotion event causes subjective experiences and then physiologic changes.
    c. the James-Lange view suggests that awareness of peripheral physiologic signals can influence our emotions.
    d. the Cannon-Bard view emphasized the importance of facial feedback for emotions.

31. Jimmy was riding on a bus that was hijacked by two armed men. During the violent ride, he experienced a rapid heartbeat and muscle trembling and noticed Jane on the seat across from him. After the ordeal, Jimmy decided to act on an impulse to ask Jane out for a date. His attraction to Jane is most consistent with
    a. drive theory.
    b. the two-factor theory of emotion.
    c. the James-Lange theory of emotion.
    d. the facial feedback hypothesis.

32. Processing of emotional information requires an intact
    a. corpus callosum.
    b. left hemisphere.
    c. cerebellum.
    d. right hemisphere.

33. Activation of the amygdala would most likely
    a. result in sadness.
    b. induce a sense of disgust.
    c. cause joy and euphoria.
    d. alter memories for emotional experiences.

34. _____ would be an example of a non-verbal cue as to the emotional state of another person.
    a. Body posture
    b. Facial expression
    c. A hand or finger gesture
    d. All of the above are correct.

35. Cross-cultural studies indicate that humans experience six basic emotions. (True-False).

36. In a recent reality show involving family conflict, a teenage daughter is seen verbally arguing with her step-mother on numerous occasions. In one instance, the daughter told her Dad that he was a "liar" at which he lost his temper and struck her repeatedly with his hands. On the side screen, the step-mother could be seen throwing shadow punches in the air with her hands. An emotion researcher would explain her behavior as
    a. expressing anger and hostility.
    b. her attempt to control her own feelings.
    c. an attempt to hide her anger.
    d. displacement behavior meant to reduce arousal.

37. If you observe a person who shows clenched fists but a smiling face, you are most likely to decide that this person is
    a. happy.
    b. experiencing the mixed emotion of disgust.
    c. confused.
    d. angry

38. Relatively mild changes in mood are referred to as affect. (True-False).

39. Match up the appropriate concept with the correct definition or best example of the concept.
    _____. "Smile and you will be happy...."
    _____. A temporary and relatively mild change in mood.
    _____. A dimension along which an emotion can be classified as positive or negative.
    _____. An example of a non-verbal emotional cue.

_____. Another name for the emotion theory proposed
by Schachter and Singer.
  a. Two-factor theory.
  b. Valence.
  c. Affect.
  d. Facial feedback hypothesis.
  e. Gesture.
40. The emotion-regulating reappraisal strategy may be
most effective because it occurs prior to the major impact
of an emotional situation.   (True-False)

Subjective Well-Being: Causes and Effects of Personal Happiness

41. For each of the comparisons below, indicate (Yes/No)
whether the first group would be expected to be happier
than the second group.
  _____. Being single rather than married.
  _____. Living in poverty versus being wealthy.
  _____. People who have high levels of positive emotion
versus those who do not.
  _____. People who have high levels of mental distur-
bance versus those who are mentally healthy.
  _____. Self-described atheists versus churchgoing reli-
gious people.

IDENTIFICATIONS

Identify the term that belongs with each of the concepts
below (place the letter for the appropriate term below in
front of each concept).
Identification   Concept:
_____1. The approval of your peers.
_____2. A cognitive strategy used to modulate emotions.
_____3. A brain structure that plays a key role in emo-
tional memories.
_____4. A person is motivated by anticipation of certain
outcomes.
_____5. The view that the body monitors and maintains
internal states at relatively constant levels.
_____6. A temporary and mild form of mood change.
_____7. A view that certain activities are inherently inter-
esting.
_____8. The preference of a person for a sexual partner of
a particular sex.
_____9. A theory of motivation that argues that we are
pushed into action by our needs.
  Identification:
  a. Homeostasis.
  b. Drive theory
  c. Intrinsic motivation.
  d. Expectancy theory.
  e. Incentive.
  f. Sexual orientation.
  g. Affect.
  h. Amygdala.
  i. Reappraisal.

FILL IN THE BLANK

1. The cognitive processes that activate, guide, and maintain behavior are termed _____.
2. Drive theory argues that we are _____ into action by
our needs.
3. Goal-setting works well when the goals are _____,
_____, and _____.
4. Maslow suggested that _____ needs are the first to be
satisfied.
5. About _____ % of U.S. adults are classified as either
overweight or obese.
6. A key environmental factor that contributes to obesity in
the U.S. is _____.
7. The capacity of a hormone to maintain a behavior is
known as an _____ effect.
8. Women are most accurate at judging a person's sex by facial cues when they are in the _____ of the menstrual
cycle.
9. A _____ person prefers partners of either sex.
10. _____ motivation is associated with rewards while
_____ motivation can actually be impaired by rewards.
11. The three components of emotion include _____,
_____, and _____.
12. The _____ theory of emotion argues that emotions
arise from our interpretation of our physiological reactions.
13. Our capacity to recognize emotions in others depends on
activity of the _____.
14. The major nonverbal cues used to judge emotion are
_____, _____, and _____.
15. _____ refers to a form of emotion regulation involving
inhibition of the expression of emotions.

COMPREHENSIVE PRACTICE TEST

1. Motivation involves forces that act on an organism to activate, guide, and maintain behavior.   (True-False)
2. The _____ approach to motivation argues that behavior is motivated by the desire to reduce unpleasant internal tension caused by unmet biological needs.
  a. psychoanalytic
  b. industrial/organizational
  c. drive
  d. incentive
3. The tendency of our body to maintain a steady level of
body temperature involves
  a. incentive motivation.
  b. instinct.
  c. homeostasis.
  d. extrinsic motivation.
4. A key problem for drive theories of motivation is to explain why hungry rats will race down an alleyway for
food.   (True-False)
5. A drive is to _____ as an incentive is to _____.
  a. "pull";   "push"
  b. instinct;   extrinsic
  c. achievement motivation;   homeostasis
  d. "push";   "pull"
6. Overeating is less likely to occur
  a. when we experience a failed exam or loss of a job.
  b. in meal settings that involve a large group of people.
  c. when we are offered large portion sizes.
  d. in people who come from wealthy families.
7. Female rats are sexually inactive after removal of the
ovaries.   (True-False)

8. The mating strategy of a human female involves
   a. a desire to have multiple sexual partners.
   b. a greater impact of physical attractiveness in their selection of potential mates.
   c. avoidance of masculine partners who like children.
   d. a preference for stable long-term relationships.

9. A homosexual orientation can be the result of having an overprotective mother or a distant father. (True-False)

10. A person who is HIGH in achievement motivation would be expected to
    a. express a strong desire for feedback on their performance.
    b. prefer moderately hard tasks.
    c. get better grades in school.
    d. All of the above are correct.

11. Match up the appropriate concept with the correct definition or best example of the concept.
    _____. The desire to meet standards of excellence.
    _____. In this theory, deficiency needs are to be met before growth needs.
    _____. A reward that is desired by a person.
    _____. The view that behavior is "pulled" by anticipated outcomes.
    _____. The capacity of the body to monitor and control its internal states.
    _____. Hungry rats will work for food.
    a. incentive
    b. achievement motivation.
    c. hierarchy of needs
    d. drive theory
    e. homeostasis
    f. expectancy
    g. deficiency need

12. Which of the following is a key requirement for effective goal-setting?
    a. The goal can be attained only with considerable effort and much luck.
    b. The person must understand the general nature of the goal.
    c. The person must be committed to the goal.
    d. All of the above are correct.

13. A person with high self esteem would be expected to be very forgiving. (True-False)

14. Extrinsic motivation is to being paid per piece produced as
    a. homeostasis is to incentive motivation.
    b. intrinsic motivation is to the pursuit of a bobby.
    c. Maslow's theory of motivation is to operant conditioning
    d. achievement motivation is to being a blue-collar worker in a large factory.

15. Damage to the posterior aspects of the right hemisphere would be expected to result in symptoms of anxiety. (True-False).

16. Which statement below is most consistent with the peripheral feedback effect?
    a. An emotion-evoking event first induces subjective reactions followed by physiologic reactions.
    b. The brain interprets the speed of our heart rate as an emotion.
    c. Subjective experiences and physiologic reactions occur at the same time to an emotion-evoking event.
    d. Facial expressions, body postures, and tone of voice can induce changes in emotional experience.

17. The statement "I am afraid because I ran" would be endorsed by
    a. James and Lange.
    b. Schachter and Singer.
    c. Cannon and Bard.
    d. Ben and Jerry.

18. A negative valence of emotion is associated with activity of the _____ while emotional arousal involves the _____.
    a. right hemisphere;   posterior aspects of the hemispheres
    b. corpus callosum;   hypothalamus and thalamus
    c. posterior aspects of the hemispheres;   left hemisphere
    d. left hemisphere;   anterior aspects of the hemispheres

19. The facial-feedback hypothesis suggests that a facial expression of a specific emotion can influence the subjective experience of that particular emotion.   (True-False).

20. A person whose gaze is averted away from you is most likely to be experiencing an emotion such as
    a. love.
    b. joy.
    c. fear.
    d. anger.

CRITICAL THINKING

1. Suppose that a researcher was able to compare the emotions experienced by persons before and after accidental transaction of the spinal cord. Imagine that persons with very low spinal cord transactions (sacral) reported no change in emotional experience, but persons with high transactions (who have little physical sensation or movement below the shoulders) reported a major decline in emotion experiences. How would the James-Lange theory of emotion deal with this pattern of results?

2. Summarize the research on subjective well-being including the role of money, power, and marital status on happiness.

NINE

Personality and Intelligence: Understanding Individual Differences

*L*et me describe my friend Nick to you. One of the first things I (Rebecca Henry) learned about Nick is that he seems to know everyone. In fact, it's hard to go anywhere with him and not get stopped by friends wanting to chat. This sociability also extends to his personal life, as he is seldom without a date. And while my husband and I enjoy socializing with him, we make sure never to go to exotic restaurants with him, as he eats only a handful of foods and gets nervous if one food gets too cozy on the plate with another. Another challenge regarding Nick is that he loves to talk about politics and social issues, ending most debates with the proclamation that he is right. He has some really diverse talents that make him fascinating, if not a bit perplexing. For example, he aced his college entrance exams, then promptly flunked out of the selective private school that admitted him. He never returned. Despite this, he has been very successful professionally, and has started several profitable companies over the years, some with products he invented. In his spare time he likes to fly his helicopter or serve as the organist at a local theater, a skill he learned without any formal training. Truly, he is an amazing character!

In this chapter, we will examine some of the essential ways in which individuals differ from one another. This topic has been important to the field of psychology not, obviously, so that people like Nick can be described, but more importantly as a means to study how the uniqueness of individuals develops and how these differences relate to behavior. Collectively, this approach in psychology is often referred to as the **individual differences perspective,** because it focuses on how individuals differ from one another. While you have seen several examples of how individuals differ in earlier chapters (e.g., susceptibility to hypnotism in Chapter 4; infant attachment style in Chapter 7), the primary focus of these chapters was to describe general principles of human cognition and behavior. Even the chapter on development (Chapter 7) focused a great deal on general principles. To put it simply, the emphasis was more on individuals' similarities than differences.

Because individuals differ in more ways than can be counted, we must organize and limit our discussion so that it doesn't simply become a laundry list of human characteristics. First of all, since this is a psychology textbook our focus is on, not surprisingly, psychological individual differences, rather than, say, physical or physiological differences such as height, weight, or blood pressure. Second, we are interested in individual characteristics that show some degree of stability over time, a topic that we will address in some depth in the next section.

To organize our discussion of individual differences we will first divide the topic of individual differences into two major categories: personality and intelligence (sometimes referred to as general cognitive ability). While this is not an exhaustive grouping, it does represent the two major categories of relatively broad and stable individual differences. What individual differences do not fit into this grouping? Specific skills such as fluency in a foreign language are one example, as they tend to be narrower than cognitive abilities and also more malleable (less stable). Similarly, people's attitudes about various things (e.g., politics, religion) can also distinguish one person from another. However, attitudes are not typically considered a type of individual difference either, because they are somewhat narrow in scope and more susceptible to change (you'll learn more about attitudes in Chapter 13).

Our discussion will first address theories that describe the nature and origins of these differences, with the first part of the chapter devoted to personality and the latter part to intelligence. Within each of these two sections we will also describe some of the tools psychologists have developed to measure various aspects of personality and cognitive ability. The importance of these tools cannot be overestimated, as they make it possible to study personality and intelligence in accordance with scientific principles you learned about in Chapter 1. Finally, our discussions of personality and intelligence will address the relevance of these differences—in other words, what they relate to in real life. For example, you probably know that certain characteristics have been linked to how well people do in school and in social relationships, but did you know that some have also been linked to such seemingly unrelated things as how long people live? This is just a glimpse of some of what we will discuss, but first we begin with a definition of personality, followed by the important question of how stable it is.

Individual differences perspective:
The approach to psychology that focuses on how individuals differ from one another.

Personality:
Individuals' unique and relatively stable patterns of behavior, thoughts, and feelings.

PERSONALITY: THE ESSENCE OF WHAT MAKES US UNIQUE

Psychologists define **personality** as an individual's unique and relatively stable patterns of behavior, thoughts, and emotions (e.g., Nelson & Miller, 1995; Zuckerman, 1995; Friedman & Schustack, 1999). In the description of Nick that began this chapter, you may have wondered if he has always been so outgoing and opinionated. Is he that way in all situations? These two thoughts address a fundamental issue about personality: How consistent is it across situations and how stable is it over time? Although there was once quite a controversy concerning this issue, growing evidence suggests that personality is quite stable. In fact, people generally show a considerable degree of consistency in their behavior across situations and over time (e.g., Heatherton & Weinberger, 1994; Roberts & DelVecchio, 2000).

But just as people differ in countless ways, they also differ with respect to such stability. In other words, some show less change in their traits over time and across situations than do others (e.g., Koestner, Bernieri, & Zuckerman, 1992). This suggests that the tendency to remain stable or change may itself be one interesting aspect of personality! However, many personality characteristics appear to change in a similar manner for most individuals, suggesting that most of us change, but we do so in similar ways. The best example of this is the personality trait of *conscientiousness*, which tends to increase for most people as they progress from adolescence into adulthood (Roberts, Walton, & Veichtbauer, 2006).

Stability in personality also can refer to people's consistency in how they behave across situations. How stable is personality in this respect? Again, there is no single answer. In some situations—ones that permit us to behave much as we wish—the preferences and tendencies that make up our personality can readily find expression in our overt behavior. In such situations, personality can be an important determinant of our actions. But other situations do *not* permit us to behave as we wish; rather, we must obey rules and do what is expected of us. In such contexts, personality is a much weaker determinant of our behavior. In other words, in many situations, our behavior is a joint function of *both* our personality and the situation itself, which may limit or restrain our actions in various ways. Perhaps a concrete example will be helpful.

Consider an individual who is very shy; she has trouble speaking up in class and avoids meeting people at parties. This is a very stable aspect of her behavior. But now imagine that she is visiting a very dear friend who is ill in the hospital. Suddenly, her friend begins to suffer some sort of seizure. Distressed, our shy friend pushes the call button and waits for a nurse to arrive, but to no avail. Will she sit quietly, continuing to wait as her friend suffers? Perhaps. But there are strong pressures in this situation toward being assertive rather than shy. What will she do? While we can't predict for certain, the chances are good that she will *not* be the shy wallflower that she typically is at parties!

In short, our behavior in any given situation is usually a complex function of both our personality (the stable internal factors that make us unique individuals) *and* situational factors in the world around us. This *interactionist perspective* is the one currently accepted by most psychologists, so keep it in mind as you read further in this chapter (see Figure 9.1; Fleeson, 2004; Vansteelandt & Van Mechelen, 1998).

Now that we've clarified the basic nature of personality, we'll provide an overview of what psychologists have learned about personality. We'll begin by describing several major *theories of personality*—sweeping frameworks for understanding personality offered by some of the true "giants" in the history of psychology. These theories represent different perspectives on personality—contrasting views about the origins and nature of human uniqueness. As you'll see, they differ greatly, but each offers insights that have added to our understanding of personality—that's why they are covered here. For each theory, we'll first describe it, then present some research evidence relating to it, and finally offer an evaluation of its current status.

FIGURE 9.1

The Interactionist Perspective: Behavior as a Function of Personality and Situational Factors

Even normally shy people can manage to act assertively when necessary. In situations like this, situational factors exert a stronger impact on behavior than personality.

FIGURE 9.2
Freud: The Source of Many Insights into the Nature of Personality
Although he was a physician, not a psychologist, Freud's views about personality have had a strong and lasting impact on the study of personality.

KEY QUESTIONS
- What is personality?
- How stable is it over time?
- What is the interactionist perspective currently adopted by most psychologists?

The Psychoanalytic Approach: Messages from the Unconscious

Quick: Before you took this course, who would you have named as the most famous psychologist in history? If you are like most students I have known, your answer would probably be *Freud*. He is, by far, the most famous figure in the history of psychology—even though he was a medical doctor. Why is this so? The answer lies in several provocative and influential theories he proposed—theories that focus on personality. Before turning to his theories, let's consider Freud as an individual—*his* personality, if you will (see Figure 9.2).

■ **Freud's background.**

Freud was born in what is now part of the Czech Republic, but when he was four years old his family moved to Vienna and he spent almost his entire life in that city. As a young man, Freud was highly ambitious and decided to make a name for himself as a medical researcher. He became discouraged with his prospects in this respect, however, and soon after receiving his medical degree, entered private practice. It was during this period that he formulated his theories of human personality and psychological disorders.

A turning point in his early career came when he won a research grant to travel to Paris to observe the work of Jean-Martin Charcot, who was then using hypnosis to treat several types of mental disorders. When Freud returned to Vienna, he worked with Joseph Breuer, a colleague who was using hypnosis in the treatment of *hysteria*—a condition in which individuals experienced physical symptoms such as blindness, deafness, or paralysis of arms or legs for which there seemed to be no underlying physical cause. Out of these experiences and his growing clinical practice, Freud gradually developed his theories of personality and mental illness (Chapter 11). His ideas were complex, and touched on many issues. With respect to personality, however, three topics are most central: *levels of consciousness*, the *structure of personality*, and *psychosexual stages of development*.

■ **Freud's theory of personality.**

Freud viewed himself as a scientist and he was well aware of research on sensory thresholds (see Chapter 3). In fact, he believed that his psychological theories were just a temporary measure that would ultimately be replaced by knowledge of the underlying biological and neural processes (Zuckerman, 1995). In any case, he applied ideas about sensory thresholds, and the possibility of responding to stimuli we can't report perceiving, to the task of understanding the human mind. He soon reached the startling conclusion that most of the mind lies below the surface—below the threshold of conscious experience.

Above this boundary is the realm of the *conscious*. This includes our current thoughts: whatever we are thinking about or experiencing at a given moment. Beneath this conscious realm is the much larger *preconscious*. This contains memories that are not part of current thought but can readily be brought to mind if the need arises. An example of a preconscious memory might be when you met a particular childhood friend. Finally, beneath the preconscious, and forming the bulk of the human mind, is the *unconscious*: thoughts, desires, and impulses of which we remain largely unaware (see Figure 9.3). Although some of this material has always been unconscious, Freud believed that much of it was once conscious, but has been actively *repressed*—driven from consciousness because it was too anxiety-

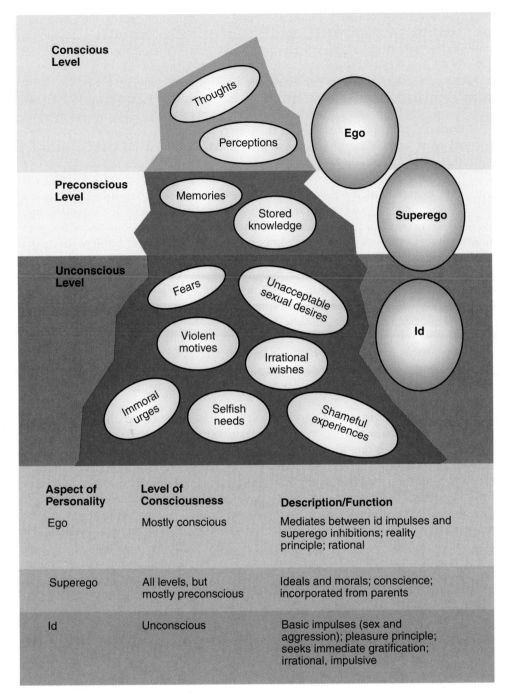

Aspect of Personality	Level of Consciousness	Description/Function
Ego	Mostly conscious	Mediates between id impulses and superego inhibitions; reality principle; rational
Superego	All levels, but mostly preconscious	Ideals and morals; conscience; incorporated from parents
Id	Unconscious	Basic impulses (sex and aggression); pleasure principle; seeks immediate gratification; irrational, impulsive

FIGURE 9.3

Freud's Views about Levels of Consciousness and the Structure of Personality

Freud believed that the human mind has three distinct levels: the conscious, preconscious, and unconscious. He also believed that personality involves three basic structures: id, ego, and superego, which correspond, very roughly, to desire, reason, and conscience.

provoking. For example, Freud contended that shameful experiences or unacceptable sexual or aggressive urges are often driven deep within the unconscious. The fact that we are not aware of them, however, in no way prevents them from affecting our behavior. Indeed, Freud believed that many of the symptoms experienced by his patients were disguised and indirect reflections of repressed thoughts and desires. This is why one major goal of **psychoanalysis**—the method of treating psychological disorders devised by Freud—is to bring repressed material back into consciousness. Presumably, once it is made conscious and patients gain insight into the early life experiences that caused them to repress it in the first place, important causes of mental illness are removed.

Psychoanalysis:

A method of therapy based on Freud's theory of personality, in which the therapist attempts to bring repressed, unconscious material into consciousness.

Id:
In Freud's theory, the portion of personality concerned with immediate gratification of primitive needs.

Pleasure principle:
The principle on which the id operates, according to which immediate pleasure is the sole motivation for behavior.

Ego:
In Freud's theory, the part of personality that takes account of external reality in the expression of instinctive sexual and aggressive urges.

Reality principle:
The principle according to which the ego operates, in which the external consequences of behavior are considered in the expression of impulses from the id.

Superego:
According to Freud, the portion of human personality representing the conscience.

Freudian slips:
Statements that seem to be simple errors in speech, but that in fact reveal unconscious thoughts or impulses.

Psychosexual stages of development:
According to Freud, an innate sequence of stages through which all humans pass. At each stage, pleasure is focused on a different region of the body.

Libido:
According to Freud, the psychic energy that powers all mental activity.

Fixation:
Excessive investment of psychic energy in a particular stage of psychosexual development. This results in various types of psychological disorders.

Freud also developed a theory regarding the *structure of personality*, and how these various structures influence our personality. He suggested that personality consists largely of three parts: the *id*, the *ego*, and the *superego* (see Figure 9.3, page 341). These correspond, roughly, to *desire, reason,* and *conscience.*

The **id** consists of all our primitive, innate urges. These include various bodily needs, sexual desire, and aggressive impulses. According to Freud, the id is totally unconscious and operates in accordance with what he termed the **pleasure principle:** It demands immediate, total gratification and is not capable of considering the potential costs of seeking this goal. In short, the id can be thought of as the *unrestrained* aspect of personality.

Unfortunately, the world offers few opportunities for instant pleasure, and attempting to gratify many of our innate urges would soon get us into serious trouble. It is in response to these facts that the second structure of personality, the **ego,** develops. The ego's task is to hold the id in check until conditions allow for satisfaction of its impulses. Thus, the ego operates in accordance with the **reality principle:** It takes into account external conditions and the consequences of various actions, and directs behavior so as to maximize pleasure *and* minimize pain. The ego is partly conscious but not entirely so; some of its actions—for example, its external struggle with the id—are outside our conscious knowledge.

The final aspect of personality described by Freud is the **superego.** It, too, seeks to control satisfaction of id impulses, but in contrast to the ego, it is concerned with *morality*—with whether various means of satisfying id impulses are right or wrong. The superego permits gratification of such impulses only when it is morally correct to do so—not only when it is safe or feasible, as required by the ego.

According to Freud, the ego must strike a balance between our primitive urges (the id) and our learned moral constraints (the superego). Freud felt that this constant struggle among id, ego, and superego plays a key role in personality and in many psychological disorders (Chapter 11). Moreover, he suggested that the struggle was often visible in everyday behavior in what have come to be known as **Freudian slips**—errors in speech that actually reflect unconscious impulses that have "slipped by" the ego or superego. An example: "She was tempting . . . I mean attempting to . . . " According to Freud, the word "tempting" reveals an unacceptable sexual impulse.

Freud also had a lot to say when it came to child development and how various developmental stages influence personality. These **psychosexual stages of development** encompass the most controversial aspects of Freud's theory of personality. According to Freud, these stages are ones through which we all pass, and that strongly shape the nature of our personality. Before turning to the stages themselves, however, we must first consider two important concepts relating to them: **libido** and **fixation.**

Libido refers to the instinctual life force that energizes the id. Release of libido is closely related to pleasure, but the focus of such pleasure—and the expression of libido—changes as we develop. In each stage of development, we obtain different kinds of pleasure and leave behind a small amount of our libido—this is the normal course of events. If an excessive amount of libido energy is tied to a particular stage, however, *fixation* results. This can stem from either too little or too much gratification during this stage, and in either case, the result is harmful. Since the individual has left too much "psychic energy" behind, less is available for full adult development. The outcome may be an adult personality reflecting the stage or stages at which fixation has occurred. To put it another way, if too much energy is drained away by fixation at earlier stages of development, the amount remaining may be insufficient to power movement to full adult development. Then, an individual may show an immature personality and several psychological disorders.

Now, back to the actual stages themselves. According to Freud, as we grow and develop, different parts of the body serve as the focus of our quest for pleasure. In the initial **oral stage,** lasting until we are about eighteen months old, we seek pleasure mainly through the mouth. If too much or too little gratification occurs during this stage, an individual may become *fixated* at it. Too little gratification results in a personality that is overly dependent on others; too much, especially after the child has developed some teeth, results in a personality that is excessively hostile, especially through verbal sarcasm.

The next stage occurs in response to efforts by parents to toilet train their children. During the **anal stage,** the process of elimination becomes the primary focus of pleasure. Fixation at this stage, stemming from overly harsh toilet-training experiences, may result in individuals who are excessively orderly or *compulsive*—they can't leave any job unfinished, and strive for perfection and neatness in everything they do. In contrast, fixation stemming from very relaxed toilet training may result in people who are undisciplined, impulsive, and excessively generous. Freud himself might well be described as compulsive; even when he was seriously ill, he personally answered dozens of letters every day—even letters from total strangers asking his advice (Benjamin & Dixon, 1996).

At about age four, the genitals become the primary source of pleasure, and children enter the **phallic stage.** Freud speculated that at this time we fantasize about sex with our opposite-sex parent—a phenomenon he termed the **Oedipus complex,** after Oedipus, a character in ancient Greek literature who unknowingly killed his father and then married his mother. Fear of punishment for such desires then enters the picture. Among boys, the feared punishment is castration, leading to *castration anxiety.* Among girls, the feared punishment is loss of love. In both cases, these fears bring about resolution of the Oedipus complex and identification with the same-sex parent. In other words, young boys give up sexual desires for their mothers and come to see their fathers as models rather than as rivals, while young girls give up their sexual desires for their father and come to see their mothers as models.

Perhaps one of Freud's most controversial suggestions is the idea that young girls experience *penis envy,* stemming from their own lack of a male sex organ. Freud suggested that, because of such envy, girls experience strong feelings of inferiority and jealousy—feelings they carry with them in disguised form even in adult life. As you can readily guess, many psychologists object strongly to these ideas, and there is virtually no evidence for them.

After resolution of the Oedipus conflict, children enter the **latency stage,** during which sexual urges are, according to Freud, at a minimum. During puberty, they enter the final **genital stage.** During this stage, pleasure is again focused on the genitals. Now, however, lust is blended with affection and the person becomes capable of adult love. Remember: According to Freud, progression to this final stage is possible only if serious fixation has *not* occurred at the earlier stages. If such fixation exists, development is blocked and various disorders, such as the ones you'll read about in Chapter 11, result. Major stages in Freud's theory of psychosexual development are summarized in Figure 9.4 on page 344.

■ **Research related to Freud's theory: Probing the unconscious.**

Freud's theories contain many intriguing ideas, and as you already know, several of these have entered into world culture—people everywhere talk about the unconscious, repressed impulses, the id and ego, and so on. It's not surprising, therefore, that psychologists have investigated several of these ideas—at least, the ones that *can* be studied through scientific means. We have already discussed the scientific status of Freud's ideas about dreams (Chapter 4), so let's consider his ideas about the unconscious.

Freud contended that our feelings and behavior can be strongly affected by information we can't bring to mind and can't describe verbally. Research in many fields of psychology suggests that, to some extent, this is true (e.g., Bornstein, 1992, 1993), although psychologists refer to such information as *nonconscious*

Oral stage:
A stage of psychosexual development during which pleasure is centered in the region of the mouth.

Anal stage:
In Freud's theory, a psychosexual stage of development in which pleasure is focused primarily on the anal zone.

Phallic stage:
An early stage of psychosexual development during which pleasure is centered in the genital region. It is during this stage that the Oedipus complex develops.

Oedipus complex:
In Freud's theory, a crisis of psychosexual development in which children must give up their sexual attraction for their opposite-sex parent.

Latency stage:
In Freud's theory, the psychosexual stage of development that follows resolution of the Oedipus complex. During this stage, sexual desires are relatively weak.

Genital stage:
The final stage of psychosexual development—one in which individuals acquire the adult capacity to combine lust with affection.

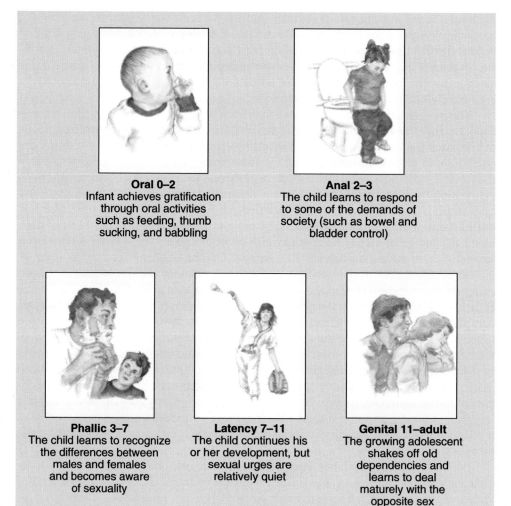

Oral 0–2
Infant achieves gratification through oral activities such as feeding, thumb sucking, and babbling

Anal 2–3
The child learns to respond to some of the demands of society (such as bowel and bladder control)

Phallic 3–7
The child learns to recognize the differences between males and females and becomes aware of sexuality

Latency 7–11
The child continues his or her development, but sexual urges are relatively quiet

Genital 11–adult
The growing adolescent shakes off old dependencies and learns to deal maturely with the opposite sex

FIGURE 9.4
The Psychosexual Stages of Development Described by Freud
According to Freud, all human beings pass through a series of discrete psychosexual stages. At each stage, pleasure is focused on a particular part of the body. Too much or too little gratification at any stage can result in *fixation*, and can lead to psychological disorders.

rather than "unconscious" to avoid assuming that such information has been repressed. Support for the existence of the impact of nonconscious information is provided by *subliminal perception*—a topic we discussed in Chapter 3—as well as by the topics of automatic processing and intuition discussed in Chapter 4. As you may recall, claims for subliminal perception have been overstated, especially with respect to its supposed value as a learning aid or marketing technique. Yet, there is no doubt that sometimes we can be influenced by, and respond to, stimuli of which we are unaware (Reder & Gordon, 1997). Findings such as these indicate that important aspects of our behavior do occur without our being aware either of the actions themselves or of the factors that caused them, just as Freud suggested.

■ **Freud's theory: An overall evaluation.**

As noted earlier, Freud's place in history is assured: His ideas and writing have exerted a profound impact on society. But what about this theory of personality? Is it currently accepted by most psychologists? As you can probably guess from our earlier comments, the answer is *definitely not*. The reasons for this rejection are clear. First, many critics have noted that Freud's theory is not really a scientific theory at all. True, as we just saw, some of his ideas, or hypotheses derived from them, can be tested. But many concepts in his theory cannot be measured or studied systematically. How, for instance can one go about observing an *id*, *fixation*, or the psychic energy contained in the *libido*? As noted in Chapter 1, a theory that cannot be tested is largely useless, and this criticism does apply to many of Freud's ideas.

Second, as we have already seen, several of Freud's proposals are not consistent with the findings of modern research—for instance, his ideas about the meaning of dreams. Third, in constructing his theory, Freud relied heavily on a small number of case studies—no more than a dozen at most. Almost all these people came from wealthy backgrounds and lived in a large and sophisticated city within a single culture. Thus, they were not representative of humans generally.

Finally, and perhaps most important of all, Freud's theories contain so many different concepts that they can explain virtually any pattern of behavior in an after-the-fact manner. If a theory can't be disconfirmed—shown to be false—then, once again, it is largely useless, and this does seem to be the case with respect to Freud's views.

For these and other reasons, Freud's theory of personality is not currently accepted by most psychologists. Yet, several of his insights—especially his ideas about levels of consciousness and the importance of **anxiety** in psychological disorders (Chapter 11)—*have* contributed to our understanding of human behavior and personality. So, while his theories don't measure up to the rigorous standards of science required by modern psychology, there is no doubt that they have had a profound and lasting impact on modern thought. (Are these effects beneficial ones? Or should you question them in your own life? For a discussion of this issue, see the **Psychology Lends a Hand** section on page 346.)

FIGURE 9.5
The Wise Old Man: An Archetype
According to Jung, all human being possess a *collective unconscious*. Information stored there is often expressed in terms of *archetypes*—representations of key aspects of human experience, such as the wise old man (shown here), mother, father, and so on.

KEY QUESTIONS

- According to Freud, what are the three levels of consciousness?
- In Freud's theory, what are the three basic components of personality?
- According to Freud, what are the psychosexual stages of development?
- Do research findings support Freud's views about the unconscious?

■ Other Psychoanalytic Views: Freud's Disciples . . . and Defectors

Whatever else Freud was, he was certainly an intellectual magnet. Over the course of several decades, he attracted many brilliant people as students or colleagues. Most of them began by accepting Freud's views. Later, however, they often disagreed with some of his major assumptions. Let's see why these individuals, often termed **neo-Freudians,** broke with Freud, and what they had to say about the nature of personality.

Carl Jung was perhaps the most bitter of all Freud's defectors and perhaps also the most famous. Jung shared Freud's views concerning the importance of the unconscious, but contended that there is another part to this aspect of personality that Freud overlooked: the **collective unconscious.** According to Jung, the collective unconscious holds experiences shared by all humans—experiences that are, in a sense, part of our biological heritage. The contents of the collective unconscious, in short, reflect the experiences our species has had since it originated. The collective unconscious finds expression in several ways, but among these, **archetypes** are the most central to Jung's theory. These are manifestations of the collective unconscious that express themselves when our conscious mind is distracted or inactive, for example, during sleep, in dreams, or fantasies (e.g., Neher, 1996). The specific expression of archetypes depends, in part, on our unique experience as individuals, but in all cases such images are representations of key aspects of the human experience—images representing *mother, father, wise old man, the sun, the moon, God, death,* and *the hero* (see Figure 9.5). It is because of these shared innate images, Jung contended, that the folklore of many different cultures contains similar figures and themes.

Another aspect of Jung's theory was his suggestion that we are all born with innate tendencies to be concerned primarily either with our inner selves or with the outside world. Jung labeled people in the first category **introverts** and

Anxiety:
In Freudian theory, unpleasant feelings of tension or worry experienced by individuals in reaction to unacceptable wishes or impulses.

Neo-Freudians:
Personality theorists who accepted basic portions of Freud's theory, but rejected or modified other portions.

Collective unconscious:
In Jung's theory, a portion of the unconscious shared by all humans.

Archetypes:
According to Jung, inherited images in the collective unconscious that shape our perceptions of the external world.

Introverts:
In Jung's theory, individuals who are hesitant and cautious and do not make friends easily.

PSYCHOLOGY LENDS A HAND

Too Much Freud for Our Own Good? Questioning Freudian Assumptions in Everyday Life

Because of his influence during the early years of psychology, many of Freud's ideas have become accepted in everyday life. Whether you realize it or not, you probably accept some of these ideas in your own life. Here, we want to raise the possibility that this is *not* necessarily a good thing. Several of these ideas have been shown to be false, so accepting them, even implicitly, can lead to serious problems. Here are some of Freud's ideas we think you should seriously question:

- **Gaining insight into the causes of our current problems will make these problems disappear—or, at least, diminish.** Do you accept this belief? Most people do. In fact, you will hear people mention this in everyday conversation: "Once I understood why I felt that way, I was able to deal with it better," or "After I figured out *why* I had those problems, they went away." In fact, a large body of research findings indicate that this is *not* necessarily the case. Gaining insight into the cause of problems, negative feelings, and personal distress can be a helpful first step. But it does not, in and of itself, guarantee that the problems will disappear. On the contrary, sometimes, thinking about them over and over again (ruminating) can have disastrous effects (see Nolen-Hoeksema & Davis, 1999). So please, do *not* accept Freud's assumption unquestioningly; doing so can be harmful to your mental health and personal happiness.

- **Dreams provide valuable insights into the unconscious, and understanding them can be very beneficial.** As we noted in Chapter 4, modern research indicates that while dreams can, indeed, reflect important events in our lives, they are *not* a direct "line" into the unconscious. On the contrary, they are more likely to represent random activity

in your nervous system, and your mind's efforts to make sense of this activity, than reflections of your hidden urges and impulses. So whatever the popular press says, or your friends tell you, do *not* place much faith in the value of interpreting dreams.

- **Once our personalities are formed, early in life, they cannot be changed; all we can do is recognize them and adapt to them.** In some ways, this may be the most dangerous assumption of all. Yes, some aspects of personality tend to be stable over time, but this in no way implies that they can never be changed. In fact, a large body of scientific evidence points to the opposite conclusion. If people genuinely want to change various aspects of their personalities, and are willing to work hard to do so, they can. They can boost their self-esteem and self-efficacy, learn to control their tempers and be less irritable, replace pessimism with optimism, and even learn to be more orderly and conscientious. Making such changes is often difficult. But modern psychology believes ardently that they *can* be made, so by all means, question the assumption that "what we are is set in stone." In this respect, Freud was definitely too pessimistic.

Please don't misunderstand: We are not suggesting that Freud's ideas should all be discarded. On the contrary, as we noted earlier, several are highly insightful and have stimulated research and thought that have greatly expanded our understanding of human behavior and personality. But the assumptions above are far too questionable to deserve the widespread, implicit acceptance they enjoy. So start today to notice them in your own thinking, and to minimize their impact.

---

described them as being hesitant and cautious; they do not make friends easily and prefer to observe the world rather than become involved in it. He labeled people in the second category **extroverts**. Such people are open and confident, make friends, and readily enjoy high levels of stimulation and a wide range of activities. While many aspects of Jung's theory have been rejected by psychologists—especially the idea of the collective unconscious—the dimension of introversion-extroversion (now usually spelled extr*a*version) appears to be a basic one of major importance, and is included in several *trait theories* we'll consider in a later section (although in these theories the term is spelled extr*a*version).

Two other important neo-Freudians are Karen Horney and Alfred Adler. Horney was one of the few females in the early psychoanalytic movement, and she disagreed with Freud strongly over his view that differences between men and women stemmed largely from innate factors—for example, anatomical differences resulting in *penis envy* among females. Horney contended that although women do often feel inferior to men (remember: she was writing in Germany in the

Extroverts:
In Jung's theory, individuals who are open and confident and make friends readily.

1920s), this is *not* a result of penis envy, but rather of how they are treated by society. She argued that if women were raised in a different type of environment, they would see themselves more favorably. In other words, it was not the male penis women envied, but rather the *power* and *autonomy* associated with "maleness." In addition, she emphasized the point that psychological disorders do not stem from fixation of psychic energy, as Freud contended, but rather from disturbed interpersonal relationships during childhood and what she termed **basic anxiety**—children's fear of being left alone, helpless and insecure. By emphasizing the importance of children's relationships with their parents, Horney called attention to the importance of social factors in shaping personality.

Adler also disagreed with Freud very strongly, but over somewhat different issues. In particular, he emphasized the importance of feelings of inferiority, which he believed we experience as children because of our small size and physical weakness. He viewed personality development as stemming primarily from our efforts to overcome such feelings, through what he termed *striving for superiority*. If these efforts go to too far, we may develop a *superiority complex*, and become a braggart or a bully (Sutton & Smith, 1999). However, under the surface, people who show this pattern still feel inferior: They are merely covering up with an outward show of strength. Like Horney and other neo-Freudians, Adler also emphasized the importance of social factors in personality; for instance, he called attention to the importance of birth order.

By now the main point should be clear: Neo-Freudians, while accepting many of Freud's basic ideas, rejected his emphasis on innate patterns of development. On the contrary, they perceived personality as stemming from a complex interplay between social factors and the experiences we have during childhood, primarily in our own families. The theories proposed by neo-Freudians are not widely accepted by psychologists, but they did serve as a kind of bridge between the provocative views offered by Freud and more modern conceptions of personality. In this respect, at least, they made an important contribution.

KEY QUESTIONS

- According to Jung, what is the collective unconscious?
- In Horney's theory, what is basic anxiety?
- According to Adler, what is the role of feelings of inferiority in personality?

Humanistic Theories: Emphasis on Growth

Id versus ego, penis envy—on the whole, psychoanalytic theories of personality take a dim view of human nature, contending that we must struggle constantly to control our bestial impulses if we are to function as healthy, rational adults. Is this view accurate? Many psychologists doubt it. They believe that human strivings for growth, dignity, and self-determination are just as important as, if not more important than, in the development of personality, the primitive motives Freud emphasized. Because of their more optimistic views concerning human nature, such views as known as **humanistic theories** (Maslow, 1970; Rogers, 1977, 1982). These theories differ widely in the concepts on which they focus, but share the following characteristics.

First, they emphasize *personal responsibility*. Each of us, these theories contend, is largely responsible for what happens to us. Our fate is mostly in our own hands; we are *not* merely rudderless ships driven here and there by dark forces within our personalities. Second, while these theories don't deny the importance of past experience, they generally focus on the present. True, we may be influenced by traumatic events early in life. Yet these do *not* have to shape our entire adult lives, and the capacity to overcome them and to go on from there is both real and powerful. Third, humanistic theories stress the importance of *personal growth*. People

Basic anxiety:
Children's fear of being left alone, helpless and insecure.

Humanistic theories:
Theories of personality emphasizing personality responsibility and innate tendencies toward personal growth.

are not, such theories argue, content with merely meeting their current needs. They wish to progress toward "bigger" goals, such as becoming the best they can be. Only when obstacles interfere with such growth is the process interrupted. A key goal of therapy (more on this in Chapter 12), therefore, should be the removal of obstacles that prevent natural growth processes from proceeding. As examples of humanistic theories, we'll now consider the views proposed by Carl Rogers and Abraham Maslow.

■ **Rogers's self theory: Becoming a fully functioning person.**

Carl Rogers planned to become a minister, but after taking several courses in psychology, he changed his mind and decided, instead, to focus on human personality. One central assumption of the theory he proposed was this: Left to their own devices, humans show many positive characteristics and move, over the course of their lives, toward becoming **fully functioning persons.** What are such people like? Rogers suggested that they are people who strive to experience life to the fullest, who live in the here and now, and who trust their feelings. They are sensitive to the needs and rights of others, but do not allow society's standards to shape their feelings or actions to an excessive degree. Fully functioning people aren't saints; they can—and do—act in ways they later regret. But throughout life, their actions are dominated by constructive impulses. They are in close touch with their own values and feelings, and experience life more deeply than most other people.

If all humans possess the capacity to become fully functioning people, why don't they all succeed? The answer, Rogers suggested, lies in the anxiety generated when life experiences are inconsistent with our ideas about ourselves—when a gap develops between our **self-concept** (our beliefs and knowledge about ourselves) and reality, or our perceptions of it. For example, imagine a young girl who is quite independent and self-reliant, and thinks of herself in this way. After her older sibling dies in an accident, however, her parents begin to baby her and to convey the message, over and over again, that she is vulnerable and must be sheltered from the outside world. This treatment is highly inconsistent with her self-concept. As a result, she experiences anxiety and adopts one or more psychological defenses to reduce it. The most common of these defenses is *distortion*— changing our perceptions of reality so that they *are* consistent with our self-concept. For example, the girl may come to believe that her parents aren't being overprotective; they are just showing normal concern for her safety. Another defense process is *denial;* she may refuse to admit to herself that as a result of being babied, she is indeed losing her independence.

In the short run, such tactics can be successful; they help reduce anxiety. Ultimately, however, they produce sizable gaps between an individual's self-concept and reality. For instance, the girl may cling to the belief that she is independent when, in fact, as a result of her parents' treatment, she is becoming increasingly helpless. The larger such gaps, Rogers contends, the greater an individual's maladjustment—and personal unhappiness (see Figure 9.6). Rogers suggested that distortions in the self-concept are common because most people grow up in an atmosphere of *conditional positive regard.* They learn that others, such as their parents, will approve of them only when they behave in certain ways and express certain feelings. As a result, many people are forced to deny the existence of various impulses and feelings, and their self-concepts become badly distorted.

How can such distorted self-concepts be repaired so that healthy development can continue? Rogers suggested that therapists can help accomplish this goal by placing individuals in an atmosphere of **unconditional positive regard**— a setting in which they will be accepted by the therapist *no matter what they say or do.* Such conditions are provided by *client-centered therapy,* a form of therapy we will consider in detail in Chapter 12.

Fully functioning persons:
In Rogers's theory, psychologically healthy people who enjoy life to the fullest.

Self-concept:
All the information and beliefs individuals have about their own characteristics and themselves.

Unconditional positive regard:
In Rogers's theory, communicating to others that they will be respected or loved regardless of what they say or do.

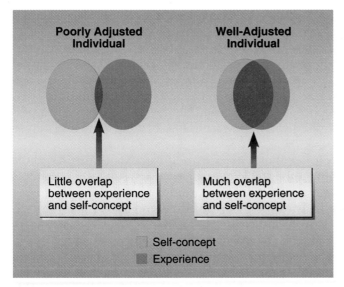

Poorly Adjusted Individual

Well-Adjusted Individual

Little overlap between experience and self-concept

Much overlap between experience and self-concept

☐ Self-concept
■ Experience

FIGURE 9.6
Gaps between Our Self-Concept and Our Experience: A Cause of Maladjustment in Rogers's Theory
According to Rogers, the larger the gap between an individual's self-concept and reality, the poorer this person's psychological adjustment.

■ **Maslow and the study of self-actualizing people.**

Another influential humanistic theory of personality was proposed by Abraham Maslow (1970). We have already described a portion of Maslow's theory, his concept of a *needs hierarchy*, in Chapter 8. This is only part of Maslow's theory of personality. He has also devoted much attention to the study of people who, in his terms, are *psychologically healthy*. These are individuals who have attained high levels of **self-actualization**—a state in which they have reached their fullest true potential. What are such people like? In essence, much like the fully functioning people described by Rogers. Self-actualized people accept themselves for what they are; they recognize their shortcomings as well as their strengths. Being in touch with their own personalities, they are less inhibited and less likely to conform than most of us. Self-actualized people are well aware of the rules imposed by society, but feel greater freedom to ignore them than do most people. Unlike most of us, they seem to retain their childhood wonder and amazement with the world. For them, life continues to be an exciting adventure rather than a boring routine. Finally, self-actualized people sometimes have what Maslow describes as **peak experiences**—instances in which they have powerful feelings of unity with the universe and feel tremendous waves of power and wonder. Such experiences appear to be linked to personal growth, for after them, individuals report feeling more spontaneous, more appreciative of life, and less concerned with the problems of everyday life. Examples of people Maslow describes as fully self-actualized are Thomas Jefferson, Albert Einstein, Eleanor Roosevelt, and George Washington Carver.

■ **Research related to humanistic theories: Links to self-esteem.**

At first glance, it might seem that humanistic theories, like psychoanalytic ones, are not readily open to scientific test. In fact, the opposite is true. Indeed, several concepts that play a key role in humanistic theories have been studied quite extensively. Among these, the one that has probably received most attention is the concept of the *self-concept*, which is so central to Rogers's theory.

Research on the self-concept has addressed many different issues—for instance, how our self-concept is formed (e.g., Marsh & Craven, 2006; Sedikides & Skowronski, 1997), how it influences the way we think (e.g., Kendzierski & Whitaker, 1997), and what information it contains (e.g., Rentsch & Heffner, 1994). Together, such research suggests that the self-concept is complex and consists of many different parts (e.g., knowledge of our own traits and beliefs, understanding

Self-actualization:
A stage of personal development in which individuals reach their maximum potential.

Peak experiences:
According to Maslow, intense emotional experiences during which individuals feel at one with the universe.

of how we are perceived by and relate to others; knowledge of how we are similar to and different from others; e.g., Baumeister & Leary, 1995).

Rogers' emphasis on the importance of the self-concept led many psychologists to focus on the closely related concept of **self-esteem**—our assessment of our overall personal worth or adequacy. Since it is virtually impossible to have beliefs about our own characteristics without also evaluating them, it is often a very short step from self-concept to self-esteem. But is self-esteem really a personality trait? In other words, does it show consistency over time and across situations?

In general, research indicates that a person's self-esteem relative to others (one's rank order) does remain quite stable over many years, suggesting that it is an aspect of personality. For example, a teenager who is near the middle during the teenage years will most likely develop into an adult who also is near the middle relative to other adults. However, there are also general patterns of change in self-esteem across the life span with the teenagers years being a time of relatively low self-esteem, marked by a steady increase through adulthood, until the last years of life. Interestingly, children tend to have higher self-esteem than teenagers, perhaps because they have yet to encounter the challenges of adolescence. This pattern, incidentally, is similar for males and females, though males on average report higher levels of self-esteem than females for all but the very first and very last years of life (Robins & Trzesniewski, 2005).

Self-esteem has also been examined across various demographic groups. For example, when examined as a group, African Americans and European-Americans do tend to differ in self-esteem (e.g., Gray-Little & Hafdahl, 2000). Specifically, this research indicates that African Americans show higher self-esteem than Americans of European descent. In contrast, members of other ethnic minorities in the United States (Hispanics, Asians, Native Americans) tend to score slightly lower than European Americans.

More recently, self-esteem has been examined in several countries outside the United States (Schmitt & Allik, 2005). In this large-scale study the self-esteem of thousands of individuals from fifty-three countries was assessed (literally, from A—Argentina—to Z—Zimbabwe). These researchers looked a little more closely at self-esteem by examining its two components: *self-competence* (beliefs that one is generally able to accomplish things) and *self-liking* (feeling that one is a good person). While it may seem as though our views about our own competence should go hand in hand with how much we like ourselves, this appears not to be the case across all cultures. The cultural dimension of *individualism-collectivism* appears to help explain these findings. This dimension describes cultural differences that reflect, in part, an emphasis on the needs of the individual versus the needs of the collective (i.e., family or larger social group). As can be seen in Figure 9.7, people from more individualistic countries (e.g., United States and the Netherlands) express higher degrees of self-competence, in contrast to self-liking, whereas people from more collectivistic countries (e.g., Pakistan, and Peru) showed the opposite pattern. Interestingly, these two aspects of self-esteem appear to compensate for each other, resulting in overall levels of self-esteem that are more similar than they are different across cultures.

■ Humanistic theories: An evaluation.

The comments above suggest that humanistic theories have had a lasting impact on psychology, and this is definitely so. Several of the ideas first proposed by Rogers, Maslow, and other humanistic theorists have entered into the mainstream of psychology. For example, in an upcoming chapter on the treatment of mental disorders (Chapter 12), you'll see how humanistic theories have been influential in guiding one approach to psychotherapy. But humanistic theories have also been subject to strong criticism. Many key concepts of humanistic theories are loosely defined. What, precisely, is self-actualization? A peak experience? A

Self-esteem:
Our assessment of our overall personal worth or adequacy.

fully functioning person? Until such terms are clearly defined, it is difficult to conduct systematic research on them. Despite such criticisms, the impact of humanistic theories has persisted, and they do indeed constitute a lasting contribution to our understanding of human personality.

KEY QUESTIONS

- How does the view of human beings proposed by humanistic theories of personality differ from that of psychoanalytic theories?
- According to Rogers, why do many individuals fail to become fully functioning persons?
- According to Maslow's theory, what is self-actualization?
- What is self-esteem? How does it vary over time and across groups?

Trait Theories: Seeking the Key Dimensions of Personality

When we describe other people, we often do so in terms of specific **personality traits**—stable dimensions of personality along which people vary, from very low to very high. This strong tendency to think about others in terms of specific characteristics is reflected in **trait theories** of personality. Such theories focus on identifying key dimensions of personality—the most important ways in which people differ. The basic idea behind this approach is as follows: Once we identify the key dimensions along which people differ, we can measure how *much* they differ and can then relate such differences to many important forms of behavior.

Unfortunately, this task sounds easier than it actually is. Human beings differ in an almost countless number of ways. How can we determine which of these are most important and stable (i.e., lasting)? One approach is to search for *clusters*—groups of traits that seem to go together. We'll now take a brief look at one contemporary theory that adopted this approach.

■ The "big five" factors: The basic dimensions of personality?

When trait theorists first began searching for the key dimensions of personality, there was a great deal of disagreement, as is often the case when a topic is first studied. Now, however, there is increasing consensus among psychologists that, in fact, there may be only five key or central dimensions of personality (e.g., Costa & McCrae, 1994; Zuckerman, 1994). These are sometimes labeled the "big five," and can be described as follows:

1. **Extraversion:** A tendency to seek stimulation and to enjoy the company of other people. (A dimension ranging from energetic, enthusiastic, sociable, and talkative on one end, to retiring, sober, reserved, silent, and cautious on the other.)
2. **Agreeableness:** A tendency to be compassionate toward others. (A dimension ranging from good-natured, cooperative, trusting, and helpful at one end, to irritable, suspicious, and uncooperative at the other.)

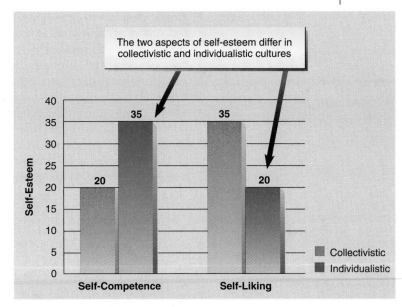

FIGURE 9.7
Cultural Differences in Self-Esteem
As shown here, people from more individualistic cultures, such as the United States and the Netherlands, tend to express higher degrees of self-competence over self-liking. In contrast, individuals in collectivist cultures, such as Peru and Pakistan, tend to show the opposite pattern.
Source: Based on data from Schmitt & Allik, 2005.

Personality traits:
Specific dimensions along which individuals' differ in consistent, stable ways.

Trait theories:
Theories of personality that focus on identifying the key dimensions along which people differ.

Extraversion:
One of the "big five" dimensions of personality; a dimension ranging from sociable, talking, and fun-loving at one end to sober, reserved, and cautious at the other.

Agreeableness:
One of the "big five" dimensions of personality; a dimension ranging from good-natured, cooperative, and trusting on one end to irritable, suspicious, uncooperative at the other.

3. **Conscientiousness:** A tendency to show self-discipline, to strive for competence and achievement. (A dimension ranging from well-organized, careful, self-disciplined, responsible, and precise at one end, to disorganized, impulsive, careless, and undependable at the other.)

4. **Emotional stability** (sometime labeled by its opposite, *neuroticism*): A tendency to experience unpleasant emotions easily (at the neuroticism end). (A dimension ranging from poised, calm, composed, and not hypochondriacal at one end, to nervous, anxious, high-strung, and hypochondriacal at the other. See Figure 9.8.)

5. **Openness to experience:** A tendency to enjoy new experiences and new ideas. (A dimension ranging from imaginative, witty, and having broad interests at one end, to down-to-earth, simple, and having narrow interests at the other.)

How basic are the "big five" dimensions? Although there is far from complete agreement on this point (e.g., Friedman & Schustack, 1999), many researchers believe that these dimensions are indeed very basic ones. For example, these dimensions are ones to which most people in many different cultures refer when describing themselves and others (e.g., McCrae, et al., 2005). In this large-scale study, cultural differences in these five traits were examined across fifty-one cultures. Results showed that people across the world use dimensions similar to those in the "big five" to describe themselves, regardless of language and culture. Even children as young as five describe themselves along these dimensions, when prompted using a creative technique called the "Puppet Interview" (Measelle et al., 2005). Other researchers, such as those interested in the evolution of personality traits, have even found evidence of these traits in other primates, such as chimpanzees and orangutans (Weiss, King, & Perkins, 2006). Interestingly, only conscientiousness does not seem to be essential in other primates. This indicates that, in an evolutionary sense, these other traits are very basic indeed!

■ **Research on trait theories.**

If the "big five" dimensions of personality are really so basic, then it is reasonable to expect that they will be related to important forms of behavior. In fact, many studies indicate that this is the case. Where people stand on the "big five" dimensions is closely linked to important outcomes, such as success in performing many jobs (e.g., Hogan, Hogan, & Roberts, 1996; Thoresen et al., 2004), running a new business (Ciavarella et al., 2004), and being helpful at work (Ladd & Henry, 2000). Some of these traits also relate to personal happiness (e.g., Steel & Ones, 2002) and the likelihood of exhibiting various psychological disorders, such as attention-deficit/hyperactivity disorder (Nigg et al., 2002). Some traits also have been linked to positive health behaviors such as the avoidance of cigarettes, alcohol, and other harmful drugs (Chassin, Flora, & King, 2004). From these results it should not be surprising that some of these traits, particularly conscientiousness, also relate to longevity (Bogg & Roberts, 2004). This is just a small sample of research suggesting that the "big five" are indeed "big"—they are basic dimensions of personality that are related to many important aspects of behavior. Thus, they are certainly worthy of further careful study.

■ **Trait theories: An evaluation.**

At present, most research on personality by psychologists occurs within the context of the trait approach. Instead of seeking to test grand theories such as the ones offered by Freud, Jung, and Rogers, most psychologists currently direct their efforts to the task of understanding specific traits and how these traits relate to behavior (Kring, Smith, & Neale, 1994). This is not to imply that the trait approach is perfect, however. On the contrary, it can be criticized in several respects. First, it is largely *descriptive* in nature. It seeks to describe the key dimensions of personality but does not attempt to determine *how* various traits develop, *how* they influence behavior, or why they are important. Second, despite several decades of careful research, there is still no final agreement concerning the traits that are most important or most basic. The "big five" dimensions are widely accepted, but they are far from *universally*

Conscientiousness:
One of the "big five" dimensions of personality; a dimension ranging from well-organized, careful, and responsible on the one end to disorganized, careless, and unscrupulous at the other.

Emotional stability:
One of the "big five" dimensions of personality; a dimension ranging from poised, calm, and composed at one extreme to nervous, anxious, and excitable at the other.

Openness to experience:
One of the "big five" dimensions of personality; a dimension ranging from imaginative, sensitive, and intellectual at one extreme to down-to-earth, insensitive, and crude at the other.

accepted, and some psychologists feel that they are not the final answer in this respect (e.g., Bandura, 1999; Block, 1995; Goldberg & Saucier, 1995).

As you can readily see, these criticisms relate primarily to what the trait approach has not yet accomplished rather than to its basic nature. All in all, we can conclude that this approach to personality has generally been a very valuable one. In short, attempting to understand the dimensions along which people differ appears to be a useful strategy for understanding the uniqueness and consistency of key aspects of their behavior.

KEY QUESTIONS

- What are the "big five" dimensions of personality?
- What behaviors are related to traits in the "big five"?
- What are the advantages and disadvantages of the trait approach?

Cognitive-Behavioral Approaches to Personality

Ultimately, all personality theories must come to grips with two basic questions: What accounts for the *uniqueness* of individuals and what underlies *consistency* in their behavior over time and across situations? Freud's answer focused on *internal* factors—hidden conflicts among the id, ego, and superego, and the active struggle to keep unacceptable impulses out of consciousness. At the other end of the continuum are approaches to personality that emphasize the role of learning and experience. While such views were not originally presented as theories of personality, they are often described as *cognitive-behavioral theories* or *learning theories of personality* to distinguish them from other perspectives (Bandura, 1997; Rotter, 1982; Skinner, 1974).

How can this perspective account for the uniqueness and consistency of human behavior? Very readily. Uniqueness, the cognitive-behavioral approach contends, merely reflects that we all have distinctive life experiences. Similarly, a cognitive-behavioral approach can explain consistency in behavior over time and across situations by noting that the responses, associations, or habits acquired through learning tend to persist. Moreover, since individuals often find themselves in situations very similar to the ones in which they acquired these tendencies, their behavior, too, tends to remain stable.

Early cognitive-behavioral views of personality emphasized the central role of learning and took what now seems to be a somewhat extreme position: They denied the importance of *any* internal causes of behavior—motives, traits, intentions, goals (Skinner, 1974). The only things that matter, these early theorists suggested, are external conditions determining patterns of reinforcement (recall the discussion of *schedules of reinforcement* in Chapter 5). At present, few psychologists agree with this position. Most now believe that internal factors—especially many aspects of *cognition*—play a crucial role in behavior. A prime example of this modern approach, is provided by Bandura's *social cognitive theory* (e.g., Bandura, 1986, 2001).

■ Social cognitive theory: A modern view of personality.

In **social cognitive theory,** Bandura places great emphasis on what he terms the **self-system**—the cognitive processes by which a person perceives, evaluates, and regulates his or her own behavior so that is appropriate in a given situation. Reflecting the emphasis on cognition in modern psychology, Bandura calls attention to the fact that people don't simply respond to reinforcements; rather, they think

FIGURE 9.8
Emotional Stability: One of the "Big Five" Dimensions of Personality
The people shown here are all low in *emotional stability* (i.e., they are high on neuroticism)—they have a strong tendency to experience unpleasant emotions.
Source: © The New Yorker Collection, 1999 Roz Chast from cartoonbank. com. All Rights Reserved.

Social cognitive theory:
A theory of behavior suggesting that human behaviors are influenced by many cognitive factors as well as by reinforcement contingencies, and that humans have an impressive capacity to regulate their own actions.

Self-system:
In Bandura's social-cognitive learning theory, the set of cognitive processes by which a person perceives, evaluates, and regulates his or her own behavior.

FIGURE 9.9
Observational Learning: An Important Source of Learning
We often acquire information and important new skills by observing the behavior of others.
Such observational learning is an important aspect of Bandura's social cognitive theory.

Self-reinforcement:
A process in which individuals reward themselves for reaching their own goals.

Observational learning:
The process through which individuals acquire information or behaviors by observing others.

Internals:
Individuals who believe that they exert considerable control over the outcomes they experience.

Externals:
Individuals who believe that they have little control over the outcomes they experience.

Self-efficacy:
Individuals' expectations concerning their ability to perform various tasks.

about the consequences of their actions, anticipate future events, and establish goals and plans. In addition, they engage in **self-reinforcement,** patting themselves on the back when they attain their goals. For example, consider the hundreds of amateur runners who participate in major marathons. Few believe that they have any chance of winning and obtaining the external rewards offered—status, fame, cash prizes. Why, then, do they run? Because, Bandura would contend, they have self-set goals, such as finishing the race, or merely going as far as they can. Meeting these goals allows them to engage in self-reinforcement, and this is sufficient to initiate what is obviously very effortful behavior.

Another important feature of Bandura's theory is its emphasis on **observational learning** (which we described in Chapter 5), a form of learning in which individuals acquire both information and new forms of behavior through observing others (Bandura, 1977). Such learning plays a role in a very wide range of human activities—everything from learning how to dress and groom in the current style of one's own society through learning how to perform new and difficult tasks (see Figure 9.9). In essence, any time human beings observe others, they can learn from this experience, and such learning can then play an important part in the development of personality.

Other learning-oriented approaches to personality have much in common with Bandura's views. For example, the *social learning theory* proposed by Julian Rotter (1954, 1982) suggests that the likelihood that a given behavior will occur in a specific situation depends on individuals' *expectancies* concerning the outcomes the behavior will produce, and the *reinforcement value* they attach to such outcomes—the degree to which they prefer one reinforcer over another. According to Rotter, individuals form *generalized expectancies* concerning the extent to which their actions shape their own outcomes. Rotter describes people who strongly believe that they can shape their own destinies as **internals** and those who believe their outcomes are largely the result of forces outside their control as **externals.** As you can probably guess, internals are often happier and better adjusted than externals.

■ Research on the social-cognitive perspective.

Perhaps the aspect of Bandura's theory that has received most attention in recent research is his concept of **self-efficacy**—an individual's belief that he or she can perform some behavior or task successfully. If you sit down to take an exam in your psychology class and expect to do well, your self-efficacy for the exam is high; if you have doubts about your performance, then your self-efficacy is lower.

Self-efficacy has been found to play a role in success on many tasks (e.g., Maurer & Pierce, 1998), health—people who expect to handle stress effectively or to get better actually do (Bandura, 1992)—personal happiness and life satisfaction (Judge et al., 1998), and success in starting a new business: Entrepreneurs tend to be higher in self-efficacy than other people and believe they can succeed, even though the odds are against them (Markman, Baron, & Balkin, 2003). Although Bandura did not initially view self-efficacy as an aspect of personality, recent findings indicate that people acquire *general* expectations about their abilities to succeed in performing many tasks—virtually any tasks they undertake. Such generalized beliefs about their task-related capabilities are stable over time, so they are now viewed by many psychologists as an important aspect of personality.

In general, learning theories of personality have been the subject of a great deal of research attention that extends beyond issues concerning personality development (e.g., Wallace, 1993). Indeed, as we'll see in Chapter 12, efforts to test these theories have led to the development of several new and highly effective techniques for treating psychological disorders. They have also been successfully applied in many educational contexts as a method for improving student learning and motivation, topics you learned about in Chapters 5 and 8.

■ **Evaluation of the cognitive-behavioral approach.**

Do all humans confront an Oedipus conflict? Are peak experiences real, and do they constitute a sign of growing self-actualization? While controversy exists with respect to these and many other aspects of psychoanalytic and humanistic theories of personality, virtually all psychologists agree that behaviors are acquired and modified through learning. Moreover, there is general agreement about the importance of cognitive factors in human behavior. Thus, a key strength of the cognitive-behavioral approach is obvious: It is based on widely accepted and well-documented principles of psychology.

Turning to criticisms, most of these have focused on older approaches rather than on the more sophisticated theories proposed by Bandura (1986, 1997) and others. Those early behaviorist theorists generally ignored the role of cognitive factors in human behavior, but this is certainly *not* true of the modern theories. A related criticism centers around how learning theories generally ignore inner conflicts, and the influence of unconscious thoughts and impulses, on behavior. However, while such issues are not explicitly addressed by theories such as Bandura's, their existence and possible impact is not in any way denied by these theories. Rather, modern learning theories would simply insist that such effects be interpreted within the context of modern psychology.

As you can readily see, these are *not* major criticisms. Thus, it seems fair to state that at present, these cognitive-behavioral theories of personality are more in tune with modern psychology than earlier theories. As such, they are certain to play an important role, along with the trait approach, in continuing efforts to understand the uniqueness and consistency of human behavior that, together, led us to consider personality in the first place.

Now that we have examined several different theories of personality, we turn to the topic of measuring personality, an issue that is fundamental to the scientific study of personality.

KEY QUESTIONS

- According to learning theories of personality, what accounts for the uniqueness and consistency of human behavior?
- In Bandura's social cognitive theory, what is the self-system?
- According to Rotter's social learning theory, what is the key difference between internals and externals?
- What is self-efficacy?

FIGURE 9.10
What Kind of Person Are You?
Personality Tests Are Everywhere
Magazines such as these often include tests promising to help you figure out what type of lover, friend, or investor you are. While many are interesting, most have not been scientifically developed, so their usefulness is questionable.

NEO personality inventory:

An objective measure of personality designed to assess individuals' relative standing on each of the "big five" dimensions of personality.

Measuring Personality

If you are like most people you have been tempted at one time or another to fill out a personality test of some sort in a magazine or online (see Figure 9.10). Tests such as these typically promise to help you "Find Out What Kind of Person (or lover, investor, friend) You Are" by having you answer a few simple questions. Scoring keys are provided at the end, allowing you to assess how you stand on the various key dimensions. This is then followed by some tips for self-improvement. Do these tests work? Like any product, some work better than others. Also, like any product, the best ones undergo extensive development and evaluation so that the tests measure what they are intended to measure.

Unfortunately, careful test development, which we address later in the chapter, typically is not done with many tests that you see in magazines and online. In addition, many psychological tests may be developed for use in one context and then inappropriately used in an entirely different context. This is equivalent to using a hammer to paint a wall simply because one is so pleased with how effectively it drove nails into a piece of wood. While this may seem like an extreme metaphor, such misuses are very common, primarily because many personality tests are readily available. Now with these cautionary words in mind, we describe below some of the ways in which psychologists have measured personality.

■ Self-report personality tests.

One way to measure personality involves asking individuals to respond to a *self-report* inventory or questionnaire. Such measures (sometimes known as *objective* tests of personality) contain questions or statements to which individuals respond in various ways. For example, a questionnaire might ask respondents to indicate the extent to which each of a set of statements is true or false about themselves, the extent to which they agree or disagree with various sentences (e.g., "I often feel that I can do everything well," "At root, I am a strong person."), or to indicate which of a pair of activities they prefer. (Incidentally, the two items listed here are from one widely used measure of self-efficacy.) Answers to the questions on such objective tests are scored by means of special keys. The score obtained by a specific person is then compared with those obtained by hundreds or even thousands of other people who have taken the test previously. In this way, an individual's relative standing on the trait being measured can be determined.

One of the most widely used self-report tests is the **NEO Personality Inventory** (NEO-PI; Costa & McCrae, 1989), used to measure the "big five" dimensions of personality described earlier in this chapter. Because it was carefully developed, the NEO Personality Inventory is widely used in research.

Self-report personality tests are also used extensively to assess psychological disorders, such as those you will learn about in Chapter 11. Such tests—for instance, the MMPI (short for Minnesota Multiphasic Personality Inventory) and the MCMI (short for Millon Clinical Multiaxial Inventory; Millon, 1987, 1997)—will be discussed in that chapter after you have learned more about various psychological disorders. These tests are especially usefully to clinical psychologists who must first identify individuals' problems before recommending specific forms of therapy for them.

■ Projective personality tests.

In contrast to questionnaires and inventories, *projective tests* of personality adopt a very different approach. They consist of a series of ambiguous stimuli—stimuli that can be interpreted in many different ways. For instance, these can be inkblots such as the one shown in Figure 9.11. People taking the test are then asked to indicate what they see or to make up a story about the stimulus. Since the stimuli themselves are ambiguous, it is assumed that the answers given by respondents will reflect various aspects of their personality. In other words, people "project" different aspects of their personality in the things they see in the stimuli. For example, someone viewing ambiguous scenes in the Thematic Apperception Test (TAT) may make up stories that consistently refer to achievement themes, such as winning a competition or achieving great feats. Another person viewing the same pictures may focus on relational themes (e.g., how individuals in the scenes get along). Because the pictures are designed to be ambiguous, people with different personality characteristics supposedly see different things, thus revealing different aspects of who they are.

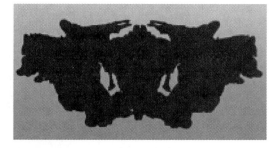

FIGURE 9.11

The Rorschach Test: One Projective Measure of Personality

Persons taking the *Rorschach test* describe what they see in a series of inkblots. Supposedly, individuals' responses reveal much about their personalities. However, recent findings cast doubt on the validity of this test.

Do such tests really work? For some projective tests, such as the TAT, the answer appears to be "yes": Such tests, when administered and scored by trained professionals, do yield scores that seem to measure what they are intended to measure (Spangler, 1992). For others, such as the famous **Rorschach test,** which uses inkblots such as the one in Figure 9.11, the answer is more doubtful (Exner, 1993; Wood, Nezwosky, & Stejskal, 1996).

In sum, many tools for measuring personality exist. None are perfect, but together, they provide psychologists with many useful techniques for investigating the stable patterns of behavior that make each of us a unique human. In fact, in recent years personality tests specifically designed for employment purposes have been used increasingly by many companies as a way to identify the best people to hire. If you want to learn more about what you should expect if you are ever asked to take such a personality test, see the following **Psychology Goes to Work** section.

KEY QUESTIONS

- What are self-report tests of personality?
- What are projective tests of personality?

Modern Research on Personality: Beyond "Grand" Theories

Grand theories such as those proposed by Freud, Rogers, Jung, and others have provided important insights into the nature of personality. From these theories subsequent researchers have examined essential questions about the role of personality in various aspects of life. We provided a few glimpses of this earlier in the chapter, such as the association between various traits in the "big five" and career success, longevity, and happiness. To provide you with a sample of what modern research on personality is like, we conclude our discussion by addressing two distinct issues that have received growing research attention: (1) What is the role of self-esteem in various aspects of life? (2) What is the role of biology in personality?

■ Self-esteem: Is more always better?

Our earlier discussion of self-esteem focused on its stability across the life span as well as gender, ethnic, and cultural differences. Implicit in these investigations is the assumption that self-esteem matters, that it relates to various aspects of adaptive behavior. What is the evidence for this? Is high self-esteem always a good thing? Below we provide some answers from recent research. You will also learn more about self-esteem in later chapters, as it plays a key role in psychological adjustment (see Chapter 12) and in our relations with others (Chapter 13).

The link between self-esteem and antisocial behaviors, such as aggression, is one that has been debated for some time, with some research indicating that individuals with high self-esteem are more aggressive and other research suggesting the opposite. While the issue is not fully resolved, the most recent evidence indi-

Rorschach test:
A widely used projective test of personality in which individuals are asked to describe what they see in a series of inkblots.

cates that individuals with low self-esteem engage in more antisocial behavior, such as aggression and delinquency, than those with high self-esteem (Donnellan et al., 2005). What is the reason for the earlier discrepancy? Apparently, it is only when self-esteem becomes excessive to the point of narcissism that aggression and other antisocial behaviors become more likely. (We'll discuss narcissism, a personality disorder characterized by excessive self-love, in Chapter 11).

The relationship between self-esteem and success in life has also received a lot of research attention. Interestingly, doing well in life and feeling good about oneself (i.e., self-esteem) do not always go hand in hand. More intriguing is that success *feels* different to people with high versus low self-esteem—individuals with high self-esteem get more pleasure from their successes. In fact, success often causes negative reactions among those with low self-esteem (Wood et al., 2005). This finding is one of the more perplexing ones. After all, doesn't everyone enjoy success? Apparently not. In several studies, individuals with low self-esteem reported heightened levels of anxiety and increased negative thoughts about themselves following success. In fact, simply *imagining* success caused similar negative reactions among those with low self-esteem! From these findings, it is easy to see how low self-esteem can be difficult to remedy, as it seems to ignore even the joys of victory (see Figure 9.12).

Though high self-esteem is an asset in these contexts as well as in a host of others, it is important to note that the single-minded *quest* for high self-esteem is often associated with negative outcomes, particularly when it is made contingent on achieving high levels of success (e.g., Crocker & Knight, 2005). These studies suggest a more balanced view of self-esteem, reminding us that while it may generally be a good thing, relentlessly pursuing it, to the point of perfectionism, may not be (Flett & Hewitt, 2005).

PSYCHOLOGY GOES TO WORK

Taking, Not Faking, Employment Tests

Taking tests of any kind can be a little nerve-racking even if you have studied. But when it comes to certain types of employment tests, especially those that focus on personality rather than ability, you really can't study for them. Added to this is the pressure of really wanting the job. Like it or not, tests such as this are now being used by most Fortune 1,000 companies and many smaller companies to screen applicants for jobs from retail clerk to executive (Wessel, 2003). Even the government uses these tests to screen applicants. Given this trend, it is likely that many of you will soon run into one of these tests when applying for a job. What is the best approach? Here are a few things for you to remember if you ever find yourself in this situation.

Be honest: While this may sound like advice that helps your potential employer more than it helps you, that is not the case. By responding honestly you are less likely to be identified as someone who is faking answers.

Be consistent: Many tests have similar questions dispersed throughout. This is done for statistical reasons rather than to trick you.

Responding consistently shows that you are reading the questions carefully and giving honest responses.

Be wary: If you generally get a bad feeling about a job because of a test or other assessment procedure, ask yourself whether this is really the type of company you want to work for. While there are legal issues regarding the use of any test, some companies disregard these requirements by using poorly developed tests. So, if your gut tells you that this is a symptom of a larger problem, you may want to consider working elsewhere.

Be relaxed: This is easier said than done and may sound like a contradiction to the last suggestion. Just remember that most tests like this are generally used only to screen out a few "bad apples." It is very unlikely that you would miss out on getting hired simply on the basis of your responses to one test.

By following these suggestions, you will not only be better informed about employment testing, but you also will more likely be hired for the type of job that suits your preferences best.

■ The biology of personality: The role of neural systems and genes.

As you read this heading we can almost hear you saying: "Are they about to tell me that I have an area of my brain that makes me extraverted?" or "Good! Now I can blame my lack of agreeableness on my genes!" Well, not quite, though researchers are beginning to get a much clearer picture of the biological bases of some aspects of personality from the fields of neuropsychology and behavior genetics.

From neuroimaging research, for example, there is strong evidence for two opposing systems in the brain that are associated with many aspects of personality. One, referred to as the **behavioral activation system (BAS)**, controls the anticipation and experience of positive experiences. It is the system that relates to the experience of rewards, and is often referred to as the approach system. The other system, referred to as the **behavioral inhibition system (BIS)**, monitors and controls our avoidance of negative experiences, and so is often referred to as an avoidance system

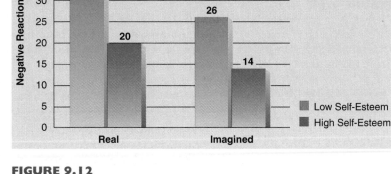

FIGURE 9.12

People with High Versus Low Self-Esteem Experience Success Very Differently

As shown here, people with low self-esteem have more negative feelings both with actual success as well as with imagined success.

Source: Based on data from Wood et al., 2005.

(Gray, 1994). These complementary systems vary in dominance from one individual to the next, thus resulting in spontaneous and sometimes impulsive behavior when the behavioral activation system is in charge, versus inaction or withdrawal when the behavioral inhibition system is dominant. These systems also may vary in dominance from one situation to the next, thus accounting for different reactions one individual may have across different situations.

Consistent with this two-system view is evidence from brain imaging studies that have identified which distinct areas of the brain are activated when individuals experience approach versus avoidance. In both systems, cortical and subcortical areas of the brain appear to be involved (see Chapter 2). The BAS, for example, seems to reside in those areas of the brain that have a heavy concentration of neurons susceptible to the neurotransmitter dopamine. Different parts of the prefrontal cortex also appear to be involved in each behavioral system.

Studies of brain-damaged individuals yield findings consistent with this view. In these studies, CT scans provide information on the location of each individual's brain damage. The behaviors of these individuals is then compared to those of people without such damage. From these comparisons, it is common to find impulse control problems in people with brain damage in one part of the prefrontal cortex, suggesting that the inhibition system has been compromised.

Thus far, we have linked brain anatomy to behavioral inhibition and activation, but we have not linked these systems to personality. To do so, one must address how various personality traits may be influenced by the tendency either to act on impulses or to suppress them. In fact, several personality traits (e.g., conscientiousness, extraversion, and agreeableness) have been viewed as a tug of war of sorts between these two systems (Carver, 2005). Even Freud's concepts of id and ego can be thought of in this way, with the ego suppressing the id's impulses. While these studies do not result in a complete picture of personality, they do show how certain areas of the brain may be partially responsible for the development of some stable personality characteristics (see Figure 9.13, page 360).

We now turn to another issue concerning the biological bases of personality: the role of genetic factors. This question has received a good deal of attention during the

Behavioral activation system (BAS):
The neural system that controls the anticipation and experience of positive experiences.

Behavioral inhibition system (BIS):
The neural system that monitors and controls our avoidance of negative experiences.

FIGURE 9.13
Neural Systems Related to Personality
Various cortical and subcortical parts of the brain are involved in two opposing systems, the behavioral activation system and the behavioral inhibition system. These systems play a role in the expression of several personality traits, such as extraversion, conscientiousness, and agreeableness.
Source: Adapted from Carver, 2005.

last twenty years and the results may surprise you. The question of genetic versus environmental origins of individual differences is as old as the field of psychology itself (often referred to as the "nature–nurture debate"). As we will cover in our discussion of intelligence, most of this research focused on the genetic basis of intelligence. More recently, however, the role of genetics in personality has been examined using the same research methodologies. These studies indicate strong evidence that genes influence personality to a moderate degree. Specifically, for each of the traits in the "big five," genes on average account for 42–57 percent of the individual variation in these traits, with openness to experience and extraversion being the most heritable and agreeableness the least heritable. The remaining two traits, conscientiousness and emotional stability, were in the midrange (Bouchard, 2004).

This does not mean, however, that there is a single gene for these traits or any other complex psychological characteristic, but it does indicate that patterns of genes, working in conjunction, may influence genetic expression in the form of personality differences. What is also important to remember, however, is that these numbers leave plenty of room for environmental influences on personality, such as childhood experiences. They also do not reveal how various genes may influence the environment that individuals choose. For example, someone who is genetically predisposed to be extraverted probably seeks out more social situations than someone who is introverted, thus resulting in more opportunities to develop successful social skills. In this way, we can see how genetic factors may get the ball rolling, but we still get a good deal of freedom to choose which environments we seek out and which we avoid. This pattern of development can also be applied as a way to understand how genetically influenced cognitive abilities affect a child's choice of activities, resulting in a unique pattern of skills.

This discussion of genetic influences concludes our discussion of personality and sets the stage for discussing the other main category of individual differences we'll examine: cognitive abilities. In closing, we should note that the research described in the previous sections represents only a tiny sample of current efforts by psychologists to understand the nature of personality and its influence on behavior. But we hope it will leave you with the idea that personality *is* important and that studying it involves much more than theories such as those proposed by Freud, Rogers, and others.

KEY QUESTIONS

- What links are there between self-esteem and behavior? Is high self-esteem always a good thing?
- What biological factors play a role in personality?

INTELLIGENCE: THE NATURE OF COGNITIVE ABILITIES

Do you recall the description of Nick at the beginning of the chapter? Would you describe him as intelligent? Your response to this probably depends a great deal on how you define intelligence, an issue that has intrigued psychologists for more than a century. In this section we'll discuss several issues related to intelligence: what it is, how it is measured, and the potential contributions of heredity and environment. In the course of our discussion of intelligence, we'll raise some of the ethical and social issues relating to the use of intelligence tests. We will also consider the extent to which intelligence tests—or any other psychological tests, such as the personality tests discussed earlier in this chapter—measure what they are designed to measure consistently and accurately—the important issues of reliability and validity. Finally, we'll describe some intriguing evidence concerning *emotional intelligence*—our ability to deal effectively with the emotional side of life.

Intelligence: Contrasting Views of Its Nature

Intelligence, like love, is one of those concepts that may be easier to recognize than to define. We often refer to others' intelligence, describing people as *bright, sharp,* or *quick* on the one hand, or as *slow, dull,* or even *stupid* on the other. And slurs on one's intelligence are often fighting words where children—and even adults—are concerned. But again, what precisely *is* intelligence? Psychologists don't entirely agree, but as a working definition we can adopt the wording offered by a distinguished panel of experts (Neisser et al., 1996): The term **intelligence** refers to individuals' abilities to: understand complex ideas; adapt effectively to the environment; learn from experience; engage in various forms of reasoning; and overcome obstacles by careful thought.

Why do we place so much importance on evaluating others' (and our own) intelligence? Partly because we believe that intelligence is related to many important outcomes: how quickly individuals can master new tasks and adapt to new situations; how successful they will be in school and in various kinds of jobs; and even how well they can get along with others. To some extent, our commonsense ideas in this respect are correct. There is, in fact, a wealth of research showing that intelligence is related, modestly at least, to wide range of life outcomes, including how well one does in school and in various jobs (e.g., Hulin, Henry, & Noon, 1990; Lubinski et al., 2006). Amazingly, it has even been shown to correlate with how long we live (e.g., Deary et al., 2004; Gottfredson & Deary, 2004), though many additional factors are important. But although intelligence *is* related to important life outcomes, this relationship is far from perfect. Many other factors, too, play a role, so predictions based on intelligence alone can be misleading.

■ Intelligence: Unitary or multifaceted?

Is intelligence a single characteristic, or does it involve several different components? In the past, psychologists who studied intelligence often disagreed sharply on this issue. In one camp were scientists who viewed intelligence as a single characteristic or dimension along which people vary. One early supporter of this view was Spearman (1927), who believed that performance on any cognitive task depended on a primary *general* factor (which he termed *g*) and one or more *specific* factors relating to particular tasks. Spearman based this view on the following finding: Although tests of intelligence often contain different kinds of items designed to measure different aspects of intelligence, scores on these items often correlate highly with one another. This fact suggested to him that no matter how intelligence was measured, it was related to a single, primary factor.

In contrast, other researchers believed that intelligence is composed of many separate abilities that operate more or less independently. According to this *multifactor* view, a given person can be high on some components of intelligence but low on others, and vice versa. One early supporter of this position was Thurstone (1938), who suggested that intelligence is composed of seven distinct primary mental abilities. Included in his list were *verbal meaning*—understanding of ideas and word meanings; *number*—speed and accuracy in dealing with numbers; and *space*—the ability to visualize objects in three dimensions.

Which of these views of intelligence has prevailed? Most modern theories of intelligence adopt a position somewhere in between these extremes. They recognize that intelligence may involve a general ability to handle a wide range of cognitive tasks and problems, as Spearman suggested, but also that intelligence *is* expressed in many different ways, and that people can be high on some aspects of intelligence but low on others. As examples of this modern approach, let's briefly consider three influential views of intelligence.

Intelligence:
Individuals' abilities to understand complex ideas, adapt effectively to the environment, learn from experience, engage in various forms of reasoning, overcome obstacles by careful thought.

FIGURE 9.14
Great Musical Skill: A Kind of Intelligence?
Gardner's theory of multiple intelligences views exceptional musical talent as one of several types of intelligence.

■ **Gardner's theory of multiple intelligences.**

In formulating their views of intelligence, most researchers have focused primarily on what might be described as "normal" children and adults: people who neither greatly exceed nor fall far below what most of us would view as "average" levels of intelligence. In addition, they have restricted their view of intelligence to verbal, mathematical, and spatial abilities. Howard Gardner (1983) argued that this approach was limiting psychology's view of intelligence. A better tactic, he suggested, would be to study not only people in the middle of the intelligence dimension, but also ones at the extremes—acclaimed geniuses and those whose cognitive functioning is impaired, as well as experts in various domains and those who might be described as possessing special mental "gifts." For instance, consider young musicians, some of whom are asked to perform as soloists with professional symphonies at a very young age. Is their ability to play the piano simply the result of extensive training (see Figure 9.14)? Or does their performance also show a special kind of intelligence—something very different from the verbal fluency we usually associate with the term *intelligence*, but perhaps just as important?

Gardner would argue strongly for the latter view. In fact, to aspects of intelligence most of us readily recognize—such as the verbal, mathematical, and spatial abilities studied by Thurstone—Gardner added such components as *musical intelligence*—the kind of intelligence described above; *bodily–kinesthetic intelligence*—the kind that allows athletes to perform amazing feats; and *personal intelligence*—for instance, the ability to get along well with others. In sum, as its name suggests, Gardner's theory of multiple intelligences proposes that there are several important types of intelligence, and that we must understand each in order to get the big picture where this important human characteristic is concerned.

■ **Sternberg's triarchic theory.**

Another important modern theory of intelligence is one proposed by Robert Sternberg (Sternberg, 1985; Sternberg et al., 1995). According to this theory, known as the **triarchic theory** of intelligence, there are actually three basic types of human intelligence. The first, called *componential* or *analytic* intelligence, involves the abilities to think critically and analytically. People high on this dimension usually excel on standard tests of academic potential and make excellent students. The second type of intelligence, *experiential* or *creative* intelligence, emphasizes insight and the ability to formulate new ideas. People who rate high on this dimension excel at zeroing in on what information is crucial in a given situation, and at combining seemingly unrelated facts. This is the kind of intelligence shown by many scientific geniuses and inventors. For example, Johannes Gutenberg, inventor of the printing press, combined the mechanisms for producing playing cards, making wine, and minting coins in his invention; thus, he showed a high level of creative intelligence.

Sternberg terms the third type of intelligence *contextual* or **practical intelligence,** and in some ways, it is the most interesting of all. People high on this dimension are intelligent in a practical, adaptive sense—they have what many would term "street smarts" and are adept at solving the problems of everyday life. Like Gardner, Sternberg suggests that there is more to intelligence than the verbal, mathematical, and reasoning abilities that are often associated with academic success. Practical intelligence, too, is important and contributes to success in many areas of life.

■ **Cattell's theory of fluid and crystallized intelligence.**

Yet another view of intelligence was offered by psychologist James McKeen Catell (1963). Cattell examined scores on many different ability tests and concluded that performance on these tests reflects two major clusters of mental ability, which he termed *fluid* and *crystallized intelligence. Fluid intelligence* refers to our largely inherited abilities to think and reason—in a sense, the hardware of our brains that

Triarchic theory:
A theory suggesting that there are three basic forms of intelligence: componential, experiential, and contextual.

Practical intelligence:
Intelligence useful in solving everyday problems.

determines the limits of our information-processing capabilities. In contrast, *crystallized intelligence* refers to accumulated knowledge—information we store over a lifetime of experience, plus the application of skills and knowledge to solving specific problems.

Longitudinal studies of intellectual abilities show that once people mature and reach adulthood, fluid intelligence seems to decrease slowly with age, but crystallized intelligence stays level or even increases (e.g., Baltes, 1987; McArdle, et al., 2002). This is why older, more experienced individuals can sometimes outperform younger ones on cognitive tasks ranging from scientific research to chess.

Is there anything we can do to slow the age-related declines observed in fluid intelligence? Fortunately, the answer seems to be "yes." Research indicates that regular aerobic exercise can help reduce age-related declines in fluid intelligence (e.g., Kramer & Willis, 2002). Although psychologists have not yet determined why such effects occur, it appears as though general cardiovascular health plays a role, as it not only keeps our heart working well, but also helps maintain healthy arteries allowing optimum blood flow to the brain. This is encouraging, as research on "mental exercise" (discussed in Chapter 7) has not yielded such positive results.

KEY QUESTIONS

- What is intelligence?
- What is Gardner's theory of multiple intelligences?
- What is Sternberg's triarchic theory of intelligence?
- What is fluid intelligence? Crystallized intelligence?

Measuring Intelligence

In 1904, when psychology was just emerging as an independent field, members of the Paris schoolboard approached Alfred Binet with an interesting request: Could he develop an objective method to identify the children who were described, in the language of that era, as being mentally retarded, so that they could be given special education? Binet was already at work on related topics, so he agreed, enlisting the aid of his colleague, Theodore Simon.

In designing this test, Binet and Simon were guided by the belief that the items used should be ones children could answer without special training or study. They felt that this was important, because the test should measure the ability to handle intellectual tasks—*not* specific knowledge acquired in school. The original test asked children to perform the following tasks: follow simple commands or imitate simple gestures; name objects shown in pictures; repeat a sentence of fifteen words; tell how two common objects are different; complete sentences begun by the examiner.

The first version of Binet and Simon's test was published in 1905 and was seen as quite effective. With it, schools could readily identify children in need of special help. Encouraged by this success, Binet and Simon broadened the scope of their test to measure variations in intelligence among all children. The revised version, published in 1908, grouped items by age, with six items at each level from three to thirteen years. Items were placed at a particular age level if about 75 percent of children of that age could pass them correctly.

Binet's tests were soon revised and adapted for use in many countries. In the United States, Lewis Terman, a psychologist at Stanford University, developed the **Stanford–Binet test,** which was soon put to use in many different settings. Over the years the Stanford–Binet has been revised several times. One of the features of the Stanford–Binet that contributed to its popularity was how it yielded a single score assumed to reflect an individual's level of intelligence—the now famous (some would say *infamous*) IQ.

Stanford–Binet test:
A widely used individual test of intelligence.

■ **IQ: its meaning then and now.**

Originally, the letters **IQ** stood for *intelligence quotient,* and a "quotient" is precisely what the scores represented. To obtain an IQ score, an examiner divided a student's mental age by his or her chronological age, then multiplied this number by 100. For this computation, mental age was based on the number of items a person passed correctly on the test: Test takers received two months' credit of "mental age" for each item passed. If an individual's mental and chronological ages were equal, an IQ of 100 was obtained; this was considered to be an average score. IQs above 100 indicated that a person's intellectual age was greater than her or his chronological age—in other words, that the individual was more intelligent than typical students of the same age. In contrast, numbers below 100 indicated that the individual was less intelligent than her or his peers.

Perhaps you can already see one obvious problem with this type of IQ score: At some point, mental growth levels off or stops, while chronological age continues to grow. As a result, IQ scores begin to decline after the early teenage years! Partly because of this problem, IQ scores now have a different definition. They simply reflect an individual's performance relative to that of people of the same age who have taken the same test. Thus, an IQ of more than 100 indicates that the person has scored higher than the average person in her or his age group, while a score below 100 indicates that the person has scored lower than average.

■ **The Wechsler scales.**

As noted earlier, the tests developed by Binet and later adapted by Terman and others remained popular for many years. They do, however, suffer from one major drawback: All are mainly verbal in content. As a result, they pay little attention to how intelligence can be revealed in nonverbal activities as well. For example, an architect who visualizes a majestic design for a new building is demonstrating a high level of intelligence; yet, no means for assessing such abilities was included in early versions of the Stanford–Binet test.

To overcome this and other problems, David Wechsler devised a set of tests for both children and adults that include nonverbal, or *performance,* items as well as verbal ones, and that yield separate scores for these two components of intelligence. Thus, Wechsler began with the view that intelligence is *not* a unitary characteristic, shown only through verbal and mathematical reasoning. However, he developed these tests at a time when the multifaceted nature of intelligence was not yet well understood, and it is not clear that Wechsler's various subtests actually do measure different aspects of intelligence. Despite such problems, the Wechsler tests are currently among the most frequently used individual tests of intelligence. For a description of the subtests in the Weschler Adult Intelligence Test, see Table 9.1.

■ **Basic requirements of tests.**

How can we tell whether intelligence tests such as these or any other tests really work? This was an issue first raised in our earlier discussion of personality tests. It is an essential issue, as it is necessary to be able to measure individual differences precisely and accurately before we can study the role they play in various aspects of life. Briefly, a test must meet three crucial requirements before we can conclude that it provides an accurate and useful measure of intelligence: The test must be carefully *standardized;* it must be *reliable;* and it must be *valid.* This process involves the collection of lots of data, as the test is "tested out," so to speak. Using statistical procedures the test is then refined (i.e., questions added, dropped, or modified) until it meets established professional guidelines. Below we provide a little more detail about what is involved in test standardization, as well as in establishing test reliability and validity.

In order for the scores obtained on a psychological test to be useful, the tests must be carefully *standardized.* This involves giving the test to a large sample of individuals who are representative of the population for whom the test is designed. Data are then analyzed to determine the average and the distribution of scores. If

IQ:
Originally, "intelligent quotient," a number that examiners derived by dividing an individual's mental age by his or her chronological age and multiplying it by 100. Now IQ simply indicates an individual's performance on an intelligence test relative to those of other people.

TABLE 9.1 Subtests of the Wechsler Adult Intelligence Scale

The widely used test of adult intelligence includes the subtests described here.

Test	Description
Verbal Tests	
Information	Examinees are asked to answer general information questions, increasing in difficulty.
Digit span	Examinees are asked to repeat series of digits read out loud by the examiner.
Vocabulary	Examinees are asked to define thirty-five words.
Arithmetic	Examinees are asked to solve arithmetic problems.
Comprehension	Examinees are asked to answer questions requiring detailed answers; answers indicate their comprehension of the questions.
Similarities	Examinees indicate in what way two items are alike.
Performance Tests	
Picture completion	Examinees indicate what part of each picture is missing.
Picture arrangement	Examinees arrange pictures to make a sensible story.
Block design	Examinees attempt to duplicate designs made with red and white blocks.
Object assembly	Examinees attempt to solve picture puzzles.
Digit symbol	Examinees fill in small boxes with coded symbols corresponding to a number above each box.

the test is well constructed, the distribution of scores will approach the *normal curve* in shape—a bell-shaped function with most scores in the middle and fewer scores as we move toward the extremes (very low scores or very high scores). The normal curve is very useful because it helps us determine just where an individual stands relative to other people who also took the test. This information then helps us to interpret an individual's performance as being relatively low, average, or high. Most widely used intelligence tests are designed to yield an average score of about 100, so the score of each test taker can be compared with this value to determine just where the person stands, in a relative sense, with respect to intelligence. The procedure for *administration* of the test should also be standardized so that people taking the test do so under the same set of conditions. This issue of standardized administration has become an increasingly important issue with the use of computer administered tests that are not, in many cases, equivalent to the same test taken under paper-and-pencil conditions (Drasgow, Luecht, & Bennett, 2005).

In addition to being carefully standardized, tests must also have high **reliability:** they must yield the similar results (the more similar the better) each time they are administered. If they don't, they are essentially useless. You may be familiar with an informal assessment of reliability every time you stand on a bathroom scale, particularly if it is an old one. If within a few moments you get very different readings (perhaps by leaning this way or that), the bathroom scale has low reliability. Doctor's scales and digital scales tend to have higher reliability, meaning that they provide more consistent readings than older scales.

Reliability:
The extent to which any measuring device (including psychological tests) yields the same result each time it is applied to the same quantity.

With psychological tests two basic forms of reliability are important. First, tests must possess what psychologists call *internal consistency:* All the items on the test must actually measure the same thing. For example, if you took a history test that had a few math problems thrown in by mistake, this test would not have high internal consistency. One way to assess such internal consistency involves dividing the test in two equivalent parts, such as the first and second halves or odd- and even-numbered items, and then comparing people's scores on each part. If the test measures intelligence reliably, then the correlation between the two parts should be positive and high. If it is, then the test is said to be high in **split-half reliability.** If it is not, then some of the items may be measuring different things, and the test may be unreliable in one important sense.

Second, to be viewed as reliable, tests must yield scores that are stable over time. Psychologists measure such **test–retest reliability** by having the same people take the test at different times. The more similar a group of people's scores are on these two occasions, the higher is the test–retest reliability. It is important to remember that reliability must be examined using a large number of people in the sample. Simply having one person score differently from one time to the next is not sufficient.

Validity is the third requirement that a test must meet. For a test to be valid, it must measure what it is intended to measure. Some early tests of intelligence, for example, especially when given to groups of immigrants, measured not intelligence, but the ability to read English. On the basis of such tests, members of various groups were labeled as "idiots" and "imbeciles" and were prevented from immigrating during the early part of the twentieth century. For a contemporary example, look at the machine shown in Figure 9.15. A sign on the front reads, "Test Your Sex Appeal!" Do you think that such a machine is really capable of measuring sex appeal? The answer is obvious, if a little disappointing: No way! After all, how could this device tell people who used it how they would be perceived by others? Psychologists would say that machines such as this one—and any other measuring devices that claim to measure something they do not—are low in **validity:** the degree to which they measure what they are supposed to measure.

The same principle applies to psychological tests: They are useful only to the extent that they really measure the characteristics they claim to measure. How can we determine whether a test is valid? Through several different methods. One of these, known as **content validity,** has to do with the extent to which items on a test are related in a straightforward way to the characteristic we wish to measure. For example, if an intelligence test consisted of measurements of the circumference of people's heads (which actually was done in the nineteenth century before the scientific study of intelligence began), we would probably conclude that it was low in content validity, because the measure seems totally unrelated to what we mean by the term *intelligence.*

Another type of validity is known as **criterion-related validity** and is based on the following reasoning: If a test actually measures what it claims to measure, then people attaining different scores on it should also differ in terms of behaviors that are relevant to the characteristic being measured. For example, we might expect that scores on an intelligence test would be related to such aspects of behavior (i.e., criteria) as grades in school and success in various occupations, either right now (this is known as *concurrent validity*) or in the future (this is known as *predictive validity*). In sum, any psychological test is useful only to the extent that it has been carefully standardized and is both reliable and valid. Keep in mind that these procedures apply to all psychological tests, not just intelligence tests.

The Cognitive and Neural Bases of Intelligence

With the development of increasingly sophisticated instrumentation, psychologists are beginning to gain a better understanding of the cognitive and neural processes that are the basis for differences in intelligence. This research, which builds on work in memory and cognition (Chapter 6) and the biological bases of

Split-half reliability:
The correlation between scores on two parts of a test.

Test–retest reliability:
A measure of the extent to which scores on a test remain stable over time.

Validity:
The extent to which a test actually measures what it claims to measure.

Content validity:
The extent to which items on a test are related in a straightforward way to the characteristic the test aims to measure.

Criterion-related validity:
The extent to which scores on a test are related to behaviors (criteria) relevant to the characteristics the test purports to measure.

cognition (Chapter 2), is beginning to give us a glimpse of what intelligence is, at the most basic level.

■ Intelligence and processing speed.

"Quick study," "quick-witted," and "fast learner" are all phrases used to describe people who are high in intelligence, both academic and practical. They suggest that being intelligent involves being able to process information quickly. Is there any scientific evidence to support this idea? In fact, there is. For example, a growing body of research has focused on the finding that the speed with which individuals perform simple perceptual and cognitive tasks (e.g., reaction time) is often correlated with scores on intelligence tests (e.g., Deary & Stough, 1996; Neisser et al., 1996). In fact, reaction time appears to be so closely related to intelligence in many studies that it helps explain the earlier finding we reported showing a link between intelligence and longevity. This research suggests that one of the reasons intelligent people tend to live longer is that they have quicker reaction times, something that presumably helps them think quickly on their feet, particularly in the face of danger (Deary & Der, 2005). So when we describe an intelligent person as "quick," we may not be that far from the truth.

Other cognitive psychologists have suggested that differences in intelligence are based on differences in *working memory capacity*. As you may recall from our discussions in Chapter 6, working memory refers to a cognitive system that stores information temporarily and also has an attentional component that regulates content. Working memory allows individuals to store complex mental representations in active memory and perform complex transformations on these representations. Some studies have shown that the complexity of one's representations and transformations in working memory are highly correlated with intelligence test scores (e.g., Friedman et al., 2006). Other research shows that measures of working memory capacity correlate highly with performance on several higher-order cognitive tasks that reflect fluid intelligence, such as planning, scheduling, and complex learning (e.g., Engle, 2002). However, a metaanalysis that examined these and other studies as a whole suggests that the link between working memory and intelligence is positive, but not strong enough to equate it with intelligence (Ackerman, Beier, & Boyle, 2005).

In sum, cognitive processing speed (e.g., reaction time) and working memory capacity appear to offer some insights for probing the nature of human intelligence by examining the basic cognitive processes that underlie this important characteristic. And since understanding a process is often an essential first step to being able to change it in beneficial ways, this is valuable progress.

FIGURE 9.15
Low Validity: An Example
Devices like this one really can't help you find your "perfect match," so the scores they provide have no validity; that is, the devices do not measure what they claim to measure.

■ Biological building blocks of intelligence.

If there are cognitive processes related to intelligence, that raises the question that there may be a biological basis for it, as there was in the case of personality, discussed earlier in this chapter. Can we trace individual differences in intelligence to differences in neural functioning? The answer suggested by a growing body of evidence is "yes" (e.g., Matarazzo, 1992; Vernon, 1993). Such research suggests, first, that *nerve conduction velocity*—the speed with which nerve impulses are conducted in the visual system—correlates significantly with measures of intelligence (Reed & Jensen, 1993).

Related research has examined metabolic activity in the brain during cognitive tasks (e.g., Haier, 1993). Presumably, if intelligence is related to efficient brain functioning, then the more intelligent people are, the less energy their brains should expend while working on various tasks. This prediction has generally been confirmed: The brains of people scoring highest on written measures of intellectual ability do expend less energy when these individuals perform complex cognitive tasks. The data in these studies have been gathered by means of the PET technique of brain imaging described in Chapter 2. Using similar imaging technologies, scientists have identified an area in the lateral prefrontal cortex of each brain hemisphere that may play an important role in intelligence by providing a global work space for organizing and coordinating information and carrying it back to other parts of the brain as needed (Duncan et al., 2000). Apparently, the relative performance of this "work space" determines how adept a person is at solving cognitive problems—precisely the characteristic that intelligence tests attempt to measure.

More recent findings point to yet another intriguing possibility: Individual differences in intelligence may stem from individual differences in **neural plasticity**—the ability of neural connections to adapt dynamically to their environments. According to psychologist Dennis Garlick (2002), intelligence develops during childhood when neural connections in the developing brain change rapidly in response to environmental cues. This view suggests that individual differences in intelligence stem from differences in how quickly, and to what degree, our brains can make these new nerve connections. Garlick notes that this process stops at maturity, implying the existence of a *critical period* for the development of intelligence. Although additional research will be needed to confirm the precise relationship of neural plasticity to intelligence, it does seem to provide an accurate accounting of much of what we know about intelligence. For example, neural plasticity helps to explain why children are particularly adept at acquiring new skills, and why development in certain mental abilities (e.g., fluid intelligence) stops at a certain point, whereas others (e.g., crystallized intelligence) seem to continue well into old age.

In sum, it appears that the improved methods now available for studying the brain and nervous system are beginning to establish the kind of links between intelligence and neural structures that psychologists have long suspected to exist. Such research is very recent, so it is still too soon to reach firm conclusions. It does appear, though, that we are on the verge of gaining a much better understanding of the cognitive and neural bases of intelligence.

KEY QUESTIONS

- What was the first individual test of intelligence, and what did scores on it mean?
- What are the Wechsler scales?
- What are standardization, reliability, and validity?
- What cognitive processes are related to intelligence?
- What findings suggest that intelligence is related to neural functioning?

Intelligence: Heredity, Environment, and Group Differences

That people differ in intelligence is obvious. *Why* such differences exist is quite another matter. Are they largely a matter of heredity—differences in the genetic materials and codes we inherit from our parents? Or are they primarily the result of environmental factors—conditions in the world around us that affect our intellectual development? Human intelligence is clearly the result of the complex interplay between genetic factors and a wide range of environmental conditions (e.g., Plomin, 1997), but the relative importance of the two still sparks debate. Let's now consider some of the evidence pointing to this conclusion.

■ Evidence for the influence of heredity.

Several lines of research offer support for the view that heredity plays an important role in human intelligence. First, consider findings with respect to family relationship and measured IQ. If intelligence is indeed determined by heredity, we would expect that the more closely two people are related, the more similar their IQs will be. This prediction has generally been confirmed (e.g., Bouchard, 2004;

Neural plasticity:
The ability of neural connections to adapt dynamically to environmental cues.

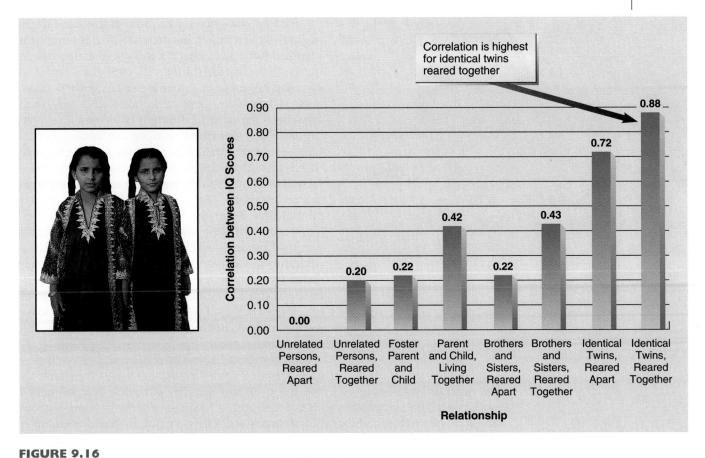

FIGURE 9.16
Family Relationship and IQ
The closer the biological relationship of two individuals, the higher the correlation between their IQ scores. This finding provides support for the role of genetic factors in intelligence.

Neisser et al., 1996). For example, the IQs of identical twins raised together correlate almost +90, those of brothers and sisters about +50, and those of cousins about +.15 (see Figure 9.16). (Higher correlations indicate stronger relationships between variables.)

Support for the impact of heredity on intelligence is also provided by studies involving adopted children. If intelligence is strongly affected by genetic factors, the IQs of adopted children should resemble those of their biological parents more closely than those of their adoptive parents. In short, the children should be more similar in IQ to the people from whom they received their genes than to the people who raised them. This prediction, too, has been confirmed (Jencks, 1972; Munsinger, 1978; Plomin et al., 1997).

Additional evidence for the role of genetic factors in intelligence is provided by studies focused on the task of identifying the specific genes that influence intelligence (e.g., Rutter & Plomin, 1997; Sherman et al., 1997). These studies have adopted as a working hypothesis the view that many genes, each exerting relatively small effects, probably play a role in general intelligence—that is, in what many aspects of mental abilities (e.g., verbal, spatial, speed-of-processing, and memory abilities) have in common (e.g., Plomin, 1997). In other words, such research has not attempted to identify *the* gene that influences intelligence, but rather has sought *quantitative trait loci* (QTLs): genes that have relatively small effects and that influence the likelihood of some characteristic in a population. The results of such studies suggest that certain genes are indeed associated with high intelligence (e.g., Chorney et al., 1998).

FIGURE 9.17
Identical Twins Reared Apart
The IQ scores of identical twins separated at birth and raised in different homes are highly correlated. This provides evidence for the impact of genetic factors on intelligence.

Finally, evidence for the role of genetic factors in intelligence has been provided by research on identical twins separated as infants (usually, within the first few weeks of life) who were then raised in different homes (e.g., Bouchard et al., 1990). Because such people have identical genetic inheritance but have been exposed to different environmental conditions—in some cases, sharply contrasting conditions—studying their IQs provides a powerful way to compare the roles of genetic and environmental factors in human intelligence. The results of such research are clear: The IQs of identical twins reared apart (often from the time they were only a few days old) correlate almost as highly as those of identical twins reared together. Moreover, such individuals are also amazingly similar in many other characteristics, such as physical appearance, preferences in dress, mannerisms, and even personality (see Figure 9.17). Clearly, these findings point to an important role for heredity in intelligence and in many other aspects of psychological functioning, as we discussed earlier in the context of personality.

On the basis of these and other findings, some researchers have estimated that the **heritability** of intelligence—the proportion of the variance in intelligence within a given population that is attributable to genetic factors—ranges from about 35 percent in childhood to as much as 75 percent in adulthood (McGue et al., 1993), and may be about 50 percent overall (Plomin et al., 1997). Why does the contribution of genetic factors to intelligence increase with age? Perhaps because as individuals grow older, their interactions with their environment are shaped less and less by restraints imposed on them by their families or by their social origins, and are shaped more and more by the characteristics they bring with them to these environments. In other words, as they grow older, individuals are increasingly able to choose or change their environments so that these permit expression of their genetically determined tendencies and preferences (Neisser et al., 1996). Whatever the precise origin of the increasing heritability of intelligence with age, there is little doubt that genetic factors do indeed play an important role in intelligence throughout life.

■ Evidence for the influence of the environment.

Genetic factors are definitely *not* the entire picture where human intelligence is concerned, however. Other findings point to the conclusion that environmental variables, too, are important. One such finding is that performance on IQ tests has risen substantially around the world at all age levels in recent decades. This phenomenon is known as the *Flynn effect* after the psychologist who first reported it (Flynn, 1987, 1996). Such increases have averaged about three IQ points per decade worldwide, but, as shown in Figure 9.18, in some countries they have been even larger. A study of children in rural Kenya found an estimated gain of 12 IQ points over a fourteen-year period (Daley et al., 2003). As a result of these gains in performance, it has been necessary to restandardize widely used tests so that they continue to yield an average IQ of 100; what is termed "average" today is actually a higher level of performance than was true in the past.

What accounts for these increases? It seems unlikely that massive shifts in human heredity occur from one generation to the next. A more reasonable explanation, therefore, focuses on changes in environmental factors. What factors have changed in recent decades? The following variables have been suggested as possible contributors to the continuing rise in IQ: better nutrition; increased urbaniza-

Heritability:
The proportion of the variance in any trait within a given population that is attributable to genetic factors.

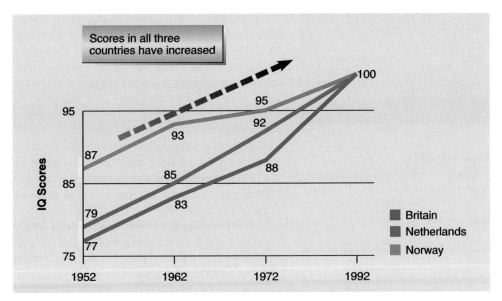

FIGURE 9.18
Worldwide Gains in IQ: Evidence for the Role of Environmental Factors in Intelligence
Performance on intelligence tests has risen sharply around the world in recent decades. Because it is very unlikely that genetic factors have changed during this period, these higher scores must be due to environmental factors. Current average IQ is set at 100; in this graph the gain is shown by how average scores in previous years would, by current test standards, be lower than 100.
Source: Based on data from Flynn, 1999.

tion; the advent of television; more and better education; more cognitively demanding jobs; and even exposure to computer games. The Kenyan study referenced above found that increases in nutrition and parents' literacy, along with a decrease in family size, coincided with the gain in IQ points. These changes seem plausible as explanations for the rise in IQ, but, as noted by Flynn (2003), there is not sufficient evidence to conclude that any or all of these factors have played a role. In any case, whatever the specific causes involved, the steady rise in performance on IQ tests points to the importance of environmental factors in human intelligence.

Additional evidence for the role of environmental factors in intelligence is provided by the findings of studies of *environmental deprivation* and *environmental enrichment*. With respect to deprivation, some findings suggest that intelligence can be reduced by the absence of key forms of environmental stimulation early in life (Gottfried, 1984). In terms of enrichment, removing children from sterile, restricted environments and placing them in more favorable settings seems to enhance their intellectual growth (e.g., Ramey & Ramey, 1998; Skeels, 1938, 1966). These findings have been confirmed in studies of adopted children, which show that their intellectual development is positively impacted by adoption, in comparison to institutional living (van IJzendoorn, Juffer, & Poelhuis, 2005).

You may be familiar with a specific example of environmental enrichment that has garnered a great deal of media attention: the so-called Mozart effect. Proponents of this view assert that simply listening to Mozart, or other classical music, will make babies smarter. Now *that* would be a powerful environmental effect! This claim was so well received in the popular press that some state governments sent out Mozart CDs to every baby born in their state (Schnellenberg, 2005). A very successful company, Baby Einstein, also built its initial success, in part, on this claim. But what does the research on music and intelligence actually suggest? Is the Mozart effect real?

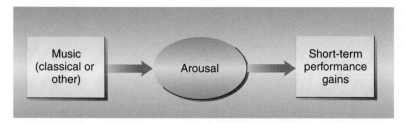

FIGURE 9.19
Mozart Effect: Does Music Enhance Intelligence?
As shown here, the apparent increase in intelligence due to music is really just a temporary increase in performance on cognitive tasks due to arousal. This arousal can result from listening to music, but can also occur when people listen to other things that they like (e.g., narrated books).
Source: Adapted from Schellenberg, 2005.

Fortunately, this is not going to be one of those cases where we frustrate you by saying, "It depends." The evidence is quite clear. Listening to Mozart does, in fact, improve *short-term* performance on a wide range of cognitive tasks. The effects, however, are short-term, and also occur when people listen to other music they like (or even listen to favorite books being read, a phenomenon that is called, tongue in cheek, the "Stephen King effect"). So, there is nothing really special about listening to Mozart, or even music in general. In fact, it appears that the effect is caused by a general increase in *arousal* that subsequently improves short-term performance on various cognitive tasks (see Figure 9.19). So, the Mozart effect is "real" in the sense that music often increases arousal and subsequent short-term performance, but certainly not in the sense that it has any long-term effects on intelligence.

In contrast to these somewhat disappointing findings, there *is* good evidence that taking music lessons (not simply listening to music) does have more stable effects on intelligence scores in the long term (Schellenberg, 2005). This study deserves attention because it controlled for other potentially relevant variables and used random assignment to determine who took music lessons and who didn't (i.e., it used principles of good experimentation discussed in Chapter 1). Results suggest positive effects of taking music lessons on intelligence, an effect that was not simply short term in nature. So if someone asks you if music makes children smarter, it appears to depend on whether the child is passively listening to it, or actively involved in doing it.

In sum, there is considerable evidence that both environmental and genetic factors play a role in intelligence. This is the view accepted by almost all psychologists, and there is little controversy about it. Greater controversy continues to exist, however, concerning the relative contribution of each of these factors. Do environmental or genetic factors play a stronger role in shaping intelligence? As we have already noted, existing evidence seems to favor the view that genetic factors may account for more of the variance in IQ scores within a given population than do environmental factors (e.g., Bouchard, 2004; Plomin, 1997), although the amount of variance may vary by socioeconomic group (Terkheimer et al., 2003). However, the recognition that genetic factors play an important role in intelligence in no way implies that intelligence is etched in stone—and definitely does not constitute an excuse for giving up on children who, because of poverty, prejudice, or neglect, are seriously at risk.

KEY QUESTIONS

• What evidence suggests that intelligence is influenced by genetic factors?
• What evidence suggests that intelligence is influenced by environmental factors?

■ **Group differences in intelligence test scores.**

In the United States and elsewhere, members of some minority groups score lower, on average, than members of the majority group. Why do such differences occur? This has been a topic of considerable controversy in psychology for many years, and currently there is still no final, universally accepted conclusion. However, it seems fair to say that at present, most psychologists attribute such group differences in performance on standard intelligence tests to environmental variables. Let's take a closer look at the evidence pointing to this conclusion.

One strong argument supporting environmental reasons for group differences in intelligence test scores is the assertion that the tests themselves may be biased against test takers from some minority groups. Why? In part because the tests were standardized largely on middle-class white people; thus, interpreting the test scores of people from minority groups in terms of these norms is not appropriate. Even worse, some critics have suggested that the tests themselves suffer from **cultural bias:** Items on the tests are ones that are familiar to middle-class white children and so give them an important edge in terms of test performance. Are such concerns valid? Careful examination of the items used on intelligence tests suggests that they may indeed be culturally biased, at least to a degree. Some items do seem to be ones that are less familiar—and therefore more difficult to answer—for minority test takers. To the extent that such cultural bias exists, it is indeed a serious flaw in IQ tests.

There is also evidence that motivational differences may account for some differences in IQ test scores. This research indicates that minority group members may perform worse on IQ tests because they are aware of negative stereotypes about members of their group (Steel & Aronson, 1996). This finding has also been found among women when performing math tests, because of the negative stereotype that women are supposedly worse at math. Collectively, these studies show that when a negative stereotype is made salient to members of a minority group, performance by members of that group declines. Further evidence has confirmed this finding, indicating that this *stereotype threat*, as it is called, has a negative influence, in part because it increases negative thinking, which interferes with performance (Cadinu et al., 2005).

On the other hand, it is important to note that most intelligence tests are generally about as successful in predicting future school performance by children from all groups. So while the tests may be biased in terms of content, this in itself does not make them useless from the point of view of predicting future performance (e.g., Rowe, Vazsonyi, & Flannery, 1994). However, it is also important to remember that intelligence is only one factor that influences performance in school and that other factors, such as self-discipline, may play an even larger role (Duckworth & Seligman, 2005). And while the debate about group differences in IQ test scores continues, many researchers, particularly those who specialize in genetics, have argued persuasively that studying racial differences in the traditional manner, by putting people into one of a few discrete categories, is an outdated approach. Instead, they advocate using more detailed genetic evidence to understand individual differences and abandoning questions that focus on race. In fact, this approach, using data from the Human Genome Project, is already under way in the field of medicine (see Anderson & Nickerson, 2005).

KEY QUESTIONS

- What evidence suggests that group differences in intelligence stem largely from environmental factors?
- Is there any evidence for the role of genetic factors in group differences in intelligence?

Emotional Intelligence: The Feeling Side of Intelligence

Can you think of people you know who may not score well on standardized intelligence tests, but who are really smart when it comes to people? They seem really in tune with what others are feeling. They also are good at monitoring their own feelings, particularly in stressful circumstances. We conclude our discussion of intelligence by describing this kind of intelligence. **Emotional intelligence,** as it is called, refers to a set of abilities related to the emotional side of life. While it has been referred to as "EQ" in books that you may find in the self-help section of bookstores, these ideas have received little scientific support. Instead, what we provide below is a summary of what is known about emotional intelligence from

Cultural bias:
The tendency of items on a test of intelligence to require specific cultural experience or knowledge.

Emotional intelligence:
Abilities relating to the emotional side of life—abilities such as perceiving, using, understanding, and managing one's own emotions, as well as the emotions of others.

FIGURE 9.20
Recognizing the Emotions of Others
As illustrated in this cartoon, one can perceive the emotions of others via body language or other nonverbal cues. Being good at this is one important aspect of emotional intelligence.
© Grimmy, Inc. King Features Syndicate.

the latest research on the topic. We examine first what it consists of, and second, what role it plays in success in various aspects of life.

■ **Major components of emotional intelligence.**

A leading expert on this topic, psychologist Peter Salovey (Salovey & Mayer, 1990; Grewal & Salovey, 2005), suggests that emotional intelligence consists of four major parts: perceiving emotions; using emotions; understanding emotions; and managing emotions. This framework focuses not only on how "in tune" we are with our own emotions, but also on how well we perceive and manage the emotions of others. The first dimension, *perceiving emotions,* relates to how well we are able to assess the emotions we are experiencing, as well as how well we can perceive the emotions of others. This dimension is viewed as the foundation on which the other dimensions are built, since it is essential to perceive emotions accurately to use, understand, or manage them. On first glance, perceiving our own emotions may seem rather straightforward, but perhaps, surprisingly, people vary a great deal in their ability to do this and it is not uncommon to misread our own emotions. I (Rebecca Henry) recall a recent instance of this in which I began crying after something had happened. Was I sad? Isn't that what one does when one is sad? After the event had passed, what I realized was that I wasn't sad at all—I was angry, fuming, in fact. If perceiving our own emotions is difficult at times, then it is easy to see how perceiving the emotions of others can be even more challenging. How do we do it? We do so primarily through nonverbal cues such as facial expression, voice intonation, and body language. Those who are most accomplished at it can even perceive the emotions of others who may be attempting to hide or mask what they are feeling (see Figure 9.20).

The second dimension, *using emotions,* relates to our ability to make use of our emotions, both positive and negative, when we need to in order to do our best in a situation. For example, if you have ever felt anxious and nervous before giving a speech or presentation you may have used this energy, negative though it was, to add vigor and enthusiasm to your delivery. The third dimension, *understanding emotions,* refers to how we make sense of the complex relationships among different emotions, both our own and others. For example, one may feel angry and guilty at the same time, and one emotion may fade over time while the other may not. In contrast, someone else in this same situation might simply report "feeling bad," a description that conveys little understanding of one's own emotions. People who are high on emotional intelligence tend to have a good understanding of the complexity of emotions, both their own and those of others.

The last dimension, *managing emotions*, refers to our ability to control our own emotions and influence the emotions of others. For example, if you have ever been in a stressful situation, you may have been able not only to calm yourself, but also to do so in a way that also calmed those around you. To manage emotions appropriately one must not only be able to change one's own emotion, but also to do so wisely. For example, I once had a colleague who was masterful at throwing a fit in such a way that he almost always got what he wanted. He once confided in me that on these occasions he often didn't really feel that angry; he simply knew that acting that way would get him what he wanted. As you can probably imagine, this set of abilities can be very useful in almost any social setting, from work to interpersonal relationships. And, like other forms of intelligence, it can be used for either good or evil, depending on one's goal (we suggest using it for good). In fact, some of the most successful political leaders of our time have relied on this skill extensively to build commitment and enthusiasm among their followers (see Figure 9.21).

FIGURE 9.21
Managing the Emotions of Others
Successful politicians are often very adept at managing their own emotions as well as the emotions of others. This skill helps them gain support for various causes, including their reelection.

- ■ Emotional intelligence: Evidence of its effects.

Much of the evidence initially offered for the existence of emotional intelligence was anecdotal or indirect in nature (e.g., Goleman, 1995, 1998). At that time, no good measure of it existed, making it impossible to address fundamental questions about how emotional intelligence might be related to success in various aspects of life. In the last few years, however, a reliable and valid measure has been developed (Mayer, Salovey, & Caruso, 2002). With this measure, psychologists now have a much better sense of the importance of emotional intelligence. For example, research indicates that social relationships are more positive for individuals who score high on this test of emotional intelligence. Specifically, those with high emotional intelligence have fewer negative interactions with friends and have closer relationships with their parents (Lopes, Salovey, & Straus, 2003). Even couples get along better, ideally when both members of the couple are high in emotional intelligence.

Not surprisingly, relationships at work are also more positive for those high in emotional intelligence. Employees high in emotional intelligence even appear to get promoted faster and actually receive higher wages than those lower in emotional intelligence (Lopes et al., in press). What is most impressive about these findings is that the results control for the effects of many other variables that might also have an influence (e.g., personality variables), thus ruling out the possibility that it is these traits, rather than emotional intelligence, that are responsible for the effects.

While these results are encouraging, they are just a beginning. Little is known yet, for example, about how stable emotional intelligence is and debate continues about whether it should be considered a type of intelligence at all. Salovey (2004), in fact, describes it as a set of skills, implying that they can be learned and developed with appropriate training and experience. If this turns out to be true, it is an encouraging note on which to end. So stay tuned: The idea of emotional intelligence is an appealing one with important implications for many aspects of life.

- What is emotional intelligence?
- What evidence is there for its effects?

SUMMARY AND REVIEW OF KEY QUESTIONS

Personality: The Essence of What Makes Us Unique

- **What is personality?**
  Personality consists of the unique and stable patterns of behavior, thoughts, and emotions shown by individuals.

- **How stable is it over time?**
  Research findings indicate that personality is quite stable over time, although some people show more stability than others.

- **What is the interactionist perspective currently adopted by most psychologists?**
  The interactionist perspective supports the view that our behavior in any given situation is a joint function of our personality and various aspects of the situation.

The Psychoanalytic Approach: Messages from the Unconscious

- **According to Freud, what are the three levels of consciousness?**
  These levels are conscious, preconscious, and unconscious.

- **In Freud's theory, what are the three basic components of personality?**
  The three basic parts of personality are id, ego, and super-ego, which correspond roughly to desire, reason, and conscience.

- **According to Freud, what are the psychosexual stages of development?**
  Freud believed that all humans move through a series of psychosexual stages during which the id's search for pleasure is focused on different regions of the body: the oral stage, anal stage, phallic stage, latency stage, and, finally, the genital stage.

- **Do research findings support Freud's views about the unconscious?**
  Research findings indicate that our behavior is sometimes influenced by stimuli or information we can't describe verbally, although there's no support for his view that such information has been driven from consciousness by repression.

Humanistic Theories: Emphasis on Growth

- **How does the view of human beings proposed by humanistic theories of personality differ from that of psychoanalytic theories?**
  Humanistic theories of personality suggest that people strive for personal development and growth; in contrast, psychoanalytic theory views humans as constantly strug-

gling to control the sexual and aggressive impulses of the id.

- **According to Rogers, why do many individuals fail to become fully functioning persons?**
  Rogers believed that many individuals fail to become fully functioning people because distorted self-concepts interfere with personal growth.

- **In Maslow's theory, what is self-actualization?**
  Self-actualization is a stage in which an individual has reached his or her maximum potential, and has become the best human being she or he can be.

- **What is self-esteem and how does it vary over time and across groups?**
  Self-esteem is a person's overall feeling of worth. In general, self-esteem decreases during the teenage years and increases during adulthood, with males having higher levels than females on average. Self-esteem also varies by ethnic group, both within and outside the United States.

Trait Theories: Seeking the Key Dimensions of Personality

- **What are the "big five" dimensions of personality?**
  Research findings point to the conclusion that there are only five basic dimensions of personality: extraversion, agreeableness, conscientiousness, emotional stability, and openness to experience.

- **What behaviors are related to traits in the "big five"?**
  Several traits in the "big five" are related to a wide range of life outcomes, including career success, happiness, and longevity.

- **What are the advantages and disadvantages of the trait approach?**
  Advantages of the trait approach include that it is the basis for most current research on personality, and that the traits it has uncovered are related to important aspects of behavior. Disadvantages include that the trait approach offers no comprehensive theory for *how* certain traits develop and *why* they are so important.

Cognitive-Behavioral Approaches to Personality

- **According to learning theories of personality, what accounts for the uniqueness and consistency of human behavior?**
  These theories of personality suggest that uniqueness derives from the unique pattern of learning experiences each individual has experienced. Such approaches ex-

plain consistency by noting that patterns of behavior, once acquired, tend to persist.

- **In Bandura's social cognitive theory, what is the self-system?**
  The self-system is the set of cognitive processes by which individuals perceive, evaluate, and regulate their own behavior.

- **According to Rotter's social learning theory, what is the key difference between internals and externals?**
  Internals believe that they can control the outcomes they experience, while externals do not.

- **What is self-efficacy?**
  Self-efficacy is belief in one's ability to perform a specific task.

Measuring Personality

- **What are self-report tests of personality?**
  These are questionnaires containing a number of questions individuals answer about themselves. An example is the NEO-PI, which measures traits in the "big five."

- **What are projective tests of personality?**
  Such tests present individuals with ambiguous stimuli. Their responses to these stimuli are assumed to reflect various aspects of their personalities.

Modern Research on Personality Beyond Grand Theories

- **What links are there between self-esteem and behavior? Is high self-esteem always a good thing?**
  Low self-esteem is related to antisocial behavior. People low in self-esteem also react to success more negatively. However, the pursuit of high self-esteem also has its costs.

- **What biological factors play a role in personality?**
  Various neural systems appear to be involved in basic tendencies linked to personality. Evidence also shows a moderate genetic influence on personality.

Intelligence: Contrasting Views of Its Nature

- **What is intelligence?**
  The term *intelligence* refers to individuals' abilities to understand complex ideas, to adapt effectively to the environment, to learn from experience, to engage in various forms of reasoning, and to overcome obstacles by careful thought.

- **What is Gardner's theory of multiple intelligences?**
  Gardner's theory suggests that there are several different kinds of intelligence, such as verbal, mathematical, musical, and bodily–kinesthetic.

- **What is Sternberg's triarchic theory of intelligence?**
  Sternberg's theory suggests that there are three basic kinds of intelligence: componential, experiential, and contextual (practical).

- **What is fluid intelligence? Crystallized intelligence?**
  Fluid intelligence has to do with our inherited abilities to think and reason. Crystallized intelligence consists of accumulated knowledge—information and skills stored over a lifetime.

Measuring Intelligence

- **What was the first individual test of intelligence, and what did scores on it mean?**
  The first individual test of intelligence was devised by Binet and Simon. It yielded a "mental age," and testers then derived an IQ (intelligence quotient) score obtained by dividing mental by chronological age and multiplying by 100.

- **What are the Wechsler scales?**
  The Wechsler scales are individual tests of intelligence for children and adults that seek to measure several aspects of intelligence—performance components as well as verbal components.

- **What are standardization, reliability, and validity?**
  Standardization is the process of establishing the average score and distribution of scores on a test so that the scores of people taking the test can be meaningfully interpreted. Reliability is the extent to which a test yields consistent results. Validity is the extent to which a test measures what it is supposed to measure.

The Cognitive and Neural Bases of Intelligence

- **What cognitive processes are related to intelligence?**
  Research indicates that both reaction time and working memory capacity are related to intelligence.

- **What findings suggest that intelligence is related to neural functioning?**
  Research findings indicate that scores on standard tests of intelligence are correlated with nerve conduction velocity and with efficiency in brain functioning. Neural plasticity, the ability of neurons to form connections in response to environmental cues, may also play a role in intelligence.

Intelligence: Heredity, Environment, and Group Differences

- **What evidence suggests that intelligence is influenced by genetic factors?**
  Evidence for the role of genetic factors is provided by the findings that the more closely related people are, the higher the correlation in their IQ scores; by research on adopted children; and by research on identical twins separated early in life and raised in different homes.

- **What evidence suggests that intelligence is influenced by environmental factors?**
  Evidence for the role of environmental factors is provided by the worldwide rise in IQ scores in recent decades (the Flynn effect), studies of environmental deprivation and enrichment, and the finding that many environmental factors, such as music lessons, can affect children's intelligence.

- **What evidence suggests that group differences in intelligence stem largely from environmental factors?**
  There is some indication that many intelligence tests suffer from cultural bias. Other sources of evidence include the Flynn effect—worldwide rises in IQ over time—and direct evidence indicating that when minority children are raised in enhanced environments, their IQ matches that of nonminority children.

- **Is there any evidence for the role of genetic factors in group differences in intelligence?**
Very little if any evidence indicates that group differences in intelligence have a genetic basis.

Emotional Intelligence: The Feeling Side of Intelligence

- **What is emotional intelligence?**
Emotional intelligence is a cluster of skills or abilities relating to the emotional side of life. It includes the ability to perceive, use, understand, and manage our own emotions as well as the emotions of others.

- **What evidence is there for its effects?**
Preliminary evidence indicates that emotional intelligence is related to success in many aspects of life, including relationships and work. However, only a few studies have been done so far, using a new measure of emotional intelligence, so much is yet to be learned.

KEY TERMS

PSYCHOLOGY: UNDERSTANDING ITS FINDINGS

How Basic Are the "Big Five"?
Similarity of Self and Other Ratings

Research on the "big five" personality theory suggests that the traits of conscientiousness, extraversion, emotional stability, agreeableness, and openness to experience are ones that are well understood across cultures and age groups. Additional evidence suggests that the basic nature of these traits also show up when people compare how they rate on these traits to how others rate them. Try the following exercise to test this idea:

1. Find a close friend or family member and show him or her the definitions of the "big five" traits discussed earlier in the chapter.

2. Rate yourself on a scale from 1 to 10 on each of the five traits. A 1 should indicate that you have very little of this trait and a 10 should indicate that you have a great deal of this trait.

3. Now, without showing your ratings to the other person, have him or her also rate you using the same scale.

4. Compare the two sets of ratings and examine them for consistency. Is there much agreement? If not, where is there the most disagreement?

While it is certain that your ratings won't be identical, it is likely that there is a good deal of similarity, particularly if this person knows you well and you were both as honest as possible. Of course, these ratings don't constitute a valid measure of these traits, so that needs to be kept in mind, also.

MAKING PSYCHOLOGY PART OF YOUR LIFE

Environmental Influences on Personality and Intelligence: How Our Choices Influence What We Become

Earlier, we noted that research indicates that personality and intelligence are determined by a mix of genetic and environmental factors (Bouchard, 2004). Evidence further suggests that genetic factors may play a role in the environments we choose, such as the situations we enjoy most or the activities that suit our abilities. With this in mind, try the following exercise:

1. Think of one personality trait and one cognitive ability that describe you. Ideally, one characteristic should be something that you feel you possess a lot of and the other should be a characteristic that you feel you possess very little of. Use specific terms from any of the theories presented earlier to describe how much of this or that characteristic you feel you have.

2. Now identify various activities or situations that you either seek out or avoid on the basis of these characteristics. Also think about why you tend to gravitate toward one activity or situation versus another, and how you feel when you are not in a situation that you have chosen.

3. Describe how your choices of environment (situations, activities) may have accentuated these characteristics over time.

4. Finally, evaluate your choices: Would you like to have more of a particular characteristic or less of another? If so, think about your future choices of environment carefully, because genetics is only part of the picture.

If you are using MyPsychLab, you have access to an electronic version of this textbook, along with dozens of valuable resources per chapter—including video and audio clips, simulations and activities, self-assessments, practice tests and other study materials. Here is a sampling of the resources available for this chapter.

EXPLORE

The Id, Ego, and Superego

Sternberg's Triarchic Theory of Intelligence

Gardner's Multiple Intelligences

WATCH

Intelligence

Memory & Exercise

Demographics and Intelligence Testing

Are Intelligence Tests Valid?

If you did not receive an access code to MyPsychLab with this text and wish to purchase access online, please visit www.MyPsychLab.com.

STUDY GUIDE

CHAPTER REVIEW

Personality: The Essence of What Makes Us Unique

1. Personality is defined as a relatively stable pattern of
   a. emotions.
   b. thoughts.
   c. behaviors.
   d. All of the above are correct.
2. The _____ view argues that whether we act in a given situation is a function of our personality and the situation.
   a. psychoanalytic
   b. interactionist
   c. humanistic
   d. homeostatic
3. Early in his career Freud used hypnosis for the treatment of anorexia nervosa. (True-False)
4. Freud would argue that our part memories of childhood friends exist within our
   a. conscious.
   b. unconscious.
   c. preconscious.
   d. postconscious.
5. Freud argued that in order for us to remain free from anxiety, our unacceptable impulses are _____ by keeping these below the _____ level of awareness.
   a. rehearsed;   preconscious
   b. enhanced;   postconscious
   c. repressed;   conscious
   d. suppressed;   unconscious
6. In considering Freud's model of consciousness; the tip of the iceberg is _____ while the base is _____.
   a. unconscious;   preconscious
   b. postconscious;   conscious
   c. preconscious;   conscious
   d. conscious;   unconscious
7. According to Freud, the function of _____ is to operate according to the _____ principle.
   a. ego;   pleasure
   b. superego;   reality
   c. id;   social reality
   d. id;   pleasure
8. The function of superego is to gratify id impulses only when it is morally correct.   (True-False)
9. Freud would suggest that a child who has an excessive amount of libido tied to a particular stage of psychosexual development will
   a. repress this fact from their conscious experience.
   b. sublimate this libido by doing good works.
   c. fixate at that stage.
   d. grow up to have an excessively violent temper.
10. The ego operates according to the pleasure principle. (True-False)
11. The Freudian term _____ refers to a psychic energy that motivates our behavior.
    a. libido
    b. reaction energy
    c. drive
    d. incentive
12. Darcy is overly concerned with being neat and tidy. Freud would most likely suggest that Darcy is fixated at the _____ stage of psychosexual development.
    a. oral
    b. phallic
    c. anal
    d. latent
13. Subsequent research has confirmed Freud's view that
    a. girls experience penis envy.
    b. humans can act on thoughts and feelings of which they are largely unaware.
    c. boys experience castration anxiety.
    d. personality is made up from id, ego and superego.
14. Carl Jung argued that we have tendencies to be concerned with portions of our environment which are reflected in the _____ versus _____ types.
    a. neurotic;   psychotic
    b. introverted;   extraverted
    c. oral;   anal
    d. secure;   anxious
15. In contrast to Freud, Alfred Adler argued that humans are motivated to resolve
    a. oedipal complex.
    b. id/superego conflicts.
    c. their archetype anxiety.
    d. feelings of inferiority.
16. Which of the following is a valid criticism of Freud's theory of personality?
    a. His theory is based on observations of a small number of patients.
    b. It is difficult to define the concepts of his theory.
    c. His theory can explain all observations and thus none.
    d. All of the above are correct.
17. A key contribution made by Freud was his view that mental processes can occur outside of conscious awareness.   (True-False)
18. The humanistic theories of personality emphasize the importance of
    a. personal growth.
    b. unconscious motivation.
    c. constant control of our darker impulses.
    d. feelings of inferiority.
19. Match the appropriate personality theorist or personality approach with each statement below.
    _____. Humans share a common set of unconscious experiences.
    _____. A view of personality that emphasizes unconscious impulses.
    _____. Social factors are a key reason as to why women feel inferior to men.
    _____. An approach that emphasizes the positive aspects of personality.
    _____. A theorist who emphasized the self-concept and peoples need for positive regard.

_____. A medical doctor who proposed a model of personality that emphasized different levels of consciousness.
a. Karen Horney.
b. Sigmund Freud.
c. Carl Jung.
d. Carl Rogers.
e. Humanistic personality theory.
f. Psychoanalytic personality theory.

20. The concept of _____ is most closely associated with the work of _____.
a. positive regard; Karen Horney
b. self-actualization; Abraham Maslow
c. self-concept; Sigmund Freud
d. superiority complex; Carl Jung

21. Carl Rogers argued that humans strive to become fully functioning persons. (True-False)

22. Which of the following would be classified by Maslow as an example of a self-actualized person?
a. Albert Einstein.
b. Boy George.
c. Charles Manson.
d. George Jefferson.

23. Which of the following is true of self-esteem?
a. Self-esteem changes dramatically during adolescence.
b. Females report higher levels of self-esteem across the life span than do males.
c. African Americans report higher levels of self-esteem than do Americans of European descent.
d. All of the above are correct.

24. Self-_____ refers to what we believe we can accomplish.
a. loathing
b. esteem
c. liking
d. competence

25. A person from a collectivist culture such as Pakistan or Peru would be expected to be high on the dimension of self-liking but lower on self-competence. (True-False)

26. A major criticism of the humanistic personality theories is that these theories tend to overemphasize the positive (True-False).

27. A(n) _____ is a stable dimension of personality that can vary from low to high.
a. archetype
b. cluster
c. trait
d. type

28. A person who treats others in a mean fashion would be said to be low in the trait of
a. agreeableness.
b. emotional stability.
c. openness to experience.
d. conscientiousness.

29. A person who is careful, well-organized, responsible, and precise would be said to be high in the trait of
a. agreeableness.
b. emotional stability.
c. openness to experience.
d. conscientiousness.

30. Another name for _____ is _____
a. extraversion; agreeableness
b. openness to experience; introversion
c. emotional stability; neuroticism
d. conscientiousness; compulsivity

31. The big five personality traits have been identified in primates. (True-False)

32. The relative profile of a person with regard to the "Big-Five" traits can be used to predict
a. how long they will live.
b. their positive health behaviors.
c. their success in business.
d. All of the above are correct.

33. Albert Bandura focused attention on the role of _____ learning, which involves noting the behavior of others.
a. stimulus-response
b. basic
c. instrumental
d. observational

34. Julian Rotter argued that whether a behavior occurs or not in a specific situation is a function of _____ and _____.
a. rewards; observational learning
b. expectancies; reinforcement value of outcomes
c. classical conditioning; operant conditioning
d. perceived efficacy; self-concept

35. A person who believes that their future is in the their control would be classified by Rotter as having a(n) _____ orientation.
a. psychotic
b. external
c. neurotic
d. internal

36. Self-efficacy is a strong predictor of personal happiness. (True-False)

37. A(n) _____ is an example of an objective measure of personality
a. projective test
b. measure of hair color
c. self-report inventory
d. unstructured job interview

38. The Behavioral Inhibition System functions as an approach system (True-False)

39. The function of the Behavioral Arousal System (BAS) is associated with the neurotransmitter
a. dopamine
b. serotonin
c. acetylcholine
d. GABA

40. The least heritable of the "Big-Five" traits is that of
a. agreeableness.
b. conscientiousness.
c. extraversion.
d. emotional stability.

Intelligence: The Nature of Cognitive Abilities

41. How long a person lives is related to their level of intelligence. (True-False)

42. Which theorist argued that intelligence is composed of seven distinct primary mental abilities?

a. Spearman.
b. Bandura.
c. Darwin.
d. Thurstone.

43. Which of the following is NOT one of the forms of intelligence identified by Howard Gardner?
    a. Musical.
    b. Personal
    c. Spatial
    d. Emotional

44. Longitudinal studies indicate that _____ intelligence decreases with age whereas _____ intelligence remains static.
    a. contextual;   analytical
    b. fluid;   crystallized
    c. emotional;   empirical
    d. crystallized;   fluid

45. An IQ score of 100 is assumed today to be
    a. the cutoff for mental retardation.
    b. a score that is at the top end of the distribution of scores.
    c. an average score.
    d. a very low score.

46. A key development of the Wechsler intelligence tests was the inclusion of nonverbal material.   (True-False)

IDENTIFICATIONS

Identify the term that belongs with each of the concepts below (place the letter for the appropriate term below in front of each concept).

Identification   Concept:

_____ 1. A person who thinks that they are a pawn of life.
_____ 2. The portion of the personality concerned with the immediate gratification of primitive needs.
_____ 3. The final stage of Freud's theory of psychosexual development.
_____ 4. A portion of the unconscious that is shared by all persons
_____ 5. A Jungian concept in which a person is cautious and does not easily make friends.
_____ 6. The feeling a person has when they are "one with the universe."
_____ 7. The situation when test scores are related to behaviors relevant to the intent of the test.
_____ 8. The id operates according to this concept.
_____ 9. A person who is always smoking or chewing gum is fixated at this stage.
_____ 10. A person who is high in this dimension of personality is able to get along with others.
_____ 11. The psychic energy that powers all mental activity.
_____ 12. The portion of the personality that operates according to the reality principle.
_____ 13. A test with this quality yields the same answer when applied to the same quantity.
_____ 14. This functions to anticipate and enjoy positive experiences.
_____ 15. A person who is unable to manage their feelings or to understand those of others would be low in this.

Identification:
a. Behavioral activation system.
b. Ego.
c. Genital stage.
d. Libido.
e. Agreeableness
f. Oral stage.
g. Externals.
h. Emotional intelligence.
i. Peak experience.
j. Pleasure principle.
k. Reliability.
l. Collective unconscious.
m. Id.
n. Introverts.
o. Content validity.

FILL IN THE BLANK

1. _____ refers to a psychic energy that motivates our behavior.
2. Emotional intelligence involves the abilities to _____, _____, _____ and _____ emotions.
3. A person who is careful, well-organized, responsible, and precise is high in the trait of _____.
4. The neo-Freudian _____ argued that psychological disorders arise from _____.
5. The _____ is the view that listening to classical music will make for a smarter baby.
6. The proportion of variance in intelligence that can be attributed to genetic factors is _____.
7. An instance in which a person misspeaks in such as a way to reveal their true feelings would be termed a _____.
8. Jung defined the _____ as that portion of the unconscious that is shared by all persons.
9. A _____ test gives the same answer when applied to the same quantity.
10. A stable dimension of personality is known as a _____.
11. _____ argued that intelligence is composed of seven distinct primary mental abilities.
12. Sternberg argues for a _____ view of intelligence.
13. _____ is defined as a relatively stable pattern of behavior, thoughts and emotions.
14. Carl Rogers suggested that therapists use _____ when dealing with clients.
15. The humanistic theories of personality emphasize the importance of _____.
16. The function of superego is to gratify _____ impulses only when it is morally correct.
17. Emotional stability is another name for _____.

COMPREHENSIVE PRACTICE TEST

1. Freud argued that our current thoughts and ideas exist at the _____ level.
   a. conscious
   b. unconscious
   c. preconscious
   d. postconscious

2. In Freud's personality theory, desire is to _____ as conscience is to _____.
   a. preconscious;   unconscious
   b. ego;   id
   c. id;   superego
   d. conscious;   unconscious

3. Paris lives life to do whatever she wants; no desire or need is left unfilled. According to Freud, Paris has an overdeveloped
   a. reality show.
   b. id.
   c. ego.
   d. superego.

4. Freud suggested that psychological difficulties in adulthood can be traced to conflict between
   a. the id and the superego.
   b. good and evil.
   c. the conscious and the preconscious.
   d. the ego and social norms.

5. Match up the appropriate concept with the correct definition or best example of the concept.
   _____. A personality component that operates according to the pleasure principle.
   _____. The location of the conscience in Freud's theory of personality.
   _____. A woman steps out of the house to call her husband to dinner—"Ralph come and get it." The problem is that her husband is named Bob whereas Ralph is the next door neighbor.
   _____. The function of this personality structure is to rein in the impulses of the id.
   _____. The view that the ego tries to maximize pleasure and minimize pain.
   _____. The view that a person may be "stuck" at one of the psychosexual stages of development.
   a. Fixation.
   b. Id.
   c. Reality principle.
   d. Freudian slip.
   e. Pleasure principle.
   f. Superego.
   g. Ego.

6. According to Carl Jung, the _____ is a portion of the unconscious mind shared by all people.
   a. libido
   b. superiority complex
   c. collective unconscious
   d. oedipal complex

7. The inferiority complex is to the unconscious as _____ is to _____.
   a. Alfred Adler;   Sigmund Freud
   b. Karen Horney;   Carl Jung
   c. Neil Miller;   Karen Horney
   d. Carl Jung;   Alfred Adler

8. A person who has "street smarts" would be said to be high in what Sternberg termed _____ intelligence.
   a. creative
   b. contextual
   c. empirical
   d. analytical

9. _____ is to psychoanalytic theory as _____ is to social learning theory.
   a. Bandura;   Jung
   b. Freud;   Rotter
   c. Maslow;   Skinner
   d. Adler;   Horney

10. Which of the following terms DO NOT belong together?
    a. objective personality measures; inkblots
    b. MMPI;   prediction of abnormal personality
    c. internals;   externals
    d. projective test;   inkblots

11. A key criticism of trait theories is that this approach
    a. is unable to predict future behavior.
    b. cannot explain the development of personality.
    c. can identify which traits are important and which are trivial.
    d. appeals to unconscious motivation.

12. A person who is low in self-esteem is likely to
    a. engage in less antisocial behavior
    b. engage in high levels of narcissism.
    c. dislike success.
    d. greatly enjoy success.

13. The crucial requirement(s) for an intelligence test relate to
    a. validity.
    b. standardization.
    c. reliability.
    d. All of the above are correct.

14. Which of the following NOT an attribute of intelligence?
    a. The ability to understand complex ideas.
    b. The capacity to create.
    c. The ability to profit from experience.
    d. The ability to think through and overcome problems.

15. The intent of the first intelligence developed by Binet was to
    a. screen immigrants for mental retardation.
    b. rapidly classify Army recruits in WWI as to military occupation.
    c. determine which students should be admitted to prep school.
    d. determine which school children would profit from special education.

16. Match up the intelligence concept with the person most closely associated with the concept.
    _____. His work argued for a single factor underlying intelligence.
    _____. His theory denoted "fluid" versus "crystallized" forms of intelligence.
    _____. The creator of the first intelligence test.
    _____. His view is that there are eight distinct forms of intelligence.
    a. Binet
    b. Cattell.
    c. Spearman.
    d. Gardner

CRITICAL THINKING

1. Discuss three major pieces of evidence that support Freud's view that humans can think without awareness.
2. Explain how psychologists are able to tease apart the biological and environmental contributions to intelligence.

TEN

Health, Stress, and Coping

*O*ne aspect of human behavior that has always intrigued me (Michael Kalsher) is how people react to good and bad events. Some people wilt at the slightest hint of adversity, whereas other people—the most resilient ones—take even the worst personal tragedies in stride. Perhaps the best example of this latter group of people that i've witnessed involves my brother-in-law Paul. Several years ago, he was diagnosed with a relatively advanced case of cancer. Although he was initially shocked by the news, as we all were, Paul quickly took an active role in managing his illness by reading everything pertaining to his form of cancer that he could get his hands on and participating in decisions concerning his treatment options. Surgery and several months of chemotherapy failed to eradicate the disease and Paul is currently receiving periodic hormone injections that keep his cancer at bay. Unfortunately, the therapy has a number of unpleasant side effects and it is likely to stop working in just a few years. While many people might be defeated by this type of situation, Paul's reaction has been quite different. He has become even more passionate about his golf game, playing several times per week; he has altered his diet and routinely seeks out new and alternative treatment possibilities; and the most interesting reaction of all— he has created an elaborate list of the things he wants to do in his life and is actively working to experience every item on the list. Moreover, through all of this, he has retained his keen sense of humor and good cheer.

This is a moving and inspiring story, and perhaps even more importantly, it highlights a key theme of this chapter: the intimate relationship that exists between psychological variables and health. Indeed, several decades of research suggest that good health is determined by a complex interaction among genetic, psychological, and social factors. Throughout this chapter, we'll encounter findings that show how these factors combine to produce good—and poor—health.

We'll begin by describing the exciting branch of psychology known as *health psychology*. The primary aim of health psychology is to identify important relationships between psychological variables and health. Second, we'll consider the nature of *stress*, a major health-related problem. Here, we'll focus on both the causes of stress and some of its major effects—how it influences health and performance. Next, we'll consider how some of our *beliefs* and *attitudes* influence the way in which we interpret certain health symptoms, and thus affect our willingness to seek necessary medical assistance. Fourth, we'll look at *behaviors* that can directly affect our risk of contracting certain lifestyle-related illnesses, such as cancer, cardiovascular diseases, and AIDS. Finally, we'll consider various ways in which psychologists work to promote personal health by encouraging healthy lifestyles.

HEALTH PSYCHOLOGY: AN OVERVIEW

Health psychology, the branch of psychology that studies the relation between psychological variables and health, reflects the view that both mind and body are important determinants of health and illness (Taylor, 2002). Specifically, health psychologists believe that our beliefs, attitudes, and behavior contribute significantly to the onset or prevention of illness (Ray, 2004). A closely related field, known as *behavioral medicine*, combines behavioral and biomedical knowledge for the prevention and treatment of disorders ordinarily thought of as being within the domain of medicine (Epstein, 1992; Keefe et al., 2002).

Health psychology and behavioral medicine have experienced tremendous growth since their beginnings in the early 1970s. Perhaps the most fundamental reason for the increased interest in health psychology and behavioral medicine is the dramatic shift observed in the leading causes of death during the twentieth century. In 1900, many of the leading causes of death could be traced to infectious diseases, such as influenza, pneumonia, and tuberculosis. However, the development of antibiotics, vaccines, and improved sanitation practices has significantly reduced these health threats, at least in this country.

As shown in Table 10.1, the current leading causes of death are attributable to a significant degree to characteristics that make up **lifestyle**—the overall pattern of decisions and behaviors that determines a person's health and quality of life. This fact suggests that psychologists can make a difference in people's quality of life by helping them eliminate behaviors that lead to illness and adopt behaviors that lead to wellness. Indeed, a majority of the conditions that now constitute the leading causes of death could be prevented if people would eat nutritious foods, reduce their alcohol consumption, practice safe sex, eliminate smoking, and exercise regularly.

To illustrate the contribution of health psychology research, let's consider a classic decade-long study conducted in Alameda County, California. The researchers asked a large group of adults whether they followed certain health practices, including sleeping seven to eight hours each night, eating breakfast regularly, refraining from smoking, drinking alcohol in moderation or not at all, maintaining their weight within normal limits, and exercising regularly (Wiley & Camacho, 1980). The results revealed that participants who reported practicing all

Health psychology:
The study of the relation between psychological variables and health, which reflects the view that both mind and body are important determinants of health and illness.

Lifestyle:
In the context of health psychology, the overall pattern of decisions and behaviors that determine health and quality of life.

TABLE 10.1   Top 10 Leading Causes of Deaths in the United States: 2003

Many of the important causes of death shown here are related to lifestyle. Thus, they can be prevented by changes in behavior.

Rank	Cause of death	Deaths	Percentage of Total Deaths
1	Heart disease	685,089	35.7
2	Cancer	556,902	29.1
3	Stroke	157,689	8.2
4	Chronic lung disease	126,382	6.6
5	Accidents (unintentional injuries)	109,277	5.7
6	Diabetes mellitus	74,219	3.9
7	Influenza and pneumonia	65,163	3.4
8	Alzheimer's disease	63,457	3.3
9	Kidney disease	42,453	2.2
10	Blood poisoning	34,069	1.8
Total		1,914,700	100

Source: Based on data in the National Vital Statistics Report, March 9, 2006.

or most of these behaviors were much less likely to die during the study period than those who practiced few or none of these behaviors. These results highlight the intimate connection between lifestyle and good health.

But how likely is it that people can be persuaded to adopt healthier lifestyles? Results from the Healthy People 2000 Initiative, a nationwide health promotion and disease prevention agenda, are encouraging, but they also point out how difficult it is to change certain behaviors. The aim of this program, initially begun in 1979, was to promote good health among U.S. citizens by identifying the most significant preventable threats to health and then focusing public and private resources to address those threats effectively. It was an ambitious project that targeted specific health indicators (e.g., physical activity, obesity, tobacco use, responsible sexual behavior) for improvement and sought to make preventive health services available to all Americans. Significant progress was made on some of the objectives, including increases in the number of children receiving immunizations and women receiving mammography screening, an increase in consumption of fruits and vegetables, and a reduction in infant mortality rates. In addition, there was a slight decrease in the percentage of adult smokers.

Unfortunately, there are a number of areas in which we have actually lost ground. Nearly 65 percent of adult Americans continue to be overweight as well as 16 percent of children ages six to eighteen (see Chapter 8) (National Center for

Health Statistics, 2002). And little progress has been made in increasing Americans' level of physical activity and fitness. Only 26 percent of adults engage in vigorous leisure-time physical activity three or more times a week, and 59 percent don't exercise at all (National Center for Health Statistics, 2005). The work toward a healthier nation continues with a new national initiative, Healthy People 2010, which focuses on twenty-eight areas in which quality of life can be improved. You can examine the particulars of the Healthy People 2010 Initiative at http://www.healthypeople.gov/document/html/uih/uih_1.htm.

KEY QUESTIONS

- What is health psychology?
- What is the field of behavioral medicine?
- To what can we attribute today's leading causes of premature death?

STRESS: ITS CAUSES, EFFECTS, AND CONTROL

Have you ever felt that you were right at the edge of being overwhelmed by negative events in your life? Or felt so overwhelmed that you just gave up? If so, you are already quite familiar with **stress**—our response to events that disrupt, or threaten to disrupt, our physical or psychological functioning (Lazarus & Folkman, 1984; Taylor, 2002). Unfortunately, stress is a common part of modern life—something few of us can avoid altogether. Partly for this reason, and partly because it seems to exert negative effects on both physical health and psychological well-being, stress has become an important topic of research in psychology. Let's examine the basic nature of stress and some of its major causes.

Stress: Its Basic Nature

Stress is a many-faceted process that occurs in reaction to events or situations, termed **stressors,** in our environment. An interesting feature of stress is the wide range of physical and psychological reactions that different people have to the same event; some may interpret an event as stressful, whereas others simply take it in stride. Moreover, a particular person may react quite differently to the same stressor at different points in time.

■ Stressors: The activators of stress.

What are stressors? Although we normally think of stress as stemming from negative events in our lives, positive events, such as getting married or receiving an unexpected job promotion, can also produce stress. Despite the wide range of stimuli that can potentially produce stress, it appears that many events we find stressful share several characteristics: (1) they are so intense that they produce a state of overload—we can no longer adapt to them; (2) they evoke incompatible tendencies in us, such as tendencies both to approach and to avoid some object or activity; and (3) they are uncontrollable—beyond our limits of control. A great deal of evidence suggests that when people can predict, control, or terminate an aversive event or situation, they perceive it to be less stressful than when they feel less in control (Kemeny, 2003).

■ Physiological responses to stressors.

When exposed to stressors, we generally experience many physiological reactions. If you've been caught off guard by someone who appears out of nowhere and grabs you while screaming "Gotcha," then you are probably familiar with some common

Stress:
The process by which we appraise and respond to events that disrupt, or threaten to disrupt, our physical or psychological functioning.

Stressors:
Events or situations in our environment that cause stress.

FIGURE 10.1
Physiological Reactions to Stressors
When we encounter stressors that frighten or surprise us, we experience a wave of physiological reactions, as illustrated in this photo. These are part of a general pattern of reactions referred to as the fight-or-flight syndrome, a process controlled through the sympathetic nervous sytem.

physical reactions to stress (see Figure 10.1). Initially, your blood pressure soars, your pulse races, and you may even begin to sweat. These are part of a general pattern of reactions referred to as the *fight-or-flight syndrome*, a process controlled through the sympathetic nervous system. As we saw in Chapter 2, the sympathetic nervous system prepares our bodies for immediate action. Usually these responses are brief, and the physical reactions pass. When we are exposed to chronic sources of stress, however, this reaction is only the first in a longer sequence of responses activated by our efforts to adapt to a stressor. This sequence, termed by Hans Selye (1976) the **general adaptation syndrome (GAS),** consists of three stages.

The first is the *alarm stage,* in which the body prepares itself for immediate action; arousal of the sympathetic nervous system releases hormones that help prepare our bodies to meet threats or dangers. If stress is prolonged, however, the *resistance stage* begins. During this second stage, arousal is lower than during the alarm stage, but our bodies continue to draw on resources at an above-normal rate to cope effectively with the stressor. Continued exposure to the same stressor or additional stressors drains the body of its resources and leads to the third stage, *exhaustion*. During this stage, our capacity to resist is depleted, and our susceptibility to illness increases.

Selye's general adaptation syndrome provides a framework for understanding our physiological responses to stressful events and suggests at least one reasonable explanation for the relation between stress and illness. Few experts would disagree that chronic stress can lead to a lowered resistance to disease. However, one weakness with Selye's model is that it seems to imply that stressors impact the body uniformly. More recent findings indicate that stressors elicit a patterned array of physiological changes that prepare humans and other animals to deal with the specific nature of the threat (Kemeny, 2003; Weiner, 1992).

■ Cognitive appraisal of our stressors.

Another problem with Selye's model is that it fails to consider the importance of cognitive processes in determining whether we interpret a specific event as stressful. The importance of these processes is made clear by the following fact: When confronted with the same potentially stress-inducing situation, some people experience stress, whereas others do not. Why? One reason involves individuals' cognitive appraisals (see Figure 10.2, page 390). In simple terms, stress occurs only to the extent that the people involved perceive that (1) the situation is somehow threaten-

General adaptation syndrome (GAS):
A profile of how organisms respond to stress; it consists of three phases: a nonspecific mobilization phase that promotes sympathetic nervous system activity; a resistance phase, during which the organism makes efforts to cope with the threat; and an exhaustion phase, which occurs if the organism fails to overcome the threat and depletes its coping resources.

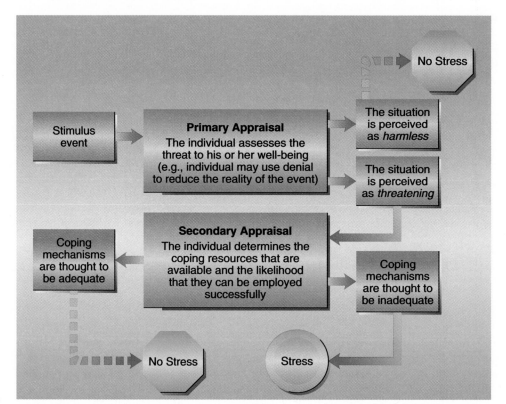

FIGURE 10.2
Stress: The Role of Cognitive Appraisals
The amount of stress you experience depends in part on your cognitive appraisals of the event or situation—the extent to which you perceive it as threatening and perceive that you will be unable to cope with it.
Source: Based on data from Hingson et al., 1990.

ing to their important goals (often described as *primary appraisal*), and (2) they will be unable to cope with these dangers or demands (often described as *secondary appraisal*) (Croyle, 1992; Lazarus & Folkman, 1984). Stress will be low when either an event is perceived as a challenge rather than a threat, or when a person is confident in his or her ability to cope with a perceived threat (Blascovich & Tomaka, 1996).

In short, cognitive and social processes have a significant impact on our responses to stress. We'll turn next to some of the causes of stress.

KEY QUESTIONS

- What is stress?
- What is the GAS model?
- What determines whether an event will be interpreted as stressful or as a challenge?

Stress: Some Major Causes

What factors contribute to stress? Unfortunately, the list is a long one. A wide range of conditions and events seems capable of generating such feelings. Among the most important of these are major stressful life events (e.g., the death of a loved one or a painful divorce), the all-too-frequent minor hassles of everyday life, and conditions and events relating to one's job.

■ Stressful life events.

Death of a spouse, injury to one's child, failure in school or at work—unless we lead truly charmed lives, most of us experience traumatic events and changes at some time or other. What are their effects on us? This question was first investigated by Holmes and Rahe (1967), who asked a large group of people to assign arbitrary points (to a maximum of one hundred) to various life events according to how much readjustment each had required. It was reasoned that the greater the number of points assigned to a given event, the more stressful it was for the people experiencing it. As shown in Table 10.2, participants in Holmes and Rahe's

TABLE 10.2 Life Events, Stress, and Personal Health

When individuals experience stressful life events, such as those near the top of this list, their health often suffers. The greater the number of points for each event, the more stressful it is perceived as being.

Event	Points	Event	Points
1. Death of spouse	100	23. Son or daughter leaving home	29
2. Divorce	73	24. Trouble with in-laws	29
3. Marital separation	65	25. Outstanding personal achievement	28
4. Jail term	63	26. Wife beginning or stopping work	26
5. Death of close family member	63	27. Beginning or ending school	26
6. Personal injury or illness	53	28. Change in living conditions	25
7. Marriage	50	29. Revision of personal habits	24
8. Getting fired at work	47	30. Trouble with boss	23
9. Marital reconciliation	45	31. Change in work hours or conditions	20
10. Retirement	45	32. Change in residence	20
11. Change in health of family member	44	33. Change in schools	20
12. Pregnancy	40	34. Change in recreation	19
13. Sex difficulties	39	35. Change in church activities	19
14. Gain of new family member	39	36. Change in social activities	18
15. Business readjustment	39	37. Taking out a loan for a lesser purchase (e.g., car or TV)	17
16. Change in financial state	38	38. Change in sleeping habits	16
17. Death of close friend	37	39. Change in number of family get-togethers	15
18. Change to different line of work	36	40. Change in eating habits	15
19. Change in number of arguments with spouse	35	41. Vacation	13
20. Taking out loan for major purchase (e.g., home)	31	42. Christmas	12
21. Foreclosure of mortgage or loan	30	43. Minor violation of the law	11
22. Change in responsibilities at work	29		

Source: Based on data from Holmes & Masuda, 1974.

study assigned the greatest number of points to such serious events as death of a spouse, divorce, and marital separation. In contrast, they assigned much smaller values to events such as change in residence, vacation, and minor violations of the law (e.g., receiving a parking ticket).

Holmes and Rahe then related the total number of points accumulated by individuals during a single year to changes in their personal health. The results were dramatic—and did much to stir psychologists' interest in the effects of stress. The greater the number of "stress points" people accumulated, the greater was their likelihood of becoming seriously ill. Although this study had a number of flaws (e.g., the correlational design did not allow for causal inferences), it suggested that accumulated stress, rather than stress emanating for any specific stressor, is associated with health problems.

Newer research has begun to identify the specific effects of accumulated stress—or *allostatic load* as it has been termed—on health (McEwen, 2005). For example, in one study, Cohen and colleagues (2003) asked a group of volunteers to describe stressful events they had experienced during the previous year and to indicate the temporal course (the onset and offset) of each event. The stressful events participants described ranged from acute stressors that were brief in duration (e.g., a severe reprimand at work or a fight with a spouse), to more chronic ones that typically lasted a month or more and involved significant disruption of everyday routines (e.g., ongoing marital problems or unemployment). Then the researchers gave these people nose drops containing a low dose of a virus that causes the common cold. The results showed that volunteers who reported experiencing chronic stressors were more likely to develop a cold than volunteers who had experienced only acute stressors. Moreover, the longer the duration of the stressor, the greater was the risk for developing a cold.

Before concluding, however, it is important to note that this picture is complicated by the existence of large differences in individuals' ability to withstand the impact of stress (Oulette-Kobasa & Puccetti, 1983). While some people suffer ill effects after exposure to a few mildly stressful events, others remain healthy even after prolonged exposure to high levels of stress. One individual difference that appears to be especially important in buffering against the harmful effects of chronic stress is *sociability*, defined as the quality of seeking others and being agreeable (Cohen, 2004). As you know from your own experience, sociable people tend to enjoy interacting with other people and generally have an agreeable nature. Why should sociable people be more resistant to disease than their less sociable counterparts? Although more research is needed to determine the precise reasons, existing evidence points to the following possibilities. First, because sociability is an inherited characteristic, it is possible that the genes that contribute to sociability may also contribute to biological processes that play a role in the body's immune system. Second, research has shown that sociability is associated with more and better social interactions, performance of health-enhancing behaviors, and better regulation of emotions and stress-hormone levels—all elements important for maintaining proper immune system functioning (Cohen et al., 2003).

■ Tragedy and catastrophe.

By now it should be evident that accumulation of stressful events may adversely impact health. However, the stress associated with a single catastrophic event—an earthquake, a hurricane, a terrorist bombing—can also exert negative effects on our health. Studies show that a significant portion of survivors of natural disasters (major hurricanes and earthquakes) report symptoms of **post-traumatic stress disorder (PTSD),** a severe psychological disorder that occurs after experiencing or witnessing a life-threatening event (see Chapter 11 for more discussion of this disorder). One of the most significant events in this country occurred on the morning of September 11, 2001, when terrorists hijacked three commercial aircraft and intentionally crashed them. More recently, in August 2005, Hurricane Katrina killed nearly 2,000 people and caused an estimated $75 billion in damages along the coastlines of Louisiana, Mississippi, and Alabama (see Figure 10.3).

As we've already noted, events like these are associated with negative health outcomes. However, research indicates that acts of mass violence, such as the September, 2001 terrorist attacks and the Oklahoma City bombings that occurred in 1995, are by far the most disturbing type of catastrophe (Norris, 2002; Tucker et al., 2002). Mass violence and terrorism have elements that may make them even more psychologically damaging than natural disasters. They are highly unpredictable, they lack a clear ending or low point that signals when the worst is over, and knowledge about how to respond to the event and its aftermath is limited (Baum, 1991).

It is too soon to comprehend the full impact of the events that occurred on

Post-traumatic stress disorder:

A psychological disorder in which people persistently re-experience a life-threatening traumatic event in their thoughts or dreams, feel as if they are reliving the event from time to time, persistently avoid stimuli associated with the traumatic event, plus several other symptoms.

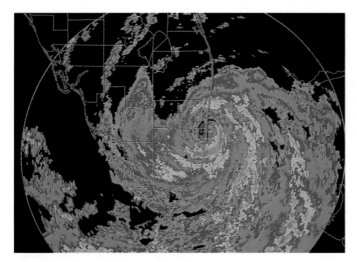

FIGURE 10.3
Post-Traumatic Stress Disorder: The Effects of Life-Altering Events
Survivors of traumatic events often report symptoms of post-traumatic stress disorder (PTSD), a severe psychological disorder that occurs after experiencing or witnessing a life-threatening event. One of the most significant natural disasters to strike the United States was Hurricane Katrina, a massive storn that struck the southeastern United States in 2005.

September 11, 2001, but research conducted thus far suggests that even people who were not directly involved in rescue and recovery efforts experienced short-term declines in their health. For example, Piotrkowski and Brannen (2002) interviewed a group comprised of staff members of New York City after-school programs and found that about 20 percent of them reported significant levels of PTSD. PTSD was highest among those who had expressed worries about a future attack (a threat appraisal). However, the *resilience* of individuals, the tendency to bounce back from negative experiences, can never be underestimated. In a study of more than 2,700 randomly selected New York City residents interviewed about six months after the September 11 attack (Bonanno, 2006), about 65 percent were characterized by resilience and only 6 percent exhibited symptoms of PTSD. Of those study participants who had personally witnessed the attack or had lost someone close to them, more than half exhibited resilience, as did about 54 percent of those who had actually been in the World Trade Center at the time.

■ **The hassles of daily life.**

Although certain events, such as terrorist attacks or natural disasters, are clearly stressful, they occur relatively infrequently. Does this mean that people's lives are mostly a serene lake of tranquility? Hardly. As you know, daily life is filled with countless minor annoying sources of stress—termed **hassles**—that seem to make up for their relatively low intensity by their much higher frequency. That such daily hassles are an important cause of stress is suggested by the findings of several studies by Lazarus and colleagues (see DeLongis, Folkman, & Lazarus, 1988; Kanner et al., 1981; Lazarus et al., 1985). These researchers developed a Hassles Scale on which individuals indicate the extent to which they have been "hassled" by common events during the past month. The items included in this scale deal with a wide range of everyday events, such as having too many things to do at once, misplacing or losing things, troublesome neighbors, and concerns over money. One group that can truly appreciate the impact of daily hassles is parents—particularly when both parents work. Thus, it is not surprising that a Parenting Daily Hassles Scale has been developed to measure the frequency and intensity of annoying experiences that parents collectively find stressful.

Hassles:
Annoying minor events of everyday life that cumulatively can affect psychological well-being.

TABLE 10.3 Measuring Daily Hassles

Many people experience "hassles" at some time or another. For each item listed, indicate how much it has been a part of your life during the past month using the following scale: Put a "0" in the space next to an experience if it was **not at all** part of your life over the past month; "1" for an experience that was **only slightly** part of your life over that time; "2" for an experience that was **distinctly** part of your life; and "3" for an experience that was **very much** part of your life over the past month. Next, add up the total. In general, the more stress people report as a result of daily hassles, the poorer their psychological well-being.

Survey of Recent Life Experiences

_____ 1. Disliking your daily activities	_____ 20. Not enough time to meet your obligations
_____ 2. Disliking your work	_____ 21. Financial burdens
_____ 3. Ethnic or racial conflict	_____ 22. Lower evaluations of your work than you think you deserve
_____ 4. Conflicts with in-laws or boyfriend's or girlfriend's family	_____ 23. Experiencing high levels of noise
_____ 5. Being let down or disappointed by friends	_____ 24. Lower evaluations of your work than you hoped for
_____ 6. Conflicts with supervisor(s) at work	_____ 25. Conflicts with family member(s)
_____ 7. Social rejection	_____ 26. Finding your work too demanding
_____ 8. Too many things to do at once	_____ 27. Conflicts with friend(s)
_____ 9. Being taken for granted	_____ 28. Trying to secure loans
_____ 10. Financial conflicts with family members	_____ 29. Getting "ripped off" or cheated in the purchase of goods
_____ 11. Having your trust betrayed by a friend	_____ 30. Unwanted interruptions of your work
_____ 12. Having your contributions overlooked	_____ 31. Social isolation
_____ 13. Struggling to meet your own standards of performance and accomplishments	_____ 32. Being ignored
_____ 14. Being taken advantage of	_____ 33. Dissatisfaction with your physical appearance
_____ 15. Not enough leisure time	_____ 34. Unsatisfactory housing conditions
_____ 16. Cash flow difficulties	_____ 35. Finding work uninteresting
_____ 17. A lot of responsibilities	_____ 36. Failing to get money you expected
_____ 18. Dissatisfaction with work	
_____ 19. Decisions about intimate relationship(s)	

Source: "The Survey of life experiences: A decontaminated hassles scale for adults," by P. Kohn and J. E. MacDonald, _Journal of Behavioral Medicine_, 15, pp. 221–225. Copyright © 1992. Reprinted by permission of Kluwer Academic/Plenum Publishers.

While such events may seem relatively minor when compared with the life events discussed earlier, they appear to be quite important. When scores on the Hassles Scale are related to reports of psychological symptoms, strong positive correlations are obtained (Lazarus et al., 1985). In short, the more stress people report as a result of daily hassles, the poorer their psychological well-being. You can assess the extent of your own exposure to daily hassles using the Hassles Scale provided in Table 10.3. Let's turn now to a discussion of the effects of work-related stress.

■ Work-related stress.

Most adults spend more time at work than in any other single activity. It is not surprising, then, that jobs or careers are viewed by 25 percent of employees as the top source of stress in their lives (NIOSH, 1999). Research also shows that people with an unstable career history are much more likely to experience long-term health effects as compared to those with a stable career (Kinnunen et al., 2005). Some of the factors producing stress in work settings are obvious; for example, blatant sexual harassment or discrimination, or extreme *overload*—being asked to do too much in too short a time. Interestingly, being asked to do too little can also cause

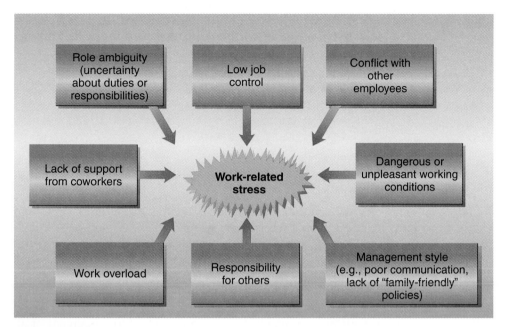

FIGURE 10.4
Sources of Work-Related Stress
Many factors contribute to stress at work. Several of the most important are summarized here.

stress. Such *underload* produces intense feelings of boredom, and these, in turn, can be very stressful.

Several other factors that play a role in work-related stress may be less apparent. One of these is *job control*—the ability to influence decisions about how and when one's job is performed. Controllability is a shared and basic need among humans. Feeling in control is usually a positive experience for most of us, whereas losing control is a negative experience. A lack of control is a major source of stress, dissatisfaction, and more frequent absences among workers (Bakker et al., 2003) and may even have an impact on their health (Bosma, Stansfeld, & Marmot, 1998).

Another factor that influences work-related stress is *role conflict*—being the target of conflicting demands or expectations from different groups of people. For example, consider the plight of many beginning managers. Their subordinates often expect such people to go to bat for them with the company to improve their work assignments, pay, and conditions. In contrast, the managers' own bosses often expect them to do the opposite—to somehow induce the employees to work harder for fewer rewards. The result: a stressful situation for the managers. Workplace stress may also be related to cultural values. For example, industrialized nations, such as the United States, tend to encourage formation of a strong work ethic, as well as high levels of performance and productivity. Unfortunately, cultural norms that give rise to phrases such as "working harder brings success" or "time is money" can lead to unhealthy work habits (*workaholism*) and the stress that accompanies work overload (see Peterson & Wilson, 2004). Additional factors that have been found to contribute to stress at work are summarized in Figure 10.4.

Can anything be done to reduce such effects? Fortunately, several lines of research suggest the answer is "yes." First, employers can reduce workplace stress by providing workers with greater autonomy and decision-making capabilities, factors that contribute to employees' feelings of control. Family-friendly policies—such as flexible work schedules or allowing work to be done from home whenever possible—can reduce stress and the conflict that can frequently follow (Voydanoff, 2005). Second, organizations can consider the **person–environment (P–E) fit.** Making sure that workers are well suited in terms of temperament and

Person–environment (P–E) fit:
This approach suggests that a misfit between a person and his or her work environment may produce stress.

ability for the demands of their jobs will reduce the stress that they experience. Steps that you can take to reduce your job stress are presented in the **Psychology Goes to Work** section below.

KEY QUESTIONS

- Which types of events are likely to create stress?
- Are daily hassles harmful?
- What are some sources of work-related stress?

Stress: Some Major Effects

By now you may be convinced that stress stems from many different sources and exerts important effects on people who experience it. What is sometimes difficult to grasp, though, is just how far-reaching these effects can be. Stress can influence our physical and psychological well-being and our performance on many tasks.

■ Stress and health: The silent killer.

The link between stress and personal health is very strong (Kiecolt-Glaser et al., 1994). According to medical experts, stress plays a role in 50 to 70 percent of all physical illness (Frese, 1985). Stress has been implicated in the occurrence of some of the most serious and life-threatening ailments known to medical science, including heart disease, high blood pressure, hardening of the arteries, ulcers, and

PSYCHOLOGY GOES TO WORK

Job Stress: What Can You Do to Control It?

Most of us will experience stress in our jobs. What can we do to control it? Psychological research suggests the following general guidelines:

1. **Set realistic goals and time frames.** Setting specific goals helps direct effort, increases persistence on tasks, and provides important feedback that allows you to chart your progress. But be realistic: Sometimes we create our own stressors by trying to accomplish too much in a day.
2. **Don't try to be a superhero.** When you already are busy and feeling overloaded, don't take on more projects. You will not impress your boss by how much you take on, but by how much you accomplish.
3. **Schedule and organize.** Use a daily planner and organize your activities. A critical component of organization is to prioritize tasks. When faced with several tasks, many of us will complete the little, unimportant tasks first simply because they are easy and their completion makes us feel good. Unfortunately, this leaves less time for the most important tasks. Make sure you invest your time wisely by tackling the most important tasks first.

4. **Anticipate stress and be ready to respond.** Analyze the likely causes of stress in your job and plan a response to them. For example, if an abrasive coworker is making work unpleasant, think of a productive way to handle your next altercation and rehearse it ahead of time.
5. **Maintain a positive attitude.** Negative thoughts and emotions often add to our stress by disrupting task focus and decreasing motivation. Think positively about your work and seek self-satisfaction in what you do.
6. **Reduce procrastination.** People procrastinate for several reasons. Often it's because they either don't know how to do the task or they are indecisive about how to approach it. Overcome self-doubt by breaking the overall task into smaller, more manageable chunks.
7. **Reconsider the necessity of meetings.** Although they are essential at times, many meetings are great time wasters. Meetings should be held only when important information needs to be shared and discussed.

even diabetes. Stress appears to exert additional, indirect effects as well; for example, people with high blood pressure perform more poorly on several important measures of cognitive performance than do people with normal blood pressure (Waldstein, 2003).

How does stress produce such effects? The precise mechanisms involved remain to be determined, but growing evidence suggests that the process goes something like this: By draining our resources and keeping us off balance physiologically, stress upsets our complex internal chemistry. In particular, it may interfere with efficient operation of our *immune systems*—the mechanisms through which our bodies recognize and destroy potentially harmful substances and intruders, such as bacteria, viruses, and cancerous cells. When functioning normally, the immune system is nothing short of amazing: Each day it removes or destroys many potential threats to our health.

Unfortunately, prolonged exposure to stress seems to disrupt this system. Chronic exposure to stress can reduce circulating levels of lymphocytes (white blood cells that fight infection and disease) and increase levels of the hormone *cortisol*, a substance that suppresses aspects of our immune system (McEwen, 2005; Segerstrom & Miller, 2004). Eventually, chronic stress can lead to development of chronic disease and speed aging of the immune system (Robles, Glaser & Kiecolt-Glaser, 2005).

The physiological effects of chronic stressors—such as a stressful job, a poor interpersonal relationship, or financial concerns—also take their toll on people's cardiovascular systems (Melamed et al., 2006; Matthews, K. A., 2005). Evidence also suggests that racial and gender differences exist in stress-induced heart disease. For instance, there is a greater prevalence of hypertension and **cardiovascular disease** among African Americans than whites, perhaps because they are exposed to more stressors in their lives and have stronger physiological reactions to stressors (Anderson, 1989). One study of African American and white women found that African American women experienced higher levels of chronic stress due to critical life events, discrimination, and economic hardship (Troxel et al., 2003). Furthermore, chronic stress was related to evidence of heart disease for African American women but not for white women. This evidence suggests that African American women may be particularly vulnerable to the burdens of chronic daily stress.

■ The effects of social support on health.

Several studies on humans and animals have led some psychologists to speculate that **social support,** the emotional and task resources provided by others, may serve to buffer the adverse effects of chronic stress. Research shows a positive correlation between a person's sources of social support and his or her health (House, Landis, & Umberson, 1998). Indeed, a lack of a reliable social support network can actually increase a person's risk of dying from disease, accidents, or suicide. People who are divorced or separated from their spouse often experience reduced functioning in certain aspects of their immune system, compared to individuals who are happily married (Kiecolt-Glaser et al., 1987, 1988).

Recent research suggests that loneliness and social isolation are associated with a weaker immune system response (Pressman et al., 2005). In a study of college freshmen (many away from home for the first time), participants were given a flu shot and then antibody levels were periodically measured to determine their body's response to it. Students who viewed themselves as lonely and having a small social network had the lowest immune system response. In addition, loneliness was associated with an elevation in levels of cortisol, which, as noted earlier, suppresses the immune system. It is also noteworthy that the *feeling* of being alone can be just as important as actually *being* alone. When a person believes that others in his or her social network will be on hand to provide support, one's coping skills can be strengthened as the person's appraisal of the stressful situation is

Cardiovascular disease:
All diseases of the heart and blood vessels.

Social support:
The emotional and task resources provided by others that may serve to help buffer the adverse effects of chronic stress.

changed (Cohen, 2004). As the philosopher Epictetus said nearly two thousand years ago: "People are disturbed not by things, but by their perception of things."

Although it is clear that receiving social support is important to health, research seems to indicate that providing social support to *others* may be just as important. In one study, Brown and colleagues (2003) isolated and compared the unique effects of giving and receiving social support on mortality in a sample of 846 elderly married people. The researchers initially measured the extent to which participants received and gave support to their spouse and to others (friends, relatives, neighbors), and then monitored mortality rates during a five-year period. Participants who reported providing high levels of support to others were significantly less likely to die during the five-year period than participants who had provided little or no support to others. By contrast, receiving social support, from one's spouse or from others, did not appear to affect mortality among people in this group. These findings suggest it may be better to give than to receive—especially when it comes to health!

Other research suggests that there may be gender differences in the effectiveness of social support offered to others. For example, Glynn, Christenfeld, and Gerirn (1999) had males and females give impromptu speeches, after which they received supportive or nonsupportive feedback from male or female observers. Cardiovascular changes such as blood pressure and heart rate were monitored during and after the speech. Social support from men had no effect on the blood pressure or heart rate of the speakers. Social support from women, however, had a calming influence on both male and female speakers. Perhaps women are better able to express empathy and support than are men, and do so in a way that men as well as women appreciate—and find useful.

■ Stress and task performance.

Psychologists once believed that the relationship between stress and task performance takes the form of an upside-down U: At first, performance improves as stress increases, presumably because the stress is arousing or energizing. Beyond some point, though, stress becomes distracting, and performance actually drops.

While this relationship may hold true under some conditions, research indicates that even low or moderate levels of stress can interfere with task performance (Motowidlo, Packard, & Manning, 1986; Steers, 1984). There are several reasons why this is so. First, even relatively mild stress can be distracting. People experiencing stress may focus on the unpleasant feelings and emotions it involves, rather than on the task at hand. Second, prolonged or repeated exposure to even mild levels of stress may exert harmful effects on health, and this may interfere with effective performance. Finally, a large body of research indicates that as arousal increases, task performance may rise at first, but at some point it falls (Berlyne, 1967). The precise location of this turning or inflection point seems to depend to a great extent on the complexity of the task performed. The greater the complexity, the lower the level of arousal at which the downturn in performance occurs. Many observers believe that the tasks performed by today's working people are more complex than those in the past. For this reason, even relatively low levels of stress may interfere with performance in today's complex work world.

Together, these factors help explain why even moderate levels of stress may interfere with many types of performance. However, stress does not always produce adverse effects. For example, as shown in Figure 10.5, people sometimes do seem to rise to the occasion and turn in sterling performances at times when stress is intense. Perhaps the most reasonable conclusion, then, is that while stress can interfere with task performance in many situations, its precise effects depend on many different factors, such as the complexity of the task being performed and personal characteristics of the individuals involved (see Suinn, 2005). As a result, generalizations about the impact of stress on work effectiveness should be made with considerable caution.

KEY QUESTIONS

- What role does stress play in physical illness?
- How does social support influence stress?
- What is the relationship between stress and performance?

UNDERSTANDING AND COMMUNICATING OUR HEALTH NEEDS

There is no doubt that modern medicine has provided the means to alleviate many types of disease and illness considered incurable until recent decades. Yet all the available medicine and technology still does not ensure that we will seek proper treatment when necessary, or that we possess the knowledge or skills necessary to realize when help is required. Moreover, because of the beliefs and attitudes we hold, it's often difficult for health professionals to get us to comply with health-promoting advice. Most of us know the behaviors that are responsible for the common health problems in our society (e.g., alcohol and drug abuse, poor diet, lack of exercise, smoking). We are also aware of changes that we can make to our lifestyle that would improve our health (e.g., better diet, more exercise, stopping or reducing smoking, reducing alcohol consumption). Yet, few of us actually change our behavior despite being aware of the benefits of doing so. In essence, many people simply do not have sufficient motivation to change (Hetzel & McMichael, 1987). This seems to indicate an important role for health psychologists: not only to help people achieve a better understanding of their health needs and to inform them about the risks of specific unhealthy behaviors, but also to identify techniques to reduce or eliminate unhealthy behaviors and to promote the adoption of healthy lifestyles.

FIGURE 10.5
The Effects of Stress on Performance
Even relatively low levels of stress may interfere with performance in today's complex world. However, these effects are often most evident among people who are under tremendous pressure to perform well. Still, some people are able to rise to the occasion at times when stress is intense.

Health Beliefs: When Do We Seek and Listen to Medical Advice?

As we discovered in Chapter 3, we all experience bodily sensations, such as the steady beating of our hearts or the rush of air flowing in and out of our lungs as we breathe. But certain sensations—like irregularities in heartbeat, tiny aches and pains, a slight queasiness, or a backache—are often termed *symptoms* because they may reflect an underlying medical problem. How do we decide that a symptom is severe enough to require medical attention? You might think that people would report symptoms or seek out medication attention when they sense a serious problem, but this is not always true. Research shows that people frequently do not seek appropriate help even when they know that something is seriously wrong (Locke & Slaby, 1982). Why is this so?

The **health belief model,** initially developed to help explain why people don't use medical screening services, may help us to understand the reasons. This model suggests that our willingness to seek medical help depends on (1) the extent to which we perceive a threat to our health, and (2) the extent to which we believe that a particular behavior will effectively reduce that threat (Rosenstock, 1974). The perception of a personal threat is influenced by our health values, specific beliefs about our susceptibility to a health problem, and beliefs concerning the seriousness of the problem. For example, we may decide to use sunscreen at the beach if we value our health highly, if we feel that sunscreen effectively

Health belief model:
A theory of health behaviors; the model predicts that whether a person practices a particular health behavior can be understood by knowing the degree to which the person perceives a personal health threat and the perception that a particular health practice will be effective in reducing that threat.

reduces the chances of skin cancer, and if we don't like what we hear about death from cancer.

Our perceptions that our behavior will be effective in reducing a health threat—in this case, the risk of contracting skin cancer—depend on whether we believe that a particular practice will reduce the chances we will contract a particular illness and whether the perceived benefits of the practice are worth the effort. For example, whether a person concerned about contracting skin cancer will actually use sunscreen depends on two beliefs: (1) that the use of sunscreen will reduce the risk of cancer, and (2) that the benefits of doing so will outweigh the perceived rewards associated with having a tan (see Figure 10.6.)

The health belief model helps explain why certain people, especially young people and adults who have never experienced a serious illness or injury, often fail to engage in actions that would be effective in preventing these outcomes—such as wearing a condom during sexual intercourse or using a safety belt when driving a car (Taylor & Brown, 1988). They don't engage in such preventive, health-protecting actions because, in their minds, the likelihood of experiencing illness or injury, their *perceived* risk, is very low—so why bother? Take, for example, a study conducted among female adolescents that measured their perceived risk for HIV (Kershaw et al., 2003). Despite engaging in the high-risk behavior of unprotected sex with multiple partners, 65 percent of participants perceived their behavior as only slightly risky or not risky at all. The perceived risk was even lower for those involved in a long-term relationship, even though their partners could potentially be high-risk.

Research on the health belief model has uncovered some interesting gender differences in the extent to which health beliefs influence intentions and behavior. According to the National Center for Health Statistics (2001), women are more likely to have yearly physical examinations, more likely to intend to schedule them on a regular basis in the future, and less likely to miss medical appointments than are men (Neal et al., 2005). Compliance with preventive health behaviors, such as self-examination, is lower in men as well, perhaps because they see themselves at lower risk for illness than females do (Courtenay et al., 2002).

Interestingly, Asian Americans are much less likely to engage in preventive health behaviors than other ethnic groups, such as seeing their health-care professional regularly for cholesterol screening, vaccinations, and mammograms (Liao et al., 2004). This might stem from the fact that Asian Americans have the lowest mortality rates of any ethnic group in the United States, lending itself to a low perception of risk within that group (Courtenay et al., 2002). Additionally, beliefs about the effectiveness of medical screening and obstacles to attending the examinations predicted attendance behavior for women but not for men. Perhaps women adopt a more rational approach to their medical care than do men.

Doctor–Patient Interactions: Why Can't We Talk to Our Doctors?

How satisfied are you with your doctors? Do you feel that they understand you as a person and how you might be feeling when you are sick? Or do they seem to talk "at" you, limiting conversation to their diagnosis and what procedures you should follow to regain or maintain your health? Unfortunately, many patients report that their doctors lack a "human touch" (see Figure 10.7, page 402). Doctors tend to restrict conversations to the physical examination itself and an explanation of the nature of prescribed medication. Psychological issues, such as what the patient knows or how he or she feels about the illness, are rarely discussed, even when these conversations center on the painful nature of cancer treatments and the possibility that the patient might die (Ford, Fallowfield, & Lewis, 1996). As a result, patients seldom feel like partners in treatment and become disillusioned with their medical care. Fortunately, more physicians are including patients in their

FIGURE 10.6
The Health Belief Model
According to the health belief model, we are more likely to take precautionary actions, such as using sunscreen, if we value our health highly, if we feel that sunscreen effectively reduces the chances of skin cancer, and if we don't like what we hear about death from cancer.

treatment decisions, including decisions concerning options for cancer care. How a doctor explains a diagnosis and therapy options can influence the treatment preferences of cancer patients. Interpersonal skills and trust between patients and their health-care providers become very important, particularly when the diagnosis may be life-threatening, and the interaction should allow time for the patient to express his or her concerns and provide input into decisions concerning therapy options. Patients also tend to be more satisfied when they receive information in simple language from a compassionate, concerned physician who does not appear rushed and interrupted (Siminoff & Step, 2005).

Why is patient satisfaction important? Research shows that patients who are more satisfied are more likely to adhere to their treatment regimens and are less likely to change physicians, thereby ensuring continuity of their treatment (Di-Matteo & Di Nicola, 1982). Greater patient satisfaction is also associated with additional beneficial outcomes, including better emotional health and fewer hospitalizations (Hall, Roter, & Milburn, 1999). Together, these studies underscore the importance of training in communication skills for health-care professionals. To be effective in treating patients and promoting their wellness, doctors, nurses, and other health professionals need to know how to get their message across—how to communicate effectively with the people who come to them for help.

■ **Surfing for solutions to medical problems on the Internet.**

Frustrated by busy doctors and the cumbersome managed-care system, many people are quietly taking matters into their own hands by consulting the Internet. Patients anxious to participate in decisions about their own treatment are turning increasingly to the Internet to confirm diagnoses, validate physician-recommended treatments, or seek alternative therapies. The World Wide Web has become a clearinghouse of information where, with the click of a mouse, people can get instant access to medical and mental health advice. Unfortunately, this practice can prove to be risky business.

Why? One reason is that the Internet is, for the most part, unregulated, and the quality and accuracy of the information contained there varies considerably. Some of the nation's top medical research facilities have created publicly accessible web sites, but so, too, have unethical people and businesses trying to sell drugs or therapies that do not have scientific evidence to support their use.

FIGURE 10.7
The Importance of Communication Skills for Health-Care Providers

As illustrated by the situation depicted in this cartoon, this person is unlikely to be satisfied with the treatment he's receiving from his doctor. Why is patient satisfaction important? Greater patient satisfaction is associated with a host of beneficial outcomes, including better emotional health and fewer hospitalizations.

Source: Reprinted with permission from Universal Press Syndicate. All rights reserved.

"Yep, that's a crocodile, all right!
They've got narrower snouts than alligators,
and they're a bit lighter in color."

Another reason why it is risky to depend solely on medical advice found on the Internet is the unpredictable effects it can have on our health. Web sites that hype new, untested cures for deadly diseases may fill patients with false hope, prompting them to abandon treatments already under way or delay urgently needed procedures that could save their lives. Conversely, sites that offer accurate but graphic details about an illness may cause people already anxious about their health to avoid seeking medical treatment altogether. In other words, without the benefit of specialized medical training or someone trained to guide them, a little knowledge can be a dangerous thing.

Still, with all its problems, the Internet is a useful medical tool. With a little effort, patients can find their way to the best doctors, cutting-edge research, information about prescription drugs, and sources of social support at a time when they need it the most (Landro, 1998). Patients may also quickly develop a working knowledge of their illnesses and, as a result, take a more informed and active role in their treatment.

KEY QUESTIONS

- What is the health belief model?
- What factors determine our willingness to make lifestyle changes or seek medical help?
- What are the advantages and disadvantages of seeking medical advice on the Internet?

Cancer:
A group of illnesses in which abnormal cells are formed that are able to proliferate, invade, and overwhelm normal tissues, and to spread to distant sites in the body.

BEHAVIORAL AND PSYCHOLOGICAL CORRELATES OF ILLNESS: THE EFFECTS OF THOUGHTS AND ACTIONS ON HEALTH

Cancer is often viewed as a purely physical illness. However, growing evidence suggests that psychological variables can play an important role in determining cancer's progression (McGuire, 1999). In other words, aspects of our behavior, perceptions, and personality can affect the onset and course of this life-threatening

FIGURE 10.8
Carcinogens: Cancer-Producing Agents in the Environment
Cigarette smoke, chemicals in the food we eat and the air we breathe, alcohol, and sun exposure have all been implicated to some extent as carcinogens.

illness. One common characteristic among individuals from families with high cancer rates is a diminished efficiency of their *natural killer cells*—cells designed specifically for the surveillance and destruction of cancerous tumor cells (Kiecolt-Glaser & Glaser, 1992). In most cases, though, whether we actually develop a cancer or other illness is moderated by **risk factors**—aspects of our lifestyle that affect the chances that we will develop or contract a particular disease, within the limits established by our genes.

Behaviors that increase our exposure to **carcinogens**—cancer-producing agents in our environment—are among the most important risk factors. Tobacco and the smoke it produces, chemicals in the food that we eat and the air that we breathe, and the radiation we receive from overexposure to the sun have all been implicated to some extent as carcinogens (see Figure 10.8).

Because people create these risks through their behaviors, psychologists can play a crucial role in preventing cancer and other health problems by developing interventions that reduce our exposure to potential carcinogens and promote healthy behaviors such as exercise and a proper diet. Before we look at several behavioral risk factors that may contribute to the development of certain illnesses, see the **Psychology Lends a Hand** section on page 404 for information on another potential danger that has recently been identified and is especially relevant in our fast-paced society—effects of the long-term use of cell phones.

Smoking: Risky for You and Everyone around You

Smoking is the largest preventable cause of illness and premature death (before age sixty-five) in the United States, accounting for about 440,000 deaths annually. This means that smoking causes approximately one of every five deaths—more than deaths from HIV, illegal drug use, alcohol use, car accidents, suicide, and murders combined (CDC, 2005). It is the leading cause of several types of cancer. In fact, an American male's risk of dying from lung cancer is about twenty-two times higher for a smoker than a nonsmoker. A smoker is up to four times more likely to develop coronary heart disease and has twice the risk for stroke (CDC,

Risk factors:
Aspects of our environment or behavior that influence our chances of developing or contracting a particular disease, within the limits established through our genetic structure.

Carcinogens:
Cancer producing agents in our environment.

PSYCHOLOGY LENDS A HAND

What Are the Risks of Long-Term Cell Phone Use: Can You Hear Me Now?

In Chapter 3, we examined the dangerous practice of using a cellular phone while driving. Now let's consider the possible *health risks* of cell-phone use. With more than 200 million cell phones in use in the United States at the end of 2005 (Cellular Telecommunications & Internet Association, 2005), cell phones have become an essential convenience for most of us (see Figure 10.9). But, as with many good things in life, there is a potential downside. The long-term effects of the use of cell phones are just beginning to be determined. A recent study conducted in Sweden uncovered a relationship between mobile phone use and brain tumors on the side of the head where the phone is held and electromagnetic radiation is absorbed (Hardell, Carlberg, & Mild, 2006). Evaluation of more than three thousand participants showed that the hazard appears greater for those who have used a cell phone for over a decade. Results pointed to a 240 percent increased risk for tumors in individuals with at least two thousand hours of cell-phone use. At first glance, this might seem like a lot of conversation. However, it translates to only about one hour of cell-phone use per day over a six-year period. Clearly, many current cell phone users already exceed this usage rate, and it is likely to increase further as many people are canceling traditional telephone service in favor of cell phones. What is even more frightening is that many parents are allowing their adolescent and preadolescent children to use cell phones. These children clearly do not appreciate the risks associated with cell phones and they could easily rack up two thousand hours of phone use or more at a relatively young age.

Researchers suggest that the health risks of cell phone use may be reduced by using hands-free devices, but more research is needed to verify this possibility. Research continues as well into the effects of using desktop cordless phones. Because these devices have a lower power output, the amount of use necessary to produce detrimental effects is much higher. So what can you do to reduce your health risk? The answers aren't necessarily desirable ones in our convenience-oriented society:

- Research indicates that the dangers may be reduced through the use of hands-free phones. Obtain one of these devices and use it whenever it's an available option.
- Use a "land-line" telephone whenever possible, particularly when the call looks like it may be lengthy.
- Don't give up a traditional telephone provider in favor of cell-only service.
- When using a cell phone, say what you have to say in the shortest time possible, thus reducing the hours of use. A pleasant side effect may be a lower cell phone bill!

FIGURE 10.9
Potential Negative Health Effects of Long-Term Cell Phone Use
Cell phones have become an essential convenience for most of us. However, as with many good things in life, overuse of these devices can have a potentially dangerous downside—the possibility of producing brain tumors on the side of the head where the phone is held.

2005). Despite the numerous risks associated with smoking—and the numerous health benefits of quitting—approximately 45 million Americans, about 21 percent of the U.S. population age eighteen and older, currently smoke (CDC, 2004). Unfortunately, the harmful effects of smoking do not end with the smoker. Smoking during pregnancy can have harmful effects on the developing fetus and can contribute to stillbirth, low birth weight, and sudden infant death syndrome (U.S. Department of Health and Human Services, 2001). And exposure to secondhand smoke (or **passive smoke**) causes about three thousand nonsmoking Americans to die of lung cancer and up to 300,000 children to suffer from asthma and other respiratory tract ailments annually (CDC, 2005).

Given the evidence against smoking, then, why do people do it? Genetic, psychosocial, and cognitive factors all seem to play a role. Individual differences in our reaction to **nicotine,** the addictive substance in tobacco, suggest that some people are biologically predisposed to become addicted to nicotine, whereas others remain unaffected. Psychosocial factors also play a role in establishing smoking behavior, especially among young people. Nearly 22 percent of U.S. high school students currently smoke (CDC, 2003). Studies have concluded that adolescents whose best friends smoke are twice as likely to take up the behavior than those whose close friends are nonsmokers (Choi, et al., 1997). The presence of family members who smoke can present a positive image of smoking as can the social image of "coolness" and the popularity it provides (Evans et al., 2006). In addition, smoking by role models in movies has been linked to an increase in the initiation of smoking among adolescents (Sargent et al., 2005; Dalton et al., 2003). A report by the U.S. Surgeon General suggests that about 90 percent of smokers report having smoked their first cigarette by age eighteen, but very few people begin to smoke after age twenty (CDC, 1998). These data highlight the urgent need for prevention programs targeting people in this age group.

For many people, smoking is a way to cope with stressful life events. Unfortunately, the temporary relief provided by cigarettes comes at a considerable cost in terms of long-term health risks and consequences. Recent research suggests that women may be more likely than men to rely on cigarettes as a coping mechanism for stress. In a study of former smokers who had quit, women were more likely to relapse and resume smoking in response to stressful life events than were men (McKee et al., 2003). This was particularly the case when the major source of stress was financial problems. Similar findings occurred when the researchers examined who among current smokers was likely to successfully quit smoking: Women experiencing financial or health problems were more likely to continue smoking than were men. These results suggest that women may be particularly likely to rely on cigarettes as a way to cope with stress in their lives.

Finally, cognitive factors appear to influence people's tendency to continue smoking. Smokers tend to hold inaccurate perceptions with regard to the risks of smoking (Weinstein, 1998). Smokers consistently acknowledge that smoking increases their health risks, but they underestimate these risks compared to nonsmokers. Smokers also tend to minimize the personal relevance of the risks of smoking; they tend not to believe that they are as much at risk as other smokers of becoming addicted or suffering negative health effects.

Unfortunately, efforts to get people to quit smoking have not been very effective. Although it's estimated that 70 percent of American smokers would like to quit, and more than 40 percent of adult smokers make an attempt to quit each year, only a small percentage are able to maintain abstinence, even for short periods of time (CDC, 1998). What makes a treatment program effective? Research suggests the following answers. First, interventions delivered by trained health-care providers tend to be more effective than self-help programs. Second, the content of smoking cessation interventions and the specific behavior change procedures used also seem to make a difference (see Table 10.4, page 406). Aversive smoking procedures, ones designed to associate smoking stimuli with feeling ill (rapid smoking), seem to be most effective, followed by interventions that include either a supportive component or training in problem solving to help smokers identify and cope with events or problems that increase the likelihood of smoking. Third, the amount of time the clinician spends with smokers has a direct influence on treatment effectiveness, with more contact leading to higher cessation rates. Finally, the use of nicotine replacement therapies (e.g., patch, gum), when combined with an intensive psychosocial intervention, tends to improve smoking cessation rates consider-

Passive smoke:
The smoke that we inhale from the smokers around us.

Nicotine:
The addictive substance in tobacco.

TABLE 10.4 Relative Effectiveness of Smoking-Cessation Interventions

A comparison of different types of smoking-cessation interventions shows they differ in their ability to help smokers kick the habit.

Type of intervention	Estimated smoking-cessation rates
No-intervention comparison group	8.8%
Aversive smoking	17.5%
Social support (providing support or encouragement as a component of treatment)	15.2%
General problem solving	13.7%
Quit smoking on a specific date	11.5%
Motivational programs	9.8%
Weight, diet, or nutrition management	9.8%
Exercise or fitness programs	9.6%
Contingency contracts (rewards for compliance; costs for noncompliance)	9.1%
Relaxation or breathing techniques	7.5%
Cigarette fading (gradually reducing number of cigarettes smoked or amount of nicotine)	6.4%

Source: Based on data from Wetter et al., 1998.

ably (Molyneux et al., 2003). In addition, newer research indicates that adding antidepressant medications to counseling and nicotine replacement therapy could play a role in increased abstinence for light smokers (Cinciripini, 2005).

Diet and Nutrition: What You Eat May Save Your Life

Poor dietary practices can dramatically increase the risk of developing chronic diseases. A poor diet has been most closely linked with cancers of the colon and rectum. Colorectal cancer is one of the leading causes of cancer deaths in the United States, killing more than 56,000 people annually (National Vital Statistics Report, 2004). Fortunately, regular consumption of certain foods, particularly fresh fruits and vegetables, may reduce the risk of developing these cancers. Regular exercise also exerts a protective effect against the development of colorectal cancer.

Diet is also a significant risk factor in the development of *cardiovascular disease*, a term used to describe all diseases of the heart and blood vessels. High levels of a certain type of **serum cholesterol,** or blood cholesterol, are strongly associated with increased risk of cardiovascular diseases (Allred, 1993; Klag et al., 1993). "Bad" or *LDL cholesterol* clogs arteries and is therefore the kind that places us most at risk of heart disease. *HDL cholesterol* helps clear LDL from the arteries and es-

Serum cholesterol:
The amount of cholesterol in our blood; it is directly proportional to the amount of cholesterol in our diets.

corts it to the liver for excretion. In other words, the more LDL you have, the more HDL you will need. The amount of cholesterol in our blood is affected by the amount of fat, especially saturated fat, and cholesterol in our diets. Serum cholesterol can be greatly reduced through a diet that is low in fats, cholesterol, and calories, and high in fiber, fruits, and vegetables.

Newer evidence suggests *trans-fatty acids*, found naturally in dairy products and meats, and also in margarine, salad dressings, fried foods, and baked goods, are particularly dangerous to health. Like saturated fat, *trans*-fat raises heart disease risk by boosting levels of LDL. But some researchers consider trans-fat worse than saturated fat because it also raises other detrimental blood fats, lowers HDL levels, and increases insulin resistance—a key step toward developing diabetes.

Although the link between dietary practices and good health is clear, it is difficult to get people to adhere to a healthy diet. One reason is that people tend to prefer the taste of high-fat foods over healthier alternatives (see Chapter 3 for additional information). High-fat foods are energy-dense—they contain more calories than foods high in carbohydrate or protein—and tend to elevate natural opiate levels in the body. If you recall our discussions in Chapter 2, natural opiates have pain-killing properties that can be extremely pleasurable for some people. Thus, because of these effects, it is not surprising that people learn to prefer eating high-fat foods. Interestingly, when people are given a drug that blocks the effects of opiates and are allowed to choose between different foods, they tend to reduce their intake of fat relative to carbohydrates (Schiffman et al., 1998).

The National Center for Health Statistics (2002) has reported that nearly 65 percent of U.S. adults are overweight. About one-third are considered obese, that is, having a Body Mass Index over 30. Consider the fact that the obesity figure in the United Kingdom is about 22 percent, in Canada 15 percent, in France 11 percent, and in Japan is only about 3 percent (International Obesity Task Force, 2003).

Most interventions designed to help people lose weight seem to work, at least initially. For example, a comparison of four of the most popular diets—Atkins, Ornish, Weight Watchers, and the Zone—revealed that all were effective in helping dieters to shed weight, thereby lowering their risk of heart disease (Dansinger, 2003). Unfortunately, the weight loss achieved through most programs does not typically last. Why? As noted in Chapter 8, a variety of factors have been shown to play a role, including genetic, behavioral, and environmental ones. One factor we did not discuss previously, however, involves the type of motivation behind the decision to begin dieting (Williams et al., 1996).

According to the **self-determination theory** (Deci & Ryan, 1985), long-term maintenance of weight loss depends on whether the motivation for doing so is perceived by the dieter as autonomous or controlled. Overweight people frequently begin dieting on the advice of their doctor or at the insistence of concerned family members. Under these circumstances, people may feel coerced into losing weight; this is an example of *controlled motivation*. However, people who begin a weight-loss program because they want to do it for themselves may experience the same activity (dieting) quite differently; this is an example of

FIGURE 10.10
Fast Food and Our Health
During the past decade, the number of Americans who are overweight has more than doubled. Why? Because many people simply eat too much. Unfortunately, this can lead to serious health problems, as is evident in this photo. Recently, people have initiated lawsuits against several well-known fast-food restaurant chains because they claim they didn't realize that eating too much fast food would be bad for them.

Self-determination theory:
When applied to health-related issues, this theory suggests that motivation to perform health-preventive behaviors is highest when we have autonomy over the decision to do so, and lowest when we do these behaviors at someone else's request.

autonomous motivation. Self-determination theory predicts that autonomously motivated weight loss will be maintained over time, whereas maintenance of weight loss achieved at the urging of others is less likely. This is exactly what Williams and colleagues (1996) found in a study of individuals entering a six-month weight-loss program. Participants who reported entering the program for themselves (autonomous motivation) attended the program more regularly, lost more weight during the program, and were more likely to maintain the weight loss nearly two years later than were people who reported joining the program because of other people's wishes (controlled motivation). More recent findings seem to confirm the useful role of self-determination theory for helping people to manage their weight (Georgiadis, Biddle, & Stavrou, 2006).

KEY QUESTIONS

- What determines who will become addicted to smoking?
- What are the effects of poor dietary practices?
- How do feelings of self-determination influence adherence to an exercise regimen?

Alcohol Consumption: Here's to Your Health?

Moderate alcohol consumption—typically defined as a daily glass of an alcoholic beverage—has been associated with significant health benefits, such as a reduced risk of coronary heart disease (Launer et al., 1996; Hennekens, 1996). Too much alcohol, however, is harmful and can have damaging effects on our health. Chronic excessive alcohol consumption can lead to deficits in many different cognitive abilities, including learning and memory, perceptual–motor skills, visual–spatial processing, and problem solving. Drinking can also lead to stomach disease, cirrhosis of the liver, cancer, impaired sexual functioning, cognitive impairment, and fetal alcohol syndrome, a condition of retardation and physical abnormalities that occurs in children of mothers who are heavy drinkers (see Chapter 7). Heavy drinking has also been implicated as a risk factor for suicide and suicide attempts (see Markowitz et al., 2002) and for the transmission of the virus that causes AIDS, by interfering with aspects of our immune system and by increasing the likelihood that people will engage in unprotected sex (LaBrie et al., 2005; Stein et al., 2005).

Given these facts, why do people continue to drink? Research suggests that genetic factors play an important role. Animal studies show that genetically engineered "knockout" mice, so named because they lack the gene responsible for production of a brain chemical called neuropeptide Y, drink more alcohol than normal mice and appear to have a greater tolerance for its effects (Koob et al., 1998). Because neuropeptide Y also appears to calm anxiety, at least in animals, these findings both suggest that some alcoholics may drink excessively to relieve stress, and also help explain the high rates of alcoholism among people with anxiety disorders. Studies with humans also highlight the role of genetic factors in drinking. Studies investigating rates of alcoholism among adopted children raised apart from their natural parents show, for example, that the sons of male alcoholics raised in adoptive homes have higher rates of alcoholism than the sons of nonalcoholics who grow up under similar circumstances (McGue, 1999). Studies that have compared the concordance rate for alcoholism among genetically identical (monozygotic) twins and fraternal (dizygotic) twins also provide support for a genetic link. Concordance refers to the probability of co-occurrence of alcoholism among twin siblings. Concordance rates are generally higher among identical twins than among fraternal twins, thus suggesting that genetic factors do indeed play a role.

But genetic factors are definitely not the only determinants of excessive drinking. Environmental factors are also involved. Ironically, the strongest evidence for the role of environmental factors in drinking also comes from studies of adoption.

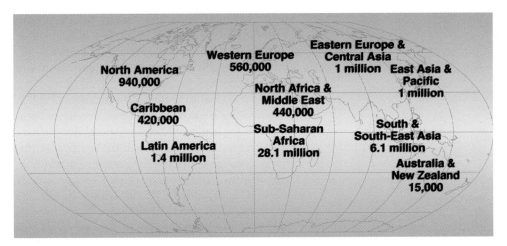

FIGURE 10.11
Distribution of AIDS Worldwide
More than 25 million people have died from AIDS since it was first recognized in 1981. At the end of 2005, an estimated 40 million people were living with HIV, with nearly 5 million new infections in 2005. *Source:* "World Map Distribution of AIDS" from Aids Epidemic Update, December 2005. Reproduced by kind permission of UNAIDS, www.unaids.org

Children reared in an adoptive family containing an alcoholic member are at significant risk of becoming alcoholics themselves (Cadoret, Troughton, & O'Gorman, 1987). The effects of this source of influence appear to be strongest when the alcoholic family member is a same-sex sibling of about the same age. Unrelated siblings who are raised together also tend to exhibit similar drinking practices (McGue, Sharma, & Benson, 1996). Together, these studies provide evidence that environmental factors play a significant role in drinking.

AIDS: A Major Assault on Public Health

Acquired immune deficiency syndrome (AIDS) has become a major health concern around the world. AIDS is the syndrome of illnesses caused by the human immunodeficiency virus (HIV). The process by which HIV produces AIDS symptoms is complex but essentially involves the devastation of aspects of the infected person's immune system, making the person extremely vulnerable to diseases, such as tuberculosis, pneumonia, and several forms of cancer. A frightening thing about AIDS is that the incubation period—the time it takes for the disease to develop—can be several years in length. This means that infected individuals can spread the disease to others without even realizing that they are infected. Because individuals can be infected only if the virus is introduced directly into the bloodstream, most HIV infections are acquired through unprotected sexual intercourse and infected blood or blood products. Unfortunately, this means that women can pass the disease to their unborn children during pregnancy or delivery, or through breastfeeding.

Based on estimates from the United Nations AIDS program (UNAIDS), more than 25 million people have died from AIDS since it was first recognized in 1981. At the end of 2005, an estimated 40.3 million people worldwide were living with HIV infection or AIDS, more than double the number ten years prior (UNAIDS, 2005). There were 4.9 million new cases reported in 2005, as well as 3.1 million deaths. It is especially alarming to note that half of the new global HIV infections are in young people aged fifteen to twenty-four. Figure 10.11 shows the relative distribution of cases of AIDS throughout the world. Although the new incidents of AIDS have begun to level off since 2000 in the United States to about

Acquired immune deficiency syndrome (AIDS):
A viral infection that reduces the immune system's ability to defend itself against the introduction of any foreign matter.

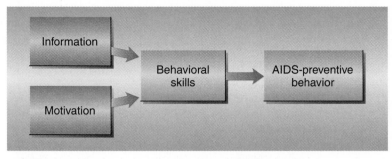

FIGURE 10.12
AIDS-Preventive Behaviors: A Model
Growing evidence suggests that prevention programs are more effective when they are tailored to meet the needs of specific target groups and when they provide people with the knowledge, motivation, and behavioral skills necessary to perform AIDS-preventive behaviors.
Source: Based on Fisher et al., 1994.

40,000 annually, the number of people living with HIV in the United States is now over 1 million (CDC, 2004). And that figure is increasing at a much more rapid rate in many other countries, especially in Africa.

In the United States, the incidence of AIDS is showing a marked increase among several groups, including women, African Americans, and Hispanic males. Although African Americans comprise only 12.5 percent of the U.S. population, they represented 48 percent of new HIV cases in 2003, and half the deaths from AIDS in the United States (CDC, 2004). AIDS is now one of the top three causes of death for African American men aged twenty-five to fifty-four. And African American women are twelve times more likely to contract HIV than white women (UNAIDS, 2005).

■ **How psychologists can help prevent the spread of AIDS.**

Why are psychologists relevant to the AIDS epidemic? One reason is that most people contract HIV as a result of certain behaviors, such as unprotected sex and intravenous drug use with contaminated needles. Thus, the only effective means of combating AIDS is to change the behaviors that place people most at risk for acquiring HIV. Health psychologists recognize that developing effective AIDS-prevention programs is a complicated business. They know, for example, that information campaigns alone—merely teaching people the facts about HIV and AIDS—are often ineffective (Helweg-Larsen & Collins, 1997). They also recognize that techniques effective for a particular target group are not necessarily effective for all groups of people (Coates & Collins, 1998). One model that is useful in developing interventions that accommodate individual and group differences is the *information–motivation–behavioral skills (IMB)* model (Fisher et al., 1994) (see Figure 10.12). According to the IMB model, people are more likely to perform HIV-preventive behaviors to the extent that they (1) know how HIV is acquired and the specific actions they must take to avoid it; (2) are motivated to perform HIV-preventive behaviors and omit risky ones; and (3) possess the skills necessary to perform relevant HIV-preventive behaviors, such as the ability to communicate with and to be appropriately assertive with a potential sexual partner.

The IMB model serves as a framework in which to conduct what is known as elicitation research. This kind of research is performed to attain specific information about a target group, including their current knowledge of HIV and AIDS, the factors that determine their motivation to reduce their personal risk, and their existing HIV-preventive behavioral skills (Fisher & Fisher, 2000; Fisher et al., 1994). Elicitation research and the IMB model are useful tools for developing effective behavior change programs. Why? Because they help researchers uncover the reasons why certain groups of people do not perform AIDS-preventive behavior.

As we've already noted, one group that is currently at risk with regard to HIV and AIDS is women. Indeed, HIV infection rates among women are growing at a rapid rate. In 2005, about 17.5 million women across the globe were infected with HIV, a million more than in 2003. It is the leading cause of death of women in some countries (UNAIDS, 2005). According to the Centers for Disease Control (CDC), AIDS cases among women in the United States have increased from 7 percent in 1985 to 27 percent in 2004. What is the reason for this increase? One in five new cases for women is linked to intravenous drug use. Another part of the answer is a risk factor unique to women: The chances of male-to-female transmission of HIV are about twelve times greater than female-to-male transmission (Padian, Shi-

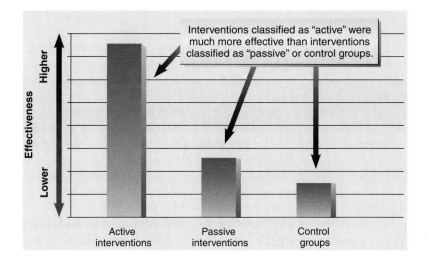

FIGURE 10.13
The Impact of Differing Strategies to Promote Safe Sex
Research suggests that *active* interventions, ones that include activities designed to increase the knowledge, motivation, and behavioral skills necessary to perform AIDS-preventive behaviors, are more effective than interventions that are primarily informational in nature or no intervention at all (control groups).
Source: Based on data from Albarracin et al., 2005.

boski, & Jewell, 1990). Elicitation research suggests that gender role differences between men and women may also play a role. For example, adherence to traditional gender roles may increase the chances that some women will succumb to pressure to engage in unprotected sex (Amaro, 1995). A related problem involves differences in the skills required to ensure safe sex. Consider, for example, the skills necessary to ensure the use of a condom during sex. For the man, this simply means putting on the condom. For the women, however, it means persuading her partner to use a condom or, perhaps, choosing not to have sex if he refuses. Finally, fear may be an important factor, especially among inner-city women and among women in abusive relationships marked by physical violence (Gomez & Marin, 1996). Under conditions like these, in which the potential for personal injury is high, it is understandable that women are reluctant to negotiate safe sex with their partners, let alone refuse to have sex with them.

Can anything be done to reverse this trend? Fortunately, the answer is "yes." A recent large-scale analysis of seventeen years of HIV-prevention interventions (Albarracin et. al, 2005) compared the impact of differing strategies to promote safer sex. Interventions labeled as *passive* are primarily informational, providing, for example, relevant facts about the dangers of unprotected sex, the benefits of condom use, what action to take when a partner doesn't want to use a condom, and an individual's personal risk of HIV infection. While the messages are designed to promote procondom attitudes, there is minimal participation by the individual in a passive procedure. *Active* interventions, which are consistent with the IMB model, include not only the comprehensive information of the passive approach, but also include personal counseling, HIV testing, and behavior training, which might include role play situations, practice sessions to increase condom use skills, and lessons in decision making, such as what to do to avoid unsafe situations. The active approach advocates the importance of advance preparation, such as having a condom readily available and talking about its use with a potential partner. As illustrated in Figure 10.13, a review of 194 reports indicated that *active* interventions, those that combine information with training, are more successful in motivating HIV-preventive behaviors than interventions classified as *passive* or no intervention (control groups). Active interventions become even more beneficial when they are presented by "expert" facilitators who share the gender and ethnicity of the target audience and when combined with distribution of condoms (Albarracin, Durantini, & Earl, 2006). Interestingly, the interventions that were least effective in promoting a change in attitude and behavior were those that induced a threat or fear. These results highlight the value of models like IMB in guiding development of more effective interventions. Let's turn now to a discussion of emotions and health.

Emotions and Health

The previous sections looked at behaviors (smoking, drinking, unprotected sex) that put people at risk for certain illnesses. Our mood states and emotions can also put us at risk for certain illnesses. Inadequate emotional expression—especially of negative feelings—can have an adverse effect on the progression of certain types of illness, such as cancer (Levy et al., 1985, 1988). People who tend to experience negative emotions and who also inhibit self-expression in their social interactions are exhibiting a pattern of behavior termed the **Type D**—or *distressed*—**personality** (Denollet, 1998). Individuals who cope with stress by keeping their negative emotions to themselves are likely to experience suppressed immune systems, greater recurrence of cancer, and higher mortality rates. In contrast, patients who demonstrate positive affect— especially joy, well-being, and happiness—increase the likelihood of recovery.

An intriguing finding is the relation between expression of distress and treatment outcome. Open expression of negative affect and a willingness to fight illness (as demonstrated by my brother-in-law Paul in the introduction to this chapter) are sometimes associated with greater immune function, decreased recurrence rates, and increased survival time, even among patients at advanced stages of cancer. For example, combative individuals—those who express anger about getting cancer and hostility toward their doctors and family members—often live longer than patients who passively accept their fate and quietly undergo treatment (Levy, 1990).

Emotion can also play a role in the progression of **hypertension,** or high blood pressure, a condition in which the pressure within the blood vessels is abnormally high. Prolonged hypertension can result in extensive damage to the entire circulatory system. Indeed, about 30 percent of cardiovascular disease deaths each year are attributable to hypertension. Negative emotions such as anxiety and hostility arouse the autonomic nervous systems and produce increases in heart rate, blood pressure, and neurotransmitters. Although the effects of emotional stressors are usually brief, extreme reactivity to anxiety, hostility, and anger may indicate a predisposition to develop hypertension (Rosenman, 1988). Not surprisingly, the strongest relations between emotions and blood pressure have been found for unexpressed anger and hostility (Rutledge & Hogan, 2002; Yan et al., 2003). Individuals who exhibit these negative emotions are also at increased risk of developing coronary heart disease, artery disease, and premature death (Smith et al., 2004, Gallo & Matthews, 2003).

Research conducted by Niaura and colleagues (2002) found that hostility in elderly men predicted coronary heart disease (CHD) over a three-year period. What is significant about this study is that the researchers included measures of other known predictors of CHD, including cigarette use, alcohol consumption, and blood lipids. Individuals who scored high on the hostility measure had substantially higher chances of CHD, even when the other risk factors were considered. Based on these results, health psychologists should develop more effective interventions for individuals who exhibit high levels of hostility.

While negative emotions can increase risks of illness, positive emotions have beneficial effects and can even reverse the lingering cardiovascular effects produced by hostility. Positive emotions—such as contentment, gratitude, hope, and love—are also associated with psychological resilience. To illustrate the important link between resiliency and positive emotions, consider a study by Frederickson and colleagues (2003). These researchers surveyed college students early in 2001 and again a few weeks after the terrorist attacks of September 11, 2001. As you might expect, many students expressed symptoms of depression after the attacks. However, students high in psychological resilience reported frequent experiences of gratitude and love, among other positive emotions, because they were grateful for their safety and that of their loved ones. These positive emotions, in turn, appeared to exert a buffering effect in that their presence was associated with lower levels of depression.

Do you recall the old adage "Laughter is often the best medicine"? The **Psychology Lends a Hand** section on page 413 examines the question of whether laughter can exert beneficial effects on our health.

Type D personality:
A term used to describe a general tendency to cope with stress by keeping negative emotions to oneself. People who exhibit this behavior pattern are more likely to experience suppressed immune systems and health-related problems.

Hypertension:
A condition in which the pressure within the blood vessels is abnormally high.

PSYCHOLOGY LENDS A HAND

Laughter—the Best Medicine?

Like me, you may have wondered whether this was just one of your grandparents' sayings or if there is, in fact, some truth to it. But how can laughter influence physical health? The following possible mechanisms have been suggested.

First, laughter puts us in a good mood, which may help to counteract the detrimental effects that negative emotions (e.g., anger, hostility) exert on the cardiovascular system. Second, laughter and its associated positive moods may counteract the negative effects of stress by allowing us to distance ourselves from the stressful events or to gain perspective in the face of problems.

Third, laughter may induce healthful physiological changes, such as exercising and relaxing muscles, improving respiration and circulation, and increasing the production of pain-killing endorphins. In fact, each of these physiological changes has been linked to a stronger immune system. Recent research by Miller and colleagues (2005; 2006) attempted to link laughter with the healthy performance of blood vessels and a subsequent decrease in cardiovascular disease. Participants' reactions to both stressful and humorous stimuli were measured by having them view segments of movies that generated mental stress and laughter. Arterial blood flow was then determined by means of an ultrasound device. It was found that the endothelium, the tissue forming the inner lining of blood vessels, either dilated or narrowed, depending on the subject matter of the movie clip. Blood vessels constricted and blood flow decreased by 35 percent following the disturbing movies, while the flow was boosted by 22 percent during laughter brought on by the humorous segments. Because the endothelium is active in the development of hardening of the arteries, these results suggest that laughter may help reduce the risk of cardiovascular disease.

Finally, laughter and good humor may indirectly improve health by improving interpersonal relationships; humorous people tend to be socially competent and attractive to other people (see Figure 10.14). A large social network may help individuals cope more effectively with stressful situations.

Interestingly, it seems there are differences between males and females in the appreciation of humor. In one recent study by Azim and colleagues (2005), men and women rated a series of cartoons for funniness while their brains were monitored by functional magnetic resonance imaging (fMRI). Overall, the results showed a great deal of similarity between men and women in the areas of the brain that were activated in response to the cartoons. However, there were some important differences. Compared to men, more activity was observed in areas of the women's brains that were previously found to be associated with processes key to appreciating humor: comprehension and integration of humorous stimuli (e.g., cartoons) and the feelings of amusement we experience when viewing or hearing something funny. These differences may help explain why men and women do not always share the same tastes when it comes to humor. Additional research will no doubt help psychologists to understand such differences more fully.

So what can you do to put more laughter into your life? Here are some tips that may help:

1. Figure out what makes you laugh, then read it, watch it, or do it more often.
2. Surround yourself with funny people and be with them as often as you can.
3. Develop your own sense of humor; start by learning how to tell a joke or story.
4. Be funny every chance you get—as long as it is not at someone else's expense.

As noted above, research is just beginning to pinpoint the relationship between laughter and good health, and there's no doubt that investigations will be ongoing into these claims. So until then, laugh often—but don't throw away your running shoes just yet if you are concerned about staying healthy.

FIGURE 10.14
Is Laughter the Best Medicine?
Laughter has several possible beneficial effects. It puts us in a good mood, it may counteract the negative effects of stress by allowing us to distance ourselves from the stressful events or to gain perspective in the face of problems, and it may indirectly improve health by improving interpersonal relationships. More research will be needed, however, to confirm the beneficial effects of laughter.

KEY QUESTIONS

- What are the consequences of heavy consumption of alcohol?
- What is AIDS? How is HIV transmitted?
- How does the IMB model attempt to change risky behaviors?
- How is the way in which we express our emotions related to our health?

PROMOTING WELLNESS: DEVELOPING A HEALTHIER LIFESTYLE

Have you ever wondered why some individuals live to be more than one hundred years old, while most people live only seventy or eighty years? Studies of people who live to be more than one hundred years old indicate that several factors may play a role in their extended life spans. One of these factors is diet: Long-lived people often show a pattern involving greater-than-average consumption of grains, leafy green and root vegetables, fresh milk, and fresh fruits, and they tend to eat low to moderate amounts of meat and animal fat. In addition, they maintain low to moderate levels of daily caloric intake (1,200 to 3,000 calories) and consume only moderate amounts of alcohol each day. Long-lived people also tend to make regular physical activity an integral part of their lives, continuing well into old age. Additional factors include continued sexual activity, adaptive personality characteristics and family stability, and continued involvement in family and community affairs during advanced years (see Chapter 7 for additional information on older adults).

In sum, while genetic factors certainly play a role in determining life span, research suggests that people may be able to extend their lives significantly by adhering to a lifestyle that includes these factors: a balanced, low-fat, low-calorie diet; regular exercise; and continued activity during later years (Pelletier, 1986). Evidence from a recent study (Small et al., 2006) indicates that it's never too late to make lifestyle changes. Study participants aged 35–69 followed a regimen of a healthy diet, relaxation techniques, cardiovascular workouts, and mental exercises for just fourteen days. The use of positron emission tomography (PET) scans (see Chapter 2) showed an improvement in brain function and enhancement of verbal skills even in this short period of time. So clearly, the benefits of a healthy lifestyle aren't just physical, but mental as well.

On the basis of such findings, a growing number of health professionals and psychologists have adopted an approach to health and wellness that is based on **prevention strategies,** techniques designed to reduce the occurrence of illness and other physical and psychological problems. The goal of *primary prevention* is to reduce or eliminate the incidence of preventable illness and injury. Primary prevention strategies usually involve one or more of the following components: educating people about the relation between their behaviors and their health; promoting motivation and skills to practice healthy behaviors; and directly modifying poor health practices through intervention.

Secondary prevention focuses on early detection to decrease the severity of illness that is already present. Thus, individuals learn about their health status through medical tests that screen for the presence of disease. Although early detection of certain diseases is increasingly carried out by health professionals and often requires sophisticated medical tests, exciting research is under way to teach patients methods of self-examination, especially for early detection of breast and testicular cancer.

Primary Prevention: Decreasing the Risks of Illness

In most instances, our initial attempts to change our health behaviors are unsuccessful. Typically, we become aware of the need to change behaviors; we initiate

Prevention strategies: Techniques designed to reduce the occurrence of disease or illness and the physical and psychological problems that often accompany them.

change; we experience a series of failed attempts to change these behaviors; and sometimes—only sometimes—we succeed. The nature of this process indicates that we need help in the form of a variety of intervention programs to meet our varied needs and purposes.

■ Health promotion messages: Marketing healthy lifestyles.

We are constantly bombarded with messages about health risks. Numerous non-profit organizations use television commercials, newspaper articles, magazine ads, radio advertising, and now the Internet to warn us about unhealthy behaviors such as smoking, unprotected sex, and alcohol and drug abuse and their associated risks, including cancer, heart disease, and AIDS. These campaigns typically provide information about symptoms that may indicate the presence of a health problem, such as shortness of breath or chest pains in the case of heart attacks, and information about the relation between specific behaviors and disease; for example, "Smoking is the number one cause of heart disease."

But can mass media campaigns alone produce widespread changes in behavior? There is little evidence that they can (Meyer, Maccoby, & Farquhar, 1980). One reason for the limited success of these programs may be the media's depiction and promotion of *un*healthy habits, which counteract health promotion messages. For example, Story and Faulkner (1990) computed the frequency of commercials advertising healthy versus unhealthy food and beverages. Most of the prime-time commercials were for unhealthy foods and beverages. Moreover, consider that the advertising dollars spent on breakfast cereals, candy and gum, soft drinks, and snacks tally up to more than one-third of all food advertising expenditures (Story & French, 2004).

Another reason for the limited success of these programs is that they ignore important individual differences that exist among people, such as their readiness to change. As you might expect, interventions tailored to meet the interests and needs of specific target groups are significantly more effective than general, one-size-fits-all interventions (Azer, 1999). For example, in an attempt to change adolescents' attitudes toward smoking, a campaign titled "*truth*," tailored for teenagers, provided unflattering facts about tobacco and that industry's marketing techniques. The ads featured "hip" youths challenging the tobacco companies' advertising strategies while proclaiming their own positive tobacco-free individuality. Teenagers in the areas targeted by the "*truth*" campaign tended to endorse statements such as "Cigarette companies try to get young people to start smoking." Evidence showed a significant decline in teen smoking in those areas, much more than the results of a similar campaign by a tobacco company, which used a "Just Say No" approach. In fact, teens exposed to the tobacco company's ads seemed to be more favorably disposed toward the tobacco industry and smoking (Farrelly et al., 2002).

Third, research suggests that the effectiveness of health prevention messages depends on the way they are framed (Rothman & Salovey, 1997). Some health prevention messages seem to work best when they emphasize the benefits of a certain health practice (gain framing), whereas others work best when they emphasize the costs (loss framing). The relative effectiveness of a gain-framed or loss-framed message depends, at least in part, on whether the function of the recommended behavior is on prevention or detection. Gain framing tends to work best for prevention behaviors that help people avert the onset or development of a health problem, such as the consistent use of sunscreen or refraining from smoking cigarettes (Detweiler et al., 1999). In contrast, loss framing seems to work best for messages intended to motivate detection behaviors, such as encouraging women to perform regular breast self-examinations or obtain a yearly mammography screening (Meyerowitz & Chaiken, 1987; Meyerowitz, Wilson, & Chaiken, 1991; Banks et al., 1995).

A final reason has to do with the nature of these types of campaigns—large-scale field projects that lack the tight experimental controls usually present in laboratory settings. Take, for example, mass-media promotions intended to reduce drinking and driving. One recent review by Elder and colleagues (2004) attempted to compare the effectiveness of different mass-media approaches to this problem. One style focused on fear, emphasizing the legal consequences or the danger of personal harm, while another presented social consequences, such as labeling drunken drivers as irresponsible or reckless. Still another portrayed relatively mild negative consequences associated with drinking and driving along with a greater focus on examples of more appropriate behavior. All seemed equally effective in reducing drinking and driving, as evidenced by a median 13 percent decrease in alcohol-related crashes in the respective areas in which these programs were deployed. The difficulty arises when attempting to draw conclusions about what contributed to the observed change in behavior. A media campaign could be just one of many factors that could potentially influence a reduction in crashes. Many other variables could also play a role, such as how frequently a particular message is viewed by the target audience, stepped-up law enforcement practices in a certain area, legislative initiatives to govern the behavior, or related news coverage, all of which make it challenging to assess the true effectiveness of mass-media campaigns.

■ **Primary prevention of cancer: The Pool Cool program.**

What is the most common form of cancer in the United States? You may be surprised to learn the answer: skin cancer, which accounts for about 50 percent of all reported cases of cancer. The incidence of melanoma, the most deadly form of skin cancer, has more than doubled since 1970, and each year 1.3 million new cases are reported. Fortunately, skin cancer is also one of the most preventable forms of cancer, making it a prime candidate for primary prevention programs. The behavioral recommendations for prevention of skin cancer are clear: Use sunscreen with a sun protection factor of fifteen or higher; limit the amount of time you spend in the sun; avoid the sun during the middle of the day (10 A.M.– 4 P.M.); and wear protective clothing such as sunglasses, hats, shirts, and pants (American Cancer Society, 2006).

In the summer of 2000, a study was begun to test the impact of a primary skin cancer prevention program—the *Pool Cool* program—on sun protection behaviors (Glanz et al., 2005). The pilot program began with twenty-eight swimming pools in two U.S. states that received either the Pool Cool sun protection training or an injury-prevention training program. The Pool Cool program was comprised of educational components that emphasized the behavioral recommendations for prevention listed previously. During the summer, researchers recorded changes in the sun protection behaviors of swimmers, parents, and aquatic staff. Significant changes were observed. For example, over time, the availability of sunscreen increased at the Pool Cool sites, but not at the other pools. The increased availability—and use—of the sunscreen by the Pool Cool kids made a significant difference in the number of sunburns they reported. There was no change in the reported number of sunburns at the other sites. The success of the initial program resulted in an expansion to four hundred pools in twenty-nine states, with 97 percent of the locations putting the skin-cancer prevention program into practice.

Secondary Prevention: The Role of Early Detection in Disease and Illness

Psychologists are taking an active role in developing motivational strategies to get people to take part in early detection procedures—techniques used to screen for the presence of disease and other serious health conditions. The identification of these conditions at an early stage can make an enormous difference in the chances for treatment success—in some cases the difference between life and death.

■ **Screening for disease: Seeking information about our health status.**

The fact that early detection and treatment of an illness is more effective than later detection and treatment is the foundation for screening programs. The widespread use of available screening techniques could decrease the incidence of cardiovascular disease through the early detection of high blood pressure and cholesterol, and could significantly reduce the number of cervical, colon, and prostate cancer deaths (Murray, 1999; Rothenberg et al., 1987).

Many companies, colleges, community organizations, and hospitals have screening programs to test for high blood pressure and serum cholesterol. Unfortunately, many people either fail to take advantage of screening programs or do not get screened regularly. Forgetting and underestimating the time since the last test are the primary reasons people wait too long between screenings. Interventions that heighten awareness or serve a reminder function, such as physician reminder systems and local advertising campaigns, can increase the frequency of screening visits (Mitchell, 1988). As with educational messages used to promote primary prevention, research indicates that educational messages used to promote *screening* procedures are most effective when they are tailored to meet people's varying levels of knowledge and styles of processing information. One way in which people vary is the extent to which they respond to personally threatening health-related information. For example, "monitors" tend to be concerned

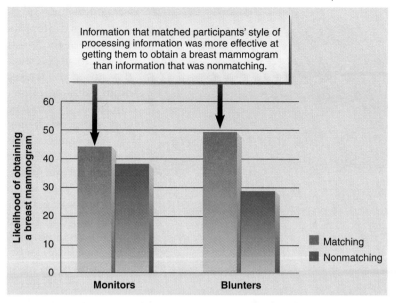

FIGURE 10.15

Increasing Participation in Screening Programs: Matching Health Information to Information Processing Styles

Health information is more effective in getting people to take part in early detection procedures when the message matches their information-processing styles. "Monitors" are more likely to obtain a breast mammogram when the information they receive contains detailed information about the risks of breast cancer and the benefits of mammography. "Blunters" are more likely to take part in screening when they receive information that is less comprehensive and presented in simple, nonthreatening language.

Source: Based on data from Williams-Piehota et al., 2005.

about their risk for disease and they tend to scan for and amplify threatening cues in health information (Miller, 1995). By contrast, *"blunters"* do not seek detailed information about their health risks or medical conditions, and instead are more likely to follow basic, nonthreatening information that suggests a simple course of action (Miller, 1996). Research suggests that health-related information can be more effective when it "matches" people's style of processing information. For example, Williams-Piehota and colleagues (2005) developed two different versions of a pamphlet designed to encourage women to obtain breast mammography screening. The pamphlet designed for "monitors" provided detailed information about the threat and risks of breast cancer as well as the benefits of mammography. The pamphlet designed for "blunters" contained much less comprehensive information that was presented using simple, nonthreatening language. As shown in Figure 10.15, information tailored to meet the women's coping styles was more effective in getting them to obtain a breast mammography than information that was not.

■ Self-examination: Detecting the early signs of illness.

Self-examination can be instrumental to the early detection of both testicular and breast cancer. The cure rate associated with testicular cancer is extremely high—over 90 percent—if the cancer is detected early. Unfortunately, in nearly half of the testicular cancers diagnosed, the presence of the disease is not detected until it has spread from the testes to the abdomen and other organs, when the chances of a full recovery are significantly less. Despite the fact that testicular self-examination techniques are available and are effective in detecting the early signs of cancer, many males remain unaware of their existence or how to perform these procedures correctly (Finney, Weist, & Friman, 1995; Steffen, 1990).

It is noteworthy that public awareness of this form of cancer has increased dramatically following cyclist Lance Armstrong's string of an unprecedented seven

FIGURE 10.16
Battling Back from Cancer
Cyclist Lance Armstrong gained instant notoriety following is first Tour de France victory in 1999. Why? One reason is that several years earlier he had nearly died of an advanced case of testicular cancer. Armstrong's dramatic comeback has significantly raised the public's awareness of this form of cancer and the importance of performing regular cancer self-examination to detect the disease at an earlier—and more curable—stage. Amazingly, Armstrong has since gone on to win the race six more times before retiring, after his most recent victory in 2005.

straight victories in the grueling Tour de France (see Figure 10.16). Why would this capture the public's attention? Just three years before he won this race for the first time in 1999, Armstrong was diagnosed with an advanced form of testicular cancer that nearly killed him. By the time he was diagnosed the cancer had already spread to his abdomen, lungs, and brain. Although given only a 50 percent chance of survival, Armstrong miraculously survived a year of painful treatment, going on to win one of sports' biggest challenges.

The dangers associated with breast cancer pose a similar challenge for women. With more than 40,000 deaths from breast cancer annually, it is the second leading cancer killer of U.S. women (American Cancer Society, 2005). Some researchers suggest that women with breast cancer detected early through secondary prevention programs—such as breast self-examination, clinical breast examination, and mammography—have a survival rate of 86 percent at five years after diagnosis (American Cancer Society, 2002).

Women are most likely to obtain mammography screening when their physician recommends it, highlighting the critical role these professionals play in promoting the importance of early detection. Programs designed to change certain beliefs are also effective in getting women to obtain mammography screening: for example, beliefs concerning their susceptibility to breast cancer, the severity of breast cancer, and the potential benefits of mammography screening (Aiken et al., 1994; Miller et al., 1996).

KEY QUESTIONS

- What role does the mass media play in our health?
- What is primary prevention?
- What is secondary prevention?

SUMMARY AND REVIEW OF KEY QUESTIONS

Health Psychology: An Overview

- **What is health psychology?**
  Health psychology is the study of the relation between psychological variables and health.

- **What is the field of behavioral medicine?**
  Behavioral medicine, a field closely related to health psychology, combines behavioral and biomedical science knowledge to prevent and treat disorders.

- **To what can we attribute today's leading causes of premature death?**
  Many of today's leading causes of premature death can be attributed to people's lifestyles.

Stress: Its Causes, Effects, and Control

- **What is stress?**
  Stress is the process that occurs in response to situations or events (stressors) that disrupt, or threaten to disrupt, our physical or psychological functioning.

- **What is the GAS model?**
  The general adaptation syndrome (GAS) describes how our bodies react to the effects of stress and includes three distinct stages: alarm, resistance, and, finally, exhaustion.

- **What determines whether an event will be interpreted as stressful or as a challenge?**
  Cognitive appraisals play an important role in determining whether we interpret potentially stressful events as stressful or as a challenge.

- **Which types of events are likely to create stress?**
  Both positive (getting married) and negative (death of a spouse) life events may be stressors. Catastrophic events (terrorism, natural disasters) may be especially stressful, even to observers.

- **Are daily hassles harmful?**
  Yes, the accumulated strain of minor annoyances such as commuting problems and waiting in lines while shopping can cause stress and affect our health.

- **What are some sources of work-related stress?**
  Sources of work-related stress include work overload and underload, low job control, and role conflict.

- **What role does stress play in physical illness?**
  Stress may play a role in 50 to 70 percent of all physical illnesses, primarily through its effect on the immune system.

- **How does social support influence stress?**
  Social support increases the contact we have with others and may improve coping skills. Providing support, as opposed to receiving it, may have stronger effects.

- **What is the relationship between stress and performance?**
  Even relatively low levels of stress may interfere with task performance. Prolonged exposure to high levels of stress may lead to illness.

Understanding and Communicating Our Health Needs

- **What is the health belief model?**
  The health belief model suggests that our willingness to seek medical help depends on the extent to which we perceive a threat to our health and the extent to which we believe that a particular behavior will effectively reduce that threat.

- **What factors determine our willingness to make lifestyle changes or seek medical help?**
  Our willingness to make lifestyle changes or seek medical help depends on our beliefs concerning our susceptibility to an illness, the severity of the illness, and the effectiveness of steps taken to deal with the illness.

- **What are the advantages and disadvantages of seeking medical advice on the Internet?**
  Some of the nation's top medical research facilities have created publicly accessible web sites, so patients can learn more about their symptoms and take a more active role in their treatment. However, the Internet is not policed; therefore, the information found at many sites is inaccurate.

Behavioral and Psychological Correlates of Illness: The Effects of Thoughts and Actions on Health

- **What determines who will become addicted to smoking?**
  Genetic, psychosocial, and cognitive factors all seem to play a role in determining who will become addicted to smoking.

- **What are the effects of poor dietary practices?**
  Poor dietary practices can increase the risks of colon and rectal cancer, breast cancer, and cardiovascular disease.

- **How do feelings of self-determination influence adherence to an exercise regimen?**
  Health-preventive behavior that we initiate and determine ourselves is more likely to be maintained over time, whereas maintenance of these behaviors achieved at the urging of others (controlled motivation) is less likely.

- **What are the consequences of heavy consumption of alcohol?**
  Chronic excessive alcohol consumption can lead to deficits in many different cognitive abilities, including learning and memory, perceptual–motor skills, visual–spatial processing, and problem solving. Drinking can also lead to stomach disease, cirrhosis of the liver, cancer, and impaired sexual functioning, and can result in fetal alcohol syndrome.

- **What is AIDS? How is HIV transmitted?**
  Acquired immune deficiency syndrome (AIDS) is a reduction in the immune system's ability to defend the body against invaders and is caused by HIV. HIV is transmitted primarily through unprotected sex and infected blood.

- **How does the IMB model attempt to change risky behaviors?**
  According to the IMB model, people will not change risky behaviors unless they know how diseases are acquired and the specific actions they must take to avoid them. Interventions based on the IMB use elicitation research to identify misinformation that individuals have and then teach the skills necessary to engage in safe behavior.

- **How is the way in which we express our emotions related to our health?**
  Failure to express our emotions can adversely affect the progression of cancer and other illnesses. Emotions can also lead to an increase in a person's blood pressure.

Promoting Wellness: Developing a Healthier Lifestyle

- **What role does the mass media play in our health?**
  The mass media, when combined with other health promotion programs, can have a beneficial impact on health behaviors.

- **What is primary prevention?**
  Primary prevention emphasizes disease prevention by educating people about the relation between their behavior and their health, promoting healthy behavior, and directly modifying poor health practices.

- **What is secondary prevention?**
  Secondary prevention techniques emphasize early detection of diseases and attempt to decrease the severity of illness that is already present.

KEY TERMS

Acquired immune deficiency syndrome (AIDS), p. 409
Cancer, p. 402
Carcinogens, p. 403
Cardiovascular disease, p. 397

Cognitive restructuring, p. 421
General adaptation syndrome (GAS), p. 389
Hassles, p. 393
Health belief model, p. 399

Health psychology, p. 386
Hypertension, p. 412
Lifestyle, p. 386
Nicotine, p. 405
Passive smoke, p. 405

PSYCHOLOGY: UNDERSTANDING ITS FINDINGS

Changing Our Explanatory Style

As was noted in this chapter, people differ considerably in their resistance to adversity in their lives. How do such persons differ? One answer involves the personality dimension of *optimism–pessimism*. Optimists and pessimists differ in variety of ways, including in their general expectancies for good outcomes and in their approaches to dealing with problems in their lives. Psychologists have learned that another important difference is their beliefs about the causes of events in their lives.

Pessimists tend to believe the causes of the negative events in their lives are permanent—"I'm a loser"—and that these will persist and spread to other areas of their lives. This helps to explain why pessimists tend to give up easily and are less resistant to the effects of stress. In contrast, people with an optimistic outlook believe that such events are the result of factors that are temporary and specific to that event.

When it comes to positive events, the opposite is true: Optimists tend to believe the causes of the positive events in their lives are permanent—"I'm smart"—and that they will spill over into other areas of their lives. Pessimists, as you might predict, tend to ascribe good fortune to transitory forces outside themselves.

We have all adopted a pessimistic explanatory style at least once in our lives. Fortunately, there are steps you can take to build a more optimistic style. First, recognize that your beliefs are just that—beliefs! An effective way to defeat a negative belief is to show that it is factually incorrect. Second, remember that most events have many causes. For example, if you performed poorly on a test, a number of factors probably played a role. To dispute your own beliefs, focus on the contributing factors that are changeable (e.g., the amount of time you studied) and specific (e.g., this particular exam was really difficult). Please note, however, that the facts won't always be on your side and the negative beliefs you hold may sometimes be true. In these instances, try to put the event into perspective. For example, you might change the belief to "I performed poorly on this exam, but I have three more exams left to take!" Finally, it is important to stop dwelling on the belief and focus on the actions that will change the situation, such as arranging your schedule to allow you to study harder for the next exam.

Whenever you find yourself feeling pessimistic about events in your life, try using these tips. To chart your progress, write down a description of each event, your initial reactions to it, and the steps you took to address the problem. Over time, you may find that you are less susceptible to pessimistic thoughts and beliefs.

MAKING PSYCHOLOGY PART OF YOUR LIFE

Managing Stress: Some Useful Tactics

Stress is a fact of life. It's all around us: at work, in our environment, and in our personal lives. Because stress arises from so many different factors and conditions, it's probably impossible to eliminate it completely. However, there are a number of techniques that you can use to lessen its harmful effects.

Physiological Coping Techniques

One of the most effective physiological coping techniques involves reducing muscle tension through **progressive relaxation.** Begin by alternately flexing and relaxing your muscles to appreciate the difference between relaxed and tense muscles. Next, relax your shoulders by slowly rolling them up and down. Now, relax your neck. Step by step, extend this process until your body is completely relaxed. Relaxation procedures are effective in reducing emotional as well as physical tension. Regular vigorous exercise is another important technique to reduce stress; it does not eliminate the problems that sometimes lead to stress, but it may increase your capacity to cope with the stress.

Behavioral Coping Techniques

There are plenty of things you can do to reduce the stress in your life. One method is time management: learning how to make time work for you instead of against you. Adhering to a well-planned schedule can help you make more efficient use of your time and eliminate behaviors that interfere with your main goals. Table 10.5 offers several tips to help you get the most out of your day.

Progressive relaxation:
A stress reduction technique in which people learn to relax by alternately flexing and relaxing their muscles in a particular muscle group and then progressively to other muscles throughout the body.

TABLE 10.5 Getting the Most Out of Your Day: Psychology in Action
One behavioral coping strategy is time management. Here are some tips to help you get the most out of your day.
Basic Principles of Time Management
1. Each day, make a list of things you want to accomplish.
2. Prioritize your list. Plan to do the toughest things first, and save the easier tasks for later in the day when you are low on energy.
3. Arrange your work schedule to take the best advantage of the hours when you work best.
4. Always set aside a block of time when you can work without any interruptions.
5. Be flexible about changes in your schedule so that you can handle unexpected events.
6. Set aside time in your daily schedule for exercise, such as jogging, aerobics, or brisk walking. You'll find that the time spent is well worth it and may even increase your productivity.
7. Set aside some time each day or week in which you always do some planned leisure activity—everybody needs a break.

Cognitive Coping Techniques

When exposed to a stressful situation, you can think about it in different ways. The process of replacing negative appraisals of stressors with more positive ones is called **cognitive restructuring** (Meichenbaum, 1977). To use this technique, start to monitor what you say to yourself during periods of stress. Begin modifying these thoughts by thinking more adaptive thoughts, such as imagining something humorous about the situation or creative ways to reduce or eliminate the source of stress. Having adequate sources of social support is also important. Because cognitive appraisal plays a crucial role in the way we interpret stressors, it is a good idea to be in contact with people who can suggest strategies for dealing with the sources of stress that you might not generate yourself. Finally, as we learned in this chapter, providing social support to others may also be beneficial to your health.

Cognitive restructuring:
A method of modifying self-talk in stress-producing situations. Clients are trained to monitor what they say to themselves in stress-provoking situations and then to modify their cognitions in adaptive ways.

If you are using MyPsychLab, you have access to an electronic version of this textbook, along with dozens of valuable resources per chapter—including video and audio clips, simulations and activities, self-assessments, practice tests and other study materials. Here is a sampling of the resources available for this chapter.

LISTEN

Problem-Focused Coping
Emotion-Focused Coping

SIMULATE

How Stressed Are You?

WATCH

Women, Health and Stress
Men and Stress
Stress and Your Skin
Smoking Damage
Drunken Buggy Behavior

If you did not receive an access code to MyPsychLab with this text and wish to purchase access online, please visit www.MyPsychLab.com.

STUDY GUIDE

CHAPTER REVIEW

Health Psychology: An Overview

1. Researchers in the field of _____ assert that a positive attitude can delay illness.
   a. health psychology
   b. chronomedicine
   c. biobehavioral medicine
   d. wellness prevention

2. Lifestyle is an important determinant of health and longevity.   (True-False).

3. Which of the following was an improvement in health promoted by the Healthy People 2000 Initiative?
   a. An increase in the number of people who regularly exercise.
   b. A slight reduction in the number of smokers.
   c. A reduction in the number of obese persons.
   d. All of the above are correct.

Stress: Its Causes, Effects, and Control

4. Which of the following it true of stress?
   a. Stress has positive effects on health.
   b. Most people find it easy to avoid stress.
   c. Stress was more common in the early colonial days.
   d. Stress follows an event that disrupts our physical or psychological functioning.

5. John is on his way to Los Angeles from Washington to Los Angeles. While trying to hail a cab, he was robbed of his watch, was overcharged by the cabbie and now he is about to be strip-searched at the airport security line. We would term his negative emotional reaction to these situations as
   a. anti-American.
   b. a series of stressors.
   c. stress.
   d. emotional stasis.

6. A key aspect of stressors is that they are
   a. easy to ignore.
   b. simple to terminate.
   c. beyond our control.
   d. able to immunize us against overload.

7. Our susceptibility to disease increases during the _____ of the General Adaptation Syndrome.
   a. alarm
   b. exhaustion
   c. distress
   d. resistance

8. Secondary threat appraisal involves the occurrence of stress for
   a. events that will impede our progress toward a goal.
   b. events that we believe we will be unable to control.
   c. recurrent pleasant situations.
   d. controllable situations.

9. Another term for accumulated stress is
   a. homeostatic burden.
   b. posttraumatic anxiety disorder.
   c. allostatic load.
   d. tertiary appraisal.

10. Persons high in sociability are resistant to disease because social persons
    a. have better social interactions.
    b. exert better control over their negative emotions.
    c. are better at performing health-enhancing behaviors.
    d. All of the above are correct.

11. Whether a person will experience PTSD after an event like that of September 11, 2001
    a. is less likely if the person expects a future attack.
    b. depends on the resilience of the person.
    c. is more likely if that person saw televised accounts as opposed to being in the World Trade Center.
    d. All of the above are correct.

12. Minor annoying events in our daily lives are known as
    a. irritants.
    b. annoyers.
    c. hassles.
    d. aggravators.

13. If Jim and Mary Jones, a young couple with children, score _____ on the daily hassles scale, we would expect them to show_____.
    a. low;   resistance to drug abuse
    b. high;   lower psychological well-being
    c. low;   psychological pathology
    d. high;   higher psychological well-being

14. Sources of stress related to work include
    a. work overload or underload.
    b. sexual harassment.
    c. an unstable job history.
    d. All of the above are correct.

15. Having a measure of control over our life is a positive experience.   (True-False)

16. Stress plays a role in _____ of all physical illness.
    a. 5%
    b. 15%
    c. 65%
    d. 95%

17. A key pathway through which stress has direct and indirect negative physical effects involves the
    a. psyche.
    b. unconscious.
    c. hippocampus and frontal cortex.
    d. immune system.

18. A new student on campus who has few friends and who feels lonely would be expected to
    a. show low levels of cortisol.
    b. have low immune function.
    c. show improved immune function.
    d. improve their degree of social support.

19. Recent research suggests that mild stress
    a. improves immune function.
    b. alters sensory memory.
    c. can reduce task performance.
    d. is more harmful that severe stress for task performance.

Understanding and Communicating Our Health Needs

20. The "health belief model" was developed in order to explain
    a. how teenagers learn to smoke.
    b. why some people refuse to seek medical treatment for minor health problems.
    c. why we engage in unhealthy behaviors.
    d. why people fail to use medical screening services.

21. The "health belief model" argues that we will change a health-related behavior if we perceive a threat to our health AND believe that this behavior change will reduce that threat.   (True-False)

22. _____ are more likely to have yearly medical exams than are _____.
    a. Men;   women
    b. Rural residents;   urban dwellers
    c. Women;   men
    d. Urban dwellers;   rural residents

23. Asian Americans rarely engage in preventative health behaviors and thus have the highest mortality rate of any American ethnic group.   (True-False)

24. Patient satisfaction with their physician is increased when
    a. their doctor talks straight at them.
    b. their doctor takes the time to use simple language to explain treatment issues.
    c. their health appointment is limited to diagnostic and treatment issues.
    d. they feel like they are being rushed out of the treatment room.

25. Surfing the internet for medical information is risky because
    a. it is free.
    b. good medical advice costs money.
    c. untested treatments are difficult to distinguish from sound medical advice.
    d. patients can find information on doctors and new treatments.

Behavioral and Psychological Correlates of Illness: The Effects of Thoughts and Actions on Health

26. Risk factors modulate whether a person who has a family history of cancer will actually develop cancer.   (True-False).

27. Which of the following is a health risk for smokers?
    a. Smoking is the leading cause of several types of cancer.
    b. A smoker has five times the risk for having a stroke.
    c. Smoking slightly increases the risk of developing lung cancer.
    d. Alcohol consumption is as likely to lead to death as is smoking.

28. The government has restricted cigarette advertising directed at children in part because
    a. most smokers report having their first cigarette between the ages of 18 and 21.
    b. of the belief that such ads are a waste of valuable advertising time.
    c. smoking is firmly established by age ten.

d. smoking is a habit picked up during adolescence.

29. Which of the following is a key factor for continuing to smoke?
    a. Overestimating the health risks of smoking.
    b. Being female with financial problems.
    c. Being male with low stress.
    d. Overreacting to the personal consequences of smoking.

30. A person who wants to quit smoking should seek a self-help program rather than looking for help from a medical program.   (True-False).

31. People prefer a diet rich in fat because fat
    a. increases opiate levels in the body.
    b. makes sugars taste better,
    c. decreases opiate levels in the body.
    d. fat lowers their risk of cardiovascular disease.

32. A person who is motivated to lose weight at the urging of their doctor or family members
    a. will keep the weight off for more than a year.
    b. is more likely to attend program meetings.
    c. is likely to lose a lot of weight.
    d. would be low in autonomous motivation.

33. Moderate alcohol consumption is defined as drinking _____ of an alcoholic beverage per day.
    a. one glass
    b. three glasses
    c. five glasses
    d. more than six glasses

34. Some alcoholics drink to relieve anxiety.   (True-False)

35. Which of the following is an example of a biological determinant of alcoholism?
    a. Unrelated brothers raised together have similar drinking patterns.
    b. An identical twin who has an alcoholic twin is unlikely to be alcoholic.
    c. An identical twin who has an alcoholic twin is likely to be alcoholic.
    d. A child adopted into a family with an alcoholic member is likely to become alcoholic.

36. An increased transmission of AIDS from one person to another is related to
    a. engaging in unprotected sexual intercourse.
    b. limited use of condoms by married couples.
    c. receiving tainted blood products.
    d. A and C are correct.

37. The only effective technique to reduce the risk of acquiring AIDS is to
    a. show documentaries on the horrible consequences of developing AIDS.
    b. encourage intravenous drug addicts to share their needles.
    c. change AIDS-related behaviors.
    d. create programs in which teenagers are taken to meet with dying AIDS victims.

38. An example of a passive AIDS-prevention intervention would be
    a. providing personal counseling.
    b. giving out fliers about the dangers of AIDS
    c. providing role-playing training that increases condom use.
    d. telling someone that AIDS will kill you.

39. A type _____ personality is more likely to die from can-cer than people who express positive emotion.
    a. A
    b. B
    c. D
    d. F
40. Negative emotions increase cardiac risk through an ac-tion on
    a. immune function.
    b. brain activity.
    c. eating habits.
    d. blood pressure.

Promoting Wellness: Developing a Healthier Lifestyle

41. Extended life span is associated with
    a. abstinence from consumption of alcohol.
    b. a diet low in fat but high in grains.
    c. an unstable family.
    d. avoidance of sexual activity.
42. Mass media programs are mostly unsuccessful because these compete with commercial advertising promoting unhealthy diets.   (True-False)
43. Cancer involving the _____ is the most common form of cancer in the United States.
    a. skin
    b. colon
    c. lungs
    d. brain
44. Match up the appropriate concept with the correct defin-ition or best example of the concept.
    _____. A person who is mostly unconcerned about their health.
    _____. A health strategy that focuses on providing edu-cation materials to people.
    _____. A person who is highly concerned about their health.
    _____. A health strategy aimed at early detection of dis-ease.
    a. Primary prevention
    b. "Blunters"
    c. Secondary prevention
    d. "Monitors"

IDENTIFICATIONS

Identify the term that belongs with each of the concepts below (place the letter for the appropriate term below in front of each concept).
Identification   Concept:
_____ 1. Events that can induce stress.
_____ 2. A health strategy that focuses on providing edu-cation materials to people.
_____ 3. The most common form of cancer in the US.
_____ 4. Having a group of friends can buffer the risks posed by chronic stress.
_____ 5. A condition that increases the likelihood of devel-oping a disease.
_____ 6. Minor annoying events that can add to diminish health.

_____ 7. A health strategy aimed at early detection of disease.
_____ 8. A health worker passes out pamphlets that de-tail the risks for contracting AIDS.
_____ 9. An environmental agent capable of causing can-cer.
_____ 10. A person who bottles up their negative feelings during the experience of stress.
_____ 11. A person exposed to a severe stressor may reex-perience that event.
_____ 12. A person who is highly concerned about risks to their health.

Identification:

    a. Hassles.
    b. Post-traumatic stress disorder.
    c. Skin cancer.
    d. Primary prevention.
    e. Carcinogen.
    f. Passive AIDS-prevention intervention.
    g. Stressor.
    h. Type D personality.
    i. Risk factor.
    j. Social support.
    k. Monitor.
    l. Secondary prevention.

FILL IN THE BLANK

1. An important determinant of health and longevity re-lates to _____.
2. _____ follows an event that disrupts our physical or psychological functioning.
3. _____ are minor annoying events in our daily lives that can disrupt out health.
4. The accumulated effects of stress is termed _____.
5. The _____ is a key pathway though which stress has direct and indirect negative physical effects.
6. The _____ argues that we will change a health-related behavior if we perceive a threat to our health AND be-lieve that this behavior change will reduce that threat.
7. A _____ modulates whether a person who has a fam-ily history of a disease will actually develop that disease
8. Hans Selye proposed the _____ to account for the neg-ative effects of stress on physical health.
9. The capacity of a person to bounce back from a severe stressor is known as
10. Work _____ refers to the situation n which a person is asked to do too little at their job.
11. _____ refers to the emotional resources from others that can buffer stress effects.
12. A _____ is a physical complaint made by a person to their physician.
13. An environmental chemical that has the capacity to in-duce cancer is known as a _____
14. A _____ is a person who is mostly unconcerned about their health.

COMPREHENSIVE PRACTICE TEST

1. _____ is the leading cause of death
   a. Alcoholism
   b. Heroin addiction
   c. Lifestyle
   d. Prostitution

2. _____ is our response to a(n) _____.
   a. Despair;   stressful situation
   b. Stress;   stressor
   c. The fight-or-flight syndrome;   stimulus that activates the parasympathetic system
   d. Exhaustion;   stress appraisal

3. Stress is evoked by negative situations and reduced by positive situations.   (True-False)

4. Which of the following terms DO NOT go together?
   a. exhaustion;   greater chance of becoming sick
   b. stressor;   negative life events
   c. General Adaptation Syndrome;   Sigmund Freud
   d. unavoidable events;   stressor

5. Judy is outgoing and easily makes friends. We would expect that Judy
   a. would be more likely to develop flu during the winter season.
   b. is low in social desirability.
   c. will develop a compromised immune system.
   d. would be less likely to develop flu during the winter season.

6. Minor annoying events in our daily lives are known as
   a. irritants.
   b. annoyers.
   c. hassles.
   d. aggravators.

7. Elevated levels of _____ will in turn _____ our immune system.
   a. cortisol;   suppress
   b. leptin;   suppress
   c. cortisol;   enhance
   d. leptin;   enhance

8. Thinking that you are lonely is NOT as important as actually being lonely in terms of suppression of immune function.   (True-False)

9. Physicians define a(n) _____ as a physical sensation that can be reported by a patient.
   a. syndrome
   b. disorder
   c. disease
   d. symptom

10. Studies of patient satisfaction indicate that improved communication leads to
    a. better compliance with the treatment program.
    b. better patient emotional health.
    c. fewer hospitalizations for the patient.
    d. All of the above are correct.

11. High levels of serum LDL cholesterol are associated with
    a. higher rates of smoking.
    b. higher rates of heart disease.
    c. lower rates of heart disease.
    d. lower rates of smoking.

12. The risk of a female contracting AIDS has increased due to
    a. intravenous drug use.
    b. abuse of prescription weight-loss drugs.
    c. the reduced risk of male-to-female sexual transmission.
    d. All of the above are correct.

13. The goal of secondary prevention is to
    a. educate people about the role of exercise for extended life.
    b. promote healthy behaviors.
    c. provide for early detection of disease.
    d. modify poor health behaviors.

14. _____ do not seek details health status information whereas _____ are highly concerned about risks to their health.
    a. "Monitors";   "obsessors"
    b. "Hypochondriacs";   "blunters"
    c. "Monitors";   "blunters"
    d. "Blunters";   "monitors"

15. Which of the following is a toxic effect of heavy alcoholic consumption?
    a. Stomach disease.
    b. Increased risk of suicide.
    c. Impaired sexual functioning.
    d. All of the above are correct.

16. Which of the following is an example of a carcinogen?
    a. Alcohol.
    b. Tobacco smoke.
    c. Radiation from the sun.
    d. All of the above are correct.

CRITICAL THINKING

1. Explain why it would be advantageous for a person to find ways to minimize the amount of stress that they experience in their daily lives.

2. Compare and contrast the primary and secondary prevention strategies for the promotion of health.

ELEVEN

Mental Disorders: When Behavior Goes "Over the Edge"

My wife and I (Robert Baron) have a very pretty and peaceful backyard, and during the warm weather, we like to eat dinner on our screened-in porch so we can look into the garden while dining. We love listening to the birds singing and to the gentle sounds of the breeze as it rustles the leaves on the trees. But many evenings, just as we are start our meal, our neighbor Joe gets busy. There are a lot of annoying sounds in the world, but among the worst, we think, are lawn mowers and leaf blowers. And those are exactly the sounds coming from Joe's yard for what seems like hours on end. The interesting thing is that he mows and blows his lawn almost every night, and does it even though it looks perfect to me when he starts! Why does he do this? I have asked Joe this question in a very gentle way many times, and his answer is always something like, "I just hate a messy lawn." And by "messy" he means a lawn in which one blade of grass is too long, or on which a few stray leaves have landed. So Joe is certainly a fanatic about neatness—much neater, where his lawn is concerned, that anyone else I know. This strong tendency in his behavior is also visible in that Joe has cut down almost all the tall and beautiful trees that once surrounded his house. Why? Again, to quote Joe himself, "Trees are dirty—they drop so much stuff on the grass!" And if Joe is not working on his lawn, he is up on a ladder cleaning windows, applying touch-up paint to his house, or cleaning litter from his rain gutters. Truly, Joe is a very nice person and a great neighbor in most respects, but sometimes, on a beautiful summer evening, I do wish that he were not quite so neat . . .

W̲hy do we begin with this tale of peaceful summer evenings disturbed by an overly neat neighbor? Because although it describes very ordinary and everyday events, it sets the stage for several important themes we will emphasize throughout this chapter—one that focuses on what psychologists previously termed "mental illnesses" or **"psychological disorders,"** but now are generally described by the term **mental disorders** (see Nietzel et al., 1998). Such disorders involve disturbances in an individual's behavioral or psychological functioning that are not acceptable in that person's society and that lead the people involved to experience distress and, usually, impaired functioning (Nietzel et al., 1998).

Does Joe show a mental disorder? Most psychologists would probably answer "no." His behavior is certainly unusual; very few people devote so much time and effort to making their lawns perfect. But mowing one's lawn or blowing away leaves are certainly acceptable behaviors in the United States. However, it seems clear that Joe's desire for a perfect lawn and perfect house do cause him considerable distress: He can't relax and enjoy himself like most other people. Instead, he spends many hours trimming, blowing, cleaning, and painting—time he could, perhaps, spend with his family and friends. And his actions annoy not only my wife and myself, but other neighbors, too. So although most psychologists would probably conclude that Joe is not suffering from a full-blown mental disorder, they would recognize that he is, in some respects, showing *tendencies* toward developing one—a disorder we'll discuss in detail in a later section. (For the record, it is known as *obsessive-compulsive disorder;* see pages 445–447.)

The main point of this example—and the one we want to make very strongly—is simply this: Deciding whether a specific person is or is not suffering from a particular mental disorder is *a very complex judgment,* one that must take several key elements into account: How unusual is the behavior? How acceptable or unacceptable is it in a given culture? How much distress does it cause the people involved? And to what extent does it impair their functioning—prevent them from enjoying happy, full lives (see Figure 11.1)? Such judgments are truly complex, so they should be made only by a qualified professional such as a psychologist or a psychiatrist, using tools and procedures we'll soon describe.

To provide you with a broad introduction to the nature and causes of mental disorders, the remainder of this chapter will proceed as follows. First, we'll briefly describe the tools used by psychologists and other mental health professionals to identify and assess mental disorders. Obviously, clear identification of such disorders is essential for choosing the best means to treat them, so these tools are very important. After that, we'll describe major forms of mental disorders and what we currently know about their origins. Techniques for treating or alleviating these problems are described in detail in Chapter 12.

Psychological disorders: Maladaptive patterns of behavior and thought that cause the people experiencing them considerable distress.

Mental disorders: Disturbances of an individual's behavioral or psychological functioning that are not culturally accepted and that lead to psychological distress, behavioral disability, or impaired overall functioning.

K E Y   Q U E S T I O N S

• What are mental disorders?
• What role do cultural factors play in defining them?

ASSESSMENT AND DIAGNOSIS: THE DSM-IV TR AND OTHER TOOLS

Suppose that one day your car won't start. What do you do? The first step is probably to gather information that will help you figure out why the engine doesn't start when you turn the ignition key. You might check to see if the headlights were left on; you might try turning on the radio—it if plays, then the battery is not totally dead; next, you might open the hood and check the connections to the

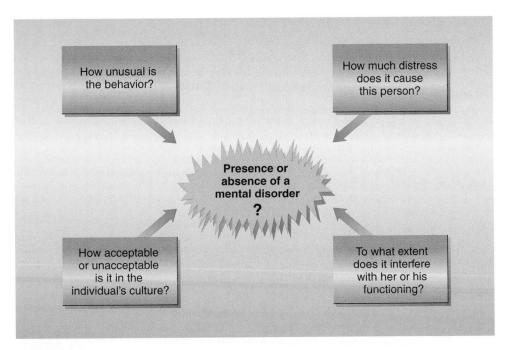

FIGURE 11.1
What Constitutes a Mental Disorder?
Most psychologists agree that in deciding whether a particular person is or is not suffering from a mental disorder, several factors must be considered: (1) How unusual is the behavior this person is showing? (2) How acceptable or unacceptable is it in her or his culture? (3) How much distress is this behavior causing the person in question? (4) To what extent does it impair his or her functioning? Taking account of all these criteria—and others, too—requires a high degree of training, so only qualified professionals such as psychologists can make it accurately.

battery. After gathering such information, you would make an initial decision about what's wrong: The battery is dead, the starter isn't working, and so on.

In a similar manner, a psychologist might go through a comparable set of steps when seeing a new patient for the first time. The psychologist would first gather information on the kind of problems the person is experiencing, conditions in her or his current life, the person's responses to various psychological tests (see Chapter 9), and so on. These information-gathering steps are known as **assessment,** and they are directed toward the goal of formulating an accurate **diagnosis**—identification of the person's problem(s). This is a crucial step, because identifying these problems often determines what the psychologist should do next—how she or he can best help this individual.

But how does the psychologist identify the specific disorder or disorders a given person is experiencing? In general, by comparing the information gathered through assessment to standard definitions of various mental disorders. In other words, psychologists and other mental health professionals have an agreed-upon system for describing and classifying mental disorders. Such a system is very useful, because without it, different psychologists or psychiatrists might refer to the same disorder with different terms or might use the same terms to describe very different problems (Millon, 1991).

Actually, several different systems for classifying mental disorders exist. However, the one that is the most widely used in the United States is the ***Diagnostic and Statistical Manual of Mental Disorders-IV-Text Revision*** (or DSM-IV-TR for short), published by the American Psychiatric Association (2000). (The phrase "text revision" refers to changes in descriptions of some of the major mental disorders that were made in this revision—the most recent one—to

Assessment:
Efforts by psychologists or other professionals to gather information on the problems individuals are experiencing. Psychologists conduct interviews in which they seek information about individuals' past and present behaviors, current problems, interpersonal relations, and personality.

Diagnosis:
Identification of the specific problems (mental disturbances) currently being experienced by individuals.

Diagnostic and Statistical Manual of Mental Disorders-IV-TR:
A manual designed to help all mental health practitioners to recognize and correctly identify (diagnose) specific disorders.

TABLE 11.1   Major Diagnostic Categories of the DSM-IV-TR

The DSM-IV classifies mental disorders according to the categories shown here.

Diagnostic Category—Axis	Examples
Adjustment disorders	With depressed mood, with anxiety
Anxiety disorders	Panic disorder, specific phobias, post-traumatic stress disorder, generalized anxiety disorder
Dissociative disorders	Dissociative amnesia, dissociative fugue, dissociative identity disorder
Eating disorders	Anorexia nervosa, bulimia nervosa
Factitious disorders	With predominantly psychological signs and symptoms; with predominantly physical signs and symptoms
Impulse-control disorders not elsewhere classified	Kleptomania, pyromania, pathological gambling
Mood disorders	Depressive disorders, bipolar disorders
Other conditions that may be a focus of clinical attention	Medication-induced movement disorders, relational problems, problems related to abuse or neglect
Schizophrenia and other psychotic disorders	Schizophrenia, schizoaffective disorder, brief psychotic disorder
Sexual and gender identity disorders	Sexual dysfunctions, paraphilias, gender identity disorders
Sleep disorders	Primary sleep disorders, sleep disorders related to another mental disorder
Somatoform disorders	Somatization disorder, conversion disorder, hypochondiasis
Substance-related disorders	Alcohol-related disorders, cocaine-related disorders, opioid-related disorders
Diagnostic Category—Axis II	**Examples**
Personality disorders	Paranoid personality disorder, schizotypal personality disorder, antisocial personality disorder
Mental retardation	Mild mental retardation, moderate mental retardation, severe mental retardation, profound mental retardation

eliminate possible sources of confusion that existed in the descriptions of several disorders [e.g., autism, certain sexual problems, depression].) Although this manual is published by the American Psychiatric Association, psychologists played an active role in its development, and are contributing in important ways to the development of the DSM-V—the next full revision, which will appear in 2011.

The major diagnostic categories of the DSM-IV-TR are shown in Table 11.1, and among them are all the major kinds of disorders covered in this chapter. In fact, the manual describes hundreds of specific disorders—many more than we'll consider here. These descriptions focus on observable features and include *diagnostic features*—symptoms that must be present before an individual is diagnosed as having a particular problem. In addition, the manual also provides much additional background information on each disorder, for instance, information about biological factors associated with the condition, and variations in each disorder that may be related to age, cultural background, and gender.

An important feature of the DSM-IV-TR is that it classifies disorders along five *axes*, rather than merely assigning them to a given category. This means that a person is described along several different dimensions (axes) rather than only one. Different axes relate to mental disorders and to physical health, social, and occupational functioning. For our purposes, two of these axes are most important: Axis I, which relates to major disorders themselves, and Axis II, which relates to *mental retardation* and to *personality disorders*—extreme and inflexible personality traits that are distressing to the person or that cause problems in school, work, or interpersonal relationships. The third axis pertains to general medical conditions relevant to each disorder, while the fourth axis considers psychosocial and environmental factors, including specific sources of stress. Finally, the fifth axis relates to a global assessment of current functioning. By evaluating people along each of these various axes, the DSM-IV-TR offers a fuller picture of their current state and psychological functioning.

Another important feature of the DSM-IV-TR it that it reflects efforts to take greater account of the potential role of cultural factors in mental disorders. For example, the description of each disorder contains description of *culturally related features*—aspects of each disorder that are related to, and may be affected by, culture. For instance, some disorders seem to occur only in some cultures. A disorder known as *Windigo,* which occurs among Native Americans in North America, involves intense anxieties that the victims will turn into monsters who literally devour other human beings! Symptoms specific to a given culture and unique ways of describing distress in various cultures are included whenever available. This information is designed to help professionals recognize the many ways in which an individual's culture can influence the form of psychological disorders.

Is the DSM-IV-TR a useful tool for psychologists? In several ways, it is. Strenuous efforts were made by the psychiatrists and psychologists who developed the DSM-IV-TR to improve it over previous versions, and in many respects these efforts succeeded: The DSM-IV-TR appears to be higher in *reliability* than earlier versions, and rests more firmly on careful, empirical research. However, it's important to note that it is still largely *descriptive* in nature: It describes psychological disorders but it makes no attempt to explain them. This is deliberate; the DSM-IV-TR was specifically designed to assist in diagnosis. It remains neutral with respect to various theories about the origins of psychological disorders. Since psychology as a science seeks *explanation,* not simply description, however, many psychologists view this aspect of the DSM-IV-TR as a shortcoming that limits its value. In addition, the DSM-IV-TR attaches specific *labels* to people, and this may activate stereotypes about them. Once a person is labeled as having a particular mental disorder, mental health professionals may perceive the person largely in terms of that label, and this can lead them to overlook important information about the person.

A third criticism is that the DSM-IV-TR may be gender-biased. Females are diagnosed as showing certain disorders much more frequently than males, and some critics suggest that this is because descriptions of such disorders seem to reflect society's views about women (sex-role stereotypes).

Finally, the DSM-IV-TR has been criticized because, as suggested by my neighbor Joe's actions, mental disorders occur on a continuum, not in discrete categories. People don't simply have a disorder or not have it; they may have it to various degrees, and show different aspects of it in varying proportions. Joe, for instance, has tendencies toward an obsessive-compulsive disorder, but is not showing this disorder fully—at least not yet! For this reason, many psychologists prefer a **dimensional approach** in which individuals are not simply assigned to specific categories, but rather are rated in many different dimensions, each relevant to a specific mental disorder. While many psychologists would prefer such an approach, and recognize the other potential problems with the DSM-IV-TR noted above, they continue to use it because of the benefits of having a single,

Dimensional approach: An approach to diagnosing mental disorders in which individuals are not simply assigned to specific categories, but rather are rated in many different dimensions, each relevant to a specific mental disorder.

TABLE 11.2 Clinical Scales of the MMPI-2

The MMPI-2 is designed to measure many aspects of personality related to psychological disorders.

Clinical Scale	Description of Disorder
Hypochondriasis	Excessive concern with bodily functions
Depression	Pessimism; hopelessness; slowing of action and thought
Hysteria	Development of physical disorders such as blindness, paralysis, and vomiting as an escape from emotional problems
Psychopathic deviance	Disregard for social customs; shallow emotions
Masculinity-femininity	Possession of traits and interests typically associated with the opposite sex
Paranoia	Suspiciousness; delusions of grandeur or persecution
Psychasthenia	Obsession; compulsions; fears; guilt; indecisiveness
Schizophrenia	Bizarre, unusual thoughts or behavior; withdrawal; hallucinations; delusions
Hypomania	Emotional excitement; flight of ideas; overactivity
Social introversion	Shyness; lack of interest in others; insecurity

widely used framework for describing and discussing mental disorders. Reflecting this fact, the DSM-IV-TR will serve as the basis for our discussions of various disorders throughout this chapter.

Psychological Assessment: Other Techniques for Assessing Mental Disorders

While the DSM-IV-TR is by far the most widely used framework for describing and identifying mental disorders, we should mention that others exist as well. One that is well validated and has been used by psychologists for many years is known as the **MMPI** (short for **Minnesota Multiphasic Personality Inventory**). This test was developed during the 1930s, but underwent a major revision in 1989 (Butcher, 1990). The current version, the MMPI-2, contains ten *clinical scales* and several *validity scales*. The clinical scales, which are summarized in Table 11.2, relate to various forms of mental disorder. Items included in each of these scales are ones that are answered differently by people who have been diagnosed as having this particular disorder and a comparison group of people who do *not* have the disorder. The validity scales are designed to determine whether, and to what extent, people are trying to "fake" their answers—for instance, whether they are trying to seem bizarre or, conversely, to give the impression that they are extremely "normal" and well adjusted. If people taking the test score high on these validity scales, their responses to the clinical scales must be interpreted with special caution.

Another test widely used to identify mental disorders is the **Millon Clinical Multiaxial Inventory** (MCMI; Millon, 1987, 1997). Items on this test correspond more closely than those on the MMPI to the categories of psychological disorders currently used by psychologists—the categories of the DSM-IV-TR. This makes the test especially useful to clinical psychologists, who must first identify an individual's problems before recommending specific forms of therapy.

Minnesota Multiphasic Personality Inventory (MMPI):
A psychological test widely used by psychologists to assess specific mental disorders.

Millon Clinical Multiaxial Inventory (MCMI):
A psychological test used in diagnosing the presence of specific mental disorders.

FIGURE 11.2
Oppositional Defiant Disorder
Disruptive behaviors are the most common reason why children are referred to psychologists for diagnosis and treatment.

One final point: How accurate are these tests in identifying various mental disorders? Recent findings suggest an encouraging answer: They are *highly* accurate. In fact, recent research comparing these tests with purely medical tests, and even MRI scans, indicates that the tests are just as accurate in predicting outcomes (Clay, 2006). Indeed, the power of these tests in successfully identifying various mental disorders seems to be so high that it even surprised many experts in the field. An important benefit of such tests is that they are efficient and less costly than assessments performed by psychiatrists and psychologists. In the current environment, where efforts to reduce medical costs has become a top priority for many companies and many individuals, this is an important benefit.

KEY QUESTIONS

- What is the DSM-IV-TR?
- In what ways is it an improvement over earlier versions?
- What other techniques for assessing mental disorders exist?

DISORDERS OF INFANCY, CHILDHOOD, AND ADOLESCENCE

Often, the problems people experience as adults are visible earlier in life, when they are children or adolescents. Recognition of this basic fact is one reason behind the increasing importance of a developmental perspective on mental disorders—the view that problems and difficulties experienced during childhood or adolescence can play an important role in the emergence of various disorders during adulthood. The DSM-IV-TR takes note of this fact, and lists a number of disorders that first emerge during childhood or adolescence. We'll consider several of these here.

Disruptive Behavior and Attention Deficit Disorders

Disruptive behaviors are the most common single reason why children are referred to psychologists for diagnosis and treatment. And such problems are quite common: As many as 10 percent of children may show such problems at some time or other. Disruptive behaviors are divided, by the DSM-IV-TR into two major categories: *oppositional defiant disorder* and *conduct disorder.*

Oppositional defiant disorder involves a pattern of behavior in which children have poor control of their emotions or have repeated conflicts with parents and other adults (e.g., teachers; see Figure 11.2). Children showing this pattern have problems getting along with others and, as a result, may start on a road that

Disruptive behaviors:
Childhood mental disorders involving poor control of impulses, conflict with other children and adults, and, in some cases, more serious forms of antisocial behavior.

leads them to more serious difficulties later in life, one of which may be *conduct disorder* (or CD). While oppositional defiant disorder usually starts when children are quite young (ages three to seven), conduct disorder begins somewhat later, often when children enter puberty. CD involves more serious antisocial behaviors that go beyond throwing tantrums or disobeying rules; it involves actions that are potentially harmful to the child, to others, or to property.

What are the causes of these disruptive patterns of behavior? Biological factors appear to play a role. Boys show such problems much more often than girls, thus suggesting a role for sex hormones, and some findings suggest that children who develop CD have unusually low levels of general arousal—and thus seem to crave the excitement that accompanies their disruptive behaviors (e.g., Raine, Venebles, & Williams, 1990). But psychological factors, too, play a role. Children with conduct disorder often show insecure attachment to their parents, and often live in negative environments involving poverty, large family size, and being placed in foster care (Biederman et al., 1990). In addition, their parents often use coercive child-rearing practices, which may actually encourage disruptive behavior (e.g., Campbell et al., 1986). Whatever the precise causes, it is clear that CD is a serious problem that can well pave the way to additional problems during adulthood.

Attention-Deficit/Hyperactivity Disorder (ADHD)

When you were in school, did you have a classmate who couldn't sit still? I did, and I remember how our teacher struggled to get Stuart to stay in his seat and pay attention to the lesson. Looking back, I'm now confident that Joseph suffered from **attention-deficit/hyperactivity disorder (ADHD)**—another important childhood mental disorder. Three patterns of ADHD exist: One in which children simply can't pay attention (inattention), another in which they show hyperactivity or impulsivity—they really *can't* sit still and can't restrain their impulses—and a third pattern that combines the two. Unfortunately, ADHD is *not* a problem that fades with the passage of time: 70 percent of children diagnosed with ADHD in elementary school still show signs of it when they are sixteen (Barkley et al., 1990).

The causes of ADHD appear, again, to be both biological and psychological. For instance, such factors as low birth rate, oxygen deprivation at birth, and alcohol consumption by expectant mothers have all been associated with ADHD (Streissguth, 1994). In addition, deficits in the reticular activating system (RAS) and in the frontal lobes may be linked to ADHD. With respect to psychological factors, risk factors seem to include parental overstimulation—parents who just can't seem to let their infants alone.

Fortunately, ADHD can be treated successfully with several drugs, all of which act as stimulants. *Ritalin* is the most frequently used, and it amplifies the impact of two neurotransmitters—norepinephrine and dopamine—in the brain. While taking this drug, children are better able to pay attention, and often become calmer and more in control of their own behavior. The effects of these medications last only four to five hours, so they must be taken quite frequently. Since Ritalin and other drugs produce potentially harmful side effects (e.g., decreased appetite, insomnia, headaches, increased blood pressure), they are definitely *not* an unmixed blessing. For this reason, many psychologists recommend treating ADHD not just with drugs (a purely medical approach), but also with *behavioral management programs* in which children are taught to listen to directions, to continue with tasks, to stay in their seat while in class, and other important skills.

Feeding and Eating Disorders

When I (Robert Baron) was in high school, the ideal female figure was one that could be described as *well-rounded*; curves were definitely in! Beginning in the mid-1960s, however, this standard of beauty changed drastically, shifting toward a

Attention-deficit/hyperactivity disorder (ADHD):
A childhood mental disorder in which children simply can't pay attention (inattention), show hyperactivity or impulsivity, or both of these symptoms.

FIGURE 11.3

Changing Ideals of Feminine Beauty: Do They Contribute to the Alarming Rise of Eating Disorders?

Until the 1960s, well-rounded female figures were considered attractive. After that time, however, a trend toward being *thin* developed and grew stronger (e.g., today's supermodels). Research findings suggest that this shift is one factor that has contributed, along with many others, to the rising incidence of eating disorders in recent decades.

much slimmer shape (see Figure 11.3). Yet despite this fact, a growing proportion of adults in the United States and other countries are actually overweight. Given this increasing gap between the image of personal beauty portrayed by the mass media and physical reality, it is not surprising that **feeding and eating disorders**—disturbances in eating behavior that involve maladaptive and unhealthy efforts to control body weight—are increasingly common. Although these obviously occur among adults (indeed, most people think of these as adult disorders), eating disorders often begin in childhood or adolescence, so it makes sense to consider them here, even though adult forms of these disorders are also classified separately on the DSM-IV-TR. In addition, the trend in recent decades has been for these disturbing disorders to start at earlier and earlier ages—as young as age eight (Nietze et al., 1998; Stice, 2002). Two eating disorders, **anorexia nervosa** and **bulimia nervosa,** have received most attention.

■ Anorexia nervosa: Yes, you *can* be too slim.

Anorexia nervosa involves an intense and excessive fear of gaining weight, coupled with refusal to maintain a normal body weight. In other words, people with this disorder relentlessly pursue the goal of being thin, no matter what this does to their health. They often have distorted perceptions of their own bodies, believing that they are much heavier than they really are. As a result of such fears and distorted perceptions, they starve themselves to the point where their weight drops to dangerously low levels.

Why do people with this disorder have such an intense fear of becoming fat? Important clues are provided by the fact that anorexia nervosa is far more common among females than males. This has led many researchers to propose that because many societies place greater emphasis on physical attractiveness for females

Feeding and eating disorders: Disturbances in eating behavior that involve maladaptive and unhealthy efforts to control body weight.

Anorexia nervosa: An eating disorder involving intense fears of gaining weight coupled with refusal to maintain normal body weight.

Bulimia nervosa: An eating disorder in which individuals engage in recurrent episodes of binge eating followed by some form of purging.

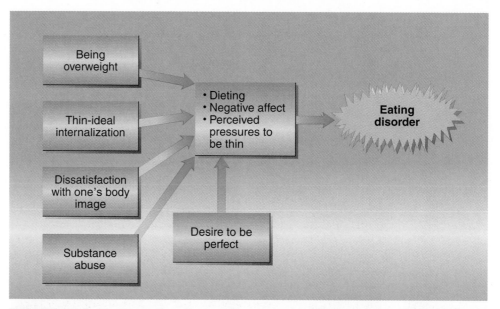

FIGURE II.4
Factors that Contribute to Eating Disorders
As shown here, several factors—including being overweight, internalizing the ideal of being thin, being dissatisfied with one's body image, a tendency to seek perfection, and substance abuse—contribute to the occurrence of serious eating disorders. Together, these factors cause many people to diet and to experience strong pressures to be thin, and these actions, in turn, can lead to anorexia nervosa and bulimia. Source: Based on suggestions by Stice, 2001.

than for males, adolescents and young women feel tremendous pressure to live up to the images of beauty shown in the mass media—to be as thin as the models who are held up as paragons of female desirability. If they are not this thin, they reason, they will be viewed as unattractive. In other words, many young women show a pattern known as *thin-ideal internalization*—they cognitively accept socially defined ideals of attractiveness which emphasize being extremely thin, and engage in behaviors designed to attain this ideal, such as dieting.

■ Bulimia: The binge–purge cycle.

If you found anorexia nervosa disturbing, you may find a second eating disorder—*bulimia nervosa*—even more unsettling. In this disorder, individuals engage in recurrent episodes of binge eating—eating huge amounts of food within short periods of time—followed by some kind of compensatory behavior designed to prevent weight gain. This can involve self-induced vomiting, the misuse of laxatives, fasting, or excessive exercise.

The causes of bulimia nervosa appear to be similar to those of anorexia nervosa: Once again, the "thin is beautiful" ideal seems to play an important role (e.g., Thompson, 1992; Williamson, Cubic, & Gleaves, 1993). Another, and related, factor is the desire to be perfect in all respects, including those relating to physical beauty. Recent findings indicate that women who are high on this trait are at risk for developing bulimia, especially if they perceive themselves to be overweight (Joiner et al., 1997). And in fact, bulimics—like anorexics—do tend to perceive themselves as much heavier than they really are (Williamson, Cubic, & Gleaves, 1993).

Overall, existing evidence indicates that both anorexia nervosa and bulimia can be understood in terms of the factors shown in Figure 11.4: Being overweight, being dissatisfied with one's body image, a desire to be perfect, substance abuse, and the thin-ideal internalization put individuals (especially young women) at risk for serious eating disorders, in part because these factors increase tendencies to experience negative affect, to diet, and to experience strong pressures to be thin

(Stice, 2002; Thompson & Stice, 2001). In short, the "thin is beautiful" stereotype encouraged by the entertainment and advertising industries may contribute to tragic results for many people.

Fortunately, some interventions, such as showing individuals how photos in magazines have been altered to make the models appear thinner—can help reduce thin-ideal internalization (Stormer & Thompson, 1998). But eating disorders remain a serious problem, and one that appears to be spreading throughout the world.

Autism: A Pervasive Developmental Disorder

Of all the childhood disorders, the ones that may be most disturbing of all are described on the DSM-IV-TR as **pervasive development disorders.** Such disorders involve lifelong impairment in mental or physical functioning, and among these, the one that has received most attention is **autistic disorder** (or autism). This term is derived from the Greek word *autos* (self), and is an apt description for children with this disorder, for they seem to be preoccupied with themselves and live in an almost totally private world. Children with this disorder show three major characteristics: marked impairments in establishing social interactions with others (e.g., they don't use nonverbal behaviors such as eye contact, don't develop peer relationships, and don't seem to be interested in other people); nonexistent or poor language skills; and stereotyped, repetitive patterns of behavior or interests. In short, children with autistic disorder seem to live in a world of their own. They make little contact with others, either through words or nonverbal gestures, show little interest in them, and when they do notice them, they often seem to treat them as objects rather than as people.

Recently, there has been a tremendous upsurge of public interest in autism, and for a very good reason: Major studies seemed to suggest that the frequency of this mental disorder was increasing tremendously. For instance, one large-scale study that was quoted frequently on the evening news and in leading newspapers suggested that the number of children with this disorder had almost tripled between 1987 and 1998, at least in the state of California (California Department of Developmental Services, 1999). If this were true, it would certainly be alarming and justify newspaper headlines such one in the *New York Times* that called attention to "A mysterious upsurge in the prevalence of autism" (October 20, 2002). So, are we really experiencing a major rise in the frequency of this serious mental disorders?

Many psychologists (e.g., Gernsbacher, Dawson, & Goldsmith, 2005,) urge caution, and for a very good reason: The description of autism in the DSM-IV and DSM-IV-TR has been broadened so as to include a much wider range of behavior. For instance, in earlier versions of the DSM, major deficits in language development were required before a child was diagnosed as showing autism. In later versions, in contrast, "difficulty in sustaining a conversation" or "lack of social imitative play" were added. Broadening the definition of a mental disorder—or almost anything else—will generally produce an increase in its frequency. For instance, suppose that we described as "tall" only people seventy-six inches or taller. A relatively small number of people would meet this criterion. If, instead, we described as "tall" anyone seventy inches or taller, a much higher number would meet the criterion. In the same way, broadening the description of autism has resulted in many more children being diagnosed as showing this condition! So yes, autism is a very serious mental disorder, but is it rising alarmingly? Many psychologists would suggest that we do not have any convincing evidence for this conclusion.

■ **The roots of autism: Genetic factors, children's theory of mind, and the role of mirror neurons.**

Autistic children often seem to live in a world of their own—they seem unable to forge the personal bonds with others that most children do effortlessly. When

Pervasive development disorders:
Disorders that involve lifelong impairment in mental or physical functioning.

Autistic disorder:
A serious childhood mental disorder involving major impairments in establishing social interactions with others, nonexistent or poor language skills, and stereotyped, repetitive patterns of behavior or interests.

smiled at by adults, they don't smile back, and they don't look in the directions where others are gazing. In short, they seem sadly isolated from basic forms of human contact. What are the origins of this heart-wrenching separation from others? One possibility is that autistic children have deficits in their *theory of mind*—their understanding of their own and other's mental states (see Chapter 7). Autistic children seem unable to realize that other people can have access to different sources of information than they do, and are unable to predict the beliefs of others from information that should allow them to make such predictions (e.g., Shulman et al., 1995). In addition, genetic factors may play a role. Twin studies show a higher concordance rate for identical than for fraternal twins (e.g., Rutter et al., 1990). Psychological factors also contribute; autistic children often suffer from attentional deficits—they fail to pay attention to such social stimuli as their mother's face and voice, or to others' calling their own names (Osterling & Dawson, 1994). Perhaps the most intriguing findings of all relate to the discovery of what are known as **mirror neurons** (Dingfelder, 2005). These are neurons that seem to play a key role in imitation—in the ability to match the actions of others. Imitation, in turn, seems to be important in forming bonds with others, so if this system fails to operate normally, children don't form these connections and may be started on the road to autism. Recent findings indicate that these neurons—the mirror system that they produced—are less active in autistic children than they are in other people (Theoret et al., 2005). For instance, when autistic people watch hand movement made by other people, their mirror-neuron areas are less active than those of normal people. And when they imitate the facial actions of others because they are told to do so, they don't use their brains' mirror system, which would allow them to do this effortlessly. Instead, they consciously analyze the actions and imitate them by doing this. In sum, autism, like many other mental disorders, seems to have multiple roots, and although this means that we can't point to one single cause for their occurrence, this fact also suggests that there be many ways to treat or alleviate them. That will be the theme of Chapter 12, which focuses on these forms of treatment.

KEY QUESTIONS

- What is oppositional defiant disorder? Conduct disorder?
- What is attention-deficit/hyperactivity disorder?
- What are anorexia nervosa and bulimia nervosa?
- What is autistic disorder?
- What are mirror neurons and what possible role do they play in autism?

MOOD DISORDERS: THE DOWNS AND UPS OF LIFE

Have you ever felt truly "down in the dumps"—sad, blue, and dejected? How about the opposite—have you ever felt so good that you seemed to be "floating on air"? You can probably bring such experiences easily to mind, because everyone has swings in mood or emotional state. For most of us, these swings are usually moderate in scope so that periods of deep despair and wild elation are rare. Some people, however, experience much wider and prolonged swings in their emotional states. Their highs are higher, their lows are lower, and they spend more time in these states than most people. Such people are described as suffering from **mood disorders.**

Depressive Disorders: Probing the Depths of Despair

Unless we lead a truly charmed existence, our daily lives expose us to some events that make us feel sad or disappointed. A poor grade, breaking up with one's

Mirror neurons:
Neurons in the brain that play a key role in imitation of others' behavior. These neurons may be important in the development of autism.

Mood disorders:
Psychological disorders in which individuals experience swings in their emotional states that are much more extreme and prolonged than is true of most people.

romantic partner, failure to get a promotion—these and many other events tip our emotional balance toward sadness. When do such reactions constitute depression? Most psychologist agree that several criteria are useful for reaching this decision.

First, people suffering from **depression** experience truly profound unhappiness and they experience it much of each day. Second, people experiencing depression report that they have lost interest in all the usual pleasures of life. Eating, sex, sports, and hobbies all fail to provide the enjoyment they did at other times. Third, people suffering from depression often experience significant weight loss (when not dieting) or gain. Depression may also involve a feeling of fatigue, insomnia, feelings of worthlessness, an inability to think or concentrate, and recurrent thoughts of death or about suicide. When individuals experience five or more of these symptoms at once during the same two-week period, they are classified by the DSM-IV-TR as showing a *major depressive episode* (see Figure 11.5).

While the symptoms described above are relatively clear and easy to spot, there is one important complication: Many men who are suffering from depression do *not* show these symptoms. Because they view "feeling sad" as a sign of weakness or laziness, they mask their feelings and often show anger instead of despair. Anger, after all, can be "managed," while sadness is something "real men" should not feel—or, at any rate, show openly. As a result, large numbers of men suffering from depression don't realize that this is their problem. Further, they are often so good at concealing their depression that even psychologists may fail to detect it (Healy, 2006). This is one reason why efforts are now under way to add "male-based" depression to the next version of the DSM—the DSM-V. Whether that does or does not happen, though, it is clear that men and women may show different symptoms when experiencing depression, just as they often show different symptoms in response to physical illnesses, for example, heart disease.

Unfortunately, depression is very common in both sexes. In fact, it is experienced by 21.3 percent of women and 12.7 percent of men at some time during their lives (Kessler et al., 1994). This nearly two-to-one gender difference in rate of experiencing depression has been reported in many studies (see Culbertson, 1997), especially those conducted in wealthy, developed countries, so it appears to be a real one. Why does it exist? As noted by Strickland (1992), several factors account for this finding, including the fact that females have traditionally had lower status, power, and income; must worry more than males about their personal safety; and are much more often than males the victims of sexual harassment and assaults. Gender differences in rates of depression may also stem from the fact that females are more willing to admit to such feelings than are males or more likely than men to remember such feelings (Wilhelm & Parker, 1994).

Sad to relate, episodes of major depression are not isolated events; most people who experience one such episode also experience others during their lives—an average of five or six (Winokur, 1986). And other experience what is known as *double depression*—they recover from major depression, but continue to experience a depressed mood (*dysthymic disorder*) or, in some cases, unusual irritability.

Bipolar Disorders: Riding the Emotional Roller-Coaster

If depression is the emotional chasm of life, then **bipolar disorder** is its emotional roller-coaster. People suffering from bipolar disorder experience wide swings in mood. They move, over varying periods of time, between deep depression and an emotional state known as *mania,* in which they are extremely excited, elated, and energetic. During manic periods, such people speak rapidly, show a sharply decreased need for sleep, jump from one idea or activity to another, and show excessive involvement in pleasurable activities that have a high potential for harmful consequences. For example, they may engage in wild buying sprees or make extremely risky investments. Clearly, bipolar disorders are very disruptive not only to the individuals who experience them but to other people in their lives as well.

FIGURE 11.5
Depression: The Emotional Chasm of Life
People experiencing a *major depressive episode* show such symptoms as an intensely negative mood, loss of interest in all the things that usually give them pleasure, significant loss (or gain) of weight, intense feelings of fatigue, and insomnia. Truly, they are in the depths of despair.

Depression:
A mood disorder in which individuals experience extreme unhappiness, lack of energy, and several related symptoms.

Bipolar disorder:
A mood disorder in which individuals experience very wide swings in mood, from deep depression to wild elation.

The Causes of Depression: Its Biological and Psychological Roots

Depression tends to run in families (Egeland et al., 1987) and is about four times more likely to occur in both members of identical twins than in both members of fraternal twins (Bowman & Nernberger, 1993). Overall, however, existing evidence suggests that genetic factors play a stronger role in bipolar than in unipolar depression. Other findings suggest that mood disorders may involve abnormalities in brain biochemistry. One possibility is that low levels of serotonin (an important neurotransmitter) may allow other neurotransmitters such as dopamine and norepinephrine to swing out of control, and this, in turn, leads to extreme changes in mood. However, this is just one possibility, and at present the precise nature of the neurochemical mechanisms that result in depression is uncertain.

Several psychological factors have been found to play a role in depression. One of these is **learned helplessness** (Seligman, 1975)—beliefs on the part of individuals that they have no control over their own outcomes. Such views often develop after exposure to situations in which such lack of control is present, but then generalize to other situations where individuals' fate *is* at least partly in their hands. One result of such feelings of helplessness seems to be depression (e.g., Seligman et al., 1988).

Another psychological mechanism that plays a key role in depression is negative views about oneself (Beck, 1976; Beck et al., 1979). Individuals suffering from depression often possess negative *self-schemas*—negative conceptions of their own traits, abilities, and behavior. As a result, they tend to be highly sensitive to criticism from others (Joiner, Alfano, & Metalsky, 1993). Since they are more likely to notice and remember such negative information, their feelings of worthlessness strengthen, and when they are exposed to various stressors (e.g., the break-up of a romantic relationship, a failure at work), their thinking become distorted in important and self-defeating ways. Depressed people begin to see neutral or even pleasant events in a negative light—for instance, they interpret a compliment from a friend as insincere, or someone's being late for an appointment as a sign of rejection. These distortions in thinking make it difficult for depressed people to make realistic judgments about events, and they begin to engage in thinking characterized by automatic, repetitive, and negative thoughts about the self, the world, and the future (what Beck describes as the *negative cognitive triad*). In sum, depressed people see themselves as inadequate and worthless, feel that they can't cope with the demands made on them, and dread the future that, they believe, will bring more of the same.

Another factor—and one that seems to play a very important role in depression—is the tendency to *ruminate*—to think repeatedly about negative events, disappointments, and in general the "dark side of life." People who tend to ruminate often drive others away with their negative views of life. As a result, when they reach out for help, no one is there (Nolen-Hoeksema & Davis, 2004). In fact, the tendency to ruminate is a very strong predictor of major depression: The more people ruminate, the more likely they are to develop depression at a later time (Law, 2005). Some researchers (e.g., Nolen-Hoeksema, 2005) report that people who tend to ruminate are more than four times as likely to experience major depression than people who do not ruminate. These findings indicate that ruminating is not merely a result of depression—it is one cause of it. (An overview of the factors that influence depression is presented in Figure 11.6.)

But why, you might be wondering, do individuals engage in rumination? Why dwell on the negative side of life? There are many reasons, but among the most important are tendencies toward perfectionism (wanting to be perfect), and an excessive focus on relationships—to the point where relationships with others are more important to some people than anything else and they will even sacrifice their own feelings or well-being for the sake of the relationships. As a result, such people experience frequent disappointments and frustrations, and these reactions

Learned helplessness:
Beliefs on the part of individuals that they cannot influence the outcomes they experience.

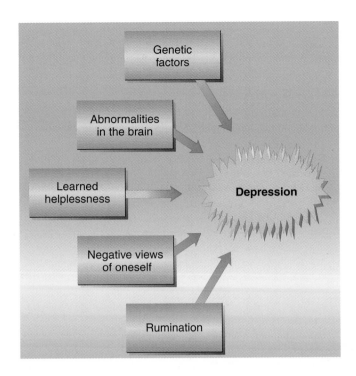

FIGURE 11.6
Factors that Play a Role in Depression
As shown here, many factors play a role in depression—biological factors, genetic factors, and several cognitive factors (e.g., the tendency to ruminate).

start them on the road toward rumination. In addition, people who ruminate believe that they face chronic, uncontrollable sources of stress and have a history of traumatic events in their lives—rejection by a spouse or lover, loss of several jobs, the death of people they love. Fortunately, the tendency to ruminate *can* be counteracted. What steps can *you* take to reduce or avoid this potentially dangerous pattern? See the **Psychology Lends a Hand** section on page 442 for some concrete suggestions.

■ Suicide: When life becomes unbearable.

Hopelessness, despair, negative views about oneself—these are key features of depression. Given such reactions it is not surprising that many persons suffering from this disorder seek a drastic solution—*suicide,* or taking of their own lives. In the United States, about 40,000 people commit suicide each year. This figure may be an underestimate because many people who die in high-risk behaviors, such as speeding on the highway or using dangerous drugs, may have intended to end their own lives. In addition, more than 300,000 people attempt suicide but don't succeed (Andreason & Black, 1995). More than two times as many women as men attempt suicide, but men are three to four times more likely to succeed when they take this course of action, mainly because men use no-fail methods such as jumping from high places, guns, or hanging; women tend to use less certain tactics, such as poison or drug overdose (Kaplan & Sadock, 1991). Also, as we noted above, men tend to conceal their depression and so are much less likely than are women to get help in dealing with it (Healy, 2006). Suicide is the tenth most frequent cause of death in the United States. Suicide rates vary with age and by nation. The highest rates occur among older people, but suicide has been on the rise among young people and is now, disturbingly, high even among teenagers. Why do people seek suicide? Notes left by people who commit suicide, and information provided by people who attempt suicide, suggest that they do so for many different reasons. However, problems with relationships seem to head the list.

Suicide varies across different cultures. In some northern European countries and Japan, the suicide rate is as high as 25 per 100,000 inhabitants. In countries with strong religious prohibitions against suicide, such as Greece and Ireland, the rate is about 6 per 100,000. In the United States, it is about 12 per 100,000. In the

PSYCHOLOGY LENDS A HAND

Stop Ruminating *Now*—and Feel Better Soon!

As we have just seen, the tendency to ruminate—to think long and hard about the negative events in our lives—often plays an important role in depression. In fact, once individuals begin to ruminate, they may start down a very slippery slope in which they find it increasingly difficult to escape from their own dark and gloomy thoughts. There *is* hope, however. Research on rumination and related "mental traps" indicates that rumination is not necessarily a one-way street. On the contrary, it can be greatly reduced by following several relatively simple steps. Here are ones that have been shown to be effective:

1. **Distraction.** It is hard to focus on past setbacks, disappointments, and failures if, instead, other thoughts fill your mind. So, one way of stopping rumination cold is to begin thinking about other things—especially positive experiences and events. For instance, if you ever find yourself thinking about painful rejection by another person (e.g., a romantic partner, a spouse, a family member), resist the temptation to dwell on this distressing experience. Instead, think about other things—activities you enjoy, instances in which you have *not* been rejected, exciting projects on which you are working. The key point is to get your own mind *off* unpleasant and negative events. To the extent you do, rumination can be effectively blocked.

2. **Reevaluate your expectations of others and your perceptions of negative events.** In other words, ask yourself, "Did I expect too much?" and "Were these events truly negative or devastating as I assumed?" Doing this can put things in perspective and suggest that the "dark side" of life is really not all that dark—there is almost always room for hope mixed in with the disappointments. By readjusting our expectations and our perceptions, we can come to see past events in a more balanced way—as offering benefits as well as costs—and as

something we can, in fact, survive. This, in turn, can help stop the cycle toward deeper and darker rumination.

3. **Develop multiple sources of self-esteem.** Many people begin to ruminate because their self-esteem is tied closely to one activity or one source of support. For instance, women tend to be somewhat more prone to rumination than men because they tend to place greater importance on personal relationships (Law, 2005). As a result, disappointments in these relationships start a cycle in which the women begin to question their own self-worth and competence, and that, in turn, can lead quickly to rumination. One effective way to prevent this cycle is to develop multiple sources of self-esteem and gratification aside from relationships. In other words, taking pride in accomplishments other than those relating to loved ones and family can help protect self-esteem by assuring that it derives from several different sources. This, too, can help reduce the tendency to ruminate.

4. **Take actions to solve various problems.** People who ruminate often sit around thinking about problems in their lives that are causing them distress, but don't take action to directly address or solve these problems. Even small steps in this direction can help, because they shift attention away from rumination over the distress caused by the problems and into efforts to develop strategies to deal with them. In other words, in such instances, *action* can help to change *thought*—and if this change reduces the tendency to ruminate, that is a very positive outcome.

One word of caution: All the techniques described here are best applied with the help of a trained psychologist. So although individuals can certainly help themselves toward the goal of reduced tendencies to ruminate, it is wise to do so in the context of ongoing therapy—one of the kinds we'll describe in detail in Chapter 12.

United States, suicide is more common among people of European descent than among those of African descent, but this gap has narrowed in the past twenty years (Bongar, 1991). Suicide rates are low among Americans of Hispanic descent, but is high among Native American males—as high as 24 per 100,000. Perhaps most disturbing of all, suicide rates have increased sharply among adolescents in recent decades and are now about 15 per 100,000 for boys and 3 per 100,000 for girls (Robins & Rutter, 1990). Indeed, suicide is the third leading cause of death for adolescents fifteen to nineteen years old, accounting for fully 12 percent of all deaths in this age group (Garland & Zigler, 1993).

Adolescents who commit suicide often do so impulsively, soon after a highly stressful event—for instance, being "dumped" by a boyfriend or girlfriend, being humiliated in some other way in public, failing a major exam in school. Suicide pacts, too, play a role: teenage lovers agree to kill themselves if they can't be together, and the two young men who killed more than a dozen of their teachers and classmates at Columbine High School in Colorado in 1999 had agreed, in advance, to take their own lives. From every perspective, suicide is a tragic event. Can anything be done to prevent it? Research by psychologists suggest that the answer is "yes." See the Making Psychology Part of Your Life section on page 462 for a summary of these steps.

KEY QUESTIONS

- What are the major symptoms of depressions? Of bipolar disorder?
- What factors play a role in the occurrence of mood disorders?
- What is rumination and what role does it play in depression?

ANXIETY DISORDERS: WHEN DREAD DEBILITATES

At one time or another, we all experience **anxiety**—a diffuse or vague concern that something unpleasant will soon occur. If such feelings become intense and persist for long periods of time, however, they can constitute another important form of mental disorder. Such **anxiety disorders** take several different forms (see Zinberg & Barlow, 1995).

Phobias: Excessive Fear of Specific Objects or Situations

Most people express some fear of snakes, heights, violent storms, and buzzing insects such as bees or wasps. Since all of these can pose real threats to our safety, such reactions are adaptive, up to a point. If such fears become excessive in that they cause intense emotional distress and interfere significantly with everyday activities, they constitute **phobias,** one important type of anxiety disorder.

While many different phobias exist, most seem to involve fear of animals (e.g., bees, spiders, snakes), the natural environment (e.g., thunder, darkness, wind), blood illness and injections (e.g., blood, needles, pain, contamination), and various situations (e.g., enclosed places, travel, empty rooms). One very common phobia is that of snakes. We seem to possess a strong tendency to easily learn to fear snakes (e.g., Ohman & Mineka, 2001). In fact, many studies indicate that we may possess genetically determined tendencies to notice snakes, to fear them, and to respond negatively to them (e.g., Ohman & Mineka, 2003). For instance, when photos of snakes are shown in such a way that people can't tell what they have seen (the photos of snakes are *masked* by another visual stimulus presented immediately after the snake photos), they still show signs of emotional arousal to the snake photos (Ohman & Soares, 1994). Similarly, if a snake is shown among other, more neutral stimuli (e.g., pictures of flowers), it is detected more quickly than other stimuli in the same context (Ohman, Flykt, & Esteves, 2001). Together, such findings suggest that we may possess a biologically determined module in our brains for fear of snakes. This module has evolved since noticing and fearing snakes is beneficial for our survival (Ohman & Mineka, 2001). As Ohman and Minkea (2003) put it, this and related modules might constitute the basic ways in which our brains represent *evil* (see Figure 11.7 on page 444).

Another common phobia is *social phobia*—excessive fear of situations in which a person might be evaluated and perhaps embarrassed. It is estimated that 13 percent of people living in the United States have had a social phobia at some time in their lives, and almost 8 percent report having had such fears during the past year (Kessler et al., 1994).

It is interesting to note that social phobias take different forms in different cultures—a clear illustration of the powerful impact of culture on mental disturbances. For instance, in Western countries, social phobias focus on being embarrassed in front of others or being rejected by them. In several Asian cultures (e.g., Japan, Korea), they focus on fears of having an external appearance that is somehow offending to others (see Jilek 2000, 2006). In other words, in these cultures

Anxiety:
Increased arousal accompanied by generalized feelings of fear or apprehension.

Anxiety disorders:
Psychological disorders taking several different forms, but which are all related to a generalized feeling of anxiety.

Phobias:
Fears that become excessive in that they cause intense emotional distress and interfere significantly with everyday activities.

FIGURE 11.7
Fear of Snakes: A Genetically Determined Phobia?
How do you react to this photo? If you are like many people, with feelings of fear. A large body of evidence suggests that we possess strong tendencies to notice snakes, to fear them, and to respond negatively to them—tendencies that may involve an evolved fear module.

what people fear is not so much embarrassment as looking bad in ways that others find disturbing or unpleasant. In short, phobias related to social situations exist across cultures, but they take different forms depending on the values and traditions of each society.

What are the causes of phobias? One possibility involves the process of *classical conditioning*, described in Chapter 5. Through such learning, stimuli that could not initially elicit strong emotional reactions can often come to do so. For example, an intense fear of buzzing sounds, such as those made by bees, may be acquired by an individual after being stung by a bee or wasp. In the past, the buzzing sound was a neutral stimulus that produced little or no reaction. The pain of being stung, however, is an unconditioned stimulus, and as a result of being closely paired with it, the buzzing sound acquires the capacity to evoke strong fear (e.g., Mulkens, deJong, & Merckelbach, 1996).

Recent findings, however, also suggest that a sense of control over the events that happen to us also plays an important role in the development of phobias, and fear generally (Dingfelder, 2006). For instance, in one well-known study (Mineka et al., 1984), rats heard a tone and then, shortly afterward, received mild shocks to their feet. Some of the rats could stop the shock—control it—by stepping on a ledge in their cages; others could not. Later, when the warning tone was sounded, those who could control the shock by stepping on the ledge showed less tendency to stop and freeze—a typical reaction of rats and many other animals to intense fear. One interpretation of these findings is that the rats who knew they could control their own exposure to shocks were, in fact, less fearful. As we'll see in Chapter 12, this principle of giving people a sense of control now plays an important role in therapy designed to counteract phobias.

Panic Disorder and Agoraphobia

The intense fears associated with phobias are triggered by specific objects or situations. Some individuals, in contrast, experience intense, terrifying anxiety that is *not* activated by a specific event or situation. Such *panic attacks* are the hallmark of **panic disorder**—periodic, unexpected attacks of intense, terrifying anxiety, known as panic attacks. Panic attacks come on suddenly, reach peak intensity within a few minutes, and may last for hours (e.g., Barlow, 1988). They leave the people who experience them feeling as if they are about to die or are losing their minds. Among the specific symptoms of panic attacks are a racing heart, sweating, dizziness, nausea, chills, and trembling; palpitations, pounding heart; feelings of unreality; fear of losing control; fear of dying; numbness or tingling sensation; chills or hot flashes.

Although panic attacks often seem to occur out of the blue, in the absence of any specific triggering event, they often take place in specific situations. In that case, panic disorder is said to be associated with **agoraphobia**—intense fear of open spaces, being in public, and traveling—or, commonly, having a panic attack while being away from home! People suffering from panic disorder with agoraphobia often experience anticipatory anxiety—they are terrified of becoming afraid.

What causes panic attacks? Existing evidence indicates that both biological factors and cognitive factors play a role. With respect to biological factors, it has been found that there is a genetic component in this disorder: About 50 percent of people with panic disorder have relatives with who have it, too (Barlow, 1988). In addition, PET scans of the brains of people who suffer from panic attacks suggest

Panic disorder:
Periodic, unexpected attacks of intense, terrifying anxiety, known as panic attacks.

Agoraphobia:
Intense fear of specific situations in which individuals suspect that help will not be available should they experience an incapacitating or embarrassing event.

that even in the nonpanic state, their brains may be functioning differently from those of other people (see Reiman et al., 1989). A portion of the brainstem, the **locus coeruleus** (LC), may play a key role in panic experiences. This area seems to function as a primitive "alarm system," and stimulating it artificially in animals results in paniclike behavior (Gorman et al., 1989). It seems possible that in people who experience panic attacks, the LC may be hypersensitive to certain stimuli (e.g., lactic acid, a natural by-product of exercise), and as a result, they may experience intense fear in situations where other people do not (e.g., Papp et al., 1993). No conclusive evidence on this mechanism yet exists, but it seems worthy of further study.

Another factor is cigarette smoking. Research findings indicate that in the United States, 40.4 percent of patients with panic disorder smoke cigarettes—a much higher proportion than in the general population. Further, this figure is higher than the proportion of smokers among people with other mental disorders (McCabe et al., 2004). Further, among lifetime smokers, 7.6 percent show signs of panic disorder, while among nonsmokers the figure is only 2.4 percent (Zvolensky & Bernstein, 2005). Does this mean that smoking causes panic attacks? Not at all! What it does suggest is that people who experience high levels of anxiety often engage in behavior they believe will reduce this anxiety, and many smokers believe that smoking will produce such effects. It may also indicate that both smoking and the tendency to develop panic disorder are related to underlying factors, such as a tendency to experience negative moods or feelings. In any case, one thing is clear: People who smoke are indeed more likely to experience panic disorder than those who do not (see Figure 11.8).

Cognitive factors, too, play a role in panic attacks. People suffering from this disorder tend to show a pattern in which they tend to interpret bodily sensations as being more dangerous than they really are—for instance, they perceive palpitations as a sign of a heart attack—and so experience anxiety, which itself induces further bodily changes and sensations (Barlow, 1988, 1993). In sum, as is true of virtually all mental disorders, panic disorder, too, stems from many different contributing factors.

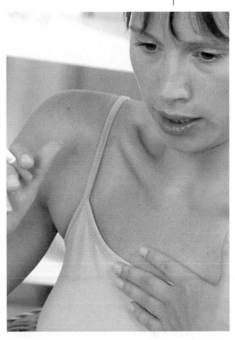

FIGURE 11.8
One More Reason Not to Smoke
Research findings indicate that panic disorder is more common among smokers than among nonsmokers. While there is no conclusive evidence that smoking actually causes panic disorders, the fact that the smoking and panic disorder tend to co-occur provides yet another reason to avoid becoming a smoker.

Obsessive-Compulsive Disorder: Behaviors and Thoughts outside One's Control

Have you ever left your home, gone halfway down the street, and then returned to see if you really locked the door or turned off the stove? Have you ever worried about catching a disease by touching infected people or objects? Most of us have had such experiences, but some people experience intense anxiety about them. They have disturbing thoughts or images about such events that they cannot get out of their minds (*obsessions*) unless they perform some action or ritual that somehow reassures them and helps to break this cycle (*compulsions*). Persons who have such experiences may be experiencing **obsessive-compulsive disorder,** another important type of anxiety disorder. What kind of disturbing thoughts or images do such people have? Among the most common are fear of dirt or germs, or of touching infected people or objects; disgust over body waste or secretions; undue concern that they have not done a job adequately, even though they know quite well that they have; and fear of having antireligious or sexual thoughts. Common compulsions—actions people perform to neutralize obsessions—include repetitive hand-washing and other kinds of cleaning (see Figure 11.9), checking doors or windows repeatedly, counting objects a precise number of times or repeating an action a specific number of times; and hoarding old mail, newspapers, and other useless objects.

What is the cause of such reactions? We all have repetitious thoughts occasionally. For example, after watching a film containing disturbing scenes of violence, we

Locus coeruleus (LC):
A portion of the brainstem that appears to play a key role in panic experiences.

Obsessive-compulsive disorder:
An anxiety disorder in which individuals have recurrent, disturbing thoughts (obsessions) they can't prevent unless they engage in specific behaviors (compulsions).

FIGURE 11.9
Obsessive-Compulsive Disorder
Like the person shown in this cartoon, individuals who develop *obsessive-compulsive disorder* often engage in actions designed to help eliminate anxiety-provoking thoughts—for instance, thoughts about dirt and avoiding its harmful effects. Reproduced by permission of Harley Schwadron.

"YOU WON'T GET ME to SIT ON THE COUCH AND DISCUSS MY OBSESSION UNTIL I STRAIGHTEN THINGS UP, DR. HUNTER."

Consistent (global and local level match)		
H	H	TTTTTTTTT
H	H	T
H H H H H		T
H	H	T
H	H	T

Inconsistent (global and local level do not match)		
T	T	H H H H H
T	T	H
T T T T		H
T	T	H
T	T	H

FIGURE 11.10
Perceptual Style and Obsessive-Compulsive Disorder
Because they tend to focus on small details, people with obsessive-compulsive disorder respond more slowly when asked to name large (global) letters when these letters are composed of different smaller (local) letters than when the large and small letters match.
Source: Based on information in Yovel, Revell, & Mineak, 2005.

may find ourselves thinking about these over and over again. Most of us soon manage to distract ourselves from such unpleasant thoughts. But individuals who develop obsessive-compulsive disorder are unable to do so. They are made anxious by their obsessive thoughts, yet they can't dismiss them readily from their minds. Moreover, they have had experiences—for instance, embarrassment—suggesting to them that some thoughts are so dangerous they must be avoided at all costs. As a result, they become even more anxious, and the cycle builds. Only by performing specific actions can they ensure their "safety" and reduce this anxiety. Therefore, they engage in complex repetitive rituals (e.g., hand-washing, checking things over and over again) that can gradually grow to fill most of their day. Since these rituals do generate reductions in anxiety, the tendency to perform them grows stronger. Unless they receive effective outside help, such people have little chance of escaping from their self-constructed, anxiety-ridden prisons.

Another factor, uncovered in recent research, relates to basic ways in which we perceive the world around us. Individuals who develop obsessive-compulsive disorder often show a strong tendency to focus on small details—to see the trees rather than the forest. As a result, they notice that tiny bit of dust or worry about some trivial problem, such as the possibility that they left the lights on when they left their home. Most other people, in contrast, see the "bigger picture" and avoid these obsessive thoughts, or experience them only in passing. Direct evidence for this perceptual basis of obsessive-compulsive disorder is provided by research conducted by Yovel, Revelle, and Mineka (2005).

These researchers asked a large group of students to complete psychological tests designed to measure obsessive-compulsive disorder. Then, they asked the students to perform a task in which they saw letters on a computer screen. The letters—for instance, H or T—were composed of smaller letters, and the small letters could be consistent or inconsistent with the large ones. For instance, a large letter H could be made up of small Hs (the large and small letters were consistent), or small Ts (the large and small letters are not consistent; see Figure 11.10). Their task was pressing a key to indicate which letter was presented, and further, on different trials to identify either the large letters (global level) or the small ones (the local level). It was predicted that people showing obsessive-compulsive disorder (or tendencies toward it) would experience more interference between the small (local) letters and the large (global) ones. In other words, because of their tendency to focus on details, they would find it hard to ignore the small letters when naming the large ones; this is known as a *local interference effect*. That's exactly what was found: The higher individuals scored on the test of obsessive-compulsive disorder, the worse their performance when interference existed— when the large letters were composed of different small letters. This suggests that a basic tendency to focus on details and to see the "trees" instead of the "forest" may be one factor that predisposes specific people toward developing obsessive-compulsive disorder.

Post-traumatic Stress Disorder

Imagine that you are sleeping peacefully in your own bed when suddenly the ground under your home heaves and shakes, and you are thrown to the floor. Once awakened, you find yourself surrounded by the sounds of objects, walls, and even entire buildings crashing to the ground—accompanied by shrieks of fear and pain from your neighbors or your own family. This is precisely the kind of experience reported by many people during earthquakes.

FIGURE 11.11
Traumatic Events: One Cause of Psychological Disorders
Some individuals who experience traumatic events such as Hurricane Katrina, which flooded New Orleans in 2005, develop post-traumatic stress disorder: they show heightened arousal, have intrusive thoughts and memories of the traumatic event, and make efforts to avoid or eliminate these thoughts.

Such experiences are described as *traumatic* by psychologists because they are extraordinary in nature—and extraordinarily disturbing. It is not surprising, then, that some people exposed to them experience **post-traumatic stress disorder**—a disorder in which individuals experience three kinds of symptoms for at least one month following a traumatic event. The three groups of symptoms are labeled *intrusive*—unwanted thoughts or flashbacks of the traumatic event; *avoidant*—attempts to avoid any thoughts of the event or stimuli that remind one of it; and *arousal*—sleep disturbances, irritability, an exaggerated startle response (e.g., people literally "jump" when unexpected events occur, suggesting that they are in a heightened state of arousal [Brady, Back, & Coffey, 2004]. Post-traumatic stress disorder can stem from a wide range of traumatic events—natural disasters, accidents, rape and other assaults, torture, or the horrors of war (see Figure 11.11; Basoglu et al., 1996; Layman et al., 1996; Vernberg et al., 1996).

Since all people exposed to traumatic events do not experience this disorder, a key question is what factors lead to its occurrence? Research suggests that many factors play a role. The amount of social support trauma victims receive after the traumatic event seems crucial (see Vernberg et al., 1996): The more support, the less likely such people are to develop PTSD. Similarly, the coping strategies chosen by trauma victims are important: Effective strategies, such as trying to see the good side of things (e.g., they survived!), help to prevent PTSD from developing, while ineffective strategies, such as blaming themselves for the traumatic event ("I should have moved away from here!"), increase its likelihood. Individual differences, too, play a role: PTSD is more likely among people who are passive, highly sensitive to criticism, and show poor social adjustment prior to the trauma (e.g., legal difficulties, irresponsibility) than among people who don't show these traits (Schnurr et al., 1993). In sum, it appears that whether individuals experience post-traumatic stress disorder after a traumatic event depends on several factors.

How do individuals attempt to cope with PTSD? Unfortunately, one way is by engaging in *substance abuse*—excessive use of alcohol, drugs (legal or illegal), or other substances that can harm their health. In fact, a high proportion of people who seek therapy for substance abuse (40 to 50 percent) show signs of PTSD, and have

Post-traumatic stress disorder:
A disorder in which people persistently reexperience the traumatic event in their thoughts or dreams, feel as if they are reliving these events from time to time, persistently avoid stimuli associated with the traumatic event, plus several other symptoms.

experienced the kind of traumatic events that produce it. One reason for the link between substance abuse and PTSD may be that these individuals use alcohol and other substances to escape from their painful symptoms—for instance, the traumatic memories they find so disturbing; this is known as the *self-medication hypothesis*. Another possibility is that common factors underlie both PTSD and substance abuse; in other words, individuals who are susceptible to one of these disorders are also susceptible to the other. Whatever the cause, it is clear that substance abuse is *not* the best way to deal with PTSD. We'll describe forms of therapy that are much safer, and more effective, in alleviating this serious mental disorder in Chapter 12.

KEY QUESTIONS

- What are phobias?
- What is panic disorder?
- What is obsessive-compulsive disorder?
- What is post-traumatic stress disorder?

DISSOCIATIVE AND SOMATOFORM DISORDERS

As we have just seen, traumatic events sometimes result in post-traumatic stress disorder. Two other major types of disorder seem to be related to dramatic, unexpected, and involuntary reactions to traumatic experiences: **dissociative disorders** and **somatoform disorders.** Although these disorders are classified separately in the DSM-IV-TR, we'll cover them together here because, historically, they have been viewed as stemming from similar causes and involving similar symptoms.

Dissociative Disorders

Have you ever awakened during the night and, just for a moment, been uncertain about where you were or even who you were? Such temporary disruptions in our normal cognitive functioning are far from rare; many people experience them from time to time as a result of fatigue, illness, or the use of alcohol or other drugs. *Dissociative disorders,* however, go far beyond such experiences, and involve more profound losses of identity or memory, intense feelings of unreality, of being depersonalized (i.e., separate from oneself), and uncertainty about one's own identity.

Dissociative disorders take several different forms. In **dissociative amnesia,** individuals suddenly experience a loss of memory that does not stem from medical conditions or other mental disorders. Such losses can be localized, involving only a specific period of time, or generalized, involving memory for the person's entire life. In another dissociative disorder, **dissociative fugue,** an individual suddenly leaves home and travels to a new location where he or she has no memory of his or her previous life. In **depersonalization disorder,** the individual retains memory, but feels like an actor in a dream or movie.

As dramatic as these disorders are, they pale when compared with the most amazing—and controversial—dissociative disorder—**dissociative identity disorder.** This was known as *multiple personality disorder* in the past, and it involves a shattering of personal identity into at least two—and often more—separate but coexisting personalities, each possessing different traits, behaviors, memories, and emotions. Usually, there is one *host personality*—the primary identity who is present most of the time, and one or more *alters*—alternative personalities who appear from time to time. *Switching,* the process of changing from one personality to another, often seems to occur in response to anxiety brought on by thought or memories of previous traumatic experiences.

Until the 1950s, cases of dissociative identity disorder were rare. Interest in this disorder, and its reported frequency, skyrocketed after the publication of the book *The Three Faces of Eve* (Thigpen & Cleckley, 1957). In 1973, a book describing one case,

---

Dissociative disorders: Disorders involving prolonged loss of memory or identity.

Somatoform disorders: Disorders in which individuals have symptoms typically associated with physical diseases or conditions, but in which no known organic or physiological basis for the symptoms can be found.

Dissociative amnesia: Profound amnesia stemming from the active motivation to forget specific events or information.

Dissociative fugue: A sudden and extreme disturbance of memory in which individuals wander off, adopt a new identity, and are unable to recall their own past.

Dissociative identity disorder: A condition labeled as *multiple personality disorder* in the past, in which a single person seems to possess two or more distinct identities or personality states, and these take control of the person's behavior at different times.

one case, *Sybil* (Wilbur, 1973) became a best seller and was soon made into a TV program; it offered an interpretation of the causes of this disorder that soon became famous—and highly controversial. This explanation suggested that dissociative identity disorder occurs as a response to traumatic events early in life, especially sexual abuse. To deal with such events, the theory contended, children create alternate personalities who can cope with such experiences more effectively than they, and might also be able to protect them from further harm.

In the years that followed, thousands of new cases of dissociative identity disorder were diagnosed by psychiatrists and some psychologists. The overwhelming majority of these cases were women who, during therapy sessions (and often under hypnosis), developed dozens or even hundreds of alters, and also suddenly had "recovered memories" of horrible sexual abuse and satanic rituals when they were children. This led many to bring legal charges against their parents (mothers as well as fathers) and other relatives, thus shattering families.

Were these charges based on fact? As we noted in Chapter 6, many mental health professionals have expressed a degree of skepticism in this respect, mainly because a number of such cases involved therapists who engaged in actions such as instructing their patients to work hard at recalling scenes of childhood sexual abuse, and to read books about multiple personality disorders. Many psychologists believe that these experiences generated false memories for events that never occurred in the minds of at least some patients. This by no means suggests that all cases of dissociative identify disorders are false; in fact, it is included in the DSM-IV-TR as a real psychological disorder. But it does seem best to approach such disorders with considerable caution. Traumatic experiences early in life—including childhood sexual abuse—certainly *do* produce harm; of that there can be no doubt. But whether such experiences lie behind many or even most cases of dissociative identify disorder remains an open question.

FIGURE 11.12

Hypochondriasis: Symptoms without Illness

Is this woman suffering from real medical ailments or showing signs of hypochondriasis—a somatoform disorder in which individuals experience symptoms of diseases they don't really have? Some findings indicate that the figure may be as high as 50 percent!

KEY QUESTIONS

• What are dissociative disorders such as dissociative amnesia?
• What is dissociative identity disorder?

Somatoform Disorders: Physical Symptoms without Physical Causes

Several of Freud's early cases involved the following kind of events. An individual would show some physical symptom (for example, deafness or paralysis of some part of the body), yet careful examination would reveal *no underlying physical causes* for the problem. Such disorders are known as *somatoform disorders*—in which individuals have physical symptoms in the absence of identifiable physical causes for these symptoms.

One common somatoform disorder is **hypochondriasis**—preoccupation with or fear of having a serious disease. People with this disorder do not actually have the diseases they fear, but they persist in worrying about them, despite repeated reassurance by their doctors that they are healthy. Many hypochondriacs are not

Hypochondriasis:
A disorder involving preoccupation with fears of disease or illness.

simply faking; they feel the pain and discomfort they report and are truly afraid that they are sick or will soon become sick (see Figure 11.12). Other people who seek medical help *are* faking. For instance, people who show **Munchausen syndrome** devote their lives to seeking—and often obtaining—costly and painful medical procedures they realize they don't need. Why? Perhaps because they relish the attention, or enjoy fooling physicians and other trained professionals. In any case, such people waste precious medical resources and often run up huge bills that must be paid by insurance companies or government programs. Munchausen syndrome, no matter how strange, is definitely no laughing matter.

Yet another somatoform disorder is known as **conversion disorder.** People with this disorder actually experience physical problems such as *motor deficits* (poor balance or coordination, paralysis or weakness of arms or legs) or *sensory deficits* (loss of sensation to touch or pain, double vision, blindness, deafness). While these disabilities are quite real to the people involved, there is no medical condition present that would produce the problems.

As is true with almost all mental disorders, a number of factors seem to play a role in the occurrence of somatoform disorders. Individuals who develop such disorders seem to have a tendency to focus on inner sensations. In addition, they tend to perceive normal bodily sensations as more intense and disturbing than do most people. Finally, they have a high level of negative affectivity—they are pessimistic, fear uncertainty, experience guilt, and have low self-esteem (Nietzel et al., 1998). Together, these traits create a predisposition or vulnerability to stressors (e.g., intense conflict with others, severe trauma) and, operating together, these factors contribute to the emergence of somatoform disorders.

In addition, of course, people who develop such disorders learn that their symptoms often yield increased attention from family members, and better treatment from them: These relatives are reluctant to give the patient "a hard time," since he or she is already suffering so much! In short, they gain important forms of reinforcement from their disorder.

KEY QUESTIONS

• What are somatoform disorders?
• What factors contribute to their occurrence?

SEXUAL AND GENDER IDENTITY DISORDERS

Freud believed that many psychological disorders can be traced to disturbances in *psychosexual development*—successive stages in our sexual development that, he suggested, are experienced by all human beings (see Chapter 9). While this view is not widely accepted by psychologists today, there is little doubt that individuals experience many problems relating to sexuality and gender identity. Several of these are discussed below.

Sexual Dysfunctions: Disturbances in Desire and Arousal

Sexual dysfunctions include disturbances in sexual desire, sexual arousal, disturbances in the ability to reach orgasm, and disorders involving pain during sexual relations. **Sexual desire disorders** involve a lack of interest in sex or active aversion to sexual activity. People experiencing these disorders report that they rarely have the sexual fantasies most people generate, that they avoid all or almost all sexual activity, and that these reactions cause them considerable distress.

In contrast, **sexual arousal disorders** involve the inability to attain or maintain an erection (males)—a condition that Viagra and other heavily advertised

Munchausen syndrome:
A syndrome in which individuals seem to devote their lives to seeking—and often obtaining—costly and painful medical procedures they realize they don't need.

Conversion disorder:
A somatoform disorder in which individuals experience actual physical impairment such as blindness, deafness, or paralysis for which there is no underlying medical cause.

Sexual desire disorders:
Disorders involving a lack of interest in sex or active aversion to sexual activity.

Sexual arousal disorders:
Involve the inability to attain or maintain an erection (males) or the absence of vaginal swelling and lubrication (females).

drugs claim to cure—or the absence of vaginal swelling and lubrication (females). **Orgasm disorders** involve the delay or absence of orgasms in both sexes. This may include *premature ejaculation* (reaching orgasm too quickly) in males. Needless to say, these problems cause considerable distress to the people who experience them (e.g., Rowland, Cooper, & Slob, 1996).

Paraphilias: Disturbances in Sexual Object or Behavior

What is sexually arousing? For most people, the answer involves the sight or touch of another human. But many people find other stimuli arousing, too. The large volume of business done by Victoria's Secret and other companies specializing in alluring lingerie for women stems, at least in part, from the fact that many men find such garments mildly sexually arousing. Other people find either inflicting or receiving pain during the sex act increases their arousal and sexual pleasure. Do such reactions constitute sexual disorders? According to most psychologists, and the DSM-IV-TR, they do not. Only when unusual or bizarre imagery or acts are *necessary* for sexual arousal (that is, it cannot occur without them) do such preferences qualify as a disorder. Such disorders are termed **paraphilias** and take many different forms. It is important to note that one of the most important changes in the DSM-IV-TR involved changes to the descriptions of paraphilias. The wording now includes the criterion that the individual has acted on bizarre or unusual urges and/or is markedly distressed by them. The reason for this change was to avoid confusion over the fact that some people experiencing paraphilias are not distressed by these disorders—by their unusual or bizarre sexual urges. For instance, many *pedophiles*—people who experience sexual urges and fantasies involving children—are often not at all upset by these urges. Clearly, though, they do indeed show a dangerous form of mental disorder.

Paraphilias are very varied in nature. For instance, in *fetishes*, individuals become aroused exclusively by inanimate objects. Often these are articles of clothing, but in more unusual cases they can involve animals, dead bodies, or even human waste. *Frotteurism*, another paraphilia, involves fantasies and urges focused on touching or rubbing against a nonconsenting person. The touching, not the coercive nature of the act, is what people with this disorder find sexually arousing. Perhaps the most disturbing paraphilia of all is *pedophilia*—a condition we mentioned above in which individuals experience sexual urges and fantasies involving children, generally ones younger than thirteen. When such urges are translated into overt actions, the effects on the young victims can be devastating (see Ambuel, 1995). Two other paraphilias are *sexual sadism* and *sexual masochism*. In the former, individuals become sexually aroused only by inflicting pain or humiliation on others. In the latter, they are aroused by receiving such treatment. Recently, it has been suggested that sadism—or at least sadistic tendencies—may be related to a serious problem many individuals encounter at work: *abusive supervisors*. Please see the **Psychology Goes to Work** section on page 452 for a discussion of this harmful pattern of behavior.)

Gender Identity Disorders

Have you ever read about a man who altered his gender to become a woman, or vice versa? Such individuals feel, often from an early age, that they were born with the wrong sexual identity. They identify strongly with the other sex and show preferences for cross-dressing (wearing clothing associated with the other gender). They are displeased with their own bodies and request—often from an early age—that they receive medical treatment to alter their primary and secondary sex characteristics. In the past, there was little that medicine could do satisfy these desires on the part of people suffering from **gender identity disorder.** Advances in surgical techniques, however, have now made it possible for such people to undergo *sex-change operations* in which their sexual organs are actually

Orgasm disorders:
A sexual disorder involving the delay or absence of orgasms in both sexes.

Paraphilias:
Disorders in which sexual arousal cannot occur without the presence of unusual imagery or acts.

Gender identity disorder:
A disorder in which individuals believe that they were born with the wrong sexual identity.

altered to approximate those of the other gender. Several thousand individuals have undergone such operations, and existing evidence indicates that most report being satisfied with the results and happier than they were before (Green & Blanchard, 1995). However, it is difficult to evaluate such self-reports. Perhaps after waiting years for surgery and spending large amounts of money for their sex-change operations, such people seem little choice but to report positive effects. Clearly such surgery is a drastic step, and should be performed only in cases where potential patients fully understand all potential risks.

PSYCHOLOGY GOES TO WORK

Abusive Supervisors and How to Deal with Them

Have you ever had a boss who frequently shouted at you and other subordinates? Who ridiculed your work? Who always seemed to be in an irritable mood, and whose mere presence seemed to tie your stomach in knots? If so, you may have experienced a specific kind of workplace aggression known as abusive supervision (Taylor, 2004). Unfortunately, this pattern is far from rare. As much as 10 percent of all employees indicate that their current boss engages in the sustained displayed of hostile verbal and nonverbal behaviors that characterize abusive supervision, and fully 30 percent report that they have had such a boss at some point during their careers (Hornstein, 2004).

Why do abusive bosses do it? Unlike the bullies we have all encountered as children, abusive supervisors are not seeking power: they already have it. As a result, they don't seek weak or helpless victims the way child bullies do. Rather, they heap their abuse on everyone. One researcher who has studied such bosses believes that they engage in abusive behavior partly to vent their own frustrations, but mainly for the sheer pleasure of exercising their power (Hornstein, 2004, p. 26). As he puts it: "It is a kind of low-grade sadism . . . They'd start on one person then move on to someone else."

When abusive supervision occurs—when bosses bully their subordinates—the effect is more than merely creating a hostile work environment. This kind of supervision damages not just the employees on the receiving end, but the entire organization as well (Duffy, 2004). Recent findings (Tepper et al., 2004) indicate, for example, that abusive supervision may reduce the incidence of helping among employees—their willingness to lend others with whom they work a hand when it is needed. And the abusive supervisors also greatly reduce employees' job satisfaction.

How should you cope with such a boss? Unfortunately, many employees seem to do so not by confronting abusive bosses or complaining about them, but instead by retreating into their own informal work groups where "misery finds company" and they can mutually support one another. Others try to placate the boss and win her or his approval. And recent findings indicate that many become less sensitive to others, coming to share the bosses' hostile style and frequent put-downs of other employees. As a result, abusive supervisors frequently continue to intimidate and terrify their subordinates.

What should you do if *you* are unlucky enough to encounter an abusive boss? While no steps can guarantee that the situation will improve, here are several we think are worth considering:

1. *Let this person know that you view her or his behavior as inappropriate.* Sometimes abusive supervisors don't realize that they are "out-of-bounds"; letting them know that you feel their actions are truly unjustified and unfair can serve as a "splash of cold water," at least for some office bullies.
2. *Find out what the grievance procedures are in your organization.* Almost every company has such procedures—a formal set of actions employees can take to file complaints about inappropriate or unfair behavior. Abusive supervision certainly falls under this heading, although most complaints have to do with harassment, sexual or otherwise. If your bosses' actions are causing you considerable stress and discomfort, do check out the procedures and find out how you can pursue them.
3. *Keep out of this person's way.* There is a Japanese proverb that says, "When you encounter an obstacle, try to push it; then try to pull it; if those approaches don't work, go around it." This is sometimes the best thing to do when faced with an abusive supervisor. The more you can avoid contact with this person, the better where your own mental and physical health is concerned.
4. *If none of these steps work, let your supervisor know that you are going to ask for help.* In general, it is unwise to threaten others—especially those with authority over us. But if you simply let your supervisor know that you cannot stand still for abusive treatment and will pursue your rights, this can cause many office or factory bullies to back off: they know that there are laws and regulations protecting the well-being of employees, and generally realize that if you do file a complaint against them, it will be a blot on their record no matter how the matter turns out.

Again, none of these steps are certain to succeed. At the least, though, they will help you cope with a very difficult situation and give you hope that it can be changed. And in fact, it *can* be altered because even supervisors have their own bosses to whom they must answer, so while they have most of the power, they by no means have it all!

KEY QUESTIONS
- What are sexual dysfunctions and paraphilias?
- What is gender identity disorder?

PERSONALITY DISORDERS: TRAITS THAT HARM

Have you ever known someone who was highly suspicious and mistrustful of others in virtually all situations? How about someone who seemed to believe that the world revolved around him or her—that he or she was the most important person on earth? Someone who seemed to have no conscience whatsoever, never experiencing guilt or regret not matter how much others were hurt? Or, for a fourth example, someone who was so dependent on others that he or she could not make decisions or take independent actions? If so, you have encountered someone experiencing another type of mental disorder—**personality disorders.** These are defined, by the DSM-IV-TR, as extreme and inflexible personality traits that are distressing to the people who have them or cause them problems in school, work, or interpersonal relations. These traits go beyond what we usually mean by this term (e.g., traits such as "kind," "honest," or "irritable") and refer to pervasive patterns of experience and behavior that are unusual and bizarre with respect to mood, personal relations, and the control of impulses.

The DSM-IV-TR divides personality disorders into three distinct clusters, so let's take a look at some of the traits that fit under these categories. The first is described as involving *odd, eccentric* behavior or traits, and includes three personality disorders: *paranoid, schizoid,* and *schizotypal*. People suffering from *paranoid personality disorders* believe that everyone is out to get them, deceive them, or take advantage of them in some way. In contrast, the *schizoid personality disorder* involves a very different pattern. People with this disorder show little or no sign of emotion, and lack basic social skills. As a result, they form few if any social relationships, and they often end up existing on the fringes of society. The third type, *schizotypal personality disorder,* also shows a pattern of social isolation and avoidance of close relationships. People with this disorder are highly anxious in social situations and often act in bizarre or strange ways; for instance, they may wear strangely out-of-date or mismatched clothes, or show up in a wool sweater in August. Research findings suggest that such people may show deficits in working memory and in the ability to shift from automatic to controlled processing (Raine et al., 1999). This may account, in part, for their strange behavior in many contexts.

The other two clusters of personality disorders include disorders involving *dramatic, emotional, and erratic forms of behavior,* and disorders involving *anxious fearful behavior.* Disorders in these categories are summarized in Table 11.3 on page 454. One of these—the **antisocial personality disorder**—is worthy of special attention. Individuals showing this disorder are chronically callous and manipulative toward others; ignore social rules and laws; behave impulsively and irresponsibly; fail to learn from punishment; and lack remorse or guilt over their misdeeds. Such people often become criminals or confidence artists—and some may even become politicians.

Existing evidence suggests that both genetic and environmental factors play a role in the occurrence of antisocial personality disorder (Rhee & Swaldman, 2002). Genetic factors may predispose specific people toward *impulsivity* and low ability to delay gratification (e.g., Sher & Trull, 1994). Moreover, people with antisocial personality disorder show reduced reactions to negative stimuli—for instance, ones that are related to unpleasant experiences such as punishment (Patrick, Bradley, & Lang, 1993). This suggests that they may be less capable than are others of experiencing negative emotions and less responsive to stimuli that serve as

Personality disorders:
Disorders involving extreme and inflexible personality traits that are distressing to the people who have them or cause them problems in school, work, or interpersonal relations.

Antisocial personality disorder:
A personality disorder involving deceitfulness, impulsivity, callous disregard for the safety or welfare of others, and a total lack of remorse for actions that harm others.

TABLE II.3 Personality Disorders

Personality disorders are extreme and inflexible personality traits that are distressing to the people who have them or cause them problems in school, work, or interpersonal relations. They refer to pervasive patterns of experience and behavior that are unusual and bizarre with respect to thought, mood, personal relations, and the control of impulses. The major types included in the DSM-IV-TR are described here.

Odd and Eccentric Personality Disorders

Paranoid personality disorder	Pervasive distrust and suspiciousness of others.
Schizoid personality disorder	Pervasive pattern of detachment from social relationships and restricted range of emotions.
Schizotypal personality disorder	Intense discomfort in interpersonal relationships, cognitive or perceptual distortions, and eccentric behavior.

Dramatic, Emotional, Erratic Personality Disorders

Antisocial personality disorder	Deceitfulness, impulsivity, irritability, reckless disregard for safety and welfare of others, and lack of remorse.
Borderline personality disorder	Pervasive pattern of instability in interpersonal relationships, self-image, and moods.
Histrionic personality disorder	Pervasive pattern of excessive emotionality and attention seeking.
Narcissistic personality disorder	Pervasive pattern of grandiosity in fantasy or behavior, plus lack of empathy.

Anxious and Fearful Personality Disorders

Avoidant personality disorder	Pervasive pattern of social inhibition, feelings of inadequacy, and hypersensitivity to negative evaluation.
Obsessive-compulsive personality disorder	Preoccupation with orderliness, perfectionism, and mental and interpersonal control.
Dependent personality disorder	Pervasive and excessive need to be taken care of.

warnings to most people to "back off"—for example, angry facial expressions on the part of others (Ogloff & Wong, 1990). Whatever its origins, one point about the antisocial personality disorder is clear: people who show this disorder often pose a serious threat to themselves and to others.

KEY QUESTIONS

- What are personality disorders?
- What characteristics are shown by people who have the antisocial personality disorder?

SCHIZOPHRENIA: LOSING TOUCH WITH REALITY

Schizophrenia:
A complex disorder characterized by hallucinations (e.g., hearing voices), delusions (beliefs with no basis in reality), disturbances in speech, and several other symptoms.

We come now to what many experts consider to be the most serious mental disorder of all: **schizophrenia.** This can be defined as a complex disorder (or cluster of disorders) characterized by fragmentation of basic psychological functions (attention, perception, thought, emotions, and behavior). As a result of such fragmentation, people with schizophrenia have serious problems adjusting to the demands of reality. They misperceive what's happening around them, often seeing or hearing things that aren't there. They have trouble paying attention to what is going on around them, and their thinking is so confused and disorganized that they cannot communicate with others. They often show bizarre behavior and blunting of emotion and motivation, so that they are unable to move or take action. And when they do show emotion, it is often inappropriate in a given situation. Schizophrenia is so disruptive that people who develop it must often be removed from society, at least temporarily, for their own protection and to undergo treatment. Clearly, then, schizophrenia involves a wide range of effects—ways in which people suffering from this serious mental disorder differ from others. It's important to note that recent findings suggest that the most important of these differences involve deficits in cognitive functioning. In fact, these deficits in cognitive performance remain even when schizophrenia is treated with powerful drugs and when other symptoms disappear (Heinrichs, 2005). Further, cognitive deficits, measured through basic psychological procedures, distinguish between schizophrenics and other people more accurately than do brain scans (PET scans, MRI). These findings have led one well-known psychologist to state (Heinrichs, 2005, page 229): "Cognitive deficits are not only part of the schizophrenia syndrome; they are the *primary expression of the schizophrenic brain*" (italics added).

The Nature of Schizophrenia

Let's begin with a closer look at the major symptoms of schizophrenia—the criteria used for the DSM-IV-TR for diagnosing this disorder. These are often divided into *positive* and *negative* symptoms. As these terms suggest, positive symptoms involve adding something that isn't normally there—excess and bizarre behaviors, seeing and hearing things that don't exist; negative symptoms, in contrast, involve absence or reduction of normal functions.

■ **Positive symptoms of schizophrenia.**

These include *delusions,* **hallucinations,** *disordered thought processes,* and *disordered behaviors.* **Delusions** involve misinterpretations of normal events and experiences—misinterpretations that lead schizophrenics to hold beliefs with little basis in reality. Delusions can take many different forms. One common type is *delusions of persecution*—the belief that one is being plotted against, spied on, threatened, or otherwise mistreated. Another common type is *delusions of grandeur*—belief that one is extremely famous, important, or powerful. People suffering from such delusions may claim that they are the president, a famous movie star, or even Jesus, Mohammed, or Buddha. Delusions, like most positive symptoms of schizophrenia, are *phasic*—they come and go. Thus, at any given time they may be present to varying degrees. When delusions are strong, however, people with schizophrenia have truly tenuous ties to reality. About 70 percent of schizophrenics experience *hallucinations:* They see or hear things that aren't really there. These often take the form of voices telling them what to do.

In addition, people with schizophrenia do not think or speak normally. Their words jump about in a fragmented and disorganized manner. There is a loosening of associations, so that one idea does not follow logically from another; indeed, ideas often seem totally unconnected. Schizophrenics often create words of their own—words that resemble real words but do not exist in their native language, for instance "littlehood" for childhood or "crimery" for bad actions. Their sentences often begin with one thought and then shift, abruptly, to another (see Barch & Berenbaum, 1996). In extreme cases, their words seem to be totally jumbled into what are sometimes termed a *verbal salad.*

These problems, and several others, seem to stem from a breakdown in the capacity for *selective attention.* Normally, we can focus our attention on certain stimuli while largely ignoring others. This is not true for schizophrenics. They are easily distracted. Even the sound of their own words may disrupt their train of thought and send them wandering off into a mysterious world of their own

Hallucinations:
Vivid sensory experiences that have no basis in physical reality.

Delusions:
Firmly held beliefs that have no basis in reality.

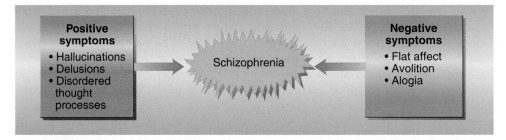

FIGURE 11.13
Major Symptoms of Schizophrenia
As shown here, major symptoms of schizophrenia fall into two headings: positive symptoms (e.g., delusions, hallucinations) and negative symptoms (e.g., flat affective reactions, avolition, alogia).

creation. As we noted earlier, these cognitive deficits seem to be a defining feature of schizophrenia—perhaps the most significant aspect of this disturbance.

The behavioral disorders shown by schizophrenics, however, are even more bizarre. For instance, they may make odd movements or strange gestures, or remain immobile in an awkward position for long periods of time—*catatonia.* They may also show disorganized behavior that makes it impossible for them to dress themselves, prepare food, or perform other daily chores.

■ **Negative symptoms of schizophrenia.**

As noted above, these symptoms reflect the absence of functions or reactions that most people show. One such symptom is *flat affect*—many people with schizophrenia show no emotion. Their faces are like emotionless masks, and they stare off into space with a glazed look. Is this because they feel nothing, or merely because they show no emotion outwardly? Some findings suggest that, in fact, schizophrenics do experience emotional reactions, but don't show any sign of them on the outside (e.g., Berenbaum & Oltmanns, 1992). Some schizophrenics do show emotion, but their reactions are inappropriate. They may giggle when describing a painful childhood experience, or cry after hearing a joke.

Another negative symptom of schizophrenia is *avolition*—a seemingly total lack of motivation or will. People showing this symptom may sit doing nothing hour after hour, and if they do start to do something, will stop in the middle of the activity and wander off. A third, related symptom is *alogia:* a lack of speech. Schizophrenics often have little or nothing to say; they may answer direct questions, but otherwise tend to remain silent, withdrawn into their own private worlds. People showing mainly positive symptoms are sometimes described as showing Type I schizophrenia, while those showing negative symptoms are described as showing Type II schizophrenia. (Figure 11.13 summarizes the major symptoms of schizophrenia.)

The Onset and Course of Schizophrenia

Schizophrenia is a *chronic* disorder, as defined by the DSM-IV-TR: it lasts at least six months. For most people, however, this disorder lasts far longer, and symptoms come and go. They have periods when they appear almost normal, and long periods when their symptoms are readily apparent. Schizophrenia can occur among adolescents, but it generally begins in the early twenties, with males showing the onset of this disorder at earlier ages than females (Remschmidt et al., 1994).

Schizophrenia is often divided into five distinct types. The most dramatic of these is the **catatonic type,** in which individuals show marked disturbances in motor behavior. Many alternate between total immobility—they sit for days or

Catatonic type:
A dramatic type of schizophrenia in which individuals show marked disturbances in motor behavior. Many alternate between total immobility and wild, excited behavior in which they rush madly about.

TABLE 11.4 Major Types of Schizophrenia

The DSM-IV-TR divides schizophrenia into the major types shown here.

Type	Symptoms
Catatonic	Unusual patterns of motor activity, such as rigid postures; also speech disturbances, such as repetitive chatter
Disorganized	Absence of affect, poorly developed delusions, verbal incoherence
Paranoid	Preoccupation with one or more sets of delusions, often centering on the belief that others are "out to get" the schizophrenic in some way
Undifferentiated	Many symptoms, including delusions, hallucinations, incoherence
Residual	Withdrawal, minimal affect, and absence of motivation; occurs after prominent delusions and hallucinations are no longer present

even weeks frozen in a single posture—and wild, excited behavior in which they rush madly about. Other types are described in Table 11.4.

Causes of Schizophrenia

Schizophrenia is one of the most bizarre, and serious, psychological disorders. It is also more common than you might guess: Between 1 and 2 percent of all people in the United States have the disorder (Wilson et al., 1996). What are the causes of the disorder? Research findings point to the role of many factors.

■ **Genetic factors.**

Schizophrenia, like several other psychological disorders, tends to run in families. The closer the family tie between two individuals, the higher the likelihood that if one develops schizophrenia, the other will show this disorder too (see Gottesman, 1991). Schizophrenia does not appear to be traceable to a single gene, however; on the contrary, research findings suggest that many genes and many environmental factors operate together to produce a tendency toward this disorder (see Conklin & Iacono, 2002: Fowles, 1994). Other evidence for the role of genetic factors in schizophrenia is provided by adoption studies. For instance, in one large-scale study conducted in Finland (Tiernari, 1991), 124 children born to schizophrenic mothers, and who were adopted shortly after birth, were compared with adopted children born to nonschizophrenic mothers. Results indicated that 9 percent of those with schizophrenic mothers showed this disorder; in contrast, less than 1 percent of those born to nonschizophrenic mothers were diagnosed as schizophrenic.

■ **Neurodevelopmental factors: Disruption in normal brain development.**

Additional evidence suggests that people with schizophrenia show several types of brain dysfunctions, including ones that develop prior to birth. In particular, several studies indicate that damage to the brain resulting from oxygen deprivation, either during or before birth, can increase the likelihood of schizophrenia later in life (Cannon et al., 1999). The fact that the incidence of schizophrenia is higher among people born during the winter months, when viral epidemics that might result in brain damage are more frequent, is consistent with this reasoning. Neuroimaging studies, too, suggest that abnormalities exist in the medial-temporal lobe and frontal lobes of people who develop schizophrenia. In fact, disruption of normal functioning in the frontal-temporal brain systems may produce the cognitive deficits that are such an important aspect of schizophrenia, and play a key role in this serious mental disorder (Heinrichs, 2005). These abnormalities do not always produces schizophrenia so, as a **diathesis-stress model** suggests, genetic factors may predispose individuals to develop schizophrenia, but this disorder will develop only if they are exposed to certain kinds of stressful environmental conditions. (A diathesis-stress model of mental disorders suggests that genetic factors may predispose individuals to develop such disorders, but the disorders develop only if they are exposed certain kinds of stressful environmental conditions.)

■ Biochemical factors.

Several findings point to the possibility that disturbances in the functioning of certain neurotransmitters—especially *dopamine*—may play a role in schizophrenia. Originally, it was suggested that schizophrenia results from a diffuse excess of dopamine in the brain. However, more recent findings indicate that it may stem from an excess of dopamine in temporal areas and a depletion of dopamine in frontal areas (More, West, & Grace, 1999). Interestingly, these are the same brain areas identified by neuroimaging studies as the ones involved in schizophrenia.

■ Psychological and environmental factors.

Among identical twins, when one develops schizophrenia, the probability that the other will also develop it is only about 50 percent. This suggests that schizophrenia is influenced by environmental and psychological factors as well as genetic and biological ones. What kind of environments place individuals at risk for schizophrenia? Intriguing clues are provided by research on *relapses* among schizophrenic patients—recurrences of the disorder after periods of relative normality. These are more common when patients' families show certain patterns of expressing emotion. Specifically, patients are more likely to suffer relapses when their families engage in harsh criticism, express hostility toward them (e.g., "I'm sick and tired of taking care of you!"), and show too much concern with their problems ("I'm trying so hard to help you!"). The relapse rate in families showing this pattern over the course of a year is fully 48 percent, while in families who do not show this pattern it is only about 20 percent (Kavanagh, 1992).

In sum, just as is true with other, less devastating mental disorders, schizophrenia, too, seems to stem from a convergence of several different factors—biological, social, environmental, and sociocultural. Together, these put some people—those with underlying predispositions—at risk for developing a mental disorder that sometimes seems to totally dissolve their links to the external world.

KEY QUESTIONS

- What is schizophrenia?
- What are positive and negative symptoms of schizophrenia?
- What factors play a role in the occurrence of schizophrenia?

SUBSTANCE-RELATED DISORDERS

Before concluding, we should consider a group of disorders that are extremely common and are related to the use of consciousness-altering drugs (see Chapter 4)—**substance-related disorders.** Do you know a heavy smoker who has tried, over and over again, to quit this habit? And do you know anyone who can't get through the day without several drinks or beers? If so, you already have first-hand experience with some of the obvious effects of these substance-related disorders. Such disorders are further divided by the DSM-IV-TR into two categories:

Diathesis-stress model:
A model suggesting that genetic factors may predispose individuals to develop schizophrenia, but this disorder will develop only if they are exposed to certain kinds of stressful environmental conditions.

Substance-related disorders:
Disorders related to the use of psychoactive substances.

FIGURE 11.14
The Two Faces of Alcohol
Ads often link alcohol consumption to having a wonderful time, and for many persons, alcohol *is* a part of enjoyable social occasions. However, when it is abused, alcohol can have the tragic consequences shown here; in fact, more than half of all fatal traffic accidents involve alcohol consumption..

substance-induced disorders—impaired functioning as a direct result of the physiological effects of the substance in question—and *substance-use disorders*—repeated frequent use of substances resulting in harmful behaviors or impairments in personal, social, and occupational functioning.

According to the DSM-IV-TR, then, **substance abuse** is a maladaptive pattern of substance use that results in repeated, significant adverse effects and maladaptive behavior—failure to meet obligations at work, school, or home, repeatedly using a psychoactive substance in hazardous ways (e.g., while driving), experiencing recurrent legal problems related to the substance, and continuing to use the substance despite its negative effects on social relationships.

Unfortunately, substance abuse is very common. Many different substances are involved (amphetamines, nicotine, opioids), but by far the one that is most frequently abused is alcohol. In the United States, it is estimated that more than 7 percent of the population shows alcohol abuse or dependence (Grant et al., 1994). And the costs of such abuse are truly shocking. More than half of all fatal traffic accidents involve alcohol, and 25 to 50 percent of deaths due to fires, falls, and drowning involve this substance (Institute of Medicine, 1989). The bottom line is this: The average life expectancy of people who abuse alcohol is ten years shorter than those who do not. Such statistics are totally ignored by advertising, which presents alcohol consumption in a totally favorable light; the reality, of course, is something else (see Figure 11.14). These comments refer primarily to *abuse* of alcohol; many people use alcohol without abusing it, and there is no implication in the DSM-IV-TR that such drinking constitutes a mental disorder.

How common is alcohol abuse? A recent study conducted by the National Institute of Alcohol Abuse and Alcoholism (NIAAA, 2005) suggests that about 17.65 million people in the United States—about one in every twelve adults—abuse alcohol. But as you might guess, large differences exist between various cultural and ethnic groups. One clear finding is that people born outside the United States are less likely to abuse alcohol than people born inside it (Adelson, 2006; NIAAA, 2005). This is true even for people of the same ethnic background (e.g., Koreans born in the United States and outside it, Africans born in and outside the United States). A very wide range of ethnic groups were included in the survey, and preliminary results indicate that people of American Indian background have higher rates

Substance abuse:
A maladaptive pattern of substance use that results in repeated, significant adverse effects and maladaptive behavior—failure to meet obligations at work, school, or home; repeatedly using a psychoactive substance in hazardous ways; experiencing recurrent legal problems related to the substance; and continuing to use the substance despite its negative effects on social relationships.

of substance abuse than any other group. In contrast, Japanese Americans and Chinese Americans have below-average rates. It is also clear that these differences reflect different attitudes toward alcohol in various groups and different life conditions—relative wealth, education, experiences with prejudice, and so on. In short, it is clear that various ethnic groups differ with respect to alcohol abuse, but much more information is needed before any firm conclusions as to the origins of these differences can be reached.

Alcohol is not the only psychoactive substance that is abused. Hundreds of millions of people smoke cigarettes, and they often develop nicotine dependence, which makes it extremely difficult for them to stop smoking. The social costs of addiction to heroin, cocaine, "crack," and other drugs are perhaps even higher. These harmful effects, coupled with the very large numbers of people involved, suggest that substance-abuse disorders are among the most damaging of all disorders described in the DSM-IV-TR. Moreover, because they stem from many different factors—biological, social, and personal—they are often very difficult to treat.

KEY QUESTION

- What is substance abuse?

SUMMARY AND REVIEW OF KEY QUESTIONS

- **What are mental disorders?**
  Disturbances of an individual's behavioral, psychological, or physical functioning that are not culturally expected and that lead to psychological distress, behavioral disability, or impaired overall functioning.

- **What role do cultural factors play in defining them?**
  The same behavior may be viewed as acceptable or unacceptable in different cultures. Thus, to some degree cultural factors determine whether specific actions are, or are not, sufficiently unusual and unacceptable to be viewed as signs of mental disorders.

Assessment and Diagnosis: The DSM-IV-TR and Other Tools

- **What is the DSM-IV-TR?**
  The DSM-IV-TR—*Diagnostic and Statistical Manual of Mental Disorders-IV-Text Revision* is the latest version of a widely used guide to mental disorders. It provides descriptions of these disorders, plus information about biological factors associated with them.

- **In what ways is it an improvement over earlier versions?**
  It rests on a firmer basis of published research than did earlier versions and directs increased attention to the role of cultural factors.

- **What other techniques for assessing mental disorders exist?**
  Several tests developed by psychologists (e.g., the MMPI, the MCMI) provide reliable and valid procedures for assessing such disorders, and are also less costly than other procedures.

Disorders of Infancy, Childhood, and Adolescence

- **What is oppositional defiant disorder? Conduct disorder?**
  Oppositional defiant disorder involves behavior in which children have poor control of their emotions or have repeated conflicts with parents and other adults (e.g., teachers). Conduct disorder involves more serious antisocial behaviors that are potentially harmful to the child, to others, or to property.

- **What is attention-deficit/hyperactivity disorder?**
  A childhood disorder in which children show inattention, hyperactivity, and impulsivity, or a combination of these behaviors.

- **What are anorexia nervosa and bulimia nervosa?**
  Anorexia nervosa involves excessive fear of becoming fat, coupled with an inability to maintain normal weight. Bulimia nervosa involves repeated cycles of binging and purging.

- **What is autistic disorder?**
  A disorder in which children show marked impairments in establishing social interactions with others, have nonexistent or poor language skills, and show stereotyped, repetitive patterns of behavior or interests.

- **What are mirror neurons and what possible role do they play in autism?**
  Mirror neurons are neurons in the brain that seem to play an important role in imitating others. Such imitation is important in forming bonds or connections with other people. When mirror neurons don't operate normally, this may interfere with imitation and contribute to the development of the social isolation that is a key feature of autism.

Mood Disorders: The Downs and Ups of Life

- **What are the major symptoms of depressions? Of bipolar disorder?**
  Major symptoms of depressions include negative mood, reduced energy, feelings of hopelessness, loss of interest in previously satisfying activities, difficulties in sleeping, and significant changes in weight. Bipolar disorders involve wide swings in mood between deep depression and mania.

- **What factors play a role in the occurrence of mood disorders?**
Mood disorders are influenced by genetic factors, and by disturbances in brain activity. Psychological factors that play a role in such disorders include learned helplessness, negative perceptions of oneself, and a tendency to focus inward on one's shortcomings.

- **What is rumination and what role does it play in depression?**
Rumination is the tendency to dwell on negative events and experiences in life. It has been found to be an important cause of depression, because once it begins, it is very difficult for individuals to break the cycle of rumination without outside help.

Anxiety Disorders: When Dread Debilitates

- **What are phobias?**
Phobias are excessive and unrealistic fears focused on specific objects or situations.

- **What is panic disorder?**
Intense, terrifying anxiety that is not triggered by any specific situation or event, although in many cases it is associated with *agoraphobia*—fear of open spaces or being away from home.

- **What is obsessive-compulsive disorder?**
A disorder in which individuals have unwanted, disturbing thoughts or images (obsessions) they cannot control, and engage in repetitive behaviors (compulsions) to neutralize such thoughts.

- **What is post-traumatic stress disorder?**
A disorder in which people persistently reexperience a traumatic event in their thoughts or dreams, feel as if they are reliving these events from time to time, persistently avoid stimuli associated with the traumatic event, and experience symptoms such as difficulty falling asleep, irritability, and difficulty in concentrating.

Dissociative and Somatoform Disorders

- **What are dissociative disorders?**
Disruptions in a person's memory, consciousness, or identity—processes that are normally integrated.

- **What is dissociative identity disorder?**
A shattering of identity into at least two—and often more—separate but coexisting personalities, each possessing different traits, behaviors, memories, and emotions.

- **What are somatoform disorders?**
Disorders in which individuals have physical symptoms in the absence of identifiable physical causes for these symptoms.

- **What factors contribute to their occurrence?**
Individuals who develop such disorders focus on inner sensations, perceive normal bodily sensations as more intense and disturbing than other people, and have a high level of negative affectivity. In addition, they obtain important forms of reinforcement from their symptoms.

Sexual and Gender Identity Disorders

- **What are sexual dysfunctions and paraphilias?**
Sexual dysfunctions involve disturbances in sexual desire, sexual arousal, the ability to attain orgasm, or pain during sexual relations. In paraphilias, unusual imagery or acts are necessary for sexual arousal.

- **What is gender identity disorder?**
Feelings on the part of individuals that they were born with the wrong sexual identity, coupled with strong desires to change this identity through medical treatment or other means.

Personality Disorders: Traits That Harm

- **What are personality disorders?**
Personality disorders are extreme and inflexible personality traits that are distressing to the people who have them or cause them problems in school, work, or interpersonal relations.

- **What characteristics are shown by people with the antisocial personality disorder?**
Such people are chronically callous and manipulative toward others; ignore social rules and laws; behave impulsively and irresponsibly; fail to learn from punishment, and lack remorse or guilt for their misdeeds.

Schizophrenia: Losing Touch with Reality

- **What is schizophrenia?**
Schizophrenia is a very serious mental disorder characterized by hallucinations (e.g., hearing voices), delusions (beliefs with no basis in reality), and disturbances in speech, behavior, and emotion.

- **What are positive and negative symptoms of schizophrenia?**
Positive symptoms involve the presence of something that is normally absent, such as hallucinations and delusions. Negative symptoms involve the absence of something that is normally present and include withdrawal, apathy, absence of emotion, and so on.

- **What factors play a role in the occurrence of schizophrenia?**
Schizophrenia has complex origins involving genetic factors, brain dysfunction, biochemical factors, and certain aspects of family environment.

Substance-Related Disorders

- **What is substance abuse?**
A maladaptive pattern of substance use that results in repeated, significant adverse effects and maladaptive behavior (e.g., failure to meet obligations at work, school, or home, repeatedly using a psychoactive substance in hazardous ways).

KEY TERMS

PSYCHOLOGY: UNDERSTANDING ITS FINDINGS

Why Identifying Mental Disorders Is a Very Tricky Task

If there's one thing we hope you have learned from this chapter, it is this: Determining whether a particular person is experiencing a specific mental disorder is a very complex and difficult task. We believe that if you now understand why, you have really understood some of the most important themes presented in this chapter. To see how well you *do* understand this key point, please indicate below the reasons why it really *is* so difficult to determine whether a particular person is experiencing a specific mental disorder. (Hint: Some of the difficulties have to do with defining just what is involved in any mental disorder; others relate to the fact that not all people experiencing a given disorder show clear symptoms of this disorder.) After you complete your answer, go back over the chapter to see how well it reflects key themes presented. Good luck—and good thinking!

MAKING PSYCHOLOGY PART OF YOUR LIFE

Preventing Suicide: How You Can Help

When terminally ill people choose to end their lives rather than endure continuous pain, their actions are understandable, even if we disapprove of them. But when young people whose lives have just begun follow this route, nearly everyone would agree that their death is truly tragic. Can *you* do anything to help prevent suicides among people you know? Research findings suggest that you can, if you pay careful attention to several warning signs—and then take appropriate action! Here are some guidelines:

- **Be alert to important warning sides that someone is seriously contemplating suicide.** These include:

  1. Statements that life no longer has any meaning, and that the person has no strong reasons for continuing to live
  2. Agitation or excitement followed by a period of calm resignation
  3. Sudden efforts to give valued possessions away to others
  4. Statements indicating "I don't want to be a burden to others anymore"

5. Revival from a deeply depressed state, coupled with taking leave of others (saying "Good-bye" instead of "So long").

If you observe these tendencies, they may well be danger signs that a person is seriously considering suicide.

- **Do not leave the people who show these warning signs alone.** Suicide is a solitary act, so just your presence on the scene may be helpful in preventing it.
- **Discourage others from blaming themselves for failure to reach unrealistic goals.** Many people who attempt suicide do so because they feel they have failed to measure up to their own standards. If you know someone who is prone to this pattern, try to get him to focus on his good points, and to realize that his standards are unrealistic—ones no one could hope to attain.

- **Take all suicide threats seriously.** One common myth about suicide is that people who threaten to kill themselves rarely do—only those who tell no one about their plans commit suicide. *This is untrue!* Approximately 70 percent of all suicides tell others about their intentions. So when someone talks about suicide, *take it seriously.*
- **Most important of all: GET HELP!!** Where preventing suicide is concerned, it's far better to get worried or concerned for nothing than it is to look the other way while a tragedy occurs. So if you are concerned about someone you know, *get professional help.* Call a local suicide hotline, discuss your concerns with someone in the campus counseling center, or see a physician or a member of the clergy. Help *is* available, so please do seek it!

If you are using MyPsychLab, you have access to an electronic version of this textbook, along with dozens of valuable resources per chapter—including video and audio clips, simulations and activities, self-assessments, practice tests and other study materials. Here is a sampling of the resources available for this chapter.

EXPLORE

The Axes of the DSM

WATCH

Seasonal Affective Disorder

Panic Disorder

Kathy: Substance Abuse

SIMULATE

Schizophrenia

If you did not receive an access code to MyPsychLab with this text and wish to purchase access online, please visit www.MyPsychLab.com.

STUDY GUIDE

CHAPTER REVIEW

Assessment and Diagnosis: The DSM-IV TR and Other Tools

1. A mental disorder involves impaired functioning but rarely mental distress. (True-False)
2. Information gathered by a therapist in their first meeting with a new patient is used
   a. by the therapist to plan an evaluation.
   b. to make the patient to feel comfortable with the therapist.
   c. to make a diagnosis of their problem.
   d. All of the above are correct.
3. The term diagnosis refers to the formal identification of a person's mental problem. (True-False).
4. The dimensions along which a person is diagnosed in the DSM-IV-TR system are referred to as
   a. categories.
   b. axes.
   c. symptoms.
   d. factors.
5. Which of the following do NOT belong together?
   a. Axis I; major psychological disorders
   b. Axis III; general medical conditions
   c. Axis IV; sources of stress
   d. Axis II; the current functional state of the person
6. Which of the following is true of the DSM-IV-TR?
   a. The intent of the system is to diagnose disorders.
   b. It has poor reliability.
   c. The system can diagnose and explain abnormal behavior.
   d. All of the above are correct.
7. The intent of the validity scales of the MMPI is to
   a. determine which therapy would be best for a particular disorder.
   b. diagnose normal behavior.
   c. determine whether people are being honest in their answers.
   d. All of the above are correct.

Disorders of Infancy, Childhood, and Adolescence

8. The most common reason for children to seek psychological treatment involves
   a. mental retardation.
   b. drug use.
   c. disruptive behaviors.
   d. truancy.
9. About 10 percent of children exhibit disruptive behaviors. (True-False)
10. Children are most commonly seen by therapists for issues relating to disruptive behavior. (True-False)
11. A child who is unable to sit still is most likely to be diagnosed as being
    a. conduct disorder.
    b. attention-deficit/hyperactivity disorder.
    c. oppositional defiant disorder.
    d. manic-depressive.
12. The most common drug used to treat ADHD is
    a. Ritalin.
    b. haloperidol.
    c. Prozac.
    d. nicotine.
13. A bulimic person would be expected to eat and then purge their food. (True-False)
14. A key issue for both anorexics and bulimics is the tendency to
    a. overeat in order to gain weight.
    b. perceive themselves as being overweight.
    c. be more common in males than in females.
    d. abuse weight loss drugs.
15. The recent upswing in the incidence of autism is likely related to changes in how the disorder is defined by the DSM-IV. (True-False)
16. Which of the following is true of autism?
    a. The incidence of autism has decreased over the last twenty years.
    b. Autism is more common in fraternal than identical twins.
    c. Autism involves overactivity of the "mirror" neurons of the brain.
    d. Autistic children have difficulty in imitating the facial reactions of others.

Mood Disorders: The Downs and Ups of Life

17. Women are more likely than are men to develop depression (True-False)
18. Major depressive disorder involves symptoms of
    a. sadness, weight loss, and insomnia.
    b. speech disorder.
    c. perceptual hallucinations.
    d. paranoia and distrust.
19. Mood disorders include major depression and bipolar disorder. (True-False)
20. A person who cycles between sadness and elation may suffer from
    a. mania.
    b. bipolar disorder.
    c. conduct disorder.
    d. schizophrenia.
21. Genetic factors play a stronger role in bipolar disorder than in major depression. (True-False)
22. Mood disorders are thought to reflect a _____ level of _____ in the brain.
    a. low; dopamine
    b. high; acetylcholine
    c. low; serotonin
    d. high; glutamate
23. Depressed people exhibit
    a. high levels of serotonin in brain.
    b. high self-esteem.

c. protracted spending sprees.

d. negative self-schemas.

24. A person who thinks about negative events and disappointments in their life is
    a. less likely to suffer from depression.
    b. just being accurate.
    c. is better at gaining new friends.
    d. more likely to suffer from depression.

25. Rumination is the tendency to dwell on negative events in the lives of others. (True-False)

26. Which of the following is NOT true of suicide?
    a. More women attempt suicide than do men.
    b. Men are more likely to suicide using handguns or jumping from a tall building.
    c. Older people have a higher suicide rate than younger people.
    d. Women are more successful at suicide than are men.

27. Suicide is the fifth leading cause of death among adolescents. (True-False)

Anxiety Disorders: When Dread Debilitates

28. In Asian cultures social phobias involve a fear of
    a. being embarrassed in front of others.
    b. large crowds.
    c. speaking in front of an audience.
    d. having an external appearance that is offensive to others.

29. An episode of panic disorder is triggered by specific environmental stimuli (True-False)

30. During a(n) _____ a person experiences is a brief, sudden, uncontrollable episode of acute anxiety and fear that is not tied to a specific event or stimulus.
    a. anxiety reaction
    b. phobic response
    c. panic attack
    d. depersonalization attack

31. An obsession is a recurrent behavior (True-False)

32. Obsessive-compulsive persons are more likely to see the trees than the forest. (True-False)

33. A person who has substantial social support is less likely to develop PTSD in response to a trauma. (True-False)

Dissociative and Somatoform Disorders

34. _____ is a form of dissociative disorder in which a person retains their memory but feels like an actor/actress in a play.
    a. Somatoform disorder
    b. Somatoform fugue
    c. Depersonalization disorder
    d. Dissociative amnesia

35. A person who lives in fear of having a serious disease would be said to have
    a. dissociative identity disorder.
    b. hyperchondriasis.
    c. fugue disorder.
    d. hypochondriasis.

Sexual and Gender Identity Disorders

36. Match up the appropriate concept with the correct definition or best example of the concept.

_____. A person who is distressed by the fact that they can only be aroused by bizarre imagery or sexual acts.

_____. A person who enjoys inflicting pain on others.

_____. A situation in which a person is sexually aroused by an inanimate object.

_____. A person who alters their sexual organs through surgery to match their gender identity.
    a. Gender identity disorder.
    b. Paraphilia.
    c. Sadism.
    d. Fetishes.

37. The best way to deal with an abusive boss is to threaten them with physical harm. (True-False)

Personality Disorders: Traits that Harm

38. A person who has few social skills and shows little evidence of emotion is most likely to suffer from _____ personality disorder.
    a. multiple
    b. schizoid
    c. antisocial
    d. paranoid

39. A person with antisocial personality disorder is impulsive and does not show remorse for harming others. (True-False)

Schizophrenia: Losing Touch with Reality

40. A delusion is an example of a negative symptom of schizophrenia. (True-False)

41. Prozac is the first-line drug treatment for schizophrenia. (True-False)

42. The most dramatic form of schizophrenia is the _____ type.
    a. paranoid.
    b. residual
    c. disorganized
    d. catatonic

Substance-Related Disorders

43. The most common substance abused by humans is
    a. marijuana.
    b. cocaine.
    c. alcohol.
    d. methamphetamine.

44. A person who has tried alcohol once would be classified as having a substance abuse disorder. (True-False)

IDENTIFICATIONS

Identify the term that belongs with each of the concepts below (place the letter for the appropriate term below in front of each concept).

Identification   Concept:

_____ 1. An eating disorder that involves self-starvation.

_____ 2. A childhood disorder involving poor social, emotional and language skills.

_____ 3. A perception that is not related to a physical sensation.

_____ 4. The notion that genetic factors can predispose a person to develop a disorder.

_____ 5. A type of schizophrenia involving major disturbance of motor function.

_____ 6. A category of childhood mental disorders.

_____ 7. A firmly held belief that has no basis in reality.

_____ 8. A young woman travels to a new city and claims to have no memory of her past life.

_____ 9. A syndrome in which mood cycles between states of depression and elation.

_____ 10. A somatoform disorder in which a person develops blindness that has no physical cause.

_____ 11. A serious mental disorder that involves positive and negative symptoms.

_____ 12. An intense form of anxiety that is not tied to a specific stimulus.

_____ 13. A general feeling of fear and apprehension.

_____ 14. A disorder in which a person believes they have the wrong sexual identity.

_____ 15. An eating disorder in which a person overeats and then purges.

Identification:
a. Anxiety
b. Bipolar disorder.
c. Hallucination.
d. Dissociative fugue.
e. Disruptive behaviors.
f. Gender identity disorder.
g. Anorexia nervosa.
h. Schizophrenia.
i. Panic attack.
j. Catatonic schizophrenia.
k. Delusion.
l. Bulimia nervosa.
m. Conversion disorder.
n. Diathesis-stress model
o. Autism.

FILL IN THE BLANK

1. The term _____ refers to the formal identification of a person's mental problem.
2. In the DSM-IV-TR system, Axis III refers to _____ of the patient.
3. The most common drug used to treat ADHD is _____
4. _____ involves serious antisocial behaviors that are harmful to others or to property.
5. The symptoms of mania involve _____.
6. The _____ comprise major depression and bipolar disorder.
7. _____ refers to our tendency to think about the negative events in our life.
8. _____ refers to the situation in which a person lives in fear of having a serious disease.
9. An intense fear of gaining weight and a refusal to maintain normal weight is termed _____.
10. A person who has an intense fear of dirt or contamination may suffer from
11. A _____ is a firmly held belief that is not true.
12. The _____ is a brain structure that plays a role in panic disorder.

13. A(n) _____ involves a perception that occurs in the absence of a sensation.
14. Schizophrenia can be divided into _____ and _____ symptoms.
15. The neurotransmitter _____ is involved in schizophrenia.

COMPREHENSIVE PRACTICE TEST

1. Decisions about whether a person suffers from a particular mental disorder involves an assessment
   a. of whether the person is distressed by their own behavior.
   b. of how unusual is their behavior.
   c. of the extent to which the behavior is socially unacceptable.
   d. All of the above are correct.
2. Which of the following is true of the DSM-IV-TR?
   a. The intent of the system is to explain psychological disorders.
   b. It has poor reliability.
   c. The system can diagnose and explain abnormal behavior.
   d. The system may be gender-biased.
3. Psychiatrists and psychologists use the MMPI to arrive at reliable and valid diagnoses of patient problems. (True-False).
4. Conduct disorder
   a. involves repeated conflict with peers.
   b. usually starts at ages three to four.
   c. involves minor problems such as cutting class.
   d. involves serious antisocial behaviors that are harmful to others or to property.
5. Which of the following is NOT associated with ADHD?
   a. Oxygen deprivation at birth.
   b. Use of alcohol by the mother during pregnancy.
   c. Low birth weight.
   d. Nicotine use by the child.
6. An autistic child would be expected to show
   a. poor social interactions with others.
   b. poor language skills.
   c. stereotyped behavior patterns.
   d. All of the above are correct.
7. Mania involves symptoms of
   a. sadness, weight loss, and insomnia.
   b. repeated motor behaviors.
   c. excitement, high energy, and elation.
   d. paranoia and distrust.
8. A technique to avoid rumination is to
   a. develop more sources of self-esteem.
   b. focus on the positive events of our life.
   c. take action to solve various problems.
   d. All of the above are correct.
9. We would expect that a person with damage to the locus coeruleus would be less likely to experience a(n)
   a. anxiety reaction.
   b. phobic response.
   c. panic attack.
   d. depersonalization attack.

10. A person suffering from obsessive-compulsive disorder may be disturbed by fear-inducing thoughts involving about
    a. sex.
    b. body waste or secretions.
    c. dirt.
    d. All of the above are correct.

11. Match up the appropriate concept with the correct definition or best example of the concept.
    _____. An intense fear of snakes that forces a person to stay in their house.
    _____. An eating disorder in which a person diets to lose weight but does not purge.
    _____. A pattern of serious antisocial behavior in a child that is dangerous to others.
    _____. A test designed to measure abnormal behavior as well as deception.
    _____. A behavior that helps to allay anxiety.
    a. Compulsion.
    b. Conduct disorder.
    c. Phobia.
    d. MMPI.
    e. Anorexia nervosa.

12. Phobias relate to an intense fear of
    a. blood.
    b. animals.
    c. the natural environment.
    d. All of the above are correct.

13. Which of the following do NOT belong together?
    a. fugue;   loss of memory
    b. depersonalization disorder;   amnesia
    c. dissociative identity disorder;   multiple personalities
    d. dissociative amnesia;   no medical cause

14. An example of a sexual arousal disorder would be a
    a. a male who is unable to maintain an erection during sex.
    b. a female who has no interest in sexual activity.
    c. a female who reaches orgasm too quickly during sex.
    d. a male who is aroused by inanimate objects.

15. The onset of schizophrenia is most commonly in
    a. childhood.
    b. early adulthood.
    c. middle adulthood.
    d. later adulthood.

16. The main distinction between a phobia and a panic attack is that
    a. phobias induce more fear than do panic attacks.
    b. panic attacks are more common in people about to give a speech.
    c. panic attacks are learned through classical conditioning.
    d. panic attacks are not tied to specific stimuli or events.

CRITICAL THINKING

1. Explain why it is important for a diagnostic system to have clearly defined symptoms and syndromes and why changes in such a diagnostic system nay appear to alter the incidence of a particular disorder.

2. Compare and contrast the positive and negative symptoms of schizophrenia and explain the notion that different causes can contribute to the disorder.

TWELVE

Psychological Treatments: Reducing the Pain and Distress of Mental Disorders

I (Robert Baron) have had many wonderful experiences as a psychologist, but one of the saddest involves a former relative I was not able to help. He was a relative by marriage, and I first met him when he was nine years old. At the time, he seemed very nice, but a little shy. As the years passed, though, this shyness developed into a full-scale social phobia with the result that as a teenager he did not date and did not have the kind of experiences that prepare most people for serious long-term relationships and deep, long-term love. He was a nice looking young man, and seemed to excel at almost every sport he played, so many young women expressed interest in him. Somehow, though, he seemed unable to convert this interest into actual relationships.

As he grew older, his social phobia led to deep depression. In fact, he was so down and so distressed that I was asked, as the psychologist in the family, to try to get him help. I did because, in my opinion, when someone begins to talk about suicide (which he did regularly), they really do need help and there's no time for delay! So, I used my network of friends and colleagues to identify an outstanding psychologist near where he lived, and arranged for him to see this person. Soon afterward, though, I received an irritated call from this colleague: "Why did you send him to me? He seems to have no problems and is definitely not suicidal. I really have to spend my time with people who need help, and in my professional opinion, he doesn't." I was stunned. I knew that this young man was very distressed; had he concealed this from the therapist?

Time went by, and he did not improve. In fact, his family and friends became increasingly worried about him because his behavior grew stranger and stranger. So, once again, I was asked to find him a therapist, and since I believed that he really was suffering, I did so once again. He was now living in a different town, so I had to find another therapist, and I did. After he saw this second therapist—who was someone I knew personally—I called just to find out what this highly qualified psychologist thought. Again, I was shocked to learn that, in his view, my relative had no serious problems! I was puzzled: could I be totally wrong? I am not a clinical psychologist so perhaps I was making a bad judgment.

What happened in the years that followed, though, was not pleasant. My relative continued to be distressed, and a source of great concern to his parents and other members of his family. He remained isolated—in fact, increasingly so. Ultimately, he gave up trying to find love and retreated into a smaller and smaller world in which he was unhappy and troubled. He was that way the last time I saw him, several years ago. Truly, when I think about this former relative and the pain he experienced, I feel very sad and think to myself, "What a waste!"

Psychological treatments:

Procedures for alleviating mental disorders based on the findings and principles of psychology and best administered by trained psychologists.

Psychotherapies:

Procedures in which people with mental disorders interact with trained therapists who help them change certain behaviors, thoughts, or emotions so that they feel and function better.

I don't use that phrase lightly because, as you'll see in this chapter, *help is definitely available* and psychologists have developed a wide range of highly effective techniques to help people with serious mental disorders to recover from them and so to experience reduced distress, improved functioning, and happier, richer lives. In the past, these procedures were described as *therapy* or *psychotherapy*, but recently, the term **psychological treatments** has been proposed as a better label for them. The reasons for this are clear: While *therapy* can be, and is, delivered by practitioners belonging to several different professions (psychiatrists, social workers, etc.), psychological treatments—which have been found to be *very* effective in helping people to recover from mental disorders—have been developed by psychologists and should be used only by people with thorough training in psychology (Barlow, 2004).

In this chapter, then, we'll strike a much happier and optimistic note than in Chapter 11 by describing the broad range of treatments for mental disorders developed by psychologists. Since many types of psychological treatment exist, we'll begin with ones that have often been described by the term **psychotherapies**—procedures in which people with mental disorders interact with trained therapists who help them to change certain behaviors, thoughts, or emotions so that they feel and function better. After that, we'll examine forms of treatment that occur in *group settings* rather than individual one-on-one sessions. Next, we'll take a brief look at *biological therapies*, which involve the use of drugs, electroconvulsive shock, and even surgery. Finally, we'll conclude by addressing the question, "Just how effective are these various forms of therapy?" Now, back to the main topic of this discussion—different forms of psychological treatment.

PSYCHOTHERAPIES: THE THERAPEUTIC ALLIANCE AS THE FOUNDATION FOR PSYCHOLOGICAL TREATMENTS

Efforts by psychologists and other professionals to help people experiencing mental disorders take many different forms. Perhaps the one that is most familiar, though, is face-to-face meetings between therapists and the individuals they are attempting to help. This process is often described by the term *psychotherapy*, since it involves efforts to use the findings and principles of psychology to help the people in question experience less stress and less impairment of their functioning in daily life. As we'll now see, many different forms of psychotherapy exist, and each of these is based on somewhat different assumptions about the causes and nature of mental disorders. However, a key ingredient in all of them—a feature that makes them all related in basic ways—is what is known as the **therapeutic alliance**—a close and often powerful relationship between the therapist and the person seeking help, in which both cooperate to alleviate the client's mental disorders. Such relationships are marked by mutual respect and trust, and are important because within them, people experiencing intense distress and seriously impaired lives no longer feel helpless, hopeless, or alone. So, as we'll point out in more detail in a later discussion of the question, "Just how effective are psychological treatments?" the therapeutic alliance is a key ingredient in *all* major forms of psychotherapy. Now, let's take a closer look at several of the procedures that have been used successfully to reduce the pain and distress of mental disorders.

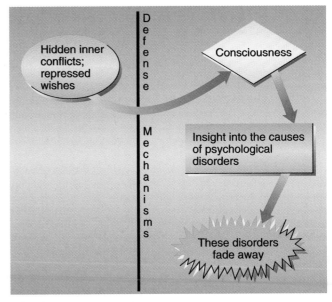

FIGURE 12.1
Psychoanalysis: How, Supposedly, It Works
Psychoanalysis, the kind of therapy developed by Freud, focuses on helping individuals gain insight into their hidden inner conflicts and repressed wishes. Freud believed that once awareness of these conflicts penetrated patients' *defense mechanisms* and became conscious, their disorders would fade away. In fact, there is little support for this view.

Psychodynamic Therapies: From Repression to Insight

Psychodynamic therapies are based on the idea that mental disorders stem primarily from the kind of hidden inner conflicts first described by Freud—for instance, conflicts between our primitive sexual and aggressive urges (id impulses) and the ego, which warns us of the dangers of gratifying these immediately, as soon as they arise (see Chapter 9). More specifically, psychodynamic therapies assume that mental disorders occur because something has gone seriously wrong in the balance between these inner forces. While several forms of therapy are based in these assumptions, the most famous is *psychoanalysis*, the approach developed by Freud.

■ Psychoanalysis.

As you may recall from Chapter 9, Freud believed that personality consists of three major parts: *id*, *ego*, and *superego*, which correspond roughly to desire, reason, and conscience. Freud believed that mental disorders occur because many impulses of the id are unacceptable to the ego or the superego, and are therefore *repressed*—driven into the depths of the unconscious. There they persist, and individuals must devote a considerable portion of their psychic energy to keeping them in check and out of consciousness. In fact, they often use various *defense mechanisms* to protect the ego from feelings of anxiety generated by these inner conflicts and clashes (see Table 12.1 for an overview of these defense mechanisms).

How can such problems be relieved? Freud felt that the crucial task was for people to overcome repression so they could recognize—and confront—their hidden feelings and impulses. Having gained such insight, he believed, they would experience a release of emotion (*abreaction*) and then, with their energies at last freed from the task of repression, they could direct these into healthy growth. Figure 12.1 summarizes these views.

These ideas concerning the causes and cure of mental illness are reflected in *psychoanalysis*, the type of therapy developed by Freud. As popular images suggest, the patient undergoing psychoanalysis lies on a couch in a partly darkened

Therapeutic alliance:
A close and often powerful relationship between the therapist and the person seeking help, in which both cooperate to alleviate the client's mental disorders.

Psychodynamic therapies:
Therapies based on the idea that mental disorders stem primarily from the kind of hidden inner conflicts first described by Freud.

TABLE 12.1	Defense Mechanisms: Reactions to Anxiety	

Freud believed that when the ego feels it may be unable to control impulses from the id, it experiences anxiety. To reduce such feelings, the ego uses various *defense mechanisms*, such as those described here.

Defense Mechanism	Its Basic Nature	Example
Repression	"Forgetting"—or pushing from consciousness into unconsciousness—unacceptable thoughts or impulses	A woman fails to recognize her attraction to her handsome new son-in-law.
Rationalization	Conjuring up socially acceptable reasons for thoughts or actions based on unacceptable motives	A young woman explains that she ate an entire chocolate cake so that it wouldn't spoil in the summer heat.
Displacement	Redirecting an emotional response from a dangerous object to a safe one	A man redirects anger from his boss to his child.
Projection	Transferring unacceptable motives or impulses to others	A man who feels strong hostility toward a neighbor perceives the neighbor as being hostile to him.
Regression	Responding to a threatening situation in a way appropriate to an earlier age or level of development	A student asks a professor to raise his grade; when she refuses, the student throws a temper tantrum.

room and engages in *free association*—he or she reports *everything* that passes through his or her mind. Freud believed that the repressed impulses and inner conflicts present in the unconscious would ultimately be revealed by these mental wanderings, at least to the trained ear of the analyst.

Freud noted that during psychoanalysis, several intriguing events often occur. The first of these is *resistance*—a patient's stubborn refusal to report certain thoughts, motives, and experiences, or overt rejection of the analyst's interpretations (Strean, 1985). Presumably, resistance occurs because patients wish to avoid the anxiety that they experience as threatening or painful thoughts come closer and closer to consciousness.

Another aspect of psychoanalysis is **transference**—intense feelings of love or hate toward the analyst on the part of the patients. Often, patients react toward their analyst as they did to someone who played a crucial role in their early lives—for example, one of their parents. Freud believed that transference could be an important tool for helping individuals work through conflicts regarding their parents, but this time in a setting where the harm done by disordered early relationships could be effectively countered. As patients' insight increased, Freud believed, transference would gradually fade away.

■ **Psychoanalysis: An evaluation.**

Psychoanalysis is probably the most famous form of psychotherapy (Hornstein, 1992). What accounts for its fame? Certainly not its effectiveness. It is fair to say that its reputation far exceeds its success in alleviating mental disorders. In the form proposed by Freud, it suffers from several major weaknesses that lessen its value. First, psychoanalysis is a costly and time-consuming process. Several years and a large amount of money are usually required for its completion—assuming it ever ends! Second, it is based largely on Freud's theories of personality and psychosexual development. As we noted in Chapter 9, these theories are provocative but difficult to test scientifically, so psychoanalysis rests on shaky scientific ground. Third, Freud designed psychoanalysis for use with highly educated people with impressive verbal skills—ones who could describe their inner thoughts and feelings with ease. Finally, its major assumption—that once insight is acquired, mental health

Transference:
Intense feelings of love or hate toward the analyst on the part of the patient.

will follow automatically—is contradicted by research findings. Over and over again, psychologists have found that insight into your own thoughts and feelings does *not* necessarily change them or prevent them from influencing behavior (e.g., Rozin, 1996). In fact, as we'll see in a later discussion of cognitive therapies, changing distorted or maladaptive modes of thought often requires great effort—and persistence. For these reasons, psychoanalysis is not a very popular form of therapy today; in fact, it has been far surpassed by newer and more effective forms that we will now consider.

KEY QUESTIONS

- What are psychotherapies?
- What is psychoanalysis and what are its major assumptions?
- What is the role of free association in psychoanalysis?

Phenomenological/Experiential Therapies: Emphasizing the Positive

Freud was something of a pessimist about basic human nature. He felt that we must constantly struggle with primitive impulses from the id. Many psychologists reject this view. They contend that people are basically good and that our strivings for growth, dignity, and self-control are just as strong as the powerful aggressive and sexual urges Freud described. Mental disorders, then, do not stem solely from unresolved inner conflicts. Rather, they arise because the environment somehow interferes with personal growth and fulfillment.

This view—plus the following three suggestions—form the basis for **phenomenological/experiential therapies** (often known as *humanistic therapies*): (1) understanding other people requires trying to see the world through their eyes (a phenomenological approach); (2) clients should be treated as equals; and (3) the therapeutic relationship with the client is central to achieving the benefits of therapy. The goal of such therapy is to help *clients* (not "patients") to become more truly themselves—to find meaning in their lives and to live in ways truly consistent with their own values and traits. Unlike psychoanalysts, humanistic therapists believe that clients must take essential responsibility for the success of therapy. The therapist is mainly a guide and facilitator, *not* the one who runs the show. Let's take a closer look at two forms of humanistic therapy.

■ Client-centered therapy: The benefits of being accepted.

Perhaps the most influential humanistic approach is **client-centered therapy,** developed by Rogers (1970, 1980). Rogers strongly rejected Freud's view that mental disorders stem from conflicts over the expression of primitive, instinctive urges. On the contrary, he argued that such problems arise mainly because clients' efforts to attain *self-actualization*—growth and development—are thwarted early in life by judgments and ideas imposed on them by other people. According to Rogers, these judgments lead individuals to acquire what he terms unrealistic *conditions of worth*. That is, they learn that they must be something other than what they really are in order to be loved and accepted—to be worthwhile as a person. For example, they come to believe that they will be rejected by their parents if they are not always neat and submissive or if they do not live up to various parental ideals. Such beliefs block people from recognizing large portions of their experience and emotions. This, in turn, interferes with normal development of the self and causes them to experience poor adjustment.

Client-centered therapy focuses on eliminating such unrealistic conditions of worth through creation of a psychological climate in which clients feel valued as people. Person-centered therapists offer *unconditional acceptance* or *unconditional positive regard* of the client and her or his feelings; a high level of *empathetic understanding;*

Phenomenological/ experiential therapies (often known as *humanistic therapies*): Therapies that assume that (1) understanding other people requires trying to see the world through their eyes (a phenomenological approach); (2) clients should be treated as equals; and (3) the therapeutic relationship with the client is central to achieving the benefits of therapy.

Client-centered therapy: A form of humanistic therapy developed by Rogers.

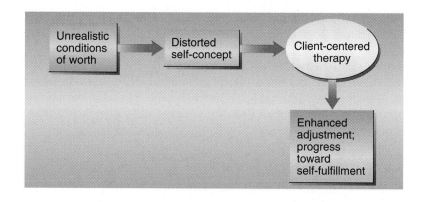

FIGURE 12.2
Client-Centered Therapy: An Overview
Rogers believed that mental disorders stem from unrealistic *conditions of worth* acquired early in life. Client-centered therapy seeks to change such beliefs, primarily by placing individuals in an environment where they receive *unconditional acceptance* from the therapist.

and accurate reflection of the client's feelings and perceptions. In this warm, caring environment, freed from the threat of rejection, individuals can come to understand their own feelings and accept even previously unwanted aspects of their own personalities. As a result, they come to see themselves as unique humans with many desirable characteristics. To the extent such changes occur, Rogers suggests, many mental disorders disappear and individuals can resume their normal progress toward self-fulfillment (see Figure 12.2).

■ Gestalt therapy: Becoming whole.

The theme of incomplete self-awareness—especially of gaps in clients' awareness of their genuine feelings—is echoed in a second humanistic approach, **Gestalt therapy.** According to Fritz Perls (1969), originator of this type of therapy, many people have difficulties in directly experiencing and expressing emotions such as anger or the need for love. As a result, they develop manipulative social games or phony roles to try—usually without success—to satisfy their needs indirectly. These games, in turn, lead people to believe that they are not responsible for their own behavior; they blame others and come to feel powerless. The goals of Gestalt therapy, therefore, are to help clients become aware of the feelings and needs they have disowned, and to recognize that these are a genuine part of themselves.

How can these goals be reached? Only by reexperiencing old hurts, jealousies, fears, and resentments. To do this, Gestalt therapists often use the *empty chair* technique. The client imagines that an important person from his or her past—parent, child, spouse—is sitting in the chair and then, perhaps for the first time, expresses his or her true feelings to this person (feelings about the imaginary person or about events or conflicts in which this person played a part). As a result, clients gain insight into their true feelings. This may actually help to reduce the emotional turmoil that brought clients to therapy in the first place—an important benefit in itself (Greenberg et al., 1994).

■ Humanistic therapies: An overview.

Phenomenological/experiential therapies certainly have a much more optimistic flavor than psychoanalysis; they don't assume that humans must constantly struggle to control inner conflicts and dark, internal forces. In addition, several techniques devised by humanistic therapists are now widely used, even by psychologists who do not share this perspective. For instance, Rogers was one of the first therapists to record therapy sessions so that they could be studied at a later time by therapists. This not only helps therapists to assist their clients; it also provides information about which techniques are most effective during therapy. Finally, some of the assumptions underlying humanistic therapies have been subjected to scientific test and found to be valid. For instance, research findings tend to confirm Rogers's view that the gap between an individual's self-image and his or her "ideal self" plays a crucial role in maladjustment (e.g., Bootzin, Acocella, & Alloy, 1993). In these ways, then, humanistic therapies have made lasting contributions to the practice of psychotherapy.

Gestalt therapy:
According to Fritz Perls (1969), originator of this type of therapy, many people have difficulties in directly experiencing and expressing emotions, such as anger or the need for love. As a result, they develop manipulative social games or phony roles to try to satisfy—usually without success—their needs indirectly.

Such therapies, however, have been criticized for their lack of a unified theoretical base and for being vague about precisely what is supposed to happen between clients and therapists. So, although they are more widely used at present than psychoanalysis, they are subject to important criticisms.

KEY QUESTIONS

- According to humanistic therapies, what is the cause of mental disorders?
- What is the major goal of Rogers's client-centered therapy?
- What is the major goal of Gestalt therapy?

Behavior Therapies: Mental Disorders and Faulty Learning

While psychodynamic and phenomenological/experiential therapies differ in many ways, they both place importance on events occurring early in clients' lives as a key source of current disorders. In contrast, another major group of therapies, known collectively as **behavior therapies,** focus primarily on individuals' current behavior. These therapies are based on the belief that many mental disorders stem from faulty learning. Either the people involved have failed to acquire the skills and behaviors they need to cope with the problems of daily life, or they have acquired *maladaptive* habits and reactions. Within this context, the key task for therapy is to change current behavior, not to correct faulty self-concepts or resolve inner conflicts. What kinds of learning play a role in behavior therapy? As we saw in Chapter 5, there are several basic kinds. Reflecting this fact, behavior therapies, too, employ techniques based on major kinds of learning.

■ Therapies based on classical conditioning.

As noted in Chapter 5, *classical conditioning* is a process in which organisms learn that the occurrence of one stimulus will soon be followed by the occurrence of another. As a result, reactions that are at first produced only by the second stimulus gradually come to be evoked by the first as well.

What does classical conditioning have to do with mental disorders? According to behavior therapists, quite a bit. Behavior therapists suggest, for example, that many *phobias* are acquired in this manner. Stimuli that happen to be present when real dangers occur may acquire the capacity to evoke intense fear because of this association. As a result, individuals experience intense fears in response to these conditioned stimuli, even though they pose no threat to their well-being. To eliminate such reactions, behavior therapists sometimes use the technique of *exposure*. This involves exposure to controlled amounts of the feared stimuli, or to mental images of them, under conditions where the people with the phobias can't escape from them. These procedures encourage *extinction* of such fears; the phobia may soon fade away (Mineka & Zinberg, 2006).

Another technique, based in part on principles of classical conditioning, is known as **systematic desensitization.** In systematic desensitization, individuals first learn how to induce a relaxed state in their own bodies—often by learning how to relax their muscles. Then, while in a relaxed state, they are exposed to stimuli that elicit fear. Since they are now experiencing relaxation, which is incompatible with fear, the conditioned link between the stimuli and fear is weakened.

Another, and closely related, technique uses *virtual environments* to reduce phobias (e.g., Winerman, 2005). In these procedures, people who are experiencing various phobias wear a special helmet—one that shows them the objects or situations they fear. Sensors in the helmet pick up even tiny head movements, so that the scene the people who are wearing the helmet see changes just as if it were real and they were turning their heads to look around in this scene (see Figure 12.3).

FIGURE 12.3

Computer-Generated Virtual Environments: A New Tool for Treating Phobias

When people suffering from phobias wear the helmet shown here, they see a computer generated virtual environment—one in which their exposure to the stimuli they fear (airplanes, spiders, snakes) can be controlled. These procedures have been found to be highly effective in helping to reduce many phobias. (Photo and copyright by Mary Levin, University of Washington. Used with permission from Hunter Hoffman, www.vrpain.com.)

Behavior therapies:
Therapies based on the belief that many mental disorders stem from faulty learning.

Systematic desensitization:
A procedure in which individuals first learn how to induce a relaxed state in their own bodies—often by learning how to relax their muscles. Then, while in a relaxed state, they are exposed to stimuli that elicit fear.

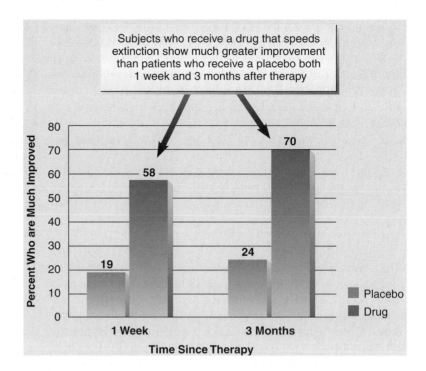

FIGURE 12.4
An Appropriate Drug and Effective Psychological Treatment: A Winning Combination
Individuals suffering from fear of heights who received both effective psychological treatment for this disorder (exposure to the stimuli they feared) *and* a drug known to facilitate extinction of conditioned fears experienced dramatic reductions in their phobias.
Source: Based on date from Davis et al., 2005).

Virtual environments offer several advantages over real ones. The amount of exposure to the feared stimuli can be carefully controlled—for instance, people who fear flying can move slowly through the many steps of a flight from takeoff to landing over the course of several sessions. Second, it is often easier to get people with phobias to be exposed to the feared stimuli when they know the stimuli aren't real. And third, it's not necessary to take them into environments where the feared stimuli really exist (e.g., into real airplanes, or to a place where they can see spiders—another common phobia).

One additional recent advance involves administration of a specific drug—*D-cycloserine*—that stimulates activity in a portion of the brain (the amygdala) that plays a key role in conditioned fears, and especially in their extinction. This drug was found to speed up extinction of fear responses among rats, and recently researchers have found that it can produce similar effects in humans. For instance, in one recent study (Davis et al., 2005), patients who showed one phobia—strong fear of heights—received virtual-reality exposure therapy. That is, they were exposed to computer-generated scenes of heights (a ride in a glass elevator). Before receiving this treatment, some of the patients were given safe doses of D-cycloserine. Other patients were given a placebo—a substance expected to have no effects on extinction of fear. Results were dramatic: When tested for fear of heights one week and again three months after the therapy, those who received the drug reported much greater improvement—much greater reductions in their fear (see Figure 12.4). Further, they were more willing to expose themselves to heights. In short, the combination of effective psychological treatment and a specific drug known to influence the neurological basis of fear produced dramatic benefits for patients—ones that could not be obtained by drugs or therapy alone.

■ Therapies based on operant conditioning.

Behavior is often shaped by the consequences it produces; actions are repeated if they yield positive outcomes or if they permit individuals to avoid or escape from negative ones. In contrast, actions that lead to negative results are suppressed. These basic principles are incorporated in several forms of therapy based on *operant conditioning*. These differ considerably in their details, but all include the following steps: (1) clear identification of undesirable or maladaptive behaviors currently shown by individuals; (2) identification of events that reinforce and maintain such responses; (3) efforts to change the environment so that these maladaptive behaviors are no longer followed by reinforcement.

Operant principles have sometimes been used in hospital settings where a large degree of control over patients' reinforcements is possible (Kazdin, 1982). Several projects have involved the establishment of *token economies* in which patients earn tokens they can exchange for various rewards, such as television-watching privileges, candy, or trips to town. These tokens are awarded for various forms of adaptive behavior, such as keeping one's room neat, participating in group meetings or therapy sessions, coming to meals on time, and eating neatly. The results have often been impressive. When individuals learn that they can acquire various rewards by behaving in adaptive ways, they often do so, with important benefits to them as well as to hospital staff (see, Paul, 1982; Paul & Lentz, 1977).

■ **Modeling: Benefiting from exposure to others.**

Many people who come to psychologists for help appear to be lacking in basic *social skills*—they don't know how to interact with others in an effective manner. They don't know how to make a request without sounding "pushy," or how to refuse a request without making the requester angry. They don't how to express their feelings clearly, how to hold their temper in check, or how to hold an ordinary conversation with others. As a result, they experience difficulties in forming friendships or intimate relationships, and encounter problems in many everyday situations. These difficulties, in turn, can leave them feeling helpless, depressed, anxious, and resentful. Behavior therapists have developed techniques for helping individuals improve their social skills. These often involve *modeling*—showing individuals demonstrations of how people with good social skills behave in many situations (see Wilson et al., 1996). (We discussed modeling in Chapter 5.)

Modeling techniques have also been used, with impressive success, in the treatment of phobias. Many studies indicate that individuals who experience intense fear of relatively harmless objects can be helped to overcome these fears through exposure to appropriate social models who demonstrate lack of fear in their presence, and who show that no harm occurs as a result of contact with these objects (e.g., Bandura & Maddux, 1977). Such procedures have been found to be effective in reducing a wide range of phobias—excessive fears of dogs, snakes, and spiders, to mention just a few (Bandura, 1986, 1995). In sum, behavioral therapies have been shown to be useful in alleviating many types of mental disorders.

KEY QUESTIONS

- According to behavior therapies, what is the primary cause of mental disorders?
- On what basic principles of learning are behavior therapies based?
- What is modeling, and how can it be used to treat mental disorders?

Cognitive Therapies: Changing Disordered Thought

At several points in this book, we have noted that cognitive processes often exert powerful effects on emotions and behavior. In other words, what we *think* strongly influences how we *feel* and what we *do*. This principle underlies another major approach to psychotherapy, **cognitive therapies.** The basic idea behind all cognitive therapies is this: Many mental disorders stem from faulty or distorted modes of thought. Change these, and the disorders, too, can be reduced or even eliminated. Here is a brief overview of several psychological treatments (types of therapy) that seek to accomplish this goal.

■ **Rational-emotive therapy: Overcoming irrational beliefs.**

Everyone I meet should like me.
I should be perfect (or darn near perfect) in every way.
Because something once affected my life, it will always affect it.
I can't bear it when things are not the way I would like them to be.

Cognitive therapies:
Therapies based on the belief that many mental disorders stem from faulty or distorted modes of thought.

Be honest: Do such views ever influence *your* thinking? While you may strongly protest that they do not, one psychologist, Albert Ellis (1987, 2005), believes that they probably *do* influence your thinking to some extent. Moreover, he contends that such *irrational thoughts* play a key role in many mental disorders. According to Ellis, the process goes something like this. Individuals experience *activating events*—things that happen to them that can potentially trigger upsetting emotional reactions. If they actually experience these strong emotional reactions, then mental disorders such as anxiety and depression may develop. The key factor determining whether this occurs, however, is the ways in which people *think* about the activating events. If they allow irrational beliefs to shape their thoughts, they are at serious risk for experiencing psychological problems.

Here's an example: Suppose one day your current romantic partner dumps you. This is certainly a sad and distressing event, but does it undermine your self-esteem and cause you to become deeply depressed? Ellis argues that this depends on how you think about it. If you fall prey to irrational beliefs, such as "Everyone must love me!" or "I can't control my emotions—I must feel totally crushed by this rejection!" you may well become depressed. If, instead, you reject these modes of thought and think, "Some people will love me and others won't, and love itself isn't always constant," or "I can deal with this—it's painful, but not the end of the world," then you will bounce back and will *not* experience depression. In essence, Ellis is saying: You can't always change the world or what happens to you, but you *can* change the ways in which you think about these experiences. *You* can decide whether, and how much, to be bothered or upset by events—being dumped by a romantic partner, losing a job, getting a lower-than-expected grade on a test, and so on.

To help people combat the negative effects of irrational thinking, Ellis developed **rational-emotive therapy (RET).** During RET, the therapist first attempts to identify irrational thoughts and then tries to persuade clients to recognize them for what they are. By challenging the irrationality of their clients' beliefs, therapists practicing RET get them to see how ridiculous and unrealistic some of their ideas are, and in this way, help them to stop being their own worst enemy.

■ Beck's cognitive-behavioral therapy for depression.

In discussing depression (pages 438–439), we noted that this extremely common but serious mental disorder has an important cognitive component: It stems, at least in part, from distorted and often self-defeating modes of thought. Recognizing this important fact, Aaron Beck (1985, 2005) has devised **Beck's cognitive-behavioral therapy** for alleviating depression. Like Ellis, Beck assumes that depressed individuals engage in illogical thinking, and that this underlies their difficulties. They hold unrealistically negative beliefs and assumptions about themselves, the future, and the world (e.g., "I'm a worthless person no one could ever love," "If good things happen to me, it's just blind luck," "My life is a mess and will never improve"). Moreover, he contends, they cling to these illogical ideas and assumption no matter what happens.

According to Beck, such distorted thinking leads individuals to have negative moods that, in turn, increase the probability of more negative thinking (see Figure 12.5). In other words, he emphasizes the importance of mood-dependent memory—how our current moods influence what we remember and what we think about (see Chapter 6). How can this vicious circle be broken? In contrast to rational-emotive therapy, Beck's cognitive approach does not attempt to disprove the ideas held by depressed people. Rather, the therapist and client work together to identify the individual's assumptions, beliefs, and expectations, and to formulate ways to test them. For example, if a client states that she is a total failure, the therapist may ask how she defines failure, and whether some experiences she defines this way may actually be only partial failures. If that's so, the therapist inquires, aren't they also partial *successes?* Continuing in this manner, the therapist

Rational-emotive therapy (RET):
A cognitive therapy based on the view that many forms of mental disorders stem from irrational thoughts.

Beck's cognitive-behavioral therapy:
A cognitive-behavioral therapy for alleviating depression. Beck, who proposed the therapy, assumes that depressed individuals engage in illogical thinking, and that this underlies their difficulties. They hold unrealistically negative beliefs and assumptions about themselves, the future, and the world.

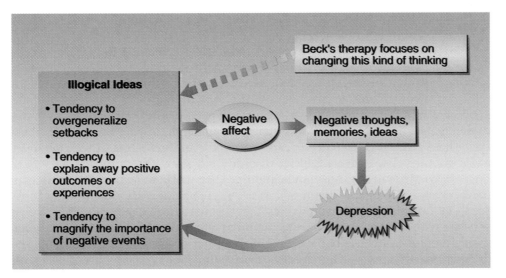

FIGURE 12.5
Beck's Cognitive-Behavioral Therapy
Beck's cognitive-behavioral therapy is designed to change cognitive tendencies (e.g., distorted thinking) that contribute to depression. Such patterns of thought often produce negative effects (moods) that then increase the likelihood of further negative thoughts. Beck's cognitive-behavioral therapy attempts to break this cycle.

might then ask the client whether there are *any* areas of her life in which she does experience success, and has succeeded in reaching goals. Recent studies indicate that as a result of these procedures, individuals learn to reinterpret negative events in ways that help them cope with such outcomes without becoming depressed (e.g., Bruder et al., 1997). So, while the specific techniques used are different from those used in RET, the major goal is much the same: helping people to recognize, and reject, false assumptions that underlie their difficulties.

■ Cognitive therapies: An evaluation.

An essential question about any form of therapy is: Does it work? Cognitive therapies pass this test with flying colors: Many studies indicate that changing or eliminating irrational beliefs can be very effective in countering depression and other personal difficulties (e.g., Blatt et al., 1996). Similarly, the procedures outlined by Beck have been found to be highly effective in treating depression (e.g., Bruder et al., 1997). Perhaps even more important, the effects they produce tend be longer lasting than those produced by other forms of therapy for depression—for instance, antidepressant drugs (we'll examine these in a later section; Segal, Gemar, & Williams, 1999). One more point: Cognitive and behavioral procedures are often combined in what is known as *cognitive-behavioral therapy*. In other words, efforts are made to change both behavior and cognition. In fact, most modern therapies fall under this heading. This reflects a basic and important fact about current forms of psychological treatment: They are eclectic and flexible in nature, and are *not* necessarily closely linked to specific theories of personality or mental disorders. In short, if modern methods for alleviating mental disorders are anything, they are diverse and pragmatic in the sense that they use whatever procedures work best for treating specific mental disorders. This is a far cry from earlier forms of therapy that were often tied closely to specific theories, such as Freud's views of psychosexual development and the origins of mental disorders.

Computer and Internet-Based Psychotherapies

All the forms of therapy we have considered so far involve face-to-face contact between a therapist and an individual seeking help. Is such contact necessary? Or can therapy occur in a less direct manner, by means of computers? This has been a topic of growing interest to psychologists, because individual therapy can be quite expensive, and this limits access to it by many people. With this thought in mind, psychologists have designed computer programs that, in a sense, perform therapy! These programs have been designed to help individuals deal with phobias, panic disorder, obsessive-compulsive disorder, and many other problems (Taylor & Luce, 2003). Growing evidence indicates that they work: In fact, in one study (Kenardy et al., 2002), people diagnosed as having panic disorder were randomly assigned to one of four groups in which they received one of the following: twelve sessions with a therapist who used cognitive behavioral techniques; six sessions with a therapist plus use of a hand-held computer programmed to help with the problem; six sessions with a therapist plus a manual telling them how to deal with their problem; or no therapy (a control group). Results indicated that the first two groups showed equal benefits, thus suggesting that a computer could substitute, at least in part, for a therapist.

Why are such techniques effective? In part because many people are less embarrassed about reporting sensitive personal information to a computer than to another person, and because computers, which are not subject to the biasing effects of mood, stereotypes, and many other factors, can sometimes make more accurate judgments about patients' conditions than can actual therapists. Please don't misunderstand: We are *not* suggesting that computer programs can replace live therapists—far from it. But it appears that, in some cases, individuals can benefit from well-designed programs used to supplement live therapy.

KEY QUESTIONS

- According to cognitive therapies, what is the primary cause of mental disorders?
- What is the major goal of rational-emotive therapy?
- What is the major goal of Beck's cognitive-behavioral therapy for depression?

PSYCHOLOGICAL TREATMENTS AND DIVERSITY: A MULTICULTURAL APPROACH TO COMBATING MENTAL DISORDERS

The United States and many other countries are undergoing dramatic shifts in the nature of their human populations. In many European countries, the proportion of people from other areas of the world—Asia, Africa, and many other locations—is growing rapidly. For instance, in France, more than 10 percent of the population is now of North African descent; in the United Kingdom, almost 15 percent of the people were born, or are the children of people born, in Asia or Africa. The United States is certainly in the front line with respect to such changes. More than 30 percent of the population belongs to cultural or ethnic minorities, and the proportion of children younger than age five in these categories is approaching 45 percent. Among these groups, Hispanics are showing the most rapid growth, and by 2035 it is estimated that they may outnumber people of European descent in several states (e.g., California, Texas).

In response to these rapid and truly gigantic changes, psychologists around the world have become increasingly aware of the importance of adopting a multicultural perspective. More specifically, they have increasingly recognized that methods of treatment *must* be adapted to reflect cultural and ethnic differences in the people served (see Figure 12.6). While mental disorders themselves are much the same throughout the world, the ways in which they are expressed, the frequency of their occurrence, and, most important of all, the best ways of treating them can, and often do, vary across different cultural or ethnic groups. Consider, for instance, Hispanics—a group of major importance in the United States. Certain values in Hispanic culture may interact in complex ways with various forms of psychological treatment (Dingfelder, 2005). For instance, people of Hispanic descent often come from tightly knit families and feel disloyal discussing family problems with an "outside" person, such as a therapist. This value is known as *familismio*. In addition, Hispanic culture emphasizes the value of *simpatia*—an emphasis on the value of interpersonal harmony. As a result, therapists may find that Hispanic patients are reluctant to follow their advice with respect to discussing sensitive topics with spouses or other family members. A third value in Hispanic culture that has relevance to psychological treatment is *personalismo*—a strong emphasis on personal relationships. This means that if a therapist attempts to maintain "professional detachment," this may be viewed negatively by Hispanic patients: They expect a more intimate give-and-take relationship.

FIGURE 12.6
Psychological Treatments Must Be Adapted to a Multicultural World
The proportion of cultural and ethnic minorities is increasing rapidly in many countries. Psychologists must adopt a truly *multicultural* perspective on psychological treatment to be of greatest help to the largest number of people.

The same kinds of issues occur with respect to Asians—another rapidly growing minority group in the United States and elsewhere. For instance, many Asians—especially older men—tend to express emotional problems in terms of bodily aches and pains. In fact, they often find psychological symptoms highly embarrassing—not something they want to reveal to others. How can psychologists get around such difficulties? Perhaps by recommending not simply medications and therapy, but perhaps also spiritual guidance and social support (e.g., a visit to a nearby Buddhist temple).

Or consider the case of a Hispanic man who suffers a disabling injury on the job. Standard treatment might involve prescriptions for painkillers and therapy aimed at developing realistic expectations about being able to return to work. In Hispanic culture, however, permanent job loss might threaten the man's position as head of the family, and so put him at risk for developing depression. Clearly, these are complex problems to which there are no simple answers (Law, 2005).

Before concluding our discussion of psychotherapies, we should note that in recent years, psychologists have become increasingly aware of the important role of cultural factors in all forms of psychological treatment. Ethical guidelines for psychologists state strongly that therapists should not provide services outside their areas of competence, and this has been interpreted to mean that they should not attempt to treat people from outside their own cultural or ethnic groups unless they are familiar both with their own cultural biases *and* differences between their cultural group and those of their patients (see Acton, 2001). With that principle in mind, therapists should definitely *not* attempt to treat all clients in the same way, regardless of their cultural background. On the contrary, they must take careful account of such factors, and assure that they build them into their relationships with clients. Findings indicate that when therapists take ethnic and cultural differences into account, they are more effective in establishing excellent working relationships with clients, and therefore in helping them (Fuertes et al., 2002). This multicultural perspective is now very strong in psychology, and is incorporated into the goals psychologists set for therapy, and in the methods they use for attaining them (e.g., Nelson-Jomes, 2002). So the multicultural perspective we have stressed throughout this book plays an important role in psychotherapy, just as it does in all activities performed by psychologists.

ALTERNATIVES TO INDIVIDUAL PSYCHOTHERAPY: GROUP THERAPIES

As we'll see in a later section, psychological treatments (including several forms of psychotherapy) really work—several of the kinds of therapy we have already considered *are* effective in alleviating mental disorders (e.g., Barlow, 2004; APA, Division of Clinical Psychology, 1995). But there are several factors that limit the usefulness of such procedures in some cases. First, individual psychotherapy is not accessible to all people who might benefit from it. It is often quite expensive (skilled therapists often receive $200, $300, or more per hour!) and—sadly—many insurance companies often won't cover such costs.

But even if individual psychotherapy were free, *cultural factors* limit its accessibility for some groups of people. For example, as we noted earlier, in many cultures it is considered unseemly to openly express one's emotions or to discuss them with other people—especially total strangers (which is what therapists are, at least initially). The result is that people from some cultures, and people from ethnic minorities (e.g., people of Hispanic or Native American descent in the United States) view individual psychotherapy as pointless or even shameful—a sign of weakness. Further, for many poor people, psychological treatment is difficult if not impossible to obtain, in part, because of the costs involved and because few facilities for delivering psychological treatments are located in areas where poor people live. In addition, however, it may stem from certain attitudes on the part of psychologists, who are largely middle-class in background and, as a result, have several false beliefs about poor people—beliefs that get in the way of their helping such people (Smith, 2005). Some of these beliefs, and their consequences for offering psychological treatments to poor people, are shown in Table 12.2. As you can see, these views—which often aren't ones recognized by the people who hold them—can truly make it difficult for people from poor backgrounds to obtain the treatment they need. No, it is *not* that psychologists are focused on making high incomes and poor people can't pay for their services. On the contrary, these attitudes lead psychologists to believe that poor people don't want their services or can't profit from them because they face much larger problems than mental disorders, and believe that these people don't know about psychology or accept it as a valid source of help.

Largely in response to these and other problems, alternative forms of treatment for mental disorders have been developed—forms that are more economical and do not require one-on-one meetings between psychologists and people in need of their help. We'll focus on two that have received, perhaps, the greatest attention: marital and family therapies.

Marital Therapy: When Spouses Are Seen as the Enemy

In the United States and many other countries, more than 50 percent of all marriages now end in divorce (Popenoe & Whitehead, 1999). While some marriages are clearly not worth saving because they are destructive to both partners, *marital therapy* (sometimes termed *couples therapy*) is designed to help couples who feel that their marriage is worth saving.

Before turning to the procedures used in such therapy, however, let's first consider a very basic question: What, in your opinion, is the number-one reason why

TABLE 12.2	When Attitudes Get in the Way of Helping People in Need of Help

Psychologists are *not* biased against poor people—or any other group for that matter! But it has recently been suggested that their own attitudes and beliefs about such people may prevent them from offering their services to these people.

Attitude	Potential Effects
Poor people have so many overwhelming problems in their lives that they have little or no use for what psychologists can offer.	Reduces motivation of psychologists to deliver psychological treatment to poor people because they believe the poor will view mental disorders as relatively trivial.
Poor people face so many major problems that the help psychologists can provide will seem unimportant to them.	Psychologists believe that the services they offer are relatively unimportant to poor people, so they feel powerless to truly help.
Working in poor neighborhoods is uncomfortable to psychologists because it forces them to see how poor people actually live.	Psychologists, who are mainly from middle-class backgrounds, are reluctant to come face-to-face with the way in which poor people actually live; this reduces their motivation to work in poor neighborhoods.
Poor people are unfamiliar with psychology and its services, so they will not use them even if they are available.	Psychologists, afraid that what they have to offer will be rejected or ignored, are reluctant to work in settings where their services will, in fact, be rejected.

Source: Based on suggestions by Smith, 2005.

couples seek professional help in the first place? If you guessed "sexual problems," guess again; such difficulties are actually far down the list. The number-one reason why couples seek therapy is *perceived unfairness* in their division of labor—each thinks that the other is not doing his or her fair share of the work. Such feelings then become the excuse for engaging in extramarital sex, for spending large amount of money, and for engaging in substance abuse (e.g., heavy drinking; Fincham, 2003).

An underlying cause of many marital conflicts can be summarized by the phrase *faulty communication*. Couples who seek marital therapy often state that their spouse never talks to them or never tells them what she/he is thinking (see Figure 12.7 for an example). Or they report that the only thing their spouse ever does is *complain* about their faults and what they are doing wrong. Even worse, each side makes *negative attributions* about the other. Here's one example: Suppose a spouse is late for dinner. How does his or her partner explain this? In marriages that are heading for serious trouble—or are already there—this action is attributed to pure inconsiderateness. Other possible causes, such as unavoidable delays in traffic, are not even considered. In other words, the partner is not given the benefit of the doubt—on the contrary, she or he is found "guilty" even before any evidence is obtained. Given that couples begin their relationships with frequent statements of mutual esteem and love, the pain of such faulty communication patterns is doubled: Each partner wonders what went wrong—and then generally blames the partner! In contrast, happy couples show a very different pattern in which they display positive problem-solving techniques and positive affect five times as often as negative problem-solving tactics (e.g., withdrawal, anger) and negative affect (Fincham, 2001; Gottman, 1993). They are also more likely to forgive

FIGURE 12.7
Marital Therapy: Help for Troubled Relationships
Clearly, the couple shown in this cartoon is experiencing major problems with respect to communication. Neither seems to know what the other is thinking—or feeling!

"None for me, thanks."

real or imagined wrongs on the part of their spouse than are couples who experience intense conflict and seek marital therapy.

How does marital therapy work? One type—*behavior marital therapy*—focuses on changing the communication problems mentioned above. Therapists work to produce such improvements in many ways, including having each partner play the role of the other person so as to see the relationship as the other does. Other techniques involve having couples watch videotapes of their own interactions. This procedure is often truly an eye-opener: "Wow, I never realized that's how I come across!" is a common reaction of a person seeing him- or herself interacting with his or her spouse. As communication between members of a couple improves, many other beneficial changes occur—for instance, they stop criticizing each other in destructive ways (e.g., Baron, 1993), express positive sentiments toward each other more frequently, and stop assuming that everything their spouse does that annoys or angers them is done on purpose (e.g., Kubany et al., 1995). Once good communication is established, couples may also find it easier to resolve other sources of friction in their relationship. The result may then be a happier and more stable relationship, and one that increases, rather than reduces, the psychological well-being of both partners.

Family Therapy: Changing Patterns That Harm

Let's begin with a disturbing fact: When individuals who have been hospitalized for serious mental disorders and who have shown improvements return home, they often experience a relapse. All the gains they have made through individual therapy vanish. This fact points to an unsettling possibility: Perhaps the problems experienced by such people stem, at least in part, from their families—from disturbed patterns of interaction among family members (Hazelrigg, Cooper, & Borduin, 1987). To the extent this is true, attempting to help one member of a family is not sufficient: unless changes are made in their family environment, too, any benefits they have experienced may disappear once they return home.

Recognition of this important fact spurred the development of several types of **family therapy,** designed to change the relationships among family members in constructive ways. Such therapies differ in form, but most are based on the following assumptions, suggested by *systems theory*—an approach that views families as social systems: *circular causality*—events within a family are interrelated

Family therapy:
Therapy designed to change the relationships among family members in constructive ways.

and cause each other in reciprocal fashion; *ecology* is crucial—families are integrated systems so that change in one member will affect all other members; and *subjectivity*—each family member has her or his personal view of family events. Together, these ideas emphasize the importance of working with all family members, because they are in constant contact with one another and create an environment in which all exist.

While family therapy focuses on making many beneficial changes within families, recent research findings indicate that, from the point of view of preventing relapses among persons recovering from serious mental disorders, one kind of change is truly crucial. This involves reducing a very destructive pattern of communication that develops in many families. This pattern is known as **expressed emotion** (EE), and involves three major components: *criticism*—one member of the family states explicitly that he or she dislikes or disapproves of something another member does (e.g., "It really annoys me when he hangs around smoking all day"); *hostility*—an extreme form of criticism in which one family member totally rejects another (e.g., "I breathe a sigh of relief every time he goes out"); and emotional overinvolvement—an over-protective, excessively devoted, self-sacrificing style (e.g., "I hate to leave him home alone even for an hour or two"; see Figure 12.8).

FIGURE 12.8
Changing Patterns of Communication That Harm: One Key Goal of Family Therapy
When individuals recovering from serious mental disorders return home, the environments they face are an important factor in determining whether they will experience a relapse (a recurrence of the mental disorder). Family therapy often focuses on reducing patterns of communication that have been shown to increase relapse rates—patterns known, collectively, as *expressed emotion*, which involves harsh criticism, hostility, and emotional overinvolvement (e.g., over protectiveness) by other family members.

Research findings (e.g., Hooley, 2004) indicate that patients who return to families with high levels of EE are two to three times as likely to suffer relapses than are patients who return to families in which levels of EE are low. So clearly, this pattern of communication is a destructive one for people recovering from mental disorders. Fortunately, it can be prevented or at least reduced. Therapy that focuses on making family members aware of their criticism, hostility, and emotional overinvolvement can, with help, reduce such communications, and the effects can be very helpful to recovering patients. A key problem is that such people are in a heightened state of vulnerability—they truly can't "take it" as they did in the past. How vulnerable are they? Recent studies (see Hooley, 2004) indicate that when people who are recovering from depression hear their mothers criticize them, a portion of the brain that often shows increased activity in response to emotion-provoking events (the dorsolateral prefrontal cortex) actually shows a *reduction* in such activity. In contrast, people who have never been depressed show *increased* activity in this region when they hear their mother criticizing them. These findings suggest that people recovering from serious mental disorders have reduced capacity to deal with emotional events, and that is one reason why, when they return to families high in EE, they are truly at risk. To the extent family therapy can prevent this pattern, it is certainly very valuable. (When individuals experience distress at home or in their relationships, this often affects their performance at work. Recognizing this fact, many companies have established programs to help employees cope with many problems. See the **Psychology Goes to Work** section below for an overview of these programs, and how they can help *you*.)

KEY QUESTIONS

- Do implicit assumptions prevent psychologists from helping at least some people who could benefit from their help?

Expressed emotion:
A summary term for conditions existing in some families involving excessive criticism, hostility, and emotional overinvolvement. High levels of expressed emotion increase the chances of relapse among people recovering from serious mental disorders.

- What is marital or couples therapy?
- What is expressed emotion and what role does it play in family therapy?

BIOLOGICAL THERAPIES

Employee assistance programs:
Programs established by companies to help employees cope with personal problems, including mental disorders.

All the psychological treatments we have described so far focus on changing behavior or thought. This makes very good sense since the more we know about mental disorders, the more we realize that they often involve patterns of behavior and thinking that cause distress to the people who show them and interfere with their leading full, happy lives. Another approach to combating mental disorders, however, involves what are known as *biological therapies*—forms of therapy that attempt to alleviate these through biological interventions. We'll now examine several of these approaches.

PSYCHOLOGY GOES TO WORK

Employee Assistance Programs: A Helping Hand from Your Company

There is an old saying that "Happy employees are productive employees." As we'll see in Chapter 14, this is not always true. But there is no doubt about the fact that "troubled employees" are *not* productive employees. Recognizing this fact, many companies have established special programs to help their employees deal with a wide range of personal problems. The companies involved do want to help their employees to lead happier lives, but in addition, they recognize that this is *good business*. Employees obviously can't do their best work when deeply distressed by personal problems or mental disorders.

These special programs—**employee assistance programs** is what they are usually called—have been established by many companies. In fact, nearly two-thirds of employers who have more than a few hundred employees have such programs in place (Wah, 2000). These programs vary greatly in scope—what problems they are equipped to handle—and in terms of their quality. But really good companies (and we hope that you work for or will work for a really good one!) offer a great deal. For instance, many large companies offer EAPs that can help employees deal with personal problems such as substance abuse, career planning, and legal or financial problems. In addition, others offer toll-free telephone access for employees who wish to talk about their problems with trained professionals—psychologists, physi-

cians, and others. This protects employees' privacy, but gives them access to the advice they need and want.

As the popularity of EAPs has grown, the range of services they offer has expanded. Some even offer *e-therapy*—two-way communication between troubled employees and trained counselors or psychologists. While this is not as effective as face-to-face meetings, it offers important benefits, such as great flexibility in terms of scheduling, and also can provide employees with access to a wide range of trained professionals.

The bottom line is simply this: Employee assistance programs are another source of help if you or someone you know is experiencing the distress and impaired functioning that derive from mental disorders. This means that when you are considering a new job, you should find out just what services are offered in the company's EAP. And once you are an employee, you should *not* be reluctant to seek help. EAPs do vary in quality, but in most cases, they are equipped to help employees cope with a wide range of problems. And if these problems are beyond their scope, the directors of these programs have ready access to psychologists and other professionals who can offer additional help. But remember: The first step must be yours, so don't hesitate. Seek help if you feel that you do need it. (By the way, we offer specific tips on how you can access the EAP in your company in a Making Psychology Part of Your Life section at the end of this chapter.)

Drug Therapy: The Pharmacological Revolution

In 1955, about 600,000 people were full-time resident patients in psychiatric hospitals in the United States. Twenty years later, this number had dropped below 175,000, and in the following years the number kept declining. What produced this dramatic shift? The answer is simple: A number of drugs effective in treating mental disorders were developed and put to use. Let's take a closer look at these drugs and their effects.

■ **Antipsychotic drugs.**

If you had visited the wards of a psychiatric hospital for seriously disturbed persons prior to 1955, you would have witnessed some pretty wild scenes—screaming, bizarre actions, nudity. If you returned a few years later, however, you would have seen a dramatic change: peace, relative tranquility, and many patients now capable of direct, sensible communication. These startling changes were largely the result of the development of *antipsychotic drugs*, sometimes known as the *major tranquilizers* or *neuroleptics*. These drugs are highly effective in reducing the *positive* symptoms shown by schizophrenics (e.g., hallucinations, delusions), but are less effective in reducing negative symptoms (e.g., withdrawal, lack of affect).

The most important group of antipsychotic drugs—*phenothiazines*—was discovered by accident. In the early 1950s, a French surgeon, Henri Laborit, used a drug in this chemical family, *Thorazine* (chlorpromazine), to reduce blood pressure in patients before surgery. He found that their blood pressure didn't drop, but that they become much less anxious. French psychiatrists tried the drug with their patients, and found that it worked: It reduced anxiety and—even more important—it also reduced hallucinations and delusions among schizophrenic patients. Chemists quickly analyzed chlorpromazine and developed many other drugs related to it (e.g., clozapine, haloperidol) that were even more effective in reducing psychotic symptoms. (Throughout this discussion we'll present brand names of drugs followed by their chemical or generic name in parentheses.)

How do the antipsychotics produce such effects? Some block the action of the neurotransmitter *dopamine* on certain receptors in the brain. As we noted earlier, the presence of an excess of this neurotransmitter, or increased sensitivity to it, may play a role in schizophrenia. Other antipsychotics, especially newer ones (e.g., Novartis, Zeneca), influence many different chemicals in the brain—neurotransmitters and others as well. In sum, many different antipsychotic drugs exist, and they do not all operate in the same way. Whatever the precise mechanism involved, however, it is clear that antipsychotic drugs are very helpful in reducing the bizarre symptoms of schizophrenia.

The use of these drugs, however, is not without drawbacks. As is true with virtually *every* drug, they often produce side effects, in this case, such side effects as blurred vision and dry mouth. Additional effects can involve uncontrollable contractions of muscles in the neck, head, tongue, and back, or uncontrollable restlessness and agitation. The most serious side effect of all, however, is **tardive dyskinesia.** After receiving antipsychotic drugs for prolonged periods of time, many patients develop this side effect, which involves loss of motor control, especially in the face. As a result, they show involuntary muscle movements of the tongue, lips, and jaw. One relatively new antipsychotic drug, Clozaril (clozapine), appears to be effective without producing tardive dyskinesia. Additional antipsychotic drugs are being developed and it is hoped that they will have even fewer side effects.

While the antipsychotic drugs are clearly of great value, and do reduce the most bizarre symptoms of schizophrenia, it should be emphasized that they do *not* cure this disorder. In the past, such drugs were more effective in treating the positive rather than negative symptoms of schizophrenia. Thus, people receiving them tended to remain somewhat withdrawn and to show the reduced levels of

Tardive dyskinesia:
A side effect of some antipsychotic drugs involving loss of motor control, especially in the face.

affect that is often part of schizophrenia. Newer drugs, however, do seem more successful in treating these negative symptoms. In any case, although drugs for treating schizophrenia are improving, the likelihood that individuals with schizophrenia will regain normal functioning and be able to live on their own is increased when they receive psychotherapy, too.

■ Antidepressant drugs.

Shortly after the development of chlorpromazine, drugs effective in reducing depression made their appearance. There are three basic types of such compounds: *selective serotonin reuptake inhibitors* (SSRIs), *MAO (monoamine oxidase) inhibitors,* and *tricyclics.* Again, as is true with virtually all drugs used to treat mental disorders, they seem to exert their effects by influencing neurotransmitters, especially serotonin and norepinephrine (Julien, 1995).

Among the SSRIs, *Prozac* (fluoxetine) is by far the most famous—and also the most commonly prescribed: More than 1.5 million prescriptions for it are written every month in the United States alone. Depressed people taking this drug often report that they feel better than they have in their entire lives. However, Prozac, like other antidepressant drugs, appears to have serious side effects. About 30 percent of patients taking it report nervousness, insomnia, joint pain, weight loss, and sexual dysfunction (Hellerstein et al., 1993). A small number report suicidal thoughts (Mendlewicz & Lecrubier, 2000).

In contrast, MAO inhibitors can produce more dangerous side effects. They seem virtually to eliminate REM sleep, and if consumed with food containing tyramine (e.g., aged cheeses, beer, red wine), can cause a sudden, extreme rise in blood pressure, thus putting patients at risk for strokes (Julien, 1992). For these reasons, these drugs are used less often than the other two types of antidepressants. Tricyclics also produce side effects, such as disturbances in sleep and appetite, but these tend to decrease within a few weeks. Widely prescribed tyrcyclics include Elavil (amitriptyline) and Tonfranil (imipramine).

One final point: While these drugs *are* often effective in treating depression, research evidence suggests that they are not necessarily more effective than cognitive-behavioral therapies (see Bruder et al., 1997; Robinson, Berman, & Meimeyer, 1990; Hollon, Shelton, & Loosen, 1991). Indeed, these forms of psychotherapy may produce longer-lasting benefits than drugs (Barlow, 2004; Segal, Gemar, & Williams, 1999). It's also important to note that antidepressants are most effective for treating major depression, and somewhat less so for milder conditions.

■ Lithium.

An entirely different kind of antidepressant drug is *lithium* (usually administered as *lithium chloride*). This drug has been found to be quite effective in treating bipolar disorder, and is effective with 60 to 70 percent of people with this disorder (Julien, 1995). Since such people are often quite agitated and even psychotic, lithium is generally administered along with antipsychotic or antidepressant medications. Unfortunately, lithium has serious side effects: Excessive doses can cause delirium, and even death. Thus, dose level must be carefully controlled for it to be effective. Exactly how lithium exerts its effects is not known, and this suggests the need for caution in its use.

■ Antianxiety drugs.

Alcohol, a substance used by many people to combat anxiety, has been available for thousands of years. Needless to say, however, it has important negative side effects. Synthetic drugs with antianxiety effects—sometimes known as *minor tranquilizers*—have been manufactured for several decades. The most widely prescribed at present are the *benzodiapezines.* This group includes drugs whose names you may already know: Valium, Ativan, Xanax, and Librium.

The most common use for antianxiety drugs, at least ostensibly, is as an aid to sleep. They are safer for this purpose than *barbiturates* since they are less addicting. However, substances derived from the benzodiazepines remain in the body for longer periods of time than those from barbiturates, and can cumulate until they reach toxic levels. Thus, long-term use of these drugs can be quite dangerous. In addition, when they are taken with alcohol their effects may be magnified; this is definitely a combination to avoid. Finally, they tend to produce dependency; individuals experience withdrawal symptoms when the medication is abruptly stopped. The benzodiazepines seem to produce their effects by acting as a kind of braking system for the nervous system, reducing activity that would otherwise result in anxiety and tension. Benzodiazepines are effective; people who take them report being calmer and less worried. However, they have potentially serious side effects: drowsiness, dizziness, fatigue, and reduced motor coordination. These can prove fatal to motorists or people operating dangerous machinery. Fortunately, such effects are much smaller for an additional antianxiety drug that is not related to the benzodiazepines: BuSpar (buspirone).

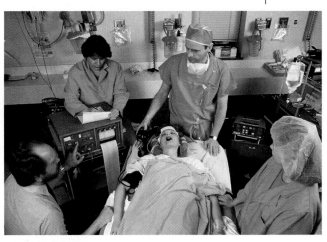

FIGURE 12.9
Electroconvulsive Therapy Today
Electric current passes through the brain for one-second intervals, eventually causing a brief seizure. This treatment seems to be effective in reducing severe depression, although how it produces such effects is still uncertain.

In sum, many drugs effective in treating serious mental disorders exist, and are being prescribed in ever-increasing quantities. And as we noted earlier, recent legislation in several states (e.g., New Mexico, Louisiana) now permits psychologists to prescribe such medicines (Stambor, 2006). Since some of these drugs are fairly new, their long-term effects remain unknown. Moreover, like all drugs, their benefits are offset, to a degree, by potentially serious side effects. Should society be more cautious in using them? This is a complex issue, but many psychologists feel that greater caution may be justified.

■ **Ethnic and racial differences in response to drugs.**

Before concluding, we should note that many of the drugs used to treat mental disorders have been found to vary in their effects in people belonging to various ethnic and racial groups. People belonging to some groups metabolize these drugs differently, benefit from them to different degrees, and show contrasting levels of side effects. Such differences *must* be taken carefully into account, and this constitutes yet another reason why all therapists must be careful to adopt a multicultural perspective on their efforts to help clients (Burroughs, Maxey, & Levy, 2002).

Electroconvulsive Therapy

Another and very different form of biological therapy is known as **electroconvulsive therapy (ECT).** This involves placing electrodes on the patient's temples and delivering shocks of 70 to 130 volts for brief intervals (approximately one second). These are continued until the patient has a seizure, a muscle contraction of the entire body, lasting at least twenty to twenty-five seconds. In order to prevent broken bones and other injuries, a muscle relaxant and a mild anesthetic are usually administered before the start of the shocks. Patients typically receive three treatments a week for several weeks (see Figure 12.9).

Surprisingly, ECT seems to work, at least for some disorders. It reduces severe depression, especially with people who have failed to respond to other forms of therapy (Effective Treatment, 1994; Fink, 1993). The American Psychiatric Association recommends it for use with patients who are severely suicidal or psychotically depressed (e.g., refusing to eat, in a stupor).

Unfortunately, there are important risks connected with ECT. It is designed to

Electroconvulsive therapy (ECT):
A from of biological therapy in which electrodes are placed on a patient's temples and strong electric shocks are then delivered to the brain.

alter the brain, and it does—producing loss of *episodic memory* in many patients. In a few cases, ECT produces irreversible damage to portions of the brain. Further, although the shocks themselves are painless, many patients find the procedures frightening, to say the least. These facts have led some researchers to criticize its use and to call for its elimination as a form of therapy. However, the fact that it works for some severely depressed people who have not responded to other forms of therapy has lead to its continued use (e.g., Fink, 1994).

Psychosurgery: From Lobotomies to Brain Implants

In 1935, a Portuguese psychiatrist, Egas Moniz, attempted to reduce aggressive behavior in psychotic patients by cutting neural connections between the prefontal lobes and the rest of the brain. The operation, known as *prefrontal lobotomy*, seemed to work: Aggressive behavior decreased. Moniz received the Nobel Prize in medicine for his work.

Encouraged by Moniz's work, psychiatrists all over the world rushed to treat mental disorders through various forms of **psychosurgery**—brain operations designed to change abnormal behavior. Tens of thousands of patients were given prefrontal lobotomies and related operations. Unfortunately, it soon became apparent that the results were not always beneficial. While some forms of objectionable or dangerous behavior did decrease, serious side effects sometimes occurred: Some patients became highly excitable and impulsive; others slipped into profound apathy and a total absence of emotion.

In view of these outcomes, most physicians stopped performing prefrontal lobotomies, and few are done today. However, other more limited operations on the brain continue. For instance, in one modern procedure, *cingulotomy*, connections between a very small area of the brain and the limbic system are severed. Results indicate that this limited kind of psychosurgery may be effective with individuals suffering from depression, anxiety disorders, and especially obsessive-compulsive disorder, and who have not responded to any other type of treatment (e.g., Cumming et al., 1995). Still newer procedures involve inserting tiny video cameras into the brain or using computer-guided imagery (e.g., MRI scans) to help surgeons make very precise lesions in the brain. It is too early to tell whether such psychosurgery will yield long-term gains.

Perhaps the most promising new technique involves implanting tiny electrodes deep within the brain (Reuters News Service, April 25, 2006). These electrodes emit pulses of electricity that block abnormal activity in nearby regions of the brain; this has been found to be effective in treating depression and obsessive-compulsive disorder. In recent studies, patients who were *not* helped by drugs or various psychological treatments did show improvement when electrodes were placed in certain regions of the brain (e.g., the ventral anterior internal capsule). Since no other form of treatment—including electroconvulsive therapy—seemed to help, this is a potential important development.

KEY QUESTIONS

- What drugs are used in the treatment of psychological disorders?
- What is electroconvulsive therapy?
- What is psychosurgery?

Psychosurgery:
A form of biological therapy in which brain operations are performed to change abnormal behavior.

PSYCHOLOGICAL TREATMENTS: ARE THEY EFFECTIVE?

Do psychological treatments really work? In other words, are they effective in alleviating mental disorders? Early research on this issue did not seem to be encouraging. In 1952, Hans Eysenck, a prominent psychologist, published a paper indicating that psychotherapy is actually quite *ineffective:* People improve at about the same rate whether they receive therapy or not. Fortunately, the findings of later, and more conclusive, studies pointed to a very different conclusion: Contrary to what Eysenck suggested, psychotherapy and other forms of psychological treatment *are* helpful (Barlow, 2004; Bergin & Lambert, 1978; Clum & Bowers, 1990). Apparently, Eysenck *over*estimated the proportion of people who recover without any therapy and also *under*estimated the proportion who improve after receiving therapy. In fact, several reviews of existing evidence—more than five hundred studies on the effects of therapy—suggest that therapy *does* work: More people who receive psychotherapy show improvements with respect to their mental disorders than people who do not receive therapy (e.g., Elkin, 1989). Further, the more treatment people receive, the more they improve, the fewer symptoms they show, and the less distress they report (Howard et al., 1986; Orlinsky & Howard, 1987). In fact, research published in prestigious medical journals such as *Journal of the American Medical Association* and the *New England Journal of Medicine* indicates that psychological treatments are actually significantly *more* effective in reducing many forms of mental disorder than routine medical care or drugs alone (see Barlow, 2004; Miranda et al., 2003; Teri et al., 2003). This is impressive evidence, and it was gathered in carefully conducted studies, so overall the following conclusions do seem justified: Psychological treatments (including many different forms of therapy) *are* effective in alleviating many kinds of mental disorder, and such treatments are at least as effective as any others for treating these disorders—and often, more effective than drugs alone. This is not to imply that psychological treatments are perfect—far from it. They are more effective in treating some disorders than others, and work better for some people than others. But overall, they *are* effective and can be of great help to people suffering from mental disorders.

Having established that basic fact, we'll now turn to two other related questions: Are some forms of therapy better than others? Why are many forms of therapy equally effective?

Are Some Forms of Psychological Treatment More Successful Than Others?

In the past, psychologists and other mental health professionals tended to choose, and stick with, one type of therapy. This meant that the specific kinds of treatment individuals received could—and did—vary greatly according to individual therapists. While that's still true to some extent, most psychologists today use a wide range of psychological treatments and are not firmly committed to one approach over the others. One reason for this shift is the finding that, although therapies differ greatly in their procedures, they do not differ greatly in the magnitude of the benefits they provide. In other words, many kinds can help if delivered by a competent and qualified therapist. Perhaps the strongest evidence for this conclusion is provided by a large-scale study conducted several years ago by the magazine *Consumer Reports*.

Once a year, *Consumer Reports* sends out a questionnaire to its nearly 200,000 subscribers, asking for information about their experience with various products. In 1994, the survey included questions about subscribers' experiences with mental health professionals. Results, which were based on the replies of more than seven thousand people, pointed to clear conclusions. First, as noted above, therapy did help: Most respondents to the survey who had participated in therapy indicated that it made them feel much better and helped eliminate the problems and symptoms they were experiencing, especially if the therapy continued for six months or more. Second, such improvements were greatest when respondents received therapy from psychologists, psychiatrists, and social workers; improvements were somewhat less when they received therapy from physicians and marriage

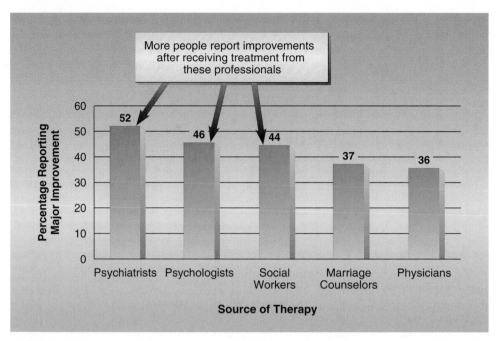

FIGURE 12.10

Evidence for the Effectiveness of Psychotherapy

The results of a recent *effectiveness study* involving thousands of participants indicate that therapy does indeed work: Large proportions of people who received psychotherapy from trained therapists (psychiatrists, psychologists, social workers) reported feeling much better as a result of such treatment. Smaller proportions reported improvements after visiting marriage counselors or physicians.
Source: Based on data reported by Seligman, 1995.

counselors (see Figure 12.10). Third, the longer therapy continued, the greater their improvement. Improvements began to occur for most people after the first six to eight sessions, and fully 75 percent of the clients showed improvement by session twenty-six. Finally, and most relevant to this discussion, it made little difference what kind of therapy respondents received: No particular approach was rated more highly than the others.

Needless to say, this study is far from perfect. First, results were based entirely on self-report—what participants *said* happened as a result of therapy. Second, the measures of change were somewhat informal, relying on questions such as, "How much did therapy help you with the specific problems that led you to therapy?" Psychologists prefer more specific and more readily quantified questions. Third, there was no control group: All participants were people who had received therapy. What happened to people with similar problems who didn't receive therapy? We can't tell.

Balanced against these important flaws, however, is the fact that this *effectiveness* study is based on responses from thousands of people who described their experiences with therapy as it actually occurs. Thus, it provides evidence that complements the findings of other research conducted under more controlled and rigorous conditions (known as *efficacy* research). In any case, putting these issues of scientific design aside, it seems clear that available evidence indicates that while therapy is indeed beneficial, there are no major differences between the various types, and no one clear winner (Hollon, DeRubeis, & Evans, 1987; Hollon, Shelton, & Loonen, 1991).

Why Are Many Different Types of Therapy Effective?

That point—the fact that many kinds of therapy seem to work about equally well—raises another intriguing question: How can this be so? How can therapies that use sharply different procedures yield such similar results? The answer that has emerged in recent years goes something like this: Various forms of therapy do differ in their rationale and in their procedures, but under the surface, all share several common, and crucial, features. It is this shared core that accounts for their simple effectiveness. What is this common core? It includes the following features.

First, all major forms of psychotherapy provide troubled individuals with a special type of setting—one in which they interact closely with a highly trained, empathetic professional. For many clients, this opportunity to interact with another person who seems to understand their problems and genuinely to care about them may be a unique and reassuring experience, and may play an important role in the benefits of many diverse forms of therapy.

Second, every form of therapy provides individuals with an explanation for their problems. No longer do these seem to be mysterious. Rather, as therapists explain, psychological disturbances stem from understandable causes, many of which lie outside the individual. This is something of a revelation to many people who have sought in vain for a clue about the causes of their difficulties.

Third, all forms of therapy specify actions that individuals can take to cope more effectively with their problems. No longer must they suffer in silence and despair. Rather, they are now actively involved in doing specific things that the confident, expert therapist indicates will help.

Fourth, all forms of therapy involve clients in what has been termed the *therapeutic alliance*—a partnership in which powerful emotional bonds are forged between people seeking help and their therapist. This relationship is marked by mutual respect and trust, and it can be a big plus for people who previously felt helpless, hopeless, and alone.

Combining all these points, the themes of *hope* and *personal control* seem to emerge very strongly. Perhaps diverse forms of therapy succeed because all provide people with increased hope about the future, plus a sense of heightened personal control—something that has been found to be very beneficial in combating several forms of mental disorder (see Mineka & Zinbart, 2006). To the extent this is the case, it is readily apparent why therapies that seem so different on the surface can all be effective. In a sense, all may provide the proverbial "light at the end of the tunnel" for people who have been struggling through the darkness of their emotional despair (see Figure 12.11 for a summary of these points). If all forms of therapy are equally effective, how can you choose a therapist? For some advice on this important issue, see the **Psychology Lends a Hand** section on page 494.

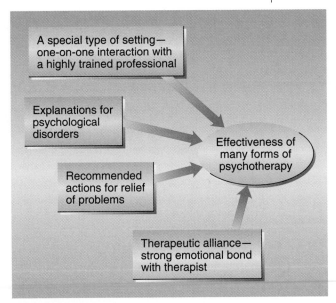

FIGURE 12.11
Factors Common to Many Forms of Therapy
The factors shown here are common to many forms of therapy, and seem to explain why, despite many differences in procedures, they all produce beneficial effects.

KEY QUESTIONS

- Is psychotherapy effective?
- Are some types of psychotherapy more effective than others?

PSYCHOLOGY LENDS A HAND

Choosing a Therapist: Some "Do's" and "Don'ts"

The odds are high that at some time in your life you, or someone close to you, will experience a mental disorder. Depression, phobias, anxiety—these are very common disorders. In fact, it is estimated that 5.4 percent of the adult population in the United States experiences a serious psychological disorder in any given year—more than 15 million people (Kersting, 2005). If there's one point we hope we have made clear, it is this: Effective help is available, and you should not hesitate to seek it. But how should you choose a therapist? Here are some basic guidelines.

- **Getting started.** The first step is usually the hardest in any task, and searching for a therapist is no exception. While you are a student, this task is fairly simple. Virtually every college or university has a department of psychology and a student health center. Both are good places to start. Visit them and ask for help. Don't be shy—the people there *want* to help, but they can't approach you—you have to take the first step. Another approach is simply to call the phone number on your health insurance card and ask for a referral to approved therapists (see Figure 12.12).

  If you are no longer a student and don't have any contact with a college or university, you can still call the psychology department of a nearby college and ask for help: The chances are good that someone there will refer you to one or more excellent therapists. But if for some reason this is not practical, you can ask your physician or some member of the clergy to direct you to the help you need. Both will almost certainly know someone you can contact. If you have no local physician and don't know any clergy, contact your local mental health association; it is probably listed in your phone book, and is another good place to start.

- **Choosing a therapist.** Let's assume that by following one of the routes above, you have obtained the names of several

therapists. How can you choose among them? Several guidelines are useful.

First, always check for *credentials*. Therapists should be trained professionals. Before you consult one, be sure that this person has a Ph.D. in psychology or an M.D. degree plus a residency in **psychiatry** or other equivalent training.

Psychiatry:
A branch of modern medicine specializing in the treatment of psychological disorders.

FIGURE 12.12
Finding a Qualified Therapist: Ask Your Local Psychologists!
If you are a student or live near a university, a good place to begin the search for a highly qualified therapist is at the department of psychology, its clinic, or at the student health center. Even if you are not a student, you can often get the help you need in these locations.

SUMMARY AND REVIEW OF KEY QUESTIONS

Psychotherapies: The Therapeutic Alliance as the Foundation for Psychological Treatments

- **What are psychotherapies?**
  Psychotherapies generally involve face-to-face meetings between therapists and the individuals they are attempting to help in which the findings and principles of psychology are used to help them experience less stress and less impairment of their functioning in daily life.

- **What is psychoanalysis and what are its major assumptions?**
  Psychoanalysis is the form of therapy developed by Freud. It assumes that mental disorders stem from hid-

den, internal conflicts and that making these conscious will lead to improved adjustment.

- **What is the role of free association in psychoanalysis?**
  Free association supposedly brings hidden urges and conflicts into consciousness.

- **According to humanistic therapies, what is the cause of mental disorders?**
  Humanistic therapies assume that mental disorders stem from factors in the environment that block or interfere with personal growth.

P S Y C H O L O G Y   L E N D S   A   H A N D

While such credentials don't guarantee that the therapist can help you, they *are* important. As noted by Barlow (2004), psychological treatments are best delivered by trained psychologists, so if you are going to receive a form of therapy, it is probably best to find a highly qualified psychologist; after all, psychological treatments are their specialty!

Second, try to find out something about the kind of disorders in which each therapist specializes. Most will readily give you this information. What you are looking for is a good *match* between your needs and the therapist's expertise.

- **Signs of progress: How long should therapy last?** If therapy is going well, both you and the therapist will know it. You'll be able to see beneficial changes in your behavior, your thoughts, and your feelings. What if it is not going well? When and how should you decide to go elsewhere? This is a difficult decision, but a rough rule of thumb is this: If you have been visiting a therapist regularly (once a week or more) for three months and see no change, it may be time to ask the therapist whether she or he is satisfied with your progress. Most forms of therapy practiced by psychologists are relatively short-term in nature. If several months have passed and your distress has not decreased, it is time to raise this issue with your therapist.

- **Danger: When to quit.** Therapy is designed to help; unfortunately, though, there are instances in which it can hurt. How can you tell if you are in danger of such outcomes? Several basic points can help. First, if you or the people around you notice that you are actually become more distressed—more depressed, more anxious, more nervous—you should ask yourself whether you are satisfied with what

is happening. At the very least, discuss these feelings with your therapist.

Second, never under any circumstances should you agree to do anything during therapy that is against your own moral or ethical principles. A great majority of therapists would never dream of making such requests but, sad to relate, there are a few who will take advantage of the therapeutic relationship to exploit their patients. The most common forms of such exploitation are sexual in nature. Unprincipled therapists may suggest that their clients engage in sexual relations with them as part of their "treatment." *This is never appropriate!* So, if your therapist makes such suggestions, *get out of there fast!*

Third, beware of exaggerated claims. If a therapist tells you that she or he can guarantee to remake your life, turn you into a powerhouse of human energy, or assure you of total happiness, be cautious. This is a good sign that you are dealing with an unprincipled—and probably poorly trained—individual. No qualified psychologist would make such claims, so again, this is a strong reason for making a fully trained psychologist your first choice.

All these suggestions are merely *guidelines* you can follow to be a sophisticated consumer of psychological services. There may be situations, for instance, where therapy requires much longer than the time period noted above, or in which a therapist has valid reasons for being reluctant to discuss procedures with you. These guidelines, however, should help you to avoid some of the pitfalls that exist with respect to finding a competent, caring therapist. Most important of all, always remember this: *Effective help is definitely out there if you take the trouble to look for it.*

- **What is the major goal of Rogers's client-centered therapy?**
Rogers's client-centered therapy focuses on eliminating unrealistic conditions of worth in a therapeutic environment of unconditional positive regard.

- **What is the major goal of Gestalt therapy?**
Gestalt therapy focuses on helping individuals acknowledge parts of their own feelings or thoughts that are not currently conscious.

- **According to behavior therapies, what is the primary cause of mental disorders?**
Behavior therapies are based on the view that mental disorders stem from faulty learning.

- **On what basic principles of learning are behavior therapies based?**
Behavior therapies are based on principles of classical conditioning, operant conditioning, and observational learning.

- **What is modeling, and how can it be used to treat mental disorders?**
Modeling is a process through which individuals acquire new information or learn new behaviors by observing the actions of others. Modeling is effective in treating several disorders, including phobias and sexual dysfunctions.

- **According to cognitive therapies, what is the primary cause of mental disorders?**
Cognitive therapies assume that the major cause of mental disorders is distorted patterns of thought.

- **What is the major goal of rational-emotive therapy?**
The major goal of rational-emotive therapy is persuading individuals to recognize and reject irrational assumptions in their thinking.

- **What is the major goal of Beck's cognitive-behavioral therapy?**
  The major goal of Beck's cognitive-behavioral therapy is persuading individuals to recognize and change irrational patterns of thought that induce negative affect and so contribute to their depression.

Psychological Treatments and Diversity: A Multicultural Approach to Combating Mental Disorders

- **What does a multicultural approach to psychological treatments suggest?**
  This approach suggests that cultural factors play an important role in mental disorders, and that treating them effectively requires sensitivity to these factors.

- **Why is it increasingly important for psychologists to adopt this perspective?**
  A multicultural perspective is increasingly important because populations of many countries are becoming much more culturally and ethnically varied than was true in the past.

Alternatives to Individual Psychotherapy: Group Therapies

- **Do implicit assumptions prevent psychologists from helping at least some people who could benefit from their help?**
  Such assumptions about the usefulness of psychological treatments to poor people can indeed deter psychologists from being as helpful to such people as they might otherwise be.

- **What is marital or couples therapy?**
  Therapy aimed at improving relations between members of couples, in situations where both members wish to preserve their relationship.

- **What is expressed emotion and what role does it play in family therapy?**
  Expressed emotion refers to a style of communication within families involving criticism, hostility, and emotional overinvolvement. Reducing EE is important because it has been found to increase relapses among people recovering from serious mental disorders.

Biological Therapies

- **What drugs are used in the treatment of psychological disorders?**
  Drugs are used to treat many mental disorders. Antipsychotic drugs reduce many symptoms such as hallucinations and delusions. Antidepressant drugs counter depression. Antianxiety drugs reduce anxiety.

- **What is electroconvulsive therapy?**
  Electroconvulsive therapy involves the delivery of strong shocks to the brain. It is used to treat depression.

- **What is psychosurgery?**
  Psychosurgery involves surgery performed on the brain to reduce or eliminate mental disorders.

Psychological Treatments: Are They Effective?

- **Is psychotherapy effective?**
  Existing evidence suggests that psychotherapy is indeed effective relative to no treatment.

- **Are some types of psychotherapy more effective than others?**
  Research findings indicate that many types of therapy are roughly equal in their effectiveness.

KEY TERMS

Beck's cognitive-behavioral therapy, p. 478
Behavior therapies, p. 475
Client-centered therapy, p. 473
Cognitive therapies, p. 477
Electroconvulsive therapy (ECT), p. 489
Employee assistance programs, p. 486

Expressed emotion, p. 485
Family therapy, p. 484
Gestalt therapy, p. 474
Phenomenological/experiential therapies (often known as *humanistic therapies*), p. 473
Psychiatry, p. 494
Psychodynamic therapies, p. 471

Psychological treatments, p. 470
Psychosurgery, p. 490
Psychotherapies, p. 470
Rational-emotive therapy, p. 478
Systematic desensitization, p. 475
Tardive dyskinesia, p. 487
Therapeutic alliance, p. 471
Transference, p. 472

PSYCHOLOGY: UNDERSTANDING ITS FINDINGS

Is Dealing with Mental Disorders Largely a Matter of Common Sense?

Many people seem to believe that dealing with mental disorders is largely a matter of common sense: Anyone who is kind, empathetic, and willing to listen can help. This is why many people who are experiencing disturbing symptoms ei-

ther keep these to themselves, or simply discuss them with their physician, clergy, family, or friends. In light of what you have learned about mental disorders and their treatment in this chapter, do you think this makes sense? Or you do you think that the treatment of such disorders can be handled better by professionals, such as psychologists? And would your answer depend on the *kind* of mental disorder in question? For instance, do you think friends and other nonprofessionals might be more helpful in dealing with such problems as depression or phobias, but less effective in helping others cope with sexual disorders or ones relating to anxiety? Make a list of various disorders you have observed in other people,

and for each rate the extent to which you think that professional treatment is definitely needed (1 = not necessary; 5 = absolutely necessary). Is there a pattern in your answers? In other words, do you find that you view some mental disorders as more serious and more difficult to treat than you do others?

MAKING PSYCHOLOGY PART OF YOUR LIFE

Seeking Help at Work: Employee Assistance Programs

As we noted earlier, many companies recognize that distressed or troubled employees are not at their best, and have established employee assistance programs to help them. How can *you* make use of such programs? Following the steps outlined below is certainly a good way to start, because they will help you learn exactly what is available to employees of the company where you work.

1. First, call the human resources office and ask whether the company has an employee assistance program (EAP for short).
2. Once you determine that it does, ask for information about the specific programs and benefits it provides.
3. Next, examine the various programs carefully; if you have any questions about what they involve, jot these down and then phone the human resources office again.

4. At this point, try to decide whether any of the programs might be helpful to you; if so, find out how you can enroll and how your privacy will be protected. (Actually, this is not a major concern: Government regulations designed to protect the health and well-being of all employees require that your company keep records of your participation in its EAP strictly confidential.)
5. Then, make an appointment, dial the phone numbers provided, or visit the web sites listed—and obtain the help you need.

The main point to keep in mind is this: More help may be available to you—for free—than you now realize. So it is definitely worth your while to find out what your company provides, and to take advantage of it if the need arises.

If you are using MyPsychLab, you have access to an electronic version of this textbook, along with dozens of valuable resources per chapter—including video and audio clips, simulations and activities, self-assessments, practice tests and other study materials. Here is a sampling of the resources available for this chapter.

EXPLORE

Coping Strategies and Their Effects
Psychotherapy Practitioners and Their Activities
Drugs Commonly Used to Treat Psychiatric Disorders

WATCH

Recent Trends in Treatment

If you did not receive an access code to MyPsychLab with this text and wish to purchase access online, please visit www.MyPsychLab.com.

STUDY GUIDE

CHAPTER REVIEW

Psychotherapies: The Therapeutic Alliance as the Foundation of Psychological Treatments

1. _____ is a proven method delivered by persons trained in psychology.
   a. Therapy
   b. Psychiatric treatment
   c. Psychological treatment
   d. Psychotherapy

2. Dr. Ralph believes that the key to helping his patients resolve their problems is to delve into and expose their unconscious conflicts. Dr. Ralph is most likely trained as a _____ therapist.
   a. humanistic
   b. psychological
   c. Pavlovian
   d. psychodynamic

3. The therapy known as _____ was developed by _____.
   a. psychoanalysis;   Freud
   b. humanism;   Pavlov
   c. psychiatry;   Maslow
   d. experiential;   Rogers

4. James constantly monitors the internet to verify that evil persons are distributing pornography. Freud would argue his behavior can be explained by the ego defense mechanism known as
   a. reaction formation.
   b. denial.
   c. repression.
   d. free association.

5. The process of free association was developed by _____ to expose the contents of the _____.
   a. Maslow;   collective psyche
   b. Skinner;   long-term memory
   c. Freud;   unconscious
   d. Rogers;   preconscious

6. A serious shortcoming of psychoanalysis is that
   a. this approach is based on shaky science.
   b. this therapy requires years of expense.
   c. insight does not automatically lead to mental health.
   d. All of the above are correct.

7. The humanistic approach known as _____ was developed by _____.
   a. humanism;   Pavlov
   b. client-centered therapy;   Rogers
   c. psychoanalysis;   Freud
   d. Gestalt;   Skinner

8. A key method for client-centered therapy is probing the unconscious of the patient for unresolved conflicts. (True-False).

9. The key task for behavior therapy is to _____.
   a. understand unconscious conflicts.
   b. change current behavior.

c. reduce the gap between a person's self-concept and how they are treated by others.
   d. accurately diagnose a disorder and then initiate drug therapy.

10. Ginny fears dogs after being bitten by one at the park. A behavior therapist would treat her phobia for dogs by
    a. instructing her to avoid parks.
    b. having Ginny view pictures of dogs.
    c. asking her if she also fears her mother and father.
    d. instructing her to avoid dogs.

11. Administration of the drug _____ increases the rate of _____ for a fear of heights.
    a. D-cycloserine;   extinction
    b. alcohol;   extinction
    c. D-cycloserine;   acquisition
    d. alcohol;   extinction

12. Setting up a token economy in a hospital would be useful in
    a. reducing physical symptoms of illness.
    b. replacing maladaptive psychotic thoughts with adaptive thoughts.
    c. promoting bathing by patients.
    d. reducing the incidence of phobias involving germs.

13. Modeling is a successful treatment for phobias. (True-False)

14. Ellis argued that _____ are key to understanding _____.
    a. activating events;   memory.
    b. diminished self-concepts;   the development of a phobia
    c. operant conditioning methods;   the formation of mental disorder
    d. irrational thoughts;   mental disorders

15. The first issue addressed by a therapist using RET is to
    a. expose the client to the object they most strongly fear.
    b. identify irrational thoughts in the client.
    c. teach the client how to retain their irrational thoughts.
    d. challenge irrational thoughts in the client.

16. The cognitive approach of Beck attempts to treat depression by disproving the irrationality of the client. (True-False).

Psychotherapy and Diversity: Multiculturalism in Helping Relationships

17. An impediment to therapy for older Asian males is their tendency to
    a. express their emotions to others.
    b. place a strong emphasis on family relationships.
    c. express emotional problems in terms of bodily aches and pains.
    d. place a strong emphasis on personal relationships

18. Dr. Franciso Gonzalez is a Hispanic clinical psychologist living in Texas. Among his clients are African-American, Asian, and Anglo persons. For him to meet ethical guidelines, Dr. Gonzalez should be familiar with

a. his own cultural biases.

b. the differences between his culture and that of his clients.

c. the culture of his clients.

d. All of the above are correct.

Alternatives to Individual Psychotherapy: Group Therapies

19. An important limitation of psychotherapy is
   a. that therapy is not effective.
   b. that the government has made psychotherapy available to the masses.
   c. that some cultures view psychotherapy as a source of shame.
   d. All of the above are correct.

20. An example of displacement is when
   a. a politician throws a fit when they do not get a valued committee assignment.
   b. a person appears to be unaware of their attraction to another person.
   c. a man explains that the woman who rejected him was really not all that attractive.
   d. an angry person kicks their car rather than their boss.

21. Much of marital discord can be traced to faulty communication.   (True-False).

22. The focus of behavior marital therapy is
   a. providing emotional support to the dominant spouse.
   b. convincing both spouses that the marriage is not worth saving.
   c. changing faulty communications between the marital partners.
   d. fairly divide the labor in the marriage.

23. Psychotherapy may produce temporary gains that are lost when the person
   a. returns to their dysfunctional family.
   b. begins to abuse alcohol and other drugs.
   c. runs out of insurance coverage.
   d. transfers to a new school.

24. Family therapy is based on the idea that
   a. all members of the family share the same values.
   b. family interactions may limit or compromise treatment of a family member.
   c. each member of the family has the same view of events that influence the family.
   d. most modern families are fragmented and isolated.

25. The statement "I do approve of you smoking pot!!!" is an example of the _____ component of expressed emotion.
   a. hostility
   b. emotional overinvolvement
   c. symbiotic
   d. criticism

26. Living in a family that is _____ in expressed emotion is considered to _____ the risk of relapse for mental disorder
   a. low;   increase
   b. high;   increase
   c. high;   decrease
   d. low;   decrease

27. Research suggests that a person who is recovering from depression has greater resilience in dealing with criticism from family members.   (True-False).

Biological Therapies

28. A major factor behind the decrease in persons residing in psychiatric hospitals after 1955 was
   a. loss of medical insurance by the families of the residents.
   b. the development of better psychotherapies for schizophrenia.
   c. the use of psychiatric drugs.
   d. All of the above are correct.

29. The term neuroleptic is another name for
   a. antianxiety medications.
   b. antidepressant drugs.
   c. psychostimulant drugs.
   d. antipsychotic medications.

30. Drug treatment of schizophrenia can produce a motor syndrome termed
   a. compulsivity.
   b. tardive dyskinesia.
   c. REM dystonia.
   d. akathisia.

31. Tardive dyskinesia involves involuntary movements of the lips, tongue, and jaw.   (True-False)

32. Which of the following is true of antipsychotic drugs?
   a. Early antipsychotic drugs were more effective for positive symptoms of schizophrenia than negative symptoms.
   b. Antipsychotic drugs do not cure schizophrenia.
   c. Modern antipsychotic drugs exert stronger effects on the negative symptoms of schizophrenia.
   d. All of the above are correct.

33. Lithium is an effective treatment for major depression but not bipolar disorder.   (True-False)

34. A serious side effect of the benzodiazepines relates to
   a. withdrawal symptoms when the drug is stopped.
   b. drowsiness and fatigue.
   c. fatal overdose when combined with alcohol.
   d. All of the above are correct.

35. Match up the appropriate concept with the correct definition or best example of the concept.
   E,D,C,B, A
   _____. Brain surgery intended to alter behavior in mentally ill persons.
   _____. The world's oldest antianxiety drug.
   _____. This treatment is effective for severe depression.
   _____. Long-term use of antipsychotic drugs can induce this motor disorder.
   _____. An example of an antidepressant drug that works by increasing brain serotonin levels.
   a. Fluoxetine.
   b. Tardive dyskinesia.
   c. Electroconvulsive therapy.
   d. Alcohol.
   e. Psychosurgery.

Psychological Treatments: Are They Effective?

36. Hans Eysenk conclusions that psychotherapy is ineffective were biased because
   a. he overestimated the proportion of people who get better without therapy.
   b. he underestimated the proportion of people who get better during therapy.

c. he used modern statistical methods to evaluate his data.

d. A and B are correct.

37. Which of the following was a result from the Consumer Reports study of psychotherapy?
    a. Treatment by a physician produced greater improvement than did treatment from a psychologist.
    b. Therapy had only brief effects on mental disorder.
    c. Cognitive types of therapy led to better improvement than did psychiatric-based therapies.
    d. Longer durations of therapy led to better improvement than did shorter durations.

38. A key flaw of the Consumer Reports study of psychotherapy is the lack of a control group.   (True-False).

IDENTIFICATIONS

Identify the term that belongs with each of the concepts below (place the letter for the appropriate term below in front of each concept).

Identification   Concept:

_____ 1. "It is the role of therapy to help people find meaning in their lives."

_____ 2. People use these to protect their ego from feelings of anxiety.

_____ 3. The state of having knowledge of one's unconscious impulses.

_____ 4. A proven method delivered by persons trained in psychology.

_____ 5. A type of therapist who refers to their "clients" rather than their "patients".

_____ 6. A situation in which a client refuses to talk to the therapist about certain topics.

_____ 7. A therapist should try to view the world through their client's eyes.

_____ 8. He developed Gestalt Therapy.

_____ 9. An irrational fear acquired through classical conditioning.

_____ 10. An arrangement in which persons can earn rewards for complying with certain rules.

_____ 11. A state of mind in which a person is able to grow and develop.

_____ 12. Having clients learn new skills by observing others using these skills.

_____ 13. "Mental disorders are caused by deep unconscious conflicts. "

_____ 14. Couples seek therapy because of this factor.

_____ 15. A form of therapy that argues that humans struggle to maintain control over their evil thoughts and internal conflicts.

_____ 16. The tendency of Hispanic family members to avoid discussion of family problems with an outside person.

Identification:
a. Sigmund Freud
b. Psychoanalysis.
c. Defense mechanisms
d. Psychological treatment
e. Insight.
f. Humanistic approaches.
g. Phobias.
h. Roger's client-centered therapy.
i. Modeling.
j. Fritz Perls.
k. Faulty communication.
l. familismio.
m. Self-actualization.
n. Token economy.
o. Resistance.

FILL IN THE BLANK

1. The interaction between a patient and a therapist is referred to as the _____.
2. The concepts known as id, ego, and superego correspond to _____.
3. _____ developed the therapy known as psychoanalysis.
4. A key assumption of _____ is that insight will lead to mental health.
5. The intense feeling of love or hate developed by the client for a therapist is known as _____.
6. Administration of the drug _____ can increase the rate of extinction for a fear of heights.
7. The empty-chair technique is used by _____.
8. _____ is a harmful pattern of communication in families.
9. A new generation antipsychotic drug that does not induce tardive dyskinesia is _____.
10. The three major classes of antidepressant drugs are the _____, _____ and the _____.
11. _____ are the most widely prescribed antianxiety drugs.
12. A major side effect of ECT involves problems in _____.
13. Severing connections of the cingulum and the limbic system may improve symptoms of _____.
14. _____ is a medical treatment in which the brain is damaged to alter behavior.
15. People report more improvement in their mental states with _____ duration of therapy.

COMPREHENSIVE PRACTICE TEST

1. The interaction between a patient and a therapist is referred to as the
   a. dynamic interaction.
   b. therapeutic alliance.
   c. mutual bond.
   d. symbiotic alliance.
2. The concepts known as id, ego, and superego correspond to
   a. reason, desire, and rationality.
   b. rage, happiness, and social custom.
   c. conscience, desire, and rationality.
   d. desire, reason, and conscience.
3. A key assumption of psychoanalysis is that insight will lead to mental health.   (True-False).
4. Match up the appropriate concept with the correct definition or best example of the concept.
   _____. A form of cooperation between client and therapist that aims to reduce the mental disorder of the client.

_____. An irrational fear of a harmless object.

_____. A type of psychotherapy devised by Freud.

_____. Perls devised this therapy to make persons aware of their feelings and needs.

_____. A type of interaction advocated by Rogers in which the therapist treats the client with respect.

_____. A process in psychoanalysis in which the client refuses to cooperate with the therapist.

  a. Resistance.

  b. Gestalt therapy.

  c. Phobia.

  d. Psychoanalysis.

  e. Therapeutic alliance.

  f. Unconditional positive regard.

5. A humanistic therapist would strongly **disagree** with the statement that
  a. It is the role of therapy to help people find meaning in their lives.
  b. Reason is overwhelmed by passion.
  c. A therapist should try to view the world through their client's eyes.
  d. A client should be treated with respect by a therapist.

6. A therapist who has an eclectic approach
  a. is trained in psychiatry.
  b. does therapy in a group setting.
  c. is trained in psychology and social work.
  d. uses a variety of approaches rather than one single treatment mode.

7. A key reason for using a multicultural approach to psychotherapy is that a treatment that is optimal for one group may not be for another group.   (True-False).

8. The tendency of Hispanic family members to avoid discussion of family problems with an outside person is known as
  a. personalismo.
  b. simpatico.
  c. machismo.
  d. familismio.

9. The most common reason that married couples seek therapy is
  a. that one spouse has had an affair.
  b. an unfair division of labor in the marriage.
  c. drug or alcohol abuse.
  d. sexual problems.

10. The statement "I cannot stand to be in the same room as my brother . . . " is an example of the _____ component of expressed emotion.
  a. hostility
  b. emotional overinvolvement
  c. symbiotic
  d. criticism

11. Antipsychotic medications reduce hallucinations and delusions through a _____ action on brain _____ receptors.
  a. blocking;   serotonin
  b. stimulatory;   dopamine
  c. blocking;   dopamine
  d. stimulatory;   serotonin

12. Which of the following terms DO NOT belong together?
  a. Chlorpromazine;   antidepressant
  b. Phenothiazines;   neuroleptic
  c. MAO inhibitor;   depression
  d. Prozac;   fluoxetine

13. The use of _____ is recommended for severely depressed and suicidal persons.
  a. barbiturates
  b. psychotherapy
  c. electroconvulsive therapy
  d. psychosurgery

14. Which of the following is the world's oldest antianxiety drug?
  a. Barbiturates.
  b. Prozac
  c. LSD
  d. Alcohol.

15. The fact that different forms of psychotherapy induce similar degrees of change may result because
  a. each form demands some financial sacrifice, which leads the client to conclude that it must have value.
  b. each requires that patients suffer in silence.
  c. psychotherapy allows a client feel reassured when interacting with a trained professional.
  d. the therapist is perceived as a "friend."

CRITICAL THINKING

1. Compare and contrast the approaches taken by psychoanalysis with that of the humanistic psychologists.

2. Explain why the Consumer Reports study indicates that different forms of therapy produce about the same degree of mental improvement.

THIRTEEN

Social Thought and Social Behavior

I'll never forget the day I (Robert Baron) met my wife—the true love of my life. I was attending a conference in Florida, and while there ran into an old friend who invited me to join him and several other people for dinner. When I arrived at the restaurant, he introduced me to two or three people in his group, and when I looked at one of them—my future wife—I felt as though a loud bell had sounded in my head. From that point on, I truly only had eyes for her. As luck would have it, I was able to sit next to her at dinner and we had a wonderful conversation, during which we discovered that we shared many interests and saw the world in much the same way. Later, after dinner, I asked her if she would like to take a stroll along the boardwalk. She agreed, and we walked and talked for what seemed like hours. The next night, we had dinner together again, accompanied by just one other friend, and as he put it years later, "I could tell that something big was happening between you two . . . It was obvious!"

But all was not smooth for us: We worked at universities more than a thousand miles apart and were both involved in serious relationships with other people, so it seemed likely that our meeting was destined to be just a magical moment that would, sadly, soon come to an end. And it did. In fact, we didn't see each other again for almost ten years! During that time, I thought about her often, and imagined what might have happened if we had met at some other time and how happy we might be if we could be together. But these were just daydreams, and I didn't see my future wife again until I was invited to give a talk at her university. When, after my arrival, she came to take me to dinner, we both knew at once that the magic between us was still there, just as if no time, rather than ten years, had passed. After dinner, we went for a drink and when, after another wonderful hour together I asked the waiter for the bill, he said: "No, this is on me . . . you are so happy it makes me happy, so it's my treat." The rest is history—our history. We were no longer in the relationships that had kept us apart ten years earlier, and although we were still separated by more than a thousand miles, we made arrangements to see each other again. Soon, we decided to make a life together and that's the end of the story—or really, the beginning, *because if life continues to be kind to us, we will have many happy years together . . .*

FIGURE 13.1
Social Psychology: Investigating the Social Side of Life
Social psychologists study all aspects of social behavior and social thought—the many ways in which we think about and interact with others. For instance, as suggested by this cartoon, some people like each other when they meet while others do not. Why? That's just one of the truly broad range of questions social psychologists seek to answer.
Source: © King Features Syndicate, January 9, 2006.

I know; this is a very romantic story, and you may be thinking something like this: "Interesting, yes, but what does it have to do with psychology?" The answer is simple: In many ways, it captures the two basic themes of **social psychology**—the branch of psychology we will examine in this chapter. Social psychologists attempt to add to our understanding of the social side of life—the many ways in which we interact with other people and form relationships with them, and the many ways in which we think about them (e.g., Baron, Byrne, & Branscombe, 2005). This story reflects both themes. When my wife and I met, we were total strangers, so our early interactions were designed, in part, to help us get acquainted. And yes, when we met there was an immediate attraction between us. Why? What was it, in addition to obvious things such as outward appearance, that led us to be drawn to each other? And remember: After meeting for the first time, we did not see each other again for almost ten years. Yet we remained in each others' thoughts, and it was these thoughts, perhaps, that kept the spark we lit during that first meeting alive through the long years that followed.

Years ago, when I (Robert Baron) taught social psychology on a regular basis, I used to tell my classes that as a field, social psychology studies everything from love and attraction on the one hand to hatred and violence on the other—plus everything in between (see Figure 13.1). That's certainly no exaggeration, because

Social psychology:
The branch of psychology that studies all aspects of social behavior and social thought.

the social side of our lives is so rich and so complex that social psychology, as a field, does indeed examine a tremendously wide range of topics and issues. To provide you with an overview of some of the most fascinating of these, we'll proceed as follows. First, we'll examine several aspects of social thought—how, and what, we think about other people. Included here will be discussions of four topics: *nonverbal communication*—how we learn about others' current feelings or reactions from facial expression, eye contact with us, and related cues; *attribution*—our efforts to understand the causes behind others' behavior—why they act as they do; **social cognition**—how we process social information, remember it, and use it in making judgments or decisions about others; and *attitudes*—our evaluations of various features of the social world.

After considering these aspects of social thought, we'll turn to several key aspects of *social behavior*—how we actually interact with other people. Under this general heading we'll first examine *prejudice*—negative attitudes toward the members of various social groups that often have powerful effects on behavior toward them. Then, we'll turn to *social influence*—the many ways in which we attempt to change others' behavior and they attempt to change ours. Finally, we'll return to the topic of the opening story above and consider *attraction and love*—why we like or dislike other people, what makes them attractive or unattractive to us, and why we fall in (and out) of love with them. (Additional aspects of social behavior are covered elsewhere in this book—in our discussions of social development [Chapter 7], and *leadership* and *teams* in Chapter 14.)

SOCIAL THOUGHT: THINKING ABOUT OTHER PEOPLE

How many times each day do you think about other people? Your answer might well be, "Who can count?" Anytime you try to figure out how other people are currently feeling (Are they happy or sad? Do they like you or dislike you?), why they have acted in various ways, or try to make judgments about them (Will they make a good roommate? Are they being honest with you about some topic?), you are engaging in *social thought* (or *social cognition*). Let's take a closer look at several important aspects of this process.

Nonverbal Communication: Unspoken Clues to Others' Moods or Reactions

One thing we want to know about other people is how they are feeling right *now*. Are they in a good mood or a bad mood? Are they responding positively or negatively to what we are saying or doing? Information of this type is often very helpful. For instance, if you want a favor from another person, when would you ask for it—when they are in a good mood or when they are in a bad mood? The answer is obvious: When they are in a good mood. Similarly, we all want to make good first impressions on others so that we can get the job—or the date! In this respect, information on how they are reacting to us can be very useful. But how, exactly, do we try to get information on others' reactions and feelings? One important way is through the use of **nonverbal cues**—information provided by others' facial expressions, eye contact, body posture and movements, and other outward expressions of what they are feeling on the inside (see DePaulo, 1992; DePaulo et al., 2003). Here, expanding on information we presented in an earlier discussion of emotion (Chapter 8), is a brief summary of what research on nonverbal cues indicates:

- *Facial expressions* can be very revealing, and generally serve as good guides to six basic emotions: anger, fear, happiness, sadness, surprise, and disgust (Izard,

Social cognition:
An area of research concerned with the ways in which we notice, store, remember, and use social information.

Nonverbal cues:
Information provided by others' facial expressions, eye contact, body posture and movements, and other outward expressions of what they are feeling on the inside.

FIGURE 13.2
Gestures: A Basic Form of Nonverbal Communication
Do you recognize the gestures shown here? In the United States and several other countries, each of these gestures has a specific meaning. However, they might well have no meaning, or different meanings, in other cultures.

1991; Ekman, 1992). Further, facial expressions are quite universal in the sense that a smile is recognized as a sign of happiness, a frown as a sign of anger, and so on, all over the world and across many different cultures.

- *Eye contact* is another useful source of information about how others are feeling. In general, a high level of eye contact is a sign of liking or positive feelings, while a low level is a sign of disliking or negative feelings. Further, as we'll note below, the direction of others' gazes (e.g., toward us or away from us) provides information on their reactions to us, and may strongly influence our reactions to them (see Mason, Tatkow, & Macrae, 2005).

- *Body movements* and *postures* are also very revealing of others' emotional states or moods. A large number of movements is often a sign of emotional arousal or uneasiness. And *gestures* often have specific meanings in a given culture (see Figure 13.2).

- *Touching* can also serve as a useful nonverbal cue. The precise meaning depends on who touches whom (it is more acceptable for high-status people to touch lower-status ones), where one person touches another (on the shoulder may be OK, but other body parts are definitely "off limits," except for people who know each other very well), and the context in which the touching takes place—for instance, touching is more acceptable at a party than at work. One specific form of touching is especially revealing—*handshakes*. Recent findings suggest that we often learn much from others' handshakes—or, at least *believe* that we learn much! For instance, in one study (Chaplin et al., 2000), assistants were trained to give handshakes to strangers that varied in strength, grip, vigor, and duration. Then, these trained assistants shook hands with many strangers, who then rated the assistants on various dimensions. Results were clear: The stronger, longer, and more vigorous the handshakes delivered by the assistants, the higher they were rated on many different dimensions (e.g., how friendly, expressive, and open to experience they were).

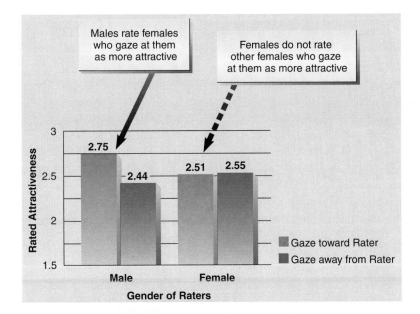

Males rate females who gaze at them as more attractive

Females do not rate other females who gaze at them as more attractive

FIGURE 13.3

The Direction of Others' Gazes: How It Influences Our Perceptions of Them

As shown here, males rated female strangers who seemed to be looking directly at them higher in terms of attractiveness than female strangers who seemed to be looking away from them. In contrast, females' ratings of the female strangers were not influenced by the direction of their gazes.

Source: Based on data from Mason, Tatkow, & Macrae, 2005.

Earlier, we mentioned that eye contact is an important nonverbal cue. In addition, others' gazes—and especially the direction of their gazes—often strongly influence our feelings about *them*. Such effects are shown very clearly in a study conducted by Mason, Tatkow, and Macrae (2005). These researchers had participants in the study look at the faces of female strangers shown on a computer screen. These images were adjusted so as to suggest that the strangers were looking directly at the participants or were looking elsewhere. When asked to rate the strangers in terms of how likable they were, participants gave higher ratings to the strangers when they appeared to be gazing in their direction. In a follow-up study using the same procedures, participants rated the *attractiveness* of the strangers whose faces they saw. Male participants rated the female strangers as more attractive when they seemed to be gazing at them. For female participants, however, the direction of a female stranger's gaze made no difference (see Figure 13.3). This suggests that gaze direction strongly influences our perception of other people, but only when we *care* whether they are looking at us—for instance, if we belong to one gender and they belong to the other. So, as is true of many nonverbal cues, our interpretation of a gaze's meaning and how this information affects other aspects of our social thought is influenced by many different factors.

In sum, nonverbal cues are often a very useful guide to others' current moods and feelings, so they provide valuable "raw materials" for social thought—for thinking about others and trying to understand just what kind of people they are. Another valuable aspect of nonverbal cues is that they can help us determine whether others are being honest with us—whether they are lying or telling the truth. For information on how *you* can use nonverbal cues for this purpose, see the **Psychology Lends a Hand** section on page 508.

Attribution: Understanding the Causes of Others' Behavior

Imagine the following situation. You're standing at a counter in a store waiting your turn when suddenly another customer walks up and hands the clerk an item she wishes to purchase. How do you react? While your first response might be, "With anger," a more accurate answer is, "It depends." And what it depends on is your perceptions of *why* this other person has cut in front of you. Did she do it on purpose? In that case, you probably *would* get angry. But perhaps she just didn't see you. In that case, you might clear your throat or otherwise indicate your presence to see what would happen next. So, it's not just what this person did that matters; your perception of *why* she did it matters, too.

PSYCHOLOGY LENDS A HAND

How to Tell When Another Person Is Lying

In many contexts, it is important to be able to tell whether others are telling the truth or lying. Research on lying indicates that it is a fact of everyday life: Most people report telling one or two lies every single day (DePaulo & Kashy, 1998). They do so for many reasons: to hide their real feelings, attitudes, or preferences; for personal gain; to "look good" to interviewers, so that they, rather than someone else, gets the job (Weiss & Feldman, 2006); or to escape punishment for misdeeds. Can we tell when others are not being honest with us? Research findings on this question suggest that we can—although doing so is far from easy (DePaulo et al., 2003). Here is a brief summary of cues—most of them nonverbal—that may indicate another person is not telling the truth:

1. **Microexpressions.** These are facial expressions lasting only a few tenths of a second. Such reactions appear on the face very quickly after an emotion-provoking event and are difficult to suppress. As result, they can be very revealing about others' true feelings or emotions. For instance, if you ask another person whether she likes something (e.g., an idea you have expressed, a new product), watch her face closely as she responds. If you see one expression (e.g., a frown), which is followed very quickly by another (e.g., a smile), this can be a useful sign that she is lying—she is stating one opinion or reaction when in fact, she really has another.

2. **Interchannel discrepancies.** A second nonverbal cue revealing of deception is known as interchannel discrepancies. (The term *channel* refers to type of nonverbal cues; for instance, facial expressions are one channel, body movements are another.) These are inconsistencies between nonverbal cues from different basic channels. These happen when persons who are lying often find it difficult to control all the channels at once. For instance, they may manage their facial expressions well, but may have difficulty looking you in the eye as they tell their lie.

3. **Eye contact.** Efforts at deception are often frequently revealed by certain aspects of eye contact. People who are lying often blink more often and show pupils that are more dilated than do people who are telling the truth. They may also show an unusually low level of eye contact or—surprisingly—an unusually high one, as they attempt to fake being honest by looking others right in the eye.

4. **Exaggerated facial expressions.** Finally, people who are lying sometimes show exaggerated facial expressions. They may smile more—or more broadly—than usual or may show greater sorrow than is typical in a given situation. A prime example: Someone says "no" to a request you've made and then shows exaggerated regret. This is a good sign that the reasons the person has supplied for saying "no" may not be true.

In addition to these nonverbal cues, other signs of deception are sometimes present in nonverbal aspects of what people actually say, or in the words they choose. When people are lying, their voice *pitch* often rises—especially when they are highly motivated to lie. Similarly, they often take longer to begin to respond to a question or to describe events. And they may show a greater tendency to start sentences, stop them, and begin again. In other words, certain aspects of people's *linguistic style* can be revealing of deception.

Perhaps even more interesting, people may actually tend to use different words when lying than telling the truth (see Vrij et al., 2000). Why would this be so? For several reasons. First, people who are lying may want to avoid directing attention to themselves so they may tend to use words such as "I" and "me" less often than people who are telling the truth. Second, they may feel guilty, so they use more words reflecting negative emotions. Third, since they are making up the events they are describing, they may use more words relating to simple actions, such as "walk" and "go," and fewer words that make the story more specific, such as "except," "but," and "without." Do such differences between lies and truthful statement exist? Research by Newman and colleagues (2003) confirms that they do. They found that, when telling lies, individuals used fewer first-person pronouns ("I" "we"), more negative emotion words, and fewer exclusive words ("except," "but"). In other words, lies were less complex, less related to the self, and more negative in nature than truthful statements.

The bottom line of all this is that detecting deception by others is a difficult task. Some people become very skilled at lying, and, in fact, after a while may begin to believe their own lies—thus making it especially hard to tell that they are not being truthful. But if you pay careful attention to the cues described above you will make their task of "pulling the wool over your eyes" much more difficult—and that is certainly worth the effort.

Attribution:
The processes through which people seek to determine the causes behind others' behavior.

This question of *why* others act as they do is one we face every day in many different contexts. The process through which we attempt to answer this question—to determine the causes behind others' behavior—is known as **attribution,** and, in general, it is a fairly orderly process. We examine others' behavior for clues as to the causes behind what they say and do, and then reach our decision. What kind of information do we consider? This depends on the specific question we

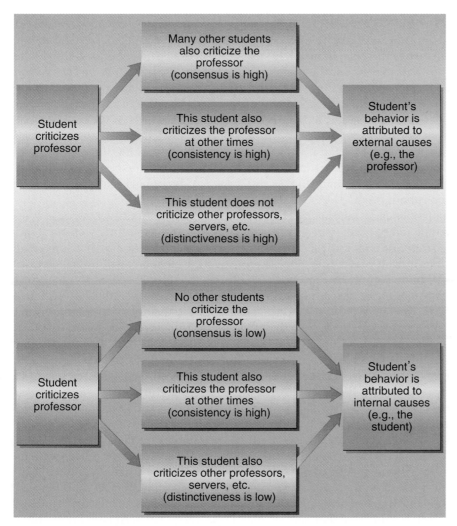

FIGURE 13.4
Causal Attribution
When consensus and distinctiveness are low but consistency is high, we attribute others' behavior to *internal* causes (upper diagram). When consensus, consistency, and distinctiveness are all high, in contrast, we attribute their behavior to *external* causes (lower diagram).

want to answer. For instance, one basic issue is: Did another person's actions stem from *internal* causes (e.g., their own traits, intentions, or motives) or from *external* causes (e.g., luck, factors beyond their control in a given situation). To answer this question, we often focus on information about: (1) whether other people behave in the same way they do (**consensus**); (2) whether this person behaves in the same manner over time (**consistency**); and (3) whether this person behaves in the same way in different situations (**distinctiveness**). If very few people act like this person (consensus is low), this person behaves in the same way over time (consistency is high), and behaves in much the same manner in many situations (distinctiveness is low), we conclude that their behavior stemmed from *internal* causes: This is the kind of person they are, and this is how they will probably remain. For instance, we'd probably draw this conclusion about a student who got up and criticized a professor harshly in class if no other students did this (consensus was low), this student criticized the professor on other occasions (consistency was high), and this student also criticized other professors and servers in restaurants (distinctiveness is low). In contrast, if all three factors are high (consensus, consistency, and distinctiveness), we are more likely to conclude that this person behaved as they did because of external causes—for instance, they might have no choice (Kelley, 1972; see Figure 13.4).

Consensus:
Information regarding the extent to which behavior by one person is shown by others as well.

Consistency:
Information regarding the extent to which a specific person shows similar behavior across time.

Distinctiveness:
Information regarding the extent to which a given person reacts in the same manner to different stimuli or situations.

■ **Attribution: Some basic sources of error.**

While attribution often involves the logical kind of reasoning described above, this is not always the case. In fact, it is subject to several kinds of errors. One of the most important is known as the **correspondence bias** or the *fundamental attribution error*, and it refers to our strong tendency to explain others' actions as stemming from (corresponding to) internal causes even in the presence of clear external (situations) causes (e.g., Gilbert & Malone, 1995). In other words, if we see someone behave in a particular way, we tend to attribute these actions to internal causes such as their own traits, even if we have no grounds for making this assumption. For instance, someone who is late for a meeting may be irresponsible, but they may also have been stuck in traffic. So the correspondence bias can lead us to false conclusions about others.

Is the tendency to emphasize dispositional causes truly universal, or is it influenced, like many other aspects of social behavior and thought, by cultural factors? Research findings indicate that while this tendency is somewhat universal, culture does indeed play a role. Specifically, the fundamental attribution error appears to be more common or stronger in cultures that emphasize individual freedom—*individualistic* cultures such as those in western Europe or the United States and Canada, than in *collectivistic* cultures that emphasize group membership, conformity, and interdependence (e.g., Triandis, 1990). This difference seems to reflect how, in individualistic cultures, there is a *norm of internality*—the view that people should accept responsibility for their own outcomes. In collectivistic cultures, in contrast, this norm is weaker or absent (Jellison & Green, 1981). For example, in one study, Morris and Pang (1994) analyzed newspaper articles about two mass murders—one committed by a Chinese graduate student and one committed by a white postal worker. The articles were published in English in the *New York Times* and in the *World Journal*, a Chinese-language newspaper published in the United States. Results were clear: The articles in English attributed both murderers' actions to dispositional factors to a greater extent than did the articles written in Chinese.

Similar findings—a strong correspondence bias in Western, individualistic countries but a much weaker one in Asian and more collectivistic ones—have been reported in several other studies (see Choi and Nisbett, 1998). So there seems little doubt that cultural factors play a role even in this very basic aspect of attribution.

Another "tilt" in our attributions is, in some respects, even worse. It is known as the **self-serving bias,** and it involves our tendency to attribute any positive outcomes we experience to our own behavior and traits (internal causes), but negative outcomes to external causes beyond our control. For instance, suppose that you receive a grade of A on an exam. You might well explain this as the result of your talent, effort, studying, and other internal causes. But suppose you receive a grade of D? In this case, you might be tempted to attribute your poor grade to the unfairness of the exam, the unrealistically high standards of your professors, and other external causes.

The self-serving bias can be the cause of much interpersonal friction. It often leads people who work with others on a joint task to perceive that they, not their partners, have made the major contributions. I see this effect in my own classes every semester when students rate their own contribution and that of the other members of their team to a required term project. The result? Most students take lots of credit for themselves when the project has gone well, but tend to blame (and downrate) their partner if it has not.

Correspondence bias (*fundamental attribution error*): The tendency to attribute behavior to internal causes to a greater extent than is actually justified.

Self-serving bias: The tendency to attribute positive outcomes to our own traits or characteristics (internal causes) but negative outcomes to factors beyond our control (external causes).

KEY QUESTIONS

• What is the correspondence bias?
• Does the correspondence bias exist in all cultures, or is it greater in some than others?
• What is the self-serving bias?

Social Cognition: How We Process Social Information

Gathering information on another person's current moods or feelings and identifying the causes behind his or her actions are important aspects of social thought, but they are far from the entire picture. Thinking about other persons involves many other tasks as well. We must decide what information is most important. We must enter such information into memory and be able to retrieve it at later times. And we must be able to combine this information in various ways to make judgments about others and to predict their future actions (Wyer & Srull, 1999). It is only by accomplishing these tasks that we can make sense out of the complex social world in which we live.

How do we perform these tasks? We have already provided part of the answer in our earlier discussions of memory and the use of *heuristics*—cognitive "rules-of-thumb" for making judgments or decisions very quickly (see Chapter 6). Those discussions, though, focused on memory and cognition generally. Here, instead, we'll focus directly on key aspects of social thought—in a sense, where our basic cognitive processes come into play with respect to the social aspects of our lives. One key finding of research on this topic closely reflects what we know about cognition generally: As human beings, we are prone to many errors and biases in our thinking about others and in our efforts to make sense of the social world in which we live. While many such errors exist, we'll focus here on two that are especially intriguing and that we didn't consider in our earlier discussion of cognition: the *negativity* bias (a tendency to pay extra attention to negative information about others) and *counterfactual thinking* (the tendency to imagine events that don't exist and outcomes that we aren't actually experiencing) (e.g., Roses & Summerville, 2005).

Negativity bias: Why, often, negative information gets extra weight. Imagine that in describing someone you haven't met, one of your friends mentions many positive things about this person—he or she is pleasant, intelligent, good-looking, friendly, and so on. Then, your friend mentions one negative piece of information: This person is also somewhat conceited. What are you likely to remember? Research findings indicate that the negative information will probably stand out in your memory (e.g Kunda, 1999). Moreover, because of this, the negative information will have a stronger influence on your desire to meet this person than any one equivalent piece of positive information. Such findings suggest that we show a strong **negativity bias**—greater sensitivity to negative information than to positive information. This is true of both social information and information about other aspects of the world, but it seems to be especially important with respect to social thought, because it can strongly—and sometimes unjustifiably—influence our judgments or decisions about other people.

Why do we have this tendency? From an evolutionary perspective, it makes a great deal of sense. Negative information reflects features of the external world that may, potentially, be threatening to our safety or well-being. For this reason, it is especially important that we be sensitive to such stimuli and thus able to respond to them quickly. Several research findings offer support for this reasoning. For instance, consider our ability to recognize facial expressions in others. The results of many studies indicate that we are faster and more accurate in detecting negative facial expressions (e.g., ones showing anger or hostility) than positive facial expressions (e.g., ones showing friendliness).

Studies conducted by Ohman, Lundqvist, and Esteves (2001) provide a clear illustration of such effects. These researchers asked participants to search for neutral, friendly, or threatening faces present among other faces with discrepant expressions (e.g., the friendly face was shown among neutral or threatening faces; the threatening face was shown among friendly or neutral faces, etc.). Results indicated that regardless of the background faces, participants were faster and more accurate in identifying threatening faces. In an additional study, participants were asked to search for several kinds of faces—threatening, friendly, scheming, or

Negativity bias:
Greater sensitivity to negative information than positive information about others.

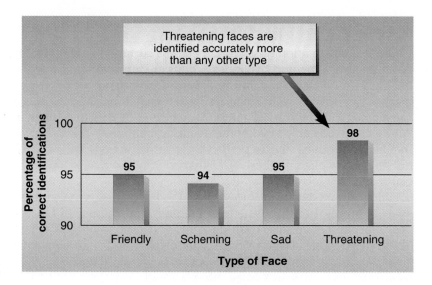

FIGURE 13.5
Evidence for the Negativity Bias: Which Face Do You Notice First?
Threatening faces shown among a background of neutral faces were identified more quickly and more accurately than friendly, scheming, or sad faces. These findings provide evidence for the existence of the *negativity bias*—enhanced sensitivity to negative stimuli or information.
Source: Based on data from Ohman, Lundqvist, & Esteves, 2001.

sad—among an array of neutral faces. Again, the threatening faces were identified faster and more accurately than any of the others (see Figure 13.5).

In sum, we appear to have a strong tendency to show enhanced sensitivity to negative information. This tendency seems to be a very basic aspect of social thought, and may, in fact, be built into the structure and functioning of our brains (Cacioppo et al., 2003). In this respect, certainly, it is an important aspect of social cognition, one worth noting with care.

■ Counterfactual thinking: The effects of considering "What might have been."

Suppose that you take an important exam; when you receive your score, it is a C-minus—much lower than you had hoped. What thoughts will enter your mind as you consider your grade? If you are like most people, you may imagine "what might have been"—receiving a higher grade—along with thoughts about how you could have obtained that better outcome. "If only I had studied more, or come to class more often," you may think to yourself. Such thoughts about "what might have been"—known in social psychology as **counterfactual thinking**—occur in a wide range of situations, not just ones in which we experience disappointments. In fact, counterfactual thinking can involve imagining outcomes that are either better (*upward* counterfactuals) or worse (*downward* counterfactuals) than we actually experience. For instance, suppose you enter an athletic contest and come in third—you receive a bronze medal. Depending on the specific circumstances, you might imagine winning the gold or silver medal—a better outcome than you received; that would be upward counterfactual thinking. On the contrary, you might imagine winning no medal at all; that would be an example of downward counterfactual thinking.

What are the effects of engaging in such thought—in imaging what did not actually happen? Neal Roese (1997), a social psychologist who has conducted many studies on counterfactual thinking, suggests that engaging in it can yield a wide range of effects, some of which are beneficial and some of which are costly (e.g., Roese & Summerville, 2005). For instance, counterfactual thinking can yield either boosts to, or reductions in, our current moods. When we imagine better outcomes than we actually receive (i.e., when we engage in *upward counterfactuals*), we often experience intense feelings of regret—especially if we think that better outcomes are unlikely in the future (Sanna, 1997; Medvec, Madey, & Gilovich, 1995). What do people regret most? Research on this topic suggests, first, that we tend to regret thing we *didn't do* but wish we had, more than things we did do that turned out badly. The reason for this seems clear: When we think about things we didn't do but wish we had done, there's no limit to the "upside"—we can imagine experiencing truly wonderful outcomes if we had done what, now, we realize we should have done! For example, we can imagine that we would now have a truly mar-

Counterfactual thinking:
The tendency to evaluate events by thinking about alternatives to them (i.e., "What might have been").

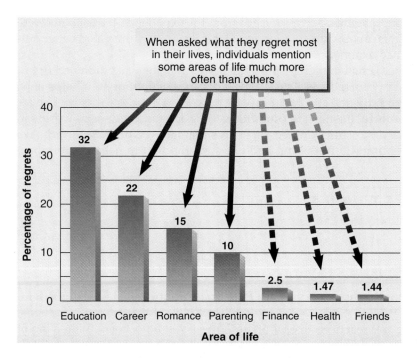

When asked what they regret most in their lives, individuals mention some areas of life much more often than others

FIGURE 13.6
What Do People Regret Most?
Research on *counterfactual thinking*—one important aspect of social thought—indicates that certain kinds of regrets—ones over education, careers, romances, and parenting—are much more common than others (e.g., regrets concerning finance, family, health, friends, etc.). This seems to be true because we are most likely to experience regrets over *missed opportunities*, and these are perceived to be more common in some areas of life than in others.
Source: Based on data from Roese & Summerville, 2005.

velous job if only we had handled a job interview differently than we did. In contrast, when we consider things we did that produced negative results, we know what these outcomes are, so there's a limit.

Additional findings indicate that people also tend to experience regret over certain aspects of life more than others. When asked to describe the things they regret most in their lives, many people tend to describe events relating to education (the school they didn't attend or course they didn't take), careers (the job they weren't offered or didn't accept), romance (especially the ones they didn't have but wish they had), parenting (things they wish they had done better as parents), and self (ways in which they could or should have improved). As you can see from Figure 13.6, regrets in these areas of life are much greater than regrets concerning finance, family, health, friends, and so on. Why do individuals regret some things more than others? According to Roese and Summerville (2005), the answer may involve how much opportunity they feel they have missed: The greater the opportunities they "blew," the more likely they are to experience regrets, and the stronger these tend to be.

Another effect of counterfactual thinking involves its impact on future performance. Engaging in counterfactual thinking after disappointing results can often help us to formulate improved strategies or tactics—ones that will yield better outcomes in the future. So in this sense, counterfactual thinking can be very helpful.

Finally, it's important to note that we often use upward and downward counterfactual thinking to deal with negative events in our lives. After such events, we may have two different goals: *self-enhancement* (to make ourselves feel better about ourselves and our past actions) or to prepare for *self-improvement* (to do better in the future). If self-enhancement is our primary goal, we are likely to engage in downward counterfactual thinking, because imaging even worse outcomes can give us comfort—we are glad things didn't turn out even worse! In contrast, if self-improvement is our key goal, then we are more likely to engage in upward counterfactual thinking; imagining better outcomes gets us prepared to seek them, even if this requires hard work. Direct evidence for this reasoning has been reported recently by White and Lehman (2005), who asked participants in their research to imagine that they had experienced a negative life events (e.g., a car accident or the ending of a romantic relationship). When told to describe how they could feel better about themselves after these events, participants generally engaged in downward counterfactual thinking—they imagined even worse outcomes than actually occurred. When told to imagine how they could improve themselves or learn from the experience, participants were more likely to engage in upward counterfactual thinking—they imagined better outcomes than they had experienced.

In sum, counterfactual thinking—the tendency to imagine what didn't occur but perhaps *could* have occurred—is a basic aspect of our social thought. It helps us to cope with disappointments, and can motivate us to work harder to achieve better outcomes in the future. In short, in our efforts to understand the social worlds in which we live, we don't simply reflect on events that have actually occurred—we also imagine ones that did not occur, and use such thought to help reach important goals.

KEY QUESTIONS

- What is the negativity bias?
- What is counterfactual thinking? How can it influence our affective states and performance?

Attitudes: Evaluating the Social World

Consider the following list: Condoleezza Rice; sport utility vehicles; Antonio Banderas; Iraq.

Do you have any reactions to each item? Unless you have been living a life of total isolation, you probably do. You may like or dislike Condoleezza Rice, believe or not believe that sport utility vehicles are wasteful and harmful to the environment, believe that Antonio Banderas is a fine actor—or one who is merely sexy—and feel that the United States should or should not be involved in Iraq. Such reactions, which social psychologists describe as **attitudes,** generally involve an emotional or affective component (for instance, liking or disliking), a cognitive component (beliefs), and a behavioral component (tendencies to act toward these items in various ways). More simply, attitudes can be defined as lasting evaluations of virtually any and every aspect of the social world—issues, ideas, people, groups, or even objects (Fazio & Roskos-Ewoldsen, 1994; Tesser & Martin, 1996).

Attitudes are an important aspect of social thought and have long been a central topic of research in social psychology, mainly because they often (but not always) influence our overt behavior (e.g., Azjen, 1991; Gibbons et al., 1998). For instance, if you have a positive attitude toward Condoleezza Rice, you might vote for her if she ran for office; if you dislike sport utility vehicles, you probably won't buy one. So attitudes are often a good predictor of present or future behavior—although far from a perfect one for reasons we'll soon explain. We'll now examine two key aspects of attitudes: *persuasion*, or how attitudes can sometimes be changed, and *cognitive dissonance*, a process through which, sometimes, we actually change our own attitudes.

■ **Persuasion: Using messages to change attitudes.**

In the early twenty-first century, efforts to change attitudes are definitely big business. Television commercials, magazine ads, billboards, warning labels on products—all are designed to change our attitudes in some way (see Figure 13.7). To what extent are such efforts at **persuasion**—efforts to change attitudes—really effective? And how does persuasion actually occur? Let's see what psychologists have learned about these issues.

Persuasion: The early approach.   Often, efforts at persuasion involve the following elements: some *source* directs some kind of *message* to one or more *recipients* (the audience). Taking note of this fact, early research on persuasion focused on these key elements, asking, "Who says what to whom and with what effect?" Key findings of this approach are summarized below:

1. Experts are more persuasive than nonexperts (Hovland & Weiss, 1951). The same arguments carry more weight when delivered by people who seem to know what they are talking about than when they are made by people lacking expertise.

Attitudes:

Lasting evaluations of various aspects of the social world that are stored in memory.

Persuasion:

The process through which one or more people attempt to alter the attitudes of one or more others.

2. Messages that do not appear to be designed to change our attitudes are often more successful in this respect than ones that seem intended to reach this goal (Walster & Festinger, 1962). In other words, we generally don't trust—and generally refuse to be influenced by—people who deliberately set out to persuade us. This is one reason why the "soft sell" is so popular in advertising and politics.

3. Attractive sources are more effective in changing attitudes than unattractive ones (Kiesler & Kiesler, 1969). This is why the models featured in many ads are highly attractive and why advertisers engage in a perpetual search for "new faces."

4. People are sometimes more susceptible to persuasion when they are distracted by some extraneous event than when they are paying full attention to what is being said (Allyn & Festinger, 1961).

5. When an audience holds attitudes contrary to those of a would-be persuader, it is often more effective for this person to adopt a *two-sided approach*, in which both sides of the argument are presented, than to adopt a *one-sided approach*. Apparently, strongly supporting one side of an issue while acknowledging that the other side has a few good points in its favor serves to disarm audience members and makes it harder for them to resist the source's major conclusions.

6. People who speak rapidly are often more persuasive than people who speak more slowly (Miller et al., 1976). So, contrary to popular belief, we do not always distrust fast-talking politicians and salespeople.

7. Persuasion can be enhanced by messages that arouse strong emotions (especially fear) in the audience, particularly when the message provides specific recommendations about how a change in attitudes or behavior will prevent the negative consequences described in the fear-provoking message (Leventhal, Singer, & Jones, 1965), and when they are *positively framed*—when they focus on potential benefits that may result from changing some behavior or attitude (e.g., Jones, Sinclair, & Courneya, 2003).

We're confident that you find all these points to be reasonable ones that probably fit with your own experience, so early research on persuasion certainly provided important insights into the factors that influence persuasion. What such work *didn't* do, however, was offer a comprehensive account of *how* persuasion occurs. Fortunately, this question has been the focus of more recent research, to which we turn next.

The cognitive approach to persuasion: Systematic versus heuristic processing. What happens when you are exposed to a persuasive message—for instance, when you watch a television commercial or listen to a political speech? Your first answer might be something like, "I think about what's happening or what's being said," and in a sense, that's correct. But how much thinking of this type do we actually do, and how do we process (absorb, interpret, evaluate) the information contained in such messages? The answer that has emerged from careful research is that, basically, we process persuasive messages in two distinct ways.

The first of these is known as **systematic processing** or the **central route,** and it involves careful consideration of message content, the ideas it contains, and so on. Such processing is quite effortful, and absorbs much of our information-processing capacity. For example, if while listening to a political speech you think very carefully about the points being made, you would be engaging in such systematic processing. The second approach, known as **heuristic processing** or the **peripheral route,** involves the use of simple rules of thumb or mental shortcuts, such as the belief that "statements by experts can be trusted," or the idea that "if it makes me feel good, I'm in favor of it." For instance, if while listening to a politi-

FIGURE 13.7
Efforts at Persuasion: Can We Resist?
Every day we are bombarded with commercials, ads, and other efforts to change our attitudes. Can we resist these efforts at persuasion? Research by social psychologists suggests several techniques that can be highly effective in this regard.

Systematic processing:
Involves careful consideration of message content, the ideas it contains, and so on. Such processing is quite effortful and absorbs much of our information-processing capacity

Central route (to persuasion):
Persuasion that occurs through careful consideration of message content.

Heuristic processing:
Involves the use of simple rules of thumb or mental shortcuts.

Peripheral route (to persuasion):
Attitude change that occurs in response to persuasion cues—information concerning the expertise, status, or attractiveness of would-be persuaders.

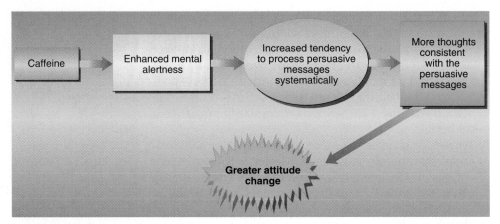

FIGURE 13.8
Effects of Caffeine on Persuasion
Research findings indicate that caffeine, a drug that increases mental alertness, also enhances the tendency to think carefully and systematically about persuasive messages. This, in turn, increases the frequency of thoughts consistent with the content of these messages, and produces increased attitude change.
Source: Based on results reported by Martin et al., 2005.

cal speech you concluded, "I like this person and believe what she is saying," you would be using heuristic processing. This kind of processing is much less effortful, and allows us to react to persuasive messages in an automatic manner. It occurs in response to cues in the message or situations that trigger various mental shortcuts (e.g., "If someone so beautiful or famous or charismatic is saying these words, then they are worthy of careful attention" or "they must be true").

Evidence that we really do use these two routes for processing persuasive messages is provided by many different studies, but one of the most interesting of these is research conducted by Martin and colleagues (2005) concerning the effects of caffeine on such processing. Caffeine, as we noted in Chapter 4, is found in coffee, tea, and many soft drinks, and is known to increase mental alertness. Given this effect, the researchers reasoned that caffeine might increase the tendency to process persuasive messages through the central route—through careful, systematic thinking. To test this prediction, the researchers gave drinks containing or not containing caffeine to volunteer participants. Then they asked them to express their attitudes about a wide range of issues, including voluntary euthanasia (a person's right to end his or her life if the person has a terminal illness). Next, all participants were exposed to persuasive messages that argued *against* their initial views. (Most students were in favor of voluntary euthanasia, so the persuasive messages argued against this position.) After reading these messages, all participants again indicated their views on this and other issues. In addition, they listed all the thoughts they had while reading the arguments against voluntary euthanasia (the persuasive message).

It was predicted that individuals who had received caffeine would process the persuasive messages more carefully than those who had not and so would show more attitude change. Further, it was also reasoned that this would occur because such systematic processing would generate more thoughts consistent with the content of the persuasive messages. Both predictions were confirmed (see Figure 13.8). Thus, caffeine—a drug that increases mental alertness—did in fact enhance the tendency of participants in the research to engage in careful, systematic processing of persuasive messages that argued against their views—and this offers strong evidence for the existence of two distinct routes to persuasion (see Petty & Cacioppo, 1996).

One more question relating to the cognitive approach to persuasion: When, precisely, do we engage in each of these distinct modes of thought? Modern theories of persuasion, such as the **elaboration-likelihood model** (ELM for short; e.g.,

Elaboration-likelihood model (ELM):
A cognitive model of persuasion suggesting that persuasion can occur through distinct routes.

Petty & Cacioppo, 1986; Petty et al., 1994) provide the following answer: We engage in the effortful type of processing (systematic processing) when our capacity to process information relating to the persuasive message is high (e.g., we have lots of knowledge about it or lots of time to engage in such thought) or when we are *motivated* to do so (the issue is important to us, we believe it is important to form an accurate view, etc.) (see Maheswaran & Chaiken, 1991; Petty & Cacioppo, 1990). In contrast, we engage in the less-effortful type of processing (heuristic processing) when we lack the ability or capacity to process more carefully (we must make our minds very quickly, have little knowledge about the issue) or when our motivation to perform such cognitive work is low (the issue is unimportant to us, has little potential effect on us, etc.). Advertisers, politicians, and salespeople wishing to change our attitudes prefer to push us into the heuristic mode of processing because it is often easier to change our attitudes when we think in this mode than when we engage in more systematic processing. Why? Because we are thinking "on automatic," and this makes it harder for us to defend against persuasion.

■ Cognitive dissonance: How we sometimes change our own attitudes.

There are many occasions in everyday life when we feel compelled to say or do things inconsistent with our true attitudes. A couple of examples: Your friend shows you his new sweater and asks how you like it. You really hate the color, but you don't say that. Instead you say "Nice . . . really nice." Your boss describes her new idea for increasing sales. You think that it is totally idiotic, but you don't tell her *that*. Instead you respond: "Sounds really interesting . . ."

The reasons for behaving in these polite—but slightly dishonest—ways are so obvious that social psychologists describe them as involving **induced** (or **forced**) **compliance**—situations in which we feel compelled to say or do things inconsistent with our true attitudes. Now, here's the most interesting part: When we behave in this way—when we engage in *attitude-discrepant behavior*, this may sometimes produce changes in the attitudes we hold. In fact, our attitudes may shift toward what we felt compelled to do or say, thus reducing the size of the gap between our true attitudes and our overt actions.

Such effects were first predicted by a very famous hypothesis known as the theory of **cognitive dissonance** (Festinger, 1957). The term *cognitive dissonance* (or *dissonance* for short) refers to the unpleasant feelings we experience when we notice a gap between two attitudes we hold, or between our attitudes and our behavior. Dissonance, it appears, is quite unpleasant (e.g., Elliot & Devine, 1994), so when we experience it, we attempt to reduce it. This can be accomplished in several ways. First, we can change our attitudes or behavior so that these are more consistent with each other. For example, we can convince ourselves that the color of our friend's sweater is not really so bad. Second, we can acquire new information that supports our attitude or our behavior. For instance, we can seek out information indicating that our boss's plan does make some sense. Third, we can engage in *trivialization*—concluding that the attitudes or behaviors in question are not important (see Simon, Greenberg, & Brehm, 1995).

Which of these tactics do we choose? As you might guess, whichever requires the least effort. In situations involving induced compliance, however, it is often the case that changing our attitudes is the easiest step to take, so it is not surprising that in such situations, our attitudes often shift so as to more closely match what we have actually said or done. In other words, we change our attitudes because doing so helps us reduce cognitive dissonance.

Dissonance and the less-leads-to-more effect. The prediction that people sometimes change their own attitudes is surprising enough. But now get ready for an even bigger surprise: Dissonance theory also predicts that the weaker the reasons we have for engaging in attitude-discrepant behavior—for saying or doing things inconsistent with our true attitudes—the greater the pressure to change these attitudes. Why is this so? Because when we have strong reasons for engaging in attitude-discrepant behav-

Induced (forced) compliance:
A technique for changing attitudes in which individuals are somehow induced to state positions different from their actual views.

Cognitive dissonance:
The state experienced by individuals when they discover inconsistency between two attitudes they hold or between their attitudes and their behavior.

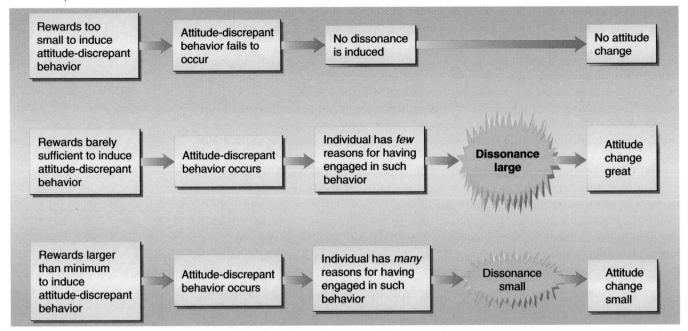

FIGURE 13.9
Why, Where Attitude Change Is Concerned, "Less" Sometimes Leads to "More"
When individuals have strong reasons for engaging in behavior discrepant with their attitudes (e.g., when they receive large rewards for doing so), they experience little or no dissonance and show little attitude change. When they have weak reasons for engaging in such behavior (e.g., when they receive small rewards for doing so), dissonance is much greater and attitude change, too, is increased. In such cases, "less" does indeed lead to "more."

Less-leads-to-more effect:
Refers to the fact that rewards just barely sufficient to induce individuals to state positions contrary to their own views often generate more attitude change than larger rewards.

ior, we realize that these are responsible for saying or doing things inconsistent with our true attitudes. As a result, we experience very little dissonance. When we have only weak reasons for engaging in attitude-discrepant behavior, however, dissonance is stronger, and so is the pressure to change our attitudes (see Figure 13.9).

Social psychologists sometimes refer to this unexpected state of affairs as the **less-leads-to-more effect:** the fact that the stronger the reasons for engaging in attitude-discrepant behavior, the weaker the pressures toward changing the underlying attitudes. Surprising as it may seem, this effect has been confirmed in many studies (e.g., Riess & Schlenker, 1977). In all these studies, people provided with a small reward for stating attitudes contrary to their own views changed these attitudes so that they became closer to the views they had been forced or induced to express.

While the less-leads-to-more effect seems to be very common, it does not occur under all conditions. Rather, it seems to happen only when several conditions exist (Cooper & Scher, 1994). First, the less-leads-to-more effect occurs only in situations in which people believe that they have a choice as to whether they will perform the attitude-discrepant behavior. Second, small rewards lead to greater attitude change only when people believe that they were personally responsible for both the chosen course of action and any negative effects it produced. And third, the less-leads-to-more effect does not occur when people view the payment they receive as a bribe rather than as a well-deserved payment for services rendered. Since these conditions do often exist, however, the strategy of offering others just barely enough to induce them to say or do things contrary to their true attitudes can often be an effective technique for inducing attitude change.

■ **Dissonance: Is it universal across all cultures?**

While many studies offer support for the suggestion that dissonance is an important aspect of social thought, it's important to note that most of this research was conducted in North America and Europe. This leaves an important question unanswered: Is cognitive dissonance a universal experience—does it occur in all cultures and influence social thought everywhere in the world? While all findings are not consistent (e.g., Yoshida, 1977), overall existing evidence points to the conclusion that dissonance is indeed a universal aspect of human thought. However, the factors that produce dissonance, and even its magnitude, can be strongly influenced by cultural factors. Perhaps a study conducted by Heine and Lehman (1997) provides the clearest evidence on these points.

These researchers reasoned that although dissonance might well occur all around the world, it might be less likely to influence attitudes in some cultures than in others. Specifically, they suggested that after making a choice between closely ranked alternatives, people from cultures such as those in the United States and Canada would be more likely to experience postdecision dissonance than people from cultures such as those in Asia. Why? Because in Western cultures the *self* is linked to individual actions, such as making correct decisions. As a result, individuals in Western cultures can experience considerable dissonance after making a choice: The possibility of having made an incorrect choice threatens their self. In many Asian cultures, in contrast, the self is not as closely linked to individual actions or choices. Rather, it is more strongly tied to roles and status—an individual's place in society and the obligations this involves. Thus, people in such cultures should be less likely to perceive the possibility of making an incorrect decision as a threat to their self-esteem, and so might be less likely to experience dissonance as a result of making such choices.

To test this reasoning, Heine and Lehman (1997) had Canadian students and Japanese students temporarily living in Canada choose ten CDs from a group of forty CDs that they would most like to own. They also evaluated how much they would like each of these ten CDs. Then, after making these choices, participants were told that they could actually have *either* the CD they ranked first or the one they ranked sixth, and were asked to choose one of these two items. After making their choice, participants rated the two CDs once again. Previous research suggests that to reduce dissonance, individuals who make such decisions often downplay the item they did not choose, while raising their ratings of the item they did choose (see Steele et al., 1993). The researchers predicted that such effects would be stronger for Canadians than for Japanese participants, and this is precisely what happened. The Canadian students boosted their ratings of the item they chose and lowered their ratings of the items they rejected, while the Japanese students did not.

These findings suggest that cultural factors do indeed influence the operation of dissonance. While all humans are made somewhat uneasy by inconsistencies between their attitudes or inconsistencies between their attitudes and their behavior, the intensity of such reactions, the precise conditions under which they occur, and the strategies used to reduce them may all be influenced by cultural factors.

KEY QUESTIONS

- What are attitudes?
- What factors were found to influence persuasion in early research?
- What is the ELM model, and how does it explain persuasion?
- What is cognitive dissonance, and how can it be reduced?
- What is induced compliance? The less-leads-to-more effect?
- Do cultural factors play a role in the occurrence of cognitive dissonance?

SOCIAL BEHAVIOR: INTERACTING WITH OTHERS

Thinking about other people is an important aspect of the social side of life, but in addition, we *interact* with others in many ways. We work with them on various tasks; we attempt to influence them—or are influenced by them; we fall in and out of love, join and leave various groups—the list goes on and on. In this section, we'll consider several important aspects of *social interaction* with others.

Prejudice: Distorted Views of the Social World . . . and Their Effects

Terrorist attacks and huge military reprisals; mass murder of one ethnic group by another; seemingly perpetual suspicion and hatred between people of different religious beliefs—the list of atrocities stemming from racial, ethnic, or religious hatred seems endless. Such actions often stem from **prejudice**—powerful negative attitudes toward the members of specific social groups based solely on their membership in that group (Dovidio & Gaertner, 1986; Zanna & Olson, 1994). Where do such attitudes come from? And what can be done to reduce their impact? These are the issues we'll now examine.

■ The origins of prejudice: Contrasting perspectives.

Many different explanations for the origins of prejudice have been proposed. Here are four that have been especially influential.

Direct intergroup conflict: Competition as a source of bias. It is sad but true that many of the things we value most—a good job, a nice home, high status—are in short supply; there's never enough to go around. This fact serves as the basis for one view of prejudice—**realistic conflict theory** (Bobo, 1983). According to this view, prejudice stems from competition between social groups over valued objects or opportunities. The theory further suggests that as such competition persists, the members of the groups involved come to view one another in increasingly negative ways (White, 1977). They label members of the other group as enemies, view their own group as superior, and draw the boundaries between themselves and their opponents ever more firmly. As a result, what starts out as economic competition gradually turns into full-scale prejudice, with the hatred and anger this usually implies. Of course, competition between groups does not always produce such effects, but it *does* produce it often enough for it to be viewed as one important cause of prejudice.

Social categorization: The us-versus-them effect and the "ultimate" attribution error. A second perspective on the origins of prejudice begins with a basic fact: Individuals generally divide the social world into two distinct categories—*us* and *them* (Turner et al., 1987). They view other people as belonging either to their own social group, usually termed the *in-group*, or to another group, an *out-group*. Such distinctions are made on the basis of many dimensions, including race, religion, sex, age, ethnic background, occupation, and even the town or neighborhood where people live.

If this process of **social categorization**—dividing the world into distinct social categories—stopped there, it would have little impact on prejudice. Unfortunately, it does not. In general, people we assign to the "us" category are viewed much more favorably than those we assign to the "them" group. In fact, out-group members are assumed to possess more undesirable traits, are seen as being more alike (homogeneous) than members of the in-group (the group we consider our own), and are often disliked (see Lambert, 1995; Linville & Fisher, 1993). This is a very basic distinction; around the world, the word used by many different cultures to refer to themselves translates, roughly, as "human beings," while the word used for other groups translates as "nonhuman" or "others." The in-group–out-group distinction also affects *attribution*—explanations for other people's behaviors. We tend to attribute desirable behaviors by members of *our* group to stable, internal causes such as admirable traits, but attribute desirable behaviors by members of out-groups to temporary factors or to external ones, such as luck (e.g., Hewstone, Bond, & Wan, 1983). This tendency to make more favorable attributions about members of one's own group than about members of other groups is sometimes described as the *ultimate attribution error*. It carries the self-serving bias described earlier into intergroup relations—with potentially devastating effects.

The role of social learning. A third perspective on the origins of prejudice begins with the obvious fact that such attitudes are *learned*: We acquire them from the people around us through the process of *social learning* (see Chapter 5). Prejudice emerges out of countless experiences in which children hear or observe their parents, friends, teachers, and others expressing prejudiced views. Because they want to be like these

Prejudice:
Negative attitudes toward the members of some social group based on their membership in this group.

Realistic conflict theory:
A theory proposing that prejudice stems, at least in part, from direct conflict between social groups.

Social categorization:
The tendency to divide the social world into two distinct categories: "us" and "them."

people, and are often rewarded for expressing the "right" views (those held by adults), they quickly adopt such attitudes themselves (see Figure 13.10).

While people with whom children interact play a key role in this process, the mass media, too, are important. If television, films, and other media present members of various social groups in an unflattering light, this may contribute to the development of prejudice on the part of children exposed to them. And in fact, this is how African Americans, Native Americans, Hispanics, and many other minority groups were presented on films and on television in the United States in the past. Fortunately, this situation has changed greatly in recent years (see Weigel, Kim, & Frost, 1995); currently, members of these groups are being shown in a much more favorable manner. So, at least one important source of prejudiced attitudes seems to be decreasing.

FIGURE 13.10
Social Learning as a Basis for Prejudice
Parents and other adults often reward children for expressing the "right" attitudes—the ones they (the adults) hold. Prejudice is often transmitted to youngsters in this manner.

Cognitive sources of prejudice: The role of stereotypes. The final source of prejudice we'll consider is in some ways the most disturbing. It involves the possibility that prejudice stems at least in part from basic aspects of social cognition (e.g., Kunda & Oleson, 1995). While several processes seem to play a role in this regard, perhaps the most important of these involves **stereotypes.** These are cognitive frameworks consisting of knowledge and beliefs about specific social groups—frameworks suggesting that, by and large, all members of these groups possess certain traits, at least to a degree (Judd, Ryan, & Park, 1991). Like other cognitive frameworks (schemas), stereotypes exert strong effects on the ways in which we process social information. For instance, information relevant to a particular stereotype is processed more quickly than information unrelated to it (e.g., Dovidio, Evans, & Tyler, 1986). Similarly, stereotypes lead us to pay attention to specific types of information—usually information consistent with the stereotypes. And when information inconsistent with stereotypes does manage to enter consciousness, it may be actively refuted or simply denied (Bartholow, Dickter, & Sestir, 2006; Bodenhausen & Macrae, 1998). In fact, recent findings indicate that when individuals encounter people who behave in ways contrary to stereotypes, they often perceive them as a new "subtype" rather than an exception to their existing stereotype (Kunda & Oleson, 1995).

What is the relevance of such effects to prejudice? Together, they tend to make stereotypes somewhat self-confirming. Once an individual has acquired a stereotype about some social group, she or he tends to notice information that fits into this cognitive framework and to remember "facts" that are consistent with it more readily than "facts" inconsistent with it. As a result, the stereotype strengthens with time and may, ultimately, become invulnerable—new information or experiences simply can't change it.

Unfortunately, stereotypes don't have to be recognized consciously by the people who hold them to influence their behavior. Indeed, a key finding of recent research on prejudice is that it often occurs at a nonconcious level: The people who are influenced by it, and by the stereotypes on which it is based, don't realize that these effects are occurring. In fact, they would often vigorously deny that they are prejudiced in any way (e.g., Grenwald, 2002). Apparently, contact with people in the stereotyped groups automatically triggers implicit, unrecognized stereotypes; these then influence reactions toward members of the stereotyped groups (e.g., negative feelings toward them), and this occurs without any conscious awareness of these processes on the part of the people involved. In other words, as we noted in Chapter 4, much of our cognitive activity occurs outside awareness—but it can still strongly influence our behavior (Bartholow et al., 2006).

Stereotypes:
Cognitive frameworks suggesting that all members of specific social groups share certain characteristics.

How strong are these effects? A recent study by Eberhardt and colleagues (2006) suggests a chilling answer. These researchers obtained photos of defendants convicted of murder in one large city between 1979 and 1999. Forty-four of the cases involved instances in which a black defendant murdered a white victim. Undergraduate students then rated the photos of the black defendants in terms of the extent to which they showed stereotypically black features. Then, the percent of the defendants who received the death penalty was examined. Results were very unsettling: Black defendants who showed stereotypical black features were more than twice as likely to receive the death penalty than those who did not (57.5 percent versus 24.4 percent). Moreover, this was true regardless of other factors that might also influence such sentences, such as severity of the murder, aggravating circumstances, and defendant's and victim's socioeconomic status. In a follow-up study, the same researchers examined murder cases in which both the defendant and the victim were black. Here, the defendant's appearance (whether they had stereotypically black features or not) made no difference. Since the jurors on such cases would almost certainly strongly deny that they were influenced by racial stereotypes, the findings of these studies offer convincing—but disturbing—evidence for the potentially powerful effects of implicit stereotypes on racial prejudice.

■ Challenging prejudice: Techniques that can help.

Whatever the precise roots of prejudice, there can be no doubt that it is a negative, brutalizing force in human affairs. Reducing prejudice and countering its effects, therefore, are important tasks. What steps can be taken to reach these goals? Here is what research findings indicate.

Breaking the cycle of prejudice: Learning not to hate.   Bigots are clearly made, not born; they acquire their prejudices as a result of experience. Given this fact, one useful way to reduce prejudice involves discouraging the transmission of bigoted views while encouraging more positive attitudes toward others. But how can we induce parents, teachers, and other adults to encourage unbiased views among children in their care? One possibility involves calling the attention of such people to their own prejudiced views. Few want to see themselves as prejudiced. Instead, they view *their* negative attitudes toward others as justified. A key initial step, therefore, is convincing caregivers that the problem exists. Once they realize that it does, many are willing to modify their words and actions.

Another argument that can be used to shift parents and other caregivers in the direction of teaching children tolerance lies in how prejudice harms not only those who are its victims, but also those who hold such views (Dovidio & Garetner, 1993). Growing evidence suggests that people who are prejudiced live in a world filled with needless fears, anxieties, and anger. As a result, they experience needless emotional turmoil that can adversely affect their health (Jussim 1991). Since most parents and teachers want to do everything possible to further children's well-being, calling these potential costs to their attention may help persuade them to transmit tolerance rather than prejudice.

Direct intergroup contact: The potential benefits of acquaintance.   At the present time many cities in the United States resemble a social donut: A disintegrating and crime-ridden core inhabited primarily by minority groups is surrounded by a ring of relatively affluent suburbs inhabited mainly by whites and a sprinkling of wealthy minority group members. Needless to say, contact between the people living in these areas is minimal.

This state of affairs raises an intriguing question: Can prejudice be reduced by somehow increasing the degree of contact between different groups? The idea that it can is known as the **contact hypothesis**, and there are several good reasons for predicting that such a strategy might prove effective (Pettigrew, 1997). First, increased contact between people from different groups can lead to a growing recognition of similarities between them. As we will see in a later section, perceived sim-

Contact hypothesis:
The view that prejudice can be reduced by increasing the degree of contact between different groups.

ilarity can generate enhanced mutual attraction. Second, while stereotypes are resistant to change, they *can* be altered when sufficient information inconsistent with them is encountered, or when individuals meet a sufficient number of "exceptions" to their stereotypes (Kunda & Oleson, 1995). Third, increased contact may help counter the illusion that all members of the stereotyped group are alike. For these and other reasons, it seems possible that direct intergroup contact may be one effective way to combat prejudice. Is it? Existing evidence suggests that it is, but only when certain conditions are met: the groups must be roughly equal in social status; the contact between them must involve cooperation and interdependence; the contact must permit them to get to know one another as individuals; norms favoring group equality must exist; and the people involved must view one another as typical of their respective groups.

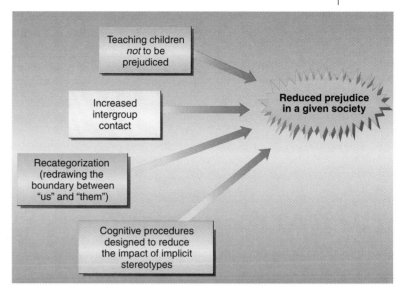

When contact between initially hostile groups occurs under these conditions, prejudice does seem to decrease (e.g., Pettigrew & Tropp, 2006). Such effects appear to be stronger for majority groups than for minority ones (Tropp & Pettigrew, 2005)—who, after all, have a lot of prior mistreatment to forgive! But, in general, increased contact between groups does seem to encourage reductions in prejudice.

FIGURE 13.11
Techniques for Reducing Prejudice
As shown here, psychological research indicates that several different techniques can be highly effective in reducing prejudice. Implementing these procedures is far from easy, but if used carefully, they *can* really help.

Recategorization: Resetting the boundary between "us" and "them." Suppose that a team from your college played against a team from a rival college. Which would be "us" and which would be "them"? The answer is obvious. Your own school's team would constitute your in-group, while the other school's team would be the out-group. But now imagine that the team from the other school had won many games and was chosen to represent your state in a national tournament. When it played against a team from another state, would you now perceive it as "us" or "them"? You would probably shift your view so that now this former "enemy" team was viewed as part of your own in-group. Situations like this suggest that the boundary between "us" and "them" is not fixed. On the contrary, it can be shifted so as to include—or exclude—various groups of people. This fact suggests another technique for reducing prejudice—one known as **recategorization** (see Gaertner et al., 1989, 1990). This involves somehow inducing individuals to shift the boundary between "us" and "them" so that it now includes groups they previously viewed as "them." The result: Their prejudice toward these people is reduced. Evidence for such effects has been obtained in several studies (e.g., Dovidio, et al., 1995; Gaertner et al., 1993), so it appears that recategorization may be a very useful technique for reducing many forms of prejudice.

Several other techniques for reducing prejudice also exist, and among these, ones based on efforts to counter the effects of implicit stereotypes—the kind of prejudice people don't even realize that they have (Olson & Fazio, 2006)—seem most promising. This can sometimes be accomplished by pairing photos of the faces of people in the stereotyped groups with positive adjectives (e.g., good, intelligent, hard-working) for periods of time that are so short that participants in the research are unaware of having seen them. Although they can't perceive these pairings between faces of groups toward whom they hold stereotypes and positive adjectives, these procedures still seem to weaken negative stereotypes.

In sum, prejudice, in one form or another, appears to have been present throughout human history and in many cultures. But we are definitely *not* powerless to reduce it and can truly make progress in this direction by using several steps identified in psychological research. (These techniques are summarized in Figure 13.11). (Does

Recategorization:
A technique for reducing prejudice that involves inducing individuals to shift the boundary between "us" and "them" so that it now includes groups they previously viewed as "them."

prejudice exist in work settings? And if so, what forms does it take? For a discussion of this important topic, see the **Psychology Goes to Work** section below.)

KEY QUESTIONS

- What are some of the major causes of prejudice?
- What techniques are effective in reducing prejudice?

PSYCHOLOGY GOES TO WORK

Prejudice in Work Settings: The Forms It Takes and What Companies Are Doing to Combat It

In the United States and many other countries, workplaces—like the rest of society—are becoming increasingly diverse. And this trend, reflecting shifts in populations, will certainly continue and grow stronger in the future. In many places, it is already here. For instance, one company—Solectron Corporation, a business in Milpitas, California, that specializes in computer assembly—has, among its 3,200 employees, people from thirty countries who speak more than forty languages (Malone, 1993).

Given such diversity, it is clear that there is no room for prejudice in workplaces; it would be a cause of interpersonal friction, get in the way of excellent work, and interfere with the careers of people who are the targets of such prejudice. In this respect, it is revealing to consider the difficulties faced by women—one group that has been the target of considerable prejudice. Although there are more women than ever in the workforce, and they are doing higher-level work than ever before, they remain highly underrepresented in the upper levels of many organizations. In fact, only about 7.9 percent of high-level executive positions are held by women in large companies even at the present time. Because such discrimination is not openly admitted, it is frequently referred to as the **glass ceiling**—a barrier that is present but cannot easily be seen.

Prejudice against women is not the only kind that exists in workplaces, however. In addition, it is clear that "all the usual suspects" are present: Prejudices based on national origin, race, and religion are common. In addition, workplaces also have some unique forms of prejudice of their own, such as prejudice based on age, physical condition (directed primarily against people who are physically or emotionally challenged), and even physical appearance—a topic to which we'll return in a later section. Clearly, then, prejudice is an important issue in workplaces and, unfortunately, you may well encounter it yourself in one form or another.

Given the potentially harmful effects of prejudice, what are companies doing to reduce it? Actually, a number of things. Many, for instance, have implemented *diversity management programs*, which focus not only on increasing diversity by hiring members of underrepresented groups, but also seek to *celebrate* diversity by creating supportive work environments for the members of such groups. Two basic kinds of diversity management programs exist—*awareness-based diversity training* and *skills-based training*—and both are based on the principles and findings of psychology.

Awareness-based diversity training is designed to raise people's awareness of diversity issues in the workplace and to get them to recognize the underlying assumptions they make about people. Typically, such training involves teaching employees about the business necessity of valuing diversity, and makes them sensitive to their own cultural assumptions and biases. This may involve using various experiential exercises that help people view others as individuals as opposed to stereotyped members of groups.

Skills-based diversity training, in contrast, is designed to help individuals acquire specific skills related to dealing effectively with diversity. This can involve building increasing understanding of other cultures, techniques for enhancing communication across cultural boundaries, and developing skills designed to reduce the likelihood of cultural misunderstandings.

Do such programs work? Results to date have been encouraging. Reducing prejudice is a complex and difficult task, so there are, unfortunately, no easy answers. But many companies are aware of the problems that can potentially arise from increased diversity, and are, with the help of psychologists, taking active steps to minimize these problems and to reduce the prejudice that often plays a role in their occurrence.

"It's the only way I can get Ted to finish projects."

FIGURE 13.12
Gaining Compliance: An Extreme Example
We all use many different techniques for gaining compliance from others—for getting them to do what we want them to do. Fortunately, few are as extreme as this one!
CLOSE TO HOME © (2005) John McPherson. Reprinted with permission of Universal Press Syndicate. All rights reserved.

Social Influence: Changing Others' Behavior

As we saw earlier, persuasion involves efforts by others to change our attitudes, and such attempts are a common part of everyday life. But persuasion is only one aspect of a much broader process known as **social influence**—attempts by one or more people to change our *behavior* in some way. Many different tactics are used for this purpose, but among these, two are especially powerful: *compliance* and *obedience*.

■ **Compliance: To ask—sometimes—is to receive.**

Suppose that you wanted someone to do something for you. How would you go about getting them to do it? If you think about this question for a moment, you'll soon realize that you probably have quite a few tricks up your sleeve for getting the other person to say "yes"—for gaining what social psychologists term **compliance** (see Figure 13.12 for an extreme example). Careful study of these tactics by social psychologists, however, suggests that most rest on a small number of basic principles. These principles, and some of the strategies for gaining compliance related to them, are described below.

Tactics based on commitment or consistency: The foot in the door. Several techniques for getting others to say "yes" to our requests are based on the principle of obtaining an initial small commitment from them. Once this is obtained, they often find it harder to refuse later requests. For instance, salespeople, fund-raisers, and other experts in gaining compliance often start with a trivial request and then, when this is accepted, move on to a larger request—the one they really wanted all along. This is known as the **foot-in-the-door technique,** and the chances are good that you have encountered it or used it yourself. Research findings indicate that it works (see Beaman et al., 1983), and that one reason it does is that people want to be consistent. Once they have said "yes" to the first request, they feel it is inconsistent to say "no" to the second. (Recall our earlier discussion of cognitive dissonance.)

A related procedure is known as the *low-ball* technique, and involves asking someone to do something under conditions that are very favorable to them. Then, once they agree, the "deal" is changed so as to make it less desirable. Salespeople at car dealers often use this tactic: They offer a great price on a car, but then, when

Social influence:
Attempts by one or more people to change our behavior in some manner.

Compliance:
A form of social influence in which one or more people attempts to influence one or more others through direct requests.

Foot-in-the-door technique:
A technique for gaining compliance in which requesters start with a small request and then, after this is granted, shift to a much larger request.

the customer accepts, indicate that the sales manager has refused to approve the deal, and that they must raise the price. If people were totally rational, they would refuse and walk away. In fact, though, they often agree to the changes, thus giving the person with whom they are dealing precisely what that individual wanted all along (Cialdini et al., 1978). Research findings indicate that this tactic works only when people have publicly accepted the initial, favorable offer; if, instead, the "deal" is changed before they have done this, the low-ball procedure does not increase compliance. This suggests that initial commitment is indeed the central principle behind this technique (Burger & Cornelius, 2003).

Tactics based on reciprocity: The door in the face.   Reciprocity is a basic rule of social life: We tend to treat other people as they have treated us. Several tactics for gaining compliance are based on this fact. One of these, which is known as the **door-in-the-face technique,** is the opposite of the foot-in-the-door technique. Instead of beginning with a small request and then escalating to a larger one, this tactic starts with a very large request that is almost certain to be rejected. After it is refused, a much smaller request is made—the one the requester wanted all along. The target person then feels a subtle pressure to reciprocate by saying "yes." After all, the requester made a concession by scaling down the first request. This technique is often successful, and its success seems to rest largely on the principle of reciprocity (Cialdini, 1994).

Tactics based on scarcity: Playing hard to get.   In general, the harder something is to obtain, the greater value it is perceived to have. This basic fact serves as the underlying principle for several tactics for gaining compliance. Perhaps the most popular of these is **playing hard to get**—a tactic in which individuals try to create the image that they are very popular or very much in demand. This puts pressure on would-be romantic partners and would-be employers to say "yes" to requests from the person using this tactic. The requests can range from "Let's get engaged" to "Pay me a high salary," but the underlying principle is the same: The people on the receiving end feel that if they don't agree, they may lose a valuable partner or employee—so they say "yes" (see Williams et al., 1993).

Tactics based on liking: Often, flattery *will* get you everywhere!   Other important tactics for gaining increased compliance are based on the principle of liking: In general, we are more willing to say "yes" to requests from others we like than to identical requests from people we don't especially like. This is the basis for **ingratiation**—somehow getting others to like you before making your request. Ingratiation, in turn, can be produced by several different tactics with which you are probably familiar. Flattery is, perhaps, the most common, but there are others, too, such as agreeing with others or emphasizing similarity to them. As we'll soon see, similarity often generates attraction, and liking others, in turn, is often an important reason for saying "yes" to requests they make.

■ Obedience: Social influence by demand.

Now we come to what is perhaps the most direct way in which one person can attempt to change the behavior of another: through *direct orders*—simply telling the target person what to do. This approach is less common than tactics of compliance, but it is far from rare, and occurs in many situations where one person has clear authority over another—in the military, in sports, and in business, to name a few. **Obedience** to the commands of sources of authority is far from surprising; military officers, coaches, and bosses have powerful ways to enforce their commands. More surprising, though, is that even people lacking in such authority can sometimes induce high levels of obedience in others. Unsettling evidence for such effects was first reported by Stanley Milgram (1963, 1974) in a series of famous experiments.

To find out whether individuals would obey commands from a relatively pow-

Door-in-the-face technique:
A technique for gaining compliance in which a large request is followed by a smaller one.

Playing hard to get:
A tactic for gaining compliance in which individuals try to create the image that they are very popular or very much in demand.

Ingratiation:
A technique of social influence based on inducing increased liking in the target people before influence is attempted.

Obedience:
A form of social influence in which one individual orders one or more others to behave in specific ways.

erless stranger, Milgram designed ingenious procedures in which participants were seated in front of the device shown in Figure 13.13, and told that each time another person (actually an assistant of the researcher) made an error on a learning task, they were to deliver an electric shock to him. Moreover, they were to raise the shock level for each error so that if he made many errors, they would soon be delivering powerful—and painful!—jolts of electricity to the learner. (Remember: This person was really an assistant who never received any electric shocks.) Would they obey these commands—and thus show obedience? If they refused, they were ordered to do so by the experimenter in increasingly severe terms. Since participants were volunteers and were paid in advance, you might predict that most would quickly refuse such "orders." In fact, though, *fully 65 percent were fully obedient*, continuing through the entire series to the final 450-volt shock.

Not surprisingly, many people protested and expressed concern over the learner's welfare. When ordered to proceed, however, most yielded to the experimenter's social influence and continued to obey. In fact, they did so even when the victim pounded on the wall and, later, stopped responding altogether, as if he had passed out! Why did the participants in Milgram's research (and in several related studies) show such high levels of obedience? Several factors seem to play a role. First, the experimenter took participants "off the hook" by explaining that he, not they, would be responsible for the learner's well-being. So, just as in many real-life situations where soldiers or police commit atrocities, participants could say, "I was only following orders" (see Hans, 1992; Kelman & Hamilton, 1989). Second, the experimenter possessed clear signs of authority and, in most societies, individuals learn that people holding authority are to be obeyed (Bushman, 1984, 1988). Finally, the experimenter's commands were gradual in nature. He didn't request that participants jump to the 450-volt shock immediately; rather, he moved toward this request one step at a time. This is similar to many real-life situations in which police or military personnel are initially ordered merely to arrest or question future victims. Only later are they ordered to beat, torture, or even to kill them.

In sum, several factors probably contributed to the high levels of obedience observed in Milgram's research and related studies. Together, these factors produced a powerful force—one that most people found difficult to resist. In fact, one well-known psychologist, Phlilp Zimbardo (2007), has recently suggested that a strong tendency to obey, plus other factors such as anonymity, may have contributed to the atrocities committed by U.S. soldiers in the Abu Ghraib prison in Iraq—atrocities in which prisoners of war were humiliated and tortured (see Figure 13.14). The fact that the power of authority is strong does not imply it cannot be resisted, however. History is filled with cases in which brave people resisted the commands—and power—of entrenched dictators and governments and, in the end, triumphed over them. The United States, of course, began with an act of rebellion

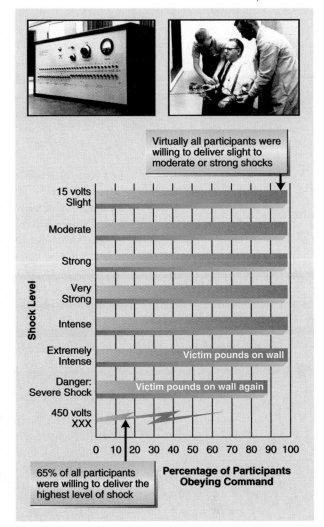

FIGURE 13.13

Milgram's Research on Obedience

The photo on the left shows the equipment used by Milgram in his famous studies. The photo on the right shows the experimenter and a participant (rear) attaching electrodes to the learner's (accomplice's) wrists. Results of the research, shown in the graph, indicated that fully 65 percent of all participants were fully obedient to the experimenter's commands—they advanced to the highest shock level (supposedly, 450 volts!).

FIGURE 13.14

Obedience to Authority in the U.S. Military

A recent study suggests that a strong tendency to obey might have contributed to the atrocities committed by U.S. soldiers in Iraq.

against the British government, and events in the former Soviet Union and throughout eastern Europe provide clear illustrations of the fact that even powerful regimes can be resisted. So while obedience is a powerful force, it *can* be resisted—and often is!

KEY QUESTIONS
- What are some of the basic principles on which tactics of compliance are based?
- What is obedience? Why does it occur?

Attraction . . . and Love

Do you remember the story at the beginning of this chapter, in which I (Robert Baron) described my first meeting with my future wife? If so, you may recall that I experienced powerful attraction to her from the very start—something that the French describe as a "coup de foudre"—literally, a stroke or blow of lightning, which translates in English—less poetically!—as "love at first sight." That such reactions occur is clear, but why? Why do people like or dislike each other when they meet, and why do these feelings sometimes become so intense that they are—or soon become—love? Let's see what social psychologists have discovered about these truly important questions.

■ **Interpersonal attraction: Why we like or dislike others.**

Think of someone you like very much, someone you strongly dislike, and someone you'd place in the middle of this dimension. Now, ask yourself this question: *Why* do you have these reactions? Revealing answers are provided by research on the nature and causes of **interpersonal attraction.**

Propinquity: Nearness makes the heart grow fonder. Many friendships and romances start when individuals are brought into contact with each other, often by chance. We tend to form relationships with people who sit nearby in class, live in our dorm or in our neighborhood, or work in the same office. So, *propinquity*—proximity or physical closeness to others—is an important factor in interpersonal attraction. In one sense, this *must* be true, because we simply can't form relationships with people we have never met. But there seems to be more to the effects of propinquity than this. Many studies indicate that the more frequently we are exposed to a given stimulus, the more—in general—we tend to like it. This is known as the **frequency of exposure effect,** and it seems to extend to people as well as to objects (see Moreland & Beach, 1992; Zajonc, 1968). The more often we encounter other people, the more we tend to like them—assuming that everything else is equal. Why? Because the more frequently we encounter a stimulus, the more familiar it becomes, and therefore the more comfortable or pleasant we feel in its presence. For this reason, propinquity is one important basis for interpersonal attraction.

Similarity: Liking others who are like ourselves. You've probably heard both of the following sayings: "Birds of a feather flock together" and "Opposites attract." Which is true? Existing evidence leaves little room for doubt: Similarity wins hands down (see Alicke & Largo, 1995; Byrne, 1971, 1992). Moreover, this is so whether such similarity relates to attitudes and beliefs, to personality traits, to personal habits such as drinking and smoking, to sexual preferences, or even to whether those involved are morning or evening people (Joiner, 1994).

Why do we like others who are similar to ourselves? The most plausible explanation is that such people provide validation for our views or our personal characteristics (Goethals, 1986). If they agree with us, or are similar to us in their behavior, this indicates that our views, preferences, and actions are correct—or at least, that they are shared by other people. This makes us feel good and our liking for them increases. Whatever the precise mechanisms involved, similarity is certainly a very powerful determinant of attraction—one of the strongest. Just how powerful are the effects of attraction? A study conducted by Roy and Christenfeld (2004) suggests that they are stronger than you might guess. These researchers

Interpersonal attraction: The extent to which we like or dislike other people.

Frequency of exposure effect: The more frequently we are exposed to a given stimulus, the more—in general—we tend to like it.

took photos of dogs and their owners and then showed the photos to people who did not know the dogs' owners. Their task was to match the dogs to their owners, and surprising as it may seem, when the dogs were purebred, the participants in the study did much better than would be expected by chance! When the dogs were of mixed breed, in contrast, they performed merely at chance level. Although these findings have recently been called into question on grounds relating to the precise methods used (Levine, 2005), they suggest that even for people and their pets, similarity may be a strong basis for attraction: People choose the pets that, in some sense, are similar to themselves!

Affective states: Positive feelings as a basis for attraction. Suppose that you meet a stranger just after receiving some really good news: You got an A on an exam when you expected only a C. Will you like this person more than if you met them for the first time after receiving bad news that put you in a negative mood? Common sense suggests that this may be so, and research findings confirm this view (see Byrne & Smeaton, 1998). Positive feelings or moods—whatever their source—cause us to like others we meet while experiencing them, while negative moods—again, whatever their source—cause us to dislike others we meet at these times. What do we mean by the phrase "whatever their source"? Simply this: If positive feelings are produced by something another person says, we will tend to like them. *But even if our positive feelings have nothing to do with this person*, we may still experience a boost in our liking for them. In short, *anything* that induces positive affect may lead us to like another person who happens to be present when we are experiencing such feelings. As you might guess, such effects are most likely to occur when we are neutral to the person to start with and when we know little about him or her (see Ottati & Isbell, 1996), but they are both strong and general enough to be viewed as one important factor in interpersonal attraction.

Physical attractiveness: Beauty may be only skin deep, but we pay lots of attention to skin. Perhaps the most obvious factor affecting interpersonal attraction is *physical beauty*. Research findings indicate that despite warnings that "Beauty is only skin deep," we are strongly influenced by it (e.g., Sprecher & Duck, 1994). Moreover, this is true for both women and men, in many different cultures, and across the entire lifespan (Langlois et al., 2000; Singh, 1993). Indeed, even one-year-old infants show a preference for attractive rather than unattractive strangers (Langlois, Roggman, & Riser-Danner, 1990.) And apparently, we can recognize faces—and categorize them in various ways (e.g., as attractive or unattractive)—in a small fraction of a second (Jacques & Rossion, 2006). This is one reason why first impressions are formed so quickly—again, in less than a second! (Willis, & Todorov, 2006). Why is this the case? One reason is that physically attractive people make us feel good—and as we just saw, this can be one important ingredient in liking (Kenrick et al., 1993). Another, suggested by evolutionary psychology (see Buss, 1999), is that physical attractiveness is associated with good health and reproductive capacity; choosing attractive mates, therefore, is one strategy for increasing our chance to contribute our genes to the next generation.

Whatever the causes, we do tend to like physically attractive people more than physically less attractive ones. But what, precisely, makes other people physically attractive? Clearly, this varies from culture to culture, but—surprisingly—less than you might guess. People tend to agree on what is or is not attractive even when judging people who differ from themselves in terms of race or ethnic background (Cunningham et al., 1995). So, what is it about some faces that makes them so attractive? One surprising possibility is suggested by research in which many faces are "averaged" by computers to produce composite faces (see Langlois & Roggman, 1990; Lemley, 2000). Results indicate that the greater the number of faces that are combined in this manner, the higher the attractiveness of the composites produced by the computer (see Figure 13.15).

Why is this so? Perhaps because "average" faces produced in this manner are closer to our schemas of each gender. In other words, we have mental frameworks

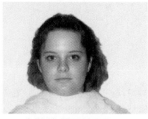

2-FACE COMPOSITE

4-FACE COMPOSITE

8-FACE COMPOSITE

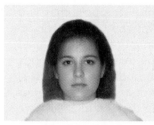

16-FACE COMPOSITE

32-FACE COMPOSITE

FIGURE 13.15
Are Attractive Faces "Average"?
When computer images of faces are combined to form a composite, this average face is rated as more attractive than the individual faces. Moreover, as the number of faces contributing to the average rises, so does the attractiveness of the composite face.
Source: Photos courtesy of Dr. Judith H. Langlois, Charles and Sarah Seay Regents Professor, Dept. of Psychology, University of Texas, Austin. Used with permission.

for faces—one for women and another for men—and composite faces are closer to these than individual faces. A related explanation is that the composite faces are more symmetrical than individual faces and that we prefer symmetry, because it is an indicator of health and reproductive capacity (e.g., Mealey, Bridgstock & Townsend, 1999). These are only two possibilities. Other aspects of faces, too, may be important. For instance, some evidence indicates that men find female faces that are either "cute" (childlike features with large, widely spaced eyes and a small nose and chin) or "mature" (prominent cheekbones, high eyebrows, large pupils, a big smile) attractive. Similarly, women seem to find two types of males faces—ones that show a big, square jaw and heavy brow, and ones that show a more youthful or "feminine" look—slender nose, small chin—attractive (Angier, 1998). Interestingly, other findings indicate that women find highly masculine faces more attractive when the women are in the middle of their menstrual cycle (and the chance of conception is high) than when they are in other phases of their cycle (Penton-Voak & Perrett, 2000). Indeed, women can distinguish more quickly between male and female faces at times when their chances of conceiving a child are high rather than when they are low (Macrae et al., 2002).

Judgments of attractiveness do not depend solely on facial features, however. They are also influenced by other aspects of people's appearance. For example, there is currently a strong bias against being overweight in many Western cultures; in view of this fact, it's not surprising that *physique* is another important determinant of attraction, at least among young people. People whose physique matches the popular model—currently, slim but muscular—tend to receive higher evaluations than people who depart from this model (e.g., Ryckman et al., 1995).

Another interesting finding relates to the belief that, in general, men are more influenced by physical appearance than women. While this may be true in certain respects, recent evidence indicates that women have a significant "edge" in remembering others' appearance (Mast & Hall, 2006). Moreover, this is true even when general memory ability, importance of appearance, and attention paid to the target people is taken into account. Why does this difference exist? One possibility, suggested by evolutionary psychology, is that attractiveness is very important for women in terms of competing with other women for the best mates; as a result, women are biologically "prepared" to notice and remember information relating to appearance to a greater extent than men. Another possibility is that women are simply better at remembering and processing many kinds of nonverbal cues and information, and appearance is, in some respects, related to this ability. Whatever the reason, however, it seems clear that women are better at remembering others' appearance than are men.

A related finding is that both women and men are better at remembering the physical location of attractive female faces than they are at remembering the physical location of attractive male faces (Becker et al., 2005). This was shown in research that used a game resembling "Concentration." Participants were shown an array of sixteen squares on a computer screen. Each square contained a face and some of the faces matched. Their task was to find the matching faces by turning over as few of the squares as possible. Four of the faces shown were highly attractive and four were average in attractiveness; this was true for both male and female faces. Results indicated that both men and women were able to remember the location of the attractive female faces better than the average female faces, but no differences occurred for the male faces: The attractive male faces were *not*

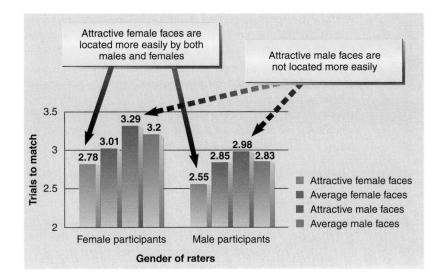

FIGURE 13.16
Attractive Female Faces Are Easier to Remember Than Attractive Male Faces
Both men and women were better able to remember the location of attractive female faces than average female faces (it took them fewer trials to locate these faces). However, the same effects did not occur for male faces: Attractive ones were not easier to locate than average faces. These findings suggest that, in one sense, attractiveness may be a more important characteristic for women than men.
Source: Based on data from Becker et al., 2005.

found more easily than the average faces (see Figure 13.16). These findings, too, may be explained within an evolutionary perspective. According to this perspective, female attractiveness is related to sexual fertility—an important dimension for mate selections for men. In contrast, male attractiveness is not related to males' status or their ability to help care for children—and these are the key dimensions women use in making *their* mate selections. Of course, this interpretation is somewhat speculative in nature; however, one thing is clear: Attractiveness may be a bigger advantage for women than for men in several different respects.

■ **Love: The most intense form of attraction.**

Have you ever been in love? If asked, most people (at least in Western cultures) will answer "yes." What do they mean by this statement? In other words, what is **love,** and how do we know that we are experiencing it? These questions have been pondered by countless poets, philosophers, and ordinary human beings for thousands of years, but it is only recently that love has become the subject of systematic research by psychologists (see Hendrick & Hendrick, 1993). Let's take a look at the answers that have emerged from this work.

Romantic love: Its nature. We should begin by noting that in this discussion, we are focusing on **romantic love**—a form of love involving feelings of strong attraction and sexual desire toward another person. However, there are several other kinds of love, too, such as the love of parents for their children, or the kind of love one can observe among couples who reach their fiftieth wedding anniversary (known as **companionate love**). While these kinds of love are not the focus of as many TV programs or films as passionate love, they, too, are recognized by psychologists as being very important (e.g., Meyers & Berscheid, 1997; Sternberg, 1988).

So what, precisely, does romantic love involve? Most experts agree that several components are crucial. First, for someone to say that they are "in love," the idea of romantic love must be present in their culture. Not all cultures have this concept, and when it is lacking, it is difficult, if not impossible, for people to say, "I'm in love." Second, the individuals in question must experience intense emotional arousal when in the presence of an appropriate person—someone defined by their culture as a suitable object for such feelings. And third, these feelings must be mixed with the desire to be loved by the object of their affection, coupled with fears that the relationship might end. Only if all of these conditions are present do individuals state—with confidence—"I'm in love."

One well-known social psychologist, Robert Sternberg (1998) emphasizes these three components in his *triangular model of love*. This model suggests love involves *passion*—powerful physical and sexual attraction; *commitment*—the desire to be loved

Love:
An intense emotional state involving attraction, sexual desire, and deep concern for another person.

Romantic love:
A form of love in which feelings of strong attraction and sexual desire toward another person are dominant.

Companionate love:
A form of love involving a high degree of commitment and deep concern with the well-being of the beloved.

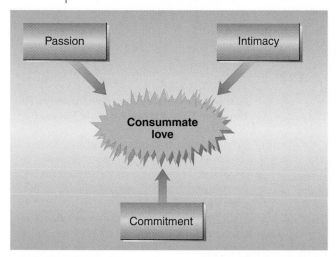

FIGURE 13.17
Sternberg's Triangular Model of Love
One well-known model of romantic love suggests that it rests on three basic foundations: passion, intimacy, and commitment. When all three exist and are in good balance, *consummate love*—the ideal form of love—can develop.
Source: Based on suggestions by Sternberg, 1986, 1998.

by the other person and to maintain a long-term relationship with that person; and *intimacy*—closeness between the partners. When all three are present, *consummate love,* the ideal form, can occur, but for this to be reached, passion, commitment, and intimacy must be in close harmony and in good balance (see Figure 13.17). This is why perfect love—of which most people dream—is indeed hard to obtain. But some people *do* attain it, and the result, at least for them, is a lifetime of happiness and fulfillment.

Love: How and why it occurs.   Although it is a powerful reaction, romantic love often develops quite suddenly. (Do you remember the chapter opening story, in which I described how strongly I reacted to my future wife on meeting her for the first time?) Many people report that they fall in love rapidly—almost as if they were struck by emotional lightning (Murray & Holmes, 1994). How can such powerful reactions develop so quickly? One explanation is that we are prepared to fall in love by our earlier relationships. As we saw in Chapter 7, infants form a powerful *attachment* to their parents or other caregivers, and in a sense, such attachment prepares us for forming powerful bonds with other people when we are adults (e.g., Hatfield & Rapson, 1993).

Another, and very different, explanation for the sudden emergence of love is provided by evolutionary psychology (Buss, 1999; Buss & Schmitt, 1993). According to this view, the reproductive success of our species depended, in the past, on two factors: (1) a desire on the part of both men and women to engage in sexual relations, and (2) an interest in investing the time and effort required to feed and protect their offspring. Love, it is further suggested, enhances both tendencies, because it leads to a lasting bond between males and females—a bond that is necessary for the prolonged child care that human beings require. Pure lust, which would assure only sexual behavior, was not sufficient, so over time humans with a propensity to form long-term relationships—to fall in love—were more successful in passing their genes on to the next generation. The result: We are genetically programmed to fall in love.

Which of these views is more accurate? At present, there is evidence for both, so the best conclusion is that both early experiences and our genetic heritage play a role in our tendency to fall in love and to form social relationships that sometimes last an entire lifetime.

Love: Why it sometimes dies.   "And they lived happily ever after." This is the way many fairy tales—and movies from the 1940s and 1950s—end, with the characters riding off into a glowing, love-filled future. If only life could match these high hopes! Some romantic relationships do blossom into lifelong commitments. But for many couples, the glow of love fades and leaves behind empty relationships from which one or both partners soon seek escape. What causes such outcomes? Research on love and on *close relationships* suggests that many factors are at work.

We have already considered one of these in our discussion of the importance of similarity in attraction. When partners discover that they are *dissimilar* in important ways, love can be weakened or even die. Such differences are often overlooked when the flames of passion run high, but become increasingly obvious when these begin to subside. Also, as time passes, dissimilarities that weren't present initially may begin emerge: The partners change and perhaps diverge. This, too, can weaken their love.

Another, and potentially serious, problem is simple *boredom*. Over time, the unchanging routines of living together may lead people to feel that they are in a rut, and are missing out on the excitement of life—and perhaps new romantic partners (Fincham & Bradbury, 1993). Such reactions can have important consequences for the relationship.

Third, jealousy can occur and undermine loving relationships. Interestingly, while both sexes experience jealousy, they differ in the pattern of such reactions.

For women, the most intense jealousy is aroused by signs that a partner is transferring his emotional commitment to another woman. For men, the most intense jealousy is triggered by evidence (or suspicions!) that a partner has been sexually unfaithful (Buunk et al., 1995).

Finally, as relationships continue, patterns of behavior that can be described only as *self-defeating* sometimes emerge. Dating couples and newlyweds frequently express positive evaluations and feelings to each other. As time passes, however, these supportive statements are sometimes replaced by negative ones. "You're so inconsiderate!" "I should never have married you!"—these kinds of feelings, either stated overtly or merely implied, become increasingly frequent. The result is that couples who once frequently praised each other shift to criticizing each other in the harshest terms imaginable (Miller, 1991). When these patterns develop, love doesn't simply die: It is literally massacred by sarcastic, hurtful remarks.

Despite such factors, many relationships *do* succeed. Such couples actively *work* at maintaining and strengthening their relationships: They practice the art of compromise, express positive feelings and sentiments toward their partners, and take their wishes and preferences into account on a daily basis. True, this requires a lot of effort, but given the rewards of maintaining a long-term intimate relationship with someone we love and who loves us it is certainly effort well spent!

KEY QUESTIONS

- What factors influence interpersonal attraction?
- Under what conditions do people conclude that they are in love?
- What factors cause love to fade and perhaps disappear?

SUMMARY AND REVIEW OF KEY QUESTIONS

Social Thought: Thinking about Other People

- **What is the correspondence bias?**
  Our tendency to overestimate the importance of internal causes of others' behavior.

- **Does the correspondence bias exist in all cultures or is it stronger in some than others?**
  The correspondence bias seems to be much stronger in individualistic cultures (ones that emphasize individual freedom and responsibility) than in collectivistic cultures (ones that emphasize group membership and interdependence).

- **What is the self-serving bias?**
  The tendency to attribute positive outcomes we experience to internal causes but negative outcomes to external causes.

- **What is the negativity bias?**
  This refers to a tendency to pay more attention to negative comments about others than to positive information about them. It can strongly influence our judgments and evaluations of others.

- **What is counterfactual thinking? How can it influence our affective states and performance?**
  Counterfactual thinking involves imagining "what might have been." If we imagine better outcomes than what occurred, this can lead to negative affect; if we imagine worse outcomes, this can lead to positive affect. Counterfactual thinking can provide insights into why negative outcomes occurred, and so can enhance our future performance.

- **What are attitudes?**
  Attitudes are lasting evaluations of various aspects of the social world—evaluations that are stored in memory.

- **What factors were found to influence persuasion in early research?**
  Early research on persuasion found that the success of persuasion was strongly affected by characteristics of the sources (e.g., their expertise), characteristics of the persuasive messages sent (e.g., whether they were one-sided or two-sided), and characteristics of the audience.

- **What is the ELM model, and how does it explain persuasion?**
  The ELM model is a cognitive model of persuasion that focuses on the thoughts people have about a persuasive communication.

- **What is cognitive dissonance, and how can it be reduced?**
  Cognitive dissonance is an unpleasant state we experience when we notice that two attitudes we hold or our attitudes and our behavior are somehow inconsistent.

- **What is induced compliance? The less-leads-to-more effect?**
  Induced compliance occurs in situations where we feel compelled to say or do something inconsistent with our true attitudes. The less-leads-to-more effect refers to the fact that the weaker the reasons we have for engaging in attitude-discrepant behavior, the more likely are we to change these attitudes.

- **Does culture play a role in the occurrence of cognitive dissonance?**
  Research findings indicate that individuals living in cultures that link self-esteem and individual action closely

(e.g., the United States, Canada) are more likely to experience dissonance after making decisions than are people living in cultures that do not link self-esteem and individual action closely (e.g., China, Japan).

Social Behavior: Interacting with Others

- **What are some of the major causes of prejudice?**
  Prejudice stems from direct competition between social groups, social categorization, social learning, and cognitive factors such as stereotypes.

- **What techniques are effective in reducing prejudice?**
  Prejudice can be reduced by socializing children to be tolerant of others, through increased intergroup contact, and through recategorization—shifting the boundary between "us" and "them" so as to include previously excluded groups.

- **What are some of the basic principles on which tactics of compliance are based?**
  Tactics of compliance are based on the principles of liking or friendship (e.g., ingratiation), commitment or consistency (e.g., the foot-in-the-door technique), reciprocity (e.g., the door-in-the-face technique), and scarcity (e.g., playing hard to get).

- **What is obedience and why does it occur?**
  In obedience, individuals follow the commands of people in authority. Obedience occurs because often the people demanding it take responsibility for any harm produced, and make their requests in a gradual manner.

- **What factors influence interpersonal attraction?**
  Among the factors that influence interpersonal attraction are propinquity, similarity, positive and negative affect, and physical attractiveness.

- **Under what conditions do people conclude that they are in love?**
  Individuals conclude that they are in love when their culture has the concept of romantic love and when they experience strong emotional arousal in the presence of a person defined as appropriate for love by their culture.

- **What factors cause love to fade and perhaps disappear?**
  Love can be weakened by such factors as jealousy, increased dissimilarity, boredom, increased levels of negative affect, and a pattern in which negative statements and attributions replace positive ones.

KEY TERMS

Attitudes, p. 514
Attribution, p. 508
Central route (to persuasion), p. 515
Cognitive dissonance, p. 517
Compliance, p. 525
Companionate love, p. 531
Consensus, p. 509
Consistency, p. 509
Contact hypothesis, p. 522
Correspondence bias (*fundamental attribution error*), p. 510
Counterfactual thinking, p. 512
Distinctiveness, p. 509
Door-in-the-face technique, p. 526

Elaboration-likelihood model (ELM), p. 516
Foot-in-the-door technique, p. 525
Frequency of exposure effect, p. 528
Heuristic processing, p. 515
Induced (forced) compliance, p. 517
Ingratiation, p. 526
Interpersonal attraction, p. 528
Less-leads-to-more effect, p. 518
Love, p. 531
Negativity bias, p. 511
Nonverbal cues, p. 505
Obedience, p. 526
Peripheral route (to persuasion), p. 515

Persuasion, p. 514
Playing hard to get, p. 526
Prejudice, p. 520
Realistic conflict theory, p. 520
Recategorization, p. 523
Romantic love, p. 531
Self-serving bias, p. 510
Social categorization, p. 520
Social cognition, p. 505
Social influence, p. 525
Social psychology, p. 504
Stereotypes, p. 521
Systematic processing, p. 515

PSYCHOLOGY: UNDERSTANDING ITS FINDINGS

When Do *You* Experience Dissonance?

Dissonance, we have suggested, is a part of everyday life: Each time we must say or do something that is not consistent with our own attitudes, we may experience unpleasant gaps between our attitudes and our actions. How often do *you* experience dissonance? And what happens when you do? To find out, complete the following exercise.

1. Keep a diary and for a week, list instances in which you notice a gap between your attitudes and your behavior—inconsistencies between what you believe and what you say or do.

2. Now, examine these incidents. Can you see any common themes? For instance, how often did you say or do something inconsistent with your true attitudes to:
   a. avoid hurting someone's feelings.
   b. avoid problems in dealing with another person.
   c. get what you wanted from someone.

3. What happened when you engaged in attitude-discrepant behavior? Did your own attitudes change? Or did you reduce dissonance in some other way?

MAKING PSYCHOLOGY PART OF YOUR LIFE

How You Can Get Other People to Like You

Being liked by others is a goal almost everyone wants to attain. But how can we reach it? Research on the basis of interpersonal attraction offers some valuable clues. Here are some steps *you* can take to increase your own likeability:

1. **Make others feel good.** One of the most important determinants of interpersonal attraction is feelings or emotions: We tend to like other people in whose presence we feel good, and dislike those in whose presence we feel bad. So, to increase others' liking for you, try to make sure that when you are with them, you help them feel good. This means that you must *not* focus on your own problems and on negative feelings; rather, you should try to say things that make others laugh and feel happy. And if at all possible, try to avoid saying or doing things that make them experience unpleasant emotions. To the extent you are associated with positive feelings and experiences, your attractiveness to others will almost certainly increase.

2. **Emphasize your similarity to other people.** Similarity, on many different dimensions, has been found to be one of the most important factors in interpersonal attraction. So if you want to be liked, call attention to the ways in which you and the people you want to like you are similar. This can mean expressing similar attitudes and preferences, or calling attention to shared experiences and beliefs. However you do it, the more similar you appear to others, the more they will tend to like you.

3. **Enhance your own appearance.** The way we look is indeed one important factor in others' liking for us. This simply means that you should do whatever you can to enhance your own appearance. No, we can't all look like movie stars, but we *can* dress and groom in ways that emphasize the positive attributes we do possess. To the extent you do this, it will almost certainly pay off in increased attractiveness to others.

4. **Make propinquity—and familiarity—work for you.** Do you want someone to like you? The first order of business is getting into contact with that person. This means that you must try to arrange your schedule and routine—where you "hang out"—so that your path and his or her path cross. And in general, the more familiar we are with people, the more we feel comfortable with them and tend to like them. So don't do this just once or twice; make sure it happens over and over again. The result may be that "familiarity breeds *content*"—greater liking for you—*not* contempt, as one old saying suggests!

None of these strategies are magic and none are guaranteed to enhance others' liking for you. But they are good steps in the right direction, and to the extent you implement them carefully and well, you may well boost others' liking for you, with all the benefits that can provide.

If you are using MyPsychLab, you have access to an electronic version of this textbook, along with dozens of valuable resources per chapter—including video and audio clips, simulations and activities, self-assessments, practice tests and other study materials. Here is a sampling of the resources available for this chapter.

EXPLORE

Bystander Intervention

Cognitive Dissonance & Attitude Change

WATCH

Lie Spy

On the Job Learning

Relationships and Love

SIMULATE

Unconscious Stereotyping

If you did not receive an access code to MyPsychLab with this text and wish to purchase access online, please visit www.MyPsychLab.com.

STUDY GUIDE

CHAPTER REVIEW

Social Thought: Thinking about Other People

1. The topic of prejudice involves the study of
   a. how we interact with other people.
   b. negative attitudes towards members of various social groups.
   c. why we like or dislike members of the opposite sex.
   d. how some people become leaders and other remain followers.

2. The fact that a person sitting across you on a bus does not maintain eye contact with you suggests that
   a. the person may not like you.
   b. the person is shy.
   c. likes you but is playing hard to get.
   d. they are about to get off the bus.

3. A person who is making a large number of body movements would be viewed as
   a. friendly.
   b. drug-addicted.
   c. nervous.
   d. outgoing.

4. An important clue that person is lying to us is when
   a. they blink less often and have a higher level of eye contact.
   b. there is a close correspondence between their tome of voice and their facial expression.
   c. the pitch of their voice becomes lower and lower.
   d. they blink more often and have a lower level of eye contact.

5. The factor of _____ refers to whether a person reacts in the same way in different situations.
   a. consensus
   b. distinctiveness
   c. consistency
   d. reliability

6. Jamey was cut off by a driver on the freeway and became quite angry at the driver about the incident. Later that week, she did the same thing to another driver but unfortunately her action resulted in her being pulled over by a traffic officer. Her claim that her action was unintentional would be consistent with
   a. correspondence bias.
   b. misattribution.
   c. the fundamental attribution error.
   d. the norm of internality.

7. Our tendency to blame external factors when we fail at a task is known as the
   a. person-perception issue.
   b. correspondence bias.
   c. fundamental attribution error.
   d. self-serving bias.

8. _____ refers to our tendency to give greater weight and attention to negative information than positive information about another person.
   a. The self-serving bias

b. The norm of internality
   c. Negativity bias
   d. The fundamental attribution error

9. People experience more regret when they engage in upward counterfactual thinking than downward counterfactual thinking.   (True-False)

10. Which of the following is NOT a key aspect of an attitude?
    a. Cognitive component.
    b. Unconscious component.
    c. Emotional component.
    d. Behavioral component.

11. A political commentator on Fox News screams "You are a liberal idiot!" at a guest who disagrees with him on an issue. This display illustrates the _____ component of an attitude.
    a. cognitive
    b. unconscious
    c. emotional
    d. behavioral

12. An attitude can be thought of as our evaluation of an aspect of our social world.   (True-False)

13. Research suggests that a message is more persuasive when
    a. we suspect that others are out to persuade us.
    b. the communicator is perceived to be an expert rather than a non-expert.
    c. the communicator is speaking slowly rather than rapidly.
    d. the communicator is perceived to be unattractive rather than attractive.

14. A fast-talking politician may be more persuasive than a slow-talking politician.   (True-False)

15. The study by Martin and colleagues found that _____ boosted the tendency of subjects to engage in _____.
    a. alcohol;   systematic processing
    b. caffeine;   peripheral processing
    c. alcohol;   peripheral processing
    d. caffeine;   systematic processing

16. We tend to engage in heuristic processing for messages on topics for which we have much experience and knowledge.   (True-False)

17. _____ involves an unpleasant state of psychological tension resulting from the discrepancy betweens out thoughts and actions.
    a. Peripheral dissonance
    b. Interchannel discrepancy
    c. Cognitive dissonance
    d. Emotional dissonance

18. Cognitive dissonance refers to the tendency to attribute one's own behavior to external, situational causes while attributing the behavior of others to internal causes. (True-False)

19. A person who is forced to take an action that is contrary to their attitudes

a. is less likely in the future to voluntarily do that behavior.

b. will experience no dissonance because the behavior was forced on them.

c. may change their attitude toward the behavior.

d. is less likely to change their attitude about the behavior

20. The weaker the reason we have for engaging in an attitude-discrepant behavior, the more likely we are to change our attitude about that behavior.   (True-False)

21. The less-leads-to-more effect does NOT occur when

a. the person is forced to take the attitude-discrepant behavior.

b. the person perceives the payment as a bribe.

c. small rewards are used as opposed to large rewards.

d. All of the above are correct.

22. Citizens from which country are least likely to experience cognitive dissonance?

a. Canada.

b. Asian.

c. United States

d. France.

Social Behavior: Interacting with Others

23. _____ involves powerful negative attitudes toward a person based on their membership in a social group.

a. Bias

b. Favoritism

c. Prejudice

d. All of the above are correct.

24. The _____ of prejudice argues that prejudice arises from competition among social groups over resources.

a. realistic conflict theory

b. social learning view

c. social categorization view

d. cognitive stereotypes view

25. According to the social categorization view of prejudice, _____ is another name for members of the out-group.

a. "us"

b. "non-human"

c. "family"

d. A and C are correct.

26. Which of the following is NOT does not contribute to social learning of prejudice?

a. Interactions of a child with peers.

b. Information from the mass media.

c. Interactions of a child with parents, teachers and other adults.

d. An inherited genetic predisposition.

27. One strategy by which to reduce the transmission of prejudice from parent to child is to point out to the parents the personal toll of having prejudiced views about others.   (True-False)

28. Contact between different groups can reduce prejudice as long as

a. the contact involves some aspect of cooperation and interdepedence.

b. the groups are about equal in social status.

c. the contact must let them get to know each others as individuals.

d. All of the above are required.

29. The situation in which a person agrees to a small favor and is then later asked to comply with a much larger request is known as the door-in-the-face technique. (True-False)

30. In Stanley Milgram's original obedience experiment only 33% of the subjects continued to shock the "learner" to the highest shock level of 450 volts.   (True-False)

31. A key characteristic that contributes to attractiveness is

a. good health.

b. extreme wealth.

c. low reproductive capacity.

d. facial symmetry.

32. Women find masculine faces most attractive when they are at the end of their menstrual cycle.   (True-False)

33. Attractiveness appears to be a bigger advantage for women than men.   (True-False)

34. In Sternberg's model of love, the _____ component involves the desire to maintain a long-term relationship with another person.

a. intimacy

b. passion

c. commitment

d. romantic love

35. A key factor in the breakup of mixed faith couples is that of

a. propinquity.

b. boredom.

c. jealousy

d. dissimilarity.

36. Match up each term below with its best definition or example.

_____. A soldier ordered by a commander to shoot an unarmed civilian does so.

_____. A behavior that is shown by most people in most situations.

_____. A football player decides that he dislikes a member of the chess club.

_____. A salesman asks a person to accept a small gift and then asks the person to purchase a more expensive item.

_____. Changes in the voice that communicate emotional state.

a. Non-verbal cue

b. Foot-in-the-door technique

c. Obedience

d. Prejudice.

e. Consensus.

IDENTIFICATIONS

Identify the term that belongs with each of the concepts below (place the letter for the appropriate term below in front of each concept).

Identification   Concept:

_____ 1. Whether a person reacts the same way in all situations.

_____ 2. This category could include body posture and movements as well as tone of voice.

_____ 3. Thinking about what might have been.

_____ 4. A negative attitude towards a member of a particular social group.

_____ 5. The weaker the reason we have for engaging in an attitude-discrepant behavior, the more likely we are to change our attitude about that behavior.

_____ 6. Another name for the correspondence bias.

_____ 7. The idea that prejudice can be reduced by increasing the amount of interaction between groups.

_____ 8. The idea that we tend to like those who are physically near us.

_____ 9. A type of love dominated by strong attraction and sexual desire for another person.

_____ 10. A person who blinks often and will not maintain eye contact.

_____ 11. A form of social influence in which one person makes a request from another.

_____ 12. Our personal evaluation of an aspect of our social world.

_____ 13. Our tendency to blame external factors when we fail at a task.

Identification:

a. Compliance.
b. Prejudice.
c. Self-serving bias.
d. Fundamental attribution error.
e. Non-verbal cue.
f. Liar.
g. Attitude.
h. Counterfactual thought.
i. The less-leads-to-more effect.
j. Romantic love.
k. Distinctiveness.
l. Contact hypothesis.
m. Propinquity.

FILL IN THE BLANK

1. _____ involve the use of simple mental short cuts to make a decision.

2. Our analysis of why others act the way that they do is termed _____.

3. _____ refer to brief facial expressions that occur just after an emotion-provoking event.

4. Our tendency to give more weight to negative information about others is called the

5. _____ refers to a type of love that involves closeness between the partners.

6. In the _____ technique, a large request is followed by a smaller request.

7. _____ is the idea that people should be responsible for their own outcomes.

8. The frequency of exposure effect says that mere exposure can increase our _____ for a stimulus.

9. The peripheral route is also known as _____.

10. Some key reasons as to why relationships fail include _____, _____, and _____.

11. A _____ is a cognitive framework in which all members of a specific social group are thought to share characteristics.

12. Social psychologists define _____ as the attempt to change attitudes.

13. A procedure that involve cognitive changes to reduce prejudice include

14. The extent to which like or dislike another person is known as _____.

15. _____ involves an unpleasant state of psychological tension resulting from the discrepancy betweens out thoughts and actions.

COMPREHENSIVE PRACTICE TEST

1. Which of the following is considered to be a non-verbal cue?
   a. Facial expressions.
   b. Tone of voice.
   c. Body posture and movements.
   d. All of the above are correct.

2. Psychologists consider that humans have six basic facial expressions. (True-False)

3. Research suggests that most people tell an average of
   a. one or two lies per day.
   b. ten to twenty lies per day.
   c. one or two lies per week.
   d. ten to twenty lies per week.

4. We are most likely to attribute a person's behavior to internal causes when consistency is high, consensus is low, and distinctiveness is low. (True-False)

5. Our tendency to evaluate some object, person, or issue in a negative or positive way is a(n)
   a. bias.
   b. implicit inference.
   c. attitude.
   d. attribution.

6. The self-serving bias involves our tendency to attribute successful outcomes of one's own behavior to _____ and unsuccessful outcomes to _____.
   a. external causes; internal causes
   b. conscious processes; unconscious processes
   c. internal causes; external causes
   d. unconscious processes; conscious processes

7. Which of the following would be an example of heuristic processing of a persuasive message?
   a. "I like this person and think that they are telling the truth."
   b. "Their first statement is true, their second statement is true, and it seems that I have heard that the third statement is also true."
   c. "If an action hero like Tom Cruise is saying that drugs do not fix mental illness, it must be true!"
   d. All but B are correct.

8. In a study of racial stereotyping in murder cases, it was found that the death penalty was assessed for those cases in which a
   a. white person was accused of killing a black person.
   b. black defendant with stereotypical black features was accused of killing a black person.
   c. black defendant with stereotypical black features was accused of killing a white person.
   d. white person was accused of killing a black person.

9. Which process of reducing prejudice most closely resembles classical conditioning?
   a. Recategorization.
   b. Teaching children not to be prejudiced.

c. Cognitive procedures designed to counter implicit stereotypes.

d. Increased intergroup conflict.

10. Stereotypical thinking may persist because it is self-confirming.   (True-False)

11. The chair of a local political action committee offers potential party workers lunch and the CD of their choice for attending a political speech by a new candidate. This would involve the persuasion technique known as the

a. door-in-the-face technique.

b. playing hard-to-get.

c. low-ball technique.

d. rule of reciprocity.

12. Which of the following pairs of terms does NOT belong together?

a. men;   better memory for details on appearance

b. women;   better memory for details on appearance

c. reduced physical attractiveness;   being overweight

d. increased physical attractiveness;   facial symmetry

13. The principle of propinquity would suggest that attraction would be most likely to develop between

a. strangers who meet at a bar during Spring Break.

b. persons who are similar in political beliefs.

c. next-door neighbors.

d. people who wait together at the same bus stop during the school year.

14. The evolutionary explanation of love is that

a. passion leads to lust.

b. lust leads to passion.

c. we are genetically programmed to fall in love.

d. consummate love occurs when passion occurs with commitment.

CRITICAL THINKING

1. Explain how behavioral observation can help to detect whether another person is attempting to deceive us (i.e. detection of lying).

2. Discuss three factors that lead to interpersonal attraction and three factors that can lead to the demise of a relationship

FOURTEEN

Industrial/ Organizational Psychology: Understanding Human Behavior at Work

When I (Rebecca Henry) think of Papa Del's Pizza, my mouth begins to water. If you were in the mood for Chicago-style pizza, theirs could not be beat. They weren't cheap, particularly for working students like me, but the pizza was certainly worth it. Then, one day the s—, or maybe we should say pizza, hit the fan. A story broke in the local paper describing rampant theft at Papa Del's. Many employees were giving away pizza to their friends who would come in as customers. Over a period of months, thousands of dollars worth of pizza went sliding out the door before management identified the problem. How did they figure out what was going on? According to the newspaper's account, the owners installed secret surveillance cameras after they suspected a problem of this sort. At the time this event occurred several years ago, cameras such as these were not commonplace, except perhaps in banks. As a result of the videotaping, the dishonest employees were identified and fired. Not surprisingly, some even faced criminal charges.

FIGURE 14.1
Employee Theft: One Example of Behavior Organizations Would Like to Minimize
While most employees do not steal, theft is common in many organizations. Like most work behaviors studied by industrial/organizational psychologists, there are many reasons why it occurs and just as many ways to try to reduce it, some more successful than others.

Industrial/organizational (I/O) psychology:
The study of human cognition and behavior at work.

We begin by describing this event because it illustrates the two major themes of this chapter. The first theme addresses the question: Why do employees do what they do? In this case it was theft, in another instance it might be years of dedicated service that goes seemingly unnoticed. We'll address some of the underlying causes of a wide range of work behavior, from the most negative to the most positive. The second theme of this chapter addresses a similar question, but from the company's point of view: Why do organizations engage in certain practices? Here, it was the installation of surveillance cameras to address the problem of theft. Was this the best way to handle this particular situation? How do other organizations cope with the same problem? In this chapter, we'll address this pair of themes (employee behavior and organizational practices) across a wide variety of workplace scenarios.

At certain points in the chapter, particularly when discussing organizational practices, our emphasis will be on what organizations *should* do if they want to be consistent with research and principles regarding human behavior. This perspective will provide you with a look "behind the scenes" of organizations, so that you can better understand how psychological principles play a role in the development of effective human resource practices. This information will also help you critique, both now and in the future, how some practices you observe at work could be improved.

As mentioned above, this chapter will also address fundamental questions regarding the underlying causes of various employee behaviors. For example, we'll examine some of the reasons why theft is such a problem in so many organizations (see Figure 14.1). We will also discuss the challenges of working as a member of a team and of being a leader. The information presented in these sections will help you understand your own behavior as well as the behavior of others with whom you work, something that will be useful regardless whether you decide to run your own company or work in an established organization.

Taken together, the topics covered in this chapter represent the field of **industrial/organizational (I/O) psychology,** the study of human cognition and behavior at work. The mission of psychologists in this field is to improve employee well-being and organizational effectiveness through research and practice. These dual missions, one focused on employees and one focused on the organization, have not always coexisted amicably, but they need not represent an either/or choice, as you will see in many instances later.

You have already read about some of the applications of I/O psychology in the various Psychology Goes to Work sections earlier in this book (see, for example, Chapters 9, 10, 12, and 13). In essence, this entire chapter could be viewed as Psychology Goes to Work, though we'll avoid covering material presented earlier. We will, however, refer back to material presented in earlier chapters. This is done so that you can see how I/O psychology fits in with, and adds to, the field of psychology as a whole. We hope that this approach will have the added benefit of helping you tie various topics together, something that is useful at the conclusion of any course.

We'll begin with a look behind the scenes at employee selection, the first contact a prospective employee has with a particular organization. We'll then move on to what most new employees experience soon after being hired: training and performance appraisal. These three topics will focus a great deal on "how to" techniques that have evolved out of the application of basic psychological research and principles. We'll then turn to the topic of work motivation, concluding with an examination of social behavior at work in the form of leadership and teams. As

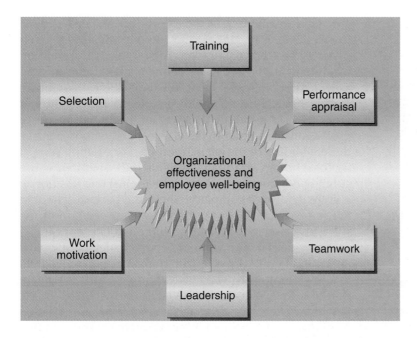

FIGURE 14.2
The Dual Mission of I/O Psychology
The science and practice of I/O psychology is concerned with both organizational effectiveness and employee well-being.

Figure 14.2 illustrates, all these topics have the dual mission of enhancing organizational effectiveness and employee well-being, though organizations may emphasize the former over the latter.

KEY QUESTIONS
- What is I/O psychology?
- What is the "dual mission" of psychologists in this field?

SELECTION: HIRING THE BEST PERSON FOR THE JOB

Most of us have a pretty good sense of what it is like to apply for a job. You may have gone through the process of answering classified ads and interviewing, or you might have observed some version of this among family and friends. My first experience with this consisted of interviewing for a position at an ice cream stand when I was in high school. The interview consisted of only one or two questions (e.g., "Are you in marching band?"). The owner called me a few days later to tell me when I should show up for training. (For the record, being in marching band was viewed negatively because it made an employee unavailable many evenings.) This certainly is not an example of a systematic, rigorous selection process, but it does highlight the general objectives of such a process (Chan, 2005). This process, in its most basic form, consists of two sequential questions that organizations must address: What information should we obtain from each job applicant? And how should the information be obtained? In this section we focus on what organizations do behind the scenes to address these two questions. Here, and in later sections, we describe the "ideal" process, allowing you to compare this process to what you might have experienced yourself.

Job Analysis: Assessing the Requirements for the Job

Long before the first job applicant is interviewed for a particular job, a systematic assessment of the job should be completed (Brannick & Levine, 2002). This sys-

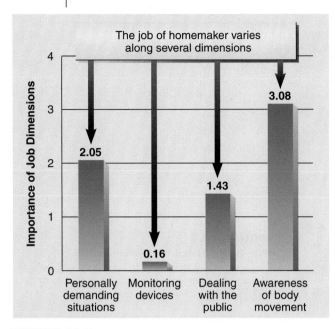

The job of homemaker varies along several dimensions

FIGURE 14.3
Job Analysis Can Reveal Surprising Results
As this classic study indicates, the job of homemaker varies along a number of dimensions. Interestingly, this job profile was most similar to the profiles of jobs that seemed on the surface to be quite different, such as airport maintenance chief and patrol officer.
Source: Adapted from Arvey & Begalla, 1975.

Job analysis:
An assessment of the tasks, duties, and responsibilities of a particular job.

Position Analysis Questionnaire (PAQ):
A specific job analysis technique that analyzes jobs along thirty-two distinct dimensions.

KSAs:
Abbreviation for the knowledge, skills, and abilities needed to perform a particular job.

tematic assessment, referred to as a **job analysis,** is done to assess the tasks, duties, and responsibilities of a job. It probably seems quite obvious to you that it is important for organizations to clearly define a job before deciding how to hire someone to do it. What may be less obvious is that this process of job analysis often requires hours of work by I/O psychologists and other human resource professionals in order to have a clear and comprehensive understanding of the job in question. For example, one of my psychology graduate students once spent an entire summer conducting a job analysis for just one position in a large insurance company! She came back to school in the fall exhausted, but with a new appreciation of the work involved in conducting a thorough job analysis.

Why does it take so much time to understand what a job entails? Can't the people in human resources just talk to a few employees who currently do the job? If you are thinking this, you are on the right track. However, the key to a systematic job analysis is to gather information from many sources in an objective manner. The data that emerge are then statistically analyzed to create an overall summary or profile of the job. This type of approach increases the likelihood of getting accurate information, something that is crucial for the design of selection systems.

Analyzing jobs in this way may take a fair bit of time, but it can often reveal subtleties of the job that were not apparent before. If you examine Figure 14.3, you can see an example of this. The researchers who conducted this classic study wanted to demonstrate that job analyses can often reveal surprising results even for the most familiar of jobs (Arvey & Begalla, 1975). To do this, they analyzed the most familiar job they could think of, the job of "homemaker," and then compared it to a database of one thousand other jobs to determine which jobs were most similar to it. Using a well-established job analysis instrument, called the **Position Analysis Questionnaire (PAQ)** (McCormick, Jeanneret, & Meacham, 1969), thirty-two job dimensions were examined to create a composite profile of the job of homemaker. Data were collected on dimensions that assessed such things as "engaging in personally demanding situations" and "awareness of body movement and balance." Figure 14.3 shows how four of these thirty-two dimensions varied in their importance for the job of homemaker. A comparison of the homemaker profile to the other one thousand jobs resulted in some surprising results, with the jobs of "patrol officer" and "airport maintenance chief" being two of the most similar to the job of homemaker. The point of the comparison is that neither of these jobs would appear on the surface to emphasize many of the same job dimensions, yet a thorough job analysis identified many similarities. This illustrates the importance of doing a job analysis even for the most familiar of jobs.

Developing Selection Techniques: Validity, Utility, and Fairness

After the completion of a thorough job analysis, we are close to answering the first question necessary for the design of a good selection system: "What information should be obtained from each job applicant?" However, job analysis information serves only as a guide for determining the knowledge, skills, and abilities (**KSAs**) that are necessary to perform a job. Before any selection instrument is used, whether it is a paper-and-pencil test, an interview, or some other type of instrument, it must be evaluated with respect to three dimensions: validity, utility, and fairness.

■ Validity: Assessing the quality of a selection instrument.

You already have some familiarity with validity from reading about it in the context of personality and intelligence tests (Chapter 9). In the context of employee selection, organizations are most concerned with one type of validity, **criterion-related validity,** because it refers to the strength of the relationship between scores on a particular selection instrument and success on the job (the criterion). Because criterion-related validity represents the strength of the relationship between two variables, it is typically assessed using correlation coefficients. As you learned in Chapter 1, correlation coefficients range from −1.00 to +1.00 with the absolute value of the correlation indicating how strong the relationship between the two variables is. For example, imagine an employer who purchases a standardized test of mechanical ability from a professional test-development firm. In the promotional materials, the test is described as having a criterion-related validity of +.40 when used to hire mechanics. In isolation it is difficult to assess whether this degree of validity is sufficient, so generally employers compare several options in order to select the test with the highest criterion-related validity.

In general, the stronger the criterion-related validity of a test (the absolute value of the correlation), the better the test will be at identifying the most qualified job applicants. At one extreme, using a test with a criterion-related validity of +1.00 would result in correctly identifying only the best applicants, whereas a test with a criterion-related validity of .00 would be equivalent to hiring employees at random. Of course these extreme values never happen in actual selection contexts, but this illustration conveys the principle linking criterion-related validity to proportion of correct hiring decisions.

■ Utility: Assessing the practical value of a selection instrument.

After identifying one or more selection instruments with a sufficient degree of criterion-related validity, the instruments are then evaluated with regard to their **utility** (Boudreau, 1991). The utility of a selection instrument refers to its usefulness, taking several factors into account, including the criterion-related validity and the cost of the testing procedure. For example, two selection instruments might have comparable degrees of criterion-related validity, but one might be more expensive to administer, giving it less utility than the other. As you can see, utility is primarily an economic concept, so we won't go into any more detail about it here. What is important to remember is that it takes psychological test information into account in order to be calculated.

■ Fairness: Avoiding discrimination, both real and perceived.

The term "fairness" can take on myriad meanings in different contexts. With regard to employee selection procedures, the term **fairness** refers both to the legality of the selection system and its fairness as perceived by job applicants. Let's consider the legal issues first. Most of you are probably somewhat familiar with various state and federal laws that protect people's civil rights in various contexts (e.g., employment, education). Among other things, these laws prohibit discrimination on the basis of certain protected classes, such as sex, race, age, and religion. What is often not stated, but what is also part of the law, is an "unless" provision that, in the context of employee selection, allows for the use of selection instruments that show "job-relatedness" and have "business necessity." In other words, the laws prohibit discrimination in hiring, but organizations can still use selection instruments as long as there is evidence that these instruments help them hire the best people.

If this sounds like what is accomplished through the careful validation of a selection instrument, you are correct. In fact, I/O psychologists working in the area of employment testing have been very influential over the years as the U.S. Supreme Court and lower courts have wrestled with these issues (see Figure 14.4). So, not only does the validity of a selection instrument help improve its utility, but it also helps it achieve the legal standards of job-relatedness and business necessity.

Beyond fairness as legally defined, why should organizations care about the *perceived* fairness of a selection system? The perceived fairness of a selection system is important because it can influence the first impressions organizations make

Criterion-related validity: The strength of the relationship between scores on a particular selection test and success on the job.

Utility: The usefulness of a selection technique that takes both the criterion-related validity and the cost of the procedure into account.

Fairness: The legality of the selection system (i.e., whether it is consistent with current employment laws) as well as its perceived fairness to job applicants.

FIGURE 14.4
I/O Psychology and Employment Law
In several important court cases, I/O psychologists have served as experts, helping the courts define such legal terms as fairness and discrimination in ways that can be objectively measured.

on prospective employees (Chapman et al., 2005; Truxillo et al., 2002). In Chapter 13 you learned about the importance of first impressions in the context of social perception. The principle is really no different in the context of a job applicant forming an impression of an organization. For example, if an organization appears to be using seemingly irrelevant or discriminatory selection techniques it will convey a very bad first impression, leading many applicants to wonder if the organization's other practices (e.g., compensation, promotion) are just as unfair. As a result, many applicants may look elsewhere for a job.

With the principles of validity, utility, and fairness in mind, we'll now turn to a discussion of several specific types of selection instruments. As you read this section, remember that these issues apply to all selection techniques, even those that may not seem like "tests" in the traditional sense of the word.

KEY QUESTIONS

- What is job analysis?
- What is criterion-related validity?
- What does the term "utility" refer to in the context of selection?
- How is the fairness of a selection system determined?

Assessing Job Applicants: Interviews, Tests, and More

The question of how to obtain information about each job applicant leads us to a vast array of options. Some selection techniques, such as standardized tests, can be purchased by organizations from companies that develop tests. Others, such as interviews, are generally developed by I/O psychologists and other human resource professionals within a particular organization. Another option for companies is to hire a consulting firm to custom-make a selection instrument to suit their needs. Below we describe a few specific selection techniques and focus on some of the advantages and disadvantages of each.

■ Interviews: Assessing job applicants face-to-face.

By far, the most common type of selection instrument is the employment interview. Here we examine it from the organization's point of view. Organizations are interested in designing interviews with a high degree of criterion-related validity, just as they would be for any other selection instrument. With interviews, the key ingredient for achieving this goal is to use a **structured interview** (see Campion, Palmer, & Campion, 1999). Several elements contribute to a structured interview, but it can be best understood by thinking of an interview as one would any other type of test. As an exercise, think about how you would feel if you learned that your classmates in this course were given different tests than you. In addition, the questions were scored by different instructors, using different scoring keys, and some students were given more time than others. Not only would this seem unfair, but it would also make you doubt the validity of the grades given to each student.

In their unstructured form, employment interviews are not unlike this sort of testing situation. However, if care is taken to select questions based on a job analysis and if the same questions are asked by the same interviewer in the same manner across all job applicants, interviews can be a very useful tool for gathering information. Many of the most valid structured interviews even have scoring keys, just like standardized tests. As you can probably imagine, the use of struc-

Structured interview:
An employment interview that is conducted in the same manner, using the same questions, for all job applicants.

tured interviews such as this can also minimize the biases that often influence one person's perception of another, such as physical attractiveness and other irrelevant personal characteristics (e.g., Baron, 1983; Ellis et al., 2002). Unfortunately, in practice, many interviews are little more than casual conversations used to determine vaguely whether a job applicant is a good "fit" with the organization. In these cases, it is not uncommon for the interview to have negligible validity and to contribute to unfair discrimination (Arvey & Campion, 1982).

Having said this, there is one exception to this rule that is important to mention. If the purpose of the interview is to assess certain aspects of the applicant's personality, then an unstructured interview can be superior to a structured one (Blackman, 2006). Why? Because a less formatted interview has the potential of allowing job candidates to "let their hair down" so that their real personalities have a chance to come out. To accomplish this, it is best that the interview be truly casual, such as dinner in a comfortable setting with no scripted questions. Of course, not all aspects of personality are likely to be revealed in this context, and some applicants will still be adept at impression management. However, certain personality characteristics, such as extraversion and dependability, can be assessed with a high degree of validity in unstructured interviews (Funder, 1995). Because of the value of both structured and unstructured interviews, it is not uncommon for organizations to use both, one for assessing qualifications and one for assessing personality. However, as you'll see below, there are other options for accomplishing this latter goal.

■ Standardized tests.

For many jobs there may be so many applicants that one-on-one interviews are out of the question during initial screening. Application blanks and resumes certainly can help with this task, but they may not be ideal for assessing specific job-relevant characteristics. In these cases, **standardized tests** are often a viable option. These paper-and-pencil tests are not unlike the standardized personality and cognitive ability tests you learned about in Chapter 9. Like these tests, they are carefully constructed so that they are reliable and valid. What differs is that tests used for selection have been validated for this specific purpose by obtaining evidence of their criterion-related validity for specific jobs. For example, several general tests of cognitive ability are commonly used to screen job applicants. Research shows that these tests are predictive of success in a wide variety of jobs (Schmidt & Hunter, 1977), though they are seldom used as the sole method for selecting employees.

Specialized personality tests are also commonly used to screen applicants. For example, research indicates that such traits as extraversion and conscientiousness have been found to be predictive of success in several types of jobs (Barrick & Mount, 1991; Sackett & Wanek, 1996). Certain personality tests have also been useful for screening out less desirable employees, such as those who might be more likely to steal (Hogan, 1991). If you recall from the chapter opening, this was a problem that the pizza restaurant dealt with after the damage had been done. By using valid tests such as this, large retailers have made significant progress in reducing employee theft before it occurs (Wessel, 2003). What is essential with regard to standardized tests like this is that they have a high degree of criterion-related validity and that they be used only for the initial screening of applicants, not for the final decision. Unfortunately, the Internet has generated a multitude of poor quality tests, many of them administered online to job applicants, making it enticing for employers to purchase tests that may promise more than they can deliver (Drasgow, 2005). And, as you learned in Chapter 9, only tests with high levels of reliability and validity have the potential for being useful.

■ Assessment centers: Selection at its most intense.

One of the most innovative selection techniques, used first to select spies during World War II, is called an **assessment center** (Lance et al. 2004). Contrary to its name, it is not really a "center" but is more of a general method of selection. Typically,

Standardized tests:
Reliable and valid tests that are used for a particular purpose and that are administered in a systematic way.

Assessment center:
A selection technique that consists of a wide variety of tests and activities administered to a small group of job applicants over a few days.

FIGURE 14.5
Assessment Center Exercise
Job applicants who participate in assessment centers
can expect to do a wide variety of group exercises
to assess their interpersonal skills, such as the lead-
erless group discussion shown here.

an assessment center consists of a wide variety of tests and activities administered
to a small group of job applicants over a few days. As this description indicates, it
can be a very intense experience for job applicants. For example, when potential
spies were assessed during World War II, one of the tests consisted of consuming
large amounts of alcohol, then identifying those who were best at keeping their
wits about them. Those who were calm and cool like James Bond were more likely
to pass on to the next level of testing. Because assessment centers tend to be a very
costly and time consuming, they are often used as the last stage of hiring, typically
for highly paid managerial and executive positions, where the benefits of hiring
the best people can be substantial.

Assessment centers typically consist of a wide variety of standardized exercises, such as working in a team or prioritizing hypothetical work activities (see
Figure 14.5). Trained assessors observe each applicant, taking careful note of
dozens of specific behaviors exhibited, such as how often applicants in a team exercise interrupt one another or compliment one another. These behavioral exercises are often supplemented with interviews and standardized tests, such as the
ones described in the preceding section. At the end, the assessors combine the
scores from each test and exercise, computing an overall rating that is used to
make the final selection decision. Because of the time and effort involved in assessment centers, consulting firms are often hired by organizations interested in
using this method.

■ Work sample tests: Showing what you know.

The last type of selection technique we describe is called a **work sample test.** As
the name indicates, a work sample test has job applicants perform a sample of the
work they would be expected to do on the job. For example, a work sample for a
clerical position might consist of a test in which various software packages are
used to create documents. Job applicants would perform the test under time
constraints to assess technical proficiency. Like any other test, the key is to stan-
dardize the administration and scoring and to evaluate the work sample test's
criterion-related validity before using it.

Work samples can be thought of as a type of audition, similar to those you
may have experienced to become part of a choir, band, or play. While work samples can be time-consuming to design and implement, they have the added advantage of giving job applicants a realistic preview of the job, something that can
help job applicants determine whether the job would suit them. However, work

Work sample test:
A selection test that requires
job applicants to perform a
sample of the work they
would be expected to do on
the job.

samples are not appropriate to assess job skills if new employees will be trained how to do most aspects of the job. We turn now to the topic of training, as it is often the first experience employees have after being hired.

KEY QUESTIONS

- What is a structured interview?
- What is an assessment center?
- What is a work sample test?

TRAINING: HELPING EMPLOYEES ACQUIRE RELEVANT SKILLS

Regardless of qualifications, most new employees go through some form of training soon after being hired. Not surprisingly, psychologists are often involved in these efforts since training is really just an example of putting principles of human learning (Chapter 5) and memory and cognition (Chapter 6) into practice. If successful, training not only helps new employees excel, but also contributes to the organization's bottom line. Motorola, for example, once estimated that every $1 spent on training results in $30 in productivity gains (Kirkpatrick, 1993). Similarly, employees who are trained well also benefit because they not only feel better about the work they do, but also have a better chance of getting raises and promotions. So if done effectively, both employer and employees benefit from effective training.

Training is also common among experienced workers at various times in their career. In fact, most jobs have changed drastically over the last several years, making training an ongoing endeavor in many professions, such as medicine and engineering. For example, some hospitals are giving experienced doctors training in how to interact with very ill patients and their families, particularly when conveying the heart-wrenching diagnosis of a terminal illness (Landro, 2006). Similarly, many large organizations that do business overseas have implemented training in cross-cultural skills, so that their employees do well when working with clients in other countries (Harris, 2006). Both examples highlight that training need not be restricted to technical job skills; it extends to interpersonal skills as well.

In the following sections we describe the procedures organizations should use for the design and evaluation of training programs. As with employee selection, a great deal typically happens behind the scenes before any training has begun.

Needs Analysis: Assessing What Skills Need to Be Trained

The first step in the design of any training program is to conduct a **needs analysis.** As the name suggests, this analysis consists of a systematic collection of data to address the question, "Who needs to learn what?" A needs analysis is conducted at three levels, beginning with an *organizational analysis*. An organizational analysis takes into account the projected costs and benefits of training various groups of employees. This type of analysis helps executives evaluate the costs and benefits of training those in one department versus another.

Once this determination as been made, a *task analysis* is done to identify the knowledge, skills, and abilities needed to perform the job. A task analysis is really equivalent in many cases to a job analysis, which you read about earlier in this chapter. So fortunately, it may not need to be redone if a thorough job analysis has recently been completed.

Lastly, a *person analysis* is done to assess the current KSAs of those who will receive the training. In recent years, particular attention has been given to the distinct training needs of different groups (e.g., older versus younger employees) with the

Needs analysis:
The first step in a training program, consisting of a systematic collection of data to address the question "Who needs to learn what?"

goal of giving every employee the training assistance needed to succeed on the job (Riggio, 2000). Cumulatively, the information gathered from a needs analysis provides the necessary foundation for assessing what training needs to be done.

Program Development: Designing a Training Method

Once training needs have been assessed, the training method is designed. As suggested earlier, research on this topic has been guided extensively by basic psychological principles in human learning, memory, and cognition, so you are already familiar with many of the basic principles that should guide the design of organizational training techniques. Rather than cover familiar ground by repeating these principles we highlight a few specific applications of these principles in the context of employee training.

■ **On-site training methods.**

Training methods are roughly categorized as those that occur either on the job site (on-site) or away from the job site (off-site). By far the most common on-site method is **on-the-job training,** in which an inexperienced employee learns the ropes in the actual work context during company hours. Under appropriate circumstances this can be a highly effective training method as it allows the new employee to engage in observational learning and to practice newly acquired skills (for a review of observational learning principles, see Chapter 5).

On-the-job training often provides the opportunity for immediate positive and negative feedback, an important part of observational learning. This helps the new employee learn from the consequences of doing a particular task either correctly or incorrectly. Employees are usually highly motivated to learn in these contexts as they are able to experience the consequences of their actions. Even now, years later, I (Rebecca Henry) remember the negative consequences I received from one of the first milkshakes I ever made. The customer returned to the window and demonstrated to me (and everyone else) how lumpy it was by spooning it onto the counter. That was very clear feedback indeed! Wow, did I learn! Never again did I let my mind wander as I used the milkshake mixer.

Despite the advantages of on-the-job training, there are some potential disadvantages. For example, new employees may learn the wrong things from the wrong employees if care is not taken to pair new hires with the most highly skilled and motivated employees. Perhaps, for example, employees at Papa Del's Pizza learned from experienced employees that it was acceptable to give away free pizza to friends. As you can see, there is no guarantee with on-the-job training that new employees will learn only the right things. For this reason, it is essential that it be carefully planned beforehand to assure that observational learning from the best employees occurs. Also consistent with observational learning principles, new employees must have the opportunity to try out the new skills they have observed, preferably not too long afterward, so that the limits of memory are not exceeded.

Another on-site option to consider is a training method called **vestibule training,** in which a separate "practice" work area is used for the trainees. This method allows for observational learning and practice while reducing some of the negative consequences that might occur as the result of employee goofs, such as lumpy milkshakes. For example, a new cashier in a grocery store may practice using the cash machine and other equipment as other trainees pose as customers. This allows the trainee to practice necessary skills in a less stressful environment, a critical element of learning any new skill.

■ **Off-site training methods.**

Employees can also be trained using a wide variety of off-site methods. Many of these methods are similar in form to educational techniques that resemble the standard classroom instruction that any student knows all too well. Some of these

On-the-job training:
Training in which an inexperienced employee learns the ropes in the actual work context during company hours.

Vestibule training:
An on-site training method that uses a separate "practice" work area, allowing for observational learning.

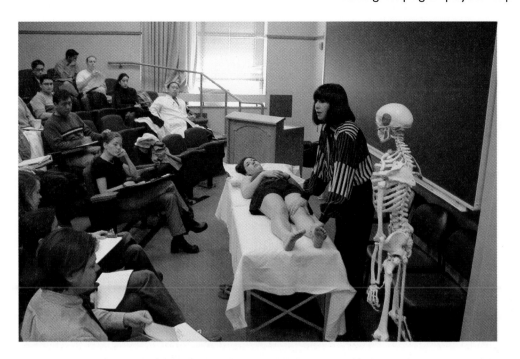

FIGURE 14.6
Using Role-Playing to Train
One highly effective training technique is for trainees to simulate an interpersonal exchange, taking turns playing both roles. Here, medical students play the role of patient to learn what it feels like to be one.

methods are not very flashy or exciting, but they may still be the best way to convey certain types of job-relevant knowledge. For example, attorneys might learn about new laws and regulations by attending a seminar. Or salespeople might learn about a new product by attending a presentation.

Another off-site method is **programmed instruction,** a technique that allows trainees to go through instructional materials at their own pace, testing themselves before proceeding to subsequent modules. You have probably used programmed instruction as a student. I first experienced it as an elementary-school student, learning spelling at my own pace. I learned the words, then tested and scored myself before going on to the next module. Not surprisingly, the ubiquity of computers and specialized software have made programmed instruction commonplace because of the ease with which feedback and scoring can be done.

Observational learning techniques are also the basis of one type of off-site training method, referred to as **behavior modeling training** (Decker & Nathan, 1985; Taylor, Russ-Eft, & Chan, 2005). This is a common technique in many managerial training programs. With behavior modeling techniques, principles of observational learning are applied so that managerial trainees can practice and learn interpersonal skills, such as how to resolve conflicts or negotiate with others (Salas & Cannon-Bowers, 2001). Behavior modeling has also been very successful in training people to use specific types of computer software (e.g., Davis & Yi, 2004). One exercise, common in behavioral modeling, is role-playing, in which trainees take turns playing both roles in an interpersonal exchange, such as doctor and patient or employee and customer (see Figure 14.6). An added benefit of role-playing is that it can help trainees empathize with the nontraditional point of view, such as that of patient or customer.

Evaluating Training Effectiveness: More Than Just Learning

Once training is complete it is important to evaluate the extent to which it has been effective. This issue is particularly of interest to organizations that may be comparing two or more training approaches, one more labor intensive and expensive than the other. For example, one study conducted at Kodak contrasted the effectiveness of two approaches for training managers how to budget and plan (Brettz & Thompsett, 1992). The first method was simply lecture-based training

Programmed instruction:
An off-site training method that allows trainees to go through instructional materials at their own pace, testing themselves before proceeding to subsequent modules.

Behavior modeling training:
A training technique that applies principles of observational learning.

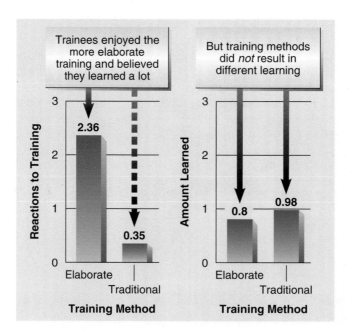

FIGURE 14.7
Comparison of Training Methods

Organizations commonly compare two or more training methods to determine which is more effective. This study shows that employee reactions to the training differed markedly, but the amount that employees learned did not.

Source: Adapted from Brettz & Thompsett, 1992.

Reaction criteria:
A measure of training effectiveness that examines how employees feel about the training experience.

Learning criteria:
A measure of training effectiveness that examines the degree of learning that occurred as a result of training.

Behavioral criteria:
A measure of training effectiveness that examines the degree of behavior change on the job.

Transfer-of-training:
The issue of whether material learned during training is demonstrated on the job.

Results criteria:
A measure of training effectiveness that examines the final outcome of the training (e.g., accident reduction).

that allowed trainees to take notes and ask questions. The contrasting training method consisted of the same factual material, but it was presented very differently, to make it more interesting. The trainers really pulled the stops out, incorporating games and skits as a way to teach the material. Classical music was played in the background with the hopes that this would reduce some of the stress of learning. Afterward, the two groups of trainees responded to a questionnaire regarding their reactions to the training and then took a test to assess what they had learned. As you can see from Figure 14.7, the more elaborate training created very positive reactions. Trainees enjoyed the games and music and they also believed they had learned more. However, the test of how much was actually learned revealed no significant differences. Given that the more elaborate training was much more expensive, it is easy to understand why the standard lecture format, boring as it was, was recommended.

This example highlights the importance of measuring several things to assess training effectiveness. Fortunately, research on training evaluation is quite specific with regard to the criteria that should be used (Kirkpatrick, 1959). The example above examined only two categories of training effectiveness criteria, **reaction criteria** and **learning criteria.** Two additional criteria, behavioral and results criteria, cannot be assessed until the trainees are back at work. **Behavioral criteria** focus on what employees actually do on the job (i.e., their behaviors) after the training. For example, equipment operators who have undergone safety training may have learned precisely how to use the equipment to prevent accidents, passing a test with flying colors that assesses their knowledge of safety procedures. However, they may not follow these steps when back at the job. Why? It could simply be that the safety procedures take a little more effort and are seen as an unnecessary bother (e.g., methodically checking various gauges or putting on safety glasses). It could also be that the new information has been forgotten. This example highlights the problem of **transfer-of-training,** the problem of demonstrating on the job what has been learned during training. This problem is one that has occupied researchers in I/O psychology just as it has the field of education for decades, though research on memory (Chapter 6) and motivation (Chapter 8) have made great strides in addressing it (De Corte, 2003).

The last of the training criteria to be assessed is the **results criterion.** This criterion addresses the question of what actually occurs as a final outcome, or result of, the training. With the safety example above, a reduction in accidents would be an example of a results criterion. In a different context, such as training customer service representatives, the results criterion might be a reduction in customer complaints. Results criteria can also take the form of economic indices, such as increases in output or reduction in waste of raw materials. So, in sum, to assess whether training has been effective, several distinct indices need to be measured.

We'll now turn to the important topic of performance appraisal, something that soon follows the training of any new employee. Like the procedures involved in selection and training, much happens behind the scenes, and whether it is done well depends, in large part, on whether psychological principles are followed.

KEY QUESTIONS

- What is a needs analysis?
- What are some examples of specific training methods?
- How are training programs evaluated?

PERFORMANCE APPRAISAL: IDENTIFYING EMPLOYEE STRENGTHS AND WEAKNESSES

When teaching courses in I/O psychology, I often ask my students at the beginning of the course to describe an unpleasant work experience they have had, to encourage them to think about the role of psychology in organizations. By far, the most common response I have received to this question over the years is a negative event that occurred when their supervisor was giving them job performance feedback. When this is done formally, as part of a **performance appraisal,** it should consist of a balanced and accurate assessment of each employee's strengths and weaknesses. My student's stories, however, tell me that often this is not the case, at least from their perspectives. They recall having their mistakes magnified and their strengths overlooked. Or they lament how the appraisal form itself did not even match the job activities that were part of their jobs. Others express anger at being evaluated by a supervisor who seemed too busy most of the time to be aware of how well each employee was doing. Why is performance appraisal such a common source of anger and dismay?

Why Performance Appraisal Is Unpopular, Yet Essential

The examples above illustrate at least some of the reasons why performance appraisal may not be something that most employees enjoy, even though research suggests that most employees generally want to receive feedback from their supervisors (Ashford, 1986). On the other side of the equation are managers who express similar dislike for this part of their jobs, because it often brings negative reactions from those they supervise (Waung & Highhouse, 1997). Indeed, one I/O psychologist who has studied performance appraisal most of his life and who now routinely does it as a department head has described it as being equivalent to root canal surgery: "It can be made relatively painless, but it is never really fun" (Murphy, 2006, page 62).

But why is this so? In part, it is because so many important decisions depend on the results of these appraisals. As can be seen in Figure 14.8, an organization's performance appraisal system can be considered the "hub" of many human resource practices, indicating that it plays a central role in these activities. For example, information from performance appraisals often serves as the basis for deciding who gets promoted. Similarly, this information is also used as the basis for determining raises. These are both *evaluative* purposes, as they serve to guide important decisions that matter to employees.

Performance appraisal:
The process of evaluating employee strengths and weaknesses.

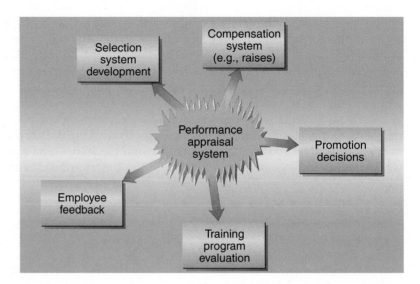

FIGURE 14.8
The Central Role of Performance Appraisal
It is important for performance appraisal systems to be accurate and fair, because they influence so many other important personnel decisions and practices.

Performance appraisal information can also provide useful information for evaluating other human resource practices, such as the effectiveness of a training program or the implementation of a new selection system. In these cases, the information about individual employees is of less importance than the overall performance of a group of employees who were part of a new training or selection system.

Other uses of performance appraisal information are more *developmental* in nature, meaning that their intent is to provide employees with individualized feedback in hopes of strengthening any weak areas. For example, a particular fast-food worker may be efficient at preparing customer orders, but may not treat people in a courteous manner. The appraisal of this employee would hopefully point out both this strength and weakness, with an accompanying plan for specialized training targeted at customer relations skills. Developmental feedback is also sometimes provided by one's coworkers, since they often have an opportunity to observe things that a supervisor may not. To learn how you can be more effective at giving feedback to your coworkers, see the **Psychology Lends a Hand** section on page 555.

Because of these important functions of performance appraisal, it is essential that the process be executed well. When this occurs, employees are more likely to feel they have been treated fairly (an important issue we return to later in the context of job satisfaction), and the organization has good-quality information on which to base important decisions.

Supervisors Are Human, Too: Errors, Biases and Memory Lapses

In its simplest form, a good performance appraisal system consists of a good appraisal form that is used appropriately. Because this is a psychology text we'll focus below on the human side of the equation rather than the construction of the appraisal form itself. First, we'll describe some common rating errors that can influence the accuracy of supervisory appraisal ratings. Then we'll discuss some methods for reducing these errors.

■ **Rating errors.**

Two of the most common errors are **leniency error** and **severity error,** the tendency for a supervisor to give employees ratings that are either higher or lower than their performance merits. As students, you have certainly seen this in the grading tendencies of various teachers you have had. In a work setting, the phe-

Leniency error:
The tendency for a supervisor to give employees ratings that are higher than their performance merits.

Severity error:
The tendency for a supervisor to give employees ratings that are lower than their performance merits.

P S Y C H O L O G Y   L E N D S   A   H A N D

How to Give Feedback to Coworkers

One of the most difficult aspects of working with others is determining when and how to give feedback to one's coworkers. Of course, giving positive feedback by telling someone they are doing well is never difficult. Negative feedback is another matter. While it is expected that supervisors and others in authority positions will give feedback, it is often not appreciated when it comes from one's peers. However, research is very clear in this regard: Being able to give constructive feedback is an essential part of working with others (Hackman, 1990). Here are some tips on how you can give constructive feedback so that it accomplishes its mission without causing friction:

1. **Be descriptive and specific, not evaluative.** When giving negative feedback, describe the behavior as specifically as you can, with a minimum of emotion and evaluation, and refrain from labeling the person (e.g., lazy, stupid).
2. **Be timely.** It is often tempting to delay saying something, hoping the problem goes away. However, it is more important for

the feedback be given soon after the behavior has occurred. This makes learning from mistakes easier and also prevents the build-up of hostilities.
3. **Be gentle.** Before you give any feedback, imagine how you would feel hearing something similar. By empathizing you will more likely deliver the feedback in a tactful manner that will be more easily received.
4. **Be accurate.** Stick to the facts when giving feedback. Be wary of the tendency to overgeneralize ("You always interrupt!") or to sarcastically gloss over problems ("So you've missed every meeting. No problem!").
5. **Be introspective.** Look honestly at your own faults and work on them before turning a critical eye on those around you.

By following these guidelines, it is more likely that the feedback you give will be listened to with a minimum of unpleasantness, and that positive change will follow.

nomenon is no different and some of the reasons it occurs may be similar. For example, a manager's ratings may suffer from leniency error because of an intentional desire to avoid unpleasant reactions from employees. After all, who is going to storm into a supervisor's office if everyone has been rated as "good" or "excellent"? While this may be an extreme example, it illustrates how a tendency to inflate ratings can easily occur even among managers who may be generally motivated to be fair.

Severity error is at the other end of the scale. What could possibly make a supervisor rate employees lower than their performance merits? Before concluding that some supervisors are just nasty, let's consider some other possibilities. Perhaps the supervisor simply has unrealistic standards. Indeed, this is thought to be one cause of severity error, and it seems to occur when supervisors use themselves as a comparison standard. For example, supervisors who have recently been promoted may remember what it was like to do the job they are now rating other people to do. They may not remember, however, how long it took them to achieve this level of excellence. As a result, the supervisor may use an unrealistic standard of comparison to rate subordinates who may be less experienced at the job.

A third common error is **central tendency error,** which represents ratings that hover around average. Supervisors who give ratings with this error may be those who have not been diligent about observing their employees during the preceding months. When given the task of rating several employees, they can't do so because they have not been paying attention. They think the "safe" response is to check the box in the middle, rather than to admit that they do not have enough information to make the judgment. Interestingly, there is also some evidence that central tendency error is more likely to occur when employees with disabilities are being rated. Specifically, this research indicates that employees with disabilities who are below average are more likely to have their ratings adjusted in a more positive direction, whereas those who are above average are more likely to have their ratings adjusted downward (Lynch & Finkelstein, 2006). The underlying

Central tendency error:
An error that represents ratings that hover around average.

FIGURE 14.9
Halo Error: One Cause of Supervisor Favoritism
When a particular employee stands out with regard to one skill or ability, such as creativity, he or she may be evaluated more favorably than is warranted across other dimensions of job performance. Distorted performance ratings of this form are referred to as halo error.

reasons for rating errors in this context is not yet clear, so future research on this topic is definitely warranted.

All three errors—leniency, severity, and central tendency—represent a pattern of evaluating most or all employees with a particular bias. The last error we consider, **halo error,** is distinct in that it represents a tendency to evaluate particular subordinates as "angels," as the term *halo* suggests. These are the employees who can be seen as doing no wrong, despite evidence to the contrary. Certainly, the concept of "playing favorites" is one with which we are all familiar. Understanding the reasons for it are more complex as it seems to stem from basic principles of social cognition, how we perceive and think about those around us (see Chapter 13).

In particular, halo error appears to stem from a general human tendency to view some characteristics as more important than others, and then to perceive those who have these characteristics in more favorable terms overall. For example, imagine a supervisor who views creativity more highly than other characteristics. This supervisor pays close attention to the creativity expressed by each subordinate. As far as this supervisor is concerned, creativity is the key to success. Now imagine one subordinate in particular who really shines when it comes to creative contributions to the team. When evaluating this subordinate along with the others, the manager rates this employee higher not only on creativity (which is appropriate) by also on unrelated dimensions, such as punctuality and teamwork skills, regardless of whether the employee is particularly noteworthy on these dimensions. This may not be favoritism in the intentional sense, but it still results in one employee receiving a more favorable evaluation than is deserved (see Figure 14.9).

■ **Techniques for reducing rating errors.**

Understanding these underlying causes for various rating errors is a helpful first step to minimize their impact. Careful development of unambiguous appraisal forms that cover all relevant dimensions of job performance is another important step to reduce rating errors. In addition to this, it is particularly important to understand the complex and often competing motives and goals supervisors may have with regard to the appraisal process (Murphy et al., 2004). For example, avoiding conflict by giving lenient ratings is one such motivation. A supervisor who has this goal is going to give much different ratings than a supervisor who is motivated to be fair. Other motives are also common, such as being seen as supportive, on the one hand, or tough, on the other. To the extent that these motives play a role, errors will occur.

In addition to conflicting motives, rating errors can also occur in more subtle ways. For example, in Chapter 13 you learned about the negative impact of stereotyping in the form of gender, race, and other characteristics. Of these, gender stereotyping has been examined the most extensively, particularly as it relates to how females and males are evaluated. Most notably, Madeline Heilman's systematic program of research suggests that women are often evaluated more negatively than men, even when these evaluations occur in the context of controlled experiments where the men and women being evaluated are trained to perform

Halo error:
A rating error that represents a tendency to evaluate particular subordinates as "angels" based on their exceptional performance along one dimension.

FIGURE 14.10
Technological Advances Make Performance Appraisal More Difficult
Technological advances, combined with other elements of virtual work environments, make it more difficult for supervisors to observe their subordinates. This is one factor that makes accurate performance appraisals a challenge.

identically (e.g. Heilman et al., 2004). This research also indicates that being helpful at work enhances how men are evaluated, but not women, suggesting that being a good citizen is optional for men, but not for women (Heilman & Chen, 2005). Similarly, research on mixed-sex teams indicates that men are more likely to get credit for what the team accomplishes than are women (Heilman & Haynes, 2005), even when the contributions of each team member are equivalent. What is particularly important to note here is that both male and female raters make these biased judgments, which underscores the pervasiveness of this form of bias. While it is unrealistic to think that organizations can eliminate all forms of stereotyping, it is possible to raise awareness of these issues as part of management training in hopes of reducing its negative effects.

Rating errors can also be reduced simply by giving supervisors ample opportunity to observe each subordinate over a period of time. While this may seem obvious, it is not uncommon, particularly in this day of virtual work environments and telecommuting, for supervisors not to see their subordinates much at all during any given week (see Figure 14.10). Lastly, appraisal systems should take into account the limits of human memory (see Chapter 6). Simply having supervisors keep a record of relevant employee behaviors can serve as set of crucial retrieval cues when the time comes to fill out the semiannual appraisal forms.

KEY QUESTIONS

- Why is performance appraisal so important?
- What are the four major types of rating errors?
- How can these errors be minimized?

WORK MOTIVATION: ENCOURAGING EMPLOYEES TO DO THEIR BEST

Our focus in this chapter is to help you understand how psychological principles are applied behind the scenes in many successful organizations. Enhancing your awareness of this can help you succeed as a job applicant and as an employee. However, this is only part of the picture. Understanding the behavior of your coworkers is at least as challenging, if not more so. For the last three topics—work motivation, leadership, and teamwork—we'll shift our attention to the behavior of others at work: Why are they motivated to behave as they do? Why are some supervisors in leadership positions more effective than others? Why do some teams have more difficulties than others? We'll begin with the topic of **work motivation,** defined as the internal processes that activate, guide, and maintain behavior directed toward work.

How does management think about work motivation? It is viewed, in combination with skills and abilities, as the second piece of a two-part puzzle. The first piece, getting highly skilled employees in place, is the primary focus of training and selection. Many selection techniques and performance appraisal systems also focus more on skills than on motivation. However, organizations realize that exceptional employees not only have the *skills*, they also have the *will* that is necessary to succeed. In this context, work motivation represents what is meant by "will."

Fortunately, theory and research on motivation, such as what you learned about in Chapter 8, have played a crucial role in helping organizations to create conditions and practices that foster high levels of motivation. These principles have been studied extensively in organizations of all kinds, resulting in many highly successful organizational techniques. For example, the most effective compensation systems are often based on principles of expectancy theory, which specify how effort is linked to performance and how performance should be rewarded. Goal-setting theory was also originally developed for application in organizations to help managers set challenging, specific goals for employees. You also read in Chapter 8 about intrinsic motivation, that comes from the pleasure and fulfillment people get from activities that they enjoy. This theory has also been applied in work settings, resulting in some very creative job design techniques that make work more enjoyable and fulfilling (Hackman & Oldham, 1976).

In this section, so as to not cover the same ground as Chapter 8, we'll focus specifically on people's feelings and attitudes about work and how these feelings motivate their behavior at work. We'll begin by discussing the link between job satisfaction and work performance. Next we'll examine how job satisfaction and its opposite, dissatisfaction, motivate employees to do positive and negative things, respectively.

Job Satisfaction: Are Happy Workers Productive Workers?

Think of a time recently when you really threw yourself into some activity. Was it something you enjoyed doing or was there some other reason, such as an important deadline, that motivated you into action? If you're like most people, you can probably think of instances in which each of these motives played a role. Sometimes we work hard at things we enjoy and sometimes we work hard for other reasons. The question posed in the heading above addresses this issue in the context of **job satisfaction,** people's attitudes about various aspects of their jobs (Smith, Kendall, & Hulin, 1969). By examining the statistical correlation between job satisfaction and performance across representative groups of employees, the question of whether happy workers are productive workers can be systematically addressed. The magnitude of the correlation indicates the degree to which job satisfaction and performance are related. Because of the importance of this question, it has been examined by researchers across hundreds of occupations and tens of thousands of employees.

For a summary of the latest, most comprehensive examination of this question, see Figure 14.11. This figure shows the results of a meta-analysis of several hundred studies that examined the job satisfaction–performance relationship (Judge et al., 2001). For simplicity, we excerpted the results of four major occupational groups to show you the range of the findings. As you can see from Figure

Work motivation:
The internal processes that activate, guide, and maintain behavior directed toward work.

Job satisfaction:
Employees' attitudes about various aspects of their jobs.

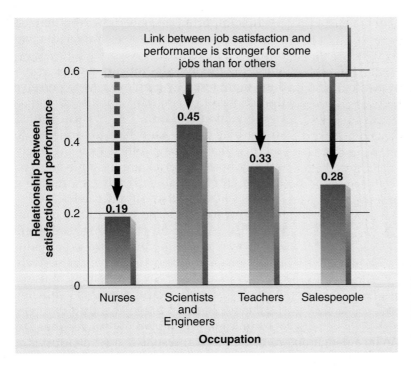

FIGURE 14.11
Job Satisfaction and Performance
Studies of the relationship between job satisfaction and performance show a modest positive correlation that varies somewhat by occupation.
Source: Adapted from Judge et al., 2001.

14.11, the researchers found a modest, positive relationship between job satisfaction and performance, but it varied somewhat across occupations. Specifically, the link between satisfaction and performance was strongest among scientists and engineers and weakest among nurses. This suggests that, for many jobs, being more satisfied does relate somewhat to performing better, but there is some variability across jobs. This variability merely reflects that other factors, such as skills and abilities, may play a more important role in performance for some jobs in contrast to others.

Organizational Citizenship and Retaliation: The Good, the Bad, and the Ugly

Organizations care about employee performance, but they also care about many other types of employee behavior. They want to retain their best employees and they want them to show up regularly and punctually. Ideally, they would also like their employees to go the extra mile, helping one another and volunteering for extra assignments. Conversely, organizations also care about minimizing destructive behaviors such as theft, sabotage, and aggression toward coworkers. What is the role of job satisfaction in these diverse behaviors?

A wealth of research evidence indicates that job satisfaction plays a significant role in each of these behaviors (e.g., Harrison, Newman, & Roth, 2006). Specifically, negative behaviors such as absenteeism, theft, and other counterproductive work behaviors show a modest but significant negative correlation with job satisfaction (i.e., more satisfied employees do fewer of these things) (Dalal, 2005; Hulin, 1990). Conversely, positive behaviors such as helping one's coworkers and volunteering for extra assignments show a modest, positive correlation with job satisfaction (i.e., more satisfied employees do more of these things) (Borman, 2004; Organ & Ryan, 1995). Particularly relevant is job dissatisfaction that stems from feelings of unfair treatment. These feelings of unfairness play an important role in a whole cluster of negative work behaviors, extending to such acts as employee theft (see Figure 14.12 on page 560) and sabotage (Ambrose, Seabright, & Schminke, 2002; Greenberg, 2002; Skarlicki & Folger, 1997).

"I do take home some office property, but only because I'm building an exact replica of the office in my home."

FIGURE 14.12
Employee Theft: One Negative Consequence of Employee Dissatisfaction
Relatively minor examples of employee theft, such as this, are common. However, when the problem gets more severe, job dissatisfaction is usually one contributing factor.

Organizational citizenship behaviors: Positive work behaviors, including helping coworkers and volunteering for extra assignments.

It is important to note, however, that job satisfaction is only one of several factors that contribute to these negative behaviors. For example, aggressive acts toward coworkers are done more often by employees who perceive the actions of others with a *hostile attribution bias* (Neuman & Baron, 1997). Those with a strong bias of this kind have a tendency to interpret the actions of others as being intentionally hostile. For example, someone who always thinks that bad drivers are being aggressive (rather than simply careless or distracted) would be someone with this attributional bias. As a result of thinking that others are always "out to get them," these individuals become more likely to behave aggressively as a way to retaliate. Not surprisingly, abuse of alcohol tends to exacerbate this tendency (LeBlanc & Barling, 2004). This distorted way of thinking, combined with feelings of dissatisfaction, can be a dangerous combination that results in a whole cluster of negative work behaviors.

Similarly, positive work behaviors, such as helping coworkers, are motivated by feelings of job satisfaction in conjunction with personal characteristics. These behaviors, referred to as **organizational citizenship behaviors,** are influenced by such personality traits as conscientiousness and empathy (Ladd & Henry, 2000; McNeely & Meglino, 1994; Organ & Ryan, 1995). Taken together, the most helpful employees tend to be those who are conscientious, empathic, and satisfied with their jobs. These examples mention only a few of the additional factors that influence positive and negative employee behaviors. What is important to remember is that job satisfaction plays a role in these behaviors, but it is not necessarily the starring role.

Creating a Satisfying Work Environment: The Essential Role of Fairness

The preceding section notes the importance of job satisfaction in a whole host of work behaviors, from the most positive to the most negative. This begs the question, "How can the job satisfaction of employees be enhanced?" This issue has received more attention from researchers and practitioners than probably any other in I/O psychology. Not surprisingly, there is no shortage of answers ranging from empirically supported techniques that focus on making work more fulfilling (Hackman & Oldham, 1976) to untested pop management fads that fill the shelves of bookstores. Between these two extremes are dozens of organizational practices and policies that attempt to make organizations more worker friendly. These include such options as alternative work arrangements (e.g., flextime) and family-friendly programs aimed at easing the often competing demands of work and family. While there is some evidence that practices such as these can be effective in attracting employees during the recruiting process, there is less evidence that they play a role in making employees happy once they are hired. In part, the problem stems from the fact that most employees do not take advantage of the wide variety of these programs. So what are organizations to do?

While there is no single method of creating a satisfying work environment, there is strong evidence that being treated in a fair manner is an essential ingredient (Brockner & Wiesenfeld, 1996). Employees who feel they are treated fairly at work (by their supervisors and by the organization in general) report higher levels of job satisfaction. Perhaps more important, being treated fairly can also lessen the otherwise negative impact of certain organizational practices, such as the implementation of smoking bans (Greenberg, 1994). Employees who are treated fairly also tend to be affected less negatively by the stresses of work–family conflict (Siegel et al., 2005).

Indeed, the positive value of fair treatment can extend well beyond feelings of satisfaction. As evidence of this, one recent field experiment examined the role of fair treatment in lessening insomnia among nurses who had just learned that they would be subjected to an undesirable change in pay policy (Greenberg, 2006). To assess the impact of fair treatment, half of the nurses' supervisors were trained in techniques promoting *interactional fairness*, a form of fairness that focuses on the interpersonal treatment that employees get from their supervisors. Results indicated, not surprisingly, that the change in pay policy had negative effects in the form of more insomnia among the nurses. More important, this negative impact was substantially lessened among nurses whose supervisors had been trained to treat them in a fair manner. While this is only one study, it is consistent with a host of others showing the same positive benefits of fair treatment. This, perhaps, is the best example of a workplace intervention that simultaneously benefits both organizations and their employees, the aforementioned dual goal of I/O psychology.

KEY QUESTIONS

- What are work motivation and job satisfaction?
- What is the nature of the relationship between job satisfaction and performance?
- What other behaviors do job satisfaction and dissatisfaction relate to?
- What role does fair treatment play in creating a satisfying work environment?

LEADERSHIP: FROM SUPERVISORS TO CEOS

At various points in this chapter we have indirectly discussed the role of those in leadership positions. For example, supervisors often play an important role in selecting, training, evaluating, and motivating their subordinates. We now focus directly on **leadership,** defined here as the process by which one member of a group (its leader) influences other group members toward attainment of shared group goals (Vecchio, 1997; Yukl, 1994). The question of how leaders exert this influence has been a topic of great interest to psychologists since the early part of the twentieth century. It is also a topic that has been studied by scholars from other disciplines, such as history and political science. While the focus in these disciplines is slightly different (e.g., political or military leaders), the central question remains the same: What contributes to effective leadership? (See Figure 14.13, on page 562.) We'll turn to that question first by examining the characteristics of effective leaders and then by examining the leaders' work context. We'll conclude with a description of one very powerful style of leadership that has been receiving much attention in recent years—transformational leadership.

Leader Characteristics: How Effective Leaders Are Different from Others

If you were taking this course several years ago, the answer to the question of what distinguishes effective leaders from others would have been, "There are no consistent findings." And, given that most of you were probably in diapers at the time, this conclusion probably wouldn't have gone against your common sense. It was, however, counterintuitive to many who studied leadership. Certainly, these

Leadership:
The process by which one member of a group (its leader) influences other group members toward attainment of shared group goals.

FIGURE 14.13
Leadership in Different Arenas
The study of leadership has spanned several academic disciplines, from political science and history to I/O psychology.

researchers thought, the best CEOs (chief executive officers) and military generals must have some unique characteristics.

■ **Early leadership research.**

Indeed, it was this belief that initiated nearly a century of research on leadership, as scholars explored a host of traits in hopes of finding some that correlated with leadership effectiveness (e.g., Terman, 1904; Yukl & Van Fleet, 1992). Are effective leaders more intelligent than others? Are they more dominant? Occasionally, an early study would report a significant relationship between one of these traits and leader effectiveness, but this pattern invariably would fail to be replicated in a subsequent study. Halfway through the century and hundreds of studies later, researchers concluded that the search for key leadership traits was not going to lead to clear answers (Stogdill, 1948).

The next avenue that researchers explored was the behavior of effective leaders. The question was modified from one that focused on traits to one that focused on what leaders actually do at work. Personality tests were put aside and clipboards were taken in hand as researchers directly observed leaders at various supervisory levels (e.g., Stogdill, 1963). These researchers did indeed begin to see distinct categories of behavior. Using sophisticated statistical analyses they were able to classify hundreds of behaviors into a reasonable number of dimensions, resulting in a final two-factor classification. This two-factor classification consisted of a set of behaviors related to the work (task behaviors) and a set of behaviors related to people (interpersonal behaviors).

This clear distinction between types of leader behaviors was encouraging, but it fell short of addressing the question of whether effective leaders do more of one type of behavior than another. Unfortunately, subsequent studies examining this question met with the same fate as the earlier trait studies: No clear pattern emerged.

■ **Leader traits and behaviors reconsidered: New findings.**

We began this section by hinting that something important must have emerged regarding the characteristics of effective leaders in the last decade or so. Indeed, there have been many recent developments in the study of personality and some of these relate to leadership. For example, in Chapter 9, you learned about a classification of personality called the "big five," which describes personality along

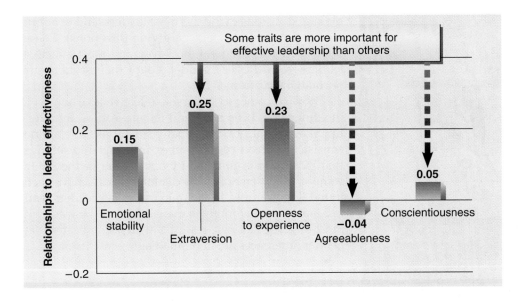

FIGURE 14.14
Traits of Effective Leaders
Meta-analyses of leadership traits show that effective leaders in business settings are different from less effective leaders in terms of some basic personality traits. *Source:* Adapted from Judge et al., 2002.

five broad dimensions (conscientiousness, extraversion, agreeableness, emotional stability, and openness to experience). The strength of this framework, combined with valid measures of each trait, has led to a reexamination of traits in the context of leadership.

One of the most conclusive studies of leadership traits examined nearly one thousand earlier studies (Judge et al., 2002). As you can see in Figure 14.14, a clear pattern emerged showing the relative importance of each of the "big five" traits in terms of their correlation with leadership effectiveness in business settings. While the correlations are modest in size, they are statistically significant for three of the five dimensions of personality. According to the results of this meta-analysis, effective leaders tend to be more extraverted and more open to experience, compared to less effective leaders. To a lesser extent, effective leaders also tend to be more emotionally stable. It is important also to note that there are two dimensions that were not related to leader effectiveness: conscientiousness and agreeableness. These traits may be important for other types of jobs, but are less so for leadership positions in business settings. We should note that these researchers also examined leadership in the military and found slightly different results (e.g., conscientiousness was correlated with leader effectiveness in this context).

This meta-analysis represents just one approach to studying effective leaders. Another recent meta-analysis has also found supportive evidence for the importance of both task and interpersonal behaviors in determining leader effectiveness (Judge, Piccolo, & Ilies, 2004). Of particular importance is the manner in which leaders reward and punish their subordinates (Podsakoff et al., 2006). As you learned in the previous section on job satisfaction, fairness comes into play in these situations, influencing how subordinates view their treatment as well as the treatment of their coworkers.

■ Gender differences in leadership.

Research on leader characteristics has also investigated whether there are any stable differences between male and female leaders. Using the same meta-analytic techniques mentioned above, Eagly and colleagues have systematically examined hundreds of studies of sex differences in leadership (Eagly & Johnson, 1990; Eagly, Karau, & Makhijani, 1995). Several consistent patterns have emerged from these studies. The question of leadership style, for example, shows that male and female leaders do tend to adopt different leadership styles on average. Female leaders tend to rely more on a participative style (e.g., getting input from others before

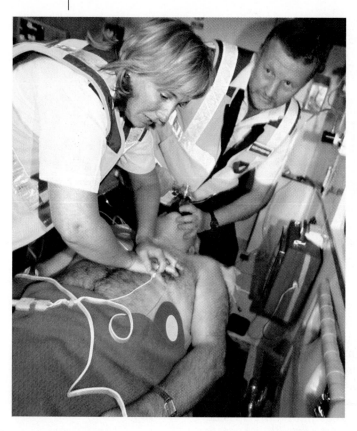

FIGURE 14.15
Leadership Style: Adapting It to Fit the Situation
Whether it is better to be directive or empowering as a leader depends on the situation. For example, when trauma teams are faced with high-level emergencies, they do better when led by a directive leader.

Path-goal theory:
A theory of leadership that examines how leaders should adapt their style of leadership in response to the situation.

Normative decision theory:
A theory of leadership that prescribes how leaders should take the situation into account when deciding how a particular decision should be made.

making decisions), whereas male leaders tend to adopt a more autocratic style (e.g., giving directions). These differences are not great, however, and most effective leaders, regardless of gender, adapt their style to the particular situation.

When it comes to leadership effectiveness, however, the differences been male and female leaders are minimal (Eagly et al., 1995). In many situations there are no consistent differences. However, in leadership settings that have been dominated by one gender or the other, some small differences in leader effectiveness have been found. For example, in the military, female leaders tend to be rated less favorably than male leaders. However, in most business settings, research evidence indicates that gender differences are minimal (Eagly et al., 1995).

Leadership in Context: How the Work Setting Influences Leaders

Everything we have discussed thus far with regard to leadership has focused on the leader with little mention of how the leader might be influenced by the work setting. Are some situations simply more challenging to leaders? Do subordinates have an impact on how leaders behave? The answer to both questions is "yes." In fact, several theories of leadership effectiveness have approached leadership in this way. One theory, called **path-goal theory,** examines how leaders should adapt their style of leadership in response to the situation (House, 1971). This theory addresses such questions as, "When is it best for a leader to be directive (i.e., to dictate exactly how things should be done) rather than empowering (i.e., to let subordinates make their own decisions and accept responsibility)?"

A recent study of trauma resuscitation teams examined precisely this question. These researchers examined the leadership styles of trauma team leaders under conditions that varied in their level of emergency. Results suggest that high-level emergencies call for a more directive leadership style, particularly if the trauma team is somewhat inexperienced (Yun, Faraj, & Sims, 2005). However, when the team is more experienced and the trauma level is lower, an empowering leadership style can be more effective (see Figure 14.15).

A related theory, called **normative decision theory,** also takes the situation into account, but does so in the context of deciding how a particular decision should be made (Vroom & Yetton, 1973). According to this theory, the central question is the degree of participation leaders should solicit from their subordinates. For example, autocratic decisions can be more appropriate when the situation dictates that the decision must be made quickly. Democracy may encourage commitment to a decision, but it is slow! However, when commitment to a decision is essential, a participative decision in which everyone has input may be more effective. This approach to leadership decision making has been very successful in management and executive training programs, because it helps future leaders learn when it is better to ask for input and when it is better to go it alone.

More recently, contemporary research on leadership has taken a novel look at leadership effectiveness by examining the impact that subordinates have on leaders. As you learned in Chapter 13, social influence is a two-way street, even when one individual has more formal authority than the other. Turning the tables in this way has resulted in some very interesting findings regarding leadership. For example, this research shows that leaders have distinct relationships with each subordinate and that the quality of the relationship varies substantially (Graen & Scandura, 1986). From this perspective, referred to as **leader-member exchange theory,** both the leader and the subordinate contribute to the creation of the relationship. Leaders and subordinates who establish a high-quality relationship tend to trust each other more, with the subordinate being given more responsibility. In contrast, low-quality relationships are characterized by formal organizational rules rather than by trust. Research has shown that subordinates benefit greatly from developing high-quality relationships with their leaders, and that these subordinates reciprocate by working harder and generally contributing more (Liden, Sparrowe, & Wayne, 1997). This approach to leadership has also shed light on how mentoring relationships develop and how having a good mentor may play a role in career success (Allen et al., 2004).

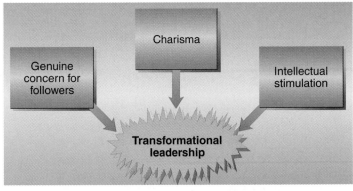

FIGURE 14.16

Transformational Leaders: A Combination of Traits and Behavior

Leaders who are described as being "transformational" possess the trait of charisma, but also behave differently than other leaders.

Transformational Leadership: Encouraging and Inspiring Others

When most of us think of truly great leaders, words like "vision," "inspiration," and "charisma" come to mind. Historical figures such as Queen Elizabeth I and Alexander the Great had these characteristics, and certain CEOs have been described in these terms as well. In recent years, psychologists have attempted to study this form of leadership, first by defining the characteristics of these leaders and then by examining how these leaders have an impact on those around them. The term **transformational leadership** has been coined to describe this type of leadership, because it captures the idea that these leaders truly transform those around them by encouraging them to think and behave in fundamentally different ways (Bass, 1985).

There are several ingredients that contribute to transformational leadership, the most central of which is **charisma.** Leaders who have charisma tend to have a clear vision for the future. Martin Luther King Jr.'s vision for social change is a good example of this. Charismatic leaders also tend to be very self-confident, expressing themselves with enthusiasm and eloquence (Riggio, 2004). This style of communication helps make their vision contagious to others. Lastly, charismatic leaders set very high standards for those who follow them. For example, religious cult leaders, often described as charismatic, expect their followers to devote their entire lives to the cult—a very high standard, indeed.

But transformational leaders are more than simply charismatic. In fact, some research shows that purely charismatic leaders can create maladaptive dependence among their followers, while those with evil intent can have disastrous effects on society (Yukl & Van Fleet, 1992). What makes transformational leaders distinctive is that they combine charisma with two additional patterns of behavior: They show genuine concern for their subordinates and they intellectually stimulate them (see Figure 14.16). This pairing of concern and intellectual challenge, combined with charisma, equips these leaders with the tools to help employees reach their potential (see Bass et al., 2003; Piccolo & Colquitt, 2006). For some specific tips on how you can become a more transformational leader at work or in an organization to which you belong, see the following **Psychology Lends a Hand** on page 566.

Leader-member exchange theory:
A theory of leadership that describes the distinct relationships that leaders form with each subordinate.

Transformational leadership:
Leadership that consists of charisma, intellectual stimulation, and genuine concern for subordinates.

Charisma:
A characteristic of transformational leaders that consists of having high self-confidence, a strong vision, enthusiasm, and eloquence. Leaders with charisma also set very high standards for followers.

KEY QUESTIONS

- What characteristics distinguish effective leaders from others?
- How does the work context influence leaders?
- What are the characteristics of transformational leaders?

P S Y C H O L O G Y   L E N D S   A   H A N D

How to Become a More Transformational Leader

Whether you are currently working or a full-time student, chances are you may find yourself in the position of leading a group or team of some sort, perhaps as a member of a volunteer organization or club. This is an ideal situation to practice leadership skills, such as those that are characteristic of transformational leaders. As you learned above, transformational leaders have charisma, but they also show consideration and attempt to intellectually stimulate those they lead. Here are some specific tips for doing each of these things:

1. **Find something you are passionate about.** The enthusiasm and vision that exemplifies charisma is easiest to demonstrate when you have a sincere interest in something. So find an organization devoted to a cause you truly believe in. Your enthusiasm will naturally show and you will find yourself beginning to think more creatively about your personal vision for the cause.
2. **Model leaders you admire.** This doesn't mean you should attempt to imitate leaders with charisma, but it would be useful to carefully observe charismatic leaders in action. By doing so you can identify which behaviors suit your personal style. This approach worked wonders for me when I was learning how to teach. I remembered what my favorite professors did and did those things that were consistent with my own personal

style of teaching. With leadership, you can learn skills in the same way.
3. **Provide intellectual challenges.** Transformational leaders are great at this. They help their team define a problem or task, but they do not tell them how to do it. Instead, they step back and encourage creativity, rather than micromanage. In the short term this can result in false starts and mistakes, but in the long term it gives team members new skills as well as a sense of ownership for what they have accomplished.
4. **Show genuine concern.** This extends beyond just being nice. What it really refers to is showing respect for each member of your team as individuals. This can best be accomplished by getting to know their strengths and weaknesses so as to help them develop to their fullest potential. This allows you to carefully gauge the intellectual challenges you provide so that they suit the particular skills of each team member. As a result, they get to achieve things on their own and to improve as a result of it.

By practicing these things you can improve your leadership skills by applying what has worked for many successful leaders. It takes time and you will probably make some mistakes along the way, but in the end you will have some very useful skills at your disposal.

TEAMWORK: THE CHALLENGES OF WORKING WITH OTHERS

"The final assignment for this course is a group project . . ." As a professor, I know that this statement will invariably bring a mixture of reactions from a class. Some typically feel relieved to share the burden of a large assignment. Others worry about whether they will be teamed up with a group of "slackers." Still others are excited about the possibility of making friends as a result of working together. Organizational work groups evoke the same diverse reactions among employees, along with a host of the same challenges. Because of these challenges, organizations should carefully consider whether a team approach is desirable.

Certainly, some activities must be performed by highly coordinated teams. A pilot cannot fly a jet without a copilot and flight engineer, nor can a surgeon remove an appendix without the efforts of nurses and technicians. However, in many instances organizations can decide whether a team approach is suitable for accomplishing a task. For example, important decisions can either be made by one individual or by a group. The decision whether to assign work to a team should take many factors into account. In this section we'll discuss some challenges of teamwork, beginning with the topic of team composition, the task of putting the team together so that it has the potential to function effectively.

Team Composition: Deciding Who Should Work with Whom

As you have no doubt observed, some people work better together than do others. This is the basic starting assumption of team composition research. The key is to identify what mixture of individual characteristics results in the most effective team functioning. Part of the answer depends on what the team is going to be required to do, and another part depends on what outcome really matters. For example, having a highly diverse work group can have a very positive impact on creative problem solving, a task that is central to many organizational teams. Unfortunately, highly diverse groups also tend to have trouble retaining members (Williams & O'Reilly, 1998), with the person who stands out being the one most likely to quit (Sacco & Schmitt, 2005). What diverse teams gain in creativity they lose in stability. However, this instability has a positive side effect. When new team members are added to an existing team, the team becomes more creative. Apparently, adding "new blood" not only brings in fresh ideas, but it can also add a spark that motivates existing team members to think more creatively (Choi & Thompson, 2005).

More generally, what appears to be most effective with regard to diversity is to have sufficient differences so that everyone can contribute something unique (Mannix & Neale, 2005). This is best accomplished by having *functional diversity*, differences that are based on training and expertise. This type of diversity also has the added benefit of allowing team members to learn from one another, something that can benefit team members over the long term. In contrast, *demographic diversity* in teams (e.g., age, sex, race) often has negative effects on team performance and team member satisfaction (Mannix & Neale, 2005), posing unique challenges for organizations committed to a creating a more diverse workplace.

Another issue related to team composition is the question of how to hire "team players," those who can work effectively with a wide range of people. This trend is gaining momentum in many team-based organizations, with consultants being awarded lucrative contracts on the condition that they help recruiters identify top-quality employees. These new hires are expected not only to be technically proficient, but also to be good at working with others. Research on the selection of team members shows once again the relevance of the "big five" personality approach. For example, teams with members who are high in conscientiousness and extraversion tend to be more effective (Barrick et al., Mount, 1998). Having highly agreeable group members is also related to team success (Barrick et al., 1998). Interestingly, this research has found evidence that even one highly disagreeable team member can have an adverse effect on an otherwise smoothly functioning group. The saying "One bad apple can spoil the barrel" certainly seems to apply to teams.

Another factor to consider is the ideal size of the team. Here, the research on motivation in teams is quite specific. According to this research, it is far better to slightly understaff a team than to make it too big (Hackman, 1990). Teams with too many members not only have more difficulties coordinating their efforts (e.g., setting a common meeting time), but they also tend to have more **social loafing,** the tendency to reduce one's efforts when working collectively (Steiner, 1972; Latane, Williams, & Harkins, 1979). Not surprisingly, when members of a team get to decide how big their team should be they often err in the direction of making it too large, in part because people understand that their own efforts can be reduced as the group gets bigger. This motive is something that organizations wrestle with as they try to create teams that are neither over- nor understaffed.

Managing Conflict: The Benefits of Some Forms of Disagreement

Once a team has been created, the potential for conflict among members arises. Conflict can come in many different forms and not all of it is destructive. For this reason, contemporary perspectives of team conflict view it as something that should be managed, rather than avoided or eliminated (Amason, 1996). One basic distinction in team conflict is **task conflict** versus **relationship conflict.** As the terms indicate, task conflict refers to disagreements about how the team's primary activity should be accomplished, whereas relationship conflict refers to interpersonal problems between individuals. For example, advertising executives might disagree about the form that a new advertising campaign should take. The executives are united on the goal of

Social loafing:
The tendency to reduce one's efforts when working in a group.

Task conflict:
Disagreement about how the team's primary activity should be accomplished.

Relationship conflict:
Conflict in the group that refers to interpersonal problems between individuals.

FIGURE 14.17

Groupthink: One Rare, but Extreme, Consequence of Too Much Agreement
Disagreement within a team can lead to positive outcomes. In contrast, too much agreement can contribute to faulty decision making resulting in disastrous results, such as the *Challenger* and *Columbia* space shuttle disasters.

doing well; they simply have different views regarding the best means of doing so. This is an example of task conflict and it is very common, particularly in functionally diverse teams. While conflicts or disagreements of this type may be unpleasant as they are occurring, they can often result in constructive outcomes, and therefore should not be squelched.

Among decision-making groups conflict can also be constructive (Henry, 1993; Sniezek & Henry, 1989). Research findings indicate that teams that have the most divergent opinions tend to make the best decisions overall. In fact, groups that experience no dissent among their members often make serious errors in judgment, sometimes referred to as **groupthink** (Janis, 1972). For example, both space shuttle disasters (the *Challenger* in 1986 and the *Columbia* in 2002) have been partially attributed to this faulty group decision process among engineers at NASA (see Figure 14.17). In fact, the importance of constructive disagreement is so generally recognized now that organizational teams will often appoint someone to voice disagreement (a "devil's advocate") to guarantee that dissenting arguments will be raised.

In contrast, relationship conflicts often serve no purpose other than to advance the agendas of the respective parties. These conflicts generally originate from personal disagreements among team members. For example, a long-feuding pair of teammates may make a point of shooting down each other's ideas merely because they dislike each other. Conflict of this variety can result in communication breakdowns, which in turn have been shown to cause the most serious of mistakes, such as airline disasters (Foushe, 1984) and surgical errors (Anand & Winslow, 2003).

Even isolated disputes can interfere with a team achieving its goal, particularly if the conflict occurs when the team first starts working together. One common dispute of this type occurs when parts of a project get divided up, with tasks assigned to each member. For example, two team members may want to do the same part of the project, leaving more boring tasks undone. Because these conflicts occur early on, they can set the tone for the entire experience and should therefore be handled as diplomatically as possible so that everyone feels as though they are an important member of the team (Henry & Landa, 2000).

Encouraging Cooperation over Competition

In addition to fostering beneficial forms of conflict, effective teams must also learn to work together. Simply putting highly trained, reasonable people together on a team is a good start, but it is not sufficient to guarantee a smoothly functioning team. Indeed, there is a great deal of evidence indicating that teams must to trained how to work collaboratively (Salas & Cannon-Bowers, 2001). Such training often includes instruction on how to communicate effectively so that information gets distributed in the most efficient manner. Communication is a particularly important aspect of training in highly diverse groups since each team member may approach the task in a different way, even using different terminology to explain similar ideas and concepts.

Another ingredient in fostering team cooperation is to have organizational reward systems that are consistent with a team approach. In other words, team members should be rewarded and recognized not when they simply perform well as individuals, but when their team performs well. For example, some compensation systems give raises and bonuses based on team performance rather than individual performance. Incentives such as this can go a long way toward creating an atmosphere that is conducive to cooperation over competition. However, research also indicates that shifting from a competitive (i.e., individual) to cooperative (team) reward system does not always go smoothly and can lead to "cutthroat co-

Groupthink:
Serious errors in group decision making that result from a lack of dissent in the group.

operation"—behavior that appears cooperative on the surface, but is actually competitive behind the scenes (Johnson et al., 2006).

These last two issues, team training and reward systems, highlight again an important theme of this chapter: The dual goals of enhancing individual well-being and organizational effectiveness can be achieved by the application of basic psychological principles. In the examples above, principles of learning (Chapter 5) and motivation (Chapter 8) were applied. We encourage you, as you review, to look for additional links to other materials presented earlier in this book because this will help you see how the science of psychology can be applied not only to one's work, but also to one's life in general.

KEY QUESTIONS

- What are some of the things to consider when putting a team together?
- What are some causes of conflict?
- How can cooperation in teams be encouraged?

SUMMARY AND REVIEW OF KEY QUESTIONS

- **What is I/O psychology?**
  I/O psychology is the study of human cognition and behavior at work.

- **What is the "dual mission" of psychologists in this field?**
  To improve employee well-being and organizational effectiveness through research and practice.

Selection: Hiring the Best Person for the Job

- **What is job analysis?**
  A systematic assessment of the tasks, duties, and responsibilities of a job.

- **What is criterion-related validity?**
  The strength of the relationship between test scores and a criterion, such as job success.

- **What does the term "utility" refer to in the context of selection?**
  The utility of a selection test refers to its usefulness, taking into account validity as well as cost.

- **How is the fairness of a selection system determined?**
  The fairness of a selection system is determined by its adherence to laws as well as by employee perceptions.

- **What is a structured interview?**
  A structured interview is one that is conducted in the same manner, using the same questions, for all job applicants. Applicant responses are also evaluated using the same standards.

- **What is an assessment center?**
  An assessment center is a selection system consisting of a wide variety of tests and activities administered to a small group of applicants over a few days.

- **What is a work sample test?**
  A work sample test requires job applicants to perform a sample of the work, just as they would be expected to if hired.

Training: Helping Employees Acquire Relevant Skills

- **What is a needs analysis?**
  A needs analysis consists of a systematic collection of information done to identify which employees are most in need of training and what they need to be trained to do.

- **What are some examples of specific training methods?**
  On-the-job training, vestibule training, programmed instruction, behavior modeling, and role-playing are all examples of specific training methods.

- **How are training programs evaluated?**
  Training programs are evaluated using four criteria: trainee reactions, learning, behavior, and results.

Performance Appraisal: Identifying Employee Strengths and Weaknesses

- **Why is performance appraisal so important?**
  Performance appraisal is important because evaluations of employees serve to influence many important human resource decisions and practices, such as promotion and raise decisions and employee feedback.

- **What are the four major types of rating errors?**
  Leniency, severity, central tendency, and halo are the four major types of rating errors.

- **How can these errors be minimized?**
  Errors can be minimized by using good appraisal forms and training supervisors with regard to their use. Supervisors should also be aware of subtle biases and motives that may affect their ratings. In addition to having ample opportunity to observe subordinates, supervisors should also keep records because of the limits of memory.

Work Motivation: Encouraging Employees to Do Their Best

- **What are work motivation and job satisfaction?**
  Work motivation is the term used to describe the internal processes that activate, guide, and maintain behavior directed toward work. Job satisfaction is the term used to describe employees' attitudes toward their jobs.

- **What is the nature of the relationship between job satisfaction and performance?**
  Research indicates that there is a modest positive correlation between job satisfaction and performance that varies somewhat by occupational group.

- **What other behaviors do job satisfaction and dissatisfaction relate to?**
  Highly satisfied employees are more likely to engage in organizational citizenship behaviors, such as helping coworkers. Highly dissatisfied employees are more likely to engage in negative behaviors, such as absenteeism, sabotage, and theft.

- **What role does fair treatment play in creating a satisfying work environment?**
  A great deal of research supports the importance of fair treatment in creating a satisfying work environment. The negative impact of unpopular workplace practices can also be lessened by fair supervisory treatment, such as interactional fairness.

Leadership: From Supervisors to CEOs

- **What characteristics distinguish effective leaders from others?**
  Research indicates that effective business leaders are more extraverted, more open to experience, and more emotionally stable than are less effective leaders.

- **How does the work context influence leaders?**
  According to various leadership theories, the work context influences the style a leader uses, the way that decisions are made, and the nature of relationships with subordinates.

- **What are the characteristics of transformational leaders?**
  Transformational leaders are highly charismatic. They also provide intellectual stimulation to their subordinates and show genuine concern for them.

Teamwork: The Challenges of Working with Others

- **What are some of the things to consider when putting a team together?**
  The amount of diversity in a team should be based on what the group's primary purpose is. Functional diversity can often be beneficial, whereas demographic diversity is often not. Also important is to staff the team with those who are conscientious and agreeable, if possible.

- **What are some causes of conflict?**
  Conflict arises from two primary sources, the task the group is doing and the relationships among group members.

- **How can cooperation in teams be encouraged?**
  Cooperation in teams can be encouraged by training teams how to work collaboratively (e.g., communicate) and by creating reward systems that give incentives for cooperative, rather than competitive, behavior.

KEY TERMS

Assessment center, p. 547
Behavior modeling training, p. 551
Behavioral criteria, p. 552
Central tendency error, p. 555
Charisma, p. 565
Criterion-related validity, p. 545
Fairness, p. 545
Groupthink, p. 568
Halo error, p. 556
Industrial/organizational (I/O) psychology, p. 542
Job analysis, p. 544
Job satisfaction, p. 558
KSAs, p. 544

Learning criteria, p. 552
Leadership, p. 561
Leader-member exchange theory, p. 565
Leniency error, p. 554
Needs analysis, p. 549
Normative decision theory, p. 564
On-the-job training, p. 550
Organizational citizenship behaviors, p. 560
Path-goal theory, p. 564
Performance appraisal, p. 553
Position Analysis Questionnaire (PAQ), p. 544
Programmed instruction, p. 551

Reaction criteria, p. 552
Relationship conflict, p. 567
Results criteria, p. 552
Severity error, p. 554
Social loafing, p. 567
Standardized tests, p. 547
Structured interview, p. 546
Task conflict, p. 567
Transfer-of-training, p. 552
Transformational leadership, p. 565
Utility, p. 545
Vestibule training, p. 550
Work motivation, p. 558
Work sample test, p. 548

PSYCHOLOGY: UNDERSTANDING ITS FINDINGS

Developing a Work Sample Test to Select Instructors

Think of the dozens of different teachers you have had throughout your life. If you are like most people, it is easiest to think of the very best and the very worst. After years of observing, you know a great deal about this profession. With this knowledge in mind, imagine that you have been appointed to a school committee to improve the hiring of math instructors, using a work sample test. Your job is to design the work sample test and develop a method for scoring each applicant. Use the following questions to guide you through

the process of developing this assessment tool. You can answer these questions on your own or work collaboratively with one or two classmates. Ideally, you should compare your answers with someone else's to see what they may have thought of that you did not.

1. What exactly would each applicant be asked to do?
2. What behavioral dimensions would you assess?
3. Who would evaluate each applicant?
4. What important characteristics would be difficult to assess with this method?

As you also learned, any selection instrument such as this should also be examined with regard to its validity, utility, and fairness. However, what you have just done is similar to what would be done during the initial development of a work sample test. Evaluating it with regard to validity, utility, and fairness would still take additional work before it could be used.

MAKING PSYCHOLOGY PART OF YOUR LIFE

Do You Like Teamwork? Good Employees Come in All Forms

People vary considerably regarding their feelings about working on a team. For example, individuals who have a very high need for achievement often prefer to work alone (Riggio, 2000). If you are curious about your own beliefs, respond to the questionnaire below, indicating on a 1 to 7 scale the extent to which you disagree (1) or agree (7) with each statement. Then use the key at the end to tally your score. Try to respond as honestly as possible, and remember that this questionnaire only tells you about your general beliefs about working with others. It says nothing necessarily about how effective you are working in a team.

_____ 1. It is easy for me to make friends when I work as part of a group.

_____ 2. Work is more significant when it is done on an individual basis.

_____ 3. Working on projects with others provides an opportunity to make friends.

_____ 4. People work harder in a group.

_____ 5. I prefer working by myself so I can decide how a project is done.

_____ 6. I find it easier to organize my ideas when working in a group.

_____ 7. Working in groups encourages people to work less.

_____ 8. Better decisions are made when working in a group.

_____ 9. Projects are more fun to do with a group of people.

_____ 10. I manage my time better when I work with others.

Key: First reverse score numbers for questions 5 and 7, giving a 1 for a 7, a 2 for a 6, etc. After reverse scoring these two items, sum across all ten. Scores range from 10 to 70, with a higher score representing more favorable attitudes about working in groups (from Henry & Olson, 2001).

If you found yourself having difficulty responding to these questions, that can be viewed as a very positive sign. It indicates that your beliefs tend to vary based on the experiences you have had in teams. If you scored very high or very low, you may want to challenge your beliefs the next time you work in a team. Perhaps you were being influenced by one particularly good or bad experience. And remember, your attitudes about teamwork don't say anything necessarily about how good a team member you tend to be. Teamwork skills, which can be developed with training and practice, are more important than attitudes.

If you are using MyPsychLab, you have access to an electronic version of this textbook, along with dozens of valuable resources per chapter—including video and audio clips, simulations and activities, self-assessments, practice tests and other study materials. Here is a sampling of the resources available for this chapter.

WATCH

Rude Atmosphere in the Workplace

If you did not receive an access code to MyPsychLab with this text and wish to purchase access online, please visit www.MyPsychLab.com.

STUDY GUIDE

CHAPTER REVIEW

Selection: Hiring the Best Person for the Job

1. The goal of industrial/organizational psychology is to improve employee well-being and organizational effectiveness.   (True-False).

2. _____ involves an assessment of the major tasks, duties and responsibilities of a job.
   a. Reliability
   b. Criterion-related validity
   c. Human factors
   d. Job analysis

3. James applied for a job as copyeditor at a newspaper and was asked to copyedit a column as part of the interview process. This would be considered to be an example of a(n):
   a. work sample test.
   b. projectives test.
   c. unstructured interview.
   d. job analysis.

4. _____ validity is the major concern for employee selection.
   a. Content-related
   b. Empirical
   c. Criterion-related
   d. Face-related

5. A paper-and-pencil test that can predict job success is said to possess
   a. face validity.
   b. minimal validity.
   c. reliability.
   d. criterion-related validity.

6. The concept of utility involves consideration of the cost of use of a test as opposed to whether that test has criterion-related validity.   (True-False).

7. Which of the following is an issue related to the validity of a selection instrument?
   a. Whether the instrument can predict job success.
   b. Whether people perceive the instrument as having utility.
   c. The actual fairness of the selection instrument.
   d. All of the above are correct.

8. Which of the following is NOT an example of a technique used to select employees?
   a. An informal interview.
   b. Standardized instrument.
   c. A structured interview.
   d. All of the above are correct.

9. Unstructured interviews are said to have low validity because such assessments are not strongly related to subsequent job performance.   (True-False)

10. Certain standardized tests can be used to screen employees who might steal from the company.   (True-False).

11. Assessment centers
    a. are usually used to screen large numbers of job applicants.

    b. consist of a variety of standardized exercises.
    c. are inexpensive to maintain.
    d. All of the above are correct.

12. A work sample test is to employee selection as
    a. an assessment center is to employee termination.
    b. an essay is to passing a course.
    c. an audition is to becoming part of a rock band.
    d. A and B are correct.

13. A good use of a work sample test is to select an employee who is to be trained on the job.   (True-False)

Training: Helping Employees Acquire Relevant Skills

14. Training of an employee
    a. will be ongoing during their career.
    b. pays off in greater profits for the company.
    c. can involve interpersonal skills as well as specific job skills.
    d. All of the above are correct.

15. The first stage of a needs analysis involves a(n)
    a. task analysis.
    b. organizational analysis.
    c. security analysis.
    d. person analysis.

16. The focus of a person analysis is to assess the current knowledge, skills and abilities of the person who is to be trained.   (True-False)

17. Which of the following is a major disadvantage of on-the job training?
    a. On-the job training is more expensive to implement that other training methods.
    b. On-the job training does not include enough observational learning.
    c. On-the job training does not provide immediate feedback to the employee.
    d. An employee may learn the wrong things while engaged in on-the job training

18. Which of the following is considered to be a form of off-site training?
    a. Attending a seminar.
    b. Vestibule training.
    c. On-the-job training.
    d. All of the above are correct.

19. A company that wants to help employees empathize with customers might use
    a. behavior modeling training.
    b. vestibule training.
    c. a role playing exercise.
    d. programmed instruction.

20. _____ criteria ask whether employees enjoyed a training seminar, whereas _____ criteria assess what, if anything, was actually learned during the seminar.
    a. Learning;   reaction
    b. Behavioral;   results
    c. Reaction;   learning
    d. Results;   behavioral

21. A consultant hired to assess the behavioral category of training would be most interested in
    a. how well the training transfers to the job.
    b. how much the person learned during the training session.
    c. whether the bottom line was increased by the training.
    d. people's emotional feelings about the training.
22. The results criterion of training involves the final outcome of training.　(True-False)

Performance Appraisal: Identifying Employee Strengths and Weaknesses

23. Which of the following is NOT a major goal of performance appraisal?
    a. Deciding on whether to provide a company officer with additional training.
    b. Deciding which employee will receive a salary increase.
    c. Determining the effectiveness of employee training.
    d. Helping an employee to strengthen their weaker areas of performance.
24. Which of the following is a reason as to why employees may resent their annual performance appraisal?
    a. The appraisal form does not measure what they do as their job.
    b. They are being rated by a supervisor who does not know them or their performance.
    c. The process may overstate their errors and understate their accomplishments.
    d. All of the above are correct.
25. The results of a performance appraisal are rarely used to decide on employee raises.　(True-False).
26. Which of the following would be an example of a developmental aspect of performance appraisal?
    a. Using performance ratings to decide who will be promoted to a new position.
    b. Deciding whether a particular training approach works better than another approach.
    c. Providing feedback to an employee who is not doing well in some areas.
    d. Using performance ratings to decide who will receive a salary raise.
27. The tendency of a supervisor to give a performance rating that is lower than the person deserved is termed the central tendency error.　(True-False)
28. Which group below is most likely to suffer from the central tendency error?
    a. Female employees.
    b. Disabled employees.
    c. Older employees.
    d. All of the above are correct.

Work Motivation: Encouraging Employees to Do Their Best

29. Which of the following would be an example of a negative employee behavior?
    a. Theft from the company.
    b. Being absent from work.
    c. Trying to sabotage a company project.
    d. All of the above are correct.

30. Negative employee behaviors such as stealing are related to low job satisfaction.　(True-False)
31. The tendency of an employee to behave in an aggressive manner can be made worse by
    a. methamphetamine.
    b. alcohol.
    c. nicotine.
    d. caffeine.
32. Which of the following is negatively related to job satisfaction?
    a. Feeling that your supervisor has treated you unfairly.
    b. Having a job as an engineer.
    c. Having a coworker offer to help you with a task.
    d. Feeling that you have too little work to do.

Leadership: From Supervisors to CEOs

33. The trait approach to leader effectiveness focuses on personal characteristics displayed by successful leaders (True-False).
34. The capacity of a person to influence other group members toward a shared goal is termed
    a. authoritarianism.
    b. guidance counseling.
    c. charisma.
    d. leadership.
35. Which of the following personality traits are NOT related to effective leadership?
    a. Conscientiousness and agreeableness.
    b. Agreeableness and introversion.
    c. Extraversion and openness to experience.
    d. Emotional stability and conscientiousness.
36. Which of the following is true of gender differences in leadership?
    a. There are few differences in leadership effectiveness between men and women.
    b. Men are more likely than women to use a participative style of leadership.
    c. The differences in leadership style and effectiveness are quite large between men and women
    d. Women are more likely than men to use an autocratic style of leadership.
37. Men are more likely than women to use a participative style of leadership.　(True-False)
38. Martin Luther King is considered to be an example of a charismatic leader.　(True-False)

Teamwork: The Challenges of Collaborative Work

39. Which of the following is a factor that will undermine the success of a work team?
    a. Having at least one disagreeable member.
    b. Being high in demographic diversity.
    c. Having too many members.
    d. All of the above are correct.
40. Task conflict refers to workplace disagreements that involve incompatible personalities.　(True-False).

IDENTIFICATIONS
Identify the term that belongs with each of the concepts below (place the letter for the appropriate term below in front of each concept).

Identification   Concept:

_____ 1. A measure of the attitudes held by an employee about their job.

_____ 2. A measure of change on the job after training.

_____ 3. The tendency of a supervisor to give high marks to an employee beyond what they deserve.

_____ 4. In this form of training, an employee learns about their job during normal work hours at the office.

_____ 5. The tendency of a supervisor to rate every person as average.

_____ 6. The process by which a supervisor rates the strengths and weaknesses of an employee.

_____ 7. A measure of training effectiveness that focuses on how an employee feels about their training experience.

_____ 8. A change in work ethic that occurs when an employee finds themselves in a large group.

_____ 9. This is the first step taken by a training program.

_____10. The tendency of a supervisor to give high marks on all categories because a person is exceptional on one dimension.

_____11. type of selection test that requires a typist to type a page of text.

_____12. A form of leadership consisting of self-confidence, a strong vision, and enthusiasm.

_____13. The usefulness of a selection technique that considers both validity and cost of implementation.

_____14. The view that a selection test should be able to predict future success on the job.

_____15. An error in judgment committed by a group that lacks the capacity for dissent.

Identification:

a. Halo error.

b. Criterion-related validity.

c. On-the-job training.

d. Reaction criteria.

e. Social loafing.

f. Charisma.

g. Behavior criteria.

h. Work sample test.

i. Utility.

j. Job satisfaction.

k. Performance appraisal.

l. Leniency error.

m. Needs analysis.

n. Central tendency error.

o. Groupthink.

FILL IN THE BLANK

1. _____ involves an assessment of the major tasks, duties and responsibilities of a job.

2. A paper-and-pencil test that can predict job success is said to possess _____

3. Vestibule training is a form of training that is conducted _____.

4. The tendency of employees working in large groups to reduce their effort is termed _____.

5. Treating employees _____ will increase job satisfaction.

6. The personality traits of _____ and _____ are NOT related to effective leadership.

7. _____ argues that a leader should take the situation into account prior to making a decision.

8. A test with _____ is useful in predicting job success and is inexpensive to implement.

9. The _____ error refers to the tendency of a supervisor to rate every person as average.

10. Stealing is considered to be a _____.

11. _____ involves an estimation of the costs and benefits of a particular form of training a group of employees.

12. The tendency of a supervisor to give a performance rating that is lower than the person deserved is termed the _____ error.

13. An appropriate use of an _____ interview would be the study of personality.

14. The relationship between job satisfaction and happiness is strongest for an _____.

COMPREHENSIVE PRACTICE TEST

1. The job selection process involves
   a. choosing which items of information to ask of each job candidate.
   b. deciding on salary increases for each employee.
   c. deciding how to obtain information from each job candidate.
   d. A and C are correct.

2. Which of the following is involved in a job analysis?
   a. Assessing the tasks, duties and responsibilities of a job.
   b. Perusing want ads for similar jobs.
   c. Asking the company CEO to specify the job duties.
   d. Having lunch with a few former employees.

3. In the job analysis reported in the textbook, the position of "homemaker" was least similar to that of "Patrolman" and "Airport Maintenance Chief."   (True-False)

4. Hans Oaf is the personnel manager for a major company and has been told to choose an employee selection test that has the best criterion-related validity. Which of the tests below should he choose?
   a. Test A: criterion-related validity = -0.60
   b. Test B: criterion-related validity = -0.30
   c. Test V: criterion-related validity = +0.60
   d. Test Z: criterion-related validity = +0.99

5. A test with utility is useful in predicting job success and is inexpensive.   (True-False)

6. A reasonable use of an unstructured interview would be to
   a. select new employees.
   b. train new employees.
   c. provide an in-depth study of personality.
   d. make recommendations about salary raises and promotions.

7. Which of the following is a key aspect of a standardized employee selection test?
   a. The test must be available on the internet.
   b. The test must be used as the final basis for choosing an employee.
   c. The test must be reliable and valid.
   d. All of the above are correct.

8. Which of the following DO NOT belong together?
   a. assessment center;   used to initially screen employees
   b. work sample;   an audition for a job
   c. standardized test;   good reliability and validity
   d. unstructured interview;   useful for learning about personality
9. Vestibule training is a form of _____ training in which _____.
   a. on-site;   trainees practice their skills in a separate work area
   b. off-site;   trainees observe other employees on the job
   c. on-site;   trainees fill out job task surveys
   d. off-site;   employers determine the requirements of the job
10. The study conducted at Kodak revealed that trainees learned more when information was provided in an interesting format as opposed to a straight lecture format. (True-False)
11. The tendency of a supervisor to give a performance rating that is lower than the person deserved is known as the _____ error.
   a. central tendency.
   b. leniency
   c. severity
   d. fundamental attribution
12. The link between job satisfaction and happiness is strongest for a(n) _____ and weakest for a(n) _____.
   a. nurse;   engineer
   b. engineer;   physician
   c. physician;   engineer
   d. scientist;   nurse
13. A key factor in creating a satisfying work environment is related to
   a. having access to many perks and benefits.
   b. whether the company provides "flex-time."
   c. being treated in a fair manner.
   d. whether the company is friendly toward families.
14. The most effective leaders are usually noted to be more outgoing and more intelligent than their followers. (True-False).
15. The key characteristic of transformational leadership is
   a. dogma.
   b. charisma.
   c. vision.
   d. social concern.
16. Highly diverse teams are likely to
   a. show decreases in creativity.
   b. show reduced work motivation.
   c. be low in job satisfaction.
   d. show a boost in creativity.

CRITICAL THINKING
1. Explain why perceived fairness is a critical aspect of job satisfaction.
2. Describe what is meant by transformational leadership and explain three ways in which you might strive toward this form of leadership.

Glossary

Absolute threshold (p. 75): The smallest amount of a stimulus that we can detect 50 percent of the time.

Accommodation (p. 253): In Piaget's theory of cognitive development, modifications in existing knowledge structures (schemas) as a result of exposure to new information or experiences.

Achievement motivation (p. 312): The desire to accomplish difficult tasks and meet standards of excellence.

Acquired immune deficiency syndrome (AIDS) (p. 409): A viral infection that reduces the immune system's ability to defend itself against the introduction of any foreign matter.

Acquisition (p. 162): The process by which a conditioned stimulus acquires the ability to elicit a conditioned response through repeated pairings of an unconditioned stimulus with a conditioned stimulus.

Action potential (p. 42): A rapid shift in the electrical charge across the cell membrane of neurons. This disturbance along the membrane communicates information within neurons.

Acuity (p. 80): The visual ability to see fine details.

Adolescence (p. 274): A period beginning with the onset of puberty and ending when individuals assume adult roles and responsibilities.

Affect (p. 315): Temporary and relatively mild shifts in current feelings and mood.

Agonist (p. 45): A chemical substance that facilitates the action of a neurotransmitter at a receptor site.

Agoraphobia (p. 444): Intense fear of specific situations in which individuals suspect that help will not be available should they experience an incapacitating or embarrassing event.

Agreeableness (p. 351): One of the "big five" dimensions of personality; a dimension ranging from good-natured, cooperative, and trusting on one end, to irritable, suspicious, uncooperative at the other.

Alpha waves (p. 133): Rapid, low-amplitude brain waves that occur when individuals are awake but relaxed.

Alzheimer's disease (p. 219): An illness primarily afflicting individuals over the age of sixty-five involving severe mental deterioration, including severe amnesia.

Amnesia (p. 217): Loss of memory stemming from illness, accident, drug abuse, or medical operation.

Amphetamines (p. 147): Drugs that act as stimulants, increasing feelings of energy and activation.

Amygdala (p. 50): A limbic system structure involved in aspects of emotional control and formation of emotional memories.

Anal stage (p. 343): In Freud's theory, a psychosexual stage of development in which pleasure is focused primarily on the anal zone.

Anorexia nervosa (p. 435): An eating disorder involving intense fears of gaining weight coupled with refusal to maintain normal body weight.

Antagonist (p. 45): A chemical substance that inhibits the impact of a neurotransmitter at a receptor site.

Anterograde amnesia (p. 218): The inability to store in long-term memory information that occurs after an amnesia-inducing event.

Antisocial personality disorder (p. 453): A personality disorder involving deceitfulness, impulsivity, callous disregard for the safety or welfare of others, and a total lack of remorse for actions that harm others.

Anxiety disorders (p. 443): Psychological disorders taking several different forms, but which are all related to a generalized feeling of anxiety.

Anxiety (p. 345, 443): Increased arousal accompanied by generalized feelings of fear or apprehension.

Apnea (p. 136): A sleep disorder in which sleepers stop breathing several times each night, and thus wake up.

Archetypes (p. 345): According to Jung, inherited images in the collective unconscious that shape our perceptions of the external world.

Assessment center (p. 547): A selection technique that consists of a wide variety of tests and activities administered to a small group of job applicants over a few days.

Assessment (p. 429): Efforts by psychologists or other professionals to gather information on the problems individuals are experiencing. Psychologists conduct interviews in which they seek information about individuals' past and present behaviors, current problems, interpersonal relations, and personality.

Assimilation (p. 253): In Piaget's theory of cognitive development, incorporation of new information into existing mental frameworks (schemas).

Attachment (p. 266): A strong affectional bond between infants and their caregivers.

Attention-deficit/hyperactivity disorder (ADHD) (p. 434): A childhood mental disorder in which children simply can't pay attention (inattention), show hyperactivity or impulsivity, or both of these symptoms.

Attitudes (p. 514): Lasting evaluations of various aspects of the social world that are stored in memory.

Attribution (p. 508): The processes through which people seek to determine the causes behind others' behavior.

Autistic disorder (p. 437): A serious childhood mental disorder involving major impairments in establishing social interactions with others, nonexistent or poor language skills, and stereotyped, repetitive patterns of behavior or interests.

Autobiographical memory (p. 212): Memory for information about events in our own lives.

Automatic processing (p. 128): Processing of information without minimal conscious awareness.

Autonomic nervous system (p. 46): Part of the peripheral nervous system that connects internal organs, glands, and involuntary muscles to the central nervous system.

Availability Heuristic (p. 17, 227): A mental shortcut suggesting that the easier it is to bring something to mind, the more frequent or important it is.

Axon terminals (p. 42): Structures at the end of axons that contain transmitter substances.

Axon (p. 41): The part of the neuron that conducts action potentials away from the cell body.

Backward conditioning (p. 163): A type of conditioning in which the presentation of the unconditioned stimulus (UCS) precedes the presentation of the conditioned stimulus (CS).

Barbiturates (p. 147): Drugs that act as depressants, reducing activity in the nervous system and behavior output.

Basic anxiety (p. 345): Children's fear of being left alone, helpless and insecure.

Behavior modeling training (p. 551): A training technique that applies principles of observational learning.

Behavior therapies (p. 475): Therapies based on the belief that many mental disorders stem from faulty learning.

Behavioral activation system (BAS) (p. 359): The neural system that controls the anticipation and experience of positive experiences.

Behavioral criteria (p. 552): A measure of training effectiveness that examines the degree of behavior change on the job.

Behavioral inhibition system (BIS) (p. 359): The neural system that monitors and controls our avoidance of negative experiences.

Behaviorism (p. 5): The view that only observable, overt activities that can be measured scientifically should be studied by psychology.

Binocular cues (p. 111): Cues to depth or distance resulting from having two eyes.

Biological constraints on learning (p. 166): Refers to how all forms of conditioning are not equally easy to establish with all organisms.

Biological rhythms (p. 123): Cyclic changes in bodily processes.

Biological sex (p. 271): Whether an individual is, biologically speaking, a male or a female.

Bipolar disorder (p. 439): A mood disorder in which individuals experience very wide swings in mood, from deep depression to wild elation.

Bisexual (p. 311): A sexual orientation in which individuals engage in sexual relations with members of both sexes.

Blind spot (p. 80): The point in the back of the retina through which the optic nerve exits the eye. This exit point contains no rods or cones, and is therefore insensitive to light.

Body language (p. 321): Nonverbal cues involving body posture or movement of body parts.

Boomerang Children (p. 285): Young adults who live at home with their parents, often after first attempting to live alone.

Bottom-up approach (p. 110): Suggests that our ability to recognize specific patterns, such as letters of the alphabet or objects, is based on simpler capacities to recognize and correctly combine lower-level features of objects, such as lines, edges, corners, and angles.

Brightness constancy (p. 106): The tendency to perceive objects as having a constant brightness when they are viewed under different conditions of illumination.

Brightness (p. 80): The physical intensity of light.

Broca's area (p. 59): A region in the prefrontal cortex that plays a role in the production of speech.

Bulimia nervosa (p. 435): An eating disorder in which individuals engage in recurrent episodes of binge eating followed by some form of purging.

Cancer (p. 402): A group of illnesses in which abnormal cells are formed that are able to proliferate, invade, and overwhelm normal tissues, and to spread to distant sites in the body.

Cannon–Bard theory (p. 316): A theory of emotion suggesting that various emotion-provoking events simultaneously produce subjective reactions labeled as emotions and physiological arousal.

Carcinogens (p. 403): Cancer producing agents in our environment.

Cardiovascular disease (p. 397): All diseases of the heart and blood vessels.

Case Method (p. 20): A method of research in which detailed information about individuals is used to develop general principles about behavior.

Cataplexy (p. 136): A symptom of narcolepsy (a sleep disorder) in which individuals fall down suddenly.

Catatonic type (p. 456): A dramatic type of schizophrenia in which individuals show marked disturbances in motor behavior. Many alternate between total immobility and wild, excited behavior in which they rush madly about.

Central nervous system (p. 45): The brain and the spinal cord.

Central route (to persuasion) (p. 515): Persuasion that occurs through careful consideration of message content.

Central tendency error (p. 555): An error that represents ratings that hover around average.

Cerebellum (p. 50): A part of the brain concerned with the regulation of basic motor activities.

Cerebral cortex (p. 50): The outer covering of the cerebral hemispheres.

Chaining (p. 174): A procedure that establishes a sequence of responses that lead to a reward following the terminal or final response in the chain.

Charisma (p. 565): A characteristic of transformational leaders that consists of having high self-confidence, a strong vision, enthusiasm, and eloquence. Leaders with charisma also set very high standards for followers.

Childhood (p. 246): The years between birth and adolescence.

Chromosomes (p. 61): Threadlike structures containing genetic material, found in nearly every cell of the body.

Chunking (p. 203): Combining separate items in some way.

Circadian rhythms (p. 123): Cyclic changes in bodily processes occurring within a single day.

Classical conditioning (p. 161): A basic form of learning in which one stimulus comes to serve as a signal for the occurrence of a second stimulus. During classical conditioning, organisms acquire information about the relations between various stimuli, not simple associations between them.

Client-centered therapy (p. 473): A form of humanistic therapy developed by Rogers.

Climacteric (p. 280): A period during which the functioning of the reproductive system and various aspects of sexual activity change greatly.

Cocaine (p. 147): A powerful stimulant that produces pleasurable sensations of increased energy and self-confidence.

Cochlea (p. 87): A portion of the inner ear containing the sensory receptors for sound.

Cocktail party phenomenon (p. 101): The effect of not being aware of other people's conversations until something of personal importance, such as hearing one's name, is mentioned and then suddenly hearing it.

Cognition (p. 200): The mental activities associated with thought, decision making, language, and other higher mental processes.

Cognitive development (p. 253): Changes in cognitive abilities and functioning.

Cognitive dissonance (p. 517): The state experienced by individuals when they discover inconsistency between two attitudes they hold or between their attitudes and their behavior.

Cognitive restructuring (p. 420): A method of modifying self-talk in stress-producing situations. Clients are trained to monitor what they say to themselves in stress-provoking situations and then to modify their cognitions in adaptive ways.

Cognitive therapies (p. 477): Therapies based on the belief that many mental disorders stem from faulty or distorted modes of thought.

Cognitive-behavioral therapy (p. 478): A cognitive-behavioral therapy for alleviating depression. Beck, who proposed the therapy, assumes that depressed individuals engage in illogical thinking, and that this underlies their difficulties. They hold unrealistically negative beliefs and assumptions about themselves, the future, and the world.

Collective unconscious (p. 345): In Jung's theory, a portion of the unconscious shared by all humans.

Companionate love (p. 531): A form of love involving a high degree of commitment and deep concern with the well-being of the beloved.

Complex cells (p. 85): Neurons in the visual cortex that respond to stimuli that move in a particular direction and that have a particular orientation.

Compliance (p. 525): A form of social influence in which one or more people attempts to influence one or more others through direct requests.

Concepts (p. 206): Mental categories for objects or events that are similar to one another in certain respects.

Concrete operations (p. 254): A stage in Piaget's theory of cognitive development occurring roughly between the ages of seven and eleven. It is at this stage that children become aware of the permanence of objects.

Conditioned response (CR) (p. 162): In classical conditioning, the response to the conditioned stimulus.

Conditioned stimulus (CS) (p. 162): In classical conditioning, the stimulus that is repeatedly paired with an unconditioned stimulus.

Conditioned taste aversion (p. 167): A type of conditioning in which the UCS (usually internal cues associated with nausea or vomiting) occurs several hours after the CS (often a novel food) leading to a strong CS-UCS association in a single trial.

Cones (p. 80): Sensory receptors in the eye that play a crucial role in sensations of color.

Confirmation bias (p. 17, 223): The tendency to pay attention primarily to information that confirms existing views or beliefs.

Confluence approach (p. 234): An approach suggesting that for creativity to occur, multiple components must converge.

Confounded (Confounding) (p. 26): Occurs when factors other than the independent variable in an experiment are permitted to vary across experimental conditions. When confounding occurs, it is impossible to determine whether changes in a dependent variable stem from the effects of the independent variable or from other, confounding variables.

Conscientiousness (p. 352): One of the "big five" dimensions of personality; a dimension ranging from well-organized, careful, and responsible on the one end, to disorganized, careless, and unscrupulous at the other.

Consensus (p. 509): Information regarding the extent to which behavior by one person is shown by others as well.

Conservation (p. 254): Understanding of the fact that certain physical attributes of an object remain unchanged, even though its outward appearance changes.

Consistency (p. 509): Information regarding the extent to which a specific person shows similar behavior to a given stimulus across time.

Constancies (p. 106): Our tendency to perceive physical objects as unchanging, despite shifts in the pattern of sensations these objects induce.

Contact hypothesis (p. 522): The view that prejudice can be reduced by increasing the degree of contact between different groups.

Content validity (p. 366): The extent to which items on a test are related in a straightforward way to the characteristic the test aims to measure.

Context-dependent memory (p. 205): Refers to how information entered into memory in one context or setting is easier to recall in that context than it is in others.

Continuous reinforcement schedule (p. 176): A schedule of reinforcement in which every occurrence of a particular behavior is reinforced.

Controlled processing (p. 128): Processing of information involving relatively high levels of conscious awareness.

Conventional level (of morality) (p. 263): According to Kohlberg, a stage of moral development during which individuals judge morality largely in terms of existing social norms or rules.

Conversion disorder (p. 450): A somatoform disorder in which individuals experience actual physical impairment such as blindness, deafness, or paralysis for which there is no underlying medical cause.

Cornea (p. 80): The curved, transparent layer through which light rays enter the eye.

Corpus callosum (p. 52): A band of nerve fibers connecting the two hemispheres of the brain.

Correlational Method of Research (p. 22): A method in which researchers attempt to determine whether, and to what extent, different variables are related to each other.

Correspondence bias (*fundamental attribution error*) (p. 510): The tendency to attribute behavior to internal causes to a greater extent than is actually justified.

Counterfactual thinking (p. 512): The tendency to evaluate events by thinking about alternative to them (i.e., "What might have been").

Crack (p. 148): A derivative of cocaine that can be smoked. It acts as a powerful stimulant.

Creativity (p. 231): The ability to produce work that is both novel (original, unexpected) and appropriate (it works—it is useful or meets task constraints).

Criterion-related validity (p. 366, 543): The extent to which scores on a test are related to behaviors (criteria) relevant to the characteristics the test purports to measure.

Critical Thinking (p. 19): Thinking that is purposeful, reasoned, and goal-directed—the kind of thinking involved in solving problems, formulating inferences when the thinker is using skills that are thoughtful and effective for the particular context.

Cross-tolerance (p. 145): Increased tolerance for one drug that develops as a result of taking another drug.

Cultural bias (p. 373): The tendency of items on a test of intelligence to require specific cultural experience or knowledge.

Curse of knowledge (p. 257): Refers to how we tend to be biased by our own knowledge when judging the perspective of people who know less about some topic than we do.

Dark adaptation (p. 81): The process through which our visual system increases its sensitivity to light under low levels of illumination.

Decision making (p. 225): The process of choosing among various courses of action or alternatives.

Delay conditioning (p. 162): A form of forward conditioning in which the onset of the unconditioned stimulus (UCS) begins while the conditioned stimulus (CS) is still present.

Delta activity (p. 133): High amplitude, slow brain waves (3.5 Hz or less) that occur during several stages of sleep, but especially during stage 4.

Delusions (p. 455): Firmly held beliefs that have no basis in reality.

Dendrite (p. 41): The part of the neuron that conducts action potentials toward the cell body.

Dependent Variable (p. 25): The variable that is measured in an experiment.

Depressants (p. 146): Drugs that reduce activity in the nervous system and therefore slow many bodily and cognitive processes. Depressants include alcohol and barbiturates.

Depression (p. 438): A mood disorder in which individuals experience extreme unhappiness, lack of energy, and several related symptoms.

Diagnosis (p. 429): Identification of the specific problems (mental disturbances) currently being experienced by individuals.

***Diagnostic and Statistical Manual of Mental Disorders-IV-TR* (p. 429):** A manual designed to help all mental health practitioners to recognize and correctly identify (diagnose) specific disorders.

Diathesis-stress model (p. 458): A model suggesting that genetic factors may predispose individuals to develop schizophrenia, but this disorder will develop only if they are exposed to certain kinds of stressful environmental conditions.

Difference threshold (p. 76): The amount by which two stimuli must differ in order to be just noticeably different.

Dimensional approach (p. 431): An approach to diagnosing mental disorders in which individuals are not simply assigned to specific categories, but rather are rated in many different dimensions, each relevant to a specific mental disorder.

Discriminative stimulus (p. 179): Signals the availability of reinforcement if a specific response is made.

Disruptive behaviors (p. 433): Childhood mental disorders involving poor control of impulses, conflict with other children and adults, and, in some cases, more serious forms of antisocial behavior.

Dissociated control, theory (p. 142): A theory suggesting that hypnotism weakens control by the central function over other cognitive and behavioral subsystems, thus permitting these subsystems to be invoked directly by the hypnotist's suggestions.

Dissociative amnesia (p. 448): Profound amnesia stemming from the active motivation to forget specific events or information.

Dissociative disorders (p. 448): Disorders involving prolonged loss of memory or identity.

Dissociative fugue (p. 448): A sudden and extreme disturbance of memory in which individuals wander off, adopt a new identity, and are unable to recall their own past.

Dissociative identity disorder (p. 448): A condition labeled as *multiple personality disorder* in the past, in which a single person seems to possess two or more distinct identities or personality states, and these take control of the person's behavior at different times.

Distinctiveness (p. 509): Information regarding the extent to which a given person reacts in the same manner to different stimuli or situations.

Door-in-the-face technique (p. 526): A technique for gaining compliance in which a large request is followed by a smaller one.

Dreams of absent-minded transgression (p. 138): Dreams in which people attempting to give up the use of tobacco, alcohol, or other drugs see themselves slipping into the use of these substances in an absentminded or careless manner.

Dreams (p. 137): Cognitive events, often vivid but disconnected, that occur during sleep. Most dreams take place during REM sleep.

Drive theory (p. 300): A theory of motivation suggesting that behavior is "pushed" from within by drives stemming from basic biological needs.

Drug abuse (p. 146): Instances in which individuals take drugs purely to change their moods, and in which they experienced impaired behavior or social functioning as a result of doing so.

Drugs (p. 145): Compounds or substances that because of their chemical structure, change the functioning of biological systems.

Ego (p. 342): In Freud's theory, the part of personality that takes account of external reality in the expression of instinctive sexual and aggressive urges.

Egocentrism (p. 254): The inability of young children to distinguish their own.

Elaboration-likelihood model (ELM) (p. 516): A cognitive model of persuasion suggesting that persuasion can occur through distinct routes.

Electro convulsive therapy (ECT) (p. 489): A from of biological therapy in which electroders are placed on a patients temples and story electric shocks are then delivered to the brain.

Electroencephalogram (EEG) (p. 132): A record of electrical activity within the brain. EEGs play an important role in the scientific study of sleep.

Electromyogram (EMG) (p. 133): A record of electrical activity in various muscles.

Embryo (p. 246): The developing child during the first eight weeks of life.

Emotional development (p. 270): Changes in the experience or expression of emotions throughout the life span.

Emotional intelligence (p. 373): Abilities relating to the emotional side of life—abilities such as perceiving, using, understanding, and managing one's own emotions, as well as the emotions of others.

Emotional stability (p. 352): One of the "big five" dimensions of personality; a dimension ranging from poised, calm, and composed at one extreme, to nervous, anxious, and excitable at the other.

Employee assistance programs (p. 486): Programs established by companies to help employees cope with personal problems, including mental disorders.

Encoding specificity principle (p. 205): Retrieval of information is successful to the extent that the retrieval cues match the cues the learner used during the study phase.

Encoding (p. 201): The process through which information is converted into a form.

Endocrine system (p. 47): A system for communication within our bodies; it consists of several glands that secrete hormones directly into the bloodstream.

Episodic memory (p. 204): Memory for factual information that we acquired at a specific time.

Escalation of commitment (p. 229): The tendency to become increasingly committed to bad decisions even as losses associated with them increase.

Evolutionary psychology (p. 12, 63): A new field of psychology, suggesting that as a result of evolution, humans now possess a large number of evolved psychological mechanisms that help (or once helped) us deal with important problems relating to survival.

Expectancy theory (p. 301): A theory of motivation suggesting that behavior is "pulled" by expectations of desirable outcomes.

Experimentation (the experimental method of research) (p. 24): A method in which researchers systematically alter one or more variables to determine whether such changes influence some aspect of behavior.

Expressed emotion (p. 485): A summary term for conditions existing in some families involving excessive criticism, hostility, and emotional overinvolvement. High levels of expressed emotion increase the chances of relapse among people recovering from serious mental disorders.

Externals (p. 354): Individuals who believe that they have little control over the outcomes they experience.

Extinction (p. 164): The process through which a conditioned stimulus gradually loses the ability to evoke conditioned responses when it is no longer followed by the unconditioned stimulus.

Extrasensory perception (ESP) (p. 112): Perception without a basis in sensory input.

Extraversion (p. 351): One of the "big five" dimensions of personality; a dimension ranging from sociable, talking, and fun-loving at one end, to sober, reserved, and cautious at the other.

Extroverts (p. 345): In Jung's theory, individuals who are open and confident and make friends readily.

Eyewitness testimony (p. 211): Information provided by witnesses to crimes or accidents.

Facial feedback hypothesis (p. 316): A hypothesis indicating that facial expressions can produce changes in emotional states.

Fairness (p. 543): The legality of the selection system (i.e., whether it is consistent with current employment laws) as well as its perceived fairness to job applicants.

Family Therapy (p. 484): Therapy designed to change the relationships among family members in constructive ways.

Farsightedness (p. 81): A condition in which the visual image entering our eye is focused behind, rather than directly on, the retina. Therefore, close objects appear out of focus, while distant objects are in clear focus.

Feature detectors (p. 85): Neurons at various levels within the visual system that respond primarily to stimuli possessing certain features in the visual cortex.

Feeding and eating disorders (p. 435): Disturbances in eating behavior that involve maladaptive and unhealthy efforts to control body weight.

Fetal alcohol syndrome (p. 248): A disorder found in newborns whose mothers have consumed large amounts of alcohol during pregnancy.

Fetus (p. 246): The developing child during the last seven months of pregnancy.

Figure-ground relationship (p. 102): Our tendency to divide the perceptual world into two distinct parts—discrete figures and the background against which they stand out.

Fixation (p. 342): Excessive investment of psychic energy in a particular stage of psychosexual development. This results in various types of psychological disorders.

Fixed-interval schedule (p. 177): A schedule of reinforcement in which a specific interval of time must elapse before a response will yield reinforcement.

Fixed-ratio schedule (p. 178): A schedule of reinforcement in which reinforcement occurs only after a fixed number of responses have been emitted.

Foot-in-the-door technique (p. 525): A technique for gaining compliance in which requesters start with a small request and then, after this is granted, shift to a much larger request.

Formal operations (stage of) (p. 255): In Piaget's theory, the final stage of cognitive development.

Fovea (p. 80): The area in the center of the retina in which cones are highly concentrated.

Framing (p. 228): Presentation of information concerning potential outcomes in terms of gains or in terms of losses.

Frequency of exposure effect (p. 528): The more frequently we are exposed to a given stimulus, the more—in general—we tend to like it.

Frequency theory (p. 90): A theory of pitch perception suggesting that sounds of different frequencies (heard as differences in pitch) induce different rates of neural activity in the hair cells of the inner ear.

Freudian slips (p. 342): Statements that seem to be simple errors in speech, but that in fact reveal unconscious thoughts or impulses.

Friendships (p. 270): Mutual dyad relationships between children involving strong affective ties.

Frontal lobe (p. 51): The portion of the cerebral cortex that lies in front of the central fissure.

Fully functioning persons (p. 348): In Rogers's theory, psychologically healthy people who enjoy life to the fullest.

Functional fixedness (p. 233): The tendency to think of using objects only as they have been used in the past.

Gate-control theory (p. 93): A theory of pain suggesting that the spinal cord contains a mechanism that can block transmission of pain to the brain.

Gender consistency (p. 271): Children's understanding that their gender will not change even if they adopted the behavior, dress, and hairstyles of the other gender.

Gender identity disorder (p. 451): A disorder in which individuals believe that they were born with the wrong sexual identity.

Gender identity (p. 271): Children's understanding of the fact that they are male or female.

Gender roles (p. 271): Beliefs about how males and females are expected to behave in many situations.

Gender schema theory (p. 274): A theory indicating that children develop a cognitive framework reflecting the beliefs of their society concerning the characteristics and roles of males and females. This *gender schema* then strongly affects the processing of new social information.

Gender stability (p. 271): Children's understanding that gender is stable over time.

Gender stereotypes (p. 271): Cultural beliefs about differences between women and men.

Gender (p. 271): A society's beliefs about the traits and behavior of males and females.

General adaptation syndrome (GAS) (p. 389): A profile of how organisms respond to stress; it consists of three phases: a nonspecific mobilization phase that promotes sympathetic nervous system activity; a resistance phase, during which the organism makes efforts to cope with the threat; and an exhaustion phase, which occurs if the organism fails to overcome the threat and depletes its coping resources.

Genes (p. 61): Biological "blueprints" that shape development and all basic bodily processes.

Genital stage (p. 343): The final stage of psychosexual development—one in which individuals acquire the adult capacity to combine lust with affection.

Gestalt psychologists (p. 102): German psychologists intrigued by our tendency to perceive sensory patterns as well-organized wholes, rather than as separate isolated parts.

Gestalt therapy (p. 474): According to Fritz Perls (1969), originator of this type of therapy, many people have difficulties in directly experiencing and expressing emotions, such as anger or the need for love. As a result, they develop manipulative social games or phony roles to try to satisfy—usually without success—their needs indirectly.

Gestures (p. 321): Movements of various body parts that convey a specific meaning to others.

Goal-setting theory (p. 302): The view that motivation can be strongly influenced by goals.

Gonads (p. 308): The primary sex glands.

Groupthink (p. 568): Serious errors in group decision making that result from a lack of dissent in the group.

Hallucinations (p. 455): Vivid sensory experiences that have no basis in physical reality.

Hallucinogens (p. 149): Drugs that profoundly alter consciousness (e.g., marijuana, LSD).

Halo Error (p. 556): A rating error that represents a tendency to evaluate particular subordinates as "angels" based on their exceptional performance along one dimension.

Hassles (p. 393): Annoying minor events of everyday life that cumulatively can affect psychological well-being.

Health belief model (p. 399): A theory of health behaviors; the model predicts that whether a person practices a particular health behavior can be understood by knowing the degree to which the person perceives a personal health threat and the perception that a particular health practice will be effective in reducing that threat.

Health psychology (p. 386): The study of the relation between psychological variables and health, which reflects the view that both mind and body are important determinants of health and illness.

Heredity (p. 60): Biologically determined characteristics passed from parents to their offspring.

Heritability (p. 63, 370): The proportion of the variance in any trait within a given population that is attributable to genetic factors.

Heterosexual (p. 311): A sexual orientation in which individuals prefer sexual relations with members of the other sex.

Heuristic processing (p. 515): Involves the use of simple rules of thumb or mental shortcuts.

Heuristics (p. 227): Mental rules of thumb that permit us to make decisions and judgments in a rapid and efficient manner.

Hierarchy of needs (p. 303): In Maslow's theory of motivation, an arrangement of needs from the most basic to those at the highest levels.

Hindsight bias (p. 223): The tendency to assume that we would have been better at predicting actual events than is really true.

Hippocampus (p. 50): A structure of the limbic system that plays a role in the formation of certain types of memories.

Homeostasis (p. 300): A state of physiological balance within the body.

Homosexual (p. 311): A sexual orientation in which individuals prefer sexual relations with members of their own sex.

Hormones (p. 47): Substances secreted by endocrine glands that regulate a wide range of bodily processes.

Hue (p. 80): The color that we experience due to the dominant wavelength of light energy.

Humanistic theories (p. 345): Theories of personality emphasizing personality responsibility and innate tendencies toward personal growth.

Hunger motivation (p. 304): The motivation to obtain and consume food.

Hypercomplex cells (p. 85): Neurons in the visual cortex that respond to complex aspects of visual stimuli, such as width, length, and shape.

Hypertension (p. 412): A condition in which the pressure within the blood vessels is abnormally high.

Hypnosis (p. 140): An interaction between two people in which one (the hypnotist) induces changes in the behavior, feelings, or cognitions of the other (the subject) through suggestions. Hypnosis involves expectations on the part of subjects and their attempts to conform to social roles (e.g., the role of the hypnotized person).

Hypochondriasis (p. 449): A disorder involving preoccupation with fears of disease or illness.

Hypohedonia (p. 180): A genetically inherited impairment in the ability to experience pleasure.

Hypothalamus (p. 50): A small structure deep within the brain that plays a key role in the regulation of the autonomic nervous system and of several forms of motivated behavior, such as eating and aggression.

Hypothesis (p. 23): A testable prediction derived from a theory.

Hypothetico-deductive reasoning (p. 255): A type of reasoning first shown by individuals during the stage of formal operations. It involves formulating a general theory and deducing specific hypotheses from it.

Id (p. 342): In Freud's theory, the portion of personality concerned with immediate gratification of primitive needs.

Illusions (p. 107): Instances in which perception yields false interpretations of physical reality.

Images (p. 224): Mental "pictures" of the external world.

Inattentional blindness (p. 103): The inability to perceive features in a visual scene if they are not being attended to.

Incentives (p. 301): Rewards individuals seek to attain.

Independent Variable (p. 25): The variable that is systematically changed in an experiment.

Individual differences perspective (p. 338): The approach to psychology that focuses on how individuals differ from one another.

Induced (forced) compliance (p. 517): A technique for changing attitudes in which individuals are somehow induced to state positions different from their actual views.

Industrial/organizational (I/O) psychology (p. 542): The study of human cognition and behavior at work.

Infantile amnesia (p. 213): Our supposed inability to remember experiences during the first two or three years of life.

Information-processing approach (p. 201): An approach to human memory that emphasizes the encoding, storage, and later retrieval of information.

Information-processing perspective (of cognitive development) (p. 258): A perspective emphasizing the importance of information processing in cognitive development.

Ingratiation (p. 526): A technique of social influence based on inducing increased liking in the target people before influence is attempted.

Insecure/ambivalent attachment (p. 267): A pattern of attachment in which children seek contact with the caregiver before separation but then, after this person returns, first seeks this person but then resists or rejects his or her offers of comfort.

Insecure/avoidant attachment (p. 267): A pattern of attachment in which children don't cry when their caregiver leaves in the *strange situation* test, and are slow to greet their caregiver when this person returns.

Insomnias (p. 135): Disorders involving the inability to fall asleep or maintain sleep once it is attained.

Intelligence (p. 361): Individuals' abilities to understand complex ideas, adapt effectively to the environment, learn from experience, engage in various forms of reasoning, overcome obstacles by careful thought.

Internals (p. 354): Individuals who believe that they exert considerable control over the outcomes they experience.

Interpersonal attraction (p. 528): The extent to which we like or dislike other people.

Intrinsic motivation (p. 313): Motivation to perform activities because they are rewarding in and of themselves.

Introverts (p. 345): In Jung's theory, individuals who are hesitant and cautious and do not make friends easily.

Intuition (p. 129): Refers to cognitive events and processes of which we are not fully aware and that we cannot readily describe in words.

IQ (p. 364): Originally, "intelligent quotient," a number that examiners derived by dividing an individual's mental age by his or her chronological age and multiplying it by 100. Now IQ simply indicates an individual's performance on an intelligence test relative to those of other people.

Iris (p. 80): The colored part of the eye that adjusts the amount of light that enters by constricting or dilating the pupil.

James–Lange theory (p. 316): A theory of emotion suggesting that emotion-provoking events produce various physiological reactions, and that recognition of these is responsible for subjective emotional experiences.

Job analysis (p. 544): An assessment of the tasks, duties, and responsibilities of a particular job.

Job satisfaction (p. 558): Employees' attitudes about various aspects of their jobs.

Just noticeable difference (jnd) (p. 76): The amount of change in a physical stimulus necessary for an individual to notice a difference in the intensity of a stimulus.

Kinesthesia (p. 99): The sense that gives us information about the location of our body parts with respect to one another and allows us to perform movement.

Korsakoff's syndrome (p. 219): An illness caused by long-term abuse of alcohol that often involves profound retrograde amnesia.

KSAs (p. 542): Abbreviation for the knowledge, skills, and abilities needed to perform a particular job.

Language (p. 259): The system we use to communicate information to others through the use of specific symbols (words, gestures), and the rules for combining them.

Latency stage (p. 343): In Freud's theory, the psychosexual stage of development that follows resolution of the Oedipus complex. During this stage, sexual desires are relatively weak.

Laws of grouping (p. 104): Simple principles that describe how we tend to group discrete stimuli together in the perceptual world.

Leader-member exchange theory (p. 565): A theory of leadership that describes the distinct relationships that leaders form with each subordinate.

Leadership (p. 561): The process by which one member of a group (its leader) influences other group members toward attainment of shared group goals.

Learned helplessness (p. 180, 440): Feelings of helplessness that develop after exposure to situations in which no effort succeeds in affecting outcomes.

Learning criteria (p. 552): A measure of training effectiveness that examines the degree of learning that occurred as a result of training.

Learning (p. 160): Any relatively permanent change in behavior (or behavior potential) resulting from experience.

Leniency error (p. 554): The tendency for a supervisor to give employees ratings that are higher than their performance merits.

Lens (p. 80): A curved structure behind the pupil that bends light rays, focusing them on the retina.

Less-leads-to-more effect (p. 517): Refers to the fact that rewards just barely sufficient to induce individuals to state positions contrary to their own views often generate more attitude change than larger rewards.

Libido (p. 342): According to Freud, the psychic energy that powers all mental activity.

Lifestyle (p. 386): In the context of health psychology, the overall pattern of decisions and behaviors that determine health and quality of life.

Limbic system (p. 50): Several structures deep within the brain that play a role in emotional reactions and behavior.

Localization (p. 90): The ability of our auditory system to determine the direction of a sound source.

Locus coeruleus (LC) (p. 445): A portion of the brainstem that appears to play a key role in panic experiences.

Logical concepts (p. 224): Concepts that can be clearly defined by a set of rules or properties.

Long-term memory (p. 203): A memory system for the retention of large amounts of information over long periods of time.

Love (p. 531): An intense emotional state involving attraction, sexual desire, and deep concern for another person.

LSD (p. 149): A powerful hallucinogen that produces profound shifts in perception; many of these are frightening in nature.

Magnetic resonance imaging (MRI) (p. 55): A method to study the intact brain in which images are obtained by exposing the brain to a strong magnetic field.

Maximizing (p. 225): A strategy for reaching decisions in which every possible alternative is considered to choose the one that is best.

Medulla (p. 49): A structure in the brain concerned with the regulation of vital bodily functions, such as breathing and heartbeat.

Memory (p. 200): Our cognitive system(s) for storing and retrieving information.

Menopause (p. 280): A cessation of the menstrual cycle.

Mental disorders (p. 428): Disturbances of an individual's behavioral or psychological functioning that are not culturally accepted and that lead to psychological distress, behavioral disability, or impaired overall functioning

Mentor (p. 279): Older and more experienced individuals who help to guide young adults.

Metacognition (p. 258): Awareness and understanding of our own cognitive processes.

Midbrain (p. 51): A part of the brain containing primitive centers for vision and hearing. It also plays a role in the regulation of visual reflexes.

Millon Clinical Multiaxial Inventory (MCMI) (p. 432): A psychological test used in diagnosing the presence of specific mental disorders.

Minnesota Multiphasic Personality Inventory (MMPI) (p. 432): A psychological test widely used psychologists to assess specific mental disorders.

Mirror neurons (p. 438): Neurons in the brain that play a key role in imitation of others' behavior. These neurons may be important in the development of autism.

Mitosis (p. 61): Cell division in which chromosome pairs split and then replicate themselves so that the full number is restored in each of the cells produced by division.

Monocular cues (p. 111): Cues to depth or distance provided by one eye.

Mood disorders (p. 438): Psychological disorders in which individuals experience swings in their emotional states that are much more extreme and prolonged than is true of most people.

Mood-congruence effects (p. 215): Refers to the finding that we tend to notice or remember information congruent with our current mood.

Mood-dependent memory (p. 215): Refers to the finding that what we remember while in a given mood may be determined, in part, by what we learned when previously in that same mood.

Moral development (p. 262): Changes that occur with age in the capacity to reason about the rightness or wrongness of various actions.

Morning people (p. 124): Individuals who experience peak levels of energy and physiological activation relatively early in the day.

Motivation (p. 300): Internal processes that activate, guide, and maintain behavior over time.

Multicultural Perspective (p. 14): A perspective that clearly recognizes the potential importance of gender, age, ethnicity, sexual orientation, disability, socioeconomic status, religious orientation, and many other social and cultural dimensions.

Munchausen syndrome (p. 450): A syndrome in which individuals seem to devote their lives to seeking—and often obtaining—costly and painful medical procedures they realize they don't need.

Narcolepsy (p. 136): A sleep disorder in which individuals are overcome by uncontrollable periods of sleep during waking hours.

Natural concepts (p. 224): Concepts that are not based on a precise set of attributes or properties, do not have clear-cut boundaries, and are often defined by prototypes.

Naturalistic Observation (p. 20): A research method in which behavior is studied in the settings where it usually occurs.

Nearsightedness (p. 81): A condition in which the visual image entering our eye is focused slightly in front of our retina, rather than directly on it. Therefore, near objects can be see clearly, while distant objects appear fuzzy or blurred.

Needs analysis (p. 549): The first step in a training program, consisting of a systematic collection of data to address the question "Who needs to learn what?"

Negative afterimage (p. 84): A sensation of complementary color that occurs after staring at a stimulus of a given hue.

Negative reinforcers (p. 172): Stimuli that strengthen responses that permit the organism to avoid or escape from their presence.

Negativity bias (p. 511): Greater sensitivity to negative information than positive information about others.

NEO personality inventory (p. 356): An objective measure of personality designed to assess individuals' relative standing on each of the "big five" dimensions of personality.

Neodisassociation theory (p. 141): A theory suggesting that hypnotized individuals enter an altered state of consciousness in which consciousness is divided.

Neo-Freudians (p. 345): Personality theorists who accepted basic portions of Freud's theory, but rejected or modified other portions.

Nervous system (p. 45): The complex structure that regulates bodily processes and is responsible for all aspects of conscious experience.

Neural plasticity (p. 368): The ability of neural connections to adapt dynamically to environmental cues.

Neurons (p. 41): Cells specialized for communicating information; the basic building blocks of the nervous system.

Neurotransmitters (transmitter substances) (p. 42): Chemicals, released by neurons, that carry information across the synapse.

Nicotine (p. 405): The addictive substance in tobacco.

Night people (p. 124): Individuals who experience peak levels of energy and physiological activation relatively late in the day.

Night terrors (p. 136): Extremely frightening dreamlike experiences that occur during non-REM sleep.

Nociceptor (p. 92): A sensory receptor that responds to stimuli that are damaging.

Nonverbal cues (p. 320, 505): Outward signs of others' emotional states. Such cues involve facial expressions, eye contact, and body language.

Normative decision theory (p. 564): A theory of leadership that prescribes how leaders should take the situation into account when deciding how a particular decision should be made.

Obedience (p. 526): A form of social influence in which one individual orders one or more others to behave in specific ways.

Object permanence (p. 254): Understanding of the fact that objects continue to exist, even when they are hidden from view.

Observational learning (p. 184, 354): The process through which individuals acquire information or behaviors by observing others.

Obsessive-compulsive disorder (p. 445): An anxiety disorder in which individuals have recurrent, disturbing thoughts (obsessions) they can't prevent unless they engage in specific behaviors (compulsions).

Occipital lobe (p. 52): A portion of the cerebral cortex involved in vision.

Oedipus complex (p. 343): In Freud's theory, a crisis of psychosexual development in which children must give up their sexual attraction for their opposite-sex parent.

On-the-job training (p. 550): Training in which an inexperienced employee learns the ropes in the actual work context during company hours.

Openness to experience (p. 352): One of the "big five" dimensions of personality; a dimension ranging from imaginative, sensitive, and intellectual at one extreme, to down-to-earth, insensitive, and crude at the other.

Operant conditioning (p. 171): A process through which organisms learn to repeat behaviors that yield positive outcomes or that permit them to avoid or escape from negative outcomes.

Opiates (p. 148): Drugs that induce a dreamy, relaxed state and, in some persons, intense feelings of pleasure. Opiates exert their effects by stimulating special receptor sites within the brain.

Opponent-process theory (p. 84): A theory that describes the processing of sensory information related to color at levels above the retina. The theory suggests that we possess six types of neurons, each of which is either stimulated or inhibited by red, green, blue, yellow, black, and white.

Optic nerve (p. 80): A bundle of nerve fibers that exit the back of the eye and carry visual information to the brain.

Oral stage (p. 343): A stage of psychosexual development during which pleasure is centered in the region of the mouth.

Organizational citizenship behaviors (p. 560): Positive work behaviors, including helping coworkers and volunteering for extra assignments.

Orgasm disorders (p. 450): A sexual disorder involving the delay or absence of orgasms in both sexes.

Panic disorder (p. 444): Periodic, unexpected attacks of intense, terrifying anxiety, known as panic attacks.

Paraphilias (p. 451): Disorders in which sexual arousal cannot occur without the presence of unusual imagery or acts.

Parapsychologists (p. 112): Individuals who study ESP and other paranormal events.

Parasympathetic nervous system (p. 47): A portion of the autonomic nervous system that readies the body for restoration of energy.

Parietal lobe (p. 51): A portion of the cerebral cortex, lying behind the central fissure, that plays a major role in the skin senses: touch, temperature, and pressure.

Passive smoke (p. 403): The smoke that we inhale from the smokers around us.

Path-goal theory (p. 564): A theory of leadership that examines how leaders should adapt their style of leadership in response to the situation.

Peak experiences (p. 349): According to Maslow, intense emotional experiences during which individuals feel at one with the universe.

Perception (p. 74): The process through which we select, organize, and interpret input from our sensory receptors.

Perfect pitch (p. 89): The ability to name or produce a note of particular pitch in the absence of a reference note.

Performance appraisal (p. 553): The process of evaluating employee strengths and weaknesses.

Peripheral nervous system (p. 45): That portion of the nervous system that connects internal organs and glands, as well as voluntary and involuntary muscles, to the central nervous system.

Peripheral route (to persuasion) (p. 515): Attitude change that occurs in response to persuasion cues—information concerning the expertise, status, or attractiveness of would-be persuaders.

Personality disorders (p. 453): Disorders involving extreme and inflexible personality traits that are distressing to the people who have them or cause them problems in school, work, or interpersonal relations.

Personality traits (p. 351): Specific dimensions along which individuals' differ in consistent, stable ways.

Personality (p. 338): Individuals' unique and relatively stable patterns of behavior, thoughts, and feelings.

Person–environment (P–E) fit (p. 395): The approach suggests that a misfit between a person and his or her work environment may produce stress.

Persuasion (p. 514): The process through which one or more people attempts to alter the attitudes of one or more others.

Pervasive development disorders (p. 437): Disorders involve lifelong impairment in mental or physical functioning.

Phallic stage (p. 343): An early stage of psychosexual development during which pleasure is centered in the genital region. It is during this stage that the Oedipus complex develops.

Phenomenological/experiential therapies (often known as *humanistic therapies*) (p. 473): Therapies that assume that (1) understanding other people requires trying to see the world through their eyes (a phenomenological approach); (2) clients should be treated as equals; and (3) the therapeutic relationship with the client is central to achieving the benefits of therapy.

Phobias (p. 169, 443): Fears that become excessive in that they cause intense emotional distress and interfere significantly with everyday activities.

Phonological awareness (p. 260): Sensitivity to the sound structure of oral (spoken) language.

Physiological dependence (p. 145): Strong urges to continue using a drug based on organic factors such as changes in metabolism.

Pinna (p. 87): The external portion of our ear.

Pitch (p. 87): The characteristic of a sound that is described as high or low. Pitch is mediated by the frequency of a sound.

Pituitary gland (p. 47): An endocrine gland that releases hormones to regulate other glands and several basic biological processes.

Place theory (p. 89): A theory suggesting that sounds of different frequency stimulate different areas of the basilar membrane, the portion of the cochlea containing sensory receptors for sound.

Placenta (p. 247): A structure that surrounds, protects, and nourishes the fetus.

Playing hard to get (p. 526): A tactic for gaining compliance in which individuals try to create the image that they are very popular or very much in demand.

Pleasure principle (p. 342): The principle on which the id operates, according to which immediate pleasure is the sole motivation for behavior.

Pons (p. 49): A portion of the brain through which sensory and motor information pass and that contains structures relating to sleep, arousal, and the regulation of muscle tone and cardiac reflexes.

Position Analysis Questionnaire (PAQ) (p. 544): A specific job analysis technique that analyzes jobs along thirty-two distinct dimensions.

Positive reinforcers (p. 172): Stimuli that strengthen responses that precede them.

Positron emission tomography (PET) (p. 55): An imaging technique that detects the activity of the brain by measuring glucose use or blood flow.

Postconventional level (of morality) (p. 263): According to Kohlberg, the final stage of moral development, one at which individuals judge morality in terms of abstract principles.

Post-traumatic stress disorder (p. 392, 447): A disorder in which people persistently reexperience the traumatic event in their thoughts or dreams, feel as if they are reliving these events from time to time, persistently avoid stimuli associated with the traumatic event, plus several other symptoms.

Practical intelligence (p. 362): Intelligence useful in solving everyday problems.

Preconventional level (of morality) (p. 263): According to Kohlberg, the earliest stage of moral development, one at which individuals judge morality in terms of the effects produced by various actions.

Prejudice (p. 519): Negative attitudes toward the members of some social group based on their membership in this group.

Premack principle (p. 172): The principle that a more preferred activity can be used to reinforce a less preferred activity.

Preoperational stage (p. 254): In Piaget's theory, a stage of cognitive development during which children become capable of mental representations of the external world.

Prevention strategies (p. 414): Techniques designed to reduce the occurrence of disease or illness and the physical and psychological problems that often accompany them.

Primary aging (p. 281): Changes in our bodies caused by the passage of time and, perhaps, genetic factors.

Proactive interference (p. 208): Occurs when information previously entered into memory interferes with the learning or storage of current information.

Problem solving (p. 223): Efforts to develop or choose among various responses to attain desired goals.

Procedural memory (p. 207) (implicit memory): A memory system the retains information we cannot readily express verbally—for example, information necessary to perform various skilled motor activities such as riding a bicycle.

Programmed instruction (p. 551): An off-site training method that allows trainees to go through instructional materials at their own pace, testing themselves before proceeding to subsequent modules.

Progressive relaxation (p. 420): A stress reduction technique in which people learn to relax by alternately flexing and relaxing their muscles in a particular muscle group and then progressively to other muscles throughout the body.

Propositional thinking (p. 275): Reasoning during the stage of formal operations, in which individuals can assess the validity of verbal assertions even when they refer to possibilities rather than actual events.

Prosopagnosia (p. 87): A rare condition in which brain damage impairs a person's ability to recognize faces.

Prototypes (p. 224): The best or clearest examples of various objects or stimuli in the physical world.

Psi (p. 112): Unusual processes of information or energy transfer that are currently unexplained in terms of known physical or biological mechanisms. Included under the heading of psi are such supposed abilities as telepathy (reading others' thoughts) and clairvoyance (perceiving objects that do not directly stimulate sensory organs).

Psychedelics (p. 149): *See* Hallucinogens.

Psychiatry (p. 494): A branch of modern medicine specializing in the treatment of psychological disorders.

Psychoanalysis (p. 341): A method of therapy based on Freud's theory of personality, in which the therapist attempts to bring repressed, unconscious material into consciousness.

Psychodynamic therapies (p. 471): Therapies based on the idea that mental disorders stem primarily from the kind of hidden inner conflicts first described by Freud.

Psychological dependence (p. 145): Strong desires to continue using a drug even though it is not physiologically addicting.

Psychological disorders (p. 428): Maladaptive patterns of behavior and thought that cause the people experiencing them considerable distress.

Psychological treatments (p. 470): Procedures for alleviating mental disorders based on the findings and principles of psychology and best administered by trained psychologists.

Psychology (p. 5): The science of behavior and cognitive processes.

Psychophysics (p. 75): A set of procedures psychologists have developed to investigate the relationship between physical properties of stimuli and people's psychological experience of them.

Psychosexual stages of development (p. 342): According to Freud, an innate sequence of stages through which all humans pass. At each stage, pleasure is focused on a different region of the body.

Psychosurgery (p. 490): A form of biological therapy in which brain operations are performed to change abnormal behavior.

Psychotherapies (p. 470): Procedures in which people with mental disorders interact with trained therapists who help them change certain behaviors, thoughts, or emotions so that they feel and function better.

Puberty (p. 274): The period of rapid change during which individuals reach sexual maturity.

Punishment (p. 173): A procedure by which the application or removal of a stimulus decreases the strength of a behavior.

Pupil (p. 80): An opening in the eye, just behind the cornea, through which light rays enter our eye.

Random Assignment of Participants to Experimental Conditions (p. 25): Assuring that all research participants have an equal chance of being exposed to each level of the independent variable (that is, of being assigned to each experimental condition).

Rational-emotive therapy (p. 478): A cognitive therapy based on the view that many forms of mental disorder-stem from irrational thoughts.

Reaction criteria (p. 552): A measure of training effectiveness that examines how employees feel about the training experience.

Realistic conflict theory (p. 520): A theory proposing that prejudice stems, at least in part, from direct conflict between social groups.

Reality principle (p. 342): The principle according to which the ego operates, in which the external consequences of behavior are considered in the expression of impulses from the id.

Recategorization (p. 522): A technique for reducing prejudice that involves inducing individuals to shift the boundary between "us" and "them" so that it now includes groups they previously viewed as "them."

Reconditioning (p. 164): The rapid recovery of a conditioned response (CR) to a CS-UCS pairing following extinction.

Reflexes (p. 45, 248): Seemingly automatic actions evoked rapidly by specific stimuli.

Reinforcement (p. 172): A procedure by which the application or removal of a stimulus increases the strength of a specific behavior.

Relationship conflict (p. 567): Conflict in the group that refers to interpersonal problems between individuals.

Relative size (p. 106): A visual cue based on a comparison of an object of unknown size to one of known size.

Reliability (p. 365): The extent to which any measuring device (including psychological tests) yields the same result each time it is applied to the same quantity.

REM sleep (p. 133): A state of sleep in which brain activity resembling waking restfulness is accompanied by deep muscle relaxation and movements of the eyes. Most dreams occurring during periods of REM sleep.

Representativeness heuristic (p. 227): A mental rule of thumb suggesting that the more closely an event or object resembles typical examples of some concept or category, the more likely it is to belong to that concept or category.

Results criteria (p. 552): A measure of training effectiveness that examines the final outcome of the training (e.g., accident reduction).

Reticular activating system (p. 49): A structure within the brain concerned with sleep, arousal, and the regulation of muscle tone and cardiac reflexes.

Retina (p. 80): The surface at the back of the eye containing the rods and cones.

Retrieval cues (p. 205): Stimuli associated with information stored in memory that can aid in its retrieval.

Retrieval (p. 201): The process through which information stored in memory is located.

Retroactive interference (p. 208): Occurs when new information being entered into memory interferes with retention of information already present in memory.

Retrograde amnesia (p. 217): Loss of memory of events that occurred prior to an amnesia-inducing event.

Risk factors (p. 403): Aspects of our environment or behavior that influence our chances of developing or contracting a particular disease, within the limits established through our genetic structure.

Rods (p. 80): One of the two types of sensory receptors for vision found in the eye.

Romantic love (p. 531): A form of love in which feelings of strong attraction and sexual desire toward another person are dominant.

Rorschach test (p. 357): A widely used projective test of personality in which individuals are asked to describe what they see in a series of inkblots.

Sampling (p. 21): With respect to the survey method, refers to the methods used to select persons who respond to the survey.

Satisficing (p. 225): A strategy for making decisions in which the first acceptable alternative is chosen.

Saturation (p. 80): The degree of concentration of the hue of light. We experience saturation as the purity of a light.

Schachter–Singer theory (two-factor theory) (p. 317): A theory of emotion suggesting that our subjective emotional states are determined, at least in part, by the cognitive labels we attach to feelings of arousal.

Schedules of reinforcement (p. 176): Rules determining when and how reinforcements will be delivered.

Schemas (p. 253): Cognitive frameworks representing our knowledge about specific.

Schizophrenia (p. 454): A complex disorder characterized by hallucinations (e.g., hearing voices), delusions (beliefs with no basis in reality), disturbances in speech, and several other symptoms.

Scripts (p. 258): Mental representations of the sequence of events in a given situation.

Secondary aging (p. 281): Changes in our bodies due to disease, disuse, or abuse.

Secure attachment (p. 267): A pattern of attachment in which infants actively seek contact with their caregiver and take comfort from her presence when she returns.

Selective attention (p. 101): The process of focusing on a particular quality, object, or event for relatively detailed analysis.

Self-actualization (p. 349): A stage of personal development in which individuals reach their maximum potential.

Self-concept (p. 348): All the information and beliefs individuals have about their own characteristics and themselves.

Self-determination theory (p. 407): When applied to health-related issues, this theory suggests that motivation to perform health-preventive behaviors is highest when we have autonomy over the decision to do so, and lowest when we do these behaviors at someone else's request.

Self-efficacy (p. 354): Individuals' expectations concerning their ability to perform various tasks.

Self-esteem (p. 350): Our assessment of our overall personal worth or adequacy.

Self-reinforcement (p. 354): A process in which individual reward themselves for reaching their own goals.

Self-serving bias (p. 510): The tendency to attribute positive outcomes to our own traits or characteristics (internal causes) but negative outcomes to factors beyond our control (external causes).

Self-system (p. 353): In Bandura's social-cognitive learning theory, the set of cognitive processes by which a person perceives, evaluates, and regulates his or her own behavior.

Semantic development (p. 262): Development of understanding of the meaning of spoken or written language.

Semantic memory (p. 204): A memory system that stores general, abstract knowledge about the world—information we cannot remember acquiring at a specific time and place.

Sensation (p. 74): Input about the physical world provided by our sensory receptors.

Sensorimotor stage (p. 253): In Piaget's theory, the earliest stage of cognitive development.

Sensory adaptation (p. 79): Reduced sensitivity to unchanging stimuli over time.

Sensory Memory (p. 201): A memory system that retains representations of sensory input

Sensory receptors (p. 74): Cells of the body specialized for the task of *transduction*—converting physical energy (light, sound) into neural impulses.

Serum cholesterol (p. 406): The amount of cholesterol in our blood; it is directly proportional to the amount of cholesterol in our diets.

Severity error (p. 554): The tendency for a supervisor to give employees ratings that are lower than their performance merits.

Sex category constancy (p. 274): Complete understanding of one's sexual identity, centering around a biologically based categorical distinction between males and females.

Sexual arousal disorders (p. 450): Involve the inability to attain or maintain an erection (males) or the absence of vaginal swelling and lubrication (females).

Sexual desire disorders (p. 450): Disorders involving a lack of interest in sex or active aversion to sexual activity.

Sexual motivation (p. 308): Motivation to engage in various forms of sexual relations.

Sexual orientation (p. 311): Individuals' preference for sexual relations with their own sex, the other sex, or both.

Shape constancy (p. 106): The tendency to perceive a physical object as having a constant shape, even when the image it casts on the retina changes.

Shaping (p. 174): A technique in which closer and closer approximations to desired behavior are required for the delivery of positive reinforcement.

Signal detection theory (p. 75): A theory suggesting that there are no absolute thresholds for sensations. Rather, detection of stimuli depends on their physical energy and on internal factors such as the relative costs and benefits associated with detecting their presence.

Simple cells (p. 85): Cells within the visual system that respond to specific shapes presented in certain orientations (e.g., horizontal, vertical).

Simultaneous conditioning (p. 163): A form of conditioning in which the conditioned stimulus (CS) and the unconditioned stimulus (UCS) begin and end at the same time.

Size constancy (p. 106): The tendency to perceive a physical object as having a constant size, even when the image it casts on the retina changes.

Sleep (p. 132): A process in which important physiological changes (e.g., shifts in brain activity, slowing of basic bodily functions) are accompanied by major shifts in consciousness.

Social categorization (p. 520): The tendency to divide the social world into two distinct categories: "us" and "them."

Social cognition (p. 505): An area of research concerned with the ways in which we notice, store, remember, and use social information.

Social cognitive theory (p. 353): A theory of behavior suggesting that human behaviors are influenced by many cognitive factors as well as by reinforcement contingencies, and that humans have an impressive capacity to regulate their own actions.

Social development (p. 265): Changes in social behavior and social relations occurring over the life span.

Social influence (p. 525): Attempts by one or more people to change our behavior in some manner.

Social loafing (p. 567): The tendency to reduce one's efforts when working in a group.

Social network (p. 276): A group of people with whom one interacts regularly.

Social psychology (p. 504): The branch of psychology that studies all aspects of social behavior and social thought.

Social support (p. 397): The emotional and task resources provided by others that may serve to help buffer the adverse effects of chronic stress.

Social-cognitive or role-playing view (p. 141): A view suggesting that effects produced by hypnosis are the result of hypnotized people's expectations about and their social role as the "hypnotized subject."

Somatic nervous system (p. 46): The portion of the nervous system that connects the brain and spinal cord to voluntary muscles.

Somatoform disorders (p. 448): Disorders in which individuals have symptoms typically associated with physical diseases or conditions, but in which no known organic or physiological basis for the symptoms can be found.

Somnambulism (p. 136): A sleep disorder in which individuals actually get up and move about while still asleep.

Split-half reliability (p. 366): The correlation between scores on two parts of a test.

Spontaneous recovery (p. 164): Following extinction, reinstatement of conditioned stimulus-unconditioned stimulus pairings will produce a conditioned response.

Stage theory (p. 264): Any theory proposing that all humans move through an orderly and predictable series of changes.

Standardized tests (p. 547): Reliable and valid tests that are used for a particular purpose and that are administered in a systematic way.

Stanford–Binet test (p. 363): A widely used individual test of intelligence.

State-dependent retrieval (p. 205): Occurs when aspects of our physical states serve as retrieval cues for information stored in long-term memory.

States of consciousness (p. 122): Varying degrees of awareness of ourselves and the external world.

Stereotypes (p. 521): Cognitive frameworks suggesting that all members of specific social groups share certain characteristics.

Stimulants (p. 147): Drugs that increase activity in the nervous system (e.g., amphetamines, caffeine, nicotine).

Stimulus control (p. 179): When a behavior occurs consistently in the presence of a discriminative stimulus.

Stimulus discrimination (p. 165): The process by which organisms learn to respond to certain stimuli but not to others.

Stimulus generalization (p. 164): The tendency of stimuli similar to a conditioned stimulus to evoke conditioned responses.

Stimulus (p. 161): A physical event capable of affecting behavior.

Storage (p. 201): The process through which information is retained in memory.

Stress (p. 388): The process by which we appraise and respond to events that disrupt, or threaten to disrupt, our physical or psychological functioning.

Stressors (p. 388): Events or situations in our environment that cause stress.

Structuralism (p. 5): An early view of psychology suggesting that the field should focus on identifying the basic structures of the human mind.

Structured interview (p. 546): An employment interview that is conducted in the same manner, using the same questions, for all job applicants.

Subjective well-being (p. 324): Individuals' global judgments of their own life satisfaction.

Subliminal perception (p. 77): The presumed influence on the behavior of a stimulus that is below the threshold for conscious experience.

Substance abuse (p. 459): A maladaptive pattern of substance use that results in repeated, significant adverse effects and maladaptive behavior—failure to meet obligations at work, school, or at home; repeatedly using a psychoactive substance in hazardous ways; experiencing recurrent legal problems related to the substance; and continuing to use the substance despite its negative effects on social relationships.

Substance-related disorders (p. 458): Disorders related to the use of psychoactive substances.

Superego (p. 342): According to Freud, the portion of human personality representing the conscience.

Suprachiasmatic nucleus (p. 124): A portion of the hypothalamus that seems to play an important role in the regulation of circadian rhythms.

Survey Method (p. 21): A research method in which large numbers of people answer questions about aspects of their views or their behavior.

Symbolic play (p. 254): Play in which children pretend that one object is another object.

Sympathetic nervous system (p. 46): The portion of the autonomic nervous system that readies the body for expenditure of energy.

Synapse (p. 42): A region where the axon of one neuron closely approaches other neurons or the cell membrane of other types of cells, such as muscle cells.

Synaptic vesicles (p. 42): Structures in the axon terminals that contain various neurotransmitters.

Systematic desensitization (p. 475): A procedure in which individuals first learn how to induce a relaxed state in their own bodies—often by learning how to relax their muscles. Then, while in a relaxed state, they are exposed to stimuli that elicit fear.

Systematic Observation (p. 20): A basic method of science in which the natural world, or various events or processes in it, are observed and measured in a very careful manner.

Systematic processing (p. 515): Involves careful consideration of message content, the ideas it contains, and so on. Such processing is quite effortful and absorbs much of our information-processing capacity.

Tardive dyskinesia (p. 487): A side effect of some antipsychotic drugs involving loss of motor control, especially in the face.

Task conflict (p. 567): Disagreement about how the team's primary activity should be accomplished.

Temperament (p. 265): Stable individual differences in the quality or intensity of emotional reactions.

Temporal lobe (p. 52): The lobe of the cerebral cortex that is involved in hearing.

Teratogens (p. 247): Factors in the environment that can harm the developing fetus.

Test–retest reliability (p. 366): A measure of the extent to which scores on a test remain stable over time.

Thalamus (p. 51): A structure deep within the brain that receives sensory input from other portions of the nervous system and then transmits this information to the cerebral hemispheres and other parts of the brain.

Theory of mind (p. 257): Refers to children's growing understanding of their own mental states and those of others.

Therapeutic alliance (p. 471): A close and often powerful relationship between the therapist and the person seeking help, in which both cooperate to alleviate the client's mental disorders.

Timbre (p. 88): The quality of a sound resulting from the complexity of a sound wave that, for example, helps us distinguish between the sound of a trumpet and that of a saxophone.

Tolerance (p. 145): Habituation to a drug so that larger and larger doses are required to produce effects of the same magnitude.

Top-down approach (p. 110): Approach to pattern recognition that starts with the analysis of high-level information, such as our knowledge, expectancies, and the context in which a stimulus is seen.

Trace conditioning (p. 162): A form of forward conditioning in which the onset of the conditioned stimulus (CS) precedes the onset of the unconditioned stimulus (UCS) and the presentation of the CS and UCS does not overlap.

Trait theories (p. 351): Theories of personality that focus on identifying the key dimensions along which people differ.

Transduction (p. 75): The translation of a physical energy into electrical signals by specialized receptor cells.

Transference (p. 472): Intense feelings of love or hate toward the analyst on the part of the patient.

Transfer-of-training (p. 552): The issue of whether material learned during training is demonstrated on the job.

Transformational leadership (p. 565): Leadership that consists of charisma, intellectual stimulation, and genuine concern for subordinates.

Triarchic theory (p. 362): A theory suggesting that there are three basic forms of intelligence: componential, experiential, and contextual.

Trichromatic theory (p. 81): A theory of color perception suggesting that we have three types of cones, each primarily receptive to different wavelengths of light.

Two-factor theory (of emotion) (p. 317): *See* Schachter–Singer Theory.

Type D personality (p. 412): A term used to describe a general tendency to cope with stress by keeping negative emotions to oneself. People who exhibit this behavior pattern are more likely to experience suppressed immune systems and health-related problems.

Unconditional positive regard (p. 348): In Rogers's theory, communicating to others that they will be respected or loved regardless of what they say or do.

Unconditioned response (UCR) (p. 162): In classical conditioning, the response evoked by an unconditioned stimulus.

Unconditioned stimulus (UCS) (p. 161): In classical conditioning, a stimulus that can evoke an unconditioned response the first time it is presented.

Utility (p. 543): The usefulness of a selection technique that takes both the criterion-related validity and the cost of the procedure into account.

Validity (p. 366): The extent to which a test actually measures what it claims to measure.

Variable-interval schedule (p. 178): A schedule of reinforcement in which a variable amount of time must elapse before a response will yield reinforcement.

Variable-ratio schedule (p. 178): A schedule of reinforcement in which reinforcement is delivered after a variable number of responses have been performed.

Vestibular sense (p. 99): Our sense of balance.

Vestibule training (p. 550): An on-site training method that uses a separate "practice" work area, allowing for observational learning.

Wavelength (p. 80): The peak-to-peak distance in a sound or light wave.

Wernicke's area (p. 59): An area in the temporal lobe that plays a role in the comprehension of speech.

Work motivation (p. 558): The internal processes that activate, guide, and maintain behavior directed toward work.

Work sample test (p. 548): A selection test that requires job applicants to perform a sample of the work they would be expected to do on the job.

Working Memory (p. 203) (previously known as short-term memory): A memory system in which information we are processing at the moment is held. Recent findings suggest that it involves more complex levels and forms of processing than was previously believed.

References

Ackerman, P. L., Beier, M. E., & Boyle, M. O. (2005). Working memory and intelligence: The same or different constructs? *Psychological Bulletin, 131,* 30–60.

Ackerman, H., Mathiak, K., Ivry, R. (2004). Temporal organization of "internal speech" as a basis for cerebellar modulation of cognitive functions. *Behavioral and Cognitive Neuroscience Reviews, 3* (1), 14–22.

Acocella, J. (1998, April 6). The politics of hysteria. *The New Yorker,* 64–79.

Acton, D. A. (2001). The "color blind" therapist. *Art Therapy, 18,* 109–112.

Adams, R. B., & Kleck, R. E. (2005). Effects of direct and averted gaze on the perception of facially communicated emotion. *Emotion, 5,* 3–11.

Adams, R. J. (1987). An evaluation of color preference in early infancy. *Infant Behavior and Development, 10,* 143–150.

Adelson, R. (2005). Feed the birds: Songbird study offers new insights into how malnutrition impairs development and cognition. *Monitor on Psychology, 36,* 16–18.

Adelson, R. (2006). Nationwide survey spotlights U.S. alcohol abuse. *Monitor on Psychology, 37,* 30–31.

Ader, R., Kelly, K., Moynihan, J. A., Grota, L. J., & Cohen, N. (1993). Conditioned enhancement of antibody production using antigen as the unconditioned stimulus. *Brain, Behavior, and Immunity, 7,* 334–343.

Adler, N. J. (1991). *International dimensions of organizational behavior.* Boston: PWS-Kent.

Adler, N. J., & Bartholomew, S. (1992). Managing globally competent people. *Academy of Management Executive, 6,* 52–65.

Adolphs, R. (2002). Recognizing emotion from facial expressions: Psychological and neurological mechanisms. *Behavioral and Cognitive Neuroscience Reviews, 1,* 21–61.

Ahmed, O. A., Ahmen, A. O., Imran, D., & Ahmed, S. (2004). Coughing to distraction. *British Journal of Plastic Surgery, 57,* 376.

Aiken, L. S., West, S. G., Woodward, C. K., Reno, R. R., & Reynolds, K. D. (1994). Increasing screening mammography in asymptomatic women: Evaluation of a second-generation, theory-based program. *Health Psychology, 13,* 526–538.

Ainsworth, M. D. S. (1973). The development of infant-mother attachment. In B. Caldwell & H. Riciutti (Eds.), *Review of child development research* (vol. 3, pp. 1–94). Chicago: University of Chicago Press.

Ajzen, J. (1991). The theory of planned behavior. Special issue: Theories of cognitive self-regulation. *Organizational Behavior and Human Decision Processes, 509,* 179–211.

Akerstedt, T., & Froberg, J. E. (1976). Interindividual differences in circadian pattern of catecholamine excretion, body temperature, performance, and subjective arousal. *Biological Psychology, 4,* 277–292.

Albarracin, D., Durantini, M. R., & Earl, A. (2006). Empirical and theoretical conclusions of an analysis of outcomes of HIV-prevention interventions. *Current Directions in Psychological Science, 15,* 73–78.

Albarracin, D., Gillette, J. C., Earl, A. N., Glasman, L. R., & Durantini, M. R. (2005). A test of major assumptions about behavior change: A comprehensive look at the effects of passive and active HIV-prevention interventions since the beginning of the epidemic. *Psychological Bulletin, 131,* 856–897.

Alexander, K. W., Quais, J. A., Goodman, G. S., Ghetti, S., Edelstein, R. B., Redlich, A. D., Cordon, I. M., & Jones, D. P. H. (2005). Traumatic impact predicts long-term memory for documented child sexual abuse. *Psychological Science, 16,* 33–40.

Alicke, M. D., & Largo, E. (1995). The role of the self in the false consensus effect. *Journal of Experimental Social Psychology, 31,* 28–47.

Allen, L. S., & Gorski, R. A. (1992). Biology, brain architecture, and human sexuality. *Journal of National Institute of Health Research, 4,* 53–59.

Allen, T. D., Eby, L. T., Poteet, M. L., & Lentz, E. (2004). Career benefits associated with mentoring for protégés: A meta-analysis. *Journal of Applied Psychology, 89,* 127–136.

Allred, J. B. (1993). Lowering serum cholesterol: Who benefits? *Journal of Nutrition, 123,* 1453–1459.

Allyn, J., & Festinger, L. (1961). The effectiveness of unanticipated persuasive communications. *Journal of Abnormal and Social Psychology, 62,* 35–40.

Alvarez-Borda, B., Ramirez-Amaya, V., Perez-Montfort, R., & Bermudez-Rattoni, F. (1995). Enhancement of antibody production by a learning paradigm. *Neurobiology of Learning and Memory, 64,* 103–105.

Ambady, N., & Rosenthal, R. (1993). Half a minute: Predicting teacher evaluations from thin slices of nonverbal behavior and physical attractiveness. *Journal of Personality and Social Psychology, 64,* 431–441.

Amaro, H. (1995). Love, sex, and power: Considering women's realities in HIV prevention. *American Psychologist, 50,* 437–447.

Amason, A. C. (1996). Distinguishing the effects of functional and dysfunctional conflict on strategic decision making: Resolving a paradox for top management groups. *Academy of Management Journal, 39,* 123–148.

Ambrose, M. L., Seabright, M. A., & Schminke, M. (2002). Sabotage in the workplace: The role of organizational justice. *Organizational Behavior and Human Decision Processes, 89,* 947–965.

Ambuel, B. (1995). Adolescents, unintended pregnancy, and abortion: The struggle for a compassionate social policy. *Current Directions in Psychological Science, 4,* 1–5.

American Academy of Otolaryngology. (2006). Noise & hearing protection. Available: www.entnet.org/healthinfo/hearing/noise_hearing.cfm.

American Academy of Pediatrics. (1998). Guidance for effective discipline. *Pediatrics, 101,* 723–728.

American Academy of Pediatrics. (2001). Media violence. *Pediatrics, 108,* 1222–1226.

American Cancer Society. (2002) *Breast Cancer Facts and Figures, 2001–2002.* Accessed from the world wide web on May 31, 2006 at www.cancer.org/downloads/STT/BrCaFF2001.pdf.

American Cancer Society. (2005). Breast cancer facts and figures, 2001–2002. Available: www.cancer.org/downloads/STT/BrCaFF2001.pdf.

American Cancer Society. (2006). Cancer facts and figures 2006. Available: www.cancer.org/docroot/PED/content/ped_7_1_Skin_Cancer_Detection_What_You_Can_Do.asp?sitearea=PED.

American Psychiatric Association (2000). *Diagnostic and statistical manual of mental disorders (text revision).* Washington, D. C.: American Psychiatric Association.

American Psychological Association. (1995). Training in and dissemination of empirically validated psychological procedures. Report and recommendations. *The Clinical Psychologist, 48,* 22–23.

Amoore, J. (1970). *Molecular basis of odor.* Springfield, IL: Thomas.

Amoore, J. (1982). Odor theory and odor classification. In E. Theimer (Ed.), *Fragrance chemistry: The science of the sense of smell.* New York: Academic Press.

Amundsen, A. H., Elvik, R., & Fridstrøm, L. (1999). Effects of the "Speak out!" campaign on the number of killed or injured road users in the county of Sogn og Fjordane, Norway. In: TØI report 425/1999.

Anand, G., & Winslow, R. (2003). Transformation in medicine is putting specialists at odds. *Wall Street Journal,* September 10.

Anderson, C. A. (2000). The impact of interactive violence on children. Hearing before the Senate Committee on Commerce, Science, and Transportation, 106th Congress, 1st Session. Available: aappolicy.aappublications.org/cgi/content/full/pediatrics;108/5/1222.

Anderson, C. A., & Bushman, B. (2001). Effects of violent video games on aggressive behavior, Aggressive cognition, aggressive affect, physiological arousal, and prosocial behavior: A meta-analytic review of the scientific literature. *Psychological Science, 12,* 353–359.

Anderson, C. A., Carnagey, N. L., & Eubanks, J. (2003). Exposure to violent media: The effects of songs with violent lyrics on aggressive thoughts and feelings. *Journal of Personality and Social Psychology, 84,* 960–971.

Anderson, J. R. (1993). *Rules of the mind.* Hillsdale, NJ: Erlbaum.

Anderson, N. B. (1989). Racial differences in stress-induced cardiovascular reactivity and hypertension: Current status and substantive issues. *Psychological Bulletin, 105,* 89–105.

Anderson, N. B., & Nickerson, K. J. (2005). Genes, race, and psychology in the genome era: An introduction. *American Psychologist, 60,* 5–8.

Andreason, N. C., & Black, D. (1995). *Introductory textbook of psychiatry* (2nd ed.). Washington, D.C.: American Psychiatric Press.

Andrews, E. A., Gosse, V. F., Gaulton, R. S., & Maddigan, R. I. (1999). Teaching introductory psychology at a distance by two-way interactive video. *Teaching of Psychology, 2,* 115–118.

Andrews, J. D. W. (1967). The achievement motive and advancement in two types of organization. *Journal of Personality and Social Psychology, 6,* 163–168.

Angier, N. (1998). Nothing becomes a man more than a woman's face. *New York Times,* September 1, p. F3.

Anthony, J. L., & Francis, D. J. (2005). Development of phonological awarness. *Current Directions in Psychological Science, 14,* 255–259.

Antrobus, J. (1991). Dreaming: Cognitive processes during cortical activation and high afferent thresholds. *Psychological Review, 98,* 96–212.

Arditi, A. (2005). Effective color contrast: Designing for people with partial sight and color deficiencies. Available: www.lighthouse.org/color_contrast.htm.

Argyle, M. (1988). *Bodily communication* (2nd ed.). New York: Methuen.

Aronoff, J., Woike, B. A., & Hyman, L. M. (1992). Which are the stimuli in facial displays of anger and happiness? Configurational bases of emotional recognition. *Journal of Personality and Social Psychology, 62,* 1050–1066.

Aronoff, S. R., & Spilka, B. (1984–1985). Patterning of facial expressions among terminal cancer patients. *Omega, 15,* 101–108.

Arvey, R. D., & Begalla, M. E. (1975). Analyzing the homemaker job using the Position Analysis Questionnaire. *Journal of Applied Psychology, 60,* 513–518.

Arvey, R. D., & Campion, J. E. (1982). The employment interview: A summary and review of recent research. *Personnel Psychology, 35,* 281–322.

Ashford, S. J. (1986). Feedback seeking in individual adaptation: A resource perspective. *Academy of Management Journal, 29,* 465–487.

Atkinson, R. C., & Shiffrin, R. M. (1968). Human memory: A proposed system and its control processes. In K. W. Spence & J. T. Spence (Eds.), *The psychology of learning and motivation: Advances in research and theory* (pp. 89–195). New York: Academic Press.

Atri, A., Sherman, S., Norman, K. A., Kirchhoff, B. A., Nicolas, M. M., Greicius, M. D., Cramer, S. C., Breiter, H. C., Hasselmo, M. E., & Stern, C. E. (2004). Blockade of central cholinergic receptors impairs new learning and increases proactive interference in a word paired-associate memory task. *Behavioral Neuroscience, 118,* 223–236.

Azar, B. (1999). Tailored interventions prove more effective. *APA Monitor, 30* (6), 38–39.

Azar, B. (2006). Wild finding on animal sleep. *Monitor on Psychology, 37,* 54–55.

Azim, E., Mobbs, D., Jo, B., Menon, V., Reiss, A. L. (2005). Sex difference in brain activation elicited by humor. *Proceedings of the National Academy of Sciences, 102,* 16496–16501.

Bachman, J. G. (1987, February). An eye on the future. *Psychology Today,* pp. 6–7.

Baddeley, A. D. (1992). Working memory. *Science, 255,* 556–559.

Baddeley, A. D., & Hitsch, G. (1994). Developments in the concept of working memory. *Neuropsychology, 8,* 485–493.

Bailey, J. M., & Pillard, R. C. (1991). A genetic study of male sexual orientation. *Archives of General Psychiatry, 48,* 1089–1096.

Bailey, J. M., & Zucker, K. J. (1995). Childhood sex-typed behavior and sexual orientation: A conceptual analysis and quantitative review. *Developmental Psychology, 31,* 43–55.

Baillorgeon, R. (2002). The acquisition of physical knowledge in infancy: A summary in eight lessons. In U. Goswami (Ed.), *Handbook of childhood cognitive development* (pp. 47–83). Oxford, England: Blackwell.

Baillorgeon, R. (2004). Infants' physical world. *Current Directions in Psychological Science, 13,* 89–94.

Baillorgeon, R., & Wang, S. (2002). Event categorization in infancy. *Trends in Cognitive Sciences, 6,* 85–95.

Bakker, A. B., Demerouti, E., de Boer, E., & Schaufeli, W. B. (2003). Job demands and job resources as predictors of absence duration and frequency. *Journal of Vocational Behavior, 62,* 341–356.

Balogh, R. D., & Porter, R. H. (1986). Olfactory preferences resulting from mere exposure in human neonates. *Infant Behavior and Development, 9,* 395–401.

Baltes, P. B. (1987). Theoretical propositions of life-span developmental psychology: On the dynamics between growth and decline. *Developmental Psychology, 23,* 611–626.

Bandura, A. (1977). Self-efficacy: Toward a unifying theory of behavioral change. *Psychological Review, 84,* 191–215.

Bandura, A. (1986). *Social foundations of thought and action: A social cognitive theory.* Englewood Cliffs, NJ: Prentice-Hall.

Bandura, A. (1992). Exercise of personal agency through the self-efficacy mechanism. In R. Schwarzer (Ed.), *Self-efficacy: Thought control of action* (pp. 3–38). Washington, D.C.,: Hemisphere.

Bandura, A. (1997). *Self–efficacy: The exercise of control.* New York: Freeman.

Bandura, A. (1999). A social cognitive theory of personality. In L. Pervin & D. John (Eds.), *Handbook of personality* (2nd ed.). New York: Guilford.

Bandura, A., & Maddux, J. E. (1977). Self-efficacy expectancy and outcome expectancy. *Journal of Personality and Social Psychology, 35,* 125–139.

Bandura, A., Ross, D., & Ross, S. (1963). Imitation of film-mediated aggressive models. *Journal of Abnormal and Social Psychology, 66,* 3–11.

Banks, S. M., Salovey, P., Greener, S., Rothman, A. J., Moyer, A., Beauvais, J., & Epel, E. (1995). The effects of message framing on mammography utilization. *Health Psychology, 14,* 178–184.

Bannon, L. (2003). Why girls and boys get different toys. *Wall Street Journal,* February 14, pp. B1, B4.

Barber, T. X., Chauncey, H. H., & Winer, R. A. (1964). Effects of hypnotic and nonhypnotic suggestions on parotid gland response to gustatory stimuli. *Psychosomatic Medicine, 26,* 374–380.

Barch, D. M., & Berenbaum, H. (1996). Language production and thought disorder in schizophrenia. *Journal of Abnormal Psychology, 105,* 81–88.

Bargh, J. A., Gollwitzer, P. M., Lee-Chai, A., Barndollar, K., & Troetschel, R. (2001). The automated will: Nonconscious activation and pursuit of behavioral goals. *Journal of Personality and Social Psychology, 74,* 1252–1265.

Bargh, J. A., Raymond, P., Pryor, J. B., & Strack, F. (1995). Attractiveness of the underling: An automatic power-sex association and its consequences for sexual harassment and aggression. *Journal of Personality and Social Psychology, 68,* 768–781.

Bar-Haim, Y., Ziv, T., Lamy, D., & Hodes, R. M. (2006). Nature and nurture in own-race face processing. (2006). *Psychological Science, 17,* 159–163.

Barkley, R. A., DuPaul, G. J., & McMurray, M. B. (1990). Comprehensive evaluation of attention deficit disorder with and without hyperactivity as defined by research criteria. *Journal of Consulting and Clinical Psychology, 58,* 775–789.

Barlow, D. H. (1988). *Anxiety and its disorders.* New York: Guilford Press.

Barlow, D. H. (1993). Disorders and emotion. *Psychological Inquiry, 2,* 58–71.

Barlow, D. H. (2004). Psychological treatments. *American Psychologist, 59,* 869–878.

Baron, R. A. (1970). Attraction toward the model and model's competence as determinants of adult imitative behavior. *Journal of Personality and Social Psychology, 14,* 335–344.

Baron, R. A. (1983). "Sweet smell of success?" The impact of pleasant artificial scents on evaluation of job applicants. *Journal of Applied Psychology, 68,* 709–713.

Baron, R. A. (1987). Mood of interviewer and the evaluation of job candidates. *Journal of Applied Social Psychology, 17,* 911–926.

Baron, R. A. (1993). Criticism (informal negative feedback) as a source of perceived unfairness in organizations: Effects, mechanisms, and countermeasures. In R. Cropanzano (Ed.), *Justice in the workplace: Approaching fairness in human resource management* (pp. 155–170). Hillsdale, NJ: Erlbaum.

Baron, R. A. (1997). The sweet smell of helping: Effects of pleasant ambient odors on helping in shopping malls. *Personality and Social Psychology Bulletin, 2,* 498–503.

Baron, R. A. (2006). Opportunity recognition as pattern recognition: How entrepreneurs "connect the dots" to identify new business opportunities. *Academy of Management Perspectives, 20,* 104–119.

Baron, R. A., & Bronfen, M. I. (1994). A whiff of reality: Empirical evidence concerning the effects of pleasant fragrances on work-related behavior. *Journal of Applied Social Psychology, 13,* 1179–1203.

Baron, R. A., Byrne, D., & Branscombe, N. R. (2005). *Social Psychology* (11th ed.). Boston: Allyn & Bacon.

Baron, R. A., & Kalsher, M. J. (1998). Effects of a pleasant ambient fragrance on simulated driving performance: The sweet smell of safety? *Environment and Behavior, 30,* 535–552.

Baron, R. A., & Richardson, D. (1994). *Human aggression* (2nd ed.). New York: Plenum.

Baron, R. A., & Shane, S. (2007). *Entrepreneurship: A process perspsective.* Cincinnati: Southwestern/Thomson.

Baron, R. A., & Thomley, J. (1994). A whiff of reality: Positive affect as a potential mediator of the effects of pleasant fragrances on task performance and helping. *Environment and Behavior, 26,* 766–784.

Barrett, L. F. (2006). Are emotions natural kinds? *Perspectives on Psychological Science, 1,* 28–58.

Barrick, M. R., & Mount, M. K. (1991). The big five personality dimensions and job performance: A meta-analysis. *Personnel Psychology, 44,* 1–26.

Barrick, M. R., Stewart, G. L., Neubert, M. J., & Mount, M. K. (1998). Relating member ability and personality to work-team processes and team effectiveness. *Journal of Applied Psychology, 83,* 377–391.

Bartholow, B. D., Dicker, C. L., & Sestir, M. A. (2006). Stereotype activation and control of race bias: cognitive control of inhibition and its impairment by alcohol. *Journal of Personality and Social Psychology, 90,* 272–287.

Bartholow, B. D., & Heinz, A. (2006). Alcohol, and aggression without consumption. *Psychological Science, 17,* 30–37.

Bartoshuk, L. M., Duffy, V. B., Fast, K., Green, B. G., Prutkin, J. M., & Snyder, D. J. (2002). Labeled scales (e.g., category, Likert, VAS) and invalid across-group comparisons: What we have learned from genetic variation in taste. *Food Quality and Preference, 14,* 125–138.

Bartoshuk, L. M., Fast, K., & Snyder, D. J. (2005). Differences in our sensory worlds: Invalid comparisons with labeled scales. *Current Directions in Psychological Science, 14,* 122–125.

Basoglu, M., Paker, M., Ozmen, E., Tasdemir, O., Sahin, D., Ceyhanli, A., & Incesu, C. (1996). Appraisal of self, social environment, and state authority as a possible mediator of posttraumatic stress disorder in tortured political activists. *Journal of Abnormal Psychology, 105,* 232–236.

Bass, B. M. (1985). *Leadership and performance beyond expectations.* New York: Free Press.

Bass, B. M., Avolio, B. J., Jung, D. I., & Berson, Y. (2003). Predicting unit performance by assessing transformational and transactional leadership. *Journal of Applied Psychology, 88,* 207–218.

Bauer, P. (1996). What do infants recall of their lives? *American Psychologist, 51,* 29–41.

Baum, A. (1991). Toxins, technology, and natural disasters. In A. Monat & R. S. Lazarus (Eds.), *Stress and coping: An anthology* (3rd ed., pp. 97–139). New York: Columbia University Press.

Baumeister, R. F., & Leary, M. R. (1995). The need to belong: Desire for interpersonal attachments as a fundamental human motivation. *Psychological Bulletin, 117,* 497–529.

Baumrind, D. (1996). A blanket injunction against disciplinary use of spanking is not warranted by the data. *Pediatrics, 98,* 828–831.

Beaman, A. L., Cole, N., Preston, M., Glentz, B., & Steblay, N. M. (1983). Fifteen years of the foot-in-the-door research: A meta-analysis. *Personality and Social Psychology Bulletin, 9,* 181–186.

Beck, A. T. (1976). *Cognitive therapy and the emotional disorders.* New York: International Universities Press.

Beck, A. T. (1985). *Anxiety disorders and phobias: A cognitive perspective.* New York: BasicBooks.

Beck, A. T. (2005). *Anxiety disorders and phobias: A cognitive perspective.* New York: BasicBooks.

Beck, A. T., Rush, A. J., Shaw, B. F., & Emery, G. (1979). *Cognitive theory of depression.* New York: Guilford Press.

Becker, D.V., Kenrick, D. T., Guerin, S., & Maner, J. K. (2005). Concentrating on beauty: Sexual selection and sociospatial memory. *Personality and Social Psychology Bulletin, 31,* 1643–1652.

Becker, H. C., Randall, C. L., Salo, A. L., Saulnier, J. L., & Weathersby, R. T. (1994). Animal research: Charting the course for FAS. *Alcohol Health and Research World, 18,* 10–16.

Begley, S. (2003). Good genes count, but many factors make up a high IQ. *Wall Street Journal,* June 26, p. B1.

Belsky, J., & Cassidy, J. (1995). Attachment: Theory and evidence. In M. Rutter & D. Hay (Eds.), *Developmental through life: A handbook for clinicians* (pp. 373–402). Oxford, England: Blackwell.

Bem, D. J., & Honorton, C. (1994). Does psi exist? Replicable evidence for an anomalous process of information transfer. *Psychological Bulletin, 115,* 4–18.

Bem, S. L. (1984). Androgyny and gender schema theory: A conceptual and empirical integration. In R. A. Dientsbier & T. B. Sondregger (Eds.), *Nebraska Symposium on Motivation* (vol. 34, pp. 179–226). Lincoln: University of Nebraska Press.

Bem, S. L. (1989). Genital knowledge and gender constancy in preschool children. *Child Development, 60,* 649–662.

Benjamin, L. T., Jr., & Dixon, D. N. (1996). Dream analysis by mail: An American woman seeks Freud's advice. *American Psychologist, 51,* 461–468.

Bentin, S., Sagiv, N., Mecklinger, A., Friederici, A., & von Cramon, Y. D. (2002). Priming visual face-processing mechanisms: Electrophysiological evidence. *Psychological Science, 13* (2), 190–193.

Berenbaum, H., & Oltmanns, T. F. (1992). Emotional experience and expression in schizophrenia and depression. *Journal of Abnormal Psychology, 101,* 37–44.

Berger, A., Sadeh, M., Tzur, G., Shuper, A., Kornreich, L, Inbar, D., Cohen, I. J., Michowiz, S., Yaniv, I., Constantini, S., Kessler, Y., & Meiran, N. (2005). Task switching after cerebellar damage. *Neuropsychology, 19,* 362–370.

Bergin, A. E., & Lambert, M. J. (1978). The evaluation of therapeutic outcomes. In S. L. Garfield & A. E. Bergin (Eds.), *Handbook of psychotherapy and behavior change: An empirical analysis* (2nd ed., pp. 139–190). New York: Wiley.

Berkowitz, L. (1984). Some effects of thoughts on anti- and pro-social influences of media events: A cognitive-neoassociation analysis. *Psychological Bulletin, 95,* 410–427.

Berlyne, D. E. (1967). Arousal and reinforcement. In D. Levine (Ed.), *Nebraska Symposium on Motivation* (vol. 15, pp. 279–286). Lincoln: University of Nebraska Press.

Berndt, T. J. (2002). Friendship quality and social development. *Current Directions in Psychological Science, 11,* 7–10.

Bernstein, I. L. (1999). Taste aversion learning: A contemporary perspective. *Nutrition, 15* (3), 229–234.

Berry, J. W., Worthington, E. L., Jr., Parrott, L. III, O'Connor, L., & Wade, N. G. (2001). Dispositional forgivingness: Development and construct validity of the Transgression Narrative Test of Forgivingness (TNTF). *Personality and Social Psychology Bulletin, 27,* 1277–1290.

Berry, J. W., Worthington, E. L., Jr., Parrott, L., III, O'Connor, L. E., & Wade, N. G. (2005). Forgivingness, vengeful rumination, and affective traits. *Journal of Personality, 73,* 183–226.

Bialystok, E., Craik, F. I. M., Klein, R., & Viswanathan, M. (2004). Bilingualism, aging, and cognitive control: Evidence from the Simon task. *Psychology and Aging, 19,* 290–303.

Biederman, I. (1987). Recognition-by-components: A theory of human image understanding. *Psychological Review, 94,* 115–147.

Biederman, I., Rosenbaum, J. F., Hirshfield, D. R., Faraone, S. V., Boldue, E. A., Gersten, M., Menninger, S. R., Kagan, J., Snidman, N., & Reznick, J. S. 1990). Psychiatric correlations of behavioral inhibitions in young children of parents with and without psychiatric disorders. *Archives of General Psychiatry, 47,* 21–26.

Birch, S. A. J. (2005). When knowledge is a curse: Children's and adults' reasoning about mental states. *Current Directions in Psychological Science, 14,* 25–29.

Birch, S. A. J., & Bloom, P. (2004). *The curse of knowledge in reasoning about false beliefs.* Manuscript submitted for publication.

Birchler, G. R. (1992). Marriage. In V. B. Van Hasselt & M. Hersen (Eds.), *Handbook of social development: A lifespan perspective.* New York: Plenum.

Biswas-Diener, R., Vitterso, J., & Diener, E. (2004). Most people are pretty happy, but there is cultural variation: The Inughuit, the Amish, and the Maasai. *Journal of Happiness Studies, 6,* 205–226.

Bixler, E. O., Kales, A., Soldatos, C. R., Kales, J. D., & Healey, S. (1979). Prevalence of sleep disorders in the Los Angeles metropolitan area. *American Journal of Psychiatry, 136,* 1257–1262.

Black, J. S., & Mendenhall, M. (1990). Cross-cultural training effectiveness: A review and a theoretical framework for future research. *Academy of Management Review, 15,* 113–136.

Blackman, M. C. (2006). Using what we know about personality to hire the ideal colleague. *The Industrial-Organizational Psychologist, 43* (3), 27–31.

Blackmore, S. (1986). A critical guide to parapsychology. *Skeptical Inquirer, 11* (1), 97–102.

Blaney, P. H. (1986). Affect and memory: A review. *Psychological Bulletin, 99,* 229–246.

Blascovich, J., & Tomaka, J. (1996). The biopsycho-social model of arousal regulation. *Advances in Experimental Social Psychology, 28,* 1–51.

Blatt, S. J., Zuroff, D. C., Quinlan, D. M., & Pilkonis, P. (1996). Interpersonal factors in brief treatment of depression: Further analysis of the NIMH Treatment of Depression Collaborative Research Program. *Journal of Consulting and Clinical Psychology, 64,* 162–171.

Block, J. H. (1995). A contrarian view of the five-factor approach to personality description. *Psychological Bulletin, 117,* 187–215.

Blumberg, M. S., & Lucas, D. E. (1994). Dual mechanisms of twitching during sleep in neonatal rats. *Behavioral Neuroscience, 108,* 1196–1202.

Bobo, L. (1983). Whites' opposition to busing: Symbolic racism or realistic group conflict? *Journal of Personality and Social Psychology, 45,* 1196–1210.

Bodenhausen, G. V., & Macrae, C. N. (1998). Stereotypes activation and inhibition. In R.S. Wyer (Ed.), *Advances in social cognition* (Vol. 11, pp. 1–2). Mahwah, NJ: Erlbaum.

Bogen, J. E. (1993). The Callosal syndromes. *Clinical Neuropsychology,* Heinemann K.M., Valenstein E., (eds.) 3rd ed. New York: Oxford University Press, pp. 337–407.

Bogg, T., & Roberts, B. W. (2004). Conscientiousness and health-related behaviors: A meta-analysis of the leading behavioral indicators to mortality. *Psychological Bulletin, 130,* 887–919.

Boling, N. C., & Robinson, D. H. (1999). Individual study, interactive multimedia, or cooperative learning: Which activity best supplements lecture-based distance education? *Journal of Educational Psychology, 91,* 169–174.

Bonanno, G. A., Galea, S., Bucciarelli, A., & Vlahov, D. (2006). Psychological resilience after disaster: New York City in the aftermath of the September 11th terrorist attack. *Psychological Science, 17,* 181–185.

Bongar, B. (1991). *The suicidal patient: Clinical and legal standards of care.* Washington, DC: American Psychological Association.

Bookstein, F. L., Sampson, P. D., Streissgarth, A. P., & Barr, H. M. (1996). Exploiting redundant measurement of dose and developmental outcome: New methods from the behavioral teratology of alcohol. *Developmental Psychology, 32,* 404–415.

Bootzin, R. R., Acocella, J. R., & Alloy, L. B. (1993). *Abnormal psychology* (6th ed.). New York: McGraw-Hill.

Borman, W. C. (2004). The concept of organizational citizenship. *Current Directions in Psychological Science, 13,* 238–241.

Borman, W. C., Penner, L. A., Allen, T. D., & Motowildo, S. J. (2001). Personality predictors of citizenship performance. *International Journal of Selection and Assessment, 9,* 52–69.

Bornstein, R. F. (1992). Subliminal mere exposure effects. In R. Bornstein & T. S. Pittman (Eds.), *Perception without awareness: Cognitive, clinical, and social perspectives* (pp. 191–210). New York: Guilford Press.

Borod, J. C. (1993). Cerebral mechanisms underlying facial, prosodic, and lexical emotional expressions: A review of neuropsychological studies and methodological issues. *Neuropsychology, 7,* 445–463.

Bortfeld, H., Morgan, J. L., Golinkoff, R. M., & Rathbun, K. (2005). Mommy and me: Familiar names help launch babies into speech-stream segmentation. *Psychological Science, 16,* 298–304.

Bosma, H., Stansfeld, S. A., & Marmot, M. G. (1998). Job control, personal characteristics, and heart disease. *Journal of Occupational Health Psychology, 3* (4), 402–409.

Bouchard, T. J., Jr. (2004). Genetic influence on human psychological traits: A survey. *Current Directions in Psychological Science, 13,* 148–151.

Bouchard, T. J., Jr., Lykken, D. T., McGue, M., Segal, N. L., & Tellegen, A. (1990). Sources of human psychological differences: The Minnesota Study of Twins Reared Apart. *Science, 250,* 223–228.

Boudreau, J. W. (1991). Utility analysis for decisions in human resource management. In M. D. Dunnette & L. M. Hough (Eds.), *Handbook of industrial and organizational psychology* (vol. 2, pp. 621–745). Palo Alto, CA: Consulting Psychologists Press.

Bowers, K. S. (1992). Imagination and dissociation in hypnotic responding. *International Journal of Clinical and Experimental Hypnosis, 40,* 253–275.

Bowles, N., & Hynds, F. (1978). *Psy search: The comprehensive guide to psychic phenomena.* New York: Harper & Row.

Bowman, E. S., & Nurnberger, J. K. (1993). Genetics of psychiatry diagnosis and treatment. In D. L. Dunner (Ed.), *Current psychiatric therapy* (pp. 46–56). Philadelphia: Saunders.

Brady, K. T., Back, S. F., & Coffey, S. F. (2004). Substance abuse and post-traumatic stress disorders. *Current Directions in Psychological Science, 31,* 207–210.

Braffman, W., & Kirsch, I. (1999). Imaginative suggestibility and hypnotizability: An empirical analysis. *Journal of Personality and Social Psychology, 77,* 578–587.

Brainerd, C. J., & Reyna, V. F. (1998). When things that were never experienced are easier to "remember" than things that were. *Psychological Science, 9,* 484–489.

Brannick, M. T., & Levine, E. L. (2002). *Job analysis: Methods, research, and applications for human resource management in the new millennium.* Thousand Oaks, CA: Sage.

Braun, K. A., Ellis, R., & Loftus, E .F. (2004). Make my memory: How advertising can change our memories of the past. *Psychology and Marketing, 19,* 1–23.

Braverman, N. S., & Bronstein, P. (Eds.). (1985). Experimental assessments and clinical applications of conditioned food aversions. *Annals of the New York Academy of Sciences, 443,* 1–41.

Brean, H. (1958). What hidden sell is all about. *Life,* March 31, pp. 104–114.

Breedlove, S. M. (1994). Sexual differentiation of the human nervous system. *Annual Review of Psychology, 45,* 389–418.

Brembs, B. (2003). Operant reward learning in Aplysia. *Current Directions in Psychological Science, 12* (6), 218–221.

Brettz, R. D., & Thompsett, R. E. (1992). Comparing traditional and integrative learning methods in organizational training programs. *Journal of Applied Psychology, 77,* 941–951.

Brickman, P., & Campbell, D. T. (1971). Hedonic relativism and planning the good society. In M. H. Appley (Ed.), *Adaptation-level theory* (pp. 287–305). New York: Academic Press.

Brickman, P. & Coates, D. (1978). Lottery winners and accident victims: is happiness relative? *Journal of Personality and Social Psychology, 36,* 917–927.

Brigham, J. C., & Barkowitz, P. (1978). Do "they all look alike"? The effects of race, sex, experience, and attitudes on the ability to recognize faces. *Journal of Applied Social Psychology, 8,* 307–318.

Brockner, J., & Wiesenfeld, B. M. (1996). An integrative framework for explaining reactions to decisions: The interactive effects of outcomes and procedures. *Psychological Bulletin, 120,* 189–208.

Brody, G. H. (2004). Siblings' direct and indirect contributions to child development. *Current Directions in Psychological Science, 13,* 124–126.

Brosnan, S., & de Waal, F. (2003). *Nature.* (Described by L. Beil, *Dallas Morning News,* September 18.)

Broussaud, D., di Pellegrino, G., & Wise, S. P. (1996). Frontal lobe mechanisms subserving vision-for-action versus vision-for-perception. *Behavioural Brain Research, 72,* 1–15.

Brown, S. L., Nesse, R. M., Vinokur, A. D., & Smith, D. M. (2003). Providing social support may be more beneficial than receiving it. *Psychological Science, 14* (4), 320–327.

Bruder, G. E., Stewart, M. W., Mercier, M. A., Agosti, V., Leite, P., Donovan, S., & Quitkin, F. M. (1997). Outcome of cognitive-behavioral therapy for depression: Relation to hemispheric dominance for verbal processing. *Journal of Abnormal Psychology, 106,* 138–144.

Burger, J. M., & Cornelius, T. (2003). Raising the price of agreement: Public commitment and the lowball compliance procedure. *Journal of Applied Social Psychology, 3,* 923–934.

Burish, T. G., & Carey, M. P. (1986). Conditioned aversive response in cancer chemotherapy patients: Theoretical and developmental analysis. *Journal of Consulting and Clinical Psychology, 54,* 593–600.

Burroughs, V. J., Randall, M. W., & Levy, R. A. (2002). Racial and ethnic differences in response to medicines: Toward individualized pharmaceutical treatment. *Journal of the National Medical Association, 94,* 1–26.

Bushman, B. J. (1984). Perceived symbols of authority and their influence on compliance. *Journal of Applied Social Psychology, 14,* 501–508.

Bushman, B. J. (1988). The effects of apparel on compliance: A field experiment with a female authority figure. *Personality and Social Psychology Bulletin, 14,* 459–467.

Bushman, B. J. (1995). Moderating role of trait aggressiveness in the effects of violent media on aggression. *Journal of Personality and Social Psychology, 69,* 950–960.

Buss, D. M. (1999). *Evolutionary psychology.* Boston: Allyn & Bacon.

Buss, D. M. (2005). *Handbook of evolutionary psychology.* New York: Wiley.

Buss, D. M., & Schmitt, D. P. (1993). Sexual strategies theory: An evolutionary perspective on human mating. *Psychological Review, 100,* 204–232.

Butcher, J. N. (1990). *MMPI-2 in psychological treatment.* New York: Oxford University Press.

Buunk, B. P. (1995). Sex, self-esteem, dependency, and extradyadic sexual experience as related to jealousy responses. *Journal of Social and Personal Relationships, 12,* 147–153.

Byrne, D. (1971). *The attraction paradigm.* New York: Academic Press.

Byrne, D. (1982). Predicting human sexual behavior. In A. G. Kraut (Ed.), *The G. Stanley Hall Lecture Series* (vol. 2, pp. 363–364, 368). Washington, D.C.: American Psychological Association.

Byrne, D. (1992). The transition from controlled laboratory experimentation to less controlled settings: Surprise! Additional variables are operative. *Communication Monographs, 59,* 190–198.

Byrne, D., & Smeaton, G. (1988). The Feeling Scale: Positive and negative affective responses. In C. M. Davis, W. L. Yarger, R. Bauserman, G. Scheer, & S. L. Davis (Eds.), *Handbook of sexuality-related measures* (pp. 50–52). Thousand Oaks, CA: Sage.

Cacioppo, J. T., Hawkley, L. C., & Berntson, G. G. (2003). The anatomy of loneliness. *Current Directions in Psychological Science, 12,* 71–74.

Cadinu, M., Maass, A., Rosabianca, A., & Kiesner, J. (2005). Why do women underperform under stereotype threat? *Psychological Science, 16,* 572–578.

Cadoret, R. J., Troughton, E., & O'Gorman, T. W. (1987). Genetic and environmental factors in alcohol abuse and antisocial personality. *Journal of Studies on Alcohol, 48,* 1–8.

California Department of Developmental Services. (1999). *Changes in the population with autism and pervasive developmental disorders in California's developmental services system: 1987–1998.* A report to the legislature. Sacramento, CA: California Health and Human Services Agency.

Campbell, J. N., & LaMotte, R. H. (1983). Latency to detection of first pain. *Brain Research, 266,* 203–208.

Campbell, S. C., Ewing, L. J., Breaux, A. M., & Szumowski, E. K. (1986). Problem three-year-olds: follow-up at school entry. *Journal of Child Psychology and Psychiatry, 27,* 473–488.

Campion, M. A., Palmer, D. K., & Campion, J. E. (1999). Structuring employment interviews to improve reliability, validity, and users' reactions. *Current Directions in Psychological Science, 7,* 1–6.

Campos, J. J., Langer, A., & Krowitz, A. (1970). Cardiac responses on the visual cliff in prelocomotor human infants. *Science, 170,* 196–197.

Cannon, T. D., Rosso, I. M., Bearden, C. E., Sanchez, L. E., & Hadley, T. (1999). A prospective cohort study of neurodevelopmental processes in the genesis and epigenesis of schizophrenia. *Development and Psychopathology, 11,* 467–485.

Cantor, N., & Sanderson, C. A. (1999). Life task participation and well-being: The importance of taking part in daily life. In D. Kahneman, E. Diener, & N. Schwarz (Eds.), *Well-being: The foundations of hedonic psychology.* New York: Russell Sage Foundation.

Capaldi, E. J. (1978). Effects of schedule and delay of reinforcement on acquisition speed. *Animal Learning and Behavior, 6,* 330–334.

Capaldi, E. J., Alptekin, S., & Birmingham, K. (1997). Discriminating between reward-produced memories: Effects of differences in reward magnitude. *Animal Learning & Behavior, 25,* 171–176.

Capaldi, E. J., & Birmingham, K. M. (1998). Reward produced memories regulate memory-discrimination learning, extinction, and other forms of discrimination learning. *Journal of Experimental Psychology: Animal Behavior Processes, 24,* 254–264.

Carlo, G., Koller, S. H., Eisenberg, N., Da Silva, M. S., & Frohlich, C. B. (1996). A cross-national study on the relations among prosocial moral reasoning, gender role orientations, and prosocial behavior. *Developmental Psychology, 32,* 231–240.

Carlson, N. R. (1998). *Physiology of behavior* (6th ed.). Boston: Allyn & Bacon.

Carlson, N. R. (1999). *Foundations of physiological psychology* (4th ed.). Boston: Allyn & Bacon.

Carpendale, J. L. M., & Krebs, D. L. (1995). Variations in moral judgment as a function of type of dilemma and moral choice. *Journal of Personality, 63,* 289–313.

Carroll, J. M., & Russell, J. A. (1996). Do facial expressions signal specific emotions? Judging emotion from the face in context. *Journal of Personality and Social Psychology, 70,* 205–218.

Carstensen, L. L., & Mikels, J. A. (2005). At the intersection of emotion and cognition. *Current Directions in Psychological Science, 14,* 117–121.

Carver, C. S. (2005). Impulse and constraint: Perspectives from personality psychology, convergence with theory in other areas, and potential for integration. *Personality and Social Psychology Review, 9,* 312–333.

Catania, A. C. (1992). *Learning* (3rd ed.). Englewood Cliffs, NJ: Prentice-Hall.

Cattell, R. B. (1963). Theory of fluid and crystallized intelligence: A critical experiment. *Journal of Educational Psychology, 54,* 1–22.

Cellular Telecommunications & Internet Association. (2005). The danger of using cellular phones while driving. Available: www.iii.org/media/hottopics/insurance/cellphones/?printerfriendly=yes.

Centers for Disease Control (1998). Cigarette Smoking Behavior of Adults: United States, 1997–1998. Accessed from the world wide web on September 25, 2006 at www.cdc.gov/nchs/data/ad/ad331.pdf.

Centers for Disease Control. (2003). Cigarette smoking among adults-United States, 2001. *Mortality and Morbidity Weekly Report, 52,* 953–956.

Centers for Disease Control. (2004). Cigarette smoking among high school students, United States, 1991–2003. *Morbidity and Mortality Weekly Report, 53,* 23, June 18. Available: www.cdc.gov/TOBACCO/research_data/youth/mm5323_highlights.htm.

Centers for Disease Control. (2004). HIV/AIDS among women. Available: www.cdc.gov/hiv/topics/women/resources/factsheets/women.htm.

Centers for Disease Control. (2005). *Adult Cigarette Smoking in the United States: Current Estimates Fact Sheet, December 2005.* Available: www.cdc.gov/tobacco/factsheets/AdultCigaretteSmoking_FactSheet.htm.

Centers for Disease Control. (2005, July). Summary health statistics for U.S. adults: National health interview survey, 2003. *Vital and Health Statistics, Series 20, 225.* Available: www.cdc.gov/nchs/data/series/sr_10/sr10_225.pdf.

Centers for Disease Control. (2006). Deaths, percent of total deaths, and death rates for the 15 leading causes of death in 5-year age groups, by race and sex: United States, 2003. *National Vital Statistics Report,* March 9. Available: www.cdc.gov/nchs/data/series/sr_10/sr10_225.pdf.

Centerwall, B. S. (1989). Exposure to television as a cause of violence. In G. Comstock (Ed.), *Public communication and behavior* (vol. 2). San Diego: Academic Press.

Chamberlin, J. (2006). Into the mouths of babes: Through policy work and a parent-education program a psychologist is helping children eat right. *Monitor on Psychology, 37,* 32–33.

Chan, D. (2005). Current directions in personnel selection research. *Current Directions in Psychological Science, 14,* 220–223.

Chang, E. C., & Asakawa, K. (2003). Cultural variations on optimistic and pessimistic bias for self versus a sibling: Is there

evidence for self-enhancement in the West and for self-criticism in the East when the referent group is specified? *Journal of Personality and Social Psychology, 84,* 569–581.

Chaplin, W. F., Phillips, J. B., Brown, J. D., Clanton, N. R., & Stein, J. L. (2000). Handshaking, gender, personality, and first impressions. *Journal of Personality and Social Psychology, 79,* 110–117.

Chapman, D. S., Uggerslev, K. L., Carroll, S. A., Piasentin, K. A., & Jones, D. A. (2005). Applicant attraction to organizations and job choice: A meta-analytic review of the correlates of recruiting outcomes. *Journal of Applied Psychology, 90,* 928–944.

Charles, S. T., Reynolds, C. A., & Gatz, M. (2001). Age-related differences and change in positive and negative affect over 23 years. *Journal of Personality and Social Psychology, 80,* 136–151.

Chassin, L., Flora, D. B., & King, K. M. (2004). Trajectories of alcohol and drug use and dependence from adolescence to adulthood: The effects of familial alcoholism and personality. *Journal of Abnormal Psychology, 113,* 483–498.

Cheng, D. T., Knight, D. C., Smith, C. N., Stein, E. A., & Helmstetter, F. J. (2003). Functional MRI of human amygdala activity during Pavlovian fear conditioning: Stimulus processing versus response expression. *Behavioral Neuroscience, 117* (1), 3–10.

Cherbuin, N., & Brinkman, C. (2006). Efficiency of callosal transfer and hemispheric interaction. *Neuropsychology, 20,* 178–184.

Chess, S., & Thomas, A. (1984). *Origins and evolution of behavior disorders.* New York: Brunner/Mazel.

Chialvo, D. R. (2004). Critical brain networks. *Physica, 340,* 756–765.

Chino, Y., Smith, E., Hatta, S., & Cheng, H. (1997). Post-natal development of binocular disparity sensitivity in neurons of the primate visual cortex. *Journal of Neuroscience, 17,* 296–307.

Choi, H., & Thompson, L. (2005). Old wine in a new bottle: Impact of membership change on group creativity. *Organizational Behavior and Human Decision Processes, 98,* 121–132.

Choi, L., & Nisbett, R. E. (1998). Situational salience and cultural differences in the correspondence bias and actor-observer bias. *Personality and Social Psychology Bulletin, 24,* 949–960.

Choi, W. S., Pierce, J. P., Gilpin, E. A., Farkas, A. J., & Berry, C. C. (1997). Which adolescent experimenters progress to established smoking in the United States. *American Journal of Preventive Medicine, 13,* 385–391.

Chomsky, N. (1968). *Language and mind.* New York: Harcourt Brace.

Christian, K. M. & Thompson, R. F., (2005). Long-term Storage of an Associative Memory Trace in the Cerebellum. *Behavioral Neuroscience, 119,* 526–537.

Cooper, J., & Scher, S. J. (1990). Actions and attitude: the role of responsibility and aversive consequences in persuasion. In T. Brock & S. Shavitt (Eds.), *The psychology of persuasion.* San Francisco: Freeman.

Chorney, M. J., Chorney, K., Seese, N., Owen, M. J., Daniels, J., McGuffin, P., Thompson, L. A., Detterman, D. K., Benbow, C., Lubinski, D., Eley, T., & Plomin, R. (1998). A quantitative trait locus associated with cognitive ability in children. *Psychological Science, 9,* 159–166.

Christman, S., Propper, R. E., & Dion, A. (2004). Increased interhemispheric interaction is associated with decreased false memories in a verbal converging semantic associates paradigm. *Brain and Cognition 56,* 313–319.

Cialdini, R. B. (1994). Interpersonal influence. In S. Shavitt & T. C. Brock (Eds.), *Persuasion* (pp. 195–218). Boston: Allyn & Bacon.

Cialdini, R. B., Cacioppo, J. T., Bassett, R., & Miller, J. A. (1978). A low-ball procedure for producing compliance: Commitment then cost. *Journal of Personality and Social Psychology, 36,* 463–476.

Ciavarella, M. A., Buchholtz, A. K., Riordan, C. M., Gatewood, R. D., & Stokes, G.S. (2004). The big five and venture survival: Is there a linkage? *Journal of Business Venturing, 19,* 465–484.

Cinciripini, P. M., Tsoh, J. Y., Wetter, D. W., Lam, C., de Moor, C., Cinciripini, L., Baile, W., Anderson, C., & Minna, J. D. (2005). Combined effects of venlafaxine, nicotine replacement, and brief counseling on smoking cessation. *Experimental and Clinical Psychopharmacology, 13,* 282–292.

Clark, R. E., & Squire, L. R. (1999). Human eye-blink classical conditioning: Effects of manipulating awareness of the stimulus contingencies. *Psychological Science, 10,* 14–18.

Clark, W. C., & Clark, S. B. (1980). Pain responses in Nepalese porters. *Science, 209,* 410–412.

Clarke-Stewart, A., Friedman, S., & Koch, J. (1985). *Child development: A topical approach.* New York: Wiley.

Clay, R. A. (2006). Assessing assessment. *Monitor on Psychology, 37,* 44–46.

Clum, G. A., & Bowers, T. G. (1990). Behavior therapy better than placebo treatments: Fact or artifact? *Psychological Bulletin, 107,* 110–113.

Coates, T. J., & Collins, C. (1998, July). Preventing HIV infection. *Scientific American,* 96–97.

Cohen, S. (2004, November). Social relationships and health. *American Psychologist,* 676–684.

Cohen, S., Doyle, W. J., Turner, R., Alper, C. M., & Skoner, D. P. (2003). Sociability and susceptibility to the common cold. *Psychological Science, 14* (5), 389–395.

Cohen, S., Doyle, W. J., Turner, R. B., Alper, C. M., & Skoner, D. P. (2003). Emotional style and susceptibility to the common cold. *Psychosomatic Medicine, 65,* 652–657.

Colcombe, S., & Kramer, A. F. (2003). Fitness effects on the cognitive function of older adults: A meta-analytic study. *Psychological Science, 14,* 125–130.

Cole, J. D. (1998). Psychotherapy with the chronic pain patient using coping skills development: outcome study. *Journal of Occupational Health Psychology, 3,* 217–226.

Cole, M. (1999). Culture in development. In M. H. Bornstein & M. E. Lamb (Eds.), *Developmental psychology: An advanced textbook* (4th ed.). Hillsdale, NJ: Erlbaum.

Collins, C. J., Hanges, P., & Locke, E. A. (2004). The relationship of need for achievement to entrepreneurship: A meta-analysis. *Human Performance, 17,* 95–117.

Colombo, J., & Richman, W. A. (2002). Infant timekeeping: Attention and temporal estimation in 40-month-olds. *Psychological Science, 13,* 475–479.

Colwill, R. M. (1993). An associative analysis of instrumental learning. *Current Directions in Psychological Science, 2,* 111–116.

Colwill, R. M., & Rescorla, R. A. (1985). Postconditioning devaluation of a reinforcer affects instrumental responding. *Journal of Experimental Psychology, 11,* 120–132.

Colwill, R. M., & Rescorla, R. A. (1988). Associations between the discriminative stimulus and the reinforcer in instrumental learning. *Journal of Experimental Psychology, 14,* 155–164.

Conklin, H. M., & Iacono, W. G. (2002). Schizophrenia: A neurodevelopmental perspective. *Current Directions in Psychological Science, 11,* 33–37.

Coren, S., Girgus, J. S., Erlichman, H., & Hakstean, A. R. (1976). An empirical taxonomy of visual illusions. *Perception & Psychophysics, 20,* 129–137.

Costa, P. T., Jr., & McCrae, R. R. (1989). *The NEO-PI/NEO-FFI manual supplement.* Odessa, FL: Psychological Assessment Resources.

Costa, P. T., Jr., & McCrae, R. R. (1994). The Revised NEO Personality Inventory (NEO-PI-R). In R. Briggs & J. M. Cheek (Eds.), *Personality measures: Development and evaluation* (vol. 1). Greenwich, CT: JAI Press.

Coulson, S., Federmeier, K. D., Van Petten, C., & Kutas, M. (2005). Right hemisphere sensitivity to word- and sentence-level context evidence from event-related brain potentials. *Journal of Experimental Psychology: Learning, Memory, and Cognition, 31,* 129–147.

Courtenay, W. H., McCreary, D. R., & Merighi, J. R. (2002). Gender and ethnic differences in health beliefs and behaviors, *Journal of Health Psychology, 7,* 219–231.

Coyle, J. T. (1987). Alzheimer's disease. In G. Adelman (Ed.), *Encyclopedia of neuroscience* (pp. 29–31). Boston: Birkhauser.

Crawford, H. J., Knebel, T., Vendemia, J. M. (1998). The nature of hypnotic analgesia: Neurophysiological foundation and evidence. *Contemporary Hypnosis, 15,* 22–33.

Crespi, L. P. (1942). Quantitative variation of incentive and performance in the white rat. *American Journal of Psychology, 55,* 467–517.

Crocker, J., & Knight, K. M. (2005). Contingencies of self-worth. *Current Directions in Psychological Science, 14,* 200–203.

Croyle, R. T. (1992). Appraisal of health threats: Cognition, motivation, and social comparison. *Cognitive Therapy and Research, 16,* 165–182.

Csikszentmihalyi, M., & Larson, R. (1984). *Being adolescent: Conflict and growth in the teenage years.* New York: Basic Books.

Culbertson, F. M. (1997). Depression and gender: An international review. *American Psychologist, 52,* 25–31.

Cumming, S., Hay, P., Lee, T., & Sachdev, P. (1995). Neuropsychological outcomes from psychosurgery for obsessive-compulsive disorder. *Australian & New Zealand Journal of Psychiatry, 29,* 293–298.

Cunningham, J., Dockery, D. W., & Speizer, F. E. (1994). Maternal smoking during pregnancy as a predictor of lung functions in children. *American Journal of Epidemiology, 139,* 1139–1152.

Cunningham, M. R., Roberts, A. R., Wu, C. H., Barbee, A. P., & Druen, P. B. (1995). "Their ideas of beauty are, on the whole, the same as ours": Consistency and variability in the cross-cultural perception of female physical attractiveness. *Journal of Personality and Social Psychology, 68,* 261–279.

Czeisler, C. A., Moore-Ede, M. C., & Coleman, R. M. (1982). Rotating shift work schedules that disrupt sleep are improved by applying Circadian principles. *Science, 217,* 460–462.

Dadds, M. R., Bovbjerg, D. H., Redd, W. H., & Cutmore, T. R. (1997). Imagery in human classical conditioning. *Psychological Bulletin, 122,* 89–103.

Dalal, R.S. (2005). A meta-analysis of the relationship between organizational citizenship behavior and counterproductive work behavior. *Journal of Applied Psychology, 90,* 1241–1255.

Daley, T. C., Whaley, S. E., Sigman, M. D., Espinosa, M. P., & Neumann, C. (2003). IQ on the rise: The Flynn effect in rural Kenyan children. *Psychological Science, 14,* 215–219.

Dalton, M. A., Sargent, J. D., Beach, M. L., Titus-Emstoff, L., Gibson, J. J., Ahrens,

M.B., Tickle, J. J., Heatherton, T. F. (2003). Effect of viewing smoking in movies on adolescent smoking initiation: A cohort study. *Lancet, 362,* 281–285.

Damak, S., Rong, M., Yasumatsu, K., Kokrashvili, Z., Varadarajan, V., Zou, S., Jiang, P., Ninomiya, Y., & Margolskee, R. F. (2003). Detection of sweet and umami taste in the absence of taste receptor T1r3. *Science, 301,* 850–853.

Dangerous Decibels (2006). Retrieved September 1, 2006, from www .dangerousdecibels .org/.

Daniel, J., & Potasova, A. (1989). Oral temperature and performance in 8 hour and 12 hour shifts. *Ergonomics, 32,* 689–696.

Dansinger, M. (2003). *One year effectiveness of the Atkins, Ornish, Weight Watchers, and Zone diets in decreasing body weight and heart disease risk.* Paper presented at the American Heart Association's annual meeting, Orlando, Florida.

Daum, I., & Schugens, M. M. (1996). On the cerebellum and classical conditioning. *Current Directions in Psychological Science, 5,* 58–61.

Davis, F. D., & Yi, M. Y. (2004). Improving computer skill training: Behavior modeling, symbolic mental rehearsal, and the role of knowledge structure. *Journal of Applied Psychology, 89,* 509–523.

Davis, M., Myers, K. M., Ressler, K. J., & Rothbaum, B. O. (2005). Facilitation of extinction of conditioned fear by D-Cycloserine: Implications for psychotherapy. *Current Directions in Psychological Science, 14,* 214–218.

Deary, I. J., & Der, G. (2005). Reaction time explains IQ's association with death. *Psychological Science, 16,* 64–69.

Deary, I. J., & Stough, C. (1996). Intelligence and inspection time. *American Psychologist, 51,* 599–608.

Deary, I. J., Whiteman, M. C., Starr, J. M., Whalley, L. J., & Fox., H. C. (2004). The impact of childhood intelligence on later life: Following up the Scottish mental surveys of 1932 and 1947. *Journal of Personality and Social Psychology, 86,* 130–147.

Deaux, K. (1993). Commentary: Sorry, wrong number-a reply to Gentile's call. *Psychological Science, 4,* 125–126.

Deci, E. L. (1975). *Intrinsic motivation.* New York: Plenum.

Deci, E. L., & Ryan, R. M. (1985). *Intrinsic motivation and self-determination in human behavior.* New York: Plenum.

Decker, P. J., & Nathan, B. R. (1985). *Behavior modeling training: Principles and applications.* New York: Praeger.

De Corte, E. (2003). Transfer as the productive use of acquired knowledge, skills, and motivations. *Current Directions in Psychological Science, 12,* 142–146.

Delis, D. C., Squire, L. R., Bihrle, A., & Massman, P. S. (1992). Componential analysis of problem-solving ability: Performance of patients with frontal lobe damage and amnesic patients on a new sorting test. *Neuropsychologia, 30,* 680–697.

DeLongis, A., Folkman, S., & Lazarus, R. S. (1988). The impact of daily stress on health and mood: Psychological and social resources as mediators. *Journal of Personality and Social Psychology, 54,* 486–495.

Dement, W. C. (1975). *Some must watch while some must sleep.* San Francisco: Freeman.

Dement, W. C., & Kleitman, N. (1957). The relation of eye movement during sleep to dream activity: An objective method for the study of dreaming. *Journal of Experimental Psychology, 53,* 339–353.

Denollet, J. (1998). Personality and coronary heart disease: The Type-D Scale-16 (DS16). *Annals of Behavioral Medicine, 20,* 209–215.

DePaulo, B. M. (1993). Nonverbal behavior and self-presentation. *Psychological Bulletin, 111,* 203–242.

DePaulo, B. M., & Kashy, D. A. (1998). Everyday lies in close and casual relationships. *Journal of Personality and Social Psychology, 74,* 63–79.

DePaulo, B. M., Lindsay, J. J., Malone, B. E., Muhlenbruck, L., Chandler, K., & Cooper, H. (2003). Cues to deception. *Psychological Bulletin, 129,* 74–118.

Desimone, R., & Ungerleider, L. G. (1989). Neural mechanisms of visual processing in monkeys. In F. Boller & J. Garfman (Eds.), *Handbook of neuropsychology* (pp. 267–299). New York: Elsevier.

Detweiler, J. B., Bedell, B. T., Salovey, P., Pronin, E., & Rothman, A. J. (1999). Message framing and sunscreen use: Gain-framed messages motivate beach-goers. *Health Psychology, 18,* 189–196.

Deutsch, D., Henthorn, T., & Dolson, M. (2004). Absolute pitch, speech, and tone language: Some experiments and a proposed framework. *Music Perception, 21,* 339–356.

DeValois, R. L., & DeValois, K. K. (1975). Neural coding of color. In E. C. Carterette & M. P. Friedman (Eds.), *Handbook of perception* (pp. 117–166). New York: Academic Press.

DeValois, R. L., & DeValois, K. K. (1993). A multistage color model. *Vision Research, 33,* 1053–1065.

De Waal, F. B. M. (2002). Evolutionary psychology: The wheat and the chaff. *Current Directions in Psychological Science, 11,* 187–191.

Dhami, M. K. (2003). Psychological models of professional decision making. *Psychological Science, 14,* 175–180.

Diamond, A., & Kirkham, N. (2005). Not quite as grown-up as we like to think. *Psychological Science, 16,* 291–297.

Dickens, W. T., & Flynn, J. R.,(2001). Heritability estimates versus large environmental effects: The IQ paradox resolved. *Psychological Review, 108,* 346–349.

Diego, M. A., Jones, N. A., Field, T., Hernandez-Reif, M., Schanberg, S., Kuhn, C., McAdam, V., Galamaga, R., & Galamaga, M. (1998). Aromatherapy positively affects mood, EEG patterns of alertness and math computations. *International Journal of Neuroscience, 96,* 217–224.

Diener, E., & Diener, C. (1996). Most people are happy. *Psychological Science, 7,* 181–185.

Diener, E., & Diener, M. (1995). Cross-cultural correlates of life satisfaction and self-esteem. *Journal of Personality and Social Psychology, 68,* 653–663.

Diener, E., Gohm, C., Suh, E., & Oishi, S. (1998). *Do the effects of marital status on subjective well-being vary across cultures?* Manuscript submitted for publication.

Diener, E., & Lucas, R. E. (1999). Personality and subjective well-being. In D. Kahneman, E. Diener, & N. Schwarz (Eds.), *Well-being: The foundations of a hedonic psychology* (pp. 213–229). New York: Russell Sage Foundation.

Diener, E., Lucas, R. E., & Scollon, C. N. (2006). Beyond the hedonic treadmill: Revising the adaptation theory of well-being. *American Psychologist, 61,* 305–314.

Diener, E., Oishi, S., & Lucas, R. E. (2003). Culture, personality, and well-being. *Annual Review of Psychology, 54,* 403–425.

Diener, E., & Seligman, M. E. P. (2002). Very happy people. *Psychological Science, 13,* 81–84.

Diener, E., & Seligman, M. E. P. (2004). Beyond money: Toward an economy of well-being. *Psychological Science in the Public Interest, 5.*

Diener, E., & Suh, E. (Eds.). (1998). *Subjective well-being across cultures.* Cambridge, MA: MIT Press.

Diener, E., Suh, E. M., Lucas, R. E., & Smith, H. L. (1999). Subjective well-being: Three decades of progress. *Psychological Bulletin, 125,* 276–302.

Diener, E., Wolsic, B., & Fujita, F. (1995). Physical attractiveness and subjective well-being. *Journal of Personality and Social Psychology, 69,* 120–129.

Dijksterhuis, A., & Aarts, H. (2003). On wildebeests and humans: The preferential detection of negative stimuli. *Psychological Science, 14* (1), 14–18.

DiMatteo, M. R., & Di Nicola, D. D. (1982). *Achieving patient compliance: The psychology of the medical practitioner's role.* New York: Pergamon Press.

Dimberg, U., Thunberg, M., & Elmehed, K. (2000). Unconscious facial reactions to emotional facial expressions. *Psychological Science, 11,* 86–89.

Dingfelder, S. F. (2005). Autism's smoking gun? *Monitor on Psychology, 36,* 52–54.

Dingfelder, S. F. (2005). Fuzzy math: A remote tribe that lacks a counting system suggests limitations on inborn representations of number. *Monitor on Psychology, 36*, 30–31.

Dingfelder, S. F. (2005). Hispanic psychology: Closing the gap for Latino patients. *Monitor on Psychology, 36*, 58–61.

Dingfelder, S. F. (2006). Fear itself. *Monitor on Psychology, 37*, 22–25.

Dion, K. K., Berscheid, E., & Walster, F. H. (1972). What is beautiful is good. *Journal of Personality and Social Psychology, 24*, 285–290.

Dobb E. (1989). The scents around us. *Sciences*, Nov.-Dec., 1989, 46–53.

Domjan, M. (2000). *The essentials of conditioning and learning* (2nd ed.). Belmont, CA: Wadsworth.

Donderi, D. C. (2006). Visual complexity: A review. *Psychological Bulletin, 132*, 73–97.

Donnellan, M. B., Trzesniewski, K. H., Robins, R. W., Moffitt, T. E., & Caspi, A. (2005). Low self-esteem is related to aggression, antisocial behavior, and delinquency. *Psychological Science, 16*, 328–335.

Douek, E. (1988). Olfaction and medicine. In S. Van Toller & G. Doll (Eds.), *Perfumery: The psychology and biology of fragrance*. London: Chapman Hall.

Dovidio, J. F., Evans, N., & Tyler, R. B. (1986). Racial stereotypes: The contents of their cognitive representations. *Journal of Experimental Social Psychology, 22*, 22–37.

Dovidio, J. F., & Gaertner, S. L. (1993). Stereotype and evaluative intergroup bias. In D. M. Mackie & D. L. Hamilton (Eds.), *Affect, cognition, and stereotyping: Interactive processes in group perception*. Orlando, FL: Academic Press.

Dovidio, J. F., Gaertner, S. L., Isen, A. M., & Lowrance, R. E. (1995). Group representations and intergroup bias: Positive affect, similarity, and group size. *Personality and Social Psychology Bulletin, 21*, 856–865.

Drasgow, F. (2005). *Computerized testing and assessment: Boon or boondoggle?* Presidential address presented at the Annual Conference of the Society for Industrial and Organizational Psychology, Los Angeles.

Drasgow, F., Luecht, R., & Bennett, R. (2005). Technology and testing. In R. L. Brennan (Ed.), *Educational Measurement* (4th ed.). Washington, D.C.: American Council on Education.

Duckworth, A. L., & Seligman, M. E. P. (2005). Self-discipline outdoes IQ in predicting academic performance of adolescents. *Psychological Science, 16*, 939–944.

Duffy, M. (2004). Unpublished study, University of Kentucky. Cited in Cary, B. (2004). Bullying bosses do it because they can. *Toronto Star*, July 2, pp. 32–33.

Dula, C. S., & Geller, E. S. (2004). Risky, aggressive, or emotional driving: Addressing the need for consistent communication among researchers. *Journal of Safety Research, 34*, 559–566.

Duncan, J., Seitz, R. J., Kolodny, J., Bor, D., Herzog, H., Ahmed, A., Newell, F. N., & Emslie, H. (2000). A neural basis for general intelligence. *Science, 289*, 457–460.

Dweck, C. S., & Licht, B. G. (1980). Learned helplessness and intellectual achievement. In M. E. P. Seligman & J. Garber (Eds.), *Human helplessness: Theory and application*. New York: Academic Press.

Eagly, A. H., Ashmore, R. D., Makhijani, M. G., & Longo, L. C. (1991). What is beautiful is good, but . . . : A meta-analytic review of research on the physical attractiveness stereotype. *Psychological Bulletin, 110*, 109–128.

Eagly, A. H., & Johnson, B. T. (1990). Gender and leadership style: A meta-analysis. *Psychological Bulletin, 90*, 1–20.

Eagly, A. H., Karau, S. J., & Makhijani, M. G. (1995). Gender and the effectiveness of leaders: A meta-analysis. *Psychological Bulletin, 112*, 125–145.

Eagly, A. H., & Wood, W. (1999). The origins of sex differences in human behavior. *American Psychologist, 54*, 408–423.

Easterbrook, G. (2003). *The progress paradox: How life gets better while people feel worse*. New York: Random House.

Eberhardt, J. L., Davies, P. G., Purdie-Vaughns, V. J., & Johnson, S. L. (2006). Looking deathworthy: Perceived stereotypicality of black defendants predicts capital-sentencing outcomes. *Psychological Science, 17*, 383–386.

Eccleston, C., & Crombez, G. (1999). Pain demands attention: A cognitive-affective model of the interruptive function of pain. *Psychological Bulletin, 125*, 356–366.

Economic Times. (2006). Body clock could be re-set. Economic Times.com, March 23.

Edwards, K., & Bryan, T. S. (1997). Judgmental biases produced by instructions to disregard: The (paradoxical) case of emotional information. *Personality and Social Psychology Bulletin, 23*, 849–864.

Effective treatment for treating depression. (1994). *Johns Hopkins Medical Letter, 6* (2), 6–7.

Egeland, J. A., Gerhard, D. S., Pauls, D. L., Sussex, J. N., Kidd, K. K., Allen, C. R., Hostetter, A. M., & Housman, D. E. (1987). Bipolar affective disorders linked to DNA markers on chromosome 11. *Nature, 325*, 783–787.

Eguiluz, V. M., Chialvo, D. R., Guillermo, A. C., Baliki, M., & Apkarian, A. V. (2005). Scale-free brain functional networks. *Physical Review Letters*, January 14, 018102–1–018102–4.

Ehrman, R. N., Robbins, S. J., Childress, A. R., & O'Brien, C. P. (1992). Conditioned responses to cocaine-related stimuli in cocaine abuse patients. *Psychopharmacology, 107*, 523–529.

Eich, J. E. (1985). Levels of processing, encoding specificity, elaboration, and CHARM. *Psychological Review, 92*, 1–38.

Eichenbaum, H., & Bunsey, M. (1995). On the binding of associations in memory: Clues from studies on the role of the hippocampal region in paired-associate learning. *Current Directions in Psychological Science, 4*, 19–23.

Eid, M., & Diener, E. (2004). Global judgments of subjective well-being: Situational variability and long-term stability. *Social Indicators Research, 65*, 245–277.

Ekman, P. (1992). Facial expressions of emotion: New findings, new questions. *Psychological Science, 3*, 34–38.

Ekman, P. (1992). Are there basic emotions? *Psychology Review, 99*, 500–553.

Ekman, P., Davidson, R. J., & Friesen, W. V. (1990). The Duchenne smile: Emotional expression and brain physiology II. *Journal of Personality and Social Psychology, 58*, 342–353.

Ekman, P., & Friesen, W. V. (1975). *Unmasking the face*. Englewood Cliffs, NJ: Prentice-Hall.

Elder, R. W., Shults, R. A., Sleet, D. A., Nichols, J. L., Thompson, R. S., Rajah, W. (2004). Effectiveness of mass media campaigns for reducing drinking and driving and alcohol-involved crashes: A systematic review. *American Journal of Preventive Medicine 27*, 57–65.

Elkin, J., Shea, T., Watkins, J. T., Imber, S. D., Stotsky, S. M., Collins, J. F., Glass, D. R., Pilkonis, P. A., Leber, W. R., Docherty, J. P., Fiester, S. J., & Parloff, M. B. (1989). National Institutes of Mental Health treatment of depression and collaborative research program. *Archives of General Psychiatry, 46*, 971–982.

Elliot, A. J., & Devine, P. G. (1994). On the motivational nature of cognitive dissonance: Dissonance as psychological discomfort. *Journal of Personality and Social Psychology, 67*, 382–394.

Ellis, A. (1987). The impossibility of achieving consistently good mental health. *American Psychologist, 42*, 364–375.

Ellis, A. (2005). *The myth of self esteem. How rational emotive therapy can change your life forever*. New York: Prometheus Books.

Ellis, A. P. J., West, B. J., Ryan, A. M., & DeShon, R. P. (2002). The use of impression management tactics in structured interviews: A function of question type? *Journal of Applied Psychology, 87*, 1200–1208.

Ellis, L. (1995). Dominance and reproductive success among nonhuman animals: A cross-species comparison. *Ethology and Sociobiology, 16*, 257–333.

Embick, D. and Poeppel, D. (2005). Mapping syntax using imaging: prospects and problems for the study of neurolinguistic computation. *Encyclopedia of Language and Linguistics 2nd ed.*, K. Brown (Ed), Oxford: Elsevier Press.

Emmons, R. A., & McCullough, M. E. (2003). Counting blessings versus burdens: An experimental investigation of gratitude and subjective well-being in daily life. *Journal of Personality and Social Psychology, 84,* 377–389.

Empson, J. A. C. (1984). Sleep and its disorders. In R. Stevens (Ed.), *Aspects of consciousness.* New York: Academic Press.

Engen, T. (1982). *The perception of odors.* New York: Academic Press.

Engen, T. (1986). *Remembering odors and their names.* Paper presented at the First Intenational Conference on the Psychology of Perfumery, University of Warwick, England.

Engen, T. (1987). Remembering odors and their names. *American Scientist, 75,* 497–503.

Engen, T., & Ross, B. M. (1973). Long-term memory of odors with and without verbal descriptions. *Journal of Experimental Psychology, 100,* 221–227.

Engle, R. W. (2001). What is working memory capacity? In H. L. Roediger, J. S. Nairne, I. Neath, & A. M. Suprenant (Eds.), *The nature of remembering: Essays in honor of Robert G. Crowder* (pp. 297–314). Washington, D.C.: American Psychological Association.

Engle, R. W. (2002). Working memory capacity as executive attention. *Current Directions in Psychological Science, 11,* 19–23.

Engle, R. W., Tuholski, S. W., Laughlin, J. E, & Conway, A. R. A. (1999). Working memory, short-term memory, and general fluid intelligence: A latent variable approach. *Journal of Experimental Psychology: General, 128,* 309–331.

Epstein, L. H. (1992). Role of behavior theory in behavioral medicine. Special issue: Behavioral medicine: An update for the 1990s. *Journal of Consulting and Clinical Psychology, 60,* 493–498.

Epstein, S. (1994). Cited in Winerman, L. (2005). Intuition: What we know without knowing how. *Monitor on Psychology, 36,* 51–53.

Erev, I. (1998). Signal detection by human observers: A cutoff reinforcement learning model of categorization decisions under uncertainty. *Psychological Review, 105,* 280–298.

Ericsson, K. A. (Ed.). (2006). *Cambridge handbook of expertise and expert performance.* Cambridge: Cambridge University Press.

Ericsson, K. A., & Kintsch, W. (1995). Long-term working memory. *Psychological Review, 102,* 211–245.

Erikson, E. H. (1950). *Childhood and society.* New York: Norton.

Erikson, E. H. (1987). *A way of looking at things: Selected papers from 1930 to 1980* (S. Schlein, Ed.). New York: Norton.

European Values Study Group and World Values Survey Association (2005). *Atlas of European Values.* Accessed from the world wide web on October 12, 2006 at www.europeanvalues.nl/index2.htm.

Evans, W. D., Powers, A., Hersey, J., & Renaud, J. (2006). The influence of social environment and social image on adolescent smoking. *Health Psychology, 25,* 26–33.

Exner, J. E. (1993). *The Rorschach: A comprehensive system: Vol. 1. Basic Foundations* (3rd ed.). New York: Wiley.

Fagot, B. I., & Kavanagh, K. (1990). The prediction of anti-social behavior from avoidant attachment classification. *Child Development, 61,* 864–873.

Fantz, R. L. (1961). The origin of form perception. *Scientific American, 204,* 66–72.

Farah, M. J. (1988). Is visual imagery really visual? Overlooked evidence from neuropsychology. *Psychological Review, 95,* 307–317.

Farrelly, M. C., Healton, C. G., Davis, K.C., Messeri, P., Hersey, J.C., & Haviland, M. L. (2002). Getting to the truth: Evaluating national tobacco countermarketing campaigns *American Journal of Public Health, 92,* 901–907.

Fawcett, A. J., & Nicolson, R. I. (2003). Children with dyslexia are slow to articulate a single speech gesture. *Dyslexia, 8,* 189–203.

Fazio, R. H., & Roskos-Ewoldsen, D. R. (1994). Acting as we feel: When and how attitudes guide behavior. In S. Shavitt & T. C. Brock (Eds.), *Persuasion* (pp. 71–93). Boston: Allyn & Bacon.

Feldman, D. C., & Tompson, H. B. (1993). Entry shock, culture shock: Socializing the new breed of global managers. *Human Resource Management, 31,* 345–362.

Ferriss, A. L. (2002). Religion and the quality of life. *Journal of Happiness Studies, 3,* 199–215.

Ferster, C. B., & Skinner, B. F. (1957). *Schedules of reinforcement.* New York: Appleton-Century-Crofts.

Festinger, L. (1957). *A theory of cognitive dissonance.* Evanston, IL: Row, Peterson.

Fibiger, H. C., Murray, C. L., & Phillips, A. G. (1983). Lesions of the nucleus basalis magoncellularis impair long-term memory in rats. *Society for Neuroscience Abstracts, 9,* 332.

Fields, H. L., & Basbaum, A. I. (1999). Central nervous system mechanisms of pain modulation. In P. D. Wall and R. Melzak (Eds.), *Textbook of pain* (4th ed., pp. 309–328). New York: Churchill Livingstone.

Fierman, J. (1995). It's 2:00 a.m., let's go to work. *Fortune,* August 21, pp. 82–86.

Fincham, F. D. (2001). Marital conflict: Correlates, structure and context. *Current Directions in Psychological Science, 12,* 23–27.

Fincham, F. D. (2003). Marital conflict: Correlates, structure, and context. *Current Directions in Psychological Science, 12,* 23–27.

Fincham, F. D., & Bradbury, T. N. (1993). Marital satisfaction, depression and attributions: A longitudinal analysis. *Journal of Personality and Social Psychology, 64,* 442–452.

Fink, M. (1994). Can ECT be an effective treatment for adolescents? *Harvard Mental Health Letter, 10,* 8.

Finkel, D., Pederson, J. L., Plomin, R., & McClearn, G. E. (1998). Longitudinal and cross-sectional twin data on cognitive abilities in adulthood: The Swedish adoption/twin study of aging. *Developmental Psychology, 34,* 1400–1413.

Finney, J. W., Weist, M. D., & Friman, P. C. (1995). Evaluation of two health education strategies for testicular self-examination. *Journal of Applied Behavior Analysis 28,* 39–46.

Fisher, J., & Fisher, W. (2000). Theoretical approaches to individual-level change in HIV risk behavior. In J. Peterson & R. DiClemente (Eds.), *Handbook of HIV prevention* (pp. 3–56). New York: Kluwer Academic/ Plenum.

Fisher, J. D., Fisher, W. A., Williams, S. S., & Malloy, T. E. (1994). Empirical tests of an information-motivation-behavioral skills model of AIDS preventive behavior with gay men and heterosexual university students. *Health Psychology 13,* 238–250.

Fivush, R., Kuebli, J., & Clubb, P. A. (1992). The structure of events and event representations: A developmental analysis. *Child Development, 63,* 188–201.

Flack, W. F., Laird, J. D., & Cavallero, R. (1999). Additive effects of facial expressions and postures on emotional feelings. *European Journal of Social Psychology, 29,* 203–217.

Flaherty, C. F., & Largen, J. (1975). Within-subjects positive and negative contrast effects in rats. *Journal of Comparative and Physiological Psychology, 88,* 653–664.

Fleeson, W. (2004). Moving personality beyond the person-situation debate: The challenge and the opportunity of within-person variability. *Current Directions in Psychological Science, 13,* 83–87.

Fletcher, G. J. O., Tither, J. M., O'Loughlin, C., Friesen, M., & Overall, N. (2004). Warm and homely or cold and beautiful? Sex differences in trading off traits in mate selection. *Personality & Social Psychology Bulletin, 30,* 659–672.

Flett, G. L., & Hewitt, P. L. (2005). The perils of perfectionism in sports and exercise. *Current Directions in Psychological Science, 14,* 14–18.

Flynn, J. R. (1987). Massive IQ gains in 14 nations: What IQ tests really measure. *Psychological Bulletin, 101,* 171–191.

Flynn, J. R. (1996). Group differences: Is the good society impossible? *Journal of Biosocial Science, 28,* 573–585.

Flynn, J. R. (2003). Movies about intelligence: The limitations of *g. Current Directions in Psychological Science, 12,* 95–98.

Folk, C. L., & Remington, R. W. (1996). When knowledge does not help: Limitations on the flexibility of attentional control.

In A. F. Kramer, M. G. H. Coles, & G. D. Logan (Eds.), *Converging operations in the study of selective attention* (pp. 271–295). Washington, D.C.: American Psychological Association.

Ford, S., Fallowfield, L., & Lewis, S. (1996). Doctor-patient interactions in oncology. *Social Science Medicine, 12,* 1511–1519.

Fordyce, W. E. (1973). Operant conditioning in the treatment of chronic pain. *Archives of Physical Medicine and Rehabilitation, 54,* 399–408.

Forgas, J. P. (1995a). Mood and judgment: The affect infusion model (AIM). *Psychological Bulletin, 117,* 39–66.

Forgas, J. P. (1995b). The role of emotion in social judgments: An introductory review and an affect infusion model (AIM). *European Journal of Social Psychology.*

Forgas, J. P. (1998). On being happy and mistaken: Mood effects on the fundamental attribution error. *Journal of Personality and Social Psychology, 75,* 318–331.

Forgas, J. P., & Fiedler, K. (1996). Us and them: Mood effects on intergroup discrimination. *Journal of Personality and Social Psychology, 70,* 28–40.

Foulkes, D. (1985). *Dreaming: A cognitive-psychological analysis.* Hillsdale, NJ: Erlbaum.

Foushee, H. C. (1984). Dyads and triads at 35,000 feet: Factors affecting group process and aircrew performance. *American Psychologist, 39,* 885–893.

Fowles, D. C. (1994). A motivational theory of psychopathology. In W. Spaulding (Ed.), *Nebraska symposium on motivation: Integrated views of motivation and emotion.* (vol 41, pp. 181–238). Lincoln: University of Nebraska Press.

Frederiksen, N. (1994). The integration of testing with teaching: Applications of cognitive psychology in instruction. *American Journal of Education, 102,* 527–564.

Fredrick, S., & Loewenstein, G. (1999). Hedonic adaptation. In D. Kahneman, E. Diener, & N. Schwarz (Eds.), *Well-being: The foundations of a hedonic psychology* (pp. 302–329). New York: Russell Sage Foundation.

Fredrickson, B. L. (2001). The role of positive emotions in positive psychology: The broaden-and-build theory of positive emotions. *American Psychologist, 56,* 218–226.

Fredrickson, B. L., & Joiner, T. (2002). Positive emotions trigger upward spirals toward emotional well-being. *Psychological Science, 13,* 172–175.

Fredrickson, B. L., Tugade, M. M., Waugh, C. E., & Larkin, G. R. (2003). What good are positive emotions in crisis? A prospective study of resilience and emotions following the terrorist attacks on the United States on September 11th, 2001. *Journal of Personality and Social Psychology, 84,* 365–376.

Frese, M. (1985). Stress at work and psychosomatic complaints: A causal interpretation. *Journal of Applied Psychology, 70,* 314–328.

Friedman, H. W., & Schustack, M. W. (1999). *Personality: Classic theories and modern research.* Boston: Allyn & Bacon.

Friedman, N. P., Miyake, A., Corley, R. P., Young, S. E., DeFries, J. C., & Hweitt, J. K. (2006). Not all executive functions are related to intelligence. *Psychological Science, 17,* 172–179.

Frisch, D. (1993). Reasons for framing effects. *Organizational Behavior and Human Decision Processes, 54,* 391–494.

Fu, H., Watkins, D., & Hui, E. K. (2004). Personality correlates of the disposition towards interpersonal forgiveness: A Chinese perspective. *International Journal of Psychology, 39,* 305–316.

Fuertes, J. N., Mueller, L. N., Chauhan, R. V., Walker, J. A., & Ladany, N. (2002). An investigation of European American therapists' approach to counseling African American clients. *Counseling Psychologists, 30,* 763–768.

Funder, D. C. (1995). On the accuracy of personality judgment: A realistic approach. *Psychological Review, 102,* 652–670.

Furman, E. (2005). *Boomerang nation: How to survive living with your parents . . . the second time around.* New York: Fireside Books.

Gaertner, S. L., Mann, J. A., Dovidio, J. F., & Murrell, J. A. (1990). How does cooperation reduce intergroup bias? *Journal of Personality and Social Psychology, 57,* 239–249.

Gaertner, S. L., Mann, J., Murrell, A., & Dovidio, J. F. (1989). Reducing intergroup bias: The benefits of recategorization. *Journal of Personality and Social Psychology, 57,* 239–249.

Gaertner, S. L., Rust, M. C., Dovidio, J. F., Bachman, B. A., & Anastasio, P. A. (1993). The contact hypothesis: The role of common ingroup identity on reducing intergroup bias. *Small Groups Research, 25,* 224–249.

Galanter, E. (1962). Contemporary psychophysics. In R. Brown, E. Galanter, E. G. Hess, & G. Mandler (Eds.), *New directions in psychology.* New York: Holt, Rinehart, & Winston.

Gallagher, M. (2000). The amygdala and associative learning. In J. P. Aggleton (Ed.), *The amygala: A functional analysis* (pp. 311–330). New York: Oxford University Press.

Gallo, L. C., & Matthews, K. A. (2003). Understanding the association between socioeconomic status and physical health: Do negative emotions play a role? *Psychological Bulletin, 129,* 10–51.

Galvin, T. (2001). Industry 2001 Report. *Training, 38(10),* 40–75.

Garcia, J., Hankins, W. G., & Rusiniak, K. W. (1974). Behavioral regulation of the milieu interne in man and rat. *Science, 185,* 824–831.

Garcia, J., & Koelling, R. A. (1966). Relation of cue to consequence in avoidance learning. *Psychonomic Science, 4,* 123.

Gardner, H. (1983). *Frames of mind: The theory of multiple intelligences.* New York: Basic Books.

Garland, A. F., & Zigler, E. (1993). Adolescent suicide prevention: Current research and social policy implications. *American Psychologist, 48,* 169–182.

Garlick, D. (2002). Understanding the nature of the general factor of intelligence: The role of individual differences in neural plasticity as an explanatory mechanism. *Psychological Review, 109,* 116–136.

Gaston, E. (2006). Nudge them out, they come back. Unmarried and debt-laden, Boomerangers just can't leave the nest. The State.Com, June 15.

Gauthier, I., Tarr, M. J., Anderson, A. W., Skudlarski, P., & Gore, J. C. (1999). Activation of the middle fusiform "face area" increases with expertise in recognizing novel objects. *Nature Neuroscience, 2,* 568–573.

Gazzaniga, M. S. (2000). Cerebral specialization and interhemispheric communication: Does the corpus callosum enable the human condition? *Brain, 123,* 1293–1326.

Gazzaniga, M. S. (2002). The split brain revisited. *Scientific American, 287,* 46–53.

Gehring, R. E., & Toglia, M. P. (1989). Recall of pictorial enactments and verbal descriptions with verbal and imagery study strategies. *Journal of Mental Imagery, 13,* 83–98.

Geier, A. E., Rozin, P., & Doros, G. (2006). Unit bias: A new heuristic that helps explain the effect of portion size on food intake. *Psychological Science, 17,* 521–525.

Geller, E. S., & Dula, C. S. (2003). *Innovative approaches to anger management.* Final report for grant #1–R43–MH62263–01A2 from the National Institutes of Health (pp. 1–40).

Georgiadis, M. M., Biddle, S. J. H., Stavrou, N. A. (2006). Motivation for weight-loss diets: A clustering, longitudinal field study using self-esteem and self-determination theory perspectives. *Health Education Journal, 65,* 53–72.

German, T. P., & Barrett, H. C. (2005). Functional fixedness in a technologically sparse culture. *Psychological Science, 16,* 1–7.

Gernsbacher, M. A., Dawson, M., & Goldsmith, H. (2005). Three reasons not to believe in an Autism epidemic. *Current Directions in Psychological Science, 14,* 55–58.

Gershoff, E. T. (2002). Corporal punishment by parents and associated child behaviors and experiences: A meta-analytic and theoretical review. *Psychological Bulletin, 128,* 539–579.

Gibbons, B. (1986). The intimate sense of smell. *National Geographic, 170,* 324–361.

Gibbons, F. X., Gerrard, M., Blanton, H., & Russell, D. W. (1998). Reasoned action and social reaction: Willingness and intention as independent predictors of health risk. *Journal of Personality and Social Psychology, 74,* 1164–1180.

Gibson, E. J., & Walk, R. D. (1960). The "visual cliff." *Scientific American, 202,* 64–71.

Gilbert, A. N., & Wysocki, C. J. (1987). The smell survey results. *National Geographic, 172,* 514–525.

Gilbert, D. T., & Malone, P. S. (1995). The correspondence bias. *Psychological Bulletin, 117,* 21–38.

Gill, J. (1985). Czechpoints. *Time Out,* August 22, p. 15.

Gilligan, C. F. (1982). *In a different voice.* Cambridge, MA: Harvard University Press.

Ginges, J. (2005). Youth bulges, civic knowledge, and political upheaval. *Psychological Science, 16,* 659–660.

Gladwell, M. (1998). The Pima paradox. *The New Yorker,* February 2, pp. 42–57.

Gladwell, M. (2005). *Blink: The power of thinking without thinking.* New York: Little, Brown.

Glanz, K., Steffen, A., Elliott, T., O'Riordan, D. (2005). Diffusion of an effective skin cancer prevention program: Design, theoretical foundations, and first-year implementation. *Health Psychology, 24,* 477–487.

Glynn, L. M., Christenfeld, N., & Gerin, W. (1999). Gender, social support, and cardiovascular responses to stress. *Psychosomatic Medicine, 61,* 234–242.

Godden, D., & Baddeley, A. D. (1975). Context-dependent memory in two natural environments: On land and under water. *British Journal of Psychology, 66,* 325–331.

Goethals, G. R. (1986). Fabricating and ignoring social reality: Self-serving estimates of consensus. In J. Olson, C. P. Herman, & N. P. Zanna (Eds.), *Relative deprivation and social comparison: The Ontario symposium on social cognition IV.* Hillsdale, NJ: Erlbaum.

Goldberg, L. R., & Saucier, G. (1995). So what do you propose we use instead? A reply to Block. *Psychological Bulletin, 117,* 221–225.

Goldstein, E. B. (2002). *Sensation and perception.* Pacific Grove, CA: Wadsworth.

Goleman, D. (1995). *Emotional intelligence.* New York: Bantam.

Goleman, D. R. (1998). *Working with emotional intelligence.* New York: Bantam.

Gómez, C. A., & Marín, B. V. (1996). Gender, culture, and power: Barriers to HIV prevention strategies for women. *Journal of Sex Research, 33,* 355–362.

Goodale, M. A., Meeman, H. P., Bulthoff, H. H., Nicolle, D. A., Murphy, K. H., & Racicot, C. L. (1994). Separate neural pathways for the visual analysis of object shape and perception and prehension. *Current Biology, 4,* 604–610.

Goodman, M. F., Bents, F. D., Tijerina, L., Wierwille, N., Lerner, N., & Benel, D. (1999). An investigation of the safety implications of wireless communications in vehicles: Report summary. Department of Transportation electronic publication. Available: www.nhtsa.dot.gov/people/injury/research/wireless/#rep.

Gorman, J., Leibowitz, M., Fryer, A., & Stein, J. (1989). A neuroanatomical hypothesis for panic disorder. *American Journal of Psychiatry, 146,* 148–161.

Gordon, W. C. (1989). *Learning and memory.* Belmont, CA: Brooks/Cole Publishing.

Gottesman, I. I. (1993). Origins of schizophrenia: Past as a prologue. In R. Plomin & G. E. McClearn (Eds.), *Nature, nurture, and psychology* (pp. 2231–2344). Washington, DC: American Psychological Association.

Gottfredson, G. D., & Holland, J. L. (1990). A longitudinal test of the influence of congruence: Job satisfaction, competency utilization, and counterproductive behavior. *Journal of Consulting Psychology, 37,* 389–398.

Gottfredson, L. S., & Deary, I. J. (2004). Intelligence predicts health and longevity, but why? *Current Directions in Psychological Science, 13,* 1–4.

Gottfried, A. W. (Ed.). (1984). *Home environment and early cognitive development.* San Francisco: Academic Press.

Gottman, J. M. (1993). The roles of conflict engagement, escalation, and avoidance in marital interaction: A longitudinal view of five types of couples. *Journal of Consulting and Clinical Psychology, 61,* 6–15.

Graen, G. B., & Scandura, T. A. (1986). Toward a psychology of dyadic organizing. In L. L. Cummings & B. M. Staw (Eds.), *Research on organizational behavior* (vol. 9, pp. 175–208). Greenwich, CT: JAI Press.

Graham, K. S., & Hodges, J. R. (1997). Differentiating the roles of the hippocampal complex and the neocortex in long-term memory storage: Evidence from the study of semantic dementia and Alzheimer's disease. *Neuropsychology, 11,* 77–89.

Granchrow, J. R., Steiner, J. E., & Daher, M. (1983). Neonatal facial expressions in response to different qualities and intensities of gustatory stimuli. *Infant Behavior and Development, 6,* 189–200.

Grant, B. F., Harford, T. C., Dawson, D. A., Chou, P., Dufour, M., & Pickering, R. (1994). Prevalence of DSM-IV alcohol abuse and dependence in United States, 1992. *NIAAA's Epidemiological Bulletin No. 35, 13,* 243–248.

Gray, J. A. (1994). Personality dimensions and emotion systems. In P. Ekman & R. J. Davidson (Eds.), *The nature of emotion: Fundamental questions* (pp. 243–247). New York: Oxford University Press.

Gray-Little, B., & Hafdahl, A. R. (2000). Factors influencing racial comparisons of self-esteem: A quantitative review. *Psychological Bulletin, 126,* 26–54.

Green, J. P., & Lynn, S. J. (1995). Hypnosis, dissociation, and simultaneous task performance. *Journal of Personality and Social Psychology, 69,* 728–735.

Green, L., Fry, A. F., & Myerson, J. (1994). Discounting of delayed rewards: A lifespan comparison. *Psychological Science, 5,* 33–36.

Green, R. (1987). *The "sissy boy syndrome" and the development of homosexuality.* New Haven, CT: Yale University Press.

Green, R., & Blanchard, K. (1995). Gender identity disorders. In H. J. Kaplan & B. J. Sadock (Eds.), *Comprehensive textbook of psychiatry/VI* (pp. 1345–1360). Baltimore: Williams & Wilkins.

Greenberg, J. (1994). Using socially fair procedures to promote acceptance of a work site smoking ban. *Journal of Applied Psychology, 79,* 288–297.

Greenberg, J. (2002). Who stole the money, and when? Individual and situational determinants of employee theft. *Organizational Behavior and Human Decision Processes, 89,* 985–1003.

Greenberg, J. (2006). Losing sleep over organizational injustice: Attenuating insomniac reactions to underpayment inequity with supervisory training in interactional justice. *Journal of Applied Psychology, 91,* 58–69.

Greenberg, J., & Baron, R. A. (2003). *Behavior in organizations* (8th ed.). Upper Saddle River, NJ: Prentice-Hall.

Greenberg, L. S., Elliott, R. K., & Lietaer, G. (1994). Research on experiential psychotherapies. In A. E. Bergin & S. L. Garfield (Eds.), *Handbook of psychotherapy and behavior change* (pp. 509–539). New York: Wiley.

Greene, J. E. (2006). What time is it? Your body knows. Herald Mail.com., March 13.

Greenwald, A. G. (2002). Constructs in student ratings of instructors. In H. I. Braun and D. N. Douglas (Eds.)., *The role of constructs in psychological and educational measurement* (p. 277–297). Mahwah, NJ: Erlbaum.

Greenwald, A. G., Draine, S. C., & Abrams, R. L. (1996). Three cognitive markers of unconscious semantic activation. *Science, 273,* 1699–1702.

Greenwald, A. G., Spangenberg, E. R., Pratkanis, A. R., & Eskenazi, J. (1991). Double-blind tests of subliminal self-help audiotapes. *Psychological Science, 2,* 119–122.

Greist-Bousquet, S., Watson, M., & Schiffman, H. R. (1990). *An examination of illusion decrement with inspection of wings-in and wings-out Müller-Lyer figures: The role of corrective and contextual information perception.* New York: Wiley.

Grewal, D., & Salovey, P. (2005). Feeling smart: The science of emotional intelligence. *American Scientist, 93,* 330–339.

Grilly, D. M. (1989). *Drugs and human behavior.* Boston: Allyn & Bacon.

Gross, C. G. (2005). Processing the facial image. *American Psychologist, 60,* 755–763.

Gross, J. J. (2001). Emotion regulation in adulthood: Timing is everything. *Current Directions in Psychological Science, 6,* 214–219.

Gruneberg, M. M., Morris, P., & Sykes, R. N. (1988). *Practical aspects of memory: Current research and issues* (vols. 1 & 2). Chichester, England: Wiley.

Guerin, D. W., & Gottfried, A. W. (1994). Developmental stability and change in parent reports of temperament: A ten-year longitudinal investigation from infancy through preadolescence. *Merrill-Palmer Quarterly, 40,* 334–355.

Guthrie, J. P., Ash, R. A., & Bendapudi, V. (1995). Additional validity evidence for a measure of Morningness. *Journal of Applied Psychology, 80,* 186–190.

Haberlandt, K. (1999). *Human memory: Exploration and application.* Boston: Allyn & Bacon.

Hackman, J. R. (Ed.) (1990). *Groups that work (and those that don't).* San Francisco: Jossey-Bass.

Hackman, J. R., & Oldham, G. R. (1976). Motivation through the design of work: Test of a theory. *Organizational Behavior and Human Performance, 16,* 250–279.

Haggerty, R. J., Garmezy, N., Rutter, M., & Sherrod, L. (1994). *Stress, risk, and resilience in children and adolescents: Processes, mechanisms, and interventions.* New York: Cambridge University Press.

Hahn, G., Charlin, V. L., Sussman, S., Dent, C. W., Manzi, J., Stacy, A. W., Flay, B., Hansen, W. B., & Burton, D. (1990). Adolescents' first and most recent use situations of smokeless tobacco and cigarettes: Similarities and differences. *Addictive Behaviors, 15,* 439–448.

Haier, R. J. (1993). Cerebral glucose metabolism and intelligence. In P. A. Vernon (Ed.), *Biological approaches to the study of human intelligence* (pp. 317–332). Norwood, NJ: Ablex.

Hajek, P., & Belcher, M. (1991). Dreams of absent-minded transgression: An empirical study of a cognitive withdrawal symptom. *Journal of Abnormal Psychology, 100,* 487–491.

Halford, G. S., Baker, R., McCredden, J. E., & Bain, J. D. (2005). How many variables can humans process? *Psychological Science, 16,* 70–76.

Hall, J. A., Roter, D. L., & Milburn, M. A. (1999). Illness and satisfaction with medical care. *Current Directions in Psychological Science, 8,* 96–99.

Halpern, D. F. (2003). *Thought and knowledge: An introduction to critical thinking* (4th ed.). Mahwah, NJ: Erlbaum.

Hamann, S. B., Ely, T. D., Hoffman, J. M., & Kilts, C. D. (2002). Ecstasy and agony: Activation of the human amygdala in positive and negative emotion. *Psychological Science, 13,* 135–141.

Hamburg, S. (1998). Inherited hypohedonia leads to learned helplessness: A conjecture updated. *Review of General Psychology, 2,* 384–403.

Hans, V. P. (1992). Obedience, justice, and the law: PS reviews recent contributions to a field ripe for new research efforts by psychological scientists. *Psychological Science, 3,* 218–221.

Hardell L., Carlberg, M., & Mild, K. H. (2006). Pooled analysis of two case-control studies on use of cellular and cordless telephones and the risk for malignant brain tumours diagnosed in 1997–2003. International Archives of Occupational and Environmental Health, DOI 10.1007/s00420-006-0088-5. Available: www.arbetslivsinstitutet.se/pdf/06033 1MildHardell_Article.pdf.

Harlow, H. F., & Harlow, M. H. (1966). Learning to love. *American Scientist, 54,* 244–272.

Harrigan, J. A., Luci, K. S., Kay, D., McLaney, A., & Rosenthal, R. (1991). Effects of expresser role and type of self-touching on observers' perceptions. *Journal of Applied Social Psychology, 21,* 585–609.

Harrington, A. (1995). Unfinished business: Models of laterality in the nineteenth century. In R. J. Davidson & K. Hugdahl (Eds.), *Brain asymmetry* (pp. 24–37). Cambridge, MA: MIT Press.

Harris, M. M. (2006). Cross-cultural skill: An emerging construct for the 21st century. *The Industrial-Organizational Psychologist, 43* (3), 43–48.

Harrison, D. A., Newman, D. A., & Roth, P. L. (2006). How important are job attitudes? Meta-analytic comparisons of integrative behavioral outcomes and time sequences. *Academy of Management Journal, 49,* 305–326.

Harrison, J. K. (1992). Individual and combined effects of behavior modeling and the cultural assimilator in cross-cultural management training. *Journal of Applied Psychology, 77,* 952–962.

Hart, D., Atkins, R., & Youniss, J. (2005). Knowledge, youth bulges, and rebellion. *Current Directions in Psychological Science, 16,* 661–662.

Hart, D., Stinson, C., Field, N., Ewert, M., & Horowitz, M. (1995). A semantic space approach to representations of self and other in pathological grief: A case study. *Psychological Science, 6,* 96–100.

Hartmann, E. L. (1973). *The functions of sleep.* New Haven, CT: Yale University Press.

Hatfield, E., & Rapson, R. L. (1993). Historical and cross-cultural perspectives on passionate love and sexual desire. *Annual Review of Sex Research, 4,* 67–97.

Haugaard, J. J., Repucci, N. D., Laurd, J., & Nauful, T. (1991). Children's definitions of the truth and their competency as witnesses in legal proceedings. *Law and Human Behavior, 15,* 253–273.

Hauser, M., Newport, E. L., & Aslin, R. N. (2001). Segmentation of the speech stream in a non-human primate: Statistical learning in cotton-top tamarins. *Cognition, 78,* B41–B52.

Hawkins, J. D., Catalano, R. F., & Miller, J. Y. (1992). Risk and protective factors for alcohol and other drug problems in adolescence and early adulthood: Implications for substance abuse prevention. *Psychological Bulletin, 112,* 64–105.

Hawkins, S. A., & Hastie, R. (1990). Hindsight: Biased judgments of past events after the outcomes are known. *Psychological Bulletin, 107,* 311–327.

Hazan, C., & Shaver, P. R. (1990). Love and work: an attachment-theoretical perspective. *Journal of Personality and Social Psychology, 59,* 270–280.

Hazelrigg, M. D., Cooper, H. M., & Borduin, C. M. (1987). Evaluating the effectiveness of family therapies: An integrative review and analysis. *Psychological Bulletin, 101,* 428–442.

Healy, M. (2006). For men, depression isn't revealed in tears. *Los Angeles Times,* January 24, D3-D4.

Heatherton, T., & Weinberger, J. L. (1994). *Can personality change?* Washington, D.C.: American Psychological Association.

Heilman, M. E., & Chen, J. J. (2005). Same behavior, different consequences: Reactions to men's and women's altruistic citizenship behavior. *Journal of Applied Psychology, 90,* 431–441.

Heilman, M. E., & Haynes, M. C. (2005). No credit where credit is due: Attributional rationalizations of women's success in male-female teams. *Journal of Applied Psychology, 90,* 905–916.

Heilman, M. E., Wallen, A. S., Fuchs, D., & Tamkins, M. M. (2004). Penalties for success: Reactions to women who succeed at male gender-typed tasks. *Journal of Applied Psychology, 89,* 416–427.

Heine, S. J., & Lehman, D. R. (1997). Culture, dissonance, and self-affirmation. *Personality and Social Psychology Bulletin, 23,* 389–400.

Heinrichs, R. W. (2005). The primacy of cognition in schizophrenia. *American Psychologist, 60,* 229–242.

Heldman, M., Russeler, J., & Munte, T. (2005). Event-related potentials in a decision-making task with delayed and immediate reward conditions. *Journal of Psychophysiology, 19.* 270–274.

Heller, W. (1997). Emotion. In M. T. Banich (Ed.), *Neuropsychology: The neural bases of mental function* (pp. 398–429). Boston: Houghton Mifflin.

Heller, W., Etienne, M. A., & Miller, G. A. (1995). Patterns of perceptual asymmetry in depression and anxiety: Implications for neuropsychological models of emotion and psychopathology. *Journal of Abnormal Psychology, 104,* 327–333.

Heller, W., Nitschke, J. B., & Miller, G. A. (1998). Lateralization in emotion and emotional disorders. *Current Directions in Psychological Science, 7,* 26–32.

Hellerstein, D., Yanowitch, P., Rosenthal, J., Samstag, L. W., Maurer, M., Kasch, K., Burrow, L., Porter, M., Cantillon, M., & Winston, R. (1993). A randomized double-blind study of fluoxetine versus placebo in the treatment of dysthymia. *American Journal of Psychiatry, 150,* 1169–1175.

Helweg-Larsen, M., & Collins, B. E. (1997). A social psychological perspective on the role of knowledge about AIDS in AIDS prevention. *Current Directions in Psychological Science, 6,* 23–26.

Hendrick, C., & Hendrick S. S. (1993). Lovers as friends. *Journal of Social and Personal Relationships, 10,* 459–466.

Hennekens, C. H. (1996). Alcohol and risk of coronary events. In *Alcohol and the cardiovascular system* (NIAAA Research Monograph). Washington, D.C.: U. S. Department of Health and Human Services.

Henry, R. A. (1993). Group judgment accuracy: Reliability and validity of post-discussion confidence judgments. *Organizational Behavior and Human Decision Processes, 56,* 11–27.

Henry, R. A., & Landa, A. (2000, April). *Delegation decisions and affective outcomes in autonomous groups.* Paper presented at the 15th Annual Conference of the Society for Industrial and Organizational Psychology, New Orleans.

Henry, R. A., & Olson, T. M. (2001, April). *Assessing general attitudes toward workgroups: Scale development and validation.* Paper presented at the 16th Annual Conference of the Society for Industrial and Organizational Psychology, San Diego.

Herman, C. P., Roth, D. A., & Polivvy, J. (2003). Effects of presence of others on food intake: A normative interpretation. *Psychological Bulletin, 129,* 873–886.

Hershberger, S. L., Lichtenstein, P., & Knox, S. S. (1994). Genetic and environmental influences on perceptions of organizational climate. *Journal of Applied Psychology, 79,* 24–33.

Herz, R. S. (1997). Emotion experienced during encoding enhances odor retrieval cue effectiveness. *American Journal of Psychology, 110,* 489–505.

Hetzel, B., & McMichael, T. (1987). *The LS factor: Lifestyle and health.* Ringwood, Victoria: Penguin.

Hewstone, M., Bond, M. H., & Wan, K. C. (1983). Social factors and social attributions: The explanation of intergroup differences in Hong Kong. *Social Cognition, 2,* 142–157.

Hilgard, E. R. (1979). Divided consciousness in hypnosis: Implications of the hidden observer. In E. Fromm & R. E. Shor (Eds.), *Hypnosis: Developments in research and new perspectives* (2nd ed). Chicago: Aldine.

Hilgard, E. R. (1986). *Divided consciousness: Multiple controls in human thought and action* (2nd ed.). New York: Wiley.

Hilgard, E. R. (1993). Dissociation and theories of hypnosis. In E. Fromm & M. R. Nash (Eds.), *Contemporary hypnosis research* (pp. 69–101). New York: Guilford Press.

Hobson, J. A. (1988). *The dreaming brain.* New York: Basic Books.

Hock, E., Schirtzinger, M. B., Lutz, W. J., & Widaman, K. (1995). Maternal depressive symptomatology over the transition to parenthood: Assessing the influence of marital satisfaction and marital sex role traditionalism. *Journal of Family Psychology, 9,* 79–88.

Hoffman, H. G., Doctor, J. N., Patterson, D. R., Carrougher, G. J., Furness, T. A., III. (2000). Use of virtual reality for adjunctive treatment of adolescent burn pain during wound care: A case report. *Pain, 85,* 305–309.

Hogan, R. T. (1991). *Personality and personality measurement.* In M. D. Dunnette & L. M. Hough (Eds.), *Handbook of industrial and organizational psychology* (vol. 2, pp. 873–920). Palo Alto, CA: Consulting Psychologists Press.

Hogan, R., Hogan, J., & Roberts, B. W. (1996). Personality measurement and employment decisions: Questions and answers. *American Psychologist, 51,* 469–477.

Hollon, S. D., DeRubeis, R. J., & Evans, M. D. (1987). Causal mediation of change in treatment for depression: Discriminating between nonspecificity and noncausality. *Psychological Bulletin, 102,* 139–149.

Hollon, S. D., Shelton, R. C., & Loosen, P. T. (1991). Cognitive therapy and pharmacotherapy for depression. *Journal of Consulting and Clinical Psychology, 59,* 88–99.

Holmes, T. H., & Rahe, R. H. (1967). The social readjustment rating scale. *Journal of Psychosomatic Research, 11,* 213–218.

Honig, W. K., & Staddon, J. E. R. (Eds.). (1977). *Handbook of operant behavior.* Englewood Cliffs, NJ: Prentice-Hall.

Hooley, J. M. (2004). Do psychiatric patients do better clinically if they live with certain kinds of families? *Current Directions in Psychological Science, 13,* 202–205.

Hoppe, R. B. (1988). In search of a phenomenon: Research in parapsychology. *Contemporary Psychology, 33,* 129–130.

Horgen, K. B, Choate M., & Brownell, K. D. (2001). Food advertising: Targeting children in a toxic environment. In D. G. Singer and J. L. Singer (Eds.), *Handbook of children and the media.* Thousand Oaks, CA: Sage, 447–462.

Hornstein, G. A. (1992). The return of the repressed: Psychology's problematic relations with psychoanalysis, 1909–1960. *American Psychologist, 47,* 254–263.

Hornstein, H. (2004). *Brutal bosses and their prey.* New York: Columbia University Press.

Horstmann, G. (2003). What do facial expressions convey: Feeling states, behavioral intentions, or action requests? *Emotion. 3,* 150–166.

House, J. S., Landis, K. R., & Umberson, D. (1988). Social relationships and health. *Science, 241,* 540–544.

House, R. J. (1971). A path-goal theory of leader effectiveness. *Administrative Science Quarterly, 16,* 321–339.

Hovland, C. I., & Weiss, W. (1951). The influence of source credibility on communication effectiveness. *Public Opinion Quarterly, 1,* 635–650.

Howard, K. I., Kopta, S. M., Krause, M. S., & Orlinsky, D. E. (1986). The dose-effect relationship in psychotherapy. *American Psychologist, 41,* 159–164.

Howard, M. O. (2001). Production and prediction of conditioned alcohol aversion: Pharmacological aversion treatment of alcohol dependence, part 1. *American Journal of Drug and Alcohol Abuse, 27,* 561–585.

Howe, M. L., & Courage, M. L. (1993). On resolving the enigma of infantile amnesia. *Psychological Bulletin, 113,* 305–326.

Hubel, D. H., & Wiesel, T. N. (1979). Brain mechanisms of vision. *Scientific American, 241,* 150–162.

Huesmann, L. R., Moise-Titus, J., Podolski, C. L., & Eron, L. D. (2003). Longitudinal relations between children's exposure to TV violence and their aggressive and violent behavior in young adulthood: 1977–1992. *Developmental Psychology, 39* (2), 201–221.

Hulin, C. L. (1990). Adaptation, persistence, and commitment in organizations. In M. D. Dunnette & L. M. Hough (Eds.), *Handbook of industrial and organizational psychology* (vol. 2, pp. 445–506). Palo Alto, CA: Consulting Psychologists Press.

Hulin, C. L., Henry, R. A., & Noon, S. L. (1990). Adding a dimension: Time as a factor in the generalizability of predictive relationships. *Psychological Bulletin, 107,* 328–340.

Hummel, J. E., & Holyoak, K. J. (2003). A symbolic-connectionist theory of relational inference and generalization. *Psychological Review, 110,* 220–264.

Hunt, E. (1993). What do we need to know about aging? In J. Cerella, J. Rybash, W.

Hoyer, & M. L. Commons (Eds.), *Adult information processing: Limits on loss* (pp. 587–598). San Diego: Academic Press.

Husband, A. J., Lin, W., Madsen, G., & King, M. G. (1993). A conditioning model for immunostimulation: Enhancement of the antibody response to ovalbumin by behavioral conditioning in rats. In A. J. Husband (Ed.), *Psychoimmunology: CNS-immune interactions* (pp. 139–147). Boca Raton, FL: CRC Press.

Huttenlocher, J., Haight, W., Bryk, A., Seltzer, M., & Lyons, T. (1991). Early vocabulary growth: Relation to language input and gender. *Developmental Psychology, 27,* 236–248.

Iacoboni, M., Rayman, J., & Zaidel, E. (1996). Left brain says yes, right brain says no: Normative duality in the split brain.. In S. R. Hameroff, A. W. Kasniak, & A. C. Scott (Eds.), *Toward a Scientific Basis of Consciousness,* pp. 197–202. Cambridge, MA: MIT Press.

Ijzendoorn, M. H. van, Juffer, F., & Poelhuis, W. K. (2005). Adoption and cognitive development: A meta-analytic comparison of adopted and nonadopted children's IQ and school performance. *Psychological Bulletin, 131,* 301–316.

Institute of Medicine. (1989). *Prevention and treatment of alcohol problems: Research opportunities.* Washington, DC: National Academy of Sciences.

Insurance Institute for Highway Safety (2005). First Evidence of Effects of Cell Phone Use on Injury Crashes. Accessed from the world wide web on September 25, 2006 at www.iihs.org/news/2005/iihs_news_071205.pdf.

International Obesity Task Force (2003). Accessed from the world-wide web on July 29, 2006 at www.iotf.org.

Isen, A. M. (2001). An Influence of Positive Affect on Decision Making in Complex Situations: Theoretical Issues with Practical Implications. *Journal of Consumer Psychology, 11,* 75–85.

Isen, A. M., & Baron, R. A. (1991). Positive affect and organizational behavior. In B. M. Staw & L. L. Cummings (Eds.), *Research in organizational behavior* (vol. 14, pp. 1–48). Greenwich, CT: JAI Press.

Iverson, J. M., & Goldin-Meadow, S. (2005). Gesture paves the way for language development. *Psychological Science, 16,* 367–371.

Ivkovich, D., Collins, K. L., Eckerman, C. O., Krasnegor, N. A., & Stanton, M. E. (1999). Classical delay eyeblink conditioning in 4- and 5-month-old human infants. *Psychological Science, 10,* 4–7.

Iwahashi, M. (1992). Scents and science. *Vogue,* pp. 212–214.

Iyengar, S. S., Wells, R. E., & Schwartz, B. (2006). Doing better but feeling worse. *Psychological Science, 17,* 143–150.

Izard, C. E. (1991). *The psychology of emotions.* New York: Plenum.

Izard, C. E. (2001). Emotional intelligence or adaptive emotions? *Emotion, 1,* 249–257.

Jacques, C., & Rossion, B. (2006). The speed of individual face categorization. *Psychological Science, 17,* 485–492.

James, W. J. (1890). *Principles of psychology.* New York: Holt.

Jameson, D., & Hurvich, L. M. (1989). Essay concerning color constancy. *Annual Review of Psychology, 40,* 1–22.

Janis, I. L. (1972). *Victims of groupthink: A psychological study of foreign-policy decisions and fiascoes.* Boston: Houghton Mifflin.

Jellison, J .M., & Green, J. (1981). A self-presentation approach to the fundamental attribution error: the norm of internality. *Journal of Personality and Social Psychology , 40,* 643–649.

Jencks, D. (1972). *Inequality: A reassessment of the effect of family and school in America.* New York: Basic Books.

Jenkins, J. G., & Dallenbach, K. M. (1924). Obliviscence during sleep and waking. *American Journal of Psychology, 35,* 605–612.

Jilek, W. G. (2000). Culturally related syndromes. In M. G. Gelder, M. G. Lopez-Ibor, & J. J. Andreasen (Eds.), *New Oxford Textbook of Psychiatry* (vol. 1., pp. 1061–1066). Oxford: Oxford University Press.

Jilek, W. G. (2006). Cultural factors in psychiatric disorders. *Mental Health Magazine,* May 9.

Johnson, B. T., & Eagly, A. H. (1989). Effects of involvement on persuasion: A meta-analysis. *Psychological Bulletin, 106,* 290–314.

Johnson, M. D., Hollenbeck, J. R., Humphrey, S. E., Ilgen, D. R., Jundt, D., & Meyer, C. J. (2006). Cutthroat cooperation: Asymmetrical adaptation in team reward structures. *Academy of Management Journal, 49,* 103–120.

Johnson, M. K., Mitchell, K. J., Raye, C. L., & Greene, E. J. (2004). An age-related deficit in prefrontal cortical function associated with refreshing information. *Psychological Science, 15,* 127–132.

Johnston, W., & Dark, V. (1986). Selective attention. *Annual Review of Psychology, 37,* 43–75.

Joiner, T. E., Jr. (1994). The interplay of similarity and self-verification in relationship formation. *Social Behavior and Personality, 22,* 195–200.

Joiner, T. E., Jr., Alfano, M. S., & Metalsky, G. I. (1993). When depression breeds contempt: Reassurance seeking, self-esteem, and rejection of depressed college students by their roommates. *Journal of Abnormal Psychology, 101* 165–173.

Joiner, T. E., Jr., Heatherton, T. F., Rudd, M. D., & Schmidt, N. B. (1997). Perfectionism, perceived with status, and bulimic symptoms: Two studies testing a diathesis-stress model. *Journal of Abnormal Psychology, 106,* 145–153.

Jones, L. W., Sinclair, R. C., & Courneya, K. S. (2003). The effects of source credibility and message framing on exercise intentions, behaviors, and attitudes: An integration of the elaboration likelihood model and prospect theory. *Journal of Applied Social Psychology, 33,* 179–196.

Jostman, N. B., Koole, S. L., van der Wulp, N. Y., & Fockenberg, D. A. (2005). Subliminal affect regulation: The moderating role of action vs. state orientation. *European Psychologist, 10,* 209–217.

Judd, C. M., Ryan, C. N., & Park, B. (1991). Accuracy in the judgment of in-group and out-group variability. *Journal of Personality and Social Psychology, 61,* 366–379.

Judge, T. A., Bono, J. E., Ilies, R., & Gerhardt, M. W. (2002). Personality and leadership: A qualitative and quantitative review. *Journal of Applied Psychology, 87,* 765–780.

Judge, T. A., Martocchio, J. J., & Thorsen, C. J. (1998). Five-factor model of personality and employee absence. *Journal of Applied Psychology, 82,* 745–755.

Judge, T. A., Piccolo, R. F., & Ilies, R. (2004). The forgotten ones? The validity of consideration and initiating structure in leadership research. *Journal of Applied Psychology, 89,* 36–51.

Judge, T. A., Thoresen, C. J., Bono, J. E., & Patton, G. K. (2001). The job satisfaction-performance relationship: A qualitative and quantitative review. *Psychological Bulletin, 127,* 376–407.

Julien, R. M. (1995). *A primer of drug action* (7th ed.). New York: Freeman.

Jussim, L. (1991). Interpersonal expectations and social reality: A reflection- construction model and reinterpretation of evidence. *Psychological Review, 98,* 54–73.

Kagan, J. (1998). Biology and the child. In W. Damon & R. M. Oerner (Eds.), *Handbook of child psychology* (vol. 1). New York: Wiley.

Kagan, J., & Snidman, N. (1991). Temperamental factors in human development. *American Psychologist, 46,* 856–862.

Kahlil Gibran (1960). *The Voice of the Master,* pt. 2, ch. 8 (1960; repr. in *A Second Treasury of Kahlil Gibran,* tr. by Anthony Ferris, 1962).

Kalivas, P. W., & Samson, H. H. (Eds.). (1992). *The neurobiology of drug and alcohol addiction.* Annals of the New York Academy of Sciences, vol. 654. New York: Academy of Sciences.

Kalsher, M. J., Cataldo, M. F., Deal, R. M., Traughber, B., & Jankel, W. R. (1985). Behavioral covariation in the treatment of chronic pain: A preliminary study. *Journal of Behavior Therapy and Experimental Psychiatry, 16,* 331–339.

Kamin, L. J. (1965). Temporal and intensity characteristics of the conditioned stimulus. In W. F. Prokasy (Ed.), *Classical conditioning: A symposium.* New York: Appleton-Century-Crofts.

Kanner, A. D., Coyne, J. C., Schaefer, C., & Lazarus, R. S. (1981). Comparison of two modes of stress measurement: Daily hassles and uplifts versus major life events. *Journal of Behavioral Medicine, 4,* 1–39.

Kanwisher, N., McDermott, J., & Chun, M. M. (1997). The fusiform face area: A module in human extrastriate cortex specialized for face perception. *Journal of Neuroscience, 17,* 4302–4311.

Kaplan, H. I., & Sadock, B. J. (1991). *Synopsis of psychiatry: Behavioral sciences and clinical psychiatry* (6th ed.). Baltimore: Williams & Wilkins.

Kavanagh, D. J. (1992). Recent developments in expressed emotion in schizophrenia. *British Journal of Psychiatry, 148,* 601–620.

Kawakami K., & Dovidio, J. F. (2001). The reliability of implicit stereotyping. *Personality and Social Psychology Bulletin, 27,* 212–225.

Kawakami, K., Dovidio, J. F., & Dijksterhuis, A. (2003). Effect of social category priming on personal attitudes. *Psychological Science, 14* (4), 315–319.

Kazdin, A. E. (1982). The token economy: A decade later. *Journal of Applied Behavior Analysis, 15,* 431–446.

Keefe, F. J., Buffington, A. L. H., Studts, J. L., & Rumble, M. E. (2002). Behavioral medicine 2002 and beyond. *Journal of Consulting and Clinical Psychology, 70* (3), 852–856.

Keefe, F. J., Lumley, M., Anderson, T., Lunch, T., & Carson, K. L. (2001). Pain and emotion: New research directions. *Journal of Clinical Psychology, 57,* 587–607.

Kelley, H. H. (1972). Attribution in social interaction. In E. E. Jones et al. (Eds.), *Attribution: Perceiving the causes of behavior.* Morristown, NJ: General Learning Press.

Kelly, D. D. (1981). Disorders of sleep and consciousness. In E. Kandel & J. Schwartz (Eds.), *Principles of neural science.* New York: Elsevier-North Holland.

Kelman, H. C., & Hamilton, V. L. (1989). *Crimes of obedience.* New Haven, CT: Yale University Press.

Kelsey, F. O. (1969). Drugs and pregnancy. *Mental Retardation, 7,* 7–10.

Kemeny, M. E. (2003). The psychobiology of stress. *Current Directions in Psychological Science, 12,* 124–129.

Kenardy, J. A., Dow, M. G. T., Johnston, D. W., Newman, M. G., Thomson, A., & Taylor, C. B. (2003). *A comparison of delivery methods of cognitive behavioural therapy for panic disorder: An international muticentre trial. Journal of Consulting & Clinical Psychology, 71* (6), 1068–1075.

Kendzierski, D., & Whitaker, D. J. (1997). The role of self-schema in linking intentions with behavior. *Personality and Social Psychology Bulletin, 23,* 139–147.

Kenrick, D. T., Groth, G. E., Trost, M. R., & Sadalla, E. K. (1993). Integrating evolutionary and social exchange perspectives on relationships: Effects of gender, self-appraisal, and involvement level on mate selection criteria. *Journal of Personality and Social Psychology, 64,* 951–969.

Kent, G. (1997). Dental phobias. In G. C. Davey (Ed.), *Phobias: A handbook of theory, research and treatment* (pp. 107–127). Chichester, England: Wiley.

Kershaw, T. S., Ethier, K. A., Niccolai, L. M., Lewis, J. B., Ickovics, J. R. (2003). Misperceived risk among female adolescents: Social and psychological factors associated with sexual risk accuracy. *Health Psychology, 22,* 523–532.

Kersting, K. (2005). Serious rehabilitation. *Monitor on Psychology, 36,* 38–41.

Kersting, K. (2006). Not biased? Despite what people say about stereotypes being bad most demonstrate implicit associations when tested. *Monitor on Psychology, 36,* 64–65.

Kessler, R. C., McGonagle, K. A., Zhao, S., Nelson, C. B., Hughes, M., Eshleman, S., Witchen, H-U., & Kendler, K. S. (1994). Lifetime and 12-month prevalence of DSM-III-R psychiatric disorders in the United States. *Archives of General Psychiatry, 5,* 8–19.

Kiecolt-Glaser, J. K., Fisher, L., Ogrocki, P., Stout, J. C., Speicher, C. E., & Glaser, R. (1987). Marital quality, marital disruption, and immune function. *Psychosomatic Medicine, 49,* 13–34.

Kiecolt-Glaser, J. K., & Glaser, R. (1992). Psychoneuroimmunology: Can psychological interventions modulate immunity? *Journal of Consulting and Clinical Psychology, 60,* 569–575.

Kiecolt-Glaser, J. K., Kennedy, S., Malkoff, S., Fisher, L., Speicher, C. E., & Glaser, R. (1988). Marital discord and immunity in males. *Psychosomatic Medicine, 50,* 213–229.

Kiecolt-Glaser, J. K., Malarkey, W., Cacioppo, J. T., & Glaser, R. (1994). Stressful personal relationships: Endocrine and immune function. In R. Glaser & J. K. Kiecolt-Glaser (Eds.), *Handbook of human stress and immunity* (pp. 321–339). San Diego: Academic Press.

Kiesler, C. A., & Kiesler, S. B. (1969). *Conformity.* Reading, MA: Addison-Wesley.

Kihlstrom, J. F (1985). Hypnosis. *Annual Review of Psychology, 36,* 385–418.

Kinnunen, M., Kaprio, J., Pulkkinen, L. (2005). Allostatic load of men and women in early middle age. *Journal of Individual Differences, 26,* 20–28.

Kinnunen, T., Zamansky, T., & Block, M. (1994). Is the hypnotized subject lying? *Journal of Abnormal Psychology, 103,* 184–191.

Kirkpatrick, D. (1993). Making it all worker-friendly. *Fortune, 128,* 44–53.

Kirkpatrick, D. L. (1959). Techniques for evaluating training programs. *Journal of the American Society of Training Directors, 13,* 3–9, 21–26.

Kirsch, I., & Braffman, W. (2001). Imaginative suggestibility and hypnotizability. *Current Directions in Psychological Science, 10,* 57–61.

Kirsch, I., & Lynn, S. J. (1998). Dissociation theories of hypnosis. *Psychological Bulletin, 123,* 100–115.

Kirsch, I., Lynn, S. J., Vigorito, M., & Miller, R. R. (in press). The role of cognition in classical and operant conditioning. *Journal of Clinical Psychology.*

Kisilevsky, B. S., Hains, S. M. J., Lee, J., Xie, X., Juang, H., Ye, H. H., Zhand, K., & Wang, Z. (2003). Effects of experience on fetal voice recognition. *Psychological Science, 14,* 220–224.

Klag, M. J., Ford, D. E., Mead, L. A., He, J., Whelton, P. K., Liang, K., & Levine, D. M. (1993). Serum cholesterol in young men and subsequent cardiovascular disease. *New England Journal of Medicine, 328,* 313–318.

Knafo, A., & Plomin, R. (2006). Parental discipline and affection and children's prosocial behavior: Genetic and environmental links. *Journal of Personality and Social Psychology, 90,* 147–164.

Knapp, R. (1987, July). When a child dies. *Psychology Today,* 60–67.

Koestner, R., Bernieri, F. & Zuckerman, M. (1992). Self-regulation and consistency between attitudes, traits, and behaviors. *Personality and Social Psychology Bulletin, 18,* 52–59.

Kohlberg, L. (1984). *Essays on moral development, Vol. 2. The psychology of moral development.* San Francisco: Harper & Row.

Kolb, B., Gibb, R., & Gorny, G. (2003). Experience-dependent changes in dendritic arbor and spine density in neocortex vary with age and sex. *Neurobiology of Learning and Memory, 79,* 1–10.

Kolb, B., Gibb, R., & Robinson, T. E. (2003). Brain plasticity and behavior. *Current Directions in Psychological Science, 12* (1), 1–5.

Koob, G. F., Roberts, A. J., Schulteis, G., Parsons, L. H., Heyser, C. J., Hyytia, P., Merlo-Pich, E., & Weiss, F. (1998). Neurocircuitry targets in ethanol reward and dependence. *Alcoholism: Clinical and Experimental Research, 22,* 3–9.

Kopp, M., Bonatti, H., Haller, C., Rumpold, G., Söllner, W., Holzner, B., Schweigkofler, H., Aigner, F., Hinterhuber, H., & Gunther, V. (2003). Life satisfaction and active coping style are important predictors of recovery from surgery. *Journal of Psychosomatic Research, 55,* 371–377.

Kosslyn, S. M. (1994). *Image and brain: The resolution of the imagery debate.* Cambridge, MA: MIT Press.

Kosslyn, S. M., & Thompson, W. L. (2003). When is early visual cortex activated during visual mental imagery? *Psychological Bulletin, 129,* 723–746.

Koutstaal, W. (2003). Older adults encode—but do not always use—perceptual details: Intentional versus unintentional effects of detail on memory judgments. *Psychological Science, 14,* 189–193.

Kozlowski, S. W. J., & Bell, B. S. (2006). Disentangling achievement orientation and goal Setting: Effects on self-regulatory processes. *Journal of Applied Psychology, 91,* 900–916.

Kramer, A. F., & Willis, S. L. (2002). Enhancing the cognitive vitality of older adults. *Current Directions in Psychological Science, 11,* 173–177.

Krestel, D., Passe, D., Smith, J. C., & Jonsson, L. (1984). Behavioral determinants of olfactory thresholds to amyl acetate in dogs. *Neuroscience Biobehavioral Review, 8,* 169–174.

Kring, A. M., Smith, D. A., & Neale, J. M. (1994). Individual differences in dispositional expressiveness: Development and validation of the emotional expressivity scale. *Journal of Personality and Social Psychology, 66,* 934–949.

Kruse, M. I., & Fromme, K. (2005). Influence of physical attractiveness and alcohol on men's perceptions of potential sexual partners and sexual behavior intentions. *Experimental and Clinical Psychopharmacology, 13,* 146–156.

Ku, G., Malhorta, D., & Murnighan, J. K. (2005). Toward a competitive arousal model of decision-making: A study of auction fever in live and Internet auctions. *Organizational Behavior and Human Decision Processes, 96,* 89–103.

Kubany, E. S., Bauer, G. B., Muraoka, M. Y., Richard, D. C., & Read, P. (1995). Impact of labeled anger and blame in intimate relationships. *Journal of Social and Clinical Psychology, 14,* 53–60.

Kübler-Ross, E. (1974). *Questions and answers about death and dying.* New York: Macmillan.

Kuhn, D. (2006). Do cognitive changes accompany developments in the adolescent brain? *Perspectives on Psychological Science, 1,* 59–67.

Kuhn, D., & Dean, D., Jr. (2005). Is developing scientific thinking all about learning to control variables? *Psychological Science, 16,* 866–670.

Kuhn, D., & Franklin, S. (2006). The second decade: What develops (and why)? In W. Damon & R. Lerner (series Eds.), and D. Kuhn & R. Siegler (volume Eds.), *Handbook of child psychology: Vol. 2. Cognition, perception, and language* (6th ed.). Hoboken, NJ: Wiley.

Kunda, Z. (1999) *Social cognition: Making sense of people.* Cambridge, MA: MIT Press.

Kunda, Z., & Oleson, K. C. (1995). Maintaining stereotypes in the face of disconfirmation: Construction grounds for subtyping deviants. *Journal of Personality and Social Psychology, 68,* 565–579.

LaBar, K. S., Crupain, M. J., Voyvodic, J. T., & McCarthy, G. (2003). Dynamic perception of facial affect and identity in the human brain. *Cerebral Cortex, 13,* 1023–1033.

LaBrie, J., Earleywine, M., Schiffman, J., Pedersen, E., Marriot, C. (2005, August). Effects of alcohol, expectancies, and partner type on condom use in college males: event-level analyses. *Journal of Sex Research, 42.*

Ladavas, E., Umilta, C., & Ricci-Bitti, P. E. (1980). Evidence for sex differences in right-hemisphere dominance for emotions. *Neuropsychologia, 18,* 361–366.

Ladd, D., & Henry, R. A. (2000). Helping coworkers and helping the organization: The role of support perceptions, exchange ideology, and conscientiousness. *Journal of Applied Social Psychology, 30,* 2028–2049.

Ladd, G. W., Kochenderfer, B. J., & Coleman, C. C. (1996). Friendship quality as a predictor of young children's early school adjustment. *Child Development, 6,* 1103–1118.

Laird, J. D. (1984). The real role of facial responses in the experience of emotion: A reply to Tourangeua and Ellsworth, and others. *Journal of Personality and Social Psychology, 47,* 909–917.

Lamb, M. E. (1977). Father-infant and mother-infant interactions in the first year of life. *Child Development, 48,* 167–181.

Lambert, A. J. (1995). Stereotypes and social judgment: The consequences of group variability. *Journal of Personality and Social Psychology, 68,* 388–403.

Lance, C. E., Lambert, T. A., Gewin, A. G., Lievens, F., & Conway, J. M. (2004). Revised estimates of dimension and exercise variance components in assessment center postexercise dimension ratings. *Journal of Applied Psychology, 89,* 377–385.

Landro, L. (1998). Alone together: Cancer patients and survivors find treatment, and support, online. *Wall Street Journal,* October 19, p. R12.

Landro, L. (2006). Pediatric hospitals teach doctors ways to convey tragic news. *Wall Street Journal,* May 2.

Langlois, J. H., Kalakanis, L., Rubenstein, A. J., Larson, A., Hallam, M., & Smoot, M. (2000). Maxims or myths of beauty: A meta-analytic and theoretical review. *Psychological Bulletin, 126,* 390–423.

Langlois, J. H., & Roggman, L. A. (1990). Attractive faces are only average. *Psychological Science, 1,* 115–121.

Langlois, J. H., Roggman, L. A., & Riesser-Danner, L. A. (1990). Infants' differential

social responses to attractive and unattractive faces. *Developmental Psychology, 26,* 153–159.

Larzelere, R. E., Sather, P. R., Schneider, W. N., Larson, D. B., & Pike, P. L. (1998). Punishment enhances reasoning's effectiveness as a disciplinary response to toddlers. *Journal of Marriage and the Family, 60,* 388–403.

Latane, B., Williams, K., & Harkins, S. (1979). Many hands make light the work: The causes and consequences of social loafing. *Journal of Personality and Social Psychology, 37,* 822–832.

Laumann, E. O., Gagnon, J. H., Michael, R. T., & Michaels, S. (1994). *The social organization of sexuality: Sexual practices in the United States.* Chicago: University of Chicago Press.

Launer, L. J., Feskens, E. J., Kalmijn, S., & Kromhout, D. (1996). Smoking, drinking, and thinking: The Zutphen Elderly study. *American Journal of Epidemiology, 143,* 219–227.

Law, B. M. (2005). Probing the depression-rumination cycle. *Monitor on Psychology, 36,* 38–39.

Law, B. M. (2005). Instilling skills for treating minority elders. *Monitor on Psychology, 36,* 50–52.

Lawless, H., & Engen, T. (1977). Associations to odors: Interference, mnemonics, and verbal labeling. *Journal of Experimental Psychology: Human Learning and Memory, 3,* 52–59.

Layman, J., Gidycz, C. A., & Lynn, S. J. (1996). Unacknowledged versus acknowledged rape victims: Situational factors and posttraumatic stress. *Journal of Abnormal Psychology, 105,* 124–131.

Lazarus, R. S., & Folkman, S. (1984). *Stress, appraisal, and coping.* New York: Springer.

Lazarus, R. S., Opton, E. M., Nomikos, M. S., & Rankin, N. O. (1985). The principle of short-circuiting of threat: Further evidence. *Journal of Personality, 33,* 622–635.

LeBlanc, M. M., & Barling, J. (2004). Workplace aggression. *Current Directions in Psychological Science, 13,* 9–12.

Lebovits, A. H. (2002). Psychological issues in the assessment and management of chronic pain. *Annals of the American Psychotherapy Association, 5.*

LeDoux, J. E. (2000). Emotion circuits in the brain. *Annual Review of Neuroscience, 23,* 155–184.

Lee, F. K., Sheldon, K. M., & Turban, D. B. (2003). Personality and the Goal-Striving Process: The Influence of Achievement Goal Patterns, Goal Level, and Mental Focus on Performance and Enjoyment. *Journal of Applied Psychology, 88,* 256–265.

Leeper, M. R., & Cordova, D. I. (1992). A desire to be taught: Instructional consequences of intrinsic motivation. *Motivation and Emotion, 16,* 187–208.

Lemery, K. S., Goldsmith, H. H., Klinnert, M. D., & Mrazek, D. A. (1999). Developmental models of infant and childhood temperament. *Developmental Psychology, 35,* 189–204.

Lemley, B. (2000, February). Isn't she lovely? *Discover,* 42–49.

Lepper, M., & Green, D. (Eds.). (1978). *The hidden costs of reward: New perspectives on the psychology of human motivation.* Hillsdale, NJ: Erlbaum.

Lerner, R. M. (1993). The demise of the nature-nurture dichotomy. *Human Development, 36,* 119–124.

LeVay, S. (1991). A difference in hypothalamic structure between heterosexual and homosexual men. *Science, 253,* 1–36.

Levenson, R. W. (1992). Autonomic nervous system differences among emotions. *Psychological Science, 3,* 23–27.

Leventhal, H., Singer, R., & Jones, S. (1965). The effects of fear and specifying of recommendation upon attitudes and behavior. *Journal of Personality and Social Psychology, 2,* 20–29.

Levine, D. W. (2005). Do dogs resemble their owners? A reanalysis of Roy and Christenfeld (2004). *Psychological Science, 16,* 83–84.

Levine, L. J., & Safer, M. A. (2002). Sources of bias in memory for emotions. *Current Directions in Psychological Science, 11,* 169–173.

Levinson, D. J. (1986). A conception of adult development. *American Psychologist, 41,* 3–13.

Levinthal, C. F. (1999). *Drugs, behavior, and modern society.* Boston: Allyn & Bacon.

Levy, S. M. (1990). Psychosocial risk factors and cancer progression: Mediating pathways linking behavior and disease. In K. D. Craig & S. M. Weiss (Eds.), *Health enhancement, disease prevention, and early intervention: Biobehavioral perspectives.* New York: Springer.

Levy, S. M., Herberman, R., Maluish, A., Achlien, B., & Lippman, M. (1985). Prognostic risk assessment in primary breast cancer by behavioral and immunological parameters. *Health Psychology, 4,* 99–113.

Levy, S. M., Lee, J., Bagley, C., & Lippman, M. (1988). Survival hazards analysis in first recurrent breast cancer patients: Seven-year follow-up. *Psychosomatic Medicine, 50,* 520–528.

Lewandowsky, S., Stritzke, W.G.K., Oberauer, K., & Moales, M. (2005). Memory for fact, fiction, and misinformation. The Iraq War 2003. *Psychological Science, 16,* 190–195.

Lewkowicz, D. J. (1996). Infants' response to the audible and visible properties of the human face. Role of lexical-syntactic content, temporal synchrony, gender,

and manner of speech. *Developmental Psychology, 32,* 347–366.

Lewy, A. J., Sack, R. I., & Singer, C. M. (1992). Bright light, melatonin, and biological rhythms in humans. In J. Montplaisir & R. Godbout (Eds.), *Sleep and biological rhythms: Basic mechanisms and applications to psychiatry.* New York: Oxford University Press.

Li, N. P., & Kenrick, D. T. (2006). Sex similarities and differences in preferences for short-term mates: What, whether, and why. *Journal of Personality and Social Psychology, 90,* 468–489.

Liao, Y., Tucker, P., Okoro, C. A., Giles, W. H., Mokdad, A. H., Harris, V. B. (2004). REACH 2010 surveillance for health status in minority communities—United States, 2001–2002. *Morbidity and Mortality Weekly Report Surveillance Summaries, 51,* 300–303.

Liddell, F. D. K. (1982). Motor vehicle accidents (1973–6) in a cohort of Montreal drivers. *Journal of Epidemiological Community Health, 36,* 140–145.

Liden, R. C., Sparrowe, R. T., & Wayne, S. J. (1997). Leader-member exchange theory: The past and potential for the future. In G. R. Ferris (Ed.), *Research in personnel and human resource management* (vol. 15, pp. 47–119). Greenwich, CT: JAI Press.

Lieberman, D. A. (1990). *Learning: Behavior and cognition.* Belmont, CA: Wadsworth.

Linville, P. W., & Fischer, G. W. (1993). Exemplar and abstraction models of perceived group variability and stereotypicality. *Social Cognition, 11,* 92–125.

Lipton, J. S., & Spelke, E. S. (2006). Preschool children master the logic of number word meanings. *Cognition, 98(3),* B57–B66.

Locke, B. Z., & Slaby, A. E. (1982). Preface. In D. Mechanic (Ed.), *Symptoms, illness behavior, and help-seeking* (pp. xi–xv). New York: Prodist.

Locke, E. A., & Latham, G. P. (2002). Building a practically useful theory of goal setting and task motivation: A 35-year odyssey. *American Psychologist, 57,* 705–717.

Loftus, E. F. (1991). The glitter of everyday memory and the gold. *American Psychologist, 46,* 16–18.

Loftus, E. F. (1997). Creating false memories. *Scientific American, 27(3),* 70–75.

Loftus, E. F. (2003). Make-believe memories. *American Psychologist, 58,* 864–873.

Loftus, E. F. (2004). Memories of things unseen. *Current Directions in Psychological Science, 13,* 145–147.

Logan, G. D. (1985). Skill and automaticity: Relations, implications, and future directions. *Canadian Journal of Psychology, 39,* 367–386.

Logan, G. D. (1988). Toward an instance theory of automotization. *Psychological Review, 95,* 492–527.

Logue, A. W. (1988). Research on self-control: An integrating framework. *Behavioral and Brain Sciences, 11,* 665–679.

Lopes, P. N., Grewal, D., Kadis, J., Gall, M., & Salovey, P. (in press). Evidence that emotional intelligence is related to job performance and affect and attitudes at work. *Psicothema.*

Lopes, P. N., Salovey, P., & Straus, R. (2003). Emotional intelligence, personality and the perceived quality of social relationships. *Personality and Individual Differences, 35,* 641–658.

Lubart, T. T., & Sternberg, R. J. (1995). An investment approach to creativity: Theory and data. In S. M. Smith, T. B. Ward, & R. A. Finke (Eds.), *The creative cognition approach* (pp. 269–302). Cambridge, MA: MIT Press.

Lubinski, D., Benbow, C. P., Webb, R. M., & Bleske-Rechek, A. (2006). Tracking exceptional human capital over two decades. *Psychological Science, 17,* 194–199.

Lubow, R. E. (1998). Latent inhibition and behavior pathology: Prophylactic and other possible effects of stimulus preexposure. In W. O'Donohue (Ed.), *Learning and behavior therapy* (pp. 107–121). Boston: Allyn & Bacon.

Luczak, S. E. (2001). Binge drinking in Chinese, Korean, and White college students: Genetic and ethnic group differences. *Psychology of Addictive Behaviors, 15,* 306–309.

Ludwig, S. (2001). The cross-race effect: Beyond recognition of faces in the laboratory. *Psychology, Public Policy, and Law, 7,* 170–200.

Luria, A. R. (1976). *Cognitive development: Its cultural and social foundations.* Cambridge, MA: Harvard University Press.

Lykken, D. T., McGue, M., Tellegen, A., & Bouchard, T. J. (1992). Emergenesis: Genetic traits that may not run in families. *American Psychologist, 47,* 1565–1577.

Lykken, D. T., & Tellegen, A. (1993). Is human mating adventitious or the result of lawful choice? A twin study of mate selection. *Journal of Personality and Social Psychology, 65,* 56–68.

Lykken, D., & Tellegen, A. (1996). Happiness is a stochastic phenomenon. *Psychological Science, 7,* 186–189.

Lynch, J. E., & Finkelstein, L. (2006). *Employee disability: Its effect on the performance evaluation process.* Paper presented at the Annual Conference of the Society for Industrial and Organizational Psychology, Dallas.

Lynn, S. J., Rhue, J. W., & Weekes, J. R. (1990). Hypnotic involuntariness: A social cognitive analysis. *Psychological Review, 974,* 169–184.

Lytton, H. (1990). Child and parent effects in boys' conduct disorders. *Developmental Psychology, 26,* 683–697.

Lyubomirsky, S., King, L., & Diener, E. (2005). The benefits of frequent positive affect: Does happiness lead to success? *Psychological Bulletin, 131,* 803–855.

Lyubomirsky, S., Sheldon, K., & Schkadae, D. (2005). Pursuing happiness: The architecture of sustainable change. *Review of General Psychology, 9,* 111–131.

Mack, A., & Rock, I. (1998). *Inattentional blindness.* Cambridge, MA: MIT Press.

Macrae, C. N., Alnwick, K. A., Milne, A. B., & Schloerscheidt, A. M. (2002). Person perception across the menstrual cycle: Hormonal influences on social-cognitive functioning. *Psychological Science, 13,* 532–536.

Magai, C., & McFadden, S. H. (1995). The role of emotions in social and personality development. *History, theory, and research.* New York: Plenum.

Maheswaran, D., & Chaiken, S. (1991). Promoting systematic processing in low-motivation settings: Effect of incongruent information on processing and judgment. *Journal of Personality and Social Psychology, 61,* 13–25.

Malone, M. S. (1993). Translating diversity into high-tech gains. *New York Times,* July 18, p. B2.

Mandel, D. R., Jusczyk, P. W., & Pisoni, D. B. (1995). Infants' recognition of the sound patterns of their own names. *Psychological Science, 6,* 314–317.

Mannix, E., & Neale, M. A. (2005). What differences make a difference? The promise and reality of diverse teams in organizations. *Psychological Science in the Public Interest, 6,* 31–55.

Markman, G. D., Baron, R. A., & Balkin, D. B. (2003). The role of regretful thinking, perseverance, and self-efficacy in venture formation. In J. Katz & D. Shepherd (Eds.), *Advances in entrepreneurship, firm emergence, and growth.* Greenwich, CT: JAI Press.

Markowitz, S., Chatterii, P., Kaestner, R., & Dhaval, D. (2002, February). Substance use and suicidal behaviors among young adults. *National Bureau of Economic Research Digest,* Paper 8810.

Markson, L., & Spelke, E. S. (2006). Infants' rapid learning about self-propelled objects. *Infancy, 9,* 45–71.

Marr, D. (1982). *Vision: A computational investigation into the human representation and processing of visual information.* San Francisco: Freeman.

Marshuetz, C. (2005). Order information in working memory: An integrative review of evidence from brain and behavior. *Psychological Bulletin, 131,* 323–339.

Martin, C. L., & Little, J. K. (1990). The relation of gender understanding to children's sex-typed preferences and gender stereotypes. *Child Development, 61,* 1427–1439.

Martin, C. L., & Ruble, D. N. (in press). Children's search for gender cues: Cognitive perspectives on gender development. *Current Directions in Psychological Science.*

Martin, P. Y., Laing, J., Marian, R., & Mitchell, M. (2005). Caffeine, cognition, and persuasion: Evidence for caffeine increasing the systematic processing of persuasive messages. *Journal of Applied Social Psychology, 35,* 160–182.

Maruta, T., Colligan, R. C., Malinchoc, M., & Offord, K. P. (2000). Optimists vs. pessimists: Survival rate among medical patients over a 30-year period. *Mayo Clinic Proceedings, 75,* 140–143.

Maslow, A. H. (1970). *Motivation and personality* (2nd ed.). New York: Harper & Row.

Mason, M. F., Tatkow, E. P., & Macrae, C. N. (2005). The look of love: Gaze shifts and person perception. *Psychological Science, 16,* 236–239.

Mason, R. B., & Just, M. A. (2004). How the brain processes causal inferences in text. *Psychological Science, 15,* 1–8.

Mast, M. S., & Hall, J. A. (2006). Women's advantage at remembering others' appearance: A systematic look at the why and when of a gender difference. *Personality and Social Psychology Bulletin, 32,* 353–364.

Matarazzo, J. D. (1992). Psychological testing and assessment in the 21st century. *American Psychologist, 47,* 1007–1018.

Mathiak, K., Hertrich, I., Grodd, W., & Ackermann, (2004). Cerebellum and speech perception: A functional magnetic resonance imaging study. *Journal of Cognitive Neuroscience, 14,* 902–912.

Matlin, M. W., & Foley, H. J. (1997). *Sensation and perception.* Boston: Allyn & Bacon.

Maton, K. I., Kohout, J. L., Wicherski, M., Leary, G.E., & Vinokurov, A. (2006). Minority students of color and the psychology graduate pipeline. *American Psychologist, 61,* 117–131.

Matsumoto, D. (2000). *Culture and psychology* (2nd ed.). Pacific Grove, CA: Brooks Cole.

Mattes, R. D. (2001). The taste of fat elevates postprandial triacylglycerol. *Physiology & Behavior, 74,* 343–348.

Mattheson, P. B., Shooenbaum, E., Greenberg, B., & Pliner, V. (1997). Association of maternal drug use during pregnancy with mother-to-child HIV transmission. *AIDS, 11,* 941–942.

Matthews, K. A. (2005). Psychological Perspectives on the Development of Coronary Heart Disease. *American Psychologist, 60,* 783–796.

Maurer, D., & Barrera, M. (1981). Infants' perception of natural and distorted arrangements of a schematic face. *Child Development, 52,* 196–202.

Maurer, T. J., & Pierce, H. R. (1998). A comparison of Likert scale and traditional measures of self-efficacy. *Journal of Applied Psychology, 83,* 324–329.

May, C. P., Hasher, L., & Foong, N. (2005). Implicit memory, age, and time of day. *Psychological Science, 16,* 96–100.

Mayer, J. D., Salovey, P., Caruso, D. R., & Sitarenios, G. (2001). Emotional intelligence as a standard intelligence. *Emotion, 1,* 232–242.

Mayes, A. R. (1996). The functional deficits that underlie amnesia: Evidence from amnesic forgetting rate and item-specific implicit memory. In D. J. Herman, C. McEvoy, C. Hertzog, P. Hertel, & M. K. Johnson (Eds.), *Basic and applied memory research: Practical applications* (vol. 2, pp. 391–405). Mahwah, NJ: Erlbaum.

Maynard, A. E. (2002). Cultural teaching: The development of teaching skills in Maya sibling interactions. *Child Development, 73,* 969–982.

Mazur, J. E. (1996). Procrastination by pigeons: Preference for larger, more delayed work requirements. *Journal of the Experimental Analysis of Behavior, 65,* 159–171.

McArdle, J. J., Caja-Ferrer, E., Hamagami, F., & Woodcock, R. W. (2002). Comparative longitudinal structural analyses of the growth and decline of multiple intellectual abilities over the life span. *Developmental Psychology, 38,* 115–142.

McCabe, R. E., Chudzik, S. M., Antony, M. M., Young, L., Swinson, R. P., & Zovlensky, M. J. (2004). Smoking behaviors across anxiety disorders. *Journal of Anxiety Disorders, 18,* 7–18.

McClearn, G. E., Plomin, R., Gora-Maslak, G., & Crabbe, J. C. (1991). The gene chase in behavioral science. *Psychological Science, 2,* 222–229.

McClelland, T. (2001). Cited in Greenberg, J., & Baron, R. A. *Behavior in organizations,* 8th ed. (2003) Upper Saddle River, NJ: Prentice-Hall.

McCormick, E. J., Jeanneret, P. R., & Meacham, R. C. (1969). *Position analysis questionnaire.* West Lafayette, IN: Occupational Research Center, Purdue University.

McCoy, S. L., Tun, P. A., Cox, L. C., Colangelo, M., Stewart, R. A., & Wingfield, A. (2005). Hearing loss and perceptual effort: Downstream effects on older adults' memory for speech. *Quarterly Journal of Experimental Psychology, 58A,* 22–33.

McCrae, R. R., Terracciano, A., & 79 members of the Personality Profiles of Cultures Project. (2005). Personality profiles of cultures: Aggregate personality traits. *Journal of Personality and Social Psychology, 89,* 407–425.

McCullough, M. E. (2001). Forgiveness: Who does it and how do they do it? *Current Directions in Psychological Science, 6,* 194–197.

McCullough, M. E., Bellah, C. G., Kilpatrick, S. D., & Johnson, J. L. (2001). Vengefulness: Relationships with forgiveness, rumination, well-being, and the big five. *Personality and Social Psychology Bulletin, 27*, 601–610.

McCullough, M. E., Pargament, K. I., & Thoresen, C. E. (2000). *Forgiveness: Theory, research, and practice.* New York: Guilford Press.

McEwen, B. S. (2005). Stressed or stressed out: What is the difference? *Journal of Psychiatry Neuroscience, 30*, 315–318.

McFarland, C., & Alvaro, C. (2000). The impact of motivation on temporal comparisons: Coping with traumatic events by perceiving personal growth. *Journal of Personality and Social Psychology, 79*, 327–343.

McGue, M. (1999). The behavioral genetics of alcoholism. *Current Directions in Psychological Science, 8*, 109–115.

McGue, M., Bouchard, T. J., Jr., Iaconon, W. G., & Lykken, D. T. (1993). Behavioral genetics of cognitive ability: A life-span perspective. In R. Plomin & G. E. McClearn (Eds.), *Nature, nurture, and psychology* (pp. 59–76). Washington, D.C.: American Psychological Association.

McGue, M., Sharma, A., & Benson, P. (1996). Parent and sibling influences on adolescent alcohol use and misuse: Evidence from a U.S. adoption cohort. *Journal of Studies on Alcohol, 57*, 8–18.

McGuire, P. A. (1999, June). Psychology and medicine connecting in war on cancer. *APA Monitor*, 8–9.

McKee, S. A., Maciejewski, P. K., Falba, T., & Mazure, C. M. (2003). Sex differences in the effects of stressful life events on changes in smoking status. *Addiction, 98*, 847–855.

McKnight, A. J., & Peck, R. C. (2002). Graduated driver licensing and safer driving. *Journal of Safety Research, 34*, 85–89.

McNally, R. J., Clancy, S. A., Barrett, H. M., & Parker, H. A. (2004). Inhibiting retrieval of trauma cues in adults reporting histories of childhood sexual abuse. *Cognition and Emotion, 18*, 479–493.

McNally, R. J., Ristuccia, C. S., & Perlman, C. A. (2005). Forgetting of trauma cues in adults reporting continuous or recovered memories of childhood sexual abuse. *Psychological Science, 16*, 336–340.

McNamara, P. (2004). *An evolutionary psychology of sleep and dreams.* Westport, CT: Preaeger.

McNamara, P., McLaren, D., Smith, D., Brown, A.,& Stickgold, R. (2005). A "Jekyll and Hyde" within: Aggressive versus friendly interactions in REM and non-REM dreams. *Psychological Science, 16*, 130–136.

McNeely, B. L., & Meglino, B. M. (1994). The role of dispositional and situational antecedents in prosocial organizational behavior: An examination of the intended beneficiaries of prosocial behavior. *Journal of Applied Psychology, 79*, 836–844.

Mealey, L., Bridgstock, R., & Townsend, G. C. (1999). Symmetry and perceived facial attactiveness: A monozygotic co-twin comparison. *Journal of Personality and Social Psychology, 76*, 151–158.

Measelle, J. R., John, O. P., Ablow, J., Cowan, P. A., & Cowan, C. P. (2005). Can children provide coherent, stable, and valid self-reports on the big five dimensions? A longitudinal study from ages 5 to 7. *Journal of Personality and Social Psychology, 89*, 90–106.

Medvec, V. H., Madey, S. F., & Gilovich, T. (1995). When less is more: Counterfactual thinking and satisfaction among Olympic athletes. *Journal of Personality and Social Psychology, 69*, 603–610.

Meehl, P. E. (1975). Hedonic capacity: Some conjectures. *Bulletin of the Menninger Clinic, 39*, 295–307.

Meeren, H. K. M., van Heijnsbergen, C.R.J., & de Gelder, B. (2005). Rapid perceptual integration of facial expression and emotional body language. *Proceedings of the National Academy of Sciences, 102*, 16518–16523.

Meichenbaum, D. H. (1977). *Cognitive-behavior modification.* New York: Plenum.

Meijmann, T., van der Meer, O., & van Dormolen, M. (1993). The after-effects of night work on short-term memory performance. *Ergonomics, 36*, 37–42.

Meissner, C. A., & Brigham, J. C. (2001). Thirty years of investigating the own-race bias in memory for faces: A meta-analytic review. *Psychology, Public Policy, and Law, 7*, 3–35.

Melamed, S., Shirom, A., Toker, S., Berliner, S., Shapira, I. (2006). Burnout and Risk of Cardiovascular Disease: Evidence, Possible Causal Paths, and Promising Research Directions. *Psychological Bulletin, 132*, 327–353.

Mellers, B. A. (2000). Choice and relative pleasure of consequences. *Psychological Bulletin, 126*, 910–924.

Mellers, B. A., & McGraw, A. P. (2001). Anticipated emotions as guides to choice. *Current Directions in Psychological Science, 6*, 210–214.

Melzack, R., & Wall, P. D. (1965). Pain mechanisms: A new theory. *Science, 150*, 971–979.

Melzack, R., & Wall, P. D. (1988). *The challenge of pain* (rev. ed.). New York: Penguin Books.

Mendlewicz, J., & Lecrubier, Y. (2000). Antidepressants section: Proceedings from a TA-SSRI consensus conference. *Acta Psychiatrica Scandinavian, 101* (Supplement 403), 5–8.

Merkelbach, H., deJong, P. J., Muris, P., & van den Hout, M. A. (1996). The etiology of specific phobias: A review. *Clinical Psychology Review, 16*, 337–361.

Metzger, A. M. (1980). A methodological study of the Kübler-Ross stage theory. *Omega, 10*, 291–301.

Meyer, A. J., Maccoby, N., & Farquhar, J. W. (1980). Skills training in a cardiovascular health education campaign. *Journal of Consulting and Clinical Psychology, 48*, 129–142.

Meyerowitz, B. E., & Chaiken, S. (1987). The effect of message framing on breast self-examination attitudes, intentions, and behavior. *Journal of Personality and Psychology, 52*, 500–510.

Meyerowitz, B. E., Wilson, D. K., & Chaiken, S. (1991, June). *Loss-framed messages increase breast self-examination for women who perceive risk.* Paper presented at the annual convention of the American Psychological Society, Washington, D.C.

Meyers, S. A., & Berscheid, E. (1997). The language of love: The difference a reposition makes. *Personality and Social Psychology Bulletin, 23*, 347–362.

Milgram, S. (1963). Behavioral study of obedience. *Journal of Abnormal and Social Psychology, 67*, 371–378.

Milgram, S. (1974). *Obedience to authority.* New York: Harper.

Millenson, J. R., & Leslie, J. C. (1979). *Principles of behavioral analysis* (2nd ed.). New York: Macmillan.

Miller, G. E., & Cohen, S. (2001). Psychological interventions and the immune system: A meta-analytic review and critique. *Health Psychology, 20* (1), 47–63.

Miller, N., Maruyama, G., Beaber, R. J., & Valone, K. (1976). Speed of speech and persuasion. 615–624.

Miller, M., Mangano, C., Park, Y., Goel, R., Plotnick, G., Vogel, G. (2005). Divergent effects of laughter and mental stress on endothelial function: Potential impact on entertainment. *Journal of the American College of Cardiology, 45* (3 Suppl.A), 408A.

Miller, M., Mangano, C., Park, Y., Goel, R., Plotnick, G. D., & Vogel, R. A. (2006). Impact of cinematic viewing on endothelial function. *Heart, 92*, 261–262.

Miller, R. S. (1991). On decorum in close relationships: Why aren't we polite to those we love? *Contemporary Social Psychology, 15*, 63–65.

Miller, S. M. (1995). Monitoring versus blunting styles of coping with cancer influence the information patients want and need about their disease: implications for cancer screening and management. *Cancer, 76*, 167–177.

Miller, S. M., Shoda, Y., & Hurley, K. (1996). Applying cognitive-social theory to health-protective behavior: Breast self-examination in cancer screening. *Psychological Bulletin, 119*, 70–94.

Millon, T. (1987). *Millon clinical multiaxial inventory-II: Manual for MCMI-II* (2nd ed.). Minneapolis: National Computer System.

Millon, T. (1991). Classification psychopathology: Rationale, alternatives, and standards. *Journal of Abnormal Psychology, 100,* 245–261.

Millon, T. A. (Ed.). (1997). *The Millon inventories: Clinical and personality assessment.* New York: Guilford Press.

Minami, H., & Dallenbach, K. M. (1946). The effect of activity upon learning and retention in the cockroach. *American Journal of Psychology, 59,* 1–58.

Mineka, S., & Zinbarg, R. (2006). A contemporary learning theory perspective on the etiology of anxiety disorders: It's not what you thought it was. *American Psychologist, 61,* 10–26.

Miranda, J., Chung, J. Y., Green, B. L., Krupnick, J., Siddique, J., Revicki, D.A., & Belin, T. (2003). Treating depression in predominantly low-income young minority women: A randomized controlled trial. *Journal of the American Medical Association, 290,* 57–65.

Mitchell, H. (1988, February). Why are women still dying of cervical cancer? *Australian Society,* pp. 34–35.

Mollon, J. D. (1993). Mixing genes and mixing colours. *Current Biology, 3,* 82–85.

Molyneux, A., Lewis, S., Leivers, U., Anderton, A., Antoniak, M., Brackenridge, A., Nilsson, F., McNeill, A., West, R., Moxham, J., & Britton, J. (2003). Clinical trial comparing nicotine replacement therapy (NRT) plus brief counseling, brief counseling alone, and minimal intervention on smoking cessation in hospital inpatients. *Thorax, 58,* 484–488.

Monahan, J. L., Murphy, S. T., & Zajonc, R. B. (2000). Subliminal mere exposure: Specific, general, and diffuse effects. *Psychological Science, 11*(6), 462–466.

Montgomery, G., & Kirsch, I. (1996). Mechanisms of placebo pain reduction: An empirical investigation. *Psychological Science, 7,* 174–176.

Moore, B. C. J. (1982). *An introduction to the psychology of hearing* (2nd ed.). New York: Academic Press.

Moore, R. Y., & Card, J. P. (1985). Visual pathways and the entrainment of circadian rhythms: The medical and biological effects of light. In R. J. Wurtman, M. J. Baum, J. T. Potts, Jr. (Eds.), *Annals of the New York Academy of Science, 453,* 123–133.

Moore-Ede, M. C., Sulzman, F. M., & Fuller, C. A. (1982). *The clocks that time us.* Cambridge, MA: Harvard University Press.

Moray, N. (1959). Attention in dichotic listening: Affective cues and the influence of instruction. *Quarterly Journal of Experimental Psychology, 11,* 59–60.

Moreland, R. L., & Beach, S. R. (1992). Exposure effects in the classroom: The development of affinity among students. *Journal of Experimental Social Psychology, 28,* 255–276.

Morewedge, C. K., Gilbert, D. T., & Wilson, T. D. (2005). The least likely of times: How remembering past biases forecasts of the future. *Psychological Science, 16,* 626–630.

Morris, M. W., & Pang, K. (1994). Culture and cause: American and Chinese attributions for social and physical events. *Journal of Personality and Social Psychology, 67,* 649–671.

Morrongiello, B. A., & Clifton, R. K. (1984). Effects of sound frequency on behavioral and cardiac orienting in newborn and five-month-old infants. *Journal of Experimental Child Psychology, 38,* 429–446.

Morse, J. M., & Morse, R. M. (1988). Cultural variation in the inference of pain. *Journal of Cross Cultural Psychology, 19,* 232–242.

Most, S. B., Scholl, B. J., Clifford, E. R., & Simons, D. J. (2005). What you see is what you set: Sustained inattentional blindness and the capture of awareness. *Psychological Review, 112,* 217–242.

Motohashi, K., & Umino, M. (2001). Heterotopic painful stimulation decreases the late component of somatosensory evoked potentials induced by electrical tooth stimulation. *Cognitive Brain Research, 11,* 39–46.

Motowidlo, S. J., Packard, J. S., & Manning, M. R. (1986). Occupational stress: Its causes and consequences for job performance. *Journal of Applied Psychology, 71,* 618–629.

Mowrer, O. H., & Jones, H. M. (1945). Habit strength as a function of the pattern of reinforcement. *Journal of Experimental Psychology, 35,* 293–311.

Mulkens, S. A. N., deJong, P. J., & Merckelbach, H. (1996). Disgust and spider phobia. *Journal of Abnormal Psychology, 105,* 464–468.

Munsinger, H. A. (1978). The adopted child's IQ: A crucial review. *Psychological Bulletin, 82,* 623–659.

Murdoch, D. D., & Pinl, R. O. (1988). The influence of beverage type on aggression in males in a natural setting. *Aggressive Behavior 4,* 325–335.

Murphy, F. C., Nimmo-Smith, I., & Lawrence, A. D. (2003). Functional neuroanatomy of emotion: A meta-analysis. *Cognitive, Affective, & Behavioral Neuroscience, 3,* 207–233.

Murphy, K. R. (2006). It does work, after all. *The Industrial-Organizational Psychologist, 43* (4), 61–62.

Murphy, K. R., Cleveland, J. N., Skattebo, A. L., & Kinney, T. B. (2004). Raters who pursue different goals give different ratings. *Journal of Applied Psychology, 89,* 158–164.

Murphy, S. T., & Zajonc, R. B. (1993). Affect, cognition, and awareness: Affective priming with suboptimal and optimal stimulus. *Journal of Personality and Social Psychology, 64,* 723–739.

Murray, B. (1999, June). Customized appeals may increase cancer screening. *APA Monitor, 35.*

Murray, S. L., & Holmes, J. G. (1999). The (mental) ties that bind: Cognitive structures that predict relationship resilience. *Journal of Personality and Social Psychology, 77,* 1228–1244.

Myers, D. (2002). *Intuition: Its powers and perils.* New Haven, CT: Yale University Press.

Myers, D. G., & Diener, E. (1995). Who is happy? *Psychological Science, 6,* 10–19.

Myers, N. A., Clifton, R. K., & Clarkson, M. C. (1987). When they were young: Almost-threes remember two years ago. *Infant Behavior and Development, 10,* 123–132.

Narayan, S. S., Temchin, A. N., Recio, A., & Ruggero, M. A. (1998). Frequency tuning of basilar membrane and auditory nerve fibers in the same cochleae. *Science, 282,* 1882–1884.

Nathans, J. (1999). The Evolution and Physiology of Human Color Vision: Insights from Molecular Genetic Studies of Visual Pigments. *Neuron, 24,* 299–312.

Nathans, J., Thomas, D., & Hogness, D. S. (1986). Molecular genetics of human color vision: The genes encoding blue, green, and red pigments. *Science, 232,* 193–202.

National Center for Health Statistics. (2001). Available: www.cdc.gov/nchs/pressroom/01news/newstudy.htm.

National Center for Health Statistics. (2002). Available: www.cdc.gov/nchs/products/pubs/pubd/hestats/obese/obse99.htm.

National Center for Health Statistics, 2005. Summary Health Statistics for U.S. Adults. Series 10, No. 225, July, 2005. Accessed from the world wide web on September 25, 2006 at www.cdc.gov/nchs/fastats/exercise.htm.

National Highway Traffic Safety Administration, (2005). Driver Cell Phone Use in 2005 Overall Results. Accessed from the world wide web on September 25, 2006 at www.nhtsa.dot.gov.

National Institute of Occupational Safety and Health. (1999). Stress at work. Available: www.cic.gov/niosh/stresswk.html.

National Television Violence Study. (1998). *Executive Summary: National Television Violence Study* (vol. 3). Santa Barbara, CA: Center for Communication and Social Policy.

National Vital Statistics Report, (2004). Vol. 53, No. 5. Accessed from the world wide web on September 25, 2006 at www.cdc.gov/CANCER/colorectal/statistics/.

Neal, R. D., Hussain-Gambles, M., Allgar, V. L., Lawlor, D. A., & Dempsey, O. (2005). Reasons for and consequences of missed appointments in general practice in the UK: Questionnaire survey and prospective review of medical records. *BioMed Central Family Practice, 6.* Available: www.pubmedcentral.nih.gov/articlerender.fcgi?artid=1291364.

Neher, A. (1996). Jung's theory of archetypes: A critique. *Journal of Humanistic Psychology, 36,* 61–91.

Neisser, U., Boodoo, G., Bouchard, T. J., Jr., Bykin, A. W., Brody, N., Ceci, S. J., Halpern, D. F., Loehlin, J. C., Perloff, R., Sternberg, R. J., & Urbina, S. (1996). Intelligence: Knowns and unknowns. *American Psychologist, 51,* 77–101.

Nelson, G., Chandrashekar, F., Hoon, M. A., Feng, L., Zhao, G., Ryba, N. F. P., & Zuker, C. S. (2002). An amino-acid taste receptor. *Nature, 416,* 199–202.

Nelson, L. J., & Miller, D. T. (1995). The distinctiveness effect in social categorization: You are what makes you unusual. *Psychological Science, 6,* 246–249.

Nelson, R. J., & Demas, G. E. (2004). Seasonal patterns of stress, disease, and sickness responses. *Current Directions in Psychological Science, 13,* 198–201.

Nelson-Jones, R. (2002). Diverse goals for multicultural counseling and therapy. *Counseling Psychology Quarterly, 15,* 133–143.

Neuman, J. H., & Baron, R. A. (1997). Aggression in the workplace. In R. A. Giacalone & J. Greenberg (Eds.), *Antisocial behavior in organizations* (pp. 37–67). Thousand Oaks, CA: Brooks/Cole.

Newman, M. L., Pennebaker, H. W., Berry, D. S. & Richards, J. M. (2003). Lying words: Predicting deception from linguistic styles. *Personality and Social Psychology Bulletin, 29,* 665–675.

Newport, E. L., & Aslin, R. N. (2000). Innately constrained learning: Blending old and new approaches to language acquisition. In S. C. Howell, S. A. Fish, & T. Keith-Lucas (Eds.), *Proceedings of the 24th Boston University Conference on Language Development* (pp. 1–21). Somerville, MA: Cascadilla Press.

NIAAA (2005). National epidemiological survey on alcoholism and related conditions. Available: www.niaaa.gov.

Niaura, R., Todaro, J. F., Stroud, L., Spiro, A., III, Ward, K. D., & Weiss, S. (2002). Hostility, the metabolic syndrome, and incident coronary heart disease. *Health Psychology, 21* (6), 588–593.

Nicolson, R. I., & Fawcett, A. J. (2005). Developmental dyslexia, learning, and the cerebellum. *Journal of Neural Transmission, 69,* 19–36.

Nietzel, M. T., Speltz, M. L., McCauley, E. A., & Bernstein, D. A. (1998). *Abnormal psychology.* Boston: Allyn & Bacon.

Nigg, J. T., John, O. P., Blaskey, L. G., Huang-Pollock, C. L., Willcutt, E. G., Hinshaw, S. P., & Pennington, B. (2002). Big five dimensions and ADHD symptoms: Links between personality traits and clinical symptoms. *Journal of Personality and Social Psychology, 83,* 451–569.

Nisan, M., & Kohlberg, L. (1982). Universality and variation in moral judgment: A longitudinal and cross-sectional study in Turkey. *Child Development, 53,* 865–876.

Nishitani, N., Schurmann, M., Amunts, K., & Hari, R. (2005). Broca's region: From action to language. *Physiology, 20,* 60–69.

Noble, J., & McConkey, K. M. (1995). Hypnotic sex change: Creating and challenging a delusion in the laboratory. *Journal of Abnormal Psychology, 104,* 69–74.

Nolen-Hoeksema, S. (2005). Interview described in *Monitor on Psychology,* November, 2005, pp. 36–38.

Nolen-Hoeksema, S., & Davis, C. G. (1994). Probing the rumination-depression cycle. *Journal of Personality and Social Psychology, 77,* 801–814.

Nolen-Hoeksema, S., & Davis, C. G. (1999). "Thanks for sharing that": Ruminators and their social support networks. *Journal of Personality and Social Psychology, 77,* 801–814.

Norman, D. A., & Shallice, T. (1985). Attention to action: Willed and automatic control of behavior. In R. J. Davidson, G. E. Schwartz, & D. Shapiro (Eds.), *Consciousness and self-regulation: Vol. 4. Advances in research and theory* (pp. 2–18). New York: Plenum.

Norris, F. H. (2002). Psychosocial consequences of disasters. *PTSD Research Quarterly, 13* (2), 1–8.

Norris, F. H., & Murrell, S. A. (1990). Social support, life events, and stress as modifiers of adjustment to bereavement by older adults. *Psychology and Aging, 5,* 429–436.

Oakley, D. (2004). Pain activation during hypnosis. *Neuroimage, 23,* 392–401.

Ogloff, J. R., & Wong, S. (1990). Electrodermal and cardiovascular evidence of a coping response in psychopaths. *Criminal Justice and Behavior, 17,* 231–245.

Ohman, A. (2002). Automaticity and the amygdala: Nonconscious responses to emotional faces. *Current Directions in Psychological Science, 11,* 62–66.

Ohman, A., Flykt, A., & Esteves, F. (2001). Emotion drives attention: Detecting the snake in the grass. *Journal of Experimental Psychology: General, 131,* 466–478.

Ohman, A., Lundqvist, D., & Esteves, F. (2001). The face in the crowd revisited: Threat advantage with schematic stimuli. *Journal of Personality and Social Psychology, 80,* 381–396.

Ohman, A., & Mineka, S. (2001). Fear, phobias, and preparedness: Toward an evolved module of fear and fear learning. *Psychological Review, 108,* 483–522.

Ohman, A., & Mineka, S. (2003). The malicious serpent: Snakes as a prototypical stimulus for an evolved module of fear. *Current Directions in Psychological Science, 12,* 5–8.

Ohman, A., & Soares, J. J. F. (1994). Unconscious anxiety: Phobic responses to masked stimuli. *Journal of Abnormal Psychology, 103,* 231–240.

Olson, M. A., & Fazio, R. H. (2006). Reducing automatically activated racial prejudice through implicit evaluative conditioning. *Personality and Social Psychology Bulletin, 32,* 421–433.

Organ, D. W., & Ryan, K. (1995). A meta-analytic review of attitudinal and dispositional predictors of organizational citizenship behavior. *Personnel Psychology, 48,* 775–802.

Orlinsky, D. E., & Howard, K. E. (1987). The relation of process to outcome in psychotherapy. In S. L. Garfield & A. E. Bergin (Eds.), *Handbook of psychotherapy and behavior change* (3rd ed.). New York: Wiley.

Osterling, J., & Dawson, G. (1994). Early recognition of children with autism: A study of first birthday home videotapes. *Journal of Autism and Development Disorders, 24,* 247–257.

Ottati, V. C., & Isbell, L. M. (1996). Effects of mood during exposure to target information on subsequently reported judgments: An on-line model of misattribution and correction. *Journal of Personality and Social Psychology, 71,* 39–53.

Oulette-Kobasa, S. C., & Puccetti, M. C. (1983). Personality and social resources in stress resistance. *Journal of Personality and Social Psychology, 45,* 836–850.

Padian, N. S., Shiboski, S., & Jewell, N. (1990). The effect of the number of exposures on the risk of heterosexual HIV transmission. *Journal of Infectious Diseases. 161,* 883–887.

Paller, K. A., Kutas, M., & McIsaac, H. K. (1995). Monitoring conscious recollection via the electrical activity of the brain. *Psychological Science, 6,* 107–111.

Papp, L., Klein, D., Martinez, J., Schneier, F., Cole, R., Liebowitz, M., Hollander, E., Fryer, A., Jordan, F., & Gorman, J. (1993). Diagnostic and substance specificity of carbon-dioxide-induced panic. *American Journal of Psychiatry, 150,* 250–257.

Passman, R. H., & Weisberg, P. (1975). Mothers and blankets as agents for promoting play and exploration by young children in a novel environment: The effects of social and nonsocial attachment objects. *Developmental Psychology, 11,* 170–177.

Pastor, D. L. (1981). The quality of mother-infant attachment and its relationship to toddlers' initial sociability with peers. *Developmental Psychology, 17,* 326–335.

Patrick, C. J., Bradley, M. M., & Lang, P. J. (1993). Emotion in the criminal psychopath: Startle reflex modulation. *Journal of Abnormal Psychology, 102,* 83–92.

Patterson, D. R. (2004). Treating pain with hypnosis. *Current Directions in Psychological Science, 13,* 252–255.

Patterson, D. R. (2005). Behavioral methods for chronic pain and illness: A reconsideration and appreciation. *Rehabilitation Psychology, 50,* 312–315.

Patterson, D. R., & Jensen, M. (2003). Hypnosis for clinical pain control. *Psychological Bulletin, 129,* 495–521.

Paul, G. L. (1982). *The development of a "transportable" system of behavioral assessment for chronic patients.* Invited address, University of Minnesota, Minneapolis.

Paul, G. L., & Lentz, R. J. (1977). *Psychosocial treatment of chronic mental patients: Milieu versus social-learning programs.* Cambridge, MA: Harvard University Press.

Pavlov, I. P. (1928). *Lectures on conditioned reflexes: Twenty-five years of objective study of the higher nervous activity (behaviour) of animals.* Trans. W. H. Gantt. New York: International Publishers. (Original work published 1923; includes original works published from 1903–1922.)

Pelletier, K. R. (1986). Longevity: What can centenarians teach us? In K. Dychtwald (Ed.), *Wellness and health promotion for the elderly.* Rockville, MD: Aspen.

Penton-Voak, I. S., & Perrett, D. I. (2000). Female preferences for male faces change cyclically: Further evidence. *Evolution and Human Behavior, 21,* 39–48.

Perls, F. (1969). *Gestalt therapy verbatim.* Lafayette, CA: Real People.

Perry, R. J., Rosen, H. R., Kramer, J. H., Beer, J. S., Levenson, R. L., Miller, B. L. (2001). Hemispheric dominance for emotions, empathy, and social behavior: Evidence from right and left handers with frontotemporal dementia. *Neurocase, 7,* 145–160.

Peterson, M., & Wilson, J. F. (2004). Work stress in America. *International Journal of Stress Management, 11,* 91–113.

Pettigrew, T. E. (1997). Generalized intergroup contact effects on prejudice. *Personality and Social Psychology Bulletin, 23,* 175–185.

Pettigrew, T. F., & Tropp, L. R. (2006). Allport's intergroup contact hypothesis: Its history and influence. In J. F. Dovidio, P. Glock, & L. Rrudman (Eds.), *On the nature of prejudice: Fifty years after Allport.* Malden, MA: Blackwell.

Petty, R. E., & Cacioppo, J. T. (1986). The elaboration likelihood model of persuasion. In L. Berkowitz (Ed.), *Advances in experimental social psychology* (vol. 19, pp. 123–205). New York: Academic Press.

Petty, R. E., & Cacioppo, J. T. (1990). Involvement and persuasion: Tradition versus integration. *Psychological Bulletin, 107,* 367–374.

Petty, R. E., Cacioppo, J. T., Strathman, A. J., & Priester, J. R. (1994). To think or not to think; Exploring two routes to persuasion. In S. Shavitt & T. C. Brock (Eds.), *Persuasion* (pp. 113–147). Boston: Allyn & Bacon.

Pfaffman, C. (1978). The vertebrate phylogeny, neural code, and integrative processes of taste. In E. C. Carterrette & M. P. Friedman (Eds.), *Handbook of perception* (vol. 6A). New York: Academic Press.

Phan, K. L., Wager, T. D., Taylor, S. F., & Liberzon, I. (2002). Functional neuroanatomy of emotion: A meta-analysis of emotion activation studies in PET and fMRI. *NeuroImage, 16,* 331–348.

Phillips, A. G., & Fibiger, H. C. (1989). Neuroanatomical bases of intracranial self-stimulation: Untangling the Gordian knot. In J. M. Leibman & S. J. Cooper (Eds.), *The neuropharmacological bases of reward* (pp. 66–105). Oxford, England: Clarendon Press.

Phillips, D. P., & Brugge, J. F. (1985). Progress in neurophysiology of sound localization. *Annual Review of Psychology, 36,* 245–274.

Piaget, J. (1965). *The moral judgment of the child.* New York: Free Press. (Originally published in 1932.)

Piaget, J. (1975). *The child's conception of the world.* Totowa, NJ: Littlefield, Adams. (Originally published in 1929.)

Piccolo, R. F., & Colquitt, J. A. (2006). Transformational leadership and job behaviors: The mediating role of core job characteristics. *Academy of Management Journal, 49,* 327–340.

Pihl, R. O., Lau, M. L., & Assaad, J. M. (1997). Aggressive disposition, alcohol, and aggression. *Aggressive Behavior, 23,* 11–18.

Pinker, S. (1997). *How the mind works.* New York: Norton.

Pinquart, M., & Sorensen, S. (2000). Influences of socioeconomic status, social network, and competence on subjective well-being in later life: A meta-analysis. *Psychology and Aging, 15,* 187–224.

Piotrkowski, C. S., & Brannen, S. J. (2002). Exposure, threat appraisal, and lost confidence as predictors of PTSD symptoms following September 11. *American Journal of Orthopsychiatry, 72,* 476–485.

Plomin, R. (1997). Genetics and intelligence: What's new? *Intelligence, 24,* 45–65.

Plomin, R., Fulker, D. W., Corley, R., & DeFries, J. C. (1997). Nature, nurture, and cognitive development from 1 to 16 years: A parent-offspring adoption study. *Psychological Science, 8,* 442–447.

Podsakoff, P. M., Bommer, W. H., Podsakoff, N. P., & MacKenzie, S. B. (2006). Relationships between leader reward and punishment behavior and subordinate attitudes, perceptions, and behaviors: A meta-analytic review of existing and new research. *Organizational Behavior and Human Decision Processes, 99,* 113–142.

Poon, L. W., & Fozard, J. L. (1980). Age and word frequency effects in continuous recognition memory. *Journal of Gerontology, 35,* 77–86.

Popenoe, D., & Whitehead, B. D. (1999). *The state of our unions.* New Brunswick, NJ: Rutgers University Press.

Poulin, F., Dishion, T. J., & Haas, E. (1999). The peer influence paradox: Friendship quality and deviancy training within male adolescent friendships. *Merrill-Palmer Quarterly, 45,* 42–61.

Pravosudov, V. V., Lavenex, P., & Omanska, A. (2005). Nutritional deficits during early development affect hippocampal structure and spatial memory later in life. *Behavioral Neuroscience, 119,* 1368–1374.

Pressman, S. D., Cohen, S., Miller, G. E., Barkin, A., Rabin, B. S., Treanor, J. J. (2005). Loneliness, social network size, and immune response to influenza vaccination in college freshmen. *Health Psychology, 24,* 297–306.

Preston, K. L., Umbricht, A., Wong, C. J., & Epstein, D. H. (2001). Shaping cocaine abstinence by successive approximation. *Journal of Consulting & Clinical Psychology, 69,* 643–654.

Principi, G. F., Kanaya, T., Ceci, S. J., & Singh, M. (2006). Believing is seeing: How rumors can engender false memories in preschoolers. *Psychological Science, 17,* 243–248.

Quinn, P. C., Bhatt, R. S., Brush, D., Grimes, A., & Sharpnack, H. (2002). Development of form similarity as a gestalt grouping principle in infancy. *Psychological Science, 13* (4), 320–328.

Raajimakers, J. G., & Shiffrin, R. M. (1981). SAM: Search of associative memory. *Psychological Review, 88,* 93–134.

Rabin, M. D., & Cain, W. S. (1984). Determinants of measured olfactory sensitivity. *Perception & Psychophysics, 39,* 281–286.

Rachlin, H. (1995). The value of temporal patterns in behavior. *Current Directions in Psychological Science, 4,* 188–192.

Raine, A., Bihrle, S., Venebles, P. H., Mednick, S. A., & Pollock, V. (1999). Skin-conductance orienting deficits and increased alcoholism in schizotypal criminals. *Journal of Abnormal Psychology, 108,* 299–306.

Raine, A., Bihrle, S., Venables, P. H., & Willams, M. (1990). Relationships between central and autonomic measure of arousal at age 15 years and criminality at age 24 years. *Archives of General Psychiatry, 47,* 1003–1007.

Ramey, C. T., & Ramey, S. L. (1998). Early intervention and early experience. *American Psychologist, 53,* 109–120.

Ray, O. (2004). How the Mind Hurts and Heals the Body. *American Psychologist, 59,* 29–40.

Raynor, J. O. (1970). Relationships between achievement-related motives, future orientation, and academic performance. *Journal of Personality and Social Psychology, 15,* 28–33.

Raz, A., Fan., & Paosner, M. I. (2005). Hypnotic suggestion reduces conflict in the human brain. *Proceedings of the National Academy of Sciences, USA, 102,* 9978–9983.

Raz, A., Kirsch, I., Pollard, J., & Nitkin-Kaner, Y. (2006). Suggestion reduces the Stroop effect. *Psychological Science, 17,* 91–95.

Redelmeier, D. A., & Tibshirani, R. J. (1997). Association between cellular telephone calls and motor vehicle collisions. *New England Journal of Medicine, 336,* 453–458.

Reder, I. M., & Gordon, J. S. (1997). Subliminal perception: Nothing special cognitively speaking. In J. D. Cohen & J. W. Schooler (Eds.), *Scientific approaches to consciousness* (pp. 125–234). Mahwah, NJ: Erlbaum.

Reed, S. B., Kirsch, I., Wickless, C., Moffitt, K. H., & Taren, P. (1996). Reporting biases in hypnosis: Suggestion or compliance? *Journal of Abnormal Psychology, 105,* 142–145.

Reed, T. E., & Jensen, A. R. (1993). Choice reaction time and visual pathway conduction velocity both correlate with intelligence but appear not to correlate with each other: Implications for information processing. *Intelligence, 17,* 191–203.

Reid, L. D. (1990). Rates of cocaine addiction among newborns. Personal communication, Rensselaer Polytechnic Institute.

Reiman, E. M., Fusselman, M. J., Fox, P. T., & Raichle, M. E. (1989). Neuroanatomical correlates of anticipatory anxiety. *Science, 243,* 1071–1074.

Reisenzein, R. (1983). The Schachter theory of emotion: Two decades later. *Psychological Bulletin, 94,* 239–264.

Remschmidt, H., Schulz, E., Mart, W., Warnke, A., & Trott, G. E. (1994). Childhood onset schizophrenia: History of the concept and recent studies. *Schizophrenia Bulletin, 20,* 727–745.

Rensink, R. A. (2005). Visual sensing without seeing. *Psychological Science, 15,* 27–32.

Rentsch, J. R., & Heffner, T. S. (1994). Assessing self-concept: Analysis of Gordon's coding scheme using "Who am I?" responses. *Journal of Social Behavior and Personality, 9,* 283–300.

Rescorla, R. A., & Wagner, A. R. (1972). A theory of Pavlovian conditioning: Variations in the effectiveness of reinforcement and nonreinforcement. In A. Black & W. F. Prokasy (Eds.), *Classical conditioning: II. Current research and theory.* New York: Appleton.

Reyna, V. F., & Titcomb, A. (1996). Constraints on the suggestibility of eyewitness testimony: A fuzzy-trace theory analysis. In D. Payne & F. Conrad (Eds.), *Intersections in basic and applied memory research.* Hillsdale, NJ: Erlbaum.

Rhee, S. H., & Waldman, I. D. (2002). Genetic and environmental influences on antisocial behavior: A meta-analysis of twin and adoption studies. *Psychological Bulletin, 128,* 490–529.

Richardson, J. T. E., & Zucco, G. M. (1989). Cognition and olfaction: A review. *Psychological Bulletin, 105,* 352–360.

Riess, M., & Schlenker, B. R. (1977). Attitude changes and responsibility avoidance as modes of dilemma resolution in forced-compliance situations. *Journal of Personality and Social Psychology, 35,* 21–30.

Rigby, C. S., Deci, E. L., Patrick, B. C., & Ryan, R. M. (1992). Beyond the intrinsic-extrinsic dichotomy: Self-determination in motivation and learning. *Motivation and Emotion, 16,* 165–185.

Rigdon, I. S. (1986). Toward a theory of helpfulness for the elderly bereaved: an invitation to a new life. *Advanced Nursing Science, 9,* 32–43.

Riggio, R. E. (2000). *Introduction to industrial/organizational psychology* (3rd ed.). Upper Saddle River, NJ: Prentice-Hall.

Riggio, R. E. (2004). Charisma. In *Encyclopedia of leadership* (vol. 1, pp. 158–162). Great Barrington, MA: Berkshire Publishing.

Roberts, B. W., & DelVecchio, W. F. (2000). The rank-order consistency of personality traits from childhood to old age: A quantitative review of longitudinal studies. *Psychological Bulletin, 126,* 3–25.

Roberts, B. W., Walton, K. E., & Veichtbauer, W. (2006). Patterns of mean-level change in personality traits across the life course: A meta-analysis of longitudinal studies. *Psychological Bulletin, 132,* 1–25.

Robin, N., & Holyoak, K. J. (1995). Relational complexity and the function of prefrontal cortex. In M. S. Gazzaniga (Ed.), *The cognitive neurosciences* (pp. 987–997). Cambridge, MA: MIT Press.

Robins, L. N., & Rutter, M. (1990). Childhood prediction of psychiatric status in the young adulthood of hyperactive boys: A study controlling for chance association. In L. Robins & M. Rutter (Eds.), *Straight and deviant pathways from childhood to adulthood* (pp. 279–299). Cambridge, MA: Cambridge University Press.

Robins, R. W., & Trzesniewski, K. H. (2005). Self-esteem development across the lifespan. *Current Directions in Psychological Science, 14,* 158–162.

Robinson, L. A., Berman, J. S., & Neimeyer, R. A. (1990). Psychotherapy for the treatment of depression: A comprehensive review of controlled outcome research. *Psychological Bulletin, 108,* 30–49.

Robles, T. F., Glaser, R., & Kiecolt-Glaser, J. K. (2005). Out of balance: A new look at chronic stress, depression, and immunity. *Current Directions in Psychological Science, 14,* 111–115.

Roese, N. J. (1997). Counterfactual thinking. *Psychological Bulletin, 121,* 133–148.

Roese, N. J., & Summerville, A. (2005). What we regret most . . . and why. *Personality and Social Psychology Bulletin, 31,* 1273–1285.

Rogers, C. R. (1970). *Carl Rogers on encounter groups.* New York: Harper & Row.

Rogers, C. R. (1977). *Carl Rogers on personal power: Inner strength and its revolutionary impact.* New York: Delacorte.

Rogers, C. R. (1980). *A way of being.* Boston: Houghton Mifflin.

Rogers, C. R. (1982, August). Nuclear war: A personal response. *American Psychological Association,* pp. 6–7.

Roney, J. R., Hanson, K. N., Durante, K. M., & Maestripieri, D. (2006). Reading men's faces: women's mate attractiveness judgments track men's testosterone and interest in infants. *Proceedings of the Royal Society B: Biological Sciences.*

Root, J. C., Wong, P. S., & Kinsbourne, M. (2006). Left Hemisphere Specialization for Response to Positive Emotional Expressions: A Divided Output Methodology. *Emotion, 6,* 473–483.

Rorick-Kehn, L. M. & Steinmetz, J. E., (2005). Amygdalar Unit Activity during Three Learning Tasks: Eyeblink Classical Conditioning, Pavlovian Fear Conditioning, and Signaled Avoidance Conditioning. *Behavioral Neuroscience, 2005,* 1254–1276.

Rosenberg, E. L., & Ekman, P. (1995). Conceptual and methodological issues in the judgment of facial expressions of emotion. *Motivation and Emotion, 19,* 111-138.

Rosenblith, J. F. (1992). *In the beginning: Development from conception to age two.* Newbury Park, CA: Sage.

Rosenfield, D., Folger, R., & Adelman, H. F. (1980). When rewards reflect competence: A qualification of the overjustification effect. *Journal of Personality and Social Psychology, 39,* 368–376.

Rosenman, R. H. (1988). The impact of certain emotions in cardiovascular disorders. In M. P. Janisse (Ed.), *Individual differences, stress, and health psychology* (pp. 1–23). New York: Springer-Verlag.

Rosenstock, I. M. (1974). The health belief model and preventive health behavior. *Health Education Monographs, 2,* 354–386.

Rosnow, R. L. (2001). Rumors and gossip in interpersonal interactions: A social exchange perspective. In R. M. Kowalski (Ed.), *Behaving badly: Aversive behavior in interpersonal relations* (pp. 203–232). Washington, D.C.: American Psychological Association.

Ross, E. D., Homan, R. W., & Buck, R. (1994). Differential hemispheric lateralization of primary and social emotions. *Neuropsychiatry, Neuropsychology, and Behavioral Neurology, 7,* 1–19.

Rothenberg, R., Nasca, P., Mikl, J., Burnett, W., & Reynolds, B. (1987). In R. W. Amler & H. B. Dull (Eds.), *Closing the gap: The burden of unnecessary illness.* New York: Oxford University Press.

Rothman, A. J., & Hardin, C. D. (1997). Different use of the availability heuristic in social judgment. *Personality and Social Psychology Bulletin, 23,* 123–138.

Rothman, A. J., & Salovey, P. (1997). Shaping perceptions to motivate healthy behavior. The role of message framing. *Psychological Bulletin, 121* (1), 3–19.

Rotter, J. B. (1954). *Social learning and clinical psychology.* Englewood Cliffs, NJ: Prentice-Hall.

Rotter, J. B. (1982). *The development and applications of social learning theory: Selected papers.* New York: Praeger.

Rowe, D. C., Vazsonyi, A. T., & Flannery, D. J. (1994). No more than skin deep: Ethnic and racial similarity in developmental process. *Psychological Review, 101,* 396–413.

Rowland, D. L., Cooper, S. E., & Slob, A. K. (1996). Genital and psychoaffective response to erotic stimulation in sexually functional and dysfunctional men. *Journal of Abnormal Psychology, 105,* 194–203.

Roy, M. M., & Christenfeld, N. J. S. (2004). Do dogs resemble their owners? *Psychological Science, 15,* 361–363.

Rozin, P. (1996). Toward a psychology of food and eating: From motivation to module to model to marker, morality, meaning, and metaphor. *Current Directions in Psychological Science, 6,* 18–20.

Rozin, P., Dow, S., Moscovitch, M., & Rajaram, S. (1998). What causes humans to begin and end a meal? A role for memory for what has been eaten, as evidenced by a study of multiple meal eating in amnesic patients. *Psychological Science, 9,* 392–396.

Rubin, D. C. (2005). A basic-systems approach to autobiographical memory. *Current Directions in Psychological Science, 14,* 79–83.

Reuters News Service. (2006). Brain implants ease depression. Described in the *Wall Street Journal,* April 26, p. B–1.

Rudestam, K. E. (2004). Distributed education and the role of online learning in training professional psychologists. *Professional Psychology: Research and Practice, 35,* 427–432.

Rushton, J. P. (2004). Genetic and environmental contributions to prosocial attitudes: A twin study of social responsibility. *Proceedings of the Royal Society, 271,* 2583–2585.

Rushton, J. P., & Bons, T. A. (2005). Mate choice and friendship in twins: Evidence for genetic similarity. *Psychological Science, 16.* 555–559.

Rushton, W. A. H. (1975). Visual pigments and color blindness. *Scientific American, 232,* 64–74.

Russell, J. A. (1994). Is there universal recognition of emotion from facial expression? A review of the cross-cultural studies. *Psychological Bulletin, 115,* 102–141.

Rutledge, T., & Hogan, B. E. (2002). A quantitative review of prospective evidence linking psychological factors with hypertension development. *Psychosomatic Medicine, 64,* 758–766.

Rutter, M., Macdonald, H., LeCouteur, A., Harrington, R., Bolton, P., & Bailey, A. (1990). Genetic factors in child psychiatric disorders, II: Empirical findings. *Journal of Child Psychology and Psychiatry, 31,* 39–83.

Ryan, R. M. (1982). Control and information in the intrapersonal sphere: An extension of cognitive evaluation theory. *Journal of Personality and Social Psychology, 43,* 450–561.

Ryckmann, R. M., Butler, J. C., Thornton, B., & Lindner, M. A. (1995, April). *Identification and assessment of physique subtype stereotypes.* Paper presented at the meeting of the Eastern Psychological Association, Boston.

Sacco, J. M., & Schmitt, N. (2005). A dynamic multilevel model of demographic diversity and misfit effects. *Journal of Applied Psychology, 90,* 203–231.

Sackett, P. R., & Wanek, J. E. (1996). New developments in the use of honesty, integrity, conscientiousness, dependability, trustworthiness, and reliability for personnel selection. *Personnel Psychology, 49,* 787–829.

Safer, M. A., Bonano, G. A., & Field, N. (2001). "It was never that bad." Biased recall of grief and long-term adjustment to the death of a spouse. *Memory, 9,* 195–204.

Safer, M. A., & Keuler, D. J. (2002). Individual differences in misremembering prepsychotherapy distress: Personality and memory distortion. *Emotion, 2,* 162–178.

Safer, M. A., Levine, L. J., & Drapalski, A. (2002). Distortion in memory for emotions: The contributions of personality and post-event knowledge. *Personality and Social Psychology Bulletin, 28,* 1495–1507.

Saffran, J. R. (2003). Statistical language learning: Mechanisms and constraints. *Current Directions in Psychological Science, 12* (4), 110–114.

Salas, E., & Cannon-Bowers, J. A. (2001). The science of training: A decade of progress. *Annual Review of Psychology, 52,* 471–499.

Salovey, P. & Grewal, D. (2005). The science of emotional intelligence. *Current Directions in Psychological Science, 14,* 281–285.

Salovey, P., & Mayer, J. D. (1990). Emotional intelligence. *Imagination, Cognition, and Personality, 9,* 185–211.

Salthouse, T. A. (2006). Mental exercise and mental aging. *Perspectives on Psychological Science, 1,* 68–87.

Samson, L. F. (1988). Perinatal viral infections and neonates. *Journal of Perinatal and Neonatal Nursing, 1,* 56–65.

Sanna, L. J. (1997). Self-efficacy and counterfactual thinking: Up a creek with and without a paddle. *Personality and Social Psychology Bulletin, 23,* 654–666.

Sansavini, A., Bertonicini, J., & Giovanelli, G. (1997). Newborns discriminate the rhythm of multisyllabic stressed words. *Developmental Psychology, 33,* 3–11.

Sargent, C. (1984). Between death and shame: Dimensions in pain in Bariba culture. *Social Science Medicine, 19,* 1299–1304.

Sargent, J. D., Beach, M. L, Adachi-Mejia, A. M., Gibson, J. J., Titus-Ernstoff, L. T., Carusi, C. P., Swain, S. D., Heatherton, T. F., Dalton, M. A. (2005). Exposure to movie smoking: Its relation to smoking initiation among U.S. adolescents. *Pediatrics, 116,* 1183–1191.

Savin-Williams, R. C. (2006). Who's gay? Does it matter? Current Directions. *Psychological Science, 15(1),* 40–44.

Schab, F. R. (1991). Odor memory: Taking stock. *Psychological Bulletin, 109,* 242–251.

Schachter, D. L., & Kihlstrom, J. F. (1989). Functional amnesia. In F. Boller & J. Grafman (Eds.), *Handbook of neuropsychology* (Vol. 3, pp. 209–230). New York: Elsevier.

Schachter, S., & Singer, J. E. (1962). Cognitive, social, and physiological determinants of emotional states. *Psychological Review, 69,* 379–399.

Schaie, K. W. (1986). *Adult development and aging* (2nd ed.). Boston: Little, Brown.

Schaie, K. W. (1990). Intellectual development in adulthood. In J. E. Birren & K. W. Schaie (Eds.), *Handbook of the psychology of aging* (3rd ed., pp. 291–309). San Diego: Academic Press.

Schaie, K. W. (1994). The course of adult intellectual development. *American Psychologist, 49,* 304–313.

Schellenberg, E. G. (2004). Music lessons enhance IQ. *Psychological Science, 15,* 511–514.

Schellenberg, E. G. (2005). Music and cognitive abilities. *Current Directions in Psychological Science, 14,* 317–320.

Schickedanz, J. A., Schickedanz, D. I., Forsyth, P. D., & Forsyth, G. A. (1998). Understanding children and adolescents (3rd ed.). Boston: Allyn & Bacon.

Schiffman, H. R. (1990). *Sensation and perception: An integrated approach* (3rd ed). New York: Wiley.

Schiffman, S. E., Graham, B. G., Sattely-Miller, E. A., & Warwick, Z. S. (1998). Orosensory perception of sensory fat. *Current Directions in Psychological Science, 7,* 137–143.

Schmidt, F. L., & Hunter, J. E. (1977). Development of a general solution to the problem of validity generalization. *Journal of Applied Psychology, 62,* 529–540.

Schmitt, D. P. (2003). Universal sex differences in the desire for sexual variety: Tests from 52 nations, 6 continents, and 13 islands. *Journal of Personality and Social Psychology, 85,* 85–104.

Schmitt, D. P., & Allik, J. (2005). Simultaneous administration of the Rosenberg self-esteem scale in 53 nations: Exploring the universal and culture-specific features of global self-esteem. *Journal of Personality and Social Psychology, 89,* 623–642.

Schnider, A., Regard, M., & Landis, T. (1994). Anterograde and retrograde amnesia following bitemporal infarction. *Behavioral Neurology, 7,* 87–92.

Schnurr, P., Friedman, M. J., & Rosenberg, S. D. (1993). Preliminary MMPI scores as predictors of combat-related PISD symptoms. *American Journal of Psychiatry, 150,* 479–483.

Schoenbaum, G., Setlow, B., Saddoris, M. P., & Gallagher, M. (2003). Encoding predicted outcome and acquired value in orbitofrontal cortex during cue sampling depends upon input from basolateral amygdala. *Neuron, 39,* 855–867.

Schwartz, B. (2004a). *The paradox of choice: Why more is less.* New York: Ecco.

Schwartz, B. (2004b) The tyranny of choice. *Scientific American, 290,* 70–76.

Seabrook, J. (1995). *In the cities of the south: Scenes from a developing world.* New York: Verso.

Sedikides, C., & Skowronski, J. J. (1997). The symbolic self in evolutionary context. *Personality and Social Psychology Review, 1,* 80–102.

Segal, N. L., & Bouchard, T. J. (1993). Grief intensity following the loss of a twin and other relatives: Test of kinship-genetic hypotheses. *Human Biology, 65,* 87–105.

Segal, Z. V., Gemar, M., & Williams, S. (1999). Differential cognitive response to a mood challenge following successful cognitive therapy or pharmacotherapy for unipolar depression. *Journal of Abnormal Psychology, 108,* 5–10.

Segerstrom, S. C., & Miller, G. E. (2004). Psychological stress and the human immune system: A meta-analytic study of 30 years of inquiry. *Psychological Bulletin, 130,* 601–630.

Seifer, R., Sameroff, A. J., Barrett, L. C., & Krafchuk, E. (1994). Infant temperament measured by multiple observations and mother report. *Child Development, 65,* 1478–1490.

Sekuler, A. B., & Bennett, P. J. (2001). Generalized common fate: Grouping by common luminance changes. *Psychological Science, 12* (6), 437–444.

Sekuler, R., & Blake, R. (1990). *Perception.* New York: Knopf.

Seligman, M. E. P. (1975). *Helplessness: On depression, development, and death.* San Francisco: Freeman.

Seligman, M. E. P., Castellon, C., Cacciola, J., Schulman, P., Luborsky, L., Ollove, M., & Downing, R. (1988). Explanatory style change during cognitive therapy for unipolar depression. *Journal of Abnormal Psychology, 97,* 13–18.

Seligman, M. E. P., Steen, T. A., Park, N., & Peterson, C. (2005). Positive psychology progress: Empirical validation of interventions. *American Psychologist, 60,* 410–421.

Shamay-Tsoory, S. G., Tomer, R., & Aharon-Peretz, J. (2005). The neuroanatomical basis of understanding sarcasm and its relationship to social cognition. *Neuropsychology, 19,* 288–300.

Shammi, P., & Stuss, D. T. (1999). Humour appreciation: A role of the right frontal lobe. *Brain, 122,* 657–666.

Shanab, M. E., & Spencer, R. E. (1978). Positive and negative contrast effects obtained following shifts in delayed water reward. *Bulletin of the Psychonomic Society, 12,* 199–202.

Shane, S. (2003). *The individual-opportunity nexus: Perspectives on entrepreneurship.* Aldershot, England: Edward Elgar.

Sharp, D .J., Scott, S. K., & Wise, R. J. S., (2004). Monitoring and the Controlled Processing of Meaning: Distinct Prefrontal Systems. *Cerebral Cortex, 14,* 1–10.

Sharp, M. J., & Getz, J. G. (1996). Substance use as impression management. *Personality and Social Psychology Bulletin, 22,* 60–67.

Shaver, P. R., & Hazan, C. (1994). Attachment. In A. L. Weber & J. H. Harvey (Eds.), *Perspectives on close relationships* (pp. 110–130). Boston: Allyn & Bacon.

Shaw, J. Y. (2005). The automatic pursuit and management of goals. *Current Directions in Psychological Science, 14,* 10–13.

Shaw, P., Greenstein, D., Lerch, J., Clasen, L., Lenroot, R., Gogtay, N., Evans, A., Rapoport, J., & Giedd, J. (2006). Intellectual ability and cortical development in children and adolescents. *Nature, 440,* 676–679.

Shepard, R. N. (1964). Circularity in judgments of relative pitch. *Journal of the Acoustical Society of America, 36,* 2346–2353.

Sher, K. J., & Trull, T. J. (1994). Personality and disinhibitory psychopathology: Alcoholism and antisocial personality disorder. *Journal of Abnormal Psychology, 103,* 92–102.

Shettleworth, S. J. (1993). Where is the comparison in comparative cognition? *Psychological Science, 4,* 179–183.

Shiffrin, R. M., & Dumais, S. T. (1981). The development of automatism. In J. R. Anderson (Ed.), *Cognitive skills and their acquisition.* Hillsdale, NJ: Erlbaum.

Shiffrin, R. M., & Schneider, W. (1977). Controlled and automatic human information processing. II. Perceptual learning, automatic attending, and a general theory. *Psychological Review, 84,* 127–190.

Shimamura, A. P., Berry, J. M., Mangela, J. A., Rusting, C. L., & Jurica, P. J. (1995). Memory and cognitive abilities in university professors: Evidence for successful aging. *Psychological Science, 6,* 271–277.

Shope, J. T., & Molnar, L. J. (2002). Graduated driver licensing in the United States: Evaluation results from the early pro-grams. *Journal of Safety Research, 34,* 63–69.

Shulman, C., Yirmiya, N., & Greenbaum, C. W. (1995). From categorization to classification: A comparison among individuals with autism, mental retardation, and normal development. *Journal of Abnormal Psychology, 104,* 601–609.

Siegel, J. (2002). Sleep deprivation and level of SOD activity. *Neuroreport, 13,* 1387–1390.

Siegel, P. A., Post, C., Brockner, J., Fishman, A. Y., & Garden, C. (2005). The moderating influence of procedural fairness on the relationship between work-life conflict and organizational commitment. *Journal of Applied Psychology, 90,* 13–24.

Siegel, S. (1984). Pavlovian conditioning and heroin overdose: Reports by overdose victims. *Bulletin of the Psychonomic Society, 22,* 428–430.

Siegel, S. (2005). Drug tolerance, drug addiction, and drug anticipation. *Current Directions in Psychological Science, 14,* 296–300.

Siegel, S., & Ramos, B. M. (2002). Applying laboratory research drug anticipation and the treatment of drug addiction. *Experimental and Clinical Psychopharmacology, 10* (3), 162–183.

Siegler, R. S., & Ellis, S. (1996). Piaget on childhood. *Psychological Science, 7,* 211–215.

Siegman, A. W., & Boyle, S. (1993). Voices of fear and anxiety and sadness and depression: The effects of speech rate and loudness on fear and anxiety and sadness and depression. *Journal of Abnormal Psychology, 102,* 430–437.

Siminoff, L. A., & Step, M. M. (2005). A communication model of shared decision making: Accounting for cancer treatment decisions. *Health Psychology, 24* Suppl., S99–S105.

Simon, L., Greenberg, J., & Brehm, J. (1995). Trivialization: The forgotten mode of dissonance reduction. *Journal of Personality and Social Psychology, 68,* 247–260.

Simpson, E. (1974). Moral development research: A case study of scientific cultural bias. *Human Development, 17,* 81–105.

Sinclair, R. C., Hoffman, C., Mark, M. M., Martin, L. L., & Pickering, T. L. (1994). Construct accessibility and the misattribution of arousal: Schachter and Singer revisited. *Psychological Science, 5,* 15–19.

Singer, M. A., & Goldin-Meadow, S. (2005). Children learn when their teacher's gestures and speech differ. *Psychological Science, 16,* 85–89.

Singh, D. (1993). Adaptive significance of female's physical attractiveness: Role of waist-to-hip ratio. *Journal of Personality and Social Psychology, 65,* 293–307.

Skarlicki, D. P., & Folger, R. (1997). Retaliation in the workplace: The roles of distributive, procedural, and interactional justice. *Journal of Applied Psychology, 82,* 434–443.

Skeels, H. M. (1938). Mental development of children in foster homes. *Journal of Consulting Psychology, 2,* 33–43.

Skeels, H. M. (1966). Ability status of children with contrasting early life experience. *Society for Research in Child Development Monographs, 31* (3), 1–65.

Skinner, B. F. (1938). *The behavior of organisms.* New York: Appleton-Century-Crofts.

Skinner, B. F. (1971). *Beyond freedom and dignity.* New York: Knopf.

Skinner, B. F. (1974). *About behaviorism.* New York: Vintage Books.

Small, G. W., Silverman, D. H. S., Siddarth, P., Ercoli, L. M., Miller, K. J., Lavretsky, H. H., Wright, B. C., Bookheimer, S. Y., Barrio, J. R., & Phelps, M. E. (2006). Effects of a 14-day healthy longevity lifestyle program on cognition and brain function. *American Journal of Geriatric Psychiatry, 14,* 538–545.

Smith, L. (2005). Psychotherapy, classism, and the poor: Conspicuous by their absence. *American Psychologist, 60,* 687–696.

Smith, P. C., Kendall, L. M., & Hulin, C. L. (1969). *The measurement of satisfaction in work and retirement.* Chicago: Rand McNally.

Smith, T. W., Glazer, K., Ruiz, J. M., & Gallo, L. C. (2004). Hostility, anger, aggressiveness, and coronary heart disease: An interpersonal perspective on personality, emotion, and health. *Journal of Personality, 72,* 1217–1270.

Sniezek, J. A., & Henry, R. A. (1989). Accuracy and confidence in group judgment. *Organizational Behavior and Human Decision Processes, 43,* 1–28.

Snyder, S. (1991). Movies and juvenile delinquency: An overview. *Adolescence, 26,* 121–132.

Spanos, N. P. (1991). A sociocognitive approach to hypnosis. In S. J. Lynn & J. R. Rhue (Eds.), *Hypnosis theories: Current models and perspectives* (pp. 324–361). New York: Guilford Press.

Spearman, C. E. (1927). *The abilities of man.* London: Macmillan.

Spence, C., & Read, L. (2003). Speech shadowing while driving: On the difficulty of splitting attention between eye and ear. *Psychological Science, 14* (3), 251–256.

Sperry, R. W. (1968). Hemisphere deconnection and unity of conscious experience. *American Psychologist, 29,* 723–733.

Spiegel, K., Leproult, R., & Van Cauter, E. (1999). Impact of a sleep debt on metabolic and endocrine function. *Lancet, 354,* 1435–1439.

Spirduso, W. W., & MacRae, P. G. (1990). Motor performance and aging. In J. E. Birren & K. W. Schaie (Eds.), *Handbook of the psychology of aging* (3rd ed., pp. 184–200). San Diego: Academic Press.

Sprecher, S., & Duck, S. (1994). Sweet talk: The importance of perceived communication for romantic and friendship attraction experienced during a get-acquainted date. *Personality and Social Psychology Bulletin, 20,* 391–400.

Springer, S. P., & Deutsch, G. (1985). *Left brain, right brain.* San Francisco: Freeman.

Squire, L. R. (1995). Biological foundations of accuracy and inaccuracy of memory. In D. L. Schachter (Ed.), *Memory distortions* (pp. 197–225). Cambridge, MA: Harvard University Press.

Stambor, Z. (2006). Psychologists help predict potential executives' success. *Monitor On Psychology, 37,* 26–27.

Stambor, Z. (2006). Psychology's prescribing pioneers. *Monitor on Psychology, 37,* 30–32.

Staw, B. M., Barsade, S. G., & Koput, K. W. (1997). Escalation at the credit window: A longitudinal study of bank executives' recognition and write-off of problem loans. *Journal of Applied Psychology, 82,* 130–142.

Steel, P., & Ones, D. S. (2002). Personality and happiness: A national-level analysis. *Journal of Personality and Social Psychology, 83,* 767–781.

Steele, C. M., & Aronson, E. (1996). Stereotype threat and the intellectual test performance of African Americans. *Journal of Personality and Social Psychology, 69,* 797–811.

Steele, C. M., & Josephs, R. A. (1990). Alcohol myopia: Its prized and dangerous effects. *American Psychologist, 45,* 921–933.

Steele, C. M., Spencer, S. J., & Lynch, M. (1993). Self-image resilience and dissonance: The role of affirmational resources. *Journal of Personality and Social Psychology, 64,* 885–896.

Steers, R. M. (1984). *Organizational behavior* (2nd ed.). Glenview, IL: Scott Foresman.

Steffen, V. J. (1990). Men's motivation to perform the testicular self-exam: Effect of prior knowledge and an educational brochure. *Journal of Applied Social Psychology, 20,* 681–702.

Stein, M., Herman, D. S., Trisvan, E., Pirragalia, P., Engler, P., Anderson, B. J. (2005). Alcohol use and sexual risk behavior among human immunodeficiency virus-positive persons. *Alcoholism Clinical and Experimental Research, 29,* 837–843.

Steiner, I. D. (1972). *Group process and productivity.* New York: Academic Press.

Sternberg, R. J. (1985). *Beyond IQ.* Cambridge: Cambridge University Press.

Sternberg, R. J. (1988). Triangulating love. In R. J. Sternberg & H. J. Barnes (Eds.), *The psychology of love* (pp. 119–138). New Haven, CT: Yale University Press.

Sternberg, R. J. (1998). *Cupid's arrow.* New York: Cambridge University Press.

Sternberg, R. J. (2004). Successful intelligence as a basis for entrepreneurship. *Journal of Business Venturing, 19,* 190–201.

Sternberg, R. J., Wagner, R. K., Williams, W. M., & Horvath, J. A. (1995). Testing common sense. *American Psychologist, 50,* 912–927.

Stevenson, R. J., & Boakes, R. A. (2003). *Psychological Review, 110,* 340–364.

Stewart, A. J., Copeland, A. P., Chester, N. L., Malley, J. E., & Barenbaum, N. B. (1997). *Separating together: How divorce transforms families.* New York: Guilford Press.

Stewart-Williams, S., & Podd, J. (2004). The placebo effect: Dissolving the expectancy versus conditioning debate. *Psychological Bulletin, 130,* 324–340.

Stice, E. (2002). Risk and maintenance factors for eating pathology: A meta-analytic review. *Psychological Bulletin, 128,* 825–848.

Stickgold, R. (2005). Sleep-dependent memory. *Nature, 437,* 1272–1278.

Stogdill, R. M. (1948). Personal factors associated with leadership: A survey of the literature. *Journal of Psychology, 25,* 35–71.

Stogdill, R. M. (1963). *Manual for the leader behavior description questionnaire, form XII.* Columbus: Ohio State University, Bureau of Business Research.

Stormer, S. M., & Thompson, J. K. (1998, November). *Challenging media messages regarding appearance: A psychoeducational program for males and females.* Paper presented at the annual meeting of the Association for the Advancement of Behavior Therapy, Washington, DC.

Story, M., & Faulkner, P. (1990). The prime time diet: A content analysis of eating behavior and food messages in television program content and commercials. *American Journal of Public Health, 80,* 738–740.

Story, M., & French, S. (2004). Food advertising and marketing directed at children and adolescents in the U.S. *International Journal of Behavioral Nutrition and Physical Activity, 1,* 3. Available: www.ijbnpa.org/content/1/1/3.

Straus, M. A., & Stewart, J. H. (1999). Corporal punishment by American parents: National data on prevalence, chronicity, severity, and duration, in relation to child and family characteristics. *Clinical Child and Family Psychology Review, 2,* 55–70.

Straus, M. A., Sugarman, D. B., & Giles-Sims, J. (1997). Spanking by parents and subsequent antisocial behavior of children. *Archives of Pediatric and Adolescent Medicine, 151,* 761–767.

Strayer, D. L., Drews, F. A. Crouch, D. J., & Johnston, W. A. (2005). *Why do cell phone conversations interfere with driving? In* W. R. Walker and D. Herrmann (Eds.), Cognitive technology: Essays on the transformation of thought and society *(pp. 51–68).* Jefferson, NC: McFarland.

Strean, H. S. (1985). *Resolving resistances in psychotherapy.* New York: Wiley Interscience.

Streissguth, A. P. (1994). A long-term perspective of FAS. *Alcohol Health and Research World, 18*, 74–81.

Streissguth, A. P., Bookstein, F. L., Sampson, P. D., Olson, H. C., & Barr, H. M. (1995, March). *Measurement and analysis of main effects, covariates, and moderators in the behavioral teratology of alcohol.* Paper presented at the Biennial Meetings of the Society for Research in Child Development, Indianapolis.

Strickland, B. R. (1992). Women and depression. *Current Directions in Psychological Science, 1*, 132–134.

Stroessner, S. J., & Mackie, D. M. (1992). The impact of induced affect on the perception of variability in social groups. *Personality and Social Psychology Bulletin, 18*, 546–554.

Stroud, M. W., Thorn, B. E., Jensen, M. P., & Boothby, J. L. (2000). The relation between pain beliefs, negative thoughts, and psychosocial functioning in chronic pain patients. *Pain, 84*, 347–352.

Suinn, R. (2005). Behavioral intervention for stress management in sports. *International Journal of Stress Management, 12*, 343–362.

Sutton, J., & Smith, P. K. (1999). Bullying as a group process: An adaptation of the participant role approach. *Aggressive Behavior, 25*, 97–111.

Swets, J. A. (1992). The science of choosing the right decision threshold in high-stakes diagnostics. *American Psychologist, 47*, 522–532.

Tanaka, K. (1993). Neuronal mechanisms of object recognition. *Science, 262*, 684–688.

Tanaka, K., Siato, H. A., Fukada, Y., & Moriya, M. (1991). Coding visual images of objects in inferotemporal cortex of the Macaque monkey. *Journal of Neurophysiology, 66*, 170–189.

Tangney, J. P., Miller, R. S., Flicker, L., & Barlow, D. H. (1996). Are shame, guilt, and embarrassment distinct emotions? *Journal of Personality and Social Psychology, 70*, 1256–1269.

Tataranni, P. A., Gautier, J. F., Chen, K., Ueckers, A., Bandy, D., Salbe, A. D., Pratley, R. E., Lawson, M. Reiman, E. M., & Ravussin, E. (1999). Neuroanatomical correlates of hunger and satiation in humans using positron emission tomography. *Proceedings of the National Academy of Sciences of the United States of America, 96*, 4569–4574.

Taylor, C. B., & Luce, K. H. (2003). Computer- and internet-based psychotherapy interventions. *Current Directions in Psychological Science, 12*, 18–22.

Taylor, P. J., Russ-Eft, D. F., & Chan, D. W. L. (2005). A meta-analytic review of behavior modeling training. *Journal of Applied Psychology, 90*, 692–709.

Taylor, S. E. (2002). *Health psychology* (5th ed.). New York: McGraw-Hill.

Taylor, S. E., & Brown, J. (1988). Illusion and well-being: A social psychological perspective on mental health. *Psychological Bulletin, 103*, 193–210.

Taylor, S. E., Pham, L. B., Rivkin, I. D., & Armor, D. A. (1998). Harnessing the imagination: Mental stimulation, self-regulation, and coping. *American Psychologist, 55*, 429–439.

Tellegen, A., Lykken, D. T., Bouchard, T. J., Wilcox, K. J., Segal, N. L., & Rich, S. (1988). Personality similarity in twins reared apart and together. *Journal of Personality and Social Psychology, 54*, 1031–1039.

Tennen, H., & Eller, S. J. (1977). Attributional components of learned helplessness. *Journal of Personality and Social Psychology, 35*, 265–271.

Tepper, B. J., Duffy, M. K., Hoobler, J., & Ensley, M. D. (2004). Moderators of the relationships between coworkers' organizational citizenship behavior and fellow employees' attitudes. *Journal of Applied Psychology, 89*, 455–465.

Teri, L., Gibbons, L. E., McCurry, S. M., Logsdon, R. G., Buchner, D. M., Barlow, W. E., Kukull, W. A., LaCroix, A. Z., McCormick, W., & Larson, E. B. (2003). Exercise plus behavioral management in patients with Alzheimer Disease: A randomized controlled trial. *Journal of the American Medical Association, 290*, 2015–2022.

Terkheimer, E., Haley, A. Waldron, M., D'Onofrio, B., & Gottesman, I. I. (2003). Socioeconomic status modifies heritability of IQ in young children. *Psychological Science, 14*, 623–628.

Terman, L. M. (1904). A preliminary study in the psychology and pedagogy of leadership. *Journal of Genetic Psychology, 11*, 413–451.

Tesser, A., & Martin, L. (1996). The psychology of evaluation. In E. T. Higgins & A. W. Kruglanski (Eds.), *Social psychology: Handbook of basic principles* (pp. 400–432). New York: Guilford Press.

Théoret, H., Halligan, E., Kobayashi, E., Fregni, F., Tager-Flusberg, H., & Pascual-Leon, A. (2005). Impaired motor facilitation during action observation in individuals with autism spectrum disorder. *Current Biology, 15*, R84–R85.

Thigpen, C. H., & Cleckley, H. (1957). *The three faces of Eve.* New York: Mcgraw-Hill.

Thomas, A., & Chess, S. (1989). Temperament and development. In G. A. Kohnstamm, J. E. Bates, & M. K. Rothbart (Eds.), *Temperament in childhood.* New York: Wiley.

Thomas, J. L. (1992). *Adulthood and aging.* Boston: Allyn & Bacon.

Thomas, K. (2000). Structural and functional brain development and its relation to cognitive development. *Biological Psychology, 54*, 241–257.

Thompson, J. K. (1992). Body image: Extent of disturbance, associated features, theoretical models, assessment methodologies, intervention strategies, and a proposal for a new DSM-IV diagnostic category-Body Image Disorder. In M. Hesen, R. M. Eisler, & P. M. Miller (Eds.), *Progress in behavior modification* (pp. 3–54). Sycamore, IL: Sycamore Publishing.

Thompson, J. K., & Stice, E. (2001). Thin-ideal internalization: Mounting evidence for a new risk factor for body-image disturbance and eating pathology. *Current Directions in Psychological Science, 10*, 181–183.

Thompson, R. F., Bao, S., Chen, L., Cipriano, B. D., Grethe, J. S., Kim, J. J., Thompson, J. K., Tracy, J. A., Weninger, M. S., & Krupa, D. J. (1997). Associative learning. In R. J. Bradley, R. A. Harris, & P. Jenner (series Eds.) & J. D. Schmahmann (vol. Ed.), *International review of neurobiology: Vol. 41. The cerebellum and cognition* (pp. 152–189). San Diego: Academic Press.

Thompson, R. F., & Krupa, D. J. (1994). Organization of memory traces in the mammalian brain. *Annual Review of Neuroscience, 17*, 519–549.

Thoresen, C. J., Bradley, J. C., Bliese, P. D., & Thoresen, J. D. (2004). The big five personality traits and individual job performance growth trajectories in maintenance and transitional job stages. *Journal of Applied Psychology, 89*, 835–853.

Thurstone, E. L. (1938). *Primary mental abilities.* Chicago: University of Chicago Press.

Tice, D. M., & Baumeister, R. F. (1997). Longitudinal study of procrastination, performance, stress, and health: The costs and benefits of dawdling. *Psychological Science, 8*, 454–458.

Tiernari, P. (1991). Interaction between genetic vulnerability and family environment: the Finnish adoptive family study of schizophrenia. *Acta Psychiatrica Scandanavica, 84*, 460–465.

Tiffany, S. T. (1990). A cognitive model of drug urges and drug-use behavior: Role of automatic and nonautomatic processes. *Psychological Review, 97*, 147–168.

Tisserand, R. B. (1977). *The art of aromatherapy.* Rochester, VT: Healing Arts Press.

Todd, J. J., Fougnie, D., & Marois, R. (2005). Visual short-term memory load suppresses temporo-parietal junction activity and induces inattentional blindness. *Psychological Science, 16*, 965–972.

Toglia, M. P., Neuschatz, J. S., & Goodwin, K. A. (1999). Recall accuracy and illusory memories: When more is less. *Memory, 7*, 233–256.

Tolman, E. C., & Honzik, C. H. (1930). Introduction and removal of reward, and maze performance in rats. *University of California Publications in Psychology, 4*, 257–275.

Took, K. S., & Weiss, D. S. (1994). The relationship between heavy metal and rap music and adolescent turmoil: Real or artifact? *Adolescence, 29,* 613–621.

Topka, H., Valls-Sole, J., Massaquoi, S. G., & Hallett, M. (1993). Deficit in classical conditioning in patients with cerebellar degeneration. *Brain, 116,* 961–969.

Towles-Schwen, T., & Fazio, R. H. (2001). On the origins of racial attitudes: Correlates of childhood experiences. *Personality and Social Psychology Bulletin, 27,* 162–175.

Tracy, J., Ghose, S. S., Stecher, T., McFall, R. M., & Steinmetz, J. E. (1999). *Psychological Science, 10,* 9–13.

Tracy, J. L., & Robins, R. W. (2004). Show your pride: Evidence for a discrete emotion expression. *Psychological Science, 15,* 194–197.

Treisman, A. (1998). The perception of features and objects. In R. D. Wright (Ed.), *Visual attention* (pp. 26–54). New York: Oxford University Press.

Triandis, H. C. (1990). Cross-cultural studies of individualism and collectivism. In J. J. Berman (Ed.), *Nebraska symposium on motivation,* 1989 (pp. 41–133). Lincoln: University of Nebraska Press.

Tropp, L. R., & Pettigrew, T. F. (2005). Relationships between intergroup contact and prejudice among minority and majority status groups. *Psychological Science, 16,* 951–956.

Troxel, W. M., Matthews, K. A., Bromberger, J. T., & Sutton-Tyrrell, K. (2003). Chronic stress burden, discrimination, and subclinical carotid artery disease in African American and Caucasian women. *Health Psychology, 22,* 300–309.

Truxillo, D. M., Bauer, T. N., Campion, M. A., & Paronto, M. E. (2002). Selection fairness information and applicant reactions: A longitudinal field study. *Journal of Applied Psychology, 87,* 1020–1031.

Tucker, P., Pfefferbaum, B., Doughty, D. E., Jones, D. E., Jordan, F. B., & Nixon, S. J. (2002). Body handlers after terrorism in Oklahoma City: Predictors of posttraumatic stress and other symptoms. *American Journal of Orthopsychiatry, 72* (4), 469–475.

Tulving, E., & Psotka, L. (1971). Retroactive inhibition in free recall: Inaccessibility of information available in the memory store. *Journal of Experimental Psychology, 87,* 1–8.

Tulving, E., & Watkins, M. J. (1973). Continuity between recall and recognition. *American Journal of Psychology, 86,* 739–748.

Tun, P. A., O'Kane, G., & Wingfield, A. (2002). Distraction and competing speech in younger and older listeners. *Psychology and Aging, 17,* 453–467.

Turban, D. B., & Keon, T. O. (1993). Organizational attractiveness: An interactionist perspective. *Journal of Applied Psychology, 78,* 184–193.

Turin, L. (1996). A spectroscopic mechanism for primary olfactory reception. *Chemical Senses, 21,* 773–791.

Turk, D. C., & Okifuji, A. (2002). Psychological factors in chronic pain: Evolution and revolution. *Journal of Consulting and Clinical Psychology, 70* (3), 678–690.

Turner, J. C., Hogg, M. A., Oakes, P. J., Richer, S. D., & Wetherell, M. S. (1987). *Rediscovering the social group: A self-categorization theory.* Oxford, England: Blackwell.

UNAIDS AIDS epidemic update: December 2005. Available: www.unaids.org/epi/2005/doc/EPIupdate2005_pdf_en/epi-update2005_en.pdf.

U.S. Census Bureau (2003). Available: www.census.gov/prod/2003pubs/c2kbr-29.pdf; www.census.gov/mso/www/rsf/hisorig/sld004.htm.

U.S. Department of Health and Human Services (1989). *Aging in the eighties: The prevalence of comorbidity and its associations with disability.* (DHHS Publication No. PHS 89–1250). Washington, D.C.: U.S. Government Printing Office.

U.S. Department of Health and Human Services. (2001). *Women and smoking: A report of the surgeon general.* Centers for Disease Control. Available: www.cdc.gov/tobacco/sgr/sgr_forwomen/index.htm

U.S. National Institutes of Health (2005). Available: www.clinicaltrials.gov/ct/show/NCT00170703?order=7.

U. S.National Institutes of Health (2005). *Observational learning in stroke patients.* Available: www.clinicaltrials.gov/show/NCT00083642.

Unger, R. K., & Crawford, M. (1992). *Women and gender: A feminist psychology.* Philadelphia: Temple University Press.

Usher, J. A, & Neisser, U. (1995). Childhood amnesia and the beginnings of memory for four early life events. *Journal of Experimental Psychology: General.*

Usichenko, T.I., Pavlovic, D., Foellner, S., & Wendt, M. (2004). Reducing venipuncture pain by a cough trick: A randomized crossover volunteer study. *Anesthesia & Analgesia, 98,* 343–345

Van den Bulck, J. (2004). Media use and dreaming: The relationship among television viewing, computer game play, and nightmares or pleasant dreams. *Dreaming, 14.* 43–49.

Vansteelandt, K., & Van Mechelan, I. (1999). Individual differences in situation-behavior profiles: A triple typology model. *Journal of Personality and Social Psychology, 75,* 751–765.

Vasquez, M. J. T., & Jones, J. M. (2006). Increasing the number of psychologists of color? Public policy issues for affirmative diversity. *American Psychologist, 61,* 132–142.

Vecchio, R. P. (Ed.) (1997). *Leadership.* South Bend, IN: Notre Dame University Press.

Vernberg, E. M., LaGreca, A. M., Silverman, W. K., & Prinstein, M. J. (1996). Prediction of posttraumatic stress symptoms in children after hurricane Andrew. *Journal of Abnormal Psychology, 105,* 237–248.

Vernon, P. A. (1993). *Biological approaches to the study of human intelligence.* Norwood, NJ: Ablex.

Von Békésy, G. (1960). *Experiments in hearing.* New York: McGraw-Hill.

Voydanoff, P. (2005). Consequences of boundary-spanning demands and resources for work-to-family conflict and perceived stress. *Journal of Occupational Health Psychology, 10,* 491–503.

Vrij, A., & Baxter, M. (2000). Accuracy and confidence in detecting truths and lies in elaborations and denials: Truth bias, lie bias, and individual differences. *Expert Evidence: the International Digest of Human Behaviour, Science and Law, 7,* 25–36.

Vroom, V. H., & Yetton, P. W. (1973). *Leadership and decision making.* Pittsburgh: University of Pittsburgh Press.

Wade, N. (2003). Y chromosome depends on itself to survive. *Wall Street Journal,* June 19, pp. A1, A20.

Wade, N. G., Bailey, D. C., & Shaffer, P. (2005). Helping clients heal: Does forgiveness make a difference? *Professional Psychology: Research and Practice, 36,* 6341–641.

Wade, N .G., & Worthington, E. L. (2005). In search of a common core: A content analysis of interventions to promote forgiveness. *Psychotherapy: Theory, Research, Practice, Training.* 42, 1601–177.

Wagenaar, W. A. (1986). My memory: A study of autobiographical memory over six years. *Cognitive Psychology, 18,* 225–252.

Wah, L. (2000). The emotional tightrope. *Management Review, 26,* 38–43.

Waldstein, S. R. (2003). The relation of hypertension to cognitive function. *Current Directions in Psychological Science, 12* (1), 9–12.

Walker, L. J. (1989). A longitudinal study of moral reasoning. *Child Development, 60,* 157–166.

Wallace, B. (1993). Day persons, night persons, and variability in hypnotic susceptibility. *Journal of Personality and Social Psychology, 64,* 827–833.

Wallace, R. K., & Fisher, L. E. (1987). *Consciousness and behavior* (2nd ed.). Boston: Allyn & Bacon.

Wallen, K. (2001). Sex and Context: Hormones and Primate Sexual Motivation. *Hormones and Behavior, 40,* 339–357.

Waller, P. F. (2002). The genesis of GDL. *Journal of Safety Research, 34,* 17–23.

Walster, E., & Festinger, L. (1962). The effectiveness of "overheard" persuasive communication. *Journal of Abnormal and Social Psychology, 65,* 395–402.

Waltz, J. A., Knowlton, B. J., Holyoak, K. J., Boone, K. B., Mishkin, F. S., de Menezes,

M., Thomas, C. R., & Miller, B. L. (1999). A system for relational reasoning in human prefrontal cortex. *Psychological Science, 10,* 119–125.

Wang, L., McCarthy, G., & Song, A. (2005). Amygdala activation to sad pictures during high-field (4 Tesla) functional magnetic resonance imaging. *Emotion, 5,* 12–22.

Ward, A., & Mann, T. (2000). Don't mind if I do: Disinhibited eating under cognitive load. *Journal of Personality and Social Psychology, 78,* 753–763.

Ward, G. R., & Krebs, D. L. (1996). Gender and dilemma differences in real-life moral judgment. *Developmental Psychology, 32,* 220–230.

Ward, T. B. (2004). Cognition, creativity, and entrepreneurship. *Journal of Business Venturing, 19,* 173–188.

Wardle, J., Robb, K. A., Johnson, F., Griffith, J., Brunner, E., Power, C., & Tovee, M. (2004). Socioeconomic variation in attitudes in eating and weight in female adolescents. *Health Psychology, 23,* 275–282.

Waung, M., & Highhouse, S. (1997). Fear of conflict and empathic buffering: Two explanations for the inflation of performance feedback. *Organizational Behavior and Human Decision Processes, 71,* 37–54.

Webb, W. (1975). *Sleep: The gentle tyrant.* Englewood Cliffs, NJ: Prentice-Hall.

Weigel, R. H., Kim, E. L., & Frost, J. L. (1995). Race relations on prime time television reconsidered: Patterns of continuity and change. *Journal of Applied Social Psychology, 25,* 223–236.

Weiner, H. (1992). *Perturbing the organism: The biology of stressful experience.* Chicago: University of Chicago Press.

Weinstein, N. D. (1998). Accuracy of smokers' risk perceptions. *Annals of Behavioral Medicine, 20,* 135–140.

Weiss, A., King, J. E., & Perkins, L. (2006). Personality and subjective well-being in orangutans (*Pongo pygmaeus* and *Pongo abelii*). *Journal of Personality and Social Psychology, 90,* 501–511.

Weiss, B., & Feldman, R. S. (2006). Looking good and lying to do it: Deception as an impression management strategy in job interviews. *Journal of Applied Social Psychology, 36,* 1070–1086.

Weiss, H. M., & Cropanzano, R. (1996). Affective events theory: A theoretical discussion of the structure, causes, and consequences of affective experiences at work. In B. M. Staw & L. L. Cummings (Eds.), *Research in organizational behavior* (vol. 19, pp. 1–745). Greenwich, CT: JAI Press.

Weiss, H. M., Nicholas, J. P., & Daus, C. S. (1999). An examination of the joint effects of affective experiences and job beliefs on job satisfaction and variations in affective experiences over time. *Organizational Behavior and Human Decision Processes, 78,* 1–24.

Weissberg, M. (1999). Cognitive aspects of pain. In P. D. Wall & R. Melzak (Eds.), *Textbook of pain* (4th ed.) (pp. 345–358). New York: Churchill Livingstone.

Wells, G. L. (1993). What do we know about eyewitness identification? *American Psychologist, 48,* 553–571.

Wen, S. W., Goldenberg, R. L., Cutter, G. R., Hoffman, H. J., Cliver, S. P., Davis, R. O., & DuBard, M. B. (1990). Smoking, maternal age, fetal growth, and gestational age at delivery. *American Journal of Obstetrics and Gynecology, 162,* 53–58.

Werker, J. F., & Desjardins, R. N. (1995). Listening to speech in the 1st year of life: Experiential influences on phoneme perception. *Current Directions in Psychological Science, 4,* 76–80.

Werts, M. G., Caldwell, N. K., & Wolery, M. (1996). Peer modeling of response chains: Observational learning by students with disabilities. *Journal of Applied Behavior Analysis, 29,* 53–66.

Wessel, H. (2003). Personality tests grow popular. *Wall Street Journal,* August 3.

Wexley, K. N., & Latham, G. P. (2002). *Developing and training human resources in organizations* (3rd ed.). Upper Saddle River, NJ: Prentice Hall.

Wheatley, T., & Haidt, J. (2005). Hypnotic disgust makes moral judgments more severe. *Psychological Science, 16,* 780–784.

White, R. K. (1977). Misperception in the Arab-Israeli conflict. *Journal of Social Issues, 25,* 41–78.

White, K., & Lehman, D. R. (2005). Culture and social comparison seeking: the role of self-motives. *Personality and Social Psychology Bulletin, 31,* 232–242.

Wilcoxon, H. C., Dragoin, W. B., & Kral, P. A. (1971). Illness-induced aversions in rats and quail: Relative salience of visual and gustatory cues. *Science, 171,* 826–828.

Wiley, J. A., & Camacho, T. C. (1980). Lifestyle and future health: Evidence from the Alameda County study. *Preventive Medicine, 9,* 1–21.

Wilhelm, K., & Parker, G. (1994). Sex differences in lifetime depression rates: Fact or artifact? *Psychological Medicine, 24,* 97–111.

Williams, A. F. (2002). The compelling case for graduated licensing. *Journal of Safety Research, 34,* 3–4.

Williams, B. F., Howard, V. F., & McLaughlin, T. F. (1994). Fetal alcohol syndrome: Developmental characteristics and directions for further research. *Education and Treatment of Children, 17,* 86–97.

Williams, D. P., Going, S. B., Lohman, T. G., Harsha, D. W., Srinivasan, S. R., Weber, L. S., & Berenson, G. S. (1992). Body fatness and risk for elevated blood pressure, total cholesteral, and serum lipoprotein ratios in children and adolescents. *American Journal of Public Health, 82,* 338–363.

Williams, G. C., Grow, V. M., Freedman, Z., Ryan, R. M., & Deci, E. L. (1996). Motivational predictors of weight loss and weight-loss maintenance. *Journal of Personality and Social Psychology, 70,* 115–126.

Williams, K. B., Radefeld, P. A., Binning, J. F., & Sudak, J. R. (1993). When job candidates are "hard" versus "easy-to-get": Effects of candidate availability on employment decisions. *Journal of Applied Social Psychology, 23,* 169–198.

Williams, K. Y., & O'Reilly, C. A. (1998). Demography and diversity in organizations: A review of 40 years of research. In L. L. Cummings & B. M. Staw (Eds.), *Research on organizational behavior* (vol. 20, pp. 77–140). Greenwich, CT: JAI Press.

Williams-Piehota, P., Pizarro, J., Schneider, T. R., Mowad, L., & Salovey, P. (2005). Matching health messages to monitor-blunter coping styles to motivate screening mammography. *Health Psychology, 24,* 58–67.

Williamson, D. A., Cubic, B. A., & Gleaves, D. H. (1993). Equivalence of body image disturbances in anorexia and bulimia nervosa. *Journal of Abnormal Psychology, 102,* 177–180.

Willis, C. M., Church, S. M., Guest, C. M., Cook, W. A., McCarthy, N., Bransbury, A. J., Church, M. R. T., & Church, J. C. T. (2004). Olfactory detection of human bladder cancer by dogs: Proof of principle study. *British Medical Journal, 329,* 712–714.

Willis, J., & Todorov, A. (2006). First impressions: Making up your mind after a 100-ms exposure to a face. *Psychological Science, 17,* 592–598.

Willis, W. D. (1985). *The pain system: The neural basis of nociceptive transmission in the mammalian nervous system.* Basel: Karger.

Wilson, G. T., Nathan, P. E., O'Leary, K. D., & Clark, L. A. (1996). *Abnormal psychology: Integrating perspectives.* Boston: Allyn & Bacon.

Wilson, S., & Reutens, D. (July, 2002). Using musical training to examine brain plasticity and cognitive development. Presentation at the 7th International Conference on Music Perception & Cognition. Sydney, Australia.

Winerman, L. (2005). Figuring out phobia. *Monitor on Psychology,* 92–96.

Winerman, L. (2006). From the stage to the lab. *Monitor on Psychology, 37,* 26–27.

Winerman, L. (2006). On the other hand, maybe I do remember . . . *Monitor on Psychology 37,* 18–19.

Wingfield, A., Tun, P. A., & McCoy, S. L. (2005). Hearing loss in older adulthood. *Current Directions in Psychological Science, 14,* 144–148.

Winkielman, P., Berridge, K. C., & Wilbarger, J. L. (2005). Unconscious affective reactions to masked happy versus angry faces influence consumption of behavior and judgments of value. *Personality and Social Psychology Bulletin, 31*, 121–135.

Winn, P. (1995). The lateral hypothalamus and motivated behavior: An old syndrome reassessed and a new perspective gained. *Current Directions in Psychological Science, 4*, 182–187.

Winokur, G. (1986). Unipolar depression. In G. Winokur & P. Clayton (Eds.), *The medical basis of psychiatry* (pp. 60–79). Philadelphia: Saunders.

Witelson, S. (1991). Sex differences in neuroanatomical changes with aging. *New England Journal of Medicine, 325*, 211–212.

Wixtel, J. T. (2004). The psychology and neuroscience of forgetting. *Annual Review of Psychology, 55*, 235–269.

Wixtel, J. T. (2006). A theory about why we forget what we once knew. *Current Directions in Psychological Science, 16*, 6–9.

Wolfe, D. A. (1987). *Child abuse: Implications for child development and psychopathology.* Newbury Park, CA: Sage.

Wolfe, J. M., Kluender, K. R., Levi, D. M., Bartoshuk, L. M., Herz, R. S., Klatzky, R. L., & Lederman, S.J. (2006). *Sensation & perception.* Sunderland, MA: Sinauer Associates.

Wolfmaier, T. (1999). Designing for the color-challenged: A challenge. Available: www.internettg.org/newsletter/mar99/accessibility_color_challenged.html.

Wood, J. M., Nezworski, M. T., & Stejskal, W. J. (1996). The comprehensive system for the Rorschach: A critical examination. *Psychological Science, 7*, 3–10.

Wood, J. V., Heimpel, S. A., Newby-Clark, I. R., & Ross, M. (2005). Snatching defeat from the jaws of victory: Self-esteem differences in the experience and anticipation of success. *Journal of Personality and Social Psychology, 89*, 764–780.

Wood, W., Wong, F. Y., & Chachere, J. G. (1991). Effects of media violence on viewers' aggression in unconstrained social interaction. *Psychological Bulletin, 109*, 373–383.

Woodruff-Pak, D. S. (1999). New directions for a classical paradigm: Human eye-blink conditioning. *Psychological Science, 10*, 1–3.

Woody, E. Z., & Bowers, K. S. (1994). A frontal assault on dissociated control. In S. J.

Lynn & J. W. Rhue (Eds.), *Dissociation: Theoretical and clinical perspectives* (pp. 52–79). New York: Guilford Press.

Wright, R. W. (1982). *The sense of smell.* Boca Raton, FL: CRC Press.

Wright, T. A., & Cropanzano, R. (2000). Psychological well-being and job satisfaction as predictors of job performance. *Journal of Occupational Health Psychology, 5*, 84–94.

Wyer, R. S., Jr., & Srull, T. K. (Eds.). (1999). *Handbook of social cognition* (3rd ed.). Mahwah, NJ: Erlbaum.

Yan, L. L., Liu, K., Matthews, K. A., Daviglus, M. L., Ferguson, T. F., & Kiefe, C. I. (2003). Psychosocial factors and risk of hypertension: The coronary artery risk development in young adults (CARDIA) study. *JAMA, 290*, 2138–2148.

Yankner, J., Johnson, S. T., Menerdo, T., Cordell, B., & Firth, C. L. (1990). Relations of neural APP-751/APP-695 in RNA ratio and neuritic plaque density in Alzheimer's disease. *Science, 248*, 854–856.

Yonas, A., Arterberry, M. E., & Granrud, C. E. (1987). Four-month-old infants' sensitivity to binocular and kinetic information for three-dimensional object shape. *Child Development, 58*, 910–927.

Yoshida, T. (1977). Effects of cognitive dissonance on task evaluation and task performance. *Japanese Journal of Psychology, 48*, 216–223.

Yovel, H., Revelle, W., & Mineka, S. (2005). Who sees the trees before the forest? The obsessive-compulsive style of visual attention. *Psychological Science, 16*, 123–129.

Yukl, G. (1994). *Leadership in organizations* (3rd ed.). Englewood Cliffs, NJ: Prentice-Hall.

Yukl, G., & Van Fleet, D. D. (1992). Theory and research on leadership in organizations. In M. D. Dunnette & L. M. Hough (Eds.), *Handbook of industrial and organizational psychology* (vol. 3, pp. 147–197). Palo Alto, CA: Consulting Psychologists Press.

Yun, S., Faraj, S., & Sims, H. P., Jr. (2005). Contingent leadership and effectiveness of trauma resuscitation teams. *Journal of Applied Psychology, 90*, 1288–1296.

Zaidel, D. W. (1994). A view of the world from a split-brain perspective. *Neurological Boundaries of Reality, 11*, 161–174.

Zajonc, R. B. (1968). Attitudinal effects of mere exposure. *Journal of Personality and*

Social Psychology Monograph Supplement, 9, 1–27.

Zajonc, R. B., & McIntosh, D. N. (1992). Emotions research: Some promising questions and some questionable promises. *Psychological Science, 3*, 70–74.

Zajonc, R. B., Murphy, S. T., & Inglehart, M. (1989). Feeling and facial efference: Implications of the vascular theory of emotion. *Psychological Review, 96*, 395–416.

Zanna, M. P., & Olson, J. M. (1994). The psychology of prejudice. *The Ontario Symposium* (vol. 7). Hillsdale, NJ: Erlbaum.

Zatzick, D. F., & Dimsdale, J. E. (1990). Cultural variations in response to painful stimuli. *Psychosomatic Medicine, 52*, 544–557.

Zeelenberg, R., Wagenmakers, E., & Rotteveel, M. (2006). The impact of emotion on perception: Bias or enhanced processing. *Psychological Science, 17*, 287–291.

Zigler, E., & Hall, N. (1989). Physical child abuse in America. In D. Cicchetti & V. Carlson (Eds.), *Child maltreatment* (pp. 38–75). New York: Cambridge University Press.

Zillmann, D., Schweitzer, K. J., & Mundorf, N. (1994). Menstrual cycle variation in women's interest in erotica. *Archives of Sexual Behavior, 23*, 579–597.

Zimbardo, P. (2007). *The Lucifer effect: How good people turn evil.* New York: Random House.

Zinberg, R. E., & Barlow, D. H. (1995). Structure of anxiety and the anxiety disorders: A hierarchical model. *Journal of Abnormal Psychology, 105*, 181–193.

Zou, Z., & Buck, L.B. (2006). Combinatorial effects of odorant mixtures in olfactory cortex. *Science, 311*, 1477–1481.

Zuckerman, M. (1994). *Behavioral expressions and biosocial bases of sensation seeking.* New York: Cambridge University Press.

Zuckerman, M. (1995). Good and bad humors: Biochemical bases of personality and its disorders. *Psychological Science, 6*, 325–332.

Zuvolensky, M. J., & Bernstein, A. (2005). Cigarette smoking and panic psychopathology. *Current Directions in Psychological Science, 14*, 301–305.

Study Guide Answer Keys

CHAPTER 1

CHAPTER REVIEW

Psychology: What it is—Aand What it Offers

1. True 2. c. 3. a. 4. c. 5. d. 6. d.
7. b. 8. a. 9. False 10. d. 11. a.
12. True 13. B,F,G,E,D,A,C

Psychology in the 21st Century: Expanding Horizons

14. True 15. c. 16. b. 17. d.
18. False 19. d.

Psychology and the Scientific Method

20. E,C,D,A,B 21. b. 22. d. 23. C,A,D
24. b. 25. True 26. d.

Research Methods in Psychology: How Psychologists Answer Questions about Behavior

27. b. 28. c. 29. D,B,A,C 30. c.
31. False 32. b. 33. d. 34. True

Psychology: What's in It for You?

35. a.

IDENTIFICATIONS

1. G 2. C 3. H 4. E 5. I 6. A
7. J 8. K 9. B 10. D

FILL IN THE BLANK

1. the method of introspection
2. stability versus change; nature versus nurture; rationality versus irrationality
3. the role of evolutionary factors in behavior; the exportation of psychology; consideration of multicultural factors.
4. Evolved psychological mechanisms.
5. Pattern recognition.
6. Science
7. Objectivity
8. Confirmation bias
9. "Sunk costs"
10. Critical thinking skills.
11. Observation, correlation, experimentation.
12. Case observation
13. predictions
14. causal
15. dependent; independent
16. Random assignment of subjects to experimental conditions; the capacity to hold constant all variables other than that varied by the experimenter.

COMPREHENSIVE PRACTICE TEST

1. False 2. d. 3. c. 4. d. 5. a.
6. d. 7. d. 8. c. 9. True 10. True
11. c. 12. c. 13. a. 14. c. 15. False

CHAPTER 2

CHAPTER REVIEW

Neurons: Building Blocks of the Nervous System

1. True 2. d. 3. a. 4. d. 5. a. 6. b.
7. b. 8. c. 9. d. 10. True
11. C,B,E,D,B,A,F,A 12. True 13. c.

The Nervous System: Its Basic Structure and Function

14. b. 15. True 16. b. 17. a.
18. False 19. c. 20. d. 21. d

The Brain: Where Consciousness Dwells

22. F,D,G,I,A,E,C,H 23. True 24. b.
25. d. 26. c. 27. d. 28. a.
29. True. 30. d. 31. A.

The Brain and Human Behavior: Where Biology and Consciousness Meet

32. d. 33. b. 34. c.

Heredity and Behavior: Genetics and Evolutionary Psychology

35. True 36. b. 37. d.

IDENTIFICATIONS

1. C 2. E 3. G 4. F
5. B 6. H 7. D 8. A

FILL IN THE BLANK

1. Neuron 2. Dendrites; axon terminals
3. vesicles 4. acetylcholine
5. spinal cord; brain
6. parasympathetic
7. control of bodily and survival functions; motivation and emotion; cognitive functions such as language, planning, and reasoning.
8. jerky uncoordinated movements.
9. Homeostasis 10. thalamus
11. frontal 12. temporal 13. right
14. electroencephalogram (EEG)
15. parallel 16. Broca's 17. Identical
18. heritability

COMPREHENSIVE PRACTICE TEST

1. axon 2. True 3. motor

4. Sensory neurons directly control muscle contraction. (True-*False)
5. d. 6. True 7. d 8. b.
9. F,C,E,B,A,D
10. c. 11. microelectrodes
12. provide interconnections between the two hemispheres.
13. b. 14. c 15. a. 16. c.

CHAPTER 3

CHAPTER REVIEW

Sensation: The Raw Materials of Understanding

1. b. 2. d. 3. a. 4. c. 5. b.
6. b. 7. True 8. c. 9. b. 10. a.
11. True 12. d. 13. a. 14. c.
15. D,H,A,C,B,F,E
16. a. The blind spot of eye is
17. c. 18. a. 19. a. 20. True
21. c. 22. b.

Hearing

23. a. 24. a. 25. a.

Touch and Other Skin Senses

26. d. 27. True 28. b. 29. False

Smell and Taste: The Chemical Senses

30. c. 31. d. 32. a. 33. b.

Kinesthesis and Vestibular Sense

34. a.

Perception: Putting It All Together

35. c. 36. True 37. d. 38. E,A,B

Psi: Perception without Sensation

39. c.

IDENTIFICATIONS

1. B 2. K 3. F 4. I 5. C 6. H
7. E 8. J 9. G 10. A 11. L

FILL IN THE BLANK

1. sensitivity 2. sensory adaptation
3. pupil
4. 400-700
5. Prosopagnosia
6. the mixture of frequencies and intensities that make up the sound wave.
7. Planum temporale (or right temporal cortex)
8. Nociceptors 9. coughing
10. odorants 11. inner ear
12. Select, organize, and interpret.

13. Gestalt psychologists
14. Recognition-by-components
15. Monocular cues
16. Clairvoyance; precognition

COMPREHENSIVE PRACTICE TEST

1. False 2. d. 3. b. 4. False 5. b.
6. b. 7. d. 8. c. 9. d. 10. False
11. d. 12. c. 13. False
14. E,D,G,A,F,C,B 15. a.

CHAPTER 4

CHAPTER REVIEW

Biological Rhythms: Tides of Life- and Conscious Experience

1. c. 2. True 3. a. 4. b. 5. d.
6. True 7. c. 8. False 9. b.
10. False

Waking States of Consciousness: From Controlled Processing to Intuition

11. c. 12. a. 13. b. 14. d.
15. True 16. b.

Sleep: The Pause that Refreshes?

17. c. 18. d. 19. c. 20. False 21. c.
22. False 23. a. 24. c.

Hypnosis: Altered State of Consciousness or Social Role Playing?

25. b. 26. C,E,A,B 27. b. 28. False
29. c. 30. a. 31. True

Consciousness-Altering Drugs: What They are and What They Do

32. d. 33. d. 34. d. 35. b. 36. False
37. a. 38. b. 39. True 40. d. 41. b.

IDENTIFICATIONS

1. H 2. J 3. I 4. E 5. G
6. A 7. B 8. F 9. C

FILL IN THE BLANK

1. States of consciousness.
2. electromyogram 3. REM sleep
4. stimulant 5. binge drink
6. Marijuana 7. narcolepsy
8. hypnosis 9. absorption
10. seasonal 11. depressant
12. psychedelic 13. morphine
14. Automatic processing 15. insomnia

COMPREHENSIVE PRACTICE TEST

1. a. 2. d. 3. d. 4. False 5. b. 6. False 7. b. 8. d. 9. d.
10. F,E,A,D,B,C, 11. d. 12. c.
13. a 14. a. 15. c.

CHAPTER 5

CHAPTER REVIEW

Classical Conditioning: Learning That Some Stimuli Signal Others

1. d. 2. b. 3. b. 4. c. 5. d.

6. C,F,A,G,D,B,E 7. c. 8. d. 9. c.
10. False 11. d. 12. b. 13. c.
14. True 15. d. 16. a.

Operant Conditioning: Learning Based on Consequences

17. b. 18. c. 19. d. 20. D,F,G,F,H,B,C
21. b 22. True 23. d. 24. c. 25. d.
26. c. 27. c. 28. False

Observational Learning: Learning From the Behavior and Outcomes of Others

29. d. 30. True

IDENTIFICATIONS

1. H 2. A 3. D 4. I 5. J 6. K
7. G 8. L 9. F 10. B

FILL IN THE BLANK

1. classical conditioning; operant conditioning; observational learning
2. backwards conditioning
3. obsession 4. resistant
5. conditional compensatory response
6. Delay 7. discriminative
8. impulsive behavior 9. variable ratio
10. variable ratio
11. spontaneous recovery
12. Learned helplessness
13. Procrastination 14. Backwards
15. intermittent

COMPREHENSIVE PRACTICE TEST

1. c. 2. b. 3. a. 4. a. 5. True 6. a.
7. b. 8. d. 9. a. 10. a. 11. b.
12. False 13. d. 14. A,C,D,F,A,E,B
15. d. 16. a.

CHAPTER 6

CHAPTER REVIEW

Human Memory: How We Remember, Why We Forget

1. c. 2. c. 3. c. 4. b. 5. c. 6. a.
7. B,E,D,F,A,C 8. d. 9. c. 10. c.
11. d. 12. True 13. b. 14. a.
15. True 16. c. 17. b. 18. c. 19. c.
20. True 21. a. 22. True 23. d.
24. b. 25. D,C,A,B 26. b. 27. a.
28. True 29. c. 30. c. 31. b. 32. c.
33. c. 34. d. v35. c. 36. d. 37. a.

Cognition: Thinking, Deciding, and Creating

38. True 39. a. 40. c. 41. b.
42. D,C,A,B 43. a. 44. c. 45. True
46. b. 47. d.

IDENTIFICATIONS

1. G 2. H 3. J 4. M 5. C 6. E
7. O 8. A 9. K 10. N 11. I 12. F
13. L 14. D 15. B

FILL IN THE BLANK

1. Cognition 2. elaborative rehearsal

3. semantic 4. explicit
5. Retroactive interference
6. long-term memory 7. satisficer
8. procedural memory
9. hippocampus
10. rumors, photos, media reports
11. Infantile amnesia
12. Logical concepts 13. chunking
14. heuristic 15. confluence
16. our own personal life.
17. Bugs Bunny

COMPREHENSIVE PRACTICE TEST

1. a. 2. b. 3. a. 4. False 5. d.
6. False 7. a. 8. False 9. a. 10. b.
11. d. 12. True 13. d. 14. False
15. c. 16. F,E,D,C,B,A

CHAPTER 7

CHAPTER REVIEW

Physical Growth and Development during Childhood

1. c. 2. True 3. c. 4. False
5. d. 6. d. 7. b.

Perceptual Development during Childhood

8. d. 9. d. 10. c.
11. A. At birth.
B. Six months.
C. At birth.
D. Two months.
E. Two months.
F. At birth.

Cognitive Development during Childhood: Changes in Our Ability to Understand the World around Us

12. c. 13. c. 14. True 15. False
16. c. 17. True 18. d. 19. c.

Moral Development: Reasoning about "Right" and "Wrong"

20. b. 21. d. 22. False 23. C,A,B,A

Social Development during Childhood: Forming Relationships with Others

24. d. 25. b. 26. True 27. d. 28. c.

From Gender Identity to Sex Category Constancy: How Children Come to Understand That the Are Female or Male

29. b. 30. b. 31. False 32. E,D,A,G,C

Adolescence: Between Child and Adult

33. d. 34. a.

Development during Our Adult Years

35. d. 36. b. 37. d. 38. c.
39. b. 40. True

Death and Bereavement
41. c. 42. True

IDENTIFICATIONS

1. L 2. N 3. J 4. H 5. E 6. B
7. F 8. O 9. G 10. C 11. K 12. D
13. M 14. A 15. I

FILL IN THE BLANK

1. physical, cognitive, social
2. fetal alcoholism 3. zygote
4. visual cliff 5. Moro 6. assimilation
7. theory of mind 8. Metacognition
9. easy 10. gestures
11. preconventional 12. puberty
13. FAS 14. postconventional
15. Metacognition 16. Secondary aging.

COMPREHENSIVE PRACTICE TEST

1. a. 2. b. 3. a. 4. c. 5. True 6. a.
7. H,D,B,E,G,A,C,F 8. False 9. a.
10. b. 11. d. 12. c. 13. c. 14. d.
15. True 16. D,F,B,E,A 17. d.

CHAPTER 8

CHAPTER REVIEW

Motivation: The Activation and Persistence of Behavior

1. True 2. a. 3. a. 4. c. 5. d.
6. True 7. b. 8. d. 9. b. 10. b.
11. True 12. b. 13. d. 14. c. 15. a.
16. False 17. c. 18. c. 19. True
20. d. 21. a. 22. True 23. c. 24. b.
25. b. 26. False 27. d.

Emotions: Their Nature, Expression, and Impact

28. b. 29. c. 30. c. 31. b. 32. d.
33. d. 34. d. 35. True 36. a. 37. d.
38. True 39. D,C,B,F,A 40. True

Subjective Well-Being: Causes and Effects of Personal Happiness

41. No,No,Yes,No,No

IDENTIFICATIONS

1. E 2. I 3. H 4. D 5. A 6. G
7. C 8. F 9. B

FILL IN THE BLANK

1. motivation 2. pushed
3. specific, challenging, and attainable.
4. physiological 5. 65%
6. portion size 7. activation
8. ovulatory 9. bisexual
10. Extrinsic; intrinsic
11. Physiological changes; subjective cognitions; emotional behaviors
12. James-Lange 13. Right hemisphere
14. Facial expressions, body movements, and posture. 15. Suppression

COMPREHENSIVE PRACTICE TEST

1. True 2. c. 3. c. 4. False 5. d.

6. d. 7. False 8. d. 9. False
10. d. 11. B,C,A,F,E,D 12. c. 13. True
14. b. 15. False 16. d. 17. a.
18. a. 19. True 20. c.

CHAPTER 9

CHAPTER REVIEW

Personality: The Essence of What Makes Us Unique

1. d. 2. b. 3. False 4. c. 5. c. 6. d.
7. d. 8. True 9. c. 10. False 11. a.
12. c. 13. b. 14. b. 15. d. 16. d.
17. True 18. a. 19. C,F,A,E,D,B
20. b. 21. True 22. a. 23. c. 24. d.
25. True 26. False 27. c. 28. a.
29. d. 30. c. 31. False 32. d. 33. d.
34. b. 35. d. 36. True 37. c.
38. False 39. a. 40. a.

Intelligence: The Nature of Cognitive Abilities

41. True 42. d. 43. d. 44. b.
45. c. 46. True

IDENTIFICATIONS

1. g 2. m 3. c 4. l 5. n 6. i
7. o 8. j 9. f 10. e 11. d 12. b
13. k 14. a 15. h

FILL IN THE BLANK

1. Libido
2. Perceive; understand; use; manage
3. conscientiousness 4. basic anxiety
5. Mozart effect 6. heritability
7. Freudian slip.
8. collective unconscious 9. reliable
10. trait 11. Thurstone 12. triarchic
13. Personality
14. unconditional positive regard
15. personal growth 16. id
17. neuroticism

COMPREHENSIVE PRACTICE TEST

1. a. 2. c. 3. b. 4. a.
5. B,F,D,G,C,A 6. c. 7. a. 8. b.
9. b. 10. a. 11. b. 12. c. 13. d.
14. b. 15. d. 16. C,B,A,D

CHAPTER 10

CHAPTER REVIEW

Health Psychology: An Overview

1. a. 2. True 3. b.

Stress: Its Causes, Effects, and Control

4. d. 5. c. 6. c. 7. b. 8. b. 9. c.
10. d. 11. b. 12. c. 13. b. 14. d.
15. True 16. c. 17. d. 18. b. 19. c.

Understanding and Communicating Our Health Needs

20. d. 21. True 22. c. 23. False
24. b. 25. c.

Behavioral and Psychological Correlates of Illness: The Effects of Thoughts and Actions on Health

26. True 27. a. 28. d. 29. b.
30. False 31. a. 32. d. 33. a.
34. True 35. c. 36. d. 37. c.
38. b. 39. c. 40. d.

Promoting Wellness: Developing a Healthier Lifestyle

41. b. 42. True 43. a. 44. B,A,D,C

IDENTIFICATIONS

1. G 2. D 3. C 4. J 5. I 6. A
7. L 8. F 9. E 10. H 11. B 12. K

FILL IN THE BLANK

1. lifestyle 2. Stress 3. Hassles
4. allostatic load. 5. immune system
6. "health belief model"
7. risk factor
8. General Adaptation Syndrome
9. Resilience. 10. underload
11. Social support 12. symptom
13. carcinogen 14. "blunter"

COMPREHENSIVE PRACTICE TEST

1. c. 2. b. 3. False 4. c. 5. d. 6. c.
7. a. 8. False 9. d. 10. d. 11. a.
12. a. 13. c. 14. d. 15. d. 16. d.

CHAPTER 11

CHAPTER REVIEW

Assessment and Diagnosis: The DSM-IV TR and Other Tools

1. True. 2. c. 3. True. 4. b.
5. d. 6. a. 7. c.

Disorders of Infancy, Childhood, and Adolescence

8. c, 9. True 11. b. 12. a. 13. True
14. b. 15. True 16. d.

Mood Disorders: The Downs and Ups of Life

17. True 18. a. 19. True. 20. b.
21. True. 22. c. 23. d. 24. d.
25. False 26. d. 27. False

Anxiety Disorders: When Dread Debilitates

28. d. 29. False 30. c. 31. False
32. True 33. True

Dissociative and Somatoform Disorders

34. c. 35. d.

Sexual and Gender Identity Disorders

36. B,C,D,A 37. False

Personality Disorders: Traits that Harm

38. b. **39.** True

Schizophrenia: Losing Touch with Reality

40. False **41.** False **42.** d.

Substance-Related Disorders

43. c. **44.** False

IDENTIFICATIONS

1. G **2.** A **3.** C **4.** N **5.** J **6.** E
7. K **8.** D **9.** B **10.** M **11.** H
12. I **13.** A **14.** F **15.** L

FILL IN THE BLANK

1. diagnosis
2. general medical conditions
3. Ritalin **4.** Conduct disorder
5. excitement, high energy, and elation
6. Mood disorders **7.** Rumination
8. Hypochondriasis
9. anorexia nervosa
10. Obsessive-compulsive disorder.
11. delusion **12.** locus coeruleus
13. hallucination **14.** positive; negative
15. dopamine

COMPREHENSIVE PRACTICE TEST

1. d. **2.** d. **3.** False **4.** d. **5.** d.
6. d. **7.** c. **8.** d. **9.** c. **10.** d.
11. C,E,B,D,A, **12.** d. **13.** b. **14.** a.
15. b. **16.** d.

CHAPTER 12

CHAPTER REVIEW

Psychotherapies: The Therapeutic Alliance as the Foundation of Psychological Treatments

1. c. **2.** d. **3.** a. **4.** a. **5.** c. **6.** d.
7. b. **8.** False **9.** b. **10.** b. **11.** a.
12. c. **13.** True **14.** d. **15.** b.
16. False

Psychotherapy and Diversity: Multiculturalism in Helping Relationships

17. c. **18.** d.
Alternatives to Individual Psychotherapy: Group Therapies
19. c. **20.** d. **21.** True **22.** c. **23.** a.
24. Family therapy is based on the idea that
25. d. **26.** b. **27.** False

Biological Therapies

28. c. **29.** d. **30.** b. **31.** True **32.** d.
33. False **34.** b. **35.** E,D,C,B,A

Psychological Treatments: Are They Effective?

36. d. **37.** d. **38.** True

IDENTIFICATIONS

1. F **2.** C **3.** E **4.** D **5.** F **6.** O
7. H **8.** J **9.** G **10.** N **11.** M **12.** I
13. A **14.** K **15.** B **16.** L

FILL IN THE BLANK

1. therapeutic alliance.
2. desire, reason, and conscience.
3. Freud **4.** psychoanalysis
5. transference **6.** D-cycloserine
7. Gestalt therapists
8. Expressed emotion **9.** clozapine
10. SSRI's, MAO inhibitors, tricylics
11. Benzodiazepines
12. episodic memory
13. Obsessive-compulsive disorder.
14. Psychosurgery **15.** longer

COMPREHENSIVE PRACTICE TEST

1. b. **2.** d. **3.** True **4.** E,C,D,B,F, A
5. b **6.** d. **7.** True **8.** d. **9.** b.
10. a. **11.** c. **12.** a. **13.** c. **14.** d.
15. c.

CHAPTER 13

CHAPTER REVIEW

Social Thought: Thinking about Other People

1. b. **2.** a. **3.** c. **4.** d. **5.** b. **6.** c.
7. d. **8.** c. **9.** True **10.** b. **11.** c.
12. True **13.** b. **14.** True **15.** d.
16. False **17.** c. **18.** False **19.** c.
20. True **21.** b. **22.** b.

Social Behavior: Interacting with Others

23. c. **24.** a. **25.** c. **26.** d. **27.** True
28. d. **29.** True **30.** False **31.** d.
32. False **33.** True **34.** c. **35.** d.
36. C,E,D,B,A

IDENTIFICATIONS

1. K **2.** E **3.** H **4.** B **5.** I **6.** D
7. L **8.** M **9.** J **10.** F **11.** A
12. G **13.** C

FILL IN THE BLANK

1. Heuristics **2.** attribution.
3. Microexpressions **4.** Negativity bias.
5. Intimacy **6.** Door-in-the-face
7. The norm of internality **8.** liking
9. heuristic processing
10. dissimilarity; boredom; jealousy.
11. stereotype **12.** persuasion
13. Recategorization and altering the impact of implicit stereotypes
14. Interpersonal attraction
15. Cognitive dissonance

COMPREHENSIVE PRACTICE TEST

1. d. **2.** True **3.** a. **4.** True **5.** c.
6. c. **7.** d. **8.** c. **9.** c. **10.** True
11. d. **12.** a.' **13.** c. **14.** c.

CHAPTER 14

CHAPTER REVIEW

Selection: Hiring the Best Person for the Job

1. True **2.** d. **3.** a. **4.** c. **5.** d.
6. True **7.** d. **8.** d. **9.** True
10. True **11.** b. **12.** c. **13.** False

Training: Helping Employees Acquire Relevant Skills

14. d. **15.** b. **16.** True **17.** d. **18.** a.
19. c. **20.** c. **21.** a. **22.** True

Performance Appraisal: Identifying Employee Strengths and Weaknesses

23. a. **24.** d.
25. The results of a performance appraisal are rarely used to decide on employee raises. (True-*False).
26. c. **27.** False **28.** b.

Work Motivation: Encouraging Employees to Do Their Best

29. d. **30.** True **31.** b. **32.** a.

Leadership: From Supervisors to CEOs

33. True **34.** d. **35.** a. **36.** a.
37. False **38.** True

Teamwork: The Challenges of Collaborative Work

39. d. **40.** False

IDENTIFICATIONS

1. J **2.** G **3.** L **4.** C **5.** N **6.** K
7. D **8.** E **9.** M **10.** A **11.** H
12. F **13.** I **14.** B **15.** O

FILL IN THE BLANK

1. Job analysis
2. criterion-related validity
3. on-site, but in a separate work area.
4. social loafing **5.** fairly
6. conscientiousness; agreeableness
7. Normative Decision theory
8. utility **9.** central tendency
10. negative employee behavior.
11. Organizational analysis.
12. severity **13.** unstructured
14. engineer.

COMPREHENSIVE PRACTICE TEST

1. d. **2.** a. **3.** False **4.** d. **5.** True
6. c. **7.** c. **8.** a. **9.** a. **10.** False.
11. c. **12.** d. **13.** c. **14.** False.
15. b. **16.** d.

Name Index

Subject Index

Credits